PROCEEDINGS

OF THE

NATIONAL COMMUNICATIONS FORUM

VOLUME XXXXII

BOOK II

HYATT REGENCY O'HARE
HOLIDAY INN O'HARE
ROSEMONT, ILLINOIS

OCTOBER 3, 4, AND 5
1988

NCF88 GENERAL CHAIRMAN

Bernard F. Sergesketter
Vice President, Central Region
Business Markets Group
AT&T

The 1988 National Communications Forum is sponsored by the National Engineering Consortium, Inc., a nonprofit corporation affiliated with 33 major universities. NCF88 is cosponsored by the United States Telephone Association. USTA represents independent and Bell Operating Companies in a broad range of activities and services.

ISSN 0886-229X

ISBN 0-933217-04-8
National Communications Forum
303 East Wacker Drive Suite 739
Chicago, Illinois 60601
312-938-3500

BOOK II CONTENTS

NEW TECHNOLOGIES INSTITUTE SEMINARS

CELLULAR INSTITUTE SEMINARS

OPS-01

BASICS OF TELEPHONY

E.J. Moore - Chairperson
Bell Northern-Research
P.O. Box 3511
Station C
Ottawa, Canada K1Y 4H7

ABSTRACT

   Modern telecommunication networks carry voice, video and data signals. The methods used range from analog and digital techniques for encoding the information, frequency and time multiplexing for optimizing bandwidth utilization, to circuit and packet switching for routing the message. This seminar addresses the basic principles behind these techniques.

   The figures following have been selected from among those discussed in the seminar. Figs. 1 to 3 illustrate the salient features of the present day North American routing and numbering plan. Figs. 4 to 9 illustrate the functions of the basic telephone set and the variety of outside plant methods used to connect it to the switching office. Figs. 10 to 19 highlight analog and digital trunk transmission hierarchies and outlines the basic concepts for converting analog signals to a digital bit stream. Figs. 19 to 26 cover the range of switching control techniques from Step-by-Step to Stored Program Control. Figs. 27 to 35 introduce signaling concepts used both in analog and digital environments. In addition, the concepts of packet switching and Cellular Mobile Radio are shown in Figures 36 to 39.

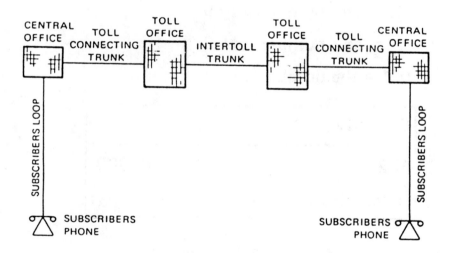

Fig. 1 Typical Switched Network

Fig. 2   Regional Boundaries

Area code	telephone number
N 0/1 X	NNX · XXXX

X = any number 0 to 9

N = any number 2 to 9

0/1 = the number 0 or 1

Capacity		
152	640	10,000
(excluding N11 codes)		

Fig. 3   Numbering Plan

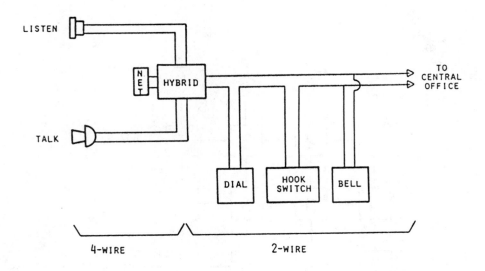

Fig. 4 The Telephone Set

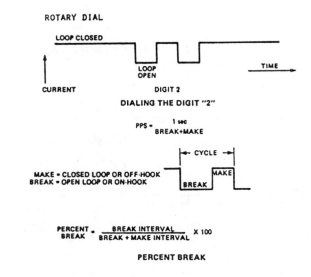

Fig. 5 Rotary Dial

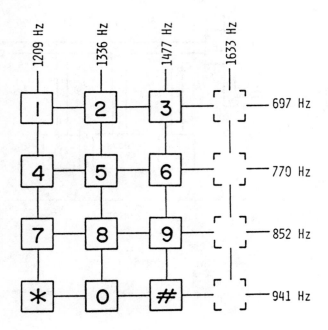

Fig. 6   Tone Dial Frequencies

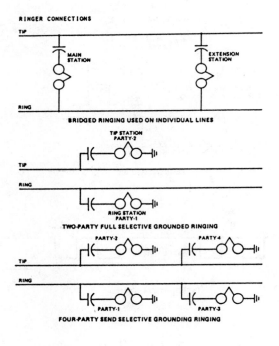

Fig. 7   Ringer Connections

Single party   20 Hz North America

Multiparty   coded ringing 20 Hz Canada

Multifrequency ringing USA

Decimonic	Harmonic	Synchromonic
20 Hz	16 2/3 Hz	16 Hz
30	25	30
40	33 1/3	42
50	50	54
60	66 2/3	66

Fig. 8 Predominant Ringing Supply Frequencies

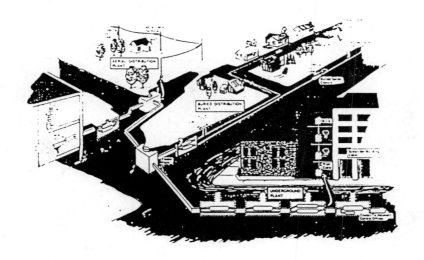

Fig. 9 View of Outside Plant

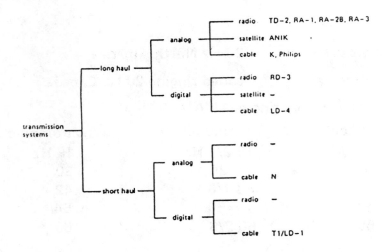

Fig. 10   Transmission Subdivisions

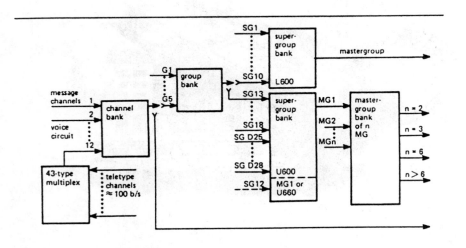

Fig. 11   Long Haul FDM Hierarchy

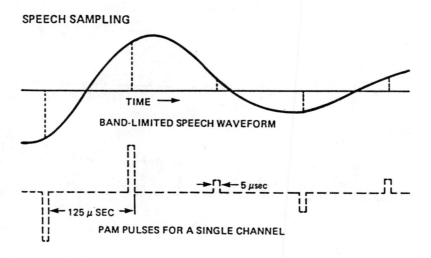

SPEECH SAMPLING

TIME →

BAND-LIMITED SPEECH WAVEFORM

5 μsec

125 μ SEC

PAM PULSES FOR A SINGLE CHANNEL

Fig. 12   Speech Sampling

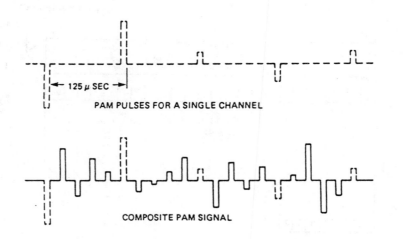

125 μ SEC

PAM PULSES FOR A SINGLE CHANNEL

COMPOSITE PAM SIGNAL

Fig. 13   Combining Sampled Signals

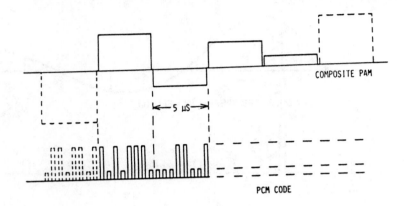

COMPOSITE PAM

5 μS

PCM CODE

Fig. 14   Encoding

FRAME FORMAT

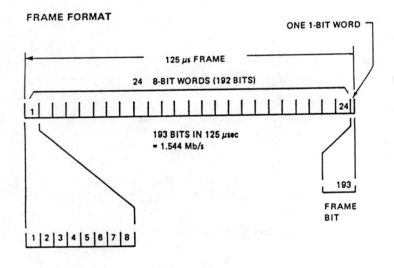

ONE 1-BIT WORD

125 μs FRAME

24   8-BIT WORDS (192 BITS)

1 · · · 24

193 BITS IN 125 μsec
= 1.544 Mb/s

193

FRAME
BIT

1 2 3 4 5 6 7 8

Fig. 15   Frame Format

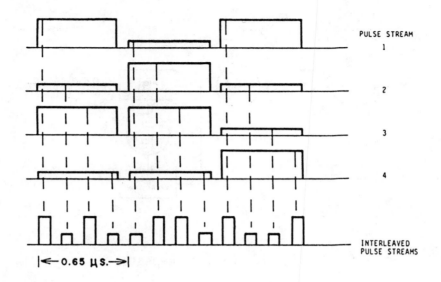

Fig. 16   PCM Multiplexing

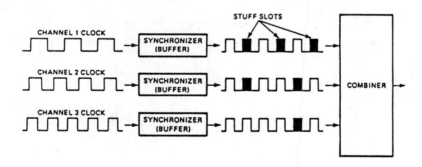

Fig. 17   Pulse Stuffing

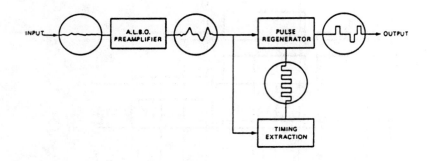

Fig. 18   Digital Repeater

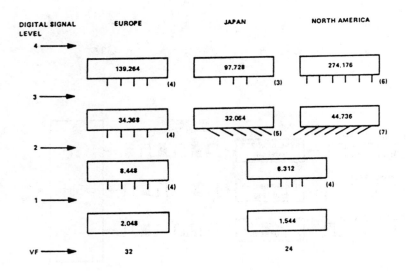

Fig. 19   Digital Transmission Hierarchy

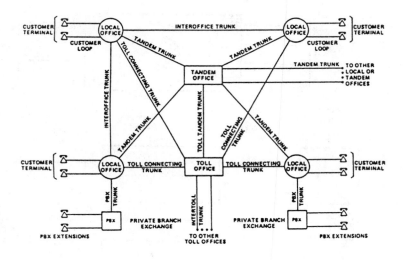

Fig. 20   Types of Switching Offices & Interconnections

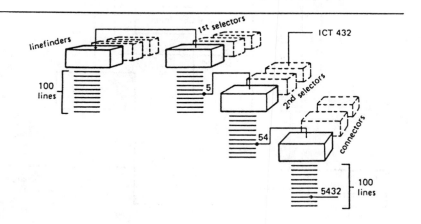

Fig. 21   S x S Trunking

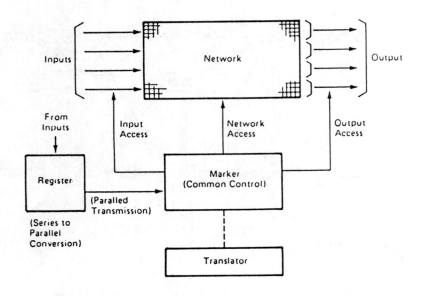

Fig. 22 Common Control System

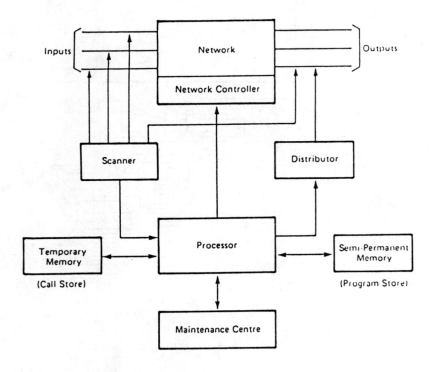

Fig. 23 Stored Program Control

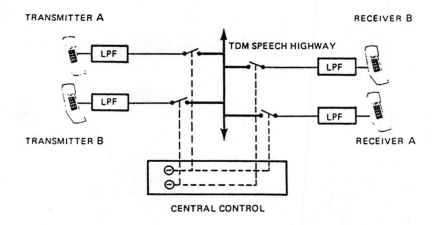

Fig. 24 Principles of TDM/PAM

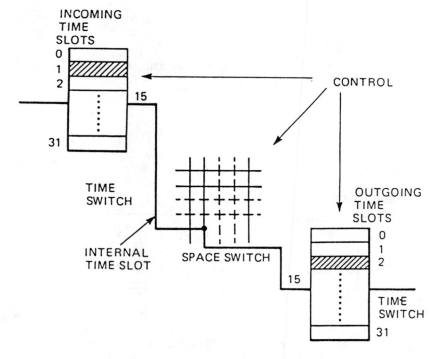

Fig. 25 Time-Space-Time Switching

942

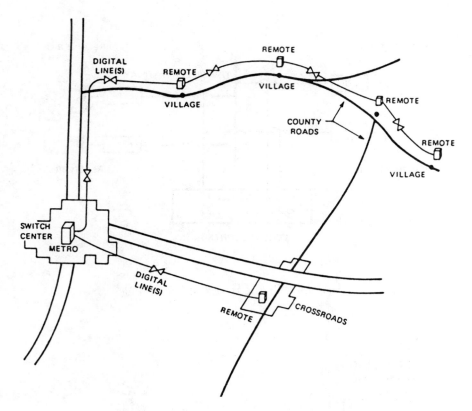

Fig. 26 Remote Switching

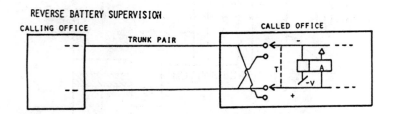

Fig. 27 Reverse Battery Supervision

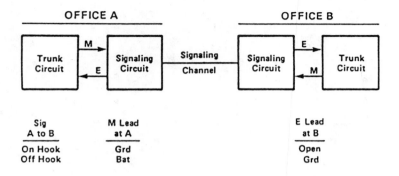

Fig. 28 E & M Lead Signaling

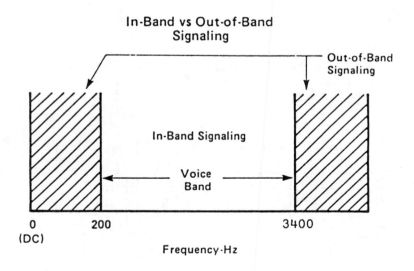

Fig. 29 In-Band vs Out-of-Band Signaling

FREQUENCY	ASSIGNED VALUE	1	2	3	4	5	6	7	8	9	0	KP	ST
700	0	•	•		•			•					•
900	1	•		•		•			•				
1100	2		•	•			•		•		•		
1300	4				•	•	•			•	•		
1500	7							•	•	•	•	•	
1700	10											•	•

COIN COLL.   COIN RET   RING BACK

Fig. 30 Multifrequency Signaling

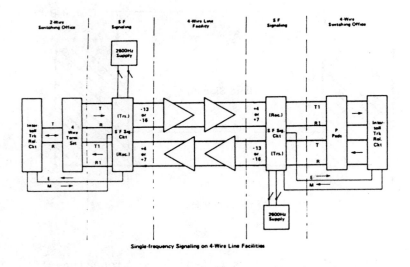

Single-frequency Signaling on 4-Wire Line Facilities

Fig. 31 Single Frequency Signaling on 4 Wire
Line Facilities

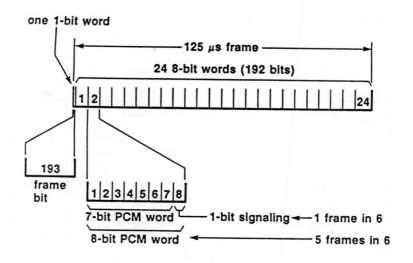

Fig. 32   Frame Format

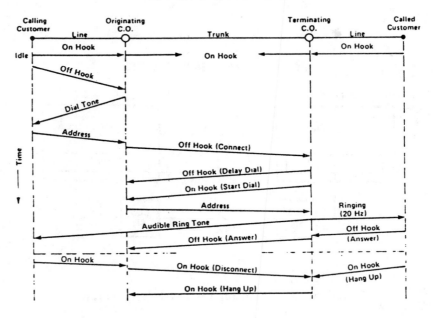

Signaling on a Typical Connection

Fig. 33   Signaling on a Typical Connection

946

PER-TRUNK SIGNALING

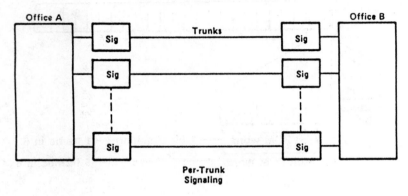

Fig. 34   Per-Trunk Signaling

COMMON CHANNEL SIGNALING

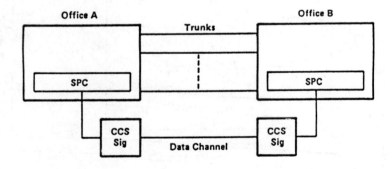

Fig. 35   Common Channel Signaling

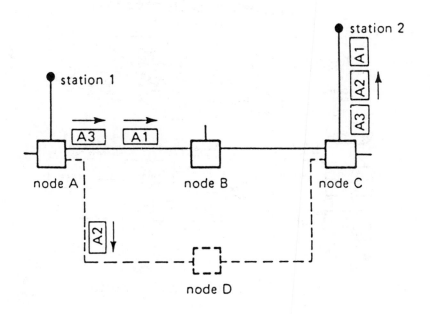

Fig. 36 Packet Network Nodal Structure

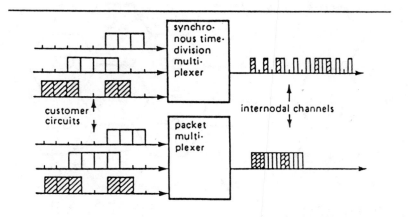

Fig. 37 Internodal Channel Utilization

948

Network architecture

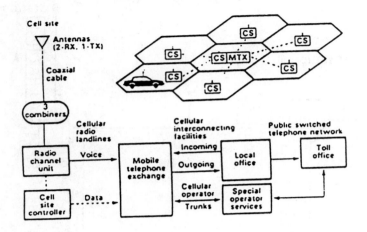

Fig. 38 Cellular Mobile Radio

Seven cell cluster

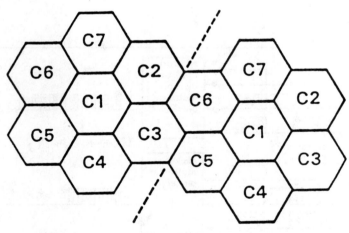

C-1:FREQ. A,B,C.
C-2: FREQ. D,E.

C-1:FREQ. A,B,C.
C-2:FREQ. D,E.

Fig. 39 Frequency Separation in Adjacent
Clusters

CUSTOMER ACCESS AND CONTROL

Evan B. Richards, Chairperson

General Manager-Network Operations

Illinois Bell

225 West Randolph
Chicago, Illinois 60606

ABSTRACT

Evolving customer access and control
technology and end user needs present the
telecommunications industry with many
challenges and opportunities. This
seminar examines the issues and
requirements introduced by customer access
and control from the user, RBOC and
manufacturer's perspectives. Emerging
technology is described, specific
applications are highlighted, and the
challenges and opportunities are explored.

L. Bernstein -- AT&T Bell Laboratories

E. Gillespie -- Ameritech Services

I. Kerr -- Bell Northern Research

P. Krause -- McDonald's Corporation

R. Williams -- IBM
ISDN IMPACT ON CUSTOMER ACCESS AND CONTROL

Patrick Krause
Director of Telecommunications

McDonald's Corporation
McDonald's Plaza
Oakbrook, Illinois 60521

ABSTRACT

Network Control and Management (NCM) in a
multi-vendor, mutli-application
environment is becoming increasingly
difficult. Integrated Service Digital
Network (ISDN) offers a promising
alternative for network transport and
management in this kind of environment.
The ability for the customer and service
providers to access and control their
networks will be enhanced as ISDN's
potential is developed and realized.

INTRODUCTION

Networking has become an increasingly
complex area as new technologies emerge,
disparate standards proliferate, required
levels of integration increase,
applications multiply, and number of
elements/nodes/components rise
exponentially. It is useful to think
about networking in terms of a three
dimensional model with each axis being an
important aspect of the networking issue
(refer to Figure 1). These three
dimensions are intimately related and
intertwined with equal importance. Any
effective network must consider all three
of these extremely important aspects and
properly factor them into the network
design. The TRANSPORT/CONNECTIVITY axis
(which primarily deals with the lower four
layers of the OSI model) represents basic
connectivity over various network
topologies such as Wide Area Networks
(WAN), Local Area Networks (LAN), and
Metropolitan Area Networks (MAN) for any
information type (i.e., voice, data,
message, and image). The COOPERATIVE
PROCESSING axis (which primarily deals
with the upper three layers of the OSI
model) represents inter-system operability
where processing and data are shared
across multiple network nodes/elements
supporting distributed applications or
integrated systems. This paper's primary
focus will be on the NETWORK CONTROL axis
which represents those capabilities which
allow the network manager to support and
maintain the network connectivity and
interoperability provided in the other two
dimensions. Obviously, any network which
ignores or overlooks any one of these
three dimensions will be self-limiting.

Within any network there are many
different elements, components, and
sub-systems which must be monitored in
order to provide for proper NCM. Refer to
Figure 2 for a picture of some of the
commonly deployed generic network
components. NCM in terms of this generic
diagram is a very complex and
multifaceted issue, too large to be dealt
with in a single paper. While most of the
elements shown overlap to some degree with
each other and most certainly with any
network control capability, this paper
will focus on ISDN based networks and
particularly the Customer Premise
Equipment (CPE) portion. McDonald's ISDN
trial experience and plans for transition
to commercial service will serve as the
basis for the treatment of NCM in a pure
ISDN environment.

ISDN BASED NETWORK CONTROL AND MANAGEMENT

There are several key considerations in an
ISDN based network which have a direct
bearing on NCM. First, ISDN offers the
potential of providing an information
outlet at every desktop or end-point in
the network. This implies that the
network may deliver any combination of
voice, data, message, and image formation
and that any NCM capability must deal with
multiple information types. Secondly,
ISDN will be synonymous with a
multi-vendor environment since its status
as an emerging standard should promote

non-proprietary solutions. This implies that any NCM capability must deal with multiple equipment types, models and manufacturers. Thirdly, ISDN implementations will result in more intelligence at the desktop or end-point in the network because of the sophisticated nature of ISDN compatible equipment relative to analog predecessors. This implies that any NCM capability must deal with multiple levels of protocol layers similar to the OSI model. Network control information to/from all layers should be relayed to the NCM system in order to allow proper management of the network. Finally, ISDN, within a single network architecture, offers many of the benefits normally associated with distinct network topologies such as WANS, MANS, and LANS. This implies that any NCM capability may treat the ISDN compatible portions of the network as a single fabric versus interconnected subnetworks. Refer to Figure 3 for an illustration of these concepts. These implications are a formidable set of requirements for any NCM and beyond the capability of most commercially available NCM alternatives. Fortunately, within the ISDN architecture there exists a mechanism for addressing these issues from a technical standpoint using the out-of-band signaling channel referred to as the "D" channel. The ISDN standards bodies have set the foundation for NCM within the "D" channel using Q931 messaging capabilities between CPE, switches, and other network components. NCM functions can be performed over this channel concurrent with normal information transmission without disruption. Once standard message formats have been agreed upon, this channel will offer a very powerful tool to customers and service providers and allow them to determine the "health" of their network and manage it more effectively.

One of the most important components of any network (but especially within the ISDN network) is the CPE. ISDN CPE could be any equipment on the customer premise which attaches to the network and provides any combination of voice, data, message, or image service. For conceptual purposes any CPE consists of four major interfaces as shown in Figure 4, all of which must be monitored and managed by the NCM system. In general, each of the ISDN compatible CPE will represent some form of call processing, either self-contained or on behalf of a Data Terminal Equipment (DTE) client (e.g., host, controller, PBX, phone, terminal, facsimile, etc.). As mentioned previously, the key to NCM capability is the out-of-band "D" channel inherent within all ISDN compatible equipment. Centralized NCM capability could be derived from this channel allowing a network manager to intelligently message with all ISDN CPE in order to perform traditional categories of NCM functions as listed below:

1. FAULT DETECTION AND CORRECTION
2. PERFORMANCE MONITORING AND ANALYSIS
3. CONFIGURATION MANAGEMENT
4. ACCOUNTING SERVICES
5. OPERATIONS/SECURITY MANAGEMENT

An illustration of how NCM might be accomplished in an ISDN environment after standards have been developed and implemented is shown in Figure 5. This matrix lists many desirable NCM functions on the vertical axis and the four major CPE interfaces on the horizontal axis. Sample entries in the matrix for an ISDN network of CPE providing voice and data services show the kind of information which could be provided either by the CPE itself or by the ISDN switch on behalf of the CPE. While this matrix is merely an example, it shows that a very rich array of NCM functions/features could be implemented using the native intelligence contained in the ISDN CPE and the powerful out-of-band messaging capability available via the "D" channel.

CONCLUSION

ISDN will enhance the customers ability to access and control the network for three basic reasons. First, ISDN will allow customers to consolidate many of their existing diverse local area and wide area networks and avoid the proliferation of multiple, incompatible networks. Fewer networks should result in more effective network management and administration. Secondly, ISDN is an emerging international standard with fairly well-defined protocols and interfaces. This will allow customers to deploy the best price-performance equipment/services from a wide array of suppliers and still maintain uniform access to the network. Thirdly, ISDN offers a unique out-of-band messaging capability with the "D" channel and Q931 signaling protocols which will facilitate implementations of increasingly sophisticated NCM capability. While NCM in an ISDN world will require much standards work and technical development, its importance to successful networking and widespread deployment of ISDN is doubted by none. The acceptance of NCM as one of the highest priorities for the ISDN industry has secured the commitment necessary for realization.

THREE DIMENSIONS OF NETWORKING
FIGURE 1

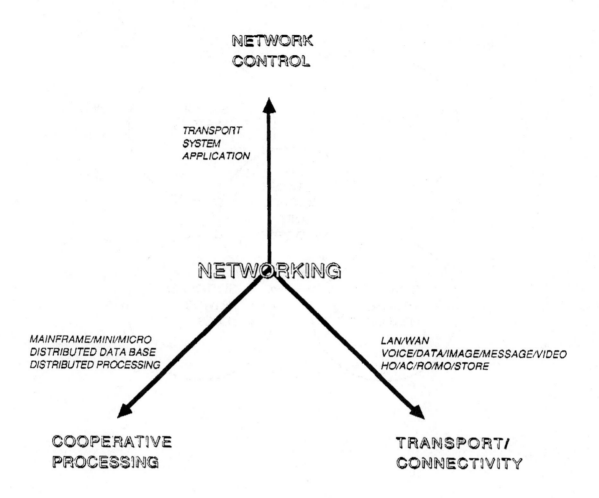

GENERIC NETWORK ELEMENTS/COMPONENTS
FIGURE 2

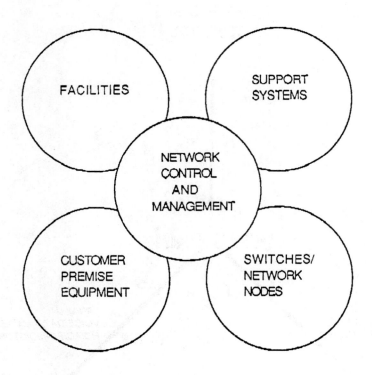

ISDN NCM IMPLICATIONS
FIGURE 3

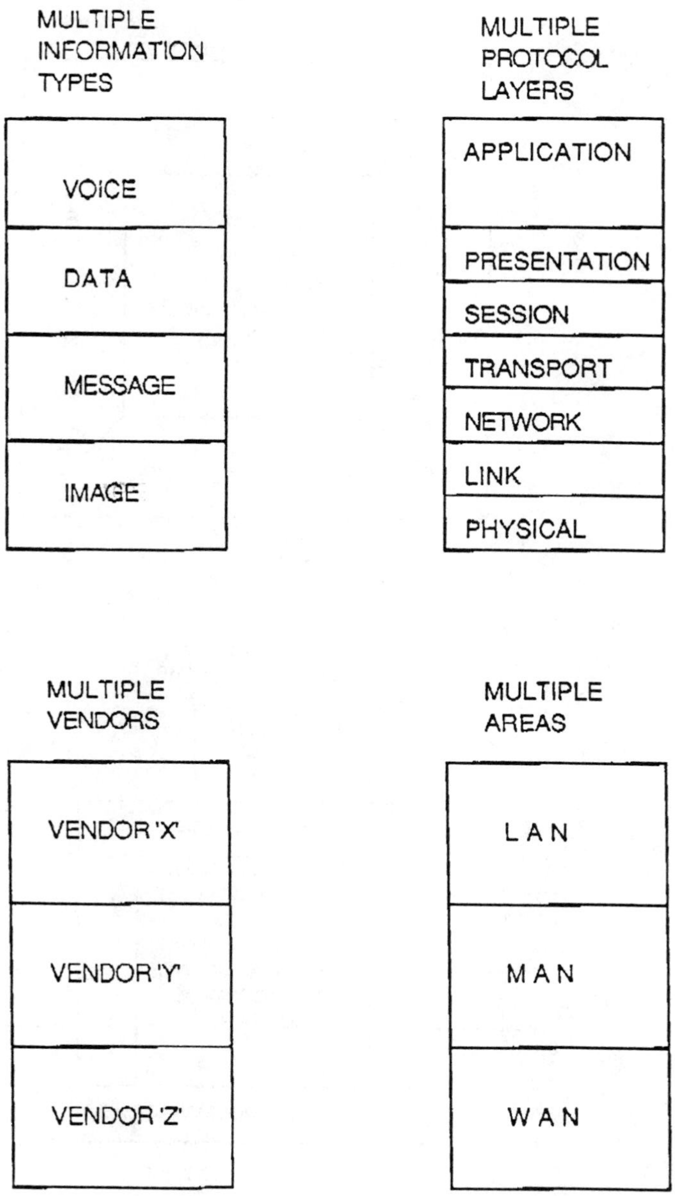

MULTIPLE
INFORMATION
TYPES

VOICE
DATA
MESSAGE
IMAGE

MULTIPLE
PROTOCOL
LAYERS

APPLICATION
PRESENTATION
SESSION
TRANSPORT
NETWORK
LINK
PHYSICAL

MULTIPLE
VENDORS

VENDOR 'X'
VENDOR 'Y'
VENDOR 'Z'

MULTIPLE
AREAS

L A N
M A N
W A N

954

ISDN CPE INTERFACES
FIGURE 4

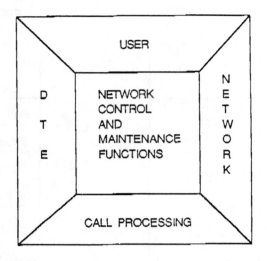

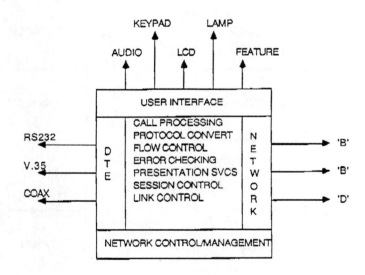

INTERFACE / NCC FUNCTION	USER	DTE	NETWORK	CALL PROCESSING
TRACE	LAST 3 BUTTONS ENTERED LAST 3 LAMPS ACTIVATED/DEACT. PREVIOUS LCD DISPLAY	LAST STATE OF RS232 INTERFACE	LAST 3 Q.931 MSG TO/FROM NET LAST X.25 PACKET TO/FROM NET	LAST STATE OF VOICE CALL (B1/B2) LAST STATE OF DATA CALL (B1/B2/D)
STATUS	CURRENT LCD DISPLAY CURRENT LAMP/LED ON/OFF	CURRENT STATE OF RS232 INTERFACE FLOW CONTROL CONDITION (ON/OFF) LOOPBACK CONDITION (ON/OFF)	CONDITION OF LEVEL 1 (T) CONDITION OF LEVEL 2 (LAPD/B)	CURRENT STATE OF VOICE CALL CURRENT STATE OF CS/PS DATA CALL CALL APPEARANCE STATUS
CONFIG INFO	TEMPLATE OF BUTTON SETUP CPE SET TYPE/MODEL	INTERFACE TYPE (RS232, V.35, COAX) DTE OPTIONS (PARITY, RS232, ETC.)	DSL PROFILE OF B1, B2, AND D COPY OF X.3 PROFILE	FIRMWARE VERSION LEVEL SOFTWARE VERSION LEVEL
TIME STAMP (MIN/MAX/AVG)	FEATURE RESPONSE TIME AP RESPONSE TIME	TURNAROUND TIME BETWEEN SEND AND RECEIVE AND SEND	GENERATE NETWORK TRANSIT TIME MESSAGE TO NCC	CALL SETUP TIME (CS+PS)
TRAFFIC STATS	BUTTON/FEATURE FREQUENCY	# OF BYTES XMIT/RCV	# OF PACKETS XMIT/RCV	# OF CS CALLS IN/OUT # OF PS CALLS IN/OUT
CALL ROUTING	SPEED DIAL NUMBERS CALL FORWARDING ACTIVATED	N/A	CALLED NUMBER OF ANY ACTIVE CS/PS CALLS	CALLING NUMBER OF ANY ACTIVE CS/PS CALLS
ERROR LOG	N/A	UNEXPECTED CONTROL LEAD CHANGE PARITY ERROR COUNT STREAMING DATA CONDITION	LEVEL 2 AND 3 TIMEOUTS, RNR, REJECTS, RETRANSMISSIONS, AND SEQUENCE ERROR COUNTS	UNSUCCESSFUL CALL ATTEMPTS
EVENT REPORT *				
RECONFIG				
RESET	CLEAR ALL DISPLAYS AND LAMPS CLEAR PROGRAM MODE	CYCLE STATE OF CONTROL LEADS	MASTER CLEAR ALL LOGIC, BUFFERS, SEQUENCE NUMBERS, ETC.	DISCONNECT ALL CALLS, RESET TO IDLE CONDITION, AND MASTER CLEAR ALL LOGIC
THRESHOLD				
ENABLE				
TEST	TURN ON ALL LAMPS/LEDS TEST/DISPLAY ALL KEYSTROKES	LOOPBACK RS232 TO DTE OR TO NET	LOOPBACK EACH B CS TO DTE OR TO NETWORK	TEST ALL CPUS AND MEMORY

FIGURE 5

956

AMERITECH'S VIEW

Eileen A. Gillespie
Director-Provisioning Planning
Operations Services

Ameritech Services
1900 East Golf Road, Floor 2
Schaumburg, Illinois 60173

ABSTRACT

Customer Network Management has presented
a "Challenge" to the Telecommunication
Industry. This seminar will focus on 1)
Ameritech's approach to the "challenge",
2) changes Ameritech views as needed in
telecommunications, enabling a more
flexible, automated, and cost effective
means of Network Management and 3)
Ameritech's architecture for Customer
Access and Control.

TECHNOLOGIES AND APPLICATIONS

R. Williams
Senior Programmer
CPD Division

IBM
P.O. Box 12195, RTP 12195
F77/062-3
Durham, North Carolina 27707

ABSTRACT

Network management of private and hybrid
networks embraces all the functions of
telco operations, administration and
maintenance. This session examines the
technologies and applications available to
the private network operator in the
future, and the impact of these
technologies and applications on Network
management and expense reduction and
enhanced customer control.

NETWORK MANAGEMENT DIRECTIONS

"CUSTOMER ACCESS AND CONTROL"

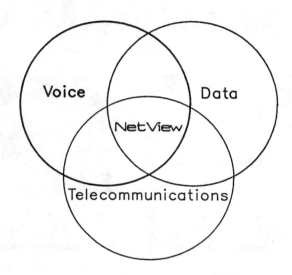

INFORMATION SYSTEM ENVIRONMENT

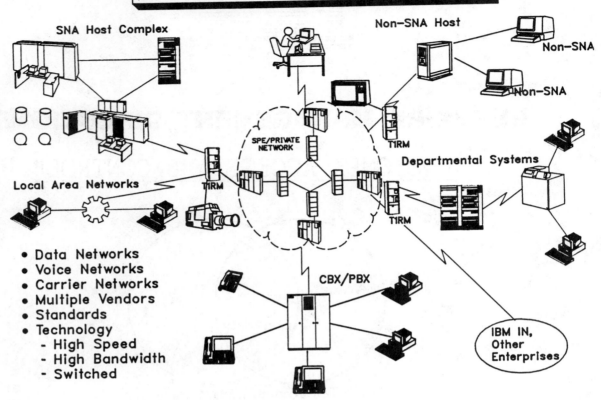

SNA Host Complex

Non-SNA Host

Non-SNA

Non-SNA

SPE/PRIVATE NETWORK

T1RM

Departmental Systems

Local Area Networks

T1RM

T1RM

- Data Networks
- Voice Networks
- Carrier Networks
- Multiple Vendors
- Standards
- Technology
  - High Speed
  - High Bandwidth
  - Switched

CBX/PBX

IBM IN, Other Enterprises

NETWORK OPERATION   TODAY AND TOMORROW

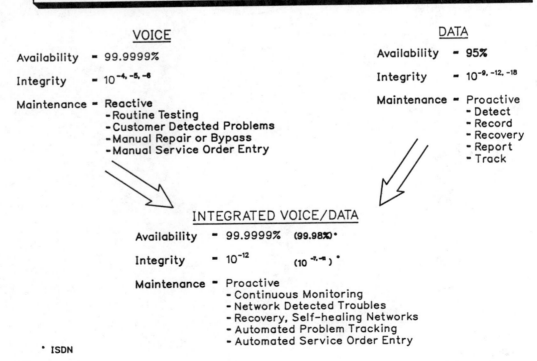

VOICE

Availability = 99.9999%

Integrity = $10^{-4, -5, -6}$

Maintenance = Reactive
- Routine Testing
- Customer Detected Problems
- Manual Repair or Bypass
- Manual Service Order Entry

DATA

Availability = 95%

Integrity = $10^{-9, -12, -18}$

Maintenance = Proactive
- Detect
- Record
- Recovery
- Report
- Track

INTEGRATED VOICE/DATA

Availability = 99.9999%   (99.98%) *

Integrity = 10^{-12} $(10^{-7, -8})$ *

Maintenance = Proactive
- Continuous Monitoring
- Network Detected Troubles
- Recovery, Self-healing Networks
- Automated Problem Tracking
- Automated Service Order Entry

* ISDN

959

NETWORK MANAGEMENT SYSTEM CONCEPT

"COHESIVE/COMPREHENSIVE APPROACH"

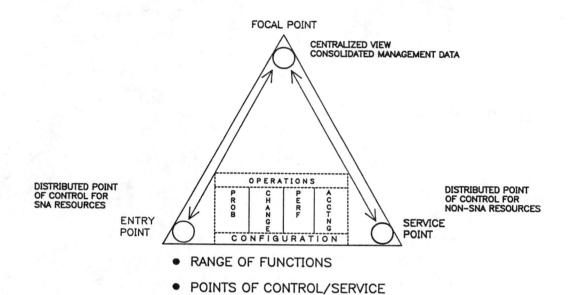

- RANGE OF FUNCTIONS
- POINTS OF CONTROL/SERVICE

NETWORK MANAGEMENT ARCHITECTURES

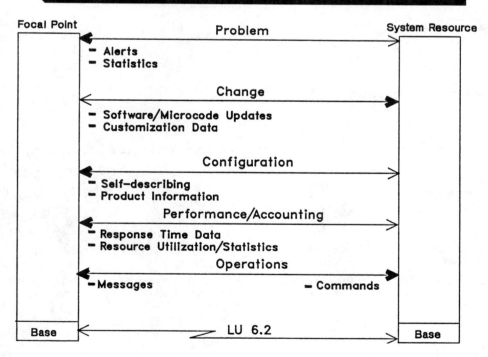

ENTERPRISE-WIDE NETWORK MANAGEMENT DIRECTION

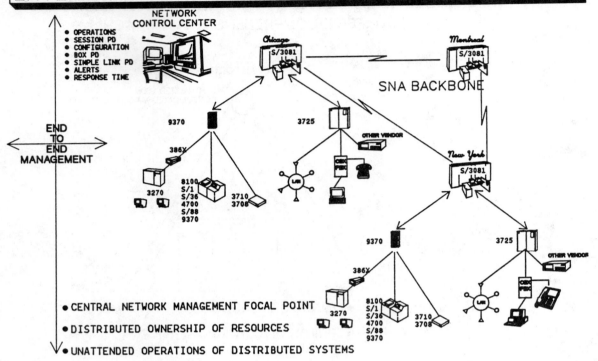

- OPERATIONS
- SESSION PD
- CONFIGURATION
- BOX PD
- SIMPLE LINK PD
- ALERTS
- RESPONSE TIME

NETWORK CONTROL CENTER

END TO END MANAGEMENT

SNA BACKBONE

- CENTRAL NETWORK MANAGEMENT FOCAL POINT
- DISTRIBUTED OWNERSHIP OF RESOURCES
- UNATTENDED OPERATIONS OF DISTRIBUTED SYSTEMS

NON-SNA NETWORK--PROBLEM MANAGEMENT

FUNCTION
- Identification
- Trend Analysis
- Reporting
- Tracking
- Notification
- Automated Response

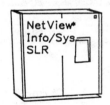

NetView*
Info/Sys
SLR

NetView/PC*

Database Management	Operator Support	Customization Capabilities	Network Interface
• Errors • Trends • Performance • Logging	• Presentation Services	• Tailor to Network • Automated Responses • Specialized Notification • Procedures	• Architecture • Open Interface • Generic Alerts

*Trademark of the IBM Corporation

961

TOTAL SYSTEM MANAGEMENT

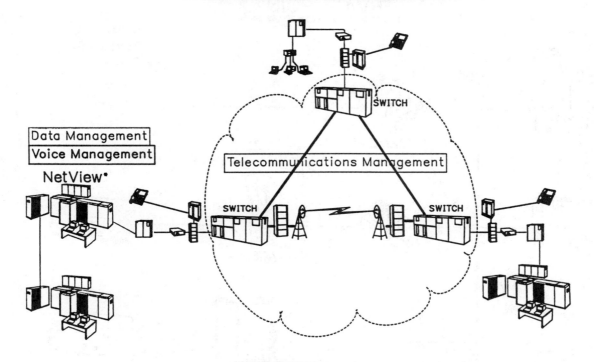

Data Management
Voice Management

NetView*

Telecommunications Management

SWITCH

SWITCH

SWITCH

*Trademark of the IBM Corp.

SNA NETWORK MANAGEMENT

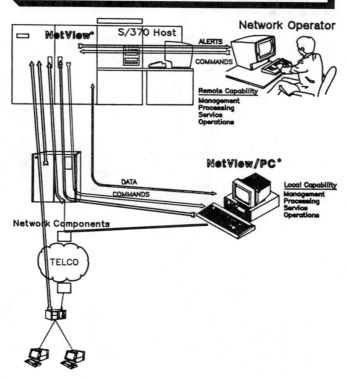

NetView*   S/370 Host

Network Operator

ALERTS

COMMANDS

Remote Capability
Management
Processing
Service
Operations

NetView/PC*

DATA

COMMANDS

Local Capability
Management
Processing
Service
Operations

Network Components

TELCO

*Trademark of the IBM Corporation

962

SERVICE POINT

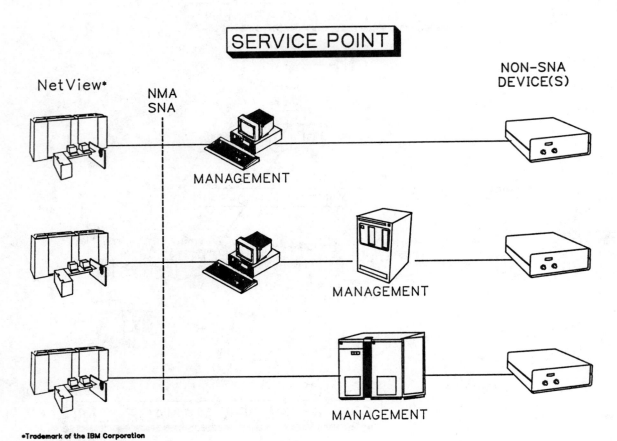

NON-SNA
DEVICE(S)

NetView*

NMA
SNA

MANAGEMENT

MANAGEMENT

MANAGEMENT

*Trademark of the IBM Corporation

963

NetView/PC* VENDOR APPLICATIONS

Vendor	P/I	Application
Applied System Technologies	P	"C" Language Application Building
Avanti Communications Corporation	P	T1, CSU/DSU
BBN Communications Corporation	P	T1
Bytex Corporation	P	Matrix Switch
Carl Vanderbeek & Associates	P	Generic Network Management Gateway
Cincinnati Bell (CMS, Inc.)	I	PBXs
Codex	I	Modems
Computer Communications, Inc.	P	T1
Cylix	P	Satellite-based Network
DataSwitch (T-Bar)	P	Matrix Switch, Performance Monitor
Datatel, Inc.	P	T1, DDS
DCA/Cohesive	I	T1-SYS9000
Diederich & Associates	P	Network Mgmt. Application Aid
Digital Commun. Products, Inc.	P	Automatic Remote Monitoring System
DMW Group, Inc.	P	PBX
Doelz Networks, Inc.	P	Network Manager, Resource Manager
Dynatech Communications, Inc.	I	T1, CSU/DSU
Dynatech Data Systems	P	Matrix Switch, T1, Performance Monitor
Emcom Corporation	I	Network Performance Monitor
General DataComm, Inc.	P	T1, Stat Mux, CSU/DSU, Modem, LAN
Granger Associates(DSC)	P	T1
Harris Farinon	P	Fiber Optic/Microwave Networks
INFINITE	I	Response Time Monitor
Infotron Systems	P	T1, Stat Mux
KAPTRONIX	I	Application Development
MCI	P	DDN, VNET
MICOM Digital	I	T1
MICOM Systems, Inc.	I	Network Manager
Network Equipment Technologies	P	T1
Newbridge Networks Corporation	P	T1
Octocom Systems, Inc.	P	Modems
OMNEE INTERNATIONAL	I	T1, PBX, STAT MUX
Paradyne	P	Modems, T1, CSU, DSU, STAT MUX
Racal-Milgo	P	CMS-Modems, Mux, DSU
Racal-Vadic	P	Management System, Modems
ROCKWELL International	I	T1, Switching Protocol Converter
StrataCom, Inc.	P	T1
Telenex Corporation	I	Matrix Switch
Teleprocessing Products, Inc.	P	DSU, CSU
TELINDUS	P	Modems
TelWatch	P	Network Monitoring System
Timeplex	P	T1
TSB INTERNATIONAL	I	PBX Alerts, Traffic Data
TYMNET	I	X.25 Packet Switched Network
Ungermann-Bass, Inc.	P	LAN
Vector Software, Inc.	P	PBX

*Trademark of the IBM Corporation

P = Product
I = Intend to provide product

Physical Network Management

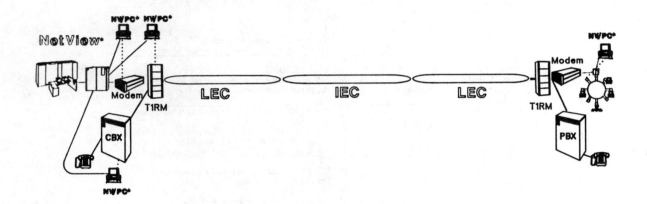

MCI – DDN Transmission Facility Monitoring

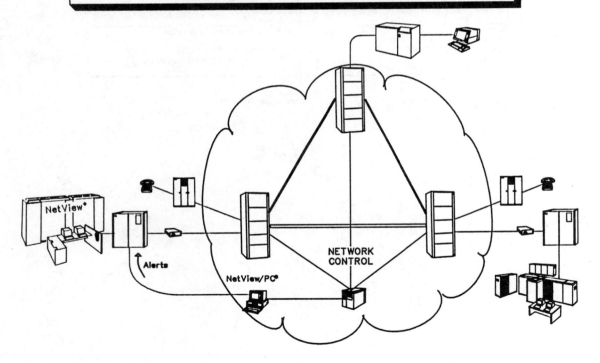

MCI – Switch VNET Alarm Reporting

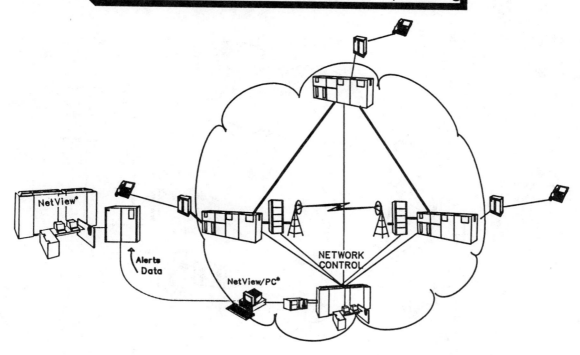

NetView*

Alerts
Data

NetView/PC*

NETWORK
CONTROL

•Trademark of the IBM Corp.

SPE GATEWAY

POSSIBLE FUNCTIONS

* ALERTS
* SMDR COLLECTION
* TROUBLE TICKETS
* TRAFFIC REPORTS
* BANDWIDTH ON DEMAND
* BANDWIDTH ALLOCATION
* DYNAMIC RECONFIGURATION
* MOVES AND CHANGES

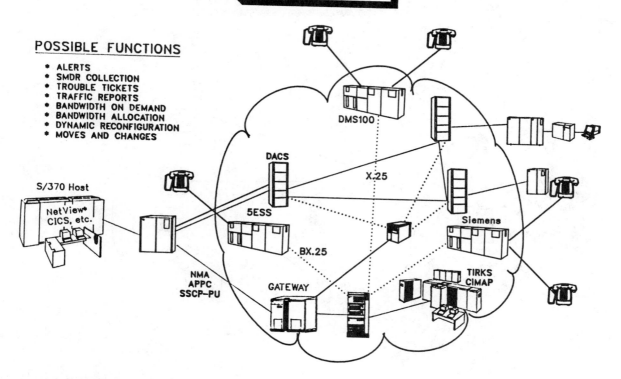

DMS100

DACS

X.25

S/370 Host

NetView*
CICS, etc.

5ESS

Siemens

BX.25

NMA
APPC
SSCP–PU

GATEWAY

TIRKS
CIMAP

•Trademark of the IBM Corporation

966

BANDWIDTH ALLOCATION

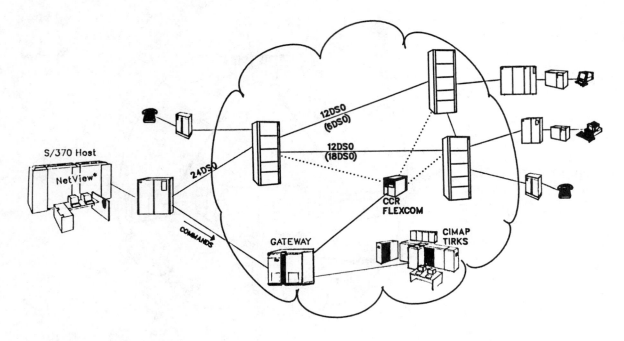

•Trademark of the IBM Corporation

TROUBLE TICKETS

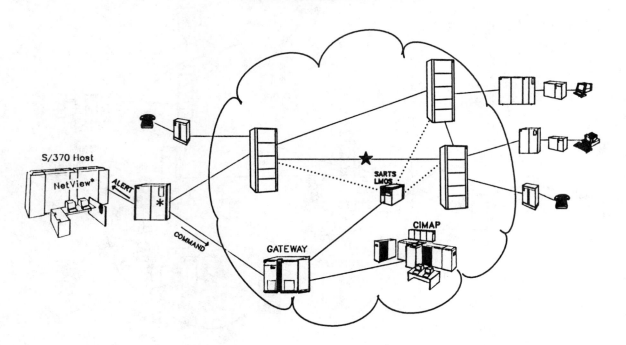

•Trademark of the IBM Corporation

967

MOVES AND CHANGES

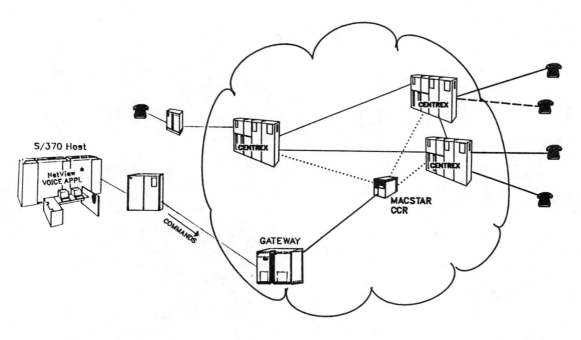

•Trademark of the IBM Corporation

BANDWIDTH ON DEMAND

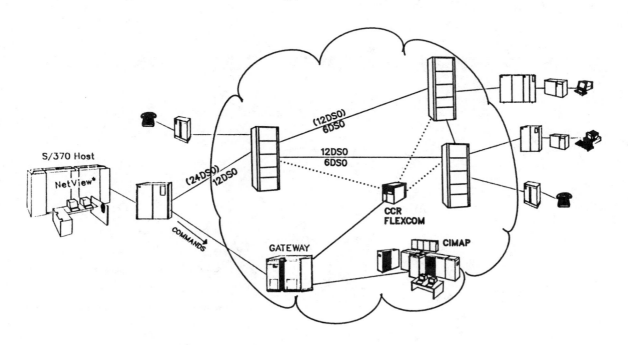

•Trademark of the IBM Corporation

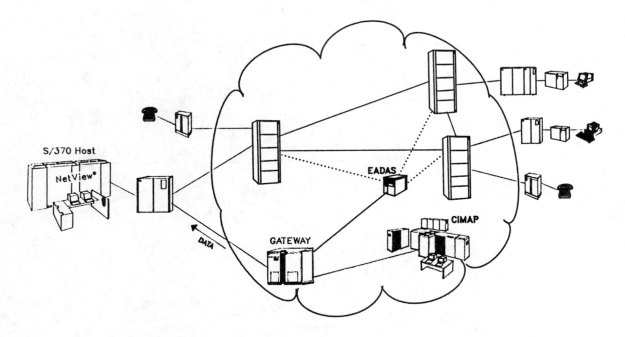

•Trademark of the IBM Corporation

Summary

NETWORK MANAGEMENT DIRECTIONS

"TOTAL NETWORK MANAGEMENT"

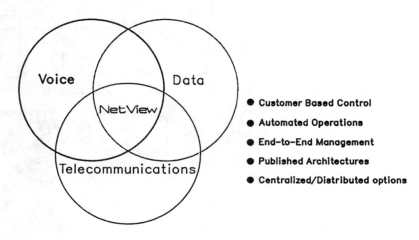

- Customer Based Control
- Automated Operations
- End-to-End Management
- Published Architectures
- Centralized/Distributed options

•Trademark of the IBM Corporation

969

CUSTOMER NETWORK MANAGEMENT OF NETWORK BASED BUSINESS SERVICES

Ian H. Kerr
Manager, Business Network Management
Development
Network Products Group

Bell Northern Research
P.O. Box 3511, Station "C"
Ottawa, Ontario K1Y 4H7
Canada

ABSTRACT

Meridian Network Control(NMC) provides businesses with the ability to manage their Centrex and ISDN based network services. The flexible, open NMC architecture supports a wide range of integrated network management applications permitting businesses and service providers to tailor configurations to meet their requirements.

Introduction - Setting the Stage

Northern Telecom's Business Network Management (BNM) program, is oriented towards public network business services and their corporate users. The management capabilities being demanded for the public environment are the same as are needed by private network services. The challenge in the public arena is to develop functionality that addresses the shared nature of the public network in an efficient, secure manner while providing the functionality needed by the end-customers. In response to this need, BNM was introduced to provide Centrex communication management functionality to corporate Centrex customers.

In general, a corporation's ability to effectively manage its network has been hampered by the nature of the network itself. Typically, these networks are hybrid in nature, that is: made up of leased and dedicated, public and private components; and, in many cases, these components have been purchased from many different vendors and operate with a great variety of interfaces. In the past, corporations have managed the dedicated elements of their networks with a variety of systems operating in isolation, while the leased elements of the hybrid corporate network were managed by the telephone companies. Corporations were, therefore, only able to gain partial control of their total network, and only by deploying a variety of standalone network management systems.

Focus on Public Network Services

Business service offered from the public network have undergone significant changes over the past decade. Individual telephone companies are now looking for opportunities to introduce new and innovative network based services aimed directly at the business market.

While not a new service, the Centrex resurgence, beginning in 1984, can be directly attributed to the desire of the Telcos to compete in the sophisticated business communications service market, beyond providing simple public network access and intra-LATA facilities. The ability of Telcos to provide the required level of business features is strengthened by the availability and excellence of the Northern Telecom Meridian Digital Centrex features on the DMS-100 Central Office switch. Evolution within the Centrex area has been rapid. At ISS '87 in Phoenix, Mountain Bell announced the successful introduction as the first working in-service ISDN Basic Rate Access service utilizing the Northern Telecom DMS-100 with Meridian ISDN Centrex services. Area Wide Centrex and Private Virtual Networking will be trialed and introduced in 1988.

New network capabilities such as these offer the business customer more efficient means of communication and increasing overall corporate productivity from the public network services. From the outset, the ability of the customer to control and manage these new capabilities has been a priority system feature. As these services are introduced into the network, end-customer control of them will be incorporated into Northern Telecom's BNM system.

In discussing businesses managing and controlling their own communications networks, this paper will first define the market in terms of network management requirements, focusing on general market characteristics and the implications of end-user network management in the public network. Then the major network management functions and how BNR and Northern Telecom deliver these capabilities will be reviewed.

Network Management Functions

A model of the customer network management functional environment has been developed (see Figure 1) to illustrate the range of responsibilities that must be addressed when corporations are performing comprehensive network management. The four main areas of Planning, Traffic & Application Management, Trouble Management and Administration have been broken down into twelve generic applications with each application again being composed of many individual features or services.

Northern Telecom's BNM system provides the means for telecommunication system managers to operate and control their communication systems as a network. The BNM system was initially introduced in

1985 and provided Centrex customers the basic network traffic and surveillance capabilities. Since that time the BNM system has continued to evolve and grow and now addresses most network management applications for Centrex.

Dynamic Change Management refers to the ability of the business' communications manager to make changes to their communications systems without the intervention of the system vendor. As an example, BNM supports a feature called Station Administration that allows an end-customer to make station moves and feature changes on Meridian Digital Centrex lines directly. The BNM system provides the security, validation rules and all the other required features through a convenient, easy-to-use Man Machine interface. Changes are implemented by the system without any direct involvement by the telco operational personnel. The Station Administration capabilities given to each customer are controlled by the telco according to their service definitions and tariffs. For example, if a customer has purchased a set quantity of Speed Call lists, this value is set by the telco in a limits table. The customer can then rearrange the feature as they wish but cannot add more than the purchased number.

Another aspect of Dynamic Change Management supported by BNM is Network Administration. The end-customer can select from a number of network routing plans set up on the BNM system in consultation with the Telco. The selected plan is then implemented automatically on the switch routing tables.

Traffic Surveillance is an important function for Corporations which spend a lot on their trunk networks, and depend on them for the success of their daily business operations. BNM has a comprehensive set of surveillance capabilities using traffic data extracted directly from the network. This data can be thresholded to indicate trouble or overload status, and the results displayed graphically on a network map. In addition, a variety of reports and analyses are produced in character or graphic form.

Trouble Surveillance is provided by the thresholding of traffic data and by the direct collection of test and exception data from the switches. Trouble Isolation is also supported by the on-line analysis of Station Message Detail Records (Call Tracking), which allows the Trunk groups and members involved in a particular problem call to be identified.

It would be a mistake, however, for Northern Telecom and BNR to attempt to develop comprehensive features and capabilities in all the twelve generic application areas. In some areas there are many already existing sophisticated telemanagement products providing a useful and functional service. In these cases the BNM application will provide a standard interface to existing telemanagement products.

An example of this type of functionality is Cost Allocation. BNM has implemented this particular function in a manner that provides both the end-customer and the Telco the most flexibility. BNM provides the real-time collection of Station Message Detail Records (SMDR, also called Call Detail Records or CDR) from the network. SMDR records are partitioned based on customer ownership and recorded in the individual customer database. BNM enables third-party cost allocation and billing applications to process call detail records by delivery of call detail records to customer premises. A variety of communications protocols, or magnetic tape, can be used so that the customer can run cost allocation applications in their own downstream processing computers.

Defining the Market

The priorities and emphasis associated with customer network management, change dramatically depending upon the type and size of customer. For example, (see Figure 2) the smaller single location voice customer may want to monitor and control communication expenses and abuse; the larger single site business may also have a dynamic requirement to move or relocate personnel within the business complex making station administration (Moves and Changes) a mandatory communications management tool. At the top end of the business spectrum, corporations with large national or international communications networks usually require access to the tools from all the twelve Network Management Functions.

Requirements Changing with User Size

The BNM system has been developed using Northern Telecom's Dynamic Network Controller (DNC) as the base technology. To date there have been three versions introduced, the Telco based DNC-500 and DNC-50, and the DNC-100 end-customer located vehicle. (The DNC-50 is similar to a DNC-500 configured for SMDR collection and delivery only.) With this configuration the BNM-500 (DNC-500 with BNM applications software) provides a secure interface into the Network Elements; partitions the data by customers; secures communications interfaces for end-customer access; generates network performance and other reports; etc. The BNM-100 (a DNC-100 with BNM applications software) provides the

971

corporate customer with the ability to interface and process information from multiple BNM-500 systems, potentially from more than one telco, on their premises. The architecture of BNM systems is illustrated in Figure 3. Through the networking capabilities and modular design of the DNC, a wide range of functional capabilities and network sizes can be accommodated. These range from a single-switch, SMDR-only application, to a nation-wide multi-carrier, comprehensive network management capability.

Conclusion

The importance of Corporate Network Management functions has been emphasized for Centrex customers. In particular, the need for a wide variety of capabilities as well as interfaces to end-customer or third-party systems has been explained. In response to these requirements, the capabilities of Northern Telecom's BNM system for customers of Meridian Digital Centrex has been described.

Figure 1. Network Management Function

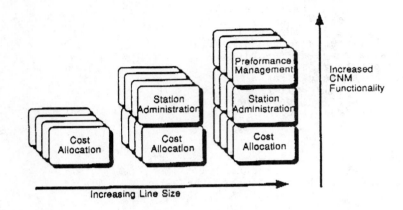

Figure 2. Examples of CUSTOMER NETWORK MANAGEMENT

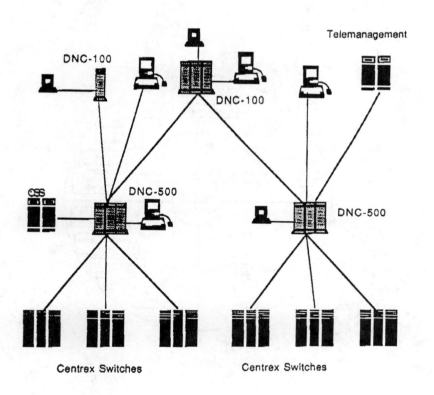

Figure 3. BNM System Architecture

EXPERIENCE WITH NETWORK MANAGEMENT SYSTEMS IN THE LOCAL EXCHANGE

L. Bernstein
Executive Director
Switching & Network Operations

AT&T Bell Laboratories
480 Red Hill Road, Room 2N206
Red Hill, New Jersey 07748-3072

ABSTRACT

Customers of local exchange carriers (LECs) Centrex demand control functions. Control is provided by permitting customers to access embedded LEC Operations Systems (OSs). These OSs permit LECs to administer existing networks and network elements (for example, switches or transmission equipment).

A unified secure access to a subset of the functions available in those OSs must be able to be determined by an LEC. This approach is a first step toward a unified network management architecture (UNMA) with which the LEC in conjunction with premises products and interlata control systems, may offer telecommunications consumers end-to-end network management. Underpinning this approach is a flexible platform based on emerging international standards on which the LEC can interconnect a variety of OSs.

This paper will review recent experience with one such system, the NetPartner Network Management System, and describe the benefits to the Local Exchange Carrier and the telecommunications consumer.

OVERVIEW

Many local exchange carrier customers today demand more information about and control over their communications systems. They need end-to-end management of their entire networks, regardless of whether they reach into a PBX, central office with centrex, long distance carrier, logical network within host computers, or even a private network. Customers also want access to Operations, Administration, and Maintenance (OA&M) capabilities that once were solely within the purview of the service provider. AT&T's new NetPartner[TM] Network Management System (NMS) answers most of these needs for local exchange customers. (Examples of customers are nationwide retailers and state governments.)

In September 1987, AT&T gave integrated network management a boost with its Unified Network Management Architecture (UNMA)[1]. UNMA integrates management systems that now control separate pieces of a network. Through UNMA, AT&T provides a blueprint for end-to-end management and control of voice and data networks, customer premises equipment, the local exchange carrier network, and AT&T interexchange services.

For customers seeking the benefits of UNMA, NetPartner NMS meets network management and control needs. It gives customers the advantages of local telephone company central office switching without forcing them to maintain an entire telecommunications system.

NetPartner NMS gives customers control of network elements through secure access to existing operations systems that are embedded within the phone company's manner of doing business. These operations systems were originally installed to enable phone companies to administer existing networks and their elements, such as switches and transmission equipment. NetPartner NMS exports these administrative capabilities to the customer. NetPartner NMS also can accommodate customers with privately owned operations systems, by providing a single workstation for accessing those and phone company's systems.

With more and more customers demanding control of their networks, it is no surprise that local phone companies are seeking to provide UNMA capabilities to new and existing Centrex customers. NetPartner NMS has been specifically designed to establish parity between the network control capabilities offered to Centrex, ISDN, and PBX customers. It is no longer necessary for customers to abandon Centrex solutions to obtain the control they need.

Security and screening of data are done in the centralized NetPartner NMS host computer complex; consequently, up to 10 different customers can share one NetPartner NMS without seeing each other's proprietary information. To each customer, NetPartner NMS looks like a private system.

The Centrex-supporting capabilities of NetPartner NMS are well suited for ISDN customers; in fact, some capabilities apply only to them. NetPartner NMS took the lead and paved the way as a prototype for customer control in an ISDN trial with Illinois Bell Telephone Co.

Customer Experience

Network Management is the buzzword for 1988. Too many of the Network Management solutions have focused solely on the sizzle and not enough on the meat. Indeed, customers want fancy graphics but they need basic technical features of robust logging, browsing, network inquiry, network control and configuration detail. It would be great if there were a single user interface across all network and host elements but it is not yet needed. Customer operations people can handle the different dialects of up to 10 network management systems today, but they require easy access from a common terminal. They find the ability to initiate tests extremely valuable and come to rely on the Network Management System when it can correlate the flood of data that often accompanies an outage. They like the ability to do simple functions simply, like swapping people's data and voice service.

The issue is "more in the matter and less in the art". Customers need access to host data and network data conveniently and rapidly so that they may have confidence in their networks. Such capability will give the MIS and telecommunications executives the confidence to integrate voice and data on single public or private networks.

SYSTEM DESCRIPTION

The NetPartner NMS architecture shown in Figure 1 has three parts: NetPartner NMS host equipment at the phone company, equipment on the customer's premises, and operations systems spread across the phone company and customer premises.

At the phone company there are three 3B2/600 host computers, a communications processor, and a workstation for administration. NetPartner NMS also requires a Datakit^R Virtual Circuit Switch (VCS) which serves as a local area network through which to access the operations systems. The host computer architecture is shown in Figure 1.

The only equipment required on a customer's premise is either a SUN$^+$ Series 3 workstation for full functionality (including windowing and graphics), or an AT&T MS-DOS* based personal computer if fewer functions will suffice.

CAPACITY

One NetPartner NMS can support 5 to 10 customers, and up to 20 users simultaneously; the phone company determines the number of users per customer. (Users are the customer's data or telecommunications managers.) A system handles up to 40,000 analog or digital lines-in any combination-and 7,500 trunks, and provides access to multiple instances of the operations systems shown in the next section.

NetPartner NMS has a set of basic messages (commands or reports) that enable it to work with these switches: 1 ESS^{TM} and 1A ESS^{TM} Centrex switches, 5ESS^{TM} Centrex and ISDN switches and DMS$^+$-100 switches providing Integrated Business Network

(IBN) services. One NetPartner NMS handles up to 25 switches serving that system's customers.

OPERATIONS SYSTEMS

The first generic of NetPartner NMS provides customer control through access to these phone company operations systems.

Engineering and Administrative Data Acquisition System

The Engineering and Administrative Data Acquisition System (EADAS) monitors network traffic by collecting and analyzing traffic data from a phone company's switches. The EADAS makes scheduled connections to the NetPartner NMS host computer and delivers User Defined Reports to be stored in NetPartner NMS. This capability gives phone companies control over report structure, content, and availability. It also enables the phone company to generate customized reports using a spreadsheet program that accesses raw data with generalized keywords.

Access to these reports will help customers determine capacity requirements. This will enable them to accommodate changing conditions, brought on by such things as business cycles, and will result in more efficient operations.

One customer discovered via one of these reports that the anguished cries of her MIS department were justified - their modem pool was overloaded during 90 percent of the business day.

Switching Control Center Systems

The Switching Control Center System (SCCS) centralizes maintenance of switch and network terminal equipment. Functions include logging messages, browsing, alarming, and indicating status. A high-speed link to the SCCS delivers switch data to the NetPartner NMS host computer for storage, and allows the user to access 1 ESS, 1A ESS, 5ESS, and DMS-100 switches.

NetPartner NMS contains a surveillance log that gathers information from the switch via the SCCS. The NetPartner NMS core set of messages supplies performance data in the form of line and trunk status messages. The phone company, however, can send other maintenance messages that a customer wants to see to NetPartner NMS thereby customizing the data for each customer.

A customer will also be able to take limited actions, such as make digital loopback tests and line- and trunk- status queries, through SCCS to the switch; this will show whether a line is in or out of service. The information the SCCS interface provides will help the customer determine responsibility for telecommunication failures and thereby facilitate making repairs.

In the new, and often complicated, world of ISDN, this surveillance and testing capability was used by one customer to determine when to dispatch repair personnel to an office in response to a complaint, and when to sit back and wait, comfortable in the knowledge that the problem belonged to his telephone company.

The LMOS Complex: LMOS, Predictor and MLT

The Loop Management Operations Systems (LMOS) complex is a family of operations systems that includes LMOS, Predictor, and the Mechanized Loop Testing (MLT) system. The customer uses the LMOS Complex to enter and check the status of trouble tickets and to test metallic lines. The customer alerts the phone company to a trouble by entering a trouble ticket through NetPartner NMS and having it processed as if it was entered by phoning the Centralized Repair Service Answering Bureau, i.e., as though the customer dialed 611. An experienced customer estimated that they saved about 10 minutes per trouble by bypassing the human interaction with the telephone company's clerk.

Similarly, customers can see the status of trouble tickets associated with their lines. Status includes such things as

pending dispatch, pending screen, dispatched in, or dispatched out. The customer also may obtain a list of all outstanding trouble tickets associated with their lines. In addition, the customer can make mechanized loop tests that verify the electrical characteristics of the loop.

1A ESS or 5ESS Switch Applications Processor

A customer uses telephone company based Applications Processors to request Station Message Detail Recording Reports.** These reports contain details of calls made by employees. The reports can be used for internal billing and to curtail misuse of company resources.

An oft-quoted story relates the surprise (and shock!) encountered by one executive when, shortly after acquiring the SMDR feature for his company, he discovered a close friend of his at the company was placing and inordinate number of calls to the executive's wife!

NetPartner NMS supports three forms of the Applications Processor: the 1A ESS switch Advanced Communications Package, the 5ESS switch Applications Processor, or the

Basic Communications Package.

Macstar End Customer Management System

A customer uses the Macstar^R End Customer Management System (ECMS) to do the following:

- Rearrange and/or move Centrex and ISDN lines and change features on them.

- Control the sequencing of outgoing route choices by alerting established automatic route selection patterns.

- Match telephone numbers with phone company-definable attributes such as equipment, name, and location.

Macstar has been in place for a few years now; periodic perusals of the usage log indicates that customers spend as much time performing queries to find out what they have in terms of features as they do in changing the features themselves.

NCCF/NPDA or NetView***

NetPartner NMS also can interface with operations systems that customers already own such as NCCF/NPDA. The Network Communication Control Facility (NCCF) is part of IBM's network management system family. It runs as an application subsystem and provides a software interface for Systems Network Architecture (SNA) network operators, enabling them to issue configuration and diagnostic commands to devices in the network. The Network Problem Determination Application (NPDA), which runs as an application under NCCF, records failures and degrading conditions on the physical SNA network and can start trace programs to find the sources of network hardware problems.

The connection to IBM's NCCF and NPDA is over a dedicated link or a property configured digital subscriber line to the customer's workstation. To the IBM host computer, NetPartner NMS looks like a cluster controller. Within the customer's various workstations, multiple programs can be run, with each workstation acting like a 3278-type terminal.

NetView is a network management system for IBM's Systems Network Architecture. It combines NCCF, NPDA, and several other small packages into one product. NetPartner NSM's support of NetView is the same as that for the smaller packages.

Phone Company Operations Systems

NetPartner NMS has also been proven able support phone company-developed operations systems such as Illinois Bell Telephone's ISDN-Mate. The first generic of NetPartner NMS also includes a general access port that gives each customer access to one additional operations system. A phone company that has a system deemed valuable to its customers can use this feature of NetPartner NMS to provide customer access without requiring any additional development by AT&T.

This general access port is an early solution to a problem that plagues all who would attempt to provide all-encompassing network management: the complexity of today's network and the plethora of vendors offering partial network management solutions.

As noted earlier, NetPartner generic 1 supports cut-through or native protocol access to operations systems. While such an approach provides a strong entry point in order to be able to support multiple vendors changing environments, and sophisticated customers, additional technologies must be applied. Two of these will be prominent in subsequent NetPartner releases: access management tools and support of a standard network management protocol.

Access management tools are being developed in support of AT&T's Universal Operations System (UOS). These tools provide customizable, user-programmable means for telephone companies to be able to chain together sequences of commands and the resultant actions in a manner so as to isolate the user interface and devices from the underlying applications. NetPartner will be one of the first products utilizing a practical application of access management.

The international network management protocol addresses the same problem but from an alternate viewpoint. This protocol is currently being defined by both national and international standards bodies and, when complete, will specify the details necessary to allow operations systems from multiple vendors to communicate. AT&T has committed to supporting the network management protocol as part of its Unified Network Management Architecture; it is the glue that allows many different pieces of the network management puzzle to be coherently interconnected and provide an end-customer with a unified point of access and control over their entire network.

CUSTOMER INTERACTIONS

The user interface--a workstation with specialized software for interacting with system functions--is the window to NetPartner NMS. As such, it translates many traditional phone company OA&M functions into the customer's language. The interface includes a set of core capabilities, plus additional functions that are provided via direct connections to remote operations systems.

The user interface includes a menu-driven, graphics-enhanced, multiwindow workstation. If a PC is used, simpler graphics and a single window display will be available. The phone company customizes a customer's menu to show only the functions that have been purchased from the phone company. NetPartner NMS's functions fit in these four categories, which serve as top-level menu items.

- Network management,

- Customer systems,

- Alarm/status, and

- Utilities.

All network management functions that the phone company offers customers are integrated in the network management category. For example, the customer has access to trouble entry and testing capabilities, as well as performance, configuration, and fault management.

Customer systems are grouped by system, rather than function, in the private-systems menu/category; for example, NetView might appear as a menu item here.

Included as part of the system's surveillance capability are the alarm/status displays, which are listed separately so that they may be accessed quickly and easily. Through this category, customers can see a text-based alarm window and a graphical network status display. The phone company can redefine alarm levels or alarm descriptions as necessary. Alarms may be cleared or acknowledged from the status displays.

Utilities are general tools furnished by NetPartner NMS. They fall into two categories: those that are accessed from the screen and used with other NetPartner NMS functions, such as window operations, and those that are accessed from the menu and serve as stand-alone functions, such as sending bulletins.

PHONE COMPANY INTERACTIONS

System Administration

NetPartner NMS provides a workstation position for an administrator that's linked through a 3BNet connection to the 3B2/600 computers. A full set of capabilities, including customer startup and continuing support, are supplied to the phone company system administrator at this position. Most of the system administrator's tasks are done through interactive terminal screens; the tasks include:

- Setting up NetPartner NMS's interfaces to the Datakit VCS,

- Initializing new customers and supporting them on an ongoing basis,

- Assigning operations systems capabilities to customers,

- Assigning permission for allowable and/or restricted commands per customer group,

- Controlling switch messages that customer groups are allowed to see,

- Determining alarm levels for various customers,

- Building tables to translate phone company switch messages into a format that the customer can understand (if the default set is not adequate or the phone company wishes to change, add, or delete any messages), and

- Customizing screen content (if changes in the default content are desired), including building displays, defining icons, and altering color choices.

Maintenance and Alarms

NetPartner NMS is connected to a system console, located next to the host computer. A full complement of maintenance capabilities are available to the computer operator/maintainer at this position. Most of the maintainer's tasks are performed through interactive screens; the person also has a primary menu for selecting the function to be performed, which includes:

- Sending messages to customers about special conditions or difficulties,

- Backing up the host database onto diskettes or tape,

- Restoring the host database from diskettes or tape,

- Reviewing operations system usage,

- Turning off power and rebooting the system,

- Performing audits and tests on the system, and

- Restoring the system in the event of failure.

Alarms for operations systems already are in place, typically in a place like the Minicomputer Maintenance Operations Center. Therefore, NetPartner NMS contains mainly secondary alarms for each of the remote operations systems and,

should any of these go down, NetPartner NMS will alert phone company personnel via a visual and (optional) audible alarm. Similarly, if the Datakit VCS goes down, an alarm will be generated at the NetPartner NMS host computer. An alternative alarm for the Datakit VCS could be tied into SCCS.

An alarm also will be generated at the NetPartner NMS host computer if any connecting link in NetPartner NMS is lost. This includes a link to any remote operations system, a link to the Datakit VCS, or a link to any customer.

An alarm relay unit for the NetPartner NMS's host computer complex is in the system cabinet. The alarms from this device can be used locally, or can be remotely tied into the building alarms on an SCCS. The NetPartner NMS host computer can also be hooked into a CompuLert[R] Computer Administration and Maintenance System, which provides for remote polling, reboot, logging, and alerting. Or, the 3B2/600 computer consoles for the NetPartner NMS host computer could be remoted to the SCC, with logging capabilities also provided.

SECURITY AND SCREENING

All security and screening for phone-company-owned operations systems connected to NetPartner NMS is done at the phone company premises via the host computers. Customers are allowed to view and touch only their own network data. All interactions are translated and screened at least once at the host. This security access is based on the customer configuration in NetPartner NMS defined by the phone company.

BENEFITS

Both the telephone company and the end customer will see significant benefits from the NetPartner NMS (in specific) and the Unified Network Management architecture approach (in general).

Telephone Company Benefits

The benefits to the telephone company of having NetPartner NMS consist of Centrex revenue retention, new revenue generation, operational savings, and the flexibility to offer customized services.

The benefits from Centrex revenue retention are estimated to be quite large. The Centrex services offered by the telephone companies currently support approximately six million lines each of which generates an average of $20/line/month. As many as 80 percent of those Centrex customers are considering moving to a PBX system. Thus NetPartner NMS is a powerful draw to help the telephone company retain Centrex customers, by leveling the playing field.

Besides helping to retain revenue, NetPartner NMS generates it. Market studies show customers are willing to pay phone companies for the control facilities they get through NetPartner NMS.

The benefits in operational savings consist of cost reduction from the telephone companies not having to do as much work -- they and handing off parts of surveillance, testing, trouble sectionalization, and other OS tasks to the end-customer through NetPartner NMS.

Finally, the telephone companies are often faced with responding to requests for specific services (in the form of RFP's) from their large customers. With the flexibility inherent in NetPartner they can now respond with customized service without accruing the overhead associated with specialized development.

End-Customer Benefits

Besides meeting existing end-customer demands for increased control over Centrex services, NetPartner NMS provides additional benefits.

NetPartner insures the privacy of the customer's data while providing a single point of control for network services and access to customer owned systems. This security will become increasingly important as the customer moves toward the goal of total end-to-end network management as promised by AT&T's Unified Network Management Architecture blueprint.

With an increased view of the network, the customer will be able to minimize impacts of service downtime. The costs of such outages can be as high as several millions of dollars per hour in the airline, retail, and investment industries.

The customer will also benefit from reduced operating expense; by being able to sectionalize troubles, they can avoid costly service calls.

THE FUTURE

NetPartner NMS, Generic 2, will have additional features and interfaces to support the private/virtual private line special services market needs plus new ISDN features.

Generic 3 will add interfaces to support additional operations systems, and will offer open interfaces based on international standards--to any operations system via the network management protocol. As part of AT&T's commitment to end-to-end network management, generic 3 will include an international standards-based interface to specific premises-based and interexchange carrier products such as AT&T's ACCUMASTER product family. Some artificial-intelligence-based capability, which would be needed for example, to start tests in intelligent-customer-premises equipment, is also planned.

NetPartner NMS plays a major part in AT&T's long range goal of providing the telephone company with the ability to offer a customer end-to-end unified network management.

REFERENCES

(1) J. W. Timko, "AT&T Systems Architecture," AT&T Technology, Vol. 2 No. 3 1987.

+SUN is a trademark of SUN Microsystems, Inc.

*MS-DOS is a trademark of Microsoft Corporation
+DMS is a trademark of Northern Telecom, Ltd.

**If the AP is located on customer premises, various other functions are also available.

***NetView is a trademark of the International Business Machines Corporation

FIGURE 1: NETPARTNER NMS ARCHITECTURE

The NetPartner NMS architecture is based primarily on already existing operations systems in the customer's and the phone company's networks.

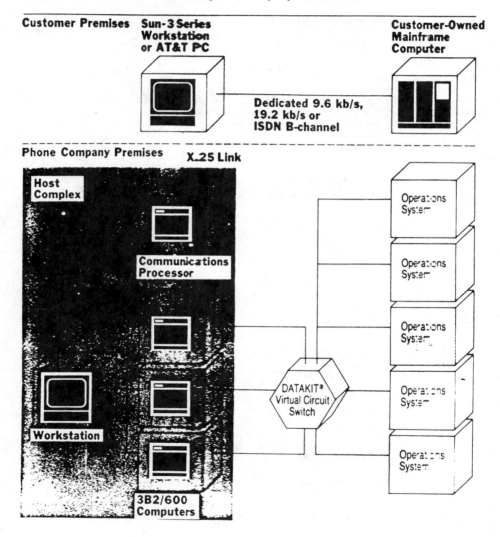

Customer Premises | **Sun-3 Series Workstation or AT&T PC** | **Customer-Owned Mainframe Computer**

Dedicated 9.6 kb/s, 19.2 kb/s or ISDN B-channel

Phone Company Premises — X.25 Link

Host Complex

Communications Processor

Workstation

3B2/600 Computers

DATAKIT® Virtual Circuit Switch

Operations System
Operations System
Operations System
Operations System
Operations System

CENTRAL OFFICE ENVIRONMENT - WILL YOUR EQUIPMENT SURVIVE?

Michael G. Kern - Chairperson
Manager
Quality Assurance

U S West Communications
100 S. 19th Street
Omaha, NE 68102

ABSTRACT

Survivability of the network is directly dependent on the environment in which its pieces reside. This seminar examines the impact that various environmental conditions have on today's technology. It explores specific equipment sensitivity issues and provides first-hand examples of how service affecting failures can be minimized. You will have an opportunity to discuss your particular concerns with four nationally recognized experts in a panel discussion following their presentations.

Frank N. Graff, Jr.   AT&T Bell
                         Laboratories

Dr. Barbara T. Reagor   Bell Communications
                         Research

Kenneth E. Ross   AT&T

Ray Whinery   U S West
                         Communications

DUST - WHAT, WHERE, WHY AND HOW
Dr. Barbara T. Reagor

Bellcore
331 Newman Springs Road
Red Bank, NJ 07701

Today, telecommunication systems are in the process of transforming from the electromechanical systems of the past to the electronic/digital office of today. These digital systems incorporate the leading edge of technology and are more compact than their electromechanical counterparts. The circuit boards contain products mounted on a multi-layered substrate from a wide variety of vendors. Physical spacings have been reduced both within components as well as between adjacently mounted components to the point where they almost touch. This makes contamination of utmost concern during the manufacture and use of the equipment. Dust accumulation on equipment is currently posing a serious threat to the long-term reliability of this new technology.

In the typical telecommunication environment we observe three classes of contaminants that can adversely impact digital technology. These are 1) Dust - various sizes of particulate matter of both organic or inorganic composition which can accumulate on and interact with equipment surfaces; 2) Gases - various chemical species such as ozone, sulfur dioxide, nitrous oxide, hydrogen chloride, chlorine, etc., which can directly react with equipment leading to effects such as corrosion of metal surfaces or stress-cracking of plastics; and 3) Vapors - various organic compounds or water which are at equilibrium with a solid or liquid source and which can adhere to dust and surfaces within switching equipment leading to a variety of failure mechanisms.

This presentation will provide an understanding of WHAT dust is, WHERE it comes from, WHY we are concerned about it, and finally, HOW we can monitor and control it. The adverse effects of dust contamination on telecommunications equipment will be illustrated through discussion of actual field failures.

Airborne dust is usually bimodally distributed by mass (or volume). Particles in the so-called "fine mode" have a median diameter in the range of 5 - 10 microns. In a typical central office, the average number of particles present in the air is less than 100,000 particles 0.5 microns or greater and less than 100 particles 5 to 10 microns or greater in size. As would be expected these two particulate modes have quite different sources. The fine mode particles arise from combustion and gas-phase condensation processes. For example, particulate ammonium sulfate is formed by neutralization of sulfuric acid aerosols by ammonia. It represents a major constituent of fine mode particles along with carbon, nitrates from automobile emissions and many other water soluble compounds. Coarse particles on the other hand are the result of soil erosion by wind, sea salt spray, and from anthropogenic mechanical processes.

In order to understand the environment in which telecommunications equipment must operate in, it is useful to compare the differences and similarities between the contaminants found in outdoor and indoor air. The typical composition of outdoor and indoor particles is presented in the slide attachments. They represent the environment at a typical central office. A comparison of indoor and outdoor composition clearly shows us that, for coarse particles, our buildings effectively remove what is outside.

Indoor coarse particles, although containing some of the outdoor materials (namely, the dust brought in on shoes or clothing or through the door) are mainly composed of materials generated by activity within the building. Indoor fine particles contain a large fraction of the same materials found in outdoor fine particles, with the exception of the organic content. The indoor concentrations of fine particles are directly related to the amount of outside air brought into the building and the efficiency of the air filters. In our offices we generate large volumes of organic vapors that originate from our extensive use of plastics, cleaning materials, paints, and people. Organic vapors can easily absorb onto the surface of fine particles. Our only way to minimize the organic vapor content of indoor air is to provide adequate ventilations. However, this brings in more outdoor air and more fine particles. To control the fine-mode particles we must employ good air filtration practices which will be discussed in the presentation.

In electromechanical equipment, our main concern has been the coarse-mode particles which could produce insulating films "opens" between contacts or produce abrasion and early wear-out of mechanical parts. In the digital equipment of today, we have begun to realize that the fine-mode particles, that contain water soluble salts or organic compounds are posing even more of a threat to the long-term reliability of the network. We have seen acute problems with computers where fine particles and organic vapors have lead to head crashes and disk drive failures. We have found that if the dust contains conductive metal or carbon particles and is allowed to accumulate on surface mounted devices on circuit boards, failures will occur. Accumulation of the fine-mode particles on circuit board components (in particular, the water soluble salts) coupled with a humidity rise can cause failures. We have even seen large amounts of the non-conducing, innocuous dust building up and cause contact problems. The best way to combat these problems is through adequate protection of the equipment both through vendor design and environmental controls.

During the lifetime of a digital switch, there are four major events that can impact its overall reliability from the stand point of dust exposure. The first is initial installation. Here, both the preparation of the space and the construction of the equipment can generate tremendous amounts of dust. Next, old equipment most often be torn out as part of the office renovation and switch upgrade. Old equipment has already accumulated dust from its years of operations, and special precautions must be taken not to contaminate the new equipment that is replacing it. The normal operating environment of the new switch can be critical to its future operation. And finally, as the network expands, we are again concerned with new installation issues. Careful planning and control during all of these stages is imperative for continued equipment reliability. Control of all sources of dust contamination is necessary with digital technology. The fine-mode particles can be controlled by adequate filtrations of the outdoor air. Indoor sources can be controlled by continuous fan operation of the HVAC system which translates into continuous air filtration. Sources such as smoking should be eliminated. Filtration is required for both the building and the equipment. With these controls in place, very good air quality can be provided which will provide for long-term equipment reliability.

In summary, it is critically important to minimize dust contamination in digital offices. Control of the environment requires an understanding of the normal working environment, building equipment to work in that environment (robustness), adequate building environmental controls and adequate equipment protections. This presentation will be illustrated through discussions of actual field failures resulting from dust.

TELECOMMUNICATIONS A.C. AND D.C POWER INTEGRATION

Kenneth E. Ross
Senior Engineer - Power, Protection
and EMC

AT&T - Federal Systems
Burlington, NC 27215

ABSTRACT

Today's successful performance and protection of Digital Telephone Switching Equipment has been enhanced mainly by the employment of a Single Point Grounding network and the inception of an isolated ground zone installation. Further isolation and protection is afforded the digital switching equipment by operating from a large bulk D.C. power plant which isolates the switch from abnormal A.C. utility power voltage variations and transients.

With the inception of Centrex, Toll Traffic Operation Positions, ISDN and other communications networks, the use of A.C. powered equipment has become more prevalent. In most all cases the A.C. powered equipment and operator positions lie in the "integrated ground plane", but must interface with the D.C. powered equipment in the isolated ground plane. Due to the nature of this extension to the digital communications equipment, the A.C. powered equipment (i.e. workstation positions) can be located some distance from the D.C. powered switch as well as be in a "commercial business office" environment.

This session and paper covers a practical approach to the integration of A.C. and D.C. powered equipment with a common bilateral signal interface that can be found in today's telephone business. It is intended that the necessary protection is provided by the inherent system design with installation restrictions rather than secondary add-on features to a lesser thought-out design. Because of the personally manned workstation positions involved, personnel hazard protection is of primary importance as well as ESD protection for the equipment being used.

INTRODUCTION

Both areas of equipment power integration and installation must be given initial design attention. It is intended that those vital aspects of the overall system design be covered in this paper as listed:

1) Integration of separate A.C. and D.C. power source that must be referenced to a single point ground (SPG) for the system.
2) Isolation and grounding of operator position A.C. powered equipment and furniture outside the isolated ground plane (IGP).
3) Miscellaneous equipment (i.e. interface and controlled access equipment) power and ground requirements.
4) Single floor and multi-floor installation requirements.
5) Compliance to the National Electrical Code for separately derived A.C. sources, raised floor installations and air plenum wiring restrictions.

As the digital telephone business expands into the areas of data acquisition, networking, etc., more systems will be required to use A.C. powered equipment. Quite often the A.C. powered operator position equipment is separated by a sizable distance (i.e. one floor or several hundred feet) requiring additional peripheral interface equipment to be supplied. It is intended that the system configurations described provide both personnel hazard safety for the operators and long term protection for all equipment during power and lightning faults.

D.C. POWERED ISOLATED GROUND PLANE (IGP) EQUIPMENT

The IGP is defined as that area dedicated to digital switching equipment that is isolated from incidental ground contact, has battery return (BR) insulated from equipment frame and is typically powered from a large bulk isolated type -48 volt power plant. The digital switching equipment and power plant are then intentionally grounded to a single point ground (SPG), sometimes referred to as main ground bar (MGB) in a telco installation.

When data communications services or toll office traffic functions are provided, operator data terminal positions exist which sometimes are raised floor installations as indicated in Fig. 2. Workstations can also contain A.C. powered printers, modems and other equipment that must provide a safe and reliable interface to the digital switching equipment as well as to the operator. Workstation furniture must be versatile and functional to support the task intended, but still provide the necessary protection for the operator and equipment.

WORKSTATION FURNISHING

Various types of furniture can be found at the ever increasing communications workstations, none of which was intended for the application. As a result, insufficient protection is provided to the operator and the equipment under the environmental conditions encountered.

Figure-1 depicts what is essential at a typical workstation to provide versatility and adequate protection. The main elements necessary are:

1) A working base or table with all metal fabrication intentionally grounded and an ESD working surface.
2) An ESD floor mat under the operator position or ESD floor tile permanently installed.
3) An ESD preventative operator's chair with low static treated fabric and graphite coaster wheels.
4) All A.C. powered equipment (e.g. modems, printers, CRT displays, etc.) in plastic housing or cases.

Items 2, 3 and 4 are self-explanatory and quite common in the industry. Item 1 needs more attention and not until recently, has commercially available furniture, custom designed for a workstation application, become available. Some of the important features the main furniture working base or table should have are:

a) The working surface should be continually adjustable in height to accommodate a sitting or standing person or a handicapped person in a wheelchair.
b) The working surface should be a permanent ESD surface and all metal parts should be shielded from operator exposure by plastic shields or epoxy coated metal shields.
c) The display CRT should be mounted on a swivel base that is continually adjustable in height to satisfy an operator's viewing level.
d) All structural metal and the ESD working surface are intentionally grounded via a ground stud connection at the base.
e) Filtered/protection A.C. receptacles should be provided at the rear to accommodate A.C. power requirements for modems, printers, CRT displays, etc.

OPERATOR POSITION POWER AND GROUNDING REQUIREMENTS

Three obstacles must be overcome with the operator positions to become safe and compatible to the rest of the system. (1) The equipment is A.C. powered and the usual large number of positions do not make local power inverters a practical solution. (2) The positions are remote from the digital switch and located in the integrated ground plane (i.e. outside the IGP) at a site or premise. (3) The operator furniture and surroundings must be adequately grounded to the SPG for ESD and personnel hazard reasons.

Due to the abundance of A.C. power required at the operator positions and the desire to be divorced from commercial power problems, a separately derived A.C. power source is desirable to maintain system isolation and operator safety. When a large bulk D.C. power plant with storage batteries already exists, a 3-10KVA DC/AC power converter can be installed as shown in Fig. 3. The inverter is installed as a dedicated A.C. source with only D.C. battery input power supplied to it. The A.C. output is grounded to the SPG per the National Electrical Code, article 250-26 for a separately derived source and should be located within one floor of the SPG if not on the same floor. The inverter output is distributed from a dedicated A.C. distribution panel as shown, to the operator positions in isolated ground (IG) receptacles to maintain separation and isolation from commercial A.C. power. The receptacles can be either a keyed or twist-lock type to distinguish it from commercial power in the same facility and to prevent undesirable equipment from being plugged into it.

Because the operator equipment is powered from an isolated power source from the digital system it is insulated from the integrated ground plane surroundings by the plastic encased equipment. The green-wire ground is isolated from integrated ground and the isolation is maintained through the use of IG receptacles back to the A.C. panel and separately derived source which is intentionally grounded to the system SPG.

COMMERCIAL BUSINESS OFFICE SPACE

In a commercial office environment where operator positions are sometimes located, a large D.C. bulk power plant would not usually be in place or required from the operator positions and A.C. power can be more practically derived by using a separate isolation transformer powered from a commercial A.C. power source as shown in Fig. 4. The secondary output of the transformer is isolated from the commercial A.C. grounding network and intentionally grounded to the SPG. The transformer output is then fed to a dedicated A.C. distribution panel, as with the inverter source, and distributed to the operator positions via conduit and IG receptacles as described previously.

To provide the same emergency power capability as the DC/AC inverter, an uninterrupted power system (UPS) is required for continuous operation of the operator positions during commercial A.C. power outages. It is also recommended to install a surge arrestor of adequate size for the system power capacity as shown, at the input to the isolation transformer. The surge arrestor is intended to suppress commercial power variations and transients and switching transients caused when the UPS switches on and off line. The surge arrestor should have fail indicators to indicate when it has failed on one or more of the power phases.

NATIONAL ELECTRICAL CODE REQUIREMENTS

In a hybrid system as described using both A.C. power and D.C. power sources referenced to a common SPG, provisions that are applicable in the National Electrical Code must still be adhered to. The more unfamiliar articles that need mentioning are sited below with the key factors mentioned:

1) For grounding of separately derived A.C. system. NEC article 250-26. - shall be grounded at any point on the separately derived system between the source and the first disconnect or overcurrent device; or shall be made at the source for a system which has no disconnect means.

2) Wiring methods in air handling space. NEC articles 300-21 - ventilation or air-handling ducts shall be so made that the possible spread of fire or products of combustion will not be substantially increased, and 300-22(c) - only mineral-insulated, type MC (metal clad) or type AC (armored cable) cable shall be used for control or power cables in systems installed in other space used for environmental air. Other type cables and conductors shall be installed in electrical metallic tubing, intermediate metal conduit, rigid metal conduit, or metal raceway ---.

3) Data processing systems. NEC article 645-1 thru 5.
   -1 Power supply wiring, interconnect wiring and grounding of data processing systems, including data communications equipment

used as a terminal shall comply with this article.
   -2 (c) Under Raised Floors
      - Be of suitable construction
      - Branch circuit supply conductors to receptacles are in rigid metal conduit ----- or type MC or AC cable is used.
      - Ventilation in the under floor area is used for the data processing area only.
   -3 A disconnect means shall be provided to disconnect the power to all electronic equipment in the room ----- readily accessible to an operator at the principal exit door.
   -4 All exposed noncurrent carrying metal parts of a data processing system shall be grounded in accord with art. 250.
   -5 Marking; each unit shall carry a nameplate listing voltage, frequency and total load current in amperes.

REFERENCES

(1)   BELL COMMUNICATIONS RESEARCH
      TYS-ESC-0000295
(2)   SURGE PROTECTION OF ELECTRONICS
      Norman H. Haskell, Member continuing engineering education, University of South Carolina
(3)   NATIONAL ELECTRICAL CODE
      1987 Handbook

DEFINITIONS

AC	- Alternating current (e.g. 120V, 60Hz)
DC	- Direct current (e.g. -48VDC or +24VDC)
GRD	- Ground (Earth Potential)
BR	- Battery return (DC load carrying conductor(s))
SPG	- Single point ground
MGB	- Master ground bar
PGP	- Principal ground point
LOG GRD	- Logic ground (isolated) or digital electronics signal ground
FR GRD	- Frame ground for insulated equipment frames
ACEG	- A.C. equipment ground (i.e. termination for "green-wire" grounding conductors)
IG	- Isolated ground (connection or termination)
IGP	- Isolated ground plane
NON-IGP	- Non-isolated ground plane (i.e. integrated ground plane)
FGB	- Floor ground bar

PVC — Poly vinyl chloride (plastic)

ESD — Electro-static discharge

UPS — Uninterrupted Power Source (AC
       power derived from batteries)

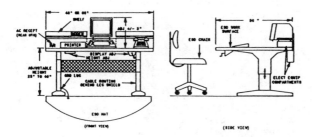

TYPICAL WORKSTATION
FIGURE - 1

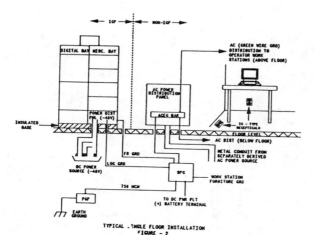

TYPICAL SINGLE FLOOR INSTALLATION
FIGURE - 2

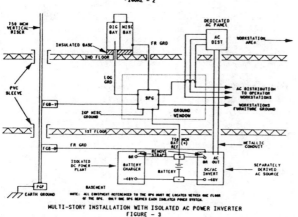

MULTI-STORY INSTALLATION WITH ISOLATED AC POWER INVERTER
FIGURE - 3

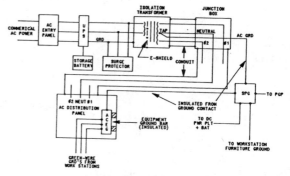

COMMERICAL POWER WITH ISOLATION TRANSFORMER
UTILIZED AS SEPARATELY DERIVED AC SCOURCE.
FIGURE - 4

ENVIRONMENTAL CONDITIONS
Frank N. Graff, Jr.

Supervisor
Quality, Methodology and
System Physical Design Group

AT&T Bell Laboratories
1200 East Warrenville Road
Naperville, IL

ABSTRACT

The deployment of high technology switching systems has generated concern over the degree of environmental control that needs to be exerted to maintain reliable operation under abnormal operating conditions. Seemingly benign environments have experienced higher than desired circuit pack failure rates during commercial power outages or when building air conditioning systems fail. The growth of the high technology digital switches has created an awareness of the need for a better understanding of the central office environment and how to control that environment when catastrophic events occur. This paper describes those measures that need to be taken to better understand "ambient" environments and how to control the central office environments when the worst happens.

INTRODUCTION

All switching systems clearly states in their requirements the operating ranges that the switch will work most effectively in. For the 5ESS Switch, as was the case for earlier electronic switches, the operating conditions are +40 to 100oF with a relative humidity range of 20 to 55 percent. Short term operating conditions are also defined for

986

72 hour periods occurring no more than fifteen days per year. In these situations the temperature range becomes 35 to 120oF with a relative humidity of 20 to 80 percent. The normal operating temperature are also further defined for occupied and unoccupied space.

Additional consideration must also be given to the cleanliness of the environment. What we have become accustom to as being a "normal" switch room environment may often contain contaminants that can be detrimental to switch operation. It is widely known that metallic dust can cause shorts between pins on a circuit pack in nearly any environment. Certain types of "dust" can be harmless under normal operating conditions while becoming conductive in the presence of higher relative humidities. Central offices can exhibit lower than normal or normal circuit pack drop out rates and experience significantly higher drop out rates when power outages occur causing the loss of the central office cooling system.

Means of controlling contaminants in the air during normal operating conditions and controlling the environment during extreme conditions are needed to maintain the integrity of the switching system. These are not necessarily high tech methods but rather require an understanding of what to do, what to look for and what not to do.

THE ENVIRONMENT

The first step is to simply understand the area surrounding the central office building. Will the surrounding environment produce significant amounts of contamination? If the answer is affirmative, then extra precautions are needed to filter this air before it enters the switch room. In all cases maintaining positive pressure within the switching area will aide in maintaining the cleanliness of the environment. By maintaining positive pressure within the switch room contaminants will be kept out of the switching area when doors are opened by the craft.

Central offices are normally maintained at temperature and humidity levels within the normal operating range that optimize switch performance and building maintenance costs. When central air conditioning systems fail and the office temperature rises, actions are generally taken to counteract the rise in temperature. Often, windows and doors of the building are opened to introduce outside air and portable fans are brought

in to circulate the air. The effects of these actions are largely a function of the "condition" of the outside air. If it is humid outside at the time the actions are taken, the normal operating limits could be exceeded for both temperature and humidity. If the air is contaminated or if dust within the office is hygro conductive, the integrity of the switch can be adversely affected. To better understand how these actions can adversely affect switch performance, one must first understand the fundamentals of the environment and how changes impact the basic properties of the environment.

The properties of air water mixtures can be presented in graphical form on psychrometric charts as shown in Figure 1. The basic psychrometric chart consists of dry-bulb temperature (x-axis) and humidity ratio (y-axis). The atmospheric pressure is fixed at 1 atmosphere. Lines of constant relative humidity are plotted as curves on the chart. If one were to imagine an operating environment of 75oF at 50 percent relative humidity, the psychrometric chart indicates an actual humidity ratio of 0.01 (Kg water/Kg air). An increase in temperature to 82oF would see a drop in relative humidity to 40 percent). In order to increase both temperature and relative humidity, the air must be heated and moisture added through humidification. The NEBS environment specifications are graphically depicted in Figure 2. Both the current normal operating and short term operating ranges are shown. It should be noted that these operating ranges have been constrained somewhat in recent years. Previous specifications permitted short term relative humidities of 10 to 90 percent. Increased knowledge of the affects of electro-static discharge (ESD) and hygro-conductive dust has brought about the changes in short term relative humidity specifications. The maximum absolute humidity ratio of 0.026; this specification provides a cap of the relative humidity at temperatures greater than 30oC (short term) and 34oC (long term).

In Figure 3 point A depicts what the environment might be inside a switch room on a typical day. Point B shows what the outside conditions might be on an extremely hot and humid summer day. Note that the outside air conditions exceed that allowed by the product specification.

The necessity of keeping the inside and outside environments separated is depicted in Figure 4. If outside air is

987

introduced into the inside environment, the mixing process will result in condensation within the switch room until temperatures and humidity levels equilibrate. If the switch office's air conditioning system fails, it is extremely important that outside air is not immediately introduced into the office environment.

When an air conditioning failure occurs, the switch room temperatures should be allowed to rise until the inside temperature exceeds that of the outdoor temperature (Figure 5). Use fans to equalize temperatures within the switch room so that isolated hot spots do not develop. During this process, the office's relative humidity will DROP. The maximum rate of change allowed for the 5ESS Switch is 8oC, or roughly 15o per hour. When temp in switch room exceeds that of the outside air, slowly introduce outside air into the switch environment. The temperature will decrease and humidity will slowly climb to the outside levels. Finally, when the air conditioning becomes available, the air conditioning should be slowly restored and dehumidification should take place to minimize the shock of returning from point B to point A. If the air conditioning air is cooled too fast, water will condense near the duct outlets. It is important that the air conditioning ducts not blow directly onto equipment because the local humidity near these outlets will be significantly greater than that of the general office area.

To understand how quickly the office temperature will rise under these conditions, the characteristics of the building must be know in advance. When the air conditioning system fails, the office temperature follows an exponential rise. The transition time is governed by the effective thermal capacitance and resistance of the building. The thermal capacitance and resistance defines how quickly the office will reach equilibrium and depends on the room size, heat source location, and building thermal resistance.

Several tools are available to estimate buildings' thermal characteristics. These tools include US Army construction program (BLAST). For information, call BLAST Support Office, 144 Mechanical Engineering Building, 1206 West Green Street, Urbana, IL 61801 on (217) 333-3977.

The building characteristics can be experimentally determined by performing no-cool tests. The characteristics of the exponential time rise can be experimentally determined at a lower noncritical temperature so that the office characteristics will be known when the outside temperature and humidity would be critical. The temperature rise and time constant characterizing the cool to no-cool process will be relatively independent of the outside temperature.

CONCLUSION

The outside environment impacts on the switch in a variety of ways. Higher temperatures are equivalent to accelerating circuit pack failure rates. For every 10oC increase in temperature, failure rates will roughly double. As the temperature increases without limit, the thermal design of the switch may be exceeded and catastrophic failures result.

Higher failure rates can be associated with high office humidity levels when circuit packs have accumulated dust on them over time. Moderate humidity levels (25 to 45 percent) yield the lowest failure rates. Low humidity levels can be associated with relatively high failure rates if adequate ESD precautions are not taken.

Contamination effects can be separated into three categories. The introduction of conductive particles into the switch will result in circuit pack failures under any conditions. Hygro-conductive particles may become conductive in the presence of high humidity. When hygro-conductive particles are combined with humidity, relatively high failure rates can occur. Nonconductive particles would be associated with relatively low circuit pack failure rates.

These affects can become more prevalent during abnormal operating conditions, such as the loss of air conditioning systems, if the appropriate measures are not taken. To minimize these affects, care must be taken when it becomes necessary to introduce outside air to lower office temperatures. If not done correctly, the resulting increases in humidity will adversely affect the operation of the switch.

Psychrometric Chart

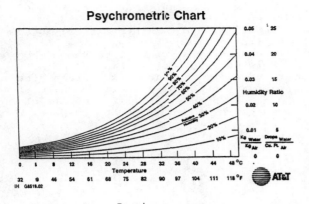

Figure 1

Psychrometric Chart

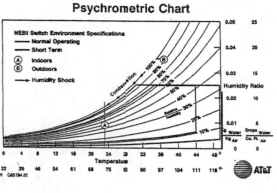

Figure 4

Psychrometric Chart

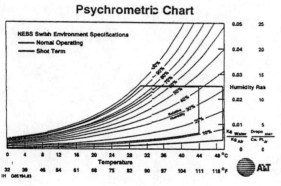

Figure 2

Psychrometric Chart

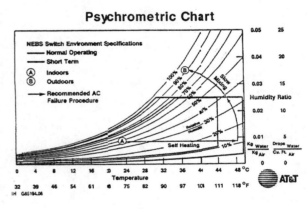

Figure 5

Psychrometric Chart

Figure 3

IMPORTANCE OF PHYSICAL DESIGN
Ray Whinery
Director
Transport Technical Support
and Analysis

U S WEST Communications
3033 N 3rd Street
Room 705
Phoenix, Arizona

ABSTRACT

This paper discusses the growing importance of reviewing the physical design aspects of new network equipment. Physical design is critical to the long term reliability and maintainability of equipment. There are several excellent references currently available through Bellcore which provide detailed physical design criteria. Many of the major manufacturing companies utilize Bellcore

989

Technical Publications to help prevent any potential physical design problems. However, several smaller manufacturing companies have little or no knowledge of physical design requirements and subsequently, utilize poor physical design practices. This ultimately reflects on the reliability of their equipment and affects the performance of our network. It is the policy of U S WEST Communications to review new equipment that is being considered for physical design. Areas of non compliance are documented and shared with vendors to secure corrective action. Many product purchase decisions are directly related to the physical design of the equipment.

INTRODUCTION

Prior to divestiture, most of the equipment purchased by the "Bell System" was designed and developed by Bell Laboratories. At that time, Bell Laboratories was an industry leader in designing long term, reliable products. Much of the design effort was focused on the physical aspects of the equipment. This included circuit board and component layout, as well as shelf assembly and bay framework requirements. Bell Labs developed stringent physical design criteria which was incorporated in all of the "Bell System" products. A simple example is the 400 type telephone set. The 400 type telephone set is sturdy, durable, and reliable. As compared to other commercially available telephone sets manufactured after divestiture, the 400 type set was obviously designed to meet stringent physical design requirements.

Subsequent to divestiture, the Regional Bell Operating Companies have been purchasing network equipment from a myriad of vendors. In an effort to help evaluate the equipment, one important criteria examined is the overall physical design. Since much of the expertise surrounding physical design remained with Bell Labs, the Bell Operating Companies have turned to Bellcore and other consulting firms for technical assistance. U S WEST Communications recognized the need to develop this expertise. Since divestiture, our corporation has identified a few key individuals that are responsible for the overall review of physical design. Our experts review the equipment during the early stages of product evaluation. During the review, any areas of non-compliance are documented and shared with the vendor. It has been our experience that the vendors are very willing to

change their design criteria to meet our special needs. In turn, the vendor also improves the overall reliability of their product.

There are many specific items that are audited during the physical design review. The following sections of this paper will provide additional details of our requirements, how the review is conducted, and some examples of improvements to products.

PHYSICAL DESIGN REQUIREMENTS

The majority of our physical design requirements can be found in the following Bellcore publications:

TR-TSY-000078   Generic Physical Design Requirements for Telecommunications Products and Equipment

TR-TSY-000228   Generic Human Factors Requirements for Network Terminal Equipment

TR-EOP-000083   Network Equipment-Building System General Requirements (NEBS)

TA-TSY-000057   Component Reliability Assurance Requirements for Telecommunications Equipment

Each publication provides specific requirements that should be considered during the initial design stages of any new product. To better understand some of the specific requirements and their importance, discussion on each of the technical publications will be provided:

GENERIC PHYSICAL DESIGN REQUIREMENTS

TR-TSY-000078 - Provides design standards and requirements, engineering and manufac-turing requirements, and manufacturing and workmanship standards. A sample of the information contained in this document includes materials and finish requirements, separable connector requirements, printed wiring board requirements, etc.

Contained within TR-78, are several mandatory specifications which are reviewed by our physical design experts. A few examples are as follows:

Fluxes - Specific fluxes must be used during the manufacturing process. We require that a non-corrosive flux be used. In addition, we specify tests that must be performed to ensure the overall compliance to the requirements that are found in TR-78. In the past, we have experienced problems with equipment manufactured using a corrosive flux. The problems are primarily associated with corrosion of the printed circuit board and components, contributing to intermittent connections.

Separable Connector Requirements - The same metal will be used for all separable contacts. This requirement pertaining to edge finger connectors as well as Integrated Circuit to Socket connections. The problem is associated with tin oxide fretting corrosion, which results in high resistance failures of components. It has been a well documented problem that has resulted in service affecting situations in different equipments.

Wire and Cable Requirements - One of the primary concerns observed in the past is associated with wire and cable dress. In many instances, wire/cable used to interconnect shelf assemblies, is dressed over sharp metal edges. We have seen instances where a plastic insulation cold flow is experienced, resulting in a short circuit condition of the wire conductor to the metal surface. We constantly audit new equipment to ensure that cable dress does not contribute to this problem.

Electrostatic Discharge - ESD has been responsible for many failure situations. In an effort to help reduce the potential from ESD damage, we require our suppliers to add an ESD jack to the equipment. In addition, we specify that the jack be visually marked as the termination point for a wrist strap. This requirement has helped our organization combat the latent affects of ESD damage.

There are several additional requirements that must be met to comply with TA-78. I have only provided a sample of those requirements to better understand how they apply to our product evaluation process.

GENERIC HUMAN FACTORS REQUIREMENTS

TA TSY-000228 - Provides criteria to help improve the maintainability of equipment. Much of the criteria is focused on specifications for equipment which support a "user friendly" environment. Since TA-228 was developed as a result of requests from craft people using the equipment, much of the information is very useful and supports the needs of our field operations people. The following information represents samples of the criteria:

Displays and LEDS - To properly maintain equipment, it is important that displays and LEDS be physically located in the equipment to allow easy visibility from the front of the equipment. In the past, we have experienced difficulty in observing an alarm display due to the location alarm indicator. This not only hinders troubleshooting activities, but can contribute to a service interruption.

Circuit Board and Shelf Assembly Labels - All circuit board identification should be marked on the faceplate or ejector latch using a label that describes that circuit board. All supporting documentation for that equipment should also refer to the same nomenclature that is found on the label. In addition, all shelf assembly slots should be labeled to help identify where circuit boards should be placed in the shelf assembly. There is a potential for placing a circuit board in the wrong shelf assembly slot when identification is not provided. This can in turn cause substantial circuit board damage and a potential fire hazard condition in some arrangements.

Safety Hazards - In addition to the safety/fire hazard described above, there are several additional items that require review. One situation involves sharp metal edges which may result from the manufacturing process. Sharp edges result in many injury situations within our Central Office environments. A second concern is associated with exposed power terminals. In a typical situation, a craftsperson might sustain injury from electrical shock of accidently shorting a tool across exposed electrical terminals.

Craft Interface Device Requirements - Several requirements for the Craft Interface Device (CID) are found throughout TA-228. The requirements were developed to help otimize the use of the hand held CID. During our design reviews, a substantial amount of time is devoted to the use of the CID and its operational features. We work with various suppliers to help develop standard interfaces which will allow our corporation to use one CID on various vendor equipment.

NEBS REQUIREMENTS

TR EOP-000068 - Provides generic requirements associated with Environmental Considerations, Spatial Considerations, Hardware and Craftsperson Interfaces, and Environmental test methods. The document is used primarily by our space planning organization, but several items are included in our physical design review process. The following represents a few specific items:

Flammability - In all of our design reviews, one of our primary requirements is associated with flammability. We currently require all plastics, cables, etc., used in equipment to meet a UL 94VO or V1 rating and to meet an oxygen index of 28%. By specifying these requirements, we can lessen the impact of a serious Central Office fire by helping to eliminate sources of ignition from our Central Office environment.

Packaging - The packaging arrangement is reviewed to ensure proper protection of the equipment during shipment. The packaging material must also be protected against any potential ESD problems.

Physical Size - Equipment must be able to fit into existing Central Office lineups. In order to ensure compatibility, many of the dimensions for bay frameworks, shelf assemblies, etc., can be found in the NEBS document.

COMPONENT RELIABILITY

TA-TSY-000357 - Provides a set of practices for manufacturing companies to use during the component selection, qualifications, and lot acceptance procedures. In the past, the selection and testing of components has varied from vendor to vendor. With the release of this TA, we are in a better position to analyze each vendors' component selection and acceptance procedure.

During the physical design review, we normally request pertinent information regarding vendor component selection and acceptance. Although there is no true way to verify compliance with the requirements in TA-357 during a design review, we feel by specifying compliance to the criteria listed in TA-357, we send a strong message to the vendor community that we in U S WEST Communications are quality conscious.

CONDUCTING A DESIGN REVIEW

In order to provide technical support to the many organizations within U S WEST, our group has designed a detailed checklist of various items that must be audited during a physical design review. As previously discussed, the items listed above as well as numerous additional items are included in the detailed checklist. During a typical design review, we work from our checklist to ensure a complete and standard audit of the equipment. When items of non-compliance are observed, we note on the checklist that further review is required. After the review has been completed, a detailed memo is prepared for the vendor, identifying the non-compliance areas.

We periodically work with the vendor technical organizations to help them better understand our requirements. After the non-compliant areas have been corrected, a follow up review is conducted. At the conclusion of the follow up review, a recommendation is forwarded to the U S WEST organization requesting our assistance which provides our findings and subsequent vendor corrective action. This information is then used in the overall product evaluation process to help rate the different products.

IMPROVEMENT TO PRODUCTS

We have several documented examples of where changes have been made to vendor products based on our requests. The majority of the changes focus around flammability, dissimilar metals, cable dress and labeling. In some instances, we've had vendors that have had to replace many components, ejector latches, ty wraps, etc., to meet our flammability requirements. We have had several situations where vendors did not understand the importance of similar metals in an Integrated Circuit to Socket combination. In these instances, we have had to provide various technical papers on that subject to secure the vendors' cooperation and understanding of the problem.

In the case of cable dress, we have had several instances where the vendors have redesigned the inter-bay cabling arrangement to protect against sharp edges and potential pinched conductors. We also have several cases where inaccurate or no labeling was used on equipment and had to be corrected.

CONCLUSIONS

In conclusion, it can be shown that a review of the physical design of new equipment is of great benefit. The review can help identify, document and correct potential problems that will ultimately affect the long term reliability of the equipment. When performed prior to equipment deployment, we can assist our field operations people by ensuring that the equipment is easily maintainable. Since we are Regional Bell Operating Company, we tend to carry more clout in obtaining cooperations from the vendors and compliance to our requirements. The work we performed in U S WEST Communications is of benefit to all purchasers of the new equipment as well as the vendor since the requirements used were developed to help design, manufacture and support a high quality and reliable product.

QUALITY MANAGEMENT: A PROFIT STRATEGY

Ed H. Tharp - Co-Chairperson
Vice President
Quality Management

U S WEST Communications, Inc.
1801 California St., Ste. 5200
Denver, Colorado 80202

Marian M. Steeples - Co-Chairperson
Director
Quality Management

U S WEST Communications, Inc.
1801 California St., Ste. 3340
Denver, Colorado 80202

ABSTRACT

In today's rapidly changing business
environment, the key to success for an
organization is contingent on its
ability to offer quality services and
products that meet or exceed customer
requirements and expectations. The
telecommunications industry is becoming
increasingly aware of the need for a
management oriented approach to
improving quality.

Improved quality results in less waste
and heightened productivity. Operating
costs are reduced leading to more
competitive pricing. Increased sales
are generated along with higher
profits. Quality is a profit strategy
because it eliminates waste, errors,
rework, and redundancies. It is
estimated that 25-40% of business
operating costs are the cost of poor
quality. Operational Quality Management
functions to reduce and eliminate waste
thereby maximizing a company's profit.
Those organizations that lead in quality
will lead in market share. This seminar
addresses the critical need of providing
a systematic process to ensure the
success of an organization's quality
imperatives. Requisite methodologies
and techniques are described.

The seminar also presents practical,
descriptive examples of quality
management in action.

THE QUALITY MANAGEMENT PLAN

Ed H. Tharp - Co-Chairperson
Vice President
Quality Management

U S WEST Communications, Inc.
1801 California St., Ste. 5200
Denver, Colorado 80202

ABSTRACT

The practical significance of Quality as
a corporate priority is explored.

Quality Management (QM) is a structured,
highly effective process that enables a
company to focus on the vital factors
requisite in providing value to
customers. Key elements in quality
planning are explained. This planning
provides an integrated approach and
leads to the resolution of critical
system issues which are at the core of
the quality problems. This session
describes major long range and short
term benefits of Quality Management.
The connection of productivity and
quality is examined. Quality has a
leverage on profits that few
organizations have fully considered.

INTRODUCTION

U S WEST Communications Group is a
telecommunications company formed as a
result of the divestiture of AT&T in
1984 (one of seven holding companies
resulting from that action).

Headquartered in Englewood, Colorado
and employing nearly 68,000 people,
U S WEST is made up of three principal
telephone operating companies, Mountain

Bell, Northwestern Bell and Pacific
Northwest Bell plus a number of other
diversified subsidiaries.

BACKGROUND: DIVESTITURE OF THE BELL
SYSTEM

The world standard for telephone
networks is, without question, the Bell
telephone network in the United States.
Designed and built as a single system,
the Bell network has long been noted for
its speed, accuracy, and cost-efficiency
in switching and completing millions of

telephone calls everyday. The 1984 breakup of the Bell System divided that network into seven regional operations. In one of those regional companies, U S WEST, Inc., management felt that the breakup and its primary causes--new technology and growing competition--called for a reexamination of the company's relationship with its customers.

For fifty years, Bell's definition of quality service had been rooted in the policy goals defined by the Communications Act of 1934. The primary thrust of those goals was to put "a phone in every home," and to assure that each phone had access to every other phone. This was achieved by providing local monopolies to the telephone companies and by substituting regulation for competition. Since the goals were to make phone service both affordable and reliable, regulators encouraged long-term depreciation of equipment and measurable standards for service. These, combined with the natural propensity of engineers to set standards, led to a highly internalized concept of quality service.

Anyone who worked in the Bell System during the past thirty or forty years does not think of an index as something in the back of a book. They know an index is something posted on the wall, such as 98. In an operator service office, this might mean that 98% of all calls were answered within ten seconds. In a business office, it might mean that the installation dates promised to customers were met 98% of the time. In a repair bureau, it might mean that 98% of trouble reports were resolved within twenty-four hours. Everyone knew that a 98 was good. A 97 was not.

In other words, the company had very rigid standards of quality, but they were based on management's (and regulators') perceptions of quality. The target of the prescribed levels was internal efficiency. This resulted in an averaged treatment of customers, with little attempt to judge the seriousness of a customer's need. (One cannot say there was no attempt to do so, because extraordinary efforts, such as an after-hours' mission to repair a disabled person's phone, were often reported and rewarded. But, generally speaking, customers were told the rules rather than granted the exception. Those rules were seen as necessary to maintain control of the vast Bell network of wires--and workers.)

Furthermore, the sometimes-conflicting goals of low cost and high quality led to elaborate mechanisms to size the force. Instead of focusing on customer satisfaction, management monitored the level of customer complaints. When complaints reached unacceptable levels, they hired a few more people to get those installations or repairs done, or to get those calls answered faster.

None of these observations is meant to suggest that the Bell System lacked a service ethic. Indeed, there was constant emphasis on the spirit of service. Its symbol was Angus McDonald, a lineman who donned snowshoes and walked for miles through a blizzard to repair broken lines. His effort was immortalized in a painting that hung on office walls across the company. In fact, Bell people even measured their performance in blizzards, fires, and floods against comparable restoration efforts after previous blizzards, fires and floods.

So the Bell culture provided a long list of standards against which employees, managers, and regulators measured almost every step of every task. There was a lot of emphasis on quality--as defined by everyone but the customer. Thus, nobody knew that the customer was less than satisfied, perhaps not even the customer himself or herself, until some eager entrepreneurs introduced new technology (much of it developed by the Bell System) faster than Bell did.

At the same time, the distinctions between communicating and computing were fading. In short order, this new environment outgrew the parameters of the Communications Act. And this new competition not only alarmed the Bell System--it also caught regulators and policymakers almost totally unprepared.

While they debated, technology marched onward, creating an environment in which divestiture of the Bell System was perhaps inevitable, (as it seems now in 20-20 hindsight).

MARKET-BASED MANAGEMENT

As noted earlier, divestiture created seven regional companies to manage the local Bell networks. Reacting to this environment in which U S WEST originated, its management undertook a reexamination of the company's relationship with its customers: Who are they? How can our network not only carry their voices, but also help them manage their time and improve their lives? How can we do a better job of listening to customers and responding to them?

As that examination progressed, the company's managers and strategists developed a new concept of quality. They sought to redefine the company's output in terms that went beyond rigid, generic, internal expectations of specific customers. For example, meeting a Wednesday installation date 98% of the time is good; but making the customer stay home all day Wednesday because you cannot name a specific hour, or will not come after hours, is not good. This process has led not only to a new emphasis on listening to customers and responding to their individual wishes, but also to a completely new corporate strategy and corporate structure.

A key element of U S WEST's new strategy is managing markets instead of managing products, services, or territories. In this way, managers can focus on meeting customers' needs with whatever mix of products and services, at whatever locations, are necessary to solve the customers' information-management problems. Another element in the company's strategy is performing effectively, both to control internal costs and to respond to the customer's definition of quality. In fact, the creation of this author's job--vice president of quality management--was a step toward fulfilling both the market strategy and the effectiveness strategy: this position is charged not only with drawing together all programs for quality in the company, but also with ensuring that a market approach to quality is shared throughout the organization. Creation of this position was one of many measures in the company's new approach to customers and to quality, an approach known as market-based management.

An internal report described the process as follows: "We have to let the markets we serve define the way we serve them. We've called this focus market-based management and we've adopted it as our new management philosophy." In other words, the company decided it must redefine quality as going far beyond an excellent adherence to engineering (or regulatory) standards. It had to define quality, instead, as satisfying the customer's needs with the right solutions to the customer's problems. That includes good products and good services. But it starts with good listening.

By 1986 U S WEST faced the challenge of pushing this idea into every part of the organization. Planners began restructuring the company's existing businesses into lean, effective market units. At the same time, it was building efficient, centralized groups to support those market units with common services. As a first step in this process, strategists brought many Mountain Bell, Northwestern Bell, and Pacific Northwest Bell functions under common management. This allowed the development of better focus and consistency in meeting customers' needs. The company also began a market unit planning process. Planners were asked to determine the markets U S WEST served, the appropriate strategies for succeeding in those markets, and the opportunities that existed to meet customer needs in new ways.

Many of the changes were invisible. More apparent to the company's customers was bringing under common management the groups that provide connections to long-distance carriers, coin telephone service, and services to customers in government and education. Large customers began almost immediately to comment on the improved quality of U S WEST's service. What they were noticing, initially, were simplification (especially, having one point of contact) and consistency (that is, having the same procedures at Northwestern Bell in Minneapolis as in Mountain Bell at Boise).

By 1987 the company began naming specific market units, such as home and personal services, government and education markets, large business, and general business. In each of these market units, management is charged with determining how customers use and distribute information, and how U S WEST can improve those processes--at a profit to the customer and to U S WEST. Today, all functions of the three Bell companies and leadership of the market units are under common management. They operate under the umbrella name U S WEST Communications. In short, the essence of U S WEST's move to market-based management is redefining quality from the customer's point of view. This effort is becoming apparent throughout the organization.

IMPLEMENTATION OF SERVICE QUALITY IMPROVEMENT
Here are a few examples, some old and some new, of U S WEST's approach to quality management.

Service Measurement
In the past, a sampling of customers was asked how well the company was meeting its standards: for example, Did the installer arrive on Wednesday, as scheduled? The results were reported in the indexes discussed earlier. After divestiture, U S WEST developed a new management tool it called the Market Perception Survey. This study is based on customers' definitions of good service: Were you satisfied or dissatisfied with our service? Why? Customers' verbatim comments are used not only to measure but also to guide the company's behavior.

Employee Input
U S WEST operates a widely recognized employee suggestion plan, which received and evaluated 5,481 employee suggestions in 1987, accepting 689. These ideas were credited with either reducing expenses or increasing revenues by a total of twelve million dollars and with improving service in dozens of small but important ways. Another vehicle for developing employee ideas is call The Aviary. This facility offers employees both time and money to develop ideas that show promise for improving the quality of U S WEST's products, services, or processes, as well as for developing new products.

Resource Allocation
More than half the jobs in America involve the creation, distribution, processing, and interpretation of information. It is a big business, nationally and internationally. To monitor this gigantic market, to assess what it means to the company and particularly to its customers, U S WEST created a separate, strategy-level organization reporting to the office of the chairman. Known as U S WEST Strategic Marketing, the organization includes market researchers and other specialists who focus on the information-management functions that customers will want in the years ahead.

A companion organization focuses on the technology customers will need to fulfill those functions. Known as U S WEST Advanced Technologies, this group of scientists, engineers, and technicians both evaluate and develop new technology. The office of the chairman has approved spending up to 3% of the company's total sales on research and development by 1990.

Management Behavior
The acid test of market-based management, with its new emphasis on quality from the customer's point of view, is the behavior of management. From the beginning, U S WEST has made it clear that quality service and customer focus are more than just buzzwords or just another program from headquarters. Management bonuses are based on two components, service and earnings, weighted equally.

Workshops in market-based management are taught by the officers themselves to hundreds of senior managers and professionals. The company's new vice president of sales in home and personal services, has visited every service representative in the fourteen states the company serves. She stays in touch with those service reps through newsletters and reply forms. When the company's officers gathered for a planning retreat last summer, the featured speakers were customers--not only business customers, but also ordinary residential customers. The company's magazine features success stories of people who focus on quality, both inside and outside the company. One was Mrs. B., a 92-year-old who sold her family's furniture during the Depression and eventually built the largest single-store furniture business in the nation.

U S WEST's president has made it clear that Monday-morning meetings and management appraisals are to spend more time discussing customer items than business items. When customer-contact employees suggested that they themselves dress more professionally, management said yes. When customers suggested longer hours, management said yes. In fact, the three Bell companies today offer 24-hour home-phone centers, where customers can call, toll-free, with questions and requests about their service, their bills, or U S WEST's products and services.

Employees are empowered to make many decisions on their own, because the customer is more important than the rules. Instead of Wednesday installations, the company will schedule appointments for 3 p.m. Wednesday—or even 3 a.m. Among other steps in 1988, the company is contemplating sending each of its nine million customers a report card. On a smaller scale, several years ago, one of the U S WEST companies used the card to find customers with little irritations that could be resolved before they became big irritations. When the company fixed these problems, the most common customer response was "Here's a company that cares about the quality of its work."

CONCLUSION
U S WEST viewed the breakup of the Bell System not as an ending, but as a beginning. Reevaluating a hundred-year heritage of carefully measured, averaged service, the company has redefined quality from the customer's point of view.

The company's primary strategies today are to effectively focus upon and meet customers' needs for quality products and services in the information age. The key is enabling employees to provide the kind of service they know the customer wants, needs, and deserves. The word is quality.

STRATEGIES FOR IMPROVING QUALITY

Marian M. Steeples - Co-Chairperson
Director
Quality Management

U S WEST Communications, Inc.
1801 California St., Ste. 3340
Denver, Colorado 80202

ABSTRACT

Achieving solid quality gains requires: designing methods that prioritize quality concerns; examining root causes of problems; and providing for resolving issues. Measurement and tracking techniques are demonstrated which illustrate the power of developing information from data. This information is integral in providing a solid base from which to make decisions. Systems for determining the cost of poor quality are presented. Quality-Profit optimization concepts are discussed along with actual descriptions of successful applications.

INTRODUCTION

U S WEST established the Quality Management organization to further its emphasis as to the importance of quality in today's increasingly competitive marketplace. The objective of Quality Management is to provide the structures and expertise needed to manage the quality process. The purpose of the quality process is to make it feasible for U S WEST to be the preeminent provider of quality communications products and services.

The Quality Management organization directs, consults, and monitors the quality process to provide support for the most effective, efficient methods of improving quality; assistance to business units to accelerate the incorporation of the quality process; and formation of a system of continuous improvement that yields superior customer service, competitive advantage, and enhanced profitability.

QUALITY MANAGEMENT PROCESS

The Quality Management Process (QMP) is a well organized and effectively implemented methodology that improves quality. Improved quality leads to improved productivity because there are fewer errors and less rework. This results in enhanced customer satisfaction which leads to competitive prices and this translates into repeat business, improved market share, and increased profitability.

Productivity drives profitability. What then drives productivity? Quality. Quality improvement has a leverage on profits that few American businesses have considered. Due to a company's dependence on profit margin, the positive impact of a single dollar of cost saved through quality improvement has a far greater effect than does an increase in sales of the same magnitude. A dollar brought in from the sale of a product or service has the burden of production/delivery costs; overhead; error correction; and so on. Where, a dollar saved through quality improvement goes straight to the bottom line.

The vast majority of quality problems in an organization are system problems. It is estimated that 85 to 90% of quality issues are the result of procedures and policies, that are allowed for inefficiencies, redundancies, or discrepancies. These are system problems. Only 10 to 15% of quality problems are the result of employee ineffectiveness.

Recognizing that most quality problems are in fact systematic to an organization, the thrust of quality improvement is to attack the system not the worker. There then needs to be a legitimate way to identify and resolve these system oriented quality problems. In order to provide for a specific methodology to improve quality, the U S WEST Quality Management organization has created a Project-by-Project approach.

The objective of the quality process is to establish a plan to assess quality, develop a quality strategy, deliver quality improvement and measure the resulting gains.

The quality project approach puts into action the quality process.

First, the appropriate Quality Council establishes quality goals to meet the objectives of the organization. Next major quality problems are identified. Then, a project team is assembled to investigate and resolve the quality problem. Many problems are cross functional in nature. Thus, the project team needs to contain appropriate representation from applicable work units that will be required to resolve the problem.

The quality project teams are provided with Just-in-Time training to meet their specific needs. The training not only gives awareness of the significance of the quality process, it also provides the understanding and skills necessary to identify and solve problems.

DESIGNING STRUCTURES FOR QUALITY MANAGEMENT

In order to succeed in quality improvement, it is essential to establish a structure that supports the organization's strategic and tactical objectives. The design of a system for quality management needs to provide both a superstructure and an infrastructure. Infrastructure is the underlying base or foundation needed to make the system function. Superstructure is what is built above, that gives form, and rests on the fundamental base. The benefits of structuring quality management are that an organizational framework is then in place that undergirds the quality process, unifies the organization, and provides a means to achieve quality results.

The superstructure includes upper management and the union. A primary form the support takes is through a system of quality councils. The purpose of quality councils is to formulate policy; establish project system; and review and support quality improvement project work.

The infrastructure is the underlying base or foundation needed to make the quality process function. It centers on project-by-project implementation. The purpose of a quality project is to diagnose problems, identify causes, develop corrective actions, and provide for a system of continuous improvement.

There are a number of elements that need to be included in designing the Quality Management organization. These include: quality councils, education and training, quality project teams, and tracking and measurement methodologies. The Quality Management organization unifies these various elements into a cohesive whole.

In structuring Quality Management there are critical success factors. Of primary concern are the following: fitting the structure to the uniqueness of the organization; dealing with major corporate problems and opportunities; and involving and training employees to have an active role in the quality process. In order to fit the structure to the organization the quality process must be customized to the specific corporate situation. The system has to be that of the company's, not one of the guru's: Deming, Juran, or Crosby; not a consulting company's prescription, but rather a structure most appropriate for the needs of the organization. While many sources of ideas should be investigated for inclusion the quality organization must be specific for the company. The structure must be built to include methods to get the pulse of the employees. Building such a system requires an investment of resources and providing staff with quality operations experience. The benefit to the corporation of proceeding in this manner far outweighs the costs involved.

Of critical importance is that the Quality Management Process be designed to deal with the major quality problems of the corporation. Existing problems must be targeted for solution. The role of quality councils is to gather data on corporate problems then prioritize these problems on the basis of their importance to the corporation. Project teams need to be organized to investigate and solve quality problems. It is essential that employees be actively involved in researching problems, that they be trained in the quality processes and then provided project structure to solve problems. Tracking and measurement methodologies need to be developed to provide the accurate information needed to resolve quality problems.

ELEMENTS OF THE QUALITY MANAGEMENT PROCESS

There are a number of basic elements that comprise the Quality Management Process. The following is the way we at U S WEST are utilizing the Quality Management Process.

1. Quality Council System
   Form, organize, and implement a system of Quality Councils for management, employees and union leadership. The purpose of quality councils is to coordinate the establishment of quality goals, review progress against these goals, and to participate in the recognition of quality improvement successes.

2. Quality Project
   (Project-by-Project)
   Organize projects so they are consistent with U S WEST's strategic and tactical plans. Investigate problems to define the project direction. Develop the project team and conduct diagnosis of the quality problem.

3. Customer Requirements
   Utilize customer surveys that are designed to measure perceptions of service and product quality. Customer satisfaction must become the focus of corporate thought and action.

4. Quality Operational Plan
   Develop the sequence of activities needed to resolve the quality issue, including the development of a phased implementation plan, description of methods and procedures, selection and training of employees, and provision for tracking and measurement.

5. Employee Training and Education
   Ensure that employees are trained in the quality process. The Quality College for U S WEST employees includes a curriculum specifically designed to provide new methods of quality education, training, motivation and team building.

6. Tracking and Measurement
   Construct, then help implement, a quality tracking and

measurement system. This includes the development of objectives and measurements that will be tracked and reported. Generate progress reports.

7. Quality Improvement

Analyze symptoms of the quality problem.
Formulate and arrange theories of the causes of symptoms.
Test theories and identify root causes of problems. Determine solution and implement corrective action.

8. Cost of Quality

Design and implement a system to calculate the cost of quality, both effective quality and poor quality.
Quality costs quantify specific quality levels and ultimately aid in the improvement of quality.

9. Customer Satisfaction and Improved Profitability

Operate quality systems to meet the needs of the customer both internally and externally.
Continually adjust the quality efforts to reflect current and future needs of the customers.

10. Recognition

Develop systems that recognize and encourage ongoing quality improvement efforts. Emphasize the accomplishments of teams as well as the individual.

11. Process Refinement

Monitor and evaluate the Quality Management Process.
Recognize the successes.
Review measures and standards.
Identify failures and areas for improvement.
Refine the system for optimal effectiveness. Provide for a system of continuous improvement.

12. Quality Management Support

Identify specific projects for quality improvement. Utilize Quality Management staff consultants to assist work areas in resolving quality issues. Organize to guide the projects. Organize to discover causes, solve problems, and ensure that remedies are effective.

QUALITY MANAGEMENT TRAINING AND EDUCATION

In order for the Quality Management organization to provide the necessary educational support, we have contracted with U S WEST's internal training organization, Learning Systems, to assist in the development of a quality curriculum. This series of courses is known as the U S WEST Quality College. To date the course offerings include: Quality Awareness Training; Quality Team Training; Quality Consultant Training; Management and Leadership Skills; and Skills and Techniques. Other courses will be added to the curriculum as the Quality Management process continues to evolve. The purpose of each is as follows:

Quality Awareness Training: To create an awareness of the Quality Management Process (QMP), including what QMP encompasses and what the specific impacts are to individual employees.

Quality Team Training: To provide skills to identify and resolve quality issues and problems.

Quality Consultant Training: To provide the Quality Consultants with the skills required to effectively lead the quality process.

Quality Management/Leadership Skills: To focus management on quality issues; to give understanding of corporate goals on quality; to describe what is expected of managers; to give understanding of what quality means (individual employee quality and corporate competitive position); and to describe quality/profit optimization.

Quality Skills and Techniques: To provide the specific skill modules to be employed during the quality improvement process.

Prior to the development of the courses, all members of the Learning Systems project group were themselves trained in quality. This was accomplished by a structured program that included work with experienced Quality Management staff; exposure to quality books and periodicals; and attendance in a variety of quality seminars.

The rollout of the courses began with Quality Awareness in August. Followed by Consultant and Team Training in September; Skills and Techniques in October; Management and Leadership will be offered in December.

Training is scheduled on a Just-in-Time basis. This phrase was adopted to describe this new method of delivering training. The concept of "Just-in-Time" borrowed from manufacturing refers to making materials available to production at the time they are needed for use. Materials are not purchased and stored.

Frequently, the practice of providing training for the entire corporation at the beginning of a new initiative or program has created a false sense of security. The belief has been that training in and of itself would cause a change for the better. Actual results show us that this is seldom the case. In truth, if there is no organized process for people to put their training to use, "sheep dip" training (where all a corporation's employees are cycled through the same course) can create problems.

These problems include: employee's heightened expectations followed by lowered morale when there is little or no positive change; the perception that this is a program not a process since this type of training parallels a program (it has a beginning and an end) the expense involved can be considerable with little or no results to justify the cost.

To avoid these and other problems, U S WEST's system of Just-in-Time Training provides education at the point in quality project work where it can be put to immediate use. Sequencing course offerings in this manner has allowed us to efficiently and effectively train our people in quality practices and methods.

QUALITY PROJECTS AT U S WEST

Quality is defined as conformance to customer expectations and requirements. Quality is measured in terms of timeliness and accuracy. If things worked perfectly, quality would be perfect. And there are high costs associated with this non-perfection, this non-conformance to requirements.

Many organizations have attempted to improve quality. Currently, there are considerable numbers of companies both manufacturing and service engaged in various methods of quality improvement. However few corporations are succeeding in obtaining the desired results. A primary reason for this frustrating lack of success can be found in lack of sound methods to identify and resolve major corporate quality issues.

The project-by-project approach instituted at U S WEST gives structure and legitimacy to the process of quality improvement. The project approach succeeds, in part, because it conforms to recognized business practices. The superstructure and infrastructure, described earlier in this work, provide the requisite framework. The Quality Management organization at the hub of the quality process provides the expertise needed for effective coordination and implementation of quality projects. The project approach succeeds because significant quality issues are addressed. The project nomination and selection process ensures the most critical concerns of the organization will be targeted.

Project nominations come from throughout the organization, from the management hierarchy (managers, supervisors, professional specialists, project teams), from the strategic and tactical goals and objectives, from the market place (sales, customer service), from the work force (formal and informal ideas presented to supervisors and other means), from data on the cost of poor quality).

The project selection machinery screens all nominations and agreement is reached on which are to become projects. This is coordinated by quality councils.

Project teams are formed to resolve quality problems. Since the majority of an organization's critical problems tend to involve the work of a number of work units, most projects are interdepartmental. The project teams are comprised of cross-functional team members.

Generally, the average savings from a single project is approximately $100,000. The cost of producing that result tends to be about $20,000. Major breakthroughs are produced when a solution to a quality problem in one area of the company can be replicated in other areas. This reduces the investment cost and increases the yield.

Current project work at U S WEST is being conducted in the following units: Carrier, Claims and Access Marketing Support; Network, Distribution Services and Switched Services; and Technical Services to name a few.

An important example that illustrates the effectiveness of the quality project system is that from a software quality work area. The quality problem there persisted and grew over a period of fourteen months. The work area involved was faced with producing a sophisticated product on a tight production schedule. There were repeated failures. Unfortunately many of these failures were discovered after the product was shipped. In effect, the customer was functioning as the final inspector and was not at all pleased with this role. A quality process was initiated to provide a remedy. Project work was conducted. The successful resolution to the problem centered on developing a more effective method of tracking and measuring system throughout the production cycle. The root cause of the problem was discovered by use of statistical analysis. It was revealed that 83% of the problem was coming from one source. Remedies were developed that significantly reduced this level to one that was more satisfactory to the customer in that the deliverable was greatly improved in its level of quality. The solution was also of considerable benefit to the work unit, as much of the costly rework was eliminated.

Cost of quality techniques are being used by the Quality Management organization to detail the quality improvement profit contributions of projects. These quality costs measure the costs specifically associated with the achievement and non-achievement of product and service quality. Quality costs are the total costs incurred by: the failure to meet requirements (both internal and external), appraising a product or service for conformance to requirements, and investing in the prevention of non-conformance to requirements.

Examples of prioritizing quality issues, examining root causes, measurement and tracking, quality-profit optimization will be fully expanded at the National Communications Forum, October 3, 1988.

CONCLUSIONS

Through managing quality, U S WEST is achieving solid, tangible results - improved customer satisfaction and increased profitability. The project-by-project approach legitimizes the quality process by providing the methodologies needed for continuous system improvement. Additionally, the process gives the organization a constancy of purpose.

A company's viability can be improved by increasing income, reducing expenses, or a combination of both. The Quality Management Process (QMP) implemented at U S WEST, addresses both these areas.

The QMP reduces expenses by operating efficiently and effectively. Cost savings result from developing systems that allow workers to do things right the first time. Workers take pride in producing a job well done. The costs of errors, rework and redundancies are reduced or eliminated.

The QMP also increases income by improving customer satisfaction. Systems are designed to meet customer expectations and requirements. This leads to superior customer relationships and competitive advantage.

In summary, improved quality reduces the cost of doing business and increases the opportunity for increasing market share. The goal of Quality Management is to make quality the competitive point of difference. We are moving in the direction of realizing our full quality potential.

NETWORK OPERATIONS: THE PLANNING PERSPECTIVE

Frederick M. Lax - Chairperson
Director
Switching Operations Systems

AT&T Bell Laboratories
6200 E. Broad Street
Columbus, Ohio 43213

ABSTRACT

During the years since divestiture there have been tremendous changes in telecommunications services, technologies, equipment, and overall strategies. Fundamental to the growth and success of these innovations is the ability to support and maintain the network commensurate with customers' performance expectations and the cost demands placed on the network providers. This seminar explores network support issues from various perspectives including evolution of architectures and data bases in support of users by providers and suppliers. This seminar and the two associated seminars, "The Outside Operations Perspective" and "The Inside Operations Perspective," discuss current and future operations support problems, implications, alternatives, and solutions.

James Bielanski   - Illinois Bell Telephone

Elizabeth Eastland   - Bell Northern
                         Research

Michael Grisham   - AT&T Bell Laboratories

Luke Kane   - Bell Communications
                         Research

A LAYERED APPROACH TO NETWORK OPERATIONS ARCHITECTURE

Elizabeth Eastland
Manager, DMS Base OAM

Bell Northern Research
P. O. Box 13478
Research Triangle Park, N. C.
27709-3478

William Kozel
Product Manager,
Switching Marketing

Northern Telecom, Inc.
4001 E. Chapel Hill - Nelson Hwy.
Research Triangle Park, N. C.
27709

ABSTRACT

The following paper defines a logical OAM architecture by dividing the OAM activities into four layers: 1) generation of raw OAM data, 2) real-time collection, medication, and integration of that data at the service node level, 3) network management applications, and 4) off-line databases which store customer and network inventory records.

The architecture follows the OSI model's intent to keep interfaces well-defined: a standard architecture is proposed to allow multiple OS and NE suppliers to efficiently accommodate the future OAM requirements of ONA and the evolving intelligent Network. In addition, the incorporation of Custom Programming into the proposed layers allows a telephone operating company to control service velocity of network management tools to ESPs, corporate network managers, and end-users.

INTRODUCTION

As the current telecommunications networks evolve to offer the information services of tomorrow, Telecommunications Operating Companies are in need of network management capabilities which are simultaneously flexible, robust and quick to respond to new services as they are deployed in the network. As local telephone operating companies face increasing competition for their markets, they need to exploit their greatest asset, the embedded network. However, this asset is only as strong as the capabilities they have to maintain it.

The telecommunication network is a complex array of transmission and connection processing equipment. The control and administration of these network elements (NE) has required the development of an equally complex array of mechanized systems known as Operations Support Systems (OSS). Customer and equipment records are stored in large databases which are often duplicated, and many times inconsistent. Generally, each operations group responsible for a specific network control or administrative function has been supported by a unique OSS. Communications between systems was often paper based, or proprietary. When all network elements were supplied by the same vendor and all operations groups part of the same company, this operations architecture performed quite adequately. However, due to divestiture and an evolving regulatory environment, the network is changing dramatically. Telephone Telecommunications Companies are being required to open up the network to provide Comparably Efficient Interconnection (CEI) to Enhanced Service Providers (ESP) creating a more Open Network Architecture (ONA).

As a result, entirely new and varied demands are being placed on today's OSS. Besides the Operating Company, the OSS must serve two new "customers" of OAM: Enhanced Service Providers and the corporate communications managers of both large and small businesses. Clearly a new architecture is needed.

A FUNCTIONALLY LAYERED OAM ARCHITECTURE

With the increasing complexity of telecommunications networks, there has been a resultant increase in the complexity of OAM (Operations, Administration and Maintenance) capabilities, procedures and systems. The architecture that is proposed in this paper attempts to structure this functionality into four functional layers (see Fig. 1): 1) generation of "raw" OAM data, 2) real-time collection, mediation, and integration of that data at the service node level, (3) on-line network management applications that are capable of multinode interaction, and 4) off-line database applications which store customer and network information necessary for the business end of managing the telecommunications network. The intent of these layers is to keep interfaces between functional layers constant, but allow appropriate flexibility for implementation and product differentiation of the functionality.

The methodology of this approach, originated with the OSI model of defining communication layers and interactions within a protocol suite. However, the two models are not to be confused; their scopes are different. The proposed OAM architectural model defines functional responsibilities across network components which is not a part of the OSI model.

The OSI seven layer protocol can be used for communication between applications within the four functional layers of the proposed OAM architecture; NTI fully endorses the OSI model for communication between applications.

The added value of the suggested architectural model is that it makes available to network management applications a consistent, standard interface to the NE and thus reduces the complexity, and hence the cost, of conforming to multiple interfaces. It incorporates the required flexibility by including custom programming to allow the Operating Company to control service delivery. It also suggests the conservation of the processor real-time by moving non-call-completion tasks to unshared processors: the processors in Layer Two which manage the access to the NE.

LAYER ONE:

This layer performs the base OAM functionality associated with call processing. It performs low level sensing such as trouble detection, raw billing measurement generation and service performance monitoring as well as the implementation of controls and data entry from higher level system. Any information in the upper three layers is either sourced or performed here. It includes the collection of information leading to operational measurements, log messages, traffic data and message accounting. The base utilities in this layer are used in provisioning, system memory administration and maintenance as directed by higher levels in the architecture.

LAYER TWO:

This layer utilizes the basic OAM building blocks ("services") of layer one in sophisticated real-time processes that perform trouble correlation, alarm to customer correlation, service affecting thresholding and so on. These tasks are not inherently related to the completion of a call and can be logically separated from layer one.

In this way, layer 2 off-loads non-essential processing tasks from layer 1 call processing, while at the same time, sends only relevant information in standard format to the Operations System (OS). This layer includes customization capability so that OAM functionality can be accessed and utilized by non Operating Company users in a secure, partitioned environment.

Layer 2 allows selected changes to be made to network resources by end-users without Operating Company intervention. It also provides end-users with service performance data in near real-time. NT's Business Network Management application is an example of such a system. To ensure integrity each end user is limited to the systems and element data related to their services only. In turn, layer 2 provides relevant updates to the layers above (e.g. OS), regarding end-user changes. Positioning OAM as a service to end-users increases the speed of service deployment and reduces unnecessary Operating Company involvement.

LAYER 3:

This layer of functionality is typically carried out at a work center. By taking advantage of the "self-healing" capabilities that layer 1 and 2 provide, the network can be monitored and provisioned remotely, relieving the telco of the need for 24-hour on-hand maintenance. It is at layer 3 that centralization of nodal OAM functionality takes place. By relating the intelligence from multiple nodes, alarms can be related to a single event such as single facility trouble triggering alarms in several network elements. Layer 3 provides functionality to allow a single service order to implement changes in all relevant network elements (e.g. PVN (Private Virtual Network) service requires updates in SSPs

(Service Switching Points) as well as SCPs (Service Control Point). NTs Dynamically Controlled Routing application is an example of such a sophisticated, real-time level 3 functionality.

LAYER 4:

This layer consists of the off-line databases which are used to keep information about the business end of the network and are generally not related to the network in real-time. These are the larger databases that house information about customers, billing records, inventory databases, circuits, service orders, et. These databases are used for functions that do not interact with the network on a real time basis such as network planing, engineering, billing, and design.

EXAMPLE ONE: PROVISIONING

The following examples will hopefully illustrate the functionality at each level. The process begins when a customer sets up an account with the Operating Company. The service representative has access to inventory databases at level 4, and based on this, can inform the customer if facilities are available for service. A customer profile is recorded in the necessary databases at this level. In the future, when the telephone company wishes to provide a service which requires certain base capabilities in multiple NE, sophisticated planning tools such as NT's PLANET will be necessary before implementation to ensure capacity and functionality exist in the network (e.g. Bellcore defined PVN Services which require SSP, STP (Signal Transfer Point) and SCP functionality). Circuit design, equipment assignment and translation all take place off-line at this layer.

Conceivably this functionality could be automated (i.e. for those services not requiring network provisioning) speeding up provisioning time for enhanced service to compare with that of POTS. After the equipment is assigned and translations are performed, messages in a standard format are passed to the various network elements affected (e.g. for PVN, the SSP and SCP could both require updates). Level 2 interprets these and does translation to vendor or equipment specific commands. When multiple pieces of the same node need updated, then this layer of functionality ensures this data is consistent. Layer 1 functionality actually activates the service.

EXAMPLE TWO: SURVEILLANCE

To illustrate the levels and their interaction further, an example of a trouble in a facility and the resultant alarm reporting is shown in Fig. 2. At layer 1 a bit error ratio on a facility has surpassed a threshold set previously at layer 2. Layer 2 would be able to correlate this event to a level of service and ultimately a customer group. A service affecting alarm is formatted into a standard message with as much detail as possible about the exact cause of the trouble and sent across a standard interface to the centralized layer 3 systems. At layer 3 a trouble ticket or similar report is issued and the appropriate testing, dispatch or change order functions are carried out. Layer 2 or 3 would be responsible for updating any off-line databases at layer 4 to eliminate billing for an out-of-service condition. As service is restored, layer 2 provides this status indication to the affected customers.

OAM AS SERVICE

As the Enhanced Service Provider (ESP) looks for OAM capabilities to support their services, the Operating Company will be in an ideal position to lease these OAM capabilities and manage end-user access to ESP services. ESPs will be looking for functionality to provide quick responses to service demand, specialized billing information and collection streams, and enhanced maintenance capabilities to ensure their service is being provided. New customers who don't have the embedded base of OAM capabilities, such as Specialized Common Carriers, may also wish to "buy" OAM capabilities from the telephone company.

For the end-user, layer 2 provides a valuable source of information and control. In turn, the ability to put the user "in charge" of the network has significant implications for the Operating Company operator. Service response time is greatly improved, and bulk billing for resource use and feature changes can be provided direct to end-user premises. Within the Operating Company, the customer oriented view of the network can be extended to cover functional, geographic or equipment management groups; each user group in effect becomes a "customer" of Layer 2 functionality.

A closer look at the sub layers of the layered architectural model (See Fig. 2), shows how basic OAM functional components could be used by end-users, ESPs and the Operating Company alike. Database partitioning capabilities and custom programmability allow layer 2 to lever functionality provided by basic OAM functions from layer 1 by customizing these for new users. For example:

- The basic function of downloading directory number information is used by the Operating Company when processing service orders; it is also used by the customer when performing station moves and changes.

- Call processing data can be formatted for AMA for the Operating Company or partitioned off for specific customers as SMDR.

- The Operating Company line and trunk monitoring data can be used to assure specific customers of a certain level of service performance on their network circuits.

For the network element, layer 2 can consolidate OS interfaces, provide a unified user-system interface, and provide cluster control of site specific or technology specific network elements; in effect acting as an OAM service node. The Northern Telecom DMS SuperNode is a case in point where a multi-function network node is created from previously separate network functions. Separate OAM functions are integrated so both the customer and the Operating Company share OAM functionality to implement more instant line changes, capture call details and monitor facilities status for several dissimilar network elements at the same node.

CONCLUSIONS

The benefits of the proposed functionality in the network operations architecture are clear. Layer 2 off-loads the processing of raw OAM data from the increasingly complex function of call processing. It addresses the difficult transition from the current OSS environment to the ONA environment of the future by giving the telephone operating company the tools to customize OAM for resale, a traditional non-revenue source. The telephone company, end-users and enhanced service providers share the management of public network resources in a win-win scenario - speeding up service response while reducing the administrative and maintenance costs.

In summary the proposed architecture provides the Telecommunications Operating Company with a structured environment within which to position and interwork current and new OAM applications, as well as providing the tools to customize and position OAM as a new source for revenue.

The authors would like to acknowledge Paul Brand, co-author of "A Network Operations Architecture for ONA" presented at NOMS 88' in New Orleans February 1988 from which the major ideas of this paper are derived.

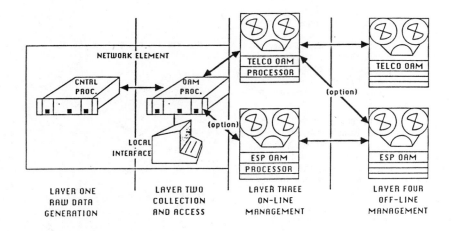

FIGURE 1.   LAYERED OAM ARCHITECTURE

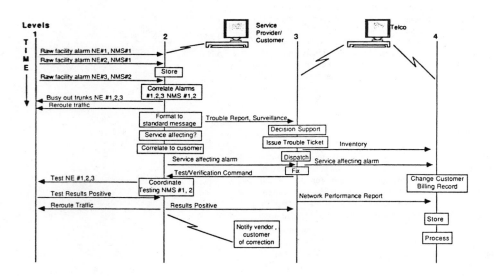

FIGURE 2.   ALARM SURVEILLANCE

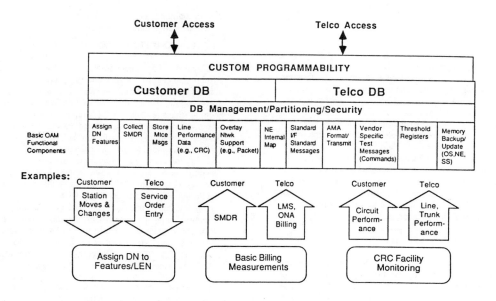

FIGURE 3.   OAM AS SERVICE

NETWORK DATA STORAGE AND PROCESSING

Michael G. Grisham
Supervisor

AT&T Bell Laboratories
480 Red Hill Road
Middletown, New Jersey 07748-3052

ABSTRACT

Prior to the development of processor-controlled network elements (NEs) and processor-based network operations systems (OSs) in telecommunications, telephone subscribers were served by the arrangement shown in Fig. 1. Because all telephones were functionally equivalent and provided no optional features, only inventory records were needed to administer customer premises equipment (CPE). Manual cross-connects on the loop side of the switch were needed to provision plain old telephone service (POTS), and manual cross-connects on the trunk side of the switch were needed to provision interoffice facilities. All equipment and service provisioning, then, was manual, relying indirectly on data stored on paper in manual filing systems. Maintenance also relied on this mass of paper records, together with manual testing and fault location methods.

TWO ROLES OF OPERATIONS SYSTEMS

During the last two decades, a number of operations systems (OSs) were deployed to mechanize the processes of provisioning and maintaining the telecommunications network and its services. As shown in Fig. 2, the Facility Assignment and Control System (FACS) and the Loop Management Operations System (LMOS) now manage data for provisioning and maintaining loops, respectively, while the Trunks Integrated Records Keeping System (TIRKS) manages data for facilities. FACS, LMOS, and TIRKS use large mainframe computer systems to store and retrieve necessary data. Testing, monitoring, and analysis functions were also mechanized with Mechanized Loop Testing (MLT), the Switching Control Center System (SCCS), Telecommunications Alarm Surveillance and Control (TASC), and the T-Carrier Administration system (TCAS), using networked minicomputer systems and specialized testing, monitoring, and telemetry hardware. The mechanization of operations functions was also partly accomplished in the network itself, as processor-controlled NEs took on self-monitoring and self-testing. And processor-controlled NEs began to rely on their own data storage capability to support both network service and some network operations functions.

THE INTEGRATED SERVICES DIGITAL NETWORK

As shown in Fig. 3, the Integrated Digital Services Network will emerge from a more complex architecture than early POTS. ISDN intelligent customer premises equipment will offer a number of features that require coordinated administration of ISDN switch capabilities. These new premises equipment and ISDN switch features will be added to a network already made more complex by processor-controlled transmission equipment in both the loop and interoffice plant. Specifically, subscriber loop carrier (SLC) equipment, with its own remotely-controlled functions and configuration data, will often intervene between ISDN premises equipment and the switch, and switches will be interconnected increasingly with an interoffice facilities network that includes digital access and cross-connect systems (DACS). In summary, ISDN will emerge on processor-controlled premises equipment and processor-controlled NEs, all relying directly on self-stored data. (Corresponding developments based on signaling systems will be ignored here for simplicity).

How will OSs support the ISDN? As shown in Fig. 4, the POTS OSs are evolving. MLT/ISDN will extend testing capabilities to include loopbacks at customer premises equipment and to use digital testing functions and status information from ISDN switches. SCCS will monitor and process NE messages from SLC and DACS, as well as new ISDN messages from switches. TASC and TCAS continue to monitor facilities, increasingly between DACS. Both FACS and LMOS must accommodate new ISDN subscriber equipment and services. TIRKS maintains and administers facilities between SLC and the switch, as well as interoffice facilities.

OS DATA AND FUNCTIONS REVISITED

Against this backdrop of changes in both the telecommunications network and the operations systems that help manage it, the two historical roles of OSs need to be considered anew. Again, the primary role of FACS, LMOS, and TIRKS has been to manage data. MLT, SCCS, TASC, and TCAS (and others not discussed here, such as SARTS) rely on these data to provide functions -- configuration, testing, monitoring, and analysis. As the network has changed, quite different trends are apparent for data versus functions. In general, more and more functions have migrated from stand-off (OS) processors into processor-controlled NEs. Examples of this trend include built-in monitoring capabilities in SLC, switches, and DACS, built-in analog and digital testing capabilities in switches, and even built-in reprovisioning in transmission systems -- one way of viewing protection switching. In contrast, data has not migrated from OS processors into NEs. Rather, redundant databases have been created, so that OSs and NEs contain supposedly identical copies of some portion of the overall network database.

THE NEED FOR A DATA ARCHITECTURE AND A DATABASE ARCHITECTURE

Some data redundancy is desirable. For example, data are duplicated when one processor needs to provide back-up for another, in cases of NE processor failure. Similarly, data are duplicated when performance considerations require it. But the problems of keeping multiple independent databases consistent are well known; two supposedly identical databases rarely stay identical for long, requiring constant audits and expensive resynchronization efforts. The solution to this problem lies in a data architecture that identifies all data entities, their relationships, and their attributes, and in a database architecture that specifies where these data are stored, how they are updated, and how they are recovered in the event of a failure. For network operations, a database architecture would explicitly allocate data between OSs and NEs, identify redundant data, and specify update mechanisms such that redundancy, where necessary, is ensured.

EXAMPLES OF DATA FLOW AMONG OSs AND NEs

Several possible ways to update redundant OS and NE data can be considered. Common to all of the examples that follow is the notion of primary versus secondary databases. For any data item that appears in multiple databases, one database is designated primary and the other database(s) secondary. All updates are accomplished by updating the primary database, and then propagated from the primary database to the secondary database(s). Fig. 5 shows one such arrangement; an OS primary database is updated, and then secondary databases are updated from the OS.

Another possible data flow is shown in Fig. 6. Here, the update is performed at a primary database in the switch, and propagated to SLC, CPE, and an OS from the switch. A final example is given in Fig. 7, which shows part of the data flow for an automatic customer station rearrangement. Upon being installed, the ISDN CPE in Fig. 7 informs the switch of its identity so that the switch can properly associate this terminal's features with its new location. The diversity of these examples is an indication of the complexity of deciding on a database architecture for network operations, and an indication of the priority which the telecommunications industry needs to give to the data architecture that is a prerequisite.

DATA AND OPERATIONS FUNCTIONS

NEs already contain data needed to support network functions; these data are stored in the NE itself because the highest performance can be obtained when the NE data and NE functions reside in the same processor (or processor complex). The network will contain much more data in the future as more processor-controlled NEs are deployed and as services grow more diverse and complicated. Because NEs are designed for very high reliability and 24-hour availability, network data is an attractive candidate for the primary source of redundant operations data. And for the same reason that network data and network functions are co-located in NEs -- maximal performance -- those operations functions that rely on data in NEs are likely to migrate to NEs. Explicit separation of data and application is in no way compromised by this trend, given a clear data architecture and database architecture.

SUMMARY

With the deployment of processor-controlled network elements, the network itself has become capable of both storing data and processing it. However, our traditional approach to operations systems allocates both data storage and processing to computer systems external to the network. To take advantage of the reliability and inherent validity of data now found in the network itself, explicit and systematic allocation is needed. In this session, the prior evolution of operations systems and factors relevant to future allocation of functions and data will be considered.

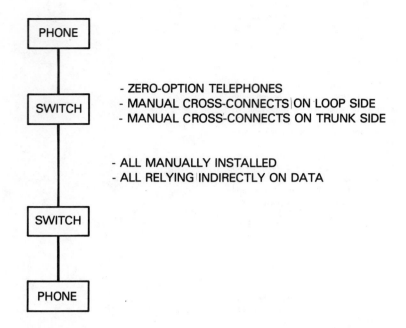

- ZERO-OPTION TELEPHONES
- MANUAL CROSS-CONNECTS ON LOOP SIDE
- MANUAL CROSS-CONNECTS ON TRUNK SIDE

- ALL MANUALLY INSTALLED
- ALL RELYING INDIRECTLY ON DATA

FIG. 1. PLAIN OLD TELEPHONE SERVICE

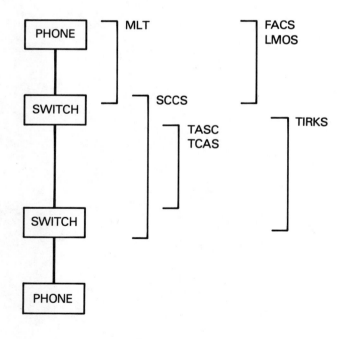

FIG. 2. SOME POTS OPERATING SYSTEMS

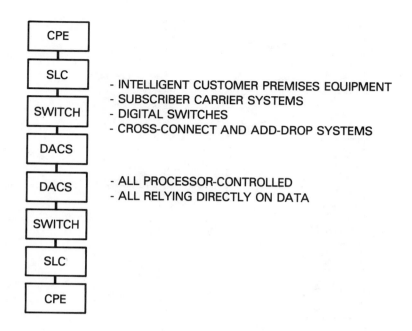

FIG. 3. INTEGRATED SERVICES DIGITAL NETWORK

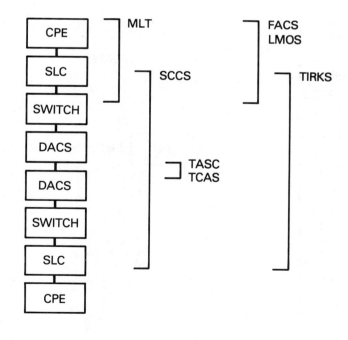

FIG. 4. SOME ISDN OPERATIONS SYSTEMS

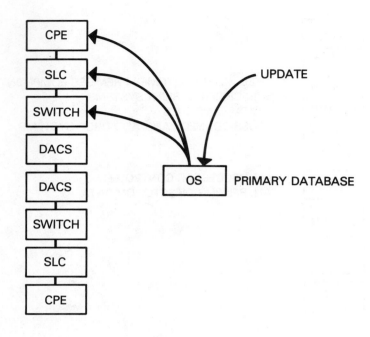

FIG. 5. ONE POSSIBLE DATA FLOW

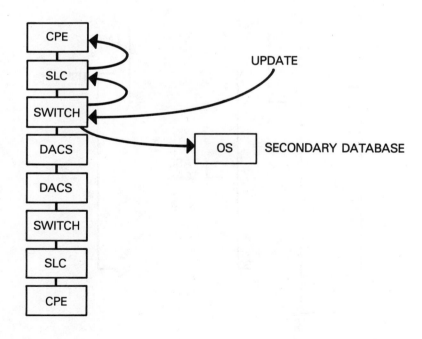

FIG. 6. ANOTHER POSSIBLE DATA FLOW

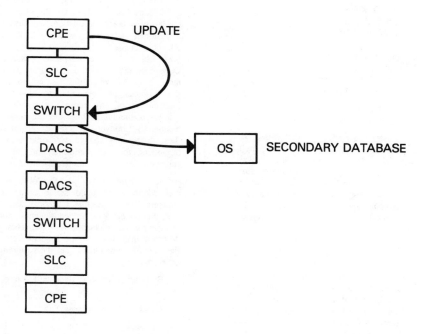

FIG. 7. AUTOMATIC CUSTOMER STATION REARRANGEMENT DATA FLOW

TELECOMMUNICATIONS DATA ARCHITECTURE PLANNING

Luke D. Kane
Member of Technical Staff
New Architecture Planning

Bell Communications Research
331 Newman Springs Road
Box 7020
Red Bank, New Jersey 07701-7020

ABSTRACT

The telecommunications industry has recognized that data is an important corporate resource to be shared by a company's application systems. Organizing data in a unified logical way gives a firm a competitive advantage, by making its information resources more responsive to change and less costly to administer. This session will review the process that was used to develop Bellcore's Strategic Data Architecture and present some of the underlying philosophy of data-driven telecommunications system development.

INTRODUCTION

Systems analysis has historically been approached from a process orientation, focusing on the particular business tasks to be mechanized. Such an approach treats data indirectly, identifying the data needed to support the particular application under development. As applications proliferate, many databases are developed with redundant information, or with similar information organized and encoded incompatibly. Information rapidly becomes inconsistent across systems; introducing new systems becomes difficult since data must be drawn together and reconciled from many partially redundant sources.

A more effective set of systems[1] can be developed by viewing data as a shareable corporate resource important to many business functions. Organizing the data in a unified logical way leads to the development of minimally redundant and consistent databases which can support a wide spectrum of business functions. Database updating activities are reduced, data storage costs are minimized, data consistency and accuracy are maximized, and the introduction of new applications is greatly improved.

Implementing this approach begins with the development of a strategic data architecture, that identifies the fundamental objects about which the corporation stores information and the relationships among objects. The objects are grouped into sets, called subject data areas, by object-to-object affinities usually measured by the degree of common usage by business tasks.

Bellcore has recently completed a Strategic Data Architecture (SDA) that analyzed the data requirements of major parts of the operation of the exchange and exchange access telephone business. This architecture provides the framework for extensive database design work to support the applications being developed for Bellcore's clients. The SDA has also provided the context for the development of a Logical Data Model, which provides significantly more detail and more rigorous rules for defining objects and their relationships.

BUILDING A DATA ARCHITECTURE

To get this integrated data modeling plan, subject matter experts built a functional architecture that spanned the operation of a telephone company, and developed from it a data architecture with the same global scope. A functional architecture is a decomposition of the telephone company's business information processes. Given a functional architecture, subject matter experts then identified objects, the relationships between the objects, and the connection between the objects and functions.

The objects represent the most important element of the data architecture because these are the classes of things about which the business stores information. For instance, a switch, a service, a customer, a project, and a vehicle may be objects of the telephone business. Notice that the objects in the above list have been objects of the telephone business since its inception. Organizing the corporation's data around the objects leads to the most stable and robust database environment since the objects of the business are stable over time. Modeling the objects independent of any computing technology also enhances the stability of the data architecture; the model is insulated from rapid technology turnover. Of course, the information we store about these things may change over time, as will the technology, but organizing the information around the objects will allow for easier evolution and minimize the need for total restructuring.

As shown in Fig. 1, the objective of a strategic data architecture is to build stable corporate databases. From a strategic data architecture a Logical Data Model, a user-oriented, machine-independent, unified semantic structure of the telephone company's data elements, is built. Then physical databases are designed from parts of the Logical Data Model combined with the technology available, and the requirements of applications in development.

Building a strategic data architecture then yields five basic results -

- A model of the business;
- An identification of the objects of the business;
- An identification of the relationships among the objects;
- A grouping of the objects into subject data areas;
- A mapping of the business functions into the data objects.

the input for the efficient development of corporate databases. The specific techniques we used to gain these results are outlined in the following sections.

STRUCTURED ANALYSIS

We began to build a model of a telephone company by modifying the Data Structured System Design (DSSD*) method. The DSSD model consists of actors, messages, objects, and functions. These components are captured in a series of structured analysis representations[2] we called Information Exchange Diagrams (IEDs) and Functional Flow Diagrams. IEDs and Functional Flow Diagrams capture the flow of information at two different levels of detail.

INFORMATION EXCHANGE DIAGRAMS

Information Exchange Diagrams (IEDs) represent the flow of messages between actors. Subject matter experts draw an actor of interest, define all the actors with which it exchanges information, define all the messages exchanged, and associate objects to messages. These actor-centered diagrams are connected in a sequence of reconciliation meetings into a chain of messages flowing across the enterprise.

Actors are the people, places, or things, both internal and external to the telephone company which transmit or receive information. External actors are given by the business environment like *Customer* and *Vendor*. Internal actors were defined from a functional architecture, the Operations Systems Strategic Plan (OSSP/3).[3]

---

* DSSD is a registered trademark and was developed by Ken Orr & Associates, Inc.

Messages and objects are the other ingredients of an IED. Messages carry the facts about an object and objects, as discussed earlier, are the fundamental strategic units of corporate data. Each message must have at least one object.

Unlike most forms of structured analysis, DSSD does not allow the use of stores of data. Using such stores at this point would preempt the purpose to data architecture, to design corporate stores of data.

An example of an IED is given in Fig. 2, of the Purchase Order Processing Actor. For example, this actor transmits a purchase order to a vendor. Recorded, though not shown here, are the objects of that message, namely Vendor Transaction and Unit Inventory. IEDs serve as a starting point for the more richly detailed Functional Flow Diagrams.

FUNCTIONAL FLOW DIAGRAMS

Functional Flow Diagrams identify the information activities which create the messages identified in the IEDs. DSSD differs from other methods for drawing data flow diagrams in that DSSD constrains a function to creating only one output message. It can have one or many input messages.

These many-to-one data flows focus on the input messages needed to produce a single output message. Each of the these elemental functions is so constrained to simplify the requirements for development.

RESULTS OF STRUCTURED ANALYSIS

Structured analysis has put all the pieces of the business model on the table. Actors, messages, elemental functions, attributes, and message flows have all been identified. The messages have suggested candidates for objects.

Any of the commonly practiced methods of structured analysis could be modified to collect the same information we did with the DSSD method. Multiple layers of data flows can be captured using techniques developed by DeMarco,[4] Gane and Sarsen,[5] IBM,[6] and others. All that needs to be added is the focus on data. Subject matter experts must map messages to objects. In our case, we used IEDs and functional flows to map the business functions to the data objects of a telephone company.

Given the ubiquitous nature of data, these subject matter experts must also agree completely on the flows and the objects. This is more of a logistical problem then one of method. We approached consistency by organizing a series of meetings between differing groups of subject matter experts who acted as arbitrators. Facilitators set the agenda based on consistency checks made by the tools we developed. As a result, we had a consensus of the parts that made up the business model. It made the really hard part of putting the pieces together much easier.

DATA ABSTRACTION

Having completed the structured analysis, we had an extensive list of candidate objects. In order to formulate the data architecture, we made use of several important ideas from data modeling[7] and database design[8] including generalization and aggregation, characterization, and Entity-Relationship modeling. While these constructs could not be applied with the same level of rigor as they can be when dealing with individual data elements in the Logical Data Model, they did provide a means of gaining significant insight into how to understand and organize the objects.

GENERALIZATION AND AGGREGATION

The structured analysis identified many candidate objects, many were obvious synonyms and data elements. These were culled by the abstraction techniques of generalization and aggregation.[9] For instance, both analog circuits and digital circuits appeared as candidate objects; network elements, operations systems, stocked items, and plug-ins were also suggested.

Working at the strategic level, we recognized that we could not identify all of the kinds of circuits or all of the kinds of items the telephone company owns. Thus we abstracted these into higher level objects which represented a generalization of these more specific objects. We thus created an object called Circuit which did not distinguish between analog and digital at the strategic level, as shown in Fig. 3. Similarly, we created an object called Unit Inventory which did not distinguish among kinds of items. In each of these cases, we recognize that in specifying the Logical Data Model, it may become important to specify the things that were generalized to these higher levels of abstraction.

As another example (see Fig. 3) of the use of abstraction, many objects were distinguished by geographical boundaries such as loop, central office, or interoffice. In all of these cases, we aggregated them to form one object since new technology is clearly blurring these boundaries and in meeting the new business planning needs it is imperative that we model and store our data in ways which are more independent of the standard network boundaries.

CHARACTERIZATION

Another concept utilized was the notion of characterization, a process defined by Flavin,[10] which splits candidate objects to reduce redundancy. While we could not apply characterization with the level of rigor that can be applied to logical database design, the concept still allowed us to partition and better understand some sets of information used by the enterprise.

In our analysis, we identified information required about network elements which was very specific to particular pieces of equipment located in particular places in the network, while other information was independent of any particular piece of that equipment. For example, many applications need to know electrical and physical characteristics of a switch. This information is true of the switch regardless of which central office it occupies. Other applications need to know specific information about particular switches such as which trunks are connected to it or what its maintenance history is. If the generic information were stored with the particular information, the generic information would be repeated for every instance of the particular switch.

We separated data into two categories of objects, either generic objects about which we store type information, or specific objects about which we store instance information. type information is germane to all occurrences of an object, i.e., it characterizes the object, while instance information pertains only to one occurrence. For example, in Fig. 4, we separated two objects - one called Catalog Item which provides generic information and the other called Unit Inventory which contains information about particular instances of Catalog Items. A real, tangible switch is a Unit Inventory object while the concept, design, and characterization of a certain type of switch is a Catalog Item object.

ENTITY-RELATIONSHIP MODEL

Entity-Relationship modeling[11] recognizes that there are entities which represent real or abstract things of our business, and there are relationships between or among these entities. Information, called attributes, is stored about both entities and relationships. This construct was helpful in communicating the definitions of many of the objects and examining a sample set of information about the object or its relationships, much greater clarity was provided.

For example, the notion of circuit which generally carries many different definitions by personnel within the telephone company, was clarified by identifying its relationships to a customer, to a service, and to a collection of pieces of hardware. Thus in our architecture, circuit is defined to be the complete path from the customer through the network which is required to provide the customer their requested network service.

SUBJECT DATA AREA CONSOLIDATION

At the end of the analysis of objects, we had identified 30 fundamental objects and their relationships. These objects were grouped into 12 Subject Data Areas, primarily driven by the object-to-object affinities, the separation of type from instance objects, and the function to object matrix. Functions are listed down the rows of the matrix while objects are listed over the columns. In the simplest case an x appears across from the function and underneath the object whenever a function uses information about that object. Object affinities were calculated from the matrix and the E-R diagrams.[12] Several Subject Data Area hypotheses were automatically generated. These were analyzed by the group using their best engineering judgement to come to the final conclusion. As Logical Data Modeling proceeds within this strategic context, new objects are likely to be introduced and some changes to these object groupings may become necessary.

The twelve Subject Data Areas recommended in the Bellcore's Strategic Data Architecture are: Customer, Customer Account, Designs & Descriptions, Enterprise, Finance, Forecast & Guidelines, Inventory, Location, Product Offering, Project, Vendor and Work Force. These subject data areas represent logical groupings of data whose physical implementation will be driven by the known and anticipated application and user views of the data, and will take into consideration performance and technical computing constraints.

SUMMARY

Efforts continue at Bellcore to extend the existing Strategic Data Architecture. The Logical Data Model work, a project driven by the software system life cycle, has begun to influence the Strategic Data Architecture. Parts of the Logical Data Model are currently being constructed that are necessary to start replacing systems currently in their mature phase. It is the goal of building real databases which drives the development of data architecture. A data architecture is not a goal in itself, but a plan to reach the goal of integrated systems development.

We are expanding this strategic architecture beyond operations and into the network areas of the business. We will be including views of how the business may look in the next decade and the next century. In this way we will build a business model of the telephone company which can serve as a blueprint for long-term, integrated systems development.

REFERENCES

1. E. P. Gould and C. D. Pack, Communication Network Planning in the Evolving Information Age, IEEE Communications, Vol. 25, No. 9, Sept., 1987, pp. 22-30.

2. Ken Orr, Structural Systems Development, New York, Yourdon Press, Inc. 1977.

3. Jerome S. Fleischman, "Operations Systems Strategic Plan for Exchange and Exchange Access Operations," Proceedings of the IEEE International Conference on Communications, Vol. 1, June 1987.

4. Tom DeMarco, Structured Analysis and System Specification, Yourdon Press, 1978.

5. Chris Gane and Trish Sarsen, Structured Systems Analsysis: Tools and Techniques, Prentice Hall, 1979.

6. IBM Corp., Business Systems Planning - Information Planning Guide, GE20-0527-3, White Plains, NY, 1975.

7. James Martin, Strategic Data Planning Methodologies, Prentice-Hall, Englewood Cliffs, New Jersey, 1982.

8. C. J. Date, An Introduction to Database Systems, Fourth Edition, Addison-Wesley Publishing, Reading, Massachusetts, 1986.

9. J. M. Smith and D.C.P. Smith, "Database Abstractions: Aggregation and Generalization," ACM Transactions on Database Systems, Vol. 2, No. 2, June 1977, pp. 105-133.

10. Matt Flavin, Fundamental Concepts of Information Modeling, Yourdon Press, 1981.

11. Peter Chen, "The Entity-Relationship Model - Toward a Unified View of Data," ACM Transactions on Database Systems, Vol. 1, No. 1, March 1987.

12. Diane E. Duffy, Edward B. Fowlkes, and Luke D. Kane, "Cluster Analysis in Strategic Data Architecture Design," Bellcore Database Symposium, 1987.

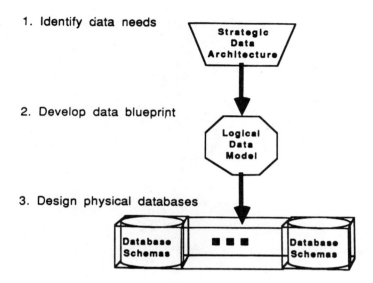

1. Identify data needs

2. Develop data blueprint

3. Design physical databases

Figure 1. Top-Down Database Development

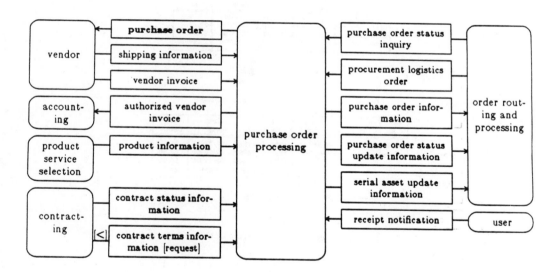

Figure 2. Purchase Order Processing Information Exchange Diagram.

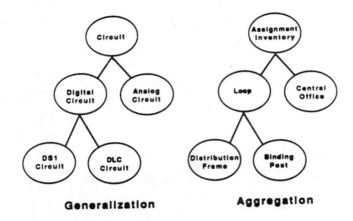

Figure 3. Generalization and Aggregation

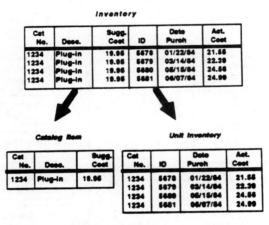

Figure 4. Characterization

OPERATIONS SUPPORT FOR ISDN AND
McDONALD'S TRIAL EXPERIENCE

James E. Bielanski
Manager - Technical Evaluation ISDN

Illinois Bell Telephone
225 W. Randolph - HQ 26 C
Chicago, Illinois 60606

ABSTRACT

This paper describes how applications are derived from the Integrated Services Digital Network (ISDN) Basic Rate Interface (BRI) and how operation support systems (OSS) have been extended to the customer to support these applications. When operations support is extended to the customer, network rearrangements associated with moves and changes can be completed in minutes instead of days.

The ISDN operations support challenges require innovative solutions and increased communications with the customer. While operations costs must be minimized, it is paramount that the support solutions recognize that the ISDN protocols extend beyond the traditional physical network interface into the customer's intelligent premises equipment. Illinois Bell's customer support commitments and experience with the McDonald's Corporation ISDN introduction trial will be reviewed.

INTRODUCTION

Corporate telecommunications managers are currently faced with a complex web of voice and data communications systems provided by multiple vendors. These systems typically have proprietary protocols that cannot support other vendors' terminal equipment. ISDN was developed to meet customer demands for the integration of multiple voice and data services. The integration of multiple networks will reduce communications expenses and increase equipment flexibility.

ISDN is a digital communications service offering which provides various combinations of voice, circuit switched and packet switched connections over a two wire loop between a customer and a local central office. Two 64 Kbps channels and one 16 Kbps channel are provided on the BRI. The 64 Kbps channels are referred to as the "Bearer" or B channels. The 16 Kbps channel is referred to as the "Data" or D channel and provides signaling and control. For simplicity, the BRI's channel carrying capability is normally represented as 2B+D.

The transport facilities used to provision ISDN are the same as those used to provide "Plain Old Telephone Service" (POTS) today. The POTS like service order flow includes a BRI ISDN service order, billing, distribution, assignments, switch translation input and outside plant maintenance support. Provisioning POTS and ISDN loops in a standardized manner eliminates the need for special facility design.

To fully benefit from the new services and applications available with ISDN, the customer must have maximum control over the provisioning of ISDN voice and data features. Although the transport facility is simple in nature (i.e., twisted pair), the information being transported via the 2B+D serving arrangement is very complex. To assist the customer in sorting out the features and functionality of ISDN, two major customer interface support systems were developed:

- Service Negotiation System (SNS)

- End Customer Control (ECC)

The Service Negotiation System was developed to assist Illinois Bell order negotiators in working with customers to establish ISDN service. With SNS, the ISDN network configurations can be identified quickly and accurately based upon the terminal equipment (CPE) the customer intends to use.

Although the SNS is well suited for the initial establishment of ISDN service, customers need the ability to rearrange their network without the delays associated with a service order. Enhancements to various telephone company Operations, Administration and Maintenance (OA&M) systems allowed End Customer Control (ECC) to be offered as a service to customers. With ECC, customers have the ability to monitor and control their ISDN network directly. Most rearrangements on an ISDN BRI can be performed within minutes instead of days.

APPLICATION SUPPORT ON ISDN

Fig. 1 (rewritten as D+2B) illustrates how the individual channels on the BRI can be utilized for customer applications.

D CHANNEL SERVICES

The D channel can be broken down into two components (i.e., Signaling and Packet Services). The signaling portion of the D channel performs the call control function for both B channels. By performing signaling and call control on the D channel, each B channel can offer a clear 64 Kbps data stream for voice or data oriented applications. The D channel also supports signaling for digital electronic key telephone functions.

Other services such as Calling Line ID, Electronic Directory and Electronic Messaging utilize the information bearing capability of D channel signaling. Electronic Directory and Electronic Message Waiting services require an Applications Processor (AP). The AP is external to the ISDN switch. Establishment of the AP data base and the management of the associated records is the responsibility of the end user. Specifications are published on how an AP is interfaced to the 5ESS[TM] ISDN switch.

X.25 PACKET SERVICES

Packet services are available on the D or B channel. For D channel X.25 packet services, the user can access a total of 15 Logical Channel Numbers (LCNs) with a data throughput of 9600 bits per second under LAPD control. B channel X.25 packet services support a maximum of 127 LCNs under LAPB control. The current throughput is defined as 19.2 Kbps and is expected to be increased with future enhancements to the ISDN switch.

Packet services are used to provide end users with the following services:

- Host Access for Data Processing

- Host Access for Word Processing

- File Transfer between Personal Computers (PCs)

- File Transfer between PCs and Host Systems

- RS 232 Local Area Network (LAN) Services

- Still Video Image Transfer

Option settings for X.25 packet services are simplified when the functions of X.28 and X.29 are utilized. X.28 and X.29 enable Host applications to down load the proper Packet Assembler/Disassembler (PAD) configurations to the ISDN CPE when the session is established. By utilizing X.28 and X.29, end users can access various Host applications without manually reconfiguring their CPE PAD parameters.

B CHANNEL SERVICES

ISDN circuit switching requires a B channel and can support either data or voice. For data services, a rate adaption scheme is required to enable slower terminals (either asynchronous or synchronous) to transmit data over an ISDN B channels at a 64

Kbps data rate. Recent standards activities (in T1D1) have been finalized establishing V.120 (V. Tad) as the U. S. rate adaption scheme for a circuit switched connection over ISDN. Preliminary indications from BELLCORE are firm that all seven regional Bell Operating companies will support the V.120 rate adaption scheme for ISDN terminal equipment.

Circuit switched services provided to end users on the B channel include:

- Multiple Call Appearances
- Shared Directory Numbers
- Enhanced Centrex Features
- Extended Call Coverage Capability
- Host to Host Computer Communications
- Group IV Facsimile
- Compressed Video
- Gateways to Other Data Networks

SERVICE NEGOTIATION SYSTEM (SNS)

By analyzing the serving capabilities of ISDN from a network and CPE perspective, Illinois Bell was able to define the requirements for a Service Negotiation System. BELLCORE developed a prototype negotiation system based upon the defined requirements. With SNS, ISDN lines are efficiently provisioned during service establishment. Fig. 2 represents the various ISDN channel configurations available with the 5ESS^{TM} utilizing generic 5E4.2.

When a customer calls to establish ISDN, the service negotiator has a wide variety of information readily available such as:

- ISDN Availability
- Loop Qualification Status
- Bearer Service Options (see Fig. 2)
- Feature Options
- Tariff Pricing
- Packet Services Supported
- Network versus CPE Terminal Management
- Call Appearance and Button Layout

Once the service order is processed, the customer is able to plug the ISDN CPE into a working BRI for service.

The system has proved to be very useful since it allows the service negotiator to work with the customer to determine the appropriate network options based upon the CPE being used. With the information stored in SNS, we minimize the customer burden of sorting through all the service options.

END CUSTOMER CONTROL (ECC)

The architecture of ISDN allows the power of a central office based switching technology to be offered directly to the customer over a standard interface. Although ISDN CPE is connected to the network via a standard interface, changes to the serving arrangements may be required.

Unlike the initial service establishment, customers want to make changes to their network without the typical delays associated with standard service order intervals (i.e., several days). Since ISDN was developed to meet customer demands for the integration of voice and data networks, it is only natural that these customers have control over their network. A timely response to changes in network functionality is very important as voice and data applications are fine tuned by the customers.

Existing end customer Operations Support Systems can be interfaced to the ECC:

Netview (SNA Network Management)
Station Message Detail Recording (SMDR)
(via an Applications Processor)

The following network OA&M functions are currently exported to the end user to enable more efficient management of their networks:

Switch Maintenance Status	- Switch alarm/Status Data Digital Test Access
Loop Maintenance Status	- Metallic Test Access Line Performance Data Trouble Ticket Status
Traffic Data	- Traffic Data
Line Rearrangement	- Modify Serving Features on a BRI (e.g.; Rearrange Call and Closed User Groups, Modify Service and Features Associated With X.25 Packet Services, etc.)
Line Status	- Terminal Change Management Automatic Route Selection

Fig. 3 identifies the network and customer operations support systems that are interfaced to the ECC.

The extension of our Operations, Administration and Maintenance capabilities also ensures a high degree of consistency between our operations and those of our customers and thus facilitates problem resolution in a timely manner. A key element of any extension of central office functionality however, is the provision of security for the service provider (network) and for the customer.

An Illinois Bell system administrator is responsible for insuring the proper partitioning of the network host processor for all customers subscribing to this capability. All customer interactions are screened and verified for proper authorization before any transactions are enabled. The integrity of the customer's networks and those of the telephone company are thus protected.

CONCLUSION

Coax elimination equipment, single and multiple directory number digital station sets (with various combinations of data connectors for packet and/or circuit switched connections). data terminal adapters, integrated voice/data terminals (IVDT) and attendant services equipment are some of the types of CPE that may be connected to the ISDN network. The Service Negotiation System allows the service negotiator to quickly and accurately match customer CPE applications with the correct network services and features.

It is a well recognized fact that major business customers are more sophisticated in the use and expectations of their communications systems today than they were a few short years ago. Customers should be given maximum direct control over the provisioning of both voice and data features, subject to switch resource restrictions.

Enhancements to Illinois Bell's mechanized switch memory recent change update system, and to its customer controlled feature change support system, allow the customer to correctly match the switch provisioned options with the corresponding CPE options. This approach minimizes costs by vastly reducing expensive service order involvement and greatly improves service delivery response times.

Several benefits are obtained by exporting our traditional OA&M capabilities to our customers.

- Customers are provided with limited, direct control of their virtual network.

- Deployment intervals for ISDN services are decreased by directly extending new support capabilities to the customer.

- The customer's diverse telecommunications environment (multiple vendors, equipment types and services) are supported via a standardized interface.

- New revenue generation opportunities are created by utilizing embedded OA&M systems for end customer control.

- There is minimal impact on our operations because service administration is centralized.

Although the ISDN interface is simple, the network support behind the interface is very elaborate and extremely powerful. It is important to recognize that lower level ISDN protocols extend beyond the standard interface directly into the CPE.

The ISDN protocols sent over the D channel directly link the internal management of the ISDN CPE to the 5ESS^{TM} switch. This capability is very similar to that of a Host application updating the X.25 PAD parameters in the CPE via the services of X.28 and X.29.

New services (both network maintenance and applications oriented) must utilize the protocol capability of ISDN to maximize the benefits of universal connectivity over ISDN. The D channel alone represents a vast untapped potential for new features and customer control.

BASIC RATE INTERFACE (BRI)

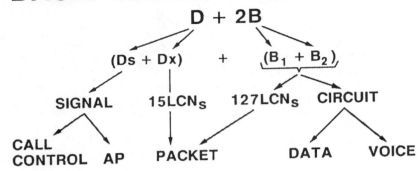

- BASIC VOICE
- KEY
- DATA

- MESSAGE DESK
- CALLING NAME ID
- CALL COVERAGE

- HOST ACCESS
- FILE TRANSFER
- STILL VIDEO

- HOST-HOST
- GROUP IV FAX
- COMPRESSED VIDEO

- CENTREX FEATURES
- MULTIPLE CAs
- SHARED DNs

FIGURE 1

OPERATIONS SUPPORT FOR ISDN AND McDONALD'S TRIAL EXPERIENCE

5ESS

CHANNEL CONFIGURATION OPTIONS

FOR GENERIC 5E4.2

	B	B	D
1	----	----	Packet Switched
2	Voice	----	(Packet Switched)
3	Circuit Switched	----	(Packet Switched)
4	Packet Switched	----	----
5	Circuit Switched	Circuit Switched	(Packet Switched)
6	Voice	Circuit Switched	(Packet Switched)
7	Voice	Packet Switched	----
8	Circuit Switched	Packet Switched	----
9	Voice - Circuit Switched	----	(Packet Switched)
10	Voice - Circuit Switched	Circuit Switched	(Packet Switched)
11	Voice - Circuit Switched	Packet Switched	----

Figure 2

ISDN/ECC PROTOTYPE
FUNCTIONAL ORGANIZATION

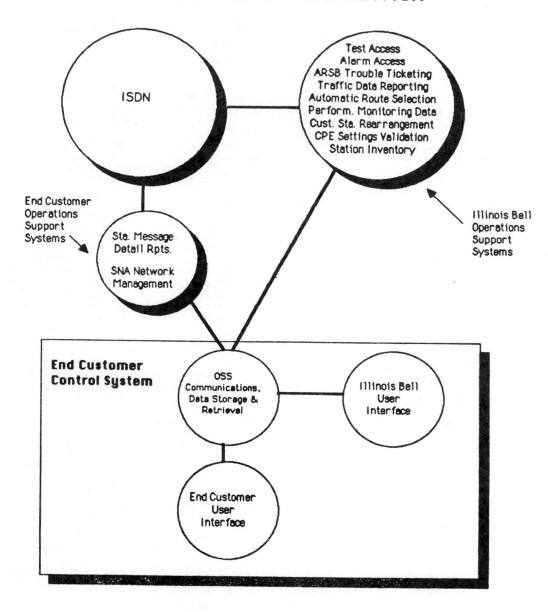

FIGURE 3

EFFECTS OF TECHNOLOGY ON WORKFORCE MANAGEMENT

S. Brad Harsha - Chairperson
Director, Service and Operations
United Telecommunications, Inc.
P.O. Box 11315
Kansas City, MO 64112

ABSTRACT

One of the most exciting opportunities in the telecommunications industry today is using technological advances to aid in how we service our customers. A vast array of solutions to today's workforce management problems is available to those who want to take advantage. This seminar provides four different views of how this can be accomplished whether in a rural environment, premise workforce, outside plant workforce or the central office.

Karen A. Krepps   -- United Telephone System, Inc., Midwest Group

David L. McCrosky -- AT&T

Jerry L. Neal   -- Contel

Van H. Taylor   -- Southwestern Bell

USE OF TECHNOLOGY

IN THE RURAL WORKFORCE

Karen A. Krepps

Assistant Vice President - Service

United Telephone System Inc., Midwest Group

600 Industrial Parkway
Industrial Airport, KS 66031

ABSTRACT

This session discusses practical applications of advanced technology by telephone company installation and repair forces implemented to improve productivity, reduce operating costs, and increase customer satisfaction.

INTRODUCTION

To the telephone technician, rural America is comprised of wide spaces, sparse populations, and long loops. In reality, rural America is also comprised of agri-business, county seats, consolidated school districts, resorts, universities, state capitols, military bases, and manufacturing plants. Its community leaders can have personal wealth and political influence matched by few telephony executives. Rural America, therefore, is a community with a variety of voice and data transmission needs. With its vast terrain, diversified economy and subtle influence, rural America requires innovative and cost effective service provisioning.

The concept of combining outside plant and service center work groups, supported by tailored automated systems, has service provisioning benefits particularly adaptable to the needs of rural America. The results of implementing such a program at United Telephone have been savings in headcount, improved productivity and reduced double dispatch.

COMBINED PLANT FUNCTIONS

Job specialization is no longer practical in numerous areas. The combining of functions so one person can maintain the loop and provide service from the central office to the customer, up to and including the instrument, is a reality. The one-person-out concept eliminates or reduces double dispatches and results in a more cost efficient, customer focused operation. Average clearing time on service problems improves and so does customer satisfaction.

However, some activities will always require specialists. Balancing these needs is our future challenge. Large PBX installations, hard digital or analog trouble, complex data network or carrier problems--all of these require special training and continued practice for good service. A traveling team of technicians for these activities will probably always be necessary.

At United, we designed our first series of cross-training classes to address the I&R/cable repair and splicer populations. Courses in fault locating, customer relations and use of other specific test gear were offered repetitively. At the same time, we instituted organizational changes, assigning our first and second level management personnel responsibility for all plant disciplines in a geographic area.

Combining of functions is not necessarily limited to service technician/cable splicer activities. Cross-training central office skills for service technicians and cable splicers to perform selected analog and digital routines and maintenance has also been accomplished. This ultimately provides a work force cross-trained to handle most dispatches, including mainframe work. Interestingly, in two of our state areas, we were able to reduce travel time fifty minutes per dispatch.

There are standard, available tools and test equipment to support the one-person-out concept. Test equipment can be categorized by use, cost, storage requirements and the necessary user expertise. The determination then is made as to which test equipment will be carried on vehicles or centrally located.

Vehicle purchases is another factor in the one-person-out concept. The technicians' needs and the rural terrain must be considered. A study conducted by two United Telephone Companies led to adoption of the 3/4 ton van to meet the needs of the combined work force concept.

With diversified training requirements, ongoing training costs increase with the implementation of combining work functions. However, the recurring productivity and service improvements more than offset the increase in training related costs.

Dispatching the right person on the appropriate work activity by contiguous geographic areas is enhanced with a mechanized system. This system may be mainframe or personal computer based. Using data files which identify available employees and their training/abilities, a center may dispatch troubles, orders, etc., in a prioritized, efficient manner. In addition, tests of handheld terminals indicate reduced errors and less waiting time as technicians receive and clear work activities. At one United company, we have used our trouble system called ARBS (Automated Repair Bureau System) to handle overall dispatching including orders, troubles, cable locates, selected routines, and some routine work order activity.

SERVICE CENTERS

As deregulation affected the plant work forces, it also affected the service center work force. Increased productivity and load equalization are primary factors for consolidating and realigning the service center operations. Integration of receive repair and service order functions also provide the customer with one contact group for reporting trouble or ordering service, thereby improving response time.

As most telcos do, United has separate service order and trouble systems. Our answer has been to implement special software which allows a service center clerk to switch between four different systems with the touch of a PF key.

The fully automated and centralized service center receives all work inputs and administers the pricing, loading, dispatching, tracking, clearing and closing of troubles, service orders and other demand and scheduled work. Clerical labor requirements are substantially reduced. The degree and amount of intelligent electronic technology available to the service center minimizes the need for personnel.

Eventually, of course, with increased digital penetration, "instant service" will become a reality. Service center clerks will create the order, dedicated facilities will be assigned through an automated database, service will be completed through the digital switch, an automated line card will be created and billing will be established--all without human intervention other than for initiating the process.

COMMUNITY PRESENCE

We cannot ignore that a "closeness to the customer" in rural America was sacrificed with the consolidation of service centers. The McKinsey study In Search of Excellence shows that, along with service overkill, attention to the customer is paramount. A successful alternative to the maintaining of visibility through local payment facilities is the Community Relations Representative concept. This person's primary function is to be visible to the rural communities. Like the legislative and regulatory affairs positions, they are expected to be close to their audience. Mayors, members of city councils, county commissioners, and the general public know of their existence and whom they represent. In addition, craft personnel and their supervisors must become company advocates, trained in explaining a changing industry and able to market various products where dedicated marketing personnel are unavailable. To accomplish this marketing, United is designing automated pricing systems which reduce time needed for quotes on simple key systems, for example.

NETWORK

For decades, the telco network has been built to carry voice traffic, requiring a narrow bandwidth to customers. Our urban and rural customers' demands for enhanced services are inevitably becoming much broader, including capabilities for integrated data/voice transmission. To meet the demands of the market in terms of new services, we must prepare for the evolution of the loop to support new ventures. A market focus for that development and deployment of technology is critical.

In the era of POTS dominance, in a regulated monopoly marketplace, there was little doubt about rural America's needs. In a competitive and expanding communications market, these needs become unclear. Capabilities can be implemented with a variety of technologies depending on specific circumstances. Network capabilities consist of:

1. Voice transport
2. Narrowband data transport
3. Wideband data transport
4. Video transport

The industry will also have to expand its perspective to include a host of customer services as they seek to determine the technologies which they will deploy, and the capabilities which they will develop. Services such as meter reading, E911, alarm telemetry, high fidelity music, banking at home, etc., will have to be included in the planning phase. Proper consideration of such services require market research and a family of flexible technologies. These technologies must be limited enough to be manageable, yet flexible enough to support a variety of customer services.

To support the present rural customer services base at a competitive cost, an important type of leverage can occur when capacity requirements increase. In feeder reinforcements or new applications, fiber optics and/or pair gain (electronics) become the preferred transmission media. The spectrum of supportable services is progressively larger as we go from analog copper to digital copper to fiber. Our network will become predominantly fiber-based, beginning with high density feeder routes, as well as exchange access.

In addition, rural communities consistently push rural telcos to install digital switch technology to attract new industries. At United, we have adopted an overall host-remote configuration philosophy. We've found this to be not only more cost-efficient in the long and short terms, but is also allows us to offer a wider array of services to a larger base of customers.

CONCLUSION

Rural America is comprised of communities with diverse voice and data transmission needs. To provide these needs in a deregulated environment, the telephone industry must move toward methods of operations and technology that reduce non-traffic sensitive costs while modernizing facilities and improving service.

Improved methods of operation include the combining and automation of work functions to improve productivity and service. We must develop flexible technologies that will support capabilities for a variety of services. Our network will become predominantly fiber-based, beginning with high density feeder routes.

Accommodating rural America's needs also requires we maintain our presence and visibility because our success depends on our willingness, and ability to be customer focused.

THE CHANGING ENVIRONMENT

IN THE PREMISE WORKFORCE

David L. McCrosky

District Manager,
Field Operations Support

AT&T

99 Jefferson Road
Room 3A49
Parsippany, NJ   07054

ABSTRACT

New technology and growing competition have forced new service marketing and service delivery strategies. This paper will address how these changes have caused service managers of premises (on-site) technician forces to reshape their organization in the changing environment.

INTRODUCTION

A number of driving forces are changing the environment for the traditional delivery of premises (on-site) customer service in the electronic servicing industry. Specifically, the shift from a manufacturing based economy to a service based economy continually brings growing pressures on service businesses to increase corporate financial contributions. Today's service business environment demands efficient use of resources.

The impact of product reliability improvements and the evolving changes in maintenance capabilities due to technological advancements is changing the face of service delivery in the computer and telecommunications segments of the IM&M (Information Movement and Management) marketplace.

These business pressures coupled with technological changes are resulting in fewer requirements for the traditional on-site hardware technician. The trend in service support is toward remote, centrally managed, software based repair processes.

This changing environment is accompanied with new challenges for managing service headcount. Not only do we see changes occurring in the nature of the field engineer's job, but some fundamental changes in the service manager's job. Traditional approaches to managing a service force are not sufficient for the changing environment.

Subsequent sections of this paper examine in greater depth, the service market and industry trends, results of increased product reliability, changes in maintenance strategies, and the impact of these changes on managing service work forces.

THE SERVICE MARKET AND SERVICE INDUSTRY TRENDS

The shift in the American economy over the past three decades from a manufacturing based economy to a service based economy has been accompanied with large growth in all segments of the service industry. The service industry segments, ranging from trade, communications, transportation, to technical services, account for about 70% of the national income and have generated forty-four (44) million new jobs over the last thirty years.[1]

Growth rates for the electronic servicing industry during this decade have been approximately ten to twelve percent. The electronic servicing industry segment includes office products, mini-mainframes, small computers and peripherals (including telecommunications equipment) and third party maintenance.

Along with this growth, servicing has taken on a new economic importance relative to corporate strategy. Service has evolved to be recognized as a strategic line of business. In fact, development of service strategic business units and the accompanying revenues, has been a key strategy for a number of major corporations to offset the effect of flat product sales. The Association of Field Service Managers (AFSM) estimates that servicing revenues for computer systems, telecommunications and electronic instruments will reach $46 billion in 1990.[2]

In past years, the growth in servicing revenues was accompanied with a growth in servicing jobs. Now, the high technology service segment is seeing a different trend that is projected to continue. High-tech service has begun to see a decline in service jobs while continued growth of revenues is predicted. The same trend is predicted to continue into the 1990's. For example, The Ledgeway Group has projected a growth of 7.4% for computer servicing revenues from 1987-1991 with industry headcount continuing to be flat or declining slightly.[3]

In the current business environment, service organizations find themselves in an increasingly competitive marketplace, under pressure from customers and internal forces to increase and improve service at the same or lower prices while increasing revenue and profit contribution to overall corporate goals. These pressures have resulted in the constant pursuit for effective and efficient productivity increases in the utilization of service resources. Service provided by on-site field engineers has historically been a labor intensive business. The underlying motivation of today's service planner and manager is the imperative to:

Decrease the labor intensity involved with servicing customer premises equipment, while meeting the market demands of increased service levels and responding to corporate financial expectations.

How is this possible? Sophisticated technological advances are forcing and allowing changes in service support strategies and eroding traditional operational approaches. To understand the changing environment and the impact on service forces, it is necessary to examine the technological trends and contributing factors.

PRODUCT TECHNOLOGY - RELIABILITY AND DESIGN

Over the past five years, significant improvements have been made in product reliability, specifically hardware reliability. The greatest strides have been made in the computer product lines where third generation technology is present; however, improvements have also been made in telecommunications products still predominantly in second generation technology.

In their 1987 report "Managing Service Headcount", The Ledgeway Group attributes these reliability improvements to "better packaging of technology, new materials, and improved product engineering with the underlying reason being competition for a customer base that has been demanding more and more (system availability."

The renewed American focus on quality is paying off in terms of product reliability, thus the results are increased system availability for users. Service organizations have been influential in the emergence of reliable systems. The economic pressures discussed earlier have motivated service organizations to provide product designers with valid product failure data and to push for product reliability and serviceability.

Some of the effects on service forces being seen at the operational level are: decreased installation time, fewer trouble calls from customers, fewer dispatches of field engineers due to remote clearance capabilities, and decreased on-site repair time due to "board-swapping" versus on-site repair.

Given these effects, one can predict the trend relative to service force requirements. The demand for traditional on-site hardware field engineer is decreasing. In fact, the largest decreases in service headcount requirements are predicted to be for the traditional hardware technician.

TECHNOLOGY AND SERVICE OPERATIONS

The quest for increased productivity coupled with the advent of technical capabilities is also changing the operational strategies for service delivery. These changes range from new approaches in managing the basic infrastructure to replacement of on-site labor intensive tasks with applications of technology.

Changes in the approach to managing the basic delivery structure have been occurring for a number of years but ongoing improvements continue to impact the efficiency of service delivery. As corporations continue to expand, becoming less local and more regional or national, state of the art support for service operations becomes essential in order to maximize resources and respond to customer expectations.

To review a few of these evolutions and their impacts on service efficiency the following examples are offered:

Mechanized inventory control has long been prevalent in manufacturing segments. With sophisticated product technology, maintenance inventories have become one of the major financial assets managed by service organizations. key to customer satisfaction and responsible financial performance is the ability to better manage field service inventories without disproportionate dollar growth. Mechanized inventory management systems utilized by field forces have become essential to improved performance by having the right inventory on the first trip to the customer site.

Mechanized support for dispatching of field engineers lessens the individual variances that were previously inherent with the differing degrees of skills between dispatchers.

Hand held terminals and newer generation technology of the lap top computers, reduce the float time between dispatch contact with field technicians and thus decrease customer response time. Traditional telephone hold time between field personnel and dispatch centers to obtain assignment and customer information is decreased or eliminated. Utilizing these devices, work completion reporting moves to real time enabling service managers to achieve more efficient utilization of resources. In short, the flow of information is being enhanced through these tools thus increasing resource utilization.

Tools to assist force planning and scheduling against work load and skills required has moved out of the "tactical planning" domain as a modeling tool into the hands of line service managers as an operational tool.

Service vendors supporting diverse but technically sophisticated product lines continue to specialize their technician forces. Specialization allows field engineers to achieve product technology expertise in shorter periods of time. Additionally, the opportunity for improved training is created when all field engineers do not have to be trained on all products and technologies.

Of great impact on the field service force are the technological advancements and tools that are beginning to replace the historical on-site labor intensive tasks involved with maintenance support.

The ability to perform remote diagnostics on more and more products results in an increased number of customer troubles resolved without dispatching a field technician.

Products with "self diagnostic" features allow isolation to software versus hardware in many instances and further increase the ability to resolve problems remotely.

The effects of remote and self-diagnostics are multifaceted. The primary impact is the migration away from total local service support to the aggregation of resources into remote support centers. More and more, first calls from the customers go to remote support centers. Service vendors receive benefit of economies of scale and can concentrate their best technical resources. Even when field technicians must be dispatched, remote technology increases the odds of isolation to the faulty part at the board level prior to dispatch.

In addition, specially designed diagnostic tools carried by field technicians allow faster, more accurate hardware trouble identification thus decreasing on-site time.

The benefits of the above are fewer field dispatches, decreased on-site time, and increased likelihood of having the correct part on the first trip.

Technology developments are beginning to emerge that allow system monitoring to spot troubles and intermittent performance prior to failure. As this predictive technology evolves in more products, the remote fix of software problems and advanced scheduling of hardware maintenance will further effect service forces. High commitments in R&D and capital are being made to develop "predictive maintenance" abilities as a major element of remote maintenance strategies.

Before leaving the subject of current support technology and trends, a few more comments about the remote support centers is appropriate. It is important to understand these centers as more than "call receipt" centers. The teaming of individuals with specific technical expertises supported by expert tools such as problem/solution databases is the growing operational approach for service support of complex systems. Translated to business strategy, a well structured and staffed support center providing value added service is a fundamental element of many service marketing strategies.

One other support strategy effecting traditional service should be mentioned. Modular technology and more sophisticated remote support abilities from service vendors have set the stage for customer participation in maintenance. A variety of service offerings are available, ranging from depot service for parts repair to offerings of service discounts associated with customer participation in problem management. There are a number of intriguing aspects of customer participation programs that can be both good for the customer and good for the service vendor. Customer/vendor partnerships in establishing solid processes for data center controls and PBX administration for example, decrease the number of customer troubles occurring from "pilot error", shift minor trouble resolution tot he customer resulting in customer cost savings, and allow the vendor to utilize expert resources for critical trouble calls.

The following summarizes the impacts that the technology changes will have on the delivery of service:

More products will be built with remote capabilities. As more products contain these features, tradi-

tional field service will be replaced with remote service.

As "predictive maintenance" evolves, the service organization will transition from a labor intensive to an information and technology intensive business. Remedial service will be replaced with predictive service to a greater degree.

With the more sophisticated products supported by the electronic servicing industry, a merging of skills required (hardware versus software) by technicians will be necessary to develop "solutions technicians".

THE IMPACT OF CHANGE - MANAGING SERVICE WORK FORCES

The final section of this paper examines the implications for managing service resources in the changing environment. While numerous changes were discussed in the previous sections, the following overall trends emerge as significant:

"Reliability and productivity improvements are decreasing work load faster than most companies' product base is growing. The number of total jobs in service has peaked and will decline slowly over the next few years.

On the leading edge, delivery of service is evolving to remote support center effort. This trend, coupled with reliability advancements, is changing the customer site job from a hardware and software fix-it job to an account management job."[4]

Obviously both trends imply the necessity for new approaches in managing service headcount. One challenge facing service organizations is: How to manage the excess of technicians as requirements for traditional on-site service jobs decline? Service planners and managers are continually attempting to develop programs that will effectively transition the skills profile of their service force to meet the future requirements. Frequently referred to as "re-profiling force sills, the programs include: training to meet the growing need of "solutions technicians", development of the required expertise as technicians are placed in product support teams in remote support centers, and transitioning the traditional fix-it technician to also function as account managers since presence with the customer is still important (even in a remote support environment).

Any discussion on re-profiling of skills logically leads to some mention of labor relations trends. Union/management partnerships are evolving around the shared interest of finding effective means of service delivery to meet the pressures of the competitive marketplace. Jointly sponsored programs include: communications forums, mutual sharing and problem solving, training and retraining programs.

The changing service environment, has also altered the nature of the service manager's job. The first line supervisor's job contains less task management and reactive problem solving. Span of control has increased as responsibilities are pushed lower in organizations. The middle manager is expected to be a more responsible business manager, an effective partner with marketing, and frequently has profit and loss responsibility. The profile of the service manager and supervisor as only an "operations manager" is no longer adequate. The standards of service performance are higher and more sophisticated and timely management information reports point out weak performance.

While the above changes are far reaching, the more fundamental and comprehensive question for managing service forces in the changing environment is: Will traditional Human Resource Management (HRM) models be compatible or sufficient in future service organizations highly dependent upon advanced technology for delivery of service?

Some believe that advanced technology in the work place calls for new HRM models and management approaches. Richard E. Walton, Harvard Business School, submits that "The current work practices of dividing work into discreetly tasks becomes obsolete in the computerized work place. Where multiple functions are integrated by computers, it is no longer possible to define jobs individually or measure individual performance. It requires a collection of people to manage a segment of technology and perform as a team."[5]

Walton has labeled this emerging HRM trend as the "commitment model" aimed at developing committed employees and emphasizing broader job definitions, teamwork, multi-skilled workers and participative managements styles.

The emerging "commitment model" differs from current HRM models in management assumptions about workers, job designs, management organization and style, job training and security, pay determination and labor relations. The following is a comparison of characteristics indicative of the "commitment model" versus the traditional HRM models prevalent in American industry for the past several decades:

"Management assumes that workers desire challenging jobs and will seek responsibility and autonomy if permitted versus the traditional view that workers need high supervision, control or even coercion.

Jobs are designed to be multi-skilled and performed by teamwork where possible. Thinking and doing are combined as compared to fragmented, narrowly defined jobs with thinking and doing separated.

Relatively flat management structures (fewer layers), where workers make suggestions and are empowered to make change versus hierarchical structures where workers are expected to follow not lead.

Workers are considered a valuable investment/asset and are constantly retrained compared to traditional approaches of considering workers as variable assets routinely laid off during business decline.

Determination of pay is linked to skills acquired and group incentives are utilized to enhance commitment to common goals, versus pay scales geared to the job (not the person) and determined by evaluation and job classification systems.

Mutuality of interest between labor and management interests are considered incompatible."[6]

While the "commitment model" is applicable to some degree in nearly all high-tech service environments, some environments and technologies are more suitable than others. Walton points out that "those technologies that inherently require intricate team work, problem solving, learning, and self monitoring are particularly suited".[7]

Service organizations supporting mainframe computers are particularly amenable to the "commitment model" and some elements of the "commitment model" are already utilized by most other service vendors. This application in support of telecommunications technology is also worth serious consideration. As telecommunications systems become more advanced and service support becomes predominantly remote, telecommunications vendors are also challenged with providing "total system support" requiring the integration of hardware, software, and networking skills. This HRM model stands out as an appropriate means of structuring, and managing service forces to tap the total resources of the organization in a demanding marketplace.

SUMMARY

In conclusion, our examination of the impact of technology on managing service forces can be summarized as follows:

Gains in product reliability, remote diagnostics and evolving predictive maintenance abilities will result in decreasing demand for the traditional on-site "fix-it" technician. The migration of service support to remote support brings with it the challenge of new skill requirements and the continued need to remain close to the customer's business and service needs while providing remote support. These changes are occurring in a marketplace where product equality is being reached and service support is a major differentiator in buying decisions. The business imperative for tapping the best capabilities and performance of service resources, while utilizing advanced technology and nontraditional management approaches, is the challenge offered to the service manager in this changing environment.

REFERENCES

1. James L. Heskett, "Lessons In The Service Sector", Harvard Business Review, March - April 1987.

2. J. Hood and M. Angwin, "Customer Service Embraces High Technology", Field Service Manager, April 1988.

3. The Ledgeway Group, Inc., Managing Service Headcount, 1987

4. The Ledgeway Group, Inc., Managing Service Headcount, 1987

5. J. Hoerr, A. Pollock, and D. Whiteside, "Management Discovers The Human Side Of Automation", Business Week, September 29, 1986.

6. J. Hoeer, A. Pollock, and D. Whiteside, "Management Discovers The Human Side Of Automation", Business Week, September 29, 1986.

7. The Ledgeway Group, Inc., Managing Service Headcount, 1987

OPPORTUNITIES IN WORKFORCE MANAGEMENT

Van H. Taylor

Division Manager,
Facilities and Special Services

Southwestern Bell

1 Bell Center
Room 14M1
St. Louis, MO 36101

ABSTRACT

As technology has continued to evolve, it has influenced both the role of the operations work force, as well as management's ability to effectively and efficiently administer that work force. This paper will discuss the challenges facing management as it deals with this technological impact, not only from a perspective of understanding the human resource management issues that the changes in technology bring with them. A brief high-level look at the evolution of technology and its impact on work force administration will be taken. This will include a look at the network technology itself, as well as the operations support systems that will require management's attention in successfully dealing with the impact of technology on work force administration will be presented.

INTRODUCTION

Over the years there has always been a good deal of attention given to the subject of managing the work force. In a pre-divestiture time frame, the attention to this area came in the form of productivity measurements, where annual increases in productivity were viewed as valid objectives, indications of improved operations, as well as confirmation that new technology was meeting its expectations. We need merely look at the productivity gains monitored during the 1970's to see that such was the case, and that network technologies, such as electronic switching and T-Carrier, were responsible for a significant part of those productivity gains.

Within the various operating companies at the middle management levels, various techniques were developed to monitor and manage the productivity. As an example, in Southwestern Bell we had a productivity measurement based on what was termed "work units". A particular task associated with a specific technology was evaluated and assigned a work unit value. The accomplishment of the task would cause the work units to be counted, and the objective was to maximize the number of work units accomplished on a per hour basis. Needless to say, it required ongoing effort to maintain and keep accurate, but it did serve as a valid indicator within our company, particularly between comparable operating entities. Its primary weakness was that it didn't in all cases promote cost efficiency, but rather work output efficiency.

With divestiture the old Bell System saying of "Service at all costs" was replaced with the newer version of "cost effective service." While this in no way meant a change in the quality of service that was to be expected by our customers, it did signal the beginning of a focus on providing those quality services at the lowest possible cost; and with the work force being a major part of that cost, it has naturally drawn much attention. Technology has continued to improve productivity by introducing more reliable and efficiently maintained network equipment. In a similar vein, mechanization has helped to both speed up and automate many work functions, while at the same time operations support systems have made it possible to more effectively manage the work force. This trend will continue for many years to come as technology will further impact how the technician does his/her job, and it is important for us to understand first, how the changes in technology will continue to impact our work force, and secondly, and as important, the philosophy managers will need to have in order to effectively utilize the technology in managing that work force.

THE IMPACT OF TECHNOLOGY

As a baseline for this discussion a high level review of the evolution of technology is beneficial as it relates to the role of the work force. In the area of switching, the electro-mechanical era saw the need for a technician who was as much as anything a good mechanic with strong physical dexterity. Step-by-step and Crossbar equipment required regular and constant attention to the various moving parts, with oiling, adjusting and lubricating some of the labor-intensive requirements to keep the switching gear in good working order. In the late 1960's and primarily in the 1970's, electronic switching came on strong, and with it the need for a technician who not only understood telephony, but also could grasp computer logic. No longer was just being a good mechanical person enough, as the technician had to become conversant in the ESS language of 1's and 0's and comprehend the processing of a call through the ESS machine. Thus, basic knowledge of electronics and logic became a necessity for the worker in the switchroom, and with the introduction of digital switching in recent years, this knowledge continues to be invaluable to the technician of today.

In a similar sense, facility and transmission equipment have made significant strides in technology that have also impacted the technician. In the days before pulse code modulation, the old analog carrier systems required considerable attention by the technician in keeping the systems fine-tuned and aligned. With the introduction of T-Carrier, the craftsman, as in the electronic switching world, was asked to understand the 1's and 0's of pulse code modulation, and, as importantly, the reliability of the equipment was greatly increased, thus eliminating much of the tuning work required of the older systems. With fiber optics and end-to-end digital connectivity, the technician, more than ever before, must understand the basics of the electronics if he/she is to fully utilize the capabilities of the technology.

With regard to Operations Support Systems, the technological gains have afforded much in the way of elimination of manual effort, improved record keeping, quicker and more effective customer response, and better utilization of the work force. To elaborate, we need only look at some of the more significant accomplishments in the last 20 years. The ability to mechanize customer records; to handle trouble reports via a mechanized repair service bureau; and to eliminate manual test desk work via utilization of mechanized testing facilities has proven a tremendous advantage in our business. Accomplishing flow-through assignment of service orders is another significant step that has saved countless hours of labor and has improved the records process. The ability to inventory central office terminal and signalling equipment as well as interoffice facilities has proven beneficial, as well as mechanizing the design process for many Special Services.

More specifically from a technician standpoint, the capabilities afforded by the evolution of technology include centralized remote monitoring of switching machine performance with the ability to remotely analyze, control and maintain these machines. Similarly for facility equipment, as well as reconfigure in some cases to avoid costly outages, has proven its savings. In the outside plant world, the ability to correlate cable troubles on a mechanized basis and sectionalize troublesome cable for repair or replacement has been most beneficial in a rehabilitation/maintenance effort.

In the area of work force administration, the ability to handle on a mechanized basis the administration of the outside craft force for both service order and trouble reports has proven most beneficial. In a similar vein, pricing and loading of the central office work force has been mechanized to afford a more effective administration of trouble reports, service orders, and preventive maintenance routines.

All in all significant progress has been made in the area of OSS's and yet there are still opportunities to be gained. What must be remembered is that technology has and will continue to impact how the work force does their job, and as importantly how management can utilize that work force in the future. To better understand the importance of this premise, it is important to examine some of the major issues that will have to be addressed to successfully deal with the impact of technology on the work force. I would offer three:

The first issue in this regard is that of developing an effective work force. First, the technician of today and the technician of tomorrow will require more than ever before an "information age" knowledge base. This is by no means an over night proposition and in fact will require new skills set to be developed or brought to the business. While many of the existing work force may well be on their way to making the information age transition, continually changing technology will require management to address this issue for the total work force. In this regard, we in Southwestern Bell have approached the subject from several different but related points. Training has and continues to be an important part of being able to manage the business both today and tomorrow. Staff and field middle management meet regularly to insure future training needs are being identified and that current training being obtained is effective and efficient. Being able to anticipate the necessary training needs and obtain or develop the required technical training is vital in today's telecommunications business.

A second aspect of technical training which we are also addressing in Southwestern Bell is that of providing an opportunity for the present work force to improve and upgrade their technical knowledge. This becomes most pertinent in a business such as our where the technical personnel have an opportunity to upgrade to higher level technical jobs. As an example, employees are given various opportunities to learn technical knowledge that is considered essential to qualifying for the higher level position. In many cases, this may require the employee's own initiative and personal time, but it provides a very viable alternative in keeping the work force up-to-date technically.

Another aspect to be mentioned with regard to developing an effective work force is that of what we in Southwestern Bell refer to as "craft intake". This process actually goes hand in hand with the previous points of technical knowledge improvement for the existing work force, but also applies to any technicians hired new into the work force. The basic principle of "craft intake" acknowledges the need for an electronics-type technician in today's business, and establishes a baseline knowledge for qualification into a job that insures technical competence. In other words, it updates the technical knowledge requirements to match the electronic, computer-based technology of today.

All of these examples I mention really focus on the issue that the development of a technically competent work force is essential in today's telecommunications business. Equally important, there is a need today, more than ever before, for that work force to be competent in customer contact skills. The evolution of technology has to a large degree depersonalized our business, and the work force of today, particularly the outside installation and repair forces, represent the largest base of employees having daily contact with the customer. The ability for the work force to successfully handle these face-to-face, personal contacts with the customer will play an ever increasing importance in the perceptions our customers have about us as a business and the service we provide. It is, therefore, appropriate that the work force be trained to not just handle a customer contact, but to make it a positive and satisfying experience for our customers.

The second major issue that must be addressed is that of utilization of the available technology. It is assumed that network technology will, without a doubt, continue to evolve; however, the point here focuses on the utilization of technology that is specifically made to help manage the work force. This technology has developed to a great deal in the last few years, and will continue to develop even further in the years ahead. As computer technology continues to improve, and particularly allows for more integration and evolution to data-driven architectures, there will be continued improvement in the tools to more effectively manage the work force. To give you an example how we have utilized such technologies recently in Southwestern Bell, I'll discuss two pertinent examples.

The first deals with mechanizing work and force administration. After some earlier experiences with some of the first mechanized pricing and loading systems

1034

which allowed for management of the work load over an available force, Southwestern Bell deployed the CIMAP (Circuit Installation and Maintenance Assistance Package) system in both our Special Services Repair Centers and the Central Office work groups. The system provides trouble ticket administration, pricing and loading of prioritized work, mechanized time reporting, as well as various management reports. The most recent application of CIMAP just trialed this past summer was for the Special Services I & M Function, where the system helps to prioritize troubles versus installation activities and makes work assignments considering the geographic distance the technician must travel as well as the priority of the work items left to be done. The end result has been an effective mechanized system to accomplish work and force administration.

Another important area where we in Southwestern Bell have utilized available technology is that of our application of a field Technician Access Network (TAN) System. This technology has allowed us to truly mobilize our outside POTS technician, giving them the capability to dial into the TAN system and obtain customer records, perform test functions, close out trouble reports, and obtain their next case of trouble to continue their work day. In Southwestern Bell, we have combined our mobilization of the technician with another approach to doing business, that of home basing, or allowing the technician to start and end his work day directly from home. With the Technician Access Network, this mode of operation becomes easily achieved, and provides tangible results, such as more productive time for the technician and expense savings associated with work centers, not to mention some very significant intangible results, such as increased job satisfaction and improved supervisory relationships.

There is, however, a word of caution to mention regarding the networking of these various OSS's, as more and more mechanization takes place. Deployment of work force administration technology like CIMAP and TAN can produce significant savings to the operations, but at the same time it quickly emphasizes the need for highly accurate data bases, and in those cases where data resides in two or more systems, the need to maintain matched data for all applications. The integration of the various operations support systems to provide for synchronized data bases will be essential as the industry continues to rely more and more on mechanized means of managing the business. It will be critical in an integrated mechanization environment that there be an approach to a corporate or common data base that has

high availability and can be utilized by all applications.

The third and final major issue I identify is that of promoting an effective management philosophy that is truly in tune with the deployment and utilization of technology. More than ever before, the technician will be given a certain independence in doing their job while at the same time have the potential of feeling "big brother" is always looking over their shoulder in the form of a supervisor at his terminal. The successful deployment of technology in the future will be able to positively increase the accountability of the technician while at the same time effectively utilize all available information to better manage the business. Trust between management and the work force will be essential, and the successful supervisor will find himself more in a coaching role as opposed to one of direct supervision.

A couple of approaches are, in my opinion, demonstrative of the direction that needs to be taken by management in light of technology trends. The first I would offer is that of an emphasis on quality. Combined with a continuing improvement in testing capabilities and better tools for the technicians to do his/her job, an emphasis on quality can have big benefits with regard to customer service and productivity. Several such quality programs have been initiated in our company, all of which have the same basic underlying principle of "doing the job right the first time", and more importantly accepting such a principle as the everyday way of doing business. While the issue of "quality" has been around for some time, technology todays lets us address it more effectively than we ever have, and a management approach that gets work force buy-in to quality will derive significant savings and efficiencies.

The second example I would mention is that of participative management and employee involvement. The work force of today can potentially run more productively. Our recent experiences in participative management have shown that our work force is able to provide valuable input to the decision making process, and as a result take a more meaningful partnership in solving the problems we face as a business. Successful managers will take advantage of this untapped resource to enhance and improve their operations.

CONCLUSION

Technology has made tremendous strides in our industry to date and will continue to evolve and improve. In the years ahead, better and more reliable network technology will be deployed, as well as ever-improving mechanization technology to aid us in managing the business more productively. The future successful managers of our business will address the impact of this technology by dealing with three important issues: First, developing an effective work force that can maintain and operate the future technology and are sensitive to customer service. Second, utilizing the full capabilities of technology that specifically relates to managing the work force. And third and finally, promoting an effective management philosophy that allows the work force to become contributing team members in improving the business operation, and in the end, overall customer service.

USING EXPERT SYSTEMS TO AID

IN WORKFORCE MANAGEMENT

Jerry L. Neal

Network System Administrator

Contel

245 Perimeter Center Parkway
Atlanta, GA 30346

ABSTRACT

This paper describes the development and use of expert systems to aid in the area of work force management. Expert systems are relatively new to the average business environment and many of the standard rules for design, development, and implementation must be redefined for this type of system to be successful. Due to the differences in technology concerning expert systems, a discussion of the development process is required to insure that the system and it's functions meet the requirements to manage the work force. A thorough review must be made to ensure that the use of a personal computer based expert system and not a conventional approach is the best solution for the given problem. A development team must be assembled with the key team member being the domain expert. The delivery system must be developed quickly, meet all the needs to perform the specific job, and provide methods to allow quick updates to meet a rapidly changing environment. Expert systems can be developed to assist in tasks where it was once thought that only a human could perform.

INTRODUCTION

Expert systems provide the capability of representing knowledge in the exact same way an individual would actually perform a given task. Expert systems open up a new realm in work force management providing the opportunity to distribute knowledge to field locations while retaining the experts to perform detailed tasks in critical areas. To tackle the task of providing expert systems, a total new process of systems development and distribution must be put into place. There are three major components that must be clarified to insure the success of an expert system:

° Identify needs

° Development of the system

° Distribution and work force management

A detail analysis must be performed reviewing the requirements for the given application to insure that an expert system and not a conventional approach is the best solution for the given problem. The acceptance of the system by all levels of management and the end-user community is critical to insure the successful development and use of the system. The selection of a development team should consist of a knowledge programmer, knowledge engineer, domain expert, and senior staff manager. Expert system development tools are to be reviewed and selected to insure all needs are met to build and distribute the final product. The main thrust of the final product should address all requirements specified by the domain expert and be delivered on an economical platform. The expert system should be developed to allow quick changes to insure a rapid response to the needs of the end-user, as well as, staff management, thereby, insuring the system meets the ever changing requirements needed to manage the work force.

IDENTIFYING THE NEED

Expert systems are not the answer to all problems, conventional applications are still required for those areas demanding rapid calculations or containing extremely large databases. Expert systems tend to fit well in areas where expertise is in short supply, large groups are required to perform a small task, conditions are constantly changing, or where problems are solved through "rule of thumb". This is not to say that an expert system could not be used to assist the user of a large conventional system; expert systems can be imbedded into the process of a conventional system to perform tasks where human expertise is normally required. Expert systems are excellent diagnostic tools which can be used in trend analysis or in areas of configuration. If an application is suited for conventional approach, expert systems should not be used in an attempt to prove the technology. Most companies contain excellent programming shops and system engineers providing an economical approach to solving the conventional application without requiring the acquisition of specialized hardware, software, consulting, and training for the development of an expert system.

Identification of the organization structure within a company will ease in the development and implementation process of expert systems. Key supporters should be identified up front and provided with a thorough understanding of the operational benefits of the system. Both tangible and intangible benefits should be shown to dispel over expectations concerning the actual performance and the return of investment of the final product. These benefits can be difficult to show, especially with systems that require human interaction. Personal computer based systems usually fit into this category and offer no benefit if they are not used; hence the acceptance by both the management that implements and the work force that will use these systems are essential.

BUILDING THE SYSTEM

A development team is required for the knowledge acquisition, design, and implementation of an expert system. This team consists of a domain expert, knowledge engineer, knowledge programmer, and senior staff manager. The team will be required to select the development system, development tools, and the delivery platform that will provide the flexibility to meet a rapidly changing environment.

The domain expert must be a recognized authority in their field and capable of describing how they perform a given task. This individual must be willing and have the time available to see the project through from beginning to end. Their local management must be informed of the time constraints required of this individual and provide the opportunity to view them at work.

The knowledge engineer (KE) contains the necessary skills to acquire knowledge from a human expert. The KE's abilities range from cognitive skills, used during knowledge acquisitions, to the understanding of computer systems and languages to insure the proper tools will be used during the development process. Interviews with management and the end-users who will receive the final product are required to incorporate all the necessary functions into the production system. The KE will review a domain expert concerning the task they perform to clearly identify the methods and thought process an individual uses in performing their job. These day to day interview sessions that are conducted with the expert will provide the KE with information to convert into

knowledge representation maps. The knowledge programmer will take these maps and develop them into a knowledge base and a user interface for final delivery of the system.

The senior staff member is critical in the coordinating efforts of the team. This individual should be used to assist in the early identification of problems that need to be solved within a company. Due to many of the new approaches used in expert system building, the senior staff member educates and briefs management on the needs of the development team to insure the success of the final system.

During the early knowledge acquisitions between the KE and the domain expert, a prototype is developed to show the feasibility of the system. These prototypes can be put together quickly needing only a few weeks of interviews and coding requirements. Once the system is accepted, the development is continued around the prototype in a cycle method that allows the domain expert to assist in the specifications and functional design of the system (figure 1). This "cycling method" allows the domain expert to have constant input throughout the development of the system insuring the final product will perform as required. The "80/20 rule" applies to expert systems as it does to the development of conventional systems, but the final product must provide all the functions identified by the domain expert. Interfaces to reporting systems, databases, communication platforms, or other hardware are essential to insure the systems use in the mainstream of day to day operations.

MANAGING THE WORK FORCE

An expert's knowledge is one of the most important assets within today's corporations. With the rapid changes in technology, maintaining a highly trained work force is an extremely costly venture. Retaining an experienced technical work force is another difficult task due to the constant demand for this expertise within all corporations.

Experts perform their task over and over until these actions become "rules-of-thumb" or heuristics. These heuristics become complex methods embedded within an individual's memory and are performed out of habit. Heuristics require little thought to perform a given task and explaining this information to another individual can be very difficult. An abstract example of this is given in figure 2; here the concept of identifying types of ground bars found in a digital central office is shown. This example is referred to as memory segments and are implemented in expert systems as "frames".

These frames contain detailed masses of information which are developed by an individual over a long period of time. This information, many times, is derived from on-the-job-training which is learned without the benefit of formal education. Psychologists believe it can take as long as ten years to develop these complex memory segments. Expert systems can be developed to not only distribute this type of information to lesser trained individuals, but retain this information in the event that the expert is no longer available.

Selling the system as a tool to perform a job, and not as artificial intelligence or "the expert system" will help dispel the "smoke and mirrors" that can often plague the acceptance of a new technology. The end-user community must view the system as a productivity enhancement or resource tool and not as a device used to reduce manpower. With a simple user interface, little or no training will be required, thereby the systems immediate use can be utilized.

Opening the product up to all departments within a company can have a tremendous impact. Training departments can use the product to incorporate into existing course lines. This can bring the actual expertise from the field to assist individuals, new to the technology, in methods used to perform a given task. Design departments can use the same tool to perform what-if scenarios to assist in their engineering efforts.

By developing the expert system on a personal computer platform, an economical means is provided to allow virtually any department within a company access to this knowledge. The concept of "a picture is worth a thousand words" is especially important in this type of knowledge transfer. High definition graphics can be used to display information in the same format as an expert would view the problem. Using expert systems on portable computers allow field personnel to perform detailed analysis to a given problem and equipped with a communication package, transfer the results back to a centralized location for further interpretation. This provides a means to retain critical professionals at a single location to assist a greater scope of the work force instead of these individuals working on simple mundane problems.

A major benefit of developing an expert system is in the tools which allow knowledge to be represented and provide methods to generate prompt and efficient changes to the systems. This is extremely critical due to the rapidly changing environment that the technical community must contend with. These changes must be placed into the model and offered to the field to insure that the credibility of the system is maintained.

CONCLUSION

As more and more complex issues are confronted by managers, means must be provided in which the work force can be managed more efficiently and effectively. Computer processes once thought to be impossible are now available in the mainstream of day-to-day operations. Advances in technology have work stations and portable computers with CPUs operating in the same ranges that mini and mainframe computers were performing a year ago. With these continued advancements in computers and software development tools, today's managers must review expert systems and their place within their organization to insure their work force has the best resources available to perform their jobs.

PROTOTYPE CYCLE

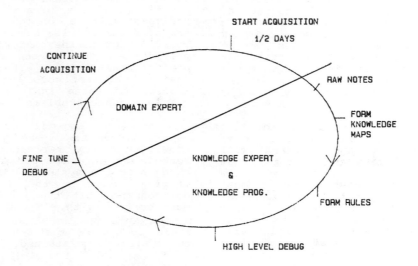

FIGURE 1

HEURISTIC INFORMATION

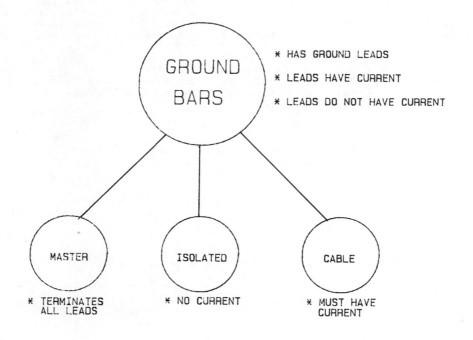

FIGURE 2

NETWORK OPERATIONS AND SUPPORT SYSTEMS:

THE INSIDE OPERATIONS PERSPECTIVE

John L. Draheim, Chairperson

Assistant Vice President -
Operations Services

Ameritech Services

1900 East Golf Road, 2nd Floor
Schaumburg, IL 60173

ABSTRACT

A world of exciting change is occurring in
Network Operations today created by the
impact of new digital technology, an
increased number of vendors, the evolution
to an intelligent, software controlled
network, and the placement of substantial
control in the hands of the customer.
This seminar will focus on the Central
Office environment and the support systems
required within it to continue to offer
new features, products and services while
reducing expenses and capital requirements.
This will be done by focusing on solving
digital switching maintenance problems,
using artificial intelligence technology
to assist in these problems, automating
translations on the line side of the
switch, and applying the automation of
Special Services to a large metropolitan
area. This seminar and the two associated
seminars, "The Planning Perspective" and
"The Outside Operations Perspective" will
discuss current and future operations
support strategies, problems,
implications, alternatives and solutions.

Paul Eng   -- Northern Telecom Inc.

Wendy Morris   -- Pacific Bell

Dennis Sassa   -- Bell Communications
                       Research

Dean Weston   -- Wisconsin Bell

PREPARING FOR THE OPERATIONS

CHALLENGES OF THE FUTURE

Paul Eng

Network Product Line Manager

Northern Telecom Inc.

Network Support Systems Division
P.O. Box 649, Concord, NH 03301

ABSTRACT

The power and flexibility needed to meet
the challenges of present and future
operations environments can only come from
new OS architectures and technology
complemented by new approaches to network
management. This paper addresses the key,
critical operations support attributes
which allow for effective adaptation to
the information and decision flows imposed
by future operations environments.

THE OPERATIONS ENVIRONMENT ... WHERE IS IT HEADED?

Much effort and energy has been spent
in defining the challenges and
opportunities confronting service
providers as a result of such forces as
technological advances in the network,
increasing service demands by the end-user
community, and the dynamic nature of the
post-divestiture environment. In response
to these changes, the operational support
needs for the present and future network
have been re-evaluated and various
conceptual models have been proposed for
consideration.

One of the critical issues facing the
industry today concerns how the existing
network, with its numerous independent
operations support systems (OSSs), can
evolve into the intelligent network of the
future supported by a full array of highly
integrated, sophisticated operations
tools. As will be explained in this
paper, a promising answer can be found in
the application of the latest advances in
artificial intelligence/expert systems,
man-machine interfaces, data base
management systems, and the ongoing
process of standardization which is
occurring in the computer industry.

In addition to the changes in the
elements that make up the network, there
is also impetus for organizational
innovations to meet the challenges of a
changing industry. In the past, the
organizational structure and operations
procedures were molded (even dictated) by
the nature of the available OSSs. In
today's dynamic environment, marketing and
business requirements must be supported by
operations procedures which can be adapted
and fine-tuned to accommodate the changing
requirements. Also, operations needs must
be allowed to evolve independent of the
support tools.

The key to achieving this operations
evolution independent of the systems
supporting the network lies in the
separation of the decision flow from the
information flow. Within the network,
information originating in network
elements flows upward through the
different equipment layers toward the
human operator, while decisions flow
downward through the different layers of
management and craft until they ultimately
impact the network elements. The
information flow depends largely on the
nature of the network elements, operations
support tools available, and the varying
abilities of humans interpreting the
information. If decisions have been
allowed to follow a path independent of
the information flow, decision flow can
depend on operational needs alone.

While the nature of information
collected is dynamic and varies with

updates and changes to the network elements, the overall operations goals and decision processes remain essentially the same. At the maintenance level, failures must be identified, service restored, and the faults repaired. From a management and planning level, network and human resources must be allocated and utilized efficiently. The OSS of the future must insulate the decision stream from any changes in content of the information gathered and the method by which it is collected from the network elements.

AN EVOLUTIONARY OPERATIONS STRATEGY

The solution to the migration of existing network support capabilities to the support of the future network can be found in judicious application of techniques and technologies available today. This is far preferable and more cost effective than waiting until certain technologies have matured or until technical advances are available to supply all required functionality. Various interim steps will obviously be necessary to maintain adequate and continuous operations support as the network evolves. Moreover, a platform based on present technology can be implemented now which provides the capabilities of embedded OSSs, and more importantly, evolves as technologies and operational needs change.

The attributes and underlying technologies of such a platform are discussed below.

PLATFORM ARCHITECTURE

In architectural terms, the basic approach is the vertical distribution of functions, data base and intelligence as show in Figure 1

As part of this partitioning, intelligence for preliminary filtering (screening), concentration, and analysis of information must be placed as close to the network elements as possible. It is inefficient and a waste of scarce network resources to bring raw data into the operations center for filtering and analysis. While these functions can be built into intelligent network elements, economics may dictate use of external devices. An external concentrator/ analyzer (called a network server) can perform the necessary storage, analysis, consolidation, and prioritization of information for a cluster of diverse network elements. Thus the cost of the intelligence required is distributed among multiple network elements.

The remote network server would typically combine the functions of a protocol/interface mediation device with filtering and information processing. In other words, the network server can be viewed as a remote extension of the host OSS providing localized support and processing for a cluster of network elements. From the standpoint of the network server, a foreign OSS can be considered a super intelligent network element.

Information from the different network servers is correlated, refined, and presented to the human users and stored in the distributed historical data base. While the network server provides for the storage of short and intermediate term information, long term analysis of the network requires the storage of historical information for months and, perhaps, a year. The various analysis modules of the OSS support both immediate network management and historical analysis functions as required. Knowledge based expert system technologies can be applied to relate disparate data and provide useful real time and historical information.

To support the decision making process of the user, the OSS architecture does not let physical location or access interfere with logical grouping of the user community. Users typically have differing interests, skills and needs in a dynamic environment. The user community is therefore fully independent of the information processing flow and depends only on the way the decision process is organized and administered. How the OSS supports the user physically imposes no restriction on the functions or information accessible.

The OSS architecture allows logical partitioning of not only the user community, but of the network and data base as well. This separation means the user community must be supported by dedicated servers providing the software and tools required for decision making. From these servers, the user community can access the network servers and historical data base as well as other embedded OSSs.

In physical terms, each logical user type is supported by its own server(s) which communicate with other components of the architecture over a local or wide area network. To provide the required flexibility, functions are implemented in software which is transportable among the different servers of the OSS. This allows for the evolution of functionality while insulating the user against hardware changes.

INFORMATION PROCESSING

As previously mentioned, information from the network elements is first processed by the network server which provides initial filtering, analysis, and concentration functions. Because the network server uses a data base management system supporting On-line Transaction Processing (OLTP), it is capable of handling high transaction rates. It also supports interfaces to diverse network elements by taking advantage of certain standard interfaces used within the telecommunications industry.

During the transition to the fully intelligent network, the network server must be able to normalize information from different sources into standard formats.

This involves not only format conversion but also the translation of the content of the messages received from network elements. The application of algorithm-based intelligence is sufficient for the conversion/translation process. However, expert system technologies are required to provide a friendly man-machine interface for user definition of the algorithms. The key to utilizing the network server as a transition device is the ability of the user to adjust and accommodate where necessary to meet current operations needs.

The next stage in the processing is provided by the various analysis modules which correlate, refine, and expand the information from the network servers. The network server focuses only on a particular network element or cluster of network elements. The view of the analysis modules is focused on the global network where the interdependency and relationships among network elements can be exploited.

To provide expeditious correlation of information from the network servers, the analysis modules emphasize the application of rule based technologies supported by OLTP capability. As with the network server, the user must be provided with the ability to modify the rules governing the correlation of information.

The last step in the processing flow is handled by the user server where the focus is on the presentation of the pertinent information in an expeditious manner to human operators. In the user server, the critical technologies are man-machine interfaces and support for both pre-programmed and ad hoc data base queries. The application of Natural Language Interface, OLTP, and high resolution color graphic workstations provide the required functions. From a man-machine interface standpoint, the user must be provided with the ability to customize the format of the information presented.

DECISION PROCESSING

Decisions within the network flow from the OSS down to the network elements. Within the OSS environment, the primary location for decision making is at the user level with secondary support at the various analysis modules.

In the present operations environment, the operator makes decisions by analyzing whatever information is available. This analysis step depends on the nature of the information received from the network and on the skill of the individual involved. With the benefit of the user server, the manual decision making process is replaced by the application of knowledge based expert system technologies which analyze network data to present the user with the most likely conclusions and the recommended solutions.

During the transition to the fully intelligent network, automated decision making allows the user to deal with information of differing clarity and meaning. It also prepares the user for a future environment where automated execution of the optimal solution can be supported.

Today, the primary challenge is to create the required knowledge base to support the automated decision making function. While the preferred solution appears to involve some type of future "self-learning" technology, immediate steps can be taken to implement a semi-automated function. In this scenario, the system records the reaction of an expert to different situations and also provides a means for the expert to correct the knowledge base.

At the level of the analysis modules and the network servers, decisions are also made on an automated basis in reaction to information received from the network. Both the network server and analysis modules must allow user manipulation/control of the reaction to a particular network event (e.g., overload condition) or other stimuli. This type of decision making functionality can be supported by the application of simple algorithms with expansion into expert system technologies. To accommodate differing operations needs, users may create and modify the algorithms as required.

SUMMARY

The most important operations challenge facing today's service provider is how to effect a graceful transition to the support environment required by the network of the future. This transition can be facilitated by the judicious integration of appropriate technologies in a single operations platform which can readily adapt to change, both technological and operational.

REFERENCES

1. Operations Systems Strategic Plan (OSSP), Bellcore publication SR-NPL-000022, Issue 2, April 1985.

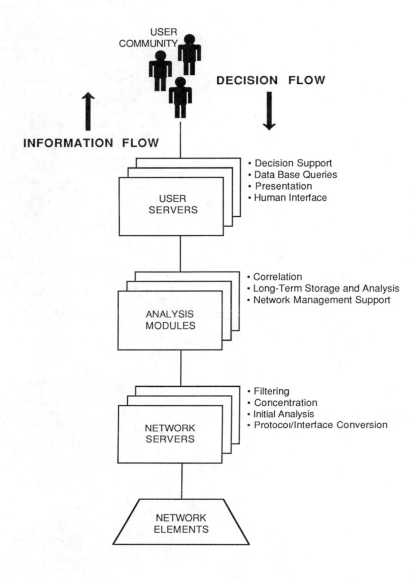

Figure 1. Distributed OSS Platform

<u>ARTIFICIAL INTELLIGENCE APPLICATION</u>

<u>FOR CENTRAL OFFICE OPERATIONS</u>

Dennis J. Sassa

District Manager –
Network Analysis Systems

Bell Communications Research

Room 22129
Red Bank, NJ 07701-7020

ABSTRACT

Opportunities exist to apply Artificial Intelligence to assist the operations people in identifying troubles, isolating faults, exercising controls, recommending repairs, and remotely correcting hardware and software troubles. Several potential central office applications of Artificial Intelligence Technologies are presented with an emphasis on Expert System Applications.

The Expert Systems and in particular diagnostic systems predominate the Artificial Intelligence Applications. The present benefits achieved by permanently capturing expertise in an Expert System include: quality improvements, productivity enhancements, consistency, reduced training expenses, and access to expert knowledge when needed. Future benefits will include machine learning, natural language processing, and automated equipment repair.

Artificial Intelligence Applications For Central Office Operations

Outline

- Artificial intelligence applications

- Maintenance operations

- Expert systems applications

- Potential benefits & promises of the future

Artificial Intelligence Applications For Central Office Operations

Artificial Intelligence Applications

- **Knowledge-based expert systems**
- **Natural language processing**
- **Robotics**
  - **Vision systems**
  - **Motion systems**
- **Machine learning**

Artificial Intelligence Applications For Central Office Operations

Typical Network Element Maintenance Operation

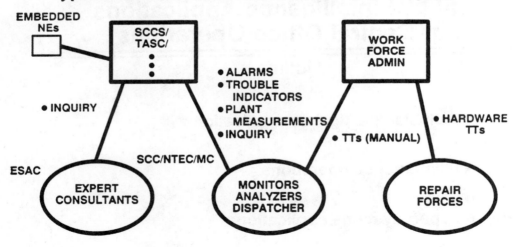

Artificial Intelligence Applications For Central Office Operations

What Is An Expert System

- A computer program/system capturing and applying a human expert's knowledge to a task

- Solve difficult problems
    - Large number of possible solutions
    - Experience and knowledge required

- Approximates expert reasoning through:
    - A knowledge base containing the experts broad range of information
    - Problem solving strategies

Artificial Intelligence Applications For Central Office Operations

Why Use Expert Systems

- Expertise is scarce
    - Human expertise is being lost
    - Expertise is needed in many locations
    - Introduction of new technology

- A small task requires a large team because no one person knows enough

- Performance degradation as a result of the complexity of the analysis

- Payoff may be large

- Retain knowledge

Artificial Intelligence Applications For Central Office Operations

When Can Expert Systems Be Used

- Genuine experts exist
- Experts can articulate their methods
- Experts agree on solutions
- Task requires symbol manipulation and uses heuristic
- Task is well bounded, well defined and stable
- Task is not too difficult and not too easy
- Task is of a manageable size

Artificial Intelligence Applications For Central Office Operations

Summary of Expert Systems In Network Operations And Management

- Generic categories of expert system applications:
  - Prediction - traffic forecast
  - Diagnosis - trouble isolation
  - Design - circuit and network configuration
  - Planning - designing actions, decision support
  - Monitoring - equipment surveillance
  - Repair - executing a plan to administer a prescribed remedy
  - Instruction - craft instruction
  - Control - interpreting, predicting, repairing, and monitoring system behaviors

Artificial Intelligence Applications For Central Office Operations

Diagnostic Systems
Network

- **NET/ADVISOR (Avant-Garde Computing Inc.)**
  - **Private networks**
- **TROUBLESHOOTER (AT&T Bell Labs)**
  - **Datakit network**
- **NTC - Network Troubleshooting Consultant (DEC)**
  - **Local area network**
- **BDS - Baseband Distribution System (Lockheed)**
  - **Switching networks**
- **NDS (Shell Development Corp)**
  - **Nationwide communications network**

Artificial Intelligence Applications For Central Office Operations

Diagnostic Systems
Switch

- **SMART - Switching Maintenance Analysis and Repair Tool (Bellcore)**
  - **1AESS™ switch**
- **COMPASS - Central Office Maintenance Printout Analysis and Suggestion System- (GTE)**
  - **GTE no. 2 Electronic Automatic Exchange**
- **MAD - Maintenance advisor (BNR)**
  - **DMS-100**
- **NEMESYS (GTE)**
  - **GTD-5 EAX central office switch**

Artificial Intelligence Applications For Central Office Operations

Diagnostic Systems
Other Areas

- **ACE - Automated Cable Expertise (AT&T Bell Laboratories)**
  - Preventive cable maintenance

- **TRACKER (British Telecom)**
  - PABX power supplies

- **ExT - The Expert Tester (Bellcore)**
  - Troubleshoots special service circuits

- **GEMS-TTA - The Generalized Expert Maintenance System**
  - Trouble trunk analyzer (AT&T Bell Laboratories)-trunks

Artificial Intelligence Applications For Central Office Operations

Monitoring/Diagnostic Systems

- **REACT - Real Time Expert Analysis and Control Tool (Bellcore)**
  - Monitors and diagnosis DMS-100 switch

- **NEMESYS - Network Management Expert System (AT&T Bell Laboratories)**
  - Fight congestion in the long distance network

Artificial Intelligence Applications For Central Office Operations

Design Systems

- DESIGNET (Bolt, Beranek and Newman)
  - Private data networks

- KAT (AT&T Bell Laboratories)
  - Network Planning

Artificial Intelligence Applications For Central Office Operations

Potential Benefits Of Applying Artificial Intelligence To Central Office Operations

- Improved service response
- Essentially eliminate monitor function
- Significantly reduce analysis function
- Retain valuable resource of operations knowledge
- Aid in training
- More efficiently utilize repair forces
- Rapid automation of operations capabilities

Artificial Intelligence Applications
For Central Office Operations

Promises Of The Future

- Increased number of categories of expert systems in network operations and management

- Integration of expert systems with traditional network operations and management systems (data base interfaces)

- Integrated expert system hardwired into equipment

- Robotics

- Natural language

AUTOMATING LINE SIDE TRANSLATIONS

Wendy Morris

District Manager

Pacific Bell

Room 4N552, 2600 Camino Ramon
San Ramon, CA 94583

ABSTRACT

This session will address central
office recent change automation from an
operating telephone company perspective.
It will take a broad look at the
mechanization of line side translations
and describe where one operating
telephone company is today, what they have
learned along the way, and how they did
it. In particular, the implementation of
new services will be examined using access
to an automated memory administration
system.

SPECIAL SERVICES - AN INTEGRATED APPROACH

Dean J. Weston

Division Manager, Business Services

Wisconsin Bell, Inc.

918 North 26th Street
Milwaukee, WI 53233

ABSTRACT

This paper will describe an integrated
organizational approach to the engineering
design, provisioning and maintenance of
special service circuits. Included will
be a definition of special service
circuits as they exist at Wisconsin Bell.
The total provisioning process will be
explained with details of organization and
operations support systems which support
the work groups provided. Impact of this
organization on results, specifically
customer due date performance will be
delineated. Maintenance results provided
by this same integrated organization will
be shown superior to that attained by
other organizational scenarios. Included
under maintenance will be differentiation
between Tier 1 and Tier 2 maintenance
support. Strong technical support to
Wisconsin Bell Marketing efforts is also
provided by the organization explained in
this paper.

INTRODUCTION

In 1981, Wisconsin Bell recognized the
need for change in the methods and
organization used for designing,
provisioning and maintaining special
service circuits. These circuits are
defined as those requiring some type of
design or design review process and are
differentiated from POTS (Plain Old
Telephone Service) by use of Common
Language Circuit Identification (CLCI).
After studying the needs of this side of
the business for several months, a new
organization was recommended and
established. The new division, initially
called the Special Services Division and
since renamed the Business Services
Division, was created with three
districts. While the three districts have
changed somewhat since 1981 because of
changing technologies and the AT&T
divestiture, the basic organization has
remained intact. The three districts are
(1) Provisioning Services: responsible
for all design activities on special
service circuits, issuance of design
documents, design technical support, TIRKS
(Trunks Integrated Record Keeping System)
system administration and TIRKS equipment
inventory; (2) Special Services
Operations - methods and procedures
support to field operations, Tier 2
maintenance support (DATRAN), new
technologies field trials and
implementation, system administration of
CIMAP (Circuit Installation and
Maintenance Assistance Package), and
internal data and terminal installation
and repair; (3) Special Services I&M -
installation and repair of special service
circuits both in the central office and on
customer premises, utilizes various
operations support systems and has
"control tower" functions in areas where
manpower resources are shared. The
geographic area covered by these three
districts is, with some exceptions, any
Wisconsin Bell exchange within the state.

SPECIAL SERVICES DEFINED

At Wisconsin Bell, a straightforward
approach to defining special service
circuits has been instituted. If a
circuit needs special equipment to work as
required, by the customer needs review
and/or design to be sure it meets
transmission loss parameters or has other
unique requirements it is designated a
special service circuit. This designation
is made during the customer ordering
process by use of Common Language Circuit
Identification $_{TM}$ (CLCI). Wisconsin Bell
is one of many companies that subscribe to
the common language standards published by
Bell Communications Research (Bellcore) of
which CLCI is one subset. Special service
circuits fall into two broad categories -
access and non-access and within each are
broken down into switched and private line
point-to-point and multi-point.

ORGANIZATION - THREE DISTRICTS

The mission of the business service
division is to focus on special service
circuits and provide premier engineering,
technical support, installation,
maintenance and marketing support for
these services. This division is part of

the Network Switched Services department with the Network Vice President's group, Provisioning Services.

PROVISIONING SERVICES

This district contains within it Systems Engineering, Circuit Provision Center, TIRKS System Administration and TIRKS Inventory Maintenance. All elements necessary for the successful design and design document issuance are vested in this group.

Systems Engineering is responsible for technical evaluation of products used to provide special services, the characterization of products in TIRKS for the circuit designers to utilize in their activities and interpretation of tariff, technical publications and other documents for circuit design requirements. Customer "special assembly" requests are developed into workable designs by this group to help Marketing retain accounts through innovative solutions.

The Circuit Provision Center (CPC) is responsible for collecting all information necessary to design special service circuits and issue a WORD (Work Order Record Details) document through TIRKS to the field forces. Design documents may be issued for installation, rearrangement or disconnect of circuits either in response to a customer service order or for an internally generated requirement such as an office conversion or cable throw. Related activities include acquisition of local loop assignments and make-up information, consultation with Marketing and technical resource on major customer conversions.

TIRKS Systems Administration personnel are responsible for release testing, training all work groups on new TIRKS-related methods and procedures, answering help-type questions from the user community and initiating maintenance and enhancements requests to Bellcore. The TIRKS software is developed and maintained by Bellcore under contract with six of the seven regional Bell Operating Companies.

Inventory maintenance of TIRKS assignable equipment is also under control of this district. While a number of different groups utilize equipment in TIRKS, special service has the predominant activity level and thus has accepted overall responsibility. Engineering groups responsible for the ordering and installation of central office equipment and interoffice facilities are the primary source of inventory data maintenance activity.

SPECIAL SERVICES OPERATIONS

The Special Services Operations group provides a number of support functions to the Special Services I&M district in addition to performing a limited line function. Methods and procedures work in today's technological climate is a never-ending process. This activity occurs in response to internal organization shifts, new products and services and changes to operations support systems. In addition to M&P activity, field trials of new equipment or systems are directed, monitored, documented and changes made as appropriate.

When troubles referred to the SSC (Special Service Center) cannot be resolved through normal testing and trouble isolation, they must be escalated to the next "Tier" of expertise. This Tier 2 maintenance group, called DATRAN, serves as a SWAT team to handle the tough trouble cases. Composed of management people with extensive background in special services with an emphasis on data transmission, they have been very effective in eliminating difficult troubles that were causing considerable customer dissatisfaction. Marketing has also used this group as a technical resource because of (DATRANs) frequent direct customer contact. Plans are to utilize this group in the pre-qualification process for potential Packet Switch, Datakit and ISDN customers.

New Technology project management/ deployment support is also provided by Special Services Operations. Most new products and services are trialed "in-house" first to gain experience and develop appropriate M&P. Since the field piece of that is handled within this group, they have been charged with the technical part of deployment support. This activity is done in concert with the Marketing Product management group with defined responsibility boundaries and hand-offs. As an adjunct to this, the installation of all internal (Wisconsin Bell) data modems, computer terminals, personal computers and voice/data networking equipment is also done in this group.

SPECIAL SERVICES I&M

The I&M district is responsible for all installation and maintenance of special services circuits (CLCI identified) in Wisconsin. This district controls all special services activities from three Special Service Centers (SSC) located in the larger metropolitan areas in the state and use LATA boundaries to delineate specific areas of responsibility between SSC's. Each SSC is fully supported with an administrative tracking system, CIMAP, and a test system, SARTS (Switched Access Remote Test System). In addition, each SSC has access to LMOS (Loop Maintenance Operation System) and MLT (Mechanized Loop Testing) for testing switched services.

The SSC also controls the loading and dispatching of all special service central office technicians and all special services systems technicians (customer premises technicians) who's activities are discussed in the next two paragraphs.

The I&M district also does all of the physical cross connect work and physical trouble shooting of special circuits in

central offices around the state. In
cities where it is not prudent to have a
special services technician, this work is
"contracted" out to the switching
technician in the switching division.

The services technician, responsible
for actual installation and maintenance
work of special services done on the
customer's premises, is also part of the
special services division, like in the
central office environment, where it is
prudent to do so, we "contract" the work
out to the distribution services
division's "POTS" technicians.

CONCLUSION

Stronger focus on special services
through this integrated organizational
scheme has proven extremely effective.
Service measurements, both internal and
external, customer satisfaction surveys
and productivity measurements have all
shown significant improvements following
the reorganization. Some specific
examples of the improvements accomplished:

Measurement Area	1981	1985	1988
Engineering/design documents issued on time	74.0	92.0	99.9
Customer Due Dates met	90.7	99.3	99.9
Special Service circuit average trouble duration (hours)	N/A	3.1	1.9
Annual circuit activity	82338	121134	116196
Employees in division	N/A	534	499

In addition to these numerical
improvements, there are the many
intangibles associated with this type
organization. The existence of a pool of
highly skilled design engineers and
technician, trained in this field is
definitely a competitive advantage. With
Marketing as a partner, we can effectively
bring to bear many resources to solve our
customers problems.

SPECIAL SERVICES - MAINTENANCE FLOW

NOTE: If either C.O. or Field is unable to repair trouble, it is escalated to Tier 2 - DATRAN.

1055

SPECIAL SERVICES - PROVISIONING FLOW

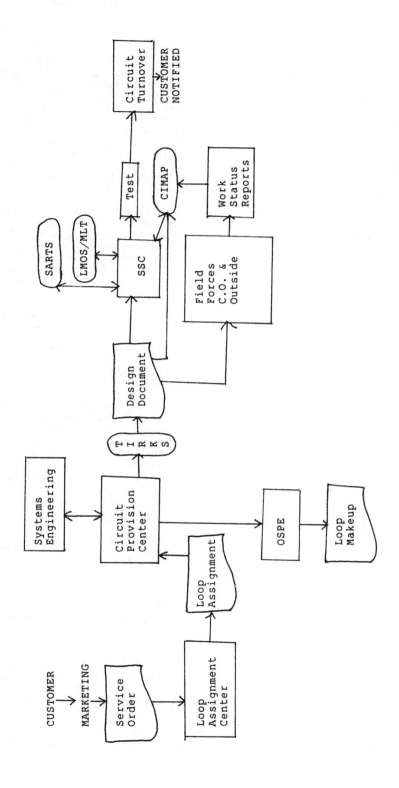

OPS-08

NETWORK OPERATIONS - THE OUTSIDE

OPERATIONS PERSPECTIVE

Wylie E. Etscheid, Chairperson

Division Manager -

Service Provisioning Support

Illinois Bell

212 W. Washington Street
Chicago, Illinois   60606

The Telecommunications Industry is undergoing some tremendous technological changes involving the methods of managing field craft for maximum productivity, and at the same time improving customer satisfaction. Already System Mechanization has brought about major productivity improvements and force reductions in the inside craft operations. This Seminar is going to focus on activities now being implemented across the country to bring similar savings and productivity improvements to the outside forces. It will start with a review of the use of hand held computers in the field and of Craft Access Technology. A specific company's strategy will be reviewed. We will then look at Craft Access and expert systems from a Preventive Maintenance perspective as well as how mobile radio can have a significant impact on an operating company's bottom line. Finally we will look at how the role of the outside technician in the year 2000 will be significantly different than it is today. This seminar addresses how to plan and implement the various technological and operational innovations to maximize the benefits to the customer, the employee and the bottom line.

Mr. D. E. Curry   - Itron Inc.
Mr. R. G. Aldridge - Illinois Bell
Ms. F. Henig   - AT&T Bell Laboratories
Ms. H. Bomengen   - Arthur D. Little, Inc.
Mr. M. A. Gicale   - Ameritech Services

Handheld Computers In A Telecom Environment

David E. Curry

Itron, Inc.

East 15616 Euclid Avenue
Spokane, Wa. 99216

Handheld computers. To many they seem to be a contradiction in terms. Typically ones experience with computers brings to mind a room full of cabinet sized processors, tape drives and disk drives. In recent years with the introduction of microprocessor technology removable and fixed data storage media, personal computers have become the reference point when one thinks of a computer. The notion of extending technology further to the point where a small inexpensive portable handheld computer equates to the processing power of a roomful of computer equipment of 15 years ago tends to stretch the limits of credibility. Yet such is the case today and industry the world over is just beginning to wake up to the reality of the technology and more importantly begin to realize the potential that handheld computing has in the work place.

If one looks at the evolution of handheld technology, among the first examples of portable computing capability occurred with calculators. The ubiquitous calculator carried by most math and science students replacing the equally ubiquitous slipstick or slide rule which replaced the abacus offers us a first look at handhelds. Technology being the inexorable monster that it is, continued to improve processing capabilities and memory storage to the point where the possibility of implementing portable handheld data collection devices became both realistic and cost effective.

We began to see some commercial applications of true handheld processing in the early 1980's. Two industries which were able to realize the early potential of the technology were the retail and utility markets. The Retail applications primarily involved inventory control systems typically food distribution and shelf stocking of supermarkets.

The utility industry applications presented a different set of challenges than retail usage. The handheld devices were used for collecting data on utility services, water gas and power consumption. The data collection process typically involved pre-loading or dispatching specific routes which included name and address, previous usage data, particular features of the account and reasonableness checks and data verification upon data entry. Data was subsequently transferred to the host billing systems through batch file transfer from reporting centers. The handheld technology and system integration is widely deployed in North America and continues to be the most cost effective means of collecting billing data despite the emergence of ISDN technology and remote Automatic Meter Reading.

The utility application of handheld technology presented substantially different operating characteristic to the manufactures of handheld technology then did the retail industry. As you would expect the telecom application of handheld computers is very similar to that of the utility industry in both the operating environment and the data collection process. At this point I would like to briefly explore the Telecom application and an emerging consensus on its benefits.

I expect all of you here today are very familiar with the fundamentals of providing field access to operational support systems. The concept and technology was first introduced by AT&T in the mid 1980's. Field access has proven itself to be both technically and economically a winner. However the technology doesn't come entirely without controversy. Technology and conceptual biases have surfaced and continue to surface resulting in some interesting polarized views of field access strategy and potential benefits.

There are two basic technical implementations of field access, voice or data. The voice implementation involves accessing a dispatch system with a butt set, the data version using a data device or handheld computer. As you might expect American enterprise being what it is, suppliers have come forth with multiple versions of field access to meet the polarized views the customer has of the access requirement. The industry is now presented with a list of options that looks like this:

- voice access only
- voice access and data printing
- data access only
- data access and printing
- data access and audio access
- data and audio and printing
- data and voice
- data and voice and printing

If these choices are not enough the industry is further presented with the option of providing the technician access via:

- wireline network
- RF (radio) network
- cellular network

It all seems simple enough to me. Well it's no wonder that when faced with the additional issues of:

- do I make the terminal a smart terminal; in effect achieving the ultimate in distributed processing?
- do I buy into the current technology and wait for more sophisticated technology to become available at a lower price?
- do I adopt a wait and see attitude and watch all the other's struggle?
- do I adopt a long term strategy based upon where I want to be in the future and take steps now to implement the first phase?

At this point I would like to briefly comment that the decision becomes very complex on the use of the field access technology and will return to the issue of the complexity of the choice facing the users a little later.

Currently field access is principally limited to providing trouble ticket dispatch, online closeout of the trouble ticket and the ability to invoke a test function from the centralized test system. Technician acceptance of the system has been widely spread and while cost justifications may vary from company to company, the economic benefits of installing the technology generally provides a very attractive return on investment. So after a years worth of experience with field access there are a number of issues that have emerged that I believe are worth examining. I would like to examine these issues form two perspectives:

- system features that are important
- terminal features that are important

Let's look first at system issues. There are currently at least two companies offering access technologies to support trouble ticket dispatch and testing. Each company has implemented access differently but all are fundamentally limited to the aforementioned functions. In the course of trialing and implementing field access there seems to be a consistent issue emerging.

The technicians are capable of and want to be able to do more than handle one trouble ticket at a time and perform MLT tests. Consequently the access system must have an architecture that supports a growth path well beyond the current limited functions.

A corollary to that issue is that the economic benefits necessary to justify the capital expenditure for field access may depend in large part in the implementation of a technology platform versatile and flexible enough to support much more than simple one at a time trouble ticket dispatch and testing.

There are many other relevant system issues that are critical to the successful implementation of field access such as security, redundancy, capacity, performance/response time, etc., but there may be no more important issue each of you are faced with than the economic one. The issue is clear. In order to get the most out of field access both short and long term you need to establish a plan to increase the functionality available to the craftsman in the field. Should you implement a system that doesn't have a clearly thought out expansion and growth plan you will be severely limiting the future and potential returns that field access promises that your field technician is capable of and will expect you to provide.

Let me now touch on the terminal features that have emerged as important. All the obvious terminal features that you would expect to be important are important.

The units need to be:

- ruggedized
- waterproof/water resistant
- portable
- able to withstand extremes of temperature
- etc.

In addition to and consistent with the requirement to provide expanded system functionality the terminals need to be able to support more than single trouble ticket dispatch. The terminals should:

- have the processing power to execute the functionality required.
- have sufficient memory or memory expansion capability to support current and future program and data requirements.
- provide the necessary technology to support bulk transfer of data and programming from the data

source to the handlelds and from the handlelds to the data source.

Once again the issue of expandability and flexibility to meet the future needs emerges as the predominant requirement. I think it was best articulated by a district manager in South Central Bell I talked to. He said, "We have to put as much thought and planning into our decision on the Field Access System and the terminal decision as we put into central office planning and outside plant provisioning."

So where does all of this leave the planners who have to make the recommendations? What are the choices? Where and when does the maximum payoff come?

Let us now consider the possibilities of a total Field Access System. I've mentioned that the industry is awakening to the fact that the economics of field access based upon simple trouble ticket dispatch are fragile. We're then left with the question, "What can we do, what functionality can be implemented to improve the payback." There are a host of OSS candidates to access that we can choose from.

- Installation service order dispatch
- facilities systems
- mechanized time reporting
- cable pressurization
- special services I&M
- access to remote test cabinets
- coin dispatch and testing
- electronic mail messaging

And how do the economics stack up? Let's consider for a moment access to a facilities system. Should you provide access to a system such as FACS, putting aside for a moment the issue of data security, the following picture emerges.

- assume a technician completes six trouble tickets a day
- assume a minimum of 1/3 of the tickets require a pair change (2 troubles)
- assume 30 minutes per pair change
- assume 250 work days per year
- assume 20 minutes per pair change in savings with direct access to FACS
- assume $30.00 per hour lab rate
- potential field savings
2 troubles X 1/3 hour per trouble X 250 days X $30.00 = $5,000.00

This simple model makes no assumptions about potential clerical labor savings or costs of providing access to FACS. If one assumed that the model is accurate to at worse case $\pm$ 30% based upon different assumptions of troubles cleared per day, quality of plant, hold time, etc. the payback still looks to be very attractive. Not every implementation of OSS access will have economics as attractive as these. However, it does begin to suggest and support the issue that limiting field access to simple trouble ticket dispatch and test

is very shortsighted.

Let us consider now the implementation of a total field access solution and think through the implications.

First the application software in the handheld needs to be fully integrated. Access to the various systems should be available to the user from the menu system whether the user is a POTS repairman, combined I&M or special services. The user should be able to view and edit data in the handheld, have access to multiple systems such as FACS, MTR, material ordering and distribution, etc. and the user should have the option of performing certain appropriate functions offline. This is an exceedingly important feature as the economics come into play.

Consider if you will for a moment the implications of having the option to perform functions offline as opposed to online connected to OSS.

If one is able to close out a trouble ticket, perform the data edits and field verifications offline the potential savings in line costs, investment in access technology to support a one minute transactions opposed to a six minute transaction begin to look enormously attractive.

We are indeed talking about the ultimate in distributed processing. Each individual using an individual personal computer performs a processing function then transmits an accurate verified data record to a host system with the complete confidence that it will be accepted. The network topography necessary to support such a technology is vastly different, less complex and less costly than a network to support each user on line performing transactions with each character being echoed and verified by the host system. If in fact you are committed to increasing the functionality available to the technician through field access then the additional network and access technology investment without an intelligent handheld device is beyond your worst budget crisis.

We've been talking about a total field access solution. There is often a fine line between what is practical and what are pipe dreams. What I have described as a total system is a reflection of the industry's emerging view of both their current and future needs. If you accept the view then the answers to the questions I raised earlier become clear.

- do I make the terminal a smart terminal in effect achieving the ultimate in distributed processing? The answer is clearly yes.
- do I buy into the current technology or wait for more sophisticated technology to become available at a lower price?
Technology always marches forward. If you endorse this theory then you never make a decision.
- do I adopt a wait and see attitude? You may be forgoing savings now.
- do I adopt a long term strategy based

upon where I want to be in the future and take the steps now to implement the plan.
The answer is clearly yes.

Returning for a moment to the issue of practicality. In addition to the realistic benefits of implementing a strategic OSS access plan let your mind wander and consider the possibilities of accessing from the field.

- expert system access
- compact disc read only memory for accessing BSP's etc.
- optical fiber testing and smart cross connect point programming
- integrated local testing capabilities

In conclusion I believe that we are experiencing the very thin edge of the wedge of the potential for enhancing the technicians work place through field access. The autonomy of the technician and hence commitment to the service concept has been a pleasant by-product of the technology. In order to build upon these early successes and maintain the field force commitment to field access it is imperative that you approach the implementation with a clear view of the future. Recognizing that clarity and the future are probably mutually exclusive the future access requirements nonetheless will require a good deal of planning and forethought. One needn't have to be an alchemist to turn field access into the pot of gold that we're all searching for. The tools and technology are available now. With spirit and vision you can all meet the goal.

Enhancing Field Productivity
A Field Access Strategy

Ronald C. Aldridge

Illinois Bell

225 W. Randolph Street
Chicago, Illinois   60606

TEXT

At Illinois Bell, we believe the evolution of computer systems includes the broad application of field access. Field Access is defined as the direct interfacing of a field technician or supervisor to Operation support Systems (OSS's) which can provide job dispatch, close, record keeping, tracking, testing and job information. Field Access plays an integral role in expediting work processes, improving the level of customer service, and enhancing field productivity.

In the maintenance arena, we have progressed from a completely manual system, heavily steeped in paper, to a system having a computerized customer record database and an assigned trouble ticket number to track customer trouble reports. With the introduction of the LMOS Mechanized Mapper Assigner (MMA) we have a paperless environment, where trouble cases are electronically routed, guided by multiple sets of rule tables and dispatched in pre-assigned geographic areas.

Field Access takes this "flow through" process one step further. Now the field technician plays a direct role in this trouble flow through the use of a hand held computer terminal. He/she participated directly, without the intervention of a third party to relay information.

This discussion focuses on the Illinois Bell view of Field Access, and how we plan to expand the capabilities of the field technician by providing access to multiple support systems.

Any successful effort to introduce new technology or new concepts must build upon existing knowledge and experience. The task of introducing Field Access requires that all technicians be at a similar threshold skill level with respect to the human interface with the various support systems. LMOS disposition codes, and Mechanized Timesheet Reporting (MTR) Work Operation Codes (WOC) were the initial targets in providing a basic level of training. A phased approach built upon this common system knowledge so that we could take advantage of the opportunities provided by Field Access.

Phase I Craft Access – Maintenance Deployment

AT&T's Craft Access system (CAS) was the pioneer vehicle in our field access strategy. The CAS system provides a proprietary dial up access network to the LMOS system, where field technicians have the capabilities of work receipt, test capability, and job closure. The primary benefits of CAS implementation were twofold:

- Force savings in the maintenance center are significant. AT&T's original estimate that a 45% reduction of the Maintenance Center forces was optimistic. Our experience demonstrated that a reduction of 45% of dispatch and field assistant personnel could be realized based upon the elimination of 80% of the calls to the center. The 80% is a reachable objective.

- There is elimination of hold time by technicians calling into the Maintenance Center. This savings differs from site to site and on an average, an increase of 1/2 trouble case per technician per day should be expected.

Additional benefits include:

- The reexamination of craft skills in the use of test data, testing techniques, and customer bill initiation identified deficiencies. A pre-testing and training course called "Building Professional Technical Proficiency" provided each technician with 8 hours of review on fault location, LMOS codes, MLT test interpretation, and customer billing codes and procedures. An additional 8 hours of training covered "how to use" the hand held terminal.

- Review opportunities for service and cost improvements that had been restricted by traditional work flows and a closed loop of computer access. These were now open for nontraditional applications such as "Home Dispatch". Home Dispatch offered the hope of increased real estate utilization and field efficiency improvements through reduction of first-job travel time. A one year trial pointed out some positives and some negatives. With all of this, came a more distributed style of management, which did not fit well in our overall management style and culture. At the end of the trial, a decision was made not to deploy Home Dispatch, with style and culture being a major consideration.

Phase II - The Smart Terminal

The successful deployment of field craft access provided insight as to what changes in strategy were necessary in order to access other systems.

One area was the AT&T Craft Access Terminal (CAT). Field technicians tended to be less specific than maintenance center personnel when inputting job narratives. Data entry with the CAT was very cumbersome. In the original form, the CAT offered a joystick to maneuver a cursor through alpha characters. The absence of an alpha keypad encouraged technicians to enter narratives that were very short and not descriptive. We felt that access to other systems would require more flexible data entry.

The introduction of the ITRON Teletech provided us with the second major component in the development of enhanced Field Access. This terminal offered a platform to access other systems as well as provide CAS functions.

There are benefits that can be derived from a smart terminal:

- VT100 terminal emulation and a standard ASCII/ANSI interface provide the initial step in access to other systems. The first application of this type will include access to the FACS system (Facility Assignment Control System - Bellcore) through the AFAP (Automated Field Assist Position - Ameritech) system. It is expected that the deployment of FACS through AFAP will provide substantial cost benefits, relative to the reduction in support staff, as did the deployment of LMOS through CAS. Future refinements will provide field access to an installation order and control system.

- Back lit screen and programmable function keys are user aids. The TeleTech screen can be read easily and program function keys expedite the input of "often repeated" data.

- A large screen for viewing data, provides for screen size of 16 lines x 21 columns compared to 4 lines x 20 columns for other devices. While this feature offers limited value in a pure CAS environment, it is very useful when scrolling through displays such as FACS facility record.

- The modular design of the TeleTech supports new features and software updates. Downloadable software from a PC, makes software changes on a per terminal basis manageable. Cords and clips are easily changed which makes for in-house maintenance of simple components.

- The capabilities of the terminal are not limited to interfacing to a host system. Terminal specific functions for future deployment include an integrated test meter to provide point meter or "offline" testing. These capabilities will include VOM functions, load coil detection and transmission/noise measurements.

- Another future capability is the ability to use the terminal as a data collector. Daily timesheet preparation can be made simple and less time consuming as data is stripped from input throughout the day to produce a time sheet. This data can then be uploaded to a Mechanized Time Reporting system (MTR) during off hours.

The decision to deploy the smart terminal introduced the need to reallocate our existing AT&T CAT terminals. We have turned this to our advantage by providing them to our forces who do not need a universal interface. Examples include:

- Coin maintenance personnel has reduced the staffing levels in the Coin Maintenance center.

- Construction splicers can now test and retrieve customer line records, eliminating calls to maintenance centers.

Phase III - Supervisor Access

A major objective in bringing Field Access to supervisors is to move activity from the "desk in the office" to a "mobile office in the field". The two components which provide this "office in the field" are the laptop terminal and cellular telephones. The "Random Colleague Plus" terminal was our choice. LMOS is accessed by dialing a protocol converter which is directly linked to the LMOS system, via the Ameritech Mobile Communications Mobile Access Data Service (MADS).

In a pure CAS environment, field supervisory capabilities were limited to the receipt of simple reports. The tracking of technician activities and trouble load status did not give the supervisor the full utilization of LMOS Generic 2 (G2). The recent change to LMOS G2, provides the field supervisor the ability to control a particular geographic "TURF". To bring this level of control to the field, it is necessary to equip the supervisor with the ability to control the load, set appointments, move technicians from one area to another, and make routine work available. In this environment, the control foreman in the Maintenance Center becomes an overall system administrator.

Other benefits of a laptop computer include:

- Laptop access is less expensive than

either the ITRON TeleTech or the AT&T CAT, while providing more functionality.

- The larger 80 X 24 screen of the laptop terminal is more adaptable to supervisory reports than the hand held terminal.

- The terminal portability is enhanced beyond Field Access. Supervisors assigned to weekend duty need not be at the office on a Sunday or holiday merely to check the status of the load, pull customer line records and answer a customer query.

- Laptop access provides access information in emergency situations and recently played an integral part in helping to operate the Maintenance Center during the fire in our Hinsdale Central Office. The dedicated LMOS data links routed through the Hinsdale hub were temporarily inoperable, and instant access was available through the laptop.

Cellular access in a Field Access environment provides field supervisors and managers with a viable means for instant, uncongested analog communications as well as data transmission capability in the CAS environment. The MADS service and a "Bridge" modem is used to provide an error correcting data transmission which can be used with a laptop terminal. The important feature of MADS is that it provides data integrity which is essential to interact with LMOS. Using the laptop terminal and cellular access, supervisors no longer are tied to a pay phone to call the Maintenance Center to check status.

Presently, we do not plan to equip craft vehicles with cellular telephones. That may well change in the future as cellular costs continue to fall. Consideration should be given to equip vehicles used primarily by technicians who do not have convenient access to land lines, such as cable locators. Also, as the use of fiber optics expands and the availability of tip and ring decreases, it will become more advantageous to deploy cellular equipment.

Phase IV - Computer Gateway

The latest technology in Field Access is a "computer gateway" by which access to any support system can be achieved through a one gate system.

Illinois Bell will be the first to sample the Craft Access Gateway system which communicates through the existing Craft Access processors and LMOS Datakit. This system provides the translation from the host to the CAS application processor which formats the information in user defined scripts.

A unique feature of the product is the user programming of the system. The users own expertise is used to program the scripts, program the system (Unix/C programming), communicate to other hosts (bisync communications) and in-host application knowledge to allow user definition of the system. The Gateway system can be an important ingredient for the development and enhancement of Field Access.

One possible Gateway/CAS main menu is:

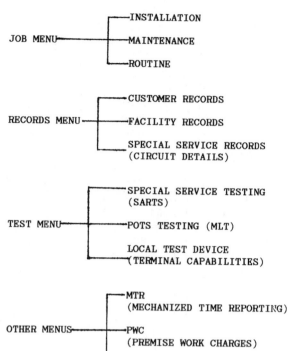

Conclusion

With a gateway system in place, a uni-tech (universally qualified technician) can move from the installation of a POTS line, to the maintenance of a special service circuit, to a cable routine job. The technician has access to information and testing devices to complete any job through the hand held terminal. Data collected throughout the day will provide precise coding for time sheet preparation as well as accurate and timely customer billing.

Field supervisors will have many of the same capabilities, and with the laptop terminals, will be able to interface as technicians. The ability to manage a multi-functional work-force from the field will facilitate better customer service and increased productivity. This strategy to equip all outside forces, both management and craft, with the latest in computer technology, will position us to meet and lead customers into the 1990's.

The Gateway System

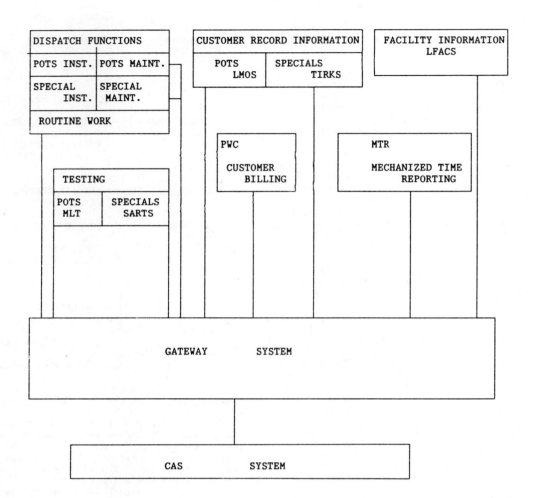

MANUAL ENVIRONMENT

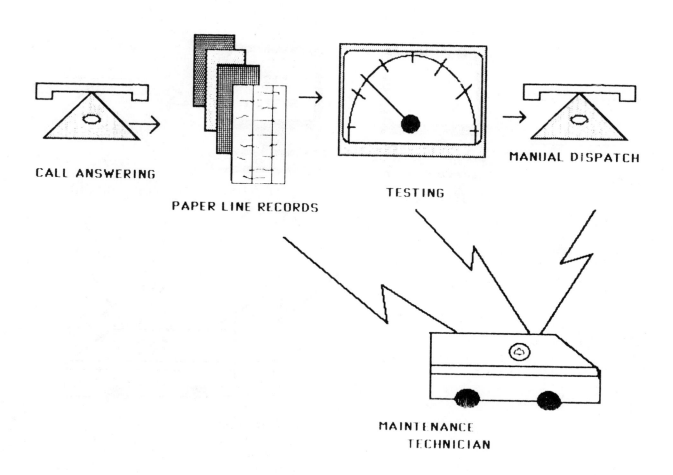

CALL ANSWERING

PAPER LINE RECORDS

TESTING

MANUAL DISPATCH

MAINTENANCE
TECHNICIAN

LMOS ENVIRONMENT

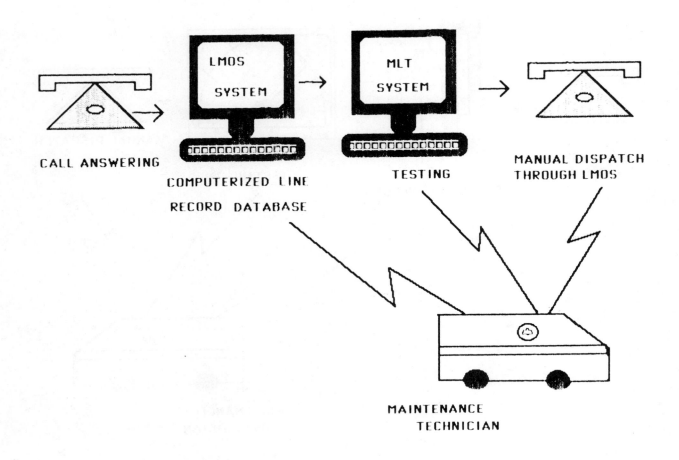

CALL ANSWERING

COMPUTERIZED LINE
RECORD DATABASE

TESTING

MANUAL DISPATCH
THROUGH LMOS

MAINTENANCE
TECHNICIAN

CAS ENVIRONMENT

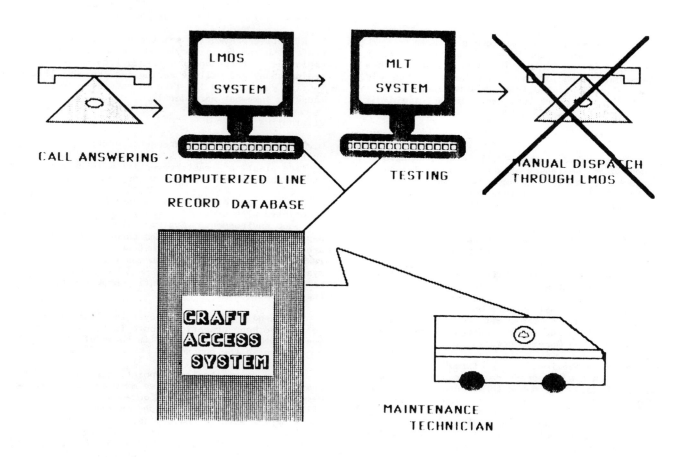

CALL ANSWERING

LMOS SYSTEM

COMPUTERIZED LINE RECORD DATABASE

MLT SYSTEM

TESTING

MANUAL DISPATCH THROUGH LMOS

CRAFT ACCESS SYSTEM

MAINTENANCE TECHNICIAN

New Technologies and Some Old Ideas

Fran H. Henig

AT&T Bell Laboratories

184 Liberty Corner Road
Warren, New Jersey   07060

ABSTRACT

Craft access networks, expert systems, and preventive maintenance systems are three relatively new technologies now being widely deployed in the field. This paper describes how these new technologies -- combined with some old and well-established ideas from Managerial Psychology -- can significantly impact field productivity.

INTRODUCTION

The last two speakers of this session have focused on the impact of what is probably the most dramatic technology to impact the outside craft since the invention of the cherry picker -- the introduction of the craft access terminal.

What I would like to do today is step back and take a somewhat broader approach, taking a look at the whole area of outside craft productivity.

My objective today is to leave you with a couple of thoughts.

First, that while we are beginning to see real changes in the way the craft are doing their jobs, we are just seeing the tip of the iceberg here -- there is a lot more to come.

We are, I believe, at the threshold of major changes in how the craft do their jobs and what that job is. That makes these both very exciting times, and somewhat uncertain times. Those of us who have been around this business for awhile know that progress doesn't come without some false starts, and in fact, some real mistakes. We have those to look forward to along with the excitement of change.

The second message I would like to leave you with is that this is a multi-dimensional problem. The opportunities to change the job of the outside craft are not **just** limited to introducing craft access systems, although that is certainly a big step, but go beyond that.

In fact, I would propose that there are at least three complementary approaches we can take to improve craft productivity.

1. The first of these is one we tend to think of last, and that is preventive maintenance -- **eliminating** work by putting in place and effectively managing preventive maintenance programs.

2. The second is providing the craft with the tools they need to do their jobs effectively. Again, I see the current craft access capabilities as a first step here, but just the beginning.

3. And last, but not least, companies are beginning to think about how they can restructure the craft job, using some established managerial and organizational techniques, to make better and more effective use of the very talented folks we already have out there. The words that get used are "empowering our employees" or "professionalizing the craft" or "participative leadership" -- but I think they are all part of the same trend.

Effective preventive maintenance, providing the craft with the tools they need, empowering our employees -- these are the trends I think we are seeing today and will be seeing for the next three to five years. And I'd like to address each of these in somewhat more detail.

Eliminating Work

The easiest way to increase productivity is just to eliminate the work entirely. For the outside plant, at least preventive maintenance is undoubtedly the most effective way of doing this.

For the last eight years, I have been associated with preventive maintenance systems for the loop environment. Systems like ACE -- an expert system which identifies chronic problem areas in the outside plant that are candidates for rehab -- and Predictor, which monitors switching system line insulation tests -- LITS -- and per call failure messages to identify problems before the customer does.

The changes in this area over the last five years have been dramatic -- both in terms of the tools that are available and in terms of their acceptance in the companies.

From an operational standpoint, most of the companies doing any preventive maintenance at all were using FAP programs, and occasionally a LIT or TRIM program. LIT sounded good in theory, but at the time was both incredibly labor intensive and unreliable. It was difficult, if not impossible, to get craft to go out on a LIT job. TRIM was more effective, but again, the analysis was very labor intensive, and, as a result, rarely done.

The times they are a-changing! Today, both Predictor and ACE systems are deployed coast to coast.

But the real changes are operational. I knew we were turning a corner when the Predictor Administrator in PacBell told me -- this was mid-1984 -- that his craft were beginning to ask for Predictor jobs, because they knew they would find something when they went out there. The found and fixed rate on Predictor dispatches was exceeding 90%.

What is the impact of all this? Let me give you a couple of examples. This first example is from one of our early ACE beta test sites. ACE had indicated that there were seven service affecting troubles in this cable complement at 3766 Harlem Avenue. What the analyzers in centers like this like about ACE is not that is is an expert system, but that when they send someone out to find the problem -- and this is one from real life -- they can go to 3766 Harlem Avenue and find a cross-box that looks fine on the outside, but like this on the inside. Now you don't have to be an outside plant expert to know that anyone who touches anything in this box is going to create more customer problems than they are fixing -- and that was exactly what was happening here.

This particular problem turned out to be an engineering job. My second example is closer to the kind of problem we see on a day-to-day basis. This is from a recent ACE installation. ACE said that four service affecting troubles had been associated with this 49A aerial terminal in the last week. This is one that could be fixed pretty quickly -- and, again, fixing it was clearly going to save future customer reports.

The bottom line here is that our objective is to get ahead of the customer. No company I'm aware of has any problem identifying bad plant that needs rehab. The problem is prioritizing the work. Tools like the preventive maintenance systems we are seeing deployed are having a real impact here.

That rat's nest of a cross-box I showed you was from one of the worst wire centers in its company. The company had purposely picked that area to test ACE. They put in ACE, a new analyzer, and a dedicated, two person, repair crew, and reduced their code 4 trouble report rate by 60% in eighteen months.

That's the good news. The bad news is that in every company I know, it is still an uphill battle to get these systems effectively used in the field. The issue is one Maintenance Center managers have to deal with on a day-to-day basis: how much of my force do I put on rehab work? Why should I dispatch Predictor-generated employee-originated reports when I have live customer troubles? These are real issues that need to be addressed.

For the future, we see two ways of addressing them. The first is by beginning to provide the MC managers with the data they need to help them make these decisions.

Let me give you a couple of examples.

One report I could provide is the cost of not doing preventive maintenance. For example, we could provide data on the Predictor and ACE jobs you elected not to dispatch . How many associated customer reports did you receive on these jobs over the next month? What did they cost you?

Another interesting piece of data is a number we have just begun to look at: how much of our live load is associated with chronic problems? It seems to me that if we can give you that information, then the managers in the Maintenance Centers can make better **business** decisions on how much preventive maintenance they should be doing.

A second major area we see for the future is trying to integrate the analysis information we have with live trouble processing. And I'll talk about that in just a minute.

Craft Tools

The next major thrust we see in improving craft productivity is giving the craft the tools they need to do their job as effectively as they can. You have heard a lot today so far about craft access systems in this context, and it is clear that there is still a lot to be done here. I think we would all like to see craft being able to access trouble history information, time reporting systems, and perhaps assignment systems so that they can do pair swaps without hanging on the phone to an assignment center. These will all happen with time.

But there is another area I would like to address, and that links the craft with some of the preventive maintenance information we have available. Today, if you think about it, we may know a whole lot more about a trouble than we use in processing it. We may know, or example, that this is the third time this customer has reported this trouble, in which case, if I were the craft, I would like to know what work was done previously. We may know there is a construction job associated with this trouble. Or that ACE has identified a bad terminal box along this run, and that is probably where I should go to clear the trouble.

This kind of information should be accessible to both the craft working the problem and the MA screening it, and we are looking at ways of doing this.

The more useful information we can give the craft to help them troubleshoot problems, the more effective and productive their work will be.

"Empowering the Craft"

And lastly, I would like to talk about some significant organizational changes. This is an area I don't feel particularly qualified to talk about -- I am a developer, not an organizational psychologist -- but there is a lot going on in the companies right now, and I think it is important for people to be aware of what is happening.

Let me give you some background.

About 20 years ago, an industrial psychologist named Frederick Herzberg did a number of studies on job satisfaction. He did something like 12 different investigations -- looking at some 1800 events that led to extreme job dissatisfaction and about the same number of events that led to job satisfaction.

What he discovered were two important things:

- First, that about 80% of the satisfiers fell into categories that he called motivators; things like achievement, recognition, the work itself, responsibility, advancement, growth.

- Secondly, about 70% of the dissatifiers were associated with things he called hygiene factors: working environments, company policies, relationships with supervisors, peers, salary, etc.

His conclusions were:

- That the opposite of dissatisfaction was not satisfaction. If I improved an employee's undesirable working environment, for example, that will make them less unhappy, but it won't make them happy -- at least on a permanent basis. At best it gets you to zero.

- And, secondly, Herzberg believed that to motivate people what was needed was something he called job enrichment, focusing on the motivators. He called this "vertical job loading" -- I think of it as adding responsibility, a sense of achievement, growth, recognition, etc.

What is happening today is that there are a number of companies throughout the country testing these ideas in one form or another. The changes range from introducing concepts like turfing and home dispatch, to more sweeping organizational changes.

At the Eastern Communications Forum last May, Chuck Johnston, A VP for the southern California area of Pacific Bell, talked about a program he has introduced where some 800 employees are participating in something they call "Participative Leadership." Some examples? He has a maintenance garage where 35 repair technicians were planning and controlling both their daily work load and fixing long standing problems. Their responsibilities included determining work schedules, overtime and vacation schedules.

In another example, the outside plant portion of a central office cutover was entirely planned, coordinated, and very successfully executed by a splicer.

Johnston noted that there had been, and continue to be, problems along the way, but, in general, he was enthusiastic about the approach.

For someone who has been around the telephone business for a long time, and in management for a long time, as I have, it will be interesting to see how far this trend goes and where it succeeds. And, as I said before, we will see some failures and mistakes along the way. At the moment, turfing seems to be working well, home dispatch gets, at best mixed reviews. But my own bet is that some of these ideas will stick, and will significantly impact the way we do business.

Summary

I would like to end by stressing that this is an important area -- that there are some real opportunities here. The average cost per access line across the country today ranges from something like $30 to over $50. Those are Outside Plant Repair costs. Of those, over 60% are directly associated with outside craft salaries. And that doesn't include things like the costs of trucks, equipment, etc., that are indirectly related to outside craft costs.

The question is, is it reasonable to assume that we can cut these costs? The answer appears to be a resounding "yes". At Bell Labs, we have done a number of studies that show that less than half of all dispatched troubles actually get found and fixed. The remainder result in repeat reports, found OK-outs or came clears, or problems cleared by pair swaps.

In summary, the opportunities abound for increasing the effectiveness of our outside craft. In this paper, we have proposed a three-pronged approach toward achieving this goal:

- First, increasing productivity by eliminating work, by putting increased emphasis on effective preventive maintenance.

- Secondly, making the craft more productive by providing them the tools they need to do their job. Again, craft access systems are an important first step here.

- And lastly, restructuring craft jobs so that we make the most of the very talented and generally very dedicated pool of people we have out there.

Mobile Radio's Impact On

Outside Plant Productivity

Heidi Bomengen

Arthur D. Little, Inc.

35 Acorn Park
Cambridge, MA   02140

ABSTRACT

Twelve operating telephone companies participated in a study aimed at determining the impact of using two-way mobile radio service in their field operation. A comparison of statistics regarding number of service calls completed per day, size of geographic territory served, average response time, and overtime as a percentage of total payroll showed that two-way mobile radio service can have a positive quantifiable impact on the productivity of maintenance, installation and construction employees and ultimately on an operating company's bottom line.

INTRODUCTION

This paper summarizes the results of telephone and personal interviews with Installation and Maintenance and Construction field staff operations of twelve operating telephone companies on the productivity of their respective organizations. The object of the study was to determine the impact of two-way mobile radio systems on the productivity of telephone company field operations. The participants of the study represented a wide geographic area and covered metropolitan, suburban, and rural areas.

The results show that two-way mobile radio service can have a positive impact on a company's bottom line in terms of enabling the completion of more service calls per day than groups without the use of radios, enabling the completion of more construction jobs per year by reducing the manpower requirements per job, and enabling the completion of installation in a shorter interval increasing the revenue generated by the implementation of new service sooner.

Methodology

The following data was collected and compared:

- Number of employees in the group
- Number of vehicles in the group
- Number of radios
- Number of access lines served
- Geographic territory -- miles covered, population density, and terrain
- Number of service calls per day per employee
- Response time = time of complaint to time of repair completion
- Distribution of time: work, travel, and dead time
- Overtime as a percentage of total payroll

In order to ensure that like scenarios were being compared, the territories of the I&M respondents were categorized into three classifications: metropolitan, suburban, and rural. The classifications were determined by the number of square miles each technician in the group was responsible for servicing. Each company classification was based upon the following criteria:

Metropolitan = each technician is responsible for less than 2 square miles.

Suburban = each technician is responsible for 2-10 square miles

Rural = each technician is responsible for more that 10 square miles

Based upon the criteria established, three respondents were classified as metropolitan, three were suburban, and five were considered rural.

In addition to collecting data, respondents were asked general questions with respect to their perception of the value of radio systems. In one case, a Construction foreman felt that the radio system was so essential to the safety of his crew that he was willing to give up two trucks (one of them was a Telsta) to offset the cost of the radio system.

Findings

To summarize the findings of the study, refer to Tables I and II. A total of fifteen interviews were conducted, some within different offices or departments of the same operating company. The interviews represented all sections of the country and all types of serving territory -- metropolitan, suburban, rural, mountains, desert, etc. Accordingly, the serving territories ranged in size from 25 to 7800 square miles and served from 20,000 to 3,000,000 access lines.

Tables III, IV and V summarize the data collected by territorial classification.

As can be seen in Table III, none of the "Metropolitan" companies used two-way mobile radio service in their Installation and Maintenance operations. They averaged 6 service calls per day per technician and 4 hour complaint to repair time for business customers. Each technician was responsible for between 1500 and 4400 access lines. Overtime ran between 5% and 13% of total payroll (no conclusion could be drawn on this subject).

Table IV illustrates that none of the company groups classified as serving "suburban" areas presently utilize two-way mobile radios. They averaged 5 service calls per day per technician and cover as much as seven times the mileage of the technicians in the "metropolitan" areas described above. If travel is assumed to be 5-10 minutes per call or 1/2 to 1 hour per day for metropolitan technicians and 15-20 minutes per call or 1-1/4 to 1-3/4 hours per day for suburban technicians, it can be illustrated given similarly equipped technicians (neither have two-way radios) that the additional hour per day spent on travel is lost productive time and its impact is an average of one less service call per day. Metropolitan technicians averaged 6 calls per day versus 5 calls per day per suburban technicians.

Five of the respondents were considered to be operating in rural environments based on the criteria described earlier. This group is shown in Table V. Technicians operating in rural areas were generally equipped with two-way mobile radio units. For the groups described as having "limited" radio use, technicians located in rural areas were generally equipped with radios and those in more densely populated sections of the territory were not provided with radios. The reason for assigning a limited number of radios was generally due to limited funding and in the cases in which funding was not a problem, all technicians were provided with radio units.

The only group that was not equipped with radios in the rural category experienced fewer service calls per day and higher response time than the other groups studied. Although technicians in these rural areas described were responsible for servicing 12 to 100 times more mileage than technicians assigned to metropolitan areas, the ones with radios were able to make an average of 5 service calls per day, the same number as the technicians in suburban areas covering less than half the territory. Average response time was approximately 4 hours, similar to that of the metropolitan area. In essence, there was no degradation in service as one might have expected would result from such a significant increase in the size of one's territorial responsibilities. There could be several reasons for these productivity statistics. Some possibilities are described below:

Technicians could be dispatched more efficiently in rural areas, grouping troubles in a particular area and assigning them to one technician minimizing travel time as much as possible.

- Troubles could be less complex than those in other areas and require less work time in proportion to travel time. There is a far greater concentration of business services in metropolitan areas than rural areas and business generally requires more complex service than residential service. Troubles and repairs would generally be more complex and require more actual service time in metropolitan areas.

- The ability to communicate directly with technicians in their vehicle or to a handheld unit could reduce the amount of unproductive time spent attempting to access a means of communication.

The last observation described above was supported by the difference in productivity within the rural category between radio users and the non-users. Table VI illustrates the amount of time spent in minutes per technician per day on travel, dead, and actual work time. "Dead" in this table represents two fifteen minute breaks and a one hour lunch break.

The table illustrates that a technician in a rural area equipped with radios spends an average of 10 minutes less time per job than a technician in a metropolitan area and an average of 12 minutes less time per job than a technician in a suburban area. This time could represent the additional time required to set up a call without the benefit of a two-way mobile radio system. Mobile service also eliminates the need to access company test centers via the customer's telephone line about which more and more technicians are feeling increasingly uncomfortable.

If Telephone Operating Companies could identify the cost of responding to a repair call after the commitment period which is generally 4 hours for business customers, a cost/benefit analysis may be performed to determine the reduction in cost to the operating company of performing one more repair per day shortening the average response time by an average of almost 15%.

Another application for two-way mobile radio systems is a means for accessing the new Craft Access Systems. Most of the companies studied are planning the implementation of an automated dispatch and test system if they have not already put one in place. Two-way mobile radio provides a means for accessing the system without the need for using customer facilities or travelling to an alternative communications facility. The combination of the two technologies could save the telephone companies even more time than if they were implemented independently. One RBOC will be trialing the implementation of their packet network over a Motorola KDT 800 Unit in a remote area.

In addition to the maintenance operations described above, we spoke to two representatives of operating telephone company Construction organizations. Both groups used two-way radio systems and expressed the fact they could not operate without them.

The only difference between the two Construction groups was the utilization of handheld radio units and externally mounted speaker systems. One company recently implemented a new radio system which may be used with handheld units and speakers. The other company's system was old and was not compatible with handheld units and speakers. The first company pulled 5 times more cable feet per person per year than the second.

In most cases, the area of greatest concern and emphasis among operating company personnel was customer service oriented -- response time to trouble reports, quality of service, etc. Productivity per se was not considered to be a major problem and in many cases, productivity statistics were no longer tracked in the sense that they were prior to divestiture. Telephone company management was concerned with improving revenues and customer service without increasing costs. The bottom line was the figure monitored!

General comments on the part of users of radios were very positive and supported the importance and benefit of the use of radios, however the comments were of such a nature as to be difficult to quantify.

CONCLUSIONS

There are many variables in the formula for determining productivity in a field service operation. Some of these variables include size of territory served, population density, and extent of development (illustrating the accessibility of alternative means of communication). By combining the statistics gathered with many general comments made during the interview program, the following conclusions can be drawn regarding the use of mobile radio for Bell Operating Companies:

- Technicians located in rural areas equipped with radios cover as much as 12 to 100 times more square mileage than technicians in suburban and metropolitan areas and complete approximately the same number of service calls per day. This conclusion is supported by the data illustrated in the graph shown in Figure 1.

- Technicians equipped with radios spend an average of 15 to 20% less time per job than technicians who are not equipped with radios. This conclusion is supported by data which is illustrated in Table VI.

- Figure 2 illustrates that the time saved on communication setup by utilizing radio access can be allocated to additional work time and consequently result in the completion of approximately the same number of service calls per day.

- There is need for two-way mobile radio systems in Construction for safety reasons in addition to possible productivity enhancements.

- Construction groups equipped with radios require less manpower for the majority of jobs than if they were not equipped with radios.

- Telephone company managers are reluctant to install two-way mobile radio systems in operations where they do not perceive a critical requirement for immediate two-way voice communication.

- Pagers are presently perceived as an alternative to mobile radio in most metropolitan and suburban areas, although many interviews pointed out their inadequacies when it is necessary to make return calls to dispatch points.

- Operations that consider pagers to be an alternative to two-way radio systems do not perceive the value of immediate two-way communications and do not track communications setup time as a percentage of the technician's day.

- There has been some indication that groups with similar responsibilities and philosophy of management experience less overtime as a percentage of total payroll when using two-way radio.

- There is a quantifiable benefit to installing service earlier and generating revenue that much sooner, however, none of the people interviewed yet utilize two-way radio service for Installation operations.

- If technicians in metropolitan and suburban areas spend the same amount of time per job as technicians in rural areas, they would have approximately one additional hour per day available for work equating to the time necessary for one more job per day.

- If technicians are able to complete one more job per day and the total number of jobs available to be worked remains constant, average response time to repair will decrease.

SUMMARY

Construction and Cable Maintenance Departments that do not presently use two-way mobile radio service appear to be the most likely candidates for its future use. The single most important quantifiable benefit to be gained by the use of two-way radio service in Construction operations is the reduction of manpower required per job. If a radio system presently exists but does not have the capability for handsfree operation, further benefits may be gained through add-ons or upgrades to the existing system.

Cable Maintenance operations are the next most likely candidate for the installation of two-way radio systems as the resolution of cable troubles is generally viewed as "time critical". Response time was consistently reported as a key concern of all field service operations. If the time spent per job without the use of two-way radio is applied to servicing more calls, the end result would be improved overall response time.

Operations which do not presently use two-way radio generally think of its applications in terms of tracking and dispatch. When studying the operations that do presently use radio systems, it was found that although some groups do use the system for tracking and dispatch, the greatest value is gained by the ability to conduct two-way conversations during the course of normal workday functions and that the system is used to resolve problem situations which would have taken longer to resolve without the accessibility to this means of communication.

TABLE I

RADIO COMMUNICATION TECHNOLOGY EMPLOYED IN REGIONAL BELL OPERATING COMPANIES

COMPANY	DEPT.	RADIO	PAGERS	C.A.T.	NONE
A	I&M	no	yes	no	no
B	Const.	yes	no	NA	no
C	I&M	no	limited	planned	limited
D	I&M	no	yes	planned	no
E	I&M	limited	yes	planned	no
F	I&M	yes	no	yes	no
G	I&M	no	yes	no	no
H	I&M	no	yes	no	no
I	I&M	no	yes	no	no
J	Const.	yes	no	NA	no
K	I&M	yes	no	yes	no
L	I&M	no	yes	no	no
M	I&M	limited	yes	no	no
N	Const.	yes	no	NA	no
O	I&M	no	yes	yes	no

TABLE II

INSTALLATION AND MAINTENANCE PERFORMANCE A REGIONAL BELL OPERATING COMPANIES INTERVI

COMPANY	RADIO	SQ. MILES PER EMPL.	AVG. SVC. CALLS /DAY/EMPL
A	no	0.1	7
B	no	0.7	5
C	no	7.4	5
D	limited	75.7	5
E	yes	12.5	4
F	no	1.7	6
G	no	2.2	5
H	no	2.5	6
I	yes	17.4	5
J	no	19.7	3
K	limited	138.6	6

TABLE III. PRODUCTIVITY OF METROPOLITAN RESPONDENTS

COMPANY	RADIO	AVG SVC CALLS/DAY	AVG RESP. TIME	OVERTIME	COVERAGE PER EMPLOYEE
A	No	7	4hrs.	8%	0.1 sq.mi.
C	No	5	4hrs.	13%	0.7 sq.mi.
G	No	6	4hrs.	5%	1.7 sq.mi.

TABLE IV. PRODUCTIVITY OF SUBURBAN RESPONDENTS

COMPANY	RADIO	AVG SVC CALLS/DAY	AVG RESP. TIME	OVERTIME	COVERAGE PER EMPLOYEE
D	No	5	16hrs.	14.9%	7 sq.mi.
H	No	5	4hrs.	2.5%	2 sq.mi.
I	No	6	30mins.	-NA-	3 sq.mi.

TABLE V. PRODUCTIVITY OF RURAL RESPONDENTS

COMPANY	RADIO	AVG SVC CALLS/DAY	AVG RESP. TIME	OVERTIME	COVERAGE PER EMPLOYEE
E	Ltd.	5	2hrs.	17%	76 sq.mi.
F	Yes	4	3hrs.	8%	13 sq.mi.
K	Yes	5	7hrs.	-NA-	17 sq.mi.
M	Ltd.	6	4hrs.	10%	139 sq.mi.
L	No	3	14hrs.	-NA-	20 sq.mi.

TABLE VI. PRODUCTIVITY COMPARISONS

Average
(Minutes/day/technician)

	METRO	SUBURBAN	RURAL
TRAVEL	45	90	150
DEAD	90	90	90
WORK (based on 8 hr/day)	345	300	240
JOBS PER DAY	6	5	5
TIME PER JOB	58	60	48

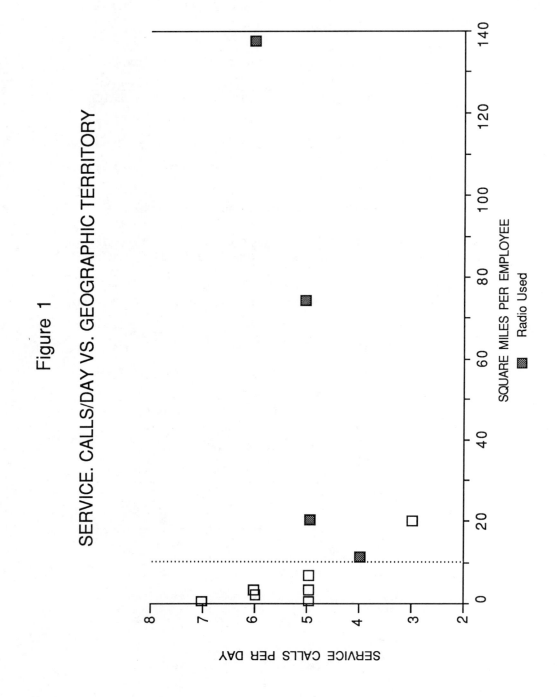

Figure 1

SERVICE. CALLS/DAY VS. GEOGRAPHIC TERRITORY

FIGURE 2

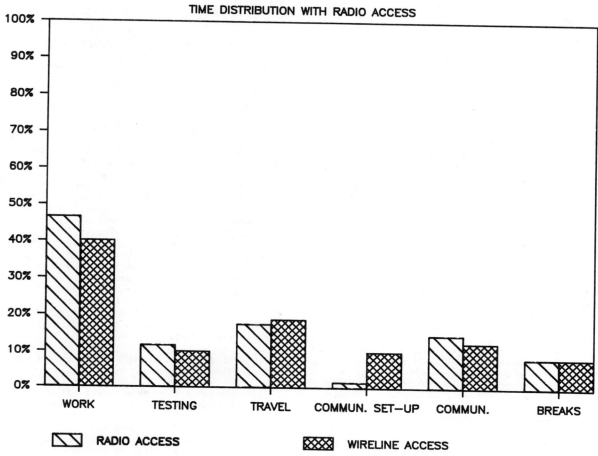

TIME DISTRIBUTION WITH RADIO ACCESS

Outside Operations The Year 2000

Mark A. Gicale

Ameritech Services

1900 East Golf Road
Schaumburg, Illinois   60173

INTRODUCTION

Today I'd like to share with you my views of
how the work performed by our communications
installation and repair forces will change by the
year 2000. To accomplish this we will concentrate
on the changes in operation systems, technology
and organizational structure.

OPERATION SYSTEMS

Advances in data communications and technology
will make possible the melding of a group of tasks
into a more efficient, coordinated process
(integration). The advance in computer technology
will make possible the modeling and development of
optimal solutions for particular goals. The
long-standing goals of the Ameritech Services and
the Ameritech Operating Companies (AOC's) are to
insure for uninterrupted service to our customers.
To accomplish this we are moving towards
end-to-end digital, dynamic control, and
integration of voice and data. With the
competitive market being as it is today and
continuing in the future, we must move to lower
costs and at the same time provide our users with
state of the art products to improve the quality,
reliability, and flexibility of service. This
will have a definite impact on how our field
forces respond to an installation and/or
maintenance work task. By the year 2000 the
outside operation will change extensively. With
the aid of the existing "Expert Systems",
integration of OS's, and a flow through
provisioning and maintenance strategy, the outside
technician will gain the expertise to resolve
problems in the field faster and more efficiently.

To an outside technician, accurate information
is of the utmost importance. In today's
environment that much needed information is not
always available. Record updates will be made on a
real time basis giving the technician the most
current and accurate information possible. This
readily available information will assist the
technician in the complexity of trouble shooting.

The outside technician will also have direct
access to the OS's. In the repair and
installation world today, the technician must rely
on information forwarded by the maintenance center
personnel. Many times the information is
incomplete or additional information is needed.
The technician will have the capability of
retrieving the additional information by
interfacing with the other OS's eliminating the
need to interact with other department personnel.
In that same vein, the technician will have the
capability of interfacing with the assignment
center via force access. They will have complete
access to all records and will be capable of
changing facility designations without conferring
with inside personnel. Today, the technician must

physically call in to the local assignment center
and request a pair change. This procedure is
somewhat cumbersome to the technician as the
chances of getting put on hold is often a common
occurrence.

To better describe what transpires in the day
of a technician in th year 2000, let me take you
on a field visit on a typical day with a
technician of the future.

Imagine this if you will:

Our technician starts the day by accessing the
dispatch system via Force Access in the comfort of
home. With a dial-up terminal, the technician
enters the assigned access identification code to
display the day's load that had been built by the
system while he/she slept. As trouble reports,
installation work orders, construction work orders
and routine jobs were being prioritized, analyzed
and categorized, the system was also tapping
resource information pertaining to force
availability for that particular day. This
algorithm also includes items such as the
technician's level of expertise, the area or
"turf" the technician is assigned to work in and
other pertinent information for the most efficient
and dynamic dispatch. The technician at this
point studies the first dispatch of the day. For
the example, we will use a typical trouble report
for our first dispatch.

The information received on the report will
include items such as:

1.   Customer telephone or circuit number
2.   Customer name, address, location of
     service
3.   Central Office equipment
4.   Loop assignment information (cable pair,
     terminal address, cross-box)
5.   Test results on initial entry
6.   Actual trouble report by the customer
7.   Type of service (Residence - Business)
8.   Class of service (1FR - 1MB - etc.)
9.   Remarks

At this point a decision must be made if
additional information is needed (the technician
would access the respective data base and
retrieve) or if sufficient information was given.
Upon that decision, the trouble analysis begins by
the technician.

This particular trouble report happens to be a
no dial tone (NDT) condition reported by the
customer. The customer reported he was out of
service. The technician reads the preliminary
test that clearly shows a ring ground (tests had
been run to assure the trouble was not in the
central office). At this point the technician
must make the decision where to start shooting the
trouble. The technician would then proceed to the
cross-box to isolate the trouble. The technician
discovers the trouble is in the distribution
cable. At this point the technician can and will
change the cable pair via the force access
terminal. The customer's records will
automatically be updated by this transaction. By
thoroughly testing the new pair and continuing
testing the customer's line to assure a working

1077

line, the technician contacts the customer to verify their line is again up and working. At this point the technician closes out the trouble report through force access. The technician will automatically receive a new work order and this routine will continue throughout the technician's work tour.

TECHNOLOGY

Another one of the major factors that will impact the outside operations installation and maintenance forces in the year 2000 will be the evolution that is currently taking place in the physical network. We will discuss three elements of the network that will have a significant impact in th local loop and how this changing network will affect the work force.

ELECTRONICS

With the emphasis of going from an analog to a digital network, the type of work that is performed by the outside operations installation and maintenance forces is becoming more like that of the current central office work forces. Network elements such as remote switches and integrated digital loop carrier are introducing new types of equipment and electronics into the local loop. The installation and maintenance functions that utilize this new sophisticated equipment. An example of this is the deployment of multiplexers into the local loop. With multiplexers now being deployed into the local loop, the installation and maintenance forces now have to be proficient in installing and maintaining services that utilize high speed data transmission up to the current DS3 level. Previously this type of high speed transmission of data was only found in the interoffice facility environment. In conjunction with the maintenance of these new types of services, the maintenance personnel must have the knowledge to test this new type of equipment utilizing testing equipment and concepts which were never used in the local loop before.

PROTOCOL

In conjunction with the high tech equipment and new services, such as ISDN, now being offered in the local loop, the ability to perform protocol analysis becomes important. In order to perform the provisioning and maintenance functions associated with ISDN, the outside operations forces must be able to perform protocol analysis. With ISDN there is currently a need to be able to analyze the X.25 protocol conversion that takes place at the customers premise. Aside from the X.25 protocol, there are additional protocols associated with ISDN. The installation and maintenance technicians must be able to perform the analysis of all these existing, and any future, types of standard types or protocols. In addition to being able to analyze this protocol, new types of testing equipment will be required by the installation and maintenance technicians in order to provide them with the required information to make decisions about the accuracy of the data being transmitted.

FIBER

With advent of the new high tech services being offered we have begun to place fiber cable into the local loop. The placement of fiber in the local loop will be not only for business customers but also for the residential customers. When fiber is placed into the local loop we will then begin to offer broadband services. With broadband services we will begin to offer not only the types of services that we offer today but will be able to offer such services as interactive television, high definition television, and high speed data transfers. These types of service offerings will change the entire concept of how the local loop is constructed and utilized. The installation and maintenance forces must now be knowledgeable in splicing techniques for fiber. In addition, with the deployment of fiber into the local loop there will be a whole new type of electronics that will be required in the customers premise.

ORGANIZATION

The last area that will be discussed is the organizational changes that will take place in the future. Today we have separate installation and maintenance forces which are organized along the lines of POTS, Special Services, and Switched Services. With the changes that are taking place from an analog to a digital network and the new switched technologies that are evolving, such as ISDN, we have begun to see minimal differences between POTS, Special Services, and Switched Services. This blurring of services will result in the despecialization of Special and Switched services. What we anticipate is that since future service offerings will become more POTS like in nature, we will require only one work force to handle the installation and maintenance functions for all services.

In today's environment, our sample company has three separate installation and maintenance forces which are supported by three different control centers. In the year 2000 we envision that we will have only one installation and maintenance force that is supported by one consolidated control center. The advantages in this type of organization is that aside from having only one work force we will have the added benefit of having a single point of contact in the control center for the technicians. This control center will provide for the coordination of all installation and maintenance activities along with assisting the installation and maintenance force in the resolution of any problems. With this type of arrangement we will have gone from today's specialized technician to that of a generic technician who will be able to handle any type of service request and will have to deal with just one control center.

CONCLUSION

With the rapid technological advances that are currently taking place, it is anticipated that the evolution of the network, along with the associated changes to operating systems and organizational structures, the communications installation and maintenance forces method of performing their functions will continue to change at an exponential rate. What this means is that we will have one communications installation and maintenance force that will perform all functions that are required to fulfill all telecommunications service requests. This will be accomplished regardless of the type service request or the type of technology that is deployed in the local loop.

In today's environment when a customer places an order for service we must decide what work force(s) will be involved with the installation. In addition, we have a wide range of mechanized and manual systems that support this installation activity. With the changes we envision in the future, these steps will no longer be required. We will only have one work force to administer which will utilize one common operating system and one universal access system. The communications installation and maintenance technician will have the necessary expertise and knowledge to either install or maintain any type of telecommunications request. This will result in an additional benefit to our customers. With the deployment of high-tech equipment into the local loop along with a universal work force we will be able to better meet our individual customers needs.

BILLING SYSTEMS OF THE FUTURE

NETWORK APPLICATIONS

Robert H. Weis - Chairperson
Staff Manager
Central Office Equipment Provisioning

BellSouth Services
Room 22P69
675 West Peachtree Street N. E.
Atlanta, Georgia 30375

ABSTRACT

The Telecommunications Network is breaking out of the basic services mode and moving into an era of new technology. Features hardly dreamed of a few years ago are being implemented on the network. Until now, the Automatic Message Accounting (AMA) billing system, to a great extent, has been overlooked in the rush of new services. We are finally realizing it must surpass all other network systems. We must be positioned to bill for all these new exotic services. Also, we now recognize the AMA system is a great source of untapped revenue and it already exists in our system. This seminar addresses the absolute requirement of the use of protocols which will permit the design of robust AMA teleprocessing networks with improved integrity and reduced costs. Customer access to billing data, on-line pricing and billing data concentration/distribution is previewed; in addition to future features which will streamline the system and generate revenues.

Richard A. Kraus -- TeleSciences CO
Systems

Sterling L. Levie, Jr.
-- Bell Communications
Research

Tom W. McEaddy   -- BellSouth Services

Bernard A. Streberger
-- AT&T Bell
Laboratories

FUTURE FEATURES IN THE NETWORK

BILLING SYSTEM

Richard A. Kraus
National Sales Manager
TeleSciences CO Systems

TeleSciences CO Systems, Inc.
5483 Crestone Circle
Boulder, Colorado 80301

ABSTRACT

The teleprocessing and Integrated Billing systems have provided the means for the telephone company to identify new services for its customers and new features within the billing operations. In order to fully comprehend these possibilities one must let your imagination explore all the possible uses for AMA billing data. Let's begin by reviewing the original justification for teleprocessing systems and the impact of the environment on these systems. This environmental impact has caused the systems to evolve and many of the original system requirements have been enhanced.

The basic benefits of a teleprocessing system have been defined in many documents during the pre-divestiture days. They centered around the elimination of the magnetic tape (or in some cases, paper tape) system widely dispersed throughout the telephone industry. Economical savings/benefits could be derived from the elimination of these systems. The central office savings centered around:

    Manpower Savings
    Transportation Savings
    Maintenance Savings
    Lost Billing Revenue

Other areas of savings were identified at the Regional Accounting Office (RAO). Some of these were:

    Tape Handling Elimination
    Elimination of Multiple
        Formats
    Call Assembly Programs
    Tape Density Changes

INTRODUCTION

Today many telephone companies, both Bell Operating Companies and independent telcos alike, are using some form of the telecommunications network to handle their automatic message accounting, or simply stated, their AMA Billing Data. The history of AMA Billing originally evolved to provide a method of recording and subsequently billing long distance toll calls. In order to accommodate this requirement, early switching systems, even the famous electro-mechanical crossbar and step-by-step switches, had to incorporate methods for recording this data.

The early AMA switch based systems depolyed two basic AMA or ticketing systems. At the local class 5 switch, the recording of this data was done by the switch with LAMA (Local) AMA Billing equipment. Another method widely deployed was CAMA (Centralized), which utilized a central toll center or tandem switch to record billing data from many subtending class 5 central offices. The CAMA Billing System used either ONI or ANI to identify the originating subscriber. The earliest of both of these systems recorded data on paper tape which was later replaced by magnetic tape units. Newer LAMA and CAMA stored program control switches came initially equipped with mag tape units for recording the billing data.

In the 70's early versions of teleprocessing systems began to appear in many telcos. Some of these systems addressed the requirements of billing records in the older electro-mechanical switches, while others addressed the capacity requirement for local measured service billing data and accurately and efficiently recording that data. Systems began to be deployed collecting both toll and measured service data over dedicated or dial up teleprocessing networks to centralized host computers. While systems were being developed to address the in-place switching systems, the newer digital switches began to have available the options of either local magnetic tape recording or teleprocessing features.

By the parallel evolution of products for the existing switch's billing system and the built-in teleprocessing capability in digital switches, teleprocessing became a "household" word in the telephone companies. By proper planning of office replacements and with an analysis of the savings for add-on (adjuncts) teleprocessing transmitters, the telephone companies are planning for a totally automated teleprocessing system utilizing the telecommunication network technology available today.

After implementing a variety of billing systems, the telephone companies have realized that they have more than just a teleprocessing or AMA data collection system. They have a totally integrated AMA network providing features and services by utilizing the near real time available AMA data. This Integrated Billing system (IBS) with the teleprocessing system at its nucleus forms a similar network to the switched network it serves. It incorporates the needs of the customers and an interface to the switch. It utilizes the switching and packet networks as its facilities while providing available network analysis data to ascertain the performance of the networks. It provides data required for the telephone companies to properly bill the inter-exchange carriers and the same data can be used to improve call completion of the interlata networks. It provides features to improve the operation and administration requirements of the people running the system while providing new data services that can generate revenue producing tariffs. In today's world switching without billing is no longer an acceptable condition.

CHANGING ENVIRONMENT

Just as the AMA manager began to get a feel for the basic teleprocessing system, the environment changed dramatically. Divestiture, equal access and increasing local measured service tariffs became requirements of the teleprocessing systems. The change impacted the billing systems with increased volumes, larger and new billing records, new recording techniques such as bulking of data, and the ability to provide new billing data services to customers.

With equal access came a nightmare of billing record requirements for the AMA manager. Heretofore non-recorded, unanswered calls and terminating calls now had to be recorded for carrier billing. Many calls such as interlata INWATS require two records for each call, one for IEC billing and one for Customer billing. Many of the new records also doubled in size. Local measured service or what is sometimes called "short haul toll" began to increase. This had a major impact on billing systems in telephone companies that had large EAS flat rate billing environments.

This environmental change, volume, new recording requirements and multiple carrier networks helped identify the features and services the teleprocessing system could offer.

EVOLUTION OF AMATPS

As the environment changed, the teleprocessing systems evolved to provide additional extended benefits to the telephone companies. Because of the complex recording/billing relationships between local telcos and interexchange carriers, the importance of minimizing data lost is a top priority. Full duplex (recording of both transmitter's disks) increases the reliability of the system.

Today's AMA records are designed for ease of processing by an RAO computer and are not very efficient for teleprocessing. Record compression techniques help reduce expenses in data link cost and on site storage. Because customers now receive bulked Local Measured Service bills, it is entirely possible to bulk these records (non Full Call Detail) at the switch's transmitter saving transmission and storage as well as RAO processing expense.

By having the ability in near real time to screen the call records, a local INWATS (EAS with Local Measured Service) feature can be provided without costly switching rearrangements. Other call screening features include SMDR and billing verification. Call screening or monitoring can also provide real time network analysis data and improved Equipment and Billing Accuracy Control (EBAC) data.

Teleprocessing systems used to their full pre-processing and analysis capability provide major savings in the RAO functions and can provide features out board the switch saving the switch's processor for switching and network requirements.

The extended benefits above are provided by the elements of the teleprocessing system:

- Collectors
- Transmitters
- Sensors
- Feature Modules
   Billing Preprocessing
   Data Screening
   System Verification

When considering the deployment of a teleprocessing system, one must identify the total variety of switching systems that will be included. This includes switching generations such as electro-mechanical, analog SPC and digital, as well as various switch manufacturers equipment. Many switching configurations and networks exist within a telephone company, such as end offices, access tandems, base and remote switches as well as a variety of IEC switches. The switches require a variety of AMA data to be recorded, some known today as well as many being identified for tomorrow. Services such as Centrex, SSP-800, Class, L.M.S. ISDN and others must be accurately recorded and billed. Properly implemented AMATPS can minimize the effect of this AMA requirement on both the network services and Regional Accounting Office departments.

Today's AMATPS billing systems must be able to integrate into the available telecommunications networks while providing expansion to tomorrow's technology. Packet network availability is beginning to reduce the requirements of a dial up switch network. New standards for transfer protocols improve the operation of the system while increased transmission speeds and data compression help reduce costs. With the utilization of packet networks comes an improvement in security and provide for disaster and recovery techniques. Other areas of network improvements come from standard administration requirements for integration into the operational support systems.

INTELLIGENT AMATPS

The teleprocessing systems help to greatly improve the efficiency of the RAO billing process. By providing a standard billing format from all types of switches, many reformatting steps are saved at the RAO. Bellcore has recently expanded this format to EBAF (Extended Bellcore AMA Format) permitting the flexibility of using the AMA records for new billing tariffs or services. By providing the data in near real time, customer bills could reflect the most current usage on their bills. Also, in the event of data corruption, recovery of lost billing data could be accomplished easily and accurately.

With today's technology, many of the heretofore functions performed by the large RAO mainframe could be accomplished by the intelligent AMATPS equipment. This is immediately evident by the functions of reformatting and call assembly currently taking place in AMA transmitters. Other RAO functions that could be done by AMATPS are:

° Bulking or summarizing local measured service or carrier access billing records.
° Reverse the calling and called numbers to provide terminating billing.
° Rating the call.
° Providing an EAS plan for an entire LATA.

Today's microprocessor controlled AMA transmitter has an almost endless amount of preprocessing billing power available for uses to be defined.

EQUAL ACCESS ENVIRONMENT

In the equal access environment, the teleprocessing system interacts with both local (LEC) and interexchange (IEC) carriers in many ways. Many telephone company switches provide the tandem switching and billing recording for many independent telco customer calls. In addition, calls placed on some carriers (ATT-COM) are recorded by the local company for both customer billing and access charging. In another case, many carriers record their own call records for customer billing and the telephone company's billing records are strictly used for access charging. This interaction among LECs and IECs requires improved methods for billing verification.
The AMATPS billing systems have the ability to monitor or audit the records and to validate the switch's translation and record content format. This, along with analyzing the call completion between the carriers, can prevent billing errors. This requirement is greatly increased with the advent of Intralata carrier implementation.

SYSTEM AND NETWORK ANALYSIS

By integrating into the switch, the network, various carriers and monitoring customer records, the telco AMA manager can perform a variety of system and network analysis. Some of these are:

° Billing switch translation verification - assuring the call is switching properly and making the correct billing record.
° Improving call completion by providing data on patterns of unanswered calls to determine

network irregularities or customer busy and don't answer conditions.
° Providing call monitoring for customer billing complaints as well as billing record traps for fraud or harassing calls.
° Provide system performance and diagnostics for correct system operation, data match and compare functions, and the ability to correct record errors.

NEW DATA SERVICES

One of the latest and most exciting new uses of the teleprocessing systems are to provide a variety of new data services from the AMA data totally separate from the basic AMA billing requirement. These include new customer features, new tariffs and new telco operation services. Several of these data services have been identified including:

° Centrex Station Message Detail Recording Data - Utilizing the AMA data found in AMATPS, SMDR data can be made readily available to the customers telecommunications manager. This will permit the Centrex customer to have real time SMDR data similar to that available from many PBXs. The teleprocessing system screens this data from the main AMA data flow and provides the SMDR to the customer's Call Accounting System equipment.
° Opinion polling or mass polling services - This incorporates the ability of the switch to terminate a customer's call on an announcement machine and make an AMA record. The teleprocessing system, when receiving this record, will store it and count the various records. This can then be passed on to a central host which will keep account of the customer voting for an opinion poll.
° Pay for View - Using the same techniques as above, data can be provided to a TV cable company to acknowledge request for program service.
° Originating 976 Calls - In todays exciting 976 market, many calls originate outside of the information providers lata or telephone company's area. These customers pay the toll charges to call a 976 number but the local company does not record these calls, not enabling them to obtain revenue for themselves or the information provider. It is possible to monitor these calls from two sources:

° The first is to monitor terminating interlata records and to check for 976 nxx codes. This could only be used to identify the carrier offering the traffic.

° The second is to monitor the called numbers at the originating telco and screen the 976 interlata calls. The originating telco could offer a service to provide the terminating telco with the customer ID placing the call.

° Marketing Studies - Better known as Subscriber Line Usage Studies (SLUS), the teleprocessing systems can screen on call records similar to the SMDR feature. These records are instantly available to the telco sales manager to analyze customers profiles and suggest new equipment and/or services.

NEW SYSTEM FEATURES

In addition to the new data services just mentioned, the AMATPS Billing systems can provide many new system features that can improve the overall performance of the system. The features being considered today are:

° Call Record compression - The AMA record formats utilized today are very efficient to RAO computer processing, but not very efficient for data transmission. There are techniques available today to reduce the size of the record for data transmission. This can be done by non data specific compression of data bits or by specific data record compression and expansion techniques between transmitter and collector. This later method has been proven to increase transmitter storage and transmission time by a factor of 6 to 1 compared to non compressed formats.

° Local Measured Service Record - When L.M.S. or other types of short-haul billing tariffs are implemented, the customer typically receives a bulked accounting of his local calls unless he pays for full call detail records. The AMA transmitter can be equipped to perform this building function at each switch location rather than at the RAO. The benefits obtained are: higher transmitter disk storage capability, considerably reduced transmission time, and reduce RAO bulking processing costs. The reduction in transmission and RAO processing costs have been estimated to yield savings of millions of dollars per year to the telephone company.

° Reverse Billing - Many telephone companies are implementing reverse billing on local calls (local 800 service) in conjunction with L.M.S. tariffs. Once again this function of billing to the terminating number can be performed by the RAO through sort programs looking for the specific called numbers from the originating subscribers billing file. The AMA transmitter can be equipped to perform this function economically at each switch location. This preprocessing function of reversing the calling and called numbers can eliminate the RAO search programs and can yield a savings of millions of dollars to the telco.

° Access Charge Bulking - Currently the local telephone company records both originating and terminating interlata call records. The purpose of these records are:

° a. Originating Records - The first purpose is to record the minutes of usage for access charging a carrier. If the carrier is recording his own billing data at his POP, no further use is required. If he is not recording the call at his Point of Presense (POP) (ATT-Com), then the record is also used to bill the customer.

° b. Terminating Record - The only purpose (except interlata INWATS) for these records is to bill the carrier for their access usage.

° Typically the telephone company will bulk all of the AMA full call detail records at the RAO into a summary of minutes of usage to bill the carrier. The AMA transmitter can be equipped to perform this function at each switch location. All terminating records can be bulked and all originating records for carriers doing their own recording can be bulked along with all Feature Group A & B call records. This preprocessing function has been estimated to save up to 90% of the required CABS processing requirements at the RAO.

SUMMARY

What started out as an efficient and accurate means of moving data from point A to point B has now become one of the most important support systems for the telephone company today. By understanding its current use as well as the potential for the teleprocessing system, the telephone company AMA manager can provide many new features and revenue generating services to benefit his company.

COMMUNICATIONS STANDARDS AND

TELEPROCESSING OF AMA DATA

Sterling L. Levie, Jr.
District Manager
Billing Systems Technology

Bell Communications Research
Room NVC-2X407
331 Newman Springs Road
Red Bank, New Jersey 07701

ABSTRACT

This article discusses the application of standard international communications protocols to the transport of Automatic Message Accounting (AMA) data from network elements to data collection centers. Use of these protocols will permit the design of robust AMA teleprocessing networks capable of handling large volumes of message billing data with improved integrity and reduced operating costs.

INTRODUCTION

This deals with a real telecommunications application called the AMA Teleprocessing System (AMATPS). The article is divided into two parts.

In the first part we will begin by getting a feel for the importance of the data handled by AMATPS. Then we'll take a look at a typical deployed AMATPS, and we'll explore some consequences of the AMATPS interface specification not having had international protocol standards available when it was designed. This part is intended to illustrate why standard communications protocols are important.

In the second part we'll look at the communications protocol structure that is proposed for use with a Next Generation AMATPS design. It is characterized by use of the FTAM application layer protocol (FTAM stands for File Transfer, Access and Management). We'll (1) take a look at some of FTAM's key characteristics, (2) introduce the concept of an AMA "index file," and then (3) walk through a description of how FTAM and the index file will be used for AMA data transfer.

We'll conclude by listing some of the advantages expected for AMATPS from use of standard communications protocols, dwelling a bit on reduced first costs and operations costs.

PART I:
AMA TELEPROCESSING SYSTEM (AMATPS)

WHAT IS AUTOMATIC MESSAGE ACCOUNTING (AMA)?

Automatic Message Accounting (AMA) is the term used by Bell Operating Companies (BOCs) to describe the network processes responsible for generating, formatting, and outputting the data needed to bill customers and carriers for their use of exchange networks and exchange network services.

Typically, each customer usage transaction with the network generates an AMA data record that contains all the information needed to bill the customer or carrier for services provided. As one might expect, an AMA record contains information such as calling telephone number, called telephone number, duration of the call, and date and time when the call was placed. It does not contain the price of the call, however. The price is calculated by an accounting office computer from currently applicable tariff rates. Priced call data are posted to customer account files, which are converted to bills once a month.

In the case of carrier access billing, an AMA record also contains the carrier's identity and the elapsed time of the carrier's connection to the exchange network. The charge for the carrier's access is calculated by an accounting office computer and posted to the carrier's account file, which is converted to a bill once per month.

In addition to billing carriers for their access to its exchange network, a BOC may also bill a carrier's customers as billing agent for the carrier. This is called an "open billing" arrangement.

These three applications of AMA data--customer billing, carrier access billing, and open billing--are responsible for approximately 45% of a typical BOC's annual revenues, based on annual reports of the seven regional companies. The annual dollar amount of these revenues is on the order of 30 billion.

WHAT IS AN AMA TELEPROCESSING SYSTEM?

The technology used to pass AMA records from the network elements that generate them to accounting office computers that bill from them is in a state of change. The older technology places AMA records on magnetic tapes that are transported from switching system locations to accounting office computers once per day. Magnetic tape technology is being replaced by the use of AMA Teleprocessing Systems (AMATPSs), which use data communications to teleprocess AMA data from network elements to centrally located collectors.

An AMATPS consists of a transmitter associated with a network element, a centrally located collector, and a communications interface between them. Although many implementations of an AMATPS are possible, generic requirements for any AMATPS are documented for the regional companies by Bell Communications Research in technical reference TR-TSY-000385. An AMATPS that conforms to these requirements is robust in the face of component or system failures.

The transmitter of an AMATPS is often referred to as an AMAT (for "AMA transmitter"). Its functions are to acquire AMA data generated by a network element, process the data as appropriate (ensuring that the data are available in a special format called Bellcore AMA Format), and store the data on a mass storage device until they are polled by the collector. The mass storage device is large enough to provide at least five average business days of AMA data.

The collector (or "AMATPS Collector") of an AMATPS functions largely automatically in acquiring the AMA data sorted at the AMATs it serves. It follows a polling schedule determined by the telephone company and at the appropriate times initiates a polling session with an AMAT. After a satisfactory communications association is established with an AMAT, the collector commands the AMAT to transmit all previously unpolled AMA data. Received AMA data are buffered on a mass storage device at the collector. When commanded by a collector operator, buffered AMA records are placed on a magnetic tape, which is the input medium to the accounting office's main frame computers.

CURRENT AMATPS COMMUNICATIONS PROTOCOL

The AMATPS interface was designed in the late 1970's, when comprehensive international protocols did not exist for communications. The X.25 network protocol existed at the time, but, for example, it did not account for peer-to-peer communications. consequently, the AMATPS specification used a modified version of X.25 called BX.25.

In the complete absence of application layer protocols, a hand-made "File Transfer procedure" was designed for AMATPS' use. This procedure was designed with an eye on the details of what was going on at the session, network, and link layers of the BX.25 protocol.

The AMATPS File Transfer procedure uses data blocks of 1531 bytes, which is a size conveniently related to packet and frame sizes, and it uses data files defined to be 100 blocks long. The file size was chosen not just because it was a round number. In case of a transmission error, a file of this size takes only about five minutes to retransmit at the then advanced modem speeds of 4800 bps.

These conventions have proved to be reliable, but they have also proved to be costly to implement and difficult for manufacturers to maintain. They provide very complex functionality which is application-specific. Consequently, there are no standard firmware or software packages available, and AMATPS manufacturers are forced to hand-code their own communications interfaces. This is a time consuming and error prone process which is frustrated by the absence of standard debugging tools such as are available for standard interfaces.

A result is that a manufacturer of a new AMATPS component cannot be sure that it will interwork successfully with existing AMATPS components, many of which are known to have small departures from the interface specification. The manufacturer therefore needs access to installed, functioning AMATPS components to finish and test his interface work.

The telephone company has corresponding difficulties, because new AMATPS components often do not work correctly, due to interface problems, and because system enhancements tend to degrade working interfaces. Communications problems range from "no response" when polling, to "hung" communications and dropped links. The telephone company experiences added costs and delays when it gives manufacturers communications access to its functioning AMATPS equipment in order to resolve interface problems. Furthermore, this access jeopardizes its billing operations to some extent.

AMATPS NEED VS. CURRENT CAPABILITIES

Beyond these interface-related problems, AMATPS needs enhanced capabilities that in many cases are difficult or impossible to implement with the current interface in place.

For one thing, AMATPS needs a data transfer rate on the order of 56,000 bps or even higher. This would permit a typical large switching office to be able to transfer a day's worth of AMA data to a collector in about 40 min. This is a manageable, human-sized interval, compared with the 8 hour period it takes today using AMATPS' current 4800 bps capabilities.

Available X.25 Public Packet Switched Networks offer a 56,000 bps transfer rate, but the current AMATPS interface is not compatible with X.25. An interface change to the X.25 standard would make packet networks available for AMATPS.

Additional capabilities needed by an AMATPS include end-to-end checks of data integrity, and capability of collectors to download software to AMATs, under full control of BOC personnel. Other needed capabilities are automatic backup of a failed collector (instead of manual backup), and automatic load-sharing between collectors, to assist in polling after unexpectedly high AMA data volumes, or after an extended collector outage.

The path to these capabilities lies in applying international protocol standards to AMATPS. A full set of such standards has been established in just the last few years. They are robust, and software and firmware for them are available commercially to AMATPS component manufacturers. Furthermore, standard implementation testing tools are also becoming available, which will simplify the development of an analysis system for testing the conformance of AMATPS components to the applicable interface specifications.

The result is that if AMATPS makes use of protocol standards, then AMATPS component manufacturers will have much improved confidence that their products will interwork with others. The manufacturers will be able to devote their development energies to AMA-related problems, and telephone companies will experience more robust and economical AMATPS implementations.

PART II:
NEXT GENERATION AMATPS
PROTOCOL HIGHLIGHTS

FTAM: FILE TRANSFER, ACCESS AND MANAGEMENT

The communications interface of the Next Generation AMATPS will conform fully to standard Open Systems Interconnection (OSI) protocol specifications. The distinguishing protocols that will be used are FTAM (File Transfer, Access and Management) at the application layer and X.25 at the network layer.

Since FTAM will give Next Generation AMATPS its real power, we will explore how it will be used. FTAM is an international standard Application Service Element for file operations. It functions at layer seven of the OSI protocol reference model. It conforms to T1M1 standards for communications between network elements and operations systems, and it has been adopted by Bellcore in its network element to operations system interface standards.

A key concept behind FTAM is that it creates an association between the file spaces of communicating entities and provides the entities with virtual access to each others' files. In effect, this divorces communications from the application functions that the entities perform.

Applied to AMATPS, the result is that a collector's application program, for example, does not focus on communications. Rather, it implements simple file utility operations, such as "copy File X from Volume O (resident at the AMAT) to Volume 1 (resident at the collector)." FTAM and the underlying communications protocols convert such file-oriented operations to the appropriate data communications exchanges.

All of the protocol actions of FTAM are file-oriented actions. For instance, an application program may select or deselect a file, open or close it, read it or write to it, or transfer it from one place to another. Different entities may be assigned different permissions with regard to these actions. Applied to AMATPS, a collector would not be permitted to write into existing AMAT files, for example.

File type is of no concern to FTAM. This brings a significant benefit to AMATPS, which must deal with many types of files. Examples are AMA data files, program files, error log files, message files, and others. Because FTAM doesn't care about file type, all types of files may be approached in a uniform manner by a collector's application program.

USING FTAM

To take advantage of FTAM, a Next Generation AMAT will organize AMA data records into files, and the record will be the fundamental unit of inventory. Data files may be closed off after a preset time interval, e.g., each half-hour, has elapsed, or after a preset quantity of records has accumulated. It will label each file by a header that includes the starting record number and the total number of records. Other parameters, such as the file's creation time, may also be included in each file's header.

A collector that establishes a communications association with the AMAT will determine what files (if any) it wishes to acquire, by consulting a new AMAT file called an index file. The index file lists all the AMAT files that the collector is permitted to access. In addition, the index file presents information about each of the listed files. For AMA data files, this information includes file name, creation date and time, primary/secondary status mark (a secondary file has previously been polled by a collector, and a primary file has not), date and time when last polled, number of the file's first data record, number of records in the file, file integrity check value, etc.

A collector's first action upon establishing a communication association with an AMAT is to acquire a copy of the AMAT's index file. The collector's application program analyzes the index file's entry for each of the files made available by the AMAT and decides which, if any, it wishes to transfer. Typically, the collector would not transfer files marked secondary. Of the primary files available, the collector might elect to transfer the oldest first, provided that sufficient transmission time and buffer space are available.

After the collector determines what files it wishes to acquire, on a file by file basis it selects the files and transfers them. After calculating an integrity check value for each transferred file and successfully matching it with the value specified in the index file, the collector deselects the file.

The protocol action corresponding to the collector's deselecting a file is critical from the AMAT's perspective. If no other action is taken by the collector, this action is interpreted as the collector's positive acknowledgment (ACK) that it successfully received the file. Before taking any further protocol-related steps, the AMAT modifies the file's entry in its index file as follows: it changes the primary status mark to secondary (if not already secondary), and it enters the current date and time as the date and time when last polled. Importantly, the AMAT does not modify the data file or any of its records. At this point the AMAT continues its normal response to the collector's deselection action.

AMATPS CHARACTERISTICS RESULTING FROM USING STANDARD COMMUNICATIONS PROTOCOLS

In the previous section, we saw how standard communications protocols, including FTAM, will be used in the Next Generation of AMATPS. We will now summarize some of the characteristics and benefits that are expected to result from this strategy.

As indicated at the end of Part I, use of standard communications protocols will make possible numerous improvements needed by today's AMATPSs. In general, use of standard communications protocols will bring benefits to Next Generation AMATPS in three categories: improved ability to handle large data volumes, improved integrity of AMA data, and improved system economics.

Improved ability to handle large data volumes will be provided in part by Next Generation AMATPS's ability to use the high data rates available with Public Packet Switched Networks. Contributing factors will be the automatic ability of collectors to share loads and for automatic backups of failed collectors.

Improved data integrity will be contributed to by several factors. Some of these are ability of AMATPS collectors to download programs to AMATs under control of the telephone company, ability of collectors to repoll files and subfiles, provision of intelligent polling logs for collectors, and simplified polling of data files that an AMAT concentrates from satellite switching locations.

The system characteristics just discussed result directly from the use of standard communications protocols. Most of them result from using FTAM at the application layer, but the ability for AMATPS to use Public Packet Switched Networks results specifically from using X.25 as the network protocol.

In closing, let's focus on system economics for Next Generation AMATPS. First costs will be significantly lower. The chief reason is that since all the protocol software needed in Next Generation AMATPS is purchasable now, suppliers will not have to build and debug their own, resulting in a very significant reduction in the time (and cost) of producing the AMATPS interface, which experience has shown is the most difficult part of the development job. This is expected to substantially reduce the protocol-related portion of the first cost of AMATPS components.

Related to this, operations costs are expected to be lower, because the interface is expected to be more robust and flexible, and because maintenance personnel will only need to acquire and maintain expertise in a single, standard interface.

Finally, in the long run, lower first costs and operations costs are expected, because the AMATPS interface will eventually be only another application of a standard interface between network elements and operations systems. That is, network elements and operations systems will eventually be equipped with a common set of communications protocol capabilities, and each application, of which AMATPS is only one of many, will draw upon these capabilities as needed, resulting in economic leveraging.

VALIDATION AND DATA INTEGRITY OF

BILLING RECORDS

A NETWORK VIEW

Tom W. McEaddy
Staff Manager
Network Operations

BellSouth Services
Room 24F57
675 West Peachtree Street N.E.
Atlanta, Georgia 30375

ABSTRACT

Technological changes are being rapidly introduced into the network to meet both today's and tomorrow's customer communication needs. These changes dictate a constant churn in office translations which directly impacts the validity and integrity of the office AMA billing records. To guard against AMA degradation, a series of checks and balances needs to be introduced into the billing stream to insure that (1) valid AMA record(s) are generated when the network is properly conditioned, (2) multiple/zero recording(s) situations are identified and properly corrected, and (3) that conversation and access timing is correct. Mechanized AMA testing and data validation is one solution to resolving AMA degradation and may be the right choice for you.

INTRODUCTION

Since Divestiture, changes to the switching environment have exploded due to equal access, new lines of business, and operator take back. During this same time frame the BOC's have been reducing operating costs. Thus, an environment has evolved where the BOC's are doing more work with less resources which has increased the risk factor for billing accuracy and integrity. The risk factor has been affected by the amount of time available for verification and testing of office and trunk translations in comparison to ongoing maintenance and provisioning activities. The time allotted to verification and testing has been minimal at best and has proven to be very costly in terms of revenues earned but not billed due to insufficient AMA recording.

Another area of concern that has contributed to revenue losses is the billing systems used to summarize, rate, and bill the customer. Customers are scrutinizing their bills more closely today primarily due to costs and the availability of off the shelf personal/micro computer hardware and software. Thus, customers are more readily contesting their bills. How sure are we that our billing systems are accurate and that there are no programming errors that are impacting the customer's bill? How sure are we that the rating systems are correct and that the usage is driven to the correct account? If our billing systems are challenged, how do we prove that our system is correct to the satisfaction of our customers? Do we adjust the customers account or do we demand payment and chance litigation?

Last but not least, how do we determine if the timing of conversation minutes and access minutes of use is correct? Aside from clock start time fluctuations, how do we prove that the call duration timing is correct for both toll and access billing? To date, the only way possible to verify timing is to go back into the central office and verify the sequence of timing events. Will this process satisfy our customers timing concerns?

WHAT CAN WE DO TO FIX THE PROBLEM?

Fixing problems are easy compared to finding and identifying problems. How does one go about verifying hundreds of central offices in search of both trunking and translations problems that are costing millions of dollars in lost revenue? How does one go about verifying hundreds of central offices that are different in both manufacturer and serving demographics? How does one validate a billing system? Do we add manpower, do we add downstream error detection programming, or do we wait for someone to report a trouble that surfaces a major revenue problem? How long or how much revenue can we afford to lose before the problems are detected and corrected? The answers to these questions are complex in terms of costs and time. The one underlying factor that always haunts corrective action is how long will the problem stay fixed or how long will it be before another problem is introduced into the network or billing system! The best solution to these problems is the deployment of a mechanized AMA testing and data validation system.

HOW CAN A MECHANIZED AMA TESTING AND VALIDATION SYSTEM HELP?

The deployment of a mechanized AMA testing and data validation system will provide the ability to perform testing of your network and billing system on a demand and routine scheduled basis. A mechanized system will permit the testing of new services for routing, AMA recording, screening (blocking and announcements) and billing to insure the accurate implementation of the service. In addition, a mechanize system will provide an audit trail for verifying billing, recording, and timing issues and historical data for resolving customer complaints. Last, a mechanized system will provide timely data and analysis, provide labor savings (Comptrollers, AMA Control Centers/Equipment and Billing Accuracy Center [AMACC/EBAC], & Switching Control Center [SCC]), and will assist in the delivery of accurate billing data to the RAO for processing.

WHAT ARE SOME OF THE PRACTICAL APPLICATIONS OF A MECHANIZED SYSTEM?

Equal Access Verification (Feature Group D):

A mechanized system can be used to perform equal access testing in both new and existing offices. New offices can establish test lines for each carrier served by the office and make test calls on either a casual dialed (10XXX) or Preferred Interexchange Carrier (PIC) basis. Test calls can include local, 976-XXXX, intra-LATA, inter-LATA, 0-, 00-, 0+, and WATS. Regressive testing can also be performed to verify blocking and screening requirements. Both originating and terminating access recordings can be obtained by controlling the test call calling and called telephone numbers.

Existing offices that are adding a new carrier or a direct office facility for a carrier can use the system to test the add activity.

Using a mechanized system to perform equal access conversions saves both the SCC and AMACC/EBAC AMA testing and validation time, insures that the testing and validation are complete, and completes the process within a minimum time frame.

Interim 800 Service:

A mechanized system can be used to verify the six digit/home NPA translators in the switches to insure that the 800 Service call is routed and PIC'd to the correct carrier. Multiple classes of service (POTS, COIN, WATS) can be set up for testing to insure that all the switches' translators are verified.

This process can be used to test any Special Access Code (SAC) code service including 900 and 700 offerings.

Central Office Routing:

A mechanized system can be used to insure that a new office can route correctly to all code points in the local rate zone (free). The system can also be used to insure that proper measured service recordings are generated for the code points in each zone/band and that intra-LATA toll points are routed and recorded correctly (BOC).

This process will eliminate the need for the SCC to manually test the office routing during an office cutover.

Verification of Call Routing and Recording:

Today, we have call routing situations that generate multiple AMA recordings (one record in two or more switches) which may impact access billing depending on the billing system logic used to extract the access records. A mechanized system can be used to generate test calls to pin point these types of routing and recording anomalies.

For example, an 800 Service call originated from a coin station could potentially be recorded four times depending on how the call is routed. There is also the potential to bill multiple access charges for the same call. A mechanized system can be used to make test calls to controlled test numbers which will enable the system to capture both the originating and terminating recordings. If the date extraction interface for the system encompasses the end office, end office LATA tandem, Traffic Operator Position System (TOPS), and Traffic service Position System (TSPS) AMA records, then the multiple recordings can be identified and the routing of the call verified.

In conclusion, a mechanized system can be used to assist you in isolating routing and billing problems.

WATS:

A mechanized system can be used to validate WATS band screening to eliminate out of band calls. In addition, the system can be used to insure that non-banded WATS service exclusions are screened correctly.

In cases where bi-directional WATS service is provided, the system can test the service class to verify that the correct AMA records are generated on both an outward and incoming basis.

Operator Services:

Operator testing has always been time consuming due to the need to interface with the operator. A mechanized system through the use of pre-recorded message tracks and/or emulator packages can make test calls to the operator (0-, 0+, and 00-) and provide the operator with the necessary instructions to place the desired call type.

This type of testing will insure that the proper end office recording was generated or not generated and that the call was recorded correctly at the operator traffic recording location.

Call Saturation Testing:

On occasion, a BOC may receive a billing complaint from a carrier that requires test calls to be made and AMA verbatims to be extracted in order to compare the carrier's AMA data to the BOC's. In these situations, a mechanized system can be used to pump test calls through the network destined for the carrier's point of presence within the LATA.

The system would compare the test call data and times recorded by the system against the BOC's AMA records and generate an error report listing the discrepancies. This type of testing would provide an unbiased source of AMA data records for resolving disputes and detecting recording problems.

End User Billing:

On occasion, a customer or Public Service Commission (PSC) may inquire about the accuracy of your billing systems. A mechanized system can be used to generate AMA test calls, rate the test calls, summarize the usage, and generate a bill for comparison purposes.

This type of feature is extremely important in providing billing accuracy information to the PSC's for rate cases and providing an audit trail for litigation situations.

SUMMARY

The bottom line for deployment of any mechanized system is how much can you save through head count reductions and other quantifiable savings. On the other hand, can you afford to continue losing significant amounts of revenue and do nothing about it? The only thing I can say for sure is that my company is concerned about its revenues and is seriously looking into mechanized AMA testing and data validation as a support system for our billing and recording functions. We know what our reported losses are today and we have taken steps to eliminate these problems. However, our main concern now is, how much are we losing that we don't know about and what lies ahead with the deployment of Integrated Services Digital Network (ISDN), Open Network Architecture (ONA), and other new service offerings?

FUTURE BILLING NETWORK ARCHITECTURE

Bernard A. Streberger
Supervisor
Billing Systems Engineering

AT&T Bell Laboratories
Room HR2J243
480 Red Hill Road
Middletown, New Jersey 07748

ABSTRACT

Since Divestiture of the Bell System an increasing number of services are being measured and billed for equitable customer results and also to better manage Telephone Company (Telco) resources. Today's AMA teleprocessing architecture features reliable store-and-forward data communications processes for billing measured services. For the 90s this design may be enhanced to include customer access, billing data concentration/distribution and on-line pricing. The smart Edge Nodes and Central Nodes of the Billing Network Architecture will promote basic and enhanced voice and data services meeting CEI and ONA requirements, while increasing Telco revenue opportunities as the billing vendor of choice.

INTRODUCTION

The Telco billing process invoices customers for their use of the network supported services. The current industry trend since divestiture of the Bell System is for pricing on a usage-sensitive basis for both voice and data switched services. The term "Usage-sensitive" implies detailed measurement of holding time or information sent, the calling and called numbers, the type of service, time of day, etc. The AMA (Automatic Message Accounting) standards insure that the network measure and record usage uniformly in order to simplify the billing process. In general, the AMA Record contains all relevant usage data for posting the detailed charges on the customer's bill.

Since 1982 the network has provisioned AMA Teleprocessing equipment for electronic transfer of AMA Records to avoid magnetic tape handling costs, delays and other incidents of lost data. AMA Teleprocessing Systems (AMATPS) insure 99.99% availability objectives for AMA recording and collection at the Telco RAOs (Revenue Accounting Offices). Network Elements (NEs) and AMATPS equipment offer MDR (Message Detailed Recording) formatting and sending capabilities for near real-time access to AMA-like usage measurements, to enable cost management, network management and bill verification processes direct to customer premises or extended to the customer premise by customer access systems arrangements. Data compression is also being featured to reduce AMATPS communication costs. Other capabilities for auditing, error detection and service specific reformatting processes are currently being planned and/or deployed.

THE 90s AND A DECADE OF CHANGE

During the 90s we anticipate a decade of change that may dramatically affect the way usage data is measured, processed and delivered. These impacts are organized into the six categories shown below.

° Usage-sensitive Pricing for Voice and
  Data Services
            Holding Time
            Information Sent
            Distance

° Customer Access
            Cost Management
            Network Management
            Bill Verification

° Real Time Pricing
            Chargeback
            Charge Quote
            Charge to Date

° Contract Billing
        Interexchange Carriers (LDS)
        Alternate Operator Services
          (AOS)
        Cellular Independent Telcos
        Billing Vendors

° Billing Management
        Information Service
          Providers (Greene 3/7/88)

° Unbundled Billing as a Basic Service
    Element
        Comparably Efficient
          Interconnection (CEI)
        Open Network Architecture
          (ONA)

BILLING NETWORK ARCHITECTURE

Since the TelCo network is responsible for recording and teleprocessing billable event information (via. AMA), it is reasonable to conclude that the "network" is a resource for processing and distributing billing data to meet the needs of the 90s. As such, the billing support network should meet current and anticipated ONA (Open Network Architecture) requirements.

The Billing Network Architecture shown in Figure 1 represents a distributed teleprocessing/data processing network with Edge Nodes close to the AMA Recording Points, and Central Nodes close to the RAO billing operations. The primary flow is the billing data sent from the Edge Nodes to one or more Central Node collection sites. The file systems insure 99.99% reliability and support the data processing and data communications requirements. In general, customer access may be provided directly from the Edge Node or from the Central Node. Customers may be end-users or network systems that support end-users. Administration and security should be distributed to the Central Node and to the Edge Nodes via the Central Nodes. The Billing Network Model is illustrated in Figure 2. Some of the billing features that should be possible include:

        Universal Data Compression
        BAF and BAF With Modules
          Support
        Bulk and Threshold Recording
          with Detail Archive
        Real Time Call Rating
        Receivers for Billing
          Management
        Access for Unbundled Billing

IN/1+ SERVICES, BULK BILLING AND REAL TIME CALL RATING

Consider the following architectural examples for Intelligent Network/1+ (IN/1+) services, Bulk Billing and Real Time Call Rating, respectively.

For IN/1+ we assume that some of the usage event information for AMA recording will be sent from the SCP (Service Control Point) to the SSP (Service Switching Point) using SSP transactions. In general, these events or billing modules will complete the formation of the standard (BAF) Bellcore AMA format in the billing record file of the Edge Node. See Figure 3. The other concept illustrated here is sorting and distributing some of the AMA/MDR information to another Central Node site for service or customer consolidation. This sorting capability may also support contract or unbundled billing requirements. In all cases, one of the Central Nodes will perform the administration and security processes.

For bulk billing we assume that the Telco will be required to keep a partial or complete archive of the detail call records. Refer to Figure 4. Archiving should be dynamically settable and independent of the bulk billing processes. In our example the bulk billing occurs in 2 stages. The first-stage may be the 24-hr. accumulation and the second-stage might be several days making up the aggregate bulk file. Special studies and audits might also be set up and collected off-line in the same manner as the archive routing and collection as performed in this example.

In the last example in Figure 5 we illustrate how on-line call rating might be performed. Here the V&H (Vertical and Horizontal) coordinates along with any other pricing related information is again administered by the Central Node, enabling the Edge Node to append pricing information to the Message Detail Recording-Customer Premise (MDR-CP) records. This enables the customer to receive verifiable pricing information for indirect billing, chargeback billing, etc. History database systems may also serve for month to date query services.

SUMMARY

As we step back to look across the '80s and the '90s, we observe that AMA formats and teleprocessing data communications are standard across the industry. The future will be driven by ONA and the need to meet expanding recording needs for a wide variety of service offerings. ONA itself will further open up the billing process with Operation Support/Network Element (OS/NE) compatible data communications and new generations of system products.

In summary we emphasize that the billing process is a major revenue stream. Usage events and billing services will drive revenues. Customers will demand access to billing information and the enhanced service provider will demand access for billing the customer. We should view billing as an opportunity to increase revenues across the board.

BILLING NETWORK ARCHITECTURE

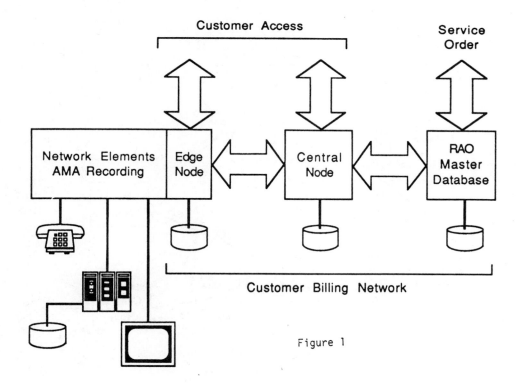

Figure 1

BIILLING NETWORK MODEL

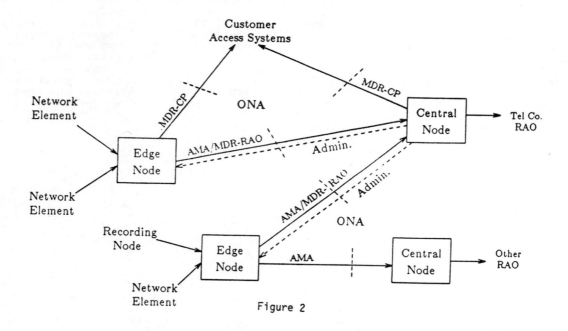

Figure 2

IN/1+ EXAMPLE

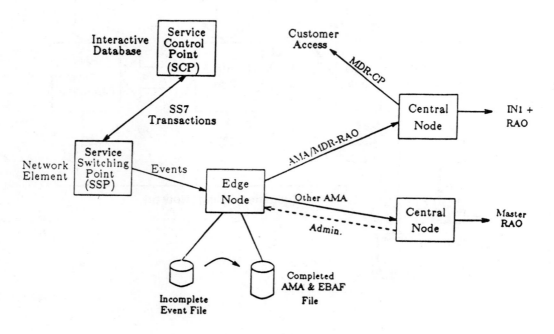

Figure 3

BULK BILLING EXAMPLE

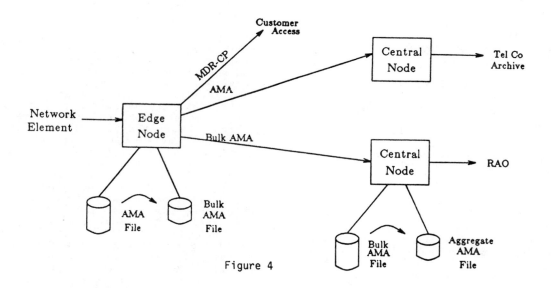

Figure 4

REAL TIME CALL RATING

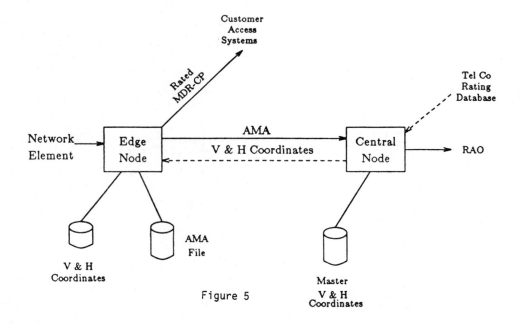

Figure 5

OPS-10

FOCUSING ON THE CUSTOMER AND SERVICE

Norman L. Cubellis, Chairperson

General Manager, Network Services

Indiana Bell

220 N. Meridian, Room 920
Indianapolis, IN 46204

In today's competitive environment telephone companies are just beginning to
understand the servicing requirements
of customers before and after the sale.
Many of these requirements have always
existed however, customers say telephone
companies have not been listening to
them. This seminar offers operations
oriented personnel a chance to hear
customer's needs on a first hand basis.
The problems encountered by an account
executive who represents the customer
to the telephone company will also be
told. The seminar will conclude with
a view of one telephone company's actions
as they attempt to respond to their
customers.

Donald C. Caramell
Ohio Bell Communications

Norman L. Cubellis
Indiana Bell Telephone

Christopher L. Davis
Rexnord Data Systems

Donald J. Zbikowski
Westinghouse Electric Corporation

FOCUSING ON THE CUSTOMER AND SERVICE

Norman L. Cubellis
General Manager - Network Services

Indiana Bell Telephone

240 N. Meridian Street
Indianapolis, Indiana 46204

This paper will address the issue of
customer service and specifically how
a telephone company can provide service
with an individual customer focus in
a competitive environment. It appears
as if the challenge is great and the
required changes in culture and operating
environments/systems will be significant.
To better understand what is required
in the marketplace, one must have an
understanding of the past, and the
drivers which have brought operating
telephone companies to their current
view as to what is proper customer
service.

The two major focus areas of technical
operating departments within telephone
companies have been operating efficiency
and a macro view of service. Today's
Marketeer, who is concerned with the
satisfaction of individual customers,
might take issue with the merits of
these objectives however, they were
worthy contributions to a monopoly
telephone environment. Equipment modernization and operating system mechniza-
permitted ever decreasing cost curves
through increased productivity. While
efficiency gains were being made, service
was still paramount in the minds of
telephone companies and their service
personnel. The measurement of service
was however, done at a macro level.
Efficient handling of the greatest
number of service requests/trouble
reports in a minimal timeframe was
the measurement of good service. This
view created a "run them in the front
door...run them out the back" approach
which while acceptable to the majority
of customers, was very painful to those
who required special attention or had
unique needs.

Even in the above described environment,
telephone companies were concerned
about individual customer service as
evidenced by the service surveys they
conducted and supporting measurement
plan the implemented. Unfortunately,
these surveys presented limited input
to guide improvements in the service
process. Customers for years, complained
that telcos did not listen to them
and were not responsive to their needs.
Whether real or perceived due to the
monopoly environment, many customers
quickly moved to competitive alternatives
as they became available because these
providers were felt to be more responsive
to identified needs.

With that brief background let's look
at today's environment and the changing
role of service departments in a telephone company. Virtually all such
companies profess a desire to be market
driven. In order to accomplish this
goal, customer needs must be identified.
This identification is achieved by
listening to customers as they delineate
current service problems and future
desires. This input can be achieved
through focus groups, face to face
interviews conducted by research firms,
meetings held between customer and
telephone company service managers,
input from field sales and servicing
personnel, and the actions of competitors. Regardless of the input utilized,

1097

servicing plans and operating systems must be developed with a strong focus on individual customer needs. Obviously a form of balance must still be struck between service and efficiency. It would be wrong to distain an efficient operation in that (1) most customers consider speed of response to be an important part of service and (2) efficiency measures hold down operating costs which lead to lower prices. The challenge then is a balance between the service needs and cost containment.

There is one other very important issue to be considered in the provision of excellent service in today's competitive environment. Managers and non-management associates must all understand their individual roles and what type of style is most effective in a customer focused setting. Generally, operations oriented personnel tend to focus on system related activities with less emphasis placed upon the people oriented aspects of the job such as problem solving and team building. in today's environment a leadership mode is required rather than a management control approach. This translates to a better informed and motivated workforce which clearly understands corporate objectives and service objectives which have been developed for <u>individual</u> customers. The practice of using overall measurement plans to determine service level, drives the wrong behavior. Employees must have a personal commitment to provide excellent service to each customer account. This is especially true for those who serve major revenue producing customers. To achieve this level of commitment, management must first provide a level of understanding which enables each employee to understand exactly what his or her role is to be. Performance must then be judged on an individual basis. All of the technical expertise will be useless unless the human expertise can be fully utilized to achieve the common service objectives.

At this point, I would like to turn my attention to some positive steps which one telephone company, in this case Indiana Bell, has taken in order to better serve the individualized needs of its customers. Our story begins with a non-operations activity. Market segmentation was our first step in the delivery of an improved service process. Indiana has segmented its customer contact operation into business and consumer markets in order to provide better focus in meeting customer needs. The Marketing Department initially asked the Operations Segment to subdivide its organization, systems and facilities into market segment related groups. Thinking back to my earlier remarks concerning efficiency such a split of plant-type functions and

support systems would be totally inefficient. In addition, expertise could be lost if operations were confined to the handling of only certain market segments. After much study, it was decided that the desired market focus could be achieved in the servicing area by creating centers within centers. By that I mean the creation of sub-groups within an existing organization which would receive additional training and support tools to accomplish their improved service objectives. These people would also be measured through the use of customer specific measurements such as individual customer surveys. An example of such an entity would be a special trouble reporting number in the Centralized Repair Bureau which is manned by personnel who are sensitized to small business customer needs through receipt of additional training in fact finding, courtesy, etc.

During the remainder of my talk I would like to relate Indiana Bell's efforts which are aimed at providing excellent customers service to our major customer segment. i would like to begin by painting a peicture which reflects the unique servicing problems presented by this market segment. Sales of switching systems or networks to these customers often involve major efforts and as such are hendled by dedicated cutover teams. These teams become familiar with the customers needs in very great detail and quite often interface with a mirror-image group made up of the customer's employees. Regular meetings are held to plan cutover activities, assign open issues to specific managers, and follow up to insure closure of outstanding issues. Minutes are issued which keep all members of this special team informed of status and action items. Generally cutovers are handled in a very professional manner and customers are thoroughly pleased with their service and our efforts.

"Through excellent effort we have raised the customers level of expectation to a very high level."

Unfortunately, once the cutover is complete we revert the customer back to our normal operation. Gone is the prior planning, the regularly scheduled joint meetings, the common objectives, the attention to detail, the follow up activity...in general we have a loss of the total commitment and the personal attention to service. In the customer's eyes we have reverted back to the uncaring telephone company which does not listen to or react to individual customer needs.

Is there a solution to this dilemma? In Indiana Bell we feel we have found the answer in the form of a Major Account

Center organization or MAC. The MAC handles the provisioning and maintenance coordination for all the services offered by Indiana Bell to our largest customers. These services include POTS, Centrex, Private Line Services, etc. Customers are given one number to call for all technical interfacing and are provided with a dedicated technician or member of a pool of dedicated technicians. These technicians interface with dedicated customer technicians in order to provide focus and understanding of problems/issues.

Let me address the steps which we undertook during the formation of the MAC:

- Our initial action was a decision as to which customers were to be served in this manner. The Marketing Department provided this answer using their segmentation philosophy. Our largest customers in terms of revenues/strategic importance were labeled as Tier I customers and scheduled for such service attention. A grouping of our next largest business customers, based upon these same criteria were also identified and will over a period of time be brought into the MAC.
- A decision had to then be made as to which functions would be performed in this Center. Indiana Bell decided to provide coordination of all service order activity within the technical segment of the business. Emphasis was placed upon the inward movement of digital services, i.e. Centrex, electronic key telephone translations, wideband facilities, etc. While none of the translations were to be performed in this Center they would be reviewed for reasonableness. The Center would coordinate field installation activity under the responsibility of the same District Manager. Finally, all repair reports would be taken in the MAC and coordi-Company-wide. All statusing with the customer would be done by the Center with special emphasis on frequent contact.
- Having determined the work to be performed, a task force reviewed the number of service orders and trouble tickets generated by these customers in order to determine projected work load and information flows.
- The task force also determined the new functions deemed necessary to truly support superlative service objectives. This information was then translated into personnel requirements.
- An extremely important function was then undertaken as operating system and interface needs were examined. An existing order and trouble ticket system was embellished

along with acceptance of major status systems such as LMOS (handles POTS services) and CIMAP (Special Services) by the MAC. People interfaces were also developed so that the flow of information between various persons responsible for portions of servicing were well established.
- Another step in the process involved the training of MAC personnel in order to provide them with the needed technical and operating system knowledge.
- An extremely important function in the establishment of the MAC was the development of a customer education package. Actually two presentations were developed so that an overview of the service concept could be given to the customer's top management personnel, while another presentation containing much more detail is presented to the customer's communication manager and staff.

Now that the Major Account Center concept has been operative for nearly one year a logical question is "what are your experiences to date"? Overall the concept has been very well accepted by our major customers however, we see an ever increasing level of expectation on the part of these customers. In essence the better individualized service we give them the more they want! We find the customer's needs are constantly changing which naturally brings about constant changes within the Center. A significant challenge to an operating group is that all of the personalized attention which we provide to MAC customers tends to destroy efficiency. A flow through of service orders with minimal human intervention is nearly impossible based upon the stated objectives of the MAC concept. Perhaps the most difficult issue which we have encountered is the ability to properly communicate with the customer regarding the status of trouble reports.

To be completely effective the Center must constantly update the customer as to trouble status. This information flow is an absolute necessity in the mind of the customer however, the information does not reside in the MAC. Personnel involved in switching maintenance, engineers, billing personnel, etc. all must regularly input the status of their work efforts to the MAC technician so that he can status the customer. A need still exists for a common customer database which would serve all departments. The management of vendors who provide the switching and transmission equipment becomes very critical in this process, i.e. solutions to problems which require software development in switching machines. Without constant status from these vendors we cannot properly communicate with our customers.

Let me finish my talk with what I view are the keys to keeping customers satisfied in today's competitive environment. Customers require that we possess a very thorough knowledge of our products which requires constant training of our servicing personnel. We must also possess information regarding future technology. While you can say this information should be communicated by Marketing personnel, the customer is very prone to ask for this information from the servicing personnel with whom they interface. We must provide personalized attention, such as Indiana Bell has attempted to provide through its Major Account Center. This personalized attention must include constant statusing of solutions to service problems and prompt escalation of difficult problems. Generally customers perceive our service personnel are slow to escalate trouble reports. Finally we must manage our vendors with a firm hand, since we cannot meet the ever increasing customer demands without a complete commitment to superlative service on the part of our suppliers.

How are these customer satisfiers accomplished? I believe the active participation of interdepartmental account teams is an absolute necessity. They must provide input as to customer needs and perceptions of our actions through listening to the customer. There must be employee commitment to provide individual customer focus and measurement plans to judge the service levels provided to market segments and in some cases to individual customers. And given all of this personalized superlative service the operations personnel must perform the difficult task of achieving efficiency so as to properly manage costs and keep our products viable in the competitive marketplace.

I wish you well in pursuit of these goals!

A MAJOR CUSTOMER'S NEEDS

Donald J. Zbikowski
Communications Manager-Central Region

Westinghouse Electric Corporation

10 S. Riverside Plaza
Chicago, Illinois 60606-3763

This session will provide an overview of the Westinghouse Corporation's local and intercity communications equipment and facilities. This multi-state customer utilizes the services of many operating companies and equipment vendors. As the Telecommunications Manager-Central Region, the speaker will focus on his expectations of vendors and suggestions as to how service levels can be improved.

A MULTI-LOCATION CUSTOMER'S NEEDS

Christopher L. Davis
Vice President - Telecommunications Policy

Rexnord Data Systems

4701 W. Greenfield Ave.
Milwaukee, Wisconsin 53214

This portion of the presentation will focus on the service and support expectations a midsized (100-400 lines) customer has of the network operations group of their local operating telephone company. Areas to be addressed: 1) Project support during the installation of a new telephone system; 2) Data Communications support - trouble shooting and problem resolution; 3) Centrex Services - what support services will be required to make Centrex a viable alternative to CPE; and 4) The benefits of involving network operations in long term communications project planning.

AN ACCOUNT EXECUTIVE'S VIEW

Donald C. Caramell
Account Manager

Ohio Bell Communications

5990 W. Creek Road
Independence, Ohio 44131

This session will stress the critical role customer service (both pre-sale and post-sale) plays in today's telecommunications environment particularly involving Centrex issues. Using past experiences, it will then transition to how optimum customer service can be attained as well outlining the optimum measurement tool.

OPS-11

COMPUTER AIDED ENGINEERING/
INTEGRATED NETWORK ENGINEERING SYSTEMS

Joyce M. Rector - Chairperson

Operations Manager,
Network Engineering

Southern Bell Telephone Company

675 West Peachtree Street, N.E.
24S79 Southern Bell Center
Atlanta, Georgia 30375

Like most businesses, utility companies have problems to solve and mainstream technologies to manage that are often linked to information technology. There is also a need to improve productivity as well as a requirement for accurate, complete and timely information for decision making. Several telephone companies' approach at dealing with these issues involves computer graphics and database technologies for managing facilities, records and land base. This seminar provides an overview of Computer Aided Engineering and Facilities Management work that is currently being deployed in the areas of central office and outside plant engineering. The economics and benefits of these projects are discussed in addition to providing integrated solutions that are necessary for success. This seminar includes an industry profile of leading edge computer technologies and strategies employed by today's most successful companies and provides insights needed to achieve similar results.

Mike Lane   -- U. S. West

Randi Olsen   -- Arthur Andersen &
                       Company

Joyce Rector   -- Southern Bell

INTEGRATION OF CENTRAL OFFICE RECORDS

R. M. (Mike) Lane
Director
Network Mechanization

U. S. West
6912 South Quentin, Suite 101
Englewood, Colorado 80112

ABSTRACT

This document presents an approach to improving the efficiency of the central office engineering forces through mechanized record keeping and improved response to the ever changing market of telecommunications. The requirements of the market place require that the engineer have real-time access to the present status of all switching equipment

in absolute detailed formats. It is not unusual to have an active telephone switching office that has several installation jobs being performed almost concurrently. As a result of this kind of activity it is imperative that all central office records, graphical prints and wiring lists depict all present and planned activity relative to each location. In the predivestiture period the dominance of mechanization support for the Bell Operating Companies came from Bell Laboratories. We have undertaken a major void in mechanization support relative to improving the response of the Network Engineering forces through integrated mechanization of the engineering functionality. This area of endeavor has been given little attention over the last decade, and only recently has gained the attention of the traditional telephone companies as a major requirement of the future.

INTRODUCTION

The switching and facility network is the backbone by which the telecommunications industry not only provides services but also plans future services to the general public. As a result it is absolutely essential that complete and accurate access to the technical makeup of this network be available to the engineers responsible for providing future services and growth.

After extensive review, we at US WEST - Communications found that there was a significant void in mechanized tools available to the engineer to improve the technical response necessary to meet the needs of the customer. It became very evident that there were numerous Operational Support Systems available, but very little to support the technical engineer in design and total management of a significant investment area--the Central Office Exchange. Most of the attention has been directed at the Planning, Provisioning and Inventory related requirements with only minimal support being provided to the "role up your sleeves" requirements of the Equipment Engineer and the Detailed Engineer. Recognizing that this area has numerous fields of endeavor encompassing not only the switch itself but also areas like mainframes, power, floor plans, transmission etc., a careful study took place to ensure that all technical requirements were being fulfilled. A course of action was developed to strategically approach addressing this problem through mechanization of not only the graphical record, but also encompassing all the technical detail information relative to each specific location throughout the region.

MECHANIZED ENGINEERING RECORDS

Our initial intentions were to position the region to control and maintain all records, graphical and technical, relevant to each switching machine. As the analysis progressed it was evident that these records provided the principal framework of data to simplify the overall engineering processes relating to the current planning efforts as well as the formation of detailed equipment specifications for purposes of ordering of material and consummating the job completion requirements. A team of Subject Matter Experts representing technical disciplines throughout the region defined the functional framework of work to be accomplished. A strategy was formulated prioritizing modules of work that outlined the definition for (1) requirements for graphical CAD data (2) the compilation of tabular wiring list information (3) a module to track job schedule information relevant to engineering activity within the switch and (4) a technical makeup of a detailed equipment specification module. These four areas became the basis for mechanization efforts focused on improving the responsiveness of the engineer. The aforementioned areas comprised essentially a two to three year development effort that we deemed unacceptable from the start of the project. Each project was then broken up into elemental modules that could be accomplished in three to five month increments that could stand by themselves at any stage of the development. By first quarter 1988 core software for each of the four emphasis areas had been developed, field tested and benchmarked to ensure that the development activity was consistent with the needs of the field organizations. It has been increasingly evident that field "buy-in" during the development was an essential key ingredient for the success of the application. During the development timeframe it became obvious that the data required to maintain accurate records of the composition of our switching systems could also be useful in other areas related to management of alarm systems engineering, maximizing the opportunities for reused switching inventories and potentially integrating with existing Operational Support Systems in Provisioning (e.g. TIRKS, PICS/DCPR), in Accounting and Engineering Support areas (e.g. DOPAC, CAMIS, etc.). These issues illustrated the important need to create an access routine backbone to reach multiple systems and share, not replicate, data essential throughout the organization. We also found that it was essential that our developmental efforts not only were compatible with our immediate needs to mechanize engineering processes but could also be (1) integrated into the mechanization future of US West (2) were compatible with other developments taking place within the region and with Bellcore and (3) were flexible enough to be adapted for other future needs that might take place.

CONCLUSION

We have been able to develop, during the last twelve months, the core software

in each of the emphasis areas described above. Each of these areas has only initially begun to present benefits to the region as of the date of this paper. The proprietary nature of these developments does not permit me to divulge the exact nature of each software design. However, the potential to provide efficiencies to our organization and the possibilities for future integration of mechanized processes appear to be almost infinite!

AUTOMATION OF THE OUTSIDE PLANT ENGINEERING PROCESS

Joyce M. Rector
Operations Manager
Network Engineering

Southern Bell Telephone Company
675 West Peachtree Street
24S79 Southern Bell Center
Atlanta, Georgia 30375

ABSTRACT

In today's environment, the user must have access to a system(s) which supports individual job functions in addition to aiding numerous downstream systems in the collection and provision of data. In the telecommunications industry, advanced interactive graphics technology is applied to the conversion of outside plant records into a digital format. The resulting intelligent data base and associated graphics can then be used in conjunction with the Work Print Generation software to create an engineering work authority. Since a majority of the information that resides on the various operational systems comes from the engineering authority, a need to automatically capture and transport information to downstream systems becomes essential. The vehicle to effect this requirement is the Work Order Manager system. This administrative and communicative system allows us to share data with heterogeneous computers having different architectures and operating systems. Integrated solutions, rather than isolated ones, are necessary for success.

INTRODUCTION

Southern Bell's strategic plans include the development and deployment of the Plant Location Record Management System (PLRMS). PLRMS is an interactive graphics system that uses a minicomputer to perform the maintenance and management of the outside plant engineering records. Initially, basic PLRMS conversion consisted of mechanizing the record keeping process. This conversion effort came from the necessity to reduce operating expenses associated with our outside plant facility records as well as effect a positive impact on the engineering environment. There is also a requirement to support the Company's need to document its continuing property record and to provide productivity improving processes.

While PLRMS provides a finished, mechanized records keeping system, the scope and potential of this technology is much broader and can have a direct and growing impact on our overall job. In order to optimize the use of this huge data base of information and in order for us to take advantage of future technology, we aimed at the Work Print Generation (WPG) design phase. The ability to generate engineering work orders from a mechanized system has long been a primary goal and driving force behind our development of PLRMS. The mechanizing of jobs allows us to automate many of the downstream functions of numerous other operational systems.

To perform this process, we propose the development of a Work Order Manager. The Work Order Manager provides for a high volume of data, transmission format, communications, high activity, inter-system isolation/protection/outage detection and diversity of system vendors and hardware. The Work Order Manager will provide system access to multiple applications through a single interface.

MECHANIZATION OF THE RECORD KEEPING PROCESS

Like most companies, Southern Bell has historically managed its outside plant network by way of a manually originated and maintained plant record or atlas plat. We have more than 157,000 of these records, exclusive of conduit and manhole laydowns, and due to the difficulty in efficiently working from this manual, often incomplete and inaccurate base of information, that we were involved in early studies using graphics technology in support of the outside plant provisioning process. Early attempts at mechanizing the record keeping processes, although attractive in theory, proved to be less than satisfactory in application. In the late 1979 and early 1980 timeframe, we decided to vigorously pursue the development of a system which would methodically address each of the shortfalls we had encountered in other attempts. At the onset, we had the desire to develop a process which in its mature state would provide the user the selection of powerful, intelligent graphic and analytical tools aimed at improving the overall job performance, e.g. productivity, quality and substance.

Time and motion studies were conducted to identify and quantify the savings possible with the deployment of a mechanized system. We embarked on gathering supporting data on the functions which could be reduced, improved or eliminated through the deployment of current graphics technology. The time and motion studies which were conducted not only identified the investment in the processes, in terms

of continuing expense charges, but also defined the target processes for graphics deployment. The results of these studies were then combined with capital investment estimates to provide the base data and the framework for economic analysis. The results of the analysis proved to be very attractive from both an economic and operational viewpoint.

In pursuing the development of the intelligent graphics technology, we first targeted the maintenance of the record base through the basic application PLRMS (Plant Location Record Management System). As noted, based upon the results of the trial and the features offered by a mechanized system, a program of company-wide implementation was undertaken. Conversion to PLRMS is scheduled to complete by June, 1989. With this, we will have accomplished our initial objective which was to provide an effective means of maintaining the records associated with the current and proposed configuration of the outside facility network. While conversion to PLRMS provides for this mechanization, it does little to automate the downstream functions.

WORK PRINT GENERATION

Although mechanized records keeping is attractive, it is not the end to our needs. At this point, we have a finished, mechanized record keeping system but we have only begun the automation process. A cursory review of the engineering cycle indicates that we basically plan, design, construct and administer the outside plant network. This cycle uses information about the existing and proposed configuration of the Network--the same data built into our records system. Since much of the information (facilities and geography) is existing, it is logical that the WPG system is an extension of the basic record keeping process. For this reason and because this approach obviously offers economies of scale in areas such as methods and procedures, equipment investment, training and administration, we decided to pursue the workprint design phase.

The purpose of WPG is to provide a means to create outside plant engineering workprints from the digitized plant location records to include assignment data access, capacity expansion and general economic evaluators as well as throughput to other operational systems. A major goal is to eliminate maintaining redundant data with separate mechanized linkages. WPG as defined by Southern Bell must encompass all facets of supporting functions from the work requirement (Service Order Driven/Planned Relief) to final closeout and records posting activities.

In the fall of 1984, a time and motion study was conducted in the Newnan office of the Columbus, Georgia

Engineering District aimed at testing the feasibility of the Work Print Generation (WPG) concept. It was evident that the technology and the technique offered potential savings. As a result of the study, we undertook to develop a mechanized WPG process for use in Southern Bell. Out of this trial, a compilation of development requirements, design requirements and operational modifications resulted. Of equal importance to these operational concerns, there are a number of features the system must address in an efficient and effective manner--data integrity, data security and user friendliness.

As the project is capital intensive with long term rather than short term paybacks, it has to be frugal in its application and use of funds. The deployment strategy is a crucial issue as to timing, sequence and scope. In order to sustain conversion, to best utilize the centralized posting groups and to place the tool into the end-users' hand as expeditiously as possible, it was determined that WPG deployment should follow basic PLRMS conversion as quickly as possible. The final major area of concern is that the system and functionality must support the ultimate objective of true systems integration. We now have a tool which addresses the significant concerns which we have reviewed.

The techniques currently adopted allow the user the ability to enter a predefined data base partition for access to an index map for identifying the area in which work is to occur. Definition of the polygon may cover all or part of one or more Plant Location Records (PLRs). Once the area of interest has been identified within the data partition, the design phase of the work authorization takes place. The posting activities within the partition utilize a Facilities Rulebased Application Model Management Environment (FRAMME) which controls the user's interaction with the facilities data base. The Rulebase includes menus, procedures and feature definitions. Work Print Generation under FRAMME provides transaction processing to separate proposed from existing facilities in the data base for data integrity and security of the master data files. An Engineer using transaction processing in the Work Print Generation FRAMME application works as if the activity is taking place directly in the master files.

Features are extracted automatically, based on the data physically being modified or added. No reference information is extracted, yet the proposed changes do not affect the master data base until the approval process has been completed and the data validated and committed. Performance is improved by eliminating time-consuming batch retrievals of large amounts of reference-only information needed for a workorder. A "nopost" file which contains all of the graphic information related solely to the EWO, a partitioned data base containing the attribute information associated with those graphic elements and also transaction files are created which contain all of the information to be passed to downstream systems.

The WPG application is screen menu driven such that the users only have to point and select the activity they wish to do. The information which is a matter of record will be written into the partitioned data base and that which is useful only to the work order will be written into the "nopost" file. Once the basic design is complete, the user then creates a plot composition request which arranges the workprint(s) in some selected order. Prior to plotting, the user selects final print preparation where workprint annotations and special symbols are placed, such as load blocks and print borders. Should the user subsequently wish to further divide or merge any of the resulting prints, it can be accommodated at this time. In addition, prints can be scaled up to allow for additional annotation required for jobs such as buried cable or lightguide. After the job order has the proper approval, it is automatically preposted (minimal intervention) to the master data base and the final prints for distribution are made. Also at this time, all of the information written into the transaction file(s) is available for downstream loading into the various operational systems. Upon completion, the job order is removed from the WPG system and is archived.

WORK ORDER MANAGER

Recognizing that we have now pushed the technology from the crude graphics record keeping system, through the use and continued development of the data base into a tool useful to the end user, we are now moving rapidly toward an environment where we will collect information at its point of conception and automate the delivery of that data to downstream operational systems. To do this effectively requires the development of an intelligent bulk data handling process. We are currently working under a contract for the development of such a process called the Work Order Manager. The Work Order Manager will act as a data switch to receive data, format it into new packets, transmit the data and track the status.

The Work Order Manager software includes a data element dictionary, a transaction table and a connecting system table. The data element dictionary defines the name of each data attribute recognized, the tag value name for the attribute, the systems which may need each element and the transactions which include those elements. The Work Order Manager establishes standards for data communications between operational systems as well as identifies data attributes which comprise the corporate data base. The Flexible Computer Interface Form (FCIF) language is the application layer protocol to be used for communications between each system. The Work Order Manager is capable of customer configuration to meet the needs of the geographic territory it serves. The configuration consists of identifying various system components, communications addresses and locally defined parameters.

This Work Order Manager will provide the controls and synergy necessary to begin integrating the various systems we use. In particular, it provides the necessary administrative environment so that the user only has to work with a single process to access and use data resident on a number of different systems.

CONCLUSIONS

In corporations, both large and small, there is an ever increasing need for accurate, complete and timely information for decision making. Locating and retrieving this information can be difficult. In addition, there is a requirement to exchange information with other organizations as well as to globally populate data bases of downstream systems. In our Company, we have taken advantage of advanced technology to convert our engineering records from a manual to a digital format through the PLRMS application. Recognizing PLRMS as the keystone process, through the Work Print Generation process, we built a set of tools to allow the user to become integrated into the Corporate data network. These tools provide graphics, analytical and/or inventory functions and unimpeded access to a variety of information necessary in the conduct of assigned tasks. In addition, this Work Print Generation process provides the foundation for the Work Order Manager in response to the necessity to collect large volumes of data at its point of origin and automate the loading of that data into downstream operational systems.

GLOSSARY OF ACRONYMS

CPR	Continuing Property Records
DPP	Discounted Payback Period
EWO	Engineering Work Order
FCIF	Flexible Computer Interface Format
FRAMME	Facilities Rulebased Application Model Management Environment
ISDN	Integrated Services Digital Network
ISO/OSI	International Standards Organization/Open Systems Interconnection
JMOS	Job Management Operations System
LEIM	Loop Electronic Inventory Module
LEIS	Loop Engineering Information System
LFACS	Loop Facility Assignment and Control System
LTEE	Long Term Economic Evaluator
LTROR	Long Term Rate Of Return
PLR	Plant Location Record
PLRMS	Plant Location Record Management System
SME	Subject Matter Expert
WOM	Work Order Manager
WPG	Work Print Generation

AN INDUSTRY PERSPECTIVE:
OPPORTUNITIES AND STRATEGIES

Randi L. Olsen
Marketing Director

Arthur Andersen & Company
717 17th Street, Suite 1900
Denver, Colorado 80202

ABSTRACT

Innovations in systems integration provide great opportunities for the telecommunications industry to cut its operating costs by as much as fifty percent. The telecommunications industry can learn from the experiences of manufacturers in other industries who have tried systems integration and succeeded. Systems integration, the linking of unrelated hardware and software, has enabled many manufacturers to reduce lead time, double capacity and cut costs. Results were made possible through the sharing of ideas and methodologies, and the simplify-automate-integrate approach to implementation. To illustrate how this can be accomplished in a telecommunications environment, this seminar offers an example of how systems integration has already been achieved at a telephone company and the benefits that are possible not only for this company, but also for all other such companies that are willing to make the systems integration move.

INTRODUCTION

As recently as five years ago, coast-to-coast hand wringing among economists was almost audible, as learned observers of the world marketplace all but pronounced American industry dead. We don't often hear that doleful sound anymore. Our overall national industry is rebounding to such an extent that U.S. manufacturing firms are beginning to compete keenly with the Japanese in most fields.

What caused the turnaround?

As much as anything, the turnaround began when U.S. manufacturers began finding ways to integrate information systems, support systems, and computer-aided engineering systems. In so doing, manufacturers dramatically cut costs while improving quality.

U.S. manufacturers also produced at least three valuable lessons that merit close study by the telecommunications industry:

- Multiple-vendor hardware, application software, and operating systems _can_ be integrated.
- To integrate off-the-shelf or custom-designed software and multiple operating environments, it is not necessary to reinvent techniques that already exist.
- Before extensively mechanizing or systematizing a process, the process should be simplified.

If our telecommunications industry would apply these lessons---and in so doing integrate its systems---the industry would, in my opinion, cut its cost of doing business by a third to a half!

Let me repeat that. Systems integration can cut telephone company operating costs by as much as fifty percent!

By "systems integration," I mean the linking of disparate devices so that they can communicate with each other in such a way as to minimize redundancies and the manual handling of data.

My claim that systems integration can cut telephone company operating costs in half is based largely on what has been accomplished by manufacturers. Perhaps, at this point, you feel compelled to say, "Fine, for the manufacturers, but what has manufacturing to do with the telecommunications industry?" I'm glad you asked. It has everything to do with you. Providing telecommunication and information services _is_ a manufacturing process and business. Like all manufacturers, you respond to customer demand with new products and/or services; you equip your networks to accommodate those products; you distribute your products in such a way that the customer can readily buy them; you engage in a customer service process to assure customer satisfaction, an order process, a product modification process, and so on. As an old birder once said, "If it walks like a duck, swims like a duck, flies like a duck, and quacks like a duck, then it must be a duck." Though you may not realize it, you do engage in manufacturing, and you, too, can benefit from systems integration.

COSTS CAN BE CUT SUBSTANTIALLY

The most obvious successes of systems integration can be found in the electronics and aerospace industries. For instance, a major aerospace supplier reduced its lead time for all functions of its manufacturing process by ninety percent! Incredibly, the time from design to finished product was cut from more than a month-and-a-half, or fifty days, to just two days!

Systems integration successes are everywhere among manufacturers, even in the so-called rustbelt. It might surprise you that some of the most eye-popping and innovative systems integration can be found in the steel and automobile industries. Consider the following examples:

- Walbro Corporation of Caro, Michigan, a maker of automotive fuel pumps, cut manufacturing lead time by 97 percent, reduced its need for assembly space by 40 percent and warehouse space by 20 percent. It doubled the capacity of its factory while cutting labor costs by 24 percent, work-in-process inventory by 99 percent, and defects by 14 percent.
- Harley-Davidson Motor Company's Milwaukee plant cut lead time by 80 percent, increased its annual inventory turnover from seven to twenty, reduced set-up costs by 85 percent, and cut labor costs 38 percent per unit.
- Cherry Electric, which makes automotive switches at a Waukegan, Illinois plant, cut space requirements by 40 percent, labor by 35 percent, and inventory by an average of about 50 percent.

Among instrument makers:

- Cambridge Instrument's Sparks, Maryland plant cut lead time by 60 percent, space for machining by 39 percent, labor by 21 percent, set-up and changeover costs by 55 percent, and inventory investment by an average of more than 50 percent.

In the leisure field:

- BSN, which makes weight benches and soccer goals in Dallas, cut lead time by 80 percent, space requirements by 25 percent, and inventory by an average of more than 60 percent, while improving productivity by 50 percent and greatly improving customer service.

I could go on with these successes for the rest of the day, but let me sum them up this way: Several hundred consulting clients that have implemented systems integration, all have had similar results. All have cut overall costs by reducing waste and inventory investment and using employees, equipment, and materials more efficiently. All have maintained or improved product quality, which usually resulted in greater buyer satisfaction, reduced maintenance and warranty costs, and reduced product liability. All added flexibility to their production processes, allowing a variety of products to be manufactured efficiently using the same equipment. All were able to respond better to the market due to an increased ability to change product characteristics easily.

UNRELATED COMPONENTS CAN BE INTEGRATED

One of the great lessons the telecommunications industry can learn from other manufacturers is that while components may be unrelated, they can be integrated. Some idea of what is possible can be found in the accomplishments of the Ingersoll Milling Machine Company of Rockford, Illinois, A pioneer in systems integration, Ingersoll, as long ago as 1981, began to integrate hardware that included: an IBM 3033U, a National Advanced Systems NAS-9060 corporate host, Allen-Bradley 8200 controllers used for CNS tool management, an Allen-Bradley ABC-AM distributed NC network system, a number of minis from Digital Equipment Corporation and Hewlett-Packard used for special functions and localized data processing, and microcomputers ranging from IBM to Digital, HP and Apple. Ingersoll's integration includes several data bases, high-security and high-integrity protection routines, and sophisticated disaster recovery systems.

In recent years, manufacturers have made solid progress in overcoming one of the major problems of connecting unrelated components. Several years back, because hardware costs had dropped so dramatically, many factory functions were automated, creating thousands of new workplace technologies, an uncountable number of vendors and products, and turf wars in which in-house combatants remained loyal to the death to their hardware and software. For a long time, these islands of automation actually inhibited the linking of functions; components were not compatible and there was no standardization. But while converting an entire manufacturing process to common hardware and software is not practical for many good reasons, manufactures have moved toward standardization in two ways: pressure on vendors and internally-designed links.

General Motors has been a leader in both approaches. More than a decade and a half, ago, various GM users of process control equipment pooled their experience with machines that talked to each other. That alliance of users ultimately pushed for a system that would conform to a model of the International Standards Organization, an open-systems interconnect model with seven layers of communication. Called the Manufacturing Automation Protocol (MAP), the GM program attracted wide support among other manufacturers. The MAP program has pushed as close as anything to standards and has produced the ability to create otherwise incompatible systems that use the same protocols for sending data back and forth.

NO NEED TO REINVENT WHAT ALREADY EXISTS

Another lesson telecommunications companies can learn from other manufacturers is that integration can be speeded by sharing ideas. These companies have already developed solutions and/or problem-solving methodologies to address many of the problems of linking systems. These solutions or solution approaches are readily available to members of the telecommunications industry by at least two means:

- Since they are your customers and you do not compete with them, other manufacturers will usually be glad to share their achievements with you. Just ask them.
- You can avail yourself of facilities dedicated to capturing the best-known systems integration knowledge, discovering new truths, and demonstrating how it all can be applied---one such facility is the Automation, Technical, and Operations Laboratory (ATOL), a systems integration center in London, England.

Essentially, ATOL helps information managers of large engineering projects cure their clusterheadaches. You know them well. There's the massive volume of documentation; there's the wide variety of data types; there are the complex interrelationships between drawings, specifications, QA schedules, and others; and there's the large number of players. This research facility currently integrates the hardware and software of more than 35 different suppliers, including IBM, Xerox, DEC, Tektronix, Apollo, and Apple.

ATOL has already demonstrated many systems integration benefits, several of which suggest that the wheel has already been invented for use by telecommunications companies. In a variety of ways, ATOL has:

- Reduced the elapsed time from the start of a product's design to the completion of production;
- Reduced the number of engineering changes late in a design process and their attendant costs;
- Improved control of design and fabrication;
- Eliminated numerous redundancies;
- Enabled parallel engineering and design for enhanced maintenance; and
- Improved accuracy and timeliness of documentation.

ATOL's use of existing technology, including document scanning, optical disks, expert systems, and relational data bases, has major implications for the management of technical information. Scanners capture information from paper and, with the use of Artificial Intelligence (AI), transform alphanumeric data into an electronic form. Optical disks can be used to store these vast quantities of electronic data. Thousands of drawings, documents, and images can be held on a single disk and accessed rapidly. Data bases handle complex interrelationships between various elements of engineering. Keep in mind, however, that it is not these individual technologies which enable the streamlining of the business process; it is their integration which represents the breakthrough.

ATOL developed, for example:

- A systems integration architecture for a major oil company to enable it to control and configure all the technical information associated with the design, development and operation of a North Sea platform;
- An integrated system for a utility, which involved the electronic translation of 20,000 local authority maps from paper, showing every house on the map---automated scanning techniques and AI routines have resulted in savings, over the life of the project, of 30 man-years of effort;
- A text recognition system based on AI techniques that enables a shipbuilder to transform paper-based parts data into an electronic data base; and
- Other commercial applications ranging from insurance to exhibit design.

SIMPLIFY FIRST, THEN AUTOMATE AND INTEGRATE

The telecommunications industry can also learn from other manufacturers that it is crucially important to simplify at the _front end_ of automation. Traditionally, telephone companies have automated functions as quickly as they could, no matter how complex the function. Afterward, they would apply fix upon fix, band-aid upon band-aid, in an attempt to optimize the function. As a consequence, this industry today has large operations support systems whose work processes were mechanized manually, step by step, uniquely and independently of the overall business planning process. The result has been unnecessarily complex. Had these companies understood the need for and benefits of business process planning, they would have simplified the functions first and then developed an efficient core system with which to work.

To see for yourself how the management of information can be simplified, I encourage you to visit research facilities, where you can also view the principle of flexible manufacturing in action, the application of which requires supportive communication and information technologies. In some of these facilities, you will be able to view technologies that capture and transfer data and handle and transport material. In an environment representing hardware and software vendors, you will see supervisory systems, MRP II, monitoring

and controlling processes, WAN, LAN (MAP/TOP) communications, and plantwide communications architectures. The methodology of the Systems Integration Center can be reduced to three simple steps:

- _Simplify_, which entails reducing or eliminating tasks that do not add value to the product, examining quality control, and structuring business processes so they flow smoothly.
- _Automate_, which entails applying automation discretely and effectively to logical points in the manufacturing process.
- _Integrate_, which means combining systems to cut costs, increase flexibility, cut lead times, eliminate redundant data applications, and generally gain or sustain a competitive edge.

These steps represent an evolutionary, reduced-risk approach to systems integration. It is an approach which has both long-term strategic and short-term tactical implications.

SYSTEMS INTEGRATION APPLIED TO A TELEPHONE COMPANY

As a quick demonstration of how integrated systems can help a telephone company, let us take a peek at one of your peers, whom we will disguise and refer to as Inland Telephone Company. Inland has ten million Access Lines (AL) and revenues of $5 billion. Its computer-aided engineering function consists of multiple systems: IBM PCs and XTs, IBM compatibles, VAX computers, and IBM mainframes. The mainframe data base is on an IBM 3090. The VAX systems provide the graphics and engineering design applications. The XTs run DOS as well as emulate Tektronix graphics, handle electronic mail and spread sheet applications, and run all kinds of proprietary programs. Because Inland's systems are continually becoming more integrated with other support systems, there is just one engineering data base under the IBM 3090 and one graphics data base under the VAX 8850. From the Engineering Workstation (EWS) an engineer can go into the system at any time of the day or night to determine the status of a job that is in the works and can literally complete the job without leaving the EWS.

To see how these capabilities are applied, consider this example. Based on a revised forecast for a geographical area, a Central Office (CO) reinforcement job reflects a growth rate increase. The planning engineer receives a message from the system and a common data base that updates all applications. In this case, the planning engineer discovers that a particular job now needs to be advanced. An alert to the design engineer and supervising engineer goes into the system, and because something is different, the next time each engineer works at his terminal he will be advised to look at the job and review its status. Upon seeing that the growth has changed, our design engineer decides to make a change. Working at his EWS, he moves the job ahead six months. When he does that, the data base notifies other applications to not only move the job up six months but also change and advance the material. At the same time, the system indicates a need to notify the records control that detailed design must be finished four months sooner than planned. The data base management application also alerts the procurement department that a materials order change is coming and advises the power, or special design, engineers that a drawing or specification must be made sooner than planned.

This relatively simple example is systems integration at work. With such a system, the Inland Telephone Company anticipates reductions in its engineering costs of about thirty-five percent because redundancies have been eliminated. The system is also being integrated with operations support systems. The final payoff: a reduction of engineering and administrative costs that exceeds fifty percent. The results at this company are typical of the opportunities telephone companies have through systems integration. The secret is just hard work: an understanding that integration can be achieved, a seeking out of people who have done it, and an adaptation of those methods. Inland Telephone Company simply went to several major aircraft companies and obtained knowledge from their people on how to go about integrating information systems and operations support systems. It then adapted what it discovered into a unique, integrated manufacturing system of its own.

As demonstrated by this example, the telecommunications industry can effect enormous savings by applying the lessons learned by manufacturers. Indeed, systems integration is already producing significant savings at many Regional Bell Operating Companies (RBOC). However, the best is yet to come. According to studies by the prestigious San Francisco Consulting Group, total integration of systems can save each RBOC $1.2 billion--per year!

Those incredible savings would result from a thirty percent increase in resource utilization and a fifty percent reduction of labor. If universally adopted, total integration of information systems would annually save the telecommunications industry a whopping $14 billion![1]

HOW TELEPHONE COMPANIES CAN PHASE IN SYSTEMS INTEGRATION

What then are telephone companies waiting on? The answer has to do with the enormous amount of money it would take to not only integrate systems but also replace much of their capital equipment. Although not old by telephone company standards, most of the equipment has largely been rendered obsolete by technology. However, it must eventually be replaced, and it must be integrated.

The question is how to proceed. First, let me tell you what I think it would cost to replace and integrate one of your major inventory systems. Here's the figure: $400 Million. Why that's more than the cost of all those systems you installed in the late 1960s. "Preposterous!" you say. Okay, now let me give you another figure: $50 Million. That's more like it, isn't it. It might go down hard, but you don't have to be a python to swallow it. And therein lies the strategy. You must cut the cost of totally integrating your systems down to bite size. Fifty million dollars annually is bite size. On the other hand, it's still a big bite. Thus, you must figure out a way to phase in a totally integrated system--over a relatively long period of time--and to do so in such a way that you are never outdistanced by technology. My buzz term for this is: No Sweat Migration Strategy.

This means that you do not need to immediately throw out all of your existing equipment, systems and procedures and replace them with the latest state-of-the-art technologies. Rather, you must evaluate your business objectives, rationally review your work flow, and develop a plan for implementing the right blend of solutions for your particular company.

The product life cycle of telephone equipment is approximately ten years. During those ten years, "enabling technology" breakthroughs affect the hardware and software capabilities of your systems. In addition, business conditions and competition are changing today and will change again tomorrow. Therefore, you must continually update the migration strategy and your projects to acknowledge - and even anticipate - these changes. The simplify-automate-integrate cycle is not a static, one-shot effort; it is a flexible business process.

So, what does all of this mean? What are the implications for you? What must you do next? It means that you must take a blind leap of faith, which is necessary in order to overcome what I call the "Lazy 'S' Syndrome". You may be familiar with the "S" shaped curve of the product life cycle.

The graph line starts lazily, curling downward for awhile and turning sharply upward for a long stretch, and then ending lazily in a slow downward and upward curl. Well, the "Lazy S" curves of products overlap. It's a good deal more comfortable to stay with a "Lazy S" at the top curl of its career than to jump off and change the sharp ride upward of another "Lazy S". To switch is to give up security for a roll of the dice. It's like taking a step backward to gamble on a long ride upward. But that's what must be done. The telecommunications industry must follow the example of its fellow manufacturers by implementing systems integration solutions. If each telecommunications company expects to stay competitive and take that exhilarating ride upward to greater financial performance, it must first get off its "Lazy S".

REFERENCES

1. SFC Highlights, "SOS for OSS", September 1987, pp. 5.

PERFORMANCE MONITORING AND SURVEILLANCE

Barbara A. LaGuardia - Chairperson
Supervisor
Operations, Administration & Maintenance
Planning
AT&T Bell Laboratories
200 Park Plaza
Naperville, IL 60566-7050

ABSTRACT

Rapid advancement in telecommunication technology is driving public and private communication networks to increase communication bandwidths, integrate circuit and packet technologies, and offer more sophisticated services. Switching, transmission, and operations systems approaches to network quality are more diverse than ever with products from many vendors becoming integrated into the network.

With these phenomena, operating companies and manufacturers alike must confront fundamental challenges in the cost of doing business and traditional views of the network maintenance. New technology also promises increased opportunities for pro-active and preventive network maintenance capabilities.

This seminar explores the history of facility surveillance, and current and future philosophies and applications in performance monitoring and surveillance.

Frank Denniston   -- New York Telephone

Jim Leeson   -- Bell Northern
                        Research

Joanne Wilson   -- AT&T Bell
                        Laboratories

Joseph Drzewiecki   -- GTE Communications
                        Systems

Wayne Vande Wall   -- AT&T Bell
                        Laboratories

HISTORY OF FACILITY SURVEILLANCE

Frank Denniston
General Manager
Switching and Transmission Operations

New York Telephone Company
1095 Avenue of the Americas
Room 2836
New York, New York 10036

ABSTRACT

This paper discusses the development, within the Bell System in particular, of facility surveillance and control systems from the early 1940's to the present day. It also necessarily tracks with the deployment of early analog carrier systems through current high speed optical fiber systems.

In order to understand the development of these systems, digressions are taken to explain the development of existing protocols which are important to understand for the developer or implementor of any modern surveillance systems.

INTRODUCTION

The need for facility surveillance systems has been recognized for about fifty years. Particularly as carrier systems and remote radio relay stations proliferated, economic and service requirements caused the telephone companies to consider the deployment of alarm and control systems primarily for long haul carrier systems. These systems continued to develop over time and set the pattern for future developments.

In the late 1960's and early 1970's as T1 carrier began to proliferate, various schemes were developed by various manufactures to track carrier failures in the local exchange trunking and within metropolitan the local operating companies began to organize Facility Surveillance Centers.

In the late 1970's fiber deployment began in earnest, surveillance schemes for this technology also started to develop, many of which were based on existing embedded systems.

Today fiber is the facility of choice for most inter office routes and we are nearing the point, where it will become the economic vehicle for most loop application. In order to support this, the newest generation of surveillance systems are currently beginning to be deployed or developed. These systems are beginning to break away from the embedded architecture but will necessarily also continue to support older embedded technology.

This paper will trace the evolution of this surveillance from the earliest wire line carrier to the Gigabit Fiber Systems.

COMMON FUNCTIONS

From the earliest days, the surveillance systems, showed some common architectural similarities. The names of the systems sometimes were varied (e.g., Alarm and Control, Telemetry). The common aspects were:

1. Alarm - Remote stations transmit

alarms (polled or as the event occurred) to the central station.

2. Status - The central station polls the alarm station for more detailed status at the remote location.

3. Control - The central station sends a signal to the remote station to cause some action to take place.

Over time the degree of intelligence in both the central station and the remote stations increased and the concept of a "surveillance system" developed from a true system to a transport protocol (e.g., E2A) with the system requirement being met by various operational support systems constrained by the functionality of the remote, the embedded transport protocols, and the output of the network elements.

THE BEGINNING

The first surveillance system developed in the late thirties supported the remote alarm of one J or K carrier repeater station. The system operated using step-by-step selectors at a 10 pulse per second rate, and had the capability of sending ten status indicators as well as one alarm report. No remote actions could be ordered up by this system.

B1

The second major surveillance system was B1 Alarm and Control System which was developed in the late 1940's and was initiated to supervise L carrier which was then being deployed both for telephone as well as to support the national distribution of network television. With this system, up to 10 unmanned main stations could be surveilled and controlled from a single maintenance center.

The system utilized two 16 gauge interstitial pairs; signalled at ten pulses per second to ground over 3 of the wires (called channels) using a differential DX signalling; the fourth wire was utilized to compensate for difference in ground potential between stations. Terminals would generate a major or minor alarm on channel one and send to the maintenance center. The maintenance center would query the alarmed station by dialing a 3 digit code (the first digit specifying the station) while the next two digits specified one of 100 order leads which directed the remote station to begin scanning the maximum 168 station alarms. (Some of these status points were not available as they were used for housekeeping and synchronization.)

The remote generated 168 pulses on channel 2 which were utilized to synchronize the central station. A state change would be sent on channel 3 at the point in the scan that a ground was encountered from the network elements.

Alarms were decoded by placing on a sheet over a bank of neon lights which were selected and locked by the counting circuit output "anded" with the C channel.

C

Type C alarm and control circuit was developed in the early fifties to support the development of TD-2 microwave. (It later was enhanced to surveill TD-3, TH1 and TH2.) It utilized a one way two wire VF circuit for alarms and a 4 wire full duplex VF circuit order circuit for status and control and voice order wire. Each remote station transmitted a tone (one of six) on the alarm circuit; the loss of tone indicated an alarm or circuit problem. Upon receipt of the alarm the control station would send a scan order on the order wire by sending a spurt of a minimum of two tones (actually 1600 Hz modulated sequentially by two lower frequency tones). This would cause a scan of 56 leads (42 indicators, 10 for checking, one no alarm, and three station indication). The remote would simultaneously send 900 Hz pulses to synchronize the receive station together with a 700 Hz pulse to indicate a ground lead. The output of the detectors would be "anded" to drive light displays. These would be decoded with overlay paper.

E

The E Telemetry systems began to be developed in the late 1960's. The first was the E1 status reporting and control system. It was the first solid state system. It utilized a 4 wire V. F. multipoint circuit and signalled at a rate of 75 or 150 bits/sec. The system was the first to utilize an alarm polling mode to determine both circuit continuity as well as presence of alarms, status conditions and control (remote switching) was performed as a result of addressing the remotes directly.

A 24 bit word format was utilized (16 bits of information, one control bit (bit 1) and 7 parity bits for error correction). In addition, 4 bits (3 ones followed by a zero) were used to synchronize the central and remote units at the start of each word.

Each master station could address up to 256 remotes. Up to 16 alarm status were sent from each remote in the alarm polling mode. For status polling, the master could address 16 status groups at each remote. Each status group could respond with up to 16 words per group.

In order to exercise the control function, two words were sent from the master station. This allowed up to 4096 addressable contact closures at the remote station. The system automatically responded with a "quick response" indicating that the order was accomplished. It was no longer necessary to verify with a status command. The interface to the network elements was either grounds or contact closures.

E2

E2 status reporting and control system was developed in the 70's. It differs from the E1 system in a number of ways:

- Transmission rate of 600 bits/second.

- Preparatory sequence of 6.5 bits rather than 4.

- Word structure remains the same as with E1

- Scan points and addressable contacts are similar.

The interface to the network elements was contact closures or grounds.

The E2 system introduced two central station functions. The first "Manual Alarm Central" operated as did all the systems from B1 in that the alarms, were treated separately as a higher class "status" and, details were gathered after the receipt of the alarm by a status poll. This manual system also contains a 4 word "status display" unit from which developed the 64 bit "display" terminology.

The other unit a "Status Polling System" did not utilize the alarm methodology or the specific alarm polling word allowed by the protocol. Instead all status groups were polled automatically in turn.

E2A Telemetry

This marked a major departure from the earlier systems, when this was developed, in the late 1970's the concept of a complete system was abandoned (i.e., all components of the earlier system; central station, remotes and transmission protocols were integrated).

E2A telemetry was reduced to a transmission protocol. The central station part of the overall functions of alerting, statusing, and control were incorporated as part of minicomputer application systems (i.e., SCCS, TCAS,

TASC). Multiple application specific remotes were developed (e.g., SCC Remotes, CCPMS, Advanced Telemetry Processor, General Telemetry Processor). Other remotes were developed which were more general in use and were utilized by more than one application system (e.g., Status and Command).

The protocol varied from E2 in the following manner:

a) Transmission speed was upped to 1200 baud.

b) The start sequence was 13 bits long (12 ones and one zero) used only on the first word, as well as the addition of a continue bit after the parity field. In all other matters the word structure was similar to E2.

c) A three word order protocol was added to operate relays at the far end. The "quick response" format used earlier was utilized to minimize the need for a subsequent status poll.

CARRIER DEVELOPMENT

When T Carrier started to be heavily deployed in major metropolitan areas in the late 60s through 1970's, it became obvious that some sort of operational support system would be necessary to aid in the managing and maintenance of the growing electronic facility system. TCAS (T Carrier Administrative System) was developed to monitor the contact closures from the CGA's associated with the network elements (i.e., D channel banks). This system was heavily deployed in many large metropolitan areas. Northest Electronics (now NT) developed a DFMS system which in addition to the TCAS functionality could also monitor the error rate of the DS-1 line using bipolar violations (e.g., 10-6 error rate) and thus could notify the central station of impending failures. It utilized an "E2A like" protocol from the central station to the remote.

Further developments in transmission technology drove vendors into developing more intelligence in the E2A remote. The economics of developing discrete contact closure input and output devices together with the cost of cabling to the remotes drove the vendor into developing a new interface (TBOS) from the remote to the Network Elements. TBOS (Telemetry Byte Oriented Serial) required a single 4 wire local parallel multipoint circuit. With this protocol, the telemetry remote periodically polls the network elements (NE) using TBOS words (12 bits; 1 start bit, 8 bit pay loads, 1 parity and two stop bits at 2400 baud). The NEs respond to the polls by sending the required number of TBOS words to the remote. The remote responds to the poll from the central station (e.g., E2A telemetry) with alarm or status.

In many of the more intelligent remotes the response to the polls is processed to determine whether the data should be alarmed, or thresholded (e.g., fiber error rates can be reported at any time they exceed a high level threshold or, if they exceed a lower level threshold some number of times in a 15 minute period). If the data element is considered to be an alarm indicator, the remote unit will respond to an alarm status poll from the central station.

NEWER SYSTEMS

Due to the growth of fiber systems (1.7 GB/s systems are relatively common) it has become necessary for the fiber vendor to develop their own proprietary system (e.g., NEC 8500) which provide full functionality to their systems but also, in most cases, support alarms status and some control functions for other manufacturers equipment.

TRANSMISSION PROTOCOL DEVELOPMENT

The transmission protocols between the host and remotes seem to be leaving E2A and moving towards X.25 to provide the transport function. Many of the vendors on the marketplace seem to be striving to meet these requirements as well as supporting, contact closure and other remote protocols (TBOS and TABS). The element lacking in much of the remote architecture is the lack of support for some of the remote provisioning and testing functions present in many newer NEs (e.g., DDM-1000, FT-G) which present a RS232B Snyder Protocol for local technicians access.

OPERATIONAL SUPPORT SYSTEM DEVELOPMENT

In the discussion of the E2A telemetry systems, it was pointed out that the alarm status and control functions were migrated into specialized operational support systems. The earliest facility system of this type was TCAS, which in addition to the traditional functions, added the capability to do some pattern analysis as well as to create and track trouble tickets.

The current generation of operational support systems continue to have expanded on that functionality by providing:

1) Communication links to work with other embedded OSSs (e.g., TIRKS, CIMAP).

2) E2A protocol links to pick up embedded remotes (e.g., TCAS).

3) Improved and expanded pattern analysis.

4) Superior computerized graphical depiction of network.

SUMMARY

Since the thirties, facility surveillance while functionally not varying from the alarm, status and control functions, has received increasing attention and vastly wider deployment. Its early deployment was primarily driven by economic considerations; either cost (e.g., the large amount of revenue that would be lost on a toll call if facilities were unavailable) and was early-on primarily an AT&T Long Lines function. Due to the lower incremental costs to add surveillance and control functions to the network elements, as well as the growth of exceeding complex and vulnerable networks, it expanded into the operations of the local exchange companies.

The increase of reliability of NEs and the development of network elements which are more self healing, still will require intelligent surveillance and management. Such management requires information and the capability to take action. Therefore, coupled with the customers increasing expectation for nearly faultless transmission performance, further growth and increased functionality of facility surveillance can be expected to continue.

ENSURING END-TO-END DIGITAL
PERFORMANCE THROUGH
CENTRALIZED SURVEILLANCE/MAINTENANCE

Jim Leeson, John Gruber, Allan Sand
BNR

P.O. Box 3511, Station 'C'
Ottawa, Ontario, Canada, K1Y 4H7

Don Lachance

Northern Telecom Inc.
P.O. Box 649, Concord, NH   03301

ABSTRACT

The intent of this paper is to present a performance-based process to support network maintenance activities which are related to, and thereby address, end-user needs. The process consists of an integrated view of network performance objectives, performance monitoring capabilities, and maintenance limits. There are two main parts to the process. The first is top-down/planning oriented, and involves the following steps:

- determination of end-user needs in terms of long-term, end-to-end digital transmission performance objectives, and allocation of these objectives to maintenance entities; and

- expression of objectives as shorter-term limits consistent with maintenance needs.

The second part of the process is bottom-up/operations oriented, and involves the following steps:

- continuous in-service performance monitoring of network elements, and reporting of the resulting performance data to a centralized surveillance center;

- comparison of this data to the short term maintenance limits derived as part of the top-down process; and

- initiation and support of maintenance action through additional analysis of performance data.

INTRODUCTION

In today's telecommunication networks, a number of converging trends are contributing to current concepts in network-level surveillance of digital transmission performance. Firstly, communications users are becoming more knowledgeable and demanding about their performance needs. A complementary trend is the advances in silicon/software techniques which are improving the ability of Network Elements (NE) and Mediating Devices (MD) to satisfy this new user emphasis, by means of performance monitoring. The monitoring functions in NEs will increasingly be able to take advantage of the performance indicators being built into digital signal formats. Finally, there continues to be progress in the standardization of transmission performance parameters and objectives.

Performance monitoring in the context of this paper means the capture of system performance data without impacting user information transfer (i.e., non-intrusive, in-service monitoring). It is a continuous process, including the collection, preprocessing, and accumulation of the result of performance measurement in NEs. In addition, network-level surveillance

implies an Operations System (OS) for centralized collection and evaluation of performance information. A significant use of the surveillance capability is to support network maintenance.

Efficient maintenance is one of the driving forces for performance surveillance. It is a tool which allows prioritization of trouble conditions, and a staged responses to them, determined by the level of observed performance (i.e., maintenance limits). Therefore, the intelligence incorporated in an OS is central to the prompt responses to trouble conditions as indicated by an appropriate set of maintenance limits. The accumulation of performance data (history) can help verify problems perceived by the end users of telecommunications services.

There are three aspects of transmission performance which are central to the development and application of network surveillance; objectives, monitoring, and maintenance limits.

In relation to network performance objectives, the T1Q1 subcommittee of the ECSA, is dealing with parameters and levels of performance. [1] Internationally, the basic level of digital error performance recommended in a digital network, including an Integrated Services Digital Network (ISDN), is given in CCITT Rec. G.821. However, individual network providers may need to meet higher performance levels or establish more comprehensive performance objective plans.

Monitoring features are implemented in NEs or MDs. The T1M1 subcommittee is addressing the NE functionality and interfaces with OSs.

Maintenance limits and maintenance support processes are one of the applications implemented in an OS. These may be TELCo specific to reflect operating needs, but should also be compatible with performance objectives and standardized monitoring features.

An effective strategy, with regard to performance surveillance, is one which recognizes a close relationship among the above aspects of network performance. For instance, they should be linked by a common set of performance parameters. We refer to this as an integrated performance strategy. The interaction among the three major elements of an integrated performance strategy is illustrated in Figure 1.

PERFORMANCE OBJECTIVES

The transmission performance of

all-digital connections in a communications network is specified by a number of parameters. These include:

- Percent Error Free Seconds (PEFS) (or Error Seconds, ES)

- Severely Errored Seconds (SES) (Including Short Interruptions, e.g., out-of-frame events)

- Bit Error Ratio (BER) (e.g., Degraded Minute [DM])
At 64 kb/s they are defined as follows:
  ES - a second containing one or more errors
  SES - a second having a BER $> 10^{-3}$
  DM - 1 minute having a BER $> 10^{-6}$ (excluding SESs)

The above parameters are applicable to circuit mode network connections rather than, for instance, a packet switched service. This paper treats the circuit mode specifically, although the concepts have more general application.

The format of performance objectives recognizes that the short-term behavior of digital systems may vary greatly. These systems operate with negligible impairment most of the time, but may occasionally degrade in performance. Specification of performance in terms of the number of intervals of degraded performance is consistent with both system behavior, and the way in which impairments are actually perceived by users. This implies that it is impractical to specify performance only in terms of a simple parameter threshold level which must always be met. Over time, some probability of being worse than a given threshold must be accepted, although it can be limited to a very small amount of time. This concept provides a basis for developing maintenance limits. The limits should be triggered by the accumulation of too many intervals for which performance is degraded below the parameter threshold level.

Maintenance limits apply to network elements, usually referred to as maintenance entities for this purpose. As a starting point for the development of maintenance limits, a scheme for allocating end-to-end objectives to the maintenance entity level is required. As discussed above, a time varying assumption fits most observed behavior, even in the short term. Therefore, the allocation of end-to-end (or interface-to-interface) performance is accomplished by dividing the total allowed number of degraded intervals, among the maintenance entities in a connection.

The implication of this for performance monitoring is that each monitored parameter should be evaluated for a standardized time interval, and a decision made as to whether the interval is degraded or not. With certain of the more recent OS designs, much of this analysis is done by an MD to reduce traffic and processing load on the OS.

TELECOMMUNICATIONS MANAGEMENT NETWORK (TMN)

Currently in the North American telecommunications industry, there are a variety of approaches to Operations, Administration, Maintenance and Provisioning (OAM&P), and a variety of interfaces between NEs and OSs. It is desirable that certain future maintenance capabilities (i.e., performance monitoring) and associated operations interfaces, be standardized. Standardized monitoring would provide a uniform understanding of performance measures in the industry; this is important given the multivendor environment and the need to resolve responsibility for end-to-end performance degradations at interfaces between different networks, and at interfaces between users and networks. ISDN access is one area in which standardization of this nature is actively underway in the industry.[2-4] Other areas remaining to be standardized involves transport networks.[5,6] In addition, standardized operations interfaces would make it possible for NEs procured from different manufactures, to be compatible with TELCo's OSs.[7]

The purpose of the TMN is to provide an overall operations architecture to enable the interconnection of various different types of OSs and telecommunications equipments (NEs) using a set of standardized protocols and interfaces. (See Figure 2.)[8-12]

From the perspective of this paper, which focuses on aspects of digital transmission performance, the relevant functions of each of the main components of TMN are as follows. The NEs (perhaps in cooperation with an MD) are responsible for monitoring, detecting, storing and reporting alarm, and performance-related information to a surveillance center (OS) across standard interfaces. These interfaces can either be between the NE and the surveillance center, or between an intermediate location (MD, remote interface unit) and the surveillance center. The various interfaces between NEs, MDs, and OSs, etc., depend on the type of NE and the OAM&P functions to be supported.

The third main interface types associated with TMN designated Q1, Q2, Q3, are as follows:

- The Q1 interface supports a small

set of relatively simple OAM&P functions, such as the transport of binary indications representing alarm states, loopback requests etc. Q1 is used between an NE and an MD, and is appropriate when large numbers of simple, small-scale NEs are supported by an MD. Protocols for Q1 are likely not to have all layers of the OSI model.

- The Q2 interface supports a larger set of more complex OAM&P functions, such as provisioning, alarm surveillance, and performance monitoring. Q2 is also distinguished by the ability to transport data rather than only binary indications; the data may also be concentrated. Q2 may be used between a more intelligent larger-scale NE and a MD, or between MDs, via a local communications network. Protocols for Q2 are also not likely to involve all layers of the OSI model.

- The Q3 interface is a full-capability interface which can support all OAM&P functions, and is appropriate for large scale NEs. Q3 is intended for use between an NE and OS or between an MD and OS via an operations network. Protocols for Q3 require layers 1 to 7 of the OSI model.

For the purpose of this paper, Q1 and Q2 are the sufficient and applicable interfaces.

After performance data is communicated from NEs to an OS via the interfaces just noted, the data can be compared to allocated performance objectives (maintenance limits). Appropriate maintenance actions can then be initiated which are in-line with a proactive centralized maintenance strategy. The data can also be used to verify that end-to-end service objectives are satisfied. Of the various OAM&P functions supported by TMN, the following is an elaboration of the maintenance functions relevant to this paper. Broadly, the functions include:

- alarm surveillance to rapidly capture out-of-service conditions due to equipment failures or severe performance degradations, so that service continuity is preserved, and immediate corrective action can be taken.

- performance monitoring to detect and verify on a continuous in-service basis less serious degradations, before end users are effected.

- fault location for both the causes of out-of-service conditions, as well as, the less serious degradations. This involves sectionalizing the trouble to the responsible maintenance jurisdiction, and locating the trouble within the jurisdiction. Sectionalization is supported by various levels of performance monitoring data as gathered by different types of NEs; that is those which terminate regenerator sections, transmission lines, and digit paths. [5,6,14]

- testing for detailed diagnostics, and for sectionalization and fault location (when this cannot be accomplished automatically by performance monitoring). Testing can also be used for verification of performance after service restoration following corrective maintenance (although this may also be done by performance monitoring). In general, testing can be in-service (non-intrusive), or out-of-service (intrusive) if necessary, the former being preferred.

- status and control, for checking and changing the state of an NE on demand (e.g., in/out of service, protection switch status, service restoral), initiating maintenance related activities (e.g., loopback, testing data gathering and reporting), changing the attributes associated with performance monitoring (e.g., threshold change, enabling and disabling of alerts, etc.).

The above functional capabilities provide the tools for carrying out cost-effective maintenance. However, in addition, a set of maintenance limits are required which can initiate meaningful maintenance actions using the above capabilities. This is addressed in the following section.

MAINTENANCE LIMITS

Transmission performance maintenance limits are one application of a TMN which in the broader sense is responsible for the surveillance and verification/correlation of all pertinent network information. For example, parameters not directly relatable to end-user performance, such as protection switching activity and equipment status, also form part of a maintenance scheme. However, this paper focuses on the maintenance limit application, as it relates to transmission performance.

The measure of impairment is in terms of standard performance parameters, such as ES, SES, and DM. In an integrated monitoring and maintenance

1117

approach, some or all of these parameters are monitored, collected, and reported to the OS by an NE. The parameters are accumulated over standard measurement averaging intervals of a minute, hour, and day, and are reported to the OS as alerts when parameter count thresholds are exceeded. [5]

There is a practical need, in facility maintenance operations, for performance information to be evaluated over a relatively short term. Performance objectives, on the other hand, may be specified for periods as long as 1 month. The derivation of maintenance limits as described in this paper is done through a process which links long-term network performance objectives to short-term facility maintenance limits that are practical for operations. As mentioned above, an important part of the process is the concept of accumulation of thresholded time intervals (i.e., time intervals in which performance is degraded below some threshold).

One approach to a short-term performance limit would be to allow the accumulation of the same amount of impaired intervals as specified for the long-term objective. In practice this would capture impairment Only after it was certain that long-term objectives were missed. A more effective rule is to linearly pro-rate from the long-term objective to an 'equivalent' short-term objective. With pro-rating, the idea is that performance should meet the pro-rated objective over short periods of time. This allows for reaction to impairment and, potentially, for a repair before long-term objectives are missed. However, there is some risk of over reaction since an objective derived by pro-rating is, in effect, more stringent than the long-term objective. A proposed practical short-term impairment accumulation period is 1 day.[12]

Optimum management of operations resources requires efficient use of both maintenance staff and equipment, and maintenance information. A feature of a software controlled operations center is its ability to prioritize or schedule performance-driven maintenance according to a set of rules (algorithm). Central to any maintenance prioritization policy is a set of maintenance limits which provide a measure of maintenance urgency (priority) related to the rate of accumulation of impairment.

Figure 3 illustrates a prioritization scheme based on four transmission performance maintenance limit categories. Ordered with respect to scheduling urgency and performance severity; the categories are Critical, Immediate, Deferrable, and Warning.

Table 1 summarizes maintenance limits based on these four categories.

The Critical maintenance limit is an indication of existing or imminent unavailability of service. This maintenance limit is derived from the thresholds corresponding to seriously degraded performance as provided for in the performance objective. It is the number of consecutive intervals with seriously degraded performance that would essentially render the service unusable or unavailable.

The Immediate maintenance limit is an indication that there is a high probability of impairment exceeding '10 times' the 1 day pro-rated objective. The '10 times' criterion is considered to be the threshold of impairment corresponding to significant risk of customer complaint. Figure 4 illustrates the implementation of the immediate maintenance limit, in terms of the accumulation of impaired intervals, i.e., alerts. For greater statistical confidence, this maintenance limit may be calculated as the number of bernoulli trials (x alerts) that ensures the 10 times rate of accumulation. For example, the value x for the required number of 1-minute alerts in a day is derived by:

$$(1-c) = \sum_{r=0}^{x} \left(\frac{1440}{r}\right) P^r (1 - P)^{(1440-r)}$$

where c = 9 for 90 percent confidence, P is the probability of an alert, and 1440 is the number of minutes in a day.

The Deferrable maintenance limit indicates that the 1 day pro-rated objective has been missed. At this level of performance, there is moderate impairment and maintenance (repair) priority may allow a logistical delay of up to several days if performance does not worsen. In pro-rating long-term network objectives to 1-day limits, deferrable maintenance limits are obtained directly by dividing the long-term objective by the number of days in the long-term period.

The fourth category is Warning. Performance exceeding a warning maintenance limit indicates that the maintenance entity has missed historic performance levels. This category is the first indication that end-to-end performance is tending to degrade. It is essentially a thresholded trend analysis.

A practical implementation of maintenance limits will not necessarily use all of the categories. The choice will depend on a number of factors, such as facility cross-section, expected error performance behavior of the transmission media being used, and presence of critical service.

Further enhancements of the OS maintenance limit analysis function may be expected in the future. One such enhanced analysis function that could be performed is maintenance support. This is the analysis of pertinent performance data, including performance history, to derive greater confidence for the action indicated by the maintenance limits. The analysis would check for persistency of impairment and avoidance of overreaction. Figure 5 shows a confirmation function, whereby, additional information and trend analysis indicate whether corrective action is feasible. For instance, the performance history of Figure 6 illustrates how a review of the performance trend could confirm the significance of deferrable limits.

CONCLUSION

The forward-looking integrated performance strategy presented in this paper emphasizes consistency among performance objectives, NE monitoring features, and operating system analysis to invoke maintenance actions. This strategy will allow operating companies to gain maximum benefit from the computing power of operating systems, and the performance data provided by a network with extensively deployed continuous in-service performance monitoring. Continuously evaluated maintenance limits and analysis to support repair actions will contribute to prompt and efficient response to performance degradation. By keying maintenance limits to performance objectives, through the performance allocation process, a policy of pro-active maintenance may be chosen, whereby, action is initiated before error events significantly impact the user.

REFERENCES

1. Proposed American National Standard for Telecommunications – Network Performance Parameters for Dedicated Digital Services-Definitions and Measurement Methods, T1Q1.4/88-004-R1, May 1988.

2. Draft of ISDN Maintenance Operations Standard, T1M1.2/88-00R3, June 20, 1988.

3. American National Standard for Telecommunications Carrier to Customer Installation; DS1 Metallic Interface Standard, T1E1/88-001R1, T1C1.2/87-001R3, Feb. 1988.

4. CCITT1.600 Series Recommendations on Maintenance Principle Com., XVIII-R 54(c)-E, Feb. 1988.

5. J. Gruber, "Performance Monitoring and Surveillance in Integrated Services Networks," Abstract, NCF Rec. Vol. 41, Bk. 1, Sept. 1987, pp. 650; full paper handed out at NCF. To be published in IEEE Journal on Selected Areas in Communications Issue on "Quality After the Sale for the Communications Community," 1988.

6. Contribution, T1M1.2/88-81, T1M1.3/88-38, "Proposal for Forward Looking Generic Layer 1 Transport Performance Monitoring Capabilities," NT1, June 20, 1988.

7. M. Blake-Knox and K. G. Knightson, "Network Operations Protocol – OSI Protocols for Operations, Administration and Maintenance," GLOBECOM Rec., Vol. 1, Houston, Texas, Dec. 1986, pp. 28.6.1-28.6.6.

8. Proposed American National Standard for Telecommunications – Operations, Administration, Maintenance and Provisioning – Lower Layer Protocols for Interfaces Between Operations Systems and Network Elements, T1M1/86-040R3, Nov. 1, 1987. (ANSI T1.204/1988).

9. Q Interfaces and Associated Protocols for Transmission Equipment in the Telecommunication Management Network (TMN), CCITT Draft Recommendation G.TMN, Sept. 1987. (G.771).

10. Proposed American National Standard for Telecommunications – Operations, Administration, Maintenance and Provisioning – Principles of Functions, Architectures and Protocols for Interfaces Between Operations Systems and Network Elements, T1M1.5/88-031R1, June 20, 1988.

11. CCITT Rec. M.30, "Principles for a Telecommunications Management Network." Report COM IV-R21-E, (3rd draft).

12. CCITT Revised Rec. M.20, "Maintenance Philosophy for Telecommunications Networks," COM IV-R23(c)-E.

13. CCITT Draft Rec. M.550, Bringing into Service and Maintenance Limits For Digital Sections and Paths, COM IV-R__

14. Draft of American National Standard

for Optical Interface Rate and Formats, ANSI T1.105-1988, (Draft March 10, 1988).

MAINTENANCE LIMIT CATEGORY	CUSTOMER PERCEPTION OF PERFORMANCE	1 DAY MAINTENANCE LIMIT	RECOMMENDED MAINTENANCE URGENCY
CRITICAL	UNUSEABLE	UNAVAILABILITY CRITERIA	CORRECT PROMPTLY
IMMEDIATE	WILL CAUSE COMPLAINT	FAILURE TO MEET 10 TIMES 1 DAY PRO-RATED OBJ. (MIN & HR INTERVALS)	CORRECT WITHIN A DAY
DEFERRABLE	PERCEPTIBLE IMPAIRMENTS & POSSIBLY CAUSING COMPLAINT	FAILURE TO MEET 1 DAY PRO-RATED OBJECTIVE (HR & DAY INTERVALS)	CORRECT WITHIN DAYS
WARNING	FIRST INDICATION OF DEGRADING PERFORMANCE	EXCEEDING RESIDUAL ERROR PERFORMANCE EXPECTATIONS (1 DAY INTERVALS)	CORRECT IF PERFORMANCE WORSENS

TABLE 1: SUMMARY OF 1 DAY MAINTENANCE LIMIT DESCRIPTION

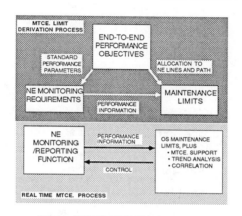

FIG.URE 1: INTERACTION OF MAJOR ELEMENTS FOR AN INTEGRATED PERFORMANCE STRATEGY

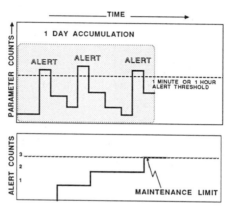

FIG 4: MAINTENANCE LIMIT ALGORITHM

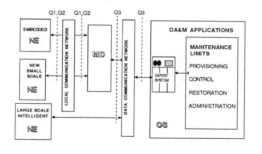

FIGURE 2: SIMPLIFIED TMN ARCHITECTURE

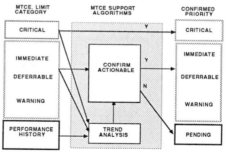

FIGURE 5: MAINTENANCE SUPPORT

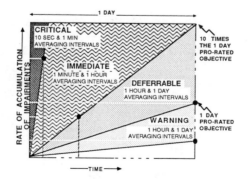

FIGURE 3: MAINTENANCE LIMIT MEASUREMENT INTERVALS AND CATEGORIES

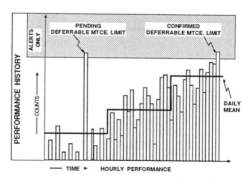

FIG 6: SUPPORT PROCESS - TREND ANALYSIS

1120

NEW MAINTENANCE STRATEGIES FOR DIGITAL FACILITIES NETWORKS

Calvin D. Cowles
Manager
Transport Technology Division

AT&T
Route 202/206 N.
Room 3C-130
Bedminster, New Jersey 07921

Joanne C. Wilson
Member of Technical Staff
Transmission Systems Engineering

AT&T Bell Laboratories
Crawford Corners Road
Room 2E-520
Holmdel, New Jersey 07733

Today AT&T is engaged in the massive and unprecedented expansion of its digital facilities network. Accompanying this growth has been an effort to develop maintenance strategies and methodologies intended to insure that these facilities provide continuously high quality digital service. This paper describes the AT&T philosophy of digital facilities maintenance, a philosophy that is based on in-service performance monitoring and coordinated facility section and DS3 path maintenance.

One approach to DS3 path maintenance uses the recently developed C-bit Parity frame format. The C-bit Parity format is an M-type DS3 frame structure that allows each frame's parity information to be embedded in the overhead bits of the following DS3 frame. By so doing, full end-to-end performance monitoring can be achieved for the DS3 path. This paper will describe the various features of the C-bit Parity format, highlighting their use within an overall digital facilities maintenance strategy.

INTRODUCTION

As the final decade of the twentieth century fast approaches, AT&T and others in the telecommunications industry, are rapidly expanding both the capacity and connectivity of its digital facilities network. This expansion is fueled by many factors, not the least of which are the burgeoning use of private computer networks by large businesses, and the technical recognition of the quality advantages of digital communications over analog. Obviously an important approach to improving the quality of digital facilities is to deploy better, more reliable transmission equipment and to improve the field engineering of the transmission system. But this, by itself, is not enough. Once in service, these systems must be maintained to a standard that will allow them to provide continuously high quality service. For this to be done it is necessary to enhance the efficiency and effectiveness of the techniques and systems used for digital facilities maintenance. After facilities are installed and turned up, these systems will be responsible for and will be a major contributor affecting the quality of the digital facilities network.

This paper describes the AT&T philosophy of network facilities maintenance. We will begin by developing a group of principles that underpin the network engineering and maintenance planning for the AT&T long distance network. Having done so, we will show how these principles are manifested in a three level maintenance strategy and will describe the tools needed to execute that strategy.

THE APPROACH

The AT&T Facility Maintenance Philosophy, stated simply, is to provide a high quality transport network using in-service performance monitoring and proactive maintenance plans and procedures. This philosophy is manifested in principles that guide network engineering and maintenance planning. These principles are applied to developing and integrating new technologies into the network, as well as to planning for and implementing maintenance activities. They are as follows:

- Treat facility maintenance from a network perspective. The service being transported over our network traverses numerous facility sections and various facility technologies. Thus, the quality of the service is determined by a network of equipment and technologies and the service should be maintained from that perspective.

- Manage a facility section as an entity, not piecewise. Thus network terminating equipment (NTE), line terminating equipment (LTE), and cross-connects are included as components within the facility sections.

- Provide remote performance monitoring and fault locating capabilities enough to identify trouble conditions and sectionalize a fault to a location.

- Use in-service testing and performance verification.

- Identify a trouble before a customer report.

- Use automatic trouble

sectionalization.

- Make one and only one dispatch for repair. Therefore, it is required that accurate remote identification of the trouble location take place the first time. This, however, should not significantly increase the lag time to dispatch for repair.

- Use the capabilities of new technologies. The network should continually evolve toward providing higher quality services as the technologies available for use in the network become better and better.

- Understand all the factors affecting the economics of maintenance. It is our belief that providing high quality service can and must be done in a cost effective way.

- Minimize the opportunities for two entities to disagree about where a trouble resides. These instances should be avoided both between AT&T regional maintenance centers, as well as between multiple vendors providing a single service.

- Use standard parameters and information sets. For ease of comparison and to simplify path maintenance, one set of performance parameters should be used for all the facilities and in all the regions.

These principles guide maintenance planning within the AT&T network. As better technologies are integrated into the digital facilities network, maintenance needs may evolve, and with them so too will these guiding principles.

APPLYING THE PRINCIPLES OF NETWORK MAINTENANCE

THE MAINTENANCE STRATEGY

The Digital Facilities Maintenance Strategy is to manage maintenance activities using performance information derived through in-service monitoring of the network. This strategy relies heavily on Operational Support Systems (OSSs) and incorporates a ''building block'' approach that assigns each maintenance function to its appropriate maintenance entity. These building blocks are, in effect, the digital signaling levels corresponding to the types of transport facilities that prevail in the network. They are:

DS1/T1:   DS1 facilities will be monitored using the

capabilities of the Extended Super Frame (ESF) Format. The primary use of this information is to allocate trouble conditions to either the access facility or to the higher level (T3) network facility. This is done through the deployment of ESF compatible NTE and stand-alone ESF monitoring units.

DS3/T3:   The focus of our digital facilities maintenance effort is at the DS3 level. DS3 facilities are monitored on both a facility section and on an end-to-end, T3 path, basis. Information on the performance of the DS3 path is obtained using the C-bit Parity Frame Format. This information is used to identify DS3 network impairments. The section data is used to sectionalize troubles to a technology or maintenance entity. The maintenance features of the transport technology are enhanced, where necessary, by deploying performance monitors to provide the section data at the DS3 level.

Line/Terminal: Performance information from facility line terminal equipment is used in those technologies where DS3 section monitoring is not feasible for either technical or economical reasons. This information may also be used to provide a means for performing autonomous fault locating, as well as, for technologies with Forward Error Correction (FEC), to provide a measure of the facility performance before FEC.

As stated earlier, this plan focuses on DS3 level network maintenance. Management of facility maintenance activity at the DS3 level provides the information needed to identify facility impairments before they affect customer service, respond quickly if a customer complains, and isolate troubles to network or access facilities. It also provides the analysis information for trending and trouble predicting, and improves our ability to render high quality support for facility level services, such as ACCUNET T1.5 and

ACCUNET T45.

THE THREE LEVEL CONCEPT

The maintenance of digital facilities, because of the capabilities of the current technologies, depends heavily on managing maintenance information and the ensuing work activities. The management process is one of collecting performance data, correlating, processing, and analyzing that data, and from that initiating maintenance actions. It can and should be directed to provide complete, concise facility performance information to support the needs of the maintenance personnel. The three levels of the concept are (1) to monitor facility performance at the DS3 level, (2) to provide monitoring on a full-time, in-service basis, and (3) to manage maintenance activities according to a proactive maintenance plan.

WHY MONITOR AT THE DS3 LEVEL?

One aspect of the digital network maintenance strategy is that monitoring of the digital facilities is to be performed at the DS3 level. Given the hierarchical structure of the network, it certainly could be argued that other levels, such as the line rate for each facility section, might be a better choice for the level at which to monitor. Monitoring of the DS3 signal provides performance information that closely reflects what is actually occurring at the facility level. Since all long haul facilities carry multiple DS3 signals, DS3 level monitoring can be uniformly deployed throughout the digital facilities network, and can be used for comparison with facility section monitoring information. In contrast, monitoring at the line rate does not provide a consistent database of performance information because the line rate changes depending on the types of facilities encountered from one section to the next. Also, the digital services provided over the network are either at or below the DS3 level. Therefore, DS3 level monitoring always captures full services, and as such simplifies determining the proper course of action should a customer complain.

Another argument for monitoring at the DS3 level is related to the way performance monitoring information will be used for trouble isolation and identification. It is well known that DS3 troubles can affect the DS1 signals within that DS3 signal. With the deployment of extended superframe format (ESF) throughout the network and with DS3 level monitoring it becomes possible to determine if a performance degradation of a DS1 line is because of a problem in either the DS1 or DS3 part of the circuit. This is much more difficult to assess without monitoring the DS3 signal. Determining the signal level that is being impaired is a first cut at isolating problems in the network. It is for these reasons that DS3 level performance monitoring is one strategy being used for maintaining the digital facilities network.

WHAT ARE THE BENEFITS OF IN-SERVICE MONITORING?

Another aspect of the digital network maintenance strategy is that performance monitoring should be done continuously on all DS3 lines, while those lines are carrying customer traffic. This approach to performance monitoring provides myriad benefits for implementing a network maintenance strategy. The first is by doing so each path or section can be benchmarked regarding how well it performs on a daily basis. Thus, degradation on a circuit can be observed and mitigated before the customer is affected. This is especially true with technologies that use forward error correction and errorless switching. For example, on some digital radio systems these features, together with monitoring the facility section at the line rate, allow protection switching to occur during microwave fading without a single bit error being experienced by the customer.

In-service performance monitoring also allows intermittent events to be captured and collected for future analysis. These kinds of impairments have been considered the most difficult to troubleshoot. Performing trending and analysis of this information can be a critical first step toward isolating the source of this type of impairment. In-service performance monitoring can also provide the best environment for troubleshooting. Out of service testing adds to the outage time of a circuit because it is made unavailable to the customer. By monitoring with a test set, the exact number of bit errors in each errored second during the monitoring period can be determined. However, for troubleshooting, often the information desired is merely the severity of the impairment --a few verses several thousand bit errors in a second--, and the frequency of the events --many in a five minute interval versus a couple over a twenty-four hour period--. Out of service testing adds no additional, useful capabilities at the expense of service availability. In addition, using this approach entails added delay in the maintenance process, thereby reducing its apparent responsiveness. Given this, clearly only by performing in-service monitoring can the maintenance process be as responsive as possible and provide the best environment for troubleshooting.

Finally, the capability for doing in-service monitoring is virtually gratis. It is de facto provided because the DS3 signal must be framed in order for the DS1 lines to be multiplexed together to form the DS3 signal. Thus, providing in-service monitoring relies on making use of the features already in place by deploying monitoring equipment to retrieve the data and OSSs to collect, correlate, format, and present information to the maintenance personnel. Regardless of the way it is implemented, in-service performance monitoring is a valuable feature of an effective strategy for maintaining a digital facilities network.

THE PROACTIVE MAINTENANCE PLAN

Maintenance management refers to using facility performance information to make informed decisions directing the activities of remote monitoring centers and field maintenance personnel. The efficient and effective use of this information is critical to meeting the ever increasing expectations of customers. The proactive maintenance plan provides the needed format for doing this, and thus for providing high quality service.

Any maintenance action can be classified as addressing one of several maintenance objectives: Trouble Detection, Trouble Verification, Trouble Sectionalization, or Repair Verification. To be manageable, the process used to accomplish these objectives effectively and efficiently needs to be both logical and simple. One way to do this is to categorize facility performance conditions in a like manner that allows maintenance responses to be both timely and accurate. We have categorized these conditions as either Good, Failed (Service Affecting or Non-Service Affecting), or Degraded.

Facility performance is ''good'' when all performance parameters are being met. No maintenance actions are required. ''Failed'' is defined as facility performance that has exceeded an acceptable error threshold. This could result from something as severe as a fiber cut or as relatively minor as a multiplexer failure. A failure is considered ''service affecting'' depending on whether a protection switch was accomplished. Maintenance activity is always begun immediately in response to a facility failure. The ''degraded'' condition is characterized by facility performance that has deteriorated to a detectable level, determined by in-service monitoring, but has of yet not failed. Analysis of the immediate and potential affect on service then determines the appropriate maintenance response.

A DS3 path is composed of one or more facility sections connected in tandem. These sections may be at the DS3 level or at the line rate of the technology, depending on the technology and its monitoring and switching hierarchy. For example, a facility with sections that are monitored and switched at the DS3 rate has ''DS3 sections,'' as opposed to one that is monitored and switched at the line rate that has ''line rate sections.''

Facility section maintenance is the first line of defense for two types of troubles in the digital network. First, when a failed condition occurs and the LTE makes a protection switch request, the OSSs notify the responsible remote maintenance center. If the protection switch completes and returns end-to-end performance to acceptable levels, the center then starts maintenance procedures to correct the trouble on the original section. If the protection switch does not complete the center sees a service affecting failure (SAF) and its first priority is to restore the service and then make maintenance decisions on the original section. Second, when performance levels in a section intermittently fall below acceptable levels, causing numerous protection switch requests, the responsible center again must start the appropriate maintenance action. For degraded performance conditions, performance information is collected and stored to support facility path maintenance, measure maintenance effectiveness, and measure the performance of specific technologies.

The sections of a DS3 path may encompass different technologies with different maintenance attributes. The goal of this maintenance plan, to deliver a high quality service from end-to-end through the network, is best done by managing degraded performance maintenance activities on an end-to-end or path basis. This is true for several reasons:

- End-to-end (NTE-to-NTE) performance information much more closely reflects the quality of the service being delivered to the customer.

- Deteriorating performance on several sections can cause the performance of the path to be degraded before any of the facility sections have a detectable performance degradation.

- Isolating troubles between DS1 and DS3 facilities is enhanced by the availability of DS1 and DS3 performance data at the multiplexer.

- Having DS3 path performance

1124

information, in addition to the ability to monitor Leased/Access facilities from an AT&T Service Node, supports having these facilities maintained as a cooperative venture between vendors.

The C-bit Parity format is the recommended format for use in performance monitoring of the DS3 path. The derived performance monitoring information will be used to manage maintenance activities and to measure network performance.

ACCESS

The maintenance philosophy for leased and access facilities is that these facilities, because they affect the quality of the service AT&T renders to its customers, are a extension of the AT&T network and therefore should be maintained using the same parameters as the remainder of the network. Therefore, continuous in-service DS3 level performance monitoring is also required for these types of facilities. The leased/access DS3 terminals must also support the C-bit Parity frame format. This format provides for single-ended performance monitoring from the AT&T Service Node and, in this application, provides a means to isolate troubles between areas of maintenance responsibility.

Quality maintenance of these facilities is critical to the delivery of high quality service. A spirit of cooperation between network and leased/access facility vendors is essential. Maintenance agreements need to be established to reflect the importance of leased/access facility maintenance.

THE TOOLS

PATH MONITORING WITH THE C-BIT PARTY FRAME FORMAT

One part of the proactive maintenance plan is simultaneous facility section and DS3 path performance monitoring. Path monitoring is a new concept made possible by the development of the C-bit Parity frame format. This format has the same basic M-type structure as the M13 frame format and, like its predecessor, is used to multiplex twenty-eight DS1 signals into a DS3 stream. The C-bit parity format differs from the M13 format mainly in the way that the 21 C bits in each frame are used. In the M13 format, on each row of the frame the C bits indicate if stuffing has occurred in that sub-frame. Multiplexers implementing the C-bit format will do the multiplexing in such a way that stuffing occurs in every sub-frame, thereby freeing the C bits to be used for other purposes (see Figures 1. and 2.).

The most important path monitoring capability is determining if an error has occurred in a frame. This can be done by comparing the parity of the received frame with that of the frame when it was transmitted. To do this the C bits in the third sub-frame have been redefined as CP bits and carry the parity information of the previous frame. At the receive terminal the parity of each frame is computed and compared with the CP bits in the succeeding frame. A parity error is declared when there is a discrepancy in the transmitted and received frame parity. The P bits in both the M13 and C-bit parity formats serve a similar purpose as the CP bits in that they carry the parity information of the proceeding frame. These bits, however, are monitored and corrected on a section by section basis and, therefore, cannot be used for path performance monitoring.

Another desirable feature in a path monitoring scheme is to be able to determine the path performance from both the receiver or near end (NE) and the transmitter or far end (FE) sides of the path. Whereas the M13 format provides for only NE monitoring, both features are available with the C-bit parity format. This was made possible through redefining the C bits in the fourth sub-frame to be far end block error (FEBE) bits. When a parity error is determined at the NE terminal this information is transmitted in the FEBE bits of the next frame transmitted in the opposite direction along the path. In a similar way far end out of frame (FE-OOF) information is transmitted by modulating the X bits in the C-bit frame structure.

Lastly, given the current proliferation of M13 type multiplexers in the field, it should be assumed that any monitoring equipment that is designed should be compatible with both DS3 frame formats. To support this the C1 bit in the first sub-frame has been redefined as the frame identifier (FID) bit. For the C-bit parity format this bit is always set to FID=1. In the M13 format this bit will vary constantly depending on whether stuffing occurs in that sub-frame. Monitoring equipment should then assume that the C-bit parity format is being implemented if vastly more of the C1 bits in the first sub-frame equal 1. It must be emphasized that whereas monitoring equipment can be made compatible with both formats, given the differences in how stuffing is handled, this can never be done with multiplexers.

OTHER TOOLS

In addition to using a new DS3 frame

format, implementing this or any other maintenance strategy requires that OSSs automate the information collecting, processing and distributing aspects of the maintenance process. As a way of realizing the various features of this proactive maintenance plan, the OSSs must perform several functions. They must use facility section monitoring data to isolate where a failure has occurred so that personnel can be deployed to the correct location.

Certainly, there are many other features that could be implemented in OSS systems to enhance the efficiency of the entire maintenance process. Executing the strategy supported in this paper entails handling and processing a large amount of performance information. The challenge to OSS development is to provide a means of intelligently filtering this copious amount of data so that the information provided is adequate to determine the next, most appropriate course of action. However, too much information can be as bad as too little, so expertise must also be applied to assure that the information provided by the OSSs is only what is necessary for the succeeding maintenance response to be effective.

CONCLUSIONS

The commitment to providing a high quality digital facilities network requires that systems and procedures be developed to enhance the management of network maintenance. By applying the principles developed here, we have put forth a strategy that encompasses in-service performance monitoring at the DS3 level and a proactive maintenance plan. A key feature of this plan is simultaneous facility section and DS3 path monitoring. Information gained from this approach can be used to enhance troubleshooting of not only technology failures, but of degraded or pre-failure problems as well. There are fundamental differences, as compared to traditional methods, in how maintenance is performed using this new strategy. Where these occur, it is often required that new techniques and OSSs be used for its implementation. One such technique is the new C-bit Parity frame format that will be implemented in the AT&T long distance network for DS3 path monitoring. We have shown how this format provides all the features necessary to do path monitoring effectively. The methods and tools developed here reflect the many years of experience AT&T has in maintaining an extensive transport facilities network. Through this experience we have learned that network maintenance is fraught with complexity and should be approached in a structured and cohesive way to fulfill its role in providing high quality digital services.

	-85 SLOT-	-85 SLOT-	-85 SLOT-	-85 SLOT-	-85 SLOT-	-85 SLOT-	-85 SLOT-	-85 SLOT-		
1	X [84]	F1 [84]	C1 [84]	F0 [84]	C2 [84]	F0 [84]	C3 [84]	F1 [0]	[S1]	[83]
2	X [84]	F1 [84]	C4 [84]	F0 [84]	C5 [84]	F0 [84]	C6 [84]	F1 [1]	[S2]	[82]
3	P [84]	F1 [84]	C7 [84]	F0 [84]	C8 [84]	F0 [84]	C9 [84]	F1 [2]	[S3]	[81]
4	P [84]	F1 [84]	C10 [84]	F0 [84]	C11 [84]	F0 [84]	C12 [84]	F1 [3]	[S4]	[80]
5	M0 [84]	F1 [84]	C13 [84]	F0 [84]	C14 [84]	F0 [84]	C15 [84]	F1 [4]	[S5]	[79]
6	M1 [84]	F1 [84]	C16 [84]	F0 [84]	C17 [84]	F0 [84]	C18 [84]	F1 [5]	[S6]	[78]
7	M0 [84]	F1 [84]	C19 [84]	F0 [84]	C20 [84]	F0 [84]	C21 [84]	F1 [6]	[S7]	[77]

NOTES:

28	F-bits (F0 = 0, F1 = 1)
2	X-bits (X = 0 or 1, but must agree)
2	P-bits (P = 0 or 1, but must agree)
3	M-bits (M0 = 0, M1 = 1)
21	C-bits (used for stuff control)
4704	Information bits
4760	Total bits

Figure 1. **M13 TYPE DS3 Frame Structure**

	-85 SLOT-	-85 SLOT-	-85 SLOT-	-85 SLOT-	-85 SLOT-	-85 SLOT-	-85 SLOT-	-85 SLOT-
1	X [84]	F1 [84]	FID [84]	FO [84]	C1 [84]	FO [84]	C1 [84]	F1 [84]
2	X [84]	F1 [84]	C1 [84]	FO [84]	C1 [84]	FO [84]	C1 [84]	F1 [84]
3	P [84]	F1 [84]	CP [84]	FO [84]	CP [84]	FO [84]	CP [84]	F1 [84]
4	P [84]	F1 [84]	FEBE [84]	FO [84]	FEBE [84]	FO [84]	FEBE [84]	F1 [84]
5	MO [84]	F1 [84]	C1 [84]	FO [84]	C1 [84]	FO [84]	C1 [84]	F1 [84]
6	M1 [84]	F1 [84]	C1 [84]	FO [84]	C1 [84]	FO [84]	C1 [84]	F1 [84]
7	MO [84]	F1 [84]	C1 [84]	FO [84]	C1 [84]	FO [84]	C1 [84]	F1 [84]

NOTES:

28	F-bits (FO = 0, F1 = 1)
2	X-bits (X = 0, OOF, X = 1, no OOF)
2	P-bits (P = 0 or 1, but must agree)
3	M-bits (MO = 0, M1 = 1)
21	C-bits (C1 = 1, CP = P, FEPE = 1 - no error, or not 1 1 1 - error)
4704	Information bits
4760	Total bits

Figure 2. **C-Bit Parity Frame Structure**

A MONITORING AND CONTROL SYSTEM FOR TELEPHONE SWITCHES

Joseph F. Drzewiecki
Derek Carlson
Members of Technical Staff

GTE Communication Systems
2500 W. Utopia Road
Phoenix, AZ 85027

ABSTRACT

A case history of a monitoring and surveillance system is presented, focusing on real-time processing of soft error and performance monitoring messages and proactive maintenance of network elements using the flexible set of provided services.

A PRACTICAL APPLICATION FOR ISDN BRI PERFORMANCE MONITORING

Wayne A. VandeWall
Member of Technical Staff
Switching Systems Engineering

AT&T Bell Laboratories
200 Park Plaza
Room 1F-426
Naperville, Il 60566-7050

William J. Wolters
Member of Technical Staff
Operational Systems Engineering

AT&T Bell Laboratories
Crawford Corners Road
Room 3G-205
Holmdel, New Jersey 07733

ABSTRACT

Integrated Services Digital Network (ISDN) is providing an evolution of services to economically fit both business and residential needs. This statement, a dream two years ago, is becoming a reality. Millions of dollars are being spent to ensure that ISDN not only becomes a reality, but becomes a success. ISDN is seen to provide the end user with a spectrum of value added services at a reasonable price. However, the success of ISDN depends on the ability to provide and maintain a high quality of service to the end customer. As ISDN evolves to offer more services with greater market penetration, there becomes a driving need to minimize the cost of maintenance for the ISDN networks. In fact, to ensure customer satisfaction and to minimize maintenance costs, prompt and accurate isolation of ISDN faults is mandatory.

In order to provide prompt and accurate fault detection and isolation, it is necessary to detect facility degradation as well as problems resulting from network or terminal protocol abnormalities. This paper presents a description of performance monitoring, why it is an important factor in ISDN maintenance, and a practical application of how it can be used for the support and maintenance of ISDN BRI facilities.

INTRODUCTION

"ISDN is the gateway to tomorrow's telephony technology" is a statement that alludes to the present day benefits for the service provider, building wire provider, and end customer. More importantly, it suggests the myriad services which can be offered in the future. In other words, the full potential of ISDN has only begun to be explored.

However, as with any service which is sold in the telephone network, a major cost, is maintenance. ISDN provides the customer with packet data, circuit switched data, voice or any combination of these three types of communications. This means that the ISDN provider must be able to maintain a consistently high quality digital network in a POTS environment. In fact, one of the greatest obstacles to the distribution and the full realization of ISDN may be the difficulty in incorporating a cost effective and reliable maintenance strategy.

ISDN, unlike POTS, is highly dependent on the capability to detect and isolate protocol problems resulting from circuit (i.e. LAPD, Q.931) and/or packet services (i.e. LAPD, LAPB, X.25) and/or facility degradation. This paper presents a scenario that illustrates how performance monitoring information can be used for the detection and isolation of an end customer trouble. Performance monitoring is only one of several maintenance tools/capabilities that are currently available and which should be utilized for a total ISDN maintenance strategy. This paper focuses on performance monitoring information provided by the ISDN digital switch and processed by the Operations System (OS).

All performance monitoring information outlined in this paper has been discussed and is in consideration in the T1M1.2 draft standard.

ISDN OVERVIEW

ISDN comes in two basic forms, Basic Rate Interface (BRI) and Primary Rate Interface (PRI). The maintenance scenario discussed in this paper addresses the BRI, although the maintenance tools outlined are also applicable to the PRI.

The BRI is composed of two 64 Kbit/sec channels (B channels) and a 16 Kbit/sec signaling link (D channel). The B channels support voice, circuit switched data and X.25 packet data on demand or continuous X.25 packet data (i.e. nail-up). The D channel uses the Q.931 protocol for the signalling control of the two B channels. The D channel can also be used for 16 Kbit/sec X.25 packet service. The BRI can be offered, based on distance constraints, on either a T (4 wire) or U (2 wire) interface (refer to figure 1). Both the T and U interface can be optioned as either point-to-point (i.e. one terminal), or multipoint (i.e. up to eight sets).

THE NEED FOR PERFORMANCE MONITORING

Performance monitoring is a vital maintenance tool for providing immediate information on a problem (i.e. degradation) and valuable isolation information once a problem is detected. For this discussion, performance monitoring refers to the detection, recording and analysis of faults in the ISDN BRI protocol at OSI model layer's 1, 2 and 3 (refer to figure 2).

Performance monitoring is needed for isolating troubles caused by BRI facility degradation and protocol discrepancies between the ISDN network and the terminal. Performance monitoring provides detailed descriptions of protocol violations that occur when a feature fails. Important aspects of continuous performance monitoring are:

⊕ It provides immediate indication of degradation or outage. This can alert crafts to problems before they are noticeable to the customer.

⊕ It provides detailed descriptions of monitored protocol information. This enables trouble isolation.

⊕ The recording mechanism (i.e. log) captures information for future analysis. This is vital for intermittent (hard to repeat) problems.

PERFORMANCE MONITORING DEFINITION

To enhance the understanding of the maintenance capabilities outlined in this paper, a brief overview of layer's 1, 2 and 3 performance monitoring information is provided. The lower three layers of the OSI model are broken down into:

A. Layer 1: physical - This is the electrical and line format needed to carry the information of the upper layers. Performance monitoring information for BRI layer 1 is:.

* CRC-6 error events: When the CRC-16 code, based on the incoming bit stream does not agree with the received CRC-16 code.

* errored seconds: A second when one or more CRC-16 error events have occurred.

* severely errored seconds: A errored second which has more than X (to be determined) CRC-16 error events.

B. Layer 2: link layer – The layer 2 protocols for the BRI are Link Access Protocol D-Channel (LAPD) and Link Access Protocol Balanced (LAPB). The performance monitoring error information for layer 2 is in the form of:

* Protocol Error Records (PERs): The PER is a record of an abnormal event in the layer 2 protocol. Once the PER is generated by the switch, it is kept in a small buffer to allow the OS to retrieve and log the records for historical analysis. Each PER contains the following information:

+ protocol type

+ date and time of abnormal occurrence

+ location (e.g., access line, channel, TEI, etc.)

+ protocol information on abnormality

* number of frames received in error

* total number of frames received

* frames retransmitted

* total number of frames transmitted

C. Layer 3: network layer – On the BRI, this is currently defined to be either Q.931 or X.25. The performance monitoring error information for layer 3 is also in the form of PERs. The format of the layer 3 PER is identical to that outlined for layer 2 PERs.

GENERAL STRATEGY

As we have seen, the ISDN switch will collect a large variety of detailed performance monitoring data. The craft will then use an OS to access, record and interpret that information. This configuration also enables the craft to utilize tools other than performance monitoring. The craft can access other switch test functions (e.g., digital loopbacks) via the OS. In the scenario that follows, performance monitoring capabilities of the switch and the OS are used synergistically to isolate the maintenance problem.

SCENARIO

The following is a scenario of a customer trouble and the steps taken for isolation using performance monitoring information. The configuration of this scenario is depicted in figure 3. The descriptions has been written from an OS craft interface point of view.

The customer has subscribed to ISDN service and has chosen the ISDN feature of establishing an X.25 packet B channel on demand through D channel set-up messages (i.e. on demand packet B channel). Installation testing has been completed with verification of all services and features. The customer has also been successfully using the ISDN service and features which were provisioned. The customer comes in one morning, tries to originate a B channel packet switching session and cannot utilize the feature. When the customer reports the trouble, additional information is provided which indicates that circuit switched data and voice are still functioning. The problem of a non-working feature can be a symptom of troubles on the BRI, terminal, ISDN switch or some combination of the three.

In the future, OS functionality of alarm/performance monitoring correlation may have the ability to detect many faults of this nature prior to customer complaint. However, for this scenario we will assume a customer report started the maintenance action. We are also assuming that the appropriate flow through mechanisms have resulted in the routing of the customer trouble to craft which have access to the information outlined in these scenarios.

The first step is to obtain the current state of the BRI and its recent history. The state of the BRI can either be in-service (IS) or out-of-service (OOS). Since the ISDN switch will periodically try to re-establish service to the BRI, it is necessary to also check the recent history of the BRI for an indication of the trouble. From the customer's complaint, it would be expected that the BRI is IS because its circuit switched capabilities are operational. When the craft queries the OS concerning the status of the BRI, the OS will automatically collect and present in a combined report the status of the BRI. This allows the craft to mentally eliminate many possible causes from a single screen.

Based on the BRI information, the craft would take designated maintenance steps based on experience and company procedures. For our discussion, we will assume that the craft needs to verify each possible fault that could cause the customer trouble.

A. Provisioning error:

One of the major causes for a feature not working is improper provisioning. Either the feature was never provisioned or the provisioning has inadvertently been changed. Our original assumption was that the feature had been verified as functional. However, the first step is to verify that the feature is still correctly provisioned for the BRI.

B. Hardware or Software failure in the ISDN switch:

Although the customer has circuit switched voice and data, failure of switch software and hardware could still affect the on demand packet B channel feature. Examples of this would be failure of the packet handler (PH) for the B channel or a problem in software that establishes the path from the line card to the PH. The craft can query the OS for the status of the BRI to get an indication of the customer trouble. The OS will retrieve and display indicate the current state and condition of the BRI, and will also, if directed retrieve and display any recent OOS history of the BRI.

C. Layer 1 failure:

Layer 1 failure indicates that the switch has detected enough layer 1 problems to remove the customer from service. It is important to note that detected layer 1 problems do not indicate that there is loss of signal. Since the customer has some features operating normally,

it is very unlikely that anything abnormal would be identified through the layer 1 performance monitoring information. However, from the current layer 1 errored second and severely errored second counts, the craft can determine if the transmission facility has operated below or hovered around the acceptable transmission level during the past hour. The OS could also develop a graphic recent history report indicating whether this particular BRI has been experiencing repetitive layer 1 problems that have gone undetected or unreported by the customer. The current CRC-6 count can be examined to see if the line is still experiencing layer 1 problems. If a layer 1 problem exists, digital loopback tests are necessary to isolate the exact section of the network contributing to the condition.

As was expected, in this scenario the layer 1 performance monitoring information does not reveal any problems.

D. Layer 2 failure:

Since layer 1 is sound, and provisioning/translations are correct, the problem is probably protocol related. The known part of the problem is the inability to send X.25 packets. Whether the cause of the trouble is layer 2 or layer 3 B-Channel X.25, or D-Channel layer 3, set-up is not known.

The craft can query the OS, using the customer's primary directory number, to see if layer 2 abnormal events have occurred. The OS could develop a report depicting the number of occurrences and a historical view of when they occurred. The report would also indicate, based on the PER, the causes of the detected layer 2 problems.

E. Layer 3 failure:

Since the craft has already checked layer 2 and found it OK, the next step is to assess the layer 3 protocol. Note that when the craft queried the OS for layer 2 problems the OS would have automatically alerted the craft to any layer 3 problems. Since the problem concerns the on demand packet B-Channel feature, the problem could be caused by layer 3 protocol discrepancies in either X.25 on the B-Channel, or Q.931 set-up on the D-Channel. The information in the PER, as with layer 2, will indicate the type of protocol problem being experienced.

We anticipate that with the information and OS capabilities presented, most customer troubles will have been isolated. However, even with the PER maintenance information, some protocol problems can not be identified. These residual problems will require the "protocol expert" for diagnosis and isolation.

F. At this stage the "protocol expert" needs access to the actual protocol interaction on the BRI. The first step would be to request the OS to direct the ISDN switch to camp-on on the BRI and trigger the sending of the hex protocol information for a specific event to the OS. The OS would automatically take the hex output from the switch and convert the output into human readable form for the expert to analyze. If more detailed or exhaustive information is needed, the craft would remotely access the BRI through the switch and direct the output to a protocol analyzer for diagnosis/isolation.

In our scenario, the problem becomes relatively simple for the protocol expert. The problem has been referred to him because no

layer 1, layer 2 or layer 3 errors have been detected. The expert's monitoring indicates that absolutely no X.25 SETUP frames are being transmitted by the CPE. The customer's set has failed in this unusual mode, where it operates normally for most features, but it fails to setup X.25 B channel communications.

CONCLUSION

This paper has presented a practical use of performance monitoring information for the detection and isolation of customer faults. It is our belief that to successfully maintain ISDN lines with "POTS LIKE" efficiency it will be necessary to successfully blend the ISDN switch monitoring capabilities, OS processing and the craft understanding of protocol information. The maintenance value of performance monitoring information relies heavily on the ability for an OS to gather the information from the network and provide the craft with network based reports that have already done much of the processing discussed in this paper.

With the use of performance monitoring and OS processing the majority of all ISDN maintenance problems will be able to be identified without the need of a "protocol expert". This will facilitate the maintenance goal of "POTS LIKE" efficiency for the ISDN network.

REFERENCES

1. T1D1.3, "Draft Standard for ISDN Basic Rate Interface for Application at the Network Side of the NT, Layer 1 Specification", April 15, 1987.

2. T1M1.2, "Draft of ISDN Maintenance Operations Standard", March 22, 1988.

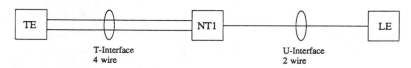

T-Interface
4 wire

U-Interface
2 wire

TE: Terminal Equipment

LE: Local Exchange

NT1: Network Termination 1

Figure 1 BRI Configuration

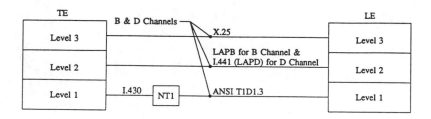

Packet Switched BRI

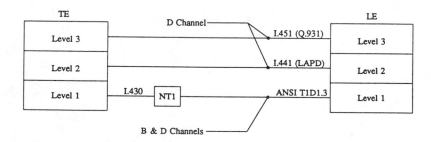

Circuit Switched BRI

TE: Terminal Equipment

LE: Local Exchange

NT1: Network Termination 1

Figure 2

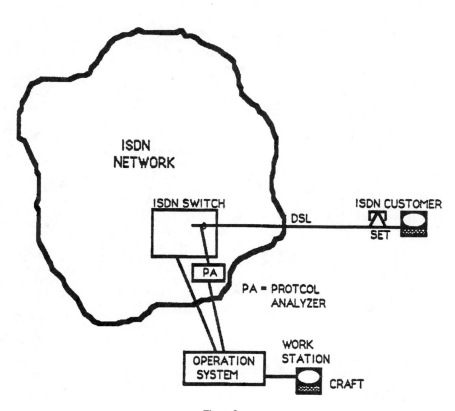

Figure 3

1132

DIGITAL TESTING STRATEGIES:

OPERATIONS   BASED ALTERNATIVES

R. P. Harrison - Chairperson

Bell Atlantic-
Network Services Inc.

New evolving technologies and the transition of the network from analog to digital has caused a void in operational testing procedures. This is further impacted by network boundaries created by divestiture between exchange and interexchange carriers. This seminar will examine the issues as identified by the industry in the various forums and standards bodies such as: The Network Operations Forum (NOF), The Interexchange Carrier Compatibility Forum (ICCF), The NOF/ICCF Digital Testing Workshop and Committee T1. Both real time as well as future, yet to be developed, solutions to these issues will be presented. This session also presents operational considerations for the transition to 64Kb Clear Channel Capability as well as a futuristic view of performance monitoring and facility maintenance.

J. C. Gutierrez Bell Communications
Research

R. P. Harrison Bell Atlantic, NSI

D. J. Hoffman US West Advanced
Technologies

P. V. Hughes U.S. West Advanced
Technologies

Session   1:   Introduction   to
NOF/ICCF Digital Testing Workshop

R. P. Harrison - Bell Atlantic

This session presents a brief history of the jointly sponsored NOF/ICCF Digital Testing Workshop, and industry group of both Exchange and Interexchange carriers that has identified and resolved many digital testing issues of national industry concern.

Session   2:   Digital   Acceptance
Tests for Switched and Special
Access

R. R. Harrison
Bell Atlantic

This session will present industry agreements developed in the NOF/ICCF Digital Testing Workshop. These agreements provide testing alternatives to embedded analog testing when the service being tested is all digital. Testing of sub-rate digital or voice grade circuits within high capacity services is also discussed.

Session   3:   Operational
Considerations For Transition to
64Kb Clear Channel Capability

J. C. Gutierrez
Bell Communications Research

The implementation of 64Kb/s Clear Channel Capability (64CCC) is essential to the introduction of digital services requiring full control of the DSO Channel. This session examines the issues associated with the evolution of 64CCC from an operational perspective. A representative sample of equipment which must be modified or replaced to provide 64CCC will be examined.

Session   4:   Operational
Considerations for Implementation
of B8ZS Line Code

P. V. Hughes
U.S. West Advanced Technologies

Binary Eight Zero Substitution (B8ZS) has been adopted by committee T1 as a method of providing 64KB Clear Channel Capability. This session covers some work being done in Committee T1 concerning the performance of AMI signals through B8ZS optioned equipment. Operational and testing considerations for B8ZS implementation will be discussed including the results of some laboratory studies that have been conducted using the B8ZS option in various circuit configurations.

Session   5:   UDSX,   a   Transport
Platform

D. J. Hoffman
U.S. West Advanced Technologies

This session presents the Universal Digital Signal Cross-Connect (UDSX) a feature rich transport platform. This platform provides an application concept and building block for DS-1 and DS-3 performance monitoring, control, testing and other attributes along with network management in support of the evolving software driven network of the future.

DIGITAL TESTING ALTERNATIVES FOR

SWITCHED VOICE GRADE SERVICES

R. P. Harrison - Co-Chairperson
NOF/ICCF Digital Testing Workshop

Bell Atlantic Network Services Inc.
One Washington Park
Newark, NJ 07102

Shortly after Divestiture it became apparent that operational interfaces between exchange carriers and interexchange carriers were severely lacking or misunderstood by the industry. Many comments regarding these interfaces were filed with the FCC, in response to the Model Tariff. In February, 1984 the FCC in Docket 83-1145 told the industry to cooperatively develope procedures to "receive, diagnose and repair troubles and allocate costs". The industry response was the formation of the Network Operations Forum (NOF).

On August 2, 1984 personnel representing Interexchange Carriers, Resellers, the seven Regional Bell Companies and a United States Telephone Association (USTA) Task Force held an organizational meeting. At this meeting key operational issues were identified and prioritized. Working committees were formed and a forum moderator was selected. On August 21 and 22, 1984 the first General Session was held. Ground rules were established as follow: Agreements would be by consensus, forum would be self policing, committees would be co-chaired jointly by ECs and ICs.

The committees kept an aggressive schedule and in November the NOF published its first documents, "Access Services Installation and Maintenance Operations Reference Documents". (This document has since been updated to issue 3 in

November, 1987) With installation and maintenance addressed, testing issues rose to the forefront and the NOF Testing Committee published the "NOF Committee Reference Document". One question was always in the background when the testing committee discussed issues - What do we do when the interface is digital? Increased deployment of digital switches brought a new question to the committee - Does it make sense to continue performing analog tests on completely digital circuits?

The operations type representatives to the testing committee felt that they had some good answers to these question however, they were not confident that their ideas were technically sound from an engineering perspective. Testing committee leadership approached the Interexchange Carrier Compatibility Forum (ICCF) and asked their help. This marriage produced th jointly sponsored NOF/ICCF Digital Testing Workshop (DTW). All workshop output would be subject to both NOF and ICCF consensus approval.

On May 25, 1985 the first Digital Testing Workshop was held in San Fransisco, California. In attendance were seventy eight representatives form thirty one companies. Participants agreed to address central office terminated access service in a digital environment as priority one issue. This was further defined as switched access service Feature Groups B, C, and D.

Three scenarios were presented for consideration: (see Figure 1, 2 and 3)

Fig. 1 (Today's Environment) Access Service provisioned with analog switches and a connecting analog facility
Fig. 2 Access Service provisioned with digital switches connected by a digital facility
Fig. 3 Access Service provisioned with at least one analog switch connected by a digital facility

It was noted that all tariffs and Technical References published to date required extensive per circuit analog testing regardless of which of the above scenarios applied. This being the case the following issues were identified:

1. What are the valid parameters to test: On pure digital access service on access service with digital interface at the Point of Termination (POT) served by an analog switch?

   a. at turnup (acceptance)
   b. on trouble referral or repair verification
   c. when adding circuits/ services on an established digital facility

2. What are the REASONABLE tests that should satisfy the above parameters?

3. Where and how do we perform this testing?

Based on these issues consensus agreement was reached on the following assumptions:

1. The full range of analog specifications and testing required today are not meaningful and not reasonable in a digital environment.

2. There is industry agreement and interest in the benefits of migrating away from analog testing in a digital environment.

3. Any proposed testing scenario should not preclude performance monitoring for digital specifications.

4. There is a need (from an operational perspective) for trunk testing to be performed on a "switch to switch" basis.

Based on the above issues and assumptions various parameters were proposed for both the purity digital and the combination analog switch digital facility cases as follow:

Existing Documented Parameters (Fig. 1) (Analog)

Standard Transmission Test Parameters (Normal Acceptance)

1. 1004Hz Loss
2. Attentuation Distortion (Gain Slope)
3. Balance (ERL-SRL)
4. C-Message Noise

Additional Transmission Test Parameters (Additional Cooperative Acceptance Testing, ACAT)

1. C-Notch Noise
2. Envelope Delay Distortion
3. Impulse Noise
4. Intermodulation Distortion
5. Phase Filter
6. Frequency Shift

Pure Digital Case (Fig. 2)
Candidate Parameter

   - 1004Hz Loss
Justification:
   To Verify

1. Software assignable pads

2. Connectivity to correct channel

3. Continuity

4. Signal Quality

Non Candidate Parameters:

1. Gain Slope

2. Envelope Delay Distortion
Justification: These are analog facility dependent

3. Balance (ERL-SRL)
Justification: Not applicable for 4-wire circuits

4. C-Message Noise

5. C-Notch Noise Intermodulation Distortion Justification: Analog Coder/Decoder dependent

6. Impulse Noise Justification: Measured as Bit Errors

7. Phase Jitter

8. Frequency Shift Justification: Analog Frequency Division Multiplex Dependent

Combination Analog Switch Digital Facility (Fig. 3)

Candidates Parameters

1. 1004Hz Loss Justification: required to verify analog trunk circuitry and channel units.

2. 3-Tone Slope

1135

3. Balance Justification: Required because of hybrid in the channel units

4. C-Message Noise

5. C-Notched Noise Justification: Noise contribution of the analog trunk circuitry.

After discussing the above traditional analog parameters, discussion turned to digital parameters and tests. Participants agreed that the digital transmission facility could be tested in lieu of individual circuit analog tests however, no standards existed for this type of testing. It was proposed that the special access HC1 parameters in PUB 62508 may apply. Many participants argued that special access HC1 is premium service and that HC1 parameters were not necessary for voice grade switched access service. Some participants proposed that existing T1 carrier manufacturer's acceptance specifications be used such as, a bit error rate test.

It became evident that further research was needed. This first meeting was adjourned so that participants could go back to their companies and further research the above issues. Another meeting was scheduled for June. In the June meeting a special task force was established to further address the digital facility test. After two more meetings the switched access agreements that follow were adopted by the DTW:

DIGITAL TESTING WORKSHOP AGREEMENTS NO DIGITAL /ANALOG (D/A) CONVERSION

Where an IC orders Switched Access Service F.G. B, C, or D with a digital interface at the POT (Interface Groups 6-10)

And the EC provides this service from a digital switch on digital transmission facilities with no D/A conversion

And the IC has no D/A conversion

The workshop recommends the following 3 Acceptance Tests:

° A Cooperative Test of the Digital Transmission Facility per October acceptance testing agreement (except in those cases where the Digital Transmission Facility has existed and is in service).

° One 1004Hz test per Trunk Group per Digroup in both directions of transmission.

° One Signalling/Operational test per trunk

NOF
ADOPTED: October 9, 1985
ICCF
ADOPTED: October 23, 1985

DIGITAL TESTING WORKSHOP AGREEMENTS WITH DIGITAL /ANALOG (D/A) CONVERSION

Where an IC orders switched Access Service F.G. B, C, or D with a digital interface at the POT (Interface Groups 6-10)

And the EC provides this service from a digital switch on digital transmission facilities with no D/A conversion and the IC has a D/A conversion

The workshop recommends either of the following acceptance test options:

Option I

All analog cooperative acceptance tests as specified in PUB 62500 except C-Message Noise (including C-Notched Noise).

Option II

° A cooperative test of the digital transmission facility (except in those cases where the digital transmission facility has existed and is in service).

° One 1004Hz test and one C-Notched Noise test per Trunk Group per Digroup in both directions of transmission.

° One Signalling/Operational test per trunk

NOF
ADOPTED: October 9, 1985
ICCV
ADOPTED: October 23, 1985

DIGITAL TESTING WORKSHOP AGREEMENTS
ACCEPTANCE TEST OF
DIGITAL TRANSMISSION FACILITIES

Cooperative acceptance test for digital transmission facilities provided in connection with an Order for voice switched access service F.G. B,C, or D

1. Bit error test in each direction of transmission using Compatible Quasi (described in PUB 62411)/ pseudo Random signal Source.

2. Acceptable bit error rate should be 10^{-6} or better for a period of one minute.

3. Test should be made at the EC DSX closest to the switch to the first IC DSX. The test shall be performed at a mutually agreed upon time during normal business hours.

NOF
ADOPTED: October 9, 1985
ICCF
ADOPTED: October 23, 1985

These agreements were passed on to the general membership of the NOF and the ICCF. All agreements were adopted however, the 10^{-6} bit error rate was questioned. The ICCF commissioned a Special Technical Meeting to further investigate the 10^{-6} bit rate test. At this Special Technical Meeting this parameter was changed to 10^{-7} bit error rate for a period for five (5) minutes. This parameter was changed due to the potential impact on voice grade data parameters, in particular, impulse noise.

The NOF took these agreements and incorporated them into Issue 2 of the NOF "Access Services Installation and Maintenance Operations Reference Documents". This document contains methods and procedures for use by the field technicians who would actually perform the work operations contained in the agreements.

Subsequent meetings of the DTW were held to address digital testing issues involving special access.

The Digital Testing Workshop has been very productive in solving existing industry digital testing concerns. We now look to the various standards bodies to pickup where we left off in the development of testing strategies, parameters and test equipment to move us into the future.

DIGITAL TESTING ALTERNATIVES FOR

SPECIAL ACCESS AND HIGH CAPACITY

DIGITAL SERVICES

W. R. Allan

Bell Communications Research
Livingston, NJ 07039

ABSTRACT

The paper will cover Digital Testing Workshop (DTW) agreements for testing sub-rate digital and voice grade services within high capacity facilities as well as testing at the DS 3 level. These testing agreements address the tests to be performed cooperatively between Exchange Carriers (ECs) and interexchange (IC) at the time of circuit acceptance. Alternatives discussed all deploy existing testing technology.

Special Access Testing Issues

The DTW Participants represent both ICs and ECs. At a meeting in August, 1985, the DTW Participants identified eight special access testing issues be addressed by the DTW. These issues were prioritized at a meeting held in September, 1985. The issues listed in priority order are:

1. What testing would apply to two point circuits at or above the DS-1 level. How should these services be tested.

2. How should non-switched VG/DS 0 tests be made on:

    ° Mux/Hub or Co/Hub
    ° Which tests
    ° Where to perform; at POT; beyond POT.

3. How to deal with WATS/FGA and Tie Lines within High Capacity Digital Access Service.

4. What tests are to be performed and how to access lower rates in higher level service, (e.g. DS 1 within DS 3).

5. Bit Error Rate (BER) application to special services, i.e. BER to EFS cross reference.

6. How to identify a digital service circuit on documentation.

7. What are the Multi EC implications within all the special access testing issues.

8. What are the Feature Group B, C, and D implications the special access issues.

The September, 1985, DTW formed a Working Group charged with defining and investigating solutions to these issues. The working group was also to draft alternative solutions or strawman proposals which would be reviewed by the DTW Participants. The working group was successful in developing proposed solutions to these testing issues. After review and modification by the DTW, consensus was reached on resolutions for all the special access issues. The resolutions have been adopted by the DTW parent forums, namely the Network Operations Forum (NOF) and the Interexchange Carrier Compatibility Forum (ICCF).

The industry consensus on how the special access testing issues should be resolved are as follows:

Issue 1A: High Capacity Digital Special Access Service HC1

High Capacity Digital Special Access Service HC1 is a point-to-point service operating at 1.544 mega bits persecond. The IC will provide, where appropriate, test access at the IC's POT location. When necessary, physical access to the IC POT will be locally arranged. Testing at the IC POT will be performed by the IC personnel. The EC will arrange testing capability at the end user POT. Testing at the end user PTO will be performed by the EC personnel.

Technical Reference (TR) PUB 62508 parameters and limits apply. The TR defines the service in terms of errored seconds. Compatible test equipment and signal source are necessary. Compatibility will be determined locally. NOF I&M specials document words apply for test access to end-user premises.

High Capacity Digital Special Access Service HC3

High Capacity Digital Special Access Service HC3 is point-to-point service operating at 44.736 mega bits per second. The agreements for HC1 service also apply for HC3 with one exception, the HC3 parameters defined in TR 62508 do not apply. TR 62508 defines HC3 service in terms of HC1 performance. Therefore, the DTW worked on developing the following HC3 acceptance test that measures the performance at the DS3 level. HC3 acceptance is to be based on 40 minute test period(s). If the first 40 minute test is less than 73 errored seconds, accept the HC3 special access service. If the first 40 minute test is more than 73 errored seconds, then additional 40 minute tests must be performed.

If three out of four 40 minute tests are each less then 84 errored seconds, accept the HC3 special access.

This HC3 acceptance test agreement has been established as an interim agreement. Carriers accepting service based on this agreement are asked to gather data to determine how reasonable these tests are.

The test is only applicable to electrical DS3 interfaces, i.e. form DSX-3 to DSX-3, or equivalent. The test can be applied whenever a HC3 goes from an IC POT to a customer premise, an exchange carrier hub, or another IC POT. The test applies to HC3 service in a framed format.

DS-0/Voice Grade Access Services Added to DS-1 Facilities Already in Service

A DS-0 or Voice Grade Signal can be extracted from a DS-1 bit stream at the IC POT with today's technology. Since this is so, joint cooperative acceptance testing can be performed from the IC POT location to the end-user POT.

In the case where the IC does not break out the DS-0 or Voice Grade Signal at the IC POT, the EC will perform test measurements of the DS-0 or Voice Grade Service from the end-user POT through the EC's digital channel unit if requested. These results will be provided to the IC, and cooperative acceptance tests will be waived.

The transmission performance for the service provided between end-user POT and the IC POT will be inaccordance with the parameters of the service ordered, not the facility.

WATS Access Lines and Feature Group A with a HC1/DS1 Interface at the POT

If the IC breaks out the DS0 or Voice Grade signal at the POT, existing methods for acceptance testing apply, e.g. the NOF I&M document. If the IC chooses not to break out the DS0 or Voice Grade signal at the POT, the EC will perform appropriate operational and transmission tests from the WATS serving office (dial tone office) through the digital channel unit. The EC will provide transmission results to the IC if requested.

Tie Lines with a HC1/DS1 Interface At the POT

Access services for tie lines are ordered and installed as special access services, i.e. IC POT to end user POT or IC POT to EC Centrex. Therefore, installation and testing of tie lines will be according to special access tariffs and DTW special access agreements.

DS-1 Service Riding within DS-3 Already in Service

When the IC demultiplexes the DS-3 signal at their POT, cooperative acceptance tests, requested will be from the end-users POT to the IC's POT at the DS-1 rate. When the IC demultiplexes the DS-3 signal to DS-1 signals at or beyond the POT in lieu of cooperative acceptance test, the EC can provide a loop-back at the DSX-1 toward the MUX and notify the IC. The IC can then verify the integrity of the DS-1 through the DS-3 multiplexer. The EC will also verify the DS-1 to the end-user POT and inform the IC of DS-1 test results. The EC will then notify the IC that the service is ready for acceptance and coordinate the removal of all loop-backs.

Multi-EC Implications of the Special Access Issue Resolutions

Multi-EC implications have been addressed in existing documents, i.e. the NOF Installation and Maintenance Document, and OBF issue resolutions. The working group recommends that these documents be used in conjunction with the DTW Special Access Issue Resolutions.

Conclusion:

The DTW has addressed all of the issues identified at the August, 1985 meeting. The resolutions have been reviewed and adopted by the NOF and the ICCF. There are no remaining open issues that the DTW is addressing. Should digital testing issues be identified by the industry in the future, they should be referred to the NOF. The NOF will determine if it is appropriate to reconvene the DTW.

These agreements are being published in the NOF publication: "Access Services Installation and Maintenance Operations Reference Documents" Issue 3. This document also addresses maintenance testing based on these DTW acceptance testing guidelines.

The DTW recognizes that its agreements are transitional, interim solutions to operational problems faced by the industry today. New technology and approved industry standards will supercede these agreements as they become available. The DTW has enjoyed a close working relationship with various T1 standards groups in hopes that our agreements will provide a smooth transition to the ultimate standards as well as providing an operations perspective in the development of such standards.

Addendum:

In April 1988 the NOF authorized the DTW to reconvene to address concerns relating to the implementation of Extended Superframe Format (ESF) as well as some new issues that are surfacing related to analog tests at digital interfaces. This work will also involve work in progress in various T1 Technical Sub-committees.

OPERATIONAL CONSIDERATIONS FOR IMPLEMENTATION OF B8ZS LINE CODE

PAUL V. HUGHES

Member Technical Staff

U S WEST Advanced Technologies
6200 S. Quebec
Englewood, CO. 80111

BACKGROUND

A significant portion of the future telecommunications market is expected to be served by the Integrated Services Digital Network (ISDN). A basic building block for ISDN is Clear Channel Capability (CCC), at 64 kb/s, and other ISDN rates. CCC allows a customer to transport digital signals with no constraint on the quantity and sequence of ones and zeros. This in turn allows the customer to utilize transmission facilities at full capacity.

Digital transmission facilities constitute the major portion of our overall interoffice networks. Of those facilities, many operate at the DS1 level (1.544 Mb/s). Twenty-four voice or data channels at the DS0 level (64 Kb/s) feed into circuitry which multiplexes the channels up to the DS1 level. At the present time, because the network constrains the digital signals by requiring a minimum ones density and limits the number of sequential zeros, the 24 DS0 channels each offer less than 64 kb/s, in terms of usable information bits for customers.

Attaining 64CCC is possible through two methods: Bipolar with Eight Zero Substitution (B8ZS) or Zero Byte Time Slot Interchange (ZBTSI). The American National Standards Institute accredited Committee T1 has recommended B8ZS and ZBTSI as two methods of providing clear channel capability.

Figure 1 is a physical model of a source/sink device capable of operating in the AMI, B8ZS, or ZBTSI mode. It is used to illustrate where the coding functions for ZBTSI and

B8ZS reside. The switch settings indicate that with AMI selected, no encoding functions for either B8ZS or ZBTSI take place. With ZBTSI selected, only encoding at the Logic Level takes place. With B8ZS selected, encoding at the Line Code level is begun.

Encoding at a particular level, i.e. logic level or line code, necessitates decoding at that same level. Figure 2 illustrates the various locations where decoding, and further encoding, would be necessary for either B8ZS or ZBTSI.

To further develop an understanding of the algorithms and behavioral models used in the T1M1 study, a discussion of the basic characteristics of B8ZS follows.

The traditional Alternate Mark Inversion (AMI) line code and the new B8ZS line code differ only in their treatment of a string of eight or more zeros (Figure 3). From a purely functional viewpoint, an AMI coder passes the zeros as zeros (today's devices are designed to deliver a DS1 signal with at least one pulse in eight pulse positions, and no more than fifteen consecutive pulse positions without pulses). A B8ZS coder with an input string of eight zeros exercises an algorithm which inserts two bipolar violations and two "1s" (the fourth and seventh zeros become marks of the same polarity as the last mark, with ones in positions five and eight completing the signature).

Figure 4 is a model and input data string for which B8ZS coding is employed. As shown, B8ZS coding can also toggle frame bits. Framing will not be directly observable at intermediate DS1 locations without B8ZS decoding. Frame error rate can be more severe compared to the AMI cases, since line errors in the B8ZS word can also cause the coded frame bit to be incorrectly decoded.

The various configurations possible with two channel banks in one direction are shown in Figure 5. With the given logic input string, the output of either an AMI or a B8ZS

coder at the DS1 is shown. The resulting data string is then shown at the receive end for both AMI and B8ZS.

AMI coded information can be successfully transmitted, within one coding-decoding section only, to a B8ZS decoder, but B8ZS-coded information cannot be successfully transmitted to an AMI decoder. An AMI decoder receiving B8ZS will see two Bipolar Violations (BPVs) and two ones which have been inserted, and decode them as four ones and errors. A B8ZS decoder will allow an AMI signal to pass in one section only because the only added design feature to the original AMI decoder is the recognition of the unique signature of B8ZS.

The input shown is used to indicate how the framing bit between words 24 and 1 is also affected. Thus the B8ZS-->AMI case not only causes errors in data, but can also result in framing errors.

On May 13, 1987, a T1 standards Ad Hoc Group met at the New York Telephone Laboratories in Rye Brook, New York. The group was charged by Technical Subcommittee T1M1.3 to prepare a technical report on the performance of AMI signals through B8ZS optioned equipment across network boundaries.

The initial setup was a D4-type channel bank connected to another D4-type channel bank (Figure 6). Where option 1, 2, 3 or 4 is shown for the channel banks, the corresponding number gives the results for BPVs, impulse noise and alarms. The two channel banks were equipped with Line Interface Units (LIUs) which could be optioned for either normal D4 format (AMI or B8ZS), or Extended Superframe Format (ESF), (AMI or B8ZS). The outputs of channels 2 and 3 on the receiving bank (B) were connected to test sets in order to measure impulse noise at a threshold of 68 dBrnC0. A 1004 Hz test tone at -13 dBm0 was inserted onto Channels 1, 2 & 3 at the transmitting bank (A). An adaptive type test set was used at the DSX-1 point to measure bipolar violations. This test setup was initially optioned for normal D4/AMI (#1), to verify proper operation. Indications were satisfactory, with no impulse noise, bipolar violations or alarms indicated.

Channel Bank "A" was then set to the B8ZS option (D4 format, #2). Impulse noise was immediately present on both Channels 2 & 3 (bank "B" receive), but no bipolar violations were indicated on the adaptive test set. Investigation revealed that the test set, being an adaptive type (automatic sensing with no operator reset), had simply indicated that B8ZS was present at the DSX-1 point. At this time, a nonadaptive type test set was substituted at the DSX-1 point, which then indicated bipolar violations (normal indication because the violations are intentional). No equipment alarms were received at any point in the system.

Channel bank "B" was then set to the B8ZS option (D4 format, #3). Impulse noise ceased, with bipolar violations still being indicated (again normal). Channel bank "A" was then set back to the AMI position (D4 format, #4). No impulse noise was generated nor were bipolar violations present.

A synopsis of the tests indicated that when both channels 2 & 3 had tone applied, channel bank "A" set for B8ZS and channel bank "B" set for AMI, impulse noise was present. If one tone was removed, then neither channel indicated impulse noise. Several variations were tried, but the end result indicates that loading adjacent channels initiates the impulse noise.

The test setup was then modified to include multiplexers. Test results again indicated that anytime the B8ZS format is sent to an AMI unit, errors will occur. Those errors will vary depending on the loading, zeros density, levels, etc. One point to be made is that intervening multiplexers will remove the bipolar violations and the logical errors will only be detected within the bitstream at the ultimate source/sink receiver, as impulse noise.

Additional tests using a quasi-random signal source (QRSS) were subsequently run. Table 1 is the results of those tests, which, although not the complete series of tests, do indicate the operational impact.

Tests were also run using ESF (Table 2). Results were the same with the addition of Cyclic Redundancy Check (CRC) 6 errors being present. The Bit Error Rate (BER) indicator on the LIU would be lit when impulse noise was present. This is not an alarm per se, but could be utilized, if so desired. Because CRC6 errors are also indicated, improper optioning is more easily detected. However the indication is only at the source/sink receiving. Incorrect options can exist at any intervening MUX.

EFFECT STATEMENTS

The following statements, each followed by a short discussion, summarize a portion of the operational, administrative, maintenance, and provisioning impacts in a mixed B8ZS/AMI network.

Improper B8ZS/AMI optioning does not generate a unique "signature."

At this time, improper optioning does not have a unique "signature," i.e. BER, AIS and dribbling error rate also relate to various other conditions within the network. A service provider may only become aware of improper optioning through customer complaint, i.e. dribbling error rate. Alarms may not be generated because the bit error rate is not high enough to trip existing alarm thresholds. If ESF is being used, a high "Cyclic Redundancy Check (CRC6) error rate" alarm is possible at the receiving source/sink. However, the following scenario presents a case in which the CRC6 does not provide the proper indications.

A simple example will be used to illustrate 1) how a recalculated CRC can indicate error-free operation in a LH section that is producing logic and line code errors and 2) indication of a CRC problem in a LH section that is operating perfectly.
Figure 7 shows a DS1 S/S device (location A) connected to one of the 28 DS1 low-speed ports of an MX3-type

multiplexer at location B. At location C, the signal again appears at the DS1 level, connected to location D. At location E, the DS1 signal then connects to the other S/S device at location F. The S/S devices and LH multiplexers all have AMI and B8ZS option switches, and the S/S devices have both Superframe (SF) and Extended Superframe (ESF) framing options.

The selected mode of operation is AMI with ESF (for error-checking capability). Both S/S devices are properly optioned in this manner. Locations D and E are also properly optioned for AMI. However, locations B and C are incorrectly optioned for B8ZS.

As was observed in the laboratory tests, idle and unequipped channel slots prevent service failure susceptibility from becoming apparent. As channel slots are equipped and the location A S/S device begins to exhibit an eight-or-more string of zeros in the DS1 bit stream, the B8ZS codec at location C will begin to generate unwanted B8ZS words. At location D, the codec will remove the bipolar violations (Violation Monitor and Removal, VMR) but the logic errors will remain (reference Figure 5). The resultant signal from the location F codec will ultimately be decoded as corrupt customer data.

A new generation test set having both ESF and B8ZS capabilities will be used to illustrate the troubleshooting problems with this scenario. Initially, a set of measurements is made at TP-1. The set is able to frame up on the signal, does not "see" any B8ZS words, and successfully recalculates a perfect CRC. The test set is moved to TP-2, where it again frames up on the signal and recalculates a perfect CRC, even though location C is the source of line code violations and logic errors due to the unwanted B8ZS words. The test set first decodes B8ZS words whenever they appear, then frames on the signal, then recalculates the CRC. Thus the test set has effectively removed the manifestation of the problem that continues to affect the far-end S/S device. While the presence

of the B8ZS light would indicate the problem, there may be no bursts of B8ZS at the time of the test which would trigger the indication. But whether or not the B8ZS indicator is lit, the set will indicate a perfect CRC 100% of the time (no other bona fide transmission problems being present).

At TP-3, the unwanted B8ZS words have been stripped of their bipolar violations (VMR characteristic). The test set will frame up on the signal (If possible) (reference figure 5, framing bit error), and attempt to recalculate the CRC. Because the signature of the B8ZS words has been removed, the test set is unable to deconvolve the the unwanted B8ZS coding. Since the errored logic one bits remain, the test set will produce a bad CRC, indicating to the operator that the transmission problem is in the D-E multiplex section. A subsequent test of this section, either looped or single-ended, will show that everything is working perfectly. The operator may conclude that the trouble is in the receiving portion of the the location F device, but again everything will check perfectly.

> Today's testing logic and techniques are inadequate to locate and isolate improperly optioned devices.

In addition to normal acceptance tests, a test must be made to determine the actual line code being transmitted and received in each direction of transmission for every line haul and source/sink section. For 64 kb/s CCC, two suggested procedures would be either a 64kHz loopback test or a DSO end-to-end test which utilizes an eight or more zeros data string (i.e. dataport channel). However, many offices do not have the resources to perform the latter test.

Test sets are available today which are adaptive in nature, i.e. will automatically switch from AMI to B8ZS without operator intervention. This set design may cause operator error when testing for AMI in a section which was inadvertently optioned for

B8ZS. The test set will indicate B8ZS but not that improper optioning may exist because it assumes that the B8ZS case is in effect and interprets the line code accordingly, thus not indicating bipolar violations or errors. For the same instance, a non-adaptive test set would indicate bipolar violations and errors. Also the test set reading may or may not indicate a bad facility i.e. if optioned for B8ZS, the readings are proper.

Improper B8ZS/AMI optioning will not normally generate alarms with average channel loading. This is dependent upon (but not limited to) the number of channels loaded, which channels are loaded, the levels used, and the ones density.

The operational impact is insidious because no alarms are issued from the incorrectly optioned line haul or source/sink equipment. The equipment may take reframe events due to the bipolar violations from B8ZS words, but (due to the random nature of the total channels' data content) this alone is not likely to be severe enough to initiate a Carrier Group Alarm (CGA). Tested separately, both line and terminal equipment will appear to be working properly.

New test signals for field use are recommended.

The subject of test signals and test equipment must be studied further. Consideration of new test signals should include, but not be limited to: existing Quasi-Random Signal Source (QRSS) w/B8ZS line code, selective two byte pattern, new stress test patterns, and the implications of framed/unframed test sequences.

Administration of internetwork line code assignments will have to be coordinated, and all carriers must have the proper optioning information.

The significance of the operational characteristics presented is that all network providers must begin the link-by-link tracking and optioning of all new B8ZS-capable source/sink and line haul elements at the time of deployment. This must be done regardless of the planned time for actually using the capability if it is desired to operate standard AMI and B8ZS networks in the same geographic area. Assignment options should be verified in all equipment being turned up that has the AMI/B8ZS option available. A positive check should be made whether AMI or B8ZS is assigned per the carrier service order.

Each carrier involved in the provisioning of a DS1 service must have the proper optioning information and the necessary order flow procedures to be implemented. This is true even if one carrier has non-optionable equipment.

In order for equipped, unassigned systems to be used for service restoration purposes, there must be agreement relative to the AMI/B8ZS option settings.

There is a need to expand the exchange of administration information about the systems that cross network boundaries. High Speed Multiplexers (MUX) available today vary in the methodology for providing B8ZS or AMI. Situations may arise where one carrier utilizes a MUX which provides B8ZS on a per DS1 basis and the connecting carrier provides B8ZS on a group basis (Typical: 4 DS1s in a group). For this case, DS1 assignments must be coordinated and the proper option setting for the low speed equipment protection will require resolution.

A methodology for automatic option verification is a viable concept.

A B8ZS-optioned source should never present more than seven consecutive zeros nor should an AMI source ever present a B8ZS "signature" word. A solution for option identification in equipment is to provide an "8 zeros received" or "B8ZS received" detector. Figure 8 indicates how the detector selection would follow option selection in the equipment. The detector would provide an indication to the surveillance/alarm equipment that would allow the sectionalization of the incorrect option.

Line haul device issues.

Digital multiplexers handle bit streams without identifying or treating framed signals or framing information in any special manner. The resulting problem is not apparent until the characteristics of today's source/sink devices are examined more closely.

Since the multiplexing equipment does not frame-align on the DS1 signal, it frequently "sees" eight or more zeros with a traditional AMI signal, because it does not use the framing reference for the identification of discrete bytes. At some predetermined number of zeros (with present and future multiplexers), a loss-of-signal and resulting "blue-signal" (AIS) condition will be declared, generally in the range of 30-80 zeros, depending on the manufacturer. Additionally, anything greater than seven consecutive zeros presented to the DS1 input port of the of a B8ZS-equipped (and optioned) multiplexer will cause the far-end B8ZS codec to produce a burst of logic ones and bipolar violations, regardless of the fact that the long zero string occurred over two adjacent bytes and all DS1 constraints were met. B8ZS-equipped (and optioned) source/sink devices should never present more than seven consecutive zeros, so there should never be a spontaneous generation of one or more B8ZS words in new B8ZS-equipped line-haul multiplexers. Again, two conditions will cause B8ZS word generation in such multiplexers: either the presentation of B8ZS words at the DS1 input ports, or the presentation of between eight and fifteen zeros, which occurs frequently with today's source/sink devices and QRSS test equipment.

Failure to properly track and option the B8ZS-capable source/sink and line-haul elements will result in random, bursty quantizing errors (impulse noise in voice channels) or massive data errors (DDS-type applications), where one or more line-haul elements inserts unwanted B8ZS words. The determination of the presence or absence of framing is not known until B8ZS is decoded and examined by the appropriate framing detector.

On total loss of receive DS3 signal, all MUX low-speed ports should produce an unframed all-ones AIS in a valid bipolar format, even when optioned for B8ZS. The Loss-of-Signal (LOS) detector at the DS3 level should be designed to inhibit all B8ZS codecs and cause AIS generators to become active for all 28 DS1 ports.

Performance Monitoring devices and techniques need to be developed for the B8ZS methodology.

With the ever-increasing implementation of new technology in our network, there follows the demand for adequate performance monitoring. The concern at this time for this particular issue deals with the adequacy of our Performance Monitoring systems to identify and locate an improperly optioned device. If B8ZS methodology is in use in a mixed environment, the Performance Monitoring/Testing (PM/TST) equipment must have the capability of identifying and verifying the line codes and options being used.

RECOMMENDATIONS

ESF should be the preferred implementation for B8ZS to take advantage of the CRC6 error checking capability.

Two methods for automatic verification of option settings are possible.

The first deals with utilizing the overhead bits in the ESF for checking option settings. This method may not require more circuitry in the physical equipment, but the drawback would be that the validation would only be for one option path, thus not ensuring end-to-end verification. Since MUXs do not find frame, this approach will not work at these points.

The second method involves the additional circuitry associated with a code detector (Figure 8). For a given circuit and with nonoptioned equipment units (source/sink or MUX), one or more status alarms could indicate immediately the option path(s) with either an improperly optioned or bad unit. Realize that while this does not indicate the B8ZS-->AMI improper option for a given path (A-->B), it will indicate the AMI-->B8ZS improper option in the reverse (B-->A) path.

The subject of test signals and test equipment should be studied further. Consideration of new test signals should include, but not be limited to: existing QRSS w/B8ZS line code, selective two byte pattern, new stress test patterns, and the implications of framed/unframed test sequences.

The capability to detect improper option selections is recommended for adaptive test sets.

DEFINITION OF TERMS

ALGORITHM: A set of rules or procedures for the solution of a problem.

ALTERNATE MARK INVERSION SIGNAL: (AMI), (BIPOLAR) A signal conveying binary digits, in which successive marks are of alternative polarity (positive and negative) but equal in amplitude, and in which spaces are of zero amplitude.

BIPOLAR VIOLATION: (BPV) A mark signal that has the same polarity as the previous mark signal in the transmission of alternate mark inversion signals.

BYTE: A group of eight binary digits handled as a unit and usually used to represent a character.

CLEAR CHANNEL: Allows the transport of digital signals with no constraint on the quantity and sequence of ones and zeros.

CODEC: A generic term for an equipment unit containing both a coder and decoder.

FORMAT: A logic-level manipulation which does not directly act on or modify the final line code.

FRAMING BIT: A non-information-carrying bit that is used for frame synchronization. The bit is placed at specific intervals in the bit stream and is used to determine the beginning and end of a frame.

LINE CODE: A particular electrical or optical representation of a digital signal as it is presented to the physical transmission medium.

LINE HAUL DEVICE: An element which transports the signals originated by source/sink devices.

SOURCE/SINK DEVICE: An element which originates (source) and terminates (sink) DS1 and DS1C signals.

QUASI-RANDOM SIGNAL SOURCE: (QRSS) A signal source, normally bay-mounted and cabled within a central office, which provides a DS1 test signal.

UNIPOLAR: Pertaining to a method of transmitting signals with one polarity, that is, positive, or negative voltage signals, but not both.

TODAY'S ENVIRONMENT

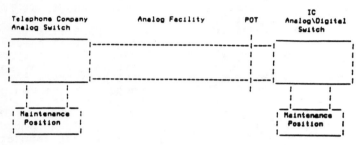

FIG 1

DIGITAL ARRANGEMENT
CASE A

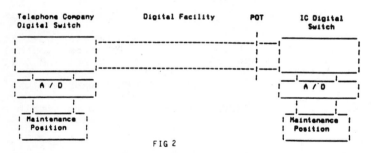

FIG 2

ANALOG ARRANGEMENT
CASE B

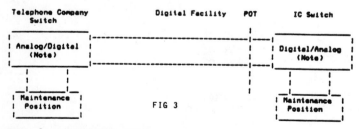

FIG 3

Note: One switch must be analog

1147

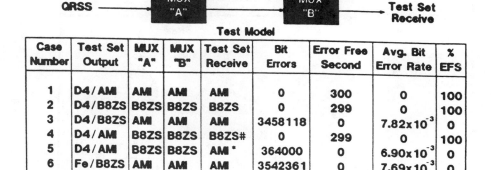

Test Model

Case Number	Test Set Output	MUX "A"	MUX "B"	Test Set Receive	Bit Errors	Error Free Second	Avg. Bit Error Rate	% EFS
1	D4/AMI	AMI	AMI	AMI	0	300	0	100
2	D4/B8ZS	B8ZS	B8ZS	B8ZS	0	299	0	100
3	D4/B8ZS	AMI	AMI	AMI	3458118	0	7.82×10^{-3}	0
4	D4/AMI	B8ZS	B8ZS	B8ZS#	0	299	0	100
5	D4/AMI	B8ZS	B8ZS	AMI *	364000	0	6.90×10^{-3}	0
6	Fe/B8ZS	AMI	AMI	AMI	3542361	0	7.69×10^{-3}	0

Notes: 1) Case Number 4 would have ~ 10^{-3} Error Rate in the Opposite Direction of Transmission
* Nonadaptive test set
# Adaptive test set

TABLE 1

B8ZS/AMI Test w/D4 Channel Bank
Channel Bank set for ESF/B8ZS, MUXs set for AMI

Analog in → BNK "A" → MUX "A" → MUX "B" → BNK "B" → Analog out

Tone on Channel	Tone Level	Results at 68 dBrnC0		CRC Errors	Average CRC Errors
2&3	-13 dBM	Ch 2-	0 hits		7.73×10
		Ch 3-	2000 hits	7719	
2&3	0 dBM	N/A		24728	2.48×10^{-1}
		N/A			
1&3	-13 dBM	Ch 1-	0 hits	0	0
		Ch 3-	0 hits	0	0
1&3	0 dBM	N/A			
		N/A			
1&24	-13 dBM	Ch 24-	0 hits		
		Ch 1 -	1900 hits	2892	2.99×10^{-2}
1&24	0 dBM	N/A		23566	2.36×10^{-1}
		N/A			

TABLE 2

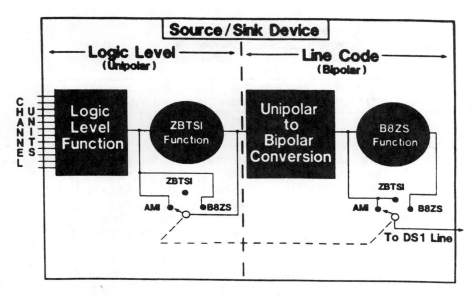

FIGURE 1

Coding Techniques
Required Locations

FIGURE 2

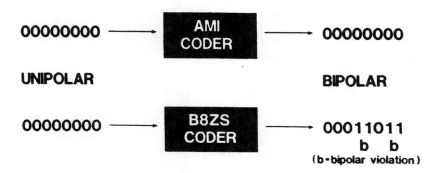

UNIPOLAR   BIPOLAR

00000000 → B8ZS CODER → 00011011
                                    b b
                         (b - bipolar violation)

FIGURE 3

AMI   B8ZS
Input Data   → B8ZS CODER →   **Coded Data**

Channel 24	frame bit	Channel 1	Channel 24	frame bit	Channel 1
10000000	0	00000001	10001101	1	00000001
01000000	0	00000001	01000110	1	10000001
00100000	0	00000001	00100011	0	11000001
00010000	0	00000001	00010001	1	01100001
00001000	0	00000001	00001000	1	10110001
00000100	0	00000001	00000100	0	11011001
00000010	0	00000001	00000010	0	01101101
00000001	0	00000001	00000001	0	00110111

FIGURE 4

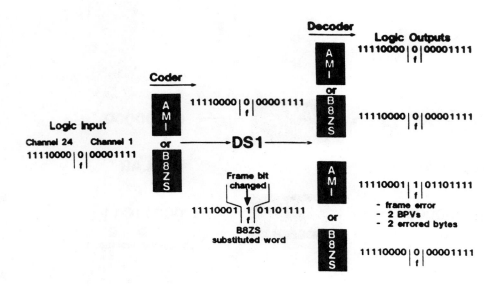

FIGURE 5

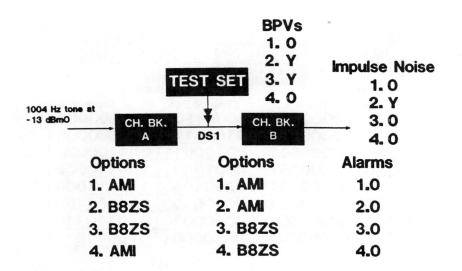

FIGURE 6

TROUBLE SECTIONALIZATION MODEL

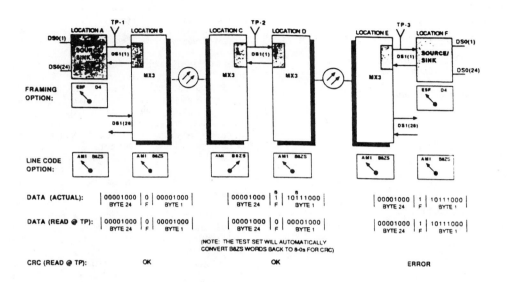

FIGURE 7

MONITOR or DECODER

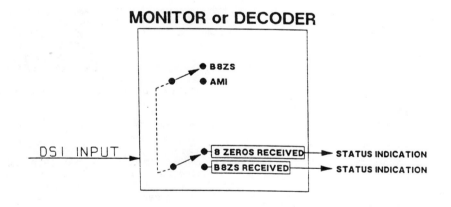

FIGURE 8

THE LAST MILE - THE FUTURE OF THE LOCAL LOOP

Louis B. Phillips
Network Manager-Business Customer Planning

GTE North Incorporated
19845 North US 31
P.O. Box 407
Westfield, Indiana 46074

ABSTRACT

The "Last Mile," that portion of the network that connects the customer to the world is, from the customer's perspective, also the "First Mile." As more and more technical demands are being made of it, the local loop takes on critical importance. Deregulation has made the picture even more complex. These presentations look at the strategies, planning techniques, service offerings, and support technologies that are all part of the industry's concerns today.

D. P. Wiater   - Central Telephone Company
                  Chicago, IL

J. M. Musser   - GTE Laboratories, Inc..
                  Waltham, MA

K. M. Corcoran - Southwestern Bell Tele. CO.
                  Fort Worth, TX

S. S. Walker   - GTE Laboratories, Inc..
                  Waltham, MA

STRATEGIES FOR A LOW RISK CUSTOMER LOOP

Daniel Paul Wiater
Assistant Staff Manager-Network & Switching

Central Telephone Company
O'Hare Plaza
8745 Higgins Road
Chicago, Illinois 60631

The design of the customer loop must be altered to meet the technical requirements of a changing environment. The costs and risks associated with the alterations can be minimized through the implementation of a few simple strategies.

There have been more major scientific advances in the last forty years than at any other period in history. These advances have had a profound effect on industries related to the storage and transport of information.

Several local carriers have aggressively capitalized on these advances and the benefits of changing technology. They, as a result, have become recognized leaders in the communications industry. The keys to their successes have been the thorough analysis of new technology and the implementation of change where warranted.

An analysis of the local telco environment indicates that the majority of the local customers needs are met, at least partially, over voice grade access lines. However, customers needs are changing. Some are developing an almost insatiable appetite for information and communications network convenience.

Communications technology is evolving to meet these changing needs. The evolution has resulted in the development of switched-access high-frequency inband signalling services such as P-Phone and Datapath. The continued evolution of customer needs and technology are already leading to a totally new network design concept, ISDN (Integrated Services Digital Network). ISDN will meet changing customer needs by providing increased bandwidth on demand. It will also provide improvements in network convenience.

The customer loop is a major component in providing voice grade, and the more sophisticated, switched access services. There are four important issues which must be addressed concerning this component, and its relationship with changing technology. They are: loading, range, customer location, and cost.

Loading is required on all voice grade circuits extending beyond 18 kilofeet. Loading is not compatible with other existing and evolving switched access services.

Range is also an issue. Voice grade service can be provided to customers well in excess of 100 kilofeet of the central office line equipment on loaded copper loops. The range of P-Phone, for example, is economically limited to 18 kilofeet because part of P-Phone is voice grade service. Therefore, beyond 18 kilofeet, loading or more costly solutions to attenuation and frequency response are required on the voice grade component of P-Phone service. The maximum range of Datapath is limited to 18 kilofeet due to propagation delay. The range of ISDN is, to a degree, gauge dependent. It can be extended beyond 18 kilofeet. However, beyond 18 kilofeet, a loop designed for ISDN will not meet the industry standards for POTS, the local telcos bread-and-butter service.

The location of the customer in relation to the serving office is also important. The range of embedded loop lengths, at Centel, runs from a low of under 500 feet to well over 150 kilofeet. An analysis of statistics, projections and current plant practices uncovered three important facts. First, the average existing Centel customer is served by a loop which is just over 14 kilofeet in length. Second, the average new customer is approximately 19.5 kilofeet from the serving line equipment. Third, neither embedded loop plant nor current loop design practices will support evolving services to the average Centel customer.

Cost is the last of the important issues. As customer needs progress from voice grade service to P-Phone, Datapath and ISDN capabilities, the cost of the materials required to build the loop also increases. It's impossible to identify which customers will request upgraded services. It is, therefore, nearly impossible to determine where limited capital resources should be spent to provide loop upgrades.

The problem Centel and other local carriers face has two components. It can be stated as: "HOW CAN THE LOCAL CARRIER DESIGN A LOOP WHICH IS CAPABLE OF PROVIDING COST EFFECTIVE POTS AND STILL MEET THE SOPHISTICATED NEEDS OF A SMALL BUT GROWING NUMBER OF CUSTOMERS?"

The available solutions to this problem are perceived as expensive. They generally involve the substitution of currently available loop electronics for copper. A strategy which involves the exclusive use of either electronics or copper is risky. Centel has developed a strategy which minimizes the risk, is relatively cost free and provides universal loop compatibility.

The strategy will make outside plant facilities look like the appropriate remotes are already in service. When they become available, they can be implemented at the proper locations to meet the new forecasted demand and reduce, as much as possible, the addition of strandable facilities.

In short, there are three simple steps to building a universally compatible loop. They are:

1. Assume there will be a universally compatible electronic device at every natural multiple of 24 kft., in order to predefine all electronic equipment boundaries at 12 kft., 36 kft., and every 24 kft. thereafter.

2. Add copper as facility shortages materialize, in order to meet the forecast, but, add that copper under the assumption that the electronic devices are already in service at the proper 24 kft. intervals.

3. Substitute currently-available electronics when the alternative is to add strandable copper, when it provides a cost advantage, or when it is the only solution to meeting the customer's needs.

EVOLUTION OF FIBER IN THE LOCAL LOOP

K. M. CORCORAN
AREA MANAGER-ENGINEERING PLANNING

SOUTHWESTERN BELL TELEPHONE COMPANY
1116 Houston, Room 1400
Fort Worth, TX 76102

ABSTRACT

Trials of fiber in the local loop have been announced across the telephone industry. This paper will discuss the driving forces, technology advancements and new services. It will deal with the evolution from copper to fiber in the local loop and will compare proposed star and bus architectures. The paper will provide a summary of announced trials and will discuss various issues and concerns yet to be resolved.

INTRODUCTION

Fiber optic technology has been playing an increasingly larger role in the evolution of the telephone network. In recent years, fiber optic systems have been deployed in interoffice and interexchange routes, loop feeder plant, point to point routes for large businesses, and local area networks. The next evolutionary step for fiber optic systems is the deployment in the local loop.

Recent advances in fiber optic technology are providing lower cost fiber cable and optoelectronic devices. These cost projections should allow economic deployment for plain old telephone service (POTS) within the early 1990's. In addition, the possibility of a new spectrum of telecommunication and video services arises.

TECHNOLOGY ADVANCEMENTS

Optical fiber represents a substantial portion of the cost of fiber in the local loop. However, single-mode fiber has decreased from $5.00/meter in 1982 to $0.23/meter in 1987. Experts predict that the cost will drop to $0.05/meter by the early 1990's if enough demand develops. Where fiber is experiencing a 20% cost decrease annually, copper is experiencing a 5% cost increase annually. Although splicing and connecting fiber is more expensive compared to copper, current emphasis is being placed upon the development of low cost splicing and low cost connectors.

Recent work in optical transmitters allow the use of either lasers or LED's with single-mode fiber. It is possible to transmit in the 400-600 Mbit/s range with LED's over single-mode fiber. It is also possible to use low-cost communication lasers mounted in a compact disk laser package.

NEW SERVICES

The second driving force in the evolution of fiber in the local loop is the potential demand for broadband services. These key services are primarily based upon video. Initially fiber could be utilized for the distribution of video, similar to current CATV distribution. Extended Quality Television (EQTV) and High Definition Television (HDTV) could be delivered as the cost of digitizing and compressing the video signal decreases. Switched video services, such as pay-per-view or video on demand, could be delivered as the cost of switching video decreases.

Additional requirements could emerge from the introduction of video telephony, home information retrieval, home shopping utilizing high quality display and arrangement of merchandise, and high fidelity audio.

EVOLUTION FROM COPPER TO FIBER

Today's local loop plant is primarily copper, and has been optimized for 4 Khz voice transmission. The 4Khz voice is digitized at 65Kbit/s. Tomorrow's services could require bit rates in the 150-600Mbit/s range. The first step in the evolution from copper to fiber is the placement of fiber from the Central Office (CO) or Remote Electronic Site (RES) to the customer. Downstream this requires the conversion of the electrical POTS signal to an optical signal at the CO or RES and transmission over fiber to the Optical Network Interface (ONI) at the home. At the ONI, the optical signal is converted to an electrical signal for POTS service. Upstream operation is merely reversed. Conversion to ISDN should not pose a problem since initial transceivers will operate much above the 144Kbit/s ISDN rate.

The next step in the evolution should be the transport of broadcast video either on separate fibers or through wave division multiplexing (WDM). Much research has been focused upon using FM analog transmission for this broadcast function.

The third step in the evolution should be the integrated transport of POTS/ISDN and digitized video utilizing the SONET format. Current NTSC video requires around 100Mbit/s non-compressed while HDTV requires around 1.1Gbit/s non-compressed. Research has indicated that compression should allow the NTSC signal to fit inside a 51.9Mbit/s SONET STS-I frame while the HDTV signal should squeeze inside a 155.5Mbit/s SONET STS-3c frame. Depending upon the service needs, the high speed fiber optic systems would operate in a multiple of 155.5Mbit/s.

COMPARISON OF DISTRIBUTION ARCHITECTURES

The most likely distribution architecture for fiber in the local loop will be similar to that of digital loop carrier, the star architecture. However, fiber introduces the possibilities of other architectures. Bus architectures, which are used in many local area network applications, are currently being researched for fiber in the local loop deployment.

Star architectures are configured where each customer has a dedicated transmission path from the CO or RES to the ONI. The advantages of the star architectures include high bit rate per customer, easier upgradability, privacy, and more traditional operations and maintenance. The disadvantages include the substantial cost for separate fibers and optical transceivers, handling a large number of fibers in the RES, and serving fewer customers per RES.

Bus architectures are configured where multiple customers are served from the same transmission path from the CO or RES to the ONI. The advantages of bus architectures include lower fiber cost due to sharing, shared transceivers, less fiber handling in the RES, and serving more customers per RES. The disadvantages include a lower bit rate per customer due to the sharing of the bus bandwidth, more difficult upgradability, and a more complex ONI transmitter due to upstream synchronization.

Preliminary work has been reported in the assessment of the different architectures. More research on the upgradability issue along with an evaluation of the operations and administration costs are needed before the final assessment can be made. A comparison of the architectures can be found in Table 1.

SUMMARY OF TELCO TRIALS

Many fiber-to-the-home trials have been announced by various telephone companies in the past two years. The first trial began in 1986 with Southern Bell providing CATV transport.

These trials should provide a focus for future vendor product performance; an indication of provisioning, maintenance, and repair expense; and in some cases insight into the market potential of new services. Table 2 provides summary of the majority of the announced trials in the U.S.

ISSUES AND CONCERNS

The first issue is that of CATV cross-ownership. Current laws prohibit a telephone company from owning a CATV operation in the same area which it operates. However, current laws do permit a CATV company to offer voice and data communications over its system. If trends in deregulation and full competition continue, it is anticipated that the CATV cross-ownership laws would be relaxed at some point in time.

Regardless of the cross-ownership issue, the deployment of fiber in the local loop would eventually create a competitive environment for the CATV operator. Third party video providers could lease capacity from the telco. Or cooperative situations could arise where CATV operators and telco's operate complementary systems; CATV operators providing video programming and telco's providing transport.

The next issue concerns the powering and ownership of the ONI. Since powering is not feasible through fiber, commercial power must be provided at the customer site. However, the outage or unavailibility of commercial power is greater than the maximum unavailability objective for POTS/ISDN services. Therefore, the development of maintenance free battery backup becomes important. In addition, it is unclear as the ownership of the ONI. As an example, the interface proposed in Pacific Bell's Project Victoria was ruled as customer equipment by the FCC.

It is important that standards for equipment be settled quickly to allow for the development of reliable, interchangeable, and competitive products. These products will need to utilize the SONET formats mentioned earlier.

Must fiber in the local loop be POTS/ISDN compensatory immediately? Some telco's have projected that fiber will be economical based upon first costs and maintenance savings by the early 1900's. If so, new copper plant placed today will not have the potential of enhanced revenues from new services.

The last concern is that the fiber in the local loop systems deployed in the near future are compatible with future technologies.

CONCLUSIONS

The future role of fiber optics is in the local loop as can be seen by the increasing number of telco trials and research projects. It is important that telco's utilize emerging fiber technology to lower maintenance costs and to offer new services. And finally, it is important that research continue in support of standard and cost effective fiber optic products for the local loop.

Table 1 - Comparison of Architectures		
	Star	Bus
Bit Rate per Customer	High	Low
Upgrade	Easy	Difficult?
Privacy	Assured	Not assured
Operations/Administration	Complex	More Complex
Fiber Costs per Customer	More	Less
CO/RES Costs per Customer	More	Less
ONI Costs per Customer	Less	More
Customers per RES	Fewer	More

Table 2 - Fiber To The Home Trials				
Telco	Location	Homes	Vendors	Services
Southern Bell	Hunter's Creek Orlando, FL	251	AT&T	CATV Transport
GTE	Cerritos, CA	5000	Various	POTS, CATV Transport Broadband
Southwestern Bell	Hallbrook Farms Leawood, KA	144	AT&T	POTS
Southern Bell	Heathrow Orlando, FL	256	NTI	POTS, ISDN CATV Transport
Contel	New York State	600	AT&T	POTS, data
Contel	California	400	AT&T	POTS, data
New Jersey Bell	Princeton Gate South Brunswick, NJ	104	AT&T	POTS, data
South Central Bell	Grove of Riveredge Memphis, TN	99	AT&T	POTS, data
Bell of Pennsylvania	Perryopolis, PA	80	CIT Alcatel	POTS, data CATV Transport
U.S. West Communications	Kensington St. Paul, MN	100	AT&T	POTS

EXCHANGE AREA PLANNING AND DESIGN IN THE 1990's

JEFFREY M. MUSSER
MANAGER, NETWORK PLANNING METHODS DEPARTMENT

GTE LABORATORIES INCORPORATED
40 Sylvan Road
Waltham, Massachusetts 02254

ABSTRACT

The telecommunications industry has seen a remarkable increase in the turnover of network and exchange area technology within the past 20 years. These technological changes have placed greater demands on the developers of network planning techniques and systems since both the increased capabilities of the underlying network technologies and the need to be able to respond quickly to changes in networking technology have placed greater demands on network planners than ever before. If anything, the speed of evolution of network technology, including the computer processing and database technology that will be used in the intelligent networks of the future, is expected to continue to increase, placing even greater demands on the ability of network services providers to rapidly and effectively plan for the evolution of their network systems, network technologies, and network configurations.

In this paper, we describe how the changing telecommunications environment is significantly altering both the requirements placed on network planning and the types of integrated network planning capabilities that are possible over the next decade and how they can be used to significantly enhance the overall network planning process. We will describe how the changes in network technology expected will radically alter the network planning problem.

In addition to the changes associated with planning for the new architectures associated with these new technologies, we will describe "design for reliability" criteria in network planning as new technologies alter the resilience and robustness of networks. For example, we will describe limitations of tree and multistar architectures when new technology is introduced and new approaches to network design to support fault-free service performance and network and network "self healing" under various failure conditions.

Ultimately, many more of the telecommunications business planning and implementation activities need to be automated in order to streamline the planning-to-provisioning process. We will describe the automation and integration of these activities, where, for example, systems measuring traffic in real-time will be feeding on-line traffic routing, network management, and network planning systems. Traffic forecasts will automatically create network plans, which will then automatically trigger engineering work orders as well as orders for capital equipment. The paper will conclude with a vision of the future of network planning, based on the previously described techniques and capabilities, where new methods and fully integrated intelligent planning systems will automate and optimize the complete planning, provisioning, and implementation process, not just the present planning task of network design.

INTRODUCTION

Planning the outside plant is a problem that has been with us for nearly as long as the telephone has existed. At least 100 years ago the problem had gotten out of hand. In those days some means of concentration would have been a blessing. Instead the decision to be made in those days was whether to add another cross arm to the pole, or had the capacity of the pole been exhausted (16 cross arms being about the limit) requiring new poles on the other side of the street. It is my understanding that the blizzard of 1888 brought about the introduction of new outside plant technology, i.e. buried cable, after all the wires came down under the weight of the snow.

What is amazing about this problem is the fact that the solution techniques have not really changed in the first 100 years of the industry. Planning is still an art not a science, and the quality of the design is a function of the skill and experience of the individual planner. To some people then the answer to automating planning is obvious -- capture the art of the planner within an Expert System. It is my intent today to show you that by bringing modern computer capability and the optimization tools of Operations Research to bear on this problem we can outdo the plans of the best expert planner.

Present policy in the GTE Telcos is to ensure that no one is further than 12kft or 2.5 miles from the first point of digitization. Therefore there could be some customers as far as 2.5 miles from the network that we are optimizing. We are specifically dealing with cables of large cross sections, not individual subscriber pairs. The problem we are addressing is how to relieve exhaust (when a particular span of cables run out, more customers exist than cable pairs), and what is the best technology to use to provide more cable pairs. We could install more cable or introduce concentrating devices which utilize cable carrier systems to provide connection between the subscriber and the central office.

In the 1960's the Bell System started using a computer program called Exchange Feeder Route Analysis Program (EFRAP) to study the long term economic impact of projected growth in telephone feeder cable requirements. A similar program called Exchange Feeder Relief Analysis Method (EFRAM) was used by the GTE Telcos, and remains as the major planning tool of the GTE Telcos. The problem with such programs today is the fact that it was not designed to include the many electronic options available today versus cable size options in the 60's. As a result the programs are often "tricked" into solving todays problems. One has to wonder about the value of a program that must be tricked in order to make it work, and the value of its results. The Telco Planners themselves began worrying about this tricking. They knew that what they had was not sufficient for the job at hand today, and surely was not up to the job as anticipated in the future. It became obvious that a new planning environment, not just a new planning computer program was needed in order to remain competitive.

WHAT IS DIFFERENT WHEN CONCENTRATORS ARE CONSIDERED?

The major assumption of the early feeder analysis programs was that the network section of cable could be planned independently of the capacities of its neighbors. In effect all that was accomplished was to introduce the notion of Net Present Value to the planners, showing them the value of delaying investment due to the opportunity cost of the money supporting the investment. Their problem was to trade off the possible economy of scale by investing in large cable cross sections early in a plan life versus the cost of the money required to make this investment before it was to be utilized. The situation changes entirely when concentrators are utilized. The assumption of independence is out the window. Placing a concentrator at the extremities of the network essentially removes from the feeder network all traffic generated beyond that concentrator (away from the central office) and homed upon that concentrator. The cable capacity closer to the central office that is no longer needed for the traffic homed upon the concentrator is now available to carry traffic from other parts of the network.

It should be obvious that the complexity of the problem, measured by the number of possible alternatives available, has increased dramatically. It is no longer a decision of what size cable to use from a finite list of 4 to 10 sizes, and when to place it. It is now a decision of what technology, cable or electronics, what size of each, what year to place them, and where. The where can be a large number up to 60 potential locations at this time. This number is in the exponent when the complexity is expressed mathematically. If we were to consider all possible plans in network of, say, 20 possible concentrator locations, and we had available 3 types of concentrators, with a planning horizon of 10 years, there would be $(3 + 1)^{20 \times 10} = 4^{200} = 10^{120}$ plans to be examined. Even if we had a super computer and could examine one plan every microsecond, it would take 10^{106} years to examine every plan in order to determine the optimum plan, the one having the least cost.

WHAT ARE TODAYS PLANNING TOOLS?

Todays planning environment begins with facility inventories buried within the bowels of a large mainframe computer. Planners access them through a myriad of screens in a hierarchical menu-driven system. These records give the planners information on cable span capacities, demands at each control point, cumulative demands on each span, locations of existing concentrators and their residual capacities. Most important the planner has paper maps of the central office under consideration, with serving areas in color. The serving areas, though arbitrarily defined, simplify the problem by decomposing it. They do not, however, have any relation to what might be an optimal plan for the total central office as a whole.

Running one of the Feeder Relief programs will tell the planner where cable exhaust is to be incurred and when, but it does not really tell the planner what to do to solve it. We then have two goals for our efforts. First, we must make it easier for the planner to go about the present task of manually planning for exhaust relief. Second, we must provide decision support systems in the form of network optimization in order to guide the planner or to do most of the job for the planner. In later years we will take on the task of automatically generating designs for new network architectures, and for networks that provide new services only to those customers where profitable.

A NEW PLANNING ENVIRONMENT

First we must get the planning tool onto the desk top of the planner. We are calling this new desk top planning environment NETCAP (NETwork Computer Aided Planning). It must be an interactive environment. The paper maps of yesterday should be replaced with modern computer graphics. The quality of the plan must not be dependent upon the skill or lack of skill of the planner. The techniques and data used by the various operating companies within a telephone company must use standard techniques. Decisions on capital investments among the telcos must be based upon common financial assumptions and analysis. A central office should be able to be planned within say two days, not the present two to six weeks.

The first step in developing such a desk top environment is to get the network facility records and customer demand forecasts down to the desk top. As you heard last year at NCF, GTE has already begun the task of computerizing and standardizing these data bases as part of its CPMS (Capital Planning Management System). It was the task of the Data Services division (GTEDS) to assemble the required data for the tool from the various existing data bases, and then transparently down-load them to the PC for the planners to access with the network planning tool. This data was incorporated within the existing mainframe EFRAM data tables, and the NETCAP data became a subset of the EFRAM data.

Once the network data was down-loaded the PC was essentially turned over to NETCAP in order to free up as much PC memory for the planning tool as possible. We have been forced to target our tool to a 640k byte machine. After the supporting application programs, such as the windows and graphics of the desk top, and the data base management system, were installed, the actual manual planning program and optimization algorithm was left with only about 200k of RAM to work with. This was accomplished through extensive use of overlays. The data base management system also helped in this regard as all network records were kept out of RAM, and error messages and helps were not placed within the in-line code but were also kept on disk and accessed through the DBMS.

HOW DOES A PLANNER SEE THE NETWORK?

A planner does not see or care about the final drop to the customer. If the planner is concerned about the individual customer, it is only with regard to how far the most distant customer is from the first point of digitization, or from the customer's digital line card. This distance ultimately determines what digital transmission rates are possible over the technology of the subscriber drop and therefore what enhanced services (2B+D, digital video, etc.) can be provided for the customer.

The planner usually sees the outside plant as a tree-type network, rooted at the central office. This might also be considered a multi-star by some persons. The outside plant is described by control points, (their location, existing electronics, its capacity, and the forecast of customers to home or terminate on that control point), the links between control points, (their technology and capacity), and the resulting forecasted demand which is accumulated from the upstream control points as the traffic gets aggregated as it is moved toward the central office. The control point is a convenient tool of the planner and usually represents sites were something changes in the cable of the outside plant or places where access is available to the individual copper pairs. It could be a manhole, an aerial splice block or a cross connect cabinet, for instance. It could also simply be where the cable gauge changes. The planners view presently is cloudy. The control points are drawn upon paper maps (Ozalid copies of city street maps) and the capacities and demands are sitting on a mainframe computer within the bowels of multiple screens in a hierarchical menu environment. Nearly all the planning is performed within the planners head as the planner tries to coordinate the tables of facilities and demands with the paper picture of the network and its interdependence.

Many Telcos (not just those of GTE) have in recent years established Electronic Service Areas (ESAs), to be served by large remote switching or concentrating units, and they are now being asked to establish smaller Fiber Serving Areas (FSAs). These help the planner because they decompose the problem into smaller subproblems, but it is the wrong approach to the problem. ESAs and FSAs were not set up based upon economic considerations. One might think of them as being established by laying cocktail glasses on the network map and drawing circles of the radius required by the ESA or FSA distant constraint. A correct approach is to simply place the distance constraint as part of the algorithm and let the optimum ESA and FSA fall where it may. We originally found ourselves trapped into obeying the predescribed boundaries but quickly found the folly in that and brought the distance constraint into the integer programming problem of the optimization algorithm.

HOW DOES AN ALGORITHM PLAN THE OSP?

The planning algorithm within NETCAP is attempting to determine the optimum schedule of what facilities to place, where to place them and when, with the optimum being determined as the plan with the maximum NPV that allows us to serve all customers forecasted to desire POTS through the next ten years. The algorithm must make decisions between placing new copper cable to provide local relief on a span or to place electronics which concentrate traffic and provide more global relief downstream from the control point at which it is placed. It must also decide between various types of electronics, multiplexers and remote switching units, as well as deciding whether to use copper or fiber for the carrier system to the central office. Each placement must also be properly sized, and this must be done with consideration of the investment opportunity cost of money, which encourages postponing large investments as long as possible. That, too, must be traded off against economies of scale achieved by placing large units in early years.

If this problem were modeled in a straight forward fashion as an integer programming problem, the model would have over 25,000 yes-no variables for a typical size central office. Clearly such as problem could not be solved by general-purpose computer programs written for solving integer programming problems. We have taken advantage of the structure of the problem and decomposed into two subproblems. Even so, each of these subproblems is of the type known as NP-complete in Operations Research jargon. This means that the time required to solve the problem grows exponentially with the size of the problem or the size of the exchange. The tree structure or multistar structure of most outside plants allow us to perform this decomposition. It also allows us to develop algorithms that require computational time that grows in a polynomial fashion with the problem size, rather than in an exponential fashion.

Our first subproblem concerns the determination of locations at which remote units should be installed to relieve exhaust rather than cable being installed. It also involves determining the set of control points whose traffic should be homed upon the installed remote unit. The development of this solution was a multiple step process. First, we solved the problem for the case where no backfeed to a remote unit was allowed. Later, backfeed was incorporated into the model. Lastly, we incorporated the existing of remote units installed before the beginning of the planning period, and finally incorporated predetermined remote unit locations in mid plan.

services that can only be provided with new technology such as a completely fiber network from the CO to the customer premise. In a non-regulated environment, our design tools will include revenues for these new services and will only design networks that serve those customers where it is cost effective to do so. The maximum NPV plan will be positive reflecting doing business for a profit. Another application of such a tool is to allow marketing to use it to determine the price required to be charged for the service in order to make it cost effective or profitable.

EXTENSIONS AND EXPANSIONS OF NETCAP

There are two directions which future work on network planning tools will take. The first is to apply new computational and algorithmic developments to the present tool in order to speed up its operation and allow the solving of larger networks than now possible. The second direction will be to expand both the systems that input to NETCAP as well as the systems that are effected by NETCAP, in other words, enlarge the role of NETCAP from simply network design to include system engineering and capital procurement. With real time input to and real time output from NETCAP we would have a "self planning and self provisioning network."

It might be suggested that the application of new massively parallel processors would be an aid to solving the planning problem. This may be true, but it will require new insights to the problem formulation and solution techniques. Straight forward application of say 1000 processors, assuming we know how to write our computer code to exploit the parallelism, would reduce the computational time to merely 10^{103} years rather than 10^{106} years, not a really terrific savings. On the other hand, application of neural net technology may only need on the order of say 600 processors to solve this same example, doing it in a manner much like pattern recognition. Each processor would need only one calculation, a yes/no decision for each of the three candidate remote units in each of the 20 candidates location in each of the 10 years of the planning horizon. Such planning tools would operate in near zero time and the computation time would not grow with the problem size. Such planning tools of course are the work for the future.

ACKNOWLEDGEMENTS

Development of NETCAP has been a real team effort, and I wish to acknowledge the work of the team, without which there would be no planning tool to report on. The team consists of M.Helme, A.Shulman, S.Kai, C.Jack, R.Primak, B.Shah, R.Vachani, C.Pucci, J.Chen, T.Magee, and P.Wang. In addition, I would like to thank the following for their support and encouragement throughout the development effort: R.Pokress and K.McMillan.

WHERE DO WE GO FROM HERE?

One might think that at this point the planning tool for the outside plant was complete. However, all that has been accomplished to date is the automation of the present method of solving today's problem: placement of pair gain devices and copper to provide service to POTS customers using existing network topology. Quality is presently the issue in our Telcos in order for them to be competitive in a nonregulated environment. This quality will be accomplished by a new network architecture that appears to be one of Zero Defects through Self Healing mechanisms. This will be accomplished by introducing fiber terminals within 4-6 kft of the customer. The network will contain sufficient intelligence to allow for alternate routing to the central office. The network architecture therefore must be different than the present tree structure of today which has only one route to the CO. It must contain loops. Placing such a constraint into the design algorithms, imbedding the concept of reliability into the design process, will be no simple task.

To date we have only been dealing with one kind of customer, POTS customers. Furthermore, we have assumed a regulated environment in which every customer must be served and served at the same price. Therefore our design tools have produced a minimum cost network, one with the maximum yet negative NPV. In the future, we will be dealing with new customers desiring new services, most likely high bandwidth video

VIDEO-ON-DEMAND OVER FIBER TO THE HOME

Stephen S. Walker
Manager, Advanced Network Technology

GTE Laboratories Incorporated
40 Sylvan Road
Waltham, MA 02254

INTRODUCTION

Telephone companies have been providing narrow band services to both homes and businesses for many years. As we enter a new phase of vast bandwidth availability over the last mile, it is time to review what should be the use of this opportunity. GTE is constructing a Video/Fiber testbed in Cerritos, California, to explore the provision of Video, including Video-on-Demand, to the home. This paper briefly describes the GTE Labs system and some of the technical choices and problems that have been encountered.

OVERVIEW OF THE CERRITOS SYSTEM CAPABILITY

A paper was presented at NCF last year (ref 1) that detailed the Labs system. Referring to Fig 1, The Central Office is connected by two fibers in a simple star (or home run) configuration. The downstream fiber supports 20 simultaneous digital video channels and a 2Mb/s voice, data and control channel. The upstream fiber is configured for 1 digital video channel and an equivalent 2Mb/s voice, data and control channel. Future network configurations will allow remote unit (RU) working with various options for switching at the RU or centrally. The chosen channel configuration for the downstream fiber is 16 unswitched and four switched digital video channels. The 2Mb/s channel is used as four 64kb/s channels reserved for local control functions and 24 channels of 64kb/s used for regular voice and data capability. (See Figure 2). This allows various combinations of voice and data separately, ISDN basic or ISDN primary, as needed.

BROADBAND SWITCHED/BROADCAST NETWORK

The traffic offered to a broadband network is assumed to be asymmetrical, as the originating broadband services tend to be few from the home, the majority being broadcast or switched services from major providers. As services change, moving towards the specifically directed services (such as Video-on-Demand), the present broadband network structures (i.e. broadcast and CATV) become impossible to use. There is expected to continue to be a demand for regular broadcast type of distribution, both free and subscription. This leaves the question open, to switch or not to switch? It is not clear whether there is a single answer, as it may change with time and with viewing habits.

DIGITAL FIBER BASED

The transmission facilities in each direction use digital encoding of the analog signals, both video and voice/data. The video encoding scheme uses 10 bits per sample at three times the color sub-carrier, and includes stereo audio. This results in a data rate of 107Mb/s, without any compression. Decoding therefore becomes relatively simple, in particular there is no need for a stereo encoder at the home so that the consumer may continue to use his regular stereo-compatible TV.

TELEPHONE SERVICE

Telephone service is supported over the fiber, for regular telephones, or may be provided for ISDN terminal equipment at either 144kb/s or at 1.5Mb/s. Initially, the analog phone will be interfaced in the in-home equipment, such that it appears as a standard CO. Similarily, the central equipment will appear to the real CO as an analog telephone. Again, the consumer uses his present terminal equipment on the system. Due to the experimental nature of the equipment, there is fall back to the copper pair. This covers any malfunction of the utility power or the system. A technique of heartbeat messages constantly checks the sanity of the system, and will initiate the fall-back, if needed. To restore to the fiber, the lines are checked for idle before switch-over, to minimize potential disturbance to a call in progress.

BROADBAND FEATURES

This system is designed to explore the provision of both present-day services (broadcast, CATV, including subscription and pay-per-view) as well as future services such as full, random Video-on-demand.

Unswitched Features: Unswitched features are those that are carried on the 16 downstream channels that are not controlled on a per-usage basis, selection of any one of these being performed at the in-home equipment. They carry programs that would normally be broadcast (the NBC's, FOX's etc) as well as the other Cable-based but non-subscription programs (C-SPAN, Weather, etc). Although the Central is informed during usage of these programs, its involvement in the selection mechanism is minimal.

Switched Features: The system provides two switching points, (see fig 3), central and local (in-home). This is the basis for a number of services that can only be achieved with difficulty, if at all, today. The four switched channels to the home allow 3 TV's and one VCR to be in use simultaneously, accessing different programs. Each user has one upstream channel, which is terminated on the central switch, allowing him to connect his sources (VCR and CamCorder) to any other user on the system. The user also has the ability, via the in-home switch, to switch his in-home sources to any (or all) of his TV's, or to his VCR. One major benefit of the central switch is the reduction in signal theft possibilities. If the signal does not even reach the consumer, it is difficult to bypass the scrambling systems to steal the signal. It is also easier for the operator to enable viewing of a one-time event (such as pay-per-view), or even enable subscription channels (HBO, etc.) on an on-demand basis.

SERVICE PROVISION

The system has many capabilities, and one problem that exists relates to the choice of services. The prototype has a state-table approach to the service logic implementation, allowing easy modification of a service. Services may be considered in various categories. The central services include replication of existing services, typically with enhancements, as well as new services. Up until now, the locally originated (i.e. from the home) services have not been possible, so there is an opportunity for creativity. One problem has been that people have created service desires quicker that they can be implemented, tending to yield a moving target. An initial set has therefore been selected for implementation and evaluation.

CENTRAL SERVICES

The central services do include the presentation and access mechanism for all programs, including broadcast type services. The description that follows applies in great part to switched and unswitched services.

Cable Based: Cable based services include subscription and pay-per-view. Instead of pre-subscription, it is possible for the system to allow access on demand. One of the major thrusts in the Cable industry is for 'impulse' buying. This allows last minute decisions on watching a program, rather than a deliberate presubscription process. The switched nature of the service provision allows immediate connection to the service, subject to appropriate checks, such as credit check.

Video-on-Demand: Video-on-Demand is a service that at least replicates the video store functionality. Video stores suffer from a number of inconveniences, not the least of which is the requirement to return the video after use. Typically, stores also have a very limited range, and a small number of copies of each available. In a very large video-on-demand system these problems can be reduced or eliminated. The implementation of video-on-demand here assigns a central VCR to the user for the duration of the transaction. This allows the user to control it as if it were in his own home. Fast forward, rewind, scan forward and back, pause, etc., are all available from the Infra-red (IR) controller. The present implementation does not support the record

function, although the technology can support it. The implications of recording centrally are twofold. This would create an interesting cassette administration problem for home video material, along with fascinating possibilities for associated database handling. It would also mean that most households would not need a VCR, so that, when their old one is retired, the decision to buy or not might depend on the economics of access to a VCR service.

The other part of a video-on-demand service, and one that increases the probability of a title being available, is the on-demand downloading. (Note, this does require the VCR in the home). A request for a title that is presently either not loaded, or not immediately available could offer the possibility of a fully-controlled download. The system, which has control of the consumer's VCR (see later section on VCR control) would instruct the user to load a blank cassette in his VCR, and that the title would be available for viewing after a certain time. This has lost one element of the impulse buying, but still avoids the trip to the video store. The system would switch to the user's VCR, start it in record mode, and download the video. If there was more than one request, the central switch would simultaneously connect to all the recipients, and perform one download, with consequent saving of network occupancy. An evolution of the present system would allow all four switched channels to be used at once, use 45Mb/s compressed, add an interface unit to the in-home equipment (decompression, memory) and download a 90 minute film in 10 minutes.

Other: Having full control of the user's VCR, and using a database approach to program selection, allows some other features to be implemented. An example is the preprogramming of the VCR to record a program. Typically people think they are programming the unit (assuming they have mastered the technique) to record a specific show. What is really done is to instruct the VCR to capture whatever is on the selected channel at the selected time. If, for any reason, the program runs late (presidential pre-empt, game runs late, etc.), then the end of the program is lost. If the programming is performed logically, the system could have the capability to resolve this anomaly.

LOCALLY ORIGINATED SERVICES

Given a full broadband channel upstream, new services are possible. The user typically has two broadband sources in his home, the VCR (play mode), and the CamCorder.

VCR Switching: The capability of the system to switch the VCR output both locally and centrally, allows a variety of different services to be implemented. (There are a number of issues involved that are not based on technology, which will not be addressed here. These include issues of security, copyright protection, and material content). Assuming that such issues are not limiting factors, the system allows a user to watch his neighbor's VCR, with full control, as if it were in his own house. It also, via the local switch, allows viewing of his, or his neighbor's, VCR in any and all rooms at the same time. Although control would be possible from any room, for service sanity it would be necessary to make one the master, at least for a specific session.

CamCorder Handling: The camcorder is typically used in a standalone manner, and not as a piece of a network based service. It would be preferable if it could be used in a wireless manner (e.g. broadband cellular), but this is not yet reasonable. For the present, the system allows the user to connect his camcorder to any TV outlet via an adapter, and then use its output as an input the system. Camcorders do not usually support any type of remote control other than remote record start, so the system will not specifically control the functionality of the unit, merely its connectivity. The service access method (using IR controllers as input, and a TV as output device) will allow a logical assignment of the camcorder to a TV, or the VCR as required, thus providing possibilities for baby monitoring (both in-home and neighbors') and for camcorder download to the user's VCR (as required by VHS-C). The camcorder is also the basis for the video telephone service.

Video Telephone: Video telephone has a history of failure, and yet continues in evolution. Most systems are trying to use the existing network and require end-user equipment that is specific to the function. Once full NTSC quality transmission is available from the home, the equipment requirements revert to consumer TV's and camcorders. The provision of the service devolves into handling the privacy/security issues and the connection. The present scenario for Video Phone takes the video as an adjunct to the regular telephone service. A typical set up would be initiated with a regular phone call. When both parties agree to "go video", a video interconnection would be made using the IR controllers, but without audio on the TV's. The telephone would continue to be used for audio, either a regular phone or a loudspeaking phone. This avoids having to handle the audio feed-around problems that exist with the camcorder being in close proximity to the TV speaker. Alternative approaches of frequency shifting, focussed microphones and speaker phone switching have been evaluated, without great hope of success.

ISSUES OF CPE CONTROL

All the foregoing has implied a significant level of device control in the home. For full service functionality, it is necessary to have system control of the TV's, and the VCR. This concept is critical to the future of network-based services, and requires significant study and industry agreement for future implementations. Practically all customer-provided equipment (CPE) functionality is driven by the manufacturers and the market. One consequence of this is a difficulty of integrating functionality across different pieces of equipment. An example "solution" is the IR learning controller with timing functions built in. This is forced on the consumer as:

1) there are not any IR standards that have become universal, hence it 'learns', and

2) the timing functionality of the VCR is not extended to the cable converter box, typically essential for scrambled channels.

Thus, this IR controller attempts to be the system integrator.

The telephone industry is accustomed to standards, and spends time and resources to ensure that standards provide the required functionality, and that the users and the manufacturers abide by them. There is little such movement in the consumer video world, while the telecommunications standards process would be too cumbersome.

VCR CONTROL

The need for VCR control has been illustrated earlier, and the difficulty of implementation explained. The central VCR's are professional models, and access is via the control port. The consumer VCR's are assumed to be just what the consumer has, typically IR controlled, no wire access, and no standards. The functionality needed includes: Play, Record, Stop, Pause, Fast forward/back and Power on/off.

Other control features would be useful, including tape end indication and speed choice. Note that the issue of power on/off is not trivial, as there is no feedback on whether the power is really on. This requires a power on detector as well as access to the power control IR code.

TV CONTROL

The TV control approach is a subset of the VCR control needs, being the power on/off control, volume control and initialization (i.e channel default is 4 in Cerritos).

IR CONTROL APPROACH

The approach chosen (see fig 4) trains the in-home equipment for each example of IR controller found. The Custom IR controllers (specially designed to match the service access techniques) will use an IR technique that is uncommon. The IR commands from the custom IR controller will be translated into device-specific IR signals at the in-home equipment. There are two types of IR command, purely local ones such as volume up and down, and service impacting commands such as new screen of program selection. These have very different requirements for responsivity as well as behavior. Volume control is typically continuous in operation, and must stop changing as soon as the button is released. Service changing may typically be allowed up to half a second reaction time, and is a single event. The system implementation recognizes these differences, by allowing local commands to be handled in the in-home controller, while the others are handled via a message to and from the central.

ISSUES OF DATABASE HANDLING

A number of service features require a database of programming material. There are a number of problems associated with providing such a feature.

CREATION AND LOADING

There are two types of data in the program database, that pertaining to externally provided programming (broadcast, cable, etc.) and that relating to system data (titles available and loaded, in-use, etc.). The more serious problem is obtaining an accurate and timely copy of the external programs data. Such data has to accessed, downloaded (hopefully it is in electronic form), and translated to appropriate form. The data should not be limited to to titles and times, but also needs additional information such as content and rating (where applicable). Loading via a dial-up link would be appropriate, but there must be some kind of consistency check before it is made available to the system and the user.

UPDATE, ON THE FLY?

The real power of this network based service is embedded in the database. The service would only be as good as the accuracy of the data, and this has to include the timeliness. The data needs to reflect the real programming situation as soon as it is known. Political pre-empts are typically known some hours or days in advance, while world crises can change the situation very rapidly. Sports events can also have impacts that are not known until the last minute. On a very large system, it would be worth 24 hour staffing, with communication channels as required to stay abreast of such situations. Small systems would have a serious problem.

ISSUES OF ENHANCED QUALITY

Another major issue facing the broadband service provider is that of quality. Most video material is available to the user having suffered NTSC transmission. Even VCR's are typically connected via channel 3 or 4, and NTSC. There are many options becoming available, and the network decisions made must be prepared to take advantage of this.

NTSC OR NOT?

The approach chosen here is to assume use of "normal" consumer equipment in the home. This implies a regular consumer VCR, camcorder and TV's that all expect to receive and/or provide NTSC on channel 3 or 4. There is an inherent limit to the quality obtainable via NTSC, and the consumer is prepared to pay for enhancements. Monitors and stereo component equipment is now in use, but there is still the limitation of the broadcast signal. NTSC cannot be ignored, but when the program material becomes available by other means, and the transmission network also supports alternatives, then a major improvement in quality of both picture and sound will become possible.

HDTV

There are a number of contenders for the HDTV area of the market. While there is a demand for such a service, there is no clear winner at present. What does become important for a network provider of broadband services is the ability to handle diverse standards on demand, and to avoid inherent limitations. Although the first implementation of Cerritos is structured around NTSC, it is expected to be able to evolve simply to a non-NTSC environment, including RGB type transport as well as HDTV capability.

AUDIO

Once the bandwidth is available, and especially when the transport is selected to be digital, there is clearly potential for much higher quality audio, such as CD quality. Despite the cheapness of CD players, access to a vast library of material would be of interest. Such quality, when coupled to HDTV and large screens, will give the consumer a quite different perspective on entertainment in the home.

CONCLUSIONS

The system is in the prototype stage now, and it is difficult to draw any conclusions about its use, either from a system point of view, or from a user's point of view. There is one conclusion that can be drawn from the design process. It seems very clear that as video entertainment services get more sophisticated, there will be a need for customer equipment to be controllable by a service-provider, and therefore there will be a need for supporting standards.

ACKNOWLEDGEMENTS

This project involves a large group of people at GTE Labs, and would not be possible without many different contributions. In particular, I would like to acknowledge the help given to me by J. Potts during the final preparation of this paper.

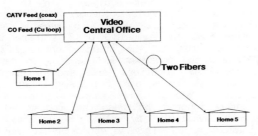

Star or Home-run Configuration
figure 1

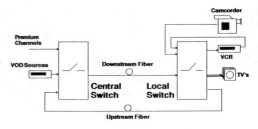

Central and Local Switching
figure 3

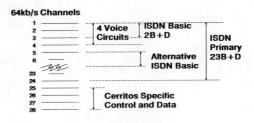

ISDN Alternatives
figure 2

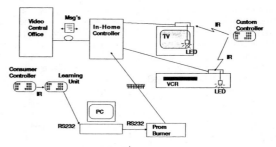

IR Handling Strategy
figure 4

DSW-01

VALUE ADDED SERVICES

Tony Loret de Mola, Chairperson

Business-Residence Services Manager
Network Systems Switching

AT&T

2600 Warrenville Rd., 52E4
Lisle, IL 60532

ABSTRACT

Generating revenue from the network has always been a prime objective of local exchange carriers (LECs). As competition increases within what was once considered secured boundaries, LECs are continually searching for ways to enhance their networks to meet their customers, and their own, objectives. The concept of adding value to an end user's business through the LEC network is both "old-hat" and revolutionary. This seminar explores how major LECs and switching manufacturers are adding value to the public network.

Richard G. Carr   -- Head, AT&T Bell Laboratories
Rose Foss   -- Manager, BellSouth Services
Michael Lach   -- Director, Ameritech Services
John Morton   -- Manager, Contel Telephone Company of Illinois

BUSINESS AND RESIDENCE SERVICES

John Morton
Manager, Sales and Marketing

Contel Telephone Company of Illinois

112 West Elm Street
Sycamore, IL 60178

ABSTRACT

This seminar examines the LEC's flagship product - Centrex. The manner in which Centrex is being molded to provide increasing value to end-users, i.e. matching feature solutions with business problems, is addressed. In addition, capabilities of the public network to enhance residence service are also explored.

VIRTUAL PRIVATE NETWORKS

Michael Lach
Director, ISDN Trial Management

Ameritech Services, Inc.

1900 East Golf Road Flr. 9
Schaumburg, IL 60193

ABSTRACT

This session explores the benefits of installing private virtual networks (PVNs) for end users. Technical considerations and end user benefits are addressed. Additionally, the future direction of PVNs are discussed.

METROPOLITAN COMMUNITY SERVICE

Rose Foss
Manager, Marketing Technical Support

BellSouth Services

675 W. Peachtree St. Room 35K67
Atlanta, GA 60375

ABSTRACT

This seminar discusses a city-wide Centrex-like service introduced by BellSouth. With a number of customers utilizing this service, it has added tremendous value to BellSouth's network. The manner of implementation and benefits to end users are addressed.

FUTURE VALUE ADDED SERVICES

Richard G. Carr
Head, Switching Services

AT&T Bell Laboratories

200 Park Place 1S-503
Naperville, IL 60566-7050

ABSTRACT

This seminar addresses how one digital switch vendor, AT&T Network Systems, plans to increase the value of the public network. Driven by LEC and end user demands, numerous capabilities are being added to the public network. These capabilities will provide LECs services designed to increase the value of their network offering.

DSW-02

BASICS OF DIGITAL SWITCHING

Jean Airey
Senior Product Training Specialist
AT&T
Corporate Education and Training
1195 Summerhill Drive
Lisle, IL 60532

ABSTRACT

This paper will provide a basic understanding and working knowledge of digital switching concepts and systems. The discussion of fundamental techniques, terminology, building blocks, hardware, software, and system design will enable practicing engineers to understand various aspects of telecommunications switching products, such as local office, toll and PBX. Several commercial digital switching systems from various manufacturers will be reviewed from the viewpoint of switching concepts and associated implementation.

Jean Airey -- AT&T

INTRODUCTION TO DIGITAL SWITCHING

ABSTRACT

The purpose of this paper is to provide you with the basic terminology and concepts of digital transmission. The paper begins with the description of analog and digital signals, progresses to the analog-to-digital conversion process, and ends with a discussion of the characteristics of multiplexing, demultiplexing, and digital-to-analog conversion.

ANALOG SIGNAL

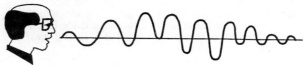

Figure 1. ANALOG SIGNAL

An Analog Signal varies in intensity matching the shape of a sound wave it represents. An Analog Signal is a continuous electrical representation of a sound wave.

The electrical signal is characterized in terms of amplitude and frequency.

Figure 2. AMPLITUDE

Amplitude is associated with loudness and intensity — the louder the sound, the higher the amplitude, and conversely, the softer the sound, the lower the amplitude.

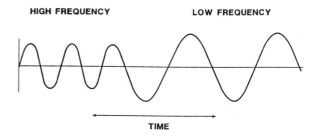

Figure 3. FREQUENCY

Frequency is associated with pitch — the higher the frequency the higher the pitch.

The pitch or frequency of sound is measured in Hertz (Hz) or the number of cycles (oscillations) per second. Hertz (Hz) is the international standard unit of frequency. It represents cycles per second or number of oscillations per second.

A high pitched sound results in a higher frequency, or number of cycles in a given period of time, than a low pitched sound.

ANALOG CONVERSATION

Today, the voice signal is the most common signal transmitted within the telecommunication network. The Analog Signal is transmitted over the telephone wire to the receiving end. At the receiving end, the signal is converted back to a sound wave which the other person can hear.

MAJOR PROBLEMS IN ANALOG TRANSMISSION

The ideal transmission channel will deliver an accurate replica of the original signal to the receiving terminal. Three major problems affect the transmission of analog signals:

— Loss - weakening of the information signal.

— Noise - unwanted electrical signals that interfere with the analog signal.

— Distortion - changing the frequency characteristics of the desired signal.

Loss can be overcome by introducing an amplifier to restore the signal to its original amplitude. However, since the amplifier cannot differentiate between signal and noise, it amplifies any noise present as well as a distortion in the signal. The amplified noise and distortion are now part of the input signal for the next section of the analog transmission line.

As the length of the analog transmission line increases, more amplifiers must be used. Noise and distortion can be minimized by proper system design and component selection. However, once they are introduced they **cannot** be eliminated.

DIGITAL SIGNAL

A Digital Signal is a series of pulses that vary between two discrete levels for a fixed period of time. An example would be telegraph clicks or turning a light switch between on and off. A transmitted digital signal generally represents a series of discrete **on/off pulses.** These discrete on/off pulses allow the Binary numbering system to be used with digital signals. This numbering system only uses the digits "0" and "1"; therefore, you can allow an "on" pulse to represent the digit "1" and an "off" pulse to represent the digit "0".

One advantage of digital transmission is the ability to regenerate signals. The digital signal is also affected by the loss, noise, and distortion characteristics of the transmission line. However, the digital signal can be regenerated (rather than amplified) at each repeater. In the process of regeneration, the effects of transmission impairments on the signal are eliminated at each repeater rather than amplified.

COMPARISON OF ANALOG AND DIGITAL SIGNALS

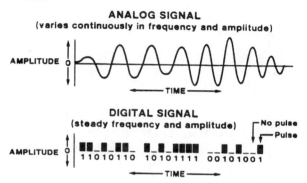

Figure 4. ANALOG AND DIGITAL SIGNALS

Figure 4 compares an analog signal to a digital signal. Notice that the analog signal is a continuous wave, changing in frequency and amplitude, and the digital signal is a series of "on" and "off" pulses.

DIGITAL CONVERSATION

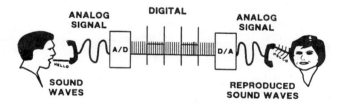

Figure 5. DIGITAL CONVERSATION

Figure 5 shows how we could have a "digital" conversation. The acoustical voice wave, converted into an analog signal through our current telephone technology, could be changed into a digital signal. This digital signal could then be transmitted over a network until, at the other end, it would be changed back to an analog signal and then to an acoustical signal again.

ANALOG-TO-DIGITAL CONVERSION

Basically, you speak and hear transmitted analog signals. In a digital switching system analog signals must be converted to digital signals.

Various techniques exist for digitizing analog signals. The following technique which is described is used with telephone transmission and switching equipment. This discussion uses the AT&T 5ESS® Switch as an example.

ANALOG TO DIGITAL CONVERSION (A TO D)

Figure 6. ANALOG TO DIGITAL CONVERSION

The process of Analog to Digital (A to D) conversion is carried out in four main steps.

1. **Filtering**
   Removing all analog signals above 4000 Hz and below 200 Hz which are beyond our frequency range of interest.

2. **Sampling**
   Testing (sampling) the analog wave 8000 times per second at repeated intervals in time. The output of this sampling step is called **Pulse Amplitude Modulation (PAM).**

3. **Quantizing**
   Measuring the amplitude of the samples and rounding off to the nearest value on a given scale.

4. **Coding**
   Converting the quantized samples into numerical values in a numbering scheme using the digits 1 and 0. The coder can recognize all of the 255 different output voltages from the quantizer. These values have a range of -127 to +127. The output of the coder is a series of pulses. The pulses form 8-bit binary words in which each bit may be either a "1" (pulse) or a "0" (no pulse).

   A binary word is a representation using the binary numbering system. The binary numbering system uses the two characters of 0 and 1, just as the decimal system uses 0 through 9 with 10 as its base. This 8-bit word represents the binary equivalent of the number from the quantizing step. This word is only one of 8000 words produced each second as the output of the coder. Once every 125μs the coder will output a digital word which represents one sample of the analog signal. The output of the coder is called **Pulse Code Modulation (PCM).**

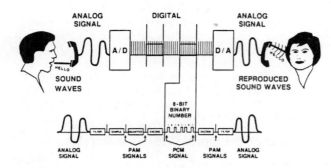

Figure 7. A to D MAJOR STEPS

DIGITAL TRANSMISSION FORMATS

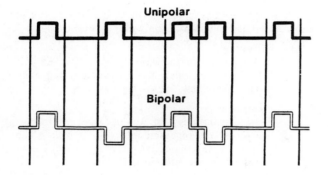

Figure 8. UNIPOLAR TO BIPOLAR CONVERSION

Characteristic of the digital signal is its format. Two common digital formats are shown in Figure 8. Although the two signals differ in appearance, the information they carry is the same

In a unipolar signal there are only two signal states, a pulse or no-pulse condition. All pulses have the same polarity. Unipolar signals are typically used in non-metallic transmission systems, such as lightwave systems.

A bipolar signal has three possible signal states: a "+" pulse, a "—" pulse or a non-pulse. The polarity of the pulses alternate from "+" to "—" to "+". Bipolar signals are typically used in metallic transmission systems.

While transmitting a digital signal from one terminal to another, the signal may be converted from unipolar to bipolar and vice-versa many times. A unipolar signal is converted to bipolar by reversing the polarity of every other pulse in the bit stream. A bipolar signal is converted to a unipolar signal by changing all the pulses to the same polarity.

The basic signal in the North American hierarchy is the DS1 signal. This signal has a capacity of 24 voice channels. In other words, this signal can carry 24 simultaneous conversations. The channel capacities of the digital signal hierarchy levels are all multiples of 24. Signal levels above DS1 are generated

by combining a number of DS1 signals through multiplexing.

A-law companding is used in most of the world except the United States, Korea, Canada, Japan and Taiwan. The A-law system uses 32 channels to yield 30 voice channels and 2 DS-0 channels for signaling and other information. The line rate for DS1 is 2.048Mb/s. When the 32 channel system interfaces with a 24 channel system the company using the 24 channel system must provide the processor to make the systems compatible.

TRANSMISSION ERRORS

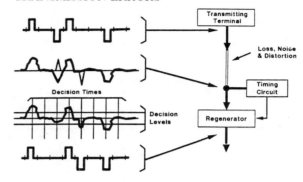

Figure 9. TRANSMISSION ERRORS

The fundamental measure of the performance of a digital transmission system is its error rate. An ERROR is defined as the change in the information content of a bit during transmission. Errors can result from:

- Excessive attenuation or distortion of the signal
- Impulse noise
- Digital crosstalk
- Timing jitter

ERROR DETECTION

A method of detecting the presence of errors in the received bit stream is needed to:

- monitor the performance of the transmission system
- initiate alarms and protection switching

Two common methods of error detection are:

1. Bipolar Violations
   Bipolar violation exists if two + pulses are received with no intervening - pulse, or two - pulses without an intervening + pulse. This enables the detection, but not the correction, of an error. The use of bipolar violations to monitor transmission performance is **in**effective if multiplexers or non-bipolar transmission lines are used.

2. Parity Check

Parity check bits can be used to monitor transmission performance. A parity bit is added to a block of data to make the total number of "1s" odd or even depending on the parity scheme employed.

ERROR PERFORMANCE OBJECTIVES

Bit Error Rate refers to the rate at which errors occur. The performance objective for telecommunications transmission systems is commonly stated as 10^6 (1 error per 1,000,000 bits transmitted).

Block Error Rate refers to the rate at which errors occur in blocks of data, typically containing 1000 data bits. A typical block error objective used is an average of no more than 1 block out of 100,000 should contain errors (or a block error rate of 10^5)

An Errored second is defined as 1 second of transmission with one or more errors. Performance is stated as a percentage of error-free seconds. As an example, a typical objective could be 99.5% error-free seconds (one errored second per 200 seconds).

MULTIPLEXING

Digital conversations can share the same path by utilizing a process called multiplexing. **Multiplexing** is the combining of multiple signals for simultaneous transmission over a common medium.

TIME DIVISION MULTIPLEXING (TDM)

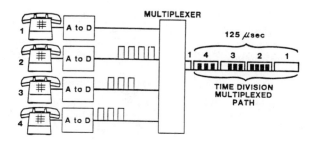

Figure 10. TIME DIVISION MULTIPLEXING

TDM is simply the sharing of a common facility in time — an extension of the principle of "taking turns".

The sampled signals at the input end are converted to pulses in a predetermined sequence and then reconstructed at the distant end.

It is the most common type of multiplexing used today with digital transmission and switching systems used in the telephone industry. TDM takes advantage of the unused time between the samples. The samples take place once every $125\mu s$, but it does not require the full $125\mu s$ to do the sample. This unused time between samples allows us to put several in one $125\mu s$ time frame or **multiplex** them together.

The four analog conversations shown in Figure 10 must go through an A-to-D conversion before they can be multiplexed. The multiplexer will first look at conversation 1 and put it on the common path. Next, conversations 2, 3, and 4 take place and by this time we have used up all of our $125\mu s$. It is now time to look at path 1 again.

One of the digital words will often be referred to as a Time Slot. Our example had four conversations, therefore, four words, therefore, four time slots. These four time slots go together to form one Time Frame.

DEMULTIPLEXING

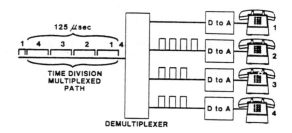

Figure 11. DEMULTIPLEXING

Demultiplexing is the next step that occurs in the conversion process from time multiplexed PCM back to analog. The Demultiplexer separates the bit stream by dropping off Time Slot 1 on Path 1, Time Slot 2 on Path 2, and so on through the last time slot in the time frame.

DIGITAL TO ANALOG CONVERSION

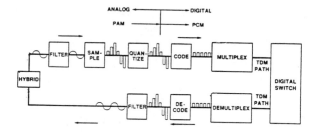

Figure 12. A/D and D/A PROCESS

Since the human ear is unable to understand digital words, Pulse Code Modulation (PCM) must be converted back to an analog signal. The two main steps in this process are:

1. Decoding

The received 8-bit word is decoded to recover the number that defines the amplitude of that sample. This information is used to rebuild a PAM signal of the original amplitude.

2. Filtering

The PAM signal is then passed through a suitably designed filter. When the 8000 PAM signals (per second) are passed through the filter, it reconstructs the analog waveform.

CONCLUSION

- An **Analog Signal** is a continuous electrical representation of a sound wave. The electrical signal is characterized in terms of amplitude and frequency.

- A **Digital Signal** is a series of pulses that varies between two discrete levels for a fixed period of time. A transmitted Digital Signal generally represents a series of discrete on/off pulses.

- The process of **Analog to Digital (A-to-D) Conversion** is carried out in the following four main steps:

  1. Filtering
  2. Sampling
  3. Quantizing
  4. Coding

- **Multiplexing** is used to let users share the available time.

- Digital transmission combines a specific number of voice channels in one time segment of 125 μs.

- **North American Digital Hierarchy** is based on a capacity of 24 voice channels

- **A-Law Digital Hierarchy** is based on 32 channels: 30 for voice and 2 for signaling

- Error detection and objectives for error performance must be established. Common methods include:

  — Bit Error Rate

  — Block Error Rate

  — Errored Second

- The **Digital-to-Analog (D-to-A) Conversion** consists of the following two steps:

  1. Decoding
  2. Filtering

DIGITAL SWITCHING TECHNIQUES

ABSTRACT

This paper looks at the various components that comprise digital switches. Typical switch "building blocks" are examined. Computer architecture will be analyzed as it relates to digital switches. Distributed processing will be explained. Various means of interfacing the digital switch with analog and digital transmission systems will be examined. The concepts of time and space switching will be explored.

COMPUTER: DEFINITION

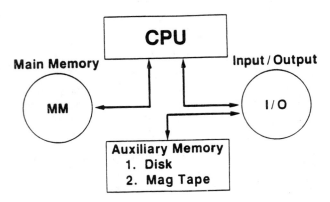

Figure 13. COMPUTER ARCHITECTURE

Computers are typically defined as *versatile, general purpose, multi-functional machines*. They contain a Central Processing Unit (CPU), Main Memory (MM), and Input/Output (I/O) components. Computers are able to perform a variety of tasks. The computer is not dedicated to any one given operation. It can be changed to perform other operations.

SOFTWARE

A computer cannot perform any task without being told specifically what to do. The commands which direct the operations within the computer are called programs. The term program is synonymous with the term software. Software directs the computer hardware on what to do, how to do it, and where to do it. The program/software resides in Memory.

Software can be divided into two categories:

- **Operating System** - Administrator or supervisor of the system, which is in complete control of activities taking place.

- **Subsystem** - Software programs which perform different functions, i.e. call processing, maintenance.

COMPUTER SYSTEM COMPONENTS

Most computer systems have three major hardware components.

1. Central Processing Unit
   The Central Processing Unit is the heart of the computer system. Its functions are:

   - Decodes instructions. In this process, the CPU performs arithmetic and logic functions.

     — Arithmetic Functions include addition, subtraction, and multiplication.

     — Logic Functions include, for example, the comparison of two numbers to determine if they are equal or non-equal.

1171

- Generates gating and timing functions. In this process, the CPU internally transfers data and performs timing to insure that instructions are performed in the correct sequence.

- Transfers data between the Main Memory and/or the Input/Output Facilities. In this process, the CPU controls the movement of data internal to the Computer System.

2. Main Memory

The hardware used to store software is called Main Memory (MM). Main Memory may contain two kinds of information:

- Instructions required to perform the task.

- Data (not necessarily instructions) such as constants required by the task software for program execution.

When initializing the system, the whole program may be loaded into Main Memory for storage. To execute an instruction, the memory is addressed and the contents are brought into the CPU where it is decoded and executed. It is important to note that instructions cannot be executed in Main Memory, only in the CPU. If you wish to "write" into Main Memory, the process is reversed.

3. Input/Output (I/O) Facilities

Main Memory, the storage area for instructions and data, is of a finite size. This means that at any given time it may not be large enough to store all of the information required.

If additional storage is required, or you wish to store programs that are not used very often, you can add storage capability in the form of hardware called Auxiliary Storage, also called **Input/Output**. This storage is usually in the form of peripheral devices called Magnetic Tape and/or Disk Drives.

Sometimes during normal program execution large amounts of data need to be transferred between the I/O and MM at a very fast transfer rate. One way to do this is through **Direct Memory Access (DMA)**.

DMA is a very useful system tool. Once a DMA transfer has been initiated or requested, it takes place over the bus and does not require further intervention from the CPU. This action allows the CPU to perform other functions.

TYPES OF MEMORY

Random Access Memory (RAM) is the primary type of Main Memory utilized in systems today. Random Access Memory means that by merely knowing the address or location of the data, it can be accessed randomly.

- RAM is read/write memory. It can be read from and written into.

- RAM contains data that may be changed.

- RAM is considered volatile.

Read-Only Memory (ROM) is not normally written into but read from only. Some examples are initialization information, diagnostics (software to check the hardware for faults), and constants required for the system program.

- ROM contains nonchangeable information.

- ROM is nonvolatile memory.

COMPUTER SPEED

Seconds are not fast enough for computer systems. Special "speed" terminology is generally used in all systems.

A millisecond (ms) is .001 of a second and is used to measure the interface with a customer. A microsecond (μs) is .000001 of a second and measures speed between components. A nanosecond (ns) is one-billionth of a second and measures memory access. A picosecond (ps) is one trillionth of a second and measures the internal working time of chips.

TIME FRAME

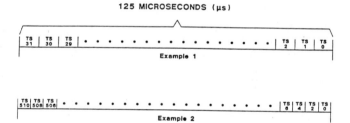

Figure 14. TIME FRAME

The term time frame is used to refer to the movement of data throughout many digital switching systems. The time frame of the digital switch is 125 microseconds. This means every time data is moved within the switch, it is compressed into this period of time. The speed with which the data is moved depends on:

a. The number of bits in the data word (8 bits of PCM data and often additional signaling bits).

multiplied by

b. The number of pieces of data (**time slots or channels**) within the 125μsec time frame.

multiplied by

c. 8000 (the sampling rate).

I.E: 16 bits x 256 channels x 8000 = 32.768 Mb/s

1172

MICROPROCESSORS

A **Microprocessor** can be defined as a miniaturized CPU on an integrated circuit chip which uses VLSI technology.

Very Large Scale Integration (VLSI) as applied in the computer industry has allowed for the reduction in the size of components to the point that they can be placed on circuit packs. This reduces power, air conditioning, space, etc., requirements greatly. The greatest advantage of utilizing this new technology is cost reduction.

Examples of microprocessor chip usage are in washing machines, refrigerators, fuel control systems, watches, etc.

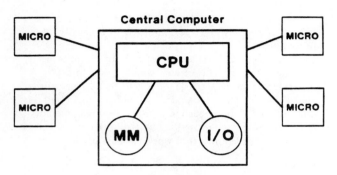

Figure 15. DISTRIBUTED PROCESSING

With the introduction of inexpensive microprocessors, menial or ancillary functions could be delegated to the surrounding microprocessors and relieve the central or "host" system to perform other more important support functions. In this mode, they only communicate with the host when necessary. Activities or events can be processed within the microprocessor. The host may not even know that the activity occurred. This type of architecture is known as **Distributed Processing.**

DIGITAL SWITCHING SYSTEM

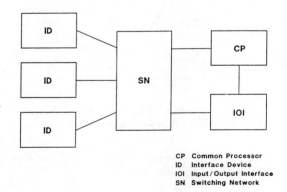

CP Common Processor
ID Interface Device
IOI Input/Output Interface
SN Switching Network

Figure 16. DIGITAL SWITCHING SYSTEM

The basic digital switching system is made up of:

- Interface Devices (IDs)
- Switching Network (SN)
- Common Processor(s) (CPs)
- Input/Output Interface (IOI)

Within the digital switch data (voice/data) is moved through

- Time Division Switching
- Space Division Switching

DIGITAL SWITCHING INTERFACE DEVICES

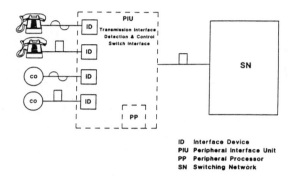

ID Interface Device
PIU Peripheral Interface Unit
PP Peripheral Processor
SN Switching Network

Figure 17. INTERFACE DEVICES

Some digital switches only handle incoming and outgoing digital signals, others handle only analog signals, and some handle both. Digital toll switches only handle trunks. An interface device must be able to handle:

1. Transmission Interface: converting the signal from analog to digital, from bipolar to unipolar, monitoring the signal for alarm conditions etc.

2. Detection and Control: watching for signaling and changes in supervision

3. Switch Interface: synchronizing the incoming signal with the switching network

In a central office switch, interface devices must provide concentration for customer lines. Concentration is provided based on analysis of the number of customers who could be expected to simultaneously require service.

A variety of interface devices can be combined in one unit -- which we will, in this discussion, call a Peripheral Interface Unit (PIU).

In switches using the distributed processing concept, a microprocessor located in the PIU or the ID will handle a percentage of the switch functions (Peripheral Processor -- PP).

Some manufacturers provide the capability of placing the ID or PIU in a remote location -- several miles from the rest of the switch.

DIGITAL SWITCH NETWORK

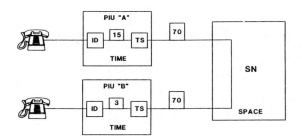

ID   Interface Device
PIU   Peripheral Interface Unit
SN   Switching Network
TS   Time Switch

Figure 18. DIGITAL SWITCH NETWORK

Within the switch network data can be moved through time division and space division switching. This is commonly used to provide connections between Interface Devices or Peripheral Units.

Time Division Switching switches the order in time of the data on a multiplexed line. Space Division Switching switches an individual time slot of one bit stream to a different outgoing bit stream.

DIGITAL SWITCH COMMON PROCESSOR

The digital switch uses some form of a common processor to oversee and control the activities of the Interface Devices, Peripheral Units, and Switch Network. Switches vary in the amount of control and responsibility assigned to the common processor. The use of distributed processing varies between switch manufacturers.

Switch manufacturers also differ in their approach to providing continuing service in case of equipment failure. Redundancy is commonly provided through one of two means:

- Load Shared

- Full Duplication (Active/Standby)

The size of the common processor required by the system will also vary. One determinate is if the switch will be expected to handle only analog or digital lines, or if it will handle both.

DIGITAL SWITCH I/O INTERFACE

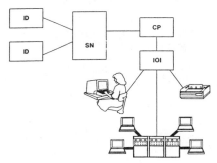

Figure 19. I/O INTERFACE

Digital switches provide some type of "user-friendly" interface with switch maintenance personnel. Maintenance personnel can monitor and maintain the whole switch from this interface.

This interface can also be used to generate reports from the common processor. Because the common processor is a computer it is capable of handling tasks beyond its primary duty of call processing.

In some switching systems the IOI provides connections for other Operation Systems.

CONCLUSION

Computers are versatile, general purpose, multi-functional machines.

Software tells the computer hardware what to do, how to do it, and where to do it. Software can be divided into two categories: Operating System and Subsystems.

Central Processing Unit (CPU) is the heart of the computer system and has three major functions:

— Decodes instructions

— Generates gating and timing functions

— Transfers data between MM and/or I/O Facilities

Main Memory (MM) is usually read/write memory used for storage of data and instructions.

Input/Output (I/O) Facilities is for storage of large programs or data and are usually disks or magnetic tapes.

Direct Memory Access (DMA) is used for swapping large amounts of data between Main Memory and I/O over a dedicated bus. DMA transfers do not require the use of the CPU and essentially provide for overlapped operation.

Random Access Memory (RAM) - Volatile semiconductor memory that can both be read from and written into.

Read Only Memory (ROM) Non-volatile memory that contains data that is not expected to change. Types of data contained in ROM would be:

— Diagnostics

— Constants

— Re-initialization routines

— Bootstrap loaders

Time Frame refers to the movement of data throughout the switch. The time frame of the switch is 125 μs.

Distributed Processing is a systems approach to mechanization that utilizes a host computer as the central system surrounded by microprocessors that perform the menial tasks of the system. The microprocessor activity de-loads the host, allowing it to perform other more important system functions.

The basic digital switching system is made up of:

- Interface devices
  - Transmission Interface -- analog and digital
  - Detection and Control
  - Switch Interface
- Switching Network
  - Connections between the periphery
  - Time/Space Division switching
- Common Processor
  - Control
  - Redundancy
- I/O Interface
  - Maintenance
  - Administrative
  - Operation Systems

DIGITAL SWITCHING SYSTEMS

ABSTRACT

This session reviews some typical state-of-the-art switching products available today from a block diagram level, relating them to the principles and techniques discussed in the previous two sessions. Several manufacturers are covered including AT&T, Northern Telecom, Ericsson, and Siemens. Digital switching with analog and digital transmission inputs are examined.

REVIEW

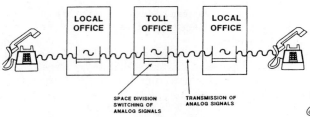

Figure 20. INTEGRATED ANALOG NETWORK

Prior to the introduction of digital transmission, the telephone network was based on space division switching and the transmission of an analog signal. This was an Integrated Analog Network

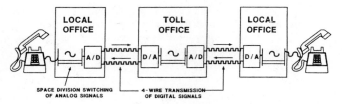

Figure 21. THE T-CARRIER SYSTEMS

The first step toward a totally digital network was the introduction of T-carrier transmission systems in the interoffice network. The advantages of better economics and technical performanance drove this conversion process.

First introduced by AT&T in 1962, T-carrier was used for interoffice trunking. It uses time division multiplexing.

- 24 channels (conversations/data)
- 8 bits per channel
- Sampled at 8000 bps
- Speed: 1.54Mbps

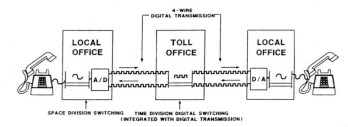

Figure 22. DIGITAL SWITCHING — TOLL OFFICE

The second step in digital switching came with the introduction of digital switching in the toll office in 1976. Space division switching of analog signals was replaced by time division switching of the to-be-transmitted digital signals. Solid state electronics had come of age, making time division digital switching faster and cheaper. Time division digital switching allowed direct connection of the switching office to the digital carriers, eliminating the need for the channel banks of A/D and D/A converters at the switch interface.

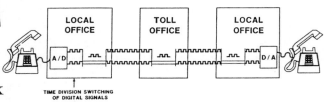

Figure 23. INTEGRATED DIGITAL NETWORK

With the conversion of the local office to time division digital switching, an Integrated Digital Network was achieved. Only the local loop remained analog.

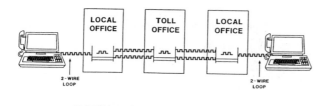

Figure 24. CONVERSION OF LOCAL LOOP

The next event in digital switching is the conversion of the analog signal at the loop plant (the subscriber loop) to digital technology. A user demand for non-voice services and the desirability of delivering this over the present loop is driving this technology.

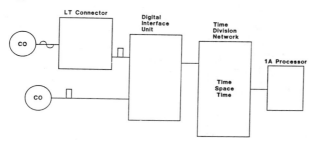

Figure 25. AT&T — 4ESS

The AT&T 4ESS was first introduced in April of 1976. It is designed to serve as a toll and access tandem switch and handles only digital and analog trunks.

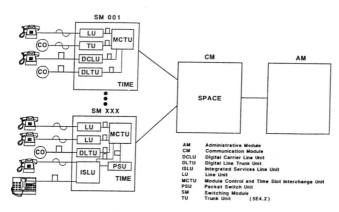

Figure 26. AT&T — 5ESS®

The AT&T 5ESS® was first introduced in March of 1982. It is designed to handle both digital and analog lines and trunks. Its modular construction allows a variety of configurations based on the customer needs.

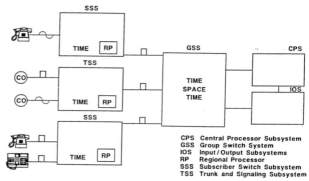

CPS	Central Processor Subsystem
GSS	Group Switch System
IOS	Input / Output Subsystems
RP	Regional Processor
SSS	Subscriber Switch Subsystem
TSS	Trunk and Signaling Subsystem

Figure 27. ERICSSON — AXE-10

The Ericsson AXE-10 added a digital group switch to its all analog SPC (Stored Program Control) switch in 1978. The AXE-10 all-digital model was introduced in May of 1982 with the addition of a digital subscriber stage. It is designed to handle digital and analog lines and trunks.

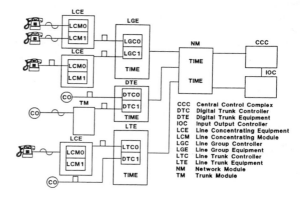

CCC	Central Control Complex
DTC	Digital Trunk Controller
DTE	Digital Trunk Equipment
IOC	Input Output Controller
LCE	Line Concentrating Equipment
LCM	Line Concentrating Module
LGC	Line Group Controller
LGE	Line Group Equipment
LTC	Line Trunk Controller
LTE	Line Trunk Equipment
NM	Network Module
TM	Trunk Module

Figure 28. NORTHERN TELECOM — DMS 100 FAMILY

The Northern Telecom DMS 200 was introduced in April of 1979. It was designed to handle toll and access tandem operations. The DMS 100 Local provides customer line service. The DMS 100/200 provides for local/toll operation. A number of other switches in the DMS family are designed for other specific applications.

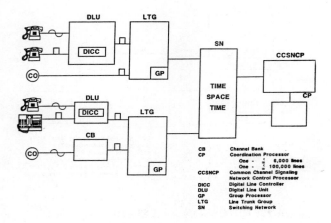

Figure 29. SIEMENS — EWSD

The EWSD was introduced in November of 1980. It was designed to handle digital and analog lines and trunks.

CONCLUSION

Early space division switching of analog signals has evolved into an integrated digital network with the digitizing of the analog signal promising to extend back to the subscriber premises. This has occurred for several reasons, including

— Cost

— Maintenance

— Control

— Consumer demand

A number of digital switches are available today. Table 1 illustrates those reviewed in this paper.

SWITCH	Lines (Total)	Trunks (Total)	Remote	Year Intr.
AT&T 4ESS	0	107,000	No	1976
AT&T 5ESS	100,000	60,000	Yes[1]	1982
Ericsson AXE-10	200,000[2]	60,000	Yes[3]	1978[4]
Northern Telecom DMS 100/200	100,000	60,000	Yes[1]	1979
Siemens EWSD	100,000[5]	60,000	Yes[3]	1980

TABLE 1. DIGITAL SWITCH SUMMARY

1 - Lines and trunks
2 - With new processor
3 - Lines only
4 - All digital model: 1982
5 - With large processor

DSW-03

SWITCHES FOR ISDN:
THE TELCO PERSPECTIVE

Joseph F. Luby, Chairperson
Asst. Vice President,
Planning & Engineering

Illinois Bell Telephone Company
225 W. Randolph Street (HQ 19F)
Chicago, Illinois 60606

ABSTRACT

This seminar will take an Operating Telephone Company's view in discussing the
switches that are available to provide an
Intergrated Services Digital Network.
ISDN is being offered by most digital
switch manufacturers. Each of these
switches uses a unique architecture to
meet the manufacturers interpretation of
the CCITT standards for ISDN. It is the
task of the operating companies to deploy
this variety of ISDN in a manner which is
cost effective, and provides an attractive, high quality service to the end
user. This seminar will relate the experiences of several operating companies in
their efforts to accomplish that implementation.

Nancy R. Daspit   - AT&T Network Systems
Dr. Daryl J. Eigen - Siemens Public
                     Switching Systems
J. David Murray   - Bell Atlantic
David S. Niles   - Michigan Bell
Michele S. Ruetty - Ohio Bell
Joan L. Shine   - Southwestern Bell
Kevin D. Williams - Illinois Bell

PREPARING FOR AN ISDN TRIAL

David S. Niles
ISDN Trial Manager

Michigan Bell Telephone
29777 Telegraph Road, Suite 3332
Southfield, Michigan 48034

ABSTRACT

This paper addresses the considerations
and planning requirements for a successful
Integrated Services Digital Network (ISDN)
trial by an Operating Telephone Company
(OTC). A successful trial requires OTC
executive management support along with
precise goal definition. Customer selection is equally important to assure that
the user of the technology has the technical sophistication and business diversification to provide a quality test of the
architecture.

The OTC can benefit from the trial both
operationally as well as expanding their
understanding of a customer's business
problems. The greatest advantage of an
ISDN trial is the close proximity of the
OTC to the user network. This affords
both entities with an enriched understanding of both their technical as well as
functional business challenges.

Documentation is a key for the OTC. The
ability to leverage the experiences of the
trial is paramount to obtaining it's full
value. Having a predetermined method for
the collection and documentation of trial
data is a must to achieving strategic
objectives.

INTRODUCTION

This paper addresses the planning and
implementation requirements for a successful Integrated Services Digital Network
(ISDN) trial. An ISDN trial affords a
Operating Telephone Company with the experience and evaluation of the ISDN technology and its ability to address customer
applications. It enables the company to
establish methods and procedures to reinforce the architecture and the services
available to customers. It builds experience in integrated voice and data environments supported using Operating Telephone
Company expertise in networking.

The motivation for a Operating Telephone
Company (OTC) trial should be threefold.
The first focus should be to develop the
required methods and operating procedures
to support the architecture and customer
needs. The second orientation should be
to build data communications and software
expertise that is based upon a switched
architecture rather than a direct facility
connection such as coaxial cable. The
final focus for the trial should be to
identify customer applications that are
appropriate for implementation within the
ISDN design and to leverage this knowledge
with the customer base.

The subsequent sections of this paper will
address the planning and implementation
requirements for a successful ISDN trial.
They include customer considerations, internal OTC requirements, external factors
to be managed and appropriate documentation guidelines.

GOAL DEFINITION & EXECUTIVE COMMITMENT

It is critical that the OTC ensure the
commitment of its senior managers to
support an ISDN trial. This support
includes the allocation of employee
resources and capital funding. The executives must be in agreement with the intent
and goals for the trial. This commitment
will then be translated into interdepartmental harmony and ensure the effort
required to achieve customer satisfaction.

The senior managers must also ensure that goals are communicated and that the trial effort is moving forward toward those ends. Having the executives tied into the process is vital in problem resolution. As the trial moves forward, unknown operating difficulties, frequently requiring funding to resolve, will arise. To ensure expedient resolution of these problem areas, the senior managers must be stakeholders in the project.

A Committee of interdiscipline executives should be established. This group would meet at least quarterly to track the progress of the trial and resolve any outstanding concerns. This format will also ensure interdepartmental commitment to objectives within defined time frames.

CUSTOMER SELECTION

It is important that the correct type of customer be chosen for the ISDN trial. A good target customer will have three major attributes. First, they should be a leading-edge customer. They should hold a reasonably prominent position in their industry. This will ensure that their applications are typical of the major entities in that industry. In addition, it affords exposure to other possible customers for the services offered by ISDN.

Second, the customer should be technically sophisticated. The technical demands of the ISDN architecture are placed upon both the OTC and the customer. OTC personnel will need to communicate effectively with user experts, especially maintenance specialists. Technical sophistication by the user aids in rapid resolution of problems by avoiding communication difficulties.

Third, the customer should be a strong, diversified data processing user. The ability to test and support a wide variety of data applications is expanded in a firm where there is a wide diversity of systems and user requirements. In addition, a mix of vendor equipment allows defined universal standard interfaces to be tested and their value confirmed to the customer. It further challenges the OTC personnel and forces their expertise to expand.

THE GUINEA PIG CONCEPT

One of the purposes of the trial is to obtain experience with the ISDN technology. However, to minimize interruption of the customer's business operations, it is strongly recommended that the technology be employed first for official communication within the OTC. The guinea pig concept focuses the test case environment within the OTC and away from the customer. The focus of this internal trial should be to emulate as many of the customer's applications as reasonably possible.

It is recommended that the deployment of ISDN within the customer's network not eliminate the current service in place. Redundant service allows the customer to continue their operations while the trouble is resolved with the ISDN technology.

Several different departments should be selected for ISDN implementation. A small quantity of lines (10-20) is sufficient to trial the technology. This minimizes investment yet still prompts experience prior to exposure with the customer. Service order, provisioning and testing procedures can all be tested using this approach.

An additional benefit of the internal trial is increased awareness by OTC employees of the capabilities of ISDN. It may be desirable to have the sales and marketing organizations as part of the internal trial to better familiarize them with the ISDN technology.

CUSTOMER PREMISES EQUIPMENT (CPE)

Customer premises equipment (CPE) is a critical component of an ISDN trial. The CPE is the most visible element of the trial to the user. They perceive the networks capabilities through the terminal equipment that fulfills their application.

It is suggested that multiple vendors be included in an ISDN trial. The diversity of user applications will force a multiple vendor environment. At the present time, most vendors are using proprietary prototype equipment and they are willing to test their equipment capabilities with the OTCs.

A CPE laboratory should be established that will facilitate the testing and verification of ISDN equipment prior to introduction in the customer environment. This laboratory provides the BOC and the vendors with a workshop that affords a controlled environment for testing the equipment. Local loop performance losses can be adjusted and the performance of the CPE determined, software problems can be resolved, and applications can be tested prior to customer involvement. Within the laboratory, the customer's applications should be attempted prior to deployment in their network. This laboratory can also serve as the test bed for maintenance and provisioning practices in conjunction with the internal OTC trial.

TECHNICAL RESOURCES

The nature of ISDN places the Operating Telephone Companies in a very close proximity with the customer network. This is especially true of their data processing network. This relationship places new technical support demands on the OTCs.

It is vital that the OTC have a qualified

pool of OSI protocol layer experts, that at a minimum, are capable of interacting through level three (network). It is recommended that this expertise extend through all seven layers including the application layer. This expertise will be used to address software related problems that cannot be resolved in the physical layers. Protocol analyzers are required to evaluate software related problems. These can be costly and do not have widespread availability.

Maintenance personnel to address local loop facility qualification for Basic Rate Interface access are required. Packet Switching personnel must manage the network through the Network Administration System including the input of packet translations into the Packet Network on an individual user basis.

All of these resources must be allocated by the OTCs if the trial will be successful. It is suggested that these personnel remain within their current organizational structures rather than establish a dedicated trial organization. This will allow for cross training of other members in the business who are not directly involved in the first ISDN installation.

PROVISIONING & MAINTENANCE

The ISDN trial should address four major operational support areas. They are switching, both Central Office and Packet, trouble resolution/maintenance, network transmission facilities, and service order and billing.

An ISDN trial provides a relatively small number of lines that can utilize mechanized service order processes yet at the same time can be completed manually in the event of system failure. This is an excellent opportunity to debug service order operating procedures. The service representative must have tools that assist in the identification of the station users requirements. This includes the necessary information for circuit and packet switched data as well as traditional circuit switched voice. This data must fill the information requirements to establish individual station translations.

The same is true of billing. While the OTC may choose not to charge the customer for participating in the ISDN trial, the OTC should generate false bills to ensure that the packaged services are capable of being invoiced. A side benefit of this approach is to determine the potential revenue stream from service packaging within the ISDN architecture based upon the customer's usage.

The most significant database support that needs to be developed is the maintenance tools. The ability to identify, define,

and isolate technical problems is critical to the success of the trial and the ISDN network. During the internal trial, simulations should be initiated to test the viability of maintenance support systems. Emulation of the customer's applications will also create software related problems that must be resolved. Combined with the simulated service outages, this should provide maintenance personnel with experience prior to service establishment with the customer.

VENDOR MANAGEMENT

The Operating Telephone Companies cannot manufacture and thus are dependent on their vendors for equipment to support the ISDN network. Managing those vendors is key to the success of an ISDN trial.

It is vital that the OTCs obtain senior vendor management support for their trial. Identify mutual goals and the value of achieving the objectives. Establish quantitative criteria for measuring performance. Find a new development or application that can be tested. In the contract with the vendor, establish identified technical support and the level and duration of that assistance. Document every interaction with the vendors and hold them to their commitments. Escalate within their hierarchy when the resolution of issues become overdue.

This vendor management is critical in three areas. They are the Central Office switch, the Packet Switch, and the Customer Premises Equipment. Due to the interactive nature of the technologies, this may require periodic multiple vendor sessions. These sessions should be well documented, the objectives for the meetings clearly defined and the outcome and commitments precisely documented.

DOCUMENTATION

Documentation is a key to a successful trial. Documentation is valuable for three purposes. The first is to ensure the success of the immediate trial. The second is to ensure that the learning experiences can be shared across departmental lines and pitfalls avoided in future deployments. The third is to facilitate effective widespread service deployment in an economical, customer applications oriented manner.

It is important that a documentation format be developed at the outset of the trial. As time moves forward, the demands of providing the service will outweigh the importance of documentation unless a process is already established. It is difficult to reconstruct past experience and information will be missed if documentation occurs after the trial has ended.

Monthly status reports to executive committees assist in ensuring appropriate documentation. In addition, separate vendor performance reports assist in tracking vendor support and technological execution. These reports should identify tasks, responsible stakeholders, targe completion dates, and current status information.

CONCLUSION

An ISDN trial can be a rewarding experience for a Operating Telephone Company and their customer. It allows them to participate in leading-edge technology, identify applications that are well suited to ISDN technology, obtain hands-on experience with ISDN capabilities, and evaluate specific vendor capabilities. It also affords a motivation for the development of data processing software expertise.

However, the greatest value to the OTC is the experience of close association to the customer's network which is required to support ISDN services. Especially true of data processing, the trial will afford the OTC with an in-depth look at the problems facing their customers and the ability of the OTC to solve those concerns using the power of the telephony network. This exposure and increased customer sensitivity reaches every department involved in the trial and establishes a pervasive environment for full ISDN service deployment.

TESTING SIEMENS'S ISDN LOOP

TECHNOLOGY

Daryl J. Eigen
Director Business Development

Siemens Public Switching Systems
Boca Raton, Florida

J. David Murray
Specialist - Technology Deployment
and Support

Bell Atlantic Network Services
Silver Spring, Maryland

ABSTRACT

Bell Atlantic and Siemens are conducting an ISDN trial at Bellcore's Navesink Research and Engineering Center. One of the distinguishing features of this trial is the use of Siemens 4B3T Line Block Code in the loop. This paper summarizes what has been learned about 4B3T technology as it was implemented over relatively long loops to serve the Navesink Center and studied through separate, rigorous tests.

INTRODUCTION

In February 1988, the first of 164 ISDN Basic Access (2B+D) lines were cutover as part of a unique Bell Atlantic/Siemens ISDN trial being conducted in Red Bank, N.J. Served from a Siemens EWSD digital switch, the Basic Access lines provide ISDN service to Bellcore's Navesink Research and Engineering Center.

This trial is unique for a number of reasons. This is the first deployment within the Bell Atlantic Region of a Siemens EWSD switch and the first time and EWSD, equipped with ISDN functionality, has been installed to serve a large Centrex customer. Customer Premises Equipment (CPE) manufactured by Siemens and Infotron for ISDN applications is being utilized for the first time as well.

To facilitate the change from 1AESS Centrex service to ISDN service without changing the users' number and in order to maintain 4-digit dialing between all Centrex/ISDN stations, an interworking adjunct arrangement between the EWSD and 1AESS was established. Successful implementation of the interworking architecture is a major trial objective. Finding an economic method of integrating ISDN capabilities into the existing network is thought to be a key to early ISDN deployment.

Another unique aspect of the trial is the role of Bell Communications Research (Bellcore). This trial is one of seven regional trials for which Bellcore has funded to provide technical support. However, in this trial Bellcore is also the customer. As a leader in ISDN planning, development, and implementation, Bellcore will have the opportunity to gain valuable hands-on experience with ISDN. In addition, Bellcore researchers will be able to test various experimental applications for ISDN which they have developed. These experiments may lead to new and advanced market applications for ISDN.

The trial was fully implemented in June 1988 and will extend to February 1989. During this period, the Siemens EWSD ISDN protocol will be tested and verified, interworking tests will be performed to verify the compatibility between the 1AESS and EWSD, and loop qualification tests will be performed. In addition, the impact of ISDN on operations will be studied, and numerous ISDN applications and configurations will be tested and evaluated.

This paper focuses on one aspect of the trial - Testing Siemens's ISDN Loop Technology. An explanation of the Siemens 4B3T Line Block Code and a detailed description of what has been learned about 4B3T technology is provided. ISDN trial service was implemented with Siemens's technology over 13 to 14 KFT loops (including CO and customer premises wiring) to serve the Navesink Center. Separate, rigorous tests of the 4B3T line code were also conducted. Results from the trial and test are discussed and briefly compared to previous Bellcore performance tests conducted for the T1E1[1] standards committee.

UNDERSTANDING SIEMENS'S ISDN TECHNOLOGY[2]

The basic components of the ISDN Basic Access arrangement are illustrated in Figure 1. The NT or Network Terminator on the customer premises side and the LT, Line Terminating equipment at the C.O., incorporate the matched transceivers which provide full duplex, digital transmission over the wire pair at 160 kbit/s.

The transmission speed of 160 kbit/s is comprised of 144 kbit/s for user data plus 16 kbit/s transmission capacity for synchronization and maintenance purposes, the latter two are not available to the user. Within the 144 kbit/s data stream are two 64 kbit/s B-channels for voice and data transmission and a 16 kbit/s channel for signalling and for the transmission of telemetry, user to user data, and packet data.

The subscriber side of the NT provides a 4-wire transmission technique which is less powerful but more economical. Up to 8 ISDN terminals or terminal adapters can be configured over the passive S bus.

The U interface is the standard nomenclature for the ISDN technology applied to the subscriber line. The subscriber line is two-wire and the ISDN technology is an advanced transmission technique allowing independent, simultaneous, digital transmission in both direction, at an error rate of less than 10^{-7}. The transmission technique for direction separation that has been agreed to in the industry is echo cancellation (2), which enables the full duplex operation. While initial deployments of the ISDN U interface have virtually all used echo cancellation technology, the line coding technique, among other attributes, differs. Siemens's initial deployment employs the 4B3T Block Code (3). Performance differences among ISDN loop systems centers strongly around the choice of the line code so a more detailed discussion on this topic is worthwhile.

Transmission Code: 4B3T

---

1 Originally the T1D1.3 Standards Committee

2 For a more complete description of Siemens's ISDN technology, see the original article from which this section was drawn. (1)

The 4B3T block code (3) provides for four binary bits to be encoded into 3 ternary digits. The 4B3T block code is particularly advantageous because at a transmission rate of 160 kbit/s it enables a reduction of the baud rate to 120 kBauds. Table 1 illustrates how each group of 4 bits is coded into three ternary symbols.

Figure 2 shows the code spectrum. It illustrates a further advantage of this technique, the restriction to lower frequencies and thus lower cable attenuation. The transmission technique is significantly simplified due to the availability of adequate capacity for a synchronization channel.

Characteristics of the U Interface Transceiver

A scrambler in the transmit path prevents any periodic patterns in the transmission line which might impair the operation of the receiver control systems. The binary data stream is converted into a three-stage signal in accordance with the code table. Synchronizing and maintenance signals are also added. After limiting the spectrum by use of a filter and then converting the digital signal into analog form, the resulting signal is fed to the transmission line.

In the receive section the incoming analog signal is first converted into a 12 bit digital signal at a sampling rate of 120 KHz. Afterwards, a compensation signal computed in the echo compensator is added to the - now quantized - input signal, suppressing the echo of the transit signal contained in the received signal.

To ensure unconditional convergence, rapid frame position recognition, and error propagation limitations, a so-called Barker code of eleven symbols serves as synchronizing patter, as shown in Figure 3. This code is inserted after every 108 symbols of user data. Including a further symbol for maintenance messages, a frame length of 120 bits and a frame duration of 1 ms is achieved. Figure 4 shows the structure of this frame.

The U transceiver implemented in VLSI is shown functionally in Figure 5. The first implementation used in this trial constitutes 4 chips. This system was matched to the impedance of the European cable (150 ohms) and not the U.S. cable (135 ohms). If optimized to the U.S. loop plant, some improvement in the working range can be expected.

Higher scale integration with the potential for improved performance is being developed. A 2-chip version is due out of production this year.

The implementation of this technology in a

field trial environment is discussed in the following section.

THE FIELD TRIAL

The 196-line Siemens EWSD was installed in the New Jersey Bell Red Bank central office and is currently operating on the generic 4.0 release. It is linked to a Siemens Packet Server Module (PSM) which provides W.25 packet data service to the ISDN users via nailed-up connections on the B-channel and multiplex connections on the D-channel. Multiple virtual circuits are provided on both.

As seen in Figure 6, the EWSD is also co-located, as an adjunct switch, with an existing 1AESS. The 1AESS provides Centrex service to the Navesink complex. Through an EWSD/1AESS interworking arrangement, Bellcore clients who were selected for ISDN service were able to maintain their existing phone number (NXX code sharing) and continue 4-digit dialing between all Centrex/ISDN stations. Connectivity and transparency between the 1AESS and EWSD were tested.

ISDN Loop Configuration

The Navesink Center is located approximately 12.5 KFT from the Red Bank CO. Digital Subscriber Loops (DSLs) serving the Navesink Center are described in Figure 7. Mixed gauge pairs available for the trial totalled 100 and were designated to serve the 50 users located in building 2, since they were served with the longest loops. The remaining mixed gauge pairs were assigned to the longest loops in the other two buildings. Straight 26 gauge pairs served the rest of the users in buildings 1 and 3. Central office cabling from the frame to the switch totalled 290 feet.

Bellcore's Navesink Center consists of three mid-rise buildings. Initially, all of the facilities serving the center terminated in building 3 which served as the Network Interface. House cables from the other two buildings were routed back to the building 3 frame. Users are located 50 to 400 feet from the cable termination point in each building. Due to the 1 KFT loop between building 3 and 1, a splice was made in the manhole serving the complex so that 26 gauge pairs could terminate directly in building 1.

In order to characterize the loops and ensure that the DSLs could operate properly, the following benchmark tests were performed on several basic access lines:

    Foreign DC Voltage
    Insulation Resistance
    Loop Resistance
    Insertion Loss
    Wideband Metallic and Impulse Noise

Power Line Noise and Longitudinal Voltage

These measurements were taken from the main frame in the CO to the network interface in building 3. Results of these tests indicated that the 26 gauge loops experiences an insertion loss measured at 40 KHz of approximately 35 dB, while mixed gauge pairs experienced a loss of about 29 dB. Additional tests on 26 gauge pairs terminated directly into building 1 yielded a loss at, 40 KHz, of 34 dB.

Bit Error Rate (BER) tests were also performed at strategic locations prior to cutover with a total sample of 100 NTs and 50 LTs to assure the upper limit of 10^{-7} was not exceeded. The entire DSL, including the NT and LT, was used in the BER tests and additional loss to test the limits of performance was added by a wire line simulator. BER test results ranged from 10^{-7} to 10^{-10}. The best performing DSLs measured 10^{-7} BER at 39.8 dB at 40KHz and 10^{-10} BER at 34 dB at 40 KHz. The worst performing DSLs measured 10^{-7} BER at 34 dB at 40 KHz which is the minimum factory qualification. The DSLs were distributed within this range and exhibited a strong correlation between the BER and loss, i.e., the higher the loss the higher the BER.

Once test results confirmed that ISDN service could be provided to Bellcore users over the 13 to 14 KFT loops, lines were cut into service. By the end of June, all 146 lines in the initial phase of the cutover were turned up for service without any problems.

Results of the field trial indicate that the early 4-chip version of 4B3T technology, in an un-optimized state, worked well. Problems with self NEXT were never encountered. While it was not an explicit objective of the service trial to stress the limits of self NEXT, 5 of the 12, 25 pair binder groups were utilized at or near capacity. These results suggest that the 4B3T technology used in this trial is limited by loss rather than by self-NEXT. To corroborate and better understand the general results found in this field trial, a separate loop test bed was created and is discussed next.

LOOP QUALIFICATION TESTS

The purpose of the Loop Qualification tests was to subject the Siemens EWSD ISDN technology to a real loop environment in a controlled and rigorous way. The operating limit of the Siemens 4B3T line code, the transmission effect of self near end crosstalk (NEXT) and various loop impairments such as unbalance and induced voltage were measured. Combined with test results from other ISDN field trials, this data will also aid in development of engineering guidelines for deploying DSLs in general.

A test bed was constructed by New Jersey Bell using cable facilities in the Red Bank wire center area separate from those serving the Navesink Center. The test bed consisted of a patch panel located in the CO and 25 pair binder groups from several existing 26 gauge cable segments. This arrangements, as shown in Figure 8, was designed so that cable segments could be configured in several ways, allowing the end-to-end circuit loss as well as the length and placements of bridged taps to be varied to simulate a variety of loop conditions.

Test Methodology

Measurement of BER was used to determine the operating limit of the DSL and to determine the range reduction in dB contributed by self NEXT, bridged taps, and transmission impairments such as 60 Hz longitudinal voltage and leakage to ground.

BER typically increases rapidly with a small increase in loop loss once the 10^{-7} BER is exceeded. Observations during tests on various loop length showed that a few hundred feet of length added to a marginally performing DSL changed the BER from 10^{-7} to 10^{-5}. The loop loss was adjusted using the wireline simulator until the BER was 10^{-5}. Self NEXT, bridged tap or a transmission impairment was then added. This caused the BER to increase. The loop loss was then reduced until the BER was approximately the same as before the impairment was added. The range reduction in dB was then defined as the difference in loop loss to achieve the same BER.

Test Results

The following test results again indicate that Siemens's early implementation of 4B3T has a minimum operating range of 34 dB. In addition, the effect of self NEXT on the DSL performance is minimal and the impact of transmission impairments, typical of voice frequency circuits in the loop, is negligible. Only bridged taps generate significant loss that contributes to a reduced range of the ISDN DSLs. The degree of error in the following tests is estimated at less than 1 dB.

Working Range
   Using single frequency loss measurements, the working range was from 34 to 38 dB at 40 KHz while maintaining a BER of 10^{-7} or better. The variance in operating range resulted from a variance in manufacturing tolerance of the LT and NT1 VLSI chips.

   The operating range or limit is defined as the minimum working range, or 34 dB,

and is the level at which all units can be used without prequalification. The operating or working limits do not include an allowance for margin and self-NEXT. Margin should be taken into account when planning the deployment of ISDN technology to account for errors in records, noise, and other transmission impairments. The amount of margin allowed will depend on whether special circuit design and testing is performed. Margin has been considered by the T1E1 Standards Committee.

Self NEXT (Near End Crosstalk)
   Self NEXT was introduced by operating 23 ISDN DSLs in the same 25 pair binder group as the pair under test. The disturbed system (pair under test) was the pair experiencing the strongest NEXT coupling. Based on theoretical and empirical considerations, we can confident that the 23 disturbers yield a crosstalk similar to a full binder group of any size. The range reduction due to self NEXT was found to be approximately 1 dB.

Effect of Bridged Taps
   These test were made using a loop configuration with a 30 dB loss and with a wire line simulator inserted to add artificial wire lengths. Range reduction measurements were made in terms of equivalent cable loss reduction to accommodate the effect of multiple lengths of 26, 24, and 22 gauge bridged taps placed at various locations in the loop. A noise insertion method was used to confirm the results.

   Test results revealed that, in some cases, the noise insertion method resulted in a 1 dB performance improvement of the DSL over the loss method. The greatest effect on range reduction due to single bridged taps was on a 4 KFT and longer taps. The maximum loss incurred as a result of a single bridged tap is: 4.0 dB for 26 gauge; 5.0 dB for 24 gauge; and 7.0 dB for 22 gauge. Shorter bridged taps had concomitantly a lesser loss.

   Range reduction due to 2 bridged taps was found to be roughly approximated by adding the loss from each of the 2 bridged taps.

Induced Voltage
   A 50 Vrms, 60 Hz longitudinal voltage transformer was connected in series with the 30 dB loop configuration, at a distance of 4.1 KFT from the NT1. The operating limit was not degraded in the presence of extraneous voltage.

Resistive and Capacitive Unbalance
   A resistive decade box was placed on one side of the 30 dB loop

configuration. The resistive unbalance was set to 30 KOHMS and then to 1 KOHM tip to ring, tip to ground, and ring to ground without producing any effect on the operating range.

A capacitive unbalance of 20 nF did not reduce the operating range using the same techniques described for resistive unbalance.

Compatibility With POTS Loops

A 500 type rotary dial telephone set and five touchtone sets were connected to the six pairs fo the connectorized cable which had the most crosstalk coupling to the pair under test at the NT1. The 1AESS switch provided dial tone and the capability to ring the phones. This configuration subjected the pair under test to the crosstalk from these POTS lines due to rotary dial pulses, switch hook flashing, ringing, and ring trip during the ringing interval. No degradation in the 34 dB operating limit was found during any test.

Note: Effects due to impulse and broadband noise were not studied explicitly.

EARLY PERFORMANCE TESTS

The field trial results and Loop Qualification tests were consistent with earlier performance measurements made in Bellcore's laboratory for the T1E1 standards committee.

A 4-chip prototype version of Siemens's MMS43 transceiver, utilizing the 4B3T line code with echo cancellation, was tested at the Bellcore laboratory on fifteen loops in mid 1986. Results were summarized in a T1E1 report. (4) These fifteen loops were chosen from a set of 300 loops in the 1983 loop survey that showed the greatest mean square loss (MSL) for transmission with the 2B1Q line code.[3] Each loop stresses the DSL by simulating operation near the limit of loop transmission characteristics.

The Bellcore report noted that the Siemens MMS43 prototype transceivers performed with some margin on all but three of the fifteen loop configurations. To meet full technical requirements, the ISDN DSL transceivers will have 6 dB margin. For the MMS43 prototype, this equates to approximately 96% of the US loop plant. THe lossiest loops over which these prototypes functioned, with non-negative marging against the crosstalk of a full binder group (the 1% worst case), had 33.8 dB MSL and about 40 dB (+ or - 1 dB) simple loss at 40 KHz. Under field trial conditions, the best measured production

---
3 MSL is a measure of loss over the full frequency range of the DSL signal.

units of the U interface chip operated at 39.8 dB at 40 KHz (with no margin and no self-NEXT) at a BER greater than 10^{-7}.

Our confidence is thus increased that the performance determined in a laboratory environment can be achieved in a real loop environment with a first production version of the U interface technology and that this technology will be able to meet full performance requirements set forth by the T1E1 Committee.

CONCLUSION

Siemens's ISDN technology using echo cancellation with the 4B3T line code was proven to be equal or better than the BER performance criteria (10^{-7} to 10^{-10}) in a real application over relatively long loops (13 to 14 KFT). Rigorous testing substantiated these findings and further demonstrated that the best performing DSLs could achieve a maximum working range of 39.8 dB at 40 KHz. It was also discovered that the only loop impairments significantly affecting performance were bridged taps.

Siemens is currently working on the US industry (DSL) standard fo echo cancellation using the 2B1Q line code. The results of the 4B3T testing are encouraging for the 2B1Q development as 4B3T and 2B1Q share certain common properties. Both are members of the block code family and both provide baud rate reduction. The general insensitivity of 4B3T to line impairments underscores the robustness of block codes. However, additional care must be taken in the design, development, and testing of 2B1Q with regard to bridged taps. Siemens is investigating possible improvements in this area including increasing the capability of the driver and the hybrid circuit in the U interface. It is also important that 2B1Q be optimized for the US loop plant.

With the knowledge gained in the trial we can be more certain that ISDN can be economically deployed without requiring costly special loop design or loop qualification.

REFERENCES

(1) Schollmeier G: The User Interface in the ISDN. Telecom Report 8 (1985), Special Issue, "Integrated Services Digital Network - ISDN", pp. 22-27.

(2) Schollmeier G: Transmission Systems for Digital Subscriber Line Circuits in the ISDN. Telecom Report 6 (1983), No. 5, pp. 207-210.

(3) Buchner, I.B.: Ternary Line Codes, Phillips Telecomm. Rev. 34 (1976), No. 2, pp. 72-87.

(4) McDonald, R.A.: Performance Measurements of Implementations of Several Line Codes. T1D1.3 Report 86-154 (8/86), pp. 9-13.

$t\rightarrow$	S1	S2	S3	S5
	$t\rightarrow$			
0001	0-+ 1	0-+ 2	0-+ 3	0-+ 4
0111	-0+ 1	-0+ 2	-0+ 3	-0+ 4
0100	-+0 1	-+0 2	-+0 3	-+0 4
0010	+-0 1	+-0 2	+-0 3	+-0 4
1011	+0- 1	+0- 2	+0- 3	+0- 4
1110	0+- 1	0+- 2	0+- 3	0+- 4
1001	+-+ 2	+-+ 3	+-+ 4	--- 1
0011	00+ 2	00+ 3	00+ 4	--0 2
1101	0+0 2	0+0 3	0+0 4	-0- 2
1000	+00 2	+00 3	+00 4	0-- 2
0110	-++ 2	-++ 3	--+ 2	--+ 3
1010	++- 2	++- 3	+-- 2	+-- 3
1111	++0 3	00- 1	00- 2	00- 3
0000	+0+ 3	0-0 1	0-0 2	0-0 3
0101	0++ 3	-00 1	-00 2	-00 3
1100	+++ 4	-+- 1	-+- 2	-+- 3

A received 3T block "000" is decoded into the 4B block "0000"

Table 1 Converting the binary data stream into three-state signals according to the MMS43 code (MMS Modified monitoring state)

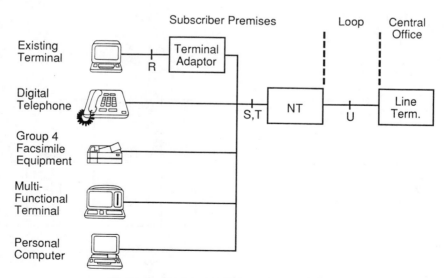

Fig. 1 Basic Access Subscriber Interface

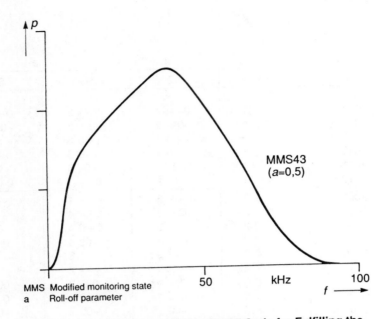

MMS Modified monitoring state
a   Roll-off parameter

Fig. 2 Performance Spectrum of the 4B/3T Code for Fulfilling the Transmission System Requirements for the Subscriber Line in the ISDN *(see Table 1)*

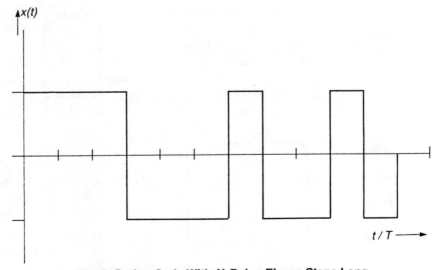

Fig. 3 Barker Code With _N_ Being Eleven Steps Long

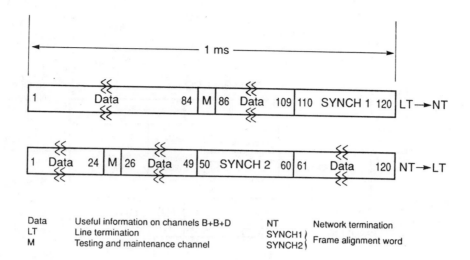

Fig. 4 Frame Structure of the Subscriber Line; the Numerical Values Identify the Symbol Position

Data	Useful information on channels B+B+D
LT	Line termination
M	Testing and maintenance channel

NT	Network termination
SYNCH1 SYNCH2	Frame alignment word

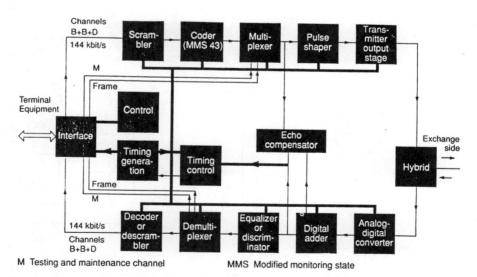

M Testing and maintenance channel   MMS Modified monitoring state

Fig. 5 Block Schematic Diagram of the Transmission Equipment at the U Interface (U Transceiver)

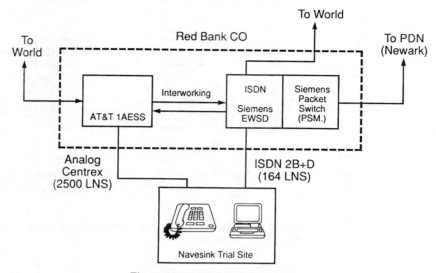

Fig. 6 ISDN Trial Configuration

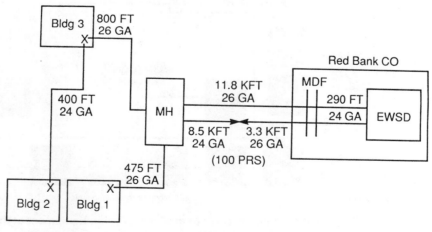

NOTE: An additional 50 to 400 feet must be allowed
from building frame to user.

FIG. 7 ISDN Trial Loops

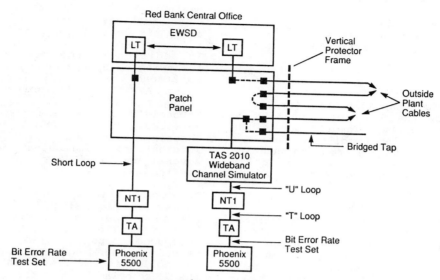

Fig. 8 NJB Loop Laboratory

5ESS^R SWITCH ISDN BETA SITE USERS GROUP

Nancy R. Daspit
Engineer Manager
ISDN Application Support

Edgar L. Vickery
Occupational Engineer

AT&T Network Systems
2600 Warrenville Road
Lisle, Illinois 60532

ABSTRACT

Through the BSUG, the joint efforts of the OTCs have made the deployment of ISDN on AT&T's 5ESS a reality. The efforts of the BSUG and its Steering Committee provide a forum for effective information sharing across all OTC functions and for early problem identification and resolution.

INTRODUCTION

Beta Sites were uniquely configured 5ESS Switches offered to the Operating Telephone Companies (OTCs) to provide the opportunity for first hand experience with the Integrated Services Digital Network (ISDN) for both telephone company personnel and their end customers. It was intended to offer opportunities for both Marketing and Operations, Administration and Maintenance organizations to trial and evaluate all aspects of ISDN working directly with their customers in a hands-on environment.

A Beta Site generally consisted of an Administrative Module (AM), Communications Module (CM) and a Switching Module (SM). The SM was engineered to contain the following hardware:

- Digital Line Trunk Unit
- Global Digital Service Unit
- Integrated Services Line Unit
- Packet Switch Unit
- Analog Line Unit
- Analog Trunk Unit
- Modular Metalic Service Unit
- Directly Connected Test Unit
- Digital Carrier Line Unit
- Digital Services Unit 2
- Integrated Services Test Function Unit

The Beta Sites ran on an early version of the 5E4 generic program which offered basic voice services in addition to Packet Switched Data (PSD) and Circuit Switched Data (CSD) features for ISDN.

Refer to Figure (1) for a layout of a typical ISDN Beta Site. Two sites elected to use Optical Remote Modules (ORMs). One of these sites had their ORM located approximately 2 miles from the 5ESS Switch; the other Beta Site had two ORMs located 4 miles and 19 miles respectively from the Switch.

The Beta Site locations are shown in Table 1.

At the time the Beta Sites were offered, the Beta Site User Group (BSUG) was formed. The purpose of the BSUG was to provide a single focal point for ISDN issues arising from the Beta Site trials. Beginning in the fourth quarter of 1986, BSUG meetings were held approximately every six weeks through February, 1988.

In addition to the six Beta Sites, the following telephone companies were invited to attend the Beta Site User Group meetings: AMERITECH (Illinois Bell, Oakbrook, IL) was a First Office Application with McDonald's as the end-customer for ISDN services. U.S. West (Mountain Bell, Phoenix, AZ) conducted a trial at the 1987 International Switching Symposium with several end customers demonstrating ISDN services.

To ensure that the BSUG addressed those issues of highest priority to the Beta Sites, a Steering Committee was formed with a single representative from each telephone company. These representatives served as the single point of contact for the collection of issues in all aspects of the ISDN trial within their company. The issues were then forwarded to the Steering Committee chairperson, who would then convene the committee to prioritize them. The chairperson worked with AT&T on the resolution of these items through presentations and/or documentation.

BETA SITE EVALUATIONS

From March 1987 through March 1988, the Beta Sites performed their evaluations of the various aspects of ISDN. These evaluations included the testing of outside plant loops used for ISDN services, the testing of operational support systems, the investigation and resolution of Automatic Message Accounting billing record formats, the development of service order questionnaires and service order processes, and the development of the maintenance support flow for customer reported ISDN troubles. Telephone company personnel also performed extensive tests of the many ISDN data features and voice services offered with the Beta Site generic. Several combinations of ISDN capabilities were available for assignment to each Basic Rate Interface. Some of those tested included:

. Coax Elimination (CSD)

. PC to Main Frame Computer Access (PSD and CSD)

. PC-to-PC File Transfer (PSD and CSD)

. Group IV Facsimile (CSD)

. Modem Pooling (PSD)

- Slow Scan Video (CSD)

- Local Area Networks using PCs and commercial software (PSD and CSD)

- Multiple logical channel calls over a single Basic Rate Interface (PSD)

The Beta Site Trials were used as preparation for the introduction of ISDN services in 1988. A three-phase process was used by many of the telephone companies in preparation for these service offerings. The first phase consisted of the evaluation of existing end-customers and the determination of the benefits they could derive from ISDN services. The second phase included evaluations of outside plant facilities, service order processes, billing, and maintenance support. The third phase consisted of hands-on training using a variety of ISDN applications and CPE equipment that provided each telephone company with the information needed to design, test, and support ISDN.

During each of these phases, the telephone companies provided information to each other through the BSUG meetings and provided AT&T with suggestions for enhancing ISDN features and operations, administration and maintenance capabilities. The knowledge gained at the completion of the Beta Site trials provided the initial learning experiences for switching equipment technicians, documentation and training developers, end customers and line-assignment, service-order and maintenance personnel to implement ISDN services.

EVALUATION OF EXISTING CUSTOMERS FOR ISDN APPLICATIONS

Evaluations of end-user configurations were accomplished in several steps. The first step involved identifying friendly end-users (e.g., Lockheed, AT&T Bell Laboratories) that are leaders in their respective industries. The second step was to have a meeting between the telephone company and the end-user to determine how their present data communications environments could benefit from and be adapted to ISDN. The third step involved identifying what ISDN CPE could best serve the end-user needs. This resulted in the determination of how ISDN can exist in a customers environment based on the ISDN features available with the 5E4 Beta Site generic. The telephone companies were interested in their customers perceptions of the ISDN services offered and the potential improvements and benefits to their business communications needs.

These steps were accomplished through the use of Pre-ISDN survey questionnaires and customer meetings.

EVALUATION OF TELEPHONE COMPANY PROCESSES

Loop qualification procedures were accom-

plished in one of two ways by the telephone companies. The first procedure required testing each individual ISDN line. The other procedure consisted of testing random loops in each binder group. Some telephone companies chose to install new cable facilities between the central office and the end-user rather than spend time testing via either of the above procedures. If it was determined that an end-user was located beyond the electrical specifications for the U Interface, Basic Rate Interface Transmission Equipment (BRITE) channel units were used to provide ISDN service using D4 Channel Banks or SLC 96 Carrier Systems. The initial prototype BRITE cards were introduced at the BSUG by AT&T and provided to the Beta Sites for evaluation.

Service Order generation was a major concern to the telephone companies involved in the Beta Bite Trials. Many operational support systems for this process were evaluated. Using these systems and some manual workarounds, the telephone companies were able to generate ISDN service orders based on the ISDN features available in the Beta Site generic. Additional work was required to include the full feature complement of the 5E4 generic in the work flow. Based on the Beta Site trials, the support systems are being enhanced to include productivity improvements as well as the additional features.

Several new billing combinations were introduced with the new ISDN features using circuit switched voice/data and packet switched data calls. Preliminary Automatic Message Accounting (AMA) call types and structure codes were provided to the Beta Sites during several BSUG meetings. AMA billing test tapes were generated at several Beta Sites for all types of ISDN calls and verified for proper billing.

Maintenance support for ISDN was a difficult area to deal with for the telephone companies. Very early in the Beta Site trials it became evident to the telephone companies that although technical support processes for the analog customer trouble reports were well established, there was no similar support structure in place for ISDN related problems. All of the telephone companies are addressing these data needs in their internal technical support organizations with additional ISDN and data training courses and hands-on experience.

Throughout the Beta Site trials, the telephone companies trialed first generation ISDN Customer Premises Equipment as well as first generation maintenance test equipment. In addition to the AT&T equipment tested, several vendors provided prototype ISDN CPE and test equipment to various Beta Sites. The BSUG facilitated the access to the other vendor equipment by inviting vendors to make presentations and demonstrations of their equipment. These vendors worked directly with the telephone companies to develop new ISDN applications and enhance protocol analysis and test equipment.

As a direct result of feedback through the BSUG, AT&T designed and provided several types of ISDN test sets to the Beta Sites for evaluation. Based on feedback, improvements have been made to many of the first generation test sets. The Basic Rate Interface Test Set (BRITS) used by the Beta Sites went through several design changes based on recommendations for additional features. Two of these features were additional incremental insertion loss and data connectivity testing capability. Additional test equipment continues to be designed and provided to many of the telephone companies for further evaluation.

The combined efforts of the BSUG members had considerable influence on the vendors who manufacture protocol analyzers. Initially protocol analyzers were equipped with only RS232 and/or V.35 interfaces. In order to protocol monitor ISDN lines, a T Interface Monitor Simulator unit was used to gain access to the two B channels as well as the D channel. Many vendors now provide a T interface connection that allows a connection directly into their unit.

Because many of the end customers were on U interface lines and the T interface access required the maintenance technician to be on the customer premises for access to the BRI line, this meant time would be lost dispatching a technician to the premises. To address this issue, AT&T developed a monitor circuit that interfaces a U line to a protocol analyzer called a U Interface Monitor (UIM). The UIM is inserted into the two wire circuit at the main distributing frame in the central office.

The UIM was provided to several Beta Sites for evaluation. As these evaluations progressed, a further enhancement to the UIM was developed. This enhancement allows the protocol analyzer to be located at a remote location such as a Switching Control Center, with access to the UIM located in the central office. BRITE units can be used on carrier facilities to increase the distance between the central office and the remote location. Refer to Figure (2)

Throughout the Beta Site trial period the telephone companies were involved with evaluating the operations, administration and maintenance capabilities of ISDN on the 5ESS Switch. Several enhancements to the switch generic were also made based on suggestions during this time frame. These enhancements included changes to the Recent Change and Verify features that enabled the telephone companies to assign ISDN features more easily. A Verify only view was added that allows for verification of Packet Handler assignments in the Packet Switch Unit (PSU). A personal computer based tool for ISDN line assignments was developed called ILAS (ISDN Line Assignment System) that provides Line Card Equipment Numbers (LCENs) and Packet Handler assignments on a mechanized basis. The ILAS system was provided to the Beta Sites for use during their trials and several modifications have been made based on their suggestions. Additional Protocol Error Record capabilities to improve maintenance capabilities were also added to the generic as a result of the BSUG feedback.

HANDS-ON TRAINING AND EXPERIENCE

The telephone companies recognized the need for ISDN training in several areas including maintenance, CPE installation, and end-user administration and feature access. Suitcased training at the Beta Sites for ISDN maintenance and the end-user feature operations were provided. In addition to the formal training classes, most telephone companies established training/demonstration areas that were used by their own personnel and their end-users to gain a working knowledge of the ISDN services offered.

ISDN hands-on experience at the Beta Sites allowed the telephone companies to develop a working knowledge of the hardware and software used in the many ISDN services. This included working with off-the-shelf components, identifying and testing terminal emulation software and file transfer software for ISDN solutions. Most telephone companies used the data expertise that was already available from their own data services personnel to support the wiring and testing of ISDN services at the Beta Sites.

BSUG SUMMARY

The Beta Site trials and the BSUG proved invaluable to the telephone companies, the end customers and AT&T. It offered first hand experience on a working 5ESS Switch with the brand new technology called ISDN. The telephone companies developed expertise in all aspects of the implementation of ISDN services as well as a better understanding of their end-user environments, and the end-user recognized that ISDN could efficiently provide their communications needs now and into the future. Based on the positive results of the Beta Site ISDN trials, all seven Regional Bell Operating Companies and several independent telephone companies are planning commercial offerings of ISDN services during 1988 and 1989.

The BSUG has now become the 5ESS Switch
ISDN User Group to continue the information interchange among the telephone
companies and vendors. This new user
group will continue to provide the telephone companies and AT&T a forum for
dialog on ISDN implementation and the
opportunity to target the future course of
ISDN development to the marketplace.

5ESS® Switch ISDN Beta Site Locations	
Company	Location
New England Telephone	Boston, MA
New Jersey Bell	Holmdel, NJ
Southern Bell	Atlanta, GA
Southwestern Bell	St. Louis, MO
Pacific Bell	Sunnyvale, CA
GTE-Florida	Tampa, FL

TABLE 1

FIGURE 1

5ESS® SWITCH
ISDN BETA SITE

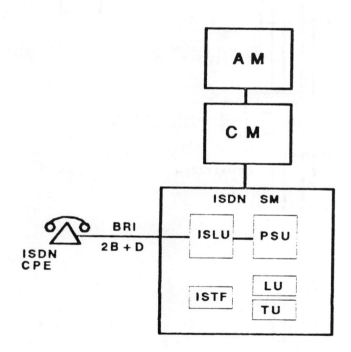

Figure 2

"U" INTERFACE
REMOTE MONITORING

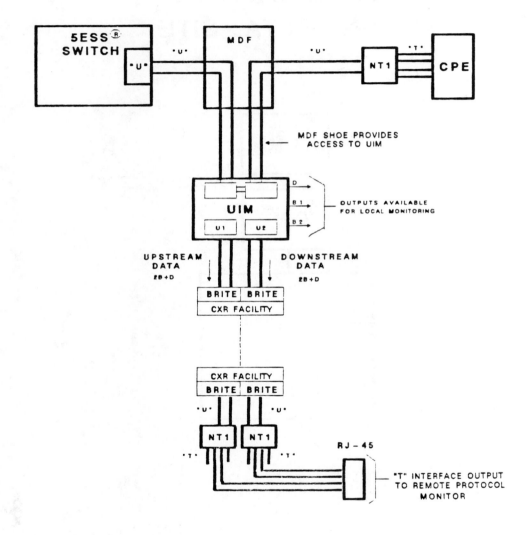

ISDN DEPLOYMENT - FROM CONCEPT TO REALITY

Kevin D. Williams
Manager
Planning & Engineering

Illinois Bell Telephone Company
225 West Randolph, HQ 26C
Chicago, Illinois 60606

ABSTRACT

A very substantial effort is required for an Operating Telephone Company to move the new technology of ISDN into the mainstream of its product offerings. It is Illinois Bell's intention to drive down the cost of ISDN by provisioning and maintaining the service on a "POTS-like" basis. This paper discusses in detail the meaning of "POTS-like" and the philosophy behind this method of providing ISDN service.

This discussion will emphasize the major strategic barriers in this deployment effort including: The development of expertise in the operations work forces; The development of Operations, Administration and Maintenance (OA&M) procedures; The interworking of ISDN based services with existing and future network services; The tariffing of ISDN as a competitive service; and the development of an understanding of ISDN applications.

INTRODUCTION

ISDN has become a common acronym in the telecommunications industry. Practically everyone is familiar with the concept of ISDN, and the proliferation of technical trials across the nation have proven that it is a viable technology. The salable attributes of an ISDN service offering will be a topic of debate for some time to come. However, there can be little argument that a successful ISDN product offering will have to offer the end user features and/or functionality which are attractive, cost effective, and reliable. It is now the responsibility of the telcos to bring this proven technology to the market. Customer acceptance of ISDN, and therefore ISDN's ultimate success, will depend entirely on this deployment effort.

A successful deployment will require the telco to develop a technical expertise with the new technology. This has been one of the primary reasons for all of the technical trials. Deployment, requires that this initial core of expertise developed during the trials be strategically utilized and expanded to accommodate large scale support requirements. In addition to the development of expertise, it will be necessary to fit ISDN into the large number of existing procedures and support systems which support the network. This area of the Operation, Administration, and Maintenance -- or OA&M -- is probably the largest obstacle to overcome in the introduction of ISDN on a commercial basis.

Even if ISDN can be adequately provisioned and maintained, it will have little customer value if it cannot support interworking with other services. Those services may be other ISDN based services provided out of another switch (of the same or a different manufacturer), or they will more likely be existing non-ISDN based services to which the end-user will require transparent communications.

In addition to all of these technical hurdles, an ISDN tariff must be filed. The rates filed in that tariff will certainly determine the attractiveness and profitability of the service. However, a thorough understanding of ISDN services and their cost characteristics is necessary to structure the tariff such that it is sound enough to meet the competitive marketplace.

All of the technology and support being poured into ISDN means nothing until the end-user identifies a need for the service. That need will manifest itself in some form of "Application". It is this word -- APPLICATION -- which is at the root of the success of ISDN. It is critical that the Telephone Operating Company understand what is meant by applications, and what are the characteristics of good (and bad) ISDN applications.

DEVELOPMENT OF TECHNICAL EXPERTISE

Although ISDN represents the integration of several digital and analog services that exist today, the support this integrated service vehicle requires a level of expertise which did not previously exist in any one work group. Therefore, it is necessary for the operating company to incrementally develop selected individuals who have a knowledge base in a particular subset of ISDN services. This development will result in a core group of ISDN expertise. This core group must serve as the primary support for the rollout of ISDN, but it will be necessary to expand the base of expertise beyond this group to support wide range deployment.

This expertise dilemma is most evident in the area of maintenance. ISDN is a switch based service. Maintenance support for trouble and service assurance will therefore be a responsibility of switching operations personnel. Until ISDN, however, these people had little to no exposure to the world of data communications technologies and protocols. Such knowledge is imperative to the maintenance support of ISDN in that even call signaling is in the form of a data communications protocol (Q.931), not to mention bearer service protocols associated with packet and circuit switched data. Therefore, it is obvious that protocol analysis will become a part of central office maintenance.

An approach which Illinois Bell is pursuing is to strategically centralize protocol analysis for ISDN. This will involve the establishment of a "Protocol Analysis Team" -- or PAT -- which will consist of several highly trained protocol experts. When a case of trouble is referred to the central office maintenance forces, they will perform some rudimentary trouble isolation procedures. If it is determined that more detailed protocol analysis will be necessary to shoot the trouble, it will be handed off to the PAT. Remote monitoring interfaces will allow the suspect line to be put up for analysis by the PAT. Upon successful analysis, the trouble will be handed back to the local maintenance forces to close out the trouble report.

The strategic development of expertise pertains not only to maintenance, but to every aspect of the telco operations. In each of these areas, a strategy similar to the PAT example above will probably be required, involving the identification and full development of a core group of deployment experts. This group will have the substantial responsibility to not only support the service rollout, but to serve as the nucleus of a larger scale development throughout the organization.

OA&M

One of the advantages of ISDN, from a telco perspective, is the simplified architecture for providing sophisticated services. To realize these benefits, it is critical that the telco support ISDN as cost effectively as possible. Specialized design and treatment of ISDN service will quickly eliminate any architectural benefits by inflating the support costs and therefore requiring a tariffed rate for the service which would be economically unattractive for the end-user. It is therefore imperative that the telco give a great deal of attention to ISDN OA&M.

ISDN OA&M can be broken down into three basic categories; Provisioning, Maintenance, Administration. Each of these categories is a topic for extensive discussion, but a few key point can be made about each.

Provisioning refers to all of the processes involved from the point when a customer decides to order ISDN service, to the point that the service is working in the customer location. The first hurdle to be overcome is in the negotiation of the customer's order. Because of the complexity of ISDN supported services, order negotiation could be extremely complicated. As an example, there are

several hundred parameter options associated with a simple X.25 packet line. It cannot be expected that every customer will understand all of the complexities of ISDN services, and for that matter, it would be unreasonable to try to train every service representative to the level of expertise necessary to walk a customer through a negotiation. In addition, the cost of this order negotiation would be prohibitive, if all options were to be explored and defined for each customer order.

To address this issue, Illinois Bell has implemented a Service Negotiation System (SNS) to assist in this process. SNS is a menu driven support system which allows a typical business service representative to walk through an ISDN order with a customer. The system mechanizes such decisions as loop qualification and parameter selections by prompting the SR for only that information relevant to the service being requested. The output of the SNS system is a fully formatted Service Order Document for input into the service order processor, and a Mate Order Document for entries into the ISDN-Mate system described below.

ISDN-Mate is an Illinois Bell developed system, which is actually an enhancement to IBT's Centrex-Mate system. These systems allow for customer control of station changes and rearrangements. This capability is not only very attractive to the end-user, but it provides a facility for the provisioning of optional features which is separate from the service order process. This allows the service order to be a simple transaction for provisioning only bearer service capabilities and "non-Matable" features. The simplified service order stream-lines the service order process and minimizes development requirements in downstream systems. If the customer chooses not to use the ISDN-Mate system, the service center personnel will have access to the system to implement Mate changes.

Maintenance involves all of the processes required to react to customer trouble reports, as well as routine maintenance for service assurance. ISDN poses additional maintenance concerns because the functionality of the service is different from traditional switched services. The protocol analysis issue addressed above is an example of the type of procedure modification which are necessary to accommodate this new service. In addition, support mechanisms for traditional trouble report flows must be modified or augmented to support the complex service. Again, it is to the operating company's advantage to force the ISDN treatment towards POTS to avoid the costly maintenance associated with special services, but expertise must be developed to make that happen.

Administration is a broad category which includes activities from the engineering of the switch to the billing of the services. The integration of various services into the ISDN package forces the integration of administrative procedures which before ISDN were completely separate. This integration results in modifications in support and billing systems and a complete revamping of long standing standard administrative procedures.

INTERWORKING

All of the various technical ISDN trials have verified the functionality of the new service. ISDN functionality alone is a major milestone for the telecommunications industry, however ISDN will not be a ubiquitous service for many years to come -- if ever. Because of this partial penetration, it is critical that ISDN supported services are capable of interworking with other services which exist in the end-user environment.

ISDN interworking take several different forms. ISDN voice services must work in a non-ISDN environment. This means more than the ability to place a call from an ISDN set to an analog station. It is necessary that the ISDN features interact properly within a non-ISDN Centrex. If a customer can not easily utilize such features as shared call appearances, intercom circuits, or call pick-up groups between ISDN and non-ISDN stations, there will be little desire to deploy ISDN.

Data services interworking become even more complex. Rate adaptation will be necessary for the connection of ISDN circuit switched data to other circuit switched data services. Packet data services must be able to reach X.75/X.75' gateways to communicate beyond the ISDN network. A critical service which must be established is modem pooling, where a common group of modems allow access out of the digital ISDN network into the word of analog data communications.

A more obvious aspect of interworking which must be addressed is that of inter-office ISDN. Even when working with a single switch manufacturer, Signaling System 7 (SS7) ISDN signaling is still early in the trial stages. Once these inter-office issues are further refined by the manufacturers, the telco will be faced with the task of implementing interoffice ISDN signaling between switch manufacturers.

TARIFF

All of a telco's hard work in preparing for ISDN will culminate with the filing of a tariff. The tariff will determine the cost of the service and those rates will be the one most important factor consid-

ered by the end-user community in deciding to deploy ISDN. It is obviously very important that the rates are attractive enough to stimulate the demand for the service. Equally as important for the telco is the profitability of those rates.

In order to ensure profitability, the telco's will have to study the characteristics of ISDN services very closely. ISDN has the potential to replace many other services -- both switched and dedicated. This migration will bring new usage characteristics into the switched environment. The determination of the costs of providing those new services must include factors for capacity utilization and feature functionality which are new to switched services tariffs.

If a tariff is to be competitive with alternative services, it will be necessary that it is structured in such a way that any service dependent costs are allocated to that particular service. The result will most likely be a tariff which breaks out access, individual bearer services, additional feature options, and usage.

APPLICATIONS/CPE

As was mentioned in the introduction, applications will drive the demand for ISDN. No two experts will agree on the definition of an ISDN application, yet this area is considered critical to ISDN deployment.

What is important for the telco is not an understanding of specific ISDN applications, but rather an understanding of how to implement and support ISDN applications. Any creative user may identify a use for ISDN in their own environment which has not been identified previously. To successfully implement an application the telco must be intimately familiar with each of the bearer services supported by ISDN, and how those services interact with the various customer premise equipment which is available. This knowledge combined with that obtained through evaluation of the interworking of the various services provides a good foundation for building new and unique ISDN applications.

CONCLUSIONS

ISDN is a complex new technology which will make substantial demands of telco personnel. It proposes alternative networking strategies to the end-user community. However, the services ISDN will replace are already proven and reliable. If the operating companies are not prepared for the deployment of this service in such a way as to provide the same (or better) reliability that the customers are used to in a more robust and cost effective manner, it will most certainly fail before it has a chance to grow. Conversely, proper preparation for the deployment may result in a demand growth rate which will be difficult to keep up with. Therefore, the telephone operating company's preparations for ISDN deployment must be thorough as well as strategic to ensure its ultimate success.

KEY ITEMS TO CONSIDER IN ISDN IMPLEMENTATION

Joan Shine
Area Manager-Switching Engineering

Southwestern Bell Telephone Company
One Bell Center
St. Louis, MO 63101

ABSTRACT

As Southwestern Bell Telephone's (SWBT) ISDN efforts migrate from the trialing stage to full scale ISDN service provisioning, numerous implementation issues and concerns have arisen which must be addressed in order to allow for a graceful evolution to the new services provided by this architecture. Where trial applications have concentrated mainly on testing ISDN functionality, features, interworking issues, and potential customer applications, SWBT has expanded its areas of concentration to include development of extensive intra-Company interdepartmental procedures necessary to ensure that ISDN service meets the expectations of its large scale early application customers.

The focus of this paper will be on identifying some of the key items to consider when implementing ISDN, and will briefly outline how SWBT has chosen to address and deal with these concerns. Particular emphasis is placed on issues related to switch engineering as they pertain specifically to the AT&T 5ESS^{tm} switch and generic 5E4.2.

INTRODUCTION

Since the very first onset of discussions addressing the introduction of ISDN into the exchange network, a great deal of concentration has been placed on identifying the advantages of this architecture including the features and services it can provide. The Telcos as well have emphasized the additional advantages of a Central Office (CO) based ISDN system, which have included the following considerations:

- Reduced capital investment and price stability including maintenance
- Reduced risk of obsolescence
- Limited floor space, power requirements, spare parts inventory, insurance, etc. for the customer
- Reliability of CO switching (fully redundant and uninterruptable power)

However, much less attention has been directed toward identifying the numerous impacts on existing Telephone Company functions, and the requirement for the introduction of new and modified procedures in almost every phase of service provisioning necessitated by the implementation of ISDN. This paper attempts to highlight the main concerns which have been raised in each of the major areas involved in the ISDN implementation process, and to briefly identify the strategy SWBT will employ to ensure the successful transition to ISDN for the early office applications.

SWBT's INITIAL DEPLOYMENT STRATEGY

SWBT's deployment of ISDN thus far has involved the equipping of central offices on an individual basis as needed to respond to specific customer requests for ISDN service. The first five early application customers include Shell and Tenneco (Houston), AT&T Technologies (St. Louis), 3M (Austin), and the AT&T Manufacturing Facility (Oklahoma City), with an estimation of over 11,000 ISDN lines in total to be installed by the end of 1988. All current sales will be provided ISDN Basic Rate Interface (BRI) 2B + D service from AT&T's 5ESS^{tm} switch.

Tariffs were filed through the Customer Specific Proposal (CSP) process, which was utilized on an individual basis to determine customer applications and general system engineering requirements. This process resulted in the determination of the cost for the service, which was used to develop the rate in each case.

With these initial sales came the recognition that each conversion would require extensive planning and interdepartmental coordination. Efforts were immediately undertaken to establish an ISDN Trial/ Early Application Management Team comprised of individuals from General Headquarters and the States, representing all of the major departments within SWBT along with Bellcore participants, involved in making ISDN a reality. Smaller teams were organized from this larger team of experts for the purpose of identifying concerns and developing new methods and procedures where necessary to support deployment of ISDN for the initial customers. As with any new service, these interim procedures would be required until such a time as SWBT's mechanized Operation Systems (OSs) have matured to the point of allowing for the flexible and complex service provisioning introduced with ISDN. Additionally, the smaller teams were designed to interface with each of the local cutover committees, and to provide assistance in resolving problems related to early deployment on a dynamic basis.

ISDN MAJOR CONCERNS AND SWBT RESOLUTIONS

The advent of ISDN has not only brought about innovation in customer applications and the promise of increased efficiency and reliability, but it has also contributed to the complexity of the design engineering, provisioning, administration and maintenance processes which the Telco provides with all network services. Although each of these areas by itself could be expanded upon to detail the extensive procedures developed to ensure the workability of ISDN, only a few of the major concerns will be highlighted here.

TRAFFIC DESIGN AND ENGINEERING CONSIDERATIONS

Immediately following Marketing's identification of a potential ISDN customer, a determination needs to be made as to the particular applications the customer plans to utilize. Where prior to ISDN, SWBT engineers were mainly concerned with sizing the switch so that it would efficiently handle the voice and circuit switched data calls as measured in hundred call seconds (ccs), they now must also contend with the impact packet switched calls have on the network, and the requirement of a second measurement of load, packets per second (pps). With the offer of simultaneous voice and data communication capability has come the introduction of new equipment components in the CO., and new load sizing and balance considerations required to maintain the efficient utilization of both a message and a packet based network.

In making the initial ISDN engineering assumptions, the overriding need of the engineer is for accurate traffic data to be used to characterize the various customer data applications. Forecasts of the quantities and types of ISDN customer applications throughout the engineering period will also be paramount, and so extreme emphasis needs to be placed on securing this information from the customer via some form of initial review process. In most cases, it should be recognized that Marketing will need assistance in interpreting customer defined applications and their relation to pps and ccs. Development of numerous application models involving various types of customer premise equipment (CPE), their interactions, and related traffic demand, may prove beneficial when attempting to identify the customer utilization required to properly size the switch.

Based on the uncertainty which most probably will be inherent in many of the initial input values, it appears to be wise to utilize a conservative engineering approach for early ISDN deployments. As we gain knowledge of ISDN customer traffic characteristics through analysis of early applications, we can refine our engineer-

ing and provide a more accurate and cost effective product.

Additionally, since the initial information on customer load estimates are expected to be speculative without actual customer traffic data available in most cases, it is extremely important that the traffic engineer communicate the engineering assumptions made on a particular ISDN customer to the individuals translating the lines. In this way, SWBT expects to avoid significant discrepancies which could result in adverse effects on call processing. The best solution is to maintain open communication among Marketing, Engineering, and Network Administration departments on an ongoing basis.

To further contribute to the already complex traffic and switching engineering jobs are the difficulties encountered with the vendor provided mechanized engineering and ordering tool. Although attempts have been made by the switch vendor to keep the system updated, the Telco engineers must often resort to manual engineering methods in cooperation with the vendor's regional engineers to determine switch requirements in complex cases.

SWBT has attempted to assist its field engineers by developing an ISDN Engineering Guide designed to address general and specific concerns where information was available. This document was not intended to supersede any switch vendor publications, but merely to provide a condensed version of many of the new facets of the engineering process involved in the introduction of ISDN. SWBT's recommendations on engineering are also noted where appropriate throughout the Guide.

A sampling of the initial engineering considerations and recommendations addressed in this Guide, which is directed specifically to use of the 5ESS^{tm} switch as the serving ISDN vehicle equipped with the 5E4.2 generic, include the following:

1) The impact on the switch based upon the utilization of the 2B + D channels of the BRI must be considered. It is especially necessary to identify the customer requirements for B-channel packet switching, since this capability requires a nailed-up connection through the switch to a dedicated packet handler (PH).

2) The Integrated Services Test Function (ISTF), a specialized circuit pack required to perform ISDN loopback tests and transmission tests, is recommended on a one per SM up to two per switch basis.

3) Modem pooling provides the capability for packet switched data communication between ISDN and

non-ISDN stations, and is a requirement for some customers while ISDN is limited to an island configuration. The engineer will need to confirm if the Telco will be providing all of the equipment associated with the modem pooling option for the ISDN customers, as well as the quantity of modem pooling members.

4) Customer requirements for shared ISDN directory numbers (DNs) must be considered, as large quantities may necessitate increasing the number of the three-port conference circuits to provide additional bridging capability. It should be noted that shared DNs reside in "loaded" switching modules (SMs) of the 5ESS^{tm}, which contain the loaded generic text for ISDN and which have a 68020 or 68012 processor with the required memory. Analog lines that reside in "loaded" SMs can also use shared DN capability.

ADVANCED TECHNOLOGY LAB

To assist further in the implementation of early application customers, SWBT has taken the ultimate step in an effort to deal with many of the complex issues and concerns arising in regard to ISDN from both the switch perspective and end-user application view. An Advanced Technology Lab (ATL) was built and opened in mid-1987, and was designed to test customer applications and to evaluate equipment made by various CPE manufacturers and switch vendors to assist in gauging how well they operate within the SWBT network. Whenever a customer requests assistance in solving problems through technology, the ATL can respond by assisting with customer analysis, application design, CPE review, switch and facilities preparation, application testing, and demonstrations. SWBT has found that lab testing of customer applications prior to their actual deployment in the Network is safer and provides a great resource for customer training as well.

To gain a better appreciation of the complexity of ISDN implementation, it is best to briefly step through some of the processes affected.

PROVISIONING PROCESS

Provisioning actually begins when a customer requests ISDN access and ends when the service is available to the customer. It includes service negotiation, service order preparation to detail the individual line requirements, network assignment of the loops, switch line equipment, and packet handlers, completion of switch translations, and installation. The main difficulties encountered in each

of these provisioning processes due to the complexity of the options offered by ISDN have been alleviated to a large degree by the interim methods developed by SWBT in conjunction with Bell Communications Research. It should be noted however that OSs are greatly affected by items such as the ability of ISDN to support multiple telephone numbers on one BRI pipe. For reasons like this, extensive modifications and enhancements to OSs will continue to be developed to eventually allow for a fully mechanized provisioning work flow designed to support the wide range of services offered with ISDN.

LOOP QUALIFICATION AND TRANSMISSION CONCERNS

Among the main concerns in the transmission and loop qualification area have been identifying the limitations imposed by deploying the pre-standard Alternate Mark Inversion (AMI) line code, as well as identifying where ISDN compatible facilities exist.

Through testing, SWBT has found that the characteristics of the AMI line code on the U-BRI line cards limits our safe deployment range to approximately 10,000 feet. This situation could potentially force us to deploy and utilize a type of remoted switching module (optically remoted module) or line unit nearer to the customer premise in order to provide ISDN. SWBT believes that the introduction of the standard 2B1Q line code with its anticipated extended operating ranges will enhance our ability to use existing facilities to the customer premise. Additionally, it is believed that the 2B1Q line code will provide a wider choice of test equipment, since multiple manufacturers are more likely to build test sets to the approved standard line code.

In order to assist in insuring satisfactory, early ISDN implementation, SWBT has developed a Loop Qualification Process designed to allow Distribution Services Outside Plant Engineers to identify loop facilities that are compatible with the services offered by ISDN. This compatibility is determined by meeting specified criteria for loss, loading, and interference with other signals carried in the same sheath. For example, SWBT feels that the allowable loop loss should be limited to 32 db at 80 Khz. Loop conditioning, if required, is recommended to be done in bulk to minimize costs, and should provide for the elimination of all known interferers such as load coils, build-out capacitors, bridge lifters, and analog carrier on ISDN loops.

Mechanized inventories of qualified loops, such as the Premises Information System (PREMIS) and Loop Facilities Assignment and Control System (LFACS), will be developed to support service negotiation and service order assignment processes as part of the overall provisioning process.

ISDN STATION REVIEWS AND SERVICE ORDER PROCESS

A new station review checklist designed to address ISDN requirements was created to assist in the station review process conducted by Marketing. Text and mechanized job aids have been provided for use in the service order negotiation process and SWBT developed a method to provision the ISDN pipe and associated features on a single service order basis. The Common Language Circuit Identification (CLCI) was selected as the access line identification to be entered on the service order as well as the Common Language Serial Field Identifier (CLS FID).

The CLS format was chosen since it was consistent with the involved operations systems' capabilities and operation's center needs. A Universal Service Order Code will also be assigned on a line basis to designate the type of termination (U or T). The customer's individual terminal capabilities in terms of channel utilization (i.e., voice, circuit-switched data, packet data) will be specified by the Bearer Services FID. ISDN service orders will be handled primarily in the Service Order Entry Center (SOEC).

LOOP ASSIGNMENT

The loop assignment process for the initial ISDN applications will be handled on a flow-through basis in the Service Order Analysis and Control (SOAC) and the Loop Facilities Assignment and Control System (LFACS) for the ISDN BRI pipe.

LINE ASSIGNMENT AND TRANSLATIONS

Two-wire loops for the BRI will be cross-connected to the switch via the main distributing frame. The Loop Assignment Center (LAC) will build records for each pipe, indicating the cable and pair, originating equipment (OE), packet originating equipment (POE), and the ISDN pipe ID. To achieve a numerical and limited load balance spreading of this equipment, SWBT utilizes the Computer System for Mainframe Operations (COSMOS) through a process involving the use of the Bellcore originated Rogan Compiler (RC) program. This program was modified by SWBT to allow assignment of the ISDN lines in conjunction with COSMOS.

Line translations should be manually handled in the Recent Change Memory Administration Center (RCMAC) via enhancements to the MIZAR application.

ORDER COMPLETION

The Circuit Installation and Maintenance Administration Package (CIMAP) was selected as the maintenance database system to support ISDN BRIs because it will be deployed throughout SWBT consistent with long range operations plans and can mechanize all the work centers involved with providing ISDN services.

Upon completion of the customer wiring and testing, a notice will be passed to CIMAP, to the Service Order Retrieval and Distribution System (SORD), and to the Customer Records Information System (CRIS), so that billing may begin and all data bases become updated.

MAINTENANCE AND ADMINISTRATION

Maintenance includes trouble detection, sectionalization, and repair functions. Since ISDN introduces end-to-end digital connectivity, a major issue has been identifying who will be responsible for testing when problems occur. It should be realized that in the early deployment stages, ISDN is difficult to treat in a completely POTS (plain old telephone service)-like fashion. Complex concerns associated with areas such as protocol analysis and testing require a modified approach to maintenance and installation.

In the initial SWBT ISDN applications, the Special Services Installation and Maintenance groups will be responsible for provisioning and repair of ISDN lines at the customer premise and for tracking each trouble report. The Special Services Center (SSC) Maintenance Tester will perform the required verification tests to sectionalize the trouble and will coordinate the repair with the appropriate work group(s). With some modifications, current procedures for processing special services trouble reports will be followed, for response to both subscriber initiated demand type trouble, as well as those problems detected through Network performance monitoring and analysis procedures. The Switching Control Center (SCC) with its emphasis on central office operations, along with the SSC, will have responsibility for monitoring data to determine when and where preventative maintenance activity is required.

With the critical nature of traffic loading being a primary concern of the Network Administrator, it is unfortunate that transport of the new ISDN traffic reports collected from the switch by the Engineering and Administration Data Acquisition System (EADAS) cannot flow automatically downstream to a system like the Traffic Data Analysis System (TDAS) in the initial ISDN deployments. In the interim, ISDN load administration will have to be monitored manually from EADAS traffic reports. In the very worst case, if any extensive delay were to be incurred, this monitoring could allow for line load balances to be initiated to evenly distribute traffic for optimum transport through the switch.

TRAINING

It is rather important to note the necessity for extensive training in preparation for ISDN deployment since in the final analysis, understanding of the services available with ISDN by the customer, along with ease of transition provided by the Telco, are the best keys to success with ISDN. For these reasons, a great deal of emphasis needs to be placed on customer training and employee development.

SWBT has demonstrated a strong commitment to ISDN by not only offering formal vendor supplied training to its employees, but also by internally developing courses to increase their knowledge level particularly in the area of data transport, including protocol analysis and testing, and customer applications. Information obtained from Bellcore's ISDN study efforts coupled with SWBT's own ATL experience and results have contributed immensely to positioning SWBT as a successful ISDN service provider.

CONCLUSION

In summary, while traffic engineering, planning, network administration, provisioning, and maintenance functions have all become more difficult and complex with the introduction of ISDN, SWBT is confident that the interim procedures it has developed will permit competent response to customer requests for early ISDN services. Although early deployment obviously carries with it some "bleeding edge" pains, SWBT believes it will also realize the incomparable benefits of knowledge derived from first-hand experience.

THE ROLE OF STANDARDIZATION IN ISDN

Michele Secoli Ruetty
Engineer

Ohio Bell Telephone Company
65 Erieview Plaza, Room 536
Cleveland, Ohio 44114

ABSTRACT

This paper will explore the importance of standardization in the development, definition and deployment of ISDN. In particular, the issues of providing vendor-independent operation of various ISDN features will be addressed. The standardization of the various interfaces (R,S,T,U and V) and their impact on the success of ISDN will also be examined. Only when standardization is complete can the LECs provide the hardware, software and features needed to support the ISDN architecture in the marketplace. Standardization is the key element to a successful deployment of ISDN.

INTRODUCTION

Integrated Services Digital Network, ISDN, is an end-to-end digital network upon which available features and applications will be carried to the customer over digital facilities. ISDN is not a service, rather, a network architecture providing end-to-end digital connectivity. ISDN will provide integrated, not simultaneous, transmission of voice and data over a single link, the digital subscriber line, DSL.

ARCHITECTURE

In order to access the network, two access interfaces are available:

BASIC RATE INTERFACE (BRI) consists of two 64kbps Bearer (B) channels and one 16kbps Delta (D) channel. The B channels may be used for circuit-switched voice, circuit-switched data or packet-switched data. The D channel may be used for low-speed packet-switched data or signaling information.

PRIMARY RATE INTERFACE (PRI) consists of twenty-three 64kbps B channels and one 64kbps D channel. This interface is particularly suited for digital PBX access and provides a 1.544Mbps data stream over T-1 facilities.

The BRI described above has been agreed upon by the telecommunications industry. Bellcore has published TR-TSY-000397 ISDN Basic Rate Access Transport System Requirements and TA-TSY-000754 ISDN Primary Rate Access Transport System Requirements in an effort to define the necessary requirements for both BRI and PRI access.

SIGNALING AND CONTROL

In order to allow communication between two devices, signaling information needs to be exchanged between the user and network on each end of the circuit. Signaling messages are used to invoke, monitor or terminate a particular call or feature. The terminal or Stored Program Control Switching System (SPCS) may use either overlap or en bloc sending signaling techniques during call processing. When overlap sending is used for call origination, all necessary information is not included in the SETUP message. Subsequent messages, known as INFORmation messages, are sent with the additional information needed to process the call. If en bloc sending is used, all necessary information is included in the SETUP message. SETUP messages are normally sent to initiate a call or feature.

With ISDN, the capability exists for the necessary tones and announcements to be provided by either the SPCS or the end user terminal. By standardizing the tones outlined in Figure 1, tones will appear the same to the end user regardless of whether they are provided by the network or generated locally by the terminal.

As a means for associating the particular user equipment attached to an ISDN access interface, service parameters or terminal service profiles are stored in the ISDN SPCS. These profiles will allow mobility within the ISDN network.

Standardization of the signaling messages and tones will allow transparency to the end user but it is required by the LECs because it will allow them to deploy a robust network of multiple vendor products and services. By standardizing the BRI and PRI interfaces, virtually any vendor's equipment may be used in the network. Vendor incompatibilities will no longer be an issue.

It is projected that geographic deployment of ISDN by the BOCs in 1990 will not be extensive, thereby limiting end-to-end applications to small ISDN islands. In order to allow the various SPCSs in these islands to communicate, Common Channel Signaling utilizing Signaling System 7 protocol will be deployed. CCS7's primary ISDN function will be to provide out-of-band signaling between ISDN network nodes. By moving the signaling out-of-band, 64 clear channel capability will be possible. CCS7 was initially deployed at the tandem level in 4Q88 to support BOC 800 database services. It is planned to begin deployment of CCS7 at the end office level by 4Q89. Standards of ISDN/CCS7 interworking are currently being defined. Most LECs are currently working on an Evolution Study to evolve their current networks into CCS compatible networks at the end office level.

INTERFACE SPECIFICATION

One of the major benefits of ISDN lies in streamlining customer premise equipment (CPE) and providing standard interfaces. Standard interfaces will allow the customer to choose among many competitively designed and priced products.

R, S, T, U AND V DEFINITIONS

Figure 2 depicts the reference configuration for the ISDN user/network interfaces.

The R Interface is located between the non-ISDN terminal and the TA. TAs will allow non-ISDN terminals to access the ISDN network.

The S Interface lies between the TE1 or TA and the NT2. The NT2 can be a PBX, LAN, electronic controller, etc. In the case

of the TA/NT2 interface, the NT2 has multi-point capability, enabling it to split the T interface into eight S interfaces.

The T Interface is an ISDN standard. Only the T reference point on the user side of the NT1 is specified in the CCITT recommendation. The interface consists of 2 pairs, one for send and one for receive. Internationally, the T interface serves as the boundary between the network and the customer's premise.

The U Interface is a single pair interface. The interface is NOT a standard. Each country may have one or more different U interfaces. In the US, the FCC is seeking to set the network boundary at the U interface, thus making NT1 customer premise equipment. This would require standardizing the U interface.

The V Interface lies between the remote and exchange reference points. The V interface for single customer termination from a remote terminal extends the range of ISDN further.

The TA adapts a terminal with a non-ISDN standard interface to an ISDN standard user-network interface.

The TE1 contains an interface in compliance with the CCITT ISDN user-network recommendations.

The TE2 contains an interface which adheres to recommendations other than those developed for ISDN.

The NT1 is a CCITT term for Network Channel Terminating Equipment (NCTE). Its function is to provide line transmission termination and layer-1 maintenance and multiplexing. The NT1 converts the four-wire T interface into the two-wire U interface, in other words, it allows compatibility between the terminal equipment and the network.

The NT2 might consist of a PBX, LAN or terminal controller. Its functions include interface termination, layer 2 and 3 protocol handling and multiplexing, switching, concentration and maintenance.

Figure 3 depicts the interface reference points, functional groupings and the status in standardizing each.

The major emphasis for the LECs when discussing Basic Rate Access lies in the U interface and the DSL. Seeing how the U interface serves as the demarcation point between the user and network, it holds great importance for the LECs. The U interface, a two-wire interface, is located on the customer's premise at the connector terminals of the Network Termination equipment. The DSL provides high quality transmission for a single

ISDN Basic Access customer over a non-loaded, two-wire metallic cable pair. Universal Digital Loop Carrier (UDLC) and placement of remote switching units (RSU) will be relied upon to extend to range of the simple DSL from the SPCS past 18,000 feet. This can only be accomplished by using 2B1Q line coding.

2B1Q LINE CODING

Standardization of the new line code to be used in ISDN, 2B1Q, is currently underway. AMI (Alternate Mark Inversion) or B8ZS (Binary 8 Zero Substitution) are currently being used in today's networks. However, current line codes will not allow the LECs to provide ISDN to customers located more than 10,000 to 12,000 feet from the Central Office. Therefore 2B1Q is being defined to allow deployment of ISDN at distances in the range of 12,000 to 18,000 feet. It is expected that initial 2B1Q prototype equipment will be available early 1989 and generally available by 1990 at the earliest.

By standardizing the interfaces and line code to be used with ISDN, any vendor's equipment may be supported by the network and operation should appear transparent to the end user. Standardization will also allow common systems of billing, service order processing, and operations support systems to be built to provision and maintain ISDN.

FEATURE SPECIFICATION

One of the many advantages of ISDN lies in the robustness of the features the LECs can provide to their customers. ISDN will allow much more flexibility in the method in which features are activated and controlled. In today's operating environment, the features the LECs can provide depend on the SPCS serving that customer. ISDN will remove this dependency and provide switch-independent features. Standardization must be complete before this may happen.

Generally, customer features available today will be available with ISDN. However, ISDN will make their operation more flexible. Also, ISDN will introduce new features which will be addressed later in this paper.

The various signaling messages, composed of information elements, required for the operation of ISDN features are specified in TA-TSY-000861. The feature operation is controlled by the exchange of messages over the D-channel between user equipment and the serving SPCS. The required messages are summarized in Figure 4.

SUPPLEMENTARY SERVICES

The following features are included in a group of features known as the Supplementary Service Features. Bellcore is heavily involved in publishing documents to define these features. Figure 5 outlines the status of each.

ACTIVATION OF FEATURES

Three types of terminals are assumed to be in use when ISDN is deployed. Terminal Adaptors will be used in conjunction with standard telephone sets to provide access to the ISDN versions of conventional features. They may not be able to take advantage of improvements to these conventional features. Simple ISDN terminals should be able to provide access to ISDN versions of conventional features, and in addition, may make use of improvements supported by feature key protocols and displays. Functional ISDN terminals should be able to access ISDN versions of conventional features and may support the improvements to those features. ISDN will allow new and more flexible methods of activating features. Features may be activated by using either dial-access protocols, contextural feature operator protocols or feature key management protocols.

For the operation of conventional multiple call handling features, the switchhook flash is used to inform the switch to perform some action. An ISDN terminal that can support at most one call appearance at a time is expected to provide the user with an equivalent to the conventional switch-hook flash to support the ISDN versions of these conventional features. This switch-hook flash equivalent, termed the Contextural Feature Operator, may be presented to the user in a variety of ways (for example, as a feature key). In dial-access activation, digits corresponding to an access code are dialed by the user to invoke the desired feature. Terminals that only present a single call to the user will provide the user with a contextual feature operator. In the case of feature key activation, feature or "function" keys may be provided on the simple or functional ISDN terminal. These function keys are programmed by the user and features are invoked by depressing the function key corresponding to the feature.

The standardization of these features, as well as activation methods, will result in feature transparency for the end user and LECs. For the end user, the operation of the features will be identical regardless of SPCS type providing the service. As an example, if a large corporation is served from several different SPCS vendors across a geographic area, it is unlikely that end users will be willing to learn multiple activation procedures to invoke similar features when traveling between locations. By standardizing interfaces and features, the LEC deployment of features using multiple SPCS vendors will be transparent to end users.

FUTURE SERVICES

DISPLAY MENU

The LECs are actively researching a new ISDN service where display terminals are controlled by the network rather than the user terminal. By designing the service in this manner, all end users will see the same display messages regardless of what vendor's equipment sits on their premise. In order to allow this type of operation, the display messages must be standardized and processing of those messages must be controlled by the network rather than the user's terminal. The attractiveness of this becomes apparent when viewed from the context of both the end user and LEC. From the end user perspective, terminals will not need to be upgraded when new information is added to the network. This is because terminals will only have to interpret network information and forward it to the network controlled display. From the LEC perspective, the service order process could be greatly simplified by giving customer's the ability to order new services or features directly from their terminal. This service could be designed to display cause, feedback and menu information. The Cause Display Feature is used to inform the user about a possible problem: what the problem is and where it occurred. The Feedback Display Feature includes call and service information such as dialed number, called number, calling number and other information related to call origination and termination. The Menu Display Feature could display information while the user is or is not on an active call. This feature could provide information about new services, general news, service ordering, as well as control and administration of services subscribed to.

USER TO USER INFORMATION EXCHANGE

Another new service which is being examined by the LECs involves user-to-user information exchange. This new service would require the user to request or invoke the service. 128 octets of user information could be processed between users during the call setup, confirmation or release stages. This data is transferred and processed whether or not the call is established. This service has many potential service implications.

Again, the base of success of these new services deals in standardization of the messages and format of the information required.

SUMMARY

The success of ISDN lies in standardization. Standardization will allow deployment of multiple CPE vendor products and

eliminate incompatibility problems in the ISDN network. Competition will reduce the price of the products making ISDN more affordable. By driving the price of ISDN downward, a larger market will result. Only when standardization is complete can full switch and vendor independence occur. Standardization, from the end user perspective, will allow products of different manufacturers and services of different providers to work together in an integrated network at a competitive price. From the LEC perspective, common billing systems, service order procedures and common operations support systems will be possible. ISDN will provide much easier maintenance of these systems. Another key aspect of standardization deals with tariff simplification. With ISDN, a common tariff may be written which precludes the idiosyncrasies between SPCS and CPE vendors the LECs have had to consider in the past. Standardization is the key to the success of the network of the future.

ACKNOWLEDGMENTS

Gerald Boyer, Bellcore
Wayne Heinmiller, Ameritech Services
Lewis Holt, Ameritech Services
Richard McDonald, Bellcore
Stephen Murphy, Ameritech Services
Lisa Yago, Bellcore

DIAL TONE	CONFIRMATION TONE
AUDIBLE RINGING TONE (OR RING-BACK TONE)	RECALL DIAL TONE
REORDER TONE (OR NETWORK CONGESTION TONE)	BARGE-IN TONE
BUSY TONE	

FIGURE 1 ISDN TONES

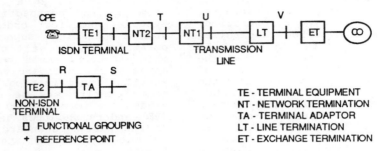

FIGURE 2 ISDN REFERENCE POINT CONFIGURATION

BASIC RATE INTERFACE		
INTERFACE OR FUNCTIONAL GROUPING	STANDARD DEFINED?	DOCUMENT
R	NO	
S	YES	I.430
T	YES	I.430
U	3Q88	TR-TSY-000393
V	NO	

FIGURE 3 ISDN INTERFACE REFERENCE POINT STANDARDIZATION

SIGNALING MESSAGES		
CALL ESTABLISHMENT MESSAGES	CALL RELEASE MESSAGES	CALL INFO PHASE MESSAGES
ALERTing CALL PROCeeding CONNECT CONNECT ACKnowledge PROGress SETUP SETUP ACKnowledge	DISConnect RELease RELease COMplete	HOLD HOLD ACKnowledge HOLD REJect RETrieve RETrieve ACKnowledge RETrieve REJect
MISC MESSAGES		NETWORK-SPECIFIC MESSAGES
INFOrmation NOTIFY		KEY HOLD KEY RELease KEY SETUP KEY SETUP ACKnowledge

FIGURE 4 ISDN SIGNALING MESSAGES

1200

SUPPLEMENTARY SERVICE FEATURES		
DOCUMENT	TITLE	RELEASED TO INDUSTRY?
TA-TSY-000205	ISDN Electronic Key Telephone Service	Y, Issue 2
TA-TSY-000847	ISDN Feature Philosophy	Y, Issue 1
TA-TSY-000848	ISDN Closed User Group	Y, Issue 1
TA-TSY-000849	ISDN Basic Business Group Structure	Y, Issue 1
TA-TSY-000850	ISDN Business Group Dial-Access Features	Y, Issue 1
TA-TSY-000851	ISDN Call Waiting Features: Utilizing a Single Call Reference	Y, Issue 1
TA-TSY-000852	ISDN Multiway Calling Features: Utilizing a Single Call Reference	Y, Issue 1
TA-TSY-000853	ISDN Call Forwarding	Y, Issue 1
TA-TSY-000854	ISDN Call Pickup	Y, Issue 1
TA-TSY-000855	ISDN Automatic Callback and Monitor	Y, Issue 1
TA-TSY-000856	ISDN Hold Capability: For Managing Multiple Independent Calls	Y, Issue 1
TA-TSY-000857	Additional Call Offering: For Managing Multiple Independent Calls	Y, Issue 1
TA-TSY-000858	Flexible Calling: For Managing Multiple Independent Calls	Y, Issue 1
TA-TSY-000859	ISDN Multiline Hunt Group	Y, Issue 1
TA-TSY-000860	ISDN Calling Number Identification Service	Y, Issue 1
TA-TSY-000861	ISDN Layer 3 Protocol Details For The Support of Supplementary Services	Y, Issue 1
TA-TSY-000862	ISDN Automatic Message Accounting Reqts	May 20, 1988
TA-TSY-000863	ISDN Collect Billing/Reverse Charging	

FIGURE 5 ISDN SUPPLEMENTARY SERVICE FEATURES

DSW-04
SWITCHES FOR ISDN: THE VENDOR'S PERSPECTIVE

John P. Delatore - Chairperson
Department Head
Advanced Systems Planning Department

AT&T Bell Laboratories
200 Park Plaza
Naperville, IL   60566-7050

ABSTRACT

In this seminar, industry experts present experiences gained during the introduction of Integrated Services Digital Network features and services. ISDN provides standardized and integrated user access to multiple transport methods and services, including simultaneous circuit switching, packet switching, and voice services. Long a goal of telecommunications planners and users, local central office switching systems which support ISDN features and services are now in service in many telephone companies. This seminar will provide feedback on the key lessons learned from these field experiences. Included in the sessions will be valuable insights obtained through interactions between the vendor, the telephone company and the end user.

Robert F. Griffith	--	Siemens Public Switching Systems, Inc.
Robert W. McDarmont	--	NEC America
David R. Richards	--	Bell Northern Research
Robert A. Sherry	--	AT&T Bell Laboratories

MODULAR DESIGN FOR ISDN DEPLOYMENT

Robert F. Griffith
Director - Sales

Siemens Public Switching Systems, Inc.
5500 Broken Sound Blvd.
Boca Raton, FL   33487

INTRODUCTION

Rapid market changes and opportunities continue to develop as a result of the merging narrow and broadband ISDN technologies and a better definition of the standards and regulatory policies. During these uncertain periods, it is a key attribute of a central office architecture, in order to ensure that these new marketing opportunities are met, that both the hardware and software be developed on a module basis. There

are three basic objectives within this modular design concept. They are:

1. Emerging ISDN features should not impact the cost of service for the non-users.

2. Emerging ISDN features should allow for full and economical retrofitting as the technologies and standards mature.

3. Emerging ISDN features should be adaptable to different market strategies.

This paper describes the ISDN modularity of the EWSD central office as being implemented to meet the network evolution of new ISDN features and concepts.

BASIC EWSD MODULAR ARCHITECTURE

The basis of modularity is through a distributed microprocessor architecture that provides for control, signaling, operations, and diagnostics. Therefore, as systems grow larger or incorporate more features, the quantity of microprocessors increases proportionally as illustrated in Figure 1.

Distributed microprocessors are incorporated within the major elements of the EWSD as illustrated in Figure 2. They are located within the Line Cards, Digital Line Unit (DLU), Line/Trunk Groups (LTGs), Switching Network (SN), Common Channel Network Control (CCNC) for Signaling System #7 (SS#7), and the Coordination Processor (CP) which is in the main processing unit of the EWSD system. The intent of this microprocessor distribution is that the peripheral processors provide the high frequency call processing functions (scanning, signaling) and the CP provides for the more complex tasks of digit analysis, routing, and operation. This is illustrated in Figure 3.

The distributed processor design technique provides for easy additions of new feature modules that may be added to the EWSD system. In addition, as the technologies and standards mature, software/hardware modifications may also be implemented, in a module basis, without affecting overall system operation.

ADDING NARROWBAND ISDN

The addition of ISDN must incorporate the objectives of not impacting the cost of service to the new users and allowing economical modifications as the standards mature. The EWSD meets these objectives by using the line cards within DLU subsystem which provides the interface to the subscriber loop. The use of an analog (SLMA) or digital ISDN (SLMD) line card provides standard analog or ISDN service, respectively. Figure 4 illustrates the Subscriber Line Module (SLM) as the loop interface that provides eight single party lines of service. The SLMA or SLMD each contain a dedicated microprocessor for signaling, control, and operations, are pin for pin compatible that may be added or removed by normal system administration procedures. In addition, the DLU is not a dedicated analog or digital line unit but may be shared for both types of service. Therefore, the EWSD meets the first objective of ISDN by not impacting the cost of ISDN service for non-users.

Figure 5 illustrates the digital (SLMD) ISDN line card which provides the majority of the processing requirements for ISDN by demultiplexing the 144 kb/s ISDN basic access line into two (2) "B" channels and one (1) "D" channel (2B+D). Figure 5 also illustrates the SLMD line card performing the level 2 function on the "D" channel and separates the "S" and "P" data into a signaling channel. The SLMD may also statistically perform the "$\sum$ P" information for "D" packet switching, as well as performing the standards multiplexed "P" information.

As the standards become more mature (2B1Q) the EWSD technology impact will be minor due to the amount of ISDN processing accomplished on the line card. The detection of level 2 information will be modified on the line card level and this will prevent any major modifications to the EWSD system. This modularity allows the EWSD to accomplish the second objective of full retrofitting on an economical basis.

Expansion of the ISDN service, from an ISDN Island into a network, may be accomplished by the addition of SS#7. The CCNC is an expansion of the modular distributive processor architecture that provides for translation of the Message Transfer Part (MTP) of the SS#7 protocol for trunk signaling. Figure 6 illustrates that the incoming signal links are terminated on the LTG and are connected through the EWSD SN to the CCNC. The CCNC performs the lower level SS#7 MTP functions to support ISDN User Part (ISUP) in order to set up calls and to provide feature activation. In addition, the CCNC will also support Transaction Capabilities (TCAP) for access to intelligent network nodes. The necessary software for the ISUP and TCAP capabilities are within the LTG and are modularly constructed to provide for easy future modification(s).

EWSD BROADBAND ISDN ARCHITECTURE

The EWSD modularity extension is particularly demonstrated by the introduction of broadband switching. Broadband switching may become the cornerstone of ISDN because it offers subscribers, on demand, the broadband channels of other interfacing subscribers. The EWSD architecture provides easy evolution of broadband by the addition of a broadband fabric that interfaces to the existing narrow band network and remains under control of the same EWSD CP. Figure 7 illustrates the addition of the Broadband Switching Network (BBSN) is to an existing EWSD host configuration. Note that the coordination processor

power to control the analog voice, narrow band ISDN and broadband ISDN requirements. Again, the addition of the BBSN is accomplished in a modular fashion without effecting the other narrow band modules.

The broadband Line/Trunk Group (LTGE) interfaces with optical subscriber loops and converts the optical signaling into the necessary electronic signaling. In addition, as illustrated by the enlarged LTGE diagram on Figure 7, the LTGE also detects the narrow band from the broadband signal. The necessary formatting is completed with the LTGE's Mux/Demux devices and then are internally routed by message buffering techniques, to the appropriate narrow band or BBSNs. It is through the LTGE router that the EWSD provides subscribers bandwidth by demand.

The BBSN will provide for a user-network interface as a gross bit rate of approximately 150 Mb/s. In addition, H4 channel considerations and subchannels that comply to the concepts of synchronous Optical Network (Sonet) operating at integer multiples of 51.84 Mb/s must also be transportable through the BBSN.

Figure 7 also illustrates the EWSD providing significant applications that range from POTS, dedicated basic rate ISDN, primary rate ISDN, narrow band and broadband ISDN, video, LAN, SS#7 signaling, and packet switching (X.75). Each of these applications were provided on a modular architecture basis that did not violate the three basic rules as established in the beginning of this paper.

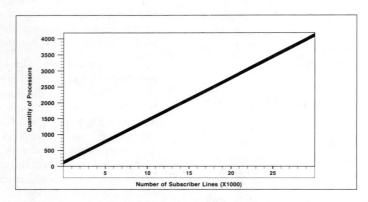

Figure 1: **Quantity of Distributed Processors vs. Number of Subscriber Lines**

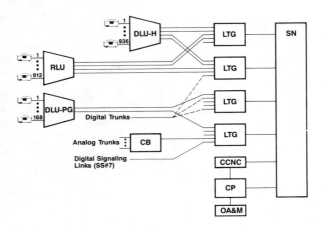

Figure 2: **EWSD — Block Diagram**

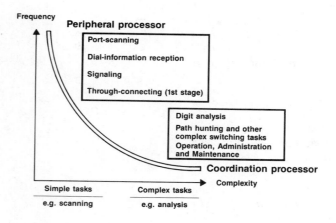

Figure 3: **System Design of Functional Split**

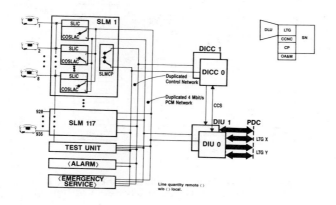

Figure 4: EWSD Digital Line Unit (DLU) —
Subsystem Configuration & Modularity

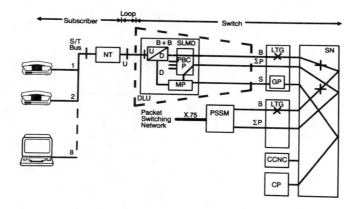

Figure 5: EWSD – ISDN Packet Transport

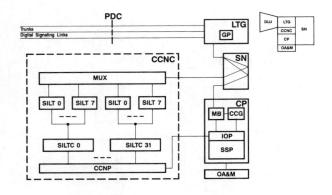

**Figure 6: EWSD Common Channel Signaling #7 —
System and CCNC Subsystem Configuration**

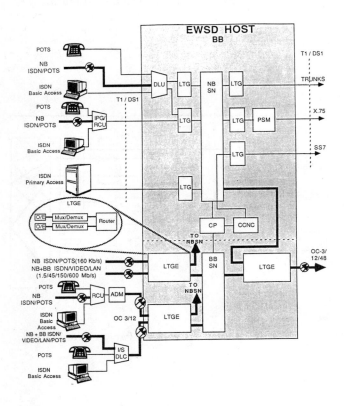

**Figure 7: Future Network Switching System With
Broadband Circuit Switch Capability**

ISDN: FROM TRIAL TO REALITY

Frederick C. Iffland
Supervisor

RBOC Studies Group

Robert A. Sherry
Supervisor

RBOC Applications Group

AT&T Bell Laboratories
200 Park Plaza
Naperville, IL 60566-7050

INTRODUCTION

Late in 1986, AT&T began its introduction of ISDN with the ceremonial first call involving Illinois Bell and McDonald's Corporation. Since that time, several steps have been taken to provide wide Local Exchange Carrier (LEC) exposure to the ISDN features on the 5ESS® Switch and, thus, facilitate the commercial introduction of ISDN.

In 1987, basic ISDN features were made available to the LECs in a series of Beta sites. These sites, described more fully in Ref. 1, consisted of a small (approximately 50) number of Basic Rate Interface (BRI) lines on a small 5ESS Switch and sufficient customer premises equipment for those lines. The sites provided a platform on which the LECs and their end users could experiment to learn more about the ISDN features, particularly in the data arena. One of the earliest sites, though not officially a Beta site, was located in Phoenix and served as a demonstration location at the International Switching Symposium in March of 1987. The primary end customer trialing ISDN features was the Intel Corporation, located in suburban Phoenix. Through the use of an optically remoted switching module, the host in Chandler was able to serve live exhibits in the downtown Hyatt Hotel, 25 miles away.

These Beta sites all had the initial version of the 5E4 generic program. They were followed by the first office application sites for the second release of 5E4. These First Office Application (FOA) sites supported the migration of ISDN features and services from the trial stage to actual commercial service early in 1988. The first customers, McDonald's in Oak Brook, Illinois, and AT&T Network Systems in Dunwoody, Georgia, marked the beginning of a rapid build-up of ISDN lines this year. By the time of this conference, more than 25,000 BRI lines will be in commercial service in more than 20 5ESS Switching Systems across the United States. These vary in degree from the trial and test locations with less than 50 to 100 BRI lines to major commercial customers in the range of 5,000 BRI lines.

All the early sites have provided valuable feedback to AT&T and the LECs and have paved the way for more orderly deployment of ISDN.

From a customer perspective, the ISDN features present a major increment in the capabilities, and complexity, of a telephone switching system. The LEC, as provider of the service, is faced with new challenges in the area of Operations, Administration, and Maintenance, as well as the areas of tariffing and data features. No longer is a simple copper tip and ring the interface to the customers' premises. There is now intelligent Customer Premises Equipment (CPE) at the end of that loop. It is typically built by a terminal equipment manufacture who has designed it to meet a lengthy published interface specification. The end customer is presented with new CPE that integrates the voice and data services that were previously completely separate. This has an obvious impact, not only on the user's daily operations, but also on the organizational structure that has historically seen separate voice and data organizations within most corporations.

This paper examines some of the experiences that have resulted from the early 5E4 sites. The information contained herein should be of interest to anyone who is involved with introducing ISDN features and services within their LEC or who will be an ISDN end user.

INITIAL ISDN INTRODUCTION

As mentioned above, ISDN features and services on the 5ESS Switch were initially deployed to the field in a small number of Beta sites using Issue 1 of the 5E4 generic program and FOA sites for the final 5E4 Issue 2. These FOA sites, a standard phase in the 5ESS Switch development methodology, allowed AT&T as the switch supplier to work in close cooperation with the purchaser of the switch, i.e., the LEC, and with the eventual end user of the new services. The FOA sites are closely supported by both AT&T Bell Laboratories and AT&T Network Systems and verified all parts of the new ISDN offering: CO hardware, software, and firmware; support programs; Operations Support Systems (OSSs) and their switch interfaces; documentation; and CPE from vendors chosen by the end user.

The complexity of the new ISDN features, particularly in the area of new and existing voice features as offered on ISDN CPE, led to detailed feature reviews with both the LEC and end user. These were held in a variety of subject areas: multibutton key system, shared directory number features, compatibility of existing (pre-5E4) Business Residence Custom Services (BRCS) features with ISDN CPE, applications processor features (electronic directory, message center), and overall OA&M issues. The reviews, typically lasting 3 to 4 hours and involving up to 30 people, produced important feedback on the design of those features. By scheduling them well in advance of first service, sufficient time existed to make modifications to the features already under development.

A second activity along these same lines was the early prototyping of actual end user feature assignments and CPE feature button layouts. In one instance, this effort uncovered a potential problem in the interaction of multiple call appearances, shared directory number, and electronic directory service in attempting to accommodate the end customer's call coverage arrangements. This particular customer, a heavy user of 1A2 key and call director equipment, wished to monitor all of a principal's call appearances at the call coverage point. This would insure that the secretary or clerk could determine if the principal was already active on a call when a new call came in. This was the philosophy currently in use with the analog key arrangement.

With each principal now having at least two or three call appearances of his or her directory number, the call coverage telephone set had insufficient number of physical buttons to monitor every call appearance. If only the first call appearance were shared to the call coverage set, the secretary or clerk would not know if the principal was using another call appearance or merely refusing to answer this new call. If the new call was of high priority and the principal was on another call, procedures dictated that the principal be buzzed to alert him or her to that new call.

A solution to this implementation problem was developed that utilized additional ISDN features. These features were the Call Forwarding/Don't Answer (CF/DA) feature, the incoming call display capabilities of the CPE set, and a new development that appended an activity flag (an asterisk) to the principal's directory number if the user is active on any of his or her call appearances. The call scenario would now be as follows:
1. The incoming call initially rings the principal's set. The caller's name and directory number may be displayed.
2. After a preset interval, the unanswered call transfers to the call coverage point.
3. The display on that set shows the incoming party's directory number, the principal's name and directory number with an asterisk if he or she is using one of the other call appearances, and the reason the call came to the call coverage point ("CF/DA").

(Note that the electronic directory display typically shows the originating party's name. This was also modified to show the terminating party's name in a CF/DA situation to facilitate personalized answering of incoming calls.)

This type of solution, identified early enough in the development process, produced a set of features that allow a more graceful transition for the typical user from analog key systems to ISDN multibutton sets equipped with displays. This feedback is a valuable result of the close working relationships that were fostered in the FOA sites.

The spirit of cooperation and teamwork was further enhanced by including LEC personnel on the AT&T FOA team. They provided an early review of the new features by personnel experienced in day-to-day switch operations and administration and suggested several significant changes, particularly in the areas of recent change and documentation. They also participated actively in the creation and reviews of the test plans that were executed at the FOA sites. This close partnering helped produce a product that better satisfied the needs of the LECs in the OA&M areas.

MIS MANAGERS AND TELECOM MANAGERS

In all of the early ISDN sites, the contractual agreement to introduce ISDN was negotiated between the corporate telecommunications manager and the local exchange carrier. These agreements were based upon the capabilities and flexibilities of ISDN, as well as the evolution potential of ISDN. Many large corporations also have a MIS manager who is responsible for the data needs of a corporation. Whereas, the Telecom manager's vendor is the LEC, the MIS manager's vendors are the large computer manufacturers. So as the Telecom manager evolves his or her implementation plans for ISDN, there must be a close cooperation between these two departments to work through the implementation plans of ISDN to coexist with embedded applications and become an integral part of future planning. In some cases, we have seen the situation where individual departments in a corporation maintain autonomy to define their data communications needs. When a corporate decision has been made to go with ISDN, then the Telecom manager has to "sell" ISDN internally to his or her customers.

The implication in these scenarios is that there is much work to be done between the time that an agreement has been signed to introduce ISDN and the time that ISDN sets get installed on the users' desks. The Telecom manager should be prepared to do the "detailed ISDN applications engineering." This requires "baselining" the embedded voice and data needs, identifying which applications can be enhanced through ISDN, and proposing new applications which ISDN makes available. In this process, the Telecom manager and MIS manager must work closely to understand not only current needs, but to plan for a 2- to 5-year evolution plan. In the early sites, AT&T, the LEC, and other vendors have worked closely with the end users to facilitate the introduction of cost-effective, efficient ISDN applications. This cooperation continues as ISDN evolves adding more capabilities in both the switch and ISDN CPE. As new ISDN applications are identified and the number of ISDN CPE choices increases, the applicability of ISDN in the office place will continue to expand.

Note that we are emphasizing the word "applications" in this discussion. It is insufficient to talk about technical capabilities, such as simultaneous voice and data or packet switching. These capabilities must be combined to form applications, such as student course registration in a college or patient care management in a hospital. This will insure that the introduction of ISDN produces the greatest possible benefits to the end users.

OA&M IMPLICATIONS OF MERGING VOICE AND DATA

In addition to its effects on the end customer, the concept of merged voice and data must be carefully considered by the LEC, particularly in the areas of Operations, Administration, and Maintenance (OA&M).

Historically, the LECs have been oriented primarily to voice services. Data has only recently begun to have direct influence on their operations. Further, most data services to date have fallen into one of two categories: voiceband or special services. Voiceband data is normally transmitted without the need for any special OA&M considerations by the serving LEC. A normal circuit-switched voice connection is established, and modems are employed to transmit data. Where voice-grade transmission is not adequate for a customer's data needs, various special services have been used. These include high-speed transmission, ranging from 19.2 kb/s to T1 speeds of 1.54 Mb/s and higher, and packet switching services that can access a variety of destinations. Generally, these special services have had support organizations devoted to them separate from the voice support groups. With ISDN, these traditionally separate worlds are quickly coming together. The central office maintenance support personnel are now challenged with the need to understand the areas of the seven layer OSI model, Q.931 signaling, and X.25 packet switching, to name just a few areas. No longer can he or she merely check the voltage and continuity of a customer's loop to clear a reported trouble. They must now be familiar with CCITT standards, the switch supplier BRI specification (Ref. 2), and X.25 services and terminology (packet size, window size, flow control, RPOA, fast select, logical circuit numbers, etc.).

Early preparation is the key to LEC management's handling of the arrival of ISDN. This preparation takes the form of planning on how to handle these new offerings in the areas of OA&M. Many LECs have expressed the intent to handle ISDN as much as possible with POTS-like procedures. In fact, this is necessary for the offering to succeed economically. However, modifications are critical in the following areas:

1. Service negotiation, including loop qualification
2. Service order preparation and input
3. Billing, especially for packet services
4. Problem resolution

A detailed analysis of these areas is beyond the scope of this paper, but other work has documented efforts in this area (Ref. 3). One example will, however, demonstrate the issues that characterize the OA&M arena for ISDN.

Consider an existing ISDN customer who purchases a new integrated voice-data telephone set to determine if it has application in their environment.

Before the customer can activate the set, supporting translations must be installed at the central office. A few considerations are as follows:

1. B- and D-channel assignment to voice, circuit-switched data, and packet-switched data.
2. Call appearance and feature button assignment. (How are the buttons numbered on the set? What features are assigned to each button?)
3. What X.25 facilities does the set support?
4. Does the set support CO-based Terminal Management Function (TMF), whereby the switch manages the call appearances on the set?
5. For circuit-switched data, what rate adaption method is used? (Although this does not impact switch translations, this will determine the set's compatibility with other manufacturer's equipment as standards are not fully resolved in this area.)

After negotiation with the customer, who is relying on documentation supplied with the new set, the translations are installed on an appropriate BRI line to the customer's premises, and the inside wiring is installed, including the NT1. The customer now begins to test this new set and finds that conferencing works all the time on the first call appearance, but only intermittently on the last call appearance.

Troubleshooting OA&M problems will utilize many of the tools provided by the 5ESS Switch. Although this appears to be a classic protocol-related problem, the craft might first perform a loop-around transmission test out to the NT1. (This test verifies the layer 1 performance of the outside plant loop, including the line card in the central office and the NT1 at the customer's premises.) The test would generally be more applicable if the customer complained of errors in data, random features not working, or lost packets of data.

Given that loop transmission is not an issue, the craft can interrogate the Protocol Error Report (PER) history on the customer's loop. This is a software buffer in the switch that registers protocol errors recognized by the switch. In this case, the switch would indicate that, indeed, errors have been seen and they can be printed for examination. Upon analysis by LEC personnel, let us assume the results are not conclusive. Full protocol analysis must now be employed by connecting a protocol analyzer to the line under test. This can be done at the customer's premises where the T interface is available, at the central office with a U interface monitor, or at a central point, such as the switching control center, using a remoting arrangement. (See Fig. 1.) Obviously, the third alternative offers the major advantage of keeping highly-trained personnel and expensive test equipment in a centralized location where they can be used most effectively.

Analysis of the protocol associated with the failing conference calls reveals that the calls are being rejected due to an apparently invalid call appearance in the call setup message. This analysis needs to then be given back to the CPE manufacturer so that their firmware can be updated.

This example is not unusual. In fact, it is typical of the challenges facing the operations area in dealing with highly sophisticated and intelligent CPE sets that can be manufactured by anyone who has purchased the BRI Specification. One of the foundations of ISDN is its open interface and eventual portability of CPE between different switching systems. This same open interface, when combined with the complexity of the sets and particularly their software, also presents one of the greatest challenges, the efficient resolution of customer trouble reports.

ISDN INTERFACE OBSERVATIONS

As the previous section outlined, there are major impacts as a result of the open ISDN CPE interface. Some of these arose in the course of the FOA sites.

One of the early issues was that AT&T, as the switch supplier, did not have access to other vendors' CPE equipment during the switch development interval. As a result, some problems, both in the switch and in the CPE, were not found until the AT&T site testing interval when the other vendors' CPE became more available through the LEC and end user. The AT&T BRI specification, although very complete, did leave some issues up to subjective interpretation. Changes have been made in the specification where necessary to remove any ambiguity for future CPE developers.

Several examples of the problems encountered will demonstrate the environment facing the industry with the introduction of very intelligent peripherals. One vendor designed a re-dial capability into their set. Rather than basing this on registering the actual digits that were dialed, the vendor chose to rely on the display element sent from the switch as the call is routed. Unfortunately, the display element contains the full seven-digit number, even for intrabusiness group calls that might only use three- or four-digit extension dialing. This situation was not found until actual testing with the switch began. In this case, no change was made in the operation of the switch.

In another instance, however, ambiguity in an intentionally erroneous message led to switch software changes. Upon initialization of a BRI line, the switch sends an intentionally faulty message toward the CPE to force a response with the Terminal Equipment Identifier (TEI). Unfortunately, the original message actually had two errors: an invalid field and a missing mandatory field. The specification called for a response to the invalid field, but allowed that the message could be ignored if the mandatory field were missing. No prioritization was specified if both errors were present. One vendor chose to ignore the message, rather than take the other path of the expected response. While a specification change could have clarified the order of error checking, this could have been led to a drawn-out process with resultant delays in CPE availability. It was more expedient to change the switch software to include the mandatory element and, thus, remove the ambiguity.

The BRI specification as released by AT&T consists of approximately 450 pages. Several revisions have occured since the original release in September, 1985. In any document of this size and complexity, it might be expected that there would be a significant number of issues resulting from either errors in the protocol specification or ambiguities in handling that protocol. It is noteworthy that such situations have been very infrequent with more than 30 vendors developing ISDN terminal equipment that have interfaces to the 5ESS switch.

An implication of these experiences is that each CPE vendor should consider a friendly user Beta site as its first application. Many LECs are establishing demonstration rooms and technology centers where new equipment can be fully verified before deployment to an end customer. AT&T-BL has also established an ISDN CPE verification facility at Holmdel, New Jersey. This laboratory, completely separated from both switch and CPE developers within AT&T, provides an exhaustive test of signaling layers 1 through 3. Confidential testing completion results are furnished directly to the vendor. When this has been used, the results have been to minimize subsequent problems in connecting the ISDN CPE to an in-service 5ESS Switch.

ISDN APPLICATIONS

In 1988, ISDN is migrating from "2B+D" to end-to-end (desk-to-desk) customer solutions. As we move from trial to reality, we move from technical feasibility studies to providing cost-effective, efficient customer communication solutions. We are moving from the capabilities of ISDN (2B+D, coax elimination, etc.) toward applications using ISDN (office automation, telemarketing, financial services, etc.).

Applications based upon ISDN must compete with existing established technologies and earn their place as viable alternatives to solve customer's voice/data communications problems. ISDN must either solve existing needs more cost-effectively or provide new features and services unique to ISDN. The underlying benefits of ISDN can be shown when end users require sophisticated voice and switched-data needs. ISDN provides the platform on which these applications are built. The underlying platform has been proven in the early trials and sophisticated ISDN application software will provide the robust applications for ISDN to migrate through the corporate structure.

Early trials set the stage for this evolution. ISDN voice features introduced in the 5E4(2) release replaced existing analog Centrex or 1A2 key applications. Multiple call appearances replaced call waiting, multiline groups, and multiple directory numbers for a single end user. Multiple analog hard-wired appearances from a 1A2 key system were replaced by shared directory numbers. The mapping from pre-ISDN voice services to ISDN voice applications requires baselining the Present Method of Operation (PMO) and identifying how ISDN can enhance the productivity of the office environment. For example, call coverage scenarios as discussed above became a major area of attention for early users. In almost all cases, ISDN enhanced the effectiveness of call handling by providing efficient call coverage capabilities, such as calling party display, reason codes for the transferred call and electronic directory.

Early data applications focused around PC-to-PC and PC-to-Host communications. Early testing of PC-to-PC communications packages showed available packages readily adaptable to ISDN. For example, many popular PC file transfer programs work over the ISDN D channel using the RS-232 PC port and an ISDN terminal adapter. The performance of these packages varies greatly depending upon the underlying protocol assumptions made in their design. Many of these packages make the assumption they will be working across modems and analog telephone lines. Therefore, their "send packet-wait for ACK" protocols hindered their performance on a highly reliable X.25 network like ISDN. Packages using YMODEM-G protocol were found to be fairly efficient in their interactions running between 6 to 7 kb/s on the 9.6 kb/s D channel. Even more effective were packages designed for digital error correcting networks such as X.25. One such package had a throughput over 12 kb/s for both ASCII and binary files.[1] In addition, the effective throughput can be increased by the use of file compression algorithms. Using data compression, this particular package has an effective performance throughput of over 18 kb/s with a binary file and over 30 kb/s for an ASCII file.[2]

---

1. Although the advertised throughput of the D channel is 9.6 kb/s, higher data rates can be obtained when signaling packets are not present on the D channel.
2. The throughput can vary based upon file format, the amount of white space, and other factors in the file.

Early PC/async terminal-to-host applications replaced slower speed dial-up access arrangements. Users were able to run existing applications, and ISDN provided additional capability for many of these. For example, ISDN supports limiting access to host ports by restricting access to members of closed user groups. This security feature protects the host from hackers accessing dial-up ports and gaining access to valuable user data. For terminal-to-host applications, 9.6 kb/s access over the D channel appears to be sufficient for most users.

For ISDN to reach its full potential, the industry must focus attention on areas that will emphasize the benefits and economics of ISDN. Within AT&T, there are several activities ongoing to flesh out these areas. One of the most significant is the TriVista studies, which are a joint partnership among end users, LECs and AT&T. In these studies, the three parties work closely together to identify ISDN applications that will improve the productivity and flexibility of the end user's operations. These studies assess the PMO to identify communications needs that can be enhanced through the introduction of ISDN. After this assessment, an ISDN communication network is proposed to provide integrated voice and data applications. This proposed ISDN solution is evaluated against competing alternatives to verify that the ISDN solution is not only technically feasible, but cost-effective. Within AT&T, these studies are reviewed to generalize the information to applications across industry segments.

CONCLUSION

As ISDN moves from the development laboratories of the world's switching system suppliers to providing end user commercial applications, the industry must be cognizant of the things needed to maximize ISDN success. These include training in both voice and data, reevaluation of organizational boundaries, assessment of how the introduction of ISDN affects current processes (e.g., service order, provisioning, etc.), and a close cooperation among vendors, service providers, and end users. The early ISDN sites using the 5ESS Switch have provided valuable feedback on specific areas that vendors, LECs, and end users should focus on to effectively roll out ISDN.

REFERENCES

1. N. R. Daspit and E. L. Vickery, "5ESS Switch ISDN Beta Site User's Group," Proceedings of the National Communications Forum, October, 1988.
2. 5ESS Switch - ISDN Basic Rate Interface Specification - 5E4 Generic Program (AT&T 5D5-900-301), AT&T, May, 1987.
3. N. J. King, "Service Provisioning Data Relationship Model for ISDN Network Maintenance," IEEE J. Select Areas Comm., Vol. 6, pp. 727-731.

4. A. Lavia, "ISDN and Data Networks," Proceedings of International Conference on Communications, 1987, pp. 9.2.1-9.2.6.

1) T INTERFACE ACCESS

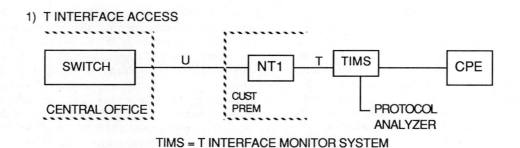

TIMS = T INTERFACE MONITOR SYSTEM

2) U INTERFACE ACCESS AT CENTRAL OFFICE

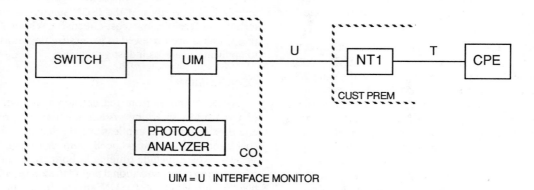

UIM = U INTERFACE MONITOR

3) REMOTE PROTOCOL ANALYSIS

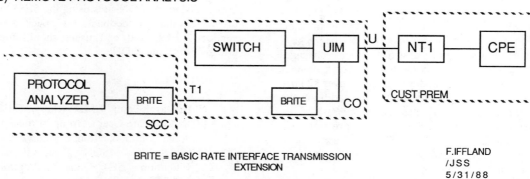

BRITE = BASIC RATE INTERFACE TRANSMISSION EXTENSION

F.IFFLAND
/JSS
5/31/88

FIG.1: PROTOCOL MONITORING ALTERNATIVES

NEAX 61E ISDN SYSTEM FIELD TRIAL PROGRESS REPORT

Robert W. McDarmont
Director of Marketing
Switching Systems Division

NEC America
1525 Walnut Hill Lane
Irving, TX   75038

ABSTRACT

This session reports on the progress and experiences gained since the first NEAX 61E ISDN System field trial, now in service for over 2 years. Several key areas are discussed, including improvements in hardware and software design, deployment strategies designed to meet a range of service demands, user reaction to ISDN, and new ISDN applications to meet user needs.

ISDN EVALUATION: PHOENIX AND PORTLAND EXPERIENCE

David R. Richards
Member of Scientific Staff

Bell Northern Research
P.O. Box 3511, Station C
Ottowa, Ontario   K1Y4H7

ABSTRACT

This session highlights user, chooser, and TELCo feedback on ISDN voice and data applications gained during the trial of Northern Telecom DMS-100 technology and customer premises equipment. Key lessons learned have been used to explore new business opportunities and to enhance customer service. The trial verified the end-user benefits derived from the various voice and data applications.

TRANSPORTING DATA VIA MODERN SWITCHING SYSTEMS

Dr. Michael P. Ludlow - Chairperson
Director, Product Management
Northern Telecom, Inc.
4001 E. Chapel Hill - Nelson Hwy.
Research Triangle Park, NC 27709-3010

ABSTRACT

ISDN is now emerging from the trial phase and volume deployment is ramping up. Data applicaions and services which justify this deployment are being successfully tested and validated. A number of supporting and evolving technologies are covered in this seminar, ranging from ISDN itself through X.25 packet data networks and Fast Packet. Specific applications are examined in detail. Compatibility and product interworking remains a major concern for many MIS/Data Communication managers. The issues and risks of standards lagging the fast pace of data access and transport technology evolution are reviewed.

Pierre Sibille -- SiemensPublic Switching Systems
Lorne Hinz   -- Northern Telecom, Inc.
David Butler   -- AT&T Bell Laboratories
Michael Ahdieh -- Northern Telecom, Inc.

TRANSPORT VIA MODERN SWITCHING SYSTEMS

Peirre Sibille

Siemens Public Switching Systems, Inc.
Broken Sound Blvd.
Boca Raton, FL 33487

ABSTRACT

Highlighting the changes in the telecommunication environment over the last several years has been the introduction of new transport mediums. New carrier concepts like ISDN, T1 and Fast Packet are here, or rapidly approaching. Even the international standard bodies are turning to new areas, and so must users and the market place. This session will focus on transport via modern switching systems, evaluating the existing packet switching technologies and T1, the new entrant ISDN and the future Fast Packet technologies. In the end, will those areas catching public attention really flourish or are they ideas whose time never really will come?

LOCAL AREA NETWORK SERVICES VIA DIGITAL SWITCHES

Lorne C. Hinz
Manager DMS Data Marketing

Northern Telecom Inc.
4001 E. Chapel Hill Nelson Hwy.
Research Triangle Park, NC 27709

ABSTRACT

Digital central office switching systems deployed in the last decade are being equipped with a range of new access technologies such as integrated voice/data modules (IVDMs), Datapath, and Integrated Services Digital Network (ISDN). These technologies are playing an important role in delivering new services in a rapidly growing data communications market. This paper presents telephone company and end user benefits of *integrated digital-switch-provided data services together with a number of applications.*

DIGITAL CENTRAL OFFICE SWITCHING SYSTEMS AND DIGITAL CENTREX

Telephone companies have deployed a large number of digital central office switching systems in the last 10 years, allowing the companies to modernize their capital equipment, reduce their operating costs and, most importantly, provide enhanced voice-based services. Today there are thousands of digital central office switching systems deployed in North America, and this number continues to grow.

These digital systems enable telephone companies to offer enhanced voice features similar to those provided on a digital private branch exchange (PBX). Digital centrex voice features such as speed calling, hot line, ring again, hunt groups, station message detail recording, class of service calling restrictions and authorization codes continue to influence the decision to install digital central office switching systems. Due to the feature-rich capabilities of these systems, digital centrex has experienced phenomenal growth in the past four years.

A telephone company subscriber using digital centrex obtains all of the advantages of a digital PBX, while eliminating the capital investment and installation, wiring and maintenance required with a PBX solution. As technologies evolve and improve, responsibility for updating centrex-based services belongs to the telephone company.

The latest evolutionary advance is the application of the technologies and features of digital centrex to traditional data communications networks.

DATA COMMUNICATIONS EVOLUTION

In traditional data communications networks, terminals are connected to one of a variety of interface devices (modems, limited distance data sets, or simply coax cable). This interface device then connects to some type of multiplexing device (cluster controller, statistical multiplexer, X.25 pad, etc.) or switching device (data PBX, voice frequency modems via telephone company voice switch, local area network, etc.) that concentrates the terminals onto a fewer number of host computer ports. Host central processing units (CPUs) are then connected to other hosts via high-capacity dedicated/private line connections.

The types of terminals that are used can be divided in three basic groups: IBM-type synchronous terminals that normally use a high speed coax interface; ASCII display terminals that predominantly have an asynchronous interface, and personal computers (PCs) that often use asynchronous interfaces. The largest market segment is composed of asynchronous ASCII terminals and PCs, and PCs, due to their rapid deployment, represent the fastest growing market segment.

Before the advent of PCs, all the intelligence in a traditional data communications network resided in the host computers. Terminals were merely input/display devices. Although some networks used switching to connect terminals to a host, their prime function was multiplexing (or concentration). All information shared between two users was always accessed through their respective host computers.

But today, PCs have brought intelligence, processing power, and storage to the users' desks. PCs also provide the base technology required to enable information exchange on a peer to peer basis without the need for an intermediate host computer. Thus, the data communications requirement with PCs as the "terminal" device is for data switching, and not just data connectivity/concentration. PCs are not only required to communicate with each other but also to call up various host computers (data bases) to retrieve or upload data.

In an environment of "dumb" terminals tied to mainframe computers, the computing department/manager defines, selects, installs and maintains the total network. Because a PC is a standalone device, however, the end user often first chooses a PC and then later requires a communications solution.

The PC user is looking for simplicity of selection, installation and use, as well as ubiquity of access and connectivity to others. A PC user normally does all data manipulation at the desk and needs only temporary connections and fast transmission times when transferring the data to another user or host computer. Many people transfer their data via a voice frequency (VF) modem on a telephone line. This method blocks all voice calls and the line can be tied up for long periods because of the transmission speeds of analog modems.

Fig. 1 shows the range of connectivity requirements a user may have. If the requirement is only to connect several PCs in an office to a common printer or file server, then a premise-based local area network (LAN) such as an AppleTalk, Ethernet, or Token Ring LAN is probably the best solution. These same premise-based solutions can be used within a single intermediate-sized building. Connectivity within large buildings, a campus of many buildings, a city, or a state, require telephone company central-office-based solutions. The telephone company-based system can be used to provide base LAN and wide area network (WAN) connectivity requirements, or the WAN connectivity requirements to tie together the small office-based LANs in each of the sites.

To address the WAN requirements, the telephone company strength for voice or data communications is geographical dispersion. The telephone system today provides universal access with a telephone jack at every office worker's desk, and in every home. The massive wiring of this network is already in place and has taken many decades to deploy. The popularity of the VF modem solution is primarily due to the ease of access (wiring and telephone jacks already in place), ease of installation, and the universality of connectivity.

Currently, the most wide-spread voice frequency modem speed is 1200 bits per second, but, with recent technology advancements, 2400 bits-per-second modems are rapidly gaining in popularity. At 1200 bits per second, a 20-page document requires 10 minutes of transmission time, or 5 minutes for the the same document at 2400 bits per second. A PC user would like to have faster transmission rates; however, modems with speeds of 9.6 to 19.2 kilobits per second have a limited market because they cost $1,000 to $3,000 each, and many can only communicate with a companion unit made by the same manufacturer. Some of these modems, including V.32s, cannot consistently approach the 19.2 kilobit-per-second speed, while some provide less than 5 kilobits-per-second throughput on typical short-haul (intraLATA) toll connections.

Why are high-speed voice frequency modems expensive, and why do they vary so dramatically in performance from one call to the next? An analog modem converts digital data into a 4 kilohertz bandwidth signal, required for switching data via analog switches, and for transmission via analog trunking systems. As the transmission speeds increase, more complex modulation and filtering techniques must be used to transmit the data through the fixed 4 kilohertz bandwidth. Increased complexity results in increased cost plus an increased susceptibility to noise or channel impairments.

DIGITAL ACCESS TECHNOLOGIES

When the analog line terminates on a digital switching system, the system's digital line card converts the low-speed analog signal to a high-speed 64 kilobit-per-second bit stream. Low-speed transmission problems could be solved with a new access technology that took full advantage of the 64 kilobit-per-second capability already in the digital switching system and digital interswitch trunking network. Several such access technologies exist, including integrated voice data modules (IVDMs), Datapath time compression multiplexing (TCM) transmission technology, and ISDN basic rate access. These interface devices use digital loop transmission to complete a fully digital connection from a user's terminal/PC, over the outside plant, through the digital central office and network, and back over another digital outside plant loop to a second user or host computer.

Digital loop transmission systems use a bandwidth of 20 to 100 kilohertz instead of the limited 4 kilohertz bandwidth because this large bandwidth is only used from the subscriber premises to the digital central office. Because these digital loop transmission systems use large bandwidths compared to voice frequency modems, the complexity of the transmission interface is reduced as the filtering is completed over a wider bandwidth, and more bandwidth is used to transmit the same number of bits. The reduced complexity translates in a lower digital system cost versus VF modem cost for comparable data rate supported. The additional benefit of a digital loop transmission system is that in most cases it can support even faster data rates with improved forward error checking.

Fig. 2 shows a typical integrated voice data module connection to a digital central office switching system. These devices leave the analog voice in its normal 4 kilohertz bandwidth, place data in the 20 to 100 kilohertz bandwidth above the voice, and the voice channel and signaling remains unmodified. The

customer premises IVDM is connected to the central office IVDM by up to 18,000 feet of outside plant telephone cable. The central office IVDM filters off the above-band data energy and feeds the unmodified 4 kilohertz voice channel into a regular digital-switch voice line card. The central-office IVDM demodulates the above-band data energy to base-band digital data.

This base-band digital data is carried to a data line card in the digital central office switch. This data line card performs a rate adaption function to map the baseband (110-19,200 bits per second) digital data into the 64 kilobit-per-second standard digital switched connection rate. These IVDM units typically transmit asynchronous data from 300-19.2 kilobits per second simultaneous with voice. Because they only transmit 19.2 kilobits per second in that total large bandwidth of 20 to 100 kilohertz, the cost of these units is relatively low (typically under $200 for each end.)

Although numerous vendors supply IVDMs, most subscriber units are only compatible with a central office companion unit made by the same manufacturer. The common data line card, however, allows any of these IVDMs to communicate through the digital central office switch. Because the data line cards provide a common interface between the IVDM and the 64 kilobit-per-second digital switch/network connection path, full data connectivity interworking is provided between users using different vendors' IVDMs.

A second commonly used transmission technology is time compression multiplexing. Northern Telecom's Datapath TCM technology provides a line burst rate of 160 kilobits per second to provide a 64 kilobit-per-second full duplex data channel and a separate 8 kilobit-per-second signaling channel over up to 18,000 feet of outside plant telephone cable. This technology essentially extends the 64 kilobit-per-second internal channel of the digital central office switch to the user's desk or computer room. Because the same 20-100 kilohertz bandwidth is used to send higher speed data than IVDMs, the level of complexity and cost is increased.

The expanded capacity of the 64 kilobit-per-second full duplex channel also supports a more extensive list of applications. In addition to asynchronous and synchronous rates of up to 19.2 kilobits per second, these applications include circuit switched 48, 56 and 64 kilobit-per-second full duplex synchronous data and switched connections for 3270- and 3194-type terminals.

The newest digital loop access technology is ISDN basic rate access (ISDN

BRA). It uses a transmission technique called echo cancellation (ECH) to enable high-speed data to be sent simultaneously in both directions over single twisted pair wiring. This technology supports two 64 kilobit-per-second voice or data channels, plus 16 kilobit-per-second signaling or data channel. The complexity and cost of the ISDN access technology has gone up significantly from the IVDM or the Datapath TCM transmission technology.

For ISDN to support existing asynchronous terminals or PCs, a terminal adapter is required to interface the 19.2 kilobit-per-second RS232 interface onto the 16 kilobit-per-second packetized "D" channel or one of 64 kilobit-per-second "B" channels. Notice that the 64 kilobit-per-second digital channel of the digital switch line card, the 64 kilobit-per-second TCM channel, or the 64 kilobit-per-second ISDN loop access system provide a common point of interworking. Using the same rate adaption protocol for each of these interfaces, full interworking is provided for all of the digital loop access systems. A user served via an IVDM line can call a user using a different vendor's IVDM, a Datapath Data Unit, or a user served via an ISDN line.

The new digital loop access products, along with the digital central-office switches, can also provide fully digital circuit-switched connections to packet-switched networks. In addition, the integrated packet handler of an ISDN-equipped digital central-office switch can provide efficient X.25 interfaces to packet networks for applications such as electronic mail or data-base access.

While the preceding has outlined the new digital loop transmission systems and how they provide high speed universal data connectivity between each other, backwards compatibility with the installed base of voice frequency modems is also required. Modem pooling on a digital central office switch allows a user on an IVDM line, a Datapath TCM line, or an ISDN line to call any voice frequency modem anywhere in the public switched telephone network. The reverse connectivity of any modem to users served on any digital loop access technology is also provided. The modem pool element provides the conversion from 64 kilobit-per-second T-LINK rate adapted data to a voice frequency modem that is compatible with the desired terminating or originating modem, providing complete analog and digital universal connectivity.

Fig. 3 provides a summary chart to use in the selection of the best digital access technology for a specific market segment requirement. Over time, the cost of ISDN BRA access products are expected to decrease. Specialized low cost ISDN BRA interface products will probably be produced for niche markets, and products with increasing functionality will be introduced at costs similar or lower than current ISDN BRA costs.

The digital central office switches will continue to evolve to support new technologies (such as frame relay), but because they are an evolution of the digital central office switch, (rather than a new stand alone customer purchased piece of equipment) these new technologies will be designed to interwork with all existing digital central office data systems.

DIGITAL CENTRAL OFFICE BASED DATA FEATURES

One attribute shared by all three of these digital transmission technologies is the ease with which they enable a user to set up a data connection. The user can either use the terminal keyboard to dial another user, or use commercially available PC communications software (the same used with VF modems) to provide automated connections to any other user or host computer. The same procedure is used by the user to call another user or host several feet away or across the city or nation. In other words, digital central office-based data services provide identical LAN-and WAN-type connectivity.

Because voice and data calls represent a 64 kilobit-per-second connection for a digital switch, many digital centrex voice features also provide powerful data communications features. The voice-based hunt group feature can be used in the data environment to provide hunting for the next free computer port. The automatic line feature can be used to provide terminal/PC power up connectivity for applications that always only terminate on a single host. Ring again can be used when all ports are busy. Station message detail recording can provide usage records. Automatic message accounting (AMA) billing provides standard integrated telephony billing.

Customer groups and class-of-service restrictions enable several customers/businesses to be served by the same central office switch and yet have their data calls secured within their respective groups. Authorization codes provide important password security features, and when used in combination with the station message detailed recording feature provide personal accountability through the logging of who reached which data base and at what time. In addition, further data-specific features such as closed user groups provide an even more extensive security capability.

Digital central office switches have a powerful set of centralized operations and capabilities required to maintain the largest network in the world, the voice network. These same powerful capabilities are available to data circuits. Features such as the ability to enable/disable a circuit, measure physical electrical chacteristics of the loop, and run bit error rate tests are all available through the digital central office switch. The customer network control of ports/services enable the entire set (or telephone company selected subsets) of these features to be used by the end customer.

In terms of networking, all the existing voice networking is used between the switches. There is no need to create a private overlay data network to provide the networking between one local area network site and another local area network site. Local area networking and wide area networking are provided via the same digital telephone network.

APPLICATIONS

Fig. 4 shows a university application of digital central office switch LAN/WAN connectivity. The university campus and surrounding city has a digital central office-based voice and data service. The cable-congested student dorms that house the cost sensitive students are provided high speed data access for their PC assignments via IVDMs. These IVDMs enable two 9.6 kilobit-per-second data connections to be provided simultaneously with the existing voice service. The host computer rooms and terminal/PC rooms in the various college buildings are equipped with rack-mount Data Units. The department head professor offices are served via ISDN lines to provide feature rich/state of art voice and data communications. By way of the digital-central-office modem pooling, students or professors at home who have voice frequency modems can communicate with any of the digitally served users. Modem pooling also enables communications to other universities, or data bases that currently only have VF-modem service. Small office-based LANs in the various buildings are also bridged together and to the full community of users, via the digital central office based data service.

As the data requirements for this university grow or evolve, some of the other applications/services which could be provided via the digital central office switch include high speed switched 56 kilobit-per-second Group IV FAX connectivity to distant sites, high speed circuit switched back up connections to dedicated lines or T-1 circuits, and 3270 terminal connectivity to cluster controllers.

There are numerous manufacturing, government, hospital, financial, and other customers who have building, campus, city or state wide voice and data communications requirements and networks similar to the university system that are also being served by digital central office switches.

CONCLUSION

Personal computers are the fastest growing data entry/display/processing device on the market, and are having a big impact on data communications networks. They are forcing data communications networks to provide peer-to-peer connectivity instead of "dumb" terminal to mainframe multiplexing of past networks. The need for universal connectivity via high-speed data switching puts the telephone companies in an ideal position to serve this market because of their installed wiring and switching networks. New digital loop access technologies in combination with the rich array of digital centrex features on such central-office switching systems as the DMS-100 present attractive data communications services to end users.

LIST OF FIGURES

Figure 1. Data Connectivity Requirements

	Premise LAN *	CO Solution †
Department	+	+
Building	+	+
Campus		+
City		+
State		+

* Apple Talk, Ethernet, Token Ring, etc.

† CO Based Solutions Provide LAN Plus WAN

Figure 2. Digital Loop Transmission Technologies

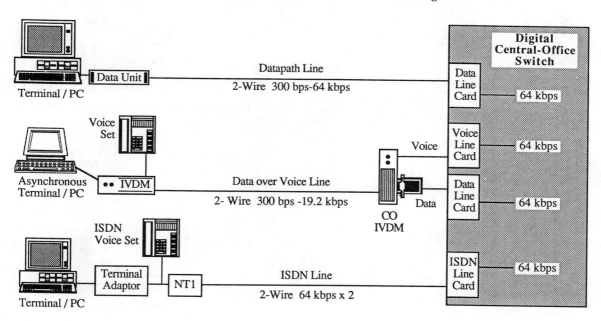

Figure 3. Digital Switch Data Access Technology Selection

	IVDM	DATAPATH	ISDN
19.2 kb/sec data	+	+	+
64 kb/sec data		+	+
3270 Services		+	+
Voice and data	+		+
Multiple Terminals	2 *		8
Low cost	+		

* Dependent upon IVDM vendor.

Figure 4. University Application—Digital Central-Office LAN/WAN

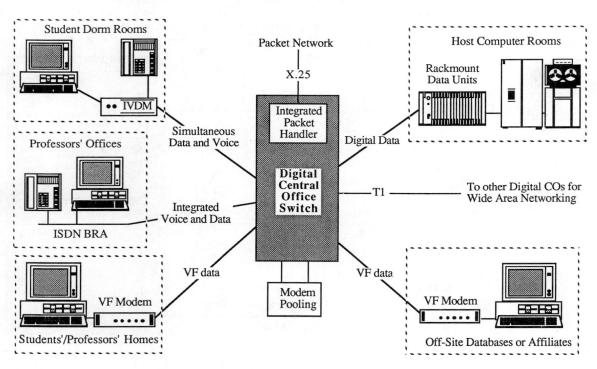

DATA NETWORK APPLICATIONS OVER AN X.25 PACKET SWITCHED NETWORK

David E. Butler
Denny P. Ko
Eberhard F. Wunderlich

AT&T - Bell Laboratories
Crawfords Corner Road, Holmdel, NJ 07733

ABSTRACT

X.25 packet switched networks have become an essential part of data network offerings in the past few years not only internationally, but in the U.S. as well. These networks provide transport services and offer data network applications a standard way of communicating with users. In this paper we will present examples of two types of applications that communicate over an X.25 packet switched network. One of these is an electronic mail application in which asynchronous device users communicate with a mail server host over the network. Another type of application has users at synchronous devices communicating with hosts through an X.25 network. The technical issues in optimizing such applications will be discussed.

INTRODUCTION

Modern packet switching networks can serve the needs of data communication users as broadly as voice telephone networks serve the needs of voice communication users. Switched data communications are required whenever multiple applications are to be supported efficiently over a single network. Packet switched networks based on the X.25 protocol are a major alternative for providing such switched data communications. CCITT RECOMmendation X.25 [1] [2] defines procedures for packet mode communication between Data Terminal Equipment (DTE) and Data Circuit-Terminating Equipment (DCE). Generally, DTEs represent the user side of the interface, and DCEs represent the network side of the interface. The X.25 protocol may be used in public packet switched networks, in private or hybrid networks, or in ISDN networks.

As Figure 1 shows, X.25 is an access protocol that does not address communication across the network. Packet switching networks generally employ proprietary protocols inside the network. Serving users who have equipment that communicates with protocols other than X.25 is easy when Packet Assemblers/Disassemblers (PADs) are used, as shown in Figure 2. The PADs and host

PADs (HPADs) convert "native" (e.g., asynchronous and 3270 BSC) data streams into X.25 packet data streams. Thus, the PADs provide the interface between a user's equipment and the X.25 packet network.

Services Under Software Control

Combinations of various software functions can be selected for each customer port on an X.25 network. A customer can change software configurations through the provisioning process X.25 packet switching services usually include Switched Virtual Circuit (SVC) and Permanent Virtual Circuit (PVC) services [2]. SVC service allows the customer to establish a circuit on demand via a virtual circuit set-up procedure. Similarly, after completion of the transaction, the customer takes down the circuit using a circuit clearing procedure. SVC service is analogous to normal telephone service. In PVC service, the logical associations are permanently established by the customer when service is ordered. These permanent logical connections remain assigned (unavailable for switched virtual circuits), whether or not communication is in progress, until changed by a customer service order request. PVC service is analogous to private line service in voice telephony.

Both SVC and PVC service are built on the concept of a logical channel, which is a full duplex path between the customer's equipment and the network. The DTE and DCE logically separate the data link into multiple logical channels. The logical channel concept is depicted in Figure 3. The logical channels are independent of one another, and each acts as the end point of a virtual circuit. Whenever a DTE or a DCE has a packet to transmit on a virtual circuit, it identifies which virtual circuit it wants by indicating which logical channel it is transmitting on. Logical channels are identified by a number in a special identification field in the packet. The logical channel number or identifier at one end of a virtual circuit need not be the same as the logical channel number at the other end. By extending the logical connection concept through the network, as shown in Figure 4, two customer DTEs become logically, though not physically, connected. Once a virtual circuit is established from customer DTE to customer DTE, data transfer can take place over the logical channels as customer activity demands it.

Applications of X.25 Packet Switching

Packet Switching is emerging as the preferred method of providing switched data service. As such, packet switching is becoming a viable means of transport for many applications. Potential applications are detailed below.

Interactive Messages

These messages are generally referred to as Inquiry/Response. These applications are two way transmissions having relatively short inputs and outputs requiring minimal delay. Depending on the magnitude of the response from the hosts, three categories can be delineated.

- low volume, such as point-of-sale, involve only a few characters of data in each direction.

- medium volume applications may involve the displaying and editing of forms; while the editing may be a local capability not utilizing the packet network, the final form is sent through the packet network.

- high volume includes information retrieval types of services, where the inquiry is a request to search a database and the response is printed at high speed with minimal delay.

Examples of Inquiry/Response applications are as follows:

- Credit check/authorization

- Reservations (airline, hotel, etc.)

- Point of sale

- Electronic order exchange

- Inventory control

- Order processing.

Non-Interactive Messages

These messages are generally one-way transmissions of information. Three potential applications are:
• Electronic Mail - Implementation using local editing capabilities would require only the final message to be sent through the packet network. In other implementations, the message is formulated using the far end processing capability, and the usage pattern is that of a short word processing session.

• Entry/Collect - This type of application involves extensive interactive communications to a local processor followed by a batch transmission across the packet network. For example, a cash register may communicate sales information to a local node throughout the business day. At the end of the day, the information is transmitted to a distant host.

• Facsimile - This is a high speed service (4.8 to 56Kbps) that provides image transmission of documents. Packet switching is becoming the preferred method of transport for many users of these machines.

Benefits

Packet networks provide many benefits over other forms of data transmissions. The primary advantage of a packet network is the efficient sharing of the network elements among multiple users thereby reducing transmission costs while increasing reliability and performance. Other benefits include:

• Shared Facilities - Packet switching allows multiple terminals to share one communications channel.

• International Standards - International standards as defined by CCITT, e.g., X.25, X.75, etc. are supported.

• Flexibility - Packet networks are flexible and easy-to-expand compared to private line networks which often require a total network reconfiguration to add new locations.

• Pricing Options - Usage sensitive pricing is available for public networks, and fixed pricing is available for private networks.

• Replaces Multiple Application Specific Networks - A single consolidated network allows better customer control and minimizes costs.

• Error Control - X.25 offers error detection and correction techniques which assure virtually error free transmission of data.

• High Performance and Availability - Packet networks offer high performance and availability via features such as alternate routing in the network, and duplex network components.

ELECTRONIC MAIL APPLICATION

Typically Electronic Mail (E-Mail) is an enhanced service accessed through an X.25 packet switching network, as shown in Figure 5. E-Mail services support gateways to various delivery mechanisms. A TELEX gateway allows subscribers to send mail to TELEX users and receive TELEX messages in the E-Mail mailbox. A paper gateway allows sending messages to non-subscribers. The paper gateway can support US Postal Service delivery, overnight courier and four-hour delivery. In addition to straight electronic mail, other services can be supported, such as a forms capability for creation, mailing and answering.

A wide variety of creation and retrieval devices can be supported by an E-Mail network. The network provides asynchronous ASCII access to any terminal using a command-line user interface for creation, sending and retrieval. Personal Computers (PCs) are becoming the most common devices used to access E-Mail services. Therefore, PC access to an E-Mail service via X.25 will be considered in detail. PCs are typically used in two different modes in this environment: as an interactive terminal, and for file transfer.

PC as Interactive Terminal

When used interactively, a PC is usually set up to emulate an asynchronous terminal. As such, its interface to the X.25 packet network is through an asynchronous PAD. The performance of asynchronous PADs are governed by a standard set of parameters (the CCITT X.3 parameters)[3] that can be used to tailor a PAD and even a single port on a PAD to a particular terminal type. When used interactively, the principal requirement is that interaction be quick, on a per character basis. The user does not want to know that there is a network between the PC and the E-Mail host.

An example of performance tuning to meet the user's expectations is provided by the procedure known as echoing. In a dial-up-to-host or private-line-to-host environment (i.e., not packet switching) the host typically sends back to the asynchronous device each character typed by the user. This action is called echoing, and causes the echoed character to appear on the screen. When an X.25 packet network and PAD are inserted between the device and the host, the PAD must operate in such a way as to not disturb the user. This can be accomplished in two ways.

The PAD's X.3 parameters can be set so that the PAD will echo each character back to the device. This will provide a very fast echo, and will be quite pleasing to the user. However, in this case the host must not echo, and therefore, the operation of the host must change. Notice that if the PAD echoes the user input, the PAD can construct relatively long packets. Packet forwarding is typically initiated by the PAD when the user types a carriage return. The specific conditions for packet forwarding are under the control of an X.3 parameter.

Alternatively, the PAD's X.3 parameters can be set so that X.25 packets containing single characters are transmitted to the host. This is accomplished by use of another X.3 parameter, the idle timer delay. This parameter governs the length of time that a PAD will wait for further user input before packetizing and forwarding what it has already received. In this case, the idle timer delay is set so that the timer usually expires after the PAD receives a character but before the next character is received. Therefore, each character is sent to the host in a separate packet, and the host must echo these characters as it normally would. The network will introduce a delay in the echo, but if the network is not overloaded, and if it uses high-speed trunks, the user will see little degradation. This scenario introduces many small packets (characters and their echoes) into the network which may have an impact on network load, and also on the cost to the customer.

The above is an example of the performance tuning that can be done to the network interface to improve the performance of an interactive application operating over an X.25 packet network.

PC File Transfer

When doing file transfer with a PC, the user wants the PC to act more like a host computer and less like an interactive terminal. The user needs reliable, high throughput data transport with flow control. High throughput is accomplished by transmitting data in large chunks into and through the network. Reliable, i.e. error free, transport with flow control is accomplished from network edge to network edge by mechanisms built into X.25 and most internal network protocols. What is needed are similar capabilities end-to-end.

The end-to-end requirement for reliable communication comes from the fact that the dial-up connections commonly employed have the possibility of interference or noise that can result in data transmission errors. A special file transfer protocol is needed to protect against these errors when the underlying link protocol is simple asynchronous transmission as is the case with most PCs File transfer protocols typically protect against errors by dividing the file transmitted into blocks, each of which contains a check sum that is checked by the receiver to detect errors in the received block. In the case of errors, the protocol provides for the retransmission of the block by the sender.

The flow control requirement is important because flow control protects against lost data due to buffer overflow. Such lost data could occur if the receiving computer system cannot handle the data as fast as it is being sent over the communication line. Flow control can be accomplished by separate flow control signals such as the common asynchronous

XON/XOFF, or by refusing to ACK in the scheme used for block retransmission.

An example of a PC file transfer protocol is Xmodem[4]. Xmodem was designed in the United States by Ward Christensen. It has gained wide acceptance as a file transfer protocol because it was an early public domain protocol incorporated into many PC communication software products. Xmodem is a simple yet effective protocol that has the following essential elements:

1. The use of 128 byte data blocks delimited by special ASCII control characters.

2. The use of a check sum and an ACK/NAK protocol for error detection and retransmission.

Since PCs, which are using Xmodem or a similar protocol for file transfer, are connected to the X.25 network through PADs, the PADs must treat the Xmodem blocks as data. The PAD parameters must be set so that the data blocks are packetized into the maximum size packets possible. Specifically, data forwarding should be done on full packets, and to accomplish this, the idle timer delay must not be set to too small a value. Therefore, we see that performance tuning is again desirable if performance is to be maximized.

SYNCHRONOUS APPLICATION

X.25 networks can also be used to advantage in synchronous environments. Here BSC or SNA are employed, and physical devices, i.e. terminals and printers, are connected to cluster controllers (CCs). The CCs are in turn connected to Front End Processors (FEPs) by point-to-point or multipoint private lines. The FEPs serve the communication processing needs of the channel attached host computers that are running the applications.

Private Line Environment

These synchronous networks operate in a private line environment where there is no network switching. Each physical device is known to the applications that it accesses. The FEPs provide the switching from application to application. They are, however, computing resources and the switching can be done more conveniently and economically in a switching network.

X.25 Environment

An X.25 network can replace the private line network that interconnects the CCs and the FEPs[5]. In addition to freeing the FEPs from the switching function, the advantages of this are in the ability of the X.25 network to shield the hosts from the physical devices. A population of virtual terminals is created that provides some advantages.

On the user side, the CCs are connected to PADs that terminate the native protocol, converting it to an X.25 packet stream. In fact, the PADs poll the connected CCs and appear to them as a FEP. The polls are not passed through the network.

On the host side, FEPs can be connected to PADs, which perform the conversion back to the native protocol. A PAD appears as a group of CCs as far as a FEP is concerned. An option is to use FEP software to perform the conversion from X.25 back to the native protocol.

The advantage of the virtual terminal concept is in its simplification of operations. Instead of having to define physical devices at each host that they access, enough virtual terminals are defined at each host to serve the number of physical devices expected to be accessing that particular host. Therefore, a contention pool of virtual terminals is created at each host. This pool is smaller than the total number of physical devices that use the host. In fact, standardized system generations can be set up for use at all hosts.

Physical devices can be added to the user side of the network without going through system generations. These additional physical devices get connected to virtual terminals in the pool. Only when the pool of virtual terminals becomes too small is a system generation necessary. So the virtual terminal population remains stable while the physical device population changes, which results in easier network growth and rearrangement.

Application Tuning

We have seen that the virtual terminal concept is very powerful, and leads to more efficient resource use. However, the switching function that underlies the virtual terminal concept requires application modification in some cases. We have seen that the native operational mode of synchronous networks is that of private line. That is, a host knows each physical device that it connects to (see above discussion). In virtual terminal operation, different physical devices are associated with a given virtual terminal at different times (the network switching function provides for this). Therefore, when the host communicates with a virtual terminal, that terminal represents different physical devices from time to time. Unless sessions are terminated carefully by the host applications, it is possible for host application sessions to lose synchronization with VC connections. To avoid this, some applications must be changed so that VC set-up and take-down to each virtual terminal is guaranteed to be in lock-step with application establishment and termination.

Here again we see how an X.25 network can provide important benefits, but some changes may be necessary to take full advantage of its strengths.

CONCLUSIONS

We have seen that X.25 networks have wide relevance in meeting the needs of data communication users. This is particularly true for supporting multiple applications on a single network. We have also seen that the X.25 interface parameters and the applications must be tuned in some situations to get the best performance at the least cost. Both asynchronous and synchronous examples of this tuning have been given in this paper. The results of such tuning are effective switched data network solutions.

REFERENCES

1.   CCITT Red Book, Volume VIII - Fascicle VIII.3, Data Communication Network Interfaces, Geneva, 1985.

2.   Mischa   Schwartz, Telecommunication   Networks: Protocols, Modeling and Analysis, Addison-Wesley Publishing Company, 1987.

3.   CCITT Red Book, Volume VIII - Fascicle VIII.2, Data Communication Networks Services and Facilities, Geneva, 1985.

4.   C. Forsberg, ed., Xmodem/Ymodem Protocol Reference: A Compendium of Documents Describing the Xmodem and Ymodem File Transfer Protocols, Omen Technology, Inc., May 30, 1985.

5.   S. Holmes and M. Fleming, Data Communications, June, 1984, "Combining the Best of SNA and X.25 Architectures".

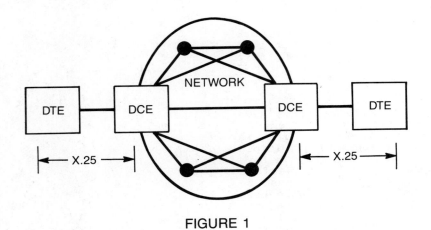

FIGURE 1

X.25 IS AN ACCESS PROTOCOL

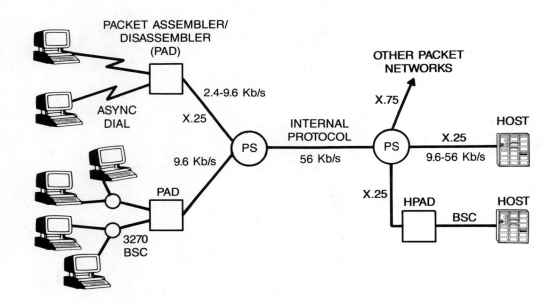

FIGURE 2

USE OF PADs

ACTUALLY ONE PHYSICAL LINK

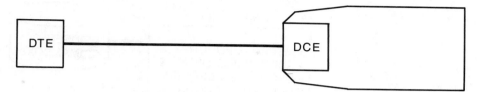

BUT LOOKS LIKE MANY SIMULTANEOUS CONNECTIONS

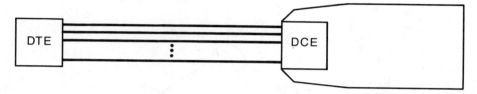

FIGURE 3

LOGICAL CHANNEL CONCEPT

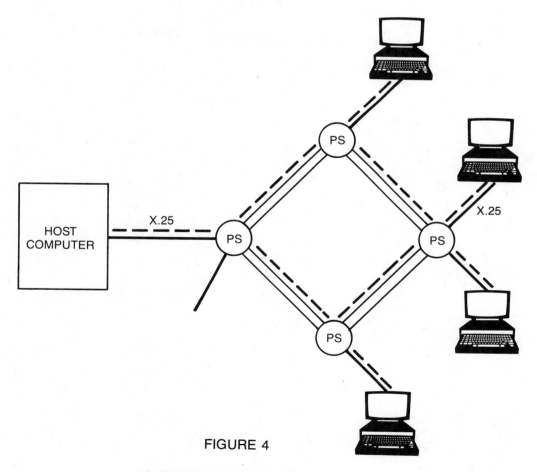

FIGURE 4

END-TO-END CONNECTIONS

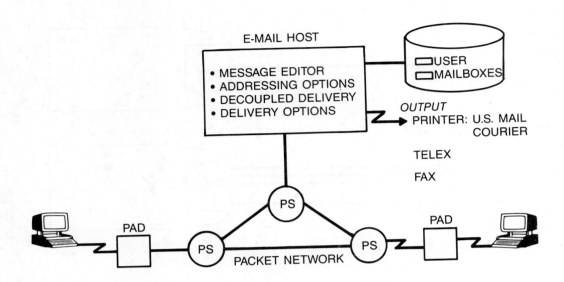

FIGURE 5

TYPICAL ELECTRONIC MAIL SERVICE

PACING STANDARDS TO TECHNOLOGY/SERVICES EVOLUTION

Michael Ahdieh

Northern Telcom, Inc.
4001 Chapel Hill-Nelson Hwy.
Research Triangle Park, NC 27709-3010

ABSTRACT

This paper addresses the accelerating pace of data-communications applications and services, as driven by the evolving needs of end-user distributed communications and data processing, and utilization of fiber bandwidth for multi-megabit data services and multi-media capabilities. It discusses the processes of standards development, and the relatively slow pace of network products and services' rollout as determined by the standards finalization cycle. The collective challenges in expediting the standards process, and product planning to ensure timely rollout of services by network providers is discussed, current activities reviewed, and further actions are recommended.

INTRODUCTION

The need for standards in telecommunications has been recognized by all industry participants including network providers, network equipment vendors, and terminal equipment suppliers. The fundamental objectives of standards development are those of equipment compatibility and interoperability, service ubiquity and efficiency, and the stimulation and growth of user application. The realization of these objectives would benefit all industry sectors, should standards be developed in a timely and effective manner. The importance of these needs, and the significance of these objectives have assumed new dimensions in a post-divestiture, multi-vendor environment in the U.S., coupled with the legislative trends toward liberalization of the telecommunications industry and increased market competition, in the U.S.A. and abroad.

The communications needs of most corporations have evolved, particularly during the last decade, from primarily voice through voice and data, to multi-media communications. The growing need for wide-area communications, across local and national boundaries, underscores the importance of inter-networking and international standards for new services, as demonstrated by the unfolding Integrated Services Digital Networks (ISDN) standards and services.

Concurrently the pace of technology evolution has been accelerating by the growing "functionality per chip", higher speeds and lowering costs of processing, and cost-effective bandwidth through the proliferation of optical fiber in the network and access plant. The rate at which new technology solutions can be applied is now outstripping the rate at which new services can be rolled out by the network providers, in particular the Regional Bell Operating Companies (RBOCs), due to the relatively sluggish process of standards development, and the associated lead times in equipment procurement and service tariffing.

The major factors determining the pace of standards, and contributing to its slow development include:

- The processes and the multiplicity of standards bodies,
- The divergences of interests within the industry sectors and at the national levels,
- The growing complexity of the interfaces and protocols encountered in the new data and multi-media services.

STANDARDS PROCESSES AND AGENCIES

The background and experience of the U.S. telecommunications industry in the formulation of standards goes back several decades. While many standards on a national level were earlier established through government and military agencies' requirements, the private sector has been active in the American National Standards Institute (ANSI) since the early 1950's. Prior to the AT&T/Bell System divestiture in 1984 the U.S. telephony and telecommunications standards for network equipment, and network to user equipment interfaces were developed through the Bell System Technical Advisory (TA) and System Requirements (SR) process. This process, with an approximate TA-release to equipment deployment cycle of 2 to 3 years, was fairly efficient in a closed market. Any interaction from the independent vendors and equipment suppliers was in reactive attempts at providing "compatible" transmission or end-system gear mostly through the independent telephone companies, and often with much longer lead times.

With the inception of digital data communications in the early 1970's, it was inevitable that the Bell System would interact with national and international standards agencies such as the Institute for Electrical and Electronics Engineers (IEEE), the Electronic Industries Association (EIA), the International Organization for Standardization (ISO). Examples are the introduction of equipment and services such as digital data service (DDS) for AT&T's private line offering, and the introduction of packet switched (X.25) service, as defined by the CCITT and offered by common carriers using Bell Systems facilities in the mid-1970's. Even then a mix of interface standards for interconnection of data circuit-terminating equipment (DCE) and data terminal equipment (DTE), ranging from proprietary (e.g. WECo 303) to North American and/or International (e.g. RS232C/V.24 and V.35), proliferated and is still in place.

AMERICAN STANDARDS FORUMS

Among the many U.S. Standards organizations, ANSI is regarded as the main national organization, and holds the U.S. membership in the ISO. For the post AT&T-divestiture era, the need for networking standards was addressed through the formation of the Exchange Carriers Standards Association (ECSA) in 1983, and the subsequent establishment of Standards committee T1-Telecommunications as accredited by ANSI in 1984. Six technical subcommittees were initially formed with the following areas of interest and expertise:

- T1C1: Carrier to Customer Premises Equipment (CPE) Interfaces
- T1D1: Integrated Services Digital Networks (ISDN)
- T1M1: Internetwork Operations, Administration, Maintenance and Provisioning
- T1Q1: Performance
- T1X1: Carrier-to-Carrier Interfaces
- T1Y1: Specialized Subjects

Two of the subcommittees (T1C1 & T1D1) were re-formed in February 1988 into T1E1 and T1S1, to better align the areas of expertise covered as follows:

- T1E1: Carrier to Customer Installation Interfaces.
- T1S1: Services, Architecture and Signaling.

Through the ANSI "due process" of open participation and consensus formalization, many standards have been moved by these subcommittees through the 'Draft Standard' and 'Letter Ballot' stages for ANSI approvals during the last year (16 standards approved by ANSI as of June 1988, with 10 others under review). Many of these are the result of successive interactions between T1 subcommittees, and liaison with other organizations. Additionally a number of other standards such as Broadband ISDN with major international significance are being prepared for release with the CCITT standards process as discussed later in this section.

Other American organizations directly involved in major aspects of telecommunications standards include:

- IEEE-802 Committee on Local Area Network (with 12 sub-committees)
- EIA-TR, & FO Groups on Information & Telecommunication Technologies (with 17 sub-committees)
- ANSC-X3 American National Standards Committees' Information Processing Systems Task Groups:
- X3S3.n on data communications aspects and OSI lower layers
- X3Tn.m on data processing aspects and OSI upper layers
- X3T9.n on system input/output interfaces

In addition a number of user-oriented forums with focus on the implementation, verification and efficacy of the standards have formed, including:

- ICCF: Interexchange Carrier Compatibility Forum
- NOF: Network Operations Forum
- COS: Corporation for Open Systems
- NIU: National Bureau of Standards ISDN User Forum

Furthermore, Bell Communications Research (Bellcore), responsible for the specifications and requirements of network equipment of the RBOCs through the process of Technical Advisory (TA), Technical Requirements (TR) and the Technology Requirement Industry Forum (TRIF), is active in defining procedures and requirements that drive, and are determined by, national standards.

The above lists only serve to identify the main forums with standards activities germane to our considerations of the standards process and inter-relationships. Detailed discussion of the associated subcommittee (SC), technical committees (TC) and working groups (WG) is beyond the scope of this paper.

INTERNATIONAL STANDARDS FORUMS:

Notable amongst the large number of international standards organization, mostly headquartered in Europe, are the CCITT (Consultative Committee for International Telegraphy and Telephony) and the ISO (International Organization for Standardization). In Europe organizations such as ECMA (European Computer Manufacturers Association) develop standards for the data processing industry, in a role like the IEEE committees in the U.S.

The CCITT is organized around eighteen study groups (SG) and approximately 64 working parties (WP) with specific study questions defined for each 4-year plenary session. The current plenary session

(1985-1988) will finalize the status of the many standards whether newly developed or updated through successive stages of "stable" and "frozen" disposition, at the plenary assembly scheduled for November 1988 in Melbourne, Australia. The activities by the CCITT's diverse working groups, particularly during the last plenary session, have experienced growing participation by not only the representatives of the nation members, but also individual trade organizations and administrations including some U.S. RBOCs, and the European CEPT.

The activities of the ISO are most widely recognized as related to the definition of the Open System Interconnect (OSI) architecture, and development of the 7-layer reference model. This work, initiated in the mid-1970's, has continued during the decade to further define and describe the concepts of the layer functionalities and inter-layer services, (Fig. 1). Much progress has been made in this work, as captured in the ISO 7498 (Note 1), and through parallel activities with other organizations including the CCITT, leading to the provisional recommendation X.200 (Note 2). Much work remains to complete the specifications required to adequately address the complex protocol structures involved in the interconnection of heterogeneous computing environments through "intelligent" networks and interworking gateways.

INTERPLAY OF STANDARDS, PRODUCTS AND SERVICES:

The role of standards in the rollout of telecommunications products and services is significantly different in a closed, vertically integrated market place, such as the U.S. pre-divestiture, and the still current environment in some European PTTs, and that of today's open-network, multi-vendor environment of the U.S.. The basic processes encountered are depicted in Figures 2-A and

2-B, respectively, and highlight the relatively earlier need for standards solidification as input into the network product implementation process.

With the inception of the ISDN principles, a set of initial standards by the CCITT (e.g. Q.900/I.400 Series) was developed, and published in the 1984 "Red Book", prior to the formation of the U.S. Committee T1. In the 1985-88 plenary session, now drawing to a close, many additions or extensions to the above standards have been developed and a majority is expected to be approved and published in the CCITT "Blue Book" after November 1988. The T1 Committees have also been active in furthering the development of North American counterparts of these interactional ISDN standards,

some examples of which will be discussed later. The desire to approach commonality of, or as a minimum, secure alignment of, both sets of proposed standards has promoted active U.S. participation, and wide representation of the Committee T1 membership in the multiferous study groups and working parties engaged in related aspects of the standard.

As an example, the development of draft standard I.122, (Note 3) has been driven by a strong and continuing process of T1 Committee (T1D1/T1S1) consensus, and successive liaisons into the SG XVIII, SG XVII, and SG XI as related to the services, data switching, and signaling aspects of the "Additional Packet-Mode" switched data capabilities of the evolving ISDN. Similar multi-faceted activities such as Interworking Standards (Draft I.500 Series) have involved numerous cycles of interaction at the North American and International levels to arrive at the set of documents likely to receive ANSI and CCITT approvals, albeit with some items for "further study".

Factors such as the differences in the established regional deployment of networks, such as the X.25 public packet switched: data networks and the circuit-switched digital data networks (PSPDNs & CSDNs) in the Nordic countries and Canada, as compared to other countries, account for the gradual pace of consensus. Northern Telecom Inc., as a major network equipment supplier, has taken an active role alongside the RBOCs and its major customers in the U.S. to expedite the development of all data networking and ISDN services standards. Cognizant, however, of the early need of the RBOCs to meet the evolving of products such as Datapath for support of circuit switched data applications is not held up by the above processes encountered for establishment of rate adaption (V.110) or terminal adaption (V.120) draft standards. Rather, through standardized procedure for interworking as embedded in I.515 (draft) standard an early deployment of products with assured forward compatibility (once the standards are finalized) the BOCs' timely rollout of ISDN compatible services will be facilitated. Similarly, the prerequisites for interworking of the stage-1, and the stage-II/II of ISDN packet mode services are being urgently addressed through the networking, and services interworking standards.in order to expedite the deployment and success of the X.25 services of the BOCs. The recent relaxation of regulatory constraints and the anticipation of the end-users' benefits of transitioning to the frame relaying services of the telcos, are assisting in this process.

Another process interacting with the standards is Bellcore's generic requirements process previously mentioned. In a number of cases TAs generated by Bellcore need to be coupled, in timing and content, to the T1 standards process to ensure final compatibility of multi-vendor products. This has the merit of strengthening the process and streamlining the product design directions. However the desire to avoid delays where possible, while details are agreed upon internationally, has led the major RBOCs and other telcos to establish "multi-vendors task force", and "nine-on-one" vendor interactions to drive early implementation agreements. Such areas as definition and prioritization of "supplementary services" for the North American market have been the main candidates. Northern Telecom Inc. has actively supported the objectives of this process within the guidelines of legislation. In similar approaches, the need to verify conformance of the protocols implemented versus the defined standard is being addressed through such forums as COS and the recently formed NIU forum mentioned above. The latter ISDN-users forum appears intent on defining conformance tests for the ISDN, and to drive implementation agreements for the connection of CPE (data terminals/hosts) to the ISDN. The number of forums now involved in such activities is becoming large, and the process unwieldy considering the overlaps with the COS, MAP/TOP, and OSI related activities, as tabulated in Figure 3.

Other recent instances of the impact of multiple standard processes on products include those of SONET, B-ISDN and Metropolitan Area Networks (MANs). While SONET's standard in the U.S. progressed rapidly, as desired by vendors and the network providers, the process of alignment with the international standards has gone through a number of reversals, and the resolution may be an agreement on a North American standard decoupled from the international standards uncertainties, to allow product rollout to proceed. Similarly the seemingly urgent need for deployment of MANs services by the RBOCs, positioned by Bellcore as the first application of broadband ISDN (B-ISDN), is moderated by the necessity of extending the related LAN standards in IEEE 802.6 to ensure compatibility with SONET in the near term, and with B-ISDN/ATM in the mid-term for early rollout of the initial data-only service (switched multi-megabit data services - SMDS), but ensuring efficient coupling and evolution to B-ISDN, as being defined in T1S1/X1 and the CCITT. While it is tempting, on occasions, to achieve faster service rollout through decoupling of the product specification from the full standardization cycle, this runs the risk of implementing a solution that deviates from the final standardized approach, thus compromising the inter-operability and compatibility objectives. This, obviously is not a complete or desirable solution and other alternatives must be sought.

EXPEDITING STANDARDS, SOME RECENT EFFORTS:

With the realization by the vendors and network providers that the pace of standards development is slower than expectations, discussions on ways of improving the voluntary standards process have begun. As a start an ANSI-sponsored seminar held in March 1988 addressed the topic and the challenge of maintaining "due process/due speed". Subsequently the T1 advisory group (T1AG) formed a "Standards Process Management" (SPM) committee, to speed up solutions for the committee T1 process. Some useful procedures already adopted include the establishment and tracking of a master schedule and related milestones for the standard development cycle. An electronic database modeled after the T1Q1 Electronic Communications System (ECS) has been established on a trial basis. A sample of the ECS's records is shown in Figure 4. Features of the trial system include bulletin board for announcements, meeting calendars, as well as the project registers for proposals, scope, contributions, reports, etc., for real-time, remote access. The trial capabilities are phased, scheduled for completion in February 1989. The results and final recommendations will then be reported by the SPM committee for T1AG review and decision towards the Phase Two.

While an encouraging and useful administrative process has been initiated for the committee T1 standards, the processes of inter-action of multiple standards bodies, the alignment of schedules and streamlining of the reporting and approval processes must be addressed. Innovative approaches extending the concepts of electronic data-bases, and greater use of our own industry's "ware", i.e. telecommunications, to reduce the elapsed time in the information dissemination and comment, can be employed and must be devised to address the process of standards development and consensus. Some basic concepts will now be presented for consideration.

RECOMMENDATIONS:

The following concepts are recommended for consideration, the implementation of which are expected to lower delays, reduce the cycles of interaction, and increase the efficiency of the standards process:

• Make greater use of Electronic Communications System to provide authorized interactive access to the on-line standards documents for real-time updating and nation-wide availability.

- Strengthen the project flow and milestone management process through coupling with other "selected set" standards organizations to optimize the "liaison and comment" cycle.

- Encourage consolidation of forums with a fair degree of overlap in their areas of interest, to minimize the interaction delays, and enhance the efficiency of the process. Such recent processes as the merger of technical committees of ISO and IEC into the joint technical committee, known as JTCI/SCG as of January 1988, and others may be used as models for considerations.

- Use telecommunications facilities to minimize delays in the contributions dissemination, and consider pre-scheduled audio/computer-conferencing in conjunction with, or as a complement to, the regular meetings to expedite the process at greater efficiency of participation without the need to travel.

- Expedite the completion of OSI definitions, and use the same principles in re-structuring the mandate of standards committees and organizations, based on well delineated responsibilities and interfaces, for optimum interaction efficiency.

- Reduce the length of "study periods" in the domestic forums, and encourage similar reduction of the CCITT plenary cycle time, to foster more frequent release of standards.

- Commit to closer interaction between all participants to avoid formation "interest groups" whose isolation may create undue delays in achieving consensus.

This reflects Northern Telecom's commitment to the OPEN World concept, and to exerting every effort to facilitate development of standards in keeping with its major customers' service rollout needs and time-frames, as guided by the technology evolution pace, and the stimulation and growth of user applications.

CONCLUSIONS

The needs for new telecommunications services, and data communications capabilities is continuing to grow at an accelerating pace. New user applications, as driven by the ever-evolving technology, demand timely rollout of services by the network providers. The ability of the network equipment vendors to react to the services needs of the RBOCs is determined by the finalization of the standards. While the efforts of the U.S. standards participants have led to the recent formulation of many standards, the initial delay, and the need to ensure multi vendor conformity has led to the establishment of a number of user forums whose efforts, while important to the overall process, may introduce additional processes and delays. In order to expedite the pace of standards development, actions have already been taken by TIAG, and other organizations to use project management tools, and to achieve consolidation of forums with overlapping interests. This process must be encouraged, while the due process of open participation and consensus supported by all participants to allow timely rollout of solid standards benefiting all industry sectors. Northern Telecom Inc. is committed to this effort with its major customers in an open market. To assist in early rollout of services while standards are in development, products with capabilities for forward compatibility through interworking features are important, and Northern Telecom Inc. is actively involved in developing standards to ensure evolvability of the telco's services and deployed equipment base.

Note 1: Information Processing Systems - Open System Interconnection, Basic Reference Model

Note 2: Reference Model of Open System Interconnection for CCITT Applications

Note 3: Frame Relaying Bearer Service - Architectural Framework and Service Description.

LAYER #	Application - related functions				
Application 7					
Presentation 6	encryption/decryption			Compression/expansion	
Session 5	session connection establishment	session connection release	session connection synchronization	session to transport connection mapping	session management
Transport 4	layer 4 connection multiplexing	layer 4 connection establishment	layer 4 connection release	error detection/ recovery	flow control	segmenting blocking
Network 3	routing/ relaying	network connection establishment	network connection release	network connection multiplexing	congestion control	addressing
Data Link 2	data link connection establishment	data link congestion release	flow control	error control	sequence control	framing synchronization
Physical 1	physical layer connection activation	physical layer connection deactivation	bit transmission		channel structure multiplex	

Figure 1: OSI Protocol Functions allocated according to layering principals of CCITT X.200.

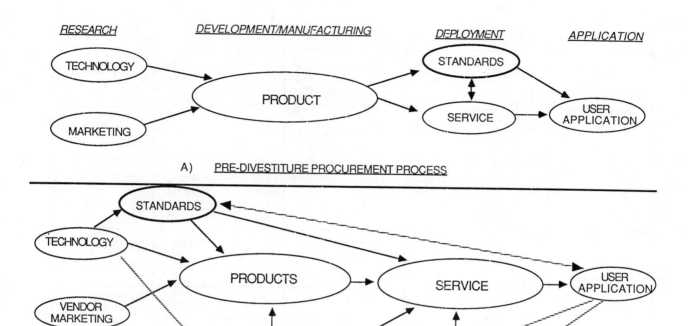

DEVELOPMENT/MANUFACTURING

DEPLOYMENT

APPLICATION

TECHNOLOGY

MARKETING

PRODUCT

STANDARDS

SERVICE

USER APPLICATION

A)   PRE-DIVESTITURE PROCUREMENT PROCESS

STANDARDS

TECHNOLOGY

VENDOR MARKETING

PRODUCTS

SERVICE

USER APPLICATION

BELLCORE

TELCO MKTNG.

NETWORK EQUIPMENT VENDOR   TELCO   CPE. VENDOR

B)   POST-DIVESTITURE PROCUREMENT PROCESS

Figure 2:   Interplay of STANDARDS, PRODUCTS, AND SERVICES

PROCESS / STANDARD		User Requirements	Standards	Implementor's Agreements	Conformance Tests
ISDN	Int'l		• CCITT SG's VII, XI, XVIII		
	U.S.	• NBS ISDN User Forum (User Workshop) • TOP ISDN SIG	• T1S1 • EIA	• NBS ISDN User Forum (Implementors Workshop) • TOP ISDN SIG • Bellcore	• Switch Vendors • Bellcore
ISDN/OSI (In Combination)	Int'l		• ISO SC6 • CCITT SG VII	• ISO SC21	• COS
	U.S.	• NBS ISDN User Forum (User Workshop) • TOP ISDN SIG		• Lower Layer SIGN of NBS OSI Workshop • TOP ISDN SIG	
OSI	Int'l	• MAP/TOP User Group	• ISO SC6, SC21 • CCITT SG VII	• ISO SC21 • MAP/TOP User Group	• COS
	U.S.		• X3S3 • X3T5	• SIGS In NBS OSI Workshop	• ITI

Figure 3: Forums Involved In End-User/ISDN Conformance Process

T1Q1 PROJECT TRACKING SHEET

WG	ANSI PROJECT	DESCRIPTION	STATUS*	TYPE** OUTPUT	PROJECTED APPROVAL DATE***	LETTER BALLOT	APPROVED DATE	COMMENTS
T1Q1.3	T1Q1 06	Packet-Switching Parameter	A	P			Q{9/84}	
						T1/LB27	T{7/85}	
		Definition and Measurement Methods		S	T[4Q88]	T1Q1/LB88-02 Closed 5/9/88		Forwarded to T1AG
				C	Q{1H88}			• CCITT SG VII
	T1Q1 09	Specification and Allocation of Packet-Switched Digital Performance	A	P			Q{9/84}	
						T1/LB30	T{7/85}	
				S	Q[88]			• Follows development of T1Q1 06 Standard
	T1Q1 10	Specification and Allocation of the Performance of an ISDN	A	P			Q{9/84}	
						T1/LB9	T{7/85}	
				S	Q[1H89]			
				C	Q[1H89]			• CCITT SG XVIII
T1Q1.4	T1Q1 01	Digital Circuit-Switched and Dedicated Service Parameter	A	P			Q{9/84}	
						T1/LB26	T{7/85}	
		Definition and Measurement Methods		S	T[3Q88]	T1LB 130 Closed 6/3/88		• Dedicated Service (ANSI/T1.503) Public Comment Closes 8/2/88
				S	Q[2H88]			• Circuit-Switched Service
	T1Q1 07	Specification and Allocation of Circuit-Switched Digital Performance	I	P			Q{9/84}	
						T1/LB28	T{7/85}	
				S	Q[89]			• Follows development of T1Q1 01 Standard
	T1Q1 08	Specification and Allocation of Dedicated-Service Digital Performance	A	P			Q{9/84}	
						T1/LB29	T{7/85}	
				S	Q[89]			• Follows development of T1Q1 01 Standard

Figure 4: Sample OF T1Q1 Electronic Communications System (ECS) Record

* A-Active, I-Inactive
** C-Contribution, P-Project Proposal, S-Standard, T-Technical Report

***T-T1, A-T1AG, C-T1C1, D-T1D1, E-T1E1, M-T1M1, Q-T1Q1, S-T1S1, X-T1X1, Y-T1Y1, I-ANSI
{ } - Historical, [ ] - Projected, < > - Targets

BASICS OF PACKET SWITCHING

Mr. C. Fred Klein, Jr., Chairperson

District Manager -
Packet Switching Requirements

Bell Communications Research

331 Newman Springs Road
Red Bank, NJ 07701

"Basics of Packet Switching"

ABSTRACT

Although circuit switching has been fundamental to telecommunications since the industry began, packet switching is being deployed as a relatively new technology. Packet switching has been made possible by the tremendous increases in processing power and the expanding need for efficient data communications. This seminar will provide a basic understanding of packet switching theory and techniques. It will compare packet switching with circuit switching and highlight some unique issues associated with this approach to switching. In addition, the regulatory issues associated with the provision of packet switching services will be discussed.

Mr. C. Fred Klein, Jr. - Bell
                          Communications
                          Research
Mr. H. Manger -   NYNEX Service Co.
Mr. William C. Tucker -   Siemens Data
                          Switching Inc.

PACKET SWITCHING FUNDAMENTALS

Mr. C. Fred Klein, Jr.

District Manager -
Packet Switching Requirements

Bell Communications Research

331 Newman Springs Road
Red Bank, NJ 07701

ABSTRACT

This paper provides a tutorial introduction to the technique of packet switching by contrasting it with digital circuit switching. Several key characteristics of packet switches are identified and a high-level design of a packet switch is discussed.

INTRODUCTION

Packet switching is a digital switching technique which has its origins in the technology of data communications. It seeks to take advantage of the fact that some data communications typically consist of bursts of data of varying length, with intervening idle periods, also of varying length. These considerations lead to switching fabric designs which are quite different from the digital switches currently used for telephony applications. It is instructive, in attempting to understand packet switching, to compare these designs, and then to look at some of the characteristics of packet-switched communications arising from the differences.

Packet switching has been evolving rapidly over the past 20 years or so. One approach uses central processors which route packets by analyzing the address information they contain and consulting routing tables. Another approach distributes the routing information in such a way that many processors share the task, each operating on a very small portion of the address and making relatively simple routing decisions. This approach allows very large-capacity switches to be designed. A local area network may be viewed as a type of packet switch as well.

CIRCUIT SWITCHING AND PACKET SWITCHING

Digital circuit switching typically employs a time-division multiplexing scheme to funnel traffic from multiple sources into the switch fabric. Each input stream is assigned a time slot from the available pool of n time slots. Since digital voice is commonly represented by 8000 8-bit samples per second, a digital circuit switch might provide n timeslots each of duration sufficient to carry 8 bits at this rate (125 μsec). When the full complement of samples from each of the n sources is stored in a buffer, switching is accomplished by mapping the incoming time slots to outgoing time slots, and outputting the n samples in the order defined by the mapping. Everything is synchronized to a common clock, so that all samples are identified by their time-slot numbers.

Most packet switches move away from the concept of synchronized time slots and fixed length samples. Instead they switch variable-length packets (up to 512 bits, 1024 bits, or more depending on design) and they handle packets whenever the sender happens to send them. The packet switch still maintains a memory map for routing inputs to outputs, but since there is no time slot permanently allocated to a user, if the user has no data to send the switch does not need to spend any time servicing that user. If packets arrive simultaneously from several users, buffering and queuing inside the switch enable them to be served.

This approach assumes that the user somehow informs the switch when data is to be sent. This is in contrast with a digital circuit switch, where a continuous digital stream is switched for the duration of the connection.

The asynchronous characteristic, along

with variability of packet-size, raises certain design and performance considerations. Delay through the switch, which in the circuit switch described above is essentially bounded when n is chosen, can be more variable in packet switches, due to queuing with variable service times based on packet length. Where traffic characteristics of circuit switches tend to balance load against delays in call setup, packet switches may also degrade in the delay of information transfer. In a non-precise but intuitive analogy, one can think of each packet almost as a separate call. For example, where overload in a circuit switch may result in lost calls, in a packet switch there might also be packet loss on existing calls, due to buffer exhaust.

PACKET SWITCH DESIGN

One of the ways packet switches cope with the large and variable sizes of packets is to separate buffering from the actual switching task. Since no time slot label exists to allow the switch to figure out to which output it should route a given packet, each packet must carry this information along with it, in a packet header. It is common for packet switches to use peripheral processors to buffer the packet, while a central processor analyzes the header and instructs the peripherals regarding the disposition of the packet. In this way, the interconnection medium between the processors becomes the actual switch fabric.

RELATION TO LANS

The evolution of packet technology has as one of its results the local area network (LAN) concept. One might think of a LAN as a packet switch, but with the peripheral units being in the users' equipment. The central unit is frequently dispensed with in LAN design. Instead whole packets are passed over the switch fabric (the interconnecting medium) and the peripherals undertake the task of recognizing which packets are addressed to them. As before, buffering while queuing for the transmission medium, with arbitration schemes to give everyone a fair shake, are key design characteristics.

CONCLUSION

Packet switching is a digital switching technique designed to meet needs significantly different from these which have driven the designs of digital circuit switches. They are characterized by asynchronicity, with variable-length packets of information being switched. This allows switching of user data only when it is presented, with idle time available to serve other users. As a result, under load the mean and variance of delay in information transfer tend to rise.

ACCESS TO PACKET NETWORKS

Mr. C. Fred Klein, Jr.

District Manager –
Packet Switching Requirements

Bell Communications Research

331 Newman Springs Road
Red Bank, NJ 07701

ABSTRACT

This paper provides a tutorial discussion of issues surrounding the support of an accurate and reliable interface to a packet network. Some of the common methods for controlling the link from user to network are explained, and relevant standards are referenced.

INTRODUCTION

The issues involved in accessing a packet network can be divided into two broad categories. The first revolves around how the user gets data from the user equipment to the packet switching equipment. These are referred to as link-level functions. The second category is concerned with how the user interacts with the network to define exactly what the network is going to do with the data. These may be referred to as network-layer issues. We will focus here on link-layer concerns. Many of the concerns are not unique to packet networks, but rather are inherent in any data link. The basic problem to be solved is that of providing reasonable assurance that packets arrive at the other end of the link exactly as they left the originating end, with all bits intact, with no packets lost, and with the packets in sequence. In addition, the equipment at either end needs a way to exert control over the volume of data being sent by the other end, so as to prevent overload. The solutions to these problems lie in surrounding a packet of data with headers and trailers which contain extra information about the packet.

ACCURATE DATA TRANSFER

To check whether all the bits in a received packet are the same as were sent, the sender attaches a check sequence to the packet. This sequence is calculated by the sender based on the binary number represented by the string of ones and zeros which makes up the packet. The algorithm for performing this calculation is carefully designed so that when the receiver repeats the algorithm and compares its answer with the one included in the packet by the sender, the probability is extremely low that the two ends would come up with the same answer unless no bits had been changed during the transmission. Algorithms in use today will detect all single-bit errors and almost all possible errors involving more than one bit.

To determine if a whole packet was somehow lost in the transmission, the control information in the header will typically contain some type of sequence numbers. While a variety of schemes exist, the principle is that each end numbers its packets from one to n, and the other end checks each received packet to see if the numbers are in sequence. If more than n packets are to be sent, the numbers cycle. That opens the possibility than n packets might be lost, and the receive would not see a break in the sequence numbers. Also, even if the receiver does detect a break, what should be done? These two cases are covered by acknowledgements of received packets. The sender can keep track of which packets are unacknowledged, and retain copies of those for retransmission if necessary. The range of sequence numbers will influence how many packets may be sent without receiving an acknowledgement of the first packet, as will other considerations such as buffer size and desired performance.

Numbering of packets is not in itself sufficient to guarantee the link will operate correctly in the presence of transmission failures. Timers also are needed to prevent failures from resulting in deadlock, as senders and receivers wait for the other side to act. Also, special messages designed strictly for control purposes must be provided to deal with instances where no user data is being sent but control information needs to be sent. Finally, most schemes for link control have some sort of "escape hatch" whereby if errors occur which cannot be corrected, both ends will be forced to reset all their counters and timers, and inform their users that they are starting over.

FLOW CONTROL

Besides the limits on how many packets may be sent before an acknowledgement is received, an explicit mechanism for limiting the flow of packets on a link is provided. This generally takes the form of additional control packets which cause the other end to stop transmitting additional data until further notice.

PACKET ACCESS FOR NON-PACKET DEVICES

The procedures described in the previous section can get rather complicated. When existing equipment cannot be economically upgraded, alternatives have been devised to translate the simpler interface into one understood by the packet switch. One of the more common cases of this is the simple asychronous start-stop terminal, frequently found in a time-sharing computer environment where lines go direct from terminal to host. When the lines are replaced by a packet network, the network may provide a packet assembler/disassembler (PAD) function to support such terminals. The PAD assembles packets from the individual characters received from the terminal, and disassembles packets coming from the network into a character-by-character stream the terminal can understand.

STANDARDS FOR ACCESS TO PACKET NETWORKS

These procedures describing precisely how information is exchanged are known as "protocols." To encourage the development of data communications, protocol standards have been developed. The CCITT has endorsed international standards recommendations for interfaces to packet networks. The most widely known CCITT recommendation in this area is X.25, which includes both a link-level protocol, Link Access Protocol B (LAP-B), and a network-layer protocol. For packet access from non-packet devices, the companion recommendations X.3, X.28 and X.29 apply.

One of the characteristics of the Integrated Services Digital Network (ISDN) is a packet-based signaling channel between the user and the ISDN, known as the D-channel. The data link standard endorsed by the CCITT for the D-channel is known as LAP-D, and is described in Recommendation Q.921. It has all the functions discussed here, plus additional mechanisms for the ISDN environment where several user devices can share a single D-channel.

CONCLUSION

Access to packet networks involves issues both at the link level and at the network level. At the link level, error detection, retransmission to recover from errors, and mechanisms to control the flow of information are provided. A number of protocol standards are in use for different applications.

PACKET SWITHCING ECONOMICS

Mr. Herbert J. Manger

Staff Director -
Product Development

NYNEX Service Co.

120 Bloomingdale Road
White Plains, NY 10605

ABSTRACT

This paper provides a tutorial introduction to the uses to which packet switched networks have traditionally been applied. The paper concentrates on the benefits of packet technology for intraLATA data communications.

INTRODUCTION

Packet switching networks were originally developed for wide area network applications in order to permit maximum utilization of long haul transmission facilities. The capital costs incurred in packet switching equipment and the expense involved in operating and maintaining the network were traded off against the savings in communication line charges.

While reduction in line charges was a prime motivator in the deployment of packet networks, it was not the only motivating factor. Elimination of the lock-in between terminals and host applications through the provision of switched virtual call services greatly reduced the need for multiple terminals and communications lines. In addition, the ability of X.25 to support multiple calls over a single access line greatly reduced the port costs and communications overhead at the host computer. The ability to charge users for the number of packets sent, rather than for holding time or distance, was very attractive to the interactive, low volume user for whom these services were designed.

At first glance, the use of packet switching networks within Local Access and Transport Areas (LATAs) does not appear to be as viable as with long haul networks. However, a combination of several factors has prompted their use as a local access offering.

- The inefficiencies of carrying interactive data on the circuit switched voice network.

- The decreasing cost of packet switching network equipment.

- The significant proportion of intra-LATA data traffic.

- The wide acceptance of X.25 protocol.

- The availability of reasonable-priced data-voice modems.

Traditionally, on the analog voice network, the basic unit of capacity has been the 3000 Hz. switched connection. When a switched call is set up, this connection is held for its duration, whether any conversation is taking place or not. With a voice call, one party or the other is typically talking about 60 percent of the time. This means that over half of the line capacity in each direction could be allocated to another conversation during the idle periods. Indeed, equipment is available on the market to permit 40 concurrent calls to be maintained over only 4 channels of a single 24 channel T-1 carrier system. However, because of the trade-off of capital equipment vs line costs, it tends to be cost effective only on long haul facilities.

If voice conversations do not allow optimum use of the switched communications channel, the inefficiencies involved with transmission of interactive data are orders of magnitude worse. In today's network, most devices are connected through the use of modems, or MOdulator/DEModulators, whose basic function is to convert the digital data signals to a voice-link signal that can be carried over the predominantly analog voice network. Because these modems transmit continuous carrier tones, they prevent the use of the channel sharing devices discussed above. The effect is that a continuous connection must be held in both directions even if absolutely no data is being transferred.

In addition, an interactive terminal session typically uses only a small percentage of available line capacity. Analysis of traffic characteristics of 1200 BPS asynchronous terminals on a major packet network indicates that the typical utilization from the terminal keyboard in towards the host computer is in the order of 1/2 of one percent. The utilization outbound from the host to the terminal's screen or printer averages about five percent. It is also instructive to compare holding times between voice and data calls. An average voice call may be in the order of 3 to 5 minutes. The average switched data call lasts between 25 and 30 minutes.

Currently, data communications accounts for approximately 10 to 20 percent of total voice and data communications expenditures in large corporations. This proportion is growing steadily with the increase in information processing applications. It is apparent that the unique characteristics of interactive data communications can severely impact the efficient engineering of circuit switched voice networks.

Furthermore, the increasing use of digital circuit switches does not provide any immediate relief. While these switch designs tend to be non-blocking, data traffic still impacts the engineering of interswitch trunk capacity. In addition, the basic increment of service is the 64 kilobit channel. The interactive data call that we discussed earlier would use only 6 bits per second inbound and 60 bits per second outbound of this total capacity of 128000 bits per second.

It is the use of packet switching technology, with its inherent statistical multiplexing capabilities that permits massive increases in efficiency by off-loading the voice network and directing the bursty, interactive data traffic onto a network that is more suitable for handling this type of transmission.

DECREASING PACKET NETWORK COSTS

Since the economic justification for packet switching networks is based on the trade-off transmission line and equipment costs, the decreasing costs of processor and memory components due to advances in VLSI technology is making packet switching attractive for even more applications.

Packet switches and access concentrators are, after all, simply specialized computers with packet switching and protocol handling software operating within them. The same advances in technology that have captured the power of a multi-million dollar IBM 360 operation from the 1970's and made it available in a Personal Computer for two or three thousand dollars are constantly improving the cost-effectiveness of packet switching networks.

INTRA-LATA DATA TRAFFIC VOLUMES

In large urban areas served by wide area packet networks, local switching of data within the urban area can account for over 30 percent of the traffic on the network. While this is not particularly cost effective for users on a network with a distance-independent tariff structure, the overriding advantages of switched calls, speed matching, X.25 lines sharing economies, and a single set of access procedures often outweigh the added cost.

An intraLATA PPSN service can serve the needs of these users at reasonable rates, as well as providing a point of access to multiple inter-exchange carriers for interLATA data transport.

WIDE ACCEPTANCE OF X.25 PROTOCOL

In the early days of packet switching, the rate of network growth was relatively slow. The primary reason for this was the unavailability of X.25 concentrators and front-end software.

Today, however, almost every large mainframe and minicomputer system has some method of X.25 support. In the Personal Computer world, X.25 cards are available for the IBM PC which allows the user to maintain multiple concurrent sessions to different destinations. In addition, a single channel X.25 adapter integrated into a 212A modem allows error-free efficient transfer of data to and from other types of PCs or other terminal devices. Terminal concentrators with Packet Assembler/Disassembler support for many types of non-packet-mode terminals are available from many manufacturers. In summary, there exists today, for virtually every type of computing system and terminal, a method of utilizing X.25 for efficient networking. X.25 protocol has become the unifying factor that allows a wide range of terminal types and computers to benefit from the efficiencies of public packet switching networks.

DATA-VOICE MODEM TECHNOLOGY

Data-voice modem technology has been in existence for quite some time. However, it is only recently that advances in Very Large Scale Integration have reduced the cost per link to the point that DVMs are cost effective. DVMs permit the simultaneous carriage of voice and data over a single non loaded cable pair at distances of up to 18,000 feet. At the central office, the voice is routed to the Class 5 switch, while data at up to 19,200 BPS is routed to the packet switch.

This approach allows the Operating Telephone Compnaies to capitalize on one of their largest investments - the local distribution system provided by their outside plant. It provides simultaneous voice and data over a single pair at less cost than the use of two pairs and conventional modems.

The sale of customer premises DVM equipment of access to the packet network provides a revenue opportunity to the unregulated subsidiary. A related opportunity is the provision of DVMs and PAD devices within a PBX. This combination can create a powerful Local Area Network at minimum cost and with minimum disruption within a corporation, and provide a cost effective X.25 connection to the packet switched network.

BENEFITS OF PACKET SWITCHING

A WORLDWIDE STANDARD FOR DATA TRANSPORT: Packet switching has emerged as the standard for transport of data on a worldwide basis. This accomplishment has been possible because of the work done by various telecommunications organizations in the world under the auspices of the International Telephone and Telegraph Consultative Committee (CCITT). The X.25 standard for interfacing terminals and host computers to the network and the X.75 standard for gateways between networks has made it possible to interface equipment supplied by various vendors and owned by different organizations. Public packet networks exist in most industrialized countries of the world.

RAPID DECLINE IN EQUIPMENT COSTS: The acceptance of CCITT packet switching standards has led to a large number of companies supplying telecommunications equipment to serve this market. In addition, all computer manufacturers support these standards. A large number of new entrants are targeting equipment for this market because of unusual universal acceptance of these standards. The net result has been both a fast growing market and very rapid decline in price for a certain level of performance. These trends are likely to continue giving further boost to this market.

A SUITABLE NETWORK TECHNOLOGY FOR PUBLIC NETWORKS: By separating the data communications function from data processing and by making it independent of the architectures of individual computer vendors, packet switched networks provide excellent mechanisms for universal access. Growth can be accomplished by adding transmission or switchng nodes and topology changes are relatively easy to implement without causing major network reconfigurations. Because of ease of growth and change, these networks are ideally suited for public network environment as compared to host based networks used for intra-company communications where extensions will create major problems.

TRANSMISSION ECONOMICS FOR BURSTY TRAFFIC: The bursty nature of data traffic leads to very poor utilization of transmission resources. Under the current circuit switch technologies the situation is made worse with the long holding times associated with the data communications between terminal and host. Line utilitzations of the order of 5 percent or less are not uncommon. With packet switching, transmission resources are not utilized until actual data communications takes place.

ROBUST TECHNOLOGY: Packet switching offers extensive error correction both on a link to link and on an end-to-end basis. Using packet switching the probability of an undetected error on a voice grade line can be improved from 1 in 10^5 to 1 in 10^{13}. In addition capability for auto- matic alternate routing in case of link or node failure provides the very high availability required for data networks.

EXTENSIVE FEATURE SET: Packet switching has implemented a very extensive set of facilities and features like closed user groups, hunt groups, reverse charging, fast select, etc. This rich feature set has considerably enhanced the capabilities of the users or the networks and the services offered by the operators of packet data networks.

PROTOCOL AND FORMAT CONVERSION: Packet switching data networks are very suitable for data communications requiring protocol and format conversions to enable communications between devices that use different formats.

SPEED CONVERSION: Packet switched data networks enable communications to take place between devices that inherently operate at different speeds. With the flow control capabilities inherent in the network it is not necessary to predefine in the host the characteristics of each device that it would be communicating with.

CONCLUSION

The attractiveness of packet switching is based upon its efficiency, low price for end users, and its ability to allow customer terminals to access multiple hosts regardless of protocol. In many instances the BOC itself derives significant cost benefits as a result of implementing packet switching as a means to transport data communications in its service area.

PACKET SWITCHING NETWORKS

Mr. C. Fred Klein, Jr.

District Manager -
Packet Switching Requirements

Bell Communications Research

331 Newman Springs Road
Red Bank, NJ 07701

ABSTRACT

This paper presents tutorial information outlining the characteristics of packet switching networks, from the perspective of the user of the service. It discusses some of the strategies employed inside the network to provide these services.

INTRODUCTION

To the user, the packet network is the provider of services such as connections to other users, charging options, end-to-end confirmation of delivery of packets, and the like. These network services are provided in a number of different ways in different types of packet networks. To appreciate the network layer it is necessary to examine some of the services to the user and also to look at the internals of networks, invisible to the user, that support these services.

CALL CONTROL

Packet protocols provide mechanisms for requesting services, setting up and tearing down connections, providing addressing and reporting error conditions.
A large number of services can be built upon this base, and different networks may provide different sets of services. Some of them are specific to the technology of packet switching. For instance, a network might allow a user to request special handling of packets to keep delay down, or to request larger maximum packet sizes to increase throughput. Other services might be analogous to services in a circuit-switched network. Call forwarding and reverse charging are two possibilities.

TRANSPORT SERVICE

The most basic service a packet network provides to a user is the transport of a packet to a desired destination. The packet as delivered by the user to the network contains all the information the network needs to route the packet. This is sometimes called a "datagram."
Built on that capability is the service by which the user identifies the desired destination in the first packet, the network assigns a simple reference number, and all subsequent packets provided by the user with that reference number are transported to the same destination, in the same order they are sent by the user, until the user terminates the service. Such a service might be described as a "packet call," or a "virtual call." The term virtual is used because, unlike the circuit-switched network, no real circuit is set up end-to-end for the duration of the call. Instead, a "virtual" circuit, consisting of memory maps in the packet switches, gives the user the appearance of a real circuit (except for the variability in delay).

MULTIPLEXING

Many virtual calls can share a link by **statistical multiplexing**. Each packet carries a logical channel number indicating

1243

the virtual call of that packet. Because the traffic is bursty, there is enough capacity on the link to carry the packets of several virtual calls. The precise number of logical channels supported depends on the speed of the link and the number of virtual calls active at any one time depends on the traffic demands.

NETWORK ROUTING

Inside the network, things do not have to be what they seem from the user's perspective. The prime example of this is in the area of routing. A network which provides virtual circuits to its users might be expected to do so by identifying, at call setup time, the route through the network that each packet is to take, and setting up mappings in each switch along the way. This approach, although valid, natural and intuitive, is not the only one in use. Some networks treat every packet as a datagram, even if the user does not see it that way. This means that once inside the network, each packet gets its own addressing information sufficient for routing through the network independent of any other packet. If there are alternate routes in the network, for example so that load can be evenly distributed across links, then packets could arrive out of order. It therefore becomes the task of the network to coordinate the sequencing of the packets in order to give the customer a virtual circuit.

The reasons for making such a design choice could be a perceived advantage in simplifying the task of intermediate switches and allowing the network to react to failures by alternate routing without a great deal of concern over individual virtual calls. This would have to offset in the designer's mind the extra burden on the switches at the edges of the network, and the extra volatility inherent in allowing traffic to be rerouted on a packet-by-packet rather than a call-by-call basis. An important part of the decision rests on what model is used for the traffic the network is to handle.

NETWORK CONTROL AND MANAGEMENT

Packet networks are ideally suited for automated network monitoring and control, since the data communications channels are readily available to the packet switches through the packet network itself. Centralized network control nodes which handle such functions as configuration management, software upgrades, and billing data collection, are included in many packet network designs.

Network management, by which we mean the immediate response to failures or congestion in the network, has been an area of much study since the early days of packet switching. There are unique problems arising from the high variability of load on packet networks as compared to voice networks. Because congestion can

arise so quickly, designers often go to great lengths to defend against potential load imbalances.

CONCLUSION

Packet networks can offer a variety of capabilities to their users, and network designers have many different approaches to supporting these capabilities. A network could support a virtual circuit service while using datagram routing, for example. Packet network designs include provisions for automated control and management of network resources.

PACKET SWITCHING REGULATORY ISSUES

Mr. William C. Tucker
Manager -
Marketing and Strategic Planning

Siemens Data Switching

5401 Broken Sound Blvd.
Boca Raton, FL 33487

ABSTRACT

This paper provides a tutorial introduction to the regulatory and legal constraints that have affected the deployment of packet switching services by the Bell Operating Companies. The regulatory overlap of the Federal Communications Commission and of the Modified Final Judgement is analyzed.

INTRODUCTION

While practically any new telecommunications service offering in the U.S. is subject to some regulatory oversight, the introduction of packet switched data transmission services by the BOCs faced unique regulatory and legal barriers. An understanding of the barriers and the prospects for their alteration is essential for any assessment of the potential for packet switching services in the U.S. data transmission services market. The two major public policy themes that will be examine briefly here are the FCCs long-standing desire to keep communications and data processing functions separate and distinct in the manner of their provision, and the information services ban of the Modified Final Judgement which precludes the BOCs from offering services which could be efficiently and economically provided via packet switching.

FEDERAL COMMUNICATIONS COMMISSION

For the past twenty years, the FCC has conducted numerous inquiries that have attempted to deal with the gradual but inexorable convergence of communications and data processing. In the First Computer Inquiry the FCC declared that while conventional "communications" services would remain regulated under the authority of the

Communications Act, "data processing" services would not be regulated and could only be offered by regulated communications carriers through a structurally separate subsidiary. A third category of services, "hybrid" services, was defined as an area of overlap between communications and data processing. These "hybrid" services were allowed to be implemented by carriers to the extent that they would facilitate communications services.

The categorization of services in the First Computer Inquiry soon became too ambiguous to implement and led to the Second Computer Inquiry in the 1970's which eliminated the prior definitions and instead attempted to subdivide all services into either "basic" or "enhanced" services. The definition of enhanced services established in Computer II included services which "...employ computer processing applications that act on the format, content, code, protocol or similar aspects of the subscriber's transmitted information...". The reference to protocol in the definition has turned out to be of critical importance to packet switched services. Although analogous protocol processing had been for some time an integral part of the signaling and stored program switching of basic voice services, the FCC in Computer II determined that protocol processing in conjunction with packet switched services was enhanced.

This decision, along with the FCCs decision in 1982 and 1983 that pure X.25 packet service without net protocol conversion is "basic" service, helped create the situation still in effect today. Packet switching service became a part basic, part enhanced service. Although the central office packet switching equipment manufactured by all vendors did not subdivide these capabilities, BOCs could not provide the enhanced functions except on a fully separated basis. In order to provide the service, the BOCs were therefore required to seek waivers of the Computer II rules.

The framework for this waiver process was set out by the FCC in 1985. The FCC at that time stated that the BOCs could provide asychronous-to-X.25 protocol conversion services using equipment collocated in their public switched network central offices provided that:

1) The interoffice channels used by the BOCs for transmission between switches must be secured at tariffed rates.

2) The basic tariffed service of X.25 to X.25 transmission must be unbundled from any protocol conversion.

3) Access by end users to the packet switched offerings of the BOCs and their competitor carriers in a non-discriminatory manner.

These three conditions eventually were included by the FCC in its Third Computer

Inquiry as conditions that must be met for the provision of any enhanced service by a BOC. In a supplemental notice to Computer III, the commission declined to change its views on protocol conversion. As a result, BOC packet switching services will continue to be part basic, part enhanced services requiring imaginative engineering and accounting rules to separate the functions for regulatory purposes. The issue will have to be considered again, however, in the context of ISDN, where the FCC will be faced with deciding whether its voice protocol rules or packet protocol rules are controlling.

MODIFIED FINAL JUDGEMENT

The definition of "information" services in the MFJ is very similar to the FCCs "enhanced" service definition. The decree describes an information service as "...the offering of a capability for generating, acquiring, storing, transforming, processing, retrieving, utilizing, or making available information which may be conveyed via telecommunications." (MFJ Section IV (J), 552 F. supp at 229). This has in effect created the situation that the BOCs are twice barred from providing services to end users that would enable them to interact with or retrieve information from a database. These types of data services, namely access to computerized databases, electronic mail, transactional services, alarm monitoring, etc., are characterized by the type of bursty data transmission which can be most efficiently and economically provided via packet switching.

Another BOC restriction in the MFJ which has affected BOC packet switching services is the ban on interLATA services. Any end user whose trnsmission destination is not in the same LATA in which it originates requires the use of an interLATA carrier. Under this scenario an end user with any type terminal other than X.25 will require a protocol conversion to the X.25/X.75 internetwork interface protocol. Thus, the FCCs protocol conversion rules and the interLATA restriction serves to cause most interLATA packet traffic to be enhanced, requiring the BOC to track both basic and enhanced costs and to recover those costs with separate rates for the basic and enhanced portions of the service provided.

The Department of Justice, in its first triennial review of the MFJ restrictions has recommended that the information services ban be lifted. DOJ is not advocating any change in the interLATA service ban.

In a decision issued on September 10, 1987, Judge Greene declined lifting any of the bans except a portion of the information services ban so that the BOCs could transport information services but not generate and sell content. Greene listed several functions he felt would be necessary for the BOCs to provide to establish an infrastructure for information services in the United States. He asked for comments on these functions from interested parties and issued a second opinion on March 7, 1988. Greene affirmed his earlier decision to allow only BOC transport of information services and not to generate content (with the sole exception of white page directories).

The five functions which comprise Judge Greene's concept of transmission, but not generation or manipulation of the content of information are data transmission, address translation, protocol conversion, billing management and introductory information content.

1) Data Transmission - includes "signal demodulation, error rate measurement, and the generation of characters on the user screen." Greene said that this would allow the network to perform functions that would otherwise require sophisticated hardware and software CPE.

2) Address Translation - means "the consumer will be enabled to use an abbreviated code or signal provided to him in order to access the information service provider instead of dialing the telephone number of the desired provider." This is simply the ability of a user to select an IP (information provider) from a list and to be connected without further dialing.

3) Protocol Conversion - Greene feels that "...a sophisticated and effective system of information transmission requires that the network perform those protocol conversion functions that are necessary to enhance transparency of communication between consumers and information service providers..." although in the September opinion Greene seemed to be saying that conversion from any protocol to X-25 is allowable, in the subsequent March opinion he specifically commented on the need to convert individual user protocols to X-400 for electronic mail applications and the need for async/sync conversions for data communication. The key to what is a Judge Greene permitted protocol conversion seems to be that it would achieve transparency or facilitate communication.

4) Billing Management - Judge Greene commented on the fact that current information services require presub-

scription which decreases accessibility and distribution. He observed that the BOC role of intermediary between information service providers and end users suggests that they are in a unique position to provide billing functions to obviate the presubscription process. The BOCs will be allowed to share revenue with IPs, which will make the service more lucrative and provide the BOCs with considerable leverage and flexibility in their negotiations with IPs desiring to be included in the BOC menu of selections.

5) Introductory Information Concept - this category of functions concerns the welcoming page or banner, the menu, and a "help" capability to assist end users in navigating within and using the BOC Gateway. In his September opinion, Greene had limited this function to the display of a welcoming page and information provider listing which were restricted to provider's names, addresses, telephone numbers, and business/service category. Subsequently, in March, Greene went to great lengths to emphasize the importance of allowing customers to search the database in any of these categories without much difficulty. He also emphasized the need to provide a help capability that would inform "how to locate different providers, how to use the listing of providers, how to select an information service, how to exit the network..." with the only condition being that this capability be limited to information about using the BOC Gateway.

CONCLUSION

During the introduction of packet switched service offerings by the BOCs, many significant legal and regulatory constraints limited the services that could be provided and affected the manner in which permissable services have been offered. The combination of FCC rules concerning enhanced services and the MFJ ban on information services resulted in very limited success. Given the FCCs conditional relaxation of its enhanced services rules and the lifting of the information services ban, it is now possible for a much more varied and attractive set of services to be offered by the BOCs.

DSW-07

DSW-08

THE AMAZING SIGNALING SYSTEM NUMBER 7

Joseph G. Rudolph

Central Region Manager

Ericsson Network Systems

400 East 22nd Street
Lombard, IL.   60148

ABSTRACT

Common Channel Signaling Number 7 is
generally regarded as the backbone to providing Intelligent Network services and a key in
implementation of ISDN. Yet, Signaling System
Number 7, in itself, provides an exciting
array of revenue generation, facilities
utilization, and call control advantages to
a wide range of stakeholders. Local exchange
carriers, Interexchange carriers, manufacturers and the business/residence users find
considerable attraction in the CCS7 technology. The benefits are no mere pipe dream.
Several trials are long underway, full-
scale deployments have been completed and
many near-term implementations underway.

This seminar examines the CCS7 technology from a balanced range of perspectives
ie., the switch manufacturer, RBOC, Bell
Operating Company, research and developer,
computer provider, user and international
telecom provider.

Ericsson has long been active in the
development and installation of Signaling
System No. 7 networks with years of successful network deployments worldwide. Presently
the Ericsson AXE switch with SS7 is in
regular service in more than 10 countries
including the United States.

The goal of providing both STP and a SSP
in the AXE was made easier because of the
Ericsson decision to use the same hardware
for both switches. The modularity of the
AXE made it the choice for both applications. This modular concept allows an STP
to be used for other functions as well.
For example, a switch serving as an STP and
an access tandem, or as an STP and an end
office/SSP. Based on their experience,
Ericsson is presenting a full line of SS7
products to the U.S. marketplace. In the
first session the nature and structure of
SS7 architectures and components are
described.

Ameritech is active in the planning and
development of SS7 networks. Their view of
service and demand forecasts, analysis of
technology and its trends along with the
related regulatory and legal issues are all
critical factors in their determination of
an architecture and deployment strategy
and are described in the Ameritech paper.

Michigan Bell discusses a Local Exchange
carriers' view of a CCS network and its
extension to end offices. The strategic
nature of SS7, the issues of existing networks and other planning considerations are
described. The definition of their SS7 plan
and the actions required to implement the
plan are also reviewed. The Michigan Bell
strategic position and guidelines for statewide deployment are then presented.

The Bellcore implementation experience
and directions offer interesting food for
thought. Current states of activity and the
challenges which are faced provide a first
hand look at the realities of SS7 deployment. The lessons which are being learned
and their influence on future directions
provide valuable insight for others.

In the IBM presentation customer premises
equipment and service provider telecommunications network management equipment are
described as having been largely independent
evolutions. The thesis of the presentation
is that with the availability of the
Intelligent Network and CCS7, a strong case
can be made to bring these two network
managements appropriately together. There
are substantial benefits that might be
realized in terms of making the combination
more efficient, offering more function, and
enabling greater capability for the network
to run itself.

British Telecom (BT) has embarked upon a
major modernization programme to replace its
existing analogue Public Switched Telephone
Network with an Integrated Digital Switching
and Signalling Network.

Their paper describes the history and evolution of the British Telecom CCITT No. 7 Common Channel Signalling (CCS7) Network, its specification and introduction into the BT Network, culminating in the establishment of a fully interconnected CCS7 Toll Network and progress toward a fully digital network for the early 1990's. An overview of the BT digital signalling network architecture and differences between the BT/CCS7 specification and that specified by CCITT in relation to BT's signalling and network requirements is also included. The evolution of CCS7 in relation to future new services and the introduction of Intelligent Networks are discussed.

Ameritech Services describes the critical signaling backbone and the robust set of services that will help meet customer communications needs during the 1990's. The implementation of a CCS/SS7 network will increase the amount of central office power the BOC can bring to help solve its' customers' communications problems. The Ameritech paper discusses the approach Ameritech Services Marketing is taking in finding answers to questions of maximizing benefits for both customers and their corporation. Solutions for four main customer segment needs are looked at: Residence, Business, Exchange Carriers and Mobile.

Michael Gray	----	Ericsson Network Systems
Eugene Wagner	----	Ameritech Services Inc.
Everette Lefler	----	Michigan Bell Telephone
Francis Duffy	----	Bell Communications Research
J. Kenneth Boggs	----	IBM Corporation
Derek Ritson	----	British Telecom
Tim Dunar	----	Ameritech Services Inc.

CCS7—FOUNDATION FOR FUTURE NETWORKS

Michael Gray

Manager, Systems Engineering

Network Systems Division

Ericsson

730 International Parkway
Richardson, Texas   75081

ABSTRACT

This session addresses SS7 as the backbone for the future network. Detailed are the capabilities which SS7 provides today and in the future as the Intelligent Network begins to increase its impact on network architecture. The nature and components of the SS7 network is demonstrated to show how new network offerings such as ISDN will be supported.

CCS7 – AN RBOC PERSPECTIVE

Eugene J. Wagner
Manager, Technology Planning

Ameritech Services, Inc.

1900 East Golf Road
Schaumburg, Illinois 60173

ABSTRACT

This session deals with the realities of CCS7 in an RBOC environment. Ameritech's view of service forecasts and technology trends along with legal and regulatory issues determined the architecture and implementation strategy for the Ameritech CCS network. Computer models were also used to determine the impact of the Signaling Point of Termination (SPOT) location in every LATA, to measure the sensitivity of the planned architecture to STP's and SCP's of varying capacities and to indicate the order of magnitude changes in related service forecasts. These and other elements of the Ameritech perspective are covered.

Planning SS7 at End Offices

Everette W. Lefler

District Manager, Network Engineering
Michigan Bell Telephone Co.
29777 Telegraph, Room 3290
Southfield, Michigan 48034

GENERAL

This paper discusses a Local Exchange Carrier's view of a Common Channel Signalling (CCS) network and its extension to end offices. Planning considerations are covered as well as some basic misconceptions regarding the infrastructure of the network deployment. The paper assumes all digital tandems have been equipped with SS7 enabling software and hardware as part of the program to position Regional companies to implement the 800 Data Base application. The paper emphasizes infrastructure versus applications primarily because many people associate the infrastructure with each application that will utilize the infrastructure to transport signaling protocols. The CCS network is not a service available to customers, it is an architecture. Many new services and network features will require the CCS network to function. Implementing Common Channel Signaling causes a very basic change in network architecture. It transforms the network from in-band signaling to out-of-band signaling and positions the network nodes, to be driven by a single data base.

STRATEGIC NATURE OF SS7

The CCS network implementation is essential to achieve the Intelligent Network (IN) of the future. The Intelligent Network features flexible structure, software controlled operation, an on-line data base common to many nodes or switches, and an extremely powerful signaling system. Signaling System 7 (SS7) is the standard protocol for communications between Intelligent Network nodes. Today, local end offices are of limited intelligence capability between nodes, because the inter-office signaling, mostly Multi-Frequency (MF), limits information transfer capability. All nodes must ultimately be converted to SS7 to support the future Intelligent Network. Once the SS7 infrastructure has been provided, new service offerings will involve primarily a software update. Each region will have a centralized data base on-line 24 hours a day. The network is analogous to a distributed packet switching network. For example, when using the network in a non-circuit related capacity, such as 800 Data Base Service, the Local Exchange Carrier can activate/deactivate 800 numbers in near real time, and offer an

entire gamut of customized 800 vertical services. Each common control end-office or tandem can quickly recognize updated 800 translations when an Inter-exchange Carrier (IC) or end-user reserves a new 800 number. It is stressed, however, that many services or features of prime importance to the Local Exchange Carriers only require Signal Transfer Points to be fully functional.

CONVERSION OF NETWORK TO SS7

Signaling provides control information between network nodes using a prescribed protocol. Today's interoffice network uses circuit associated signaling, or in-band trunk signaling. This technology utilizes 8 Kb/s of an interoffice 64 Kb/s channel for network signaling information and the remaining 56 Kb/s for customer voice or data information. Figure 1 depicts circuit associated signaling. In-band signaling has many disadvantages such as long call setup time, inefficient trunk usage, restricted signaling capability and security problems. Using SS7, the interoffice network does not require the 8 Kb/s of signaling information over the voice or data channel. It transmits the signaling data over a separate signaling network and voice or data over a separate bearer network. Figure 2 depicts a CCS network. The CCS network provides more efficient trunk usage based on reduced call setup time and reduced non-productive trunk usage. Fraud is reduced because the message and signaling paths are separated. Based on the Bellcore document titled "Impact of CCS Deployment Strategies on the Voice Trunk Network", TM-NPL-008931, Common Channel Signaling could reduce voice trunk holding times by up to 2 - 3% for IntraLATA calls and 6 - 8% for InterLATA calls. Reduced trunk requirements directly related to CCS deployment are tangible benefits to both the Local Exchange Company as well as Interexchange Companies.

CONTRAST BETWEEN INFRASTRUCTURE AND APPLICATIONS

It is important to distinguish network infrastructure from the applications. The CCS infrastructure consists of four basic elements; Signaling Nodes, Signal Transfer Points (STPs), Service Control Points (SCPs) and Signaling Links (SLKs) (see Figure 3). The Signaling Node (normally a tandem or an end-office) may either be a Signaling Point (SP) or Service Switching Point (SSP). Service Switching Points (SSPs) are Signaling Nodes associated with a data base while Signaling Points (SPs) are not associated with a data base. STP's are equipped to interact with on-line data bases, other STP's, and SPC switching nodes. Service Control Point's (SCP's) are network nodes that provide access to the centralized data bases. The

SS7 network protocol permits more network control information to be exchanged between switching nodes than the 8 Kbps of control data used with an in-band signaling network. New service applications resulting from the CCS infrastructure include Custom Local Area Signaling Services (CLASS), Integrated Services Digital Network (ISDN) services, 800 Service, Alternate Billing Service, Private Virtual Network (PVN), N911 and Metropolitan Centrex. While not considered a service, the interconnection of switched voice and data trunks is a potential cost saving application of the CCS network at the Local Exchange Carrier level. The switching node connectivity is the foundation for most other services. Thus, its importance should not be overlooked.

PLANNING CONSIDERATIONS

The Common Channel Signaling network presently consists of a regional pair of Signal Transfer Points (STPs) and Service Control Points (SCPs), Signaling Links (SLKs) and Signaling Nodes. The data base (SCP) applications involve a high degree of connectivity between regions (e.g. 800 Service, LIDB, and PVN). The applications which provide the Local Exchange Carriers the most benefit include; switched voice and data trunks between switching nodes, Interoffice ISDN and Interoffice CLASS. Since these services along with PVN, Metroplitan Centrex and N911 involve primarily end offices, the local STP is thrust into prominence since all SS7 equipped SSP offices require links to an STP. Deploying local STP's proves economical by elimination many lengthy Digital Data Service (DDS) circuits connecting the regional STPs to the local Service Switching Points (SSPs). In addition, the operation of the SS7 controlled interoffice trunking is best administered locally. STP's will be required for future IC and other large customer interconnection. Future studies will undoubtedly establish that deployment of local SCP's is economical. For example, a local SCP could be used for distributed 800, PVN or N911, billing arrangements and Metropolitan Centrex.

Two operation modes are defined for the SS7 protocol. They are data base query (non-circuit related) and inter-office trunk signaling (circuit related). Data base query mode involves the SCP receiving requests for call processing from the SSP via the STP. The SCP will access the appropriate data base to obtain call information and send the reply to the SSP via the STP. Applications requiring an SSP, STP, and SCP for data base query include 800 Service and LIDB. The regional STPs will initially support data base query applications. Applications that do not require an SCP for data base query include Custom Local Area Signaling Service (CLASS), and Integrated Services Digital Network (ISDN) services. These services are best provided by a local STP.

DEFINING THE PLAN

The purpose of a Signaling System 7 (SS7) Fundamental Plan is to define an end-office SS7 plan and describe actions required to implement the plan. Prior to the recommendation to deploy end-office SS7, consideration must be given to the physical aspects of the STP, the required end-office modifications, defining the operations support systems and the associated administration centers.
Identifying training requirements and socializing the concept of a new out-of-band signaling system is of extreme importance to the success of the study. Physical aspects of deploying a local mated pair of STPs include determining the building location, interconnecting link requirements, and actual STP performance. The best location for the STP's in the judgment of the author would be at a 24 hour manned central office. However, the decisions regarding the STP staffing should be made by Switching Personnel. The STPs should be located at geographically separated facility hubs to insure route diversity of the signaling links and to insure against a single central office failure disabling the entire network. The Signaling Links require diversely routed paths (preferably fiber) connecting appropriate network elements to insure nodal communication in the event of a single link failure. Each link is engineered to carry 40% of the signaling load under normal conditions and 100% of the load, in emergency conditions. SS7 links should meet DDS performance objectives of 99.9% availability with 99.5% error free seconds, trouble isolation within 15 minutes of a report, and two hours maximum downtime. The STP must have gateway capability to enable it to access alternative data bases or STPs. Because many smaller offices will not require the data capacity available with a 56 Kb/s circuit, the link ports should accommodate 4.8 kb/s and 9.6 Kb/s as well. The STP vendor must comply with the Bellcore document titled "STP Generic Requirements", TR-TSY-00082 and provide Signal Transfer Point component redundancy. Redundancy is imperative for a local CCS network because potentially every interoffice call will be routed by the STP. The redundant STPs, STP components, and Signaling Links have the ability to transmit messages around failed components, so a failed link will not isolate a signaling point. With the increased use of digital switches and fiber routes, there will be an increasing need to develop a non-hierarchical alternate routing capability as a network sur-

vivability measure. When reviewing end-office SS7 deployment, consideration must be given to end-office modification requirements. Each end-office must be equipped with the appropriate SS7 hardware and software to formulate SS7 messages. This will include generic updates. Converting interoffice trunks from circuit associated signaling to SS7 requires switch manufacturers to provide direction for a conversion procedure. In some cases, software and conversion procedures will be available from other RBOC's on a license basis. Choosing end-office locations to deploy SS7 does not mandate the purchase of application software for services such as Custom Local Area Signaling Services (CLASS), or Integrated Services Digital Network (ISDN) services. A plan to deploy an SS7 infrastructure which provides message trunk connectivity and compliments new services can be deployed to meet marketing needs.

An end-office CCS network requires the establishment of a local Signaling Engineering and Administration Center (SEAC) to provision, administer, and maintain the network. Figure 3 depicts the Signaling Engineering and Administration Center's (SEAC's) role in the CCS network. The SEAC provides 24 hour CCS network maintenance and surveillance. The Signaling Engineering and Administration Center (SEAC) can be co-located with one of the STP's or located at a Switching Control Center (SCC). The SEAC requires a Signaling Engineering and Administration System (SEAS) access. SEAS is the Bellcore software package developed as the primary operations support system for the CCS network. It would be appropriate to perform an economic analysis to determine if a local SEAS application would be more economical than accessing the regional SEAS.

A comprehensive Operations Plan for the CCS network must be developed by Switching Systems. This plan includes procedures for network provisioning, administration, and maintenance. CCS network provisioning involves translation assignments and link additions. CCS network administration functions include data generation, collection, service surveillance and equipment utilization. CCS network maintenance involves the maintenance of the Signal Transfer Points (STPs), Signaling Nodes (SPs or SSPs) and the Signaling Links (SLKs). The STPs are not co-located, therefore on-premise maintenance resources should be available. It is recommended that STP maintenance be considered the responsibility of local switching forces. The Signaling Nodes (SPs or SSPs) are located in the end-offices or tandems and are part of the central office equipment.

The Signaling Links should also be maintained by local switching forces. The CCS transmission links will be DDS quality circuits, and will be tested and maintained using existing procedures. Overall network administration is similar to dial administration, however, the technology differs greatly from message traffic.

Since SS7 protocol impacts every corner of the network, it is imperative that all levels of management understand the basic principles of a CCS network and identify their responsibilities to prepare for the future CCS network. This is accomplished through staff training and socializing the change at all management levels.

Developing an SS7 Implementation Plan which details the level of change expected in the network and how to handle it is very necessary. Implementing the CCS network will be a progressive activity which may span a number of years.

STUDY RESULTS

After defining the CCS network requirements, the following plan was a recommended and approved End-Office SS7 Plan. Our strategic position is to deploy SS7 statewide, within the following guidelines:

1. Equip all digital tandems with SS7 capability.

2. Establish Local STPs prior to extending SS7 to end-offices.

3. Equip all new switches purchased with SS7 capability.

4. Equip existing digital end-offices with SS7 capability. This decision is based on both message trunking and potential revenue generating applications, such as CLASS and ISDN.

5. Equip all 1AESS offices with attached processors with SS7 capability. The economic benefit achieved must be studied to determine conversion priority. It does not appear economical to equip 1AESS with IN/2 capabilities.

6. Equip remaining analog switching centers and ESS switching centers with SS7 capability. The decision to equip these offices with SS7 capability requires an economic analysis comparing upgrading versus replacement.

CIRCUIT ASSOCIATED SIGNALING

**MESSAGE/DATA TRAVEL THE SAME PATH AS
THE SIGNALING INFORMATION**

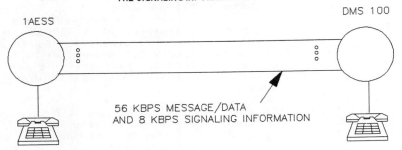

56 KBPS MESSAGE/DATA
AND 8 KBPS SIGNALING INFORMATION

Figure 1.

COMMON CHANNEL SIGNALING

**MESSAGE/DATA TRAVEL ON SEPERATE PATHS
THAN THE SIGNALING INFORMATION**

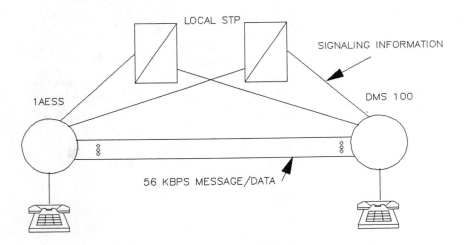

Figure 2.

COMMON CHANNEL SIGNALING NETWORK

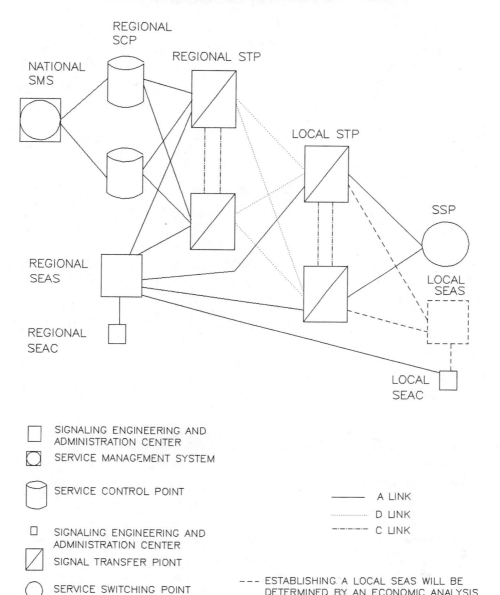

Figure 3.

1253

SS7 PROTOCOL MODEL

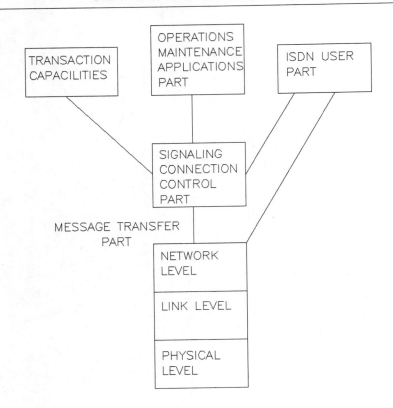

SOFTWARE LAYERS REQUIRED

INTEROFFICE TRUNK SIGNALING & CLASS
    MESSAGE TRANSFER PART
    ISDN USER PART

800 DATABASE SERVICE & LIDB
    MESSAGE TRANSFER PART
    SIGNALING CONNECTION CONTROL PART
    ISDN USER PART
    TRANSACTION CAPABILITIES

Figure 4.

SS7 IMPLEMENTATION EXPERIENCE AND DIRECTIONS

FRANCIS P. DUFFY

District Manager, CCS Project Management

Bell Communications Research

331 Newman Springs Road
Red Bank, NJ 07701

Introduction

Nationwide implementation of Common Channel Signaling (CCS) capabilities based upon the Signaling System No. 7 (SS7) protocol has been progressing steadily for the past two years. Currently, all Bellcore Client Companies (BCCs) have successfully deployed backbone CCS networks. These networks consist of Service Switching Points (SSPs), Signaling Transfer Points (STPs), and Service Control Points (SCPs). The SSPs provide entry points into the CCS network for data base queries directed to SCPs. Services such as 800 Service, Alternate Billing Services (ABS), and Private Virtual Networks (PVN) are dependent upon centralized data base capabilities for call processing support. The STPs function as CCS network packet switches interconnecting signaling points and providing access to data base capabilities. The STP functionality will be augmented with "gateway" capabilities to support CCS interconnections between independent carrier networks. The "gateway" functionality supports inter-network routing and screening for security and control purposes. The illustration in Figure 1 depicts the CCS network architecture as described.

At this time, some switches within local exchange networks are being modified to support SS7 trunk signaling for call setup. This intra-network call setup capability will become more prevalent as additional vendor products are introduced. Within two years, SS7 trunk signaling capabilities for inter-network call setup support should be available. This milestone will set the scene for CCS network interconnections and the evolution of significant new services dependent upon CCS/SS7 and Integrated Services Digital Networks (ISDN).

Implementation Experience

Initial implementation activities focused on the introduction of data base oriented services. The challenge was to deploy multiple vendor products, integrate them into a single CCS network, and evaluate the outcome from network, operation, and service views. This challenge was further complicated by the following circumstances: (1) many of the standards had been adopted in the relatively recent past or were still under consideration, (2) network element requirements became available within the past few years, and (3) vendor CCS/SS7 capabilities based on these requirements were just being introduced.

To accomplish this task, the following approach was adopted:

1. Conduct lab-to-lab tests between Bellcore and vendor laboratories as early as feasible to uncover and correct non-conformance prior to field installations.

2. Conduct stand-alone network element tests immediately after vendor delivery and acceptance testing.

3. Conduct pair-wise network element tests as associated elements become available to evaluate inter-communications and action/response behavior.

4. Conduct network integration tests from SSP to SCPs to evaluate network support capabilities under normal and failure modes of operation.

5. Conduct call processing tests to evaluate CCS/SS7 support from a service viewpoint.

6. Conduct stability tests to evaluate performance over time.

7. Conduct a "friendly user" trial to evaluate service from the user's view and ongoing network operations from an internal service provider view.

This testing scenario provided an orderly guideline for addressing the Message Transfer Part (MTP) and Signaling Connection Control Part (SCCP) of the SS7 protocol. The Transaction Capability Applications Part (TCAP) was not tested directly. Extensive call processing tests were conducted to assure that the service was supported properly. These tests covered calls launched from various types of calling party stations, serving end offices and access tandem offices under a variety of serving arrangements, e.g., originating foreign Numbering Plan Areas (NPAs).

BellSouth provided the opportunity to conduct First Application tests for Data Base 800 Service. The goal was to assure, as best possible, that the technical requirements were met, that those requirements held up under integrated CCS network conditions, and that the service operated as expected. Field testing began in July 1986 with the arrival of a single STP. By the end of October, all network elements were in place for the first time. This network is depicted in Figure 2. On November 12, 1986, the first successful 800 call was placed. Between November 1986 and the end of January 1987, network integration testing and call processing testing, which includes about 600 separate call scenarios, were completed. To accomplish other internal work, stability testing was delayed until June 1987. Upon completion of these tests, BellSouth assumed operation of the CCS network and, along with South Central Bell, sponsored and conducted a "friendly user" trial between July 6 and August 16, 1988. With only minor start-up problems, the trial was supported successfully. Completion of these First Application tests launched the introduction of similar capabilities within the operating territories of all Bellcore Client Companies.

Subsequent to the First Application tests for 800 Service, ABS has been successfully tested within the local exchange. This service concept includes (1) calling card validation, (2) collect, and (3) third party billing data base features. From a CCS/SS7 viewpoint, the ABS testing was able to take advantage of previous network testing for 800 Service. Therefore, testing centered about the switch (Operator Services System) capabilities and the data base (Line Information Data Base) capabilities. Similar tests are underway for PVN.

During 1988, Bellcore and the operating telephone companies have been deeply involved in intra-network call setup using CCS/SS7 network capabilities. These tests include stand-alone switch testing, interswitch testing, and the interworking among the various vendor products.

Test Vehicle

Due to the complexities of this implementation schedule, a number of significant obstacles had to be conquered. A rationale testing methodology, as described above, represents one such milestone attained. The most significant milestone, however, was the development within Bellcore of a test system which could facilitate such a vast testing challenge. The Network Services Test System (NSTS) was designed to provide a means for testing an entire CCS network. It not only had to provide SS7 protocol testing capabilities for the various levels of interactions, it also had to provide diagnostic capabilities which could be used to isolate problems encountered in a distributed network. In addition, it had to provide means to control the level of testing staff required in the field environment.

To accomplish these goals, the test system itself was designed to be deployed in a distributive manner, controlled centrally, and operated remotely. Its functions are to simulate network element capabilities, initiate events, monitor responses, record data, and provide time stamps. A high level view of this system is provided in Figure 2.

The NSTS is designed for in-depth technical evaluation of new CCS network architectures, elements, SS7 capabilities, and services. It can also be used to evaluate CCS network performance under in-service conditions and to diagnose intractable network problems. Its use in the Bellcore CCS/SS7 test arena has been widely recognized as invaluable.

Lessons Learned

Two important elements have contributed fundamentally to the CCS/SS7 implementation successes enjoyed to date. The first is the mutual undertaking of lab-to-lab tests between Bellcore and vendor labs at the direction of the Bellcore Client Companies. This provides an opportunity to detect and correct non-conformance items earlier in the process. Two important by-products flow from this endeavor: (1) software stability may settle in earlier and (2) more difficult field detection/isolation problems can be avoided.

The second element is the need for vendor/operating telephone company/Bellcore working interactions during the testing process. To facilitate a quicker understanding of perceived problems, a more direct channel for issue resolution, and a more streamlined process for moving ahead with the full complement of tests.

Direction

In the 1989-1990 timeframe, the expectations are to forge ahead with the introduction of STP-Gateway capabilities and SS7 trunk signaling call setup support for calls transiting multiple carrier networks. This will position the industry for CCS/SS7 interconnection to support call setup for a wide variety of existing and new services. The flowchart in Figure 3 depicts the events along the way to realize these initial CCS interconnection service goals.

Conclusion

The CCS/SS7 experiences and directions touched upon in this paper relate to the foundation of a rapidly evolving infrastructure for the modern telephone industry environment. All of the capabilities discussed belong to Phase 1 of the Intelligent Network (IN1). At this time, many Bellcore organizations are working on Phase 2 and intermediate phase concepts, architectures, requirements, operations, procedures, development planning, and so forth. These too will bring new implementation challenges and experiences. Hopefully, lessons learned today may be modified and applied tomorrow. Again, new directions will surface and the process will be replicated into the future.

References

[1] De Santos, J.M., Gandner, B. F., BOC 800 Service: Offering the Customer More Choices," Bell Communications Research Exchange, January/February, 1986, pp. 18-22.

[2] Cambron, K., "Testing the Intelligent Network," Bell Communications Research Exchange, July/August, 1986, pp. 23-27.

[3] Fineman, M. M., Huber, H. A., Moresco, T. V., Scheller, T. W., "Making it Easy: Alternate Billing Services," Bell Communications Research Exchange, November/December, 1987, pp.8-12. 16.29

Figure 1 - CCS Network Architecture

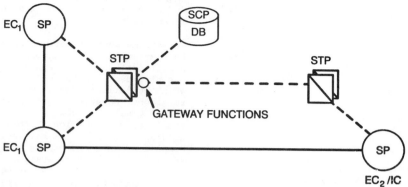

SP - SIGNALING POINT
STP - SIGNALING TRANSFER POINT
DB - DATA BASE

SCP - SERVICE CONTROL POINT
EC - EXCHANGE CARRIER
IC - INTEREXCHANGE CARRIER

NVC88 AFD226.001

Figure 2 - First Application Network Architecture For Testing

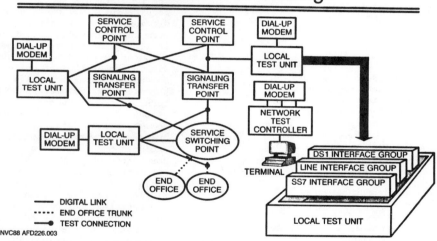

— DIGITAL LINK
···· END OFFICE TRUNK
•— TEST CONNECTION

NVC88 AFD226.003

Figure 3 - CCS Interconnection For Call Setup

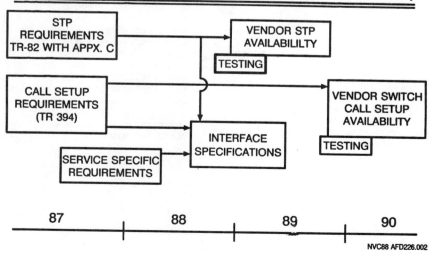

NVC88 AFD226.002

CCS7 - New Opportunities In Network Management

J. Kenneth Boggs

Senior Programmer

IBM Corp.

F75/656-1
PO Box 12195
Research Triangle Park, NC   27709

Abstract
Customer premises equipment and service provider equipment telecommunications network management have been largely independent evolutions. The thesis of this presentation is that with the availability of the Intelligent Network and CCS7, a strong case can be made to bring these two network managements appropriately together. There are substantial benefits that might be realized in terms of making the combination more efficient, offering more function, and enabling greater capability for the network to run itself.

Same but different
This paper is addressed to those who define network management products and standards. This paper is a call to unify what is today fragmented. Emphasis is given to a definition of the problem. Due to limitations of the conference format, in part, it will be left to future papers to explore the characteristics of the solution

In addition to the current network management fragmentation, our language describing the problem is also inconsistent. Different language is used for customer controlled equipment and service provider equipment. For example, note that OA&M probably covers the same scope as network management but that is not obvious.

A broad scope definition of network management is needed since it must encompass both environments: customer premises equipment (CPE) and service provider equipment (SPE). The assumption of this paper is that the definition includes all the functions that act upon the operational network, including topology definition, monitoring and reporting of status, deployment of changes, cutover and cutback, performance and flow control, and maintenance of inventory.

Network management for CPE and SPE have been evolving semi-independently for about a half-century. This separate evolution has provided a technology simplification which has allowed development of timely solutions. However, since CPE customers normally use the Public Switched Network (PSN) for some portion of their network, solutions in each area have not been completely independent. As the sophistication and capacity of both information processing and communication technologies have grown, it now appears feasible to implement combined solutions should this be needed and desirable.

Customer comes first
Although the effects of these two evolutions continues to be expressed and there continues to be motivation to solve CPE requirements independently from SPE requirements, customer requirements are driving the two together. From a short-term customer viewpoint, there is a need to allow end-to-end management of the computer based communications concurrently with state-of-the-art voice facilities. End-to-end management is a consequence of the need for customer control which, in turn, is a consequence of the commitment of the customer business on-line to the communications network. The long-term customer network management objective includes the ability to implement a highly cost-efficient, self-managing network with the characteristic of a single-failure producing a single-report and a single corrective action. Both short-term and long-term customer requirements appear to be achievable only through a creative combination of CPE and SPE network management information.

But is there a payoff for the service provider? Yes, from both the view of the service provider as well as the customer, there are advantages that may be realized. Common advantages might be realized in terms of reduced operational costs and reduced duplication, improvement in manageability through reduced confusion and strategic positioning to utilize state-of-the-art technologies as they emerge. The CPE can better utilize their networks as a corporate strategic resource which is responsive to corporate growth, focus and direction. The SPE can better capitalize on their networks through rapid introduction of new, customer specific services. In addition, this coordinated network management introduces a business growth opportunity for providing value added services by either a customer or a service provider for others.

Fences and neighbors

In all of this, new opportunities are created for both CPE and SPE. But the CPE and SPE interaction and dependencies demands some structure that protects the interests of both. One metaphor to describe a successful way to handle this is "Good fences make good neighbors." Realization of the new opportunities will depend upon definition and implementation of such mutually beneficial interfaces.

Why have we not already achieved this integration? What keeps us apart other than regulation and history? The CPE focus has been logical connectivity, largely ignoring the details of the communication channel. The SPE focus has been the physical connectivity, largely ignoring the details of how the communication channel was being used. As a consequence, we find the two blind to each other. This blindness carries over into non-technical areas such as organization, values, attitudes, interests, insight and intuition.

The telephone network has always had an effect upon the CPE customer but the reasons for that effect were generally not understood. Along with this lack of understanding goes a limited ability for the CPE customer to diagnose problems. These two factors can lead to a perception that fixing a problem requires an inordinate amount of time and is unpredictable. Alternatively, there may be the perception that since the SPE network is totally reliable it never requires any management. Coordinated actions are primarily manual or none at all. The consequences of exercising alternative connections are ambiguous and seem to require "brute force".

The CPE customer has affected the SPE network but this logical usage was private and proprietary to the CPE customer. As a result, the CPE customer may make unexpected demands without warning.

Similarly, the telephony service provider probably does not know the consequences to the CPE customer of network management actions. In addition, the telephony service provider has no means of forewarning or alerting his customers regarding actions he plans to take or is taking.

In addition, the service provider may have mixed feelings about providing the CPE customer the means for obtaining predictable service with rapid diagnosis and fixes. Traditionally there has been a management approach that implied, "I take care of the physical network and users must go thru me to receive any diagnosis or fix." Not opening up the physical network has contributed to the reliability of the telephony network. Since it may now be necessary to open up CPE access in some way to the physical network, there is a technical challenge to achieve this without giving up the reliability so hard won.

Last, but significant in the business environment, though most customers would benefit from this CPE/SPE synergy, in sheer numbers it is only the largest of customers that have these requirements as an urgent need. Of course, these are the largest organizations in the United States and probably account for a large majority of business telephone usage. These companies have solved the basic connectivity problem and are now trying to manage the rapid increase in elements brought on by the micro and mini revolution. In addition, the telephone and other communication vendors are starting to offer a large number of services such as Tx multiplexers, Software Define Networks etc. that all require network management. No clear advocate has been forthcoming, since each CPE technology gain has been largely held as proprietary as possible. Finally, the communications part of most businesses has been marked more by competition rather than cooperation. Among the many communications vendors one pundit commented that these vendors acted a lot like piranhas - small and ravenously feeding upon one another.

A new direction

A different approach is needed lest we allow ourselves to ignore our mutual customers requirements since neither CPE nor SPE can alone solve these requirements. IBM's Open Network Management Architectures is one example of how to approach these requirements, beginning from a largely CPE viewpoint. Another is AT&T's UNMA, from a largely telephony viewpoint. Yet more is needed. What technical mechanisms are needed to implement these objectives? Are there examples from which we might build?

There are two aspects involved in defining solutions, in building these "good fences." First, we need to define the data structures, conditions and events that will flow between the CPEs and SPEs. Then, we need to apply these definitions toward improving the different CPE and SPE usages of the communication facilities. This last step will also test whether the data defined is sufficiently complete and robust. Note that in this process, it is possible to take constructive steps addressing specific usages without necessarily solving all problems at one time. Thus an incremental expansion of these "fences" can be envisioned.

The data structures, conditions and events that exist can provide a starting point. The central three subtopics are alarms, alerts and actions; generic data structure; and connectivity mechanism.

Alarms and alerts are logical constructs for representing important events that occur in a communication network. Conceptually, an alarm is a minor event, possibly not causing an outage of service but leading to one. An alert is a major event, possibly one involving a service outage. It is also consistent to view an event such as the renewed availability of a communication resource as an alarm or alert. Logically an alarm or alert can be viewed as flowing to some decision-making entity. Once an interpretation or meaning has been ascribed to an alarm, alert or combination of the same, it is possible that corrective action may be initiated by that same decision-making entity. In today's networks, a lot of decisions are manual or automated with simple command languages. Before long, it may be some portion of this decision making that might be encapsulated into a knowledge-based system.

A generic data structure is required to allow an open-ended mechanism but with consideration for minimizing transmission data. This kind of encoding is already expressed in elements of SNA and OSI implementations.

All architectural elements must be interconnected. The connectivity considerations include link-segment definition, topology and provisioning references and dependencies. Relational data-base technology gives a starting point of how to define this kind of information. Basically the lowest addressable element is the link segment with topology described by interconnecting these link segments. Last, this mechanism is completed with administrative data, most importantly that about provisioning systems, SMSs and OSS dependencies.

Synergism at work

Given the preceding architectural constructs, how does this approach add value to network use? Synergistic advantages can be projected with planned SPE services such as PVN, ISDN and IN/1+. PVN resource management might be enhanced by allowing inquiries for the current availability of performance paths, anticipated resource availability by time of day, and feedback on dynamic resource allocations. ISDN could benefit if inquiries for this network management information were available via the D channel providing a subset of the full IN/1+ information. IN/1+ might be enhanced with dynamic monitoring, single network management image, and distribution of function among CPE and SPE processing.

Advantages can be projected regarding recoverability for dynamic function distribution, i.e., the ability to determine the scope of recovery control dynamically. This service would allow controlling two or more elements simultaneously executing inconsistent recovery strategies. This facility would include the ability to delegate responsibility, automate inspection of results, and provide a route for this information to other management responsibility and control.

Peer-to-peer approach

A peer-to-peer approach recognizes two, or more, authorities. This approach acknowledges these multiple authorities and thus could apply not only at the CPE/SPE interface but also at the IEC/LATA interface. This approach would achieve comprehensiveness without giving up independent realms of control and responsibility. This kind of approach may also offer an enhancement to the interface between the independent service-provider and the public switched-network service providers. Integrated equal-access is inherent along with feasibility for specialized network management unconstrained by hierarchical notions. Finally, this approach could offer added value between networks; eg., X.25, OSI, SNA.

Why bother?

Do we really need to bother doing this? I believe we cannot avoid it nor should we try. It's, sort of, be pushed into the briar patch or jump. First, technology is giving us opportunities for growth that are exceeding our ability to manage them. Second, some of these technologies, eg. ISDN and IN, are looking for high value applications. Third, extra management is a value added service with strong value that both CPE and SPE can make a good buck over. It's time to lower our quills and bring the two environments cooperatively together.

BRITISH TELECOM CCITT No.7 PLANNING, DIRECTION AND EXPERIENCE

Derek Ritson

British Telecommunications plc
UK Communications
Network Systems Engineering
151 Gower Street, London, WC1E 6BA

ABSTRACT

British Telecom (BT) has embarked upon a major modernisation programme to replace its existing analogue Public Switched Telephone Network with an Integrated Digital Switching and Signalling Network.

This paper describes the history and evolution of the British Telecom CCITT No.7 Common Channel Signalling (CCS7) Network, its specification and intro-duction into the BT Network, culminating in the establishment of a fully inter-connected CCS7 Toll Network and progress toward a fully digital network for the early 1990's. An overview of the BT digital signalling network architecture and differences between the BT/CCS7 specification and that specified by CCITT in relation to BT's signalling and network requirements is also included. BT's experience of interworking to different implementations of CCS7 both within the BT Network and to other network operators and the need for interworking validation prior to interconnect is examined. The evolution of CCS7 in relation to future new services and the introduction of Intelligent Networks are discussed.

INTRODUCTION

After extensive studies during the late 60's, British Telecom decided that an integrated Digital Switching and Trans-mission Network would be the most economical Telecommunications infra-structure for the future. In the early 70's, British Telecom embarked on a major collaborative development with our UK Switch suppliers to produce a number of compatible modular Digital Switching Systems for Local and Toll Office applications known as System X.

The signalling requirement between System X digital switches is a digital common channel signalling capability based upon the then emerging CCITT Recommendations for Signalling System Number 7.

Subsequently, during the early to mid 80's, competitive tendering for Local Office and Derived Services capabilities introduced AXE10 and 5ESS-PRX digital systems into the BT network all using CCS7 as the signalling medium between switching nodes.

BT IMPLEMENTATION OF CCS7

Standards and Specification Evolution

The signalling interface spec-ifications of the early systems reflected a combined interpretation of the Draft CCITT Recommendations as they were evolving during the 1972 - 1980 CCITT Plenary Periods.

In parallel with the further development of the CCITT recommendations during the period 1975 to 1980, British Telecom, in collaboration with our UK Switch suppliers, together, were developing the first phase of the modular Digital Switching and Signalling Systems and the first implementations were being installed for trial at a number of sites. At this time, certain capabilities such as loadsharing, ISDN and supple-mentary services which BT wished to implement had not been fully defined in the CCITT recommendations. In order to support these and other services, British Telecom felt it necessary to produce its own series of specifications based on the evolving international standards.

The Message Transfer Part differed from the international specification as BT had implemented a loadsharing algorithm between links in a linkset with an even distribution of traffic to available links.

The BT National User Part (NUP) differed from the CCITT TUP in the following areas:

* The BT NUP Supports SIM interchanges and end-to-end signalling for ISDN call set up and for first customer clear as a release protocol;
* BT NUP supports 65536 messages in 256 groups (allowed by an H1/H0 field of 8 bits instead of 4);
* capability is included for more flexible charging requirements;
* additional messages are provided to allow signalling capability to Operator Services Systems;
* provision of a "Version" indicator or compatibility mechanism is included to ensure messages from enhanced or later versions received by an earlier implementation would not result in call failure. e.g. a Red Book implementation could send a message not recognised by a Yellow Book implementation.
* It was not considered necessary for the BT NUP to provide Speech Path continuity check as BT were only intending to implement CCS7 associated with digital transmission routes which have their own inbuilt error detection algorithms.

During 1982/83 in the lead up to competitive procurement, BT produced a specification that was as near the International Standard as possible but would allow interworking to the existing BT CCS7 implementations, and allow evolution toward the International Standard. All BT Network implementations now comply to this specification. This early BT Specification contained :

* Message Transfer protocols complying with the CCITT Yellow Book;
* Basic Telephony protocols;
* ISDN protocols originated via Digital Access Signalling System (DASS), a BT implementation for ISDN;
* Operator Services Protocols.

Resultant upon the Privatisation of BT in 1984, our Telecommunications Licence required BT to allow interconnection at the digital interface with other Network Operators. The need for interworking of interprocessor signalling capabilities to different implementations of switching systems brought new problems to the interworking arrangements and I will address these issues later in the paper.

In 1985 the BT Specification was upgraded to reflect necessary operational changes and to anticipate and reflect draft CCITT recommendations being made available; and again, in 1987, to include changes to the National User Part (NUP) and to reflect the CCITT Red and draft Blue Book Recommendations.

These included :
* Customer Supplementary Services Protocols;
* Closed User Group;
* user access to Calling/Called Line Identity (CLI);
* redirection/diversion of calls;
* calls completion on busy;
* network access to use CLI for Malicious Call Identification (MCI);
* digital connectivity capability (digital path required throughout the routing of the call);
* Selective Barring;
* Network Supplementary Services e.g.
  - Call Dropback protocols
  - Virtual Private Network protocols
  - Centrex Protocols

BT will continue to require implementation of our own NUP until a CCITT Recommended stable separated ISUP is available. BT will review its use of ISUP at that time.

Early Trials and Implementations

The first British telecom working implementation of CCS7 was a point to point trial between two early First Office Applications of the System X Toll (Cambridge) and Local (Arrington) Office

applications and this was undertaken during 1980/81. This system carried test traffic initially, then opened up for controlled live traffic from our Research Department Offices; later, ordinary customers terminated on the Arrington switch were allowed Toll access over the CCS7 signalling link to Cambridge and thereon into the existing analogue Toll Network. This early trial was also used to prove that the new network would interwork with the existing analogue network.

International Trials

With the publication of the CCITT Recommendations in 1980, it was proposed that, rather than establish an International Trial under the aegis of the CCITT, individual manufacturers and Administrations should set up their own trials to prove out the Recommendations.

One of the first working international systems was the point to point trial between a System X implementation at the BT Research Laboratories at Martlesham Heath in Suffolk and an ITT System 1240 at the Bell Telephone Manufacturing Company (BTMC) plant in Antwerp, Belgium during 1982/83. This trial however, only tested MTP interworking.

The principle outcome of this trial was to confirm the general sufficiency of the Recommendations, but identified necessary specification clarifications in relation to the generation of Flags, durations of time-outs and tolerances; without these clarifications, interworking of different implementations could not be assured. These changes were considered by CCITT SG XI/2 for incorporation into the Recommendations. The trial high-lighted the fallibility of specification production and the global interpretation by implementors.

BT/UK Field Trial

During 1983 BT undertook a field trial of a number of sites prior to bringing them into public service, including all available implementations of CCS7 to be introduced into the BT/UKC Network. Included in this trial were four System X digital Toll switches (Edinburgh, Leeds, Coventry and London) and a System X Model at the BT Research Laboratories; the Interworking trial also included CCS7 interworking to one Local Office application parented off the Coventry Toll Unit.

The object of the trial was to confirm the interworking capabilities and network performance under a wide range of operating conditions prior to network modernisation. The opportunity was taken to inject faulty messages and sequences using test equipment - to be described later - and to monitor the effects of overload and recovery actions not possible on live systems.

Penetration of CCS7 into the British Telecom Network

In November 1987 British Telecom achieved its programme of a fully digitally CCS7 interconnected Toll Network comprising 53 System X Toll Switches.

By March 89, BT will have installed and brought into service 1843 Local Office Applications (299 Main Processor Sites and 1544 Remote Concentrators) all using CCS7 to access the digital Toll Network, where each Local Office is parented on two separate Toll Switches for security. By March 1989 it is planned that the Toll Network will be carrying 90% of the long distant traffic.

BT are currently installing new Digital Local Switches, using CCS7 at an average rate of two each working day, to give a fully integrated digital switching and signalling network by 1995.

Operator Services Systems which interface the Digital Local Switches via CCS7 are currently being installed and 50 are programmed to be operational by 1990.

Augmenting the digital network are approximately 500 analogue SPC Systems (TXE4) Local Switches which have been enhanced to accommodate CCS7 Signalling such that the 7 million customers on these modern analogue switches can benefit from the CCS7 capabilities.

In addition British Telecom have introduced CCS7 signalling between an AXE10 international gateway and the Toll Network during late 1986. A Digital International Switching Centre and Operator Services Complex with an International CCS7 capability interworking to the National Signalling Network using CCS7 has been installed and was brought into service early 1988; a further International Switching Gateway interfacing the Toll Network using CCS7 is currently being installed and is planned to come into service later in 1988.

We believe that BT is now operating one of the largest and most complex operational CCS7 Signalling Network in the world currently comprising, a total of 6625 CCS7 links carrying signalling for approximately 200,000 erlangs of traffic - (2915 inter Toll CCS7 Links and 3710 Toll to Local and peripheral CCS7 Links).

AN OVERVIEW OF THE BT SSC7 NETWORK

The structure of the BT Digital National Network is shown in Fig 1.

Customers gain access to the network at the Local Office node which can be either a main processor or a remote concentrator parented off a main processor. Customers can have digital ISDN access or ordinary loop/mf

signalling. The Local Switch Processors are dual parented to at least two Digital Main Network Switching Units (DMSU's) in the National Toll Network.

Specialised services, such as automatic freefone (800) service, are provided by the Derived Services Network. This consists of 10 5ESS-PRX Systems fully interconnected by CCS7 with secured CCS7 links to the Toll Network and are currently being brought into service These 10 Nodes, termed Digital Derived Services Switching Centres (DDSSC's) have access to Network Control Points via the AT&T CCIS interface.

Access to the International Switches is via CCS7 to/from the National Toll Network.

A new digital Operator Services System is currently being installed parented from System X Local Switches using a similar implementation of CCS7 as that used between the System X Main Processor and its Remote Concentrators.

It should be noted that although all BT/UKC digital switches can provide CCS7 STP facilities, currently only a very small percentage of the signalling traffic is routed via STP's and this is planned to reduce as more links are installed. Most signalling traffic is fully associated using the 64Kb/s TS16 of a 30 ch pcm and can address 4096 digital speech circuits within a signalling linkset routed with the transmission circuits.

CONVERSION OF ANALOGUE TO DIGITAL

During the transition between replacement of the analogue signalling network with digital switching and CCS7, the two networks needed to co-exist providing required interconnectivity; the aim being to maximise the use of the new network whilst limiting growth of the old and to minimise the heavy analogue/digital interworking costs of routing calls between the two networks.

The general aim has been to use the new digital network at the earliest possible point in the routing and once into the digital network to remain within it until the call destination. No routings would cross the boundary between the two networks more than once.

To plan and implement the conversion of the total network requires considerable co-ordination over all sectors of the network on a national basis so that digital links are installed in a coherent fashion. Control has been exercised by means of a Network Master Plan which contains the outline plans and objectives for all switching nodes (eg mode of conversion, conversion dates, interconnect routings and version interworking requirements etc.) thus performing a mandatory framework for the detailed implementation, planning and equipment procurement requirements.

BT EXPERIENCES WITH INTRODUCTION OF CCS7

Variety of Systems

Complex Interface Specifications can never be 100% correct, they are continually evolving to reflect the changing customer, regulatory and environmental needs; therefore there will always be specification deficiencies and scope for differences in interpretation by design teams.

With each additional system introduced into the network, the scope for interworking problems increase. Specification interpretation can cause differences in protocols, message sequences, timers, far-near end processor recovery and signalling recovery actions.

BT has ensured that the various implementations of CCS7 will interwork, to provide network wide services and facilities without prejudicing the interworking capability, security and stability of networks and interfacing nodes.

Build Enhancements

CCS7 is evolving and will continue to do so to support new customer and network features by means of new USER Parts (e.g. ISUP, SCCP TC) or enhancements to existing User Parts. The National User Part (NUP), although meeting the overall requirements of CCITT, does not support all messages and may differ in certain respects, such as message length. Interfacing versions of CCS7 must therefore be tolerant of messages from either older or more recent CCS7 version messages being received and should reject unexpected messages in a controlled fashion.

BT has produced a comprehensive set of interworking validation procedures to be established before a new software build or enhancement can be released into the Network and only allows two builds of a particular system (e.g. System X, AXE10) in its Network at any one time.

Interconnect to Other CCS7 Networks

In addition to the complexities of interworking to various implementations of CCS7 within the BT Network, the BT Operating Licence requires us to interconnect with Other UK Network Operators and Administrations Networks within the UK. Also, BT requires access to the International Network using the International version of CCS7.

These other Networks can be grouped into the following major types of operators all of which interface with BT at the digital interface using CCS7:

* Mobile Operators (two separate Cellular Radio systems currently operate in the UK);

* Other UK Licensed Telecommunications Operators (Currently Mercury Communications Limited);
* Other UK Telecommunications Administrations (e.g. Hull Telephone Corporation, Manx, Channel Isles);
* Cross border working (Irish Republic).
* Other International Network Operators using the International version of CCS7.

BT and the interfacing Network Operator must ensure the interworking capability of the different systems which in combination provides the total network services and facilities.

NEED FOR VALIDATION

For these reasons, and those previously mentioned, BT has produced a coherent testing strategy that ensures systems being introduced or enhanced:

* meet BT's Interface Specification on CCS7;
* successfully interwork with other systems in the UK and International Networks;
* ensure introduction would not jeopardise the security and stability of the network, and,
* meet the same criteria of validation.

Some of the test requirements could be provided by the Operations and Maintenance Applications Part (OMAP), however, OMAP cannot be used until full network provision of the Signalling Connection Control Part (SCCP) is implemented. Therefore alternative testing strategies were needed to give sufficient confidence that an implementation of CCS7 could be introduced into the BT network.

Test Specification

The comprehensive generic test specification identifies three types of testing:

    i)   Interface Validation Testing
    ii) Interworking Testing
    ii) Commissioning Testing

Interface Validation Testing

The purpose of Interface Validation Testing is to prove a particular realisation of the Interface conforms to the specification. The tests are divided into protocol, provocative and functional tests.

Protocol tests are concerned with the validation of the sequence and contents of messages passing over the CCS7 interface under test and to prove that these are compliant with the CCS7 interface specifications.

The purpose of a provocative test is to test the performance of the system under test when invalid messages or invalid values are sent to it, to check that it can handle these sequences in a controlled manner without affecting service.

Functional tests are those which use two switches or captive switch models. The objectives of these tests are to prove that in as near a live environment as is possible, the CCS7 realisations are fully compatible.

Interworking Tests

The interworking tests ensure that a new switch system incorporating CCS7 Signalling will interwork with the rest of the network over its CCS7 links. Test traffic is generated to exercise the necessary functions of the CCS7 interface, and, as these may include tests which could endanger the service provided by an operational switch carrying live traffic, they are performed either on a First Office Application before going live or on a non-operational switch (Captive Model).

There are also tests of an Operations and Maintenance, Provocative, and High traffic (message) Overload and Switch System Overload nature, designed to prove that actions at one end of a CCS7 link do not have undesirable effects upon a system at the other end of the link; again, these tests are performed on operational switches not carrying live traffic or on a non-operational switch or captive model.

Commissioning Tests

The purpose of commissioning Tests is to prove that CCS7 Signalling Routes can be added and removed to/from the switch data and to prove that signalling network management actions can be performed. The tests prove that the correct data has been loaded in the switches concerned such that calls can be correctly established.

Test Strategy

For new implementations, comprehensive testing is performed to prove the total implementation of the CCS7 Signalling protocols; for enhancements, an agreed level of re-test and regression testing is performed on captive units prior to loading the build onto a working live system. This is to give sufficient confidence of the implementation prior to loading the new software or installing new or modified hardware for trialling on a working unit before introduction into the network.

Test Equipment

CCS7 implementations do not have the capability to generate or receive corrupted, out of sequence or provocative messages/protocols or to modify timers running on message protocols, to test possible reactions. CCS7 implementations can contain dormant software faults or protocol incompatibilities that only become apparent on interconnection to other implementations.

To assist the test programme, BT have developed a CCS7 Tester called "Martinet (TM)" which is capable of exercising all Level 2, 3 & 4 protocols and is capable of generating messages in any sequence and to adjust timers to test how the product would perform under mis-sequencing and fault conditions. It is therefore possible to test the protocols and facilities of the Message Transfer Part, Telephony and ISDN User Parts, Signalling Connection Control Part and Transaction Capabilities. The use of this tester has proved invaluable to BT in the testing of systems before interconnection or going live and has allowed interworking difficulties to be resolved before live interconnect is established.

Examples of Problems Found from Testing

As with any new development, the testing has identified a number of problems the most significant of which could be attributed to either specification deficiencies or differences in interpretation of the specification which when implemented cause interworking difficulties or incompatibilities. The following are some examples of the types of problems found from BT's testing and in-service experience:

In situations where system software or data becomes corrupted, systems institute recovery actions to refresh their software or data from a known good source. Interworking testing during nodal recovery of different implementations has shown that it is possible for large groups of circuits to be left idle at a recovering node and blocked at an interfacing node without attention being given to maintenance personnel. This can result in large blocks of circuits being removed from service.

During nodal recovery, Blocking or Unblocking messages can be generated by the recovering node over the CCS7 signalling link, at a rate which cannot always be handled by a receiving node. This can cause the receiving node to fail and if not prevented could ripple through the network causing other nodes to fail. BT have arranged that messages are restricted to a manageable rate between systems but defined rates are not currently specified in the CCITT

Recommendations.

The CCITT Recommendation do not indicate mechanisms to relate message rate with processing power for implementors of small systems to adequately cope with receipt of high message rates. BT have found that different implementations message rates and flow control procedures can cause difficulties when signalling between nodes of different processing power. Artificial limits have been set on BT systems to ensure interworking capability but the specification needs clarifying in this area.

A number of interworking incompatibilities relating to message protocols have been resolved as a result of the level of testing performed which would have reduced network performance and would have been extremely difficult to locate once systems were in-service.

FUTURE CCS7 APPLICATIONS

CCS7 is specified to allow evolution to provide enhanced services and facilities. BT see the next stage of evolution to be the implementation of a stable ISDN User Part (ISUP) and both the Signalling Connection Control Part (SCCP) and the Transaction Capabilities Application Part (TCAP) to allow transfer of non-circuit related signalling messages. BT is planning to introduce Intelligent Network capabilities from early 1990 onwards requiring further development of the CCS7 Network to provide SCCP and TCAP capabilities.

The emergence of Intelligent Network requirements with non-circuit related message interactions to network databases will require complex signalling network management requirements.

Once introduced world-wide, CCS7 could be the largest most complex interprocessor communication network, requiring sophisticated management tools and international co-operation during its evolution and enhancement to provide future telecommunication facilities.

CONCLUSIONS

British Telecom has had a CCS7 Network operational since 1981 which now consists of 53 fully interconnected Toll Switches and by March 1989 will include 1855 Local Office Units currently being extended at an average rate of 2 units each working day.

For British Telecom, CCS7 is a considerable success and is now an established capability within our extensive digital network and inter-connects a number of implementations both within the British Telecom Network and to other operators and administrations.

The experience of British Telecom's programme of installing, enhancing and managing such a complex signalling network has highlighted the necessity for strict Software Release control procedures and the validation of interworking between different implementations of CCS7, to ensure continued network coherence.

We believe that British Telecom have one of the largest and most complex operational CCS7 signalling networks in the world and have developed significant expertise in management, enhancement and validation; however, once introduced world-wide, CCS7 will be the largest most complex interprocessor communication network which will require sophisticated management and international co-operation during its evolution and enhancement to provide the necessary new and advanced, efficient telecommunication facilities for the future.

ACKNOWLEDGEMENTS

To The Manager Network Systems Engineering Division for permission to publish this paper; and to Mr K Ward BT/UKC Ch. Eng. NPW. for permission to use extracts from a Paper presented to Aston University, (Birmingham) UK 1987 : Network Planning, Parts 1 & 2.

REFERENCES

Series of articles on CCITT Signalling System No.7: *British Telecommunications. Eng.*, Vol 7 Part 1 April 1988.

MANTERFIELD, R.J. Paper on specification and evolution of CCITT No.7 *International Switching and Signalling Symposium. 1987*

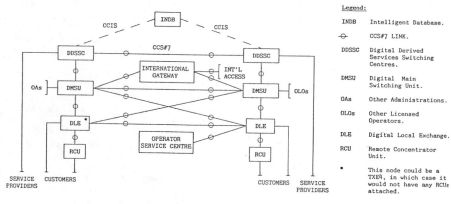

Fig 1   STRUCTURE OF THE BRITISH TELECOM DIGITAL NETWORK

CCS/SS7
WHAT DOES IT MEAN
TO THE CUSTOMERS

TIM A. DUNAR
DIRECTOR,
CONSUMER MARKET MANAGEMENT AND
PLANNING

AMERITECH SERVICES CONSUMER
MARKETING
SUITE 1219
ONE PLAZA EAST
330 E. KILBOURN AVENUE
MILWAUKEE, WI 53202-3176

ABSTRACT

The implementation of Common Channel Signaling/Signaling System 7 (CCS/SS7) technology brings the capability for a wide range of new calling features to the customer via the central office.

In the home the customer will able to redial the phone number of the call he just missed. He will be able to trace annoyance calls. He will be notified when the busy line he just dialed has become free. He will be able to permit calls dialed only from certain numbers to reach his phone.

In the office, the emergence of ISDN and many other new services will greatly enhance voice and data communications.

In short, CCS/SS7 will provide the necessary signaling backbone for a feature-rich set of services that will help meet customer communications needs of the 1990's.

INTRODUCTION

The implementation of a CCS/SS7 network will increase the amount of central office power the BOC can bring to help solve its customers' communications problems. At the same time the BOC is presented with a unique set of problems determining where, when, and how to deploy this technology to maximize the benefits to both its customers and itself.

For purposes of planning, it's important to separate the immediate promises and problems of CCS/SS7 services from the future possibilities of the technology.

CUSTOMER BENEFITS

This paper first discusses the benefits SS7 will bring to the BOC's customers and it then discusses the approach Ameritech Services Marketing is taking in finding answers to questions of maximizing these benefits to both our customers and our corporation.

We'll look at customer needs for which SS7 will provide solutions for four main customer segments: Residence, Business, Exchange Carriers, and Mobile. Our discussion will be limited to only those SS7-related services that have already been developed or are currently being developed for delivery to our customers in the next four years.

Residence/Small Business Customers' Needs

Call management and security are two basic telecommunications needs that residence and small business customers can have satisfied through SS7 services. Each will be discussed in turn below.

Need: Call Management

Residence and small business customers want to screen and manage their inbound and outbound calls. They want to eliminate missed calls, know who is calling, and determine when, if or how to answer the calls.

Evidence supporting this need is demonstrated by the increase in consumer spending levels for multi-function telephone sets and answering machines. These products and services, once thought to be appropriate only for the business consumer, are quickly becoming mass market items as customers' need for call management increases and prices drop.

Solution: Custom Local Area Signaling Services (CLASS)

CLASS is a set of call management capabilities. These central office-based features allow users to screen and manage incoming and outgoing calls. The CCS/SS7 network provides interoffice access to CLASS features, making them much more valuable to the consumer. Some of the CLASS features are outlined below.

Automatic Callback (AC) automatically redials the last incoming call whether or not is was answered. If the line to which the AC request is made is idle, the call is completed. If the line is busy the request

is queued until:
- the line becomes idle and the call can be completed. At that time a special ringback notifies the customer that their AC call is being completed.
- the system deactivates the request because it times out (usually after 30 minutes) or the initial ringback and five subsequent ringbacks are not answered.

Repeat Dialing (RD) automatically redials the last outgoing number called by the customer. If the called line is idle, the call completes immediately. If the called line is busy, the RD request is queued and monitored until:
- both the called line and the calling party's line are idle at which time the call is completed.
- the system deactivates the request because of either an unanswered ringback or the time limit for queueing is reached.

Distinctive Ringing (DR) provides a way to distinguish certain calls from all others by providing a distinctive ringing pattern. These calls may be ones the customer wants to be sure to answer, or to avoid answering. The customer programs numbers into the DR list. When a call comes in from one of those numbers, one of the following occurs:
- if the line is idle, the customer's phone is rung distinctively.
- if the line is active, and the customer subscribes to Call Waiting, the customer hears a distinctive Call Waiting tone.
- if the line is active, and the customer does not have Call Waiting, no call waiting alert is given and the calling party hears a busy signal.

Call Screening (CS) provides customers with the ability to block calls from certain numbers, which may or may not be known to the customer.

Numbers which a customer knows and wants to block are programmed by the customer into a Call Screening list. When a call from that number is made to the customer, the customer is not alerted and the calling party hears a terminating announcement provided by the local operating company.

Upon receiving a call from an unknown number, the customer can activate Call Screening and consequently deny access to further calls from that number.

Selective Call Forwarding (SCF) provides Call Forwarding customers with a means to forward only selected calls to another number. After activating Call Forwarding, the customer programs the directory numbers of the calls he wants forwarded. Incoming calls will then be screened and if they are not on the SCF list, they will not be forwarded and will receive standard treatment.

Customer Originated Trace (COT) can automatically perform a trace of the last incoming call when activated by the customer. The customer is informed that the trace feature has been activated and is told how to follow up on the trace.

Calling Number Delivery (CND) displays the incoming call's directory number on a display device provided by the customer attached to his phone. The directory number of every incoming call is displayed. If the called customer's line is busy, the calling number is displayed only if the customer is alerted to the call by a Call Waiting tone.

Calling Number Delivery Blocking (CNDB) is available to those customers who do not wish to have their number delivered to the calling party. Consequently, if the called party has Calling Number Delivery, the CNDB customer's number will not be displayed. Non-published number customers' numbers are automatically blocked.

Need: Security.

Customers are motivated to enhance home monitoring capabilities and to increase family safety and protection.

Solution: Network 911 Service

Network 911 (N 911) service allows emergency agencies to have access to more complete, accurate, and timely information without relying on the caller, who may be under considerable stress.

Medium and Large Business Customers' Needs

Medium and large business customers' communication needs fall into five areas:
- efficiency
- cost containment
- voice/data integration
- new technology
- greater transmission speeds.
Each will be discussed in turn below with solutions offered by CCS/SS7.

Need: Efficiency.

In past years, increases in productivity for white collar employees have lagged behind increases for blue collar employees. Office of the future technology promised to accelerate increases in white collar productivity and customers are anxious to see its impact.

Solution: LATA-Wide Message Desk

The LATA-Wide Message Desk service will eliminate the time wasted in current message systems. It allows a multi-location user or several users to share a single message desk. This message desk can be located at a remote site.

Need: Cost containment

Cost containment has become a major factor in nearly every business segment. Customers have made it clear that it is important to be able to predict, budget, and control their telecommunications costs.

Solution: LATA-Wide Centrex

LATA-Wide Centrex allows a Centrex system with locations in multiple central offices in a single LATA to have a common dialing plan and to share costly private facilities like WATS lines.

Solution: Virtual Network

Virtual Networks can replace existing under-utilized private lines using the public switched and CCS/SS7 networks.

Need: Voice/data integration.

Separate voice and data transmission facilities are subject to periods of idle time resulting in increased overhead. Integrating voice and data increases the overall efficiency of the network.

Need: New Technology

Large businesses are very interested in using new telecommunications technologies not for the sake of the technology but for its benefits. One example is the growing use of video conferencing for holding meetings and training sessions without the cost of bringing all participants to a common site.

Need: Greater Transmission Speed

Every year the rapid delivery of information is becoming more and more of a marketable asset. Systems sold today must meet the demands for speed and volume of transmission that will be needed over the next few years.

Solution: ISDN

An Integrated Services Digital Network (ISDN) provides an architecture designed to integrate the public network for voice, data, facsimile, and video. A customer can have 64 Kbs channels that provides for video conferencing, or high speed data transmission.

Interexchange Carriers' Needs

Interexchange carriers understand the CCS/SS7 technology and its implications perhaps better than either the residence or business customer. Their need is more directly related to the SS7 technology rather than to a single application that depends on SS7.

Need: SS7

All of the major interexchange carriers have expressed interest in widespread deployment of SS7 in the BOC and are already deploying SS7 in their own networks. The carriers are looking for ways to increase the efficiency of their networks while reducing costs and generating new revenues.

Solution: SS7 At the End Office

SS7 at the end office greatly reduces the call set-up time and consequently, trunk holding time for each call. Hence, IC's increase the efficiency of their network as well as reduce their network investment through internodal trunk saving and switch port savings.

With SS7, 900 Service could be performed without setting up the entire call. Instead, a message containing the dialed number is sent to the IC via SS7 while an announcement is played from the local central office.

SS7 allows IC's to provide interLATA CLASS feature offerings, generating additional revenue for the IC's and making CLASS an even more attractive package of services to the consumer.

Mobile Customers' Needs

Mobile customers need ways to make cellular communications even more useful.

Need: Ubiquitous access

Mobile/cellular telephone users wish to have ubiquitous telecommunications access, without geographic limitations.

Solution: Mobile Roamer Service

Mobile Roamer Service allows a mobile telephone subscriber to receive and place calls in locations other than his "home" location.

CHALLENGE TO THE COMPANIES

Now that we've stated some of the benefits of SS7 features and services to individual customers the problem remains of developing a deployment plan for CCS/SS7. How can we integrate customer information and technical capabilities to achieve effective solutions?

SPECIAL PROBLEMS

The development of a Signaling System 7 deployment plan is heavily influenced by several special problems that haven't been encountered in the analysis of most other telecommunications technologies.

Connectivity

The first special problem is connectivity. For a customer to get value from many Signaling System 7 features it necessary for SS7 capabilities to exist at both the call originating and call terminating point.

Number Delivery is a excellent example of this situation. If only several isolated wire centers in a metropolitan area are equipped with Signaling System 7 it's unlikely that a customer would subscribe to Number Delivery. Only a very limited number of his calls would come from a wire center equipped to send the calling digits. Number Delivery might be interesting but would fall short of being a real call management tool.

Any plan for deploying SS7 technology must anticipate the connectivity necessary for individual services to deliver promised benefits to customers. In an environment of unlimited resources this would pose no problem. Universal deployment could be the solution and connectivity would cease to be an issue. In today's business environment, however, both human and financial resources are limited and thus the analysis of connectivity takes on great importance.

Customer Groups

A second problem is that over time the focus of SS7 feature development will shift from residence services to business services.

In looking at services already developed to take advantage of Signaling System 7 capabilities we see that the initial benefits will come to the residence market and the interexchange carrier market. As time progresses, however, it's clear that benefits to the business customer will rapidly increase. This shifting focus of customer benefits is a factor that a planner must weigh when developing deployment plans.

Complexity

A third problem presented by SS7 services is finding a way to simplify the operation of increasingly complex services so customers will receive maximum benefits from their use. A feature not used is a useless feature.

DEPLOYMENT SOLUTION

In consideration of these problems then, how does an operating company develop an implementation plan that best serves its customer groups? At Ameritech Services Marketing our solution is to develop a modeling technique that measures geographic demand for SS7 services and then evaluates the financial result of each deployment scenario.

There are three major elements in this plan:
- Service Demand Curve Development
- Deployment Scenario Building
- Financial Modeling.

Demand Curve Development

We begin by looking at services already planned for development or already being tested in the field. We develop demand curves for each of these services. This process is more complicated than normal demand curve development because not only are price, quantity, and time variables considered but a connectivity dimension is also introduced.

Each potential service has a unique set of information sources used to develop the individual demand curves.

For example, in developing demand curve for CLASS services we use a combination of primary research and the evaluation of results from CLASS tests in Harrisburg and Orlando as well as Ameritech CLASS tests still underway in Muncie, Indiana.

In developing demand curves for LATA-Wide Centrex and LATA-Wide Message Desk we used primary and secondary research sources as well as information about concentrations of current Centrex customers and concentrations of business customers by size and industry group throughout Ameritech's major LATAs.

These individual curves then become components in the next part of our modeling technique, deployment scenario development.

Scenario Development

Over the past year and a half, Ameritech Services Marketing has developed a database that summarizes by wire center the size and characteristics of each of our important customer segments. This information, when coupled with the demand curves developed for individual SS7 services, is used to test the results of a number of SS7 implementation scenarios for each major LATA in the Ameritech region.

At least ten possible deployment scenarios for each major LATA were tested to determine overall service demand and potential revenue development. Each of these individual scenarios is then carried to the third stage of this process, financial modeling.

Financial Modeling

The cost of the deployment of SS7 for each of these scenarios is then developed. Using cost and revenue projections for each scenarios Ameritech Services Marketing is then able to analyze the best use of company resources in bringing value to our customers from SS7 services.

This process is very flexible. As additional SS7-supported services become identified their demand curves and costs can be incorporated in the process. New scenarios can be built with new financial impacts readily available for analysis.

HUMAN FACTOR PROBLEMS

As mentioned earlier in this paper, Ameritech is very concerned about finding ways to simplify the operations of some of the SS7 services.

In reviewing research from CLASS trials in Harrisburg and Orlando it was clear that problems with customer access and usage of central office features could well be a major stumbling block to bringing the value of those features to individual customers. In our Muncie, Indiana trial, Indiana Bell placed great emphasis on finding and developing network audio information techniques to make feature usage more user friendly.

Ameritech is also heavily involved with many of its business customers as they bring Intelligent Network (IN) and ISDN technologies into their operations.

Although we may not have the final answer to the best way of making features user friendly, Ameritech has a number of efforts underway that will help answer those questions.

CONCLUSION

We have discussed some customer benefits from the use of SS7 services as well as one approach to the question of how to deliver maximum benefits to both our customers and to our companies from the deployment of this technology.

There is great promise in features resulting from CCS/SS7 technology. We feel they will go a long way toward solving many of our customers' major communication problems.

This paper was developed with help from Dave Leuck, Tom Karbowski, and Don Wipfli from Ameritech Services Consumer Marketing.

APPROACHES TO DISTRIBUTED SWITCHING

Gerald J. Butters - Chairperson
Vice President, Marketing
Integrated Network Systems

Northern Telecom Inc.
4001 E. Chapel Hill-Nelson Highway
Research Triangle Park, NC 27709

ABSTRACT

Because the basic design premise of Pulse Code Modulation (PCM) has been carried over from transport into modern digital switch design, the integration of switching and transport functions has blurred the demarcation of these functions. Network systems planners now have many more options to consider when seeking network solutions. Along with more options to consider when seeking network solutions. Along with more options, of course, comes more complexity. As a consequence, the switch and facility planning disciplines often merge into one, creating new job descriptions and training requirements. This seminar will familiarize the various disciplines charged with growing, modernizing and administering an optimum network with the latest technology in distributed switching components.

David Cox   -- Northern Telecom Inc.

John P. Lodwig -- AT&T-Bell Laboratories

Robert P. McDarmont -- NEC America, Inc.

Richard K. Romanow   -- Illinois Bell

STAND-ALONE VS. REMOTE

John P. Lodwig
Director, Dallas Field Office

AT&T-Bell Laboratories
Suite 900, One Main Place
Dallas, Texas 75202

ABSTRACT

Since its introduction in 1982, the 5ESS Switch has evolved its distributed architecture to include a family of remote switching modules. This family of remote switching modules provides all of the CENTREX and ISDN services included in the same basic switching module found in the central office. In addition to the usual pair gain advantage that a remote normally provides, this family of remote switches also offers full stand-alone service. This service offering provides new opportunities for Local Exchange

Carrier (LEC) area planners when considering a Community Dial Office (CDO) replacement, or when competing with a PBX vendor for business opportunities.

This talk focuses on opportunities provided by the 5ESS Switch family of remote switches with stand-alone operational capabilities. It will examine the extension of the base architecture by use of digital T1 and fiber optic interconnection over distances in excess of 100 miles from the host environment.

INTRODUCTION

This paper addresses several scenarios where the 5ESS Switch family of remote switching modules may benefit the Local Exchange Carrier (LEC) as the switch of choice for particular applications. An overview of the 5ESS Switch (Fig.1) as the base provider for both the POTS and ISDN services is examined including:

- Direct loop access to the CO Switching Module (SM).
- Remote SMs.
- SLC access to host (CO) SMs and to remote SMs.
- PBX access to either host CO SMs or remote SMs and
- The ability to provide Stand-Alone call completion for the case of either the host CO SM or the remote SM.

No attempt is made to provide specific cost, since the cost varies depending on the vendor, the buyer, quantity, etc. In addition, cable burial cost varies dramatically, depending on company, rural, suburban, urban, required bandwidth, etc.

For the remainder of this paper the 5ESS Switch Remote Switching Module family will be called RSM except where the specific nature of the application is important. This includes the host/remote(s) arrangement with T1 access (copper or fiber multiplexors) as well as the various directly coupled Optically Remote Module (ORM) options now (or soon to be) available.

LEC CONSIDERATIONS FOR REMOTES

The ability to provide services of interest to the end user at minimal expense, and in a timely manner is extremely important to Local Exchange Carrier (LEC) area planners. These services range from Plain Old Telephone Service (POTS) required by the average home owner, to sophisticated ISDN networking capabilities that challenge advanced PBX service offerings. Although the requirements for these services vary from user to user, it is safe to say that the basic POTS service and many of the advanced ISDN services can be provided by:

- various Central Office (CO configurations
- closely coupled Remote Switching Module(s) found with the more advanced CO switching systems
- the typical digital transmission remote offerings, e.g. SLC-96
- a typical PBX
- various D-Bank plug-ins.

Even the newcomer ISDN service interface can be provided by all of the above, assuming that the host CO Switch or PBX is capable of the service. However, a major distinction associated with providing the service to the end user relates to the ability to continue service when the serving switch enters a stand-alone operational mode. Some remote offerings include stand-alone, some do not. An important question is thus: Remote Vs. Stand-Alone?

From a LEC perspective, services should be provisioned based on the specific application. However, many factors impact the selection of an appropriate customer service interface. Some basic assumptions guiding this paper that relate to these issues are as follows:

- Both residential and business customers require cost effective telephone service. However, business revenues are generally more strategic than those available in the residential market.
- The major LEC competitor for business service offerings is the PBX.
- The modern PBX is strongly oriented towards vertical voice and data services. The ability to provide integrated Local Area Network (LAN) on-site switching is a must for the modern corporate customer.
- CO based ISDN services can allow the LEC to compete with PBX services.
- Recent changes in the tax depreciation laws may encourage past PBX customers to let the LEC assume investment risks.
- Operations, Administration, and Maintenance (OA&M) is an expensive proposition for the LEC (or PBX system). Centralized switch provisioning capabilities, unstaffed

remote switches, continuity of hardware (spares) is a must if the LEC is to be cost effective.
- Positioning of remote switches as Customer Premise Equipment (CPE) is no longer a major legal or technical obstacle (if cost effective).
- Recent advances in Closed Environmental Vault (CEV) technology provides very effective CO equivalent environments.
- The small independent customer (or homeowner) is so distributed that providing the same service reliability as available to the large business customer is not cost effective to that end user.

If we accept the above as reasonable statements pertaining to the major LECs in the USA today, then the primary concerns for those LECs are cost and service reliability, (where cost includes both first cost and maintenance cost). Service reliability can be either part of the base cost or sold as a vertical service to the end user. However, providing the same service with greater reliability, lower first cost, and minimal OA&M cost is typically an important LEC goal.

5ESS SWITCH ARCHITECTURE

The 5ESS Switch is an example of a modern digital switch capable of a wide variety of deployment scenarios. Briefly, the switch has a physical architecture that provides a core administrative module (3B2OD Processor), a center stage Communications Module (CM) switch, and up to 190 local/remote switching modules for loop access. Some of the basic characteristics are as follows:

- Fully duplex processing and message paths are provided for all internal operations.
- Primary Operational Support System interfaces for OA&M are through the AM.
- The CM provides a message path between the AM and the SMs. It also provides the circuit/data path for inter-SM communications. As shown in Fig. 2 & 3, these SMs can be remoted to distances in excess of 100 miles by use of various transmission configurations.
- Each half of the duplex SM is connected to the corresponding half of the duplex CM via 2 Network Control and Timing (NCT) links, for a total of 4 NCT links per SM. Each of the NCT links connecting an SM to the CM

requires two fibers (one transmit, one receive) carrying information at the rate of 32.736 Mbit/Sec. These fibers may be extended up to a 1000 foot limit at the host CO site.

- The SM provides the loop access connections with each SM capable of terminating up to 5000 lines, or 480 digital trunks. Obviously, these numbers are (as with all switches) a function of traffic mix and holding times. But 2000 to 3000 lines/SM is a very real configuration under severe traffic loads. Each SM/RSM has a traffic capacity of 16524 CCS per hour at 90% load.
- Intra-Module call completion (stand-alone) to emergency numbers or other ports on the same SM are inherent in the design. In addition, when in the stand-alone mode, the RSMs can provide all basic CO functions including call completion for all local line and trunk groups terminating on that particular RSM, billing, route to announcement, alternate routing, etc.. This ability will be extended to the integrated Optically Remote Module (ORM) family in the 1988 time frame.
- The 5ESS SMs are capable of providing a broad range of service offerings, including analog, digital, and ISDN line and trunk services. These include the ability to directly connect SLCs and PBXs to the RSM over directly terminated digital facilities.
- The feature set is near to parity with the 1AESS Switch and is growing at a very fast pace.
- Common Channel Signaling System 7 is provided via a Common Network Interface (CNI) Ring that interfaces to the AM.
- Line and trunk testing can be provided on a per SM or RSM basis.
- The 5ESS Switch and all SM types are fully compliant with the FCC rules (part 15J) governing CPE Electro-Magnetic Compatibility (EMC) requirements.

5ESS SWITCH REMOTE SWITCHING MODULE (RSM)

Although first conceived as a remote pair gain switch, since 1985 the RSM has matured into an effective alternative for CDOs and other applications. With its stand-alone capabilities, flexible transmission arrangements, and physical consistency with the host switch, it provides a viable service alternative for many of the following applications:

- CDO substitute.

- Point of presence for private networks (PBX alternative), access tandem switches, toll switches, or CENTREX customers.
- ISDN on-premise voice/data networking.

INITIAL OFFERING

The 5ESS Switch initial RSM offering provided for a remote SM with OA&M access and call control via umbilical DS1 facilities terminating on a Facilities Interface Unit (FIU) at the RSM and on a host SM Digital Line Trunk Unit (DLTU) at the CO site. The DS1 facilities require the RSM (23 voice/data DS0 channels with 1 out of band signaling channel) format, with a minimum of 2 DS1 facilities per RSM and a maximum of 20 DS1 facilities per RSM. The number of DS1 facilities is a function of the traffic between the host and remote locations.

RSM ENHANCEMENTS

In 1985, enhancements to the RSM offering were made to:

- offer clustered (Multi-Module Remote Switching Module (MMRSM)) RSMs.
- provide host independent stand-alone call completion, with alternate routing, billing, traffic measurements, etc. for both the RSM and MMRSM configurations, and
- provide integrated Optically Remote Module (ORM) configurations.

In 1988, all RSM configurations, including the ORM, will provide vertical services in the stand-alone mode. The availability of the various transmission interfaces and specific customer requirements will govern the choice of RSM type. Also, the MMRSM with FIU connectivity offer stand-alone vertical services across site associated RSM boundaries whereas the ORM provides stand-alone vertical services only to terminations on the particular ORM. Communications between ORMs in a stand-alone situation is treated as inter-office trunk connections.

MMRSM - For the MMRSM case, one or more host CO SMs are required to terminate the umbilical DS1 facilities required for OA&M and RSM to CO communications when the RSM is not in stand-alone. The MMRSM configuration can effectively support 10,000 to 14,000 lines depending on the specific traffic criteria of the site location.

ORM - The ORM is configured with

full bandwidth capabilities between the ORM and any other SM/ORM hosted by the same 5ESS Switch. Although, more limited than the RSM in providing inter-ORM vertical services when in the stand-alone mode of operation, the limit on lines and trunk connections is truly the limit of a 5ESS Switch. Also with the availability of diverse routing, and built in protection switching of the 5ESS Switch architecture, this presents no perceptual (or even real) service problem for the end user. With the ever increasing deployment of fiber in the various LATAs, the ORM truly becomes the instrument of choice to compete with the PBX market.

TRANSMISSION INTERFACES

As shown in Fig. 2 and 3, the RSM family can be supported by various transmission interfaces.

MMRSM TRANSMISSION ALTERNATIVES

The RSM interface can be supported by any multiplexing arrangement that supports DS1 signaling, except for satellite communications. Satellite communications introduce excessive delay in the transmission path and would introduce abnormal amounts of echo in the conversation. Some examples shown in Fig. 2 depict the direct T1 connection, optical transmission multiplexing arrangements, and microwave.

5ESS SWITCH ORM ALTERNATIVES

The 5ESS Switch 5E5 (1988) generic Optically Remoted Module (ORM) offering provides for several transmission alternatives with the ability of the ORM to operate in a stand-alone (isolation) environment if the transmission path or host 5ESS Switch becomes inoperative. The term Optically Remoted Module refers to a standard 5ESS Switch Switching Module (SM) whose 4 Network Control and Timing (NCT) links are "stretched" via various optic and electrical transmission equipment beyond the constraints of the host 5ESS Switch location. Three versions of the NCT stretch are available in the 1988 5E5 generic (Fig. 3).

Two-Mile ORM (initially offered in 1985), where the NCT links are literally extended over multi-mode fiber for a distance up to two miles between the CM and the SM. No intervening transmission equipment is required for this case. It relies solely on more sensitive photo-detectors at the CM and SM than normally found when the CM and SM are located in the same physical building.

All 8 fiber paths are required end to end between the CM and ORM. The major advantage for this ORM version is zero transmission equipment cost. Also, with this arrangement and appropriate diverse routing of the fiber paths, complete protection switching of facilities exist as part of the 5ESS Switch duplicated NCT link recovery strategy for SMs.

The 5E3 (1986) ORM with DS3 compatibility provides for the conversion of the 32.768 Mbit/Sec. NCT transmission rate to a standard synchronous DS3 44.736 Mbit/Sec. rate by bit stuffing techniques. This function is provided by a Transmission Rate Converter Unit (TRCU) that outputs DS3 electrical signals to compatible fiber optic transmission equipment. This configuration is referred to as the TRCU-E. The intent is to multiplex all NCT signal paths onto a single fiber transmission path that has protected switching capabilities. With this feature, the ORM can be supported up to the same advertised distance (150 miles) as the RSM. The main advantage with this arrangement is the ability to hop onto backbone DS3 compatible fiber optic transmission networks.

In the 1988 5E5 generic offering, the TRCU is modified to provide a direct 90 Mbit/Sec. multiplexer arrangement that layers two NCT bit stuffed DS3 signals onto a single 90 Mbit/Sec. dedicated fiber optic transmission facility. This configuration is known as the TRCU-O (Transmission Rate Converter Unit – Direct Optical Interface). This version can support ORMs up to 36 miles over single-mode fiber from the host 5ESS Switch without optic regeneration. Also, only 2 transmission links (4 fibers) are required for this arrangement. As in the case of the two mile ORM protection switching is provided as part of the basic 5ESS Switch NCT recovery software. The major advantages of this offering relate to the low transmission cost for extended distances and to the use of AT&Ts DDM1000 Optical Link Interface (OLI) circuits as the optic interface. These OLIs are a proven technology, and by extending their use to the ORM application the LEC is able to reduce their overall circuit spares where they are using DDM1000 units.

In the future, other transmission equipment manufacturers may elect to provide special arrangements for a direct termination for the 5ESS Switch NCT links. However, this equipment must be transparent to the 5ESS Switch internal NCT link recovery strategies and should have a low bit error rate for effective use.

END USER CONFIGURATIONS

Many examples of an end user loop interface can be visualized. Ranging from a farm community of 500 people, with over half of the community communicating to the host switch over lines equipped with range extenders, to the large metro business community, e.g. New York City with its many distributed loop access arrangement to many wire centers within the city. The latter case presents a host of problems different than the former.

RURAL SERVICE

In the case of a rural area, with end users distributed over a large geographical area, it is more typical to find small Community Dial Office (CDO) switches providing individual drop loops to the customer than widespread use of remote loop concentrators, e.g. SLCs. Additionally, the embedded base is probably all copper with only special situations gaining consideration for fiber optic access for trunking or remotes. However, if the rural community is within serving distance of a larger mini-metro area (10,000 plus lines), the use of a remote switch that offers full stand-alone call completion, emergency number routing, centralized OA&M off the host CO, etc., may prove in as a cost effective alternative to providing an independent small CDO for the rural community.

Although the small stand-alone CDO switch can, at first blush, appear less expensive than an RSM if only POTS service is required, the area planner needs to consider sparing costs for circuit packs for a different switch, provisioning consistency, craft familiarity with the product, reliability, etc. that may outweigh the alternative offering.

METRO END USER

The metro environment offers LECs the most diversified challenge in the selection of the right switch configuration. The Chicago, Il., metro area provides service to several million lines. The many Chicago suburbs require service ranging from 1000 to 100,000 lines. The distance between non-corporate communities of interest are usually within a 10 mile radius, with inter-office transmission provided by T1

or fiber. The end user may be the average home owner with a single line appearance, or the milti-location corporate customer with each location requiring several thousand line appearances. Further, the movement of business customers to large multi-corporate park environments offers yet another variable in the selection of the serving switch. These large business customers require private networking capability, with ever increasing emphasis on data networking and uninterrupted service. In many cases the private network aspect of these corporate layouts extend well beyond a specific LATA configuration.

This environment offers many opportunities for the LEC area planners to use the flexibility of the 5ESS Switch RSM family in challenging the PBX offerings to large business customers. Also, the use of CEVs as points of presence in residential and small business areas offers another opportunity to position new services in a cost effective manner. Floor space in the CO is not cheap, and when it is exhausted the ability to place segments of a switch at a new (remote) location can be very attractive from an overall cost and maintenance viewpoint.

SERVICE RELIABILITY

Reliability to the end user has different implications depending on the customer. Basic reliability usually includes the ability to access emergency numbers, e.g. police, fire, hospital, etc. even if normal intra-community call completion has failed. The end user is of course subject to loop access failure due either to the station equipment, or to the loop connection. However, the ability of a switch to provide emergency communications for a community of interest, town, business location, private network, etc., is a significant area of advantage provided by the 5ESS Switch RSM family. Further, the ability to provide enhanced services within that community during an isolation period is becoming more the norm than before. This is especially true for the modern corporate location, with local data base access via on-premise (or protected access) switches. When normal service access to the outside world is lost, call completion for intra-location calls, and data switching capabilities are still a must in order for business to proceed effectively. For inter-location communications, LEC area planners should consider providing adequate diverse routing to minimize the possibility for access interruption. Of course this is true when provisioning for a privately owned company PBX as well as when the LEC is providing the enhanced services to business locations.

Overall call completion reliability can be considered a matter of economics. The 5ESS Switch is fully duplex, capable of providing isolation mode (stand-alone) switching with alternate routing from any serving SM (host or RSM) location. Also, isolation mode local data switching is provided as part of the basic stand-alone capability. If we can bound the question of reliability, and accept it as a cost plus offering commanding premium charges, then the LEC can compete for those PBX customers that desire the level of reliability obtainable with host CO switches or their RSMs. Further, when enhanced services are provided to a business location by the LEC instead of a

PBX, the business customer has the opportunity to redirect capital investments targeted for PBX equipment to other company activities.

CONCLUSIONS

The opportunity for area planners within the LECs is greatly expanded with the availability of RSMs such as those provided by the 5ESS Switch. The full range of CENTREX and ISDN services, initial cost, ongoing maintenance cost, craft familiarity, service reliability, flexible placement, sparing consideration, etc., make the 5ESS Switch RSM family very attractive in the LEC environment. Very key to the RSM service offering is the ability to reduce loop cost to customer premise, and at the same time offer the very important ability to operate in a stand-alone mode. For the ever changing LEC environment, this is a must for today and the future.

5ESS™ Switch System Architecture

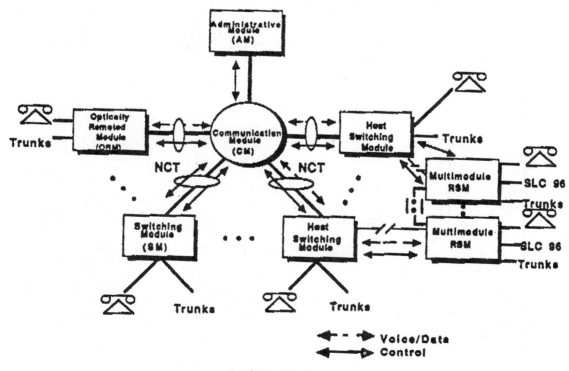

FIGURE 1

FIGURE 2

SELECTED RSM TRANSMISSION ALTERNATIVES

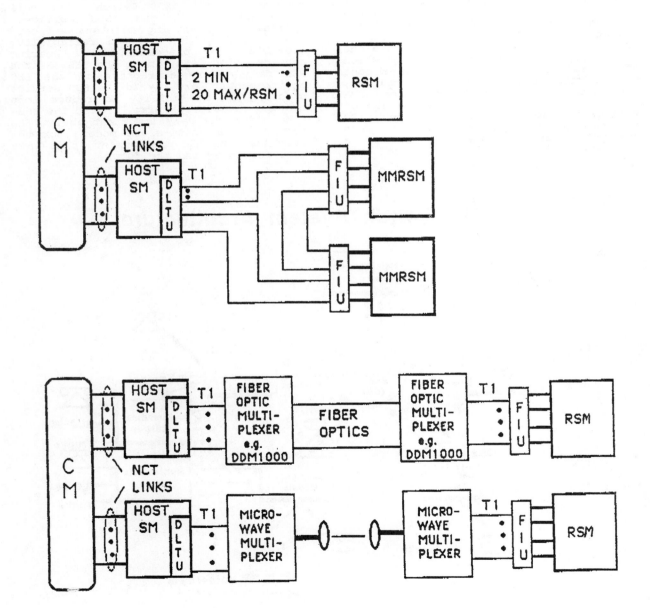

F I G U R E   3

5ESS™ Switch ORM Transmission Interfaces

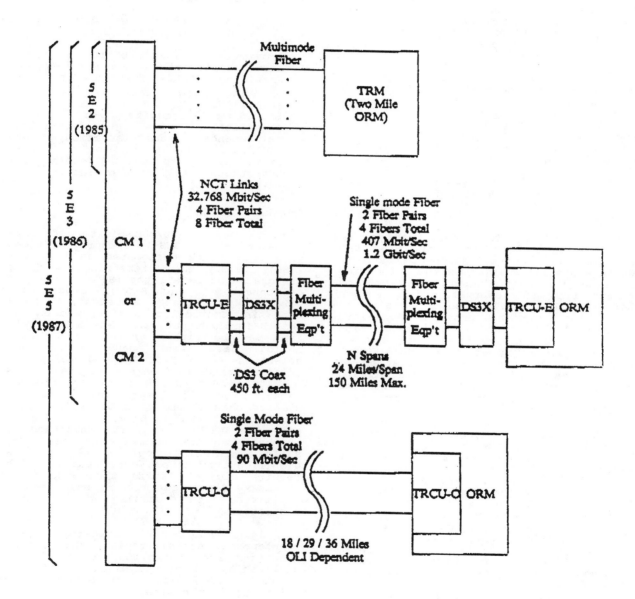

1279

HOST/SATELLITE SWITCHING OFFICE

David P. Cox
Manager, Product Management
DMS-10 Marketing

Northern Telecom Inc.
4001 E. Chapel Hill-Nelson Highway
Research Triangle Park, NC 27709

ABSTRACT

Along with ever-changing technologies in switching and transmission have come a series of unique problems and solutions for the rural network. Until recently, new technologies were designed for existing architecture developed in the 1920s and 1930s. Today, stored program control, along with digital switching and transmission facilities, make changes possible in that architecture to insure flexibility to meet the needs of today's and tomorrow's customers. This paper outlines one of Northern Telecom's solutions to provide this flexibility - the DMS-10 Host Switching Office/Satellite Switching Office (HSO/SSO) cluster configuration.

INTRODUCTION

The first significant change to rural network architecture was the addition of remote equipment modules, which essentially involves the relocation of line equipment frames to a location remote from the central office switch (host). All intelligence is located at the host, which provides complete functional control. Interconnection between host and remote is via digital carriers operating at 1.544 Mb/s (DS-1 spans). This permits centralization of maintenance, administration, and billing functions at the host, but also requires the host intelligence to perform call processing.

The primary source of difficulty with this arrangement is the span line. When span lines to the remote fail, the remote is no longer fully operational. Although most remotes are now equipped with an emergency stand-alone feature, the basic function in this mode is to provide POTS service, while enhanced services such as custom calling features and centrex are usually lost.

Additionally, some remotes provide limited trunking functions for connection to an office other than the host, which allows for emergency calling. However, the full capabilities available when the host span is operational are not possible.

In an urban network, the failure location of the span lines, or the remote itself, are usually accessed easily and repair is expedient. In the rural network, the distance between host and remote is often great, making repair slow and often difficult due to travel time to the site or bad weather conditions which make travel hazardous.

The DMS-10 HSO/SSO was developed to maximize the rural network by:

- Providing reliability and survivability of a stand-alone switch;
- Providing full functionality for trunking and services in the satellite;
- Providing benefits of remote operation; i.e., centralized maintenance, administration, and billing;
- Providing further operational advantages with future evolution.

HSO/SSO CLUSTER

The DMS-10 HSO/SSO cluster consists of stand-alone DMS-10 central offices with one office designated as the host (HSO) and the remaining offices designated as satellites (SSOs). The HSO is connected to each SSO via a dedicated data link terminated at each end to a Data Link Controller card located on the DMS-10 Input/Output (I/O) bus. This data link may be either analog or digital. Analog data link baud rates are selectable from 2400 to 9600 baud and utilize standard modems. Digital links operate at 56Kb/s and may be on channel banks, drop and insert units, or may utilize channel one of a Digital Carrier Module (DCM) in the DMS-10. If channel one of a DCM is used, the remaining 23 channels may be used for trunks. The analog data link approach can have a significant advantage over remotes which require digital links, thus making it necessary for telcos with existing analog facilities to change to digital facilities.

In HSO/SSO clusters, all maintenance, administration, and billing functions are centralized at the host, duplicating one of the major benefits of remotes. All call processing and switching in the satellites occur at the serving office, not at the host, thus providing the reliability of a stand-alone office.

Since no specific criteria exists for designating a particular office as the HSO, an existing group of offices can be converted to an HSO/SSO cluster. Additionally, satellites may be added to an existing cluster at any time, allowing a migratory approach to implementation.

The centralization requires only one I/O device at the HSO for each function, including: maintenance, administration, operational measurements, and service order activity. One I/O device could be used for all functions, depending on the size of the cluster and the ability to handle the amount of data. HSO/SSO also requires only one billing device (magnetic tape or AMA teleprocessing system) at the HSO. There is provision for storing up to five days of AMA billing on the system tape or disk at each satellite as a back-up for use when the data link is inoperable. Once the link operation is restored, the SSO will automatically transmit stored call records to the HSO for collection on the billing device. This feature, called 5-Day AMA Back-up, is included in all satellites equipped with the DMS-10 Input/Output Interface (IOI) unit.

For Operational Support Systems (OSS), functions such as Switching Control Center System (SCCS) and Engineering Administration and Data Acquisition System (EADAS) are also centralized at the HSO.

While this centralization is key to significant cost savings for telcos, the satellite will support its own stand-alone I/O interfaces in conjunction with the HSO if necessary. This will enable, for example, the performance of maintenance diagnostics from the SSO via a maintenance terminal, while service orders are entered at the HSO.

With Equal Access, the point of carrier presence can also be provided by the HSO, with all offices in the cluster being conforming end offices. The HSO can also be arranged as an Access Tandem.

The fact that all switches in the HSO/SSO cluster are stand-alone offices allows the support of trunking and the full line of DMS-10 remotes, and interfaces to subscriber carriers. This provides the telco with full flexibility to configure its network in the most cost-effective way to meet service needs.

DMS-10 HSO/SSO is supported in the 200, 300 and 400 Series. Any Series may be an SSO; however, the HSO must be either a 300 or 400 Series. An HSO/SSO cluster can consist of up to 16 offices with a total network of not more than 17,500 lines. The primary limiting factor on cluster size is the number of messages that can be handled by the HSO while still maintaining call processing integrity for its own lines and trunks. Increased network capacity may be obtained by implementing a Large Cluster Controller, which will be discussed later in this paper.

HSO/SSO CLUSTER MESSAGE TRANSFER

The Data Link Controller (DLC) circuit pack is the key component of the message transfer system between the HSO and SSOs. It provides multi-protocol, dual port control of the digital or analog link. This pack supports Level-2 Link Access Protocol-Balanced (LAPB) protocol, which is compatible with International Standards Organization (ISO) High-Level Data Link Control (HDLC) protocol.

Due to the large number and variety of messages that are possible from SSOs to the HSO, a method of controlling message transfer on the links was devised. This method, called Flow Control, allocates a pool of message buffers in the HSO. Once the SSO has sent the maximum number of messages for which buffer space is allocated, subsequent messages are queued at the SSO. The HSO signals the SSO when message transfer is to resume.

Under normal operation, a pair of duplicated data links are provisioned from each SSO to the HSO for reliability. This duplication includes two DLCs at the HSO for each satellite and two DLCs at each satellite. Each DLC in the pair is accessible by either Central Processing Unit (CPU) in the switch. It is also desirable to utilize diverse routing for the link span lines whenever possible.

However, there can be instances where, due to specific switch configurations, it is necessary to operate with simplex data links. The DMS-10 will allow implementation of single DLCs for satellites, but it is not recommended unless absolutely necessary.

CLUSTER DATA MANAGEMENT SYSTEM

A necessary evolution of the HSO/SSO

cluster concept is the transmission of bulk data between the HSO and the SSO. This capability in the DMS-10 is called Cluster Data Management System (CDMS).

With CDMS, the telco can minimize manpower requirements and travel expense to each office when a generic upgrade is executed. If the new generic program is compatible with the earlier generic program, and no hardware changes are necessary, all functions to be performed during the upgrade can be instituted at the HSO. The data that can be downloaded are all generic programs including:

- Resident program store information;
- Firmware programs;
- Overlay programs;
- Download programs to be loaded to intelligent peripherals.

In addition to downloading generic programs, CDMS also allows SSO office image data to be uploaded to the HSO and stored on a back-up tape. These tapes may be kept at the HSO and updates performed as often as required.

CDMS is designed to insure such that flexibility in call processing or trunking is maintained. The only restrictions for CDMS are that only one SSO can be downloaded at one time, and an Input/Output Interface (IOI) is required in both the HSO and SSO.

LARGE CLUSTER APPLICATIONS

The major concern in the design of HSO/SSO was to ensure call processing integrity at each SSO and at the HSO. With the added responsibilities placed on the HSO for cluster operations, as stated earlier, the cluster line size is limited to 17,500. This proves to be a difficult situation for some telcos with clusters of larger switches. To better enable customers to meet line size requirements and still take advantage of the HSO/SSO concept, Northern Telecom developed the Large Cluster Controller (LCC), increasing capacity of the cluster to 50,000 lines.

The hardware architecture for the LCC is a DMS-10 front end (CPUs, IOI tape drives or disk, and alarm system), and two General Purpose I/O (GPIO) shelves for the DLCs. This equipment is housed in two standard DMS-10 bays with additional room for billing equipment such as the Cook Electric Billing Media Converter.

The LCC becomes the HSO with no call processing responsibilities, therefore allowing full dedication to cluster functions and, in turn, increased line capacity in the cluster. All switching offices become SSOs. In the LCC concept, the LCC may be collocated with a DMS-10, which will operate as a satellite; collocated with a Northern Telecom DMS-100 or another manufacturer's switch; or located somewhere other than a central office - for example, in a telco maintenance center such as SCC or NEMAC, etc. There are three requirements for location of the LCC:

- The same environmental requirements as for a standard DMS-10;
- A central office power and ground source;
- Access to data link facilities, analog or digital.

This arrangement allows a great deal of flexibility in setting up network operations support systems.

The LCC will support 200, 300, and 400 Series SSOs and utilize the same DLCs as HSO/SSO. The data link facilities are also the same as with HSO/SSO; analog pairs, drop and insert units, channel banks, or DCM channel.

Further development has been done to allow more flexible facility access by providing nailed-up connections in the DMS-10. This allows data links to be switched through the DMS-10 network, enabling multiple data links on a single DCM. This feature is operational with or without the LCC. All features associated with HSO/SSO are also supported in the LCC, including CDMS, OSS interfaces, and simplex operation.

FUTURE APPLICATIONS

With the constantly changing needs of today's telecommunications industry, it is essential to continue to evolve the HSO/SSO concept to meet those needs. Many avenues for enhancement are being explored for the role of HSO/SSO with Common Channel Signaling 7 (CCS7) and Integrated Services Digital Network (ISDN).

CONCLUSION

It is quite apparent that the HSO/SSO concept is successful, with over 100 cluster configurations in service today and a growing percentage of requests for HSO/SSO in quotes for new offices. Northern Telecom is dedicated to the further enhancement of the concept and will continue to evolve HSO/SSO to meet the needs of today and tomorrow with CCS7, ISDN, and beyond.

REFERENCES

John M. Wallis "Solutions to Rural Area Networking", Telephone Engineer & Management, Nov. 1985.

DMS and Cook Electric are trademarks of Northern Telecom.

A DIGITAL ADJUNCT APPROACH TO NEW SERVICE PROVISIONING

Robert W. McDarmont
Director of Marketing
Switching Systems Division

NEC America, Inc.
1525 Walnut Hill Lane
Irving, Texas 75038

ABSTRACT

Adjunct systems have been developed for a variety of purposes in the telecommunications industry. Often adjunct systems introduce new technologies and capabilities to the network. This paper discusses the development of adjunct configurations of the NEC NEAX 61E Digital Switching System to provide ISDN and SS7 (Signaling System 7) services to subscribers of older technology Central Office systems. The paper presents an evolutionary path for network modernization, demonstrating how new technologies may be introduced economically and with minimal disruption to existing service.

DISTRIBUTED SWITCHING PHILOSOPHY, ARCHITECTURE AND ECONOMICS

Richard K. Romanow
Manager-Exchange Planning
Fundamental Planning Division

Illinois Bell Telephone Company
225 West Randolph
Chicago, Illinois 60606

ABSTRACT

The deployment of distributive switching architectures commonly referred to as remote switching units (RSUs) and the associated costs and concerns from an administrative and operational perspective have caused a re-evaluation of the study assumptions used to support RSU deployment. This paper addresses the philosophy, architecture and costs used to evaluate RSU deployment in their two most generally accepted configurations--that of the Extended and Modified Extended office. We will explore the established analog architecture, remote switch applications and economics and finally the merit of deploying remote switches in a Modified Extended office configuration. Insights gained through experience with current planning and implementation of these configurations will be shared.

INTRODUCTION

In the last five years remote switch deployments have been aggressively studied and deployed as cost effective vehicles to accommodate growth and provide alternatives to traditional feeder relief technologies such as metallic wire pairs and digital loop carrier systems. The remote switch extends the switching capability of the host central office into the distribution network and is an effective means of providing both standard, switched and Integrated Services Digital Network (ISDN) services where large growth demands are forecasted and the loop transmission requirements are questionable. The actual deployment of this architecture has caused concern in the Operation, Administration and Maintenance (OA&M) areas.

Distributed switching technology deployed in a loop environment raises several administrative and operational issues that should be considered during the planning process. Existing procedures that have evolved to administer traditional loop technologies need revisiting in an RSU environment. Some of the mechanized systems employed to test and provide automatic service order assignments are incapable of functioning in this new environment due to limited software capabilities. The concerns in the OA&M arena have provided the impetus to re-evaluate the study assumptions associated with deploying both Extended (EXO) and Modified Extended (MXO) offices and determine their current cost benefit relationship. Extended office deployment requires all local loops, within the serving area, be recentered to the remote switch distributing frame while the Modified Extended office requires no such recentering effort. The conclusion reached will illustrate that i) distributed switching is here to stay ii) Deployment of Modified Extended offices will continue and iii) the OA&M concerns will be alleviated.

PHILOSOPHY, ARCHITECTURE, AND ECONOMICS

The existing analog architecture consists of an analog central office which provides the switching capability between the customer local loop and the network. It interfaces to the switched network over voice grade facilities (metallic copper pairs) to the customer premise. It is limited in both the distance and services it can provide to both the residence and business customer.

The primary difference between these embedded analog switches and the digital switches which are replacing them is the method of signal transfer within the switch and as such the services which can be accommodated and the speed at which these services can be switched through the network.

In Illinois Bell the major administrative functions are mechanized and include the Loop Facility Assignment and Control System (LFACS), the Computer System for Main Frame Operations (COSMOS) and the Service Order Analysis Control (SOAC) subsystem. These computer based systems provide for the assignment of local loop pairs and central office equipment and ensure flow through operation of service orders with minimal manual assignment required. Central office technicians at both the Switching Control Center (SCC) and central office location provide maintenance and off hour support.

RSUs provide an alternative to traditional feeder relief technologies such as metallic wire pairs and digital loop carrier systems. RSU may be cost effective in areas of large growth demands for traditional switched services and which have a high potential for digital services. In some cases RSUs are deployed for specific customer requirements in lieu of the traditional facility deployment.

Loop deployment of remote switches is normally based upon economic feeder route relief considerations along with requirements for digital services. Initial architectures assumed that loop applications of RSUs would be pair gain devices. The basic components of the remote switch architecture consist of the remote switch, distribution facility and the umbilical facility that connects the remote to the host switch which is usually multiple 1.544 MB/s DS1s. Both the Extended and Modified Extended Office contain these basic components, the quantity of components vary and consequently the cost for implementing each configuration varies.

The administration of the remote configurations are basically identical to the analog environment. The same mechanized systems are employed to control order flow and to maintain minimal manual involvement. In the Extended Office application this procedure works well but as we shall see in the Modified Extended application problems exist and therefore costs increase.

The major support mechanisms perform the same functions as in the analog environment.

The RSU can be economically deployed in the local loop to provide digital services, and reduce the need for additional feeder cable or digital loop carrier for two wire, switched access services. Generally, for voice grade residential service the loop can extend to 18kf on coarse gauge cable, for ISDN 10kf limited on transmission at 32db. Because the need for two wire metallic pairs is greatly reduced in the feeder plant, pair gain with the associated cost reductions are realized.

For individual customers which have large, centrally located requirements for both voice and digital services, RSUs can be economically deployed using the same pair gain rationale. In this instance however, the deployment is usually confined to one customer's requirements and the issue of EXO VS MXO is pre-empted.

Which brings us to the discussion of the Extended Office versus the Modified Extended Office. The EXO configuration requires that all subscriber lines, within the RSA be recentered to the Remote Distributing Frame at cutover. This means that the new RSU must be capable of supporting the traffic associated with the embedded base (those lines to be recentered) in addition to the growth requirements expected within the new RSA, over the study period. The additional costs associated with equipping the new remote to accommodate the embedded lines must also be taken into consideration which include the expense to recenter the distribution plant from the host location to the new RDF.

The MXO configuration requires that we accommodate only anticipated growth and eliminates the need to recenter any existing lines. Existing customers retain the copper facility to the analog switch. Telephone number changes and the cost to equip additional line appearances are avoided, however, administrative penalties are incurred in the order flow process because the mechanized systems we employ to install switched services (LFACS, COSMOS, SOAC etc) are not capable of making automatic assignments and consequently this arrangement requires manual intervention which reduces efficiency and increases administrative costs. To determine the relative economic merit of providing an EXO or MXO configuration, certain parameters must be defined and their profiles established.

The first profile requiring definition is the particular area to be considered for RSU deployment or the Remote Serving Area (RSA). This area must be determined by using as many known inputs as possible along with engineering judgment. Proximity to an existing host switch, available vacant land, anticipated growth potential and type of community, whether business or residence, are some of the parameters used to define the initial study area. Once this overall area is defined, it is segmented into smaller areas called CSAs for an in-depth analysis.

Once the study area is defined a forecast is requested to determine the type and amount of requirements anticipated. The results of this forecast will determine whether the study should continue. Should the forecast be too low or the requirements only for switched services this area may not be a proper candidate for RSU deployment.

One major component for cost consideration is the hardware associated with the remote, its manufacture, engineering and installation. For our analysis we will assume an average line cost of $350 per line.

Loop costs include expenditures associated with the placement of additional cable, conduit, trenching and rearrangement of local facilities to the remote building. For the purpose of this study we will assume a cost of $50 per

line for new structure and copper and $30 per line for transfer of working lines into the remote. We will assume that the new switch will be located adjacent to a major conduit or facility path.

Umbilical facilities which connect the remote to the host switch is provided over fiber and at the 1.544 MB/s rate. For the purpose of this study assume 16 DS1s at 20KFT; cost is $75,000 for electronics, fiber and establishing the facility.

Building size is estimated at 30ft X 40ft with a per square foot cost of $225. These costs would be common to any alternative where reinforcement is required due to growth requirements. Land is required at a cost of $3.50 per square foot; land is estimated at $177,000 which will accommodate the future need to convert to stand alone switch operation once this remote reaches capacity exhaust.

Maintenance costs are assumed common to each alternative although under most circumstances there could be a reduction in maintenance costs associated with the placement of a RSU.

Administration costs vary with the type of deployment; for an extended office the administration costs are assumed equal to the existing arrangement for modified extended deployment the costs on average are $10,000 per year.

Additional parameters that will influence our analysis is the current number of stations within the RSA which we estimate at 2000 and the growth rate per year forecasted at 650. We anticipate conversion in 1990 at which time 3300 stations will be in service.

From this information we can construct the major cost components of the study, namely:

RSU DEPLOYMENT

SWITCH	1,610,000	$350*(3300+1300) RECENTERED
	455,000	$350*(1300) NOT RECENTERED
LOOP	230,000	$50*4600 RECENTERED
	99,000	$30*3300 RECENTERED
	65,000	$50*1300-- NOT RECENTERED
UMBILICAL FACILITY	75,000	
BUILDING	270,000	$225*(30*40)
LAND	177,000	

```
ADMINIS-      10,000   PER YR. FOR MODIFIED
TRATION.                           EXTENDED
```

PAIR GAIN DEPLOYMENT-
ASSUMES NO RECENTERING:

```
SWITCH       455,000   $350*1300
LOOP          65,000   $50*1300
PAIR GAIN    570,000   96*.72=69 AVG. FILL
                       1300/69=19 SYSTEMS*
                       $30,000=$570,000
UMBILICAL
 FACILITY     75,000
BUILDING     270,000   $225*(30*40)
LAND         177,000
ADMINIS-
 TRATION      10,000
```
Maintenance costs are assumed common to
each alternative.

AGGREGATED FIRST COST COMPONENTS

```
NEW REMOTE WITHOUT RECENTERING  1,052,000
PAIR GAIN ALTERNATIVE - NO
                  RECENTERING   1,622,000
NEW REMOTE WITH RECENTERING     2,471,000
PAIR GAIN ALTERNATIVE-
                  RECENTERING   3,107,000
```

The most economic alternative on a first cost basis is the new remote without recentering followed by the pair gain without recentering and finally the remote with recentering. The estimated costs associated with the recentering component for the pair gain solution is $1.485M and if added to the pair gain solution would bring the total to $3.107M which is the least economically feasible alternative and assumes re-use of the existing central office equipment.

We have seen the costs to implement the RSU in a modified Extended configuration is considerably less on a first cost basis than that of an Extended office application. The incremental cost difference, between these configurations, is approximately $1.4M.

The administration of the remote in a modified extended application adds approximately $10,000 a year to the cost component. Quadrupling this cost for the sake of argument still has a negligible affect on the total savings. The need to administer the local loop however has an intangible constraint which is difficult to quantify; the need to manually assign the local loop onto service orders. In our effort to mechanize the assignment process we neglected to foresee the potential remote implications and consequently do not have the flexibility

to assign local facilities based on prefix and local address. These constraints are currently being reviewed to determine software changes that will provide sufficient assignment flexibility so that our drive to mechanize does not restrict our deployment of Modified Extended offices and that our need to deploy Modified Extended offices does not impose additional cost expenditures in the service order and operations arena.

From a facility perspective the Extended office provides a neat, clean definition of where each local facility, for a specific geographical area terminates. This allows for efficiency in developing loop plans and provides for ease of maintenance, however as we have seen the costs to recenter the existing plan can be considerable from both a local loop and central office perspective.

Both the Extended and Modified configurations can accommodate digital services such as ISDN however, only loop facilities terminated on the remote distributing frame can be provided these services; those lines in the MXO configuration which are not recentered cannot directly benefit from the installation of the remote. The application of the MXO does not preclude selective recentering however, with recentering comes the issue of telephone number changes which must be considered in relation to customer impact.

SUMMARY AND CONCLUSIONS

We have seen that the basic distributed switching architecture consists of a host digital switch with one or more remote switches placed in the distribution network and connected by umbilical facilities at the 1.544 MB/s rate. One of two configurations, the Extended or the Modified Extended office is deployed. The line capacity of each of these remotes is between 5000 and 11000 POTS access lines.

In addition we have seen the major application of these configurations is when you have a moderate embedded line base in a geographical area which is forecasted to experience substantial growth in a relatively short period of time. Sizable business penetration with requirements for digital technology will enhance RSU deployment potential. The Extended office is more appropriate when line growth is large and the embedded base is small, thereby minimizing costs associated with recentering. The Modified Extended office is appropriate when a large embedded line base exists and the cost to recenter the base exceed the economic benefit derived.

Factors which will influence the study outcome include the geography, forecast, and services and costs associated with the RSU deployment. In addition the Operational, Administrative and Maintenance concerns need consideration as well as the mechanized systems which support service order installation activity.

The economic advantage of RSU deployment over pair gain systems and copper facility placement can be considerable. The cost factors discussed lead one to believe that the administrative penalties do not outweigh the benefits of MXO deployment.

In conclusion, the application of distributed switching will continue to be deployed as an economical pair gain device to support digital services and growth in the distribution network with large customer requirements being satisfied by strategically placed RSUs. MXO deployments will remain in the planning arsenal as an appropriate deployment architecture. OA&M and mechanized systems that support service order activity will need to accommodate this architecture and steps are being taken to ensure this accommodation takes place.

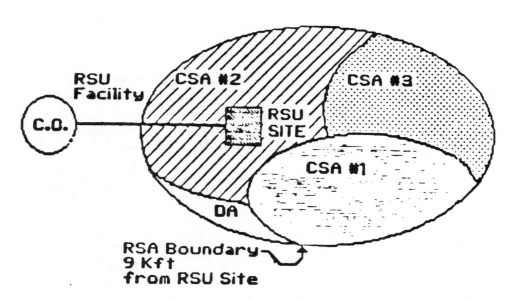

TYPICAL RSA SERVING ARRANGEMENT

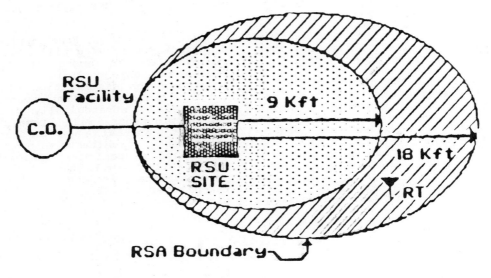

RSU EXTENDED TO 18 KFT

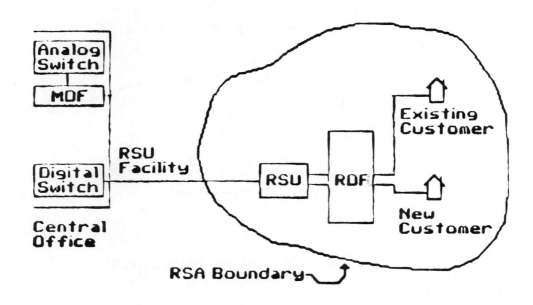

EXTENDED OFFICE APPLICATION

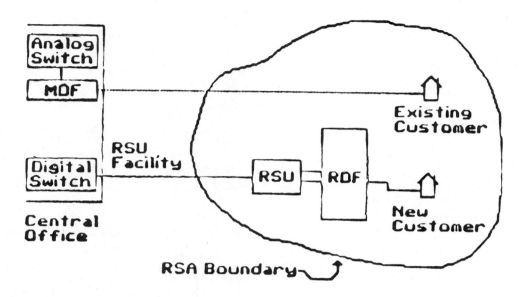

MODIFIED EXTENDED RSU APPLICATION

GLOSSARY

Acronyms and Definitions:

RSU- Remote Switching Unit; An extension of the switching capability of the host central office which provides an alternative to traditional feeder relief technologies (e.g. metallic pairs, digital loop carrier).

EXO- Extended Central Office; The application of a RSU where the defined serving area is totally recentered to the main distribution frame of the RSU. All designated facilities for this geographical area would now terminate on the RSU frame.

MXO- Modified Extended Office; In this RSU application the embedded customer facilities remain at the host switch distribution frame while new customer (e.g. new construction) are provided at the remote switch frame.

RSA- Remote Serving Area; The geographical area for which the remote switch will provide service. In the case of the Modified Extended Office service is provided to new customers (subsequent to the switch being established) only.

CSA- Customer Serving Area; A subset geographical area which for study purposes further partitions the RSA into smaller areas. The combined CSAs make up an RSA.

CUCRIT- Capital Utilization Criteria; The computer based economics program used to develop the incremental cost analysis between two mutually exclusive alternatives. Program output includes, but is not limited to Net Present Value, Net Present Worth of Expenditures and provides various reports associated with the cash flows for each alternative studied.

DSW-10

INTEGRATING PACKET SWITCHING TECHNOLOGY INTO DIGITAL SWITCHING

Richard B. Brownfield, Chairperson
Director, Sales

Northern Telecom, Inc.
Central Region
155 E. Algonquin Road
Arlington Heights, Illinois 60005

ABSTRACT

The foundation of the voice network is firmly grounded in digital switching technology, and the services provided by the network for users at all levels of sophistication have dramatically migrated from analog systems using basic switched-circuit connectivity to virtual networks imbedded in an ISDN environment.

The challenge of virtual network technology is to maximize the utilization of scarce network resources while optimizing the efficiencies of both voice and data transport. The purpose of this seminar is to explore the new ISDN network topology, to examine ISDN switch/packet applications in system applications, and discuss network applications for integrated voice/data systems in the evolving ISDN/SS7 network.

Richard Brownfield -- Sales Engineer, Northern Telecom
Richard Dillon -- ISDN Data Consultant, AT&T
Mitchell Moore -- Account Manager, Siemens Public Switching Systems

INTEGRATED ACCESS TOPOLOGY OVERVIEW

Mitchell S. Moore
Account Manager

Siemens Public Switching Systems
2136 Gallows Road, Suite G
Dunnloring, VA 22027

ABSTRACT

This session presents a detailed description of the ISDN network topology with a specific focus on the switched circuit/packet interface. The main emphasis will be on describing the flow of data through a typical node from the subscriber source (either ISDN 2B+D or ISDN 23+B) to a packet network, and on discussing the structure and functionality of interface protocols used on both the subscriber interface and the packet network interface.

The EWSD Central Office Switching Architecture - An Overview: The Siemens EWSD central office switch is a modular design that is based on multimicroprocessor technology. In its full configuration, the EWSD can interface up to 100,000 subscriber lines (@3 CCS), and is capable of performance exceeding 900,000 busy-hour call attempts (BHCA). Targeted primarily as a Class 5 central office switch in North America, the EWSD is the flagship offering in the Siemens ISDN product family.

Figure 1 shows a block diagram of the EWSD architecture. Subscriber interface modules include the Remote Line Unit (RLU), the Host Digital Line Unit (DLU-H) and the Pair-Gain Digital Line Unit (DLU-PG). The DLU-H and the RLU each interface in excess of 900 subscriber loops; the DLU-H is typically colocated with the rest of the EWSD switching elements, whereas the RLU is deployed in a location remote to the rest of the switch. The subscriber interface modules attached to the Line/Trunk Group (LTG) modules via 4 DS-1 facilities. As show in the figure, a subscriber line unit can terminate on more than one LTG for enhanced reliability. The switching function in the EWSD is performed by the switching Network (SN), which operates under the supervision of the Coordination Processor (CP). The CP also supports the Operations, Administration and Maintenance (OA&M) interface for the EWSD. Finally, digital trunks and signalling links (SS7) are supported directly by the LTGs; analog trunking facilities are derived through the use of Channel Banks (CB).

Figure 2 expands on the block diagram previously shown, with an emphasis on the internal EWSD digital interfaces. As mentioned previously, the DLUs interface to the LTGs via DS-1 facilities. The interface between the LTGs and the SN is an 8 Mbit channel.

Figure 3 shows a detailed block diagram of the DLU and of the Subscriber Line Module (SLM) cards internal to the DLU. Each SLM can interface up to 8 subscriber loops via Subscriber Line Interface Controllers (SLIC). The SLMs (and associated SLICs) are attached to a dual 4 Mbit PCM network whose output interfaces to dual redundant Digital Interface Units (DIU) for conversion to the DS-1 trunking format. A separate control network (SLMCPs and DICCs) is resident in the DLU to handle signalling and coordination of events within that DLU.

Integrating ISDN into the EWSD Architecture: Due to its modular architecture, addition of ISDN capability to the EWSD is a simple process. Figure 4 shows that support of the Basic ISDN access scheme (2B+D) is accomplished by the addition of a Digital Subscriber Line Module (SLMD) to the DLU. Primary ISDN access arrangements (23B+D) are handled directly by the LTGs in the EWSD architecture. The LTGs also provide direct interface capability for various Service Modules (SM), one of which is often a packet server module for access to packet switched data networks.

Figure 5 summarizes the components of the Basic ISDN access interface to the EWSD. The block marked "Line Terminator" in the diagram corresponds to the SLMD in the previous figure. The subscriber loop interface between the SLMD and the Network Channel Terminating Equipment (NT) on the subscriber premises is called the U interface. The U interface is non-standard, network-dependent interface. The characteristics of the U interface in the EWSD architecture are listed in Figure 6. Note that a 4B3T block encoding scheme is utilized on the U channel, permitting the 160 kbps 2B+D structure to be carried over 120 kbuad of total bandwidth.

Returning to Figure 5, it is seen that, on the customer side of the NT, the interface to various ISDN-compatible terminal devices is called the S/T interface. The S/T interface is a standard CCITT interface consisting of three protocol layers (per OSI); physical, link and network. The physical layer is described in detail by CCITT Recommendations I.430 and I.431 (1984); the link layer likewise in I.440 and I.441 (1984), and the network layer in I.450 and I.451 (1984). The characteristics of this CCITT standard "2B+D" interface are shown in Figure 7. Note that the S/T interface is a multistation configuration, capable of supporting up to 8 ISDN-compatible terminal devices.

Finally, returning again to Figure 5, it can be seen that existing non-ISDN-compatible terminal equipment can interface to the ISDN through the use of a Terminal Adaptor. A Terminal Adaptor is a device that convert non-ISDN standard protocols for transport within the framework of the 2B+D channel structure. Common Terminal Adaptor functions are shown in Figure 8. The "R" interface protocol can be any one of a number of current standard protocols, including asynchronous, bisynchronous, SNA/SDLC and X.25. Terminal Adaptor Functionality is limited only by the offerings of the vendors of the devices. In theory, any non-ISDN standard protocol can be transported over the Basic ISDN Access Interface (S/T) through the use of a Terminal Adaptor.

Figure 9 schematically illustrates the implementation if the ISDN Basic Rate

Interface in the EWSD architecture. The U link carries the Siemens-specific protocol between the SLMD in the DLU and the NT on the customer's premises. The S link carries CCITT standard protocols between the ISDN terminal(s) and the NT 2B+D format. Note that call-control procedures (layer 3, I.451) are transported between the ISDN terminal and the processor in the LTG via the S link and the U link. Support of Packet-Mode Data Transport in the EWSD ISDN Architecture: Packet mode data transport can be accomplished in two basic ways on an ISDN network. Packets can travel over the ISDN B channel at 64 kbps, or they can travel over the ISDN D channel, among the D-channel signalling information. In the EWSD architecture, a Packet Switch Service Module (PSSM) is required in each case, as shown in Figure 10. The PSSM is a LAP-D compatible packet switch that provides an interface between an LTG in the EWSD and X.25/X.75 compatible devices/networks. With the PSSM in place, data from a high-speed packet mode terminal (e.g., an X.25 host computer) can be transported over an ISDN B channel, and switched to the PSSM by the SN. For low-speed packet applications, the ISDN D channel can be used to transport end-user data packets. Figure 10 shows that, on the SLDM, the D channel is split from the 2 B channels and is sent to a microprocessor (MP) for further processing. The MP separates signalling frames from user data frames, sending the signalling data on to the CP via the appropriate LTG. The end-user packet data is multiplexed onto a nailed-up connection through the SN, and is thus forwarded to the PSSM for switching to the appropriate destination.

Figure 11 shows several packet applications as they would be implemented on an EWSD ISDN island. Note that, through the use of Tas, many different terminal types can access the PSSM. X.25-type DTEs can interface to the ISDN either directly through a Terminal Adaptor, or indirectly through the PSSM. The degree of connectivity offered to packet mode applications by the EWSD ISDN concept is indeed very high.

Figure 12 shows a specific customer application, namely telemetry of environmental information between building sensors and a remote host computer location via the EWSD ISDN. Note that the ISDN D channel is used for this low-speed data application. The EWSD routes the telemetry data to its destination via the PSSM, which in turn provides a direct X.25 interface to the telemetry host.

INTEGRATED ACCESS APPLICATION

Richard Dillon
ISDN Data Consultant

AT&T

2600 Warrenville Road
Lisle, IL 60532

ABSTRACT

The session examines an approach to the integration of packet-switched data into digital switching, using the 5ESS switch as a model. AT&T field trials are used as the source for performance date. The session provides an overview of an application, PC networking, utilizing an ISDN basic rate interface for integrated access, the performance issues involved, and the administration and maintenance of the user network.

NETWORK APPLICATIONS

Richard Brownfield
Director, Sales

Northern Telecom Inc.

155 E. Algonquin Road
Arlington Heights, IL 60005

ABSTRACT

This session explores network applications arising from the successful integration of voice and data in an ISDN environment. Specific trends examined are the synergies resulting from merging of ISDN islands, emergence of SS-7 signaling for integrated voice/data nodes, and impact of virtual networks on the switching node. The Northern Telecom DMS-SuperNode is used as a model to illustrate specific future applications.

DSW-11
USER PROGRAMMABILITY OF SWITCHES - THE FUTURE

Jerry L. Rhattigan, Chairperson
Vice President, Central Region

Northern Telecom Inc.,
155 E. Algonquin Road
Arlington Heights, IL 60005
(312) 981-5344

"User Programmability of
Switches - The Future"

ABSTRACT

There are no limits to the control, flexibility and end-user feature availability that stored program digital switches can provide. But finding the optimum balance between the market needs of the end-user and smooth operation from the perspective of the telephone company and the switch manufacturer is no simple task.

This seminar presents the various viewpoints evaluating the needs and restrictions faced by each group. Key influences are identified and the factors the identify optimum - and profitable - operation are addressed.

At the conclusion of the presentations the speakers will conduct panel a discussion to address questions raised in the session.

Raymond F. Albers
Assistant Vice President
Technology Planning

Bell Atlantic
1210 N. Court Road 3rd floor
Arlington, Virginia, 22201

Peter E. Jackson
Vice President, Applied Technology

SBC Technology Resources, Inc.,
Applied Technology
One Bell Center, Room 37-E-06
St. Louis, MO 63101

Roger Schwantes
Vice President
Product & Technology Planning

Northern Telecom Inc.,
200 Athens Way
Nashville, TN 37228

PROGRAMMABILITY FOR SWITCHED SERVICES - BELL ATLANTIC PERSPECTIVE

Raymond F. Albers
Assistant Vice President
Technology Planning

Bell Atlantic

1210 N. Court Road 3rd Floor
Arlington, Virginia, USA

ABSTRACT

Increasingly powerful computerization of switching systems, signaling systems, network data bases and terminal equipment has made possible increasing flexibility and customization of customer services. Yet BOC's like Bell Atlantic, who provide switched network services to customers but are not permitted to manufacture telecommunications equipment, are unable, today, to effect delivery of customized services. This paper explores possible evolution of switches and networks to place more control in the hands of the service provider.

SERVICE INTELLIGENCE

Designers and Providers of Telecommunications Networks, services and equipment continually make decision or develop opinions as to where the "intelligence" for telecommunications services ought to reside. Should it reside in the telephones, terminals and computer equipment connected to the network? In the switching system that serves a particular customer's premises (i.e., a PBX) or a particular geographic area (i.e., central office)? Or, as is becoming increasingly feasible in separate nodes located either within the telephone network or on service providers premises?

While the service providers continue pondering all this, most end users of course neither know nor care where the intelligence resides. The answer they would give - and we providers ought to listen to them - is that the intelligence should reside wherever it needs to provide the best and most cost effective service to meet their needs.

In fact, for most service there is no single answer. Certainly if one looks at all the services a particular customer uses, there is no single answer. The intelligence will reside more than one place, to give individual users options. My favorite simple example is speed dialing. One can buy telephone sets with built in automatic dialers, or one can subscribe to "speed calling" from the telephone company. The former might work best for a customer who makes most telephone calls from one set (e.g., in an office) and wants the convenience of having the telephone directory and the push buttons all in the same instrument. Speed calling from the central office, on the other hand, might be best for a residence customer who already has a large number of extension phones without built -in dialers, and wants the convenience of abbreviated dialing from every telephone. in the house.

NETWORK-BASED INTELLIGENCE EVOLUTION

From a network provider's perspective, Bell Atlantic is of course primarily interested in being able to provide intelligent services from within the network, in order to be responsive to its customer's needs and to complement, as well as to compete with, intelligence provided from premises products and terminal equipment.

Figure 1 represents a view of the evolution of intelligence within the network. Ever since the advent of stored program controlled switching in the late 1960's, virtually all feature functionality has been located in the software of the switch serving the individual customer. This is still the predominant situation today, although we have begun to evolve to the next two stages: switches linked via common channel signaling, and the use of centralized routing nodes within the network.

COMMON CHANNEL SIGNALING

As we begin to deploy common channel signaling, the processors of the switches serving the calling customers can begin to communicate with each other for additional call and feature control. This is typified by the family of CLASS services, which depend primarily on the ability to pass identity of the calling number to the called central office, and the ability to pass status information (e.g., busy or idle status of a particular line) between the two switch processors.

Common Channel Signaling also makes it possible for a switch processor to communicate with another network element to get additional call processing instructions. The 800 service is the first example of the use of centralizes routing nodes within the network.

NETWORK-Terminal Interaction

As we start to deploy ISDN services, we will move to the phase of increased control of network features by the customer's terminal equipment. Prior to ISDN even though the central office switch is digital, and is connected to other switches via digital facilities, the line to the customer remains analog and is limited in its signaling and control functionalities to fairly elementary DC and inband tone signaling. The ISDN separate D signaling channel with its data communication protocol orientation, presents an opportunity for an immensely rich variety of signaling, information, status, and control messages to be passed between the terminal equipment and the switching system, and thence to the rest of the network.

Control Nodes

The next phase of the evolution, which I have here labeled "switching control nodes," is an extension of the routing control node concept used for the 800 service. This is the focus of the "Intelligent Network" research currently being conducted by Bell Atlantic, the other Regional Operating Companies, and Bell Communications Research. The idea here is that telephone companies, or any agent they chose, would be able to develop software that would control switching feature of numerous connected switches in order to be able to bring customized services to individual customers, or to trial and deliver new services to a mass market.

Assuming that this major effort can be successfully carried out, a logical next step would be to partition this capability so that individual users - perhaps at first the communications managers of large multi- line customers and later even single line business and residence customers - would be able to customize features that are available on their lines without adversely impacting other people's lines.

SWITCH SOFTWARE DEVELOPMENT

Feature software today

If we examine where we are today with the feature software in switching systems, we see that it is a situation of virtually total control by the switching system vendor. Although the switch suppliers will attempt to meet the telephone companies needs, the fact is that today the assignment of develop- ment priorities, the details of feature operation, date of availability, and the price charged to the operating company is under control of the switch manufacturer.

The telephone company's role in providing features to customers is limited to one of switch administration - that is, turning on or turning off a particular feature for a particular subscriber line, or changing parameters such as the "forward-to" number for call forwarding busy/don't answer. The user - our customer - has even less control. Our customer is limited primarily to invoking features that have been made available by the manufacturer and enabled by the telephone company, for example activating or deactivating call forwarding and dialing a speed calling code. The user can also make small changes in parameters, for example changing the numbers on one's speed calling list. Independently of the switch software, we have begun to increase the customer's control by providing access to some of the switch administration systems that are uses by the telephone company. Perhaps the best example here is the Centrex Customer Rearrangement System, which allows Centrex customers to change numbers and features on individual users' lines.

BOC Control

What we need is more control of the switch features by the service providers. The intelligent network effort is aimed in this direction. Another approach being explored by some switching equipment manufacturers is the notion of allowing the telephone companies to participate in the switch software development process. The two principal paths here are partitioning to switch software in such a way as to allow the telephone companies to have access to portions of it without adversely impacting the rest of the code, and having telephone company personnel working hand in hand with the switch vendors' own software development team to accelerate the feature development process. These approaches have the potential of providing relief prior to the availability of the intelligent network, or serving as a useful complement to the intelligent network by providing a means by which feature software can be moved back into the switch when a service has been successfully trailed in the intelligent network mode.

In evaluating various proposals and alternative methods of achieving th feature development control we need Bell Atlantic has developed several metrics.

The first thing we look at is the degree of Bell Atlantic control. That is, is Bell Atlantic the final arbiter of how, when and whether the feature is implemented, and the precise definition and operation of the feature, or does the switch vendor still retain some degree of "veto power".

The second concern is the speed of implementation, and this has two facets: how quickly can the software development process be put into place, and then once it is in place, how long does it take to develop and deliver an individual feature.

Finally, and by no means least important, is the cost. Here again there are two facets: what is the cost of developing a programmable switch, or of building up a cadre of systems engineers and programmers who can do the feature definition

and software coding and secondly, once all this has been put into place, how much does it cost us to develop the next new feature or family of features.

Switch Development Process

The current switch feature development cycle is complex, takes a long time, and involves interaction at many levels among multiple engineering and development organizations. Figure 2 is an attempt to depict the stages of this process. While different vendors will have different names for the various stages, and perhaps have a lesser or greater number of individual stages named and defined, this probably represents a reasonable view of the key stages in the process. Note particularly that the process is not completely serial. That is the next step, and perhaps even the succeeding one, will begin before one step end necessitating complex interactions among the teams of people involved in each activity.

In fact, the situation is even more complex. Figure 3 is an attempt to illustrate the fact that switch manufacturers typically begin working on the next software release before the current one has been delivered to the telephone companies. in fact, at any point in time there may be several software releases in progress. This causes an enormously complex management and administrative task in maintaining forward and backward compatibility.

To insert a third party, such as a telephone company programming team, into this process and still maintain the software integrity across several releases represents an enormous challenge. The challenge is even mire profound if one consider inserting not one but several telephone company teams into the process, or perhaps even a different team for each major customer for whom customized features are being developed.

The question then is whether switch software is, or can be made to be, sufficiently modular. Can one have clean separations of functions, with a core of system software, perhaps surrounded by feature software for the "mainstream" features and call control, and then perhaps a higher layer that represents an area in which individual BOCs or individual customers could develop customized applications. Can there be clean interfaces among the layers, and well marked entrances and exits from the higher customized application layer so that customized features can be introduced without adversely affecting call processing for the rest of the switch.

From what we at Bell Atlantic have learned in discussions with switch manufacturers and others, today's switches are a long way from this ideal. Much time and resource expenditure will be needed to move to "switch programmability".

WHAT TO DO MEANWHILE?

While we are working these problems, we believe that some gains in the overall development cycle time (if not control) can be gained through improvement of the up front "service creation" process. Our efforts in this direction include better management of the Standards and Generic Requirements process so that decision on feature descriptions and protocol implementations are made more expeditiously. Also, we believe that trials, using adjunct switching frames if necessary, to test market new features and to get the important user inputs and human factors work done properly up front will lead to better Generic Requirements that (we hope) will not have to be redone in the next switch software development cycle, thus allowing us to begin generating revenues for the feature more quickly.

The importance of Generic Requirements for switch feature, ISDN capabilities, etc., cannot be over emphasized. The multi-vendor environment post-divestiture is a reality, it is also essential for our business interests, and will increase rather than decrease. While differences in feature activation and operation among vendors, and among software releases of a particular vendor, might be somewhat for single large customers, it cannot be tolerated in a mass market environment. Advertising, selling and delivering custom calling services, and educating customers in their use and operation, is already exceedingly complex in today's environment where there are very few customized services, and not too many feature differences. Having a feature work completely differently in an area served by central office Brand A versus central office Brand B or C is completely unacceptable.

EVOLUTION

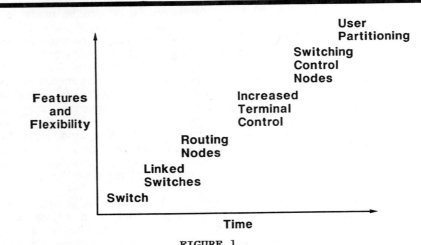

FIGURE 1

DEVELOPMENT CYCLE

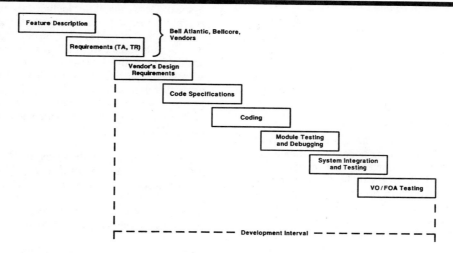

FIGURE 2

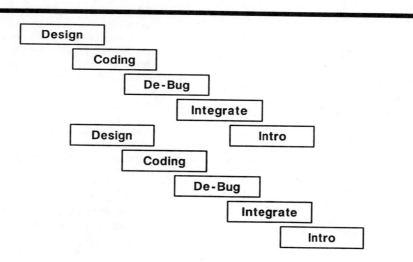

FIGURE 3

NETWORK PROGRAMMABILITY: A TECHNOLOGY PERSPECTIVE

Peter E. Jackson
Vice President, Applied Technology

Steven R. Dimmitt
Director, Network Applications

SBC Technology Resources Inc
St. Louis, MO

ABSTRACT

Increasing network intelligence through the addition of attached processors to switching nodes and through the addition of new network elements such as the SCP, service control point, in IN2 will be the next major augmentation of network functionality after ISDN. In this paper we explore the needs for network programmability in a general way and then examine some of the technology issues inherent in the distributed functionality implied by network programmability.

EXAMPLE

Imagine that five years in the future your daughter is scheduled to pick you up downtown at 6 pm and to take you home after a busy day moving between meetings at several sites in the area. As she drives toward the downtown core at 5:50 pm on the Interstate highway, she becomes trapped between exits in a traffic jam that is not moving.

Realizing that she cannot keep her appointed pickup time with you at the prearranged street corner, she decides to make an alternative plan. She quickly places a call to your **personal access number** on the cellular telephone in the car. The network, realizing that you are on foot in the downtown core, routes the call **as a voice call** to the **personal terminal** (Figure 1) in your pocket.

You agree that it would be best for your daughter to exit the highway at the next opportunity and to take a shortcut to your corner. Unfortunately, she is not familiar with the route and dubious about driving through unfamiliar streets. You call up your **map service data base** and view the route on your screen. Putting a copy into the terminal in the car, you show it to your daughter and allay her fears of taking an unknown and uncertain direction.

Finally, fifteen minutes later, and only ten minutes late, she shows up at the appointed corner, and you both head home.

The example is simple. It shows two people in an identifiable situation. Communications with people on the move in an intelligent network environment made the process seem simple and useful. Underneath the simplicity, however, was extended network functionality and intelligence beyond today's capabilities, but realizable as achievable extensions of today's technology.

Some of these capabilities included the use of a personal access number, the selection by the network of the type of media most sensible under the circumstances (routing the call as a voice call), the use of a personal, portable terminal, and the interaction with a data base with subsequent transfer, or pasting, of an image downstream to another user. Most of these capabilities are available in some form today, but require a greater investment in equipment or access protocols than described in the near-future example.

The functionality described was made easier to access and utilize with the aid of distributed network service features made possible with attached processors under IN2. Additional perspective on portable communications is given in the accompanying paper, Portable Communication, also presented at NCF88.

Next we will look at some additional motivations for moving to an intelligent architecture and then examine some of the technology implications and some of the requirements to bring this type of functionality to life.

MOTIVATION

Three primary factors appear to be the motivators for an attached processor implementation of the emerging Intelligent Network. These factors are new service needs, the service provider's absolute requirement to serve the marketplace demand for fast introduction of new features, and the desire in a competitive marketplace to find a mechanism through which to trial new service and business opportunities before cutover to full committed service.

New Network-Based Services

Distributed, programmable intelligence embedded in the network will provide a mechanism to offer "Follow-Me" services and other services such as personal access numbers which rely on large, distributed data base functionality integrated with call processing. Follow-Me communications reflects a mapping in real time across the network between a subscriber's physical location as reflected in the nearest physical access number and their personal access number, or logical access number. By updating this logical and physical relationship, the network is able to route calls to a subscriber as they change location, and could even allow the customer's chosen set of premium services to move along at the same time.

Programmable network intelligence will also be required to achieve workable implementations of information service gateways and to provide for flexible billing services. At first, these gateways and billing capabilities will be provided on an isolated, lumped basis within or attached to the network fabric. As the industry gains experience with gateway functionality, it too will be provided from processors distributed throughout the set of switching nodes.

Fast Feature Introduction

Current introduction cycles for new service capabilities as provided from switch vendors fall in the range of 14 to 30 months. These delays are frequently unacceptable to service providers to meet the needs of sophisticated customers for new services or to meet the demands of regulatory agencies. To provide an alternative, several switch vendors are beginning to offer attached processor configurations for central offices which provide for customer (i.e. service provider) or third-party programmability. These new vehicles have been discussed at length in forums over the past year, and offer a capability for service providers to product new network functionality outside of the standard switch vendor's software upgrade cycle. With a specialized team of software developers, the service provider is for the first time capable of being in control of the software development cycle and of selecting a sequence of feature introduction dates meeting local, specialized needs. This architecture and its capabilities and requirements will be examined in sections which follow.

Trial Services

In addition to offering specialized features on a cycle controlled by the service provider, the attached processor with network programmability provides a vehicle for rapid introduction on a trial basis of new services which are untested in the marketplace. As well, it allows for a cost-effective vehicle for testing user response to service presentation and to the human-machine interface with a large, untested customer base at the network level.

The attached processor will be a vehicle for gaining a fast view of the marketplace, for achieving early penetration of the market, and for shaking down evolutionary technology long before a commitment to full service.

Open Network Opportunity

Within this area of difficult technology may lie a reward which will be enabled by an open architecture approach. Assuming that processor capabilities become available widely in the network and that the network applications software environment is opened up to third-party programming, a clever programmer or entrepreneur will invent an unforeseen application which will have an impact on network services as profound as Visicalc had on personal computing. One of our goals as technologists and business people has got to be to produce the environment with the new technology which provides the open platform and competitive opportunity to allow this invention to occur and to be fully realized in the marketplace.

Subsequent sections of this paper discuss the architecture and technology of the new distributed programming environment.

NETWORK ARCHITECTURE

Two views of Intelligent Network architecture have emerged as displayed in Figures 2 and 3. Earlier views proposed the lumped technology (Figure 2) while a view which has emerged within the past year has proposed the distributed architecture (Figure 3) as an alternative.

The lumped approach won the early designation as IN2. This view called for the majority of call processing functionality to migrate to large, lumped processors in the system referred to as SCP's. It was believed that by centralizing the intelligence within each LATA or large network area, the dependence on switching machine vendor software development cycles could be reduced and that feature introduction dates could be accelerated. In addition, the lumped approach appeared to offer advantages in the provision of innovative new services based on centralized, large data bases.

One untidy feature of the proposal was that a single agency would be the development and delivery house for all the software. This flaw merely traded a dependence on a small set of switch vendors for dependence on a single R&D house. This approach is not a viable answer if it is the sole path to new network functionality. As we shall see, however, when combined with a distributed processor capability and more general network programmability by many vendors, this approach is very promising.

The distributed architecture pictured in the lower portion of the figure is a more workable approach. In this architecture, the SCP functions are distributed throughout the network on an as-needed basis according to functional needs and competitive marketplace demands. In this view, the large data base structures may still be employed, but are augmented by local intelligence and local copies of the master data base which are used by call processing software with immediate access.

The distributed processor platforms are provided throughout the network in configurations as discussed below. It is on these platforms that the third-party network services software and applications are run. In the next two sections we will discuss attributes of this technology and point out the industry path to developing requirements for effective operation within the architecture.

REALIZATION OF DISTRIBUTED INTELLIGENCE

In order to realize an Intelligent Network architecture that offers distributed control over the services that comprise that network, it is necessary to define an appropriate Nodal architecture that can effectively support a distributed processing environment. Figure 3 illustrates that Nodal architecture (with Attached Processors) which provides the framework for a Network architecture of distributed intelligence. The presence of the Attached Processors allows specific applications and new services to be developed and deployed with minimal impact on a node and thus minimal impact on the network.

When developing a Nodal architecture which supports Attached Processors, it is necessary to determine to what level the Attached Processors will be coupled to the existing switch architecture and messaging algorithms. A tightly coupled environment in which applications and new services are designed on distributed processors that are very dependent on proprietary messaging schemes, offers limited advantages over a non-distributed network. While tailored services could be developed on these nodes, deployment of these services would be limited to one type of switch node. Deployment on other nodes within the network would result in anything from small modifications to total redesign of the application.

Most service providers, however, are interested in providing the applications that are the most profitable while meeting a customer's needs. Applications that can be deployed ubiquitously over the entire network will have the greatest potential to meet a service provider's financial interests as well as meet the end user's needs. A loosely coupled general purpose Attached Processor will not only allow unique services to be offered on a single node, but will also enable applications to be deployed across the whole network, regardless of the manufacturer or vendor of the switch node. This calls for open and standard interfaces that will allow applications to be developed and executed on non-proprietary platforms.

Figure 4 sketches a software architecture that provides an open and standard Operating System environment and Application Platform. The first step towards a general purpose Attached Processor is to define a standard Operating System environment. This includes the base software "hooks", hardware access strategy (disk reads and writes), file access, inter-processor communication methodology, and other basic operating system functions. It is also necessary to design a standard Application Platform. This platform should consist of the software interfaces (procedure or system calls) that are required to allow service providers to develop distributed network applications and services. An ever growing library of interfaces will provide a common framework from which applications can be developed and could potentially reduce the complexity, manpower, and time it takes to develop applications. "State of the art" development tools, including compilers, languages (potentially object oriented), debuggers, software library systems, and documentation systems are just as important and necessary. Standardization of of the

Operating System and the Application Platform is vital to the successful implementation of an Intelligent Network offering distributed processing and control.

DISTRIBUTED PROCESSOR ISSUES

Although realization of a distributed processing environment using today's technology appears to be within reach and almost inevitable, several issues associated with a distributed environment must be resolved

Nodal

Evolving switch architectures to incorporate distributed processing presents three basic issues: Capacity, Security., and Quality. Regardless of how loosely or tightly an Attached Processor is coupled to the existing switch node, design effort must be spent ensuring that the individual components of the switch, and the switch as a whole, have significant capacity to handle additional applications. The capacity of the access methodology, either a Data Bus (in the case of a tightly coupled processor) or via network access (ISDN, SS7 in the case of a loosely coupled processor) must be looked at closely as well as the other components that play a role in providing network services.

Security, while always a concern, becomes more of an issue when control is distributed over multiple processors. The key advantages of a distributed environment: Open interfaces, New and faster service applications, reduced design complexity, also make the switch node more exposed to security problems. Thought must be taken not only to prevent unauthorized access into a distributed environment, but also provide secure and consistent interfaces for authorized users.

Successful service providers must not only be concerned with providing new and better applications but also with maintaining a very high quality of service to the end users. Secure and safe interfaces for application programmers will reduce the chances of a new service impacting the services already provided to the end user. Providing a solution to the example of the father and daughter without maintaining a high quality of service to the customer is unacceptable.

Data Base Management

The majority of applications that service providers wish to provide in a distributed environment require the use of large databases. Whether these databases exist in a single-node environment or are distributed across the network, the area of realtime database access, both read and write, must be addressed. If the network is unable to maintain a location database in real time, the daughter in the example would not be able to reach her father regardless of the technology advances that are made in the area of cellular communications. In addition, if excessive delays are experienced by customers when accessing services that require database access, that service will most likely be put on the shelf because of low demand.

Even non-realtime access into a database can pose a problem in a distributed database environment. Service providers must have the ability to change data easily in a single location and to have the changes propagated throughout the entire network.

Interworking of Functionalities

Developing a standard interface that allows distributed inter-processor communication is a mandatory step in the realization of an Intelligent Network. However, it is not sufficient just to provide a set of low level protocols that enables two processes to communicate, but it is necessary to understand the functionality of each of the processes. An application programmer, given all the necessary tools and interfaces, will be unable to design a new service unless he understands the functionality of the interfaces he must work with.Thought must be given to make sure that the semantics of distributed processes are understood to ensure an efficient interworking between a new application and the existing software.

Multivendor Environment

Today's network consists of nodes from a wide range of vendors. One of the major challenges in developing a distributed processor environment, is to ensure an application desired by a service provider, either designed by a vendor, the service provider, or a third party, can be deployed as much as possible through the entire network. Because the telecommunications industry is such a highly competitive arena, service providers cannot afford to limit the deployment of end user desired applications because of a dependency on a particular vendor's equipment. Redesigning applications to run on different platforms and operating systems is possible, but not cost or time effective. It is imperative that a distributed environment support standard and open interfaces to maximize the ability to deploy services and applications ubiquitously over the network.

Shared Resources

One of the perceived advantages of a distributed processing environment is that the service provider will have the ability to design and develop applications much quicker than a vendor can today. However, this advantage will not be fully realized if the application programmer's tool set is not adequate for the task. In order to reduce the time and cost in developing a new application on an attached processor, it is vital that a library of shared resources be developed that would give the application programmer the tools he needs. As this library grows with more and more resources, it should be able to take advantage of the most recent technological advancements in software development. Use of object oriented languages and artificial intelligence to develop software applications for the intelligent network is a natural evolution.

WHERE WE GO FROM HERE

The immediate issues are the establishment of an architecture, the agreement on system requirements and standards, the identification of security requirements, and agreement on an evolutionary plan to grow to the new architecture from today's network. Steve Dimmitt has called together an informal group from interested members in the industry to begin formulation of the issues. By the time of the NCF meeting in October of this year, we should be able to identify more crisply the items where agreement can be reached most swiftly.

PORTABLE TERMINAL

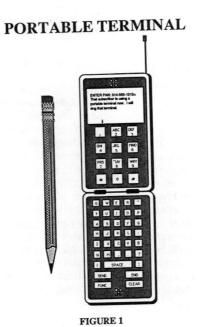

FIGURE 1

NETWORK ARCHITECTURE
LUMPED

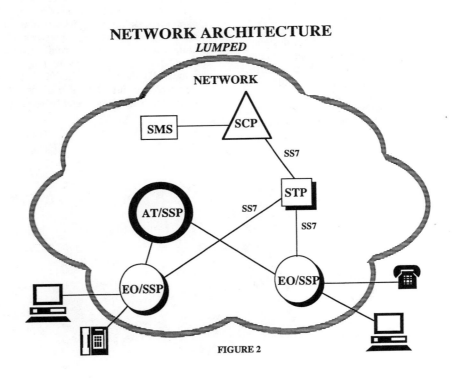

FIGURE 2

NETWORK ARCHITECTURE
DISTRIBUTED

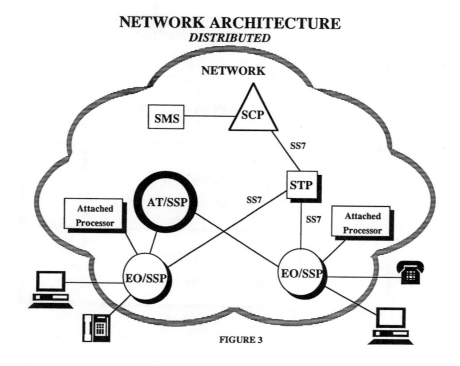

FIGURE 3

DISTRIBUTED INTELLIGENCE
NODAL ARCHITECTURE

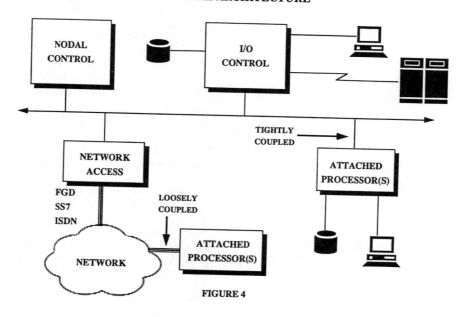

FIGURE 4

ATTACHED PROCESSOR
SOFTWARE ARCHITECTURE

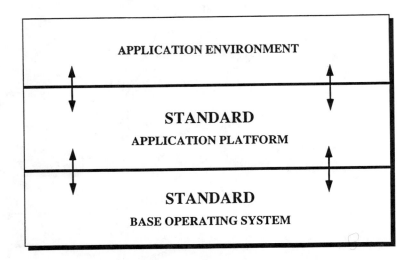

FIGURE 5

CUSTOM PROGRAMMING

Roger Schwantes, Vice President
Product & Technology Planning

Northern Telecom Inc.

200 Athens Way
Nashville, TN 37228

ABSTRACT

The telephone operating companies, and the other providers of telecommunication services, are looking for innovative ways to respond quickly to market opportunities by differentiating their services. Custom programming will allow these service providers to define and implement their own market-specific applications with great flexibility.

Northern Telecom is providing a total programming environment; hardware. software and support services for development of custom applications. Industry standard operating environment and programming languages are supported.

Two modes of programming are supported:

In the Associated mode, the service provider has complete control of and responsibility for feature definition, design, programming, deployment and support of the applications. It allows the service provider to deploy new services on Northern Telecom platforms (e.g., DMS SuperNode), based on their market and business requirements. In this mode, the service provider is not dependent on Northern Telecom's development and product release processes.

The integrated mode gives the service provider the ability to specify and define market-specific feature requirements for Northern Telecom's products. Through the use of dedicated design teams, accelerated feature development and release is achieved. Software developed in the Integrated mode is released through Northern Telecom's standard release processes.

As part of its support services, a Custom Programming laboratory has established by Northern Telecom in Research Triangle Park, North Carolina. This new laboratory is a multi-purpose facility that supports the Services portfolio as well as customer-dedicated facilities and enables the service provider planners, systems designers, and programming staff to define, implement, and deploy new services in conjunction with Northern Telecom designers.

Customer service facilities and designer work stations are provided for use by customer design staff. The laboratory provides facilities for testing and verification of the design application. The test staff is available to assist in the planning of test cases and test execution.

Northern Telecom will support the customers in establishing their own laboratory facilities through facilities planning, installation and maintenance.

This talk will focus on the status and some of the specific applications of Custom Programming.

DSW-12

ARCHITECTURES AND APPLICATIONS

Carl J. Stehman
Chairperson

Switching Systems Division
Rockwell International Corporation
1431 Opus Place
Downers Grove, Illinois 60515

Current technological and market trends place a growing emphasis on network features. The theme for this year's Architectures and Applications seminar is "Switch Architectures to Support the New Network Features." The seminar explores switching design considerations for handling open network architectures, intelligent network features, and gateway switching arrangements.

In the first paper, Ann Michaels and Doug Sink examine the impact of ONA on the future development of switching equipment and software. They identify two areas of significant impact, unbundling of capabilities and expanded interface capabilities. It appears that unbundling, in particular, will be a challenge more complex than many have imagined.

With the second paper, we move to the intelligent network. Mohamed Shabana and David Anderson itemize the criteria for a switch that supports the evolution toward the intelligent networks. To satisfy the requirements, they describe a distributed multi-processor switch architecture with integrated packet network and modular software. In the third paper, Gary Pinkham emphasizes the services-oriented destiny of intelligent networks and proposes new feature creation at the provisioning level rather than at the traditional manufacturing level. He also proposes switch architectures that permit centralization or decentralization of services as needed to fit current circumstances.

In the fourth paper, Jim Spencer describes the architecture and functionality of a gateway arrangement constructed primarily from OEM building blocks.

Gary Pinkham   Ericsson Network Systems

Mohamed Shabana DSC Communications Corp.
& David G. Anderson

Douglas D. Sink AT&T Bell Laboratories
& Ann S. Michaels

James Spencer   Integrated Communications
Systems

THE IMPLICATIONS OF ONA ON THE DESIGN OF LOCAL SWITCHING SYSTEMS

A. S. Michaels

D. D. Sink

Information Services and
CENTREX Planning Group

AT&T Bell Laboratories
200 Park Plaza
Naperville, Illinois 60566

ABSTRACT

The order to the BOCs to unbundle basic network functions and to present these concepts in their plans for Open Network Architecture (ONA) has an effect on all segments of the telecommunications community, including network providers, equipment vendors, enhanced service providers, regulators, and end customers. Its implications for the future development of switching equipment and software are the subject of this report. AT&T has identified six possible areas of impact on switching systems. Initial investigations suggest that two of these are directly attributable to ONA: (1) the unbundling of basic elements which have traditionally been embedded within network services, and (2) the development of generic. Enhanced Service Provider (ESP) interface capabilities. The other four areas are addressed either in the development of ISDN and the intelligent network or as part of ongoing feature development. Current indications are that full compliance with ONA requirements in the long run will require a general increase in complexity of switching systems. The cost of this increase must eventually be weighed against the benefits of ONA.

INTRODUCTION

In the Computer Inquiry III (CI-III) Report and Order issued in June 1986, the Federal Communications Commission (FCC) imposed a new concept of regulation which it labeled Open Network Architecture (ONA). At the heart of the ONA concept is the requirement that the Bell Operating Companies (BOCs) unbundle their basic local network functions into building blocks the FCC called Basic Service Elements, which would be made available on an equal access basis to both the carrier's own enhanced services operations and those of its competitors. The order mandated that the Regional Holding Companies (RHCs) and their BOC subsidiaries develop an initial set of key elements of this type and describe these as part of the initial ONA plan which each RHC was required to file on or before February 1, 1988. The order further required that establishment of an appropriate set of specific network functions to be unbundled and offered by the BOCs must be done with participation of the enhanced service industry.

The implementation of the ONA concept has an impact not only on the Enhanced Service Providers (ESPs), but also on essentially every segment of the telecommunications industry. In addition to the ESPs, other entities which have a stake in the development of ONA include federal and state regulators, large volume network users, the BOCs, interexchange carriers, value-added network providers, and equipment manufacturers. By the nature of the requirement, it is obvious that the BOCs and the ESPs are major stakeholders in the development of ONA: the BOCs as the providers of unbundled network capabilities and the ESPs as principal consumers of them. However, the role of other stakeholders, such as network equipment manufacturers, none-the-less vital to implementation of the ONA concept.

It is from the perspective of a supplier of switching equipment to the BOC market that this paper is written. For network equipment manufacturers, such as AT&T, ONA presents a changing market place that could have significant product line impact. In fact, current indications are that local switching system products will indeed be impacted in several ways. The challenge for network equipment manufacturers is to work actively with the BOCs toward defining a truly useful set of unbundled service offerings from both the ESP and BOC perspective. To the extent that ONA service offerings do not prove useful in the market place, resource expenditures will not be recovered. On the positive side, increased network usage means more revenue for the BOCs and can result in increased sales for network equipment vendors.

This paper focuses on the ongoing process to assess the potential impact of ONA requirements on the design and development of local switching systems. It is organized into six sections, the first of which reviews CI-III guidelines for network capabilities to be unbundled. This review is followed by a brief overview of major industry ONA activities culminating in the development of RHC ONA plans. The third section analyzes the network capabilities that have been requested at national and regional ONA forums and organizes them into categories based on

anticipated switching system impact. The fourth section discusses an internal AT&T analysis of the development impact which could be expected from unbundling network embedded within existing features and presenting them as individual tariffed service offerings. The fifth section presents some thoughts on a generic interface for ESPs, and the concluding section provides some insights into the probable impacts on local switching systems as the ONA concept is realized.

FCC UNBUNDLING GUIDELINES

Although Basic Service Elements are fundamental to the concept of ONA, the FCC provided only general guidelines in CI-III for identifying and defining these unbundled building blocks. The following summarizes specific paragraphs from the Report and Order that describe the FCC's Basic Service Element concept:

• "All basic network capabilities...including signaling, switching, billing and network management are subject to the unbundling requirement."

• Capabilities specifically cited as candidates for unbundling include: supervisory signaling, calling number identification, special alerting signal (such as stutter dial tone), abbreviated dialing, called number identification, and line status.

• Basic Service Elements are to be provided "on a tariffed basis," and competitors are to "pay only for those Basic Service Elements that they use in providing enhanced services."

• "...each set of basic services that a carrier incorporates into an enhanced service offering must be available to the public under tariff as a Basic Service Element or as a set of Basic Service Elements."

• Carriers are required to develop "an initial set of key Basic Service Elements that can be used in a wide variety of enhanced services..."

• "...we require participating carriers to make available the initial set of Basic Service Elements based on the expected market demand for such elements, their utility as perceived by enhanced service competitors, and the technical and costing feasibility of such unbundling."

INDUSTRY ONA ACTIVITIES

As of February 1, 1988, all seven RHCs had filed ONA plans with the FCC as required by the CI-III Report and Order. Two major areas of activity

1307

played a fundamental role in development of those ONA plans: (1) the collection and analysis of industry requests for network functionality, and (2) the creation of a common RHC ONA model.

Beginning in 1986 and continuing through 1987, the RHCs and their BOC subsidiaries, in response to the FCC directive, actively sought industry participation in the identification of candidate network functionality for unbundling. They individually and jointly held regional national ONA forums. They conducted specific industry and one-on-one market research. They participated in industry association meetings and generally made themselves available to discuss and receive input on the association meetings and generally made themselves available to discuss and receive input on the industry's needs. The results of these processes were compiled by the RHCs into a national list of 118 industry requests for network capabilities. These candidate capabilities were then evaluated by each of the RHCs to assess their market demand, their utility as perceived by the ESPs, and their technical and costing feasibility. The feasibility of meeting the CI-III requirement for provision within one year of ONA plan approval was a major factor in identification of initial service offerings based on these candidate capabilities. The service offerings included in the ONA plans filed by the RHCs are based on, but not limited to, this common set of 118 industry requests.

These service offerings can be described in terms of the common ONA model developed by the RHCs. This model has been structured to be technically independent for accommodation of a variety of existing architectures as well as evolving future network architectures. While specific applications of the model may vary among individual RHCs, it has in general served as a framework to facilitate communication among industry participants in the ONA process. The term Basic Service Element was introduced and loosely defined by the FCC in CI-III to describe the general concept of an unbundled building block. The RHC ONA model gives more specificity to this concept.

The Basic Service Element is defined as one of three components of the ONA model. The other two types of components are Basic Serving Arrangements and Complementary Network Services. A Basic Serving Arrangement (BSA) is defined by this model as the underlying connection of an ESP to and through the BOC's network. It is

considered the fundamental ONA connection to those networks. Example BSAs include circuit-switched voice-grade lines, circuit-switched digital lines, and dedicated private lines. A Basic Service Element (BSE) is then defined as an optional network capability that may be selected in conjunction with a BSA. Examples include call queuing and distribution functions, calling number delivery, night transfer, and control by the ESP of end customer message alerting mechanisms. Complementary Network Services (CNSs) provide the means for an ESP client to connect to the network and access the ESP in an ONA environment. Examples of possible CNSs include call forwarding and abbreviated dialing. Throughout this paper, the term service offering is used as a generic term to refer to the general components of the ONA model: BSA, BSE, or CNS. Although considered by the RHCs to be outside the ONA umbrella, a fourth service class was recognized as having considerable value to ESPs. Called Ancillary Services, this class could include BOC offerings of billing and collection services, for example.

ANALYSIS OF INDUSTRY-REQUESTED NETWORK CAPABILITIES

The primary impact of ONA on network equipment can be expected to come from changes/modifications requested by the BOCs to meet the needs of the ESPs and large volume end users. Much effort has been devoted by the RHCs and the BOCs to the collection of the requests for network capabilities identified by industry ONA processes and to analyze and evaluate these requests as candidate ONA service offerings. Determining the impact on switching systems by equipment vendors has also been part of the overall evaluation process. Current investigations have suggested six general areas of switching system impact:

1. Existing Capabilities: Some network capabilities being requested are available today with tariff or price modification and require little (or minor) development.

2. Unbundled Capabilities: Some network capabilities being requested will require development to unbundle them from existing features.

3. New Features: Some network capabilities being requested will require development of new network functions or features.

4. New Interfaces: Some network capabilities being requested will require development of new network interfaces or significant expansion of current or planned interfaces.

1308

5. Regional-Specific Features: Some network capabilities requested may vary from region to region based on individual BOC ONA plans and, thus, require customization or special feature development for specific BOCs.

6. Network Interconnection Modifications: Some network capabilities being requested require interoffice communication and, thus, require modifications to network interconnection capabilities (e.g., implementation of CCS7 to local central offices, expanded information fields, etc.).

In addition to the impact of providing ONA service offerings from Local Exchange Networks, it should be noted that the BOC's ability to offer enhanced services from their basic networks will likely provide new enhanced feature and integration requirements for equipment manufacturers. Such opportunities are not addressed here.

The first of the six areas of impact listed above, Existing Capabilities, has an insignificant effect on current switch systems. Two additional areas, New Features and Network Interconnection Modifications, can be handled by existing industry processes, both in the planning of switch development and in BOC operational processes. Moreover, they do not directly require any significant redirection of today's trends for switching systems.

A third area, Regional-Specific Features, reflects an individual BOC's need to provide increased responsiveness to its own customers through the ability to create unique or customized services. While it is to be expected that these needs will show up in the ONA process, they are not solely attributable to ONA. In fact, ONA may actually mitigate this impact by providing ESPs, end users, and CPE manufacturers with the opportunity to vocalize their needs for national uniformity and to insist on more coordination among RHCs than would have occurred otherwise.

This classification identifies two unique areas of impact on switching systems that are primarily attributable to ONA: Unbundled Capabilities and New Interfaces. Constrained by the feasibility of provision within one year of ONA plan approval, the initial RHC ONA plans tend to describe service offerings based on existing or committed network capabilities. These service offerings represent unbundling which could be accomplished by the BOCs without requiring new switch development. Future requirements for unbundling will be determined by the

ongoing ONA process. To understand the general impact of the potential future unbundling of existing services, AT&T has undertaken an analysis which will be described in the next section. Some thoughts on the need for a generic interface for ESPs will then be presented.

AT&T SWITCHING SYSTEMS ANALYSIS

Unbundling for CI-III

AT&T's analysis of the impact of unbundling was done using voice messaging services as a specific frame of reference. Generalizations were then made from the results of this specific analysis. The first step of the multi-step analysis process was to introduce and define the concept of "degree of unbundling." This concept provides a scale of unbundling against which development of specific ONA service offerings can be measured. Based on the unbundling scale, the next step was to identify network capabilities at various levels of unbundling, and to gather some specific data points of development estimates for these sample network capabilities. Finally, the specific data points were extrapolated to "rules of thumb" to provide insight into the costs associated with development of ONA service offerings.

For the purpose of this study, specific data points were obtained via analysis of the Simplified Message Desk Interface (SMDI) service on the 1A ESS^{TM} central office switch. In terms of the ONA model, the BSA associated with SMDI is a dedicated private line, and the existing Call Forwarding features can be considered CNSs. The SMDI service itself is one example of a BSE. The impact of unbundling elements of existing services was studied by decomposing SMDI into various functional units for individual consideration as BSEs.

The Degree of Unbundling

The results of the study show that the degree of unbundling is determined by three factors:

1. The unit size of the network capability being unbundled;
2. The extent to which the network capability remains service-specific;
3. The accessibility of the network capability to the ESP customer as a separately subscribable entity.

The size of the unbundled unit could vary through a considerable range of possibilities. Some of the obvious points on a continuous scale are illustrated in Figure 1. At one extreme, switch capabilities are made available to subscribers as tariffed offerings only in the form of services or features. This point corresponds, for the most part, with today's situation.

The SMDI and Call Forwarding features are representative of units of capabilities currently available under tariff. Packages of logically related capabilities represent the first step in unbundling. The Call History information supplied by SMDI is an example of such a package. In moving toward smaller unit sizes, the next obvious step in unbundling is to make individual capabilities (such as calling number) available under tariff.

At the opposite extreme of service-level unbundling is primitive-level unbundling. However, even primitives can be defined at various levels, making this a rather broad category. Possibilities range from such primitives as "make a call" to lower-level primitives such as "apply audible ringing."

The second factor in determining the degree of unbundling is the extent to which a particular network capability is service-specific. In general, for a particular network capability, the more options provided for the stimulus which causes the network to perform the required action and the more BSA alternatives accommodated, the larger the range of applications for such a network capability. Thus, the service-specificity will decrease accordingly.

The final factor in determining the degree of unbundling is ESP customer-accessibility. Customer-accessibility refers to the ability of the switch to support subscription to the network capability as a separate entity. In effect, all ONA service offerings must have the attribute of customer-accessibility to comply with CI-III.

The Impact of Various Degrees of Unbundling

The second step in the AT&T analysis of the impact of unbundling was to define possible BSEs that could be unbundled from the current SMDI on the 1A ESS switch and then to quantify the development effort required to provide that capability as a separate tariffable entity. Generally, before the technical and costing feasibility of providing a particular capability on an individual feature basis could be evaluated, specifications had to be determined for:
1. The general conditions under which the capability is to be available;

2. The stimuli which cause the network to perform the associated action;
3. The BSA mechanisms over which communication with the ESP is provided; and
4. The Operations, Administration, and Maintenance (OA&M) functions needed, such as provisioning, usage measurements, billing, and maintenance.

It became apparent quite early in the study that the definition of service offerings is not nearly as simple as it appears from the industry process of selection of network capabilities for consideration. In fact, none of the three tests for service offerings (market demand, utility for ESPs, or technical and costing feasibility) can be evaluated until the service offering is accompanied by a detailed specification of the conditions under which it can be made available.

The final step of the AT&T analysis of unbundling was to extrapolate the estimated development effort for specific BSEs representing selected degrees of unbundling in an attempt to provide generic "rules of thumb" to assess the general impact of unbundling existing services. Some of our observations are:

1. Service-specific unbundling, resulting from the strict decomposition of existing services, can be accomplished more readily than less service-specific unbundling. (In other words, generalized unbundling will typically be more costly than if capabilities are unbundled to support a narrow range of services.)
2. Service specificity appears to be a more significant factor than unit size in determining the difficulty of unbundling existing services.
3. Even if the impact on switch development of unbundling a single service offering is relatively small, the implementation of a number (30 or so) of such service offerings would be significant and must be addressed in conjunction with other customer feature needs.
4. The general impact of unbundling will be likely to result in an overall increase in options on current interfaces, in stimuli to trigger feature capabilities, and in OA&M capabilities (such as service orders, usage measurements, customer profiles and screening operations, and security provisions). These impacts will increase the complexity of switch software and feature interactions.

GENERIC ESP INTERFACE CAPABILITIES

The ongoing ONA process has revealed that many industry requested network capabilities fall into one of two categories:

1. The first is information uniquely available to the network. Examples of such network information include Calling Directory Number, Called Directory Number, Call History Package, and Call Disconnect Indication.
2. The second is functions inherently provided by the network. The ESPs wish to gain access and a degree of control of these functions in real time as the need arises. An example of such a function might be the request from an ESP to transfer a call currently connected to that ESP to another point on the network.

Preliminary examination of the list of 118 industry requests jointly compiled by the RHCs suggests that about one third of them fall into one of these categories. Both categories require some level of signaling for information exchange between the network and the ESP. In other words, the information exchange necessary to support these capabilities requires an intelligent interface. If one reviews the way in which such capabilities are supported in today's network, one finds an assortment of interfaces associated with specific services or service categories. It is clear that a proliferation of interfaces is not the most cost effective approach to providing ESP access to these network capabilities in the future. A study has recently been initiated by AT&T to further understand industry requested network functions requiring expanded ESP signaling capabilities. While this study is still in progress, it appears that a generic ESP interface can evolve from currently defined ISDN interfaces, providing cost effective delivery over both the Basic and Primary Rate Interfaces.

CONCLUSION

While the industry process addressing ONA includes considerable discussion of new features and expanded network capabilities, these aspects of the discussion must be separated from the analysis of the impact of unbundled service offerings, BSEs and BSAs, on digital switching systems. The needs for new and expanded capabilities are not a result of ONA and would have evolved without the ONA requirement.

The impact of ONA on digital switching systems is derived, for the most part, from the unbundling requirement and from the expanded signaling needs of the ESP. The resulting impact of unbundling can best be summarized as the need to support for each separately available unit a variety of options on current interfaces, a variety of stimuli to trigger features and option capabilities, and the OA&M capabilities required to present that unbundled element as a tariffed service offering. Thus, the general complexity of switch software will increase. Also, the need for expanded signaling will likely evolve into an expansion of signaling capabilities on both the Basic and Primary Rate Interfaces to provide a generic interface option for ESPs.

Impact of ONA on Switching Systems
Unbundling
A Spectrum of Possibilities

Unit Size		Definition/Example
• Service Level	+	• Availability Only as Services - Messaging Interface via SMDI
• Package Level	+	• Packages of Associated Capabilities - Call History Package (Calling DN, Called DN, Call Type)
• Capability Level	+	• Individually Subscribable Service Capabilities - Calling DN - Called DN - Call Type - MWI Control
• Primitive Level	+	• Network Primitives Available to Service Providers - Collect Information - Monitor • • • - Apply/Remove Dial Tone - Connect/Release Digit Receiver - Apply Audible Ringing

FIGURE 1.

INTELLIGENT SWITCH ARCHITECTURE

Mohamed Shabana
Director
Advanced Systems Engineering

David G. Anderson
Senior Planner

DSC Communications Corporation
1000 Coit Road
Plano, Texas 75075

ABSTRACT

Intelligent and powerful switching elements are an integral part of the evolution towards the Intelligent Network (IN). The intelligent switch hardware consists of a distributed multi-processor system architecture that utilizes an integrated packet network to provide a fast and reliable message transport. The intelligent switch software architecture consists of a modular software designed to meet integrated services required to support the IN. These capabilities support the deployment of enhanced physical or logical services devices into the hardware and software platform.

INTRODUCTION

Switch vendors and exchange carriers are developing and installing a new generation of switching elements to support the evolution towards the Intelligent Network (IN). This new generation consists of Service Switching Points (SSP), Signal Transfer Points (STP), Service Control Points (SCP), and Intelligent Gateways (IG). Certain generalized design criteria can be stated for a switching element to test the "goodness of fit" of a particular design architecture with the IN in which it must function. A switch meeting these criteria can be considered a next generation switch or an intelligent switch:

- The switch design should allow for the combination of many functions in a single device with a single network fabric (figure 1). Multifunctional switch architectures provide the capability to combine such functions as switch/SSP, STP, SCP, and IG.

- Modularity of both hardware and software provides a cost effective product covering the entire size accommodate any mix of functional combinations.

- The capacity should be well in excess of existing needs, and the design should allow future capacity expansions.

- The device architecture employed should not be real time limited. The addition of new features and capabilities should not degrade the real time performance of existing functions.

- New services and features must be able to be added quickly in order to meet market windows and maximize the revenue stream from the new services. Two key elements of this capability are: User Programmability, which gives operating companies the ability to develop and introduce features independently of the equipment vendor; and Customer Control, which allows individual customers to manage their own subdivision of the communications network.

- The design should be based on currently available technology but be able to be upgraded to new, more powerful technology when needed.

- The new network switch must operate with today's network equipment while providing a smooth transition path to the IN. This includes compatibility with Next Generation Operations Support Systems as well as today's OSSs.

- The design must meet reliability standards for hardware, and software and allow for additions of new functions, features, and capacity with no negative impact on established service.

Today's VLSI microprocessor, memory, and mass storage technologies, properly structured, offer the power (speed and capacity) and flexibility to satisfy all of the above design criteria for the IN switching elements. This is possible through the use of software intensive, microprocessor based, distributed architecture designs where each microprocessor has the inherent intelligence to perform its assigned functions without direction from a central source. This allows minimization of interprocessor communications and efficient use of the processing power available.

The following sections of this paper describe the control, software, and applications architectures for an intelligent switch. Next, this paper illustrates how these architectures are used to build applications, provide enhanced services, and construct a platform that can be expanded to accommodate growth and future services. The final section describes system capacities for SSP, STP, and combined spectrum and with the capability to SSP/STP applications.

INTELLIGENT SWITCH CONTROL ARCHITECTURE

Figure 2 shows a switch control architecture that satisfies the above requirements. This architecture is based on a network of distributed microprocessors interconnected by a high message throughput fabric. The microprocessors all have a common interface structure but vary in processor type, speed and memory. The two main elements of this architecture are the Message Transport Network (MTN) and the Application Clusters. They are described below.

1. Message Transport Network. The MTN is the high message throughput fabric that interconnects the different application clusters. The MTN consists of a square, single-stage matrix that uses a high speed message transfer protocol to transfer data packets between application clusters. Only inter-cluster data packets are transported on the MTN. Intra-cluster data packets do not enter the MTN. For reliability, all key components are strictly redundant.

2. Application Clusters. Each application cluster consists of a Transport Node Controller (TNC), microprocessors, storage devices, and hardware specific to the application being supported. The capacity of the cluster depends on the speed of the cluster bus, the capacity of the TNC, and the number of microprocessors and memory storage devices that can be connected to a single cluster bus. For reliability, the TNC, all microprocessors, all storage devices, and all critical applications hardware are duplicated. Each of these major components is described below.

- Transport Node Controller. The TNC is the interface to the MTN. All processors connected directly to the cluster bus send inter-processor data packets to the TNC for routing. The TNC discriminates between intra-cluster and inter-cluster packets by using the destination address contained in the packet. It sends intra-cluster packets directly to the destination processor on the cluster. The TNC formats inter-cluster packets into the MTN packet protocol, establishes a connection through the MTN to the TNC of the destination applications cluster, sends the packets, and confirms that the destination TNC has received them correctly.

- Microprocessors. Each applications cluster can contain a number of different types of microprocessors.

wide range of performance both in terms of raw processing power and memory that they can access. Thus, the application can be matched to the processing power required. The microprocessors are programmed using high level languages with assembly programming required only for extremely time-critical functions.

- Storage Devices. Some applications may require more memory than is available in the microprocessor. Therefore, an external, dedicated memory unit may be associated with each microprocessor. For other applications, mass memory can be provided to store large data structures requiring very fast access. All microprocessors assigned to the function supported by this mass memory element can then access it. Very large online databases can be stored on disk storage devices associated with an applications cluster.

- Applications Hardware. Application specific hardware includes such traditional telephone office equipment as the switch matrix, digit senders and receivers, trunk circuit interfaces, OSS data links, and intercept equipment. It also includes IN equipment such as CCS7 links, ISDN/packet network interfaces, and specialized interfaces to enhanced services.

INTELLIGENT SWITCH SOFTWARE ARCHITECTURE

The software architecture is based on the principles of functional relocatibility and functional replication. Functional relocatability allows a function to be located in any processor and to be relocated from one processor to another during system expansion. Functional replication is the storing of a program or function in more than one processor.

These two principles allow efficient engineering of the system processors based on traffic and capacity demands. An example of this is the provisioning of call management functions. In a small system with low capacity requirements, all call management functions, such as resource allocation, statistics, call translations, load balancing, and queueing, are packaged into a single processor. For a large system, these functions may be located in three different processors: a call manager containing the resource allocation and statistics functions, a service manager containing the load balancing and queueing functions, and a translations processor containing call translation. If a system's call translations requirements, for example, cannot be handled by a single translation processor, the translations function can be replicated to several translation processors, thus allowing

These applications processors have a additional capacity to be plugged-in as needed.

Other system software requirements are:

- The physical location, both processor and memory address, is transparent to the program.

- new or modified programs can be individually loaded into the system.

- System reconfiguration due to expansion can be done online with no service interruptions.

- All inter-program communication is via well defined logical interfaces controlled by the operating system.

- All interface to the hardware is via the operating system so that the software will not be affected by hardware evolution.

- The switch's operating system is distributed among all of the processors and uses a distributed configuration table to define the location of each program in the system.

This software supports the definition of different architectures for the microprocessors in the applications clusters. A mixture of these architectures can be used in a single cluster. Four possible configurations are described below and are shown in figure 3:

1. Each microprocessor may be assigned a unique function within the cluster. In this configuration the functional programs stored in each microprocessor are different from those stored in the other microprocessors in the cluster.

2. Several microprocessors may be assigned to the same function but work with different traffic or configuration dependent hardware devices. In this configuration the functional programs stored in each microprocessor of the group are identical. The hardware are also identical. The selection of the hardware device (e.g. trunk, service circuit, signaling link) determines which microprocessor handles the function on a particular call or transaction.

3. Several microprocessors may be assigned to the same function, with the specific processor that does the work selected by a manager. In this configuration also, the functional programs stored in each microprocessor of the group, except the manager, are identical. Since no specific hardware elements are associated with these microprocessors, any one of the group

The manager selects the specific microprocessor based on dynamic information, such as the instantaneous state of each microprocessor of the group.

4. A microprocessor hierarchy may be established, with some processors acting as slaves to others. Both the master and slave microprocessors may utilize any of the three configurations described above. All communications to or from a slave processor must pass through its master. The slave processors do not communicate among themselves.

These control and software architectures create a high degree of flexibility in the engineering of a specific system. A switch can be engineered and built for its particular size and capacity requirements. Only incremental hardware additions and a configuration table change are required to increase capacity.

INTELLIGENT SWITCH APPLICATIONS ARCHITECTURE

An IN switch can be constructed from seven different types of applications cluster as shown in figure 4. Each applications cluster is named according to the predominant application running in that cluster. The seven cluster types are described below.

1. Administration/Maintenance Cluster. This cluster provides local and remote interfaces for operation and maintenance, recent change and verify, provisioning and network management functions. This cluster also contains the interfaces required to communicate with remote OSSs and local craft terminals.

2. CCS7 Signaling Cluster. This cluster provides the interface to the CCS7 signaling links and the routing and screening functions for CCS7 messages.

3. Call Processing Cluster and Facility Interface Subsystem. This cluster includes translation and routing and trunk circuit interface functions for switch applications. The Integrated Services User Part (ISUP) and Transaction Capabilities Application Part (TCAP) processing also belong in this cluster. The digital and analog trunk interfaces controlled from this cluster form the Facility Interface Subsystem.

4. ISDN Signaling Cluster. This cluster supports the lower layers of ISDN, including D-channel interfaces and X.25/X.75 packet network interfaces. The messages received are translated into a form that can be processed by other applications clusters.

can process the functions for any call.

5. Switch Matrix and Switching Matrix Control Cluster. The switch matrix is the digital switching fabric used to transport voice and data. For IN applications, a multirate fabric, capable of switching intact signals at up to the DS3 (44.736 Mbits/sec) rate is desirable. It is also desirable to be able to expand the switch matrix to a maximum of over 100K channels in economically sized increments. The Switching Matrix Control Cluster supports the connect, disconnect and performance monitoring functions for the switch matrix.

6. Service Circuit Control Cluster. This cluster supports the transition to an all digital CCS7 network. It includes conventional DTMF/MF senders and receivers and continuity tone detectors.

7. Service Control Point Cluster. Telecommunications database functions are implemented in this cluster. It also supports multiple applications such as Virtual Private Network and Calling Card Verification.

APPLICATIONS AND ENHANCED SERVICE

Individual IN switching elements are built up from a subset of the seven cluster types. An STP (figure 5) is composed of the combination of an Administration/Maintenance Cluster and one or more CCS7 Signaling Clusters. The addition of one or more Service Control Point Clusters produces an SCP or a combination STP/SCP, depending on the configuration of the network. An existing STP can have SCP functionality added, and an existing SCP can have STP functionality added without impacting the original application since all processing is distributed.

An SSP (figure 6) is formed by combining a Call Processing Cluster, a Switch Matrix Cluster, a Service Circuit Cluster, a Common Channel Signaling Cluster, and an Administration/Maintenance Cluster. Again depending on the configuration of the network, the switch could be an SSP or a combined SSP/STP.

An IG provides a network-wide access point for enhanced services. The enhanced service providers are connected to the IG. Calls requesting the services are routed to the IG from other points of the IN. Thus, the services are available in all parts of the network, regardless of where the actual processing for the service is located. Two examples of this are audiotext and videotext (figure 7).

Audiotext service provides a voice

integrated into the intelligent switch using Intelligent Audiotext Peripherals (IAPs). The IAPs are connected to the switch matrix for network access. Administrative control is via the MTN.

Videotext service provides alphanumeric text from a database to a user with a terminal. The videotext database may be connected to the switch or the database may be located at some other place in the network. Remote videotext databases are accessed using Intelligent Videotext Peripherals.

Since the processing is distributed, several switch applications can be combined in a single system (figure 8) without reducing the capacity of any of the functions. This multifunctionality allows the exchange carrier to minimize the number of network elements, thus reducing operating costs, while providing the high processing capacities and the ability to add new services required in today's Information Age.

The modularity of the architecture shown does not require a separate physical entity for each cluster type. In small switches several applications clusters may be combined into one physical cluster. For example, in a single cluster STP, both Administration/Maintenance and Common Channel Signaling processors are connected to one cluster bus. There is no MTN in this single cluster architecture. As more signaling links are added to the single cluster STP, additional Signaling Channel Interface (SCI) processors are needed to provide the lower level interface to the additional links. Because of the increased CCS7 traffic, the Common Channel Distributor (CCD) processors are replicated to provide more translation and screening capacity for CCS7 messages.

As the STP is expanded further, the limit of the single cluster system is reached. It must now be reconfigured into two clusters and an MTN added. The SCI and CCD processors are now on a separate CCS7 Signaling Cluster. The Administration/Maintenance Cluster is also a separate physical structure. Further expansion of the STP is accomplished by adding more CCS7 Signaling Clusters.

SYSTEM CAPACITY

The processing capacity for particular functions can be selectively engineered. In an SSP trunk groups are normally engineered for a load of ten busy hours calls per trunk circuit. The call management processors for an SSP with 30,000 trunks would be configured to support 300,000 busy hour calls, and the switch would be equipped with a messaging capability. Audiotext is 32,000 port matrix. The call management processors for a maximum size SSP of 120,000 trunks would be configured for 1,200,000 busy hour calls, and the switch would be equipped with a 128,000 port matrix.

In an STP call CCS7 processing is located in the SCI and CCD processors, which form the Common Channel Signaling Clusters. There is one SCI processor for each CCS7 link. The number of CCD processors is engineered based on the level and characteristics of the CCS7 traffic. Additional CCD processors can be added as required to support increased traffic levels. A full size STP with 720 CCS7 links supports a total message throughput of up to 100,000 messages per second.

In a combined SSP/STP, as shown in table 1, the limiting factor for the size of the system is MTN port utilization. The STP function does not use either the call management or switch matrix resources of the SSP and, thus, thas no effect on SSP call processing capacity. The CCS7 links required by the SSP are an integral part of the STP. From a network perspective, the total number of CCS7 links required in the combined switch is less, and processing efficiency is higher, than for a standalone SSP and STP. This is so because the messages generated by the SSP function are transferred internally using the MTN and/or Cluster Buses to the STP function. This internal transfer causes no traffic load on the CCS7 links, unlike the case with a standalone SSP and STP in which CCS7 messages must be sent between the two.

CONCLUSION

Establishment of the IN depends, to a large extent, on the design, development and deployment of intelligent switch architectures. IN switch design and development must make maximum use of the synergies among recent developments in such technologies as microprocessors,software languages, operating systems, custom VLSI, and fiber optics. These designs must not preclude the incorporation, after initial deployment, of further advances in these technologies. At the same time, they must work smoothly with existing network elements and OSSs. A multifunctional switch based on a disctributed processor architecture with a high degree of flexibility and modularity in all aspects of its design is the best vehicle for achieving these goals.

DEX MEGAHUB

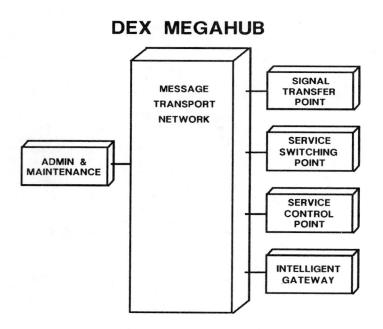

Figure 1 - Multi-Functional Application

DEX MEGAHUB

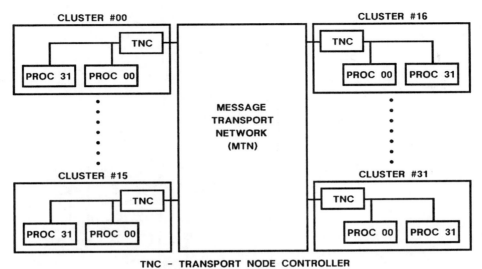

TNC - TRANSPORT NODE CONTROLLER

Figure 2 - Control Architecture

DEX MEGAHUB

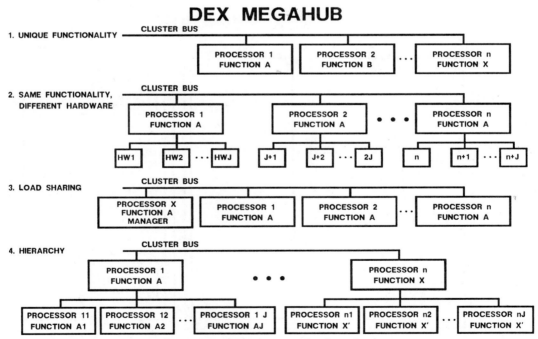

Figure 3 - Microprocessor Configurations

1317

DEX MEGAHUB

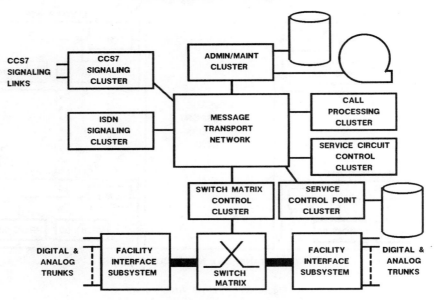

Figure 4 - Applications Cluster Architecture

DEX MEGAHUB

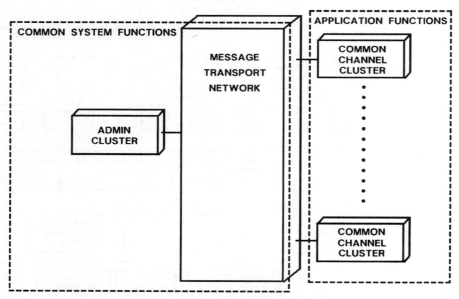

Figure 5 - Signal Transfer Point (STP) Application

DEX MEGAHUB

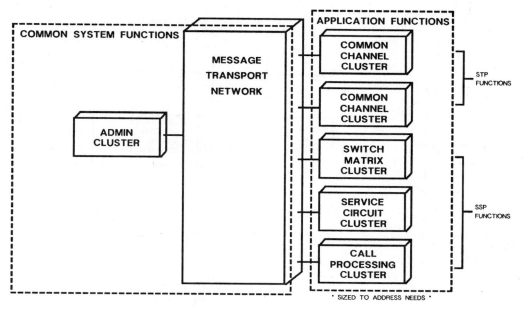

Figure 6 - Combined SSP/STP Application

DEX MEGAHUB

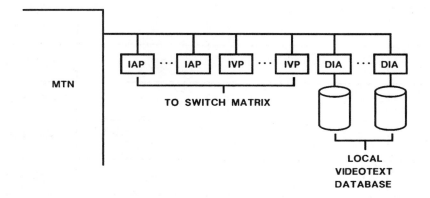

DIA - DISK INTERFACE ADAPTER
IAP - INTELLIGENT AUDIOTEXT PERIPHERAL
IVP - INTELLIGENT VIDEOTEXT PERIPHERAL

Figure 7 - IG With Audiotext/Videotext

DEX MEGAHUB

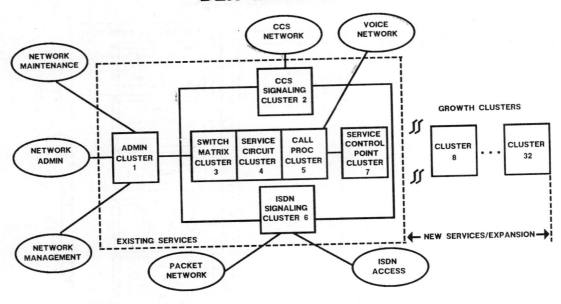

Figure 8 - Architectural Evolution

NUMBER OF TRUNKS (SSP)	NUMBER OF SIGNALING LINKS (STP)	NUMBER OF CLUSTERS	MTN PORT UTILIZATION
30,000	24	5	15.6%
30,000	672	32	100.0%
60,000	24	6	18.8%
60,000	648	32	100.0%
120,000	24	9	28.1%
120,000	576	32	100.0%

Table 1 - SSP/STP Capacities

A RATIONAL APPROACH TO INTELLIGENT NETWORKS

Gary Pinkham

Ericsson Network Systems
730 International Parkway
Richardson, Texas 75081

ABSTRACT

The concepts of an intelligent network have been receiving increasing attention for some time. In an increasingly competitive environment, they have raised expectations of a new level of flexibility in the fast and economical provisioning of new network services. This paper provides an overview of Ericsson's Intelligent Network Architecture (INA), and the rationale behind the architectural precepts.

OVERVIEW

An intelligent network is a network environment within which services can be logically provided independent of the physical structure of the network. The main requirement is that the service provider must be responsive to any market opportunity and, at the same time, able to keep service costs at a minimum. If the service providers are to meet this requirement, the network must be able to provide telecommunications services in a manner so transparent that subscribers can ignore how or even where functions are provided. The service provider must be able to optimize this partitioning according to the particular purpose, competitive demands, and regulatory requirements of each service.

From Ericsson's perspective, an intelligent network should contain the following attributes:

- Rapid service introduction with ubiquitous availability.
- Uniform service operation in a multi-vendor environment.
- Telco programmability for software-defined services.
- Feature portability across different network nodes.
- Subscriber control of network services.

UNBUNDLED SERVICE LOGIC FOR FUNCTIONAL FLEXIBILITY

The primary benefit of the Intelligent network is the quick and ubiquitous introduction of new networks. This, in turn, will allow new network services to be introduced under full service-provider control, in response to end-user requirements, in a competitive environment.

To enable new services to be introduced quickly, and to help deal with the network as a system rather than as a conglomerate of incompatible technologies, the network service logic must be unbundled from the access and transport technologies. This has several interesting implications:

- A new feature can be independent of the access arrangement, whether analog or digital so any network user may be supported.

- A new feature may be introduced into individual central network nodes and is accessable from any switching point by communicating over SS7 signaling network.

- New and existing features may be combined to create new/enhanced network services, for any access and transport technology.

Intelligent Network Architecture (INA) exploits the use of common resource management techniques to define a generic network service logic (i.e. functions) that is common across all INA elements. INA allows standard software modules to become a generic instrument for controlling not only the user-to-user channels, but also the bearer network for various other supplementary and value-added services. By unbundling service control logic, only the switch fabric and processor hardware need to be adapted to actual capacity requirements and the prevailing transmission technology. Network service logic can be used by multiple network nodes and is portable across generations of systems. Over time, this will reduce manufacturer development costs as well as operation expenses and capital investments by the network service provider.

FUNCTIONAL COMPONENTS AS SYSTEM PRIMITIVES

In order to take full advantage of the intelligent network opportunity, Ericsson has based its INA on the premise that each service provided to a subscriber can be broken down into elemental or basic components referred to as "functional components." Using this view, certain functions are specific to a particular service or subscriber; other functions appear in many or all services. Functional components implemented within a switching system may also be activated or deactivated by a software control mechanism either internally (within the system) or externally (through a SS7 communications interface).

The factors that distinguish one service from another are the functional components used and the order in which they are sequenced. Therefore, the INA concept assumes that once a set of functional components is defined and implemented, new services can be introduced by linking the appropriate subset of functional components in the required order to produce the desired service. Figure 1 - INA Concept of Functional Components to Build Services illustrates the concept of using functional components to describe a service.

The functional components are considered to be a set of primitives since they are superset of functions required across a spectrum of services. The communications interface is a control channel that uses the primitives as a command language. Thus, a service logic process can be defined independent of the switching system physically handling a call. The service logic program activates the appropriate system functions in a specified sequence to provide the desired service.

SERVICE CREATION

Today most manufacturers of telephone systems are also marketers of telephone services, developing seemingly endless feature lists based on perceived end user needs. Because the development process is in the hands of the switch vendors, not in the hands of the service providers, there is often considerable lag time in getting new features and services to market. Very often, the final feature or service package, once available, must still be tailored to specific end-user requirements. This development-design-distribution process is time consuming and expensive for system manufacturers, service providers, and end users alike.

Ericsson believes there is a more intelligent approach to this situation; an approach that lends itself to a service creation capability at the service provider level, rather than the system vendor level. Essentially, service creation is an end-user, market-driven process. Therefore, service development should take place at the service provisioning level and not at the system manufacturing level. This allows the service providers to be more responsive to customer needs and to develop more precise services at the best possible price.

Currently AXE is supporting a variety of intelligent network services such as Virtual Network Services Phone, 800 Service and Roamer Service for mobile telephone networks. These services are implemented via an Open Service Control Interface which allows AXE to utilize internal number translation service logic or to access service logic located in another node. Conversely, AXE can act as a service control point (SCP) for other network nodes as well.

With the addition of an Open Feature Programming Interface, feature programs can be unbundled from the basic call processing functions. The Open Feature Programming Interface gives network service providers (i.e. telcos) the flexibility to define entirely new services and features. For the service programmer, the Open Feature Programming Interface hides the internal structure (both hardware and software) of the AXE.

INA SIGNALING AND ADDRESSING

Signaling systems and network service logic have to increasingly cope not only with physical network ports, but also with mobile terminals and individual subscribers that can access network services from any network port. Once the network signaling capabilities have been built with the requisite service mechanisms, they provide a power infrastructure for simplified service provisioning.

With SS7 network signaling, service logic can be physically remoted from the network elements (e.g., Service Switching Point - SSP) controlled by the logic. The advent of the ISDN-D channel, a common signalling channel for digital subscriber access, indicates that even subscriber signaling will become fully disassociated from the service logic. In INA, the signaling channel can be fully disassociated from the information channel. Consequently, a call can be supported from any network element containing the required service logic.

INTELLIGENT NETWORK SCENARIOS

Ericsson's INA consists of the following logical network elements:

- Service Control Points (SCPs) - centralized notes that contain service control logic.
- Service Switching Points (SSPs) - distributed switching nodes that process calls by interacting with SCPs.
- Signal Transfer Part (STPs) - tandem packet switches that route SS7 messages between SCPs and SSPs.
- Service Switching and Control Points (SSCPs) - centralized nodes that have integrated SSP and SCP functionality.
- Service Management System (SMS) - centralized operations system for service creation, establishment, and migration.

Using these network components several basic network topologies can be developed. In all alternatives, the intelligent network is initially deployed as an overlay network. In actual practice, some combination of the two alternatives is the most probable scenario. The main objective is the flexibility to physically locate the service control logic (i.e. SCP functions) wherever it makes the most sense.

Given the objectives of an intelligent network, several different scenarios of how the intelligent network may develop can be envisioned. A simplistic view has been proposed by several groups as a likely approach. In this view, the network service logic is always centralized in general-purpose computers; the switches are depleted of service intelligence and become simply a transport switching device.

While this architectural approach does address the objectives of the intelligent network, it does not do so in an optimal way. This is especially true when a reasonable range of potential services is considered along with SS7 network overhead and service quality objectives. For these reasons, this scenario is too simplistic to be practical. Ericsson has determined that the key to intelligent networks is not an issue of centralized service logic. We believe the key requirement is the flexibility to be able to either centralize or distribute service logic based on the network parameters (economic & performance) associated with a particular service.

Pragmatic network planning methodologies consistently indicate that the best approach to any network architecture is to find the balance between the different cost aspects of providing a service and the requirements to satisfy the subscriber's needs in a timely and affordable manner. For intelligent networks, this implies that the optimal approach is the ability to migrate service intelligence from central nodes toward the subscriber access system as network capabilities and economics allow. Ericsson also believes that this is the most feasible approach.

Ericsson's Intelligent Network Architecture allows new features to be introduced in centralized nodes using a standard service representation language (Figure 2). As service usage grows and

is accepted by the market, service logic migrates toward the subscriber access point to lower the network signaling costs and improve service performance. The service logic is portable across network nodes (Figure 3). By using a standard service representation language, services can be distributed into the network, the centralized nodes become free and can be reused in a continuing process for the introduction of new services. The pace of migration is determined by the network cost for centralization versus the operation and administrative costs for distribution. The service logic migration mechanism is an integral part of the network architecture (Figure 4). The centralized service nodes are used only as a temporary resource for the introduction of new services. Thus, the network is continually optimized for cost and service provisioning.

SUMMARY

Market and technological developments have generated a need for a new level of flexibility in the definition and provisioning of a new network services. This development is welcome. It will contribute to the progressive growth of the network, as well as actively encourage the development of new, competitive services. Accordingly, Ericsson has defined the INA network architecture and developed AXE-based products that optimally help the network service provider to meet these developments.

With Intelligent Network Architecture, new services can be introduced in centralized nodes (either SCP or SSCP). As service usage grows and is accepted by the market, service logic migrates towards the subscriber access point. As services are distributed out into the network, the centralized nodes become free and can be reused in a continuing process of successive introduction of new services. The pace of migration is determined by the network cost for centralization versus the operation and administrative costs for distribution. The service logic migration mechanism is an integral part of the network architecture. Centralized service nodes are used only as a tempoary resource for the introduction of new services. Thus, the network is continually optimized for cost and service provisioning.

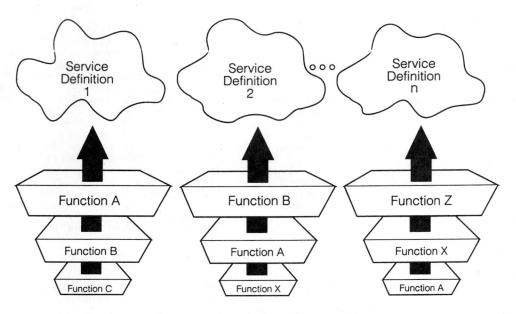

Services are built up by linking functions in different
combination and sequences to meet the service definitions

Figure   1 – INA Concept of Functional Components

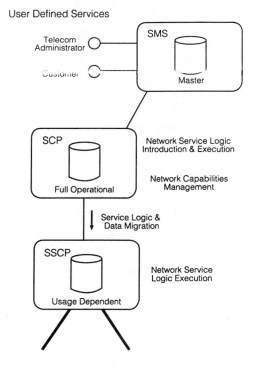

Figure   2 – INA Service Definition and Migration

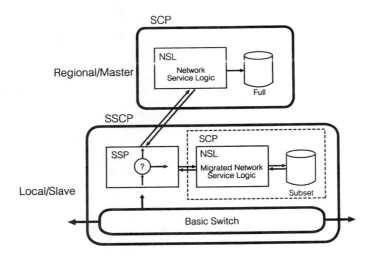

Figure 3 – INA Service Execution

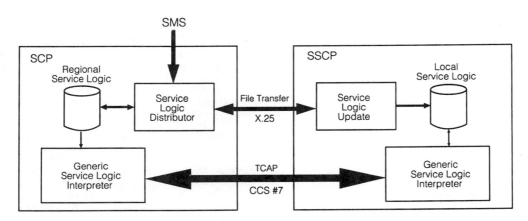

Figure 4 – INA Service Migration

GATEWAY ARCHITECTURE

James H. Spencer
Director, Gateway Services

Integrated Communication Systems
1000 Holcomb Woods Parkway, Suite 412
Roswell, Georgia 30076

ABSTRACT
Gateways to the network are gateways to the future. This session describes architecture and functionality of a gateway arrangement constructed primarily of OEM building blocks.

1325

DSW-13

FUTURE SWITCHING TECHNOLOGIES SEMINAR

Edward D. Reynolds, Chairperson

Regional Customer Services Manager

Northern Telecom, Inc.

155 East Algonquin Road
Arlington Heights, IL 60005

ABSTRACT

Ten years from now Switching Technologies
will be as different from our present
systems as Digital was to Analog. In
addition, there will be changes in
trunking configurations and the switching
process itself. This Seminar takes a
long look into the future and provides
information on how newly emerging technologies are expected to operate and
evolve. The presentations should prove
useful in anticipating and integrating
these new technologies into present
switching configurations.

Dr. Nian C. Huang
Siemans Public Switching Systems

Ronald A. Spanke
AT&T Bell Laboratories

A. Methiwalla
Bell Northern Research

Architectures and Technologies for
Broadband ISDN

N. C. Huang,
Senior Staff Engineer
Siemens Public Switching Systems, Inc.
5500 Broken Sound Boulevard
Boca Raton, Florida 33487

ABSTRACT

The future broadband network will offer integrated communications services including narrowband ISDN, high-speed
data and video services to residential and business subscribers.
This session discusses a broadband switching network architecture and advanced technologies used to implement
these services. The network architecture provides an evolu-
tional approach from the narrowband to the broadband
through modular expansion of digital switching systems and
user-network interfaces. This session also reviews current
status of broadband standards activities.

INTRODUCTION

ISDN (Integrated Services Digital Network) provides a unified
approach to handle voice, data and image services. This is accomplished through the use of integrated access and switching, message-oriented signaling protocol and multiple bit-
rate interfaces [1-3]. The service trials and initial introduction of the ISDN in the public network have taken place. The
next advance in the subscriber loop area is the deployment
of optical fibers [4] and the provision of broadband services.
Recent progress in the development of optical fibers and high-
speed electronics indicates that the cost of providing broadband services can be reduced substantially. In the near term,
the deployment of the broadband network can meet the increasing demand for high-speed data communications due to
the growing use of distributed data bases and the need for
interconnecting Local Area Networks (LANs). In the long
term, video communications may become a relatively low-cost
service and the distribution of high-quality digital video via
optical fibers to residential subscribers may become an
economically competitive alternative.

At the present time, both the international and the U.S. standards committees are working together to resolve various standards issues (e.g.,service definition, reference configuration,
video coding and band width, bit-rate and multiplexing structure of user-network interface, channel rates, and signaling
protocol) of broadband ISDN. At the end of this study period,
CCITT plans to publish the Recommendation I.121 that
describes the framework of providing broadband aspects of
ISDN. The intent of this paper is to discuss some of the major issues of broadband ISDN; in addition, we describe a
general architecture that evolves from a narrowband ISDN
to a broadband ISDN.

NETWORK ARCHITECTURE

Figure 1 shows a general broadband network architecture. The
broadband ISDN supports a variety of concurrent applications
over a single user-network interface. The narrowband and
broadband signals are multiplexed together and transmitted
via optical fibers between subscribers and broadband Central Office (CO). Similar to today's access network architecture, the subscribers are connected to the CO in a star-shaped
network. In certain areas, the use of remote electronics can
help to reduce the cost of massive deployment of fibers in
the subscriber loops. We favor the star or double star architecture because the telcos can use the existing conduits to deploy
the new fiber cables and save the cost of digging-up the
ground. At the subscriber premises, the optical fibers end in
a Broadband Network Terminator (B-NT) that contains op-
tical/electrical converters and narrowband/broadband
(de)multiplexers.

The broadband CO includes an ISDN switching system and
add-on modules: broadband switching module and broadband
distribution module. A broadband packet switching module
may be added as well. This architecture provides the flexibility
to grow from the basic ISDN structure to a full broadband
switching system. In addition, broadband modules can utilize
the signaling, control and operational capabilities of the ISDN
switching system. Thus it reduces the size and cost of broadband modules.

The broadband switching module is used to provide circuit-
switched connections for high-speed data and digital video
signals. The control is via signaling channels connecting
subscribers and the broadband central office.

The broadband distribution module receives video and stereo
sound programs from Program Provider Unit (PPU) and
transmits one-way broadband digital signals to subscribers.
In the video distribution service, subscribers can select video
channels in the usual manner using the control of the TV converter. The channel selection is transmitted through the common signaling channel to the broadband central office.

The broadband packet switching module is used to handle the growing amount of high-speed data traffic. The packet switching module will connect data subscribers to the high-throughput packet switching network. The packet switching module will initially provide direct interfaces to high-speed links at 1.544 Mbit/s. As data communications demand more bandwidth, a broadband packet switching module will be used to connect the data subscribers via the broadband channels to the broadband packet network.

USER-NETWORK INTERFACE

The broadband user-network interface is a major topic of discussion in both U.S. standard committees and international standard committee CCITT Study Group XVIII [5]. The aim is to have an international standard for broadband user-network interface to facilitate terminal portability and international connectivity. The interface issues currently under consideration include interface bit-rate, channel bit-rates, multiplexing structure, access capabilities, reference configurations, etc.

At the present time, most administrations focus on a broadband user-network interface with a gross bit-rate of about 150 Mbit/s. The interface can carry an H4 channel of about 135 Mbit/s. It is also anticipated that channels at H21 (32.768 Mbit/s) and H22 (around 44 Mbit/s) will be offered to subscribers. In addition, the interface will carry narrowband traffic. Some administrations also consider to offer a subscriber up to four H4 channels for an aggregate bit-rate of about 600 Mbit/s in the downstream direction (from CO to subscribers). The manner in which broadband user-network interface will carry traffic is currently a topic of extensive debate within CCITT Study Group XVIII. However, there is a general agreement that two modes will be offered: Synchronous Transfer Mode (STM) and Asynchronous Transfer Mode (ATM) as shown in Figure 2. In addition to these two transfer modes, the investigations of hybrid solutions accommodating both ATM and STM are in progress.

In the STM approach, the interface is divided into a number of access channels, where each channel has assigned time slots within an interface frame structure. On the other hand, the ATM approach does not assign specific time slots to a connection. Instead, the information field of the interface is divided into fixed-length cells with headers containing logical channel numbers. The headers can also be used to identify the service type and priority of the cell. This approach can be used to allocate the circuit-switched channels by periodically assigning a fixed number of cells in each frame. It can also be used to allocate the cells to bursty traffic.

The customer premises reference configuration is also a subject for standardization. Most administrations have focused on a set of reference configurations which are the extension of those defined for narrowband ISDN. Recently, it has been proposed that new reference configurations be defined to connect LANs and MANs (Metropolitan Area Networks) to the broadband network. To be compatible with the narrowband ISDN, the B-NT offers the ISDN's standardized S_o-bus interface via which all narrowband ISDN terminals are attached. In addition, it offers broadband S_b and S_d interfaces.

S_b-interface is designed for broadband communication services and is bi-directionally symmetric. It supports one H4 channel. For data applications, a broadband channel using packet mode is a market requirement. It interfaces with computers, LANs, and work-stations. This channel could also support services with information transfer rates that are lower than the broadband channel rate.

S_d-interface is designed for distribution services, therefore it must take into account the asymmetry of the traffic in the incoming (B-NT to terminals) and outgoing (terminals to B-NT) directions. In the incoming direction, S_d-interface will support up to four H4 channels. In the outgoing direction, S_d-interface also supports a D channel for program selection; the D channels will use an enhanced version of ISDN D channel protocol.

BROADBAND SWITCHING

Broadband switching is the cornerstone of the broadband ISDN because it allows any subscriber to address on-demand the broadband channels of other subscribers. With high-speed electronics (ECL, sub-micron CMOS, and GaAs), conventional switch architectures can provide circuit switching capability for high-quality video services. Recent research results indicate that new switching techniques such as Asynchronous Time Division (ATD) technique can provide flexible multiplexing and switching mechanisms for a broadband ISDN [6]. However, there are still many unanswered technical and economical questions associated with the ATD technique. Therefore it is still not clear which direction the future broadband switching technique will take. In the following, we describe an architecture that provides circuit switching capability for high-speed video services. The broadband channels with embedded ATD technique will be routed to the fast packet switch module.

Figure 3 illustrates the connection of broadband modules to EWSD switching systems [7]. The modular architecture of EWSD allows us to evolve smoothly from narrowband ISDN to a broadband network. The bottom half of the switch block diagram shows the narrowband EWSD switch. The top half of the block diagram shows the add-on switch modules. The broadband LTG (Line Trunk Group), LTGE, interfaces with optical subscriber loops and converts the optical signals into electronic signals and vice versa. It further multiplexes/demultiplexes the narrowband signals from the broadband signals. The broadband signals are routed through the broadband switching networks, while the narrowband signals are routed via internal links to the narrowband switching network (NBSN). In addition, control, operation, administration, and maintenance functions of the switching modules will be done by the Coordination Processor (CP) of the EWSD switching system.

Figure 4 illustrates an example of a switching network array for broadband communications services. Broadband modules contain three major components: Broadband Line Groups (BLG), Broadband Trunk Groups (BTG) and a Broadband Central Switching Network (BCSN). It is a three-stage space division switching network. Trunks are tied to a 64x128 expansion stage. The combination of the expansion stage with the central switching network achieves a non-blocking configuration which is also suitable for broadband transit switching systems. Broadband subscriber lines are attached to a 192x64 concentration stage. Assuming that the average traffic per subscriber line is 0.2 erlang (or equivalently 7.2 CCS), the blocking probability for an intraoffice broadband connection is less than 0.01%. The operating speed of the switching network depends on the selected broadband channel rate.

The technologies needed to implement broadband switching networks must meet the following stringent requirements:

- suitable for high speed signals up to 140 Mbit/s
- low power dissipation
- very large scale integration of the devices so that the switching unit's layout can be kept compact and the length of the signal transmission path be reduced to a minimum.

Siemens has developed two ECL switching chips (16x8 and 32x16 switching matrices) which are implemented as gate arrays. However, CMOS technology has also advanced into the speed range for broadband switching networks. An integrated circuit chip with an even greater density level (32x32) and significantly reduced power dissipation (approx. 1.5W) is under development.

TRANSMISSION SYSTEM

We propose to use single-mode fibers with very low-cost lasers (1300 nm) in the subscriber loops. However, recent development of LED technology has indicated that LED may operate at about 600 Mbit/s and transmit over 5 K meters of single-mode fiber without repeater. Among the advantages of lasers are high coupled power with single-mode fibers and high bandwidth x distance product. But lasers are still expensive for the home use at the present time; in addition, the reliability of lasers needs further improvement. On the other hand, the LED is relatively cheap, but the power coupling to the single-mode fiber is not as good as lasers.

The assessment of low-cost lasers and LEDs should be closely monitored as optical technology matures and as market demands increase. The economics of the Wavelength Division Multiplexing (WDM) technique in the subscriber access network is under study. In addition to identifying the most promising opto-electronic devices, it is important to expedite research and development efforts in compact, low-power-consumption receiver and multiplexing electronics, particularly those belonging to the user interface units at the subscriber premises.

The concept of Synchronous Optical Network (SONET) has been considered in the U.S. and international standard committees. The North American Standard Committee has defined a family of SONET interface rates which are integer multiples of 51.84 Mbit/s basic signal called ''Synchronous Transport Signal Level 1, or STS-1.'' The SONET frame structure provides a convenient vehicle to transport existing standard signal rates (e.g., DS1, DS2 and DS3) between network node interfaces. It is advantageous to use SONET (STS-3) bit-rate and frame structure in broadband subscriber loops; however, some simplification of SONET overhead and pointer mechanism may be advantageous to reduce the cost of SONET interface.

VIDEO TERMINAL AND CHANNEL RATES

The full motion video will be one of the major services provided via broadband ISDN. Although the digitization of video signals has been studied extensively, a standard has not yet evolved. In the process of determining the video coding techniques and the associated channel rates, we have taken the following considerations:

- High quality video transmission
- Trade-off between the network and terminal cost
- Compatibility between terminals for distribution video and those for videophone
- Compatibility with existing video equipment (e.g., camera, TV, VCR)

The distribution of digitally encoded TV programs over the fiber network will initially be used to supplement the over-the-air broadcast and the CATV services. To stimulate the customers' demand on this service, the video quality must be superior to the existing services. The current NTSC color video is subject to two impairments. One is the distortion of the signal in the analog domain. For this reason, digitized NTSC-quality TV is much more robust with respect to transmission impairments, and it can deliver the best picture within the NTSC constraints. The transmission of NTSC video can be achieved by codecs operating at about 45 Mbit/s. This is demonstrated by several existing products. T1Y1 committee is in the process of standardizing an NTSC-based video encoding technique with a bit-rate of 45 Mbit/s.

Another problem with the NTSC system is the technique used to add the chrominance (color) components to the basic luminance (black and white) picture. Because of the limited bandwidth available for the chrominance components and the manner in which the chrominance components are superimposed on the luminance signal, the NTSC signal format could lead to some impairments. The Extended Quality Television (EQTV) coding scheme [8] increases the bandwidth of luminance and chrominance components and encodes them separately to avoid spectral interference. The transmission of EQTV can be achieved by codecs operating at around 135 Mbit/s.

The transmission rate of the video signal is determined by the desired video quality and the complexity of the video codecs. A high bit-rate can reduce the complexity and cost of the video codecs, but it might increase the cost of transmission and switching equipment. Therefore, the cost optimization should cover all the elements involved in a connection. To ensure that the EQTV signals can be distributed over the broadband network and to minimize the overall cost, we have allowed a rate of about 135 Mbit/s in the broadband switching network. The economics and technology of providing HDTV (High Definition TV) at this bit-rate will be studied in the future.

The use of a video coding scheme for all types of services, including videophone and distribution video, has the merit of compatible terminals. But the use of different coding schemes will allow videophone service to use the network facility more efficiently. The development of broadband local network should take this issue into consideration, it should also consider the availability of different digital video codecs in the market. In the near future, the bandwidth will still be expensive for the interoffice trunking facilities. To minimize the cost of long-distance transmission, a transcoder will be used to reduce the bandwidth for communication video services.

APPLICATIONS AND EVOLUTION STRATEGY

Even though the objectives for achieving the target broadband network are the same in different parts of the country and the world, initially the network will be different due to political and legal constraints. Examples include the spread of the CATV network, monopoly vs. competition, and government regulation. An additional factor for consideration is the investment risk. These different factors have led to the different approaches in the evolution from today's network to the broadband network. We may divide these approaches into two scenarios.

The first scenario is the market driven approach. This scenario applies to the business area, where the demand for high-speed data communication is increasing. One example of this approach is the deployment of optical fibers for the interconnection of LANs in the Metropolitan Area Network (MAN). With high-speed communication network, the response time for new computer workstations with high-resolution bit-mapped screens can be significantly reduced. The trials of MAN have been conducted by a few Bell Operating Companies. Another example is the use of overlay network in the public or private networks, such as video conference for business applications and the provision of video services for special applications. In this scenario, the primary demand for broadband services comes from the business sector. Each subscriber will be cabled individually and the cost per subscriber will be rather high in the beginning.

The second scenario is a technology-driven approach, which is based on the assumption that the fiber cost will be declined to the point to compete with the combination of coaxial cable for video distribution and wire pairs for narrowband ISDN. In addition, the economics of scale can help to reduce the cost further by mass deployment of fibers in the subscriber loop areas. An initial step in this direction is to deploy fiber subscriber loops for POTS only, while the service can be naturally evolved into an ISDN. As fiber subscriber loops proliferate and the broadband communications become more attractively priced, full interactive video communications will eventually become prevalent in the residential areas. Eventually all services will be integrated together as discussed in CCITT.

Given the uncertainty of the demand for broadband services and the desire and competition to deploy optical fibers in the subscriber loops, the integration of a cross-connect system to the EWSD switching system can be used as an interim solution to evolve to a broadband network. This architecture can be used to deploy fibers in the subscriber loop areas to provide narrowband services initially. Once the traffic for the broadband services justifies, they can also be used to carry broadband traffic.

In the subscriber access environment as shown in Figure 5, one CCM (Cross-Connect Multiplexer) can be used as a remote terminal that acts as a collection hub for other remote switching modules, PBXs, and LANs. The remote CCM can be connected to the CCM or CCS (Cross-Connect System) in the CO on a ring or point-to-point basis. When it is configured on a ring architecture, the remote CCMs can be used as ADMs (Add/Drop Multiplexers), which link many Carrier Serving Areas (CSAs) on the same route to the CO. Depending on the need of each CSA, the CCM will dynamically add/drop appropriate amount of traffic to this area.

Another potential application of this network is the capability for dynamic reconfiguration. For example, the network is configured as a star architecture to route the traffic to the CO during the day, and it is reconfigured to the ring architecture to serve the data applications during the night. An integration of the interfaces of these systems to OSS (Operation Support System) can simplify the OA&M cost.

CONCLUSION

Broadband communication will be the next development task after the integration of the narrowband services in the ISDN. Its technical feasibility has already been demonstrated by a number of pilot projects [9,10]. We have developed the technologies for a broadband network and this development will be continued still further.

The introduction of the broadband ISDN will have some impact on various issues (e.g., signaling system, D channel protocol, numbering plan, and routing principles) of the telecommunication network. These issues have to be resolved by the U.S. and the international telecommunication standard committees.

REFERENCES

1. Special Issue on Integrated Services Digital Network (ISDN), Telcom Report, Volume 8, April 1985.

2. D. J. Eigen, "Bringing ISDN Closer to Reality," Telecommunications Magazine, Volume 19, No. 11, November 1985.

3. G. Arndt and H.J. Rothamel, "Communication Services in the ISDN", Telcom Report, 10-15, Volume 8, April 1985.

4. R. K. Snelling and K. W. Kaplan, "All Fiber Networks - A Reality by 1988 -1989," ICC'87, Seattle, June 1987.

5. S. E. Minzer, "'Broadband User-Network Interfaces to ISDN," ICC'87, Seattle, June 1987.

6. J. P. Coudreuse and M. Servel, "PRELUDE: An Asynchronous Time-Division Switched Network," ICC'87, Seattle, June 1987.

7. E. Knorpp and B. Schaffer, "Integration of Broadband Services in the ISDN," 1174-1180, ICC '85.

8. Encoding Parameters of Digital Television for Studios, CCIR Rec. 601 (Mod 1), November 1983.

9. E. Braun, "BIGFON Heralds the Start of a New Era in Telecommunications," Telcom Report, 189-195, Volume 5, No. 3, 1982.

10. U. Pohle, "Wideband Communication in the ISDN: Experience from BIGFON Project, Proc. ISS '84, Florence, Italy, 1984.

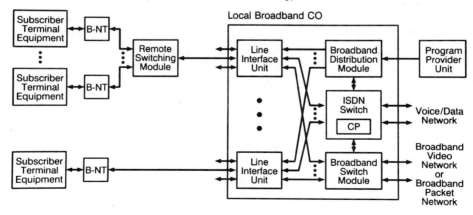

Figure 1: Network Architecture

1. Classical Approach: STD Based Multiplexing Technique

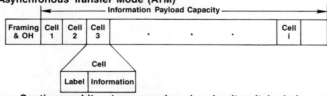

Framing & OH	D	H_4 ($3 \times H_{22}$ or $4 \times H_{21}$)	$m \times H_1$	$n \times B$

- H channels can be operated in either circuit or packet Mode
- H_4: ∼135 Mbps ; H_{22}: ∼44 Mbps ; H_{21}: ∼32 Mbps ;

2. Asynchronous Transfer Mode (ATM)

Framing & OH	Cell 1	Cell 2	Cell 3	· · ·	Cell i	

Cell

Label	Information

- Continuous bit - stream services (or circuit-switched channels) can be allocated by assigning a fixed number of cells in each frame.

Figure 2: Alternative Multiplexing Techniques

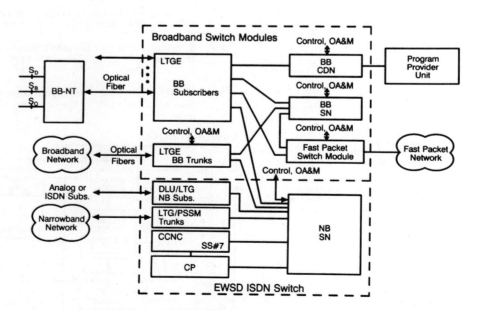

Figure 3: Broadband Switch Architecture

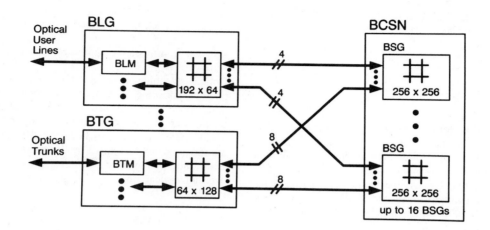

Figure 4: **Broadband Switching Networks**

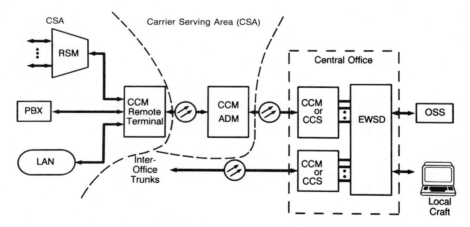

Figure 5: **An Integrated EWSD/Cross-Connect Approach**

Guided Wave Optical Switching
Ronald A. Spanke
Member of Technical Staff
AT&T Bell Laboratories
1200 E. Warrenville Rd
Naperville, IL 60566

ABSTRACT

Now that semiconductor lasers and optical fiber have become widely used for high speed digital transmission, the field of optical switching is emerging as a possible technology for future switching applications. While concepts for switching photons instead of electrons have been around for many years, the technology is still in its infancy. This presentation will review the basic concepts of how guided-wave photonic switching works and discuss various architectures suited for constructing optical switches.

INTRODUCTION

The advantages of optical data transmission are widely known. Freedom from electromagnetic interference, small physical size, low cost, long repeater spacing, and very high bandwidth make optical fibers suitable for very high data rate communications. This high bandwidth offers the potential for many new subscriber services including, but certainly not limited to, broadcast and point-to-point video, and high capacity data transfer (100's of Mbits per subscriber).

Now that we have these services on a high-speed optical transmission fiber, how do we switch all of these incoming photons to different destinations? This presentation explores various optical switching elements as a solution to this problem. The approach used to review basic optical switching concepts will be to: demonstrate the need for high bandwidth and optical switching; provide an overview of what an optical switch looks like; discuss a fundamental building block for optical switching, the directional coupler; and finally, to discuss how architectures can be constructed from these building blocks to form larger optical switching systems.

NEED FOR HIGH BANDWIDTH (OPTICAL) SWITCHING

Todays optical fiber transmission systems are adequate if every transmitter wants to talk with one and only one receiver. If a high bandwidth user wishes to communicate with two, three or more other users at various times, they must either have a dedicated optical fiber between themselves and every possible endpoint or construct some form of a central switch that connects all users.

In today's implementation of this high-bandwidth central switch, the optical information on the incoming fibers is first converted to electronics, switched through conventional electronic switching, and converted back to optics by a laser and sent out over a fiber. The drawback of this approach is the limited bandwidth of the electronic switching fabric of only a few 100's of MHz. Where do we go as transmission speeds edge up into the GHz?

Optical switching offers the ability to simply switch the photons, avoiding the optic to electronic and electronic to optic conversions. In theory, some optical switches have a bandwidth roughly equivalent to an optical fiber (several TeraHertz!). In practice, however, the data rate through an optical switch is limited by the transmitter and receiver electronics. In general, whatever data rate can be sent over an optical fiber can be switched through an optical switch.

AN OVERVIEW OF OPTICAL SWITCHING ARCHITECTURES

What does an optical switch look like? It can best be modeled as a black box with several input optical fibers and several output optical fibers. If the number of fibers is large, this optical switch can be subdivided into several smaller optical networks interconnected by optical fiber. In the limit, these networks can be constructed by interconnecting many fundamental switching elements.

The fundamental optical switching element or *Beta Cell* is a 2x2 optical switch with inputs A and B and outputs A' and B'. In one state, the light from input A goes to output A', and input B goes to output B', and in the other state, the light from input A is switched to output B' while input B is switched to output A'.

The fact that light is immune to external electric and magnetic fields is a strong selling point for interference-free optical transmission. However, in the switching field it means that a beam of light will not change its direction in the presence of an applied electric or magnetic field as a stream of electrons would. Since almost all electronic switching mechanisms are based on some microscopic or macroscopic field effect, conventional methods for steering electrons will not work for steering photons.

The one phenomenon that light responds to is a change in the index of refraction, n, of the propagating medium. Index of refraction changes account for the everyday phenomenon of reflection and refraction. A change in the index of refraction can slow down, speed up, or change the direction of an incident beam. To realize an optical switch one might somehow control the index of refraction of the medium.

MATERIALS FOR AN OPTICAL SWITCH

One now has to construct this optical *Beta Cell*. The basic requirements for a fiber optic switching medium are:

1. It must be transparent(low propagation loss) at the operating wavelength, λ.

2. It must be capable of being processed such that a waveguide can be created in the material to channel the light.

3. The material must be able to change its index of refraction, n, by applying an external stimulus such as an electric field.

One of the most promising material candidates is Lithium Niobate ($LiNbO_3$). A single mode optical channel waveguide can be fabricated into the surface of a $LiNbO_3$ crystal by diffusion of a strip of titanium.[1] This titanium diffused channel is only 5-10 microns wide and has a slightly higher index of refraction thereby confining the optical beam by total internal reflection.

THE DIRECTIONAL COUPLER AND WAVEGUIDE COUPLING

One of the basic optical switching elements that can perform the beta cell function is the directional coupler shown in figure 1.[2] When light travels down a diffused channel waveguide, most of the optical energy is confined inside the waveguide. However, part of the energy resides in an evanescent field that extends out from the waveguide several microns on each side. When two parallel diffused waveguide channels are brought close enough to each other such that their evanescent fields overlap, some of the energy in the first waveguide couples into the second waveguide.

If the two waveguides have identical propagation speeds, this evanescent field coupling continues until all of the optical energy originally in the first waveguide is coupled into the second waveguide. This complete transfer of power occurs in a characteristic coupling length, l, usually a few mm to a few cm. If the waveguides remain close together longer than this coupling length, the energy begins to couple back into the first waveguide. The optical power will continue to couple periodically back and forth between the two waveguides.

We can fabricate a directional coupler with length L, where L/l is an odd integer. This gives us an optical device where all the power that enters into the first waveguide exits from the second, and all the power that enters the second waveguide exits from the first.

DIRECTIONAL COUPLER SWITCH WITH AN APPLIED ELECTRIC FIELD

If it is desired to switch the light such that it remains in the original waveguide, an electric field can be applied to the directional coupler to change its coupling characteristics. Lithium Niobate is an electro-optic material that changes its index of refraction slightly when an electric field is present.

The electrodes are arranged so that, as the voltage increases, the index of refraction increases in one waveguide and decreases in the other. The two waveguides no longer have identical propagation speeds and the coupling between the waveguides changes.

At some value of applied voltage, the mismatch between the two waveguides will have the right value such that all of the optical power entering waveguide A returns to waveguide A and the optical power entering waveguide B returns to waveguide B. We now have a physical device capable of functioning as our optical beta element that switches state by changing the control voltage V.

CHARACTERISTICS OF OPTICAL SWITCH ARCHITECTURES

Several directional couplers can be tied together to form an optical switch. There are many possible architectures for interconnecting these *beta* elements, each possessing various characteristics. In evaluating an NxN optical switch architecture, several constraints apply:

1. *Blocking, Nonblocking, or Rearrangeable Nonblocking:*
   If any unused optical input can be connected to any unused output, the network is nonblocking. If existing connections must be torn down and rearranged to complete a call, it is rearrangeably nonblocking. If some permutation of the switch cannot be realized at all, it is a blocking network.

2. *Broadcast or Point-to-Point:*
   A point to point network maps one input to only one output. A broadcast network allows several outputs to listen to the same input.

3. *Directional Couplers:*
   The number of directional couplers required to implement an NxN switch should be minimized.

4. *Drivers:*
   The number of electronic drivers and associated control leads should be minimized.

5. *Attenuation:*
   Every directional coupler passed adds to the overall attenuation of the switch. Minimize the worst case and differential attenuation.

6. *Signal-to-Noise Ratio:*
   Every directional coupler passed leaks some optical noise into the desired signal from the other signal. Maximize the overall system signal to noise ratio(SNR).

The optimal optical switch architecture for a given situation depends on the relative importance of the above constraints. Some architectures may have a low number of directional couplers but may also exhibit a low system

SNR. Four optical switching architectures are examined in detail: The crossbar architecture, an N-stage planar architecture, and two architectures proposed by the author based on active and passive splitters and combiners.

THE CROSSBAR OPTICAL SWITCH ARCHITECTURE

The crossbar or rectangular switch matrix is a classical electronic switching architecture that can be implemented with 2x2 directional couplers for each of the crosspoints. The optical crossbar is a wide-sense, nonblocking, point-to-point switch. A crossbar switch with N inputs and M outputs requires $N \cdot M$ directional couplers and is shown in figure 2. Each directional coupler requires its own control lead and driver circuitry.

The longest path, from input N to output M, must pass through $N+M-1$ directional couplers. The worst case SNR occurs when input N is connected to output 1 and must pass through $N-1$ directional couplers each carrying a full power signal.[3] A 4x4 optical crossbar architecture can be fabricated on a single 1x6 cm $LiNbO_3$ substrate. Recently 4x4 and 8x8 optical crossbar switches have been fabricated.[4] [5]

THE N-STAGE PLANAR ARCHITECTURE

The number of directional couplers can be reduced significantly by using an N-Stage planar architecture shown in figure 3.[6] This reduction in directional couplers forces the architecture to become a rearrangeably nonblocking point-to-point switch. The NxN switch now requires only $\frac{N(N-1)}{2}$ directional couplers. A separate driver is still required for each coupler.

The worst case path through the switch is also shorter. The worst case optical signals now only pass through N directional couplers. The SNR for the N-Stage planar architecture is slightly worse than the crossbar since each signal passes through N directional couplers which can leak part of a full power signal into the desired channel.

MULTI-SUBSTRATE ARCHITECTURES

To help solve the problem with large numbers of drivers, large overall switch attenuations, and low system SNR's, the following two architectures were proposed.[7] Both architectures rely on multiple optical substrates interconnected by fiber. The substrates are either a 1xN active splitter chip, a 1xN passive splitter chip, or an Nx1 active combiner chip.

The 1xN active splitter is constructed from $N-1$ directional couplers that function as 1x2 switches arranged in a k-stage

tree structure where $k=\log_2 N$. An Nx1 active combiner uses $N-1$ directional couplers that function as 2x1 switches and also requires k stages. The 1xN passive splitter can either be fabricated on $LiNbO_3$, or 50/50 fiber splitters could be used to construct a k-stage passive splitting tree.

The first architecture, type 1, is constructed from N 1xN active splitters interconnected to N Nx1 active combiners and is shown in figure 4. This architecture requires a total of $2N(N-1)$ directional couplers to implement a full NxN switch. For control purposes, every directional coupler in the same stage of each substrate can be electrically tied together. This gives only k control leads and drivers per substrate instead of $N-1$. The total number of drivers required for an NxN architecture is $2N\log_2 N$, which represents a significant reduction for large N.

Architecture type 1 is a strictly nonblocking point-to-point switch. Every input passes through k directional couplers in the active splitter and k directional couplers in the active combiner. The SNR for this architecture is significantly improved because every possible noise term must pass through two directional couplers as crosstalk to enter a desired channel.

The second architecture, type 2, is constructed of N 1xN passive splitters and N Nx1 active combiners. Since each input is passively split, multiple outputs can listen to the same input. Architecture type 2 is a strictly nonblocking broadcast architecture. This architecture requires $N(N-1)$ passive 50/50 splitting elements and $N(N-1)$ directional couplers. Again the directional couplers in each stage of every active combiner substrate can be electrically tied together giving a total of $N\log_2 N$ drivers.

The optical path for architecture type 2 passes through k 50/50 passive splitting elements each of which incurs a 3 dB power loss and through k directional couplers. Due to the passive splitter, this architecture no longer has the advantage of the double crosstalk rejection of type 1, but still exhibits a reasonably good system SNR because each desired signal only has to pass k directional couplers that leak a full power signal into the desired signal.

Architecture types 1 and 2 can also be fabricated as a single substrate. The single substrate fabrication requires the use of passive optical waveguide crossovers located between the switching elements to give the required device interconnectivity. A 4x4 single substrate version of the type 2 broadcast architecture has recently been fabricated[8] which exhibits insertion losses between 11.6 and 13.9 dB and crosstalk values that were better than -35 dB.

COMPARISON OF OPTICAL SWITCHING ARCHITECTURES

The above architectures can be compared on many points. The first comparison criterion is nonblocking and broadcast capabilities.

Crossbar: Wide-Sense Nonblocking   Point-to-Point
N-Stage: Rearrangeable Nonblocking Point-to-Point
Type 1:   Strictly Nonblocking   Point-to-Point
Type 2:   Strictly Nonblocking   Broadcast

The total number of directional couplers and electronic drivers required for an NxN architecture are given by:

	COUPLERS	DRIVERS
Crossbar:	N^2	N^2
N-Stage:	$N(N-1)/2$	$N(N-1)/2$
Type 1:	$2N(N-1)$	$2N \cdot k$
Type 2:	$N(N-1)$	$N \cdot k$

The worst case attenuation is calculated based on the number of directional couplers a signal must pass through. Each directional coupler has an insertion loss L associated with it. Every 50/50 splitting element has an insertion loss of 3 dB + E for excess loss. Every time a fiber-to-waveguide transition is encountered, an additional insertion loss, W, is added to the attenuation. For this comparison, fiber and connector losses are ignored. The overall attenuation or insertion loss is given by:

Crossbar:	$IL = (2N-1)L + 2W$
N-Stage:	$IL = NL + 2W$
Type 1:	$IL = 2kL + 4W$
Type 2:	$IL = k(3dB + E) + kL + 4W$

The worst case system SNR is calculated based on the number of couplers that leak noise power into the desired signal. The crosstalk extinction ratio, x, represents the optical power that the directional coupler leaks into the wrong waveguide. The SNR is given by:

Crossbar:	$SNR = X - 10\log(N-1)$
N-Stage:	$SNR = X - 10\log N$
Type 1:	$SNR = 2X - 10\log k$
Type 2:	$SNR = X - 10\log k$

It is interesting to graph these characteristics against increasing switch dimension. The number of drivers for the various architectures is plotted verses switch dimension in figure 5. The overall switch attenuation is plotted in figure 6 with $L=E=1dB$, $W=2dB$. The system SNR is plotted verses switch dimension in figure 7 with $X=20dB$. The dotted horizontal line represents an 11 dB SNR that is required to maintain an overall bit error rate of 10^{-9}.

LIMITS OF OPTICAL SWITCHING

Electro-optic switching offers many potential advantages especially where very high bandwidth is desired. However, one must understand the practical limits of using this technology in a switching product.

One major constraint is the physical size of the optical devices. The directional coupler switching element previously described is very long and can range from $2-10mm$ in length. In addition, a significant amount of room must be left between devices for waveguide interconnection, since the diffused channel waveguides are limited to curves with radii greater than about $4cm$.

Today's best densities are on the order of 10-100 couplers on a standard $LiNbO_3$ crystal size (1x6 cm). A ballpark estimate indicates that an interconnected NxN optical switch takes up over 10,000 times more crystal real estate than an electronic NxN VLSI silicon switch. This alone is a heavy price to pay for high bandwidth, when silicon can run pretty fast itself.

Another constraint is the control voltage, typically anywhere from 10 to greater than 50 volts. Since the required voltages are not compatible with TTL/ECL levels, special driver circuits must be used. With the addition of the driver circuits, an optical switch requires even more physical space.

High voltage tends to increase the cost of the drivers and decrease the switching speed and reconfiguration rate of the switch. Maximum reconfiguration rates may be confined to 10's to 100's of MHz if 10 to 50 volts must be switched. Once configured in a state, the optical switch has a virtually unlimited data throughput rate (GHz-THz).

Finally, given the attenuation and SNR limits discussed previously, there is a limit on the dimensionality of an optical switch without requiring regeneration and amplification within the switch. An NxN switch can only approach dimensions of a few hundred before becoming seriously limited by attenuation or SNR.

APPLICATIONS FOR OPTICAL SWITCHING

The above constraints indicate that $Ti:LiNbO_3$ guided wave optical switching is not the ultimate solution for all switching needs. As we look into the future, we attempt to ask ourselves how and where this optical switching technology might best fit in to our overall switching framework. One can try to define the type of environment that is best suited for optical switching.

Optical switching naturally fits into high data rate environments, especially those situations where the data rates are faster than can be handled in a large electronic switch matrix(above several 100's of MHz). Because the reconfiguration rates are relatively slow(10's to 100's of MHz) compared with the possible data throughput rates (GHz-THz), optics should be used for slow speed switching of very high speed signals. One example could be a very high definition TV channel that is switched only when the customer changes stations.

Finally, size, power, attenuation, SNR and cost tend to limit optical switching applications to small switching networks. One can foresee the size of these networks perhaps reaching several hundred but not several thousand.

CONCLUSION

This talk has presented an overview of the basic concepts involved in optical switching. New materials such as Lithium Niobate and devices such as the directional coupler can permit the optical switching of heretofore unachievable data rates. The optimal architectures for switching photons are not necessarily the optimal architectures for switching electrons.

Any limits of this technology that we see today may vanish with new breakthroughs. Future research should improve the characteristics of these devices, and bring new devices and architectures to this emerging field. We are looking at a young technology, continually developing with a lot of potential for the future.

REFERENCES

1. R. V. Schmidt and I. P. Kaminow, "Metal Diffused Optical Waveguides in LiNbO₃," *Appl. Phys. Lett.*, Vol. 25 (1974), pp. 458-460.

2. R. C. Alferness, "Guided-Wave Devices for Optical Communication," *IEEE J. Quantum Electron,* QE-17 (1981) p. 946

3. Hinton, H. S., "A Nonblocking Optical Interconnection Network Using Directional Couplers," *GLOBECOM, '84*, 26.5.1-26.5.5.

4. G. A. Bogert, "4x4 Ti:LiNbO₃ Integrated Optical Crossbar Switch Array," *Appl. Phys. Lett.* 47 (1985) p. 348.

5. P. Granestrand, L. Thylen, B. Stoltz, K. Berguall, W. Doblissen, H. Heidrich and D. Hoffman, "Strictly Nonblocking 8x8 Integrated Optic Switch Matrix in Ti:LiNbO₃," *IGWO '86*, p. 4.

6. R. A. Spanke, V. E. Benes, "An N-stage Planar Optical Permutation Network," *Applied Optics*, Vol. 26, April 1, 1987, p. 1226.

7. R. A. Spanke, "Architectures for Large Nonblocking Optical Space Switches," *IEEE J. Quantum Electron.* Vol. QE-22, June, 1986, p. 964.

8. Bogert, G. A., "4x4 Ti:LiNbO₃ Switch Array with Full Broadcast Capability," *Topical Meeting on Photonic Switching*, March 18-20, 1987, Incline Village, NV., p. 68.

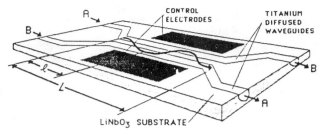

Figure 1.   Directional Coupler Optical Switching Element.

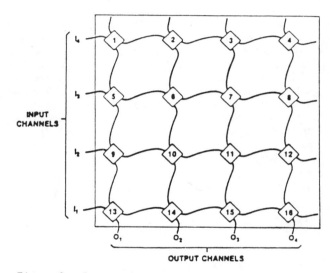

Figure 2.   Rectangular Crossbar Architecture Implemented with Directional Couplers.

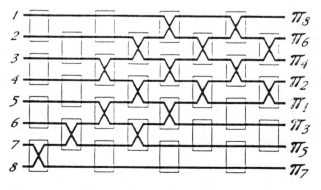

Figure 3.   N-Stage Planar Optical Switching Architecture.

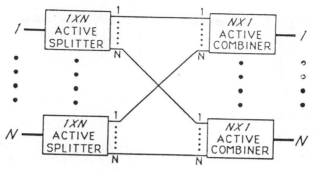

Figure 4. Architecture Type 1 constructed
From 1xN Active Splitters and
Nx1 Active Combiners.

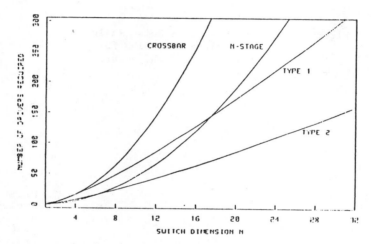

Figure 5. Number of Electronic Drivers
verses Switch Dimension for
Various Switch Architectures.

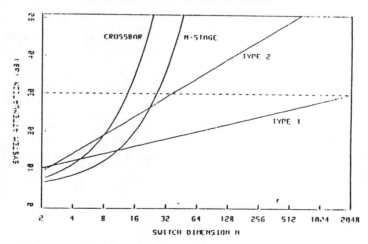

Figure 6. Overall Attenuation verses Switch
Dimension for various Optical
Switching Architectures.

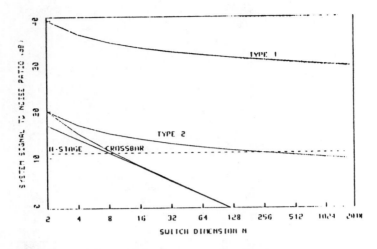

Figure 7. System Signal to Noise Ratio
verses Switch Dimension for
Various Switch Architectures.

Photonic Interconnect
For High Speed Switching
A. Methiwalla
Manager of Exploratory Systems
Advanced Technologies Laboratory
Bell Northern Research
Ottowa, Canada

The potential application of electrically
reconfigurable photonic interconnects for
high capacity switching is being made
possible by recent advances in high speed
opto-electronic and electronic devices.
Their integration with each other and with
passive optical devices will be reviewed
to evaluate the expected evolution of
photonic interconnection technology toward
a future optical crosspoint concept.

OPEN FORUM

At the conclusion of the Future Switching
Technologies presentations, the speakers
will hold an open forum and entertain
questions on any subject with which they
are familiar and information is available.

THE EVOLVING ROLE OF PREMISES BASED (PBX) DIGITAL SWITCHING SOLUTIONS

Thomas E. Mader, Chairperson

Vice President, Marketing

Northern Telecom, Inc.

155 East Algonquin, Suite 300
Arlington Heights, IL 60005

ABSTRACT

The PBX has played an increasing role in the evolution of telephony over the past ten years. Innovation and change propelled the customer premises based switch ahead of Centrex at one point in time. The two services now appear to be at parity, and even complementary positions. This seminar discusses the role of premises based digital switching technology in the marketplace, clarifies its role, and defines its future.

Robert DelPriore   -- Vice President, Northern Telecom
William Murphy   -- Director of Research and
                      Development, Ameritech
                      Communications
William Wiley   -- Project Director, AT&T

PBX ARCHITECTURES

William Murphy
Director of Research and Development

Ameritech Communications, Inc.

300 S. Wacker Drive, Floor 10
Chicago, IL 60606

ABSTRACT

AT&T, Northern Telecom, NEC and IBM/ROLM are the current market share leaders in the digital PBX business. This paper compares their products with respect to general architecture, interfaceability/ standard support, and software practices. Also discussed are several views regarding future developments in the communications marketplace.

The paper is not intended to be an endorsement of one manufacturer's product over another; nor does it imply that these four product lines are superior to other PBX alternatives. We simply feel that focusing on these market leaders will give us some insight into the market at large.

INTRODUCTION

The PBX market has been highly competitive for the past several years. Divestiture created seven new large distribution channels in 1984, and several high technology companies have entered (and left) the market since then. During the mid 1980s, the "generation war" was in full swing, and most manufacturers were busy trying to convince everyone that their particular offerings were "fourth generation." What has happened since then? Where is the market going?

Few people hype the fourth generation these days. Customers appear to have tired quickly of abstract arguments involving architectural supremacy. Most continue to be concerned, however, with bread and butter issues like simplicity, reliability, and future safety.

In this paper, we will examine the four PBX manufacturers who enjoy the largest market share. While we will touch on several general architectural issues, we will focus on areas many customers seem very concerned about: INTERFACEABILITY and SOFTWARE PRACTICES. These important areas directly affect key customer perception of simplicity, reliability, future safety, and ease of implementation.

We will also discuss these key players' view of the future PBX marketplace.

I. IBM/ROLM

  i) GENERAL. . .The new 9751 PBX family is an evolutionary design built on the matures ROLMBUS 295. The basic building blocks of the system are: two shelves/pod, two pods/cabinet, five cabinets/node, and up to fifteen nodes per system. Each node uses 2030 time slots allowing 1015 simultaneous conversations and can serve up to about 2000 users via two 32 bit processors.

  IBM/ROLM considers the architecture fully distributed in that no identifiable common equipment is required to serve a networked system. Physically, each node must be directly connected to each other node via at least one but as many as four 74 MB twin coaxial connections. Fibre can be used between 1K feet and 20K feet, and T-1 could be used in a pinch. Call control signaling is done via a separate coaxial connection running a 2.5 MB IBM proprietary protocol.

  IBM/ROLM feels strongly that five variables contribute to PBX design: memory, power, space, time slots, and busy hour call attempts (BHCAs). IBM/ROLM claims their architecture allows approximately three times as many BHCAs as their closest competitor. (BHCAs are essentially a function of efficient call control, as the call attempt must be processed before a time slot can be assigned.) As integrated data applications generate more data calls, and new feature enhancements increase call origination, BHCA capacity becomes increasingly crucial, says IBM/ROLM.

  ii) INTERFACEABILITY

    a)LAN. . .Generally, IBM/ROLM supports IBM's traditional view that three basic categories of traffic, switched, LAN, and direct connected, should be architecturally separate. To that end, high speed local area networks are not offered, integrated with the switch or multiplexed over limited pair wiring.

    b)MESSAGE CENTER. . .IBM/ROLM aggressively markets their own PHONEMAIL product, but does make the ROLMPHONE 244 interface available to anyone who wants to integrate a voicemail system. Also, a more robust interface called TAP is available to serve a message desk application similar to the one currently offered on IBM SYSTEM 36. Eventually, we expect this application to be available on OS/2 based machines.

c)ISDN...Currently, station sets are served via the proprietary ROLMLINK, which provides four 64KB streams to the desktop, so migration to 2B+D should be easily achieved. In previous switches, ROLM used a non standard 12 bit voice sampling technique which would have made ISDN migration difficult, but the 9751 has changed to a standard 8 bit scheme. IBM continues to participate in various standards discussions and has issued several position papers regarding ISDN support, so ultimate compatibility is expected.

iii)   SOFTWARE...IBM ROLM does all programming in Rolm Programming Language (RPL), which is somewhat similar to UNIX C. IBM/ROLM appears committed to making systems changes and upgrades as totally software intensive as possible. The system backup data base is installed in RAM and upgrades/updates are loaded via PS/2 floppy disk. IBM/ROLM feels this method causes least trauma for the customer, and distributor costs are lower due to decreased PROM inventory requirements.

When asked about the future, IBM/ROLM quickly answers that many integrated voice/data applications will evolve over the next few years. They believe we have yet to scratch the surface of advanced PBX applications. Also, they see the 9751 as eventually becoming a full fledged SNA node.

II.   AT&T

i)   GENERAL...The ATT SYSTEM 85 consists of a common control cabinet which can serve up to thirty one modules. Each module utilizes 512 time slots and terminates 300-800 stations. When several modules are required, they may be "star" wired via fibre to a "center stage" time multiplex switch (TMS).

The common control cabinet houses a 501CC 16 bit processor which performs most call control functions. The TMS does not include a processor and directs all intra switch/inter module traffic. Each module also includes a processor and all processors can (optionally) be redundant.

Essentially, the SYSTEM 85 design is an evolutionary design from the DIMENSION family. Cabinets are somewhat large (although newer space saving designs will likely be announced soon). Integrated office functions are provided via external applications processors, and data switching is a separate major functional component.

SYSTEM 75, however, is a new design. Unlike the SYSTEM 85, which essentially moved the DIMENSION architecture into a digital environment, SYSTEM 75 was designed to be a dual TDM bus switch utilizing multiple processors from day one. Although the 1800 port switch is currently positioned below SYSTEM 85, advanced

networking features make it possible to configure large multi node systems serving over 10,000 ports. Eventually, AT&T will merge these two products.

Although some may criticize the SYSTEM 85 by calling it a digital DIMENSION, it is important to remember that DIMENSION software is a tried and true product operating on a significant installed base. Also, both SYSTEM 75 and SYSTEM 85 support an extremely wide range of AT&T station instruments, so end user implementation is easy for current AT&T customers.

ii)   INTERFACEABILITY

a)LAN...AT&T currently offers LAN connections via STARLAN, which is basically related to the switch only via a common wiring plan and proprietary station multiplexing scheme. As with other switches, circuit switched data connectivity is also available.

It appears that AT&T believes most typical "PC" LANS will remain local in nature and that most casual users (i.e. many call attempts, short holding times) will grow most rapidly in the future. The multiple processor nature of the SYSTEM 75 architecture seems especially suited to this type of environment.

b)MESSAGE CENTER...AT&T currently markets their own voicemail system called AUDIX. The MC interface is essentially proprietary, although 1 or 2 manufacturers claim compatibility.

c)ISDN...AT&T currently delivers two 64KB bit streams and 48KB packet channels to the desktop in an ISDN (LIKE) format. Naturally, AT&T is heavily involved in the current standards discussion and already offers primary rate interfaces to the #5ESS class 4 central offices.

iii)   SOFTWARE...Currently, the SYSTEM 85 utilizes mature DIMENSION software as already noted. SYSTEM 75 uses a proprietary UNIX-like operating system called ORYX PECOS, which, according to AT&T, will ultimately serve both vehicles. Application processor programs, however, are written in UNIX C (on the SYSTEM 75), so it is likely that AT&T will encourage feature customization by VARs and sophisticated customers.

AT&T utilizes RAM memory and generally believes in soft upgrades.

AT&T's view of the future seems to allow for large increases in "casual" data traffic (e.g. executives using E-mail, etc.). The multiple application processor architecture of the SYSTEM 75 seems tailor made for VAR customization, and it is probably only a matter of time before this design replaces the more mature SYSTEM 85. Apparently, AT&T also believes that most LAN applications will continue to be "local" in nature.

III. NORTHERN TELECOM

i) GENERAL. . .The SL-1/SL-100 architecture is a tried and true hierarchal architecture which has evolved over several years. The SL-1 has been continually improved and enhanced since the mid 1970s and the SL-100 is a direct descendant of the DMS100 central office switch.

Because the SL family uses centralized call processing, several models covering several line sizes are available. The SL-1 covers the market up to about 5000 stations and the SL-100 can grow to approximately 30,000 in standard configurations.

The primary processor is the NT40 16 bit processor (fully redundant), but the SL-100 "SUPERNODE" utilized new Motorola 32 bit processors which effectively doubles its capacity to about 60,000 stations.

Because of the central processing architecture, most all calls must be carried back to the central switch, which means that local calls placed within the same peripheral "controller" must utilize two network talk paths (one out and one in), but the REMOTE SWITCHING CENTER component of the SL-100 actually does its own switching, indicating that Northern is evolving to a more distributed architecture.

ii) INTERFACEABILITY

a)LANS. . .Northern Telecom's DATA VOICE SYSTEM (DVS) computing technology is an interesting new networking concept. Basically, DVS consists of multiple backplane processors all connected by a high speed bus (or "LAN in a box") which then utilizes a 2.56 MBPS copper wire transmission scheme to the desktop to effectively allow workstation connection. Networking software was written assuming local processing at the desktop as well, so the end result is a flexible architecture which can provide fault tolerant processing power either locally or remotely, as the application demands, thus making full use of today's relatively cheap MIPs and memory.

This technology is applied in the DV1 product, a sophisticated satellite business communication and processing system in the Packet Transport Equipment (PTE), which serves as a PBX adjunct (and uses only the 2.56 MPBS transport scheme), and, finally, Northern recently announced the Data Networking System, which serves as an Intelligent Network connectivity system, (either stand alone or PBX attached).

Currently, the PTE adjunct system provides LANSTAR (Northern proprietary) connectivity to the desktop and Northern supports the BANYAN file server for PC space LAN applications but Northern is actively trying to certify other vendors as well.

b)MESSAGE CENTER. . .Northern Telecom has published their message center specification and enjoys compatibility with several prominent voice mail vendors. Currently, Northern promotes the use of their DV1 system as an attached message center (as well as office automation) adjunct.

c)ISDN. . .Northern currently delivers data to the desktop via four 64KBPS and two 16KPBS packet channels on the SL-100. Basic rate access is currently available and the M-53T telephone and PC/ISDN adaptor are supported. Northern currently uses stimulus (non-standard) call signaling, however, and plans to evolve to logical signaling in the near future.

iii) SOFTWARE. . .Northern uses an operating system called BNR PASCAL (proprietary) for all switch programming. Northern is committed to software intensive upgrades and revisions and can usually download changes from their remote center.

Northern is obviously optimistic about a future in voice/data integration and has taken care (via the DNS product) to position herself as a connectivity problem solver when the complexities of the integrated environment occur.

Northern faces two challenges: 1) Fighting the perception of old technology and 2) explaining the DVS concept so that everyone can understand its purpose.

IV. NEC

i) GENERAL. . .NEC utilizes a distributed processing architecture which includes processors in every node (or "stack") and processors on every line card. The basic systems are: IMS/364 ports/100-300 lines, IMG/768 ports/200-500 lines, MMG/5520 ports/500-4000 lines, and UMG/23184 ports/4000+ lines. NEC stresses that these are all usable ports.

In the MMG and UMG configurations, four and sixteen backup load sharing processors may be utilized respectively. Should one of the processors fail, the others automatically increase their load to compensate.

NEC claims that their architecture is truly distributed in that nodes are tied together via a 49 MB high speed bus which does not degrade port capacities. Local processors handle supervisory, status and setup functions, while main processors run the operating system, control I/O, manage system features, and interface to the time division bus. Local line card processors further offload the nodal processors and handle local feature implementations.

ii) INTERFACEABILITY

a)LAN. . .NEC currently does not offer a LAN connectivity capability but plans to introduce this service soon. When offered, the LAN module will provide 4MB to the desktop via twisted pair distribution and will meet the ETHERNET TCPIP standard. Earlier prototypes of the offering were planned to support VIANET, but NEC decided not to roll the product out until de facto standard ETHERNET could be supported.

b)MESSAGE CENTER. . .NEC originally kept its message center interface proprietary and encouraged associates to sell manufacturers messaging solutions, but now offers a robust external interface in its OA1 announcement. This interface actually follows the seven layer OSI standard and allows some measure of PBX function control from an external device.

c)ISDN. . .NEC currently delivers data to the desktop via two 64 KB channels and what they call a "big D". . .a 1.5 MB packet channel. Also supported is a 1.5 MB "big H" high capacity channel. NEC plans to begin supporting terminal adapters and ISDN station apparatus in some limited fashion in 1989. Support of PRI is also expected.

iii)   SOFTWARE. . .NEC differs from the other major PBX manufacturers in its software delivery philosophy by using PROMs for most upgrades and revisions. NEC uses bubble memory backup so that restart via floppy disk during recovery is not necessary and 15-30 minutes downtime can be alleviated. NEC also states that RAM memory is more volatile and prone to problems than their bubble memory approach.

Also unlike most other major PBX manufacturers, NEC software is currently written in assembler language. In 1984, NEC needed to get the 2400 to market in a timely fashion, and undoubtedly, assembler language was the fastest option at that time. NEC is currently converting much of its software to UNIX C.

For the future, NEC sees PBXs continuing down the cost curve. Improvements in VLSI technology will continue to make the market very competitive and margins will continue to be small.

NEC firmly believes that the profit potential will lie in vertical software intensive applications made possible by the functional integration of voice and data.

Also, NEC believes that network management will play a significant role in the battle for market share. Expect NEC to announce network management packages and NETVIEW interfaces soon.

V.   GENERAL OBSERVATIONS

i)   PBX DIFFERENTIATORS

a)ARCHITECTURE DISTRIBUTION. .Most of the newer PBX architectures tend to include main processors, network processors, nodal processors, circuit card processors (sometimes), and even telephone instrument processors (sometimes). The benefits of distributing all this processing power is flexibility. No one knows for sure what features and applications are coming in the future, so no one can say for sure whether local or central processing makes the most sense. A highly distributed architecture leaves the options open and can provide all sorts of fail safe redundancy.

Older, more hierarchal systems also have benefits. For one thing, the software is generally simpler. Since multiple processors need not communicate

with each other for certain feature implementations, there is less potential for nagging "bugs" or other malfunctions. The fact that these systems typically have long proven track records (i.e. the software is very mature) is also a plus.

b)LAN PHILOSOPHY. . .Two of the major vendors seem to have distanced typical PC LAN applications from their PBX architectures. One of these (IBM/ROLM) does not even make use of current high bandwidth twisted pair technology and discourages the intermixing of "switched, LAN, or direct connect" traffic. Both of these vendors (AT&T and IBM/ROLM) actively market multimedia building distribution systems.

Other vendors seem to take a more active stand regarding LAN and PBX integration and some vendors have created new and different architectures to do this.

c)SOFTWARE LANGUAGE. . .Most major PBX vendors use a high level structured language because it is easier to design, test, and implement new features over the long run. Also, changes in software personnel tend to be easier to live through. Some vendors, however, still use machine language, which tends to be more efficient.

d)SOFTWARE UPGRADE PHILOSOPHY. . . Again, most vendors strive for totally soft, downloadable upgrades and revisions and utilize RAM for backup memory. Ideally, this should afford the customer minimum downtime and should be most cost effective for both customer and distributor, as changes can often be done remotely and inventories remain unaffected.

Some vendors, however, claim that RAM is too volatile and utilize EPROM to deliver most upgrades. These vendors tend to believe that, even in a soft environment, downtime is often unavoidable because of such factors as memory expansions, data base updates, etc. Also, they claim that the typical reboot time lapse necessary when loading a floppy disk is unacceptable to some customers. (NEC uses bubble memory backup.)

ii)   PBX SIMILARITIES

a)TREND TOWARD MORE DISTRIBUTED ARCHITECTURES. . .Because processing power and memory are continually coming down the cost curve, all vendors are moving toward more distributed architectures. Those with mature products sometimes move a little more slowly, but everyone realizes the potential for high resource voice/data applications and wants to have the flexibility to implement features in the most efficient manner.

b)TREND TOWARD PBX AS CONNECTIVITY TOOL. . .Most data processing vendors and VARs are probably better equipped to drive voice/data applications at the functional level. In general, the data industry is better at marketing than the voice industry. Armies of VARs (value added resellers) are poised to identify, analyze, and attach sharply defined vertical markets while PBX vendors keep struggling to design the perfect system that will serve everyone. As fully distributed systems emerge and as the evolution of standards (such as ISDN, ONA, etc.) make customization possible, the role of the PBX will likely change from one of switching and feature provisioning to one of overall connectivity between several disparate subsystems.

In this environment, implementation and support of complex products (e.g. Northern Telecom's new DNs described herein) in a very complex multi-vendor environment becomes the real challenge. i.e. The challenge is more human than technological.

c)TREND TOWARD MORE OPEN ARCHITECTURES. . .Most of the large switch vendors come from an environment where a certain amount of ongoing add-on business could be counted on to follow a large PBX sale. Because mot systems were highly proprietary, ongoing adds/moves/changes revenue, station set sales, software upgrades, etc. provided a reliable source for this revenue.

As we move into the 1990s, more and more communications system standards (e.g. ISDN, SS7, ONA, etc.) will make it possible for customers to consider other alternatives for services previously controlled by their PBX vendor. Most of the systems discussed in this paper have already taken steps to insure that such things as desktop data delivery, LAN connectivity, etc. meet established documented or de facto standards. As more standards solidify, customers will probably begin to migrate from the "RFP" procurement process to an "approved vendor list" process for communications and many buying decisions will likely be driven downward in the organizations. In this environment, manufacturers and distributors will have to go about winning their ongoing business the old fashioned way.

VI. CONCLUSIONS

i) Some of the key differentiators of the market leading PBX architectures today are:

  -processing distribution
  -software philosophy
  -processor redundancy schemes
  -open vs. closed interfaces
  -LAN integration philosophy
  -backup memory
  -call control software efficiency

ii) All major vendors seem to be moving toward more distributed architectures.

iii) The PBX is undergoing a gradual role change. In the future, connectivity will be more important than end user features, which will probably be provided more via vertically oriented value added resellers. In this environment, system support requirements will become much more complex and demanding.

iv) The days of long term account control via large proprietary systems are just about over. Customers will no longer tolerate this approach.

ACKNOWLEDGEMENTS:

Dan Carlucci, Executive Program Manager, ROLM

Marcel Tesse, District Manager/Product Management and Marketing, AT&T

Cary O'Brien, Director of Product Marketing, NORTHERN TELECOM

Tom Ruddy, Manager of Product Engineering, NEC AMERICA

APPLICATIONS AND SERVICES

William Wiley
Project Director

AT&T

101 N. Wacker, Suite 1600
Chicago, IL 60606

This session focuses on the emerging applications and services available and planned for the premises based systems. It discusses the applications most requested by end users as the PBX evolves as a major component of the digital switching technologies available to end users.

NETWORKING

Robert P. DelPriore
Vice President, Networks

Northern Telecom, Inc.

2435 N. Central Expressway Palisades
Richardson, TX 75080

ABSTRACT

This session sets the stage for the seminar by addressing the growing network requirements and opportunities for end users of telecommunication services. It focuses on today's networking environment with a view toward the future evolutions of networking at the corporate level.

NETWORKING

Robert P. DelPriore
Vice President, Networks

Bill Young
Director, Network Systems

Northern Telecom, Inc.

2435 N. Central Expressway Palisades
Richardson, TX 75080

CUSTOM DESIGNED NETWORKS

This paper will examine the "why," the "what," and the "how" of a Custom Designed Network. It will emphasize that Custom Designed Networks must depend on customer involvements, satisfy user demands, and advance business interests.

It is helpful to examine "why" networks are important, as many of these factors will continue to influence the direction of Custom Designed Networks. Three factors are most relevant - market dynamics, user demands, and technological capabilities. These factors have pushed for the growth of the corporate network.

A changed work environment has pressed for new network perspectives. Such factors as consolidations and mergers result in a central view of requirements, and greater need to communicate across diverse locations. The move from being an industrial-based society to being a service-based economy has forced greater emphasis on information flow. Regulatory change, specifically divestiture, created a new perspective for Network operation. Customer options were now possible and customer control became easier. Finally, the perspective is becoming global rather than regional with emphasis on foreign markets. Therefore, there is growing acceptance and added emphasis on developing and implementing international standards.

Beyond the business/market influence, the user has become more sophisticated. There is now greater demand for access to the intelligence available in the network, without being confined to local databases. Relatedly, the user wants greater control over the operation of the network in order to ensure improved service for the network user. The customer also gained a realization that the network could be used as a time saver, time enhancer or as a lever for success. Finally, if customer demands were to be satisfied, an end-to-end perspective would be necessary to ensure transparency in Network features, applications, and services which support the business operations of the entire enterprise.

The final push for Customer Designed Networks comes from the very fact that technology and developments have made advanced networking capabilities possible and desirable. Processing time is faster, processing power is greater and processing cost is cheaper. Transmission speeds have increased exponentially. Functionality has graduated from nodal to network intelligence. Finally, the evolution of the OSI reference model makes possible Network interworking, growth and flexibility. The technology is now in place to meet market requirements and user demands, and has the ability to expand further given the greater emphasis on uniform industry standards.

It is also important to examine "what" today's Networks consist of. In essence, "what" is the service provision, and service application for Networks.

It is helpful to examine the "what" of networks in terms of Facilities and Services. Are the networks structured to work as a whole with corporate strategic directions in mind, or have they been structured to satisfy specific generic service functions and geared around particular facility solution?

Networks have grown with different points of focus. Often larger companies have decided it is imperative to own, maintain, and operate their networks to maximize control. Other companies, particularly when focus may be local and the service required is voice, have relied on alternative solutions, such as the local telephone company providing local network services and the long distance company providing nationwide network services. In reality, however, the customer has a range of Networking options which would enhance the business opportunities and effectiveness.

Another factor complicating the existing Telecommunications environment is that it has been customary for separate networks to be structured around the generic service to be provided, either voice, data, or image. While such network solutions may be the best solution for particular operations or applications, segregated independent service networks may not best advance business objectives or efficiencies. Significant opportunities for economic advantage, operating efficiencies, and new network capabilities and options may be realized by combining or integrating PBX functionality with public network services. Viewed from this new perspective, the Custom Designed Network would draw from various networking options to develop a comprehensive solution which addresses the strategic objectives of the business. In short, the solution is "hybrid" networking and is driven by customer requirements. The customer will be able to mix and match public and customer owned network components, and employ specific and integrated component options to meet business objectives and satisfy user needs.

The hybrid network integrates customer owned network elements with network services using OSI standard interfaces, and is the basis for end-to-end feature transparency, networking applications, and advanced network services. Hybrid networking is the necessary element for a Custom Designed Network. It reflects customer choice, responds to user demands, and accommodates business dynamics, e.g., growth.

The "how" of the equation must now be addressed. How does functional hybrid networking now become possible? The enabler is Open Architecture principles.

For hybrid networking to be effective, Open Architecture principles must be incorporated in a market, regulatory and technological sense. In this environment, the customer is not dependent on a single vendor solution, a single service provider solution, or an internal limitation. Open Architecture allows the greatest opportunity to advance business goals in utilizing the Custom Designed Network as a component of strategic business planning. To gain a better grasp of the relationship of Open Architecture to the Custom Designed Network, let us examine these Market, Regulatory, and Technological perspectives.

Open Architecture principles respond to Market requirements stemming from user demand and business needs. Both elements require the ability to interwork with other users or other systems within the network and/or between networks, and to enhance network intelligence, functionality, and scope. Both elements require equipment which can not only interconnect, but also be interoperative in the network without major re-work, be capable of handling expanding Network demand, and evolve to new technologies without major investment.

Open Architecture principles also address Technology developments. While many proprietary architectures still have significant market share, standards have pushed the evolution of the development of Open Architecture protocol models. The OSI, ISDN and CCS7 Reference Models all are predicated on making network operations/services more transparent throughout the system; ensuring flexible and economic growth of equipment; and providing end-to-end network features, applications and services.

Finally, Open Architecture principles respond to Regulatory direction, specifically, the FCC ONA decision. With ONA, the Commission sought benefit from OSI/ISDN open architecture concepts to ensure competition, and maximize customer options. In essence, ONA objectives make the public network an open tool by which the market place is able to satisfy diverse communications requirements. Thus, market demand, technological development and regulatory direction have pushed the introduction and requirement for Open Architecture principles.

Open Architecture therefore must be viewed from a:

Market Perspective
  o Interworking
  o Interoperability

Technolgical Perspective
  o Transparency
  o Flexibility
  o Intelligence; and

Regulatory Perspective
  o Competition
  o Options

Open Architecture principles and protocols coupled with hybrid networking are the foundation for Custom Designed Networks. But something else now becomes possible in this new networking environment. The customer gains the ability to influence network functionality on a real time basis through Customer Programmability. The Network becomes a strategic asset of the Corporation which can be expanded, enhanced and made smarter to advance the business interests of the Corporation.

Customer Programmability allows construction of intelligent components, i.e., applications software to deliver capabilities across the network as a means of gaining competitive advantage. Customer Programmability would consist of a basic tool kit. It would have the capacity to be expanded through 3rd party software of internal development. Benefits stemming from such capability would include customer services/feature introduction on an accelerated basis with direct application to actual business goals. Improved Network control capabilities for routing, network performance, and OA&M functions are possible. Customer Programmability allows the Network to be a market lever through provision of exclusive functions to markets or suppliers.

The Custom Designed Network should therefore be Hybrid in nature, structured around an open architecture, and be customer programmable. A necessary ingredient to make this possible is an Open Architecture-based network management system. The network management system must be capable of controlling the customer owned network elements, as well as that portion of the public network which

is being utilized as a component of the Corporate Hybrid Network.

Custom Designed Networks therefore consist of four basic elements: Hybrid Networking, Structured around an Open Architecture, Network Management, and customer programmability. Further, and most importantly, it incorporates customer input, enhances user control, and the Custom Designed Network addresses the strategic business objectives of the enterprise.

1343B

DSW-15

DIGITAL SWITCHING INTEGRATION AND CAPACITY

Richard N. Aurin - Chairperson
Division Manager-Switching Engineering

Southwestern Bell Telephone Company
One Bell Center, Suite 13-B-01
St. Louis, Missouri 63101-3099

ABSTRACT

Success in today's market depends on the timely introduction of new services and features. Based on past industry experience when providing these new features, switching machine capacity has been a major concern to both the Operating Telephone Company and Providers of switching equipment. This concern has now intensified due to ISDN plus the new data base services which are being deployed and planned for the future.

This seminar will identify major digital switch capacity concerns from a users perspective. It will explore how the industry views these problems and what are the plans to meet this challenge.

Leonard J. Forys -- Bell Communications Research

Robert A. Miller -- GTE Communication Systems

Brian A. Ostberg -- AT&T Bell Laboratories

John Tebes -- Siemens Communication Systems, Inc.

Roy D. Welch -- Southwestern Bell Telephone Company

DIGITAL SWITCH CAPACITY AN RBOC VIEW

Roy D. Welch
District Manager, Network Design

Southwestern Bell Telephone Company
One Bell Center, Suite 13-F-07
St. Louis, Missouri 63101-3099

ABSTRACT

During the past four years we have been deploying large digital switches in Southwestern Bell Telephone Company. During this time we have had some occasions to work closely with the switch vendors in determining the maximum traffic load carrying capacity of these switches. This paper describes some of the problems faced by an Operating Telephone Company (OTC) in determining the most limiting traffic capacity of a vendor's digital switch. It also describes what the vendor needs to provide to the OTC to enable it's engineering forces to determine pre-cutover capacity as well as perform post-cutover capacity analysis.

INTRODUCTION

A critical aspect of planning for a new or replacement switch in the message telephone network with one of newer technology is that of determining just how long the new switch will provide service before it must be relieved by an equipment addition or by another switch. This is especially true if the new switch type has not been in use in a particular OTC before that time.

Today's planning and provisioning cycles are such that by the time a new switch is being cut into service, its first growth addition is already being planned. Additionally, before it has been in service long enough to provide two busy seasons of good engineering data, the first growth addition has already been ordered from the vendor. This means that there is at least one outstanding growth addition job in the ordering stage before any in-service busy season data can be gathered upon which to base capacity estimates for a new switch.

There is nothing new in this respect from the planning and engineering problems that have been faced by the OTC engineer in the past with the electromechanical and analog store program control (SPC) switches. However, with the introduction of digital switches with distributed processing functions and interprocessor communications, this job of determining a limiting capacity becomes much more complex and critical than in the past.

TYPES OF CAPACITY LIMITS

Before stored program control switches appeared in the message telephone network there were three main areas of capacity limits in the electromechanical switches of the day. There was a physical limit to the number of customer lines which could be working before the office would have to be closed to further assignments. This was called the termination capacity. There was also a physical limit to the quantity of telephone numbers available for use. Thirdly, there was a switching capacity limit which included both common control and talking channel equipment. This third capacity had no one item of equipment that could be considered as the limiting item. It was a capacity limit derived from the probability of meeting certain grades of service criteria during the busy hour of the busy season in the various stages of network switching equipment, common control equipment and network paths. These grades of service were based on dial tone delay and path blockage in the switch.

When stored program control (SPC) switches began to appear in the network in the 1968 and 1969 time frame we found that telephone numbers were no longer an important limiting equipment item. They became a memory storage item instead. However, a new limiting switching capacity item was introduced. This was the central processor (CPU) of the SPC switch. The CPU introduced the most complex and variable capacity concerns experienced by OTCs up to that time. As part of the common control equipment in a switch, the CPU is considered a switching capacity item. The CPU is generally considered in a category by itself for capacity purposes however even though it is contained in the overall category of switching equipment.

The principles used to determine termination capacity in a digital switch are generally the same as they have been since the electromechanical switch was introduced. While the various types of common control equipment are different, the same principles of determining switching capacity apply here too. That is, with the exception of the CPU.

When the modern digital switch began to appear we started hearing words like non-blocking, virtually non-blocking and near non-blocking applied to the switching networks in these switches. Unfortunately, this has been interpreted by some people as meaning that the job of the traffic engineer would become easier and that less emphasis would need to be given to traffic engineering them.

Events have proven that this is not the case. The trade off of having a "nearly non-blocking network" has presented some new problems to the traffic engineer. The efficiency of the internal linkage of the digital switch has all but eliminated blocking in this portion of the network fabric. However, the subscriber line modules at the switch front end still perform the same old familiar concentration function we have always had in switches of all vintages. Blocking can occur in a digital switch because of this concentration. Since the rest of the network contributes little to the overall blocking in the switch, the blocking that does occur, does so in these front end modules. As such, they tend to have very steep load service curves. It then becomes very important to plan for the peak loads that will be offered to them. These front end modules require as much or more attention during the engineering phase as did the analog SPC switch. The

traffic engineering principles are not new, but the degree of effort has increased rather than decreasing as was commonly voiced.

It is possible to examine the switching architecture of a switch and arrive at a statistical model resulting in a fairly accurate load service curve for its switching fabric. On the other hand it is not possible for an OTC engineer to examine the inner most workings of the CPU of a switch and divine just what effect the vendor's generic program will have on the overall load service curve relationships in that switch. He must rely heavily on the vendor's documentation and laboratory test results. It is for this reason then that the remainder of this paper will deal with the difficulties and needs of the OTC in determining the call processing capacity of a digital switch CPU.

TYPICAL LOAD SERVICE CURVES

Load service curves show the relationship of increasing traffic load to the corresponding effect that the load has on some measurement of the service quality. These curves, for example, can be drawn to show usage versus dial tone delay. Others can show attempts versus blocking. Such curves when available are valuable tools for use by the traffic engineer in designing a particular switch. Load service curves can be drawn for each of the various traffic sensitive components of a switch if required. Generally however such curves are only required for the more costly and service critical components of the switch.

In the Step-By-Step (SXS) vintage of equipment the grade of service deteriorated in a gradual and predictable way with increased load. There was no CPU to take into account when calculating capacity.

With the arrival of Crossbar equipment we had the electromechanical counterpart of a central processing community, but processing as such was still distributed over several equipment items. The load service curve for this type of switch equipment is more pronounced than that of the SXS equipment, but is still gentle when compared to the electronic switches.

When the first analog SPC switches were deployed we found that because of the limitations of processor speeds the CPU became the ultimate limiting piece of equipment in those switches. Those switches handled call originations in a first come, first serve basis unlike their electromechanical predecessors. As long as these processors were operated within their capacity limits all origination requests were served in a timely manner. However, if they were operated at or above their capacity then all originations were treated with equally poor response. The knee of this load service curve became very pronounced. Compared to the SXS switch curve it was like running into a brick wall when the attempt capacity was exceeded. Everything depended on this one CPU for service.

In those early analog SPC days it was recognized that it was not prudent to try to specify a typical call carrying capacity that attempted to squeeze the last drop of CPU real-time out of the switch. As a result, if the engineer abided by the capacity calculations provided by the vendor there was no real reason to expect the switch to get into trouble because of CPU overload. There was generally adequate reserve capacity to allow for the minute to minute variations in the High Day Busy Hour (HDBH) load caused by random call originations. If the traffic engineer decided to probe for higher processor occupancies, he did so like a farmer plowing close to the edge of a cliff in a heavy fog, hoping for a larger crop yield and no injuries.

As time passed, faster CPUs became available. Eventually, we had enough processing capacity that the CPU was no longer the threat of limiting capacity it once was. It seemed as though the traffic engineer could stop worrying about CPU capacity. However, it was not to be. The vendor redesigned the switch to provide increased terminations and once again the CPU became a major limiting item.

When the digital switches began to come on line they were accompanied by distributed processing. No longer did we have a single processor to watch. There were multiple processors for which to calculate and track capacities. Also, at this time, fully integrated subscriber digital line equipment began to proliferate in the distribution plant. This meant that the normal load balance technique of numerically spreading classes of service across all line interfaces was no longer possible to the degree it once was. The importance of monitoring peripheral processors became as important as that of monitoring the CPU. In addition, other things began to occur. Switches from multiple vendors were beginning to be installed in the network.

PROBLEMS FACED BY THE OTC

It was not long before we discovered that different vendors specified their processor capacities in different ways. One vendor expressed maximum CPU occupancy for call processing based on the criteria to which we were accustomed. Another specified maximum CPU occupancy for call processing based on an idealized switching environment. There was no standard basis for vendors to use in specifying maximum CPU occupancy for call processing.

Terminology differences became evident. In attempting to state traffic handling capacities of the CPU it was necessary to have detailed discussions with vendors on what constituted a call versus an attempt and which terminology was being used to describe the CPU capacity. The vendors' engineering questionnaires used different terminology in describing the required inputs or various call types.

Generic program updates tend to "rob" call carrying capacity. New features and services all consume their proportional part of the total call processing occupancy. These additional capabilities often consume real time at a greater rate than the vendor is capable of recovering through processor speed-up innovations. This can lead to a trap for the OTC. The traffic engineer having calculated a theoretical call carrying capacity for the CPU of a given switch may have already placed a growth order on the vendor based on the estimated call carrying capacity he expects from some, as yet unannounced generic program issue. When the CPU real-time consumption per call is finally announced it may be too late to change the outstanding order to account for increased processor work times.

If a switch happens to have already been capped because of having reached maximum CPU capacity, a generic program update can create havoc if it includes an increase in CPU work time per call. Such a happening will necessitate either deciding to delay an upgrade to the new generic program or to remove load from the switch. The former will probably cause the loss of needed operational or revenue producing features. The second will often cause the changing of subscriber telephone numbers, a very unpopular and unlikely choice. The uncertainties associated with the real time consumption of various call types in future generic programs create the need for maintaining a real-time buffer to allow for this eventuality. This is unfortunate in that it prevents the OTC engineer from fully using the CPU capacity until he can be sure that the switch will not fall into that trap.

The OTC planning and engineering cycle is such that the OTC needs to have accurate engineering information from the vendor at a minimum of about eighteen months ahead of the required in-service date of the switch addition. One of the most critical items of information required is an accurate estimate of the CPU real-time consumption per call. This is usually stated as a milliseconds consumption per call. Unfortunately these estimates are just that, estimates, and are not always realized in practice.

Vendor estimates of call timings have tended to be overly optimistic in some cases. Call timings in those cases may have been developed using observations obtained from a laboratory switch. In some cases these switches were running in a non-loaded condition while the call timings were measured. In field conditions in a heavily loaded switch these timings can deviate from the laboratory observed conditions. In a distributed processing switch the amount of interprocessor communications required to set up and handle a call may cause queuing during high load conditions. In addition, momentary queuing can also occur at other points during call processing in a loaded switch. Each of these items can increase the effective milliseconds per call timings in a working switch.

An important point to be considered when determining the available call processing capacity for a given CPU is that non-deferrable overhead work in the CPU can invade that portion of CPU time normally considered as being available for call processing work. The vendor's estimate of the percentage of total CPU time devoted to non-deferrable work time has in some cases tended to be on the idealistic side. Equipment failures do occur. High levels of trunk originations caused by carrier failures do happen. Other conditions in the switch can cause maintenance routines to be activated. When these conditions are present the percentage of non-deferrable work can increase several fold with a corresponding reduction in available call processing time.

With each different vendor's switch there is an absolute need for practical diagnostic tools that will aid the OTC traffic engineer in analyzing CPU load problems. He must be able to measure the proportion of CPU work time being spent in the various activities of the CPU. Such tools seem to be available within the vendor's organization but are not generally known to the OTC engineer until a switch gets in trouble and the vendor is called on for help. Some of these diagnostic tools are only available as non-resident programs and are not installed in the switch where they can be used during the time they are needed. It is difficult to try to load a program tape into a switch when the switch is already under stress.

Each OTC at one time or another has had occasion to obtain help from its switch vendor on processor capacity related problems. For a period of time it appeared as though the only route into a vendor's organization was through their sales or marketing interfaces. Experience has shown that these organizations are the least equipped to assist in these types of problems. They have even provided bad information in some cases. The OTC engineer needs to be able to talk directly with the vendor's capacity experts and obtain detailed information to assist him in his capacity analysis.

From the OTC standpoint, nothing can replace good documentation for a source of expert knowledge. It can contain the collective knowledge of many individuals on a given subject. Where CPU capacity is the subject, it is doubtful that any one single person can be considered the final expert. It is for this reason that the OTC must have accurate and timely documentation with frequent updates.

WHAT THE OTC NEEDS TO DO THE CAPACITY JOB

There is a desperate need for a standard basis upon which a vendor must state his capacity. This standard should require capacity to be based on a standard mix of call types and services. It should specify a standard mix of inter and intra switch call flow. It should require capacity statements considering a range of switch environments such as multi-office city, single office city, heavy business, residential and tandem only type offices.

The vendor should specify an "all day" CPU call processing occupancy capacity. This occupancy value should be such that if it is sustained the switch will still be able to do all of its normal functions without any impairment. During this level of occupancy the switch should not be in the position of deferring maintenance routines. Output displays should not be delayed. Traffic usage measurements should not be impaired or otherwise distorted. All operations support systems should be supported. Customer service objectives should be capable of being met. Minute-to-minute variability in traffic loads should have been taken into account. In other words, the switch should be able to run twenty-four hours a day at that CPU occupancy without any abnormal conditions being experienced.

A "drop dead" CPU call processing occupancy should also be specified. This occupancy should represent the point at which all deferrable tasks have been deferred and no additional call processing occupancy can be obtained. In the area of CPU loads greater than the "all day" occupancy, the actions of the CPU should be fully documented. What functions are deferred? Which ones are non-deferrable? What portion of the overall switch service degradation is contributed by the CPU?

The OTC needs to have a detailed description of the overload strategies employed by the switch vendor. Does the switch change from a first in first out to a first in last out operation for

1347

call origination requests? In the peripheral processors? In the CPU? At what point do overload controls come into action? When is normal operation restored? What happens to call origination and call progress queues? Are originations retained in queue until served or are they dropped from queue? To what degree are traffic measurements affected? These and many other questions should be answered and described in detail in documents made available to the OTC.

Improvements in processing speed should be provided to offset the impacts of new generic program loads as they occur. Every effort should be made to reduce the effect of generic program changes. This would permit the OTC to more fully use the switch without danger of falling into the capacity trap mentioned earlier.

The capacity effects of new generic programs should be determined and provided to the OTC earlier than at present. The milliseconds per call timings should be made more accurate with respect to what will actually be experienced out of the laboratory environment.

Load service curves should be provided on all traffic sensitive components of the switch. This includes line and trunk unit modules as well as peripheral and central processor units.

Each vendor should appoint a switch capacity subject matter expert (SME) who will act as an advocate for the OTC within the vendor's organization. This person should be a highly technical person capable of grasping the OTC viewpoint of service responsibility. This SME should also be available to participate with the OTC in its training sessions. Such an arrangement will pay large dividends by creating a mutual understanding of both the OTC and vendor concerns.

The vendor should provide good capacity analysis and estimation tools. Where possible these tools should be mechanized. Backup documentation providing algorithms used in calculations must always be furnished. While the vendor is expected to furnish default input values used in the algorithms, the ability to override these values should be provided to the OTC. There should be a pre-cutover capacity estimation capability as well as one for post-cutover capacity analysis to be used on an ongoing basis with actual switch data as input.

The vendor should provide the OTC with access to some of the more sophisticated analysis programs that it uses itself for capacity problem analysis. Other excellent analysis programs that are available for use but are non-resident in the switch should be considered for candidates as resident software.

Adequate measurements should be provided within the switch as part of the regular office traffic and service measurements to enable the OTC to ascertain the health of the call processing and call progress through the switch. Field applications and office simulations have shown that ninety-five percent of all switches studied had an average fifteen minute peaking factor over the switch busy hour. Capability should be provided to measure and evaluate the degree of this peak quarter hour to total busy hour ratio.

There has been a tendency to eliminate certain call blocking measurements because "the digital switch is non-blocking." As long as any circuit switch has any concentration in its switching fabric it can block. All known digital circuit switches manufactured today can block a call because of the lack of a completing path. The traditional incoming matching loss and similar measurements should be provided in a digital switch as they were in their predecessors.

SUMMARY

The digital switch has brought us many new capabilities that were not possible just a few years ago. New service capabilities will make it possible to give the end user greater control over his own communications capabilities than ever before. These new services can be brought to the market place more quickly and deployed more easily than with earlier switches. They are truly the gateway switches into the Intelligent Network era.

It should be recognized however, that these advantages do not come without some trade-off elsewhere. Part of this trade-off is the increased need for data collection and its analysis for surveillance purposes. This surveillance must be based on good information provided by the switch vendor. The jobs of the traffic engineer and the switch administrator are more important than ever before in the digital switch environment. Capacity design and surveillance functions must not be relegated to a lesser importance based on the mistaken idea that these new digital switches do not require it.

MAJOR CAPACITY ISSUES
FROM THE USERS PERSPECTIVE

Leonard J. Forys
District Manager, Traffic Analysis I

Bellcore
331 Newman Springs Road, Room 2Z-119
Red Bank, New Jersey 07701-7020

INTRODUCTION

Two of Bellcore's functions in regards to capacity issues are to draft Generic Requirements e.g., the Local Switching System Generic Requirements (LSSGR), and to do technical analysis of vendor switches based on these requirements.

In order to draft generic requirements, analysis also is done on generic issues which could significantly impact switch capacity. This paper will provide a summary of some of these analyses and show how they impact and support the generic requirements.

We will consider four examples: synchronization effects, load box testing, traffic surging and overload control design.

SYNCHRONIZATION

Recent work on analyzing processor schedules for digital switches has resulted in the discovery of a new phenomenon which can significantly influence their capacity and performance. This phenomenon, which we have termed "synchronization" results from the processor schedule imposing batching of work. (Parts of this topic were previously documented in Ref. 1.) This phenomenon is sensitive to the variation of received digit times and can cause oscillations of occupancy. It resembles a "resonance" type of effect.

IDEALIZED PROCESSOR SCHEDULE

To understand the phenomenon, let us consider an idealized processor schedule. It may represent the central processing unit(s) or peripheral processors of a digital switch. Figure 1 represents the processor schedule we will consider.

Typically, the processor will need to perform overhead activities representing the operating system overhead, routine audits, traffic measurement activities, etc. We will make this overhead the highest priority within our schedule. Originations are often detected by microprocessor based scanning units and their responses are sent directly to our processor or by other processors and are handled by I/O programs. These determine what type of messages were sent from the scanners or other periphery, and put the messages into the appropriate queues for processing. The I/O handling will be next in our priority.

New originations are placed into an origination queue which is the lowest priority queue in our schedule. Digits are typically sent in groups to the processor and are processed at a higher priority than originations, e.g., Queue 1 in our example. Disconnects could be processed in another queue, etc. Priority is given to the various queues by the following mechanism. A running clock is initialized to zero by the overhead routines at the start of a typical cycle. When tasks are processed from the various queues, the running time is compared to a threshold, T. If the running time exceeds T, the processor will begin a new cycle by entering the overhead routines. Thus, if the running time expires while processing Queue 1, the processor will begin handling the overhead and reinitialize the running clock. If the threshold, T, is small, this schedule resembles a non-preemptive priority schedule. If T is larger, there is less priority given to the Queues at the head of the list. T will be set to 100 milliseconds in our examples.

Although our schedule is idealized, it does resemble many actual processor schedules. It is important to note that the processing time done on an origination is typically a small fraction (less than 25%) of the work done on a call. The origination task is to see to it that a receiver is connected to the sending caller, so that digits can be collected. Much of the work on a call occurs when the last digit is received. At this point, translation of the digits occurs, idle trunks (or lines) selected, outpulsing (or ringing) activated etc.

Let us now consider the following "thought experiment". Suppose that we are running at modest loads so that we are completing all of the queues within time T. Suppose further that there is a group of originations enqueued in the origination queue. If we were in an access tandem environment, MF signaling would typically be used to input digits into our office. This signaling is very regular. In fact, suppose it were constant. Then, after processing the group of originations, receivers would be connected, start dialing sent and the last digits of the calls received at a constant time in the future. This group of last digits could produce a temporary overload on the system. The processor would not complete all of the processing in its queues before T. In fact, the processing of originations could be temporarily suspended. When this happens, new originations would be enqueued in the origination queue (note that I/O would not be suspended because it has a high priority). When the temporary overload due to the occurrence of a group of last digits was over, the origination queue would (with high probability) contain a group of originations. These in turn would produce a group of last digits, etc.

The overall effect would be that the system would "synchronize" itself into a cycle of oscillations, alternating between processing groups of originations then groups of last digits, etc. (Disconnects would appear relatively randomly in all processing intervals and not significantly alter the phenomenon.)

Large delays in the processing of originations would appear at relatively modest occupancies. In addition, relatively large delays in the processing of last digits would occur because they would appear in batches.

QUANTIFICATION OF PERFORMANCE

A call by call simulation was developed to analyze the performance of our idealized schedule. Figure 2 indicates the results of some of our analysis. Call timings were chosen so that the maximum call rate that could be handled was approximately 200,000 calls/hour. Occupancy was normalized to be between 0 to 100% by deleting the overhead. The time from processing the origination to the reception of the last digit was varied by keeping the mean constant, but changing the range. Thus, the curve marked U(1,10) represents last digit times which occur uniformly between 1 and 10 seconds.

As the figures illustrates, there can be a substantial difference in performance, depending on the variability of the last digit times. The U(1,10) case might represent an end office, where there is a great variety of digit dialing times: fast dialers, slow dialers, 2 or 4 or 7 or 10 digits dialed, etc. The constant 5.5" dialing approximates the situation of an access tandem where the office is receiving MF digits (together with ANI).

If the mean time to the last digit is made shorter, the curves all move to the right. In many access tandem applications, the time to last digit is approximately 2.2". Actual field data from several access tandems indicate a sharp rise in the origination average delay at about 85% occupancy.

In fact, the results were accurately predicted by our simulation, in advance of receiving the field data.

Figure 3 indicates a sample 20 second run from our simulation for the case of dialing times being U(1.6,2.7). The average input rate was approximately 60 calls/second. Note however that the system is often admitting in excess of 200 calls in one second, then admitting no calls for a period of time (about 2 seconds later), then another large batch of originations, etc. It appears as though the system is in oscillation, a type of resonance response. The period of the oscillations appears to be related to the mean last digit time.

POSSIBLE SOLUTION

Observing the pattern of calls admitted to the system in Fig. 3 suggests that a possible solution would be to put a limit on the rate at which calls are accepted into the system per unit of time. Unfortunately, this simple solution did not work for us. The imposed limit produced delays which were about as large as the synchronization effect. Instead, a more radical solution is proposed.

Consider processing originations twice during a cycle. Once, at a priority level above Queue 1, the second time at the lowest priority as before. When serving originations at the higher priority, a maximum number of originations, 0, 1, 2, 3 will be allowed. Clearly, the origination delays would be reduced by this mechanism. This is indicated in Fig. 4. What is surprising is the effect on the delays for digit processing, which takes place in Queue 1. As indicated by Fig. 5, the "post dialing" delays (digit processing delays) are also improved as the number of high priority originations is increased from 0 to 3.

This result is somewhat counter intuitive. It is like joining a line in a theatre and trying to convince the person ahead of you that their service would be improved if you were allowed in ahead of them. This clearly does not happen. What happens is that successors to the "preempted digits" will receive improved service.

The proposed solution needs to be modified to include heavy overload considerations, but it is suggestive of a fruitful approach.

This work points out the necessity of allowing work to be presented to the system in a smooth manner. It raises questions about new switch applications such as intelligent network services. Here, responses will be elicited from data bases which will occur with computer controlled regularity. Processor schedules need to account for possible synchronization effects.

This work is very recent in nature. Through the generic requirements process, we intend to alert the switch vendor community to this phenomenon.

LOAD BOX TESTING

Load boxes are programmable devices used to provide test loads to a switching system. These devices can be programmed to simulate different call types, vary interevent times and to wait for start dial indications. They have many uses such as to determine the correctness of the call handling code, accuracy of traffic measurements, to enable estimates of the real time cost of processing the call and to test overload control logic. Another application is to determine load service relationships for the switch. We will examine this last application.

Because of the cost involved in load testing a large digital switch, the holding times associated with load boxes is often kept to a minimum. Thus, we have a "finite source" effect to consider when analyzing load box results. One of the key differences between load box traffic and real traffic is that as delays in processing increase, the holding times of the load boxes increases also (waiting for start dial, e.g.). This can cause a reduction in call attempt load per load box.

Another difference is that if the times between generations of subsequent calls on a load box is kept short, there may not be enough variability in the arrival pattern of the load boxes.

The call by call simulator described above was modified to simulate load boxes. (An analytic model for this problem was presented in Ref. 1.) The same idealized schedule was used. Consider load boxes with the following parameters: 6" constant conversation time, last digit times U(1,10) and a constant 2" pause interval between disconnect and origination of the next call.

Figure 6 illustrates a load service curves generated for a system whose maximum possible capacity is approximately 10,000 calls/hour. By "closed system" we mean the load box results, by "open system" we mean Poisson offered traffic, the standard model of "real traffic". Note that there can be a large difference in the load service relationships.

For a large system of 200,000 calls/hour maximum capacity, the differences tend to be less apparent. This is illustrated in Fig. 7.

These examples illustrate that arbitrary use of load boxes can sometimes produce misleading results. By increasing load box holding times and introducing more randomness in the "pause interval" between calls, the differences between load box results and Poisson traffic can be made arbitrarily small. The expense of doing this, however, may be prohibitive in many cases. We estimate that 3 to 4 times the number of load boxes may be needed for the small system to obtain suitable accuracy.

We are further quantifying this issue and intend to incorporate our results into generic requirements or a special analysis report.

Although the load box results for large systems can be reasonably close to that of Poisson traffic, we should point out that there is another aspect of traffic characteristics that needs to be considered: "traffic surging".

TRAFFIC SURGING

If the entire load on a processor for an hour were presented during the first minute of that hour, the performance of the system would be clearly different than if the load appeared uniformly spread throughout the hour. There are a number of situations where the traffic can "peak" or "surge" during the hour. Figure 8 illustrates the case of a tandem switch in an evening busy hour. Two minute counts were made of data for a one hour period from 7:00 pm until 8:00 pm. Although the figure only indicates the traffic pattern for one day, an average over 20 days indicates the same effects. The cause of the load surging in this case is attributable to television commercial breaks. There are a number of other situations where this can happen such as the ending of school sessions, etc.

If the load surging happens in off peak hours, it normally would not impact the performance of the switch, unless the load surges were of sufficient magnitude to drive the switch into overload.

In Fig. 9 we indicate the performance of the impact of load surging obtained by simulating the idealized processor schedule indicated earlier. References 2 and 3 indicate the impact of load surging on an analog switch with a cyclic processor schedule. The load pattern chosen was a 5 minute surge for during the first part of a 15 minute interval. The processor capacity for "flat" traffic is assumed to be approximately 200,000 calls/hour. The effects of load surging are less pronounced for small capacity systems and more apparent for high capacity systems.

We are currently engaged in a study to determine the presence of load surging in difference switch applications. It appears that for switches with evening busy hours, this phenomenon must be accounted for in determining switch capacity. As indicated in Ref. 3, the impact is sensitive to the overload control strategy of the switch.

OVERLOAD CONTROL ISSUES

Traditionally, overload control strategies have been designed to protect the integrity of switches in heavy load situations. Basically, new requests to the switch are controlled so that the processor will not accept more originations than it can handle. Otherwise, large delays would occur during call setup which could cause the loss of a call. References 3, 4, 5 and 7 indicate another consideration in design of overload controls. Overload controls need to account for customer behavior, especially in response to dial tone delays. Experiments have been done to determine customers' response to dial tone delays. The results of one of these experiments is documented in Ref. 6. Dial tone was suppressed (although a receiver connection was made) for a specified time on live calls in a switch and customer response was recorded:

waited for tone, dialed before tone, abandoned before tone. The results of one of the experiments is indicated in Fig. 10.

If the servicing of the queue for line originations were done in a First-In-First-Out (FIFO) manner, under overloads dial tone delay would occur for all calls. As the figure indicates, if dial tone were delayed 4 seconds, about 50% of customers would have abandoned, 40% would have begun dialing before tone and only 10% would be patiently waiting for tone. The implication of this is that of those customers who would be served after a delay of 4 seconds, 80% would be seen as partial dials, and 20% would be seen as properly dialed calls. A partial dial consumes an appreciable amount of processing time, which is in effect, wasted. The partial dial would, with high probability reattempt, thus further increasing the overload. The number of successfully completed calls for the switch would substantially decrease under overloads.

The LSSGR requires that the switch account for customer behavior characteristics to maintain high levels of completed calls under overloads. One method suggested is to service line originations in a Last-In-First-Out (LIFO) mechanism. This insures that under overloads, only customers who have received little dial tone delay would be served. There would be little (or none) partial dials (due to delayed dial tone). Although this strategy has the advantage of insuring high completion ratios under overloads, it suffers from the fact that patience is not rewarded. Theoretically, some customers who were patient might never obtain service.

Another mechanism is necessary to reward patience. First, customers who are enqueued for service need to be ignored if they flash their switch hooks or reinitiate their attempts. Also, the line origination queue is periodically examined. Originations which are delayed greater then, e.g., 20 seconds, are examined to see if they have abandoned. If abandoned, they are removed from the queue. If they are still present, they are artificially placed at the back of the queue as a new service attempt. In that way, they are likely to be selected as the last arrival and served. This modified strategy - LIFO with automatic reattempt insures that patience is the best strategy.

The performance of this strategy has been extensively analyzed with simulations, analytic modelling and field data (see e.g., Refs. 3, 4, 5 and 7), and has been adopted by a number of digital switch vendors. The performance has been shown to be vastly superior to that of FIFO strategies and is robust to customer behavior patterns.

Perhaps more importantly, the LIFO strategy also tends to decrease customer complaints. This follows because of several reasons. Higher completion rates result in less reattempts. Because of LIFO, a large fraction of customers may not even know that an overload is taking place. With FIFO, every customer experienced large delays and so is a possible candidate for complaints. With FIFO, dial tone delay would be apparent on every successive reattempt. With LIFO, on successive attempts it is likely that the customer would get dial tone quickly.

CONCLUSIONS

We have indicated a number of generic issues which impact digital switch capacity and performance. We are using this knowledge to update and enhance generic requirements and alerting the vendor switch community to possible pitfalls. We are building on this experience to examine new issues emerging from future service offerings including ISD, multiple function switch (combined STP, SSP, Access Tandem, Operator Services) and intelligent network architectures.

REFERENCES

(1) L.J. Forys, C.S. Im, W. Henderson "Analysis of Load Box Testing for Voice Switches", Proceedings of the 12th International Teletraffic Congress (ITC), Turin Italy, 1988

(2) L.J. Forys, "A Characterization of Traffic Variability for SPC Systems", Proceedings of the 9th ITC, Torremolinos, Spain, 1979

(3) L.J. Forys, "New Overload Issues in a Divested Environment", Proceedings of the 11th ITC, Kyoto, Japan, 1985

(4) L.J. Forys, "Performance Analysis of a New Overload Strategy", proceedings of the 10th ITC, Montreal, Canada, 1983

(5) J.W. Borchering, L.J. Forys, A.A. Fredericks, G.J. Hejny, "Coping With Overloads", Bell Laboratories Record, pp. 183-185, July/August, 1981

(6) J.J. Phelan, L. Burkard, M. Weekly, "Customer Behavior and Unexpected Dial Tone Delay", Proceedings of the 11th ITC, Kyoto, Japan, 1985

(7) L.J. Forys, "Modeling of SPC Switching Systems", 1977 ITC Seminar on Modeling of Stored Programme Controlled Exchanges and Data Networks

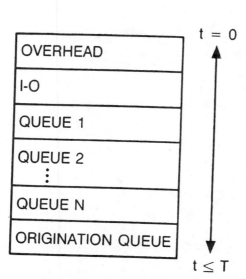

FIGURE 1: IDEALIZED PROCESSOR SCHEDULE

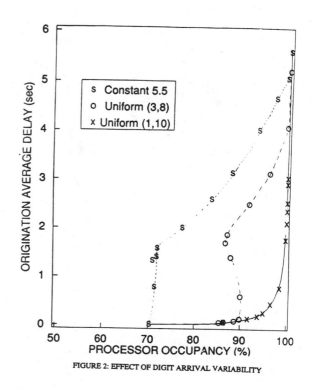

FIGURE 2: EFFECT OF DIGIT ARRIVAL VARIABILITY

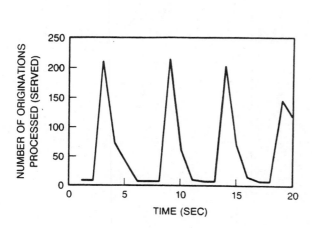

FIGURE 3: SAMPLE SIMULATION RUN

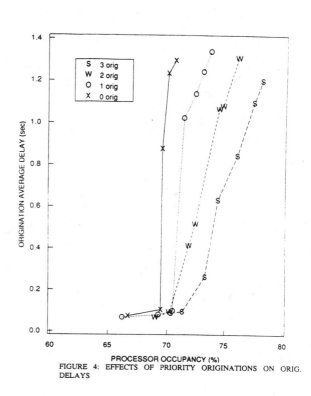

FIGURE 4: EFFECTS OF PRIORITY ORIGINATIONS ON ORIG. DELAYS

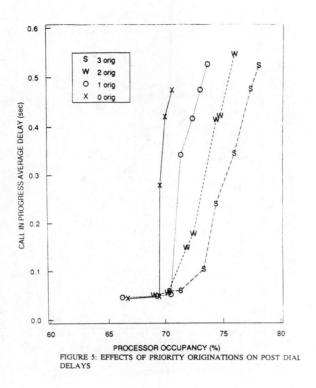

FIGURE 5: EFFECTS OF PRIORITY ORIGINATIONS ON POST DIAL DELAYS

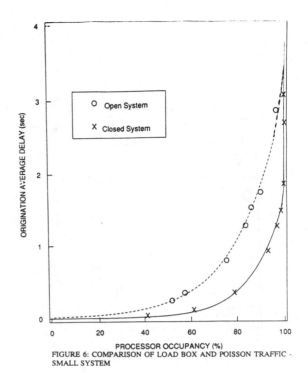

FIGURE 6: COMPARISON OF LOAD BOX AND POISSON TRAFFIC - SMALL SYSTEM

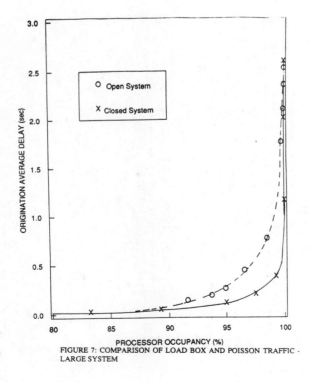

FIGURE 7: COMPARISON OF LOAD BOX AND POISSON TRAFFIC - LARGE SYSTEM

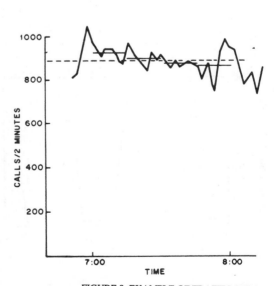

FIGURE 8: EXAMPLE OF TRAFFIC SURGING

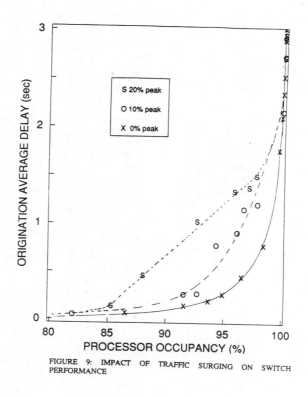

FIGURE 9: IMPACT OF TRAFFIC SURGING ON SWITCH PERFORMANCE

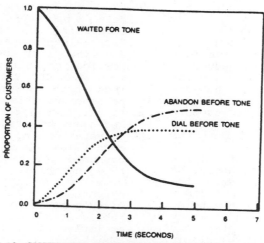

FIGURE 10: CUSTOMER RESPONSE TO UNEXPECTED DIAL TONE DELAY

THE SECOND DIMENSION
OF
SWITCHING ARCHITECTURE

Robert A. Miller
Director-Marketing Planning and Analysis

GTE Communication Systems
2500 West Utopia Road
Phoenix, Arizona 85027

ABSTRACT

Discussions of switching system architecture have often focused only on the single dimension of full centralized versus fully decentralized. To obtain an optimum architecture, however, it is necessary to exploit a second dimension of multiple processors running in parallel. Trade-offs within and among these dimensions are identified, and an optimum architecture is characterized. Application of these concepts to a current switching system architecture is cited and discussed.

INTRODUCTION

Ever since the introduction of stored program controlled systems (SPCS) in the late 1960s, network switching systems have struggled to live up to their published Busy Hour Call Attempt (BHCA) capacities. In some cases this was due to overly optimistic capacity models or inappropriate designs, but in most cases it was due to the greater "work-time-per-call" that resulted from the increased number and complexity of new services and new network capabilities that were added to the switching systems over time.

THE PROBLEM: CONTINUOUSLY INCREASING PROCESSING REQUIREMENTS

The processing requirements of a single network switching system have increased over time as a result of four primary factors: an increased number of terminations; increased service capabilities; increased network capabilities; and the increased use of synchronous data protocols to support all of these capabilities.

The demand for increasing the number of terminations per network switching system arises from the potential savings that an operating company can achieve by consolidating the multiple switching units of older technology, large offices into a single, larger system. The operating company saves the cost of all inter-unit trunking and signaling, the implicit cost of processing individual calls multiple times, and the (often hidden) cost of engineering and administering multiple systems.

The demand for increasing the scope and variety of a system's service capabilities arises from a combination of end-user market demand and the desire on the part of operating companies for continued, efficient capital utilization.

The market demand is a reflection of the increased dependency of end-users (especially business end-users) upon communication services generally, and in the language of ISDN, the "laundry list" of those services now includes: circuit-switching and packet switching; voice, data and image basic bearer services; supplementary bearer services including custom calling, CENTREX, CLASS and X.25 user facilities; both basic and supplementary teleservices including customer control, electronic messaging, electronic directories, and enhanced service gateways; and finally protocol conversions for multiple terminal signaling classes.

The efficient utilization by operating companies of invested capital depends to a considerable degree upon their ability to provide as many services as possible from the single asset of a network switching system. Generally speaking, the proliferation of service-specific capital investments lowers the overall efficiency of capital utilization and increases the risk of stranded investments.

The demand for increasing the scope and variety of a system's network capabilities also arises from a combination of factors. These include the requirement to support the increasing scope and variety of services, the requirement for more marketing, engineering and administrative data about end-user calling patterns, and the requirement for increased centralization and automation of operations generally.

And lastly, the increasing use of data protocols to support all capabilities has a significant impact on "work-time-per-call". The use of X.25 and the ISDN D-channel protocol for service capabilities, and the use of X.75 and SS7 for network capabilities adds both power and flexibility to telecommunications, but at the expense of processing performance (i.e., BHCA). And when the requirements for protocol conversions are also taken into account, even more processing power can be consumed per call. Today the scope of this capability includes conversions: from voice-band to digital; from synchronous to asynchronous; from circuit-mode to packet-mode; and from public standard to proprietary extension or implementation.

THE DEVELOPMENT GOAL: HOW HIGH IS UP?

Taking all of the above requirements into consideration, the question arises as to how to characterize an appropriate processing-power related development goal for a network switching system. History has shown that merely displaying the current "laundry list" of services is insufficient as a development guide because over the life-time of a system, the scope and variety of services can and has changed dramatically. A more generic characterization is required.

After due consideration, the following development goal was established at GTE Communication Systems: "With respect to system architectural limitations, a network switching system should exhaust its termination capacity before it exhausts its processing capacity."

This characterization is not independent of the "laundry list" of current or possible services, but it does allow development organizations to focus upon considerations such as "processing power per termination" and to avoid becoming distracted by short-term changes in the content of an increasingly volatile "laundry list" of services. This characterization is also convenient in that it scales directly with the planned size of the network switching system.

THE FIRST DIMENSION: CENTRALIZED vs. DISTRIBUTED

With respect to the current generation of network switching systems, the development base was comprised almost exclusively of older systems whose stored program control was fully centralized into a single central processor complex. The disadvantages of these older systems resulted primarily from the absolute limitations on their total processing capacity and their relatively high cost for small office applications.

Small office applications were costly because they had to bear the cost burden of a relatively expensive central processor complex necessarily designed for much larger applications. Some vendors of network switching systems addressed this problem by developing different capacity processors for different office sizes, but this put artificial constraints on the possibilities for growth in all but the largest offices. It also mandated a "heart transplant" (processor change-out) or replacement of the entire switching system when the capacity of a smaller processor was exhausted.

By the late 1970s the availability, power and relatively low cost of microprocessors made possible the consideration of distributed control architectures. By off-loading selected tasks from central to peripheral processors, a distributed architecture could significantly increase the overall processing power of a network switching system; and because peripheral

processors were packaged to control specified groups of line and/or trunk terminations, distributed control systems had lower small-office costs and relatively smooth cost/growth curves even for large applications.

Distributed control systems had their disadvantages however, and these were due primarily to the large number of processor complexes in the system. This resulted in an increased complexity of interaction within the system, not only for normal call processing, but also (especially) for maintenance related processes.

Distributed control systems also required that choices be made as to the assignment of tasks between central and peripheral processors. Some tasks were obviously appropriate for centralization. These included: the allocation of any common resource (e.g., hunting for an idle line, trunk, service-circuit, operator position, or attendant position in a group thereof); switch and network management; common channel signaling; and operational communications with the system. And some tasks were obviously appropriate for decentralization. These included: the sense and control of individual lines, trunks, service circuits and positions; and the local execution of device diagnostics.

Other tasks, including many of those in call processing, were distributed or centralized only after a case by case analysis. The selection criteria included: system reliability; local vs. global data requirements; task cohesiveness; and the overall economic impact on the system. In the final analysis it was clear that neither a fully centralized nor a fully decentralized system was optimum. Instead the optimum system architecture was somewhere in between.

THE SECOND DIMENSION: SINGLE vs. MULTIPLE

The availability, power and relatively low cost of microprocessors also made possible the consideration of multiple, parallel processor complexes within the structure of a distributed control system. GTE Communication Systems gave consideration to multiple, parallel processors both in the central control and in the peripheral control.

Redundant single processor complexes were determined to be suitable for peripheral processing due to the relatively small hardware domain involved and the related economics. However multiple, redundant, parallel processor complexes were determined to be suitable for central processing because the ability to add office-engineerable processing power over time would allow the optimum "central vs. peripheral" task distribution to be retained from generic to generic regardless of the changes that happen to occur in service or network capabilities.

One concern that was initially expressed about multiple, parallel processor architectures was related to the issue of common resource contention (primarily access to common memory). A detailed analysis of this issue determined however that a total contention losses of only a few percent was achievable even with a large number of parallel central processors.

Another concern that was initially expressed about multiple, parallel processor systems was due to their use of commercial microprocessors as the basis of their central controls. At the time of the original analysis by GTE Communication Systems, proprietary, special-purpose, central control processors were about twice as powerful as the best microprocessors then available. This led to a detailed comparison of relative price-performance between microprocessor-based central processor complexes and those based upon proprietary, special-purpose processors. Not only was the commercial microprocessor based architecture found to have better price-performance at the time of the original analysis, but technological progress in microprocessor design since that time has improved their price-performance with respect to proprietary processors.

As a result of the analysis it also became evident that the single central processor architecture has essentially no ability to retain optimum "central vs. peripheral" task distribution. It was clear that if a single central processor system reached its limit, then either the system had to be capped or some properly centralized tasks had to be improperly distributed. Generally speaking, the penalty paid for improperly distributed tasks was in terms of additional, otherwise unnecessary, message, memory or real-time overhead. It also became evident that improperly distributed tasks rapidly cannibalized the internal resources of the network switching systems. Eventually attempts to improperly distribute tasks reach a point of "no return" where the resulting inefficiencies are greater than the gain from distributing a particular task. When this point is reached, only capping the system or a "heart transplant" are available as courses of action.

In addition to eliminating the need for a "heart transplant" or the engineering of a second switching unit, multiple, parallel central processing complexes also increase system reliability, especially for large office applications. And they permit even lower cost in small offices and even smoother cost/growth curves than single central processor systems. This is because, like the peripheral processors, the cost of central processing power grows only as the system grows.

It is important to mention one other characteristic of multiple, parallel processing systems: they result in very little additional design or development complexity as long as the concept is part of the original architecture. Vendors who have attempted to convert from a single central processor architecture have found the conversion virtually impossible to do without starting over virtually from "blank paper". This result occurs because the development of a system involves many subtle dependencies that designers unconsciously include in many development decisions, and once made, these decisions cannot be disentangled from the original system architecture.

A TWO-DIMENSIONAL EXAMPLE: GTD-5 EAX

To systematically accommodate a future with continuously increasing "work-time-per-call", GTE Communication Systems chose a unique design in 1978 for its second generation digital switching system, the GTD-5 EAX^{TM}. This design incorporated multiple, parallel, central microprocessors within a distributed microprocessor architecture; and with more than six years of field experience and 10,000,000 lines of GTD-5 EAX now in public service in North America alone, this architecture has clearly demonstrated its important advantages over single central processor systems, especially for the long-term. In fact much of the basic architecture being discussed in the industry today under the label of "Next Generation Switch (NGS)" has been in-service on the GTD-5 EAX since 1982; and in addition, certain new central control designs recently announced by other vendors are clearly imitative of the GTD-5 EAX.

The central control of the GTD-5 EAX utilizes a 24 Mb/s LAN (the Message Distributor Circuit [MDC]) with up to 96 universal processor ports. Up to 64 of these ports are used for peripheral processor complexes, and the remaining 32 ports are available for central processor complexes. All of the central processor complexes have access to common memory and to the SS7 control network. One of the central processor complexes (the Administrative Processor Complex [APC]) specializes in local I/O and operational support (OS) network communication, and the remaining complexes (Telephony Processor Complexes [TPCs]) handle the actual processing of all of the different varieties of calls. (Any TPC can be involved in any phase of a call.) TPCs constitute a "full availability" pool of processing power, and they are engineered in accordance with BHCA requirements of the application office. Because of the large number of TPCs that can be engineered, the architecture of the GTD-5 EAX is especially well suited to large-office, high-traffic applications.

CONCLUSION

Network switching systems with multiple, parallel central processors have important advantages over single central processor systems, especially for the long term. Among these advantages are: better price-performance; greater, ultimate processing capacity; termination-based (rather than feature-based) exhaust; lower small-office costs; greater large-office reliability; and cost/growth curves that are more naturally linear than any alternative design.

FEATURE INTEGRATION
IN THE 5ESS^{TM} SWITCH

Brian A. Ostberg
Member of the Technical Staff

AT&T Bell Laboratories
1200 East Warrenville Road
Room 1F-365, Department 55634
Naperville, Illinois 60566

ABSTRACT

This paper describes how the 5ESS^{TM} Switch has evolved and will continue to evolve to meet the capacity and resource challenges of capabilities such as Integrated Services Digital Network (ISDN), enhanced network services, and termination growth. The graceful integration of ISDN into the 5ESS Switch will be the primary example used in the paper, with discussion on system resources and performance. In addition, information will be provided on the internal processes used by the 5ESS Switch project in planning, implementing, testing, and monitoring performance and resource objectives.

1. INTRODUCTION

Since its introduction in the early 1980s, the 5ESS Switching System has proven to be a highly reliable and evolvable switching vehicle. The system has demonstrated great flexibility, in both hardware and software design, by rapidly achieving parity with 1A ESS^{TM} Switch services and features, by early introduction of ISDN (Integrated Services Digital Network) and CCS7 (Common Channel Signaling - Version 7) capabilities, by support of multiple switching applications, and by responsiveness to the ever growing body of enhanced network services. To ensure

the graceful integration of these capabilities and future capabilities into the 5ESS Switch, hardware and software platforms have been and will continue to be incorporated into the system architecture, providing a modular and evolvable base for rapid introduction of new features and new technologies.

In addition to hardware and software platforms, the 5ESS Switch project continually monitors, analyzes, and projects the capacities and performance of the various switch components, constantly assessing if and when there is a need for processor, bandwidth, or software improvements and optimizations. This internal mechanism has evolved into a sophisticated planning, development, and verification system, ensuring the continued integrity of the 5ESS Switch capacity and performance.

2. 5ESS SWITCH ARCHITECTURE AND CAPACITY OVERVIEW

2.1 Hardware Architecture

The 5ESS Switch is based on a distributed, modular hardware architecture which provides customized switch configurations, incremental system growth, flexible remoting capabilities, high system reliability, and support of multiple applications. The distributed nature of the switch architecture enables graceful introduction and integration of new switch features and capabilities. Additionally, it ensures well-defined interfaces (in both hardware and software) and true parallel processing, resulting in significant call processing performance gains. The modular 5ESS Switch hardware can be categorized into three general areas: distributed functional processors (the Switching Modules and the Administrative Module), a processor communication backbone (the Communication Module and the fiber optic Network Control and Timing Links), and the peripheral interface units (Line and Trunk Termination Units, CCS Interface Units, and Operational Support System Interface Units).

2.1.1 Distributed Processors

Distributed processing in the 5ESS Switch is performed by a single Administrative Module (AM) and any number of SMs (up to 192) to meet the needs of the switching office. Most of call processing related work takes place in the Switching Modules, which are interconnected for voice, data, and control through the Communication Module (CM) and the Network Control and Timing (NCT) Links. At the core of the SM architecture is the SM Processor (SMP) which is based on the Motorola

Corporation 68000 family of microprocessors, providing an evolvable base for future microprocessor technology.

To support remoted switching applications, the 5ESS Switch also provides Remote Switching Modules (RSM) and RSM clusters. RSMs and RSM clusters provide full stand-alone capabilities and are connected back to a host SM in the central office via T1 transmission links. In the 5E3 generic, AT&T introduced Optically Remote Switching Modules (ORM), which are linked directly back to the CM via extended fiber optic links. As an additional enhancement to the ORM, full stand-alone capabilities will be available in the 5E5 generic.

The Administrative Module (AM) consists of an AT&T 3B20D processor, which communicates with the SMs via the CM. The AT&T 3B20D is a fully duplex processor and memory system supported by UNIX[TM] RTR, a real-time version of the UNIX operating system. The AM provides the 5ESS Switch with a reliable disk system, a human-machine interface, and interfaces for Operations Systems (OS) and the CCS7 network.

2.1.2 Processor Communication Network

The communication backbone of the 5ESS Switch consists of the Communication Module (CM) and the fiber optic NCT links. Voice paths between SMs travel over time slots on the NCT links and are switched through the Time Multiplexed Switch (TMS) in the CM. Control messages between the SMs also travel over the NCT links and are routed to the appropriate destination processor (AM or SMs) via the Message Switch (MSGS) located in the CM.

2.1.3 Peripheral Interfaces

The final major hardware category of the 5ESS Switch is the peripheral interface units, which provide switch interfaces for analog and digital lines, analog and digital trunks, human-machine communications, OS communications, and the CCS7 network. Trunk and line interface units reside on the SMs, providing switch connection and services to direct lines and trunks. The human-machine and OS interfaces connect to the switch through the Input/Output Processor (IOP) of the AM, while the CCS7 interface connects to the AM via the Common Network Interface Ring (CNI-Ring).

2.2 Software Architecture

The 5ESS Switch makes use of a common software environment to support its distributed, multi-processing capabilities. The base software which resides in all of the distributed functional processors within the system includes the operating system (Operating System for Distributing Switching), a relational and distributed Database Manager, a Communication Manager, Maintenance and System Integrity software, and a virtual switching machine. These base capabilities provide a highly reliable software application platform for switching, upon which sophisticated call processing features and services can readily be built (Ref. 1).

In addition to the set of common software shared by the multi-processing environment, where appropriate the 5ESS Switch also makes use of some global support and application software. This software provides global call processing functionality such as trunk routing and time-slot path hunt. Centralization of these functions ensures maximum call performance and minimal switch resource impact. Call processing software which at one time had been centralized, such as screening functions and line termination routing, have evolved to distributed algorithms, to increase the overall switch capacity and to provide greater stand-alone capabilities to the SMs (Ref. 2).

Other software that benefits from a centralized location includes database administration via the Recent Change interface and switch operation, administration, and maintenance (OA&M) via the Human-Machine interface. These functions reside primarily in the UNIX RTR environment of the AT&T 3B20D processor. UNIX RTR is a hardened version of UNIX, which provides high system reliability/integrity and a UNIX-like programming environment for real-time applications. The UNIX environment serves as a standardized and familiar programming platform upon which front-end application software can be built.

2.3 Switch Capacity Evolution

By taking advantage of new hardware and software technologies, the 5ESS Switch has rapidly increased its overall rated[1] capacity by almost two orders of magnitude (80 times the initial introduction) within a seven year period, providing rated call capacities of greater than 400,000 POTS call per hour by the 5E5 generic. Planned enhancements for the 5E6 generic will increase the rated switch capacity by an additional 50%, providing approximately 600,000 rated POTS calls per hour and

---

[1]Rated capacity refers to the maximum number of calls that the switch can indefinitely sustain, while maintaining switch performance requirements. The Peak capacity is generally much higher but can only be sustained for relatively short periods of time.

350,000 feature rich calls[2] per hour. Additional switch capacity enhancements are currently being studied and planned and are expected to yield even greater capacities in future generics.

Table 1 provides a generic by generic comparison of the rated POTS call capacities of the 5ESS Switch, from the 5E1(1) generic to the 5E5 generic.

Table 2 provides a generic by generic comparison of the rated capacities of the 5ESS Switch for specific switch application models, for both the 5E4(2) generic and the 5E5 generic. Each of the application models is a specific set of assumptions and observations related to office feature penetration/usage, port (line/trunk) usage, and office configuration. The Metro application model is based on feature rich metropolitan offices observed in the field. Similarly, the Tandem and OSPS models are based on data and projections for field Tandem and Operator Services Position System (OSPS) offices. Tandem applications provide interswitch hubbing services to local offices, while OSPS is a 5ESS Switch configuration which provides operator services (such as Toll and Assist, Directory Assistance, and Commercial Automatic Call Distribution) via ISDN interfaces. In addition to rated capacities, Table 2 also provides some information on the model office configurations.

3. 5ESS SWITCH FEATURE/SERVICE INTEGRATION

3.1 Integrated Services Digital Network (ISDN)

With the 5E4 generic, the 5ESS Switch provides a rich set of ISDN capabilities and services. Fundamental to this set of services is the Basic Rate Interface (BRI) which provides 2B+D services (two 64Kps voice/data channels and one 16Kps data/signaling channel) and the Primary Rate Interface (PRI) which provides 23B+D services (twenty-three 64Kps voice/data channels and one 64Kps data/signaling channel). Through these interfaces, the 5ESS Switch delivers ISDN capabilities such as Integrated Services Local Area Networks, Multibutton Feature Activation, Multiple Call Appearances, ISDN Key System, Electronic Directory, Message Services, and Operator Services Position System (OSPS).

To achieve the integration of these capabilities, AT&T built upon the hardware and software platforms inherent

in the 5ESS Switch design, evolving the switch from a conventional digital switch to a full ISDN switch. ISDN access was introduced by the development of two new peripheral interface units, the Integrated Services Line Unit (ISLU) and the Packet Switch Unit (PSU). The ISLU provides physical access for BRIs, and the Digital Line Trunk Unit (DLTU) provides physical access for PRIs. The PSU terminates D channels and packet switched B channels and also serves as an intelligent packet switch, switching X.25 data packets using Protocol Handlers (PHs) that communicate with each other and the SMP via a 10 Mbps packet bus (Ref. 3).

To provide additional SM processing support for the rich set of ISDN call processing capabilities, the SMP20 was deployed in the 5E4(2) generic. This SMP version uses the Motorola Corporation 68020 microprocessor, enabling rated call capacities more than twice that of the SMP1 (which uses the Motorola Corporation 68000 microprocessor). Additional SMP processor enhancements have already been planned for the 5E6 generic.

Other developments that support more specialized ISDN capabilities are the Application Processor (AP) BRI interface for the Message Services and Electronic Directory features, and the Remote-ISLU (RISLU) which is being used by OSPS to provide capabilities such as Toll and Assist, Directory Assistance, and Commercial Automatic Call Distribution.

3.2 Common Channel Signaling (CCS)

The Common Channel Signaling (CCS) network has evolved significantly over the past decade, standardizing on the CCITT Signaling System 7 protocol, incorporating higher speed signaling capabilities (56 Kbps), and providing datagram-like signaling services. This evolution has been spurred on by several causes, including advanced signaling needs for voice services, ISDN, Open Network Architectures (ONA), movement towards more intelligent networks, and the ever growing market for information management related services.

As an integral component of the CCS network, the 5ESS Switch began supporting CCS features, such as OSO/INWATS and Network Call Denial in the 5E2(2) generic. To provide this capability, AT&T developed the Common Network Interface Ring (CNI Ring), which enabled AT&T Switching vehicles the capability of high speed interfacing (56 Kbps) with the CCS network. On the 5ESS Switch, this interface resides on the AM (3B20D) via the Dual Serial Channel (DSCH). With the 5E3 generic, additional development provided the 5ESS Switch with the capability of handling CCS6 related trunk calls, with CCS

---

[2]Feature Rich Calls refers to a specific set of feature penetration and usage assumptions, modeled on feature rich Metropolitan switching offices.

messages traveling through the CNI Ring interface (Ref. 4).

Shortly thereafter, the 5E4(2) generic provided full CCS7 signaling capabilities in the 5ESS Switch, enabling AT&T to simultaneously introduce SSP 800 services (Service Switching Point-800). Additionally, as a means of significantly increasing the CCS7 related call capacity of the 5ESS Switch, AT&T introduced the Direct Link Node (DLN) in the 5E4(2) generic. This CNI Ring enhancement enables direct memory access (DMA) transfer for CCS7 call processing related messages to and from the 3B20D (AM), all but eliminating the AM real time necessary to handle CCS7 messages.

In terms of software structure, much of the CCS related code was constructed on the software platforms already available in the AM and the SM. An additional platform was built to handle TCAP (Transaction Capability Application Part) messages used in SSP 800 calls. This platform was again used in the 5E5 generic to provide features such as Local Area Signaling Services (LASS) and Private Virtual Network (PVN). LASS provides interswitch subscriber services, such as Auto-CallBack and Calling Party Identification; while PVN provides a powerful set of services utilizing centralized network databases and intelligent switches to provide an alternative/enhancement to existing private subscriber networks.

3.3 Capacity and Performance Verification

With the rapid introduction of features and services in the 5ESS Switch, AT&T has developed a refined internal organizational mechanism for ensuring the continued integrity of switch capacity and performance. The sections that follow provide a high level description of the organizational processes used to implement this mechanism.

3.3.1 Performance Requirements

As more and more capabilities and flexibility are incorporated into digital switching systems, switching capacity and performance requirements are becoming more complicated and more demanding. Although LSSGR, CCITT, and other standards provide a significant amount of guidance, they do not always cover all scenarios, nor are they necessarily complete when generic planning and development commences.

To resolve these problems, AT&T has specific activities in place to understand, interpret, and refine performance and capacity standards that apply to switching systems in general and to specific features/capabilities in particular. AT&T's performance requirements organizations continually study the application of industry standards to new and existing switch services, features, and capabilities. In addition, these organizations continually interact with the 5ESS Switch customers, understanding customer expectations for both switch capacity/performance and feature performance. These organizations then provide the 5ESS Switch project planners and architects the standards and requirements that the switch must be capable of supporting for each generic.

3.3.2 Performance Planning

Once provided with the generic capacity and performance related requirements, the 5ESS Switch planners and architects set about determining if, when, and where the switch will fall short of its objectives. To do this, they use field and lab data and build analytic and simulation models to provide detailed information on the system and the various system components. If any shortfalls are determined by the planners and architects, various solutions are proposed and investigated. Each of the proposals are then assessed for benefit, system impact, development costs, and costs to the customer. Based on these criteria, a few of the proposals are singled out as likely candidates and examined in great detail. After this examination, a single proposal is recommended and planned for the generic.

3.3.3 Feature Development and Verification

Once a proposal or feature is planned for the generic, it is passed to development organizations, who help to greatly refine the proposal and understand its implementation. These organizations implement the feature/proposal, using the initial set of requirements as their development and testing criteria. As development of features progress, they are continually monitored to ensure that they fall within feature and switch requirements. Once developed and tested, the feature/proposal is integrated into a Verification Package with other closely related features. The package is then passed back to the organizations that initially set the capacity and performance requirements for the generic. These organizations exhaustively test each Verification Package, to ensure that the package and its component features meet all requirements. Finally, the Verification Packages are all merged into a single load and, again, exhaustively tested.

4. FUTURE TRENDS

With regards to capacity and performance, there are four major network/switching trends that will likely influence future 5ESS Switch architecture and planning. These challenges are being carefully investigated by AT&T systems engineers, planners, and architects; and, in many instances, plans are already well underway for meeting these challenges.

4.1 Intelligent Networks

Over the past few years, more and more emphasis has been placed on incorporating greater intelligence within the switching network and on customer premises. This emphasis has been fostered by the move towards more distributed processing and the desire for both network based services and information management services.

The primary impact of Intelligent Network (IN) capabilities on the 5ESS Switch will be related to system software, since more call processing intelligence may be distributed external to the switch. The existence of the SSP 800 feature and Private Virtual Network feature in the 5ESS Switch software provides base IN capabilities, upon which future IN capabilities can be built. Also, teams of 5ESS Switch systems engineers, architects, and planners are investigating additions to existing switch platforms, to enable larger scale distribution of intelligence within the network.

To provide for the ever growing information management market, AT&T introduced the Applications Processor (AP) in the 5E3 generic. This intelligent switching adjunct was initially interfaced to the AM's IOP and provided enhanced billing services, such as Message Detail Recording (MDR). With the 5E4(2) generic, the capabilities of the AP were enhanced, by interfacing the AP to the SM via a BRI. This move gave the Application Processor ISDN capabilities, such that it was able to offer Electronic Directory and Messaging Services. Future plans for the AP point towards continued evolution, providing additional information management types of services.

4.2 Large Office Capacity & Termination Growth

Increased emphasis, in both the domestic and international markets, is being placed on larger offices with very large capacities. Domestically, this trend includes both the local office and the tandem office; and, for international markets, this trend applies especially to large gateway type offices.

To meet this large office

challenge, AT&T is planning to introduce the Communications Module Processor (CMP) in the 5E6 Generic. The CMP is a Motorola Corporation 68030 based processor which plugs into spare slots in the CM, and its primary function will be to support globally accessible call processing functions, such as trunk routing and time-slot path hunting. It is projected that the CMP will provide the 5ESS Switch with the capability of handling approximately 600,000 rated POTS calls per hour and 350,000 feature rich calls per hour, 25% greater than the capacity of the 1A ESS™ Switch. An additional CMP function will be global database administration, which is expected to significantly benefit Recent Change performance. The software that will support these CMP functions has resided in the AM from generics 5E1 through 5E5. The rapid migration of 5E5 AM-resident call processing and database software to the 5E6 CMP further emphasizes the modularity, portability, and evolvability of the 5ESS Switch software architecture.

Because of the plug-in nature of the CMP, additional CMPs can provide even greater capacities in the generics beyond 5E6. Also, due to its inherent design, the CMP has the capability to incorporate new microprocessor technologies, as they become available. Additional architectural enhancements for capacity growth that are either planned or under study include bandwidth enhancements to the Message Switch in the CM and additional evolutionary enhancements to the SMP20.

4.3 Enhanced ISDN Services

The potential of ISDN cannot be underestimated. The past few years have seen a rapid influx of ISDN related features; and, the next five to ten years will likely see many more, especially in Area ISDN Networking and ISDN Data services. As users become more familiar and comfortable with ISDN's capabilities, greater and greater demands will be placed upon the ISDN network. At this time, AT&T is currently studying several alternative proposals for providing enhancements to the integrated ISDN capabilities of the 5ESS Switch.

4.4 ISDN Broadband

Limited/Prototype ISDN Broadband capabilities have already been deployed successfully in several European markets; and, domestically, several trial applications are currently under study. Although most agree that the potential for ISDN Broadband is very large, the capability poses several challenges to the switching industry, not the least of which is related to ISDN bandwidth. Again, AT&T is working to meet this challenge. Active planning and prototyping is proceeding, which would provide the 5ESS Switch with ISDN Broadband switching capabilities.

5. CONCLUSION

The 5ESS Switch has proven itself to be a very flexible and extendible switching vehicle, upon which the features and services of the 1980's and 1990's can be built. To provide this flexibility, the 5ESS Switch makes use of a modular, distributed hardware architecture, which is complemented by a common software environment resident in each of the switch's application processors. In addition to this first level of modularity, the 5ESS Switch also possesses a second level of modularity in its hardware and software platforms. These platforms enable the switch to gracefully evolve, while rapidly exploiting new technologies and incorporating new switch/network services and features. This evolvability has been demonstrated time and again in generics 5E1 through 5E6. With additional platforms, such as those planned for the 5E6 generic, the 5ESS Switch will be further positioned to evolve with the switching/network trends of the 1990s.

6. ACKNOWLEDGEMENTS

The author would like to thank the following individuals for their many helpful comments and insights: W.K. Cline, L.A. Craven, F.L. Hinson, J.J. Kulzer, I.H. Li, R.J. Olson, J.J. Phelan, P.F. Schultz, K.J. Scott, R.A. Singer, K.R. Stanley, and G.H. Zimmerman

REFERENCES

1. T. Duncan and W.H. Huen, "Software Structure of No. 5 ESS -A Distributed Telephone Switching System", IEEE Transactions on Communications, Volume 30, No. 6, pp. 1379-1385, June, 1982.

2. L.G. Anders, C.H. Bowers, D.L. Carney, J.J. Kulzer, and W. W. Parker, "Distributed System Tradeoffs", International Switching Symposium Proceedings, Volume 1, pp. 26-33, March, 1987.

3. D.L. Carney, and E.M. Prell, "Planning for ISDN in the 5ESS[TM] Switch", AT&T Technical Journal, Volume 65, Issue 1, pp. 35-43, January-February, 1986.

4. J.J. Lawser and P.L. Oxley, "Common Channel Signaling Network Evolution", AT&T Technical Journal, Volume 66, Issue 3, pp. 13-20, May-June, 1987

TABLE 1. 5ESS® Switch Generic Nominal Capacities

Generic (Issue) Release	Rated Call/Hr (Completed POTS Calls)	Maximum Number of Local SMs	POTS Lines	Trunks
5E1(1)	5K	1	1500	250
5E1(1A)	10K	1	1500	250
5E1(2)1	130K	30	50,000	7,500
5E1(2)2	200K	30	50,000	7,500
5E2(1)	200K	192	50,000	7,500
5E2(2)	300K	192	100,000	15,000
5E3	300K	192	100,000	15,000
5E4(1)	300K	192	100,000	15,000
5E4(2)	300K	192	100,000	15,000
5E5	400K	192	125,000	20,000

TABLE 2. 5ESS® Metro Application Model Capacities

Model	Units	5E4(2)	5E5
Metro			
	BH Calls	200K	220K
	Lines	~50K	~55K
	Trunks	~11K	~13K
Tandem			
	BH Calls	200K	225K
	Trunks	~25K	~28K
	CCS7 Trunks	~50%	~50%
OSPS			
	DA Positions	512	512
	TA Positions	512	512
	ACD Positions	1000	1000

PROCESSOR ARCHITECTURE
IN THE SIEMENS EWSD SWITCH

Dr. John Tebes
Director-Product Planning
and Quality Assurance

Siemens Communication Systems, Inc.
5500 Broken Sound Boulevard, N.W.
Building 7
Boca Raton, Florida 33487

Anthony Maher
Deputy Director-Systems Engineering

Siemens AG
Boschetsriederstrasse 133
8000 Munchen 70, West Germany

ABSTRACT

Solutions to concerns of Digital Switching capacity, flexibility and accommodation of new features/services are examined thru an example system architecture. Specifically, the Siemens EWSD Switch Processor Architecture is described with emphasis on the design concepts and techniques which address the issues of capacity growth, new features/service implementation, and technology evolution.

INTRODUCTION

Inadequate Switching System capacity to meet temporary exchange needs, to enable exchange growth, or to allow for service additions had led the operating companies to numerous negative outcomes that ultimately result in poor grades of service and additional costs or investments. The major issues and concerns in regard to capacity have been discussed earlier and include:

* Replacement of Central Office (CO)
* Complicated Traffic Engineering due to limited resources
* Overload Conditions due to peaked traffic and high load traffic
* Loss of Performance with new Generic Releases
* New Features and Services require more and more processor capacity.

This article describes the SIEMENS architectural response to the capacity issue and its realization in the form of the modular performance extension possible in the CP-113, the coordination processor of the EWSD system. The essential characteristics of a switching system with respect to the capacity issue are:

* a Switching System must have a Robust Architecture, that is be designed with a future safe capacity range (i.e., more than 1 million BHCA),
* modularity must be incorporated in a qualitative and quantitative manner so that the CO can incrementally evolve to meet the increasing demands of facility and feature growth,
* reserves must be built in to carry the offered traffic for various overload conditions (i.e., peaking), and
* reliability must be designed in to provide fail safe redundancy at high capacities.

The realization of these essential characteristics will be discussed in detail but first a short overview of the EWSD system and the CP-113 architecture will be provided in order to establish a basic system understanding.

OVERVIEW OF EWSD

The EWSD system is a distributed processing digital switching system (Fig. 1). The main distributed processing units are located in the digital line unit (DLU) and line trunk group (LTG). Both digital (ISDN) and analog subscriber lines are terminated on the DLU. The DLU provides EWSD's line card functions (e.g., line supervision) for both subscriber access types and the concentration of subscriber traffic on to a primary digital carrier highway (PCM 24). The PCM 24 connections from the DLU terminate at the LTG. Here, the first level of call processing is performed for active subscriber lines and trunks. This includes digit collection and analysis. The LTGs in completing a "telephone call" communicate both speech information and commands via the switching network (SN). The LTGs in completing a "telephone call" communicate both speech information and commands via the switching network (SN). The LTGs are connected to the SN via an 8-Mbit/s secondary digital highway. The SN provides the capability to interconnect LTGs and allows the LTG to communicate with the Coordination Processor (CP) in respect to the exchange of call processing information. The CP is the system unit which coordinates all major processes basic to a central office switch: call setup, route selection, network path selection, collecting charging information, providing for craft interfaces, providing failure recognition for faulty units, etc.

EWSD has previously supported two CP types, the CP-103 and CP-112. The CP-113 has evolved from the CP-112 and CP-103 to provide another solution for the coordination processor functional unit in the EWSD system. In this respect it is fully compatible with all the other existing functional units such as the LTG and the SN.

The CP-113, however, can operate as a CP in much large configuration that its predecessors. It can support exchanges serving up to 250,000 subscribers or requiring in excess of 1.2 million BHCA call handling capability.

OVERVIEW OF CP-113

The CP-113 is not a single processor. It is a set of up to 16 physically identical processors attached to a duplicated bus (Fig. 2). Communication between the processors takes place via this duplicated 256-Mbit/s (32-Mbytes/s), four-byte-wide bus. This bus allows each processor access to a duplicated common memory (CMY) which contains among other things the mailboxes for message passing and the exchange's semipermanent and transient data which is accessed by all the processors. The common memory is divided into 4 separate memory banks (MYB 0-3). All four banks can be accessed simultaneously. The CMY can be equipped with 64 Mbytes. The task program of the CP-113 is resident in a local memory (LMY) that is replicated in each of the 16 processors. The LMY has a memory of 8 Mbytes.

In any system configuration, there are two designated base processors (BAP). One is the master and is responsible for all coordination processor functions (maintenance, administrative and global call processing). The second BAP is a backup for the master. Additional call processing capacity may be added to the system by "plugging in" additional processors, which are designated call processing processors (CAP). The BAPs and the CAPs all execute call processing in a load sharing fashion by handling messages from the periphery as transactions. The relevant call data is available to all processors in redundant form in the common memory.

The remaining processors are input/output controllers (IOC) which interface I/O devices to the CP. These I/O devices can include switching periphery, personal computers, external storage on tape and disk, data links, and generally provide the capability to add I/O extensions to the system.

The hardware, of all the processors, is identical with the minor exception that the IOCs contain two additional circuit boards. These circuit boards provide the interface to the input/output processors (IOP) and their related devices (PCs, and external memory on disk or tape or data links).

The minimum system configuration consists of two BAP's and two IOC's.

ROBUST ARCHITECTURE

The most fundamental requirement for a switching system to meet the capacity requirements is that it must have a robust architecture. By this is meant, the internal architecture must be designed to accommodate the flow of enormous data quickly and efficiently, and the system throughput should be designed to be much greater (factor of 2) than the advertised capacity.

The best perspective of the CP-113 robust architecture is provided by the table in Fig. 3 which lists some of the power statistics of the processor. In order to add to this perspective the following is a summary of the more important technology characteristics. The architecture is based on 32 bits end to end. All of the CP processors (BAP, CAP, IOC, and IOPs), the buses, the memories, and the addressing is a full 4 bytes wide. This enables the system to provide balanced thruput at this powerful bandwidth. It also enables the memory addressing to be linear up to 4 Gigabytes of RAM. In addition, since the disks are addressed in 2 kbyte blocks it allows up to 8,000 Gigabytes of disk capacity to be addressed.

The system bus clocks its 32 bits at the frequency of 8 megahertz which enables a bus throughput of 256 megabits/sec. This massive thruput allows the system to maximally access common memory and read disk at 20 megabits/sec. (max. disk speed) without any significant system bus burden. Both local and common memories will initially be deployed with 256 kilobit chip technology. The use of higher density memories require no changes to the CP-113. These boards allow extension of local and common memory maximum sizes within the same physical shelf space allocated for memory. The disks and tapes are all based on the state of the art interfaces, speeds (e.g., Disk - 20 megabits/sec.) and capacities (e.g., multiples of 300 megabytes). The advertised performance of the CP-113 is a 1.2 MBHCA. This is achieved via the use of 6 CAP's, although a total of 10 CAP's can be plugged into the common bus.

In summary, the basic architecture of the CP-113 provides a powerful foundation to building dynamic and static performance.

QUALITATIVE MODULARITY

By correctly identifying in the early design stages the system elements particularly subject to change, it was possible to design-in qualitative modularity. This allows new hardware and software technology to be incorporated via isolated modifications to the processor. In this way obsolescence due to technological progress can be avoided.

HARDWARE TECHNOLOGY

Despite the fact that the CP-113 technology is extremely advanced, the architecture provides easy accommodation of upgrading key system components. This capability was built into the processor to take advantage of the ongoing rapid progress in technology.

The following key areas were identified early in the design phase of the CP as targets for change or improvement:

* Central Processor Units (CPU) -version and speed
* Memory - chip density and speed
* I/O devices (e.g., disks, tapes) -interfaces, capacities, and speed.

As a result of anticipating technological change in these areas and of having the goal of taking advantage of progress to increase CP-113 performance whenever it is opportune, the following two design principles were formulated and carried thru:
(1) Standard interfaces were designed which decoupled (isolated the influence of) the CPU, memory, and IOP from each other and the rest of the processors as depicted in Fig. 4.
(2) Asynchronous interface timing was incorporated separately in the bus-memory complex, and the processing units and I/O area. This allows each unit to take local advantage of clock frequency progress without requiring modifications in the other units.

As a result of these two steps, it is possible to:
(1) equip the memory boards of the CP-113 with 256-kbit, 1-Mbit or 4-Mbit chips (when they become available), thereby providing increasing memory capacities without affecting any other circuit boards or the backplanes of the processor.
(2) upgrade the CPU with faster or functionally richer versions of the Motorola 68000 - 32-bit family by changing only the relevant processor executive circuits boards which now house the MC68020.
(3) introduce new types of peripheral devices via a modified IOP circuit board. No changes to the IOC or IOP backplane are necessary; the IOP is simply plugged in.

SOFTWARE TECHNOLOGY

The EWSD software has been designed for change and specifically allowing the enhancements to specific software modules and thereby localizing the change. The following key areas were identified as areas subject to change:

* Hardware related (e.g., CPU) : hardware technology improvements
* Application related : rapid introduction of new services and features (i.e., ISDN, Intelligent Networks).

As a result of anticipating these changes, the following key design principles were formulated:
(1) Provide a software environment so applications can be added rapidly to an existing software base.
(2) Segregate hardware related software from the application software.
(3) Segregate application software from

basic software.
(4) Reduce the visibility of the multiprocessor to the application software.

The software environment chosen was based on using the CCITT recommended high level language CHILL. CHILL supports software modularity and multi-programming. The decision to use CHILL was made very early in the design of the EWSD system and has proved to be essential in allowing the EWSD software to be ported from the CP-103 to the CP-112 and finally to the CP-113. The existing support tools had to be enhanced for the CP-113, such as the interactive CHILL level debugging system.

The software, related to a specific hardware component, was isolated and standardized interfaces were defined between this and the remaining software (i.e., application software). Consequently, when a new hardware component is replaced, the related software is possibly upgraded or at most needs to be replaced.

The application software was separated from the basic software (Operating System, Safeguarding, I/O) via standardized interfaces resulting in a software platform on which new applications could be introduced without affecting the base software. This means that CENTREX and ISDN could be introduced without affecting the basic software.

The visibility of the multi-processor was isolated to specific software components; in particular (1) the Operating System was enhanced to implement the new functions for the multi-processor and for hiding the hardware (CAP's, BAP's) from the application software, and (2) due to "data hiding" principles having been observed in EWSD software design from the outset, it was possible to embed control mechanisms (locks) for shared data access in a restricted set of database procedures. Therefore, only a few software modules needed to be changed and the application software remained portable within the Coordination Processor family (e.g., CP-112).

QUANTITATIVE MODULARITY

A basic architectural principle of the CP-113 is the capability to increase its performance in a modular fashion which accommodates need or demand. This principal was designed into the system to counter the unpredictability in the performance growth of exchange requirements over time. Specifically, the CP-113 performance can be grown (without service interruption) to accommodate exchange demand in the following representative areas: (1) Memory capacity; (2) I/O Periphery, and

(3) Call Handling capacity.

(1) Memory Capacity

Common memory capacity can be grown in steps. Based on the existing 256 kilobit chip design, the memory can be grown in steps of 16 megabytes up to a maximum of 64 megabytes. In this way as a CO grows in size to meet the required capacity needs, the memory can similarly keep in step. Depending on the availability of the 1 megabit chip (4 megabit chip), the CMY can be increased to 256 Mbytes (1 Gigabyte) and the LMY can be increased to 32 Mbytes (128 Mbytes).

(2) I/O Periphery

Additional tapes, data links, etc., may be added to the system by equipping the CP with their respective IOPs and cabling the respective devices. If the addition of device/IOP couplets requires the presence of an additional IOC, then this unit must be grown before the couplet is equipped. This is accomplished by equipping the IOC unit and then activating it (by MML command).

(3) Call Handling Capacity

Call handling capacity can be grown beyond the basic 2 BAP configuration in the CP-113 by the additional equipping of single or multiple CAP's (see Fig. 5). Since the local memory of a CAP contains software instructions and local process data, the unit will be loaded in background relative to other activities and then activated. This means that call processing capacity could be added to the CP-113 without disturbing service in any way. This capability allows great flexibility in dimensioning exchanges. For example, if the call processing demand of an exchange was underestimated for any reason this problem could be compensated for by simply adding a CAP. Moreover, this ability to add CAPs allows an office to grow gracefully as more and more subscribers are added such as in an expanding suburban community.

Finally, this plug-in CAP capability addresses the problem of an existing office requiring additional capacity due to the introduction of new features or perhaps maintaining its capacity when a new generic version requires more real time for existing features.

OVERLOAD RESERVE

In a switching system, the traffic behavior can frequently lead to so called overload conditions. The design of a switching system should take this into account. The CP-113 is designed for expected and random overload conditions.

A typical expected overload condition is that occurring on Mother's Day. On such a day, a spare or reserve CAP could be inserted and via MML be activated to handle the expected overload traffic.

A typical random overload condition is that occurring due to random peaked behavior of traffic, such as that occurring right after lunch. This is handled by the CP-113 in its basic architecture. The BAP spare is also executing call processing continually, although the capacity contribution is not counted in the system performance (BHCA) value (since the performance quoted must be available when 1 processor is out of service). Since BAP spare is called upon to substitute for a failed BAP master or CAP there is an effective built in overload reserve capacity of 250 KBHCA = 1 BAP capacity regardless of system configuration for such random overload conditions. This capacity can be called productive redundancy.

RELIABILITY AT HIGH CAPACITY

The virtually non-stop operation of exchanges even in failure conditions is one of the most important standards in telephony. Generally designing a system with microsynchronous operation satisfies these requirements. On the other hand, new aspects of reliability must be considered for system operating at very high capacity. The new aspect centers on the speed of recognition for a failed unit and its consequent segregation from the system in order to prevent it from causing erroneous system operation during the handling of very high traffic.

The CP-113 meets all of the specific requirements associated with this standard by utilizing some proven telephony techniques in a combination of new ways. This combination results in enhanced system behavior in the face of failure conditions. An extremely significant characteristic of the CP-113 enhanced behavior known as "microsynchronous plus" is that the processing hardware is replicated to detect and isolate hardware faults immediately and precisely. Figure 2 illustrates this replication in respect to the individual processors (BAP, CAP, etc.). Except for the local memory (which is checked by 7 Error Detection Code bits) all individual processors circuitry is duplicated and matched internally. If the matching circuitry fails the entire processor unit is removed from service. No additional software programs or probability algorithms are necessary to determine which one of a pair of units is at fault which is the contemporary necessity for non-internally duplicated microsynchronous machines. A failure in the CP-113 is immediately detected and isolated.

There is no game of chance in guessing as to which unit was faulty.

The proven method of microsynchronous operation between units for the detection of faults has been extended to internal unit use for the additional purpose of fault isolation. This technique is the same for the bus system circuitry (bus controller and arbitration logic).

In addition, the bus paths are checked by ECC and parity bits. The common memory dual units are also synchronously accessed (e.g., write) but they are checked by seven ECC bits and protected by a CP-113 specific function called access control (AC). The local memory is also protected by the AC. This is a hardware controlled memory management which defines memory access rights. That means programs are checked in real time for authorization to read or write the segments of memory they are attempting to address. This hardware prevents unauthorized memory violations by programs.

When any CP-113 unit fails a redundant unit (e.g., BAP, bus, memory) will immediately take over the faulty units responsibility. The CAPS function in loadsharing mode and therefore use n+1 pool redundancy. The call processing related data is all stored in duplicated common memories. When a processor fails the remaining processors naturally take over for the failed unit, without impact on established or transient calls.

CONCLUSION

As can be seen, in order to effectively address the issue associated with capacity a switching system must have a) a robust architecture, b) a modular design for the expected changes in technology and the demands for new services and features, c) reserve capacity built for the overload situations, and d) enhanced safeguarding measures to meet the reliability standards for very high capacity switching systems. The CP-113 is an example of a switching system designed to meet the challenge of providing capacity in incremental steps and to accommodate via evolution the diverse customer needs in new services and features.

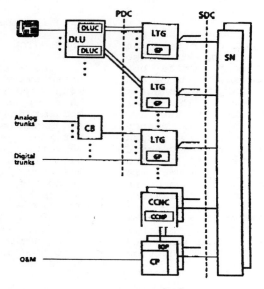

FIG. 1   EWSD block diagram

B:CMY	Access bus for common memory
B:IOC	Bus for input/output control
CI	Common interface
CMY	Common memory
IOP	Input/output processor for devices and for message buffer
LMY	Local memory
MYB	Memory bank
MYC	Memory control
PU	Processing unit

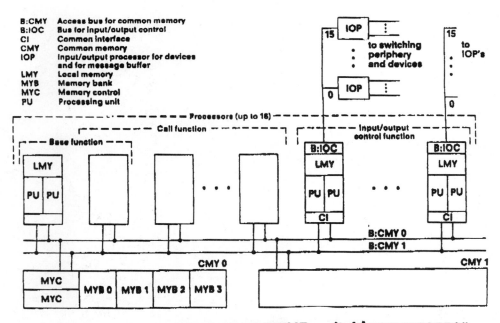

FIG. 2   Structure of CP113 switching processor

- Performance (call capacity) : 250 - 1240 KBHCA (Ref. load A)

- Number of processors : 4 - 16
  (physically connectable)

- Microprocessor : MOTOROLA MC 68020
  (4 - byte - architecture)
  Instruction set : 112 instructions
  Frequency : 16.67 MHz
  Address space : 4 Gbytes
  (Instruction -) cache : 64 words (32 bits)
  Interrupt levels : 8
  Program levels : 2

- (Internal -) bus width : 4 bytes

- Local memory (LMY)
  Capacity : 4/8 Mbytes (256 Kbit - chips)
  Word length : 39 bits (32 data + 7 ECC)
  Storage medium : RAM + EPROM (128 Kbytes)
  Access / cycle - time : 212 / 420 ns

- Technology : TTL (advanced - low - power Schottky; FAST)

Technical data: Processor (Base / CAP / IOC)

- Bus width : 32 address bits
  : 32 data bits
  : 22 control / ECC / parity - bits

- (Multiplex -) : 4 Time slots (each 125 ns)
  Mode of operation   per frame

- Frequency : 8 MHz

- Max. data rate : 32 Mbyte/s

FIG. 3-A   Technical data CP113:
            Access bus for common memory (B:CMY)

- **Storage capacity** : 16 / 32 / 48 / 64 Mbyte (using 256 Kbit - chips)

- **Memory banks** (fixed assignment to the B: CMY - time - slots) : 4

- **Word length** : 39 bits (32 data + 7 ECC)

- **Access / cycle - time** (at memory - interface) : 375 / 500 ns

- **Access - time for MC 68020** : $\approx 1.8\ \mu s$ (average)

Technical data SSP113D: Common memory (CMY)

Input / output control (IOC)

- **Number of IOC** : 2 - 4

- **Max. number of IOP (per IOC)** : 16

- **Bus width (B:IOC)** : 32 address / data bits (multiplexed)
  15 control -/ parity bits
  32 grant -/ request lines (2 for each IOP)

- **Max. data rate (B:IOC)** : 5.5 Mbyte/s

- **Max. data rate (IOP $\rightarrow$ CMY)** : 3 Mbyte/s

- **HW - structure** : see processing units

FIG. 3-B   **Technical data CP113: Input / output**

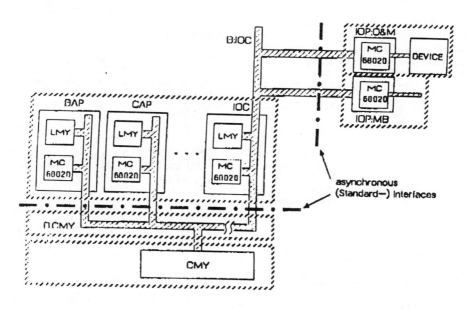

FIG. 4   CP113 : Qualitative Modularity

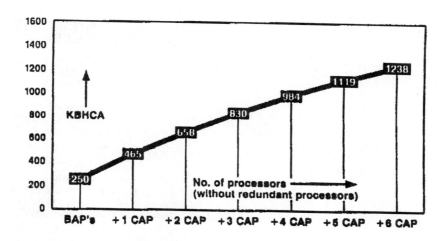

FIG. 5   **Performance CP113**

DSW-16

NEXT-GENERATION SWITCHING: REQUIREMENTS & CAPABILITIES

Mark W. Beckner – Chairperson
Senior Director
Switching Technology

Ameritech Services, Inc.
1900 East Golf Road
Schaumburg, IL 60173

There are at least three visible technical trends that will have major impact on what is being referred to as "next-generation" switching architecture. These trends are:
- the disaggregation of switching hardware/software functionality
- the increasing bandwidth of switched network applications, and
- the decreasing difference between private-line and switched communications.

Current research focuses on requirements for next-generation switched networks and the key hardware and software technologies necessary to deploy these systems. This seminar presents the current directions in the both the requirements and the technologies for next-generation switching systems.

Stephen Walters — Bellcore

Gottfried Luderer — AT&T Bell Laboratories

Bill Pennington — DSC Communications Corp.

Marek Wernik — Bell-Northern Research

NGS REQUIREMENTS OVERVIEW

Stephen M. Walters
Division Manager
Advanced Network Technology

Bell Communications Research
331 Newman Springs Rd.– Room 2Z483
Red Bank, NJ 07701-7020

ABSTRACT*

This session focuses on new capabilities such as fast packet switching and feature programmability and speculates on their future (potential) impact on NGS requirements. Traffic and architecture are also considered.

---

* NOTE: An extended summary was unavailable prior to publishing the proceedings.

THE ROLE OF FAST PACKET SWITCHING IN NEXT GENERATION SWITCHES

Gottfried W. R. Luderer
Department Head
Advanced Switching Networks

AT&T Bell Laboratories
200 Park Plaza – Room 1Z-104
Naperville, IL 60566

ABSTRACT*

Fast packet switching technology's state of the art will be reviewed, its benefits and challenges for the future network will be discussed and some speculations on its use in the future network will be made.

INTEGRATION OF CROSS CONNECT AND MESSAGE SWITCHING CAPABILITIES

William C. Pennington
Assistant Vice President
Advanced Systems Technology

Digital Switch Corporation
1000 Coit Road
Plano, TX 75075

ABSTRACT*

This session will describe a switching system architecture that can provide integrated channel and message switching from narrowband to broadband. Benefits for this integration will also be discussed.

SWITCHING FOR MULTIMEDIA COMMUNICATIONS

Marek R. Wernik
Manager
Broadband Architecture and Performance

Bell-Northern Research
P.O. Box 3511, Station C
Ottawa, Ontario K1Y 4H7

ABSTRACT

Advances in computing and storage technologies, digital imaging, and video coding are making multimedia information systems widely available in addition to existing voice and data services. This process is already visible in such industries as publishing and advertising, as well as in medicine and education. The widespread use of powerful workstations in geographically distributed customers' locations, the need for shared access to large image databases and mainframes, and the need for accelerated production processes are creating a demand for multimedia broadband communications.

Today's public switched telephony networks are increasingly based on digital technology. This has provided a base network capability suitable for a range of services beyond the traditional voice services. Further enhancements in the areas of transmission, switching, and signaling technologies are required to provide the flexibility and performance for a multimedia broadband environment.

From the user information transfer point of view, this evolution will likely entail three phases. The first, a high speed data phase, will be driven by the increasing demands for higher bandwidth and more flexibility to support distributed computing environment and provide connectivity between high -speed Local Area Networks (LAN). The second phase, a multimedia phase, will be driven by the need to support multiple types of connections with very different characteristics, ranging from voice and low-speed data to high-quality image transfer. The third phase, a broadband phase, will be driven by the need to support video services such as point-to-point videoconference and entertainment video.

Network scope and functionality should be determined by the scale and pace of these environmental changes. Transmission and switching, access and core, local area and wide area, business and residence - all these components and applications may evolve in distinct but related ways. An increase in channel transmission capacity available to the user will be needed in each of the evolution phases; requirements will likely be in the range of 1.5 Mbit/s, 45 Mbit/s, and at least 150 Mbit/s respectively, to accommodate a large range of service bit-rates. Above the underlying bit transmission, new information transfer capabilities will be required in order to satisfy a wide range of connection types, which will be compatible with the evolving transmission media standards. The frame-based transfer capability, such as Frame Relay Service and Switched Multimegabit Data Service are candidates for near-term high speed data applications. There are alternative solutions for multimedia applications ranging from Fiber Distributed Data Interface technology for integrated services LANs, and Distributed Queue Dual Bus technology for Metropolitan Area Networks, to the Asynchronous Transfer Mode (ATM) for wide area, public networks. For the third phase of evolution - the broadband phase - the alternatives also include high-capacity circuit switching. There will be a need for efficient interworking between transport technologies introduced in different evolution phases in order to make all the network changes invisible to the customer, who wants to perceive the evolution as increased flexibility, improved performance, and/or advanced network features.

ATM is a transport scheme which, by combining the advantages of synchronous time division multiplexing and statistical multiplexing, satisfies the communication requirements of a large spectrum of services, and which is well suited for high-speed hardware implementation. A communication structure based on ATM requires new system design rules, new control strategies, and new architectural approaches. This paper highlights some of these rules and design tradeoffs which take into account services performance and technology requirements. From that, the design principles for multimedia switching are derived.

Switching nodes of the future must have flexibility to provide an evolution to multimedia broadband capabilities and to network services dictated by new customer needs. The paper provides the generic functional and technology requirements for such an architecture and shows how it can support application environments in different network evolution phases.

CREATING NEW PRODUCT IDEAS

Harry F. Petty, III, Chairperson

Director - Systems Marketing

Centel Communications Systems

Two Continental Towers
1701 Golf Road
Rolling Meadows, IL 60008

ABSTRACT

The entire product life cycle begins with the product concept. Getting the right product to market is the most critical success factor facing any engineering or marketing organization. This seminar looks at the techniques that can be employed to define the market's requirement for a successful new product and provides two case studies to illustrate the proper methods employed in the creating of two new products.

Dr. Robert S. Braudy -- Quantum Group
                          International

Gregory Hawkins   -- Digital Sound
                          Corporation

Robert Lane   -- Northern Telecom
                          Incorporated

METHOD FOR PRODUCT DEFINITION

Dr. Robert S. Braudy
Senior Vice President

Quantum Group International, Inc.
7 Corporate Park Drive
Suite 101
White Plains, New York   10604

Applications of different research and analysis methods will be discussed. Case studies will be used to illustrate advantages/disadvantages of a variety of market research techniques. These techniques will cover the gamut of methodologies from limited primary research coupled with database work to a detailed quasi-experimental design for a nine month field trial.

Cases involving videotex, packet switching products, virtual private network-offerings, Centrex services and impulse-pay-per-view cable television services will be presented. The importance of defining the client's requirements, product features/functions and outputs prior to initiating research will be stressed.

PRODUCT DEFINITION FOR A HOTEL VOICE MESSAGING SYSTEM

Greg Hawkins
Director of Marketing

David Trandal
Manager, Software Development

Digital Sound Corporation
2030 Alameda Padre Serra
Santa Barbara, CA 93103

ABSTRACT

This paper describes how Digital Sound developed INNtouch(tm), its guest messaging product of the lodging marketplace. Only after the lodging industry's communications patterns were thoroughly researched and understood could the development process begin.

Few voice mail manufacturers had taken the time to truly understand the user requirements within the hotel environment, although many realized the opportunity in the guest messaging market. Digital Sound was fortunate to find a hotel chain that was willing to work together to help develop a custom application.

INNtouch is the result of a significant amount of work. With the hotel, Digital Sound defined the functional requirements necessary to assure guest acceptance and minimize administrative work for the hotel staff. The result is INNtouch(tm), a unique messaging system that integrates with the hotel's property management system (PMS). This integration eliminates mailbox administration, and provides for a fuller range of service. Additionally, INNtouch provides the hotel staff with full-featured voice mail.

CURRENT SITUATION

The lodging industry has become increasingly competitive in recent years. Any business traveler need only to look at an airline inflight magazine to appreciate the lengths hotel chains go to improve customer service and brand loyalty.

Research showed us that in this competitive environment, the only area of ongoing concern (and opportunity for differentiation) is message taking. Today's most common process does not encourage callers to leave detailed messages. Nor can it effectively deal with the growing number of international travelers who need to leave a message in a foreign language.

Staffing can also be a problem. It can be expensive and even difficult due to seasonal fluctuations and conventions. Our research showed that many properties have had difficulty taking messages and then providing easy retrieval during peak periods.

Additionally, major chains have recently instituted frequent traveler programs, resulting in more work for front desk personnel. When a guest checks in, time is now spent giving credit not only for the hotel stay, but also airline mileage and rental cars. This coupled with other extra services hotels may offer has increased the amount of time required to check guests into their rooms. This time element turned out to be an important factor in the development of our guest messaging system.

Hotels now realize there was an opportunity to offer business travelers a significant new service. However, as they began trials of standard "corporate" voice mail systems, significant problems with user acceptance became apparent.

THE PROCESS

The first step was to clearly understand the communication patterns involved in both the message taking process and the administrative steps necessary for checking guests in and out. Our process consisted of surveying hotel staff who either took messages or opened and closed guest mailboxes. Our early analysis found many of the major chains were interested in the concept of guest messaging, but were uneasy with the notion of yet another task for the front desk personnel. So for the product to be truly effective, we realized we needed to allow two things: easy outside caller and guest use; and integration with existing hotel systems. It is this integration that facilitates messaging while minimizing or even eliminating work for the front desk staff.

Message taking is still largely a manual process: Many hotels require large operator staffs to handle the volume of messages. However, our research did point to a significant use of electronic mail systems to facilitate this process. These systems also make the operator aware of any other text messages (such as federal express packages) that might be waiting for pick up. Because many hotels rely on these existing systems, the need to integrate the voice messaging system with the text messaging system became important.

As mentioned, a key problem with a traditional voice mail solution was the user interface. Initial trials quickly showed that it was too complicated for the casual user: Training would be required to allow the guest to use the system. As we examined the communications flow in message taking, we felt that the automated process should be as easy as the manual one; no training should be required. Therefore, we wanted to provide the simplest way to access the system. This meant an entirely new user interface providing limited, but essential functionality.

SIMPLIFIED USER INTERFACE

In the current hotel environment, guests can easily pick up their messages: the guests dial a single digit number that connects them to the message center. The attendant will then check for and deliver the messages to the guest. We wanted our voice messaging system to be as simple to use.

In designing INNtouch, however, we went one step further. When guests dial the message center number they are directly connected to the voice messaging system and--more importantly--their own mailbox. Unlike standard voice messaging systems, there is no log-on sequence, no need to enter passwords or room numbers. Nor is any operator assistance required. Also included was the ability to allow easy message pick up from a remote location.

An overriding objective in development was to minimize guest effort at every step. So once in the system, INNtouch announces the number of messages a guest has, and then immediately plays them. Our research also showed that some systems did not allow the guest to review a message before the next message began to play. This was found to be unacceptable: often a phone number or other important information needed to be written down. If missed the first time, the user needed to be able to go back and review it.

INNtouch prompts the user to take one of three directions after the initial review of each message:
Press (1) to review current message again
Press (*) to discard the message
Press (#) to save the message
These three actions are the only ones that a guest will use in the message retrieval process. Discussions with different hotels demonstrated that they should have the discretion of allowing the guest to save a message. This will reduce the storage requirements and therefore the cost of the system. Since our early discussions showed that flexibility would be important in areas such as this, we designed the product to give the individual hotel a variety of options.

Another option hotels have is to offer varying levels of the "human touch." An example: When a caller tries to reach a guest in their room, the system can be programmed to transfer either to the voice messaging system or to an operator in a busy/no answer situation. Some hotels wanted to give the caller the option of leaving a voice or text message, only putting them into the voice messaging system after they had expressed a desire to do so. Once in the system, the caller is informed that the guest is unavailable and so is asked to leave a message. This greeting is standard and does not give a room number or guest name for security purposes.

If the caller requires additional assistance after reaching INNtouch, they may obtain it by pressing "0." This will revert the call to the operator. It was also discovered that in some cases people would not want to have the system answer their phone. So the ability to disable the system was added. We also encountered a growing percentage of rooms with two-line phones, so the system provides a single mailbox for these situations.

Finally, each hotel likes to have its own personality. This can be accomplished in the prompts used throughout the system. This ability for the hotel to record custom prompts rounded out the user interface.

PROPERTY MANAGEMENT SYSTEM INTEGRATION

Early in our definition process of the user interface we began to uncover problems from a voice mail/PBX integration perspective that would severely limit the usefulness of the system. We also needed to automate the mailbox setup process. Another problem revolved around providing message waiting indicators (MWI) for voice messages.

The most common PBX software in hotels cannot support voice messaging. In fact, most PBX manufacturers did not envision voice messaging in this environment. As a result, standard integration techniques may not provide MWI. Our research pointed out that something needed to be developed to allow for broad industry penetration.

As a result, the INNtouch-Property Management System Interface was designed to address the specific needs of voice messaging in the hotel environment. This interface allows the hotel to centralize the day-to-day administration of the INNtouch system, while providing a means by which the PMS can arbitrate room message indicators.

As mentioned earlier, many hotels use electronic mail systems to facilitate messages. Therefore, we had to integrate these systems into any real solution that we might develop. The PMS interface provides for this integration. In a PMS integrated mode, the guest will be informed in the message summary if there are any text messages waiting. After playing all their voice messages, the system will automatically transfer the call to the attendant who can then deliver the information.

Other issues of concern centered around the administration of the mailbox set up. The solution to this also seemed to reside in the property management system. In most cases the PMS is used to check guests in and out. When integrated, the PMS automatically establishes a mailbox for the guest. In a non-integrated mode, the mailbox set up is accomplished manually, through the telephone. The front desk clerk calls a special mailbox and enters the room number to activate the mailbox.

One distinct advantage available with PMS integration is the ability to offer guests pre-check-in and post check-out mailboxes. This became an attractive feature for travelers who might be traveling from the west to east coast. The guest can have a mailbox established prior to arrival and can alert callers to leave messages at his hotel. At check in, the messages are waiting for him.

Acting as the master to the PBX and the INNtouch system, the PMS provides message waiting indication. This provides notification of voice messages regardless of the PBX or type of software that it is running.

The physical interconnection between utilizes a standard, full duplex, data link circuit operating through a 1200 baud modem. The ability to operate higher baud rates is possible, but requires the use of an optional serial card in the VoiceServer. Messages are sent from the PMS to the VoiceServer over the data link to request administrative changes to the INNtouch data base.

CONCLUSION

Creating a new simplified user interface provided the guest with the necessary functionality to assure acceptance, while the PMS integration solved many of the administrative and integration issues that the hotel chains identified as critical to assure broader penetration. Our recently completed field trial yielded important feedback that has been included in the final product. We feel the long and detailed process has resulted in a superior product and will ultimately pay off in significant sales of the system.

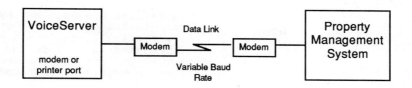

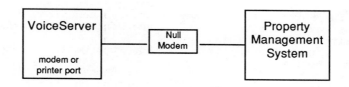

**Fig. 1. VoiceServer – Property Management System
Physical Interconnection**

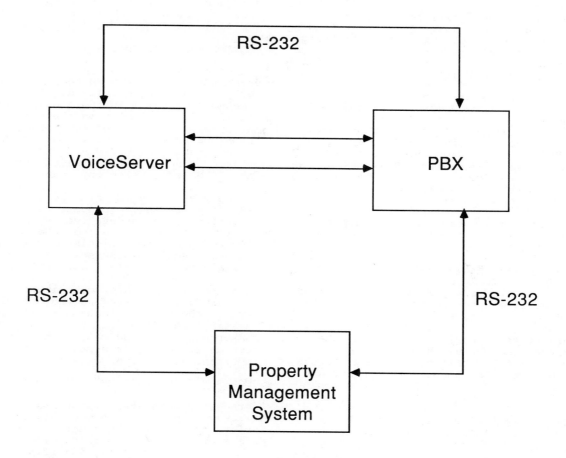

Fig. 2. INNtouch Configuration

FEATURE DEFINITION FOR A NEW GENERATION OF DIGITAL KEY SYSTEMS

Robert Lane
Product Manager
Custom Business Products

Northern Telecom, Inc.
Meridian Key Division
565 Marriott Drive
Suite 300
Nashville, TN   37210

ABSTRACT

Northern Telecom's new Norstar Digital Key System was the result of extensive market research and usability testing. This session explores how rigorous usability testing can take the guesswork out of the product definition process. In particular, a process call Co-Discovery Learning provided vital information on man-machine interface, feature interaction and documentation.

GUIDING PRINCIPLE

Product design is more than fitting technology into a box. It's understanding how people use products and then fitting those products to people.

BUILDING A DESIGN TEAM

Charged with ensuring ease of use in Meridian Norstar, Northern Telecom called into action a multi-disciplinary team of specialists from Bell Northern Research (BNR) to collect and analyze user feedback. The Design Interpretive (DI) team worked with Northern Telecom and BNR software and hardware developers to incorporate these users' insights into the design process itself.

The Meridian Norstar Design Interpretive Team was drawn from the following nine disciplines:

Usability Testing - evaluated the ability of representative users to perform the functions offered by Norstar, and worked with designers to incorporate user feedback into the final design.

User-Interface Design - developed the messages for the alphanumeric liquid crystal display that guide users through the operation of Norstar functions, and defined exactly how each function would work.

User Documentation - developed the simplified telephone user card that explains procedures to follow if people encounter difficulties in the operation of the system.

Industrial Design - packaged and created the image for the terminals and the key service unit (KSU), while meeting mechanical assembly and manufacturability requirements.

Mechanical Design - employing BNR's computer-aided design/computer-aided engineering tools, created the design files used to produce the Norstar mechanical structures, including the housing keyboards and acoustic assemblies.

Hardware Ergonomics - ensured that the Norstar terminals and KSU designs were well adapted for human use.

Consumer Research - conducted market surveys and product studies to evaluate the Norstar design and features.

Acoustic Design - developed the hands-free speaker assumably and the modular microphone, which is enclosed in a separate chamber to achieve manufacturability and maintain high audio quality.

Audio Conformance - worked closely with the acoustic, silicon, and electrical designers to ensure that the product met industry and Northern Telecom standards for audio quality.

TESTING FOR SIMPLICITY

One of the secrets behind the simplicity of Meridian Norstar - Northern Telecom's recently introduced fully digital key telephone system - is the alphanumeric liquid crystal display on the telephones. The display - 1 line by 16 characters on the M7208 telephone and 2 line by 16 characters on the M7310 - p;*rovices step-by-step guidance for accessing the more than 70 Norstar telephony features.

The display messages were the focus for usability testing, a process whereby the reactions fo representative users to a product design are studied. Secretaries, executives and receptionists from both large and small businesses were recruited to evaluate Norstar's functionality.

In a lab at BNR, this community of users was carefully observed as they tried to perform the various features offered by Norstar, including call forwarding, conference call, and call hold. In the testing stage, their mistakes were as important as their successes.

SUCCESS THROUGH FAILURE

Users never make stupid mistakes. There is always a good reason why they are not performing functions correctly. We try to determine why their understanding of the way something works may be different from our design intent.

The next step is to profit from the user's mistakes, addressing and eliminating any difficulty encountered.

Nothing on the Meridian Norstar telephones is there by accident. Every single button, every word on the display, and the exact position, size, shape, and angle of every element were carefully and deliberately thought through to incorporate feedback from users.

A PROCESS CALLED USABILITY TESTING

Team members conducting the tests were housed in a control room. In an adjacent room - empty except for two chairs and a working model of a Norstar telephone, driven by a computer - the actions and reactions of the recruits were studied and documented through two unobtrusive video cameras.

The usability testers employed a BNR-developed process call "co-discovery learning", which involves two people learning to use product features simultaneously.

When you test two people together, they tend to discuss their problems with each other. This interaction gives us more valuable feedback and makes it much easier to evaluate the products usability.

For Norstar, the team logged more than 200 hours videotaping the users. Then they documented their findings and recommendations and worked with the designers to make the terminals easy to operate.

The display is very important. It tells users what to do next. During testing, in fact, we did not provide users with any documentation. They had to rely solely on the display's guidance.

We developed what can be called a discoverable interface, which means that people can work the set intuitively by watching th e commands and following the prompts on the display to perform a function.

PRODUCT DOCUMENTATION

To design an interface that supported all the Norstar functions, BNR duplicated the features on a MacIntosh personal computer. Then, working closely with the software designers and usability testers, refined the display messages to address any problems users had during testing.

The interface was designed so that all the features operate in a similar manner. Once users figure out how any one feature works, they can transfer that knowledge to operate other features.

In fact, the consistent interface and simple prompts allowed the documentation group to develop what is probably the smallest telephone user guide in the

industry - a four-section card that replaces the typical user manual of 30 to 40 pages.

Employing data gathered during testing, the documentation team adopted a minimalist approach, providing only the information that users would need if they encountered difficulties performing functions.

ATTENTION TO DETAIL

While the user interface was being evaluated, other Norstar support groups were testing the physical design. An industrial design team was involved from the beginning of the development process, defining the design objectives with Northern Telcom's marketing divisions in Nashville, TN and Calgary, Canada.

PHYSICAL DESIGN

For example, after reaching an agreement with Northern Telecom on the design objectives of the Norstar terminals, several ideas were sketched and from these carved styrofoam models were developed.

When Northern Telecom was comfortable with initial designs, a solid model portraying the details of the telephone sets were used for studies by the consumer research group, which provided input to all the development groups. All aspects of the terminals that impact users in the field were evaluated. The challenge of the consumer research group was to translate the users; concerns into terminology that designers can respond to.

To obtain consumer feedback, the team conducted several studies aimed at evaluating the characteristics of the terminals. For example, the group took Norstar to various locales, including the University of Texas and Eastman-Kodak, to ask some 300 users to rate the functionality and visual appearance of the handset alone.

In addition to the consumer research results, input from hardware ergonomists ensured that Northern Telecom products were designed for physical ease of use. Armed with such statistics as people's arm reach and common viewing angles for th4e display, ergonomists specified and later refined critical physical characteristics of Norstar system.

At one point, ergonomists traveled through the corridors of BNR and Northern Telecom with a prototype terminal perched on a trolley to study people's reactions to the display under different lighting conditions. Because the success of the terminal depends partly on how well users can read the information on the display, it was important that we take into account

every element that may affect easy
viewing.

DESIGNING FOR SERVICE

The design team also evaluated the key
service unit (KSU), which houses the
access lines and software cartridges that
support six outside lines and sixteen
telephones. For this appraisal,
researchers went into the field to study
how a KSU would typically be installed.

Once this initial evaluation was
completed, designers returned to the field
with a model of the proposed Norstar KSU
to test the ease with which the unit could
be mounted on the wall, the software
cartridges inserted in the unit, and the
cables routed. The results were forwarded
to the KSU designers who refined the
design to ensure easy installation and
servicing.

Then, the team brought installers into the
usability lab to see whether they had
problems programming a newly installed key
system. The usability observations were
supplied to the documentation team, and
together, the groups developed a
programming sheet. The sheet is a job aid
that guies installers of the Norstar
system through configuration and
administration tasks.

MORE ABOUT CO-DISCOVERY LEARNING

The Co-Discovery Learning method has been
used by Northern Telecom/BNR since 1984.
The technique of testing two people at
once is common in usability testing
circles, but the method of testing two
people and testing without any
documentation is unique to NT/BNR. The
following are five techniques that make
our Co-Discovery Learning method
especially effective:

More Emphasis on Core Tasks - the ones
that users do most often and that are most
critical to the users. For a telephone,
the core tasks would include answering
calls, making calls, transferring calls,
setting up conference calls, programming
and using auto-dialers, etc.

Setting Behavior Criteria - defining
acceptable levels of performance. For
example, users should be able to set up a
conference call for the first time within
5 minutes, without using any documentation
or getting any "hints" from the
experimenter. If they can not, the
feature must be redesigned and re-tested.

Quantitative Measure of Performance - we
now measure the amount of time users
require to complete each task, the number
of errors they make, number of keystrokes,
number of times they accidentally drop a
call, and whether they require "hints"
from the experimenter.

Usability Classes - we classify the
usability of each core task according to
the quantitative performance measures.
For example, if any user4s drop calls or
if a certain percentage of users require
hints, the usability is Class 0, which is
unacceptable and must be fixed.

Minimal Documentation - usability testing
and the design of the documentation have
been much more closely coupled. Initial
tests are done without any documentation.
In addition to discovering interface
problems, this also helps identify the
minimal information needs to be included
in formal documentation. Once the
interface is redesigned and re-tested, the
documentation is also tested. At this
stage, problems with the coupling of the
interface and documentation are uncovered.

CONCLUSION

Usability testing, and particularly the
Co-Discovery Learning process is an
important element of the product
definition/product design process at
Northern Telecom./

Design changes which are easy to implement
early in the product development cycle
become costly and time consuming to
implement late in the cycle. Therefore
the impact of this and other testing,
modeling and consumer research activity by
Northern Telecom results in a superior
functioning product and a cost-effective
development program.

In addition to testing feature
interaction, serviceability and other
important factors, the Co-Discovery
Learning process used by NT/BNR provides
the blue-print for essential
documentation.

Finally, simple operation and simple
documentation encourage users to try
additional features and to transfer the
knowledge they have acquired to those
features.

PQR-02

The New Product Introduction Process

Tom McManus- Chairperson
Director Manufacturing Process Technology

Northern Telecom Inc.
200 Athens Way,
Nashville , Tenn. 37228

ABSTRACT

This seminar deals with the New Product Introduction Process.

The ability of a company to respond quickly and accurately to the market trends in new product requirements and features will determine the long term success of that company.

In the last decade the complexity of technology in telecommunications has increased in a non linear fashion, and has driven the need for inventive solutions in the design and manufacture of new products.

Designs now require increased amounts of data to describe their functionality, fabrication, and assembly, and this has driven the emergence of sophisticated network techniques to move the information quickly and accurately from design centers to manufacturing facilities. The effective management of the NPI information is an essential element contributing to the success of a company in terms of new product introduction capability.

Whilst the design, and the design process, have increased in complexity, the philosophy of manufacturing has altered with the emergence of flow processes in electronics assembly. "Just in Time" philosophy is being applied throughout the industry, and increased emphasis has been placed on quality. At the same time, new products are being introduced at an accelerated pace, and this has reduced the product lifetime. The focus of electronic manufacturing is reduction of the interval required to introduce new products and features into the marketplace.

These factors, combined with the pervasive introduction of computer aided tools, have forced a re-thinking of the entire product realization process. The papers in this seminar address this process management issue, from the perspective of teamwork, emphasis on operations engineering, and computer augmented communications.

The presenters of the papers in this seminar provide us with a broad perspective on the process, and the complexities involved in harnessing and redirecting the energy in the process. They are:-

Richard C. Ricks	Northern Telecom Inc.
Mike Pratt	American Telephone & Telegraph
Earl Hewitt	Northern Telecom Inc.
John Gage	Sun Microsystems
Dimitri Dimancesco	Digital Equipment Corporation

The first paper "*NEW PRODUCT INTRODUCTION- A TEAM PROCESS*" provides an overview of the product delivery process from idea formulation through deployment to customer, with emphasis on the teamwork required by the development agency, the product supplier, and the customer.

The second paper "*IMPROVING NPI "WHITE COLLAR" PROCESSES*" discusses how to identify the critical decision points in the new product introduction process, and the information required to effectively manage it. In addition a methodology, called "operation engineering", for continuously improving these basic business processes is presented, addressing process characterization, analysis, improvement and control.

The next paper "*USING PROCESS FUNCTION ANALYSIS TO MAKE NEW PRODUCT INTRODUCTION A COMPETITIVE WEAPON*" presents a powerful technique for ensuring the best use of organizational resources and perhaps the most valuable resource...time.

The fourth paper "*PRODUCT INNOVATION IN A TIME OF STANDARDS*" describes how rapid advances in technology, now forcibly coupled to emerging open standards that all competitors must follow, create new rules for product design, innovation,and introduction.

The final paper "*COMPUTER AUTOMATED COMMUNICATIONS: IMPROVING THE EFFECTIVENESS OF THE MANUFACTURING AND ENGINEERING PROCESS*" describes the impact of rapidly changing technology on the traditional manual processes and discusses the need to address the entire process in order to achieve major gains in engineering effectiveness.

NEW PRODUCT INTRODUCTION
A TEAM PROCESS

Richard Ricks
Manager New Products

Barry Bond
Manager Process Development

Northern Telecom, Inc.
4001 E. Chapel Hill-Nelson Hwy.
Research Triangle Park, N. C. 27707

ABSTRACT

In today's fast paced telecommunications market, a procedure to routinely develop and deliver high quality new products in the minimum amount of time is essential. This paper examines the product delivery process from idea formulation through deployment to the customer, with emphasis on the teamwork required by the development agency, product supplier, and customer.

INTRODUCTION

In today's marketplace, a company's continued success is dependent upon its successful execution of the product realization process.

Product realization is a process that takes an idea and turns it into a reality. This process can be thought of as a series of discrete stages: initiation, definition, development, verification and manufacturing/deployment. These stages do not progress in a smooth sequence, but rather move in a spiral sequence with continual reiterations. Reviews are held at the end of each stage to monitor and evaluate the project.

To be successful, the product realization process must be well defined with established standards. This helps to ensure continuity in the application of the process in spite of personnel turnovers and provides a platform for process development. The detailed deliverables will vary depending on the project and the evolutionary state of the process itself.

Teamwork builds agreement, understanding and cooperation that is essential for the successful introduction of a new product. Everyone works as a team to ensure that the right product is delivered, and that manufacturing, marketing, and business issues are addressed effectively. All must acknowledge accountability for tasks and roles assigned to them.

A typical team consists of a customer, a marketing interface, a development agency and a product supplier. For the purposes of this paper, the product supplier is defined as consisting of: Project Management, Marketing, Manufacturing, Production Operations, Quality, Installation, Customer Services, Maintenance, Repair, Verification, and Documentation.

Customer participation should be sought at every stage. Such an open approach from product inception to product delivery will be much more beneficial to the success of the project. The desired result is a customer relations platform that should provide not only customer feedback but an actual framework for delivering products and services.

Permeating all stages of the product realization process is the fact that projects are temporary entities that tend to develop a unique political association all their own. The dynamics of project politics are derived from these facts.

o Projects have positive benefits including high visibility, support from high level management, and much attention from many people.

o Projects go against the grain of most organizations as they are politically organized around function and staff arrangements.

o Enmity in others can be aroused because the dramatic results of the high-energy, short term, and highly visible team may make them feel inadequate. This upsets their normal operation, increases the pressure and expectations of them, and puts them in the background while the project assumes a spotlight position.

Project management must recognize these political pitfalls and react accordingly in order to maintain a focus on the project's goal.

GOALS

A company's first concern is to produce quality products that meet its customers' needs. A true measure of success is customer satisfaction with the product.

The result of the efforts of the team members must be judged to ever more exacting standards. Yesterday's standards are no longer appropriate for the error-free, self healing networks that can be software-programmed and managed by the customer. A successful company teams with its customers, suppliers, and development agency, and integrates every facet of its product realization operation to elevate product delivery to a high level of responsiveness.

Customers define quality not only by how well a product performs, but by such areas as sales and marketing services, distribution services, technical services, product maintenance and repair services, documentation, training and software. These diverse areas must be identified immediately as part of the project team, and their requirements must be considered part of the design requirement, not added after the design is fixed.

INITIATION

The initiation phase is the beginning of the product realization process. Bringing an idea from concept to delivered product is a highly iterative process. It requires many discussions, ranging from peer group meetings to formal presentations to management. (FIG. 1)

New products start with ideas. These ideas should be the result of marketing listening to the customer and communicating the customer's needs to the development agency. To listen properly marketing must understand both the customer and the market.

A new idea needs a sponsor to be transformed from a proposal into a product. In advocating a new idea, one must answer all kinds of questions about feasibility and marketability from people with expertise in different areas. When the experts are convinced of merit in a proposed product, they will back it and make it work. While they will challenge often, every criticism that is met with well-reasoned responses earns commitment from those whose support will be important for success.

Customers must be involved to make sure that the product really will have a place in the market. A customer's demonstrated interest is probably the best proof of the value of a product idea, since the new product idea must compete not only with competitor's offerings, but with customer's current methods of filling a need. Customer involvement is one of the strongest means of winning corporate backing.

DEFINITION

In the definition stage the objective of the project is defined, broken down into elements (work breakdown structure) and all resource requirements are determined. (FIG. 2)

A project team is formed and cooperatively establishes the goals, objectives and scope of the project based on the customer contract, requirements document and design specification. Time, resource, and effort plans for producing the product are developed. The time constraints, priorities and support required should be clearly understood at this stage.

Proper definition of any project requires clear identification of individual work elements and definition of sizes, risks and other component parts for management planning and control purposes. At the same time, teambuilding is crucial. People solve problems, not technology.

Required resources must be determined with respect to the constraints placed on the project. The three degrees of freedom - funding, time, and function - must be balanced to achieve the project goals. If the required resources are not available the project goals will not be attainable. These should be documented and presented to management. An honest early warning system that the project may be in jeopardy is critical.

The project management plan controls and directs the project introduction. It defines responsibilities, the ways information will be communicated, the manner in which difficulties will be resolved, and how change will be managed.

The high level design is determined in the definition stage. If extensive research is required, the team must evaluate whether this cost, in time and funding, may jeopardize the product's chances of meeting market windows, production cost targets, or other criteria affecting its commercial success.

DEVELOPMENT

In the development stage the detailed design and documentation of a new product is accomplished, and prototype units are assembled. (FIG. 3)

Development progresses as three parallel processes - hardware, software and documentation. The parts of each process are tested separately and then integrated and tested as the complete product.

As testing uncovers design problems, changes are required. Root causes, not symptoms, must be addressed to produce an excellent, as opposed to an adequate, product.

However, if changes to the product design are not performed in a controlled manner they will result in problems with schedules and costs. Controlling changes will also help in the effort to test whether new problems have been introduced through design recycles.

Prototypes are essential in the development stage as they allow testing of the product's feasibility. Specifically, prototypes are used to:

o Identify risk areas
o Assist in the costing and budgeting process
o Assist in presale efforts
o Indicate modifications needed
o Define techniques for manufacturing/deployment

Prototyping gives the product supplier an opportunity to test the manufacturability of the new product and gear up for full-scale production. The design must be tolerant enough to accommodate variances introduced in the manufacturing process while retaining a design that will allow for optimal economy. All direct and indirect cost factors must be considered.

VERIFICATION

The verification stage (FIG. 4) assesses how well a product meets the needs of the customer who inspired it. Customer involvement not only assures that the product is what the customer wants but helps build excitement about the product and earns customer commitment.

The first real product is produced during this stage. Verification of the product should consist of both static (peer reviews) and dynamic testing. Dynamic verification is done on many levels:

o Component
o Circuit pack
o Subsystem
o System integration/regression
o Customer site

An in-service field trial of the product is critical to discovering problems likely to emerge in the functioning and manufacturing of the new product. Product functionality and reliability in real-use conditions are thoroughly tested at this point. As in the development process, root causes of problems must be found and corrected to avoid poor quality and product failure.

Verification is not completed until the product functions according to criteria established by the design team. This criteria should establish both an acceptable number of errors allowed in a specified timeframe, and a period of time over which the product must operate error-free.

Schedule overruns in the development stage can encroach on time budgeted for verification. However, no new product can bypass verification. Problems arising after the general release of the product force the product supplier to devote far more customer support and servicing than should be necessary, and both the development agency's and product supplier's reputation for quality suffers.

Field trial tests also evaluate product integration with other equipment in the customer's environment. Installation, support, and service capability are also evaluated. Requirements for diagnostic tools and test equipment are also confirmed at this point.

Surveys of elements important to the end user - aesthetics, ease of use, usefulness of features - must be prepared, along with methods for collecting and analyzing the data.

Comprehensiveness and usefulness of the documentation are appraised by those who work with the new product. Technical documentation, end-user documentation, training and marketing materials should be included in the documentation package to allow the user to assess the entire presentation of the product.

MANUFACTURING AND DEPLOYMENT

In the manufacturing and deployment stage, the product's design is stabilized and optimized for volume production. (FIG. 5)

After positive results from the field trial are obtained, the product goes into limited production. This production ramp, prior to general availability, is required to allow the product supplier to acquire the capacity to produce the product and verify his processes.

The primary task at this stage is to fine-tune the manufacturing process so that the highest quality product can be manufactured as quickly as possible at the lowest cost.

To fine-tune the process, product supplier personnel need to:

o Analyze the manufacturing-yield results to evaluate the design robustness and component quality, and identify any manufacturing-process defects;

o Review manufacturing-time issues such as supplier relationships, assembly methods, mechanical-fit issues, and test and repair methods;

o Compare the manufacturing costs with those originally projected; and

o Finalize all design-transfer information.

By the time a new product is ready to manufacture in limited quantities, it has often achieved significant visibility in the market. There can be temptation and pressure to eliminate the production ramp. This should be resisted, however, since delays at this stage, (part shortages, design changes, low yields, etc.), may cause loss of long term market opportunities and customer dissatisfaction.

As the corporation begins to advertise, manufacture, and distribute the product, resource requirements peak as a broad range of activities take place concurrently. To manage manufacturing materials alone, for example, includes selecting vendors, purchasing materials, assessing quality, and moving materials to manufacturing sites.

During this stage of the introduction the design is transferred to the product supplier and the development agency's focus changes from research and development to product engineering and support. The development agency continues to work with the product supplier until they can fully support and meet customer expectations for installation, training, and service. At a point both deem appropriate, design authority for the new product is transferred to the product supplier.

Much of the value of the product from the customer's point of view lies in how well a product is supported after purchase. Training, emergency support, and additional equipment must be readily accessible to customers. Ongoing communication with sales and marketing personnel will help them keep their equipment up to date and ensure that they can take advantage of new products and features as they are developed.

The manufacturing and deployment of a product is the stage most visible to customers, and the stage that ultimately decides the success of new products.

CONCLUSION

The transformation of an idea to a product that the customer wants and needs requires the coordinated efforts of a large number of people and the completion of numerous deliverables. The complexity of the task can be reduced by breaking projects down into stages. The project progresses to the next stage only when the prior stage is successfully completed.

Regardless of the management techniques used to define, monitor and control, the project success is dependent on teamwork. The customer is a key member of the team.

Consistent application of the product realization process will result in successful projects being the norm, not the exception, and help assure the continued success of a corporation.

REFERENCES

"NEW PRODUCT INTRODUCTION, THE CHALLENGE." BELL-NORTHERN RESEARCH, DECEMBER 1987.

MERRILLS, ROY "RAISING SERVICE TO NEW LEVELS." CONNECTIONS, DECEMBER 1987.

WENIG, RAYMOND AND PARDOE, TERRY "SUCCESSFUL PROGRAM AND PROJECT MANAGEMENT." INTERNATIONAL MANAGEMENT SERVICES, INC., 1987.

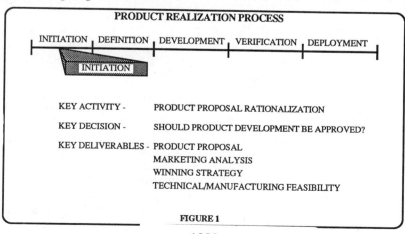

PRODUCT REALIZATION PROCESS

INITIATION | DEFINITION | DEVELOPMENT | VERIFICATION | DEPLOYMENT

INITIATION

KEY ACTIVITY - PRODUCT PROPOSAL RATIONALIZATION

KEY DECISION - SHOULD PRODUCT DEVELOPMENT BE APPROVED?

KEY DELIVERABLES - PRODUCT PROPOSAL
MARKETING ANALYSIS
WINNING STRATEGY
TECHNICAL/MANUFACTURING FEASIBILITY

FIGURE 1

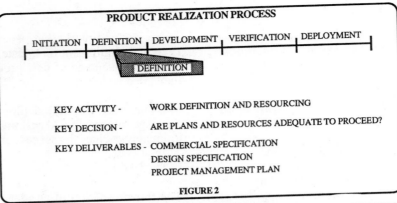

PRODUCT REALIZATION PROCESS

INITIATION | DEFINITION | DEVELOPMENT | VERIFICATION | DEPLOYMENT

DEFINITION

KEY ACTIVITY -   WORK DEFINITION AND RESOURCING

KEY DECISION -   ARE PLANS AND RESOURCES ADEQUATE TO PROCEED?

KEY DELIVERABLES - COMMERCIAL SPECIFICATION
                              DESIGN SPECIFICATION
                              PROJECT MANAGEMENT PLAN

FIGURE 2

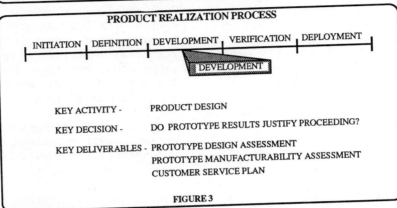

PRODUCT REALIZATION PROCESS

INITIATION | DEFINITION | DEVELOPMENT | VERIFICATION | DEPLOYMENT

DEVELOPMENT

KEY ACTIVITY -   PRODUCT DESIGN

KEY DECISION -   DO PROTOTYPE RESULTS JUSTIFY PROCEEDING?

KEY DELIVERABLES - PROTOTYPE DESIGN ASSESSMENT
                              PROTOTYPE MANUFACTURABILITY ASSESSMENT
                              CUSTOMER SERVICE PLAN

FIGURE 3

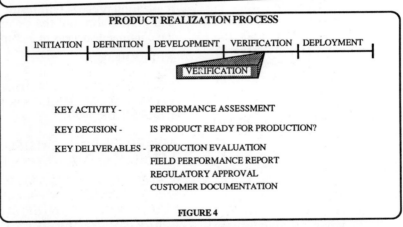

PRODUCT REALIZATION PROCESS

INITIATION | DEFINITION | DEVELOPMENT | VERIFICATION | DEPLOYMENT

VERIFICATION

KEY ACTIVITY -   PERFORMANCE ASSESSMENT

KEY DECISION -   IS PRODUCT READY FOR PRODUCTION?

KEY DELIVERABLES - PRODUCTION EVALUATION
                              FIELD PERFORMANCE REPORT
                              REGULATORY APPROVAL
                              CUSTOMER DOCUMENTATION

FIGURE 4

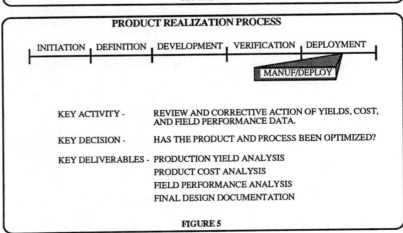

PRODUCT REALIZATION PROCESS

INITIATION | DEFINITION | DEVELOPMENT | VERIFICATION | DEPLOYMENT

MANUF/DEPLOY

KEY ACTIVITY -   REVIEW AND CORRECTIVE ACTION OF YIELDS, COST,
                              AND FIELD PERFORMANCE DATA.

KEY DECISION -   HAS THE PRODUCT AND PROCESS BEEN OPTIMIZED?

KEY DELIVERABLES - PRODUCTION YIELD ANALYSIS
                              PRODUCT COST ANALYSIS
                              FIELD PERFORMANCE ANALYSIS
                              FINAL DESIGN DOCUMENTATION

FIGURE 5

IMPROVING NPI WHITE COLLAR PROCESSES

Michael K. Pratt

Technical Supervisor
Product Realization Operations Engineering

AT&T Bell Laboratories

Crawford Corners Road, Room 3L-314
Holmdel, New Jersey 07733

ABSTRACT

This paper discusses two approaches to improve New Product Introduction (NPI). The first examines issues relevant to managing NPI projects, discussing how to identify the critical decision points in the NPI process, and the information required to effectively manage it.

The second approach explores NPI as a set of coupled information processes, producing the information necessary to plan, develop and deploy a quality product that meets the customer's needs and expectations. A methodology, called "operations engineering," for continuously improving these basic business processes will be presented, addressing process characterization, analysis, improvement and control.

INTRODUCTION

The timely introduction of new products has always been a critical factor in the success of a business enterprise. When new products embody superior technology, either in product design or manufacturing methods, a significant market advantage often develops. This allows the enterprise to recover investments in research and development of these new technologies by pricing at significantly higher margins until their competitors in the industry reach the same technological plateau. Hopefully, by the time competitors reach that point, substantial market share will have been established that can then be defended by competitive product pricing.

However, the pace of technological advance is seldom constant, and many advances are difficult to protect from immediate replication by competitors. This leads to periods when the technological distance between competitors within a mature industry is small. As the technology gulf diminishes, the relative efficiency and effectiveness of the basic business processes that realize new products and deliver them to the customer become increasingly important.

In fact, it can be argued that the relative effectiveness of these processes has become a significant differentiation between successful companies. The business strategy of employing an expeditious process for introducing new products on the heels of the industries' technological leaders, commonly referred to as "fast following," has enabled many companies to rapidly expand their market share at the expense of their competitors.

Ultimately, the long term wellbeing of an enterprise, and its ability to invest in continued research and development to maintain a competitive position, will reflect in part the efficiency and effectiveness of its NPI processes. While the U.S. still leads the world in research efforts and patents granted, its lead is diminishing (1)(2). To maintain a leadership position within an industry, a company must not only maintain a strong technological posture, but constantly improve its processes of delivering that technology to the marketplace.

The "white collar" information processes required to introduce new products, and how effectively they are managed, can have as profound an impact on market timeliness, product quality, and customer satisfaction as the production processes that manufacture them. Indeed, information itself, be it a manufacturing layout or design specification, can be viewed as logical subassemblies of a product. By improving both the effectiveness of managing NPI efforts, and the fundamental processes NPI employs, the competitive posture of an enterprise can be significantly improved. The remainder of this paper discusses how to improve the introduction of new products by addressing both of these elements.

MANAGING NPI PROJECTS

Most NPI projects can be naturally broken into several distinct stages of activity. For example, market planning, concept development, product design, manufacturing and eventual product deployment are general stages that most NPI efforts pass through. As the skills required in each stage may be highly specialized, many companies organize along similar functional lines. With a functionally oriented organizational structure, a new product will typically undergo several handoffs from inception to general availability, and communication within the project is often difficult.

Another approach to managing NPI efforts, often used by smaller companies, is to form project centered teams, bringing together all the required resources until NPI has been accomplished. While this structure improves communications and reduces handoffs, it may be less efficient in its use of specialized resources and can be an overwhelming management challenge on large projects.

However, functional organizations can enjoy many of the attributes of the project centered team approach by establishing the appropriate NPI management structure. A project management team that encompasses the key managers from each stage of NPI will improve the communications between organizations and reduce the uncertainty of handoffs. Representing their respective organizations' functional expertise and interests, these managers are collectively accountable for the course of decisions during the entire project. This larger accountability will force the assessment of project decisions on downstream stages of NPI at every step, while encouraging the continuous reassessment of earlier project assumptions.

No matter what the style, management is always responsible for the efficient and effective use of the resources dedicated to realizing a new product. The specific project management structure that best fits the needs of an enterprise will be a function of the organization, the cultural environment, and the nature of the product under development. The structure chosen should clearly identify accountabilities through all stages of NPI to prevent misunderstandings at handoffs and ensure the early assessment of downstream considerations. Of course, the vested authority to execute these accountabilities is essential to the success of any management approach.

IDENTIFYING CRITICAL DECISION POINTS

Once the project management structure has been established, it is important to identify the critical points in the project where the right decisions must be made to have the most influential impact on the project. These decision points occur where significant additional resources must be invested in the project if it is to continue to completion. The resources invested in a project usually closely track the stages of NPI and would include, for example, resources required for market planning and concept development, detailed design, prototype development, production facility development, full scale manufacturing, and distribution.

At these decision points, the NPI management team makes a go/no-go decision on whether to proceed to the next stage of NPI. Previous assumptions made at earlier control points are reexamined to make sure current conditions or new information have not altered basic project premises. While this may seem to be an obvious activity in project management, it is surprising how often projects continue to press forward with a life of their own, long after changing conditions or circumstances have eroded chances for success. With the appropriate project management structure, and a well disciplined process for assessing the project at these critical decision points, management cannot avoid making difficult decisions, even if it means the termination of the project.

DECISION POINT INFORMATION

Once these critical decision points have been identified, then the right information must be assembled to decide whether or not to invest in the next stage of the project. This information should be well documented, identifying the individual responsible for providing it. As an example, for a decision point located after market planning and conceptual development have been performed, but before detailed product design resources are committed, the following partial listing of information would be required:

- product cost target
- design specifications
- design methodology and support tool environment
- change management strategy
- system integration and test strategy
- product documentation plan
- critical technology choices

As implied, this information must be tailored to each decision point.

The following is an example of

information gathered and assessed at a prior decision point that must be reexamined to make certain that the assumptions and decisions made previously are still valid.

- sales plan and targets

- product functional requirements

- pricing strategy

- product life cycle projections

- project funding strategy

Typical questions to answer include; do the cost targets fit within the pricing strategy margins; do the design specifications satisfy the product functional requirements; has new information on the competition's product offerings altered product life cycle projections; etc.

CONTINUOUS PROCESS IMPROVEMENT

Lester Thurow, Dean of the School of Management at MIT, notes an interesting characteristic of American management (3). He states that in the American character, a problem has not been solved, perhaps cannot be solved, unless one overriding cause can be isolated. However, when analyzing NPI processes, most often there is no single cause, but rather a multitude of small, contributing causes, for poor process performance. Thurow goes on to state that "correcting each of many small causes is not part of the American style, but such small improvements are at the heart of large aggregate improvements," and that "progress is made by making thousands of incremental improvements."

Continuous process improvement is the structured set of activities that seeks to identify each of the many causes, both large and small, that together can strangle the processes employed in NPI, yielding a process of poor quality, thats too slow and costly to be competitive. Conceptually, the essence of continuous process improvement might be summed up as the iterative struggle to,

- understand,

  - simplify,

    - integrate,

      - and automate, where appropriate

the basic processes of realizing products. Without the requisite attention to the first three of these steps, investment in automation, either in automated production facilities (4) or design automation tools,

will be suboptimal. Most industries have examples of attempts to automate complex and poorly understood processes, yielding less than the expected results.

Operations engineering is a methodology that applies fundamental systems engineering and operations research principles to continuously improve information processes. The methodology is composed of the following general steps:

- establish process ownership

- characterize and analyze the process under study

- develop and implement process improvements

- establish process control

PROCESS OWNERSHIP

Continuous process improvement intrinsically means changing the way people do their jobs. Establishing a climate where change is championed is critical to to the success of these efforts. Engaging the active participation of the line management for the processes under study is essential to establishing this climate, and ensuring their buy-in to the process improvements that are identified.

To improve the end-to-end performance of many processes, it is often necessary to change the way functions are performed in several organizations. This will require establishing a sense of common ownership of the process between parties that may have parochial and conflicting concerns. Organizational consultants can often be useful in developing the appropriate campaign to establish this mutual ownership and teamwork, by helping to uncover and address sensitivities that arise.

PROCESS CHARACTERIZATION AND ANALYSIS

The most useful method of understanding a process is to characterize its elements and attributes in a manner that facilitates modeling and analysis. There are a number of process characterization techniques, with varying degrees of complexity, such as data flow diagrams, Petri nets, and IDEF0 (5), to name just a few. Attributes of these techniques can also be combined to develop a customized method that is best suited to a specific application. To maintain a level of consistency, and facilitate the integration of multiple processes, it is beneficial to establish a standard technique. At a minimum, the technique should be able to characterize basic functions and associated organizational accountabilities, including information inputs and outputs to each function. In addition, the ability to characterize value-added activity, procedural precedence, and support system relationships will enrich the understanding of the process under question. As implied earlier, actively involving the organizations that are accountable for performing these processes is important to both the quality of the characterization and the degree of buy-in to the eventual process improvements to be realized.

Using the process characterization to identify the principle inputs and outputs, the appropriate metrics to assess process performance can be determined. Metrics are a particularly sensitive issue, especially when they can be misused to reflect on the human resource instead of the process. Ownership is extremely important, and methods such as the nominal group technique (6) can be used to help participatively develop these measures.

These metrics should illustrate, at the highest level, process performance as a function of cost, interval and quality of the information produced by the process. Since it may be possible, for example, to optimize interval at the expense of quality or cost, it is important to be able to assess the combined impact. With target performance parameters in mind, these metrics can identify where the process has the greatest need of improvement. In addition, by employing root-cause and failure mode analysis techniques, chronic problems, non value-added functions, and information bottlenecks identified during characterization can serve as excellent places to begin to probe for opportunities to improve the process.

PROCESS IMPROVEMENT

Once the process is characterized and performance metrics established, proposals to change the process to realize an improvement can be developed, modeled and trialed to demonstrate their impact before any risk is taken on a specific project. The modeling and trial include both the change in functional and organizational aspects of the improvement, as well as any change in the support system environment.

After a specific improvement has been trialed and proven, then a detailed migration plan describing how and when the new process will be implemented is developed. This is an often overlooked consideration of process change that can have a significant impact because of the high coupling between the products under development and the processes and tools used to realize them. In fact, it is often best to improve a process when it is between major projects, minimizing the amount of information that must be translated or maintained in two different environments.

PROCESS CONTROL

It has long been understood that industrial processes can be more effectively managed by the application of statistical control methods (7). Few manufacturing managers, for example, could imagine effectively managing production without the use of traditional process yield and interval statistics. Now that information processes have been rendered observable by appropriate characterization and metrics, similar techniques can be used to improve our ability to manage these processes as well. Using statistical control techniques, appropriate process control limits can be established to help determine the range of process capability, and identify when the process begins to fall out of control. Process performance outside these limits identifies problems that require attention, and may lead to additional opportunities for process improvements.

Figure 1 shows a simplified example of a process control chart, identifying both the process control limits and the effects one might anticipate from implementing an improvement in the process. At the highest level, cost, interval and quality (shown as quality defects, or inverse quality for simplification) would be expected to be reduced with the implementation of a process improvement. Note the temporary degradation in performance that might accompany the training and ramp-up period in process change. This phenomenon is often seen (7) when changes are made in typical industrial processes, and they should be anticipated in changing white collar information processes, as well.

CONCLUSIONS

The ability to quickly and efficiently introduce new products and technology into the market place is essential to the competitive posture of every enterprise. Increasing the effectiveness of NPI project management, and continuously improving the processes employed in NPI, can have a significant impact on a companies' competitive position.

By facilitating common ownership through all stages of NPI, identifying the critical decision points in a project, and making sure the right information is available to make quality decisions, every NPI project can be improved. In addition, structured characterization and analysis of the information processes employed in NPI can illuminate significant opportunities for process improvement. The establishment and diligent tracking of appropriate metrics enables the continuous assessment of process performance (8), continuously raises new opportunities for improvement, and fuels the iterative application of these techniques.

REFERENCES

1. National Academy of Engineering, *Technology and Global Industry*, Bruce R. Guile and Harvey Brooks, Eds. (National Academy Press, Washington, DC, 1987), p.200.
2. National Science Foundation, *Science Indicators* (Government Printing Office, Washington, DC, 1985), appendix table 1-7.
3. Lester C. Thurow, "A Weakness in Process Technology," *Science*, p.1659, vol.238, Dec. 18, 1987.
4. R. Jaikumar, *Harvard Business Rev.*, vol.86 (Nov-Dec 1986).
5. ICAM DEFinition, *Integrated Computer Aided Manufacturing (ICAM) Architecture Part II, vol.IV - Function Modeling Manual (IDEF0)*, AFWL TR-81-4023, June 1981.
6. Ira B. Gregerman, "Knowledge Worker Productivity: Characteristics and Measurement." *Transactions of the American Association of Cost Engineers*, p.I.2.1, June 1981.
7. W. A. Shewhart, *Economic Control of Quality of Manufactured Product*, Princeton, N.J.: D. Van Nostrand Co., 1931.
8. E. E. Adams, Jr.; J. C. Hershauer; and W. A. Ruch; *Productivity and Quality: Measurement as a Basis for Improvement*. Englewood Cliffs, N.J.: Prentice-Hall, 1981.

Process Performance

Simplified Control Chart

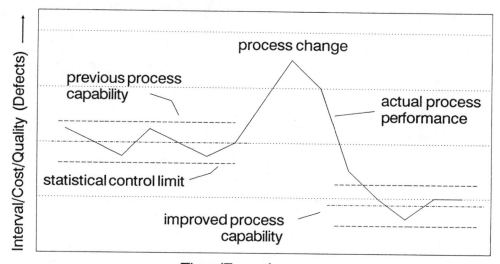

Figure 1

USING PROCESS FUNCTION ANALYSIS TO MAKE NEW PRODUCT INTRODUCTION A COMPETITIVE WEAPON

Stewart O. Davis
Manager, New Manufacturing
Processing Development
Northern Telecom Inc.
One Ravinia Drive
Atlanta, Georgia 30346

Earl Hewitt
General Manager, SL-1 Operations
Northern Telecom Inc.
2305 Mission College Boulevard
Santa Clara, California 95054

ABSTRACT

The speed and quality of the process of introducing a new product can be as important to the success of the product as the actual new product. Designing the process based on the functions that add value to the product and its introduction can produce a competitive advantage in itself. This paper presents a powerful method for ensuring the best use of organizational resources and perhaps the most valuable resource--time.

INTRODUCTION

There is a standard for New Product Introduction (NPI) in Western industry that has tended to be more myth than fact - a quality product, on-time and within costs. Until recently, the average product could qualify in only two of the three. You could produce the product on-time and within cost, but the quality suffered. You could deliver a quality product, on-time, but it wasn't cheap. For most companies, the power to deliver quality products, on-time, and within costs simply was beyond the grasp of business reality. Innovative new product introduction was seldom associated with the innovation of the new product itself. Fast and innovative approaches generally came out of entrepreneurial and start-up ventures. For big, established businesses, the very idea of using the speed and quality of the NPI process as a competitive weapon was a subject for seminars and text books--not the way business was done.

Most approaches to NPI do not focus on the real purpose of NPI: innovation, placing a good idea into the hands of an interested market quickly. In fact, NPI is probably more of a routine in most businesses, laden with overhead generating transactions, organizational "turf" battles, politics, and all the other ingredients of bureaucratic cement. Many companies, however, are finding ways to make the organization more responsive by focusing on making the product's introduction as important as the product. The old standard hasn't been reinvented. Competitive companies are simply finding ways to make the old standard happen. George Stalk of the Boston Consulting Group, writes, "Just when their Western counterparts are beginning to 'fight back' by focusing attention on their costs, the Japanese have changed the basis of competition to include expanded product variety and fast response time, in addition to low cost and high quality." (1)

Time is one of the most, if not the most, valuable of corporate resources. It is a commodity available to all who want to compete in any market. Time in an NPI process that is not consumed by functions that add to the product, service and customer value chain is money wasted. The ability to use time wisely and produce a greater variety of new products for increasingly competitive markets will characterize tomorrow's winners and losers. As in military operations, the ability to surprise your enemy is a critical success factor. Developing the process that allows you to be there first, consistently, before the competition can make NPI a competitive weapon.

NORTHERN TELECOM'S RESPONSE

Unraveling a complex and time-consuming NPI process is a challenging endeavor. It is a challenge that can be met by those willing to invest the time to do it. Stanley Davis states in Future Perfect, "Those who limit their thinking to the familiar contexts of the industrial age will never be able to exploit the essential raw materials of the new economy -- time, space, and matter. In this new economic model, we could reverse the statement that "time is money" to read "money is time". The key resource is time, and money is the way to measure whether or not you are getting as much full value out of it as you might." (2) The consequences of not optimizing the value of the time available to introduce a new product can be disastrous.

A recent McKinsey and Company study indicated that shipping a new product six months late can cause a 33% loss in after-tax profits for that product. The Thomas Group, Inc. found that over 60% of calendar cycle times critical to competition occurred outside the manufacturing arena. They also found that the value of the cash that is tied up while a product "sits" in new product "work-in-process" is significant (64% of sales revenues). This cash is tied up in functions that basically add no value to the product or service, or the customer.

In responding to the time-based pressures of NPI, Northern Telecom focused on processes in general and NPI in particular. The steps in our response are shown below:

1. Change thinking and attitudes first!

2. Understand, document and simplify the process, separating functions from deliverables, people and organizations involved.

3. Highlight non-value adding functions and activities.

4. Retain (and consider for automation) only those functions and processes that add to the customer's value chain.

5. Drive changes through the culture.

CHANGING THINKING AND ATTITUDES

Turning NPI into a competitive weapon begins with changing ways of thinking and attitudes. The awareness phase of the AIDA approach (awareness, interest, desire, action), that you have or may soon have a problem, creates a whole new mindset, and this change in perspective causes thinking and attitudes to change. Without an awareness of the need to shift NPI thinking, the interest, desire and action required to change will not materialize. Northern Telecom has gone through these steps and is now into the action phase -- streamlining NPI to make it a competitive weapon.

Northern Telecom has traditionally held to essentially one approach to new product introduction and development. It aimed at product and feature characteristics which:

• Have broad market appeal.

• Can justify the high R&D investment needed.

• Are less time sensitive.

While this approach served well in the past, a technology explosion, increasing customer demands for new features and capabilities and increasing competition all indicated that the time was right for change. Awareness that we were heading into a problem lead to a series of actions to define the problem, and make recommendations for action. The customer and competition messages were just symptoms. The problem fell into three major categories.

• The total NPI process time was too long.

• Resource limitations delaying start times.

• Not following our "Formula for Success".

The message was that the status quo was unacceptable.

IMPROVING THE PROCESS

To remain the world's leading supplier of fully digital telecommunications systems, Northern Telecom conducted a number of internal studies and researched both competitors and industry in general to discover the necessary actions to eliminate both time and non-value adding activities from NPI. The results of these studies lead to a set of actions for not only streamlining the process, but also improving resource utilization and creating a new framework or "Formula for Success". For this formula to work, it had to be transferrable to the actual process. Before doing this, however, the process had to be understood, documented, and simplified.

UNDERSTANDING, DOCUMENTING AND SIMPLIFYING THE PROCESS

Once an awareness of the time and complexity of NPI has been created, there has to be an approach that ensures the "baby isn't thrown out with the bathwater". One of Robert Hall's major precepts in "Attaining Manufacturing Excellence" is what he calls "Value-Added Manufacturing". "Do nothing that does not add value to the product or service, or to the customer....whether material, space, time, energy, systems, or human activity of any sort." (3) A tall order in itself, Hall adds his own to Shigeo Shingo's "Seven Wastes":

• The wastes of overproduction, waiting, transporting, processing, stocks, motion, and making defective products (Study of the Toyota Production System).

• The waste of unnecessary measuring, recording, and managing in an effort to deal with unnecessary complexity.

All of these wastes apply to NPI, in that they consume time and add very little value to a new product or for a customer. When observed in physical operations they often provide clues to other wastes far removed from the direct activity itself. In the case of physical inventory, concepts like "Just-in Time" allow material to be "seen" as it sits in place. The result is to challenge why the product is required to sit at all. But what about the indirect activity associated with NPI, that often spans years and crosses multiple organizational "turfs" and boundaries? It is difficult to simply "see" time wasted as it occurs much less attempt cause-and-effect analysis.

VALUE-ADDING NPI

Because it is so impractical to directly observe all operations required to introduce a new product, most improvement studies do it in a piece meal fashion which may involve a host of techniques and methods. It takes time, regardless of the technique or method, and requires positive contributions from everyone involved. A major obstacle to creating a roadmap for change to something as naturally complex as NPI, is finding a method suitable to all aspects and acceptable to those involved. Value-adding NPI is such an approach, in that it focuses on process; uses a common denominator (function); emphasizes the how and why of serving the customer (logic and common sense); and is built on the premise that the customer determines value. The final equation translates into giving the customer what they want in a quality product, faster, and for less. And it is written in the "future perfect " tense - doing it right the first time!

There is a temptation to "fix" something that is obviously wrong without taking the time to understand the "how and why" it was designed to work. Before simplifying, it is crucial that the entire process be understood and documented, to providing the "how and why" it was designed as it was, and adding context for proposed changes.

THE METHOD

Clearing away the organizational "baggage" that tends to be loaded onto NPI is essential to understanding the "how and why", and streamlining the process. Northern Telecom uses a variation of a method developed by Fairchild Communications and Electronics. This method requires that the NPI process be defined strictly in terms of the functions to be performed. The input and output deliverables and end-products the process uses are then related. Organizational resources and responsibility to perform these functions are added last. By examining functions first, and their value, the time they consume in delivering the new product can be analyzed and organizationally unbiased improvements developed. The technique for function analysis is Value Analysis/Value Engineering -- which creates a process designed in the "future perfect" tense.

THE TECHNIQUE: VALUE ANALYSIS/VALUE ENGINEERING

Value Analysis/Value Engineering (VA/VE) is a technique for getting more for less, improving quality and increasing responsiveness. In hardware products it is getting more performance, better quality and improved customer satisfaction for less cost to produce. For software, it is not only producing programs that work, it is also ensuring computer compatibility, transportability, and maintainability, faster and at less cost per line of code. Applied to organizational or service activities, like NPI, it is getting desired results faster with fewer resources.

The technique draws experts from various departments of the business together. as a business team. It is a technique that employs mind setting, problem setting, and problem solving. Through organizational team work, function analysis, cost analysis and creativity techniques, they seek out the better way that works and is faster--not just something that works but what works best and costs less. That's good value.

Value Analysis / Value Engineering (VA/VE) is an organized process to accomplish what is desired for the minimum expenditure of resources. (4)

HOW DOES IT WORK?

The VA/VE process has a six-step Job Plan that follows a specific sequence.

1. Information phase - gathers more and better information about the process and the functions required to make it work.

2. Analysis Phase - focuses on functions and further defines areas of improvement opportunity for improvement for functions that add value.

3. Creativity Phase - generates a large quantity and variety of unjudged ideas, including automation, for performing value- adding NPI functions faster.

4. Evaluation Phase - selects the best ideas that streamline the NPI process.

5. Implementation Phase - obtains the benefit of these improvements through action.

WHERE THE TIME AND VALUE IS IN NPI

New product development and introduction in the 1960's was performed in a relatively straightforward sequence. Dollars were spent exploring and formulating new product concepts. These concepts then were screened, analyzed for their profit potential and further refined, depending on performance features. Prototypes determined whether products could measure up to the design specifications. Depending on the results, these prototypes were either scrubbed, further refined. or

taken "as is" into the marketplace. During the 1970's, both consumers and product manufacturers were forced to become more sophisticated in the approaches to each other in the marketplace.(5)

Today, much new product work is still basically done by this step-to-step process, except that relative to the 1960's process, the number of steps in the process and process complexity has increased, and so has the time and overhead! The requirements for the process to work and be successful are phenomenally more complex than the process of the 1960's, and inherently based on assumptions of vastly improved leadership, project championship, communication-cation, coordination and control. Even when working smoothly, it creates an enormous amount of transactions and requires a very large overhead. Each "feedback" loop in an NPI process almost completely repeats the entire cycle, greatly extending the time. While traditionally accepted, using a series of hand-offs for product development and introduction responsibility may well have fit the process used in the 1960's. It will not fit the requirements for faster response times and reduced intervals of the 1980's and beyond.

The time in NPI that is readily identifiable for elimination is generally found in those functions that add no value to the product or service--transaction processing, waiting, recycling, etc.--things the customer knows will happen, but it not interested in paying for. A good starting point in assessing the speed of NPI is to evaluate the money being spent in individual NPI activities and steps relative to the whole process...because money is time. Then evaluate the value those activities add to the customer's value chain. Figure 1 shows results of a review that compared process time as it should have been to reality (and the cash it tied up) in the context of:

*   The amount required to work on the system (product) being introduced.

*   The amount required to work the product through the introduction process.

Figure 2 shows the impact of those same time factors on other activities in the actual product development and introduction cycle.

These functions are often thought of as "essentials that must be performed ", if a quality product is to be delivered on-time and within cost. They have almost become organizational sacred cows, addressed with "thou shalts...". Schedules are seldom built in the "future perfect tense", but tend more to reflect the organizational culture and the need to perform traditional activities. Times are allocated based on a "past tense" basis ("what did it take last time?"). It often borders on sacrilege to ask if the functions themselves are necessary at all. As examples:

*   How many functions, transactions and hand-offs are really necessary to explore, formulate, screen and analyze new product concepts?

*   Why has designing and transferring designs into manufacturing become more complex, as more powerful computer aided design and simulation tools become available?

*   Why are breadboard models necessary to debug designs with full simulation available?

• Why should four or five prototypes be built, when one built by the prime manufacturing site could serve the entire introduction community?

The point of each of these examples is that they are candidates for Parkinson's Law, which states, "all work expands or contracts to fill the time available for its completion." The truth is that even most NPI improvement efforts are attempts to fit the NPI process to the organization, and not the reverse. Once the NPI clock starts, the time on the schedule tends to be filled up with organizationally driven functions based on "we've always done it that way." This type of thinking also dictates competitive scheduling that tends to create self-fulfilling prophecies. If you believe the customer will eventually change his mind, given enough time, it will happen, thus justifying the use of old estimates. The opportunity is there for winners to create order of magnitude competitive advantages by eliminating non-value adding functions and streamlining the NPI process to deliver as fast as possible.

THE RESULTS

The use of these techniques and method produced a generic NPI process capable of being tailored to fit any particular Northern Telecom division's new product introduction needs. The emphasis throughout the entire process is doing the job right on the first pass, and doing it as fast as possible. Figure 3 offers a copy of this streamlined generic process.

The customer doesn't care about every thing that must be done to produce and deliver a new product, and likewise doesn't feel obliged to pay for more than is reasonable. It only makes good business sense that the minimum set of essential functions that have to be performed and that add value should be charged to the customer.

DRIVING CHANGES THROUGH THE CULTURE

For a business activity as naturally complex as NPI, incremental process changes must be driven in a context the organization can accept, and through the culture of the organization. Building a new initiative and direction for the company through making NPI a competitive weapon can provide the motivation as well as the roadmap for continuous change.

There are many ways to develop new processes and all have worth. In the case of NPI, the very nature and intensity of the effort requires finely tuned team work, a "Yes, if" attitude. This approach requires teamwork to be successfully applied, and it builds a winning attitude about the business and the competition. Time-based competition requires such an approach to NPI, based on ownership and teamwork.

In an age when many company cultures are threatened by change, NPI represents a tremendous opportunity to focus that energy toward a positive direction--to turn it into a competitive weapon to ensure that everybody wins, not just the customer. The management of tomorrow's winning companies must invest the time, effort, and resources to look at ways to produce a more flexible and responsive NPI process. Because NPI encompasses the entire organization of most companies, the involvement required to improve the speed and quality of the

process automatically builds ownership. And ownership builds and changes attitudes in a way that people want to look for ways to constantly make things better.

CONCLUSION

The shift is real in the basis of competition from low cost and high quality, to low cost, high quality, fast response times , and increased product variety. The Boston University Manufacturer's roundtable reported in 1987 that time-based competition is likely to increase as a focus for managerial attention in the 1990's.(6) American industry must seriously examine the situation and accept the reality of time-based competition. With an attitude of designing an NPI process described in the "future perfect tense", senior management must ask:

• How much time is required to move a new product through the process from concept to market? What is the right amount?

• How much value is added to the product by process functions that add the most time?

• What would we do differently if we had to cut NPI times by 50% to be competitive? By 90% to be the leader?

• What process functions in can be eliminated to make changes in the way we do business?

Northern Telecom's approach is working. It is taking longer than first thought, but has dedicated champions keeping the vision alive. Changing thinking and attitudes can be painful and lengthy. Understanding and documenting an NPI process before trying to simplify it requires discipline, persistence, and leadership. Without a technique like VA/VE that forces people to think by emphasizing function and value from the customer's perspective, eliminating functions that add no value and consume time can be a management nightmare. The secret to success lies in the improvement that teamwork and communications bring--through the people of the organization itself.

Western business can and must begin the process of improving response times today. The longer the delay, the more likely the competition will make the choices mentioned above for us. Time is one commodity we all possess, in equal amounts that are not devaluated on a daily basis. It is one of the most precious and often the most wasted corporate resource. It should be spent as wisely as money, because money is time. Those that do will have added the ability to surprise their competition-- through NPI.

REFERENCES

1. Stalk, George, Jr., Article, "Time-Based Competition", The Boston Consulting Group, Inc., Boston, MA (1981), p. 1.

2. Davis, Stanley M., Future Perfect, Reading, MA, The Addison-Wesley Publishing Company, Inc. (1987), pp 18-19.

3. Hall, Robert, W., Attaining Manufacturing Excellence, Homewood, IL, Dow- Jones - Irwin, (1987), p. 24.

4. Miles, Lawrence D., <u>Techniques of Value Analysis and Engineering</u>, McGraw-Hill, New York, NY (1972), p. 25.

5. Sommers, William P., "Product Development: New Approaches in the 1980's", <u>Readings in the Management of Innovation</u>, Ballinger Publishing Company, Cambridge, MA (1982), p. 53.

6. Miller, Jeffrey, G. & Roth, Aleda V., <u>Manufacturing Strategies</u>, Executive Summary of the 1987 North American Manufacturing Futures Survey, The Boston University Roundtable, Boston, MA (1987), p. 25.

SYSTEMS/PROCESS PROBLEM CONTENT

PRODUCT DEVELOPMENT AND INTRODUCTION CYCLE

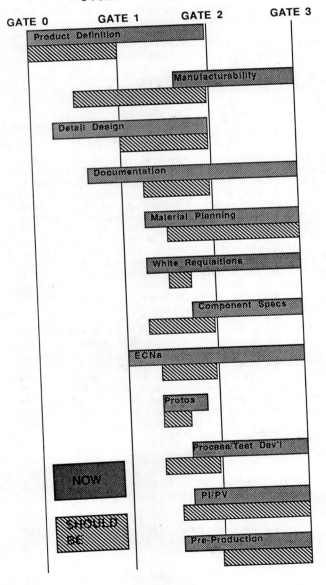

FIGURE 1

System   Process

Product Definition

Manufacturability

Detail Design

Documentation

Material Planning

White Requisitions

Component Specifications

ECNs

Prototypes

Process/Test Development

FIGURE 2

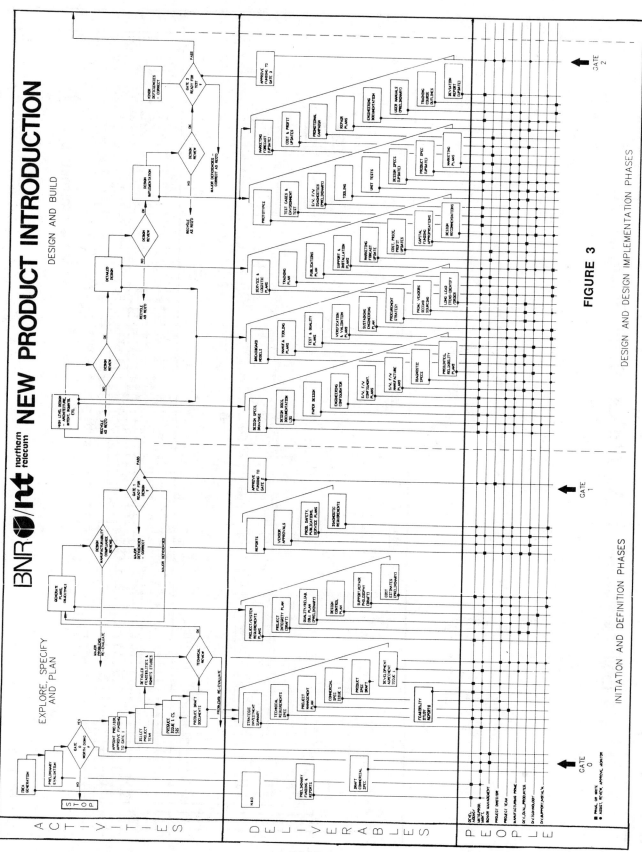

BNR/nt northern telecom **NEW PRODUCT INTRODUCTION**

FIGURE 3

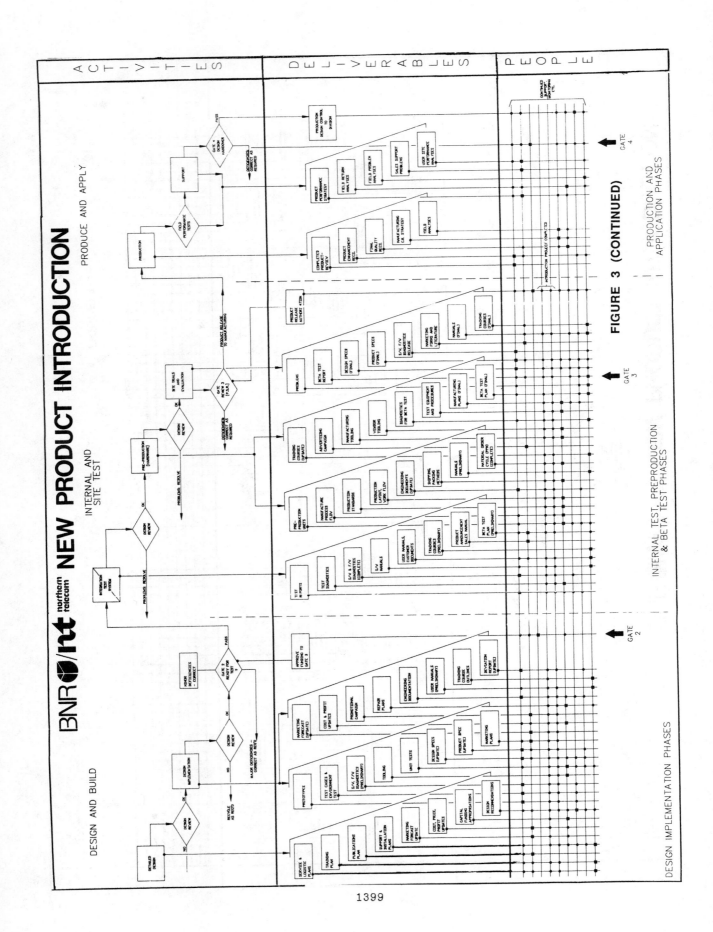

FIGURE 3 (CONTINUED)

Product Innovation In A Time of Standards

John Gage
Director, Science Office

Sun Microsystems, Inc.
2550 Garcia Avenue,
Mountain View, CA 94043
415 960 1330

1. ABSTRACT

Rapid advances in technology, now forcibly coupled to emerging open standards that all competitors must follow, create new rules for product design, innovation and creation. This development is forcing profound changes in the computer industry. The critical problem is bringing technology to market while it is new. Time to market is all-important.

The emergence of international standards in operating systems, networking protocols, languages, graphics, user interfaces, database query languages, page description languages, and computer architectures is a response to accelerating change: designers cannot build upon existing products to create new products if everything changes at once. To take advantage of the newest advances in a reasonable time, as much existing development must be preserved as possible, which implies an ever-increasing reliance on layered products, with well-defined interfaces.

This, in turn, implies that all competitors must incorporate standards into their products, or face enormous costs of idiosyncratic development across all technologies, which is clearly unrealistic for even the largest companies.

This paper describes the past, present, and future enabling technologies which have shaped the evolution of our computer product design. Most importantly, our use of standards in all areas has allowed us to integrate the overlapping waves of new technology, thus shortening the product introduction cycle.

2. INTRODUCTION

2.1. *Enabling Technologies*

Product design begins today in an environment of accelerating technical change in certain critical technologies. In these technological areas, quantitative changes are of sufficient magnitude to create qualitative differences in products. In the communication and computing industry, changes in speed, in resolution, in amount of information that can be created, communicated, stored and retrieved are doubling--not in ten years, but in one. The critical technologies that make this possible are *enabling technologies*.

2.2. *Examples of Enabling Technologies*

A fundamental example is VLSI technology, a revolution driving many other technologies. Advances in hardware design and circuit manufacturing methods have resulted in a doubling of microprocessor CPU speed each year since 1984, a development captured by Joy's Law:

$$MIPS = 2^{year-1984}$$

Similarly, VLSI advances underly a second remarkable change, with tremendous implications: memory devices are doubling in capacity every eighteen months, with four megabit and sixteen megabit DRAMs on the immediate horizon.

Another example: the advent of optical and laser devices, both for transmission and storage of information. The speed of computer local area networks in the last six years has moved from the range of a thousand kilobits per second to the ten megabits a second of Ethernet to the hundred megabits per second of FDDI. The ability of optical storage devices to archive data in near-permanent form, in massive volume, is poised to change the nature and distribution of what we communicate over networks.

These technologies enable new generations of products to be developed, and therefore their rate of change governs the speed and expense of product change.

2.3. *Effect upon Industries*

Not only new products, but new industries emerge, and at an accelerating rate, as a result of new enabling technologies.

The advent of cheap memory chips led to bit-map displays, which led to windowed high-resolution displays, which led to desktop publishing, and the proliferation of computer-aided design tools.

The advent of cheap, high bandwidth local area networks led to electronic mail systems; a desire for more closely coupled communication led to remote procedure call protocols, which led to network file systems sharing disks across thousands of computers and the beginning of distributed applications across short and long-haul networks.

2.4. *Common Elements of Enabling Technologies*

Characteristically, these critical technologies have general attributes:

- They provide a fundamental advantage--in cost, in speed, in size, in power.
- They provide a solution to a larger problem.
- They allow an existing set of solutions to be combined in new ways.
- They become part of the solution.
- They replace previous technologies.

Therefore, to ensure a steady development of products in times of change requires a careful assessment of enabling technologies, to predict when, and in which ways they will affect existing plans. Failure to anticipate changes will lead to disruptions: example after example can be found in the daily trade press of the computer industry.

2.5. *Other Identifying Marks of Enabling Technologies*

- They are often rejected at first, because they challenge existing ways of doing things
- They often go against conventional wisdom, making their supporters uncomfortable.
- They often create new companies.

2.6. *Standardization is Necessary to Minimize Disruption by New Technology*

As change occurs, elements of complicated systems no longer match the rest of the system: the new volume of information surpasses the capacity of the communication channels, or new CPU speeds swamp the bandwidth of the memory channel. These imbalances require new system design to integrate the new capabilities, but the complexity of systems makes this process extremely difficult unless each element of the system is decoupled in some way from the rest of the system.

This is the function of standardization of protocols, of layering of system elements so that an advance in performance of one element can be utilized by other elements with a minimum of adjustment to existing software and hardware.

Thus, the importance of standardization is to remove constraints inhibiting the adoption of new technology (though often this is not understood, or is accompanied by a cynical attempt to use standards to freeze technology for the benefit of existing products). Our experience is that standardization brings acceleration in time to market.

3. EXAMPLES OF PRESENT ENABLING TECHNOLOGIES AND EMERGING STANDARDS

The list of technologies worth tracking is long, but a sampling for those that affect computing and communications today are:

- CD-ROM and Digital Audio Tape, for very dense information storage.
- Fiber optics
- FAX chips

The arrival of a variety of signal processing chips, together with standards for manipulation of images

- Flat Panel Displays
- Reduced Instruction Set Computers

The simplicity of the circuitry allows remarkable increases in logic cycling time; current estimates are that the annual doubling of CPU speed can be maintained in uniprocessors for the next five to six years, using technology known today.

- Laser printers
- Postscript Page Description Language

4. SUN'S ENABLING TECHNOLOGIES (1982-1987)

Sun is an interesting example, since our product cycle can be viewed as less than six months between significant change of product. Examining our choice of fundamental technologies can be placed in perspective against the recent history of standards activity in operating systems, networking, backplane definition, graphics libraries, and computer architectures.

- Bit-mapped, high-resolution displays

Present only on a few research and high-end machines in 1981, everywhere today.

- 32-bit microprocessors
- Ethernet

Present only in a few research organizations in 1981, everywhere today.

- UNIX

An academic research system in 1981, endorsed by IBM, DEC, HP, TI, Unisys, Olivetti, Siemens, ICL, Fujitsu, NEC, Toshiba, Sony, Apple, ... today.

- Remote Procedure Call/ Network File System

Remote procedure call protocols were research topics in 1981, designed to allow all computing architectures to be combined into one resource for a user. This went directly against the product plans of IBM, DEC, DG, HP, and most of the computer industry. Today, they are the underpinning of truly distributed computing, and endorsed by all computer vendors.

5. SUN'S ENABLING TECHNOLOGIES (1987-1992)

The fundamental direction for computing and communications technology will involve integration of functions. Examples of existing devices that are now separate from the workstation will indicate what will become part of the computer: telephone, answering machine, scanner, copier, FAX, document filer and library(optical mass storage), audio and video devices.

- SPARC/RISC: Reduced Instruction Set Computer
- Postscript/NeWS: Page Description Language. Analytic Font Descriptions

The arrival of a standard page description language, incorporating a high quality font description, created desk top publishing. Much more is coming, as separate information industries--printing, publishing, database, information retrieval, archive-- are combined in a manner that will bring them much larger markets.

- User Interface/ OpenLook

A common user paradigm, that allows a quick understanding of how to use the computer to accomplish a human task, is just beginning to emerge. Only the arrival of extraordinary computational power will allow us to accomplish the normal tasks that we do each day: speak, and have our words understood; sketch with pencil, or with a gesture, and have the sketch understood; accentuate our normal communications with inflection, facial expression, and body movement.

- Object-Oriented Information Storage and Retrieval

Software systems are growing exponentially, both in size and complexity. Object-oriented techniques offer support for much more easily designed and maintained systems; the change in patterns of thought of programmers will affect the entire industry.

- VLSI/ Integrated functions in silicon:

Most elements of systems will be ASIC, with the very large gate counts possible in existing technologies to allow single-chip implementations of all major elements.

Networking speeds will be boosted to 100 MBytes/second, while ISDN allows existing local loops to provide home access to newly available information services.

6. FUNDAMENTAL FUTURE ENABLING TECHNOLOGIES

- Reduction of the speed-power constant:

One definition of a semiconductor technology is the power that a given form of logic consumes. As the time to cycle a gate goes down, the power required by the circuit goes up; the product of the speed and the power is a constant for a given technology. Currently, the pathway to reduce this constant lies in moving from CMOS to ECL to Gallium Arsenide. Superconductivity will make one of the factors in this constant-valued product go to zero; though we do not know how to do it, the impact on system design will be enormous.

- Approximation of human communication methods:

We are improving the ability of computers to convey information to human beings through improved graphics, sound, and other visualiation interfaces. Going the other way--from human to computer--is a major bottleneck. Voice recognition, together with multidimensional, tactile, gesture input will transform products.

- Powerful language and notational system understanding:

All existing software will be redone in new, more powerful, more general languages, for functionality, comprehensibility, and ease of maintenance. The concerns of application programmers will be expressed as the relations among objects; object-oriented languages and databases will dominate.

Issues that consume the bulk of programming time today will be hidden in the synatax of new languages, not in the programmer's grasp of algorithms. Programs will contain methods of proving correctness, so that an application will, at each stage of development, be capable of demonstrating that it is doing what it is supposed to.

7. CONCLUSIONS

Innovation in product stems directly from the ability to bring the newest technologies to market quickly. To do this, you must determine the interrelationship of the most important enabling technologies, and design so that an advance in one area can be incorporated without redoing the other technologies. Clearly, the existence of standard interfaces among technologies allows this in a way not possible in the past. Much of the explosion of new technology results from a new capability to build on past accomplishment, instead of reinventing new versions of old solutions.

The implications of this analysis are several: those who design based on standards have a more rapid time to market, and therefore a greater chance to displace their rivals. Those who use standard environments or platforms can benefit immediately from overlapping waves of technical advance.

Institutions who base their existence on older, non-standard technology run the risk of stagnating, since the cost of integrating new technology is high.

Countries with large installed bases of tightly coupled, highly interdependent technologies are at risk in a time of accelerating change, for the social dislocations brought about by the inability of the industrial infrastructure to change brings a high cost in economic and human terms. There is a close interrelationship between the most important enabling technologies--those that promise to transform products and industries--and the burgeoning world of international standards. Each responds to the other; each develops in response to the other.

COMPUTER AIDED COMMUNICATIONS
Improving the Effectiveness of the Engineering & Manufacturing Processes

D. Dimancesco Jr.
Programs Manager
Engineering Systems Group

Digital Equipment Corporation
2 Results Way
Marlboro, Mass. 01752

ABSTRACT

With the advent of large computer networks tying together large numbers of people across local and wide areas, computers are providing new forms of people to people communications and information exchange. Electronic mail, computer conferencing and electronic libraries, are replacing many of the inefficiencies of the telephone, meeting room, and paper documents, thereby insuring faster and more efficient flow of information. Gradually, these tools are spawning new concepts, such as electronic "book readers", and "electronic library" cards. And they are helping bring down traditional organizational barriers to the cross-organization and and cross-process flow of information. This paper discusses the growth and evolution of "computer aided communications" and its implications for the organization and for engineering and manufacturing processes.

INTRODUCTION

Originally we viewed computers as tools to help manipulate and process data very fast, as data storage devices or as "intelligent" controllers for various automated processes or devices. However, with the fairly recent advent of large networks of computers that span entire organizations and wide geographic areas, the network and the computers are emerging as a new communications utility complementing the telephone, replacing the inter-office memo or the meeting room or the library. Some have labelled this:

"Computer Aided Communications" - an environment where the computer plays a vital role as a store and forwarder and router of messages, a keeper of directories and locations of people, as repository or archiver of people-to-people communications, as a transmitter of documents, and so forth.

We now see the computer and the network creating a new dimension in the organization: vastly the improving decision making processes and vastly enhancing the sharing of knowledge.

A FIRST NEW DIMENSION: ELECTRONIC MAIL

In an age when corporations are seeking new ways to develop and bring better products to market faster, the electronic mail communications artery becomes a vital tool for speeding up or improving engineering processes. The following quote from the book "Common LISP" (by Guy L. Steele Jr., Digital Press), illustrates the value of a large electronic mail network in the design of a new product:

"...The development of COMMON LISP would most probably not have been possible without the electronic message network provided by ARPANET. Design decisions were made on several hundred distinct points, for the most part by concensus, and by simple majority votes when necessary. Except for two one-day meetings, all of the language design and discussion was done through the ARPANET message system...The message system also provided automatic archiving of the entire discusssion."

There is hardly an engineering manager, anywhere that does not have horror stories to tell about the bottlenecks, delays and errors that result from engineering change requests, change notifications, change approvals and the distribution of engineering change orders (ECO's). At a time when the most advanced technology is being applied to automating design, and performing complex simulations, the engineering change procedures are frequently still mired in morass of manual and paper-based procedures. At one highly automated aerospace company it was calculated that the process for engineering changes for one product was producing 30,000 pieces of paper per year! Electronic mail systems are now coming to the rescue. One corporation has now built a totally paperless ECO system out its electronic mail system. Another large corporation has decided that an electronic mail-based ECO system can produce the biggest impact on reducing time to market cycles for new products!

At Digital an electronic mail facility was first developed and put in place to serve our engineering department - to speed the distribution of engineering documents, to enhance the engineer-to-engineer communications, and to streamline the approval, notification and release proceses. Over time its value was perceived beyond engineering and it ultimately grew into a worldwide corporate network tieing together over 50,000 employees. It is sometimes cited as the single most significant productivity tool. It is treated as a must always-be-available utility, similar to the electric and telephone utilities

2

A SECOND NEW DIMENSION: ELECTRONIC CONFERENCING

After electronic mail become a widespread facility inside Digital, it became apparent that it was excellent for some forms of communications, but not so good for others. To distribute information, you had to know the names and locations of people. The same information was getting replicated throughout the network and stored on many discs in many places. Once again, engineers anxious to introduce new efficiencies in their work, developed computer conferencing. This has become such as useful tool, that the Digital network now carries over thousand separate active and on-going conferences, approximately 70% of which are dedicated to engineering topics! This massive conferencing network ties together project teams - not only across engineering departments - but also brings together the extended project team: engineering, manufacturing, service and marketing. Teams - the members of which have never met or who may not even know all of the participants' names - now conduct active electronic conferences on new design projects, manufacturing processes, technology issues, competitive trends and marketing issues.

Shoshanna Zuboff, a Harvard Business Professor, has extensively explored this new communcations medium and describes it in her new book - "The Age of the Smart Machine" - as creating a "universal mind" that spans time and distance - "a communications medium that offers an alternative to the constraints of geography and time associated with face-to-face meetings of telephone conversations while avoiding the formality of written correspondence."

At Digital conferencing system is serving the engineering community by allowing engineers to discuss the impact of design changes, to solicit ideas for new product features, to quickly get feedback on manufacturability and serviceability requirements from plants and from the field. All this without leaving the desk, yet quickly reaching out to and conversing with fellow employees dispersed around various parts of the country or the world.

ANOTHER DIMENSION: ELECTRONIC LIBRARIES

It is imposssible to design a product, manufacture it, install or it, or possibly even use it without a vast array of standards manuals (very, very vast if you are designing something for the the military!), manufacturing and assembly procedures, installation manuals and user guides. One large corporation, for example, prints and distributes over eight million pages of standards information to its engineers each year!

The resources required to write, illustrate, print, and distribute all this material are massive.

Often the manual steps involved in producing and distributing documents sometimes take so long that much information is outdated by the time the documentation reaches its destination. For example, it has been estimated that of 125,000 different manuals currently in use by one branch of the military, 25% are out of date at any one time!

With computer networks serving large organizations it should therefor be possible to make large sets of documents like standards manuals, manufacturing instruction sheets, and a wide variety of other corporate documents available electronically - thereby reducing the time required to print, distribute and update, and insuring more timeliness of the information.

At Digital we have put in use, precisely such a facility. Its a form of "electronic library" where a wide array of coporate documents can be accessed across the computer network from office terminals or workstations. The software - called VAX/VTX - was inspired by Videotex technology, but actually went much further than Videotex. It keeps track of pages (individual pages for one book or manual can actually be stored on any computer on the network) yet this is "transparent" to the user who simply has the impression that he or she is paging through a single volume. One advantage to this technique is that authors or individuals responsible for a segment or chapter in manual can actually maintain it and keep it up to date on their own pc, workstation or computer disk (attached to the network).

It is one thing to make documents or manuals available on a computer network, but it also important to have an easy way to electronically search across a bookshelf or within a book -- as you would if you were actually standing in a library. VTX allows you - simply from your pc, workstation or terminal keyboard - to electronically "browse" across bookshelves, "scan" tables of contents, quickly access chapters or sections, and even electronically "flip" pages backwards or forwards, insert "bookmarks", and copy or print pages.

One large manufacturer is using VTX as the basis for implementing a "paperless factory" environment - displaying machine set-up and product assembly instructions on the factory shop floor electronically.

PQR-03

PQR-04

PROCESS QUALITY MANAGEMENT IMPROVEMENT I
AND II

Dennis L. McKiernan, Chairperson

Supervisor, Quality Planning

AT&T Bell Laboratories.
6200 East Broad Street
1H305
Columbus, OH 43213

All work, no matter the type, be it R&D,
manufacturing, administration, common
labor, hardware, software, service, or
something completely different, can be
thought of as following a process.
Further, all processes produce products,
be they tangible--such as a manufactured
piece part, a typed page, or an assembly--
or intangible--such as an idea, a
decision, or a policy statement, Given
the appropriate customer focus, the
quality of the process determines the
quality of the product. Hence, improving
the quality of the process improves the
quality of the product. Processes for the
most part are the responsibility of
management, and so developing a customer-
focused, continuous process improvement
focus among managers is a vital step to
successfully competing in today's and
tomorrow's business environment. These
two seminars, introductory in nature,
focus upon the customer, quality, process,
process improvement, and the role of
management in bringing about the changes
required to achieve a quality product. It
is highly recommended that participants
attend both seminars on this vitally
important topic.

Douglas A. Brown - AT&T Bell Laboratories
Barry A. Shaffer - AT&T Bell Laboratories.

Part I
Quality and Process

Douglas A. Brown
Supervisor, Planning & Process Management
AT&T Bell Laboratories
6200 East Broad Street
1H329
Columbus, OH 43213

This session explores the elements of the
cost of quality, defines churn and
quality, demonstrates that process and
quality are inextricably entwined, and
focuses on what must be done.

Process Models
Douglas A. Brown

This session describes what we mean when
we speak of a process, presenting simple,
complex, and layered models made up of
replicas of a basic element composed of
five parts: input, value added, quality
check points, output and feedback for
improvement. External and internal
customers and suppliers are defined.

Process Baselining

Barry A. Shaffer
Supervisor, Planning
AT&T Bell Laboratories
6200 East Broad Street
0A209
Columbus, OH 43213

This session describes the steps necessary
to bring a process under control so that
continuous process improvement can begin.

Part II
Continuous Process Improvement

Barry A. Shaffer

Building upon the morning seminar, this
session describes the steps necessary to
maintain control of a system and begin
continuous process improvement.

Tools

Douglas A. Brown

This session describes the "tools" needed
to baseline a system, get it under
control, institute continuous process
improvement, and translate
customer/supplier expectations and trade-
offs into requirements.

Cultural Issues

This session explores the cultural issues
involved in adopting principles of
customer focus and of continuous process
improvement.

Summary

Douglas A. Brown
Dennis L. McKiernan
Barry A. Shaffer

This session highlights the key
philosophical principles involved and
outlines how to get started on the
"quality" journey.

PQR-05

DESIGN METHODS AND TOOLS

Andrew H. Young, Chairperson
Director, New Product Introduction

Northern Telecom
2305 Mission College Blvd.
Santa Clara, CA 95054

ABSTRACT

Ever since the beginning of the Industrial Age, design methods (management and documentation) and support infrastructure (data distribution and administration) have evolved to suit the tools available. Until very recently, pen and paper were the most commonly used tools for design, so methods and infrastructure were also pen and paper based. Today however, most design tools are computerized. In many cases design methods and infrastructure are still on paper, and using computer systems offers a new set of problems as well as new opportunities. This session will review some of the issues involved and propose some solutions for computer based design methods and infrastructure evolution.

Grant K. Garnett	-- AT & T Data Systems Group
John E. Nast	-- Technical Documentation Consulting Service
Andrew H. Young	-- Northern Telecom

Automating Design Administration Information

Andrew Young
Northern Telecom

ABSTRACT

Design administration information is 'information about information' - it is the information needed to manage, control, distribute, and organize technical data. Administration data is not the same as technical data and an opportunity exists for

significant benefits by separating it from the technical data before automation occurs. In the case of Computer Integrated Manufacturing (CIM), the opportunity to separate the data becomes a necessity due to the demands of integrated data flows.

This paper describes how administration data can be understood and automated and proposes the use of Expert Systems technology to achieve the automation. A computer based implementation of the approval process for engineering changes is used as an example of these type of systems.

INTRODUCTION

Market pressures are forcing shorter intervals on design and manufacturing. Products and production activities are becoming more complex requiring more control and administration. Most, if not all, of the tools being used today for telecommunications product design and production are computer based. In addition, the product development and production environment is becoming more integrated through the implementation of CIM and information flows between design and manufacturing are becoming electronic messages between functionally specific computer systems. Under these conditions, understanding the type of information flows being automated becomes important to the success of the business.

In a design and manufacturing environment there are two kinds of data required for product introduction, production, and delivery - technical data and administration data. Generally these two data types are tightly linked, managed together, and are significantly impacted by changes in each others domain. The two types of data, though, are very different as administration data exists to control and sometimes explain technical data in management terms. Since these two types of data are necessary to manage the business, they must be appropriately dealt with when implementing CIM. During the startup of CIM activities at Northern Telecom, we found that automating technical data, although not trivial, was relatively straight forward compared to attempting to automate administration data. We found that the administration data was not easy to understand and capture and was very difficult to automate.

How , then, does administration data differ from technical data and can administration information be automated in the same way as technical information? If not, then how can administration data be automated and what are some of the problems which might be encountered during automation? Why does CIM seem to be the cause for this opportunity? What are the benefits and impacts of automating administration information and is there an example of a successfully implemented system?

These are some of the questions this paper will address. The concepts presented are generic and can be applied by any company. Unfortunately, the specific system - engineering change approval - used as an example to describe administration information automation cannot be applied in the form Northern Telecom has implemented it. Because of the very nature of administration information, each administration system will tend to be unique to the company which develops it.

TECHNICAL and ADMINISTRATION DATA

It was suggested before that there is a significant difference between technical and administration information. These differences are found in the way the information is changed as it moves from functional area to functional area and how much of the total available information is transmitted.

Technical Data

Technical data can be defined as data which conveys design intent whether the design is a product or the information used to produce the product. An example is the product design file whether it comes from a set of drawings or from a Computer Aided Design (CAD) system. The design file contains a complete description of the product as created by the design engineer. Specific data elements might be the printed circuit board (PCB) schematic and parts stocklist. Technical data can also include the data used to drive manufacturing activities such as autoinsertation tapes for autoinsertation machines, shop aids to help build the product, or integrated circuit models for PCB simulation.

Administration Data

Administration data or 'information about the technical information' can be defined as the data used to manage, control or cause the use of, technical data. Generic examples of administration data are harder to point to because this type of data is developed to satisfy specific management processes used by a company to design, produce and deliver its products. Some examples, though, which exist in many industries would be product release control records, order entry numbers, the approval routing for a change notice, project and case numbers, customer or employee numbers, cheque requisition approval routing, etc.

Data Flow Automation Issues

In general, the content and type of technical information varies substantially in the various design and manufacturing functional areas. Only a portion of the data created or used in a functional area is transferred to other functional areas when the work has been completed. And normally on receipt, the data is transformed to another form. Therefore for technical data, the integration focus of CIM is on standardizing transmission formats and developing conversion programs to link the computer based systems available in each functional area of design and manufacturing rather than providing end-to-end systems.

Administration data, on the other hand, is generally not transformed on transmission and follows a specified process path involving a number of steps or activities through some portion of the design and manufacturing environment. Administration data is generally not restricted to one functional area and is shared among a wide range of users. Therefore the CIM focus for administration data is on systems which can be used in all functional areas using the same data.

The process paths referred to above traverse all elements of the design and manufacturing environment, are necessary for a successful business and are sometimes known as overhead processes. Unfortunately, these processes are not as well understood or controlled as product design and production activities. In every company, a specific person is responsible for a specific design and manufacturing activity within a functional area but there is generally no one responsible for an administration process which crosses functional areas.

Finally, the administration data used in a company has normally been developed over time and is almost an integral part of the company's cultural. This situation makes it difficult, sometimes, to understand the need for the data, simplify it if necessary, and capture,and automate the data as part of a system. (It should be noted that, in this area, we are dealing with an organization and territorial concerns probably contribute to this difficulty. In addition, the phrase "we've always done it that way" seems to be a very powerful weapon for constraining change.)

DESIGN and MANUFACTURING TOOL INTEGRATION

Figure 1. shows a typical data flow between functional areas of design and manufacturing for a paper based environment. New product requirements are given to product designers in the form of commercial specifications and these are then transformed and augmented to create design specifications. The design specifications are then transformed and enhanced to develop detailed engineering information for the design and manufacturing engineers. This data creation and transformation process continues until all the necessary information has been generated to produce and ship the product.

At the same time as these activities are occurring, the administration information is tracking progress and moving along in conjunction with the technical information. The major difference is that the administration information is not being significantly transformed. In a paper based manufacturing environment, all of this information conversion and recording occurs on paper and is stored on paper. Control or administration data is also kept on paper. In many cases the same piece of paper is used for both types of information.

In a CIM environment information flow will look, functionally, much the same as Figure 1. except that the activities in each functional area will be automated and, to a certain degree, integrated across functional areas through the use of a data storage and retrieval system as seen in Figure 2. In general though, the transformation interfaces between these areas are for technical data transfer with the administration data still being managed

and exchanged on paper due to the issues mentioned above.

The Influence of CIM

The issue, of course, is that the overall interval for completing an overhead process combined with a design and manufacturing activity is the longest set of intervals of all the activities or overhead processes involved. In a situation where the technical data is available at the speed of light, the paper based administration data will substantially increase the time it takes to deliver a new product.

AUTOMATING ADMINISTRATION DATA

As described previously, administration data is information about the technical data and, unlike technical data, moves between functional areas generally with the same form and content. Technical data, on the other hand, is created and used in the functional area in which it was developed and most of this data does not move between functional areas,

The creation and use of technical data, by its very nature, is seen as an 'expert' activity involving engineers and other similar specialists. The use and distribution of administration information is equally an 'expert' activity. This is not the normal view of data flows in overhead processes but it is a very useful way of looking at the question of how to automate administration information. (If the reader is not sure that administration information flow and control is an 'expert' activity, then the reader should try the following experiment. If your company has engineering changes, try to find out where a specific change is in the approval and implementation process at any specific point in time. Then identify the person who knew most about how the process worked and therefore was able to help you the most in finding the change. There should be no doubt in your mind after this experiment that this person is an 'expert'.)

Administration as an 'Expert' Activity

If managing administration data is an 'expert' activity, then it must have rules. These rules are sometimes easily found in the policies and procedures used by the company but more often than not they are ad hoc, not necessarily logical, based on experience, applied based on discretion and known in detail only to those people who spend most of their time pushing paper through the process. In actual fact, the overhead process might have been simple and well defined at one time but it changed as new requirements arose and as more information was required for dealing with management issues. The point is that there are rules and they are being applied, generally in a consistent fashion.

There are rules for dealing with the administration information within a functional area and there are also rules on how the administration information is transmitted between the various functional areas of design and manufacturing. In general, the 'expert' who acts as the information receiver or sender in a functional area knows where the data comes from or is going to and what must be dome to successfully manage the information. (It should be noted, though, that these 'experts' seem to know less about the transmission rules the farther away from their own functional area the information gets. That no one knows the entire process is the major issue to be overcome in automating administration information.)

Expert Systems Technology

If administration information is managed by definable rules, then automating this information is not only a case of providing a system that transmits the data but also one that helps the 'expert' do their jobs using the rules. The system must also be able to provide at least the same level of control as exists on paper, must be able to contribute to interval reduction as described above and must be able to easily react to potentially rapid changes in the rules.

There are a number of computer science techniques for developing sophisticated systems to satisfy the above type of requirements but a new technology, Expert Systems (ES), has recently become available which appears to be well suited to the task. ES technology can be looked at as a programming language appropriately structured to handle rules rather than just data and calculations. (ES technology is much more than this simple definition but this is as far as we need go for the purposes of this paper.)

Value Management Techniques for Rules Acquisition

It has been previously suggested that capturing the rules is difficult because there is no single source for the rules, the rules are not widely known, they are not necessarily predictable, and they are held by a group comprising 'experts' from many functional areas.

In order to capture the rules as to how administration information is managed and transmitted, these 'experts' must be interviewed and their knowledge codified. A good technique is to have all the 'experts' interviewed at the same time. This will maximize the capture of those rules relating to data transmission as well as provide insight into the relationship between process activities in each functional area. But capturing the rules of the process as it now exists and developing an administration system is not enough. The process, as it now exists, has probably grown and changed shape over time in response to all kinds of needs and demands. There is every likelihood that the process is inefficient and, in places, redundant and that it could be improved through an analysis of the valued added by each rule in the process.

At Northern Telecom, we tried a number of methods to capture the rules and Value Management (VM) proved quite successful.. Since we were dealing with information, a computer science methodology was tried first. This involved defining the creators and the users of information and then diagraming how the information flowed between all the experts. The diagram was expected to be a definition of how the process worked. The next step in this activity would have required that the existing computer systems and data bases be reorganizes to fit our new understanding of the process. This methodology did not prove very useful because the cost of making the changes was too high.

The last method we tried - Value Management, based on Value Analysis and Value Engineering - proved very suitable for understanding overhead processes, and the technique provided us with the ability to review the value added by each rule in the process. The technique involves defining the existing process rules using the 'experts' who are executing the rules. This took some time as the engineering change approval process we chose to automate is complex and is used by all design and manufacturing functional areas. Using the same team, we then asked for proposals to improve the process. This process review and modification activity continued until all rules defined for the new change management approval process seemed to be adding value. (Figure 3. shows a typical example of how Value Management charts the rules of a process. The partial process shown is for customer order entry.)

Expert Systems Technology and Administration Information

Now that we had the rules of a new process defined for the engineering change approval process, an expert system was selected. In Northern Telecom's design and manufacturing environment, though, there are data distribution integration requirements for new systems. In Figure 2., the automated data flows for technical information can be seen and we wanted to achieve the same situation for administration information. The expert system architecture we feel is necessary is shown in Figure 4. which is a partial transformation of Figure 2. With this type of architecture, administration information and process rules can be managed like other information elements. Under these conditions, ES technology plays the same role for administration information as data base technology does for technical data.

THE ENGINEERING CHANGE APPROVAL SYSTEM

The Engineering Change Management (ECM) System was our first attempt at developing administration systems and it has been a success. The system has been installed and is being used to administer and approve engineering change notices. The system executes the engineering change approval process rules and is available across all functional areas of design and manufacturing.

Expert System technology has proven to be a very useful way of automating administration process rules and ECM is now being implemented in other Northern divisions with different change approval processes. Using ES technology has allowed us to isolate the process rules from the application thus allowing different engineering change approval processes to be delivered by the same administration system. (Note that this is not a

contradiction to a point made earlier since we are still dealing with the same company.)

CONCLUSION

Automating administration information is an absolute necessity for design and manufacturing interval reduction especially when the technical data is being delivered electronically. The process rules for administration activities can be successfully capturing using Value Management techniques and Expert Systems technology can provide the mechanism for allowing users to execute those rules. Using these concepts, Northern Telecom has implemented a system which automates administration information for managing the approval process for engineering changes.

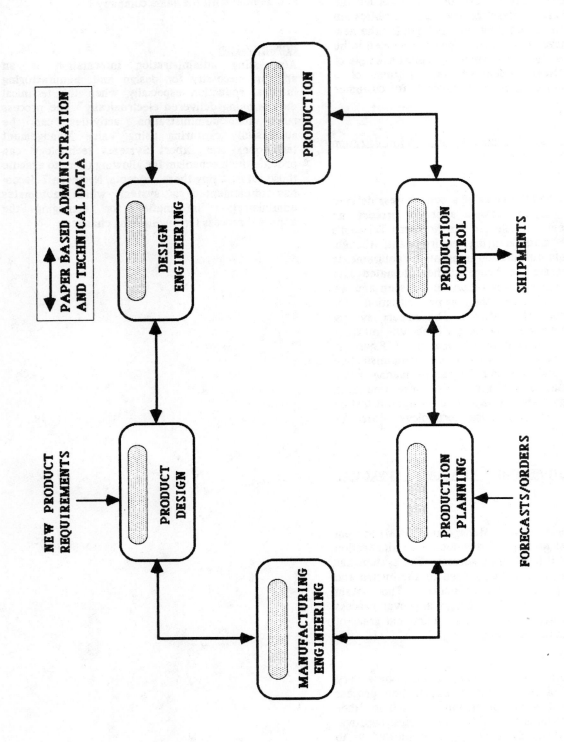

Figure 1: Paper Based Technical and Administration Data Flow

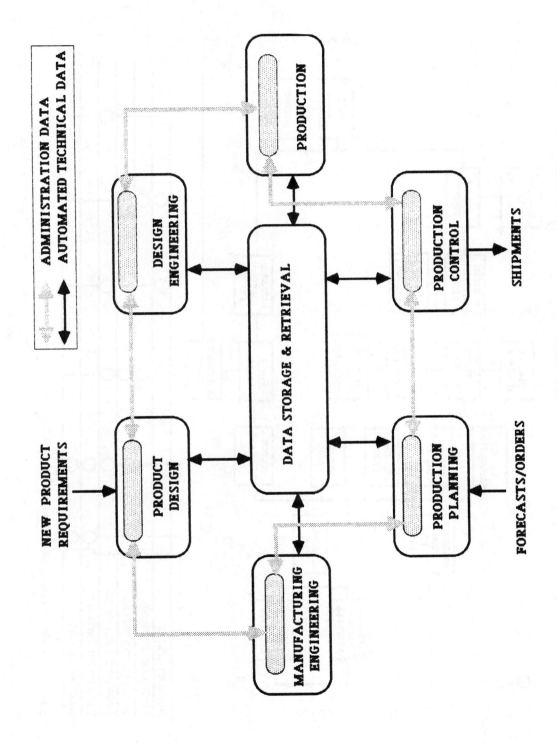

Figure 2: Paper Based Administration information and Auromated Technical Information

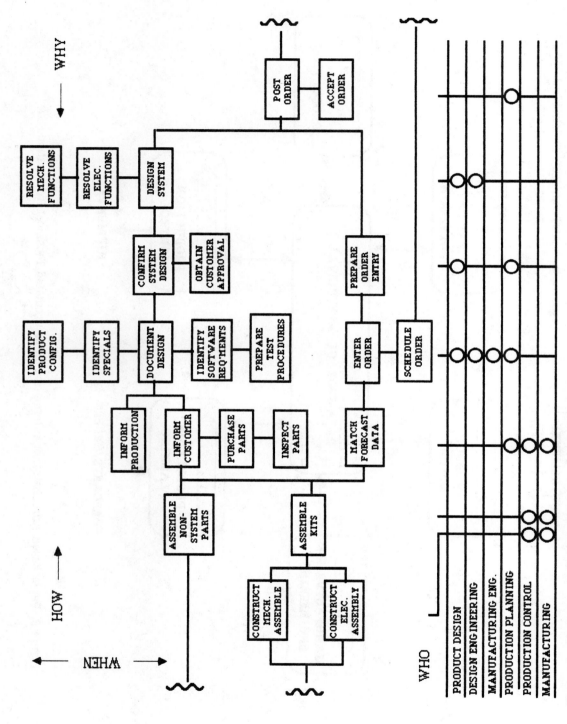

Figure 3: Customer Order/New Product Request Process

1413

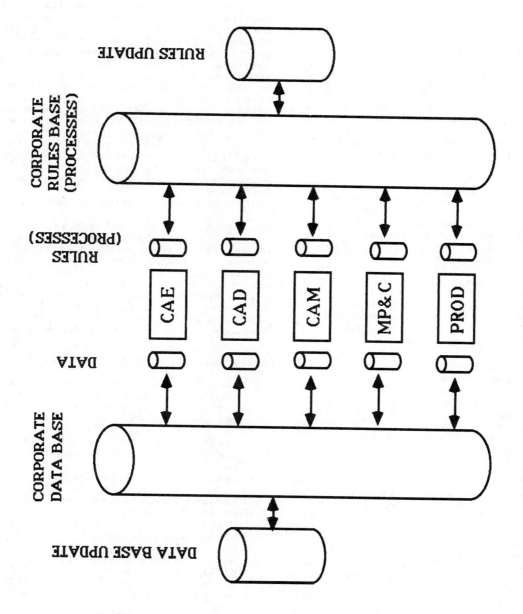

Figure 4: Design and Manufacturing Technical and Administration Tool Evolution

INTERDISCIPLINARY DESIGN MANAGEMENT

John E. Nast
Partner

TECHNICAL DOCUMENTATION CONSULTING SERVICES

15171 Lester Lane,
Los Gatos, CA 95030
(408) 356-5866

ABSTRACT

Today's high technology products are so complex that their performance cannot be fully tested or validated. They require many diverse design and process specialists. Their marketplace is fast moving and competitive. New product designs quickly become obsolete. Components, and processes are introduced at an accelerating rate.

Effective, fast reacting, design management is more essential and difficult than ever. We need management systems that are developed from a corporate perspective, using a Systems Engineering approach, to integrate data and expertise from every corner of the company. They must be fast acting, responsive, and adequately control design development and changes. This requires interactive/integrated computer systems to support effective administrative procedures. This paper presents an overview for such systems and the problems that must be resolved.

INTRODUCTION

Years ago, Design Engineers created an initial product design and then determined if and when a change was needed, what the change would be, and how it would be implemented. In those days we could expect a top level designer to know all there was to know about a product: it's design, how it was built, used, maintained, etc.

Today, multidisciplinary, high technology designs and automated production methods are too complex for an individual to fully understand in depth. This has resulted in high levels of specialization and increasingly complex products. Administrative functions that once were clerical are now supported by a variety of computer systems; many are professionalized and have become highly technical. The impact of seemingly simple decisions in this highly complex industrial environment usually involves several functional areas of the company and a number of technical specialties. Design Engineering can no longer effectively manage product design by unilaterally making design decisions. Not only do product designs influence every part of the company, but many other functional groups have requirements and information that must be included in the design to accommodate manufacturing processes, schedules, cost considerations, quality requirements, and assure that it will function as required.

Another important initial source of information and continuous feedback for design is marketing, who must assure that the ever changing needs of intended customers are met. If the product is supported after delivery an additional list of considerations must be included in design decisions.

The design of today's complex products requires decisions that are based on evaluation of information from throughout the company. When you consider the number of specialists and data systems that establish requirements, provide data, or make recommendations that influence design decisions; no designer can create an optimum design without the benefit of feedback and information. In our competitive environment, the US cannot afford ineffective, inefficient, or unreliable product designs. We must optimize our product designs. To do this we must integrate our management of product designs from their inception through their design, production, and support life-cycle.

ORIGIN OF PRODUCT DESIGN MANAGEMENT

Most production during World War II was accomplished with designs that were as simple as possible, using well established technology. Following the war, the military application of high technology to development of new ships, aircraft, missiles, and weapon systems created a product complexity far beyond our management ability. They were plagued with problems that were really symptoms of ineffective management.

DEVELOPMENT WAS OUT OF CONTROL

o Behind schedule. Products not available when needed. Development Projects often continued long after need for product was past.

o Design did not meet requirements. Could not evaluate products against original requirements. Changes made products unsuitable for intended use.

o Uncontrolled changes resulted in loss of ability to define what was tested. Unable to compare tested prototypes to production configuration.

o Coordination among design groups became difficult, interfaces not maintained, parts from different groups did not fit or function together.

PRODUCTION WAS OUT OF CONTROL

o Changes out of control. Unable to document delivered configuration. High levels of scrap and rework. Costs were out of control.

o Changes often introduced more problems than they solved. Untested changes degraded performance.

o Each system configuration was different, production units not identical.

o Quality was poor because of poor definition of requirements. Design data was often incomplete, all needed documents not available, documents incomplete, missing requirements. Designs often lacked inherent quality.

o Producibility of initial design was degraded as the number of design specialties increased. Designers less familiar with manufacturing processes.

o Lack of configuration control of the delivered hardware compromised field support. Interchangeability was not maintained, spare parts often did not fit or function as reqd.

A special military/industrial committee was established to resolve these problems. They established new management disciplines and formalized others. Among these were Project Management & Configuration Management (CM). These new management systems formalized the coordination of design management among all affected parties. Their approach to Configuration Management included the following:

CONFIGURATION IDENTIFICATION;
o Part and Document ID.
o Product Baseline ID and Management.
o Interchangeability.
o Specification and drawing practices

CONFIGURATION CHANGE CONTROL
o Change Review and Approval based on Technical, Cost, and Schedule Review.

CONFIGURATION STATUS ACCOUNTING
o Part and Document Status Records.
o Current Configuration Definition.
o Change Status Tracking.
o Serialized Configuration Tracking.

CM was based on the customers need to control the configuration of equipment supplied by contractors. Because of this it is seldom directly applicable to commercial products; however, the philosophy of its derivation provides the foundation of the approach used in this paper.

PROBLEMS IN HIGH TECHNOLOGY MANAGEMENT

Today's problems in high technology design and production are very similar to those that faced the military in the 1950's and 1960's, the same difficulties in managing development and production, aggravated by an increasing rate of change to product design.

CONTROL OF CHANGES

Design changes are perhaps the most obvious symptom of management problems. The cost of changes is not often evaluated, but when it is it is found to be very significant. One company found that about 25% of the loaded labor and material cost of the product was attributable to changes. Another found that about the same portion of their spares inventory cost was the result of change.

The problem of managing changes falls into two classic areas. The first area for improvement, often pointed out by manufacturing and quality, is to do a better job during development. Unfortunately even when the initial design was flawless, there are still a large number of changes required to accommodate external changes in areas such as: (1) component and material cost and availability, (2) customer requirements, (3) manufacturing processes, equipment, and technology, (4) new design technology, (5) laws, regulations, and standards, (6) financial considerations, etc.

To resolve these design management problems we must examine the product life cycle from a corporate perspective. We must understand the design cycle from the perspective of (1) the designer, (2) the areas that provide data and guidance for design, and (3) those that are affected by the design.

Computer systems can, and do, provide a great deal of help with different aspects of the problem, but most of them currently act as isolated systems that are unconnected with the sources of the data that they require. CAD/CAM, MRP, and CIM represent steps in the integration of these computer systems. The preceding paper presented an innovative approach to the administrative aspects of the problem that has great potential.[1] But ultimately we need to have these systems interact to share and organize data in ways that help us make informed decisions, and perhaps take action under basic and routine conditions.

In the remainder of this paper I will run through typical phases of Product Design Management, discuss the problems, recommend some solutions, and cover areas where computer is or can be helpful. My emphasis is on how we can best integrate the contributions of the technical and administrative specialists throughout the company, and at times, even from suppliers and customers.

PRODUCT DESIGN MANAGEMENT

"Product Design Management" is the term I use for the principles of "Configuration Management" adapted to commercial products. I use this term in lieu of CM because I believe that it more clearly describes the function in commercial companies, and also because it avoids the stigma of the bureaucratic requirements and delays associated with Military Contracting.

A life cycle approach to Product Design Management includes four areas of activity:

- PRE-DEVELOPMENT PLANNING,
- PRODUCT & PROCESS DEVELOPMENT MGMT,
- PRODUCTION RELEASE AND START-UP,
- PRODUCTION & POST PRODUCTION MGMT.

It applies a corporate perspective to the coordination and review of design from the initial planning for development of a new product until after production and customer support are terminated. Throughout the product life it controls the design by:

o Establishing design objectives and requirements before development. Including design rules and technical guidance for the designers.

o Establishing close coordination among all technical and administrative specialties that are involved or affected by the design.

o Holding technical and managerial reviews to assure that objectives are being met, or to consider changes when necessary.

o Assuring adequate test and evaluation of the product at appropriate times during its life cycle.

o Managing design release to production with a plan based on the users need for controlled information.

o Coordinating design decisions and activities among those that have something to contribute, and having specialists available to provide information and consult with design as needed.

The following general overview of the basic phases for management of high technology design provides a framework for this paper. Each company would implement it somewhat differently because of the unique requirements of the companies personality, its product, its position in the market, and the nature of the marketplace.

PRE-DEVELOPMENT PLANNING
As change avoidance is founded on a well executed product development, effective product development is based on the planning done before development is initiated.

Before the actual start of development, a number of preliminary activities must be done to provide a framework to manage development:

Engineering and Marketing must cooperatively define objectives and requirements for the new product; they must also establish a schedule that balances time needed for development against the early introduction of the product to gain a worthwhile marketshare. Marketing must also forecast total production and production rate so that design and manufacturing engineering can make process and capacity related tradeoffs. From this basis Manufacturing, Quality Assurance, Test Engineering and Customer Support either verify that they have capacity for the new product; or identify processes, equipment, facilities, etc. that must be

developed or changed. Customer support must define a maintenance philosophy to guide design. Manufacturing Quality and Test Engineering must identify design constraints and make recommendations to guide the designers. When all this is done, Finance must review the available resources and estimate the investment expense, anticipated cash flow, and return on investment for the project.

The product of this activity is:

(1) A development specification and envelope/style drawing(s) to document requirements and objectives of design.
(2) An initial set of design rules.
(3) A program plan (possibly using PERT/Cost^2 or equivalent) to document the schedule and financial planning.
(4) Plans for development of processes, facility changes and other activities that must parallel product design.
(5) A narrative to document the basis of tradeoffs, risk analysis, and other factors used to make program decisions.

The effectiveness of a development program and the ability to manage the many interdependent links is a direct result of this preliminary planning. The effectiveness of the planning depends to a great deal on the level of coordination between the planners and working level management throughout the company.

The first plan of this type that a company prepares is usually very difficult to do. But almost every one in which I have been involved has resulted in significant changes in the plan, improving it or resolving serious problems before they arose. The importance of documenting the technical objectives and requirements for a development program seems self evident, but surprisingly often they are either not documented, they are put aside and never looked at

(often residing in a managers desk, never to be seen by designers).

MANAGING TO THE PLAN

For the planning to remain meaningful it should be reevaluated at each management review to assure that the program is progressing according to plan. If the program is not progressing as expected changes can be made to the plan, resources reallocated, schedules can be changed, problems can be reviewed and resolved, or if the problems are sufficiently serious the project can be terminated. At the completion of Development the plan can be used to evaluate the overall performance of development and the validity of the information used to make the original program decisions.

In addition to the generally improved performance and the reduction of the program impact of problems, the experience gained by planning and managing each program will improve the validity of the next, etc. and thus over time these plans become easier to prepare and more accurate. This provides top management with more valid information for authorizing and managing subsequent programs.

Let me reflect on planning, and the maintenance and use of the plan for management. PERT, one of the earliest project management systems, was frequently required for Government contracts. It could be done manually but was most efficient when done with a computer.

It can be demonstrated that the discipline on planning invoked by PERT resulted in most of its benefits. In many programs, PERT was used as a planning tool and then was dropped, because of the difficulty in manually gathering and entering data into the program. Today it is clear that the effectiveness of project management programs (like PERT/Cost) is associated with the ease of capturing and entering the day to day data that is needed to feed it. When they are integrated with other systems to automatically capture data from payroll, procurement, design status, change control, prototype material planning, etc. they become self maintaining and much more useful as a tool for management.

The world of administrative systems was touched on by my predecessor and there are a great many of them. They can range from simple data base systems to more complex approaches that apply Artificial Intelligence (AI) or Expert Systems. MRP has made a start in manufacturing area but its scope is too limited. I am yet to find an MRP system with a truly effective Engineering Design/Change Control System.

MANAGING THE DEVELOPMENT PHASE

The development phase is typically divided into two stages, System design and Design Development.

THE SYSTEM DESIGN/LAYOUT STAGE

This stage includes the following design tasks:

o   Overall system requirements are allocated to subsystems and major components,
o   Physical and functional interface requirements are established for subsystems and major components.
o   Industrial design establishes the "look" of the new product.
o   Electronic packaging design rules are established.
o   Requirements for process, equipment, and facility developments are defined.
o   Fabrication approach for major components is established.
o   Product structure is established.
o   New design concepts are breadboarded and tested.

Accomplishing many of the tasks mentioned above involve input and guidance from almost every part of the company.

At the conclusion of System Design, the project plan should be updated to reflect breadboard test results, changes in the state-of-the-art. Delegation of tasks based on the allocation of requirements and interface requirements for major components and subsystems must be documented and assigned. These assignments should also include design constraints and interdependancies with other groups. External factors such as changes in the marketplace, cost of money, etc. should also be updated.

At the conclusion of this, a management review is held, and if successful the Design Development Stage is Authorized.

At the conclusion of the System Design Stage, a Management Design Review should be held to (1) review results of development testing, (2) reevaluate the ability of the design to meet its objectives and requirements (fully consider any needed changes) (3) review technical problems that have been identified, (4) reevaluate areas of potential risk, (5) either confirm that the program is progressing according to plan or determine what changes are needed. At the successful conclusion of the review the System Design Stage is concluded and authorization for Detail Design is given.

DETAIL DESIGN DEVELOPMENT STAGE

The primary function of this stage is to develop the detail design of the product and test it sufficiently to assure that it will function as anticipated. Testing usually involves building several prototypes for extensive testing (called "alpha" tests by some), This may also include sending prototypes to one or more favored/cooperative customers for additional testing and evaluation in an operating environment ("beta" test).

The Development Phase is completed when a management review of the test results and reevaluation of the plan is successful and production is authorized.

Many of these tasks are accomplished with interacting CAE & CAD. Someday we may also see them be directly linked with administrative systems like Document Status and Control, Project Management, and Prototype MRP. Another improvement that should not be too difficult to implement is the flagging of interface dimensions and functions, so that their special status is identified when changes are proposed.

A related area of software development is the integration of design rules with CAE and CAD to identify potential degradation of producibility, or performance. One example is a program by Valisys Corp.[3] that prepares software inspection gages for a coordinate measuring machine. When dimensioning is unclear or violates basic standards it asks questions and attempts to have the designer clarify the requirement, add missing information, or correct the condition. Some larger high tech companies are applying AI in other design review tasks, including the simulation of both mechanical and electronic tests.

DESIGN COORDINATION & REVIEWS

Design Review Meetings are an important part of the development process, but they are not a substitute for "one on one" or small technical coordination meetings.

When is the best time for the many specialists with contributions to make to provide their inputs? After it's in production? During production start-up? As part of the Review for Production Release? - or - while it is still in its formative stage? - The answer is obvious, but often overlooked.

The key to effective product design, and avoiding changes, lies in coordination during product development. (Do it right the first time.) To do this we must provide technical input from design and design support specialists to designers during the formative period, before it is finished.

A few companies accomplished this by having process specialists coordinate closely with Designers while the design was still on the drawingboard. A few others use a Product Introduction Team with representatives from Materiel, Manufacturing and Process Engineering, Quality Assurance, Customer Support, and other contributing functions.

WE MUST END THE ISOLATIONISM OF DESIGN

Although a few companies do effectively coordinate during the design process with a feeling of team cooperation, many others (often in high tech where need is greatest) have their Design Groups isolated from the rest of the company, having little or no communication with anyone. This design elitism creates a world with high walls to prevent the coordination that is badly needed. Release is spoken of as "throwing it over the wall". They may have a review at release, but the designer often feels that his "design" is submitted to inferiors for judgement and criticism. This can and often does create ill will, and does little to promote a spirit of teamwork.

TECHNICAL COORDINATION MEETINGS

Coordination meetings are another way to get the information and advice needed by the designer. To be effective these should be small, informal, meetings od working level specialists and designers that have something specific to contribute. This type of meeting should become a common event, convened for a specific purpose, perhaps called by working level design manager, supervisor, or group leader. One important benefit of this type of meeting is the synergy that arises from the discussion, often deriving innovative and effective solutions that would not otherwise have been found. The major problems with these meeting is (1) the tendency to hold them on a regular basis whether or not there is a worthwhile subject for review, allowing them to become dull and unproductive, (2) having the wrong people there, everyone should have an interest in the specific subject and should participate, (3) intimidating the participants by discouraging free introduction of new ideas or having high level managers present. A key to the success of this approach is the conference leading skill of the leader.

CAE and CAD offer an opportunity for technical review without meetings. If each technical reviewer has access to the CAD file(s) for design review they could (1) pull it up on their terminals, (2) review, and redline it on a specially designated layer, (3) contact the designer by phone to discuss requirements and alternatives, etc. Design can then (1) review the comments of the different reviewers (each on its own layer), (2) discuss technical issues and alternatives with the reviewers by phone, and (3) make the necessary changes to the basic file. Following this the reviewers can see what was done with their comments and "signoff" the design by entering a password into an administrative file for release and document control.

MANAGEMENT REVIEW MEETINGS

Formal Management Review Meetings should be held at specified milestones during the project to evaluate the status of the program, identify and resolve problems that require management action, evaluate test results, reevaluate any changes to the program plan or market, and decide on any needed corrective action. When held at the end of a phase or Stage, these meetings also consider whether or not the project should advance to the next Stage or Phase.

PRODUCTION STARTUP

PLANNING

Planning the startup of production and the introduction of the product to the market should be done during Development. The degree of overlap of Production Startup and Development should be based on evaluation of the risk of tooling up for an unproven design against the need for early introduction of the product to the marketplace. It should combine a coordinated design review and planning activity with process development, long lead procurement, publication and training, and many others. It requires much more planning than most recognize. It must consider the needs of Design, Test, Manufacturing and Process Engineering, Material Management, Quality Assurance and Customer Support to assure:

o Availability of Engineering documentation when it is needed.

o Efficient implementation of suggestions and requirements to improve the product, production, and customer support.

o A workable plan for delivery and support of the product to assure customer satisfaction.
o Early familiarity with the design by manufacturing, quality, and support personnel to significantly decrease problems and improve production and support.

o Early procurement of long lead items to avoid delays in the production schedule

This planning activity provides the benefit of a smooth production startup, including schedule improvement, lower cost and design change avoidance. The final activity of production startup should be the extensive testing of the first "Pilot" units to validate the production product.

During Production Startup there is a high level of involvement of many specialists, these is also need for an expedited change control procedure and a special status for the design to allow planning, procurement and tooling of an unproven design.

A Management Review after the Production Validation Tests would change the status of the design to "full production", which requires evaluation of changes to minimize their impact on production and delivered products.

IMPROVING CONTROL OF DESIGN CHANGES

There are two major problem areas associated with the control of design changes during production. The first is the review of proposed changes and planning of their implementation. The other is maintaining control of the simultaneous implementation of numerous changes during production.

COORDINATED CHANGE REVIEW AND APPROVAL
Review of each proposed change to include analysis of technical, cost, and schedule factors as the basis of its authorization, incorporation, and implementation.

TECHNICAL ANALYSIS of proposed changes should include the following, as needed:

o MODELING & TEST - If a change includes functionally sensitive areas it should be modeled and tested. The test report should be included in the review.

o USERS REVIEW - specialists from each affected area should be given a chance to determine if their needs are met and suggest any appropriate improvements.

o CUSTOMER REVIEW - Some customers may require an opportunity to review changes, and the right to disapprove them.

o MARKETING REVIEW of changes that affect performance of marketability.

COST ANALYSIS based on disposition and effectivity should include:

o ONE TIME COST - cost of implementing the change and rework or scrap cost.

o NET CHANGE TO PRODUCT COST

SCHEDULE ANALYSIS of change with a proposed implementation schedule should also be required for change authorization if applicable. Many changes require no scheduling, other simple changes can be quickly implemented with only one or two events. But, some changes require elaborate scheduling.

Not all of this analysis is required for every change. Many are clear cut and obvious with no question that they should be implemented. Many have no significant cost or schedule impact. There needs to be a simple process for simple changes that will allows more time for analysis of complex changes. The problem is to expedite the simple ones and assure that adequate analysis of the complex ones is bypassed.

A policy for Change Authorization should be similar to the financial policy that limits the authority to commit funds. This policy would identify the cost limit for change approval by the chairman of the change board, and establish progressively higher approval levels for more costly changes.

MANAGING CHANGE IMPLEMENTATION
Many companies have difficulty implementing changes, although many don't even know it. They may have problems meeting production schedules, unacceptably high inventory levels, constant shortages, etc. and not realize that a major contributor to these problems is a lack of control of change implementation.

Many factories process 100 or more changes per month. Each including between 1 and 50 documents. Some changes do not require implementation into production, others may require between one day and 9 months to implement. Implementation ranges from an update to an MRP record, to a project that involves 200 or more interrelated tasks or events by 10 or more different departments. A change to a part that takes 6 months or more to implement may be overtaken by an emergency change that must be implemented immediately.

Even this might be manageable if implementation was well planned and everything was on schedule (which almost never happens). Many MRP systems claim to handle change implementation but I know of none that manage the environment and detail above.

A PERT type program that handles many small concurrent projects can do a great deal to ease this problem, especially if integrated with MRP, payroll accounting, status tracking of engineering and process documents (Design, Quality, & Production), procurement, receiving, stores, and other related activities. It would identify many problems early enough for corrective action to be taken before they became severe, or impacted delivery or the production schedule. If you project our problems today into the future, with more complex higher technology products, it is hard to imagine operating without such a system.

WHERE ARE WE GOING

If you look at Design Management from the perspective just presented, it should be apparent that we need to emphasize a coordinated team approach to the development of product design and control of its changes. But it must include a clear delegation of responsibilities.

We can benefit from computer programs that use an Expert System or Artificial Intelligence approach to administrative aspects of design management, and to the development and application of design rules.

One area could be a change control system that supported the review, planning, approval, and implementation of design changes. This system would interact with MRP, drawing status records, records for Production, Quality and Test Engineering documents; and other Engineering, and Manufacturing and Customer Support systems. It could evaluate the change objective, priority, urgency, parts & processes affected, disposition of parts, etc. With that information it could assemble data on stock status, lead time, production flow, tools & fixtures affected, instructions and procedures affected, cost, design sensitivity, process sensitivity, related changes in-process, impact on customer support and spares, etc. and then conduct an analysis. This analysis could result in a list of questions, a request for additional data, etc. When the new data is entered, the system could provide a cost analysis and implementation schedule.

With this, plus reviewers technical comments, test results, etc. management could decide whether or not a change should be approved. After approval, The system could track implementation and alert management when problems arise. Other benefits would include historical data that could be used to improve new designs and production.

This is a long way from reality, but I believe it can, and will, be developed. The experience of Northern Telecom seems to support this concept. Since each company and product environment is unique and constantly changing, such a program would need to be flexible and somewhat heuristic, to keep up-to-date with its environment.

To illustrate rules and logic could be developed, consider classification of changes by their primary objective, using the following categories:

o ERROR CORRECTION - Correct design error, add missing data, etc.

o DESIGN REQUIREMENT - Make the product perform to spec.

o MANUFACTURING SERVICE - Facilitate or improve Manufacturing, Quality Assurance, or Test cost or practice.

o CUSTOMER SUPPORT SERVICE - Facilitate or Improve Customer Support cost, performance, or practice.

o PRODUCT ENHANCEMENT - Improve performance above required levels, add features or capabilities, etc.

o CUSTOMER REQUESTED - Changes to requirements that were previously requested. (Paid for by the customer.)

Each category has inherent characteristics and requirements for analysis, for example:

Cost is not usually a factor for ERROR CORRECTION or PRODUCT REQUIREMENT

Except for availability or problems that could stop production or disqualify the product, approval of a MANUFACTURING SERVICE or CUSTOMER SERVICE change is based on net cost savings.

PRODUCT ENHANCEMENTS must be justified by Marketing to assure that the benefits offset the cost.

The customer must accept the cost of a CUSTOMER REQUESTED change.

It becomes clear that each class has its individual rules for cost evaluation and justification.

This same kind of analysis can be applied to other change criteria and be used to derive a set of practices, recommendations, and rules for change analysis. Consider the consequence of not implementing a change, urgency for a change, planning the most cost effective implementation, the fastest implementation, etc.

IN CONCLUSION

Today we face problems of design deficiencies and a constant design change. These problems will not go away, in fact, they will get progressively worse as technology becomes more complex. Some companies have found that design changes represent about 25% of the production labor and material cost, other companies loose over 50% of their capacity from problems caused by poor control of changes. If we are to be successful in the future we must minimize the need for change and learn to handle them better.

Our first line of defense should be change avoidance by more effective management of development. "Doing it right the first time." In an interdisciplinary environment this requires feedback and teamwork.

Our main line of defense should be better control of changes. Modeling and testing changes before incorporation. Basing change approval on prior evaluation of technical, cost, and schedule data, as applicable.

The flavor of how these techniques are implemented differs from one company to the next, and from one industry to the next. I have attempted to provide a model that can be tailored to fit individual issues and problems. It is my hope that this paper will motivate some companies to evaluate how well they are currently managing their product design. I also hope that I may have given some ideas for new directions that computer systems companies can take to resolve some very serious problems.

Automating Design Administration Information - A. Young - Director, New Product Intro Northern Telecom Inc.

2. PERT - Program Evaluation and Review Technique, an early project management system, widely used in Government Contracting. PERT/Cost used the schedule and organization of PERT as a framework for budgeting and cost control.

3. Valisys Corporation, 2050 Martin Ave, Santa Clara, CA 95050 a division of FMC Corporation.

PRODUCT RELEASE

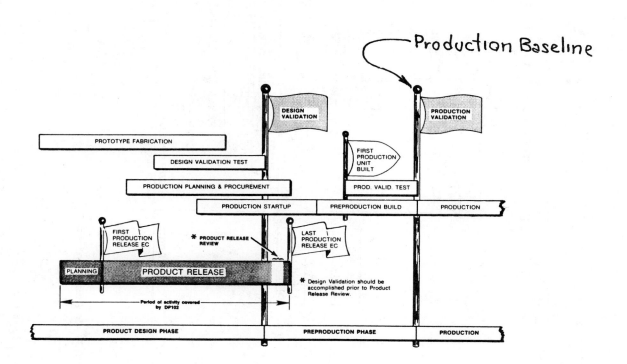

PROGRAM LIFE CYCLE

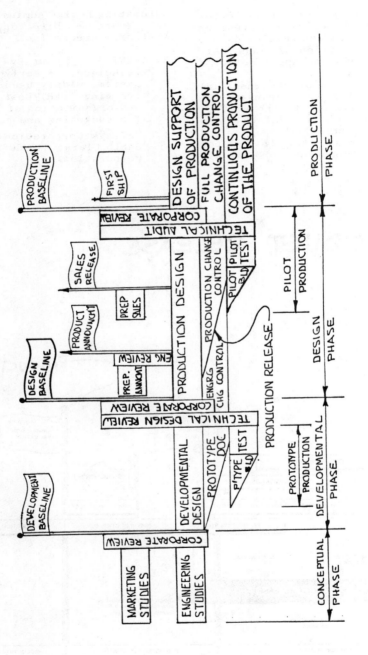

NAST & Associates

AIDD '84 - 7

1423

Integrating CAD Systems Through the Use of a Database Manager

Grant K. Garnett
Member of Technical Staff

AT&T Bell Laboratories
Naperville, Illinois

1. Abstract

AT&T's Data System Group has implemented a variety of Mechanical CAD tools to improve the quality of the computer equipment design process. The variety of user interfaces, however, makes the product data difficult to access for casual tool users. In addition, the variety of hardware platforms and operating environments complicates sharing of information. Integrating these tools with a database manager allows casual users to access information easily and enables the CAD tools to share data. By referencing meta-data, data about the design data, the database manager locates the source of the requested data, pulls the data to the requested location, and translates that data into the desired format. In this way, the information from the multiple CAD tools can be viewed on line, printed at remote locations, or pulled into manufacturing systems from a single user interface. The database manager also provides both version and configuration control for product information. This system reduces intervals, eliminates hand-offs, and makes information readily available, thus increasing the quality of the design information and improving the design process.

2. Introduction

Computer aided tools have been introduced into some corporations as a series of unrelated pieces. Often the research and development organizations and the manufacturing organizations purchase and implement different tools to serve different functions. Even within the confines of these organizations, groups with different functions may implement different tools to meet specific goals. A complex system of unrelated tools results. Such a system inhibits the effective use of design information, prohibiting novice computer users from accessing product information in its electronic form. This paper considers one such system and describes a database manager used to integrate this system.

3. Overview of CAD System

To gain an appreciation for the diversity of the CAD tools that have been implemented in the environment being considered, this section describes the characteristics and the function of each tool. Each of these tools can be categorized as either a textual tool or a graphical tool. The textual tools store data in a database structure. The graphics tools generate two-dimensional or three-dimensional views of the equipment as commonly appear in standard engineering drawings.

3.1 Textual Tools

Two different tools, FORGE and FOCUS-PDD are used to capture, store, and generate documentation for textual information. FORGE is an internally developed field oriented editor. The tool runs on AT&T computer equipment under the UNIX® operating system. FOCUS-PDD is also an internally developed CAD tool. This tool runs on AMDAHL computer equipment under the MVS-JES3™ operating system and utilizes the IMS™ database handler.

Applications written using FORGE allow engineers to generate cover sheets for manufacturing documentation packages. When packages of new information are released to manufacturing, these cover sheets serve as an introduction and a table of contents for the package. The cover sheets, and thus the data in FORGE, supply valuable meta-data.

The FOCUS-PDD tool allows engineers to capture stocklist information, configuration rules, and manufacturing notes. The tool encourages engineers to use existing components and performs audits to ensure conformance to corporate standards. In addition, the tool formats the design information for release to manufacturing. The FOCUS-PDD tool provides design data about the product that is critical to the ordering and manufacturing processes.

Both these tools allow users to request hard copy output. Hard copies are printed on a local XEROX™ 9700 high speed printer and delivered to the user's mail box. FOCUS-PDD also allows users to request microfilm output for the official release of information to the corporate distribution channels.

3.2 Graphical Tools

Two primary classifications of graphical tools are used in this environment. A small group of experts use UNIGRAPHICS®, a commercially available tool that runs on a VAX® under the VMS® operating system. These experts generate two-dimensional drawings and three-dimensional wire frame models of individual components and create assembly level graphics. Since the manufacturing organization does not generally use the electronic data and many other organizations within the corporation do not have access to the electronic data, the engineers combine two dimensional views, isometric views, borders, and title blocks to create traditional design drawings. After these drawings are created, microfilm is generated from the paper copies and released to manufacturing and other organizations within the corporation. These organizations work from paper copies that are generated from microfilm.

A larger group of casual CAD users adopted PC based CAD tools, finding both the PCs and the CAD tools readily available and easy to use. Many of the users selected VERSACAD®, however, CADKEY® and

AutoCAD® are also being utilized. These tools run on AT&T personal computers and most often run under the MS-DOS® operating system. Engineers primarily use these tools when doing conceptual design work or when three-dimensional design capture is not necessary.

The PC based CAD tools generally use a Hewlett Packard pen plotter to create hard copy output. The UNIGRAPHICS system uses either a VERSATEC® electrostatic plotter or an IMAGEN laser writer to create hard copy output.

4. Description of the Database Management System

Given an understanding of the nature of the CAD tools used in the design environment, the motivation for developing an integrated system becomes apparent. This section discusses the rationale for creating a database manager and describes the requirements that drove the development of the integrated system. The section goes on to describe the database management system that was developed and the requirements that it placed on the CAD tools and output devices. Finally, the section proposes improvements to the system that should be incorporated in the next phase of the development effort.

4.1 Rationale for Development

Without the database management system, engineers needed to access as many as four different tools to view or print all the design information. Each of these tools required the user to be familiar with different operating environments, hardware platforms, and software interfaces. As a result, plotting or viewing information was intimidating for even experienced computer users. Asking individuals who were not comfortable with computers to use several tools only increased their uneasiness with the computer.

In addition to intimidating the users, the unintegrated tool set was difficult for the design experts to use and manage effectively. When a hard copy of the drawing needed to be produced, the responsible experts would generate sections of the drawing using the different tools and output devices. Then an individual manually merged the output to create the complete engineering drawing. If the expert desired to view, print, or modify an existing graphics sheet, it was not clear where the design file resided. The location of this file could only be determined if the user or a CAD system expert searched each of several storage mediums.

Thus, a need clearly existed to organize and manage the design information residing in the various CAD tools and to provide users with easy access to all information.

4.2 Database Management System Requirements

The database management system requirements that drove the development effort were broken into three categories: functional requirements, operational requirements, and conceptual requirements. Each of these categories is discussed.

4.2.1 Functional Requirements

From a functional standpoint, the database manager was required to provide access to all design information through a single menu driven user interface. In addition, all printed output needed to be generated on local printers or laser writers and all graphics needed to be viewable from low cost workstations. In this way the novice user would only need to be familiar with one operating environment, one hardware platform, and one software interface.

4.2.2 Operational Requirements

From an operational standpoint, the designers were expected to execute a procedure to "release" information to the database manager whenever new design information became available. The database manager was expected to use this input to update its look up tables. When a user entered the system, the menu interface was required to prompt the user for a drawing number, an issue number, and the desired output device, ie. line printer, laser writer, or terminal. Finally, the database manager was expected to locate the source of the design information, translate the information to the desired format, and display the information as requested.

4.2.3 Conceptual Requirements

From a conceptual standpoint, the database manager was envisioned to be a read only, information pull system. Further, it was envisioned that the data would be stored on the CAD system where the data originated and in its native format. Upon request, the information would be pulled to the user's system and reformatted for display in real time. In addition, the system was envisioned to provide an open architecture so that additional CAD tools and output devices could be integrated into the system.

4.3 First Pass Database Management System Description

From the requirements described above, a first pass database management system was developed. Most of the system requirements were realized in the first pass system. This section evaluates the system based on each category of the requirements and describes the information flow of the system.

4.3.1 Functional Description

The first pass database management system realized all the functional requirements. With the system, users access all design information through a single, menu driven user interface. If users have access to a Postscript compatible laser writer, the system will generate hard copy output for all sections of the drawing regardless of their content or their source. If users do not have access to a laser writer, hard copy output is generated at either a line printer or a pen plotter depending on the content of the information. Textual information can be viewed on any standard terminal. Viewing graphical information, however, requires that the user possess either a TEKTRONICS®

4100 series workstation or an AT&T 630 graphics terminal. Either of these devices is a low cost alternative when compared with a UNIGRAPHICS workstation.

4.3.2 Operational Description

The first pass system also realized most of the operational requirements. When new information is released to manufacturing through the microfilm process, the designers initiate an electronic release to the database manager. The database manager then uses this information to update the tables that contain the meta-data. The database manager updates its information every 24 hours. While in most cases this interval is acceptable, the database manager can deliver files within the hour if necessary. When users enter the system, they select a drawing number, issue number, and output device. The database manager then locates the information requested, checks the current format of the information, translates the information if necessary, and displays or prints the requested information.

4.3.3 Graphical Information Flow

Figure 1 depicts the information flow for graphical information. The sourcing CAD tool postprocesses the native file to create a standard IGES file. At the same time, a small file of meta-data is generated. The sourcing CAD tool's operating system then pushes these two ASCII files to the UNIX system where the database manager resides. The database manager recognizes that new information has arrived, uses the meta-data file to update the ORACLE® tables, and initiates an IGES to TEKTRONICS translation to create a viewable format. Finally, the IGES file is compressed and both the IGES file and the TEKTRONICS file are stored in the database. When users ask to view a drawing, the TEKTRONICS file is rapidly displayed to the screen without processing time delays. When users ask to print a drawing, the database manager invokes an IGES to Postscript translation process and sends the results to the laser writer.

4.3.4 Textual Information Flow

Figure 2 depicts the flow of textual information. The sourcing CAD system postprocesses the native file to create a file of Colon Separated Data (CSD). As in the graphics process, the source system creates a small file of meta-data. Then this system pushes these files from its resident operating system to the UNIX system where the database manager resides. The database manager recognizes that new information has arrived, uses the file of meta-data to update the ORACLE tables, and stores the CSD file to disk. When users ask to either view or print the textual sections of the drawing, the database management system invokes applications that postprocess the CSD files in real time.

4.3.5 Conceptual Description

Since one purpose of the first pass system was to demonstrate its feasibility and need, the initial development made use of existing networks, communication tools, device drivers, and postprocessors whenever possible. Making optimum use of existing capabilities minimized the development cost of the first pass system. For example, since translating the data from its native format was more efficiently and more economically performed with existing IGES postprocessors, the graphics data was transferred to the database manager in the IGES format. In addition, due to the complexity of communicating between two different operating systems in real time, the pull capability was deferred to a secondary development phase. Finally, the first pass system stores both the IGES format and the TEKTRONICS format. Although it would be more desirable to store the data in a single format, the extra storage space was sacrificed to achieve reasonable viewing speeds with existing software. Thus, although the first pass system did not fulfill all the conceptual requirements, the system that currently exists is fully functional.

4.4 CAD Tool and Output Device Requirements

To maintain an open architecture, the database management system placed several requirements on the supported CAD tools and output devices. The tools providing graphical information must meet the following requirements:

1. The CAD tool must be capable of placing the standard drawing output in IGES format.
2. The CAD tool must provide a means of generating the meta-data file needed by the database manager. The meta-data file contains information such as the drawing number, sheet number, sheet title, issue number, sourcing CAD system, file format, etc.
3. The CAD tool's operating system must be capable of transferring the IGES file and the meta-data file to a UNIX system.

The tools providing textual information must satisfy the following requirements:

1. The CAD tool must be capable of translating its data into the standard Colon Separated Data (CSD) format recognized by the database management system.
2. The CAD tool must provide a means of generating the meta-data file needed by the database manager.
3. The CAD tool's operating system must be capable of transferring the CSD file and the meta-data file to a UNIX system.

The output devices must satisfy the following requirements:

1. Devices displaying graphical information must be capable of emulating a TEKTRONICS 4100 series workstation.

2. Devices printing graphical information must support either POSTSCRIPT® or HP-GL™.

3. Devices printing textual information must support either POSTSCRIPT or standard ASCII output.

If a CAD tool or output device satisfies these requirements it can be integrated directly into the first pass database management system.

4.5 Future System Development Targets

In the next phase of the database management system, several improvements are proposed. This section describes three of the most significant improvements and identifies the elements of the system that will need to be modified to realize each improvement.

4.5.1 Transforming Push to Pull

The system developed requires the sourcing CAD tools to push the meta-data file as well as an IGES design file to the database manager. A more desirable system would only require the CAD tools to push the meta-data file to the database manager and to make the new design file readable. The CAD tools would no longer download design files to another system. If performance limitations did not prohibit real time data transfer and translation, the database management system could request a file from the source on demand. This capability would minimize the fixed memory requirements of the database management system.

To provide such a capability, the communication software used to move data from one operating system to another must be enhanced. The enhanced software must allow the UNIX based database management system to execute a file transfer remotely. In addition, the sourcing CAD tools must provide access to all design files. If the source files are moved, renamed, or archived, the sourcing CAD tool must notify the database manager.

4.5.2 Real Time Data Transfer and Translation

To transfer and translate design data directly from the sourcing system in real time, both the performance of the data communications network and the translation software must be improved.

Sizes for typical design files range from 0.5 to 3 megabytes. The network being used supports a maximum data transfer rate of 9600 bits per second. Consequently, data transfer times range from 20 seconds to 2 minutes per file. Such delays are unacceptable in a production level system. To make real time data transfer acceptable the data transfer speed must be increased by two orders of magnitude. Such improvement will require the implementation of a high speed data network.

In a real time system, each file requested must be translated from its native format to IGES and from IGES to the requested output format. Currently, the performance of the translation software makes real time translation of files unfeasible. The translation to

IGES alone can require several minutes of processing. Since the CAD tool vendors own the modules that translate the native files to IGES format, the performance of this translation may be difficult to affect. Another strategy to improve performance would be to eliminate the translation to IGES and translate directly to the output format. Note however, that this strategy requires each CAD tool to provide a means of directly accessing the design data.

4.5.3 Supporting Multiple Devices with Display Postscript®

If users wish to view graphics with the first pass system, their workstation must be capable of emulating a TEKTRONICS 4100 series workstation. A more desirable system would allow the user to select from a wider range of workstations. If the workstation industry supported a standard display language, the database management system could provide postprocessors from IGES to the display language. Then users could select a workstation that supports the standard display language and meets their additional requirements. An industry standard for display languages has yet to emerge, but languages such as Display Postscript and Network Extensible Window System (NEWS™) could evolve to meet such a need. When the industry supports a standard display language, a postprocessor should be added to the database manager's capabilities.

5. System Engineering Considerations

When designing a database management system such as the one described, a system engineer weighs a variety of critical assumptions and attempts to balance the advantages and disadvantages of each option. This section discusses four of the most critical design parameters that were considered when engineering this system.

5.1 Supporting a Single System vs. an Open Architecture

When integrating a set of unrelated CAD tools, the system engineer may be tempted to consolidate the different CAD tools into a single tool. Although some consolidation may be advisable, the system engineer must strive to provide an open architecture.

Ideally, a system engineer could purchase or develop a single tool to perform all the necessary engineering, design, and manufacturing functions. The single tool would then become the "integrated" system and any existing tools would be eliminated. Although such a scenario appears desirable, realizing such a tool is seldom feasible. Although many commercial products claim to be comprehensive, a single tool that meets all the process requirements is difficult to purchase commercially. Due to the complexity of such a tool, internal development is usually uneconomical. Often a minimum of three or four systems are required for the engineering, design, and manufacturing processes. Some of these tools may be purchased commercially while others may be developed internally.

If the integration software could provide a completely open architecture, the system would be capable of accepting data from any tool and would present the data in the desired format on any output device. Due to the level of variability in tools and output devices, however, the tools supported will need to meet at least a minimum set of requirements. Obviously, as the number of supported tools increases, the complexity of the integration problem also increases. The integration complexity increases to an even greater extent if the system must support multiple operating systems.

Since several different CAD tools had been adopted in the environment being considered, the database management system was designed with an open architecture. As is frequently the case, extensive capital investment in the existing tools along with an embedded user base prohibited the system engineer from eliminating any tools. Therefore, the database management system was required to support several different tools that function under several different operating environments. Each of these tools is required to meet a basic set of requirements. Additional tools that meet these basic requirements can be directly integrated into the existing system.

5.2 Using IGES vs. Developing Custom Postprocessors

In order to provide an open architecture, some system engineers choose to take advantage of widely supported industry standards such as IGES. Due to the inconsistencies in IGES implementations, however, other engineers prefer to develop custom postprocessors for each CAD tool supported.

IGES, the Initial Graphics Exchange Specification, provides a common format for the transfer of graphical design information from one system to another. Many CAD tool vendors provide IGES translators with their software package. The problem with IGES, however, is that each CAD tool vendor interprets and implements the standard somewhat differently. As a result, when files are moved from one system to another, portions of the data may be lost. In addition, in designing postprocessors that will accept IGES files from several different sources, differences in the IGES implementations must be well understood and carefully considered.

For these reasons, some system engineers would prefer not to use the IGES format. When IGES is not used, the database management system must access graphical data directly. Unfortunately, some CAD tools do not provide direct access to the data structure. In addition, if IGES is not utilized, a new postprocessor must be created and permanently supported for each tool that is added to the system. This requirement limits the flexibility of the system and makes supporting a large number of tools uneconomical.

As a result, the system engineers chose to use the IGES format as a standard method of transferring graphical

design information to the database manager.

5.3 Duplicating Information vs. Accessing Information in Real Time

The methodology selected to transfer and translate information significantly impacts the performance and the cost of the system. If the system engineer chooses to move the data in real time, the system cost increases and performance may be sacrificed. If, on the other hand, the system engineer chooses to process the data before the information is requested, the system will duplicate design information in the downstream systems and information control must be monitored more carefully.

If the data will be transferred and translated in real time, the system engineer must provide a high speed data network and high performance translation software. These requirements increase the cost of the system. In addition, if the system will be highly utilized, several users may perform similar translations simultaneously. As a result, the system will require additional processing power. Finally, note that if a single drawing is requested many times, the data from the source will be retranslated and retransferred just as many times.

Instead, the system engineer may opt to transfer and translate the design information once and then store the translated version of the file. This increases the amount of fixed memory space required for the system but eliminates many of the other costs associated with

real time translation of the data. A disadvantage of a batch system is that the system may transfer and translate data that will never be requested from the database manager. In addition, the system engineers must ensure that users do not add value to the information that has been downloaded from the source. Instead, the new information should be added at the design source.

The system engineer may consider a combination of a real time system and downstream storage of information. In this methodology, the data would be transferred and translated from the original source in real time the first time a user requests the information. The translated format would then be saved in the database manager for future reference. Such a system would still require high performance translators, a high speed network, and additional fixed memory. Nevertheless, the demand for processing power would be reduced significantly since information would never be translated multiple times.

In the first pass system described above, the system engineer chose to duplicate the information in the downstream system. In the second phase of the development effort, a combination of downstream storage and real time data transfer and translation is proposed.

6. Capturing Information as Data vs. Graphics

In designing an integrated system, the engineer should strive to create a flexible system that allows users to define their output interactively. This forces system engineers to consider the process used to capture design information. If design engineers capture textual information as graphics, a computer may not be able to search, sort, reformat, or download the information.

In many cases, the CAD system experts used drawing boards prior to the introduction of the computer aided tools. As a result, the designers frequently capture information as graphical text that could be better managed as drawing attributes. When the information is captured as graphical text, it becomes unreadable to the computer. Consequently, the only useful output that the system can generate is paper. To modify the presentation of the material, the drawing must be restructured manually. Searching and sorting the information must also be performed manually. Downloading the information to another system requires that a user keystroke the information from paper into the downstream system.

In this case, the system engineer must work with designers to identify the common attributes that are captured as graphical text and provide a data structure for managing this information. If carefully planned, the designer can store the information as data and still generate standard drawing formats without additional work. If information is stored in a data structure, postprocessors can be written for each CAD tool to generate a standard formatted data file from the drawing files. Then, users will have the capability of reformatting the drawing output, searching and sorting the drawing information, and downloading this information directly into downstream systems.

As implied above, the database manager requires that CAD systems store textual information in a data structure. As a result, FOCUS-PDD and FORGE, used to capture the cover sheets, stocklists, notes, and tables, store the information in a data structure. Postprocessors then format a standard Colon Separated Data (CSD) file from the drawing files. The CSD file is well defined and available to applications for postprocessing. A set of standard applications for viewing and printing the data have been developed. In addition, several custom applications have been developed that provide a subset of the information needed for a particular application. Using the UNIX commands and standard applications, engineers with little programming experience can develop powerful applications.

7. Summary

The case study described in this paper demonstrates the benefits that can be realized from integrating existing CAD tools. Even when an organization uses multiple CAD tools to capture design information, users should have the capability of accessing the information easily. For this reason, the database management system was developed. As shown, the system provides access to design information that resides on four different CAD tools that operate under four different operating systems. With the database management system, users need only be familiar with one menu interface and one operating system.

Most organizations will require several different CAD tools to satisfy the requirements of all users. Nevertheless, the system engineers must continually strive to provide and integrated system. In conclusion, system engineers must not lose sight of their goal -- providing the information users with easy access to electronic design information in a timely manner.

8. Acknowledgements

The author would like to thank Mr. Bill E. Carroll and Mr. Dan E. Radke for their contributions to the concepts presented in this paper.

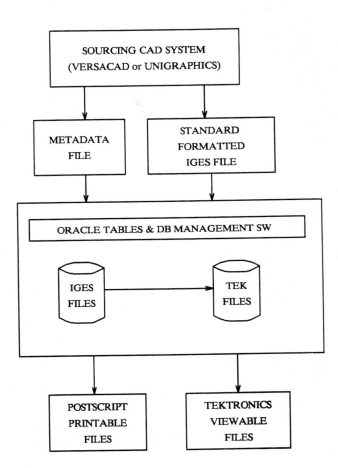

GRAPHICAL INFORMATION FLOW
FIGURE 1

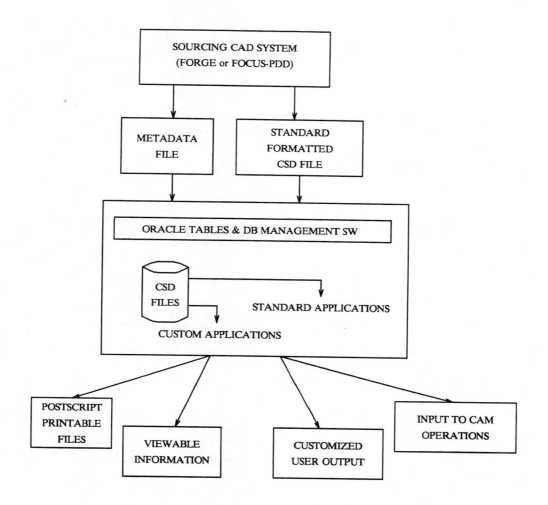

TEXTUAL INFORMATION FLOW
FIGURE 2

PQR-06

NEW PRODUCT INTRODUCTION

Dan Rafferty, Chairperson
Regional Vice President

Raychem Corporation
2100 Swift Drive
Oak Brook, Illinois 60521

ABSTRACT

The theme of this year's Product
Realization Institute is the Product Life
Cycle. Generally, there are four stages
in a product's life cycle:
1. Introduction
2. Growth
3. Maturity
4. Decline

Probably the single most important phase
of a product's life cycle is the product's
introduction. In a world where 80% of new
products fail, this portion of a product's
life cycle is also the most dangerous and
delicate. On the positive side, it is
during this phase that the product takes
on a character and reputation that will
last during its full life cycle.

Divestiture has had an important effect
on the cultural behavior of both users
and vendors. Good faith, trust and
partnership are all new roles for
suppliers and customers. These roles are
tested severely during the New Product
Introduction Phase.

The following three discussions will
focus on this New Product Introduction
Phase from a new company like Optilink
offering a new technology, to two more
established companies such as 3M and
Raychem offering new technology to both
the copper and fiber world.

Mr. Kermit Ross - Optilink Corporation

Dr. Dennis Hamill - 3M Company

Mr. Zak Manuszak - Raychem Corporation

NEW PRODUCT INTRODUCTION

IN THE NEW TELECOMMUNICATIONS MARKET

Kermit Ross
Director of Marketing

Optilink Corporation
1310-C Redwood Highway
Petaluma, California 94975

ABSTRACT

The divestiture of the Bell Operating
Companies and the consequent reorganization of the US telecommunications
industry has profoundly changed the ways
that billions of dollars are spent and
thousands of products are bought and sold.
Suppliers to this industry must understand
these changes in order to retain existing
business and, in particular, to develop
new business. This paper will examine the
pre- and post-divestiture environments and
will discuss the strategic considerations
for the introduction of new products in
each. A case history from each environment
will be used to illustrate the differences
between them.

THE REORGANIZATION OF THE US TELEPHONE INDUSTRY

Next to the invention of the telephone, the
pivotal event of January 1, 1984 is the
most significant in the history of our
industry. Many observers would say it is
the most significant and far-reaching
event in the history of business in the
United States. On January 1, 1984 a
business worth more than 100 billion
dollars was taken apart and the
relationships among it and its customers,
employees, owners and suppliers were
changed profoundly and forever. Volumes
have already been written about these
changes and this paper does not presume to
discuss them in general or in detail.
However, it does examine the process of
new product introduction both before and
after divestiture.

THE PRE-DIVESTITURE ENVIRONMENT

Before January 1, 1984 about 80 percent of
all the telephones in the U.S. were
served by the "Bell System". AT&T and the
twenty-three Bell Operating Companies
(BOCs) enjoyed regulated monopolies of the
local, long distance and customer equipment markets. Some competition began to
occur in long distance when MCI entered
the market in the 1970's, and the FCC
deregulated customer premise equipment
(CPE) and instituted the Part 68 registration program in 1976. But these
competitive inroads were fiercely and, in
large part, successfully resisted by the
BOCs and the parent AT&T.

Many forces were present in the pre-
divestiture Bell System to slow change.
Since, until the 1970's, the business was
a monopoly, there were no competitive
pressures and virtually no market
motivation for technical change. The
regulatory entities were not renowned for
promoting new technology. Telephone
companies are very capital intensive and
this investment was depreciated very
slowly, 20 to 40 year lifetimes being the
norm.

Another factor retarding change was the immense size of the organization. Change takes time and energy to overcome the inertia of such an organization. Furthermore, this organization institutionalized uniformity. A central staff organization called the AT&T General Departments developed and recommended uniform practices and procedures to the BOCs in the form of the ubiquitous "Bell System Practices".

AT&T also owned the biggest and best research and development organization in the world, Bell Laboratories, whose job was to develop proprietary solutions to the BOCs' problems. These solutions were turned into products to be manufactured by Western Electric, the manufacturing arm of AT&T. Before divestiture Western Electric supplied over 90 percent of the BOCs' needs, either with products it manufactured or with products procured, warehoused and distributed on their behalf. The BOCs had learned to expect proprietary solutions from a sole source at the deliberate pace determined by regulation and the depreciation schedule.

The remaining 20 percent of the US telephone customers were served by non-Bell, "independent" telephone companies. These telephone companies were much more open to the introduction of new products than the BOCs. Most had no integrated research or manufacturing organizations, so they were dependent on the supplier community to provide these functions. However, the independents were under the same regulatory constraints as the BOCs and were not as well financed. The independent telephone companies financed by the REA were exceptions to this general rule in that they had access to US government loans at very favorable interest rates. This enabled them to be among the most progressive of all US telephone companies in the deployment of new technologies and products. Until the formation of the "Bell System Purchased Products Division" (BSPPD), the system of REA specifications provided the industry with the only system of national performance standards for telephone products.

What were the strategic interests of the telephone companies in the pre-divestiture environment? The first of these was the control of operating costs. Telephone companies were (and still are) regulated by an allowable rate of return on assets, the "rate base". The telephone companies could reach their profitability objectives only by carefully controlling costs. Rate, i.e. price, increases and additions to the rate base, i.e. capital expenditures, were closely scrutinized by the regulators. There were only three satisfactory reasons to expend capital: to serve new customers, to reduce costs or to improve reliability, "service". Even an improvement in reliability could be looked at as a reduction of maintenance costs. When capital expenditures were made, they were planned to last for a long time; depreciation was spread over 20 to 40 years.

The pre-divestiture telephone companies took great pride (justly so) in providing excellent service. Service was defined more as reliability than as responsiveness. This, too, had an effect on operating costs. Better service meant lower costs.

Before divestiture most BOC purchases were made from or through Western Electric. This vertically integrated the manufacture of most goods and many services. The financial impact was to move money from the expense side of the regulated BOCs' income statements to the revenue line of the non-regulated Western Electric's. Purchasing from Western Electric was clearly in the strategic interest of the pre-divestiture Bell System. Some of the independent companies pursued similar strategies with affiliated manufacturing subsidiaries or supply houses.

The opportunities for outside suppliers to introduce new products, especially to the BOCs, in the pre-divestiture environment were limited. Some suppliers chose to ignore the BOCs and concentrate on the independent part of the market. Others supplied products to and/or through Western Electric. Western Electric, in addition to being the manufacturing arm of the Bell System, purchased, warehoused and distributed almost all the rest of the BOCs' needs. This worked best for suppliers who developed proprietary solutions for acute needs. The proprietary part was important since, if the need became acute enough and widespread enough, Western Electric would simply begin to manufacture a product to address it. The BOCs, however, were conditioned to accept proprietary solutions from sole sources. Once launched, such products could easily be protected from competition.

In the last half of the 1970's the Bell System Purchased Products Division (BSPPD) was formed as part of the AT&T General Departments. The formation of this organization was the result of regulatory pressure to demonstrate that the Bell System could and would purchase products from outside sources. BSPPD developed performance specifications which were made available to the supplier community. As these specifications became available, BSPPD evaluated "general trade" products to determine their suitability for use by the BOCs and published their findings. The BOCs created "general trade products" organizations to coordinate with BSPPD at the operating company level.

A CASE STUDY: DISTRIBUTION SPLICE PRETERMINATION

In the middle 1970's the telephone companies were being challenged to deal with massive and unfamiliar changes in US demography. It seemed that everybody was moving to the sunbelt states, resulting in explosive growth in population, business activity and demand for telephone service. This strained the capabilities of the existing telephone plant and required much more to be constructed very quickly. Much of the strain occurred in the distribution portion of the plant. Large quantities of new distribution plant were required quickly to respond to the demands for new service.

All this occurred at a time when many new methods, procedures and materials were being simultaneously introduced into the distribution plant. The concept of "Out of Sight Plant" was being promoted and widely adopted as the solution to many of the costly maintenance problems of traditional aerial distribution plant. But existing construction methods and materials were not readily adaptable to this new concept. New materials, like jelly-filled cable, were rapidly introduced, sometimes without a complete understanding of the systems and compatibility requirements. There was an acute need for a systems approach to distribution plant construction which would deal with the quality, reliability and productivity concerns of the telephone companies.

Some telephone companies began to experiment with non-traditional methods of distribution plant construction. Three telephone companies established factories where distribution service splices could be prefabricated for later transport to the field. The quality and productivity advantages of this approach were obvious. But the traditional materials used in these early experiments raised serious doubts related to long term reliability. Hard encapsulated splices were simply not meant to be rolled up on to a cable reel. Oil resistant materials like polyurethane encapsulants were never meant to bond to oily materials like cable filling compounds.

Raychem Corporation learned of the experiments in distribution service splice prefabrication and developed a product system which was uniquely suitable for the application. The application and Raychem's product were later named the PRETERM system. Raychem had certain proprietary technological ingredients that could be combined to address the special requirements of PRETERM. These included heat-shrinkable plastic sleeves and heat-activated adhesives that could reinstate the cable jacket with similar strength and flexibility. These were combined with heat-activated sealants with appropriate thermomechanical properties and compatibility characteristics to reinstate the cable filling material. The object was the creation of a splice that was as strong, flexible and tough as the cable, and could, therefore, be handled like the cable during placing.

An applications subsystem was provided to streamline and organize the production process, and to remove much of the human factors variability from it. This consisted of workstations, heaters and powered reel handling equipment.

The PRETERM concept and the product system developed for its implementation were widely adopted by BOCs and independent telephone companies in the last half of the 1970's. PERTERM was a proprietary system with unique advantages over more conventional methods and materials. It was also a system's approach, with the component subsystems and their relationships to each other carefully thought out and well-rationalized. It succeeded because it addressed the strategic concerns of the pre-divestiture telephone companies:

- How to meet the demands for timely service in an explosively growing environment?

- How to control (lower) the cost of constructing new distribution plant to meet those demands?

- How to insure the reliability of the new plant so as to control (lower) continuing life cycle costs?

The developers of PRETERM perceived an acute need of the BOCs. This need occurred at the intersection of strategic concerns: timely service, construction cost and reliability, with explosive growth. PRETERM focused proprietary technology, organized within a systems approach on the need.

THE POST-DIVESTITURE ENVIRONMENT

On January 1, 1984 the BOCs were officially separated from AT&T and the Regional Bell Operating Companies (RBOCs) came into being. There was no more AT&T General Departments to provide planning for the BOCs and direction for Bell Laboratories and Western Electric. Although Western Electric, now called AT&T Technologies, continues to supply the BOCs with a large fraction of their needs, the fraction immediately began to decline and was recently estimated to be less than 60 percent. The Western Electric purchasing and distribution organizations have disappeared leaving the distribution functions of inventory, order fulfillment and accounts receivable to be done by the RBOCs or the suppliers. Procurement organizations were formed by the RBOCs to assume the purchasing responsibility and take over some of the distribution functions. Bellcore was established to replace the research and engineering resource lost to the RBOCs when Bell Laboratories was dealt to AT&T. Bellcore acts as a unifying influence in the establishment of equipment requirements and testing methods used by the RBOCs to evaluate products, but does not approve products for use by them.

The strategic concerns of the post-divestiture telephone companies may be broadly categorized as:

- Deregulation

- Competition

- Market forces

The Modified Final Judgement was the instrument of restructuring and reorganization of the largest single piece of the US telecommunications industry. At the same time the forces of deregulation have been at work to vastly increase the telephone companies' freedom to expand their product offerings and to alter their ways of doing business. "Open Network Architectures" will permit the telephone companies' networks to be used to deliver more and entirely new kinds of communications products. New entrepreneurial companies will spring up to create these products that will stretch the performance capabilities of existing networks to their breaking points. This will be especially apparent in the "local loop", which is still mainly copper wire with its inherent limitations in bandwidth.

The regulators, however, are beginning to consider accelerated depreciation and ending rate of return regulation. This will permit, perhaps encourage, the telephone companies to replace the limiting elements in the network more rapidly. Switching machines are being rapidly converted to digital technology. The long distance network is already almost converted to fiber optics. The next wave of rapid change is occurring in the local loop.

The second major strategic consideration is competition. Three major long distance networks and a number of long distance resellers compete for the long haul business of residential and small business customers. Many private networks have sprung up to support the needs of large businesses. There are many and varied outlets for CPE, and sometimes CPE (private branch exchange) competes with network service (Centrex). A growing number of suppliers compete for nearly half the RBOCs' purchases. The RBOCs have abandoned the sole source concept in favor of the "multi-vendor environment".

A multi-vendor environment is the antitheses of proprietary products. But a multi-vendor environment requires

standards to unify and codify the expression of the telephone companies needs. Bellcore has emerged in a key role in facilitating the creation and promulgation of these standards. Examples of standards likely to have far-reaching effects are ISDN, SYNTRAN and SONET. Bellcore has also published forward-looking generic requirements for products like integrated digital loop carrier (IDLC) to help stimulate the multi-vendor supply of transmission equipment and switches.

Competition results from the operation of a comparatively deregulated market. Market forces are at work to create new products... network services. Technology is added to the network to increase intelligence and capacity. The key technologies of the new network are microelectronics and software, which provide intelligence; and photonics, which vastly increases capacity.

Why do the telephone companies need intelligent, high capacity networks? Such networks can increase revenues; they can handle the new services of the future, voice, data, imaging or combination thereof. They can provide carrying capacity on demand and can be quickly and easily reconfigured to put the capacity where it is needed. They can shorten lead times for new service and for restoring interrupted service. They can be inexpensive in terms of first cost, and, especially in terms of ongoing operations and maintenance costs. They also prepare the network for the future.

The telephone companies are thinking a lot about the future these days. They must do so to assure the continued growth of revenues and profits expected by their new owners. There are only two ways to increase revenues and profits: introduce new products or reduce the costs of providing existing products. To decide what products to introduce and how to introduce them requires strategic planning and marketing. The products which suppliers present to the telephone companies will be intensely scrutinized by these disciplines to determine their compatibility with the new strategic considerations of the post-divestiture environment.

A CASE STUDY: THE OPTICAL DIGITAL LOOP
          CARRIER

Demand for telephone services has always grown at a steady rate. Never has there been more demand for such diverse services as in the post-divestiture environment. The telephone companies' customers want POTS, data, T1, ISDN, local and wide area networks, telemetry, and soon, video and other imaging services. If the telephone companies don't provide these services, their competitors will. Thanks to advances in digital and optical technology, the means to provide these services is available to the telephone companies. One of the means is the expanded use of optical fiber in the loop plant. But the full capability of optical fiber can not be realized without a digital loop carrier designed specifically for the optical fiber media.

Optilink Corporation is a new company which was formed to develop an "optical digital loop carrier". The name of this new product is Litespan 2000^{TM}.

The existing loop plant was simply not designed to deliver many of the new telephone services now being contemplated. Yet telephone companies will find themselves in the new role of distributors of such advanced services. This means new equipment must be added to the telephone plant. But new equipment, no matter how advanced and attractive, must be cost justified on its ability to provide existing services as competitively as current copper wire technology.

The capacity of the Litespan 2000 closely matches the Carrier Serving Area (CSA) design standard used by the RBOCs. This minimizes the overhead costs of delivering advanced services in the areas where these services are most likely to be needed: large urban and suburban CSAs of up to 2000 subscribers and smaller decentralized CSA's consisting of 1 to 3 smaller distribution areas of 200 to 600 subscribers each.

Secondly, Litespan 2000's ability to dynamically allocate bandwidth means it can provide the full range of data rates and formats from POTS to ISDN, DS1, DS3 and beyond, directly to customers who require the services, whenever they require them. The system's central software control, timeslot interchange and SONET signal add/drop capabilities make provisioning of these services flexible, easy, and quickly accomplished. Varying bandwidths can be assigned and reassigned to any channel unit. For example, ISDN and POTS are provisioned the same way and either service can be assigned to any channel unit, reassigned at will, or mixed within channel banks. The result is advanced service capabilities to allow telephone companies to create new products and, consequently, new profits.

But the widespread use of these advanced services will not happen overnight. Neither will it happen uniformly through-out the telephone companies' networks. For these reasons, Litespan 2000 has a modular design which allows the telephone companies to evolve the usage of the system at their own pace, growing into the system's full capabilities as demand materializes.

The system's modularity also provides a high level of reliability and economy of operation. A faulty card is identified by software controlled diagnostics from a central location. Service can also be redirected to a different line card by a software-controlled assignment subsystem. Redundant common electronics and optics can be provided so even the most destructive failures do not interrupt service. A central controller provides constant and complete information regarding system status, including diagnostics, inventory, and provisioning databases.

The Litespan 2000 will allow the telephone companies to provide ISDN and other advanced services without obsoleting existing equipment. It interleaves smoothly with existing digital loop carriers, caps their growth and complements their limited capabilities. It provides the telephone company with the capacity to respond to their customer's need for advanced services, with the intelligence to manage networks of advanced services and with the responsiveness to compete in the new telecommunications market.

The completion of the optical loop carrier case study can not be reported now; it is actually just beginning. Even in the new, fast-paced telecommunications market, the telephone companies are very deliberate about adding new elements to their networks. First office trial installations of Litespan 2000 will occur in at least three RBOCs in the first half of 1989. The job of developing practices and other documentation to enable the RBOCs to introduce Litespan into their networks has already begun and will continue through the trial stages. Full production and large scale implementation is planned for early 1990.

CONCLUSION

Everybody attending this session has survived and some will prosper in the new post-divestiture telecommunications market. In order to prosper, telephone companies must create new telecommunications services products. In order to prosper, suppliers to the telephone companies must recognize and adapt to the changes that have occurred since January 1, 1984. Our customers have become strategic and market-driven in their outlook and fiercely competitive in their behavior. Suppliers must recognize the new strategic concerns of the telephone companies and develop products which address these concerns.

ACKNOWLEDGEMENTS

The divestiture of the BOCs, its consequences and effects has been the subject of many books, papers and articles since the event itself. This author has been fortunate to have read many of these writings and benefited from the knowledge therein. Acknowledgement is made to the

authors of these materials, too numerous
to name here.

Acknowledgement is also made to the
author's colleagues at Optilink who have
read and commented on this paper in draft
form and to my former employer, Raychem
Corporation, for contributing visual aids
which enliven its presentation.

INNOVATIVE NEW PRODUCT PROCESSES

Dennis W. Hamill
Marketing Operations Director
TelComm Products Division

3M Company
P.O. Box 2963
Austin, Texas 78769

ABSTRACT

This paper describes a process for new
product introduction; time tested, proven
and improved over the years at 3M, a
company labeled by some analysts as the
most successful new product company. The
process has its roots in 3M's innovation
environment and depends very strongly on
close contact with customers throughout
the product development cycle. The result
of this process is an ongoing series of
introductions of new products aimed at
meeting customers requirements globally,
but usually driven by a specific
customer's defined needs.

INTRODUCTION

In these times of major rapid changes, new
needs and new problems require new
solutions and new products on time scales
that are more demanding than ever before.
The rapid development of new products
springing from well researched customer
needs is 3M's driving pattern.

The process of new product introduction,
our emphasis in this session, really
begins with a new product concept,
continues through a series of interactions
with key potential customers and ends only
with a satisfied user demonstrating through
ongoing use that the new product works and
adds value to the user. This process
requires innovative people, working in
supportive environments, taking risks,
putting technology pieces together to
solve a well defined need. 3M has, over
the years, developed both a process and
environment to assist those entrepeneurs
to solve a customer's problem.

THE NEW PRODUCT INTRODUCTION PROCESS

3M does make innovation a priority and, in
fact, does drive for excellence in the new
product introduction process. There are
unique aspects of 3M that help the
innovational process, such as our strong
central melting pot of 86 distinct
technologies which contribute to the
variety and versatility of its innovations.
These technologies are applied to 10 major
market segments with strong successful
relationships with customers around the
world. At 3M we consider our partnership
with each customer the ultimate niche
business.

These are the visible attributes of 3M's
focus on products of which we have over
45,000. More fundamental, however, is the
environment for innovation which has been
built and refined over the company's 80
year history. This environment is a
combination of traditional freedoms for
individual action and well based support
systems which together allow an eight
billion dollar company to leverage its
size while operating like a large number
of small companies.

The first crucial aspect of that
environment is our understanding of and
support for the entrepreneurial process.
Most senior management at 3M have had
entrepreneurial successes where they, as
individuals, took risks and acted based on
their own belief in a new technology, a
new market or a new product. They now
protect and defend this environment in
which they thrived. The need to make
mistakes is understood. There is a rule
at 3M, strongly supported, that every
professional person should spend 15% of the
time on work of his or her choice, for
which the individual alone is responsible
and which need not be reported. This
early "scouting" activity is the wellspring
of innovation at 3M. It is here that ideas
are pursued through wrong paths, dead ends,
gestation periods; while the individual
is free from outside judgements and
stifling justification requirements. The
fruits of this work lead to new programs
which are strong enough to stand the
process of peer and management review as
they grow.

Besides the freedom to act, the freedom
for individual growth is assured in 3M by
a dual ladder structure in which growth
through equivalent positions on both the
professional side and the management side
of the ladder is limited only by an
individual's willingness to grasp
responsibility and deliver results.
Corresponding positions are truly
equivalent both in pay and perquisites,
but most importantly in the eyes of all
3Mers. Movement between operating units
to take advantage of growth opportunities
occurs often in this company where growth
spawns new jobs and where experiences in
multiple operating units add greatly to
an individual's 3M education. Recognition
of individuals does both cause and result
from growth in position and responsibility;
but, in addition, is enhanced and
formalized in a number of ways. Broad
exposure of individuals to their peers and
to management throughout the corporation

is assured by a system of technology and technical product audits in all laboratories and by an active organization of the 6000 members of the technical community in a Forum; with regular meetings of over 30 special interest chapters providing a format for technical discipline and technology sharing across organizational boundaries. Very often these interchanges spawn new product activities in divisions resulting from product or technology activities in other divisions totally unrelated in businesses.

Not only are business units and product teams recognized throughout 3M for exceptional achievement, but <u>individual</u> excellence in both the technical and marketing areas is recognized in formal programs that start in each operating division and end in corporate recognition of those individuals. These programs have high visibility and the selection process depends on peer judgement, thus resulting in a high level of credibility and in motivation and inspiration.

Thus, at 3M, individuals are free to act, have the liberty to explore and fail and are encouraged and recognized for their ideas, their inventions, their initiative and their enterprise!

A second major facet of the 3M innovation environment is the autonomy given to the product champion. One of the strongest themes of growth at 3M is the ability of an individual to grow an idea through informal, and then formal stages, until it becomes a stand-alone business project, then a department and then a division, of which there are now 45 at 3M. This process is self-repeating with divisions continuing to spin - off new departments which then become divisions themselves in the grow and divide style at 3M. These divisions each have world-wide responsibility for their business areas and generate their own new product and acquisition activities in support of those businesses.

Each business unit, as it is formed and headed by a champion, includes committed members of the three fundamental arms of each autonomous unit; technical, manufacturing and marketing. Support resources are available, but interference from above is minimal. Support comes from organizations not treated as staff, but as partners, with individuals assigned to that business unit management team. Each support function, in fact, is entrepreneurial as well, with innovation in their service product being key to their success.

These support systems provide the third critical aspect of 3M's innovation environment. The inherent speed and decisiveness of action which stems from autonomy must be supported with enabling

systems if new products are to be brought to market with continually shortening development time targets, but with documentation ensuring highest quality and lowest possible manufacturing cost as well as consistency with the strategic goals of the operating unit and the company.

3M's program management tools are standard and corporate wide. They are simply guidelines for assisting program managers as they both run their programs and choreograph management decisions. There are no specified time lines, only well defined decision points so that the operating division management are involved in the progress analysis and, most importantly, committed themselves, for their functional areas to the next phase in the product commercialization process. At 3M this system is more of a communications assurance process. These phases of concept, feasibility, development, scale-up and standard production work well for the wide variety of products; hardware, software and softgoods, developed each year at 3M.

During the concept stage a variety of individual actions occur; salesmen working their roles as problem solvers with customers, laboratory and marketing people pushing back the barriers to discovery in their respective disciplines and much informal interchange as ideas are tested and challenged by individuals or teams as a product definition is evolved.

During the feasibility phase, sufficient process and market testing is done to determine (again, often in teams, but sometimes by individuals) whether it is feasible that this product can be a successful business for the operating unit. The major risks and investments are made in development and scale-up, but the program management disciplines assure proper involvement of all key players throughout the cycle.

There is no specific reference in our program management system to a <u>product release point</u>. As stated earlier, in fact, product release is the involvement with key customers in the fine tuning of a product concept right up through a series of specific release activities, that parallel the product development and scale-up periods. The most critical activity in the entire process is testing; not just with respect to conformance to specification, both operationally and environmentally, but additionally through testing under real field use conditions. For TelComm this starts with our Field Service Engineers applying the product; field application of reflective decals, for example, applying our reflective sign/ license plate technology to telco symbols for marking outside plant; buried closure installation using an innovative "Armorcast" technology drawn from our health-care bone-setting cast material adapted to the demanding buried environment specifications requiring 40-year life; and fiber optic analogues to copper plant entrance terminals. In every one of these cases user evaluations began "in-house", then moved to specific customer laboratories and then into customer field applications. These trials extend beyond mere ease-of-use and are our means of evaluating effectiveness of our product literature and installation instructions. Practices are followed and critiqued, and improved at each phase of these trials.

The full release of a product to our global markets follows completion of a large number of "check-list" activities which include those mentioned above, but which are designed in total to provide assurance that the same support available to a single pilot customer is available to all customers globally who wish to trial and buy the product. This includes assurance of product in stock, technical support available, all literature and training programs available and a sales organization fully trained itself on the product.

Roll-out is often targeted to coincide with a major industry event where maximum exposure and customer feedback can be achieved quickly. At a major fiber optic showcase six weeks ago, for example, we introduced a revolutionary new mechanical fiber optic splice following all of the activities described here. In this case, sponsorship by interested operating companies of staff evaluation activities was achieved through the early hands-on evaluations by key customers.

One of the best examples of ongoing new product introduction through customer interactions is the outside plant cross-connect product history. We started years ago by responding to customer dissatisfaction with terminal blocks with introduction of a quick-connect block based on our MS^2 punch-down technology. Customer feedback that some situations required a more rugged, less craft sensitive solution led to our introduction of binding post blocks in cross-connect cabinets. Finally, customers demanded the ease and ruggedness of binding post with the contact reliability of insulation displacement contacts, and we have introduced our new self-strip blocks which provide a sealed, automatic cut-off, uniform contact every time with a 90° turn of a screwdriver. In this case, again besides exhaustive testing of the contacts, blocks and cabinets in accelerated aging and environmental as well as performance testing, actual simulated box-loading jumper running tests were run in our labs and then in telco situations through an independent test organization. These resulted in proof-by-use of the product concept and led to full product release in a short time.

A tool of growing importance at 3M, and a crucial application in my division's speedy development of new molded products like connectors, is Computer Integrated Manufacture. By Computer Integrated Manufacture, I mean the integration of computer aided design and computer assisted manufacture together with the business data necessary to schedule and produce the designed product. Complex parts, such as pluggable modular connectors, can be designed and tested for pluggability before any parts are fabricated. When the part is determined to be correct and is simulated to satisfaction, the data base is transferred to mold generation equipment and contact stamping and forming equipment where molds and dies are fabricated automatically. Finished parts are produced with the elimination of at least one interactive prototyping cycle and time to finished production parts and products is decreased dramatically. Both mechanical and electronic design at 3M are now done on CAD and the links to manufacturing are in place. This adds to our ability to react to fine-tuning the product through this product introduction process.

CONCLUSIONS

Successful introduction of new products requires disciplines, innovative product management, and tight coupling to the ultimate users of the product. The process at 3M is one of allowing great freedom for individuals while giving them support systems they can draw on to bring their products through to success with customers. While strategies and investments in opportunities differ between operating divisions at 3M, every division every year must have at least 25% new product sales; that is, sales of products which didn't exist five years earlier. This is one of 3M's four stated financial objectives. The objectives for individuals and customer relationships are demonstrated over and over in our successful new product introductions

THE TECHNICAL AND MARKETING

ASPECTS OF INTRODUCING NEW PRODUCTS TO

THE COMMUNICATIONS INDUSTRY

Zak Manuszak
National Marketing Manager
U.S. Telecom

Raychem Corporation
300 Constitution Drive
Menlo Park, California 94025

ABSTRACT

This paper and topic describes how we as professionals working in the Communications industry should respond to and deal with the opportunities we have in introducing new technology-cum-new products into the current communications network. Over the past four years external market factors have forced Regional Operating Companies to look beyond centralized research and development resources which traditionally linked end-users with product developers and suppliers. Internal R&D resources, although deep in technical understanding, were somewhat limited in scope of technical capabilities. In response to this opportunity generated by Federal Regulations brought on by antitrust legislation since 1984, end users and suppliers have gone through dramatic, albeit profound, changes in the way they interact with one another, particularly in the arena of new product development and introductions.

These changes promise to have a major impact on our industry not only in determining which products and technologies are integrated into the marketplace, but more importantly, on the long-term side, how end-users and suppliers are becoming partners in determining the future of how we do business with one another. This is generating a cultural change between customer and supplier. What was once a laborious, almost tortuous process of selling products to a Telco has now become an alliance of resources from both the perspective of the Telco as well as the supplier. More and more, Telcos are looking to vendors to solve their technical problems with cost effective solutions in order to reduce their overall operating expenses thus making them more profitable and better able to compete in providing communications services in a global economy.

INTRODUCTION

Opportunities for new or improved products arise virtually everyday in the communications industry. These opportunities require innovation as well as enhancements in technology, design, materials science, etc. Bringing materials technology and product design together with a specific technical need generates a process which in the past was tedious and time consuming, that now has proven to be most effective in coupling problems with effective solutions. That is, linking the end-user, the Telco, together with suppliers in not only innovating a solution to a problem but in introducing that particular solution within the confines of the Telco as well as to the rest of the industry. Hence we see the relationship between buyer and seller becoming a partnership in product innovation and introduction, as well as a vehicle for future product developments and subsequent commercialization.

This paper will delineate the technical and marketing aspects of how new products are developed and then introduced within the Telecom environment by focusing in on a particular problem within a Telco and how a solution (product) was developed which not only resolved a specific issue, but also opened the door for further product development and innovation in related applications and technologies.

We will see how a particular technology in the field of environmental sealing, nominally Gels, can be applied in the context of product design and application in developing an entire product line which not only led to solving a Telco's particular noise problem but also drastically reduced maintenance costs over a period of a few months and subsequent months following. The ultimate goal of the Telco!

We will look at the process and time involved to develop the final commercial product by first looking at the various stages of prototypes designed along its evolution into today's product line. This is important in order to understand the aspects of the process employed, both technical as well as commercial, which eventually led up to the product's final design, value to the customer, product position and price structure, product acceptance and approval, and customer use.

In today's marketplace, this same process or others very close to this are constantly being utilized for the development and introduction of new or related product lines employing gels sealing as one of their major features in product design. Of note on this particular point is that once the customer has convinced himself that this technology is the optimum solution to his current problem, he need not convince himself time and time again that the same technology can be applied to similar problems in different situations. Merely by enhancing or improving product design or via alternate application techniques, solutions can be innovated from a new but proven technology. In short, the customer believes that this technology of sealing (i.e. Gels) is better than any other technology (sealing) that may be available to him at this time. Hence, when environmental sealing is a desired objective, the end-user knows that he wants gels. He already has become your partner regarding this concept as well as your technical ally.

Although the case study in this paper focuses on the process of how a particular gel product was developed and introduced, there will be several points brought to light relative to the roles and responsibilities of both the end-users, the Telco, and the supplier in innovating and introducing new technology via new products. It goes without saying that we will discuss the belief that technical and product change drive business forward.

Nothing could be truer given the culture in the current Communications environment.

WHEN ADVERSARIES BECOME PARTNERS

Prior to 1984, marketing to the Bell System and the major independents was more than a challenging task. The culture that existed within the industry was not as conducive to open communication either commercially or technically. Telco Network Planning was determined many times without the benefit of the various and diverse enterprises which were capable of assisting, funding and supporting certain tactics and maneuvers in growing the business. Any cognitive, long range planning by users and suppliers was done exclusive of one another's philosophies, capabilities, objectives, etc. Although directly interrelated as buyer and seller, OTC's, product developers, manufacturers and suppliers were more adversarial than allies. Simply stated, the industry was not benefiting from the technical and commercial resources that a venture between users and suppliers could generate.

Since 1984, the Communications industry has experienced historic changes. The most significant of these are of course the giant leaps in optical transmission coupled with advances in microelectronics, increased competition, and the proactive desire to be a market-driven industry. Corporations of all sizes and diversions are all paying much closer attention to outside forces in the marketplace. They are listening to customers and suppliers, and to each other; partner or competitor. This has created a more external, market-driven industry. This cultural shift has also produced dramatic changes in relationships between customers and suppliers. The long standing adversarial relationships between buyer and seller are becoming a partnership of capabilities. Increased competition, and Telco cost-reduction programs have forced end-users to seek suppliers who can produce and deliver better, quicker, higher quality products at a lower total cost.

Along this same line, supplier competition for market segments has also driven manufacturers to take renewed interest in the quality, design, cost, and delivery schedules of their products to their customers. This not only requires innovation in product development but in product manufacturing processes as well.

Given the similarity in the objectives of both end-user and supplier and the current industry culture, alliances are being formed which bring customer and vendor together in strategic partnerships. These ventures get people thinking alike in achieving a common goal. Specific customers become targeted market segments due to their needs and objectives. Vendors become favored suppliers because of their capacity and commitment to innovate cost-effective solutions to end-user needs. Both partners benefit enormously from the alliance in respect to both immediate goal achievement as well as toward future collaborative efforts. It is this partnership which maximizes the contribution new technology via new product introductions bring to the industry. It is ipsofacto that no one succeeds without the support and assistance of others. This is indigenous to our laissez-faire culture and becoming more apparent in our global economy where so many industries are interwoven at various disciplines within their infrastructures. Hopefully, these ventures between users and suppliers drive the industry toward a more beneficial and favorable state of affairs for the entire marketplace.

PRODUCT LIFE CYCLE

Before getting into the different yet dynamic roles and responsibilities of both customer and supplier in our case study, a brief look at a rather mundane marketing concept is prerequisite. The concept of product life cycles has been around forever. (Who coined the term is unknown. Obviously not someone at any Telco.) It's nothing to get overly excited about, yet it should be the cornerstone of product and marketing strategies of any enterprise which markets or distributes products or services (See Figure 1). (This should cover just about every type of business in the private sector.) As mentioned earlier, product change drives business forward. Any business which recognizes the venerable axiom that "things change" should be deeply involved in capitalizing on that change and the best way to capitalize on change is to 1) understand that market needs are volatile and, 2) position your market strategy in order to cope with and respond to changing needs. It is important also to understand that needs can contract as well as expand at different periods during the market cycle.

As specifically related to this discussion concerning new product innovation and introduction, simply stated, new products should be tailored to be inherently suited to market volatility. This is a process which must be started early after the product need is identified in order to incorporate this adaptability as soon as possible during the product's development phase (See Figure 2). This assures that the necessary features will be designed into the product which allow for future enhancements, upgrades, downgrades, ulterior applications, etc...What this means in the long run is that the marketplace benefits from the full potential of a given technology and specific product design to the maximum, thus avoiding short-term obsolescence which is very costly to both customer and supplier.

It is noteworthy also, in understanding that every product has a predictable life cycle. The maxim reads... <u>nothing</u> <u>lasts</u> <u>forever</u>. Recent research done at the Massachusetts Institute of Technology shows that the appeal of most products is from 7 to 10 years or slightly less. Now this cycle can be slightly shorter or longer depending on the industry involved, but on average 7 years seems to be approximate. It is this writer's opinion from personal research as well as experience that the current Telecommunications industry produces product life cycles of 5 to 7 years (Figure 1). What this means is that early on in the life cycle of an existing product, ideas for future product enhancements or new product concepts should be entertained as well as innovated. Customers and suppliers should begin work on new models or designs before existing ones show their age (See Figure 3). As allies in new product introduction end-users and vendors should get one another looking beyond the current product applications and successes and think in terms of "life cycles"...to focus on the next generation of products. This leads to a degree of cognizant effort being put into future market planning for tomorrows challenges. The moral of all this discussion on product life cycles is again to optimize product design and introduction in order to maximize the contribution of new technology in the marketplace.

The graph in Figure 3 may look complex, but the thought behind it is simple...if you are not looking to develop something new you are living on borrowed time. Time where product obsolescence means reduced revenues and diluted market presence for the supplier, but also the inefficient use of resources for the end-user, thereby reducing his capacity to compete, his competitive edge. Both customer and supplier are in a sense retrenching instead of competing as well as they can.

The whole process of product life cycle planning is of course a dynamic concept. The cycle should never end. (Unless of course one choses not to compete in a particular market). The success of how poorly or how well companies employ the product life cycle concept can be ascertained by looking at your industry leaders in a particular market segment. As a matter of fact, leaders in almost any human endeavor employ the latest techniques, technology, information, etc... Anything that gives them a competitive edge. It's axiomatic. Remember the whole idea is to compete with all the resources you can...You'll need them. The application of this concept of life cycle planning as well as the aspects of new product innovation and introduction will be expounded upon in the following sections of this paper when we review the roles and responsibilities of customers and suppliers in bringing a new product to the marketplace. The discussion will focus on how a specific new technology such as "Gels" gets integrated into product designs and eventually introduced into the marketplace.

GELS TECHNOLOGY

In the communications industry, particularly related to Outside Plant, environmental protection is the key for various components that constitute the Network. This is especially true when we consider the effects that moisture have on the electrical components of the network. A category of materials which are classified as GELS offer many advantages over more traditional materials used for providing environmental protection.

A gel can be described as a highly swollen macromolecule. It is differentiated from a solution state by virtue of a process known as crosslinking (See Figure 6). The crosslinks are induced either physically, by hydrogen bonding via electron beam radiation exposure, or chemically. For example, Flexgel, which is used for filling telephone cables, is an example of a gel material. Gels can be formulated and produced with a varying range of material properties which allow them to be used as environmental sealing materials and can be integrated into product designs whose objectives are to provide substantial environmental sealing but which are also re-enterable and reusable. Material properties such as adhesive and cohesive strength are important for the proper gel composition given a specific application.

From Figure 6 you will note that the gel state of a macromolecule has discerning properties from a solution vis-a-vis the ability of a gel to move freely. The macromolecular structure of the gel has restricted movement. The molecular chains no longer move as units and are unable to change positions within the structure. This restricted movement gives gels the distinctive physical property that they do not flow. The gels will wet and seal like a liquid yet they behave like solid bodies relative to their elasticity.

The desired degree of movement can be controlled by the polymer concentration employed as well as the polymer structure. Therefore gels of different polymers will offer different degrees of movement or stiffness for a given concentration.

It should also be noted that movement is also restricted by the degree of cross-linking in the macromolecule. The greater the number of crosslinks, the smaller the possibility of movement. By increasing the number of crosslinks, the gels become harder and tougher, or more brittle as the case might be. Again, this depends on the type of polymer and the concentration level of the polymer.

In summary, gels can be described as materials which are; a) macromolecules in the swollen state, b) Which do not flow, yet are deformable, and c) exhibit elastic properties similar to elastomers.

ADVANTAGES OF GELS

Many types of materials are used in the Communications industry for environmentally sealing components in Outside Plant. They range from the application of greases to curable two part resin systems. Examples of each are used daily by thousands of technicians in the industry. Greases are employed by various types of wire connectors and two part resins are used exclusively in buried filled closure applications. Grease systems tend to be easily installed yet are limited by poor environmental sealing under compression. The grease tends to "flow" out from its containment device particularly with increased temperature exposure. Also, greases have no elastic memory and tend to behave as liquids rather than elastomers. Re-entry is also a messy, unclean, "greasy" experience.

Two part resin systems are limited in that they require a mixing and filling process. They also have shelf life and are craft sensitive during application. They allow re-entry but result in somewhat of a "destructive" experience.

On the other hand, gels can be viewed as soft elastomers. They are deformable under compression and give a very good seal. Gels can deform to their elastic limit and are good void fillers in applications. They exhibit excellent temperature properties and have indefinite elastic memory. Therefore, removal of the compressive force causes the gel to retract. For use in the communications industry gels provide the benefits of excellent electrical properties, have good molecular stability, and generate a good environmental seal.

FROM GEL TO PRODUCT

Gels have been around the communications industry since the early 1970's. The one application we are all most familiar with of course, Flexgel cable filling compound, has already been mentioned. Beyond this, not very much Gel Technology has been integrated via new product introduction since then. This fact however, excludes what has been introduced into the marketplace over the past five years by several new product innovations within the industry. For the sake of our discussion here we will focus primarily on one of these product lines, a gel filled device for environmentally sealing terminal lugs, called TermSeal™ (See Figure 7).

Any interconnect point is one of the most problematic components of the Outside Plant Network. Nothing could be truer when it comes to terminals. The metallic nature of terminals makes them very vulnerable to corrosion problems resulting from humidity, salt or chemical sprays, fog, flood conditions, industrial pollutants, dust contaminants, etc. Insects and vermin also have access to building, buried, and aerial terminal housings. The occurrence of insect nests and webs between or among terminal lugs is quite a common source of trouble reports. This very problem was the source of a cost reduction program which generated the innovation of the TermSeal™ gel device.

Figures 4 and 5 depict the case history of how the TermSeal product was innovated and eventually introduced. The timing basically parallels the idea and development phases of the product life cycle process shown in Figure 2.

The duration of innovation and introduction processes took approximately 24 months from the definition of the market need, through the product idea conceptualization, and then eventually leading to the commercialization of the TermSeal™ product line. It is omitted from the graphical representation of this product introduction, but the manufacturing scale-up procedures usually take place during year two of the product life cycle. Exactly when depends upon how technically complex the manufacturing processes are as well as upon the market demand for the product, and design sophistication. For clarification regarding the TermSeal™ product introduction, manufacturing scale-up took place between months eighteen and twenty-four.

The overriding events in the product innovation and introduction procedures which quickly deemed the product a success in the eyes of both the customer and supplier were that the prototype designs worked so well in testing as well as field trials that the customer immediately saw reductions in maintenance costs wherever the gel devices were installed. The prototype designs had been so well defined that initial testing established the products capabilities as well as application limits. These parameters far exceeded the requirements identified by the Corrosion Task Force.

Major field testing took place in a harsh industrial environment near a salt water coastline. The area is defined as one which is highly vulnerable to corrosion caused by salt air and fog, chemical, as well as flood water exposure. The results of this field trial are shown in Table 1. They show that over a period of five months the trouble report rate was reduced by over 70%! This generated a gross savings of $60,360 on a total installed cost of $23,298, or a net savings of $37,062. You can see how these types of results brought some wide-eyed attention to the TermSeal product line. In actuality, the trouble report rate dropped immediately from month 1 to month 2 of the field trial by almost 50%! It is this kind of product innovation and introduction which reduces the overall cost to compete and drive our industries forward in the current global economy.

Since the product was first introduced, TermSeal has found its way into virtually every major OTC in the United States. Various international PTT's and Telcos are evaluating the gel devices' merits for their networks. Suffice it to say that literally millions and millions have found their way to environmentally seal and protect the communications networks at home and abroad.

PARTNERSHIP PROCESS

It is important to note here in the paper, after reviewing our gel technology case study, that the roles and responsibilities of each partner in this process, both customer and supplier, are still distinct by definition, yet are very much inter-related and always converging based on desire to compete. What has taken place in today's communications environment is that there has been an alliance of resources in order to solve a specific problem or achieve a stated objective.

This alliance between customer and supplier should begin as early as possible in the product life cycle and always conclude in an orientation position ready for the next opportunity. Prior to this litigated evolution in the communication industry culture, customer and vendor behaved more like Reagan and Gorbachev, out to achieve the same objective but by different means. Things were just out of sync!

Figure 8 depicts a flow chart diagram of the partnership process as it relates to the major points of interreaction between the customer and supplier. The first interaction stage is based upon the business philosophy of each enterprise. Each entity, customer and supplier, must identify the common ground between them. The second stage will require resource sharing and understanding the capabilities of one another. The third stage, mutual task and funding interaction, is where the job really gets "done" (or doesn't get done as the case might be!). Finally, the solution is carried forward into the marketplace where commercial leveraging factors proliferate the solution through-out the industry.

CONCLUSION

The introduction and proliferation of gel technology-cum-gel products has benefited tremendously from a communications environment which is qualitatively different from what proceeded it. Customers and suppliers have positioned themselves to see that the next generation of products conclusively solve the limitations of their forerunners. And that as partners in this industry, they have committed themselves to serve the rapid growth together. And we all know that partners work harder than employees.

ACKNOWLEDGEMENTS

Special acknowledgement goes out to Dr. Keith Dawes, Mr. Chris Debbaut and Dr. A.A.P. Sutherland for their work in gels technology over the past few years as well as their contributions in consultation for this paper. In particular, the author would like to recognize Ms. Emily Hope, Mrs. Chris DeNoyo and Mr. Mark Toomey for their dedicated and compassionate assistance in compiling the information contained herein.

REFERENCES

Harvard Business Review, March/April 1988

Thriving on Chaos, Tom Peters

Passion for Excellence, Tom Peters

In Search of Excellence, Tom Peters

The Microelectronics Race, (excerpts) by George Gilder, (1988 release)

Inc. Magazine, Issues January 1988 - July 1988

Business Week Publication, Issues January 1988 - July 1988

Marketing Masters, Lessons in the Art of Marketing, Paul E. Brown

Telephony Publications, May-June, 1988

Corporate Combat, William E. Peacock

TNS, The New Salesmanship, Steve Salerno

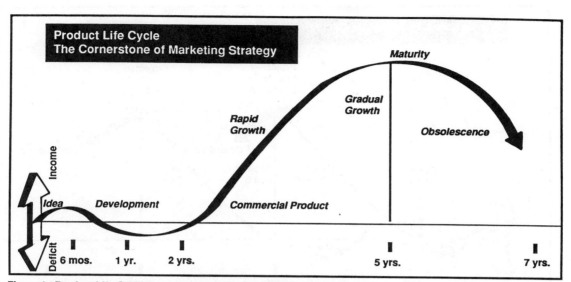

Figure 1 - Product Life Cycle (assume 7 years from conception to obselescence)

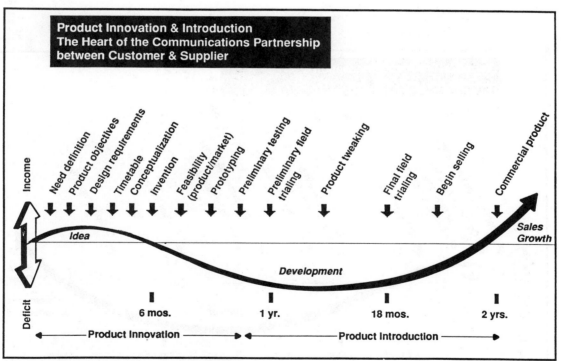

Figure 2 - Idea and Development Phase of Product Life Cycle

1444

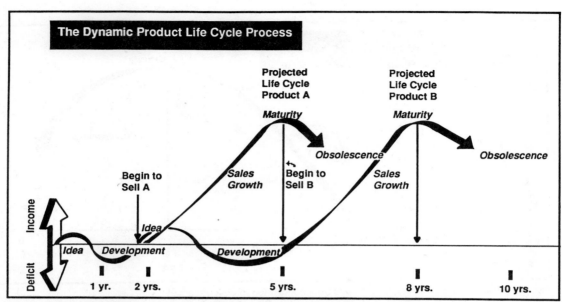

Figure 3- Product A is beginning to be sold. Ideas and enhancements for its replacement are already underway...
When it reaches its maturity, Product B will then be introduced. (Based on 7-year life cycle.)

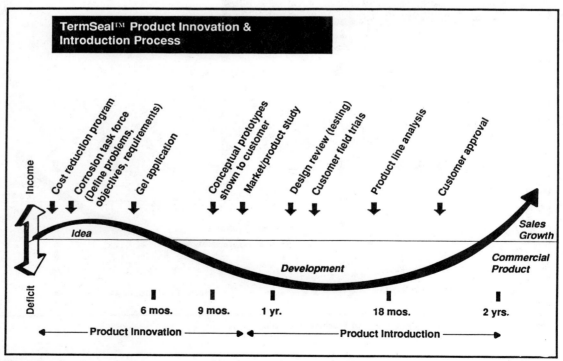

Figure 4

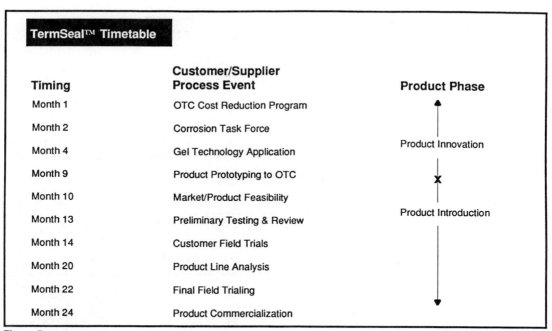

TermSeal™ Timetable

Timing	Customer/Supplier Process Event	Product Phase
Month 1	OTC Cost Reduction Program	
Month 2	Corrosion Task Force	
Month 4	Gel Technology Application	Product Innovation
Month 9	Product Prototyping to OTC	
Month 10	Market/Product Feasibility	
Month 13	Preliminary Testing & Review	Product Introduction
Month 14	Customer Field Trials	
Month 20	Product Line Analysis	
Month 22	Final Field Trialing	
Month 24	Product Commercialization	

Figure 5

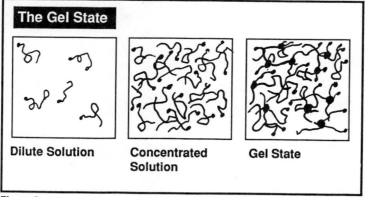

The Gel State

Dilute Solution   Concentrated Solution   Gel State

Figure 6

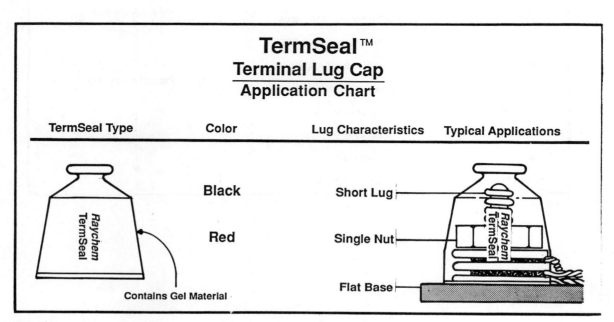

TermSeal™
Terminal Lug Cap
Application Chart

TermSeal Type	Color	Lug Characteristics	Typical Applications
Raychem TermSeal — Contains Gel Material	Black Red	Short Lug Single Nut Flat Base	

Figure 7

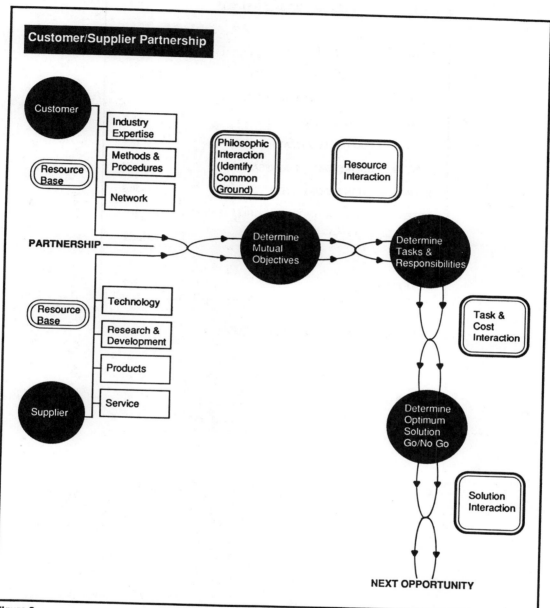

Figure 8

1448

```
┌─────────────────────────────────────────────────────┐
│              TERMSEAL FIELD TRIAL                    │
│                                                      │
│            COST /SAVINGS  ANALYSIS                   │
│                                                      │
│                                                      │
│   TOTAL NUMBER OF LINES                      1,000   │
│                                                      │
│   TOTAL REHAB COST USING TERMSEAL         $ 23,298   │
│                                                      │
│   TROUBLE REPORT RATE PER 1000 LINES                 │
│                                                      │
│     - MONTH 1 (BEFORE TERMSEAL)               68.7   │
│                                                      │
│     - MONTH 6 (AFTER TERMSEAL)                18.4   │
│                                                      │
│   COST OF LABOR/REPORT = $100.00/EA                  │
│                                                      │
│   IMPROVEMENT IN REPORT RATE                  50.3   │
│                                                      │
│   POTENTIAL GROSS SAVINGS (50.3 x $100 x 12 Months) $ 60,360 │
│                                                      │
│   REHAB COST                              $ 23,298   │
│                                                      │
│                                                      │
│     NET SAVINGS                           $ 37,062   │
└─────────────────────────────────────────────────────┘
```

TABLE I. - TERMSEAL FIELD TRIAL ECONOMICS

Managing the Product Life Cycle

Martin H. Singer, Chairperson
Director of Marketing, Communications Systems

Tellabs, Inc.
4951 Indiana Avenue
Lisle, Illinois 60532

Abstract

Life cycle management varies for different types of Telecommunication products. Increasingly, software products (e.g., Network management) and services (ACCUNET; MEGASTREAM; WATS) represent the bailiwick of the telecommunications product manager. Pricing, feature enhancements, and rules for upgrading these products are important elements to managing the life cycle of these "products" as well as the more traditional products in our industry.

Separate reviews on the management of hardware, software, and service products will be delivered in this session with a focus on the aforementioned variables. Network Management software, T1-based services, and voice transmission products will be specific areas of discussion.

William D. Schindel - - Applied Computing Devices

Arthur R. Meierdirk - -   Tellabs, Inc.

Walter B. Blackwell - - Telecom Canada

Planning the Life Cycle: Special Problems of Software Intensive Products

William D. Schindel
President

Applied Computing Devices
100 North Campus Drive
Terre Haute, Indiana 47802

Abstract

The life cycle of any product can be influenced by the planning of enhancements, pricing changes, and service. Software products are particularly amenable to these influences and can realize long life spans if planned correctly. Methods for influencing their life cycle will be reviewed.

Managing Product Life Cycles - A Mature or Declining Market

Arthur R. Meierdirk
Group Product Manager, Network Access Systems

Tellabs, Inc.
4951 Indiana Avenue
Lisle, Illinois 60532

Abstract

THE PURPOSE OF THIS PAPER IS TO DISCUSS THE MANAGEMENT OF PRODUCTS DURING THEIR MATURE OR DECLINING LIFE CYCLE. THE MANAGERIAL PROBLEMS ENCOUNTERED DURING THESE STAGES CAN BE VERY DIFFERENT FROM PREVIOUS BUSINESS EXPERIENCE AND ARE QUITE OFTEN TERMINAL. THE FOCUS WILL BE ON PRACTICAL EXPERIENCES RATHER THAN TEXTBOOK THEORY. IN MY EXPERIENCE, UNDERSTANDING THE PHASES OF A PRODUCT'S LIFE, SHIFTS IN CUSTOMER ATTITUDE, AND VARIABLES FOR FORECASTING ARE ESSENTIAL TO SUCCESS IN A MATURE OR DECLINING MARKET. I WOULD LIKE TO EXPAND ON THOSE TOPICS AND FINISH WITH STRATEGIES FOR SUCCESS IN THIS VERY TOUGH MARKET.

PHASES OF A PRODUCT'S LIFE

THE FIRST STEP IS TO CATEGORIZE THE PHASES OF A PRODUCT'S LIFE. THE TERMS "PIONEERING", "GROWING", "MATURING", AND "DECLINING" REPRESENT THE ACTIVITIES EXPERIENCED.

PIONEERING IS THE FIRST PHASE OF A PRODUCT'S LIFE. IT IS PROBABLY A BRAND NEW TECHNOLOGY OR APPLICATION OF TECHNOLOGY. THE CUSTOMER HAS TO BE SOLD ON THE TECHNOLOGY, APPLICATION, HARD-WARE, SUPPLIER, ETCETERA. IT IS A VERY LONG SALES PROCESS, FULL OF OBSTACLES AND SETBACKS. THIS MARKET IS, HOWEVER, AN UNTAPPED MARKET WITH (PROBABLY) NO COMPETITORS. THIS IS USUALLY LEADING EDGE" TECHNOLOGY, OF GREAT INTEREST TO THE CUSTOMER, AND OFFERS THE POTENTIAL FOR GREAT SUCCESS. EMPLOYEES ARE EXCITED BY THE OPPORTUNITIES AND NEWNESS OF THE MARKET.

GROWTH MARKETS BEGIN WHEN PIONEERING ENDS. CUSTOMERS BELIEVE IN THE VALUE OF THE PRODUCT OR SERVICE OFFERED TO THE EXTENT THAT DEMAND EXCEEDS SUPPLY. THIS MARKET COULD SUPPORT MANY COMPETITORS SUCCESSFULLY. BUSINESSES IN THIS MARKET ENJOY PROFITS AND OPPORTUNITIES FOR EMPLOYEE ADVANCEMENT GENERATED BY GROWTH. EMPLOYEE MORALE IS PROBABLY FAIRLY HIGH, THERE IS CONFIDENCE IN MANAGERIAL SKILLS, AND COMPETITORS MAY BE ON FRIENDLY TERMS. COMPANIES MAY EXPERIENCE MOST OF THEIR SUCCESS IN GROWTH MARKETS.

MATURE MARKETS RESULT WHEN THE AGGREGATE MARKET STOPS GROWING. ALL POTENTIAL CUSTOMERS ARE IDENTIFIED, UNTAPPED MARKETS REACHED, AND APPLICATIONS COVERED. AT THIS TIME, SUPPLY EQUALS

DEMAND. IT IS NOW TOUGHER TO EXPAND YOUR BUSINESS , GROWTH MUST COME AT THE THE EXPENSE OF A COMPETITOR. BUSINESS MANAGEMENT SKILLS BECOME INCREASINGLY IMPORTANT SINCE YOU NO LONGER HAVE GROWING REVENUES TO MASK POOR BUSINESS DECISIONS. WITH THE MARKET SIZE CLOSING IN, SOME SUPPLIERS MAY BEGIN PRICE CUTTING TO KEEP MARKET SHARE. CONFIDENCE IN MANAGERIAL SKILLS MAY BEGIN TO ERODE, OPPORTUNITY FOR EMPLOYEE GROWTH MAY BE REDUCED, AND KEY EMPLOYEES MAY BE VULNERABLE TO "HEADHUNTERS". EMPLOYEES WHO ARE MOST SUCCESSFUL IN A PIONEERING OR GROWING MARKET MAY NOT BE SUCCESSFUL IN A MATURE MARKET, CONSEQUENTLY, THEIR MOTIVATION MAY SUFFER. AT THIS POINT, COMPETITORS ARE BEGINNING TO SENSE HOW TOUGH THE MARKET WILL BECOME.

DECLINING MARKETS ARE THE RESULT OF SIGNIFICANT CHANGES IN CUSTOMER DEMAND. THERE HAS BEEN A SHIFT IN TECHNOLOGY, FASHION, THE ENVIRONMENT, ETC. THAT IS CAUSING A SERIOUS DECLINE IN DEMAND. THE SUPPLY OF PRODUCTS USUALLY EXCEEDS DEMAND. THIS DISCREPANCY IS OFTEN THE RESULT OF MANAGEMENT'S RELUCTANCE TO CUT FORECASTS AND CORRESPONDING BUDGETS IN THE BELIEF THAT, "WE CAN STILL MAKE IT HAPPEN". IN ADDITION, SOME CUSTOMERS MAY REACT TO PRICE CUTS BY SHOPPING AROUND MORE. THIS INCREASED ACTIVITY IS OFTEN MIS-INTERPRETTED AS REAL DEMAND AND CORRESPONDING FORECASTS ARE ENTERED. THE RESULTING INCREASES IN INVENTORIES BECOME A GREAT CONCERN TO MANAGEMENT. EXPECT INTENSE COMPETITION IN THIS MARKET PLACE. THE SHRINKING REVENUE BASE, EXPANDING INVENTORIES, AND PREDICTIONS OF THE END OF THE MARKET WILL CAUSE SERIOUS PRICE CUTS AND A FLURRY OF SALES ACTIVITY. BUSINESSES ARE NOW LOCKED INTO A BITTER BATTLE WHERE THE WINNERS MERELY SURVIVE AND LOSERS DIE! A VERY SERIOUS THREAT TO THE HEALTH OF YOUR BUSINESS IS THE POTENTIAL LOSS OF MANY KEY MANAGEMENT, SALES, AND SUPPORT PERSONNEL. THERE ARE USUALLY SOME SERIOUS CHALLENGES OF MANAGERIAL SKILLS OR DECISIONS, LOSS OF ADVANCEMENT OPPORTUNITY, HIRING FREEZES, LOSS OF LONG-TERM GOALS, AND MORALE DROPS TO ZERO. ALL THIS MAKES YOUR BUSINESS A GREAT RESOURCE FOR EMPLOYMENT AGENCIES.

IT IS IMPORTANT TO RECOGNIZE THE DIFFERENCES IN EACH OF THE PRODUCT LIFE CYCLES AND ANTICIPATE THEIR EFFECTS AS A BUSINESS MOVES FROM ONE TO THE NEXT. MANY OF THE STRENGTHS THAT LEAD TO SUCCESS IN ONE STAGE MAY ACTUALLY BE A HINDERENCE IN THE NEXT.

FORECASTING IN MATURE/DECLINING MARKETS

FORECASTING PRODUCT DEMAND IS A VERY BASIC MARKETING FUNCTION.DETERMINATION OF THE TOTAL MARKET POTENTIAL, EXPECTED ANNUAL SALES, PERCENT OF MARKET SHARE, OUTSIDE INFLUENCES, AND OTHER VARIABLES ALL GO INTO FORECASTS. ERRORS IN FORECASTING RESULT IN EITHER EXCESS OR INSUFFICIENT INVENTORY AND THEIR CONSEQUENCES.THESE INVENTORY FLUCTUATIONS ARE A CONCERN IN ALL BUSINESSES,BUT ARE A MORE SERIOUS PROBLEM IN A MATURE OR DECLINING MARKET.SINCE THE PRODUCT'S LIFE IS NEARING THE END OF ITS CYCLE, THERE IS THE DANGER THAT INCORRECT FORECASTS WILL LEAD TO OBSOLETE PRODUCT INVENTORY THAT MUST BE WRITTEN OFF.CUSTOMERS, ON THE OTHER HAND, WILL HAVE FEW SUPPLIERS FOR THESE PRODUCTS AND WILL BE VERY DISTRESSED BY SUPPLY SHORTAGES.

ALTHOUGH I DO NOT INTEND TO DISCUSS FORECASTING IN DETAIL, THERE IS ONE ASPECT OF FORECASTING THAT IS ESPECIALLY IMPORTANT WHEN WORKING IN A MATURE OR, MORE IMPORTANTLY, DECLINING MARKET. WHETHER A PRODUCT IS A PERISHABLE OR NON-PERISHABLE HAS A VERY SERIOUS IMPACT ON PURCHASES AND A DRAMATIC EFFECT ON THE LIFE OF ITS MARKET.PERISHABLES ARE PRODUCTS THAT CANNOT BE REUSED. CONSUMPTION IS SUCH THAT THE USED PRODUCT HAS NO VALUE IN THE MARKET-PLACE. ANNUAL USAGE OF THESE PRODUCTS SHOULD EQUAL TOTAL ANNUAL DEMAND. NON-PERISHABLES, ON THE OTHER HAND, HAVE A POTENTIAL RE-USE MARKET. THE RE-USE OF THESE PRODUCTS POSE NEW VARIABLES INTO THE FORECASTING PROCESS. SINCE THESE PRODUCTS CAN BE REUSED, THE PRESENCE OF THE INSTALLED BASE BECOMES A NEW SOURCE OF PRODUCTS IN A DECLINING MARKET. EACH UNIT THAT IS REMOVED FROM SERVICE MAY BE PLACED IN THE CUSTOMERS INVENTORY FOR USE IN PLACE OF A NEW UNIT YOU MAY HAVE ALREADY FORECAST AND PUT IN INVENTORY.IN A DECLINING MARKET, IT IS ENTIRELY POSSIBLE FOR REUSE TO EQUAL TOTAL DEMAND FOR NEW PRODUCTS. AT THIS POINT, ALTHOUGH THERE IS DEMAND FOR THE PRODUCT, THERE MAY BE NO DEMAND FOR NEW PRODUCTS.

STRATEGIES FOR MATURE/DECLINING MARKETS

WITH ALL THESE VARIABLES IN MIND, LET'S FOCUS ON STRATEGIES FOR MARKETING IN A MATURE OR DECLINING MARKET. SOME COMPANIES MAY EXIT AS SOON AS A MARKET MATURES, SOME WILL STAY UNTIL PROFITS DWINDLE, AND ONLY A FEW WILL ATTEMPT TO STAY UNTIL "THE END". REGARDLESS OF WHICH STRATEGY IS CHOSEN, THERE WILL BE A DAY THAT ALL VENDORS WILL EXIT FROM A DECLINING MARKET, THE ONLY QUESTION IS WHEN IT WILL OCCUR. EACH CHOICE REQUIRES PREPARATION AND CONTROLS TO MAKE TRANSITIONS AS SMOOTH AS POSSIBLE WITH LITTLE IMPACT ON YOUR CUSTOMER BASE.EXITING FROM THE MARKET AS SOON AS IT MATURES ALLOWS YOU TO AVOID MANY OF THE PROBLEMS ASSOCIATED WITH TOUGH MARKETS.MANY ENGINEERING DRIVEN COMPANIES USE THIS STRATEGY; DEVELOP A NEW TECHNOLOGY, SELL THE CONCEPT, BE A MARKET LEADER AND THEN, WHEN GROWTH SLOWS, INTEREST WANES, AND PROFITS DWINDLE, THEY APPLY RESOURCES TO NEW TECHNOLOGY. IT IS PRIMARILY A MATTER OF MARKET ANALYSIS AND FORECASTING. BY REMAINING IN ONLY PIONEERING AND GROWING MARKETS, OPPORTUNITIES ABOUND, THE FUTURE LOOKS BRIGHT, AND EMPLOYEE MOTIVATION REMAINS HIGH. UNFORTUNATELY SOME OF THE CUSTOMERS MAY BE TAKEN BY SURPRIZE WHEN PRODUCTS ARE SUDDENLY DROPPED FROM PRODUCTION. THIS COULD LEAD TO FUTURE PROBLEMS WHEN TRYING TO SELL THESE

SOME COMPANIES ELECT TO STAY IN THE MARKET THROUGH THE MATURE STAGE AND WELL INTO THE DECLINE. THESE COMPANIES MAY FORECAST THE DECLINE AND SIMPLY FOLLOW THE DOWNWARD TREND, EXITING AT SOME PREDETERMINED POINT IN REVENUES OR PROFIT. TO MAINTAIN PROFITABILITY, ONLY PRODUCTS WITH GOOD PROFIT MARGIN OR HIGH VOLUME CUSTOMERS CAN BE MAINTAINED. THIS CAN LEAVE SOME CUSTOMER NEEDS UNSATISFIED AND FORCE THEM TO LOOK TO YOUR COMPETITORS FOR OTHER PRODUCT NEEDS. THESE COMPETITORS WILL

ALSO PURSUE YOUR HIGH VOLUME PRODUCTS, SO PRICE WARS COULD BE AN EXPECTED CONSEQUENCE OF NOT BEING A FULL-LINE VENDOR. WHEN PROFITABILITY DECLINES TO THE MINIMUM ACCEPTABLE LEVEL, SELL OFF THE INVENTORY AND EXIT THE MARKET. AGAIN, THIS MAY LEAD TO THE SAME CUSTOMER PROBLEMS THAT SIMPLY EXITING EXITING THE MARKET WOULD HAVE CAUSED.

KEY SUPPLIERS

THERE IS ROOM, IN A DECLINING MARKET, FOR ONE OR TWO KEY SUPPLIERS. THESE SUPPLIERS WILL HAVE TO PROVIDE A FULL LINE OF PRODUCTS OR SEVICES FOR THEIR CUSTOMER'S NEEDS. ALTHOUGH DEMAND FOR THEIR PRODUCTS MAY HAVE DECLINED, SPECIFIC CUSTOMER NEEDS ARE AS CRITICAL NOW AS EVER. MANY VENDORS HAVE SOLD OFF INVENTORY, REDUCED PRODUCT OFFERINGS, AND "TURNED THEIR BACK" ON SOME CUSTOMER NEEDS. COMPANIES THAT INTEND TO REMAIN IN THIS MARKET AS A KEY VENDOR WILL NOT BE ALLOWED TO USE THESE OPPORTUNISTIC STRATEGIES. THEY MUST PROVIDE FULL MARKET SUPPORT TO EARN THEIR POSITION. THIS IS A MUCH MORE COMPLEX PROCESS WITH SEVERAL CRITICAL OBJECTIVES TO BE REACHED.

INDUSTRY LEADER

FIRST, ESTABLISHMENT OF THE POSITION AS AN INDUSTRY LEADER MAY BE REQUIRED TO CONTROL AS MUCH MARKET SHARE AS NECESSARY TO BE PROFITABLE IN THIS MARKET. IT MAY BE NECESSARY TO REACH FIFTY TO SEVENTY PERCENT OF THE TOTAL MARKET TO REMAIN PROFITABLE.ATTAINMENT OF THIS LEVEL OF CREDIBILITY MAY REQUIRE SUPPORT AS A CONSULTANT TO BOTH THE INDUSTRY AND THE CUSTOMERS. IN ADDITION, HIGH QUALITY PRODUCTS AND SERVICES WILL HAVE TO BE OFFERED.

MARKET CONTROL

CONTROL OF THE MARKET IS VERY IMPORTANT TO SUCCESS IN THE DECLINING MARKET. MANY "ILLEGITIMATE" SUPPLIERS WILL BE REDUCING INVENTORIES BY SELLING ONLY KEY PRODUCTS OR KEY ACCOUNTS, OR CUTTING PRICES TO GRAB MARKETS. THESE ACTIVITIES ARE A SERIOUS THREAT TO A FULL-LINE SUPPLIER AND ANY CHANCE FOR PROFITABLE SALES. STRATEGIZE TO ELIMINATE THESE KINDS OF COMPETITORS BY USING TECHNOLOGY, QUALITY, SUPPORT, AVAILABILITY, OR (AS A LAST RESORT) PRICE.COMPANIES HAVING GREAT ENGINEERING RESOURCES AVAILABLE MAY BE ABLE TO DESIGN PRODUCTS THAT CREATE TECHNOLOGICAL PROBLEMS TO ANY COMPETITORS THAT MAY TRY TO ENTER THE MARKET. IN LINE WITH THIS STRATEGY IS QUALITY. IT MAY BE POSSIBLE TO SELL CUSTOMERS ON LEVELS OF QUALITY IN PRODUCTION PROCESSES THAT ARE IMPOSSIBLE FOR COMPETITORS TO MEET WITHOUT MAKING SIGNIFICANT INVESTMENTS IN CAPITAL AND/OR TRAINING. ANOTHER STRATEGY WOULD BE TO FOCUS ON BEING A FULL-LINE SUPPLIER. SOME COMPANIES HAVE A GOOD HISTORY OF PRODUCT SUPPORT, HIGH QUALITY SERVICE, AND PRODUCT AVAILABILITY. FOCUSING ON THESE FUNCTIONS AND GETTING CUSTOMERS TO DEMAND THIS FROM ALL VENDORS MAY KEEP SOME OPPORTUNISTS OUT OF THE MARKET.PRICE COMPETITION SHOULD ALWAYS BE A LAST RESORT SINCE IT REDUCES YOUR ABILITY TO IMPLEMENT THE PREVIOUS STRATEGIES AND MAY GIVE COMPETITORS MORE CREDIBILITY. THERE ARE TIMES, HOWEVER, WHEN THE QUICKEST WAY TO ATTACK A COMPETITOR IS WITH PRICE. THE MOST LIKELY TARGET WOULD BE A FINANCIALLY VULNERABLE COMPETITOR. CHOOSING A KEY ACCOUNT AND USING A LOW PRICE TO GET ATTENTION MAY SUCCEED IN EITHER GETTING THE BUSINESS OR CAUSING THE COMPETITOR TO CUT ITS PROFITS. EITHER RESULT WILL CAUSE GREAT CONCERN TO SHAKY COMPETITION AND HOPEFULLY REDUCE THEIR INTEREST IN THE MARKET. QUITE SIMPLY, PRICE SHOULD BE USED TO TAKE KEY ACCOUNTS FROM SELECT COMPETITORS BUT, ONLY AS A LAST RESORT. IT IS DOUBTFUL THAT "INDUSTRY LEADERS" WILL BE ABLE TO SUPPLY THE REQUIRED QUALITY AND SUPPORT AND, AT THE SAME TIME, USE PRICE-CUTS TO CAPTURE SALES.

DESIGN CHANGES

PRODUCT DESIGN CHANGES MAY ALSO BE NECESSARY TO STAY COMPETITIVE IN A DECLINING MARKET. UNIVERSAL PRODUCTS, ONES PROVIDING MULTIPLE FEATURES ON SINGLE PRODUCTS, ARE ATTRACTIVE TO THE CUSTOMER AND THE VENDOR. MODULAR DESIGN OF THE PRODUCT SHOULD ALSO BE CONSIDERED AS IT MAY REDUCE INVENTORY REQUIREMENTS AND MAKE IT EASIER TO RECOGNIZE APPLICATIONS. THIS IS VERY IMPORTANT SINCE THERE WILL BE FEWER AND FEWER "EXPERTS" AVAILABLE FOR APPLICATION/SALES ENGINEERING. OTHER REDESIGNS MAY BE NECESSARY TO REDUCE BOTH MANUFACTURING LABOR AND PIECE-PARTS COST IN PREPARATION OF THE PRICE WARS THAT MAY FOLLOW. ESTABLISHMENT OF A POSITION AS THE MARKET LEADER WILL ATTRACT CHALLENGES FROM CUSTOMERS AND COMPETITORS ALIKE. THE PRODUCT SHOULD BE OF A QUALITY TECHNOLOGY, AND PRICE ONE WOULD EXPECT FROM THE INDUSTRY LEADER.AS DISCUSSED EARLIER, REUSE OF EXISTING PRODUCTS MAY REACH THE POINT THAT THEY EQUAL THE DEMAND FOR NEW PRODUCTS. IF USED PRODUCTS ARE ACCEPTABLE, THERE IS A SERIOUS DANGER THAT ALL NEW PRODUCT SALES WILL END. TO PROLONG THE NEW PRODUCT MARKET, SOME VALUABLE FEATURES WILL HAVE TO BE ADDED TO THE PRODUCT TO PROVIDE DIFFERENTIATION FROM REUSEABLE PRODUCTS. IN THIS WAY, EVEN THOUGH THE REUSE PRODUCTS ARE "FREE", THE FEATURES OF THE NEW PRODUCTS ARE VIEWED AS WORTH THE NEW INVESTMENT. THE MOST LOGICAL FEATURES TO ADD WOULD REDUCE INSTALLATION AND MAINTENANCE COSTS SINCE THEY ARE EASIEST TO COST JUSTIFY. OTHER ENHANCEMENTS MUST BE CAREFULLY RESEARCHED AS ANY R&D SPENT ON DECLINING MARKETS MAY HAVE LIMITED REWARDS WITH HIGH OPPORTUNITY COSTS.

EMPLOYEE CONSIDERATIONS

THE FINAL CONSIDERATION IS THE EMPLOYEE. THE KEY PEOPLE ARE ESPECIALLY VULNERABLE TO TURNOVER IF THEY SEE NO FUTURE FOR THEMSELVES. THEY ARE AWARE OF REDUCED BUDGETS, HAVE HEARD PREDICTIONS OF FURTHER MARKET DECLINES, AND MAY SEE LITTLE FUTURE FOR THEMSELVES. EMPLOYEE MOTIVATION WILL BE DIFFICULT IN THIS KIND OF ENVIRONMENT AND KEY PEOPLE ARE OFTEN FIRST TO GO SINCE THEY HAVE THE MOST OPPORTUNITY. SPECIAL EFFORTS WILL BE NECESSARY TO PROVIDE THE PERSONAL GROWTH AND LONG-TERM GROWTH MOST EMPLOYEES NEED. MANAGERS SHOULD BEGIN PLANNING BEYOND THEIR CURRENT DECLINING MARKET. UNLESS THE COMPANY WILL SIMPLY "GO OUT OF BUSINESS" WHEN THE MARKET FOR CURRENT PRODUCT ENDS, THERE MUST BE PLANNING FOR THE FUTURE PRODUCTS. KEY PEOPLE ARE PROBABLY PLANNED TO MOVE INTO THOSE MARKETS, MANAGEMENT OFTEN FAILS TO CONVEY THESE PLANS TO THOSE INVOLVED. SIMPLE COMMUNICATION REGARDING LONG-RANGE GOALS AND PLANS CAN HELP REDUCE THE RISK OF LOSING THE PEOPLE MANAGEMENT NEEDS FOR THE FUTURE.MANY OF THE CURRENT PEOPLE ARE DEVELOPING SPECIAL SKILLS THAT WILL BE OF VALUE IN THE FUTURE. ONE OF THE CHARACTERISTICS OF MATURE/DECLINING MARKETS IS INTENSE

COMPETITION. MANAGERS THAT HAVE SUCCESSFULLY COMPETED IN A DECLINING MARKET PROBABLY DEVELOPED MANY SOLID BUSINESS SKILLS. THESE MANAGERS HAVE EXPERIENCED A WIDE VARIETY OF BUSINESS PROBLEMS THAT HAD TO BE SOLVED; THERE WERE NO "GROWTH REVENUES" TO COVER MISTAKES. MANAGERS SHOULD TAKE THESE SKILLS INTO ACCOUNT AND PLAN TO MAKE BEST USE OF THESE SKILLS FOR FUTURE MANAGEMENT OPPORTUNITIES.IN CASES WHERE THE MARKET DECLINE IS CAUSED BY A NEW TECHNOLOGY, THE CUSTOMER MAY HAVE TROUBLE KEEPING UP WITH THE CHANGE. THIS IS OFTEN OVER-LOOKED BY MANAGEMENT AND MARKETING PEOPLE. THE TIMES HAVE CHANGED, BUT THE CUSTOMER IS HAVING TROUBLE KEEPING UP WITH THE CHANGES. THE EMPLOYEES MARKETING THE CURRENT "OBSOLETE" TECHNOLOGY MAY SERVE AN IMPORTANT FUNCTION BY ACTING AS A "BRIDGE" BETWEEN THE NEW AND OLD PRODUCTS. WHEN "FAMILIAR VOICES" EXPLAIN THE TRANSITION FROM THE "OLD TO THE NEW", IT MAY BE MORE READILY RECEIVED. TO ACCOMPLISH THIS, EMPLOYEES WILL NEED TRAINING FOR THEIR NEW POSITIONS AND, AT THE SAME TIME, CONTINUE AT THEIR CURRENT POSITIONS. THIS HIGHLIGHTS THE IMPORTANCE OF MAKING DESIGN CHANGES TO MATURE/DECLINING PRODUCTS TO MAKE THEM EASIER TO ADMINISTER AND THUS FREE UP EMPLOYEE TIME FOR LEARNING NEW TECHNOLOGIES OR APPLICATIONS.THIS FOCUS ON EMPLOYEES MAY HELP MOTIVATION AND REDUCE TURNOVER BY IDENTIFYING OPPORTUNITIES FOR PERSONAL GROWTH AND A LONG-TERM FUTURE EVEN THOUGH THE MARKET IS ON THE DECLINE.

SUMMARY

WE LOOKED AT FOUR PHASES OF PRODUCT LIFE CYCLES; PIONEERING, GROWING, MATURING, AND DECLINING.

EACH HAS DIFFERENT CHARACTERISTICS FOR FORECASTING, MANAGING, CUSTOMER EXPECTATIONS, COMPETITION, AND EMPLOYEE MOTIVATION. IN A MATURE OR DECLINING MARKET, FORECASTING AND EMPLOYEE MOTIVATION ARE OFTEN OVERLOOKED. WHEN FACED WITH THE PROSPECT OF A MATURE MARKET, A STRATEGY FOR MARKETING MUST BE CHOSEN. EXIT IMMEDIATELY, STAY IN UNTIL PROFITS DWINDLE, OR PLAN TO BE THE KEY PLAYER FOR THE LONG-TERM.THE CHOICE SHOULD REFLECT BOTH THE LONG-TERM ORGANIZATIONAL GOALS AND BE COMPATIBLE WITH THE HISTORY IN THE MARKET.

Managing the Services Life Cycle

Walter B. Blackwell
Director, Service Planning and Development

Telecom Canada
160 Elgin Street
Floor 23G
Ottawa, Ontario PS K1G3J4

Abstract

Megastream, a public network T1 offering in Canada, has been managed as a service that competes with private network offerings. Services have life cycles that must be managed in ways that ways that are both similar to and different from products. Specific experiences with Megastream will be discussed.

MANAGING LIFE CYCLE COST OPTIMIZATION

Jo Anne H. Miller - Chairperson
Head, Small Computer Development
and Management Department

AT&T Data Systems Group
1100 E. Warrenville Road
Naperville, IL 60566

ABSTRACT

As concerns with both customer focused quality and corporate productivity and profitability rise, managing all aspects of product cost over the complete product life cycle becomes increasingly important. Life cycle costs include those that are expended in the design, development, manufacture, sale and customer arenas. How these are dealt with during the life span of a product and the interactions between these components are dealt with in this seminar. The customer view of life cycle cost optimization as well as the development and manufacturing issues are addressed. An informal panel will conclude the seminar.

Donald Jester   -- Rockwell International

Jo Anne Miller   -- AT&T Data Systems
                     Group

Burgess Oliver   -- Northern Telecom Inc.

Roger Patel   -- AT&T Network Systems

E911 SYSTEM
LIFE CYCLE COST OPTIMIZATION
THROUGH PRODUCT DESIGN

Don J. Jester
Manager, Product Line Planning

Rockwell International
Downers Grove, IL 60515

ABSTRACT

This paper addresses life cycle costs by considering the impact that knowledge of a system's cost elements can have on product design. The example system is an area E911 service, chosen because of the author's familiarity with 9-1-1 systems, and because they involve a wide range of expenditures over their life cycle, not atypical of other large telecommunications systems.

SYSTEM DEPLOYMENT

Increasingly, states are recognizing the value of providing uniform 9-1-1 policies together with providing methods of funding 9-1-1 systems. At present, thirty states have pending or in-force legislation promoting 9-1-1, with provision for local or state funding to establish service. The most common funding mechanism is through a surcharge on phone bills, authorized for collection by the local exchange carrier on behalf of the state. Application of collected monies varies, but generally includes first costs for new network equipment, database equipment, plus database creation and maintenance. Also covered may be answering point equipment, and more infrequently, telephone trunking charges and answering point personnel charges.

Regardless of whether supported through a funding mechanism or not, the cost items mentioned above are necessary in all E911 systems. Product designs that reduce these costs while maintaining high service levels benefit all parties.

9-1-1 DEFINED

There are a number of 9-1-1 system arrangements, here briefly described to aid understanding of cost and design factors.

The common feature of all 9-1-1 systems is the ability of a citizen to reach a trained public safety agency call taker by dialing the digits 9-1-1, instead of needing to remember a seven digit number that changes for each community and often for each agency within a community.

Early systems used an arrangement that has become known as Basic 9-1-1. Many are in operation today. Exhibit 1 depicts a basic system composed of end offices in the served area, each capable of recognizing the dialed digits 9-1-1 and forwarding all such calls to a predesignated answering point. Ringback, called party hold, switchhook monitor, and forced disconnect are common features in basic systems. They give the call taker some control over the call and some ability to determine the originating location if the calling party doesn't provide it (through ringback and call trace).

Hybrid systems are recognized in many current pieces of legislation. They provide two very useful additional features; ANI and ALI. ANI, or Automatic Number Identification, is the ability of an end office to forward the calling parties' phone number to the Public Safety Answering Point ("PSAP") for display to the answering call taker. ALI, or Automatic Location Identification, is the provision of a data record for each telephone number in the served area, which contains the address (location) of the telephone, class of service, name of business or in some cases residential occupant at that address, and names of the serving public safety agencies. These records may reside in a central database serving all communities in the area or they may be distributed, with storage, at each answering point. If distributed, there is generally a master centralized database that downloads the distributed units. ALI records are accessed using the calling party ANI as a key. A hybrid system is shown in Exhibit 2. Note that end offices still directly forward calls to a single answering point.

In handling 9-1-1 calls, speed and accuracy are essential. Speed in call handling means getting the call to the point where it can be responded to as rapidly as possible. Where central office and jurisdiction boundaries do not coincide, the calls of some subscribers in basic and hybrid systems will go to the wrong answering point. The call must then be transferred to the proper point, typically where the emergency vehicles are dispatched. Enhanced 911 systems add a third feature to ANI and ALI; Selective Routing. Selective Routing gets calls to the proper jurisdiction by routing them through a second switch acting as a tandem. The caller's ANI is passed from the end office to the tandem, which uses it to select a route from translation tables maintained within it. The tables contain a list of all served telephone numbers with the proper answering point route for each number, and with alternative routes should the initial be blocked. The ANI used to route the call is then passed forward to the answering point for use as in a hybrid system. Exhibit 3 shows an Enhanced 9-1-1 (E911) system arrangement.

Some larger answering points (perhaps 15 or more answering positions) enjoy additional benefits by using an ACD to distribute the calls. The ACD may be dedicated to 9-1-1 service in the very large centers. For smaller centers an ACD adjunct to an existing PBX is often used. Networked ACD is beginning to be offered for 9-1-1 service, provided from the same tandem that provides the selective routing. Regardless of the source of service, FIFO treatment of calls, equitable distribution between answering personnel, detailed traffic reports, and administrative tools are distinct advantages of ACD systems.

RELATIVE LIFE CYCLE COSTS

With the preceding information as reference, relative costs of providing elements of an E911 system can be examined. Exhibit 4 provides a rank ordering of life cycle cost elements for a hypothetical model of a moderate-sized system, consisting of a central metro area and its surrounding suburbs and counties. The system is fully Enhanced throughout, with a single E911 tandem routing all calls, and a centralized ALI database serving this and a number of other such areas. Ongoing costs are combined using discounted present worth of future expenditures over a medium term (say 5 years) planning horizon. Only incremental costs are considered.

The model is not intended to represent a particular area. Indeed, any cost could easily move one or two positions in relative ranking depending on circumstances. However, the table depicts a typical situation with enough fidelity to permit inferences. Note also that the list contains only direct out-of-pocket costs. Other less tangible costs, but nonetheless important costs, are considered later.

LIFE CYCLE COST ANALYSIS

There is a tendency to focus on hardware elements when discussing 9-1-1 system costs. However a large portion, in some cases over half of all expenses, is for personnel and a significant amount of these costs pertain to database creation and maintenance. The combined capital and expense costs associated with the ALI database can be more than half the total. Since ALI data and selective routing tables - a by-product of ALI creation - are the fundamental benefits of Enhanced 9-1-1, it seems appropriate that the bulk of the costs support these primary benefits of the service. However, an examination of costs can lead to concepts for products or aspects of product design, which can reduce them without affect on service.

The largest cost element is often the initial creation and purification of the ALI records. Generally, the first step is to extract relevant fields from an existing database; the local exchange carrier's customer records or, in some cases, other utilities' data. Whichever the source, purification is a major effort. Purification is the resolution of incorrect record entries such as billed-to address rather than physical address, OPX, stations behind PBXs, and so forth. The target is better than 97% accuracy at cutover. To achieve this takes much legwork, but powerful database utility packages can help. Alias file tools, rapid sorting and searching routines, and good human/system interfaces are examples of features that can reduce the average purification hours per record while promoting accuracy. And, these same features aid in the ongoing maintenance of the data. ALI database vendor's literature typically highlights user features such as record layout and comment capability which are important, but more attention could be paid to the design and benefits of support tools.

ALI database hardware is itself a large proportion of a system's total cost. In the example table, the ALI system capital is assumed allocated between a number of served areas, say three to five. To allocate the total cost of an entire database machine to one area might offset the benefit of even such an important service. However, the local carrier must develop tariffs using a conservative view which can mean allocating ALI equipment of large capacity to an area or areas requiring only a fraction of it. Modularity is a key factor in addressing this first cost. Systems which can start small and be easily expanded as capacity needs increase have a distinct advantage. Currently ALI databases are physically and administratively separate entities. Ultimately ALI data can be integrated into master line information databases serving the Intelligent Network. This evolution will lead to significant cost savings through sharing of administrative overheads.

The master routing guide or MSAG (Master Street Address Guide) is the document that assigns each address in the served area to a specific set of agencies, one agency of each type (law, fire, medical). What might seem a trivial task of creating an MSAG is typically not so. Many locations do not have precise addresses, streets are not known by their "official" names, and there is often disagreement on jurisdictional boundaries, especially for medical services. Mechanization is not as potent here. Helpful items include a clear plan and useful job aids. These are best developed from experience. The consultant, or local carrier acting as a consultant, can be of great help in doing things right the first time.

Answering point equipment benefits from advances in technology. Electronics improvements can reduce not only first costs, but also maintenance and sparing life cycle costs. A key factor in optimizing costs is again modularity. If a large amount of fixed capacity common equipment is needed, smaller suburban answering points will pay substantially more per position than will larger ones. Some totally modular equipment is now available, but it is limited in the maximum number of positions that can be interconnected. This means having a second type of equipment for the few large centers, an additional life cycle expense. The best solution is modular units that can grow from one to a very large number of positions without common equipment overhead.

A tandem switch, or an adjunct performing tandem services from a Class 5 office, is the only current means of providing selective routing on an area basis. Off-premises extensions from a PBX or ACD are used for limited transfers, but no CPE system, to the author's knowledge, automatically selectively extends calls based on incoming ANI. Intelligent Network (IN) deployment may eliminate the tandem function per se, but it is relatively far off. In the interim there is significant social benefit to deploying E911 systems now. The optimization requirement is in being able to migrate to IN without a complete reinvestment.

Other tangible expenses constitute a relatively small part of total life cycle costs. Some can be reduced as a by-product of other improvement, such as with ALI support mechanization. Others, such as call-through test expense, are intrinsically reduced with better ALI and translation data at the beginning of the test.

OTHER COSTS

Beyond tangible costs are a set of others that must be considered in E911 product design. Because E911 systems deal with saving human life there is a very high opportunity cost of not completing the mission. Emergency call handling effectiveness is not measured in the same way as inbound information service or telemarketing applications, where the emphasis is on saving parts of a second per call. Rather, the emphasis is on call handling accuracy and on reducing the stress of the call taker.

A factor in achieving improved accuracy is in the human factors design of the call-taking position equipment. Under stress there is less tolerance for remembering complex key sequences. A larger number of single purpose keys, each unambiguously labeled, aids in producing correct actions, especially for infrequently used commands. A large number of customizable keys is an aid to accommodating the unique aspects of an answering point's operation without resorting to complex command sequences.

Another factor which must be considered is fallback or workaround arrangements to deal with failure of each element of the system. Products designed to complement these plans are first highly reliable and second provide alternate service capability. For example, a commercial-powered position console that reverts to battery or telephone line power if necessary, and with provision for switching to an alternate local line, reduces the risk of employing it as the sole interface for 9-1-1 calls.

CONCLUSION

Knowledge of the life cycle costs of deploying a system can aid vendors in reducing those costs through product design. In this case the optimization of costs is from the user's point of view. In E911 systems, as with others, cost optimization is not simply a matter of minimization. There are less easily quantified, but nonetheless real, factors that enter into the decision. Exhibit 5 summarizes the factors discussed in this example.

BASIC 9-1-1

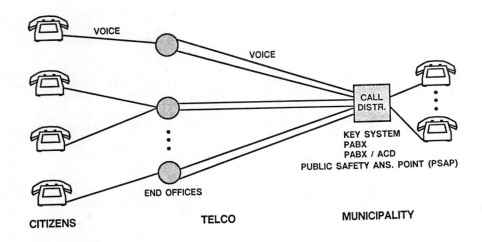

EXHIBIT 1

MS1249

HYBRID 9-1-1

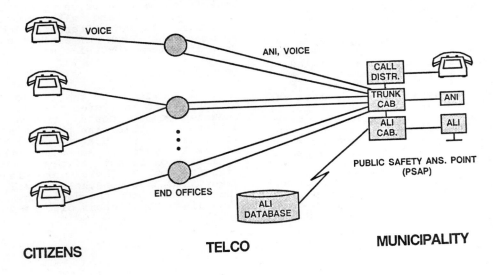

EXHIBIT 2

MS1250

ENHANCED 9-1-1

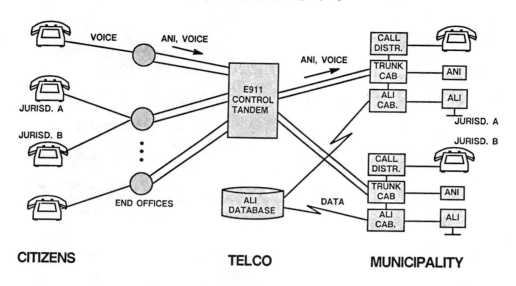

CITIZENS   **TELCO**   **MUNICIPALITY**

MS1251

EXHIBIT 3

RELATIVE LIFECYCLE COSTS
E911 SYSTEM

COST ELEMENT	PERCENT TOT. L.C.C.
CREATE AND PURIFY ALI RECORDS	18
ALI DATABASE EQUIPMENT – ALLOCATED	16
ANSWERING POINT EQUIPMENT	15
PREPARE AND VALIDATE MASTER ROUTING GUIDE	12
TANDEM SWITCHING EQUIPMENT	10
ALI RECORD MAINTENANCE	8
END OFFICE (ANI) EQUIPMENT	5
MASTER ROUTING GUIDE MAINTENANCE	5
TRANSFER CALLS TO APPROPRIATE SECONDARY	5
CALL THROUGH TESTING	3
NETWORK ADMINISTRATION AND BILLING SERVICES	3

MS1252

EXHIBIT 4

E911 SYSTEM DESIGN ASPECTS
INFLUENCED BY KNOWLEDGE OF LIFECYCLE COSTS

COST	DESIGN
ALI RECORD CREATION	DATABASE TOOLS
ALI DATABASE EQUIPMENT	EQUIPMENT MODULARITY
ANSWERING POINT EQUIPMENT	EQUIPMENT MODULARITY
TANDEM SWITCHING EQUIPMENT	AUTOTRANSFER FROM CPE
OPERATION ERRORS	SINGLE KEYPRESS COMMANDS
OPERATION ERRORS	CUSTOMIZABLE KEYS
SYSTEM FAILURE	ALTERNATIVE SERVICE MODE

EXHIBIT 5

MS1253

MANAGING THE COST OF THE TELECOMMUNICATION SYSTEM

Roger R. Patel
Senior Engineer, New Product
Review & Long Range Planning -
5ESS® Switching Equipment

AT&T Network Systems
2600 Warrenville Road
Lisle, IL 60532

ABSTRACT

In today's cost-conscious and competitive environment, the cost of the telecommunication system has, in a real sense, become one of the most important management challenges of the 1980s. The cost of the electronic components is the dominant factor in a telecommunication system and hence, complex selection scenarios confront the designer, purchaser, supplier, and equipment manufacturer in their striving for the highest possible quality component for the lowest cost. Thus, the cost of the telecommunication system becomes the lifeblood for the profitability and needs a staff of innovative professional management.

Over the past 3 years, a group of professionals called "Cost Management Engineering (CME)" at AT&T Network Software Center have developed and implemented many technical and management procedures. They have made significant contributions to the profitability of AT&T Network Systems Equipment Division (NSED) during their short tenure. The success of CME has primarily been accomplished through the following three Product Realization Processes (PRP):

1. Product Review Team (PRT) - focuses on activities dealing with product modeling and content analysis.

2. Cost Management Engineering (CME) - encompasses a cradle-to-grave viewpoint of all critical design decisions, along with a product development cycle.

3. Component Utilization Committee (CUC) - brings prime focus on all aspects of the component cost reduction.

This paper analyzes the subset of the functions and organizations that deal most directly with these three PRPs of Cost Management.

INTRODUCTION

Over the past 10 years, the electronic component industry has experienced continued expansion in their product offerings. This has been fueled by technological advances and global business expansion. Most high technology telecommunication systems have been designed with new state-of-the-art electronic components and, hence, they are more material intensive rather than the labor. Due to the competitive digital switch market, much attention in the last 5 years has been given to the system cost, and in a real sense, it has become one of the most important management challenges of the 1980s. As a result, a complex selection scenario confronts the designer, purchaser, and equipment manufacturer in their striving for the highest possible quality component for the lowest cost.

Over the past 3 years, a group of

professional CME, both at AT&T Bell Laboratories and Network Software Center, have contributed a significant cost reduction to the components through many special technical and management procedures. The success of effective cost management of CME has become increasingly recognized as a critical ingredient in the development and manufacture of the AT&T Network System Equipment Division products as shown in Exhibit 1. This paper emphasizes the subset of the functions and organizations that deal most directly with Cost Management.

COST MANAGEMENT THROUGH PRODUCT REALIZATION PROCESS

Cost Management itself may be defined as the acquisition, distribution, maintenance, and control of the cost contents of a particular product so that the organizations that play a role in the Product Realization Process have the product cost information they need to do their part. A second aspect of Cost Management is tracking and overseeing product cost and maximizing profitability primarily through value engineering and cost improvement.

The success of Component Management, through which many savings are effected, has been accomplished through the following three Product Realization Processes:

1. PRT - focuses on activities dealing with product modeling and content analysis.

2. CME - encompasses a cradle-to-grave viewpoint of all critical design decisions, along with a product development cycle.

3. CUC - brings prime focus on all aspects of the component cost reductions.

PRT AND PRODUCT MODELING

The primary element needed to manage the cost is the identification of the cost contents of the product during its life cycle. The prime function of the PRT Group is to engineer a typical annual average model of a product including design changes and cost improvement, if any, for 3 to 5 years. A software system called "Cost Analysis and Product Evaluation" (CAPE) has been developed to aid in the periodic review of cost progression and price implication for the current and future planning horizon.

Basically, CAPE manipulates the three main files - Design Master, Part Cost, and Labor Value - and generates a variety of reports shown in Exhibit 2. A brief description of the contents of these files is as follows:

1. Design Master: This file contains various assemblies and lists the components/parts and their quantities per assembly [i.e., Bill of Material (BOM)]. It is important

to know the design evolution for at least 3 to 5 years. This requires the identification of the development milestones of the major subsets and generation of BOMs accordingly.

2. Component/Part Cost: This file includes the part number, source, and cost of all assemblies and parts. The expected cost trends and/or the cost of any cost-reduced substitute must be identified for at least 3 to 5 years.

3. Labor Value: This file contains the number of manufacturing hours at each process assembly stage along with the appropriate loaded rates.

Based on the typical model configuration, cost improvement model for 3 to 5 years is developed.

COST MANAGEMENT ENGINEERING

CME is a professional component engineering discipline which encompasses a cradle-to-grave viewpoint of all critical component cost-related decisions along with a product development cycle. Major responsibilities of CME are focused on six areas: a) identify high-cost impact components, b) identify cost reduction opportunity and risk, c) fund cost reduction developments, d) prepare executive overview, e) negotiate financial profitability forecasting, and f) monitor progress. The details of these functions are highlighted as follows:

Identify High Cost Components

This can be obtained by three sources:

1. Identify top 59 to 100 components from the CAPE cost report which would typically be 80 to 90 percent of the total product cost;

2. Manually obtain the component forecast and incurred cost and identify top 50 to 100 components; or,

3. as a worst case, obtain Bill of Materials and circuit pack requirements for the product and compute the component needs, and subsequently obtain the incurred component cost and then identify top 50 to 100 components.

Identify Cost Reduction Opportunity and Risk

The key to identifying the cost reduction opportunities is to apply systematic value engineering, cost improvement, and purchase economy techniques for a variety of alternatives to each high cost component. To complement this process, CME has developed a novel approach.

This approach has proven to be

simplistic, yet highly effective. The cost of any expensive component can be reduced by analyzing its cost content and selecting an alternative through one of the alternatives listed in Exhibit 3.

Furthermore, CME assesses the probability of success for each cost-effective alternative so that its development can be prioritized. Three common probabilities of success used are: H (High) - most likely, M (Moderate) - likely, and L (Low) - most unlikely.

Fund Cost Reduction Developments

A unique funding procedure called "Cost Reduction Development Management" (as shown in Exhibit 4) was established to provide the funding needs for the Laboratories' cost reduction developments. This procedure is similar to traditional AT&T Engineering Cost Reduction procedure; however, it applies primarily to designs/products requiring less than 2 years' development for a cost-reduced design change initiated by the Laboratories' designers. There are five major areas in which the design changes occur, those being - custom device shrink (i.e., VLSI), technology upgrade, functional consolidation (i.e., smart shrink), improved manufacturing yield and performance enhancement.

As a part of administrating the developments, CME can become involved in several areas: economic evaluation/ justification, approval of development funds from Product Line Management (PLM), authorization of the development through purchase orders, and monitoring and administration of the cost reduction development and its funds.

As a result of this work, typically a ten fold return has been achieved on expenses versus savings.

Prepare Executive Overview

The cost of the telecommunication system drives the profitability of the corporation. Therefore, a senior management-level committee has been organized to review and resolve critical decisions which impact profitability. In order to assist the committee, CME has prepared a document which summarizes the overall system cost improvement plans in a very concise format. Typically, 3 to 5 years of cost improvement plans are documented in this book. The major 1987 cost improvement resolutions were Film Wound versus Ceramic Capacitor, Optical Data Links, Multilayer Interconnect Products, Integrated Secondary Protector and Digital Signal Processor - 32.

Negotiate Financial Profitability Forecasting

The key to meeting the cost reduction goals is to convince financial management to include the planned cost improvement into the fiscal year financial profitability of a manufacturing location. In this role, CME develops the cost reduction opportunities 6 to 7 months in advance of the fiscal year impact and participates in the negotiation of the fiscal year profitability with organizations such as: Product Line Management, Product Engineering, and Accounting. Once the financial commitment is made, management support for the implementation is a reality.

Monitor Progress

Traditionally, it takes 3 to 18 months to implement any material cost reduction due to the complexity of the procedures and, hence, the cost reduction can be 'bogged down'. In order to remedy this situation, CME succeeded in assigning a dedicated procedural observer (i.e., one who should not relax or quit until proof of a milestone completion or bottom line is seen).

Thus, a team of individuals dedicated to monitor and track milestones and process steps assuring the financial profitability is proven to be essential.

COMPONENT UTILIZATION COMMITTEE

Beginning in 1981, a group of professional Component Engineers initiated the analysis of major product cost contents and provided the ways and means to reduce the cost of hardware elements and/or components. As a result, a formal committee, called the Component Utilization Committee, was formed to focus on all aspects of the component cost reductions. The CUC is composed of approximately 25 technical and management members and includes representation from - Component Engineering, Product Engineering, PRT, Bell Laboratories Component Management, CME, New and Change, Standard Engineering, Engineering Purchased Integrated Circuits, Purchased Product Engineering as well as Purchasing.

Beginning in 1985, the CUC enjoyed an increased support by management which led to the development and introduction of an efficient process flow as a tool for evaluating and implementing the best quality component at the lowest cost. Periodically, the cost contents of major products are analyzed, and the potential cost-reduction components are added to the component substitution process flow shown in Exhibit 5. A weekly working level meeting is held to prioritize and monitor the status of each cost-reduced component which has to progress through at least 16 analysis steps prior to formal approval.

CONCLUSION

As stated earlier, world-wide competitive pressures dictate that AT&T's ability to compete in global markets can only be successful by obtaining or designing the components which have the highest quality and lowest cost suppliers anywhere in the world. The cost management techniques discussed in this paper have proven to be a powerful and effective way of meeting the 1990's challenges ahead for the company.

EXHIBIT 1

Cost Management Engineering

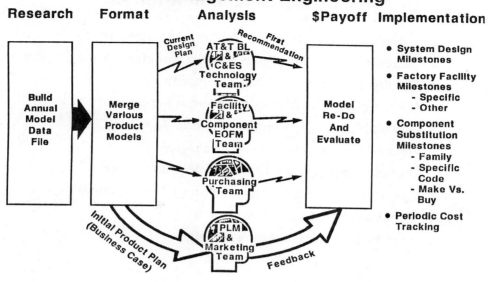

EXHIBIT 2 - CAPE ANALYSIS REPORTS

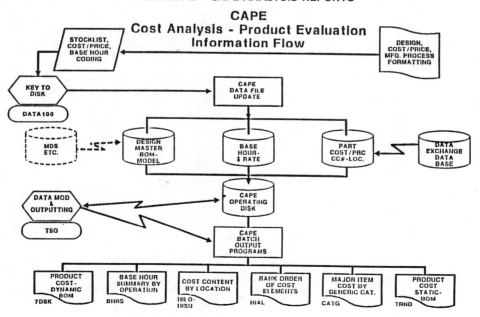

EXHIBIT 3

Material Selection Alternatives

- Substitute Cost Reduced Equivalent Component
- Convert Application From Military Specification To Commercial
- Qualify 2nd Source / Create Competition
- Make vs Buy - Challenging Internal Suppliers
- Buy vs Make - Challenging Outside Suppliers
- Relax Costly Requirement / Packaging
- Manufacture Military Specifications In-House
- Quantity Price Break Through Long Term Commitment
- Consolidate / Or Re-Allocate
- Negotiate Contract Aggressively

EXHIBIT 4

CR DEVELOPMENT MANAGEMENT
(FUNDING PROCEDURE)

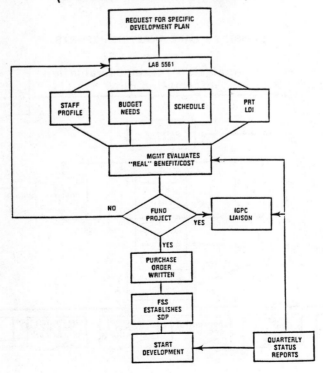

EXHIBIT 5

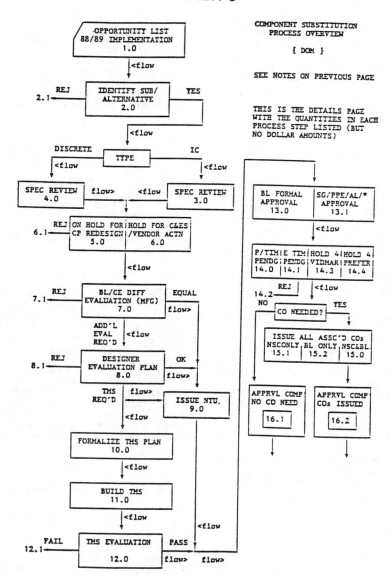

LIFE CYCLE COST
PURCHASED MATERIAL IMPACT

Burgess G. Oliver
Corporate Director of Materials Management

Northern Telecom Inc.
200 Athens Way
Nashville, TN   37228

ABSTRACT

Approximately 65% of the cost to manufacture electronic equipment for the telecommunication marketplace is generated by the value of purchased materials, including its associated attracted cost.

This presentation will examine Northern Telecom's Materials and Purchasing Group effort to reduce Life Cycle Cost, that portion of end to end cost associated with the manufacture and reliability of products, while reducing overhead cost by linking the firm through Logistics Management.

Attracted costs, also known as "life cycle cost", are those costs resulting from activities that don't add value to the product as it moves through the different stages of the manufacturing process. As these non-value-added activities are explicitly related to the organizational structure and overall manufacturing environment, actions toward attracted cost reduction are often represented by the adoption of general manufacturing policies and philosophies (i.e., "Just-In-Time (JIT)", "Fast Flow" Manufacturing), rather than with minor adjustments to the existing manufacturing and materials logistics management practices.

We will examine the various facets of attracted cost in the procurement segment of the total life cycle chain, show findings at divisional level within NTI and look at demonstrated process changes which will minimize these total life cycle costs from both customer and vendor view. We will use Exhibit A to move from a macro view to a micro view of these costs.

INTRODUCTION

Linking the firms through logistics management involves the availability and positioning of materials at the lowest cost; whether they are raw material or finished goods, original customer orders or installed base service, and the moving to process based strategies - to identify cost and where value is added or created in terms of impact on their market.

On the inbound side of this definition it includes procurement, inbound transportation, raw material and raw material inventory control. On the outbound side would be finished goods inventory, customer service, order entry, outbound transportation, warehousing and installed base service. Truly integrated logistics balances all these activities and ties them strategically and operationally together.

As companies find it increasingly difficult to ignore the manufacturing part of the flow and total cost reduction, manufacturing will also become just one more component in the integrated logistics staffing process. We need to look at our business from the standpoint of the value added chain to identify cost and where value is added or created in terms of impact.

A great manufacturing myth assumes our customers want speed of delivery. Actually, what they want is reliability, so they can depend on the right amount of a product arriving at the right time. Suppliers equate speed with good service. Reliable service also keeps total cost down and quality improves. A service that customers value is easier to provide. A key to accomplishing this is reliable information, received on a timely basis by the right person, who can interpret it correctly and then act on it expeditiously.

PHILOSOPHY

The Attracted Costs of purchase parts are those non-value-added costs incurred from the moment a purchase order is initiated to the moment the part leaves the stockroom. The basic philosophy behind attracted costs is that the real cost, or Life Cycle Cost, of an item consists of:

1. The item unit cost, including the net purchase price plus all duties and incoming freight charges required to land the item on the receiving dock.

2. The Procurement/Acquisition Cost, including requisitioning, purchasing, expediting, receiving, inspection, and accounting costs.

3. The holding costs associated with inventory such as capital costs, service costs, storage space cost and inventory risk costs.

4. Inventory shortage or stock-out costs, usually dealt with directly through a specified target service level.

5. The inventory management system operating cost. This cost is related to the sophistication of the inventory management system and is, therefore, usually beyond the influence of daily operational decisions.

EARLY INVESTIGATION

1986 Film Resistor Study: In 1986 a team analyzed the acquisition and handling of Film Resistors in six Northern Telecom locations throughout the United States. Film resistors, with $1 million Annual Gross Receipts (AGR) spread over nearly 100 million items, were chosen to represent all Class "C" inventory items. This team investigated the Purchasing, Receiving, Incoming Inspection, Stocking/Disbursing, Cycle Counting, and Invoice Processing functions and concluded that to purchase and store the $1 million AGR of film resistors required:

- 16.5 people

- 8,000 square feet of storage space

- Total attracted costs of $610,000 or 61% of the AGR.

They noted that "the bulk of attracted costs are incurred in functions where policies for A, B and C items are virtually identical; receiving inspecting and stocking/disbursing... They recommended that procedures be changed to reduce the time and effort spent on purchasing, shipping, receiving, inspecting and tracking low AGR CPCs. Specific recommendations included:

- Use of an expense-as-ordered accounting system for "C" items.

- Establishing a relationship with one or more key supplier(s) that result in short (2 weeks) lead times for low-volume (less than $100K AGR) resistors.

- Use phone-in (no paperwork) purchasing and monthly payment for these items.

- Ship resistors directly to the

sequencing area bypassing traditional receiving, inspection and stockroom activities.

1987 DIVISION STUDY

In the summer of 1987 a University of North Carolina Business School Team analyzed high dollar and low dollar categories of production part numbers at a Northern Telecom Division. Using the Film Resistor study as a starting point, they initiated a comprehensive survey of the purchasing function and a detailed analysis of computer-based purchase order information. From this base they developed a Lotus 1-2-3 spreadsheet model to simulate the purchased material life cycle. The model includes inputs for department staffing and budgets and can be used to predict a division's total attracted costs based on annual gross purchases, balance on hand and the number of line items for each inventory class. (See Exhibit B.) They concluded that for the division:

- The annual attracted cost is estimated to be more than $6 million.

- The attracted cost rate for the division is 13%.

- The attracted cost rate for "C" items is 65%.

- Stockroom (46%), freight (14%) and incoming inspection (13%) are the most significant attracted costs for "C" items.

- Holding costs represent more than a third of stockroom costs.

See Table 1 for the division's total attracted cost.

Specific recommendations included:

- Increased purchasing automation

- Source inspection and vendor certification to reduce incoming inspection

- Better component packaging to support reduced pick-times and reduced lot-sizes

- Floor stock and ship-to-WIP to reduce material and information transactions

- Minimize incoming freight charges through Traffic Analysis

- Implementation of changes to support JIT and Fast Flow

Purchasing

At the local level, purchasing should be the lead group for identifying and facilitating change due to purchasing practices impact on downstream groups. Purchasing should be responsible for analyzing the effects of changes in purchasing practices, such as ordering policies and lot sizes on other areas.

Increased automation of routine purchasing transactions through information systems like electronic purchasing is essential to reducing total attracted costs. Expense and capital purchasing should be automated along with production materials.

Buyers should concentrate on selecting competent vendors and maintaining effective relationships with those vendors rather than performing clerical or expediting tasks. Purchasing should also develop effective systems for tracking and controlling vendor performance. Increased single source purchasing and vendor reduction are also important.

Corporate purchasing has a goal of extending contract coverage to 80% by 1988, including 98% of electronic components. As well as performing this important function, corporate purchasing should take the lead in supporting effective local purchasing, especially in the implementation of changes like JIT which require extensive NT/supplier coordination.

Incoming Inspection

Incoming inspection is a prime target for attracted cost reduction. Incoming inspection requirements should be minimized so that incoming inspection audits vendor performance rather than duplicating vendor outgoing inspection. Quality at the source should be emphasized and 100% inspection eliminated.

Vendor certification programs must be fully utilized to reduce 100% inspection and reduce attracted costs. Vendor certification will also relieve bottlenecks and help develop suppliers for JIT.

Stockrooms

Stockroom management and purchasing should work together on identifying and implementing changes in component packaging to make selecting, sequencing, kitting, and production faster and more efficient and reduce waste.

Floor Stocking and Ship-to-WIP

Floor stocking and ship-to-WIP are two approaches to reducing attracted costs for purchased parts. Floor stocking reduces the time and labor hours for part selection for high-usage parts. Select and kitting costs must be balanced off against material costs, inventory investment and production floor space. For floor stock items with a common vendor or local distributor, vendor floor stocking should be considered. Vendor involvement can range from consignment areas in the warehouse, periodic vendor review and stocking to other programs. Ship-to-WIP also reduces purchased parts acquisition costs and materials handling along with supporting JIT and Fast-Flow production.

Incoming Freight

Incoming freight costs on C items should be reduced through analysis of current incoming freight practices for C level items by commodity code and shipping method. C items should be shipped by the lowest cost method which supports production requirements.

Cost Accounting and Accounts Payable

Information transactions and data processing should be reduced in cost accounting and accounts payable through electronic data transfer and data integration. Monthly invoicing from vendors with high transactions volume and centralization of some transaction processing should also be implemented.

Inventory Reduction

As divisions gain better control over materials requirements they can reduce safety stock and safety lead times as well as reducing inventory levels. These reductions can be tracked through life cycle cost analysis to determine the optimum inventory balance with dynamic simulation.

THE CHALLENGE OF THE FUTURE

Individual functional areas and divisions within Northern Telecom can no longer operate independently of each other. In the future, increased linkages through shared databases, real-time processing of operations and other technology will be increased.

Introduction of JIT techniques to the factory floor with lot size reduction will increase transactions volume beyond the capability of current systems including MRP and shop floor control. Routine transactions will be handled through computer to computer transactions as well as manual systems like Kanban, with exceptions only requiring human intervention. Many transactions will be tracked only at the aggregate level, with transactions on individual items not tracked.

Procurement will become increasingly oriented towards single source suppliers, long-term supply commitments, and monthly frozen schedules to support Fast-Flow production. Suppliers will link directly into Northern Telecom information systems such as MRP, reducing errors, lead time, and manual clerical work for routine transactions.

Production operations may be increasingly outsourced to offshore and specialized vendors as Northern Telecom concentrates on its competitive strengths and rationalizes production. Incoming inspection will be mainly random sampling to audit vendor performance and provide feedback.

Attracted costs identification and reduction should be part of the ongoing process of never ending improvement. Northern Telecom should constantly strive to improve the abilities of its people, its procedures, and its computer support.

People are the key to Northern Telecom's future, especially in the implementation of changes required to meet future needs. Training, communication, and awareness are the three tools which will allow effective use of this important resource.

This, in effect, is a movement far beyond our feeble attempt of Just-In-Time inventory. It must be a kind of synchronized manufacturing and logistics flow that looks at the process in a new uninhibited way. Our goal must be to create an environment in which costs are continuously going down, quality is continuously going up, and the ever evolving needs of customers are being met with greater flexibility and responsiveness TIME BASED BUSINESS approach...

Information, or access to information, is the glue that bonds the entire process together. Information systems make Just-In-Time operation possible, and allows companies to be successful with greatly reduced inventories. It further allows us to create value added strategic differentiation, and shorten customer response times. We must look at our customers, internal, and external needs and help them to accomplish their goals of reduced cost, improved quality and time based management.

Since information is the key driver in cementing the strategic alliance relationships, in effect, information itself will become an ultimate value added (time based) ingredient. We must maximize our information technology as a tool for realizing this value added strategic advantage.

WHERE ARE YOU

A recent article from A. T. Kearney, Inc., talked about the degree of information integration and how it varies from company to company. Very few companies have managed to integrate every logistic function and tie logistics into their strategic management. To accomplish this, in Peter Drucker's words, a "sea" change, that is, a far-reaching, evolutionary change in management philosophy and technique is required.

In their studies of the degree of integration of different companies, they were able to identify three discrete stages. Companies in stage one typically see their management mission as controlling only finished goods transportation and warehousing. They emphasize expediting today's workload and minding the store operationally. Efforts to improve operations are phenomenal with little or no systems analysis. The focus is almost entirely on cost reduction.

Companies in stage two of developing integrated logistics take a more tactical approach to distribution control management. The mission is to integrate finished goods distribution with the ultimate goal of satisfying customer demand. Integration of inbound materials transportation often occurs at this stage, as does involvement in customer service and order processing. Stage two companies' managers often team with other departments, such as marketing or manufacturing, to achieve tactical improvements in the physical distribution system. The focus in these companies is on firm profitability.

Stage three companies confirm physical distribution and materials management to integrate the total logistics process. They take a strategic approach to making logistic management part of the firm's total business, increasing the interaction with and support to other functions. The process now includes sales forecasting, production planning, overall sourcing decisions including international sourcing, makes versus buy, and raw material and work-in-process management. Stage three companies tie logistics together to bring strategies into action. A time based oneness with all operations.

As stated earlier, the great manufacturing myth assumes our customers want speed of delivery. Actually from an attracted cost standpoint, they want reliability so they can depend on the right amount of products arriving at the right time. A company which is reliable in delivery and quality drives cost down. Service that the customer values is easier to provide. And reliability is the goal of integrated logistics management.

SUMMARY

Purchased parts attracted costs can be identified, and quantified, through the application of simple analytic techniques. The cost of purchased parts to Northern Telecom must be seen as the total life cycle costs rather than purchase costs. Also, the interdependence of departments and importance of communication between departments should be recognized as important in implementation of changes and new procedures.

Attracted costs analysis may also be used to facilitate the changes in planning, procurement, and production required to support Just-In-Time and Fast-Flow Production. These findings should be incorporated into studies of attracted costs upstream and downstream of the areas researched to ensure integrated logistic management and true improvements to life cycle cost.

Simple improvements in process sometimes provide the greatest payback in total cost reduction.

TABLE 1 - DIVISION TOTAL ATTRACTED COST

	HIGH $	LOW $	TOTAL
STOCKROOMS			
SELECTS	7.43%	7.21%	7.32%
KITTING	2.41%	0.32%	1.34%
CYCLE COUNT	1.16%	4.06%	2.63%
PUTAWAY	0.73%	0.84%	0.79%
COMP PREP	1.44%	15.37%	8.51%
SEQUENCING	0.71%	2.06%	1.39%
HOLDING (CAPITAL)	18.40%	12.93%	15.62%
RECEIVING	3.35%	3.87%	3.62%
STORAGE (SPACE)	6.40%	4.50%	5.43%
STOCKROOM TOTAL	42.01%	51.14%	46.65%
PURCHASING	7.02%	14.46%	10.79%
FREIGHT DUTIES	22.23%	5.93%	13.96%
INCOMING INSPECTION	11.60%	13.40%	12.51%
CHANGE/ERROR	12.26%	8.62%	12.42%
ACCOUNTING	4.87%	6.45%	5.67%
TOTAL	100.00%	100.00%	100.00%
TOTAL AS % MATERIAL	10.08%	64.94%	16.60%

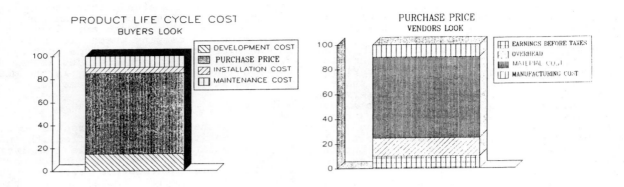

MATERIAL COST

ATTRACTED COST

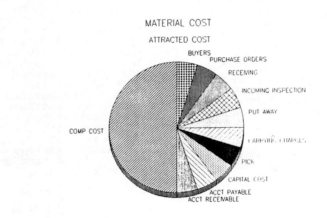

EXHIBIT A

NT-10 ATTRACTED COSTS 1/1/87 - 5/31/87

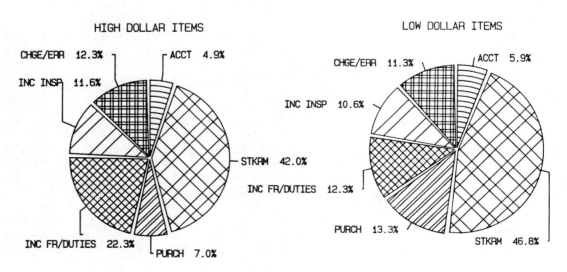

HIGH DOLLAR ITEMS

CHGE/ERR 12.3%
INC INSP 11.6%
ACCT 4.9%
STKRM 42.0%
INC FR/DUTIES 12.3%
INC FR/DUTIES 22.3%
PURCH 7.0%

LOW DOLLAR ITEMS

CHGE/ERR 11.3%
ACCT 5.9%
INC INSP 10.6%
PURCH 13.3%
STKRM 46.8%

EXHIBIT B

1469

OPTIMIZING DEVELOPMENT COSTS WHILE
EVOLVING A MINICOMPUTER FAMILY

Jo Anne H. Miller
Head, Small Computer Development
and Management Department

AT&T Data Systems Group
1100 East Warrenvillle Road
Naperville, IL 60566

ABSTRACT

This paper addresses the role of design and development in the life cycle cost optimization of a minicomputer family. The product management process that was utilized to trade-off various design alternatives in order to minimize development cost and maximize system performance is elaborated. Emphasis is given to the requirement of dynamic interaction between product management, development and manufacturing personnel to achieve this goal. The role of design innovation within the constraints of cost, quality and time to market is also explored.

INTRODUCTION

While product life cycle cost optimization is most usually thought of in terms of manufacturing and product costs, appropriate management of the design and development activities can also positively impact the total cost optimization over a product's life cycle. The AT&T 3B2 minicomputer family was first introduced in April 1984 and has had new, evolving members on a 12-18 month cycle since that time. Each development cycle has increased the cost effectiveness of the development staff and the product development management process.

DEVELOPMENT - IMPACTED COMPONENTS OF COST

The most obvious development-related component is the total cost of the product development cycle itself. For a minicomputer product this component consists of the staff time and direct and indirect expenses that are associated with the design, implementation, debugging and preparation for high volume manufacturing of the circuit packs (system board, memory, backplane, I/O controllers), specialized hardware such as power supplies, cabinetry as well as operating system and communications system software. The principal factors that influence this cost component are the size and complexity of the design, the experience level and skill of the staff, the size of the software to be developed, the thoroughness of the development review process to catch errors, the effectiveness of the debugging tools, the newness of the component technology, the stability of the product requirements, and the effectiveness of the project management team. Additionally, if the development is spread over many organizations the interface complexity increases and with it the cost of the product development cycle.

There are several other components to life cycle product cost that are impacted/influenced by the development organization. A key one is the selection of the components that determine product cost of goods. Nearly everyone is familiar with the scenario of the over-engineered/ over-designed product that clearly performs the function required, but does it with such state-of-the-art or gold-plated components that the product can't be priced competitively. The component selection is in turn impacted by the skill and experience of the designer as well as the designer's understanding of the impact of component selection on the manufacturability, testability and saleability of the product.

Another element of development-impacted cost is the opportunity cost of a product that is late into the marketplace or perhaps finds its market window shut altogether. Again the items that make a development costly also tend to lengthen it. A sloppy development team will make errors that will take a long time to correct, multiple iterations of circuit packs or software loads. However, the biggest cause of market window opportunity costs is changing requirements or a failure to properly interpret the requirements due perhaps to staff inexperience, arrogance, or failure to communicate effectively with product management and marketing.

A third additional development-impacted element of cost is the manufacturability of the product. Although labor is not a large component of most electronic products, including minicomputers, the design can have impacts on board yields as well as special test requirements that can directly affect the product cost. As stated previously, design complexity, developer skill and experience and appreciation of the manufacturing process and needs are some of the fundamental factors influencing this element of total product cost. Introduction of a new manufacturing technology such as surface-mount devices that will ultimately reduce costs, must be carefully timed so that life cycle costs can be minimized.

A final area of cost that is impacted by the development organization is the design component of customer-perceived quality. Hardware and software errors that are not found and corrected during the development cycle are the principal culprits here. Additionally, the physical design of skins and cables can have a direct impact on customer-perceived quality. There is also that fundamental functionality aspect of quality that could be compromised by a development organization out of touch with its market in an effort to meet a schedule, reducing or eliminating a critical function. A problem here can result in poor market acceptance, an opportunity cost of the highest magnitude.

1470

AT&T introduced the 3B2 minicomputer product line in 1984 with the Model 300. This model was part of AT&T's initial commercial computer line. As the first member of a new computer family, the Model 300 was completely developed from scratch. All hardware from the system board through the floppy tape controller to the sheet metal skins was a new design. The operating system was a port of UNIX® System V (the initial release of that product), but hardware dependent software such as I/O controller drivers had to be developed from scratch. Sufficient forethought was included in the design of the 3B2/300 so that the next model, the 3B2/400, could be introduced approximately 1 year later as a set of modifications rather than a total from-scratch design. See Exhibit 1 for a System Architecture diagram. The 400 pushed the architecture of the 300 to its evolutionary limit, to get more main memory, more disk capacity or more I/O slots, architectural changes would have to occur. The 3B2/600 introduced in March of 1987 was the result of these changes. While building on the same I/O system bus and utilizing some of the same memory arrays, and I/O controllers, much of the 3B2/600 was new. See Exhibit 2 for a System Architecture diagram. A new microbus and buffered microbus improved memory access times. A new system board for increased frequency chips as well as accommodating more main memory was introduced. The industry standard Small Computer System Interface (SCSI) bus was introduced as a mechanism for rapid incorporation of new mass storage peripheral technology for greater capacity and performance. The 3B2/600 was designed to be an evolutionary platform for additional performance enhancements, both in hardware and software. Some of these enhancements have been realized as additions such as a VME auxiliary I/O bus interface, or the MultiProcessor Enhancement (MPE) co-processing element to increase the performance of CPU-bound tasks. The 3B2/700, introduced in May 1988, is an evolution of the 600 with a higher speed system board and support for additional main memory (up to 64 Mbytes) and larger internal disks. Follow-on evolutionary developments are underway, all using the 3B2/600 as the base.

PRODUCT DEVELOPMENT MANAGEMENT PROCESS AND IMPROVEMENTS

The appropriate management of the development cycle for the particular evolutionary stage of a product family such as the 3B2 minicomputer is critical if the life cycle development costs are to be optimized. As was pointed out above, many of the development-impacted development costs are associated with an improper understanding of the customer needs, specific product requirements as well as the manufacturing restrictions. Interaction between product management, development, manufacturing and even sales are critical for the optimization of total cost.

The product development management process as it is currently practiced in AT&T's Data Systems Group is seen in Exhibit 3. In general, the process of new product development can be initiated from three sources. The design/development organization can have a bright new idea that might be triggered by a new technology or a technical innovation – this is the technology driven or pushed product. The 3B2/300 and 600 were of this flavor. The marketplace can be seen to be demanding a particular set of features or price/performance ratio that is perceived by the marketing and sales organization and in turn becomes a request from the product management organization to develop a product with a particular set of characteristics. This is the market driven or pulled product. The 3B2/400, 500 were in this category. Finally, there is the need to significantly improve the margins of the product or the manufacturability of the product. This push also comes from the product management organization and has been the driving force behind many of the modifications in the 3B2/700. Whatever the source, there is an initial product proposal known within AT&T's Data Systems Group as the Functional Product Need (FPN) statement. This is a working definition that allows several organizations to initiate activity to determine if a product will in fact be committed. Many different activities have to take place prior to a commitment to proceed, especially for a brand new product, i.e., market acceptance studies, competitive analysis, salesforce acceptance, financial estimates, development estimates, and manufacturing estimates. For an evolutionary product, some of these steps may be shortened. Once formal approval has been obtained product, project and manufacturing plans are developed and tracked and monitored on a regular basis, ranging from a week to a month as the interval.

No matter what the particular process there are a number of critical elements that must be in place in order for cost optimization and sales success to result. Probably the single most important element is a set of goals shared among product management, development, manufacturing and marketing as to what the product is supposed to accomplish, what value it will add for a jointly held view of a market segment. A second critical element is a jointly understood view of the financial requirements/constraints on product cost of goods. A third critical element is a jointly understood time to market. Underneath all of these shared views among the various organizations must be a sense of mutual respect and trust if the objectives are to be met.

These critical elements, and indeed the current structure of the product development management process, were not in place when AT&T launched the 3B2/300. The initial version of that model was nearly completely developed before there were joint goals established.

As a result, there were critical missing features such as a Math Accelerator Unit (MAU) to handle floating point operations in a competitive manner and a second release of the product was required to bring about full-functionality. As the 3B2 product line has evolved, so has the process of product development management so as to reduce those critical development-impacted costs. With the 3B2/700, the process described here had come to fruition and the result is the highest performing member of the 3B2 family for the lowest development cost.

In addition to the regularly scheduled tracking meetings, frequent informal working meetings by development product management and manufacturing personnel are required to assure that the goals are met. This will generally result in changes and deviations from the intermediate milestones in the project plan, but frequently results in a higher quality, more cost-effective product. As an example, the 3B2/700 was originally envisioned as a change to the system board to allow the new WE® 32200 chipset to operate at 22 MHz - a modest performance enhancement over the 18 MHz operation of the WE32100 in the 3B2/600 and 500. Additionally, a new UNIX release, System V Release 2.2, was to be incorporated. After discussions with marketing, the product management organization determined that in order to have sufficient value-added over the 3B2/600, the ability to support greater than 16 Mbytes of main memory and larger mass storage peripherals should be core 3B2/700 features. If these would have been developed as add-ons, there would have been additional testing time required and there might have been market opportunity costs from a delayed market entry.

In addition to evolving the relationship between product management, manufacturing and development, over the 3B2 product life cycle, a number of improvements have been made to the internals of the development process. Both the development management and staff have grown in experience. Although few of the original 3B2/300 developers were directly involved in the 3B2/700 many were its technical supervisors. Because the architectures have evolved rather than being totally new, new staff could be brought in without additional cost penalties. Because of the relative stability of the architecture, changes for cost reductions and performance enhancements have been able to be made in a cost-effective manner. The project management aspects of planning and tracking both major and intermediate milestones have been enchanced and tightened. A significant investment has also been made in computer aided design verification techniques for the circuit pack designs. This effort has allowed a reduction of the average number of artmasters (the full iteratives of a pack design) to go from 4 to 2 saving both direct development dollars and time. See Exhibit 3.

CONCLUSION

Over the past 5 years an expanding 3B2 product line has been introduced. During that same timeframe, the product development management process has been evolved so that both direct and indirect development-impacted costs can be optimized.

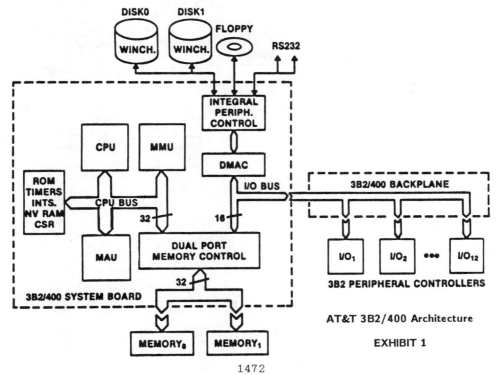

AT&T 3B2/400 Architecture

EXHIBIT 1

AT&T 3B2 PROCESSORS

3B2/600
System Architecture

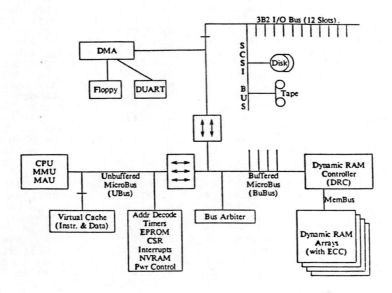

EXHIBIT 2

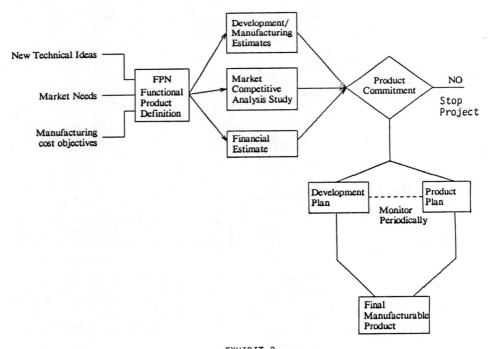

EXHIBIT 3

Product Development Process

PQR-09

THE REVOLUTION IN CUSTOMER EXPECTATIONS

Ronald Martin, Chairperson
Vice President-Quality
ADC Telecommunications, Inc.
4900 West 78th St.
Minneapolis, Minnesota 55435

Survival and success in the 1990's will require a new perspective on QUALITY in the Communications Industry. The Industry has seen unprecedented change in the last five years. This change will continue, especially in the understanding and implementation of Quality. This seminar explores customers' new definition of TOTAL QUALITY and how it is reshaping customer expectations. In this evolving new world, customers' definition of Quality covers all aspects of doing business, not just product quality, so every member of an organization-- engineering, sales, product and marketing management, purchasing, and credit -- are all part of the Total Quality Organization. This series explores this issue from the perspective of the end customers, suppliers to the industry, and the regulatory role.

Margaret Lulic - ADC Telecommunications, Inc.

Cliff Miller - GTE Corporation

Sharon L. Nelson - Washington State Utilities and Transportation Commission

Terrance A. Wilhelms - Hewlett-Packard Co.

THE NATURE OF THE REVOLUTION IN CUSTOMER EXPECTATIONS

Margaret A. Lulic
Public Network Market Manager

ADC Telecommunications, Inc.
4900 West 78th St.
Minneapolis, Minnesota 55435

ABSTRACT

This paper describes a fundamental change that is already underway in the Telecommunications Industry. Customers' expectations of their suppliers are becoming more encompassing. They expect quality in all aspects of their relationship not just in products. The strategic implications of this for the customer and supplier are reviewed to demonstrate the benefits to both parties if Total Quality thinking is implemented. A framework for undertaking this new direction is also described.

INTRODUCTION

A revolution is a sudden fundamental change in the political, social or economic structure of any population. This definition certainly applies to our industry. The Telecommunications Industry has experienced dramatic upheaval in recent years. The changes in the economic and competitive structure of the industry bear little resemblance to what they did just a few short years ago. Customers' expectations are changing dramatically and rapidly. There are few signs that this rate of change is abating, and some signs indicate that it is accelerating. This seminar focuses on Total Quality as one of the prime elements of the continuing revolution for the next decade.

Quality has always been a critical aspect in the industry as it related to the quality of network services and, therefore, the quality of network equipment. There are four primary approaches to defining quality that one can see in the industry today. They are: 1) a product approach which emphasizes performance and features, 2) a process approach which emphasizes conformance to specifications, 3) a user approach which focuses on the total package of product, service and image as perceived by the customer; and 4) the value approach which looks at total perceived benefits divided by the total cost of doing business. The concept of Total Quality is best reflected in the latter.

The role of quality is changing to become a larger part of strategic positioning and competitive advantage. The degree to which participants in the industry select and adopt one of the concepts of Quality will determine the future competitive and economic structure of the industry, and that company's role in the industry. This first session focuses on defining the nature of Total Quality relative to what it is and its strategic role and, secondly, describes the critical elements necessary for its implementation.

THE TOTAL QUALITY CONCEPT

There are a number of leaders in the field of quality, such as Dr. W. Edwards Deming, Philip B. Crosby, and Dr. Joseph Juran, who have provided insight into the concept of Total Quality. Though each has a different emphasis, they seem to agree on several basic issues as to what Total Quality is.

- It is giving the customer what they have a right to expect in all aspects of doing business. This leads to customer satisfaction and loyalty.

- It is a continuous effort to improve. It is never done. This is the way to stay competitive and maintain market share.

- It is meeting customer needs right the first time through design and processes, not by rework of a defective part or process. This reduces costs and eliminates waste.

Corporations that accept this definition and implement Total Quality will also find that a change in definition leads to a change in the role of Quality in strategic plans, operations, customer relations and supplier relations. Quality becomes everyone's responsibility; the way decisions are made changes, and quality becomes part of competitive advantage. These have significant strategic implications and are discussed in the next section.

THE STRATEGIC IMPLICATIONS

The strategic implications of implementing Total Quality, as just defined, are related to the three areas of market share, customer satisfaction and cost structure. Measurable evidence is available from across many industries that demonstrates that Quality is a key strategic issue in these three areas. They show there will be substantial return to the customer, the customers' customer and the Total Quality supplier.

The Profit Impact of Market Strategies Program at the Strategic Planning Institute provides data on the issue of market share. They have studied over 450 companies on the issue of profit, share, and strategies. The primary principle that has evolved from the PIMS database is "In the long run, the most important single factor affecting a business unit's performance is the quality of its products and services, relative to those of competitors." This is explained in detail in the book The PIMS Principles by Robert Buzzell and Bradley Gale. Two key points are also made about the definition of quality that correlate to the Total Quality concept. They emphasize it is the customer's total perception of the product, services and supplier (versus only conformance to specifications) and that these perceptions are measurable. This is seen in Fig. 1.

This flows into the second strategic area of customer satisfaction. The results for the customer are greater satisfaction and value because all their needs are being addressed and monitored. The results for the supplier are loyalty, repeat business, less vulnerability to price wars, higher market share, and higher prices. The role of quality, therefore, is at the core of the business strategy.

It now becomes clear why defining quality as conformance to product specifications is a piece rather than the whole. A conformance focus, as PIMS points out, has problems. Specifications can be flawed and frequently are oblivious to competition and the customers' comparison standards. It leads to too much inward focus. Instead, we need to review all aspects of the relationship and seek continuous improvement of them.

There is a tendency to assume that if there are few or no complaints, customers are satisfied. Then complacency sets in. Hard data, again, suggests that the assumption is wrong. Research by the Forum Corporation and others finds that 25% of the customer base of the average business is at risk of switching suppliers. Only 4% of the dissatisfied customers, however, will complain to the supplier. Other research finds that the primary reasons that people switch are poor treatment and indifference by a supplier's employee (68%), dissatisfaction with the product (14%) and competition (9%).

Continuous improvement is necessary to keep these existing customers happy. It includes pro-active efforts to evaluate their satisfaction and identify new needs as well as internally generated efforts to improve. This is well worth the effort. Capturing new customers is typically five times more expensive than keeping existing ones.

The third strategic implication relates to cost structure. Total Quality focuses on the elimination of waste and rework, on doing things right the first time. National estimates from Philip Crosby and others are that the average business loses 25-40% of their gross revenues in scrap and rework as a result of not utilizing a statistically driven Total Quality approach. Confirmation of these numbers has been made by several telecommunications companies. Approximately half of these costs are due to their supplier base and the other half to their own internal processes. Elimination of that kind of waste would benefit everyone, including subscribers, and dramatically affect competitiveness in the international market as well.

A FRAMEWORK FOR CHANGE

There are four areas in which change is needed if one is to adopt a Total Quality approach as shown in Figure 2. The four types are Management Leadership, Corporate Values, Company Capabilities, and Operating Principles. We'll review each.

A new direction in leadership is required at the highest management levels in customer, government, and supplier organizations. Leaders are needed to create an atmosphere of trust and cooperation within their operations and with their customer and supplier base. The management role of monitoring performance against arbitrary numbers needs to be replaced. The commitments that are necessary to move in the direction of Total Quality require education and decision making at this level. As Dr. Deming often points out, "Only top management can establish constancy of purpose, make policy, establish core values, and create the road map for implementation." The selection of what role quality has in strategy and which definition of quality is implemented significantly affects the nature of the customer-supplier relationship. Government leaders can facilitate this or hinder this as well through legislation.

A change or reinforcement of Values is also necessary. Suppliers must value their customers more and customers must value their suppliers more. Signs that a supplier values its customers include:

- Making all types of internal decisions only after looking at it from the customers' perspective. This includes more than product decisions. Items like invoicing, packaging, and shipping procedures affect customers. The organization and management of sales administration functions and high quality contacts are all critical to the customer.

- Telling the customer the truth as to what your processes can do and what they cannot do.

- Pro-actively seeking measurements of performance and needs from the customer's perspective.

No one would disagree with the idea of valuing the customer but some may disagree with valuing the supplier. This is a critical element, too. To implement Total Quality requires long term commitments between suppliers and customers. Suppliers must be able to invest with some sense of security that the customer is serious about its stated needs and that those needs have a value. The investment will yield a return. Signs that the supplier is valued by the customer include:

- A willingness to clarify and share information about all types of needs and to rank priorities. Specify levels of performance without over specifying how the supplier should achieve them.

- Loyalty to suppliers over time if performance is maintained and to providing them with larger pieces of

the business. Reducing the number of suppliers is usually part of this.

- A willingness to help develop suppliers through formal and statistically driven evaluations.

- Adopting a procurement evaluation system that looks at life cycle costs in all its facets rather than only purchased price. Weighing the total value received versus price.

Third, two capabilities need to be developed or enhanced by a company striving for Total Quality. First, the use of Statistical Methods must be acquired to monitor processes, identify stability, and measure continuous improvement. These are critical. Second, the supplier and the customer need to improve communication capabilities in defining and understanding needs and value. Examples of the existence of and growth in these areas include:

- Decision making and evaluations based on data versus impressions.

- Communicating key customer requirements throughout the organization and systematically using them to shape the design of new products and services.

- Regular quantitative and qualitative market research on customer satisfaction.

Finally, review and modification of processes in all functions are necessary in an organization in reference to four Principles. They are Prevention, Design in Quality, Reduce Variation and Continuous Improvement. We'll review each of these briefly.

- The emphasis must be on Prevention versus Detection.

- Quality must be designed into the product or service, not left to chance or manufacturing to be added afterwards.

- The emphasis must be on reducing variation, not just conforming to specifications.

- The pursuit must begin for continuous improvement. The story of Total Quality is a never ending one.

REFERENCES

1. Dr. W. Edwards Deming, _Out of the Crisis_, Massachusetts Institute of Technology Center for Advanced Engineering Study, Cambridge, MA, 1986.

2. Philip B. Crosby, _Quality Without Tears_, McGraw-Hill Book Company, New York, 1984.

3. Robert Buzzell and Bradley Gale, _The PIMS Principles_, The Free Press, New York, 1987.

4. Jerry G. Bowels, "Rediscovering the Customer", _Fortune_, January 18, 1988.

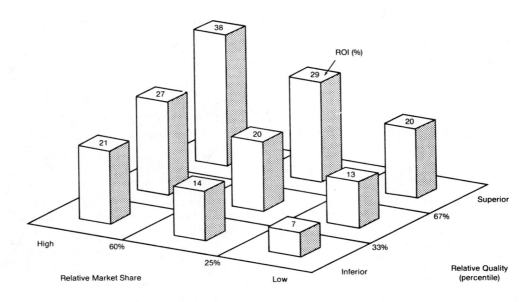

PIMS Principles, Buzzell & Gale, pg. 109.

Figure 1

IMPLEMENTATION FOR CHANGE

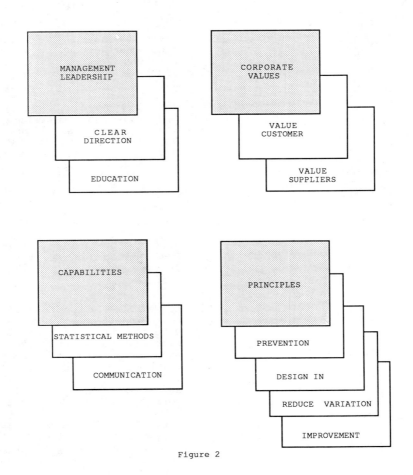

Figure 2

QUALITY STARTS WITH CUSTOMER FEEDBACK

Terrance A. Wilhelms
Quality Analyst

Hewlett Packard
Midwest Sales Region
5201 Tollview Drive
Rolling Meadows, IL 60008

ABSTRACT

This paper reviews the critical role of customer input in achieving successful new products and services. The essential elements of a quality customer feedback strategy are explored and defined, as well as the importance of management commitment to the success of such feedback strategies.

INTRODUCTION

Over the last decade as global competition has become stronger the traditional definition of quality in the United States has been challenged by our foreign competitors. In order to compete in this arena we must change our definition of quality in this country to meet this challenge.

The traditional definition of "QUALITY" in the U.S. is "the product or service meets or exceeds the specifications". The danger with this definition is that it fosters an illusion that the company will be successful because they provide "QUALITY" products, and doesn't consider the fact that there may be no market for that product because the specifications don't reflect any real customer need. A more appropriate definition of "QUALITY" is "the product or service satisfies the customers' needs." Using this second definition requires companies to understand their customers' needs before they design a product or service. This is where a "CUSTOMER INFORMATION SYSTEM" comes in.

There are five key elements which are essential to a customer information system; they are:

1. Data Collection Strategy
2. Formal Acknowledgment System
3. Formal System for Action
4. Employee Commitment
5. Management Commitment

DATA COLLECTION STRATEGY

Why do we need to collect customer information? There are many new techniques to ensure quality products/services which are being written about such as QFD, PD, TQC, and so forth (see note). The common thread which drives all of these programs is customer information, thus making collection of this information paramount to the successful implementation of these programs.

How do we collect customer information? There are numerous ways to go about collecting data: customer surveys, employee interviews, customer interviews, market research, and so on. A total data collection strategy will utilize as many forms of data collection as appropriate to capture the voice of your customer without duplicating effort.

There are several key points to keep in mind when developing a data collection strategy. 1. Don't collect data unless you have a strategy for using that data. Data is costly to collect and of no value if not put to use. This strategy must take into account the needs of the various systems which the company is using to design in, or assure quality within the organization, some of these being QFD, PD, Quality Circles, SPC, etc. 2. The value of the data to the company must offset its collection cost. 3. The cost to the person supplying the data must be offset by some benefit, be it actual or perceived.

---

note) QFD - Quality Function Deployment, PD - Policy Deployment, TQC - Total Quality Control, SPC - Statistical Process Control

FORMAL ACKNOWLEDGEMENT SYSTEM

Once the data has been collected the people who have supplied the data must be made aware of what is being done with the data. If this is done poorly or not at all, the flow of data will quickly cease as there will be no perceived value by the person supplying the data. There is a personal cost to those who supply data in the form of time and personal commitment. People need some compensation for this cost if they are to continue to participate. The compensation can take many forms from a simple acknowledgement letter to some monetary gain. Without this element, however, the program is doomed to failure.

FORMAL SYSTEM FOR ACTION

As stated earlier data has no value if it's not used for action. If we collect data yet have no system for supplying that data to the departments which can use it for process improvements, we have wasted our time and resources. There must be a formal problem handling plan for immediate corrective action when customer complaints are received, as well as channels for product/service enhancement data to flow to the appropriate departments within the organization. This is essential for maximizing the value of the data we have collected.

EMPLOYEE COMMITMENT

The first, most frequent, and often times only contact a customer has with a company is through the first line employees. Every contact a customer has with these employees is an opportunity to build a loyal customer. If these contacts are mishandled, not only do you potentially lose the customer involved, but he will likely tell 8 to 16 of his acquaintances. (see Fig. 1). Therefore the quality of each customer contact is very important to a company's future. Also this is the group within the company who have the best feel for what your customers want and their commitment to supplying this information to management is vital to the success of an information program. The keys to getting this group involved are training and management commitment.

MANAGEMENT COMMITMENT

This is the most important yet most difficult element of the puzzle to put together. In today's U.S. business climate, management focuses on results,(i.e. number of units shipped, number of invoices collected, has quota been met, etc.) rather than on whether the needs of the customers have been met. If this type of philosophy is not changed within the organization, the success of a customer information system will be minimal at best. Customer satisfaction must be the number one priority of every manager and employee within the organization. This can only be accomplished by direct involvement of all levels of management in training employees, participating in process improvement activities, and in incorporating these goals in job descriptions and performance evaluations.

A policy deployment management style must be adopted if a company is truly going to be successful at integrating customer input into their organization. In policy deployment, strategies are developed which ensure results by focusing on the means by which the results are obtained, thus focusing on entire processes and fostering teamwork between departments rather than the sub-optimization and competition which current result oriented management produces.

CONCLUSION

Most managers will acknowledge the need for this type of program but lack the active commitment which is needed. In today's companies the key focus is on short term profits; this focus has to be changed if true progress in quality improvement is to be made. This short term focus on profits puts tremendous pressure on employees and middle level management to focus on quick fixes, and short term, band-aid, solutions to problems which show immediate results, as opposed to putting resources into analyzing and correcting the real problems in our businesses which dissatisfy our customers. (See Fig. 1)

The success of a customer information system relies on the long term commitment to customer satisfaction from all levels within the organization. A company wide integrated data collection strategy, acknowledgement strategy, and plan for action are vital to the success of companies into the next decade. Those who embrace these strategies and listen to their customers will survive and prosper.

REFERENCES

1. Quality Progress Magazine, 25th Anniversary Issue/1987.

2. Quality Progress Magazine, June, 1988.

3. Milind M. Lele and Jagdish N. Sheth, The Customer is Key, John Wiley and Sons, New York, NY, 1987.

4. Masaaki Imai, Kaizen, The Key to Japan's Competitive Success, Random House Business Divsion, New York, NY, 1986.

5. Kaoru Ishikawa, What is Total Quality Control? The Japanese Way, Prentiss-Hall, Englewood Cliffs, NJ, 1985, 6th printing, 1987. Translated by David J. Lu.

THE HIGH COST OF LOSING A CUSTOMER

- In the average business, for every customer who bothers to complain, there are 26 others who remain silent.

- The averaged "wronged" customer will tell 8 to 16 people.

- 91 percent of unhappy customers will never purchase goods or services from you again

- If you make an effort to remedy customers' complaints, 82 to 95 percent of them will stay with you.

- It costs about five times as much to attract a new customer as it costs to keep an old one.

(From studies conducted by Technical Assistance Research Programs, Washington, DC)

Figure 1

EVALUATING CRITICAL ASPECTS OF SUPPLIER PERFORMANCE

Clifton Miller
Director - Product Standardization
Administration

GTE Service Corporation
Dallas/Ft. Worth Airport, Texas

Customers have always had high expectations of the telecommunications industry. Before deregulation, we could characterize the industry with two observations:

1. high customer expectations, and
2. no competition.

Today customer expectations continue to be high. Customers are bombarded with information about what competitors have to offer. In a deregulated environment, the cost of providing quality service is an important issue. Customer costs must be kept competitively low.

With deregulation, low costs are achieved through quality products -- products that are not defective and do not require repair, servicing, or substitutions.

As a major provider of telecommunications and information transport services, GTE must continue to meet critical new challenges. These challenges, which face our telephone operations management team and employee body alike, stem from the changes in our industry resulting from technological, political, and regulatory influences.

Chief among the primary challenges we face are three:

• The need to meet increasingly sophisticated end-customer expectations.

• Accomplishing the transition from a regulated utility to a dynamic enterprise in a highly competitive market environment.

• Effectively managing the cost and quality performance of the business while we attend to the other two.

Recognizing that we cannot meet these challenges alone, GTE Telephone Operations has instituted a Partners in Quality program with our suppliers. Before describing this program in greater detail, let me place the entire matter of quality at GTE in perspective.

According to the terms of our published company quality policy, "Quality is conformance to the requirements and expectations of the internal and external customers, throughout the expected period of use of the product or service."

Also, under the terms of the same corporate policy, GTE is dedicated to achieving the highest quality in all the market segments we serve. What's more, every company, group, and strategic business unit within the corporation is charged with developing its own supporting policies and quality-improvement programs.

We believe that quality products begin with carefully prepared specifications to vendors. Rigorous testing by GTE determines which products will be standardized and selected. Vendor performance to those specifications will be closely evaluated.

Let us examine more closely, then, GTE's Partners in Quality program. Together with other internal efforts, this program will -- in a controlled manner -- reduce the number of vendors, standardize most products, and mean that GTE will only be working with preferred vendors of high quality. As of today, approximately 85 percent of our capital budget product expenditures -- including 56 products and 51 suppliers -- is covered under the Partners In Quality program. We have already begun reducing the cost of poor quality, which in 1986 amounted to several hundred million dollars.

Vendors who are identified as "preferred" by the new program benefit in two ways:

• They get a larger share of GTE's business.

• They receive feedback from us to help them maintain peak performance.

Organizationally, different groups have been established within GTE to handle various phases of product planning, selection, evaluation, and after-sales support.

Our Partners In Quality program concentrates on strengthening vendors' roles and responsibilities in terms of quality and customer satisfaction. The program focuses on three areas:

• Education
• Product Management
• Vendor Management

Education refers to internal and external training about the purpose and procedures behind the Partners In Quality program. Internally, GTE works with employees -- particularly those in vendor-contact jobs -- to communicate how the program works. Our people know what responsibilities and expectations are assigned to them.

Externally, GTE conducts a series of seminars for our top vendors throughout the country. The purpose of these sessions is to introduce the Partners In Quality program and to explain its requirements.

Changes in product management have affected vendors in a number of ways. We now use life cycle management as a guiding concept. The emphasis is on determining the true costs of products and services. Given that emphasis, it was logical that we should further centralize the handling of specific products with specific product managers. Therefore, one product manager is responsible for a given product for the duration of its life cycle. The benefit to our vendors is that they now have one focal point -- a single point of entry -- to sell telecommunications products to all seven GTE telephone companies.

Planning is now an especially important part of product management. In the past, problems existed because of lack of timely information regarding customer needs. Today, however, GTE is committing additional resources to obtain critical information about customer needs. This information is presented to vendors so they can respond pro-actively to GTE's requirements.

Product management has benefitted greatly from improved standardization procedures. Many times the delivery of quality products depends on the quality of communication prior to delivery. Through GTE's efforts in the areas of education and product management, communication with vendors has been greatly improved.

Communication also plays an important role in vendor management. Vendor management means there is now a system in place to track and rate a vendor's performance -- and that good performers will be rewarded. Vendor management is a significant step for GTE. It is our way of controlling the number of vendors we deal with by identifying those who consistently provide quality products and services.

Vendor quality is measured carefully through the use of the "weighted point categorical method." It incorporates both objective and subjective ratings. The vendor evaluation process gathers fundamental information that can be used to judge the quality of a vendor's products or services.

- Was the material delivered on time?
- Were the proper items and quantities received?
- Was it a high quality product?
- Was there quality after-sales support?

The actual evaluation is divided into four primary categories:

- Quality of delivery.
- Quality of pricing.
- Quality of customer service.
- Quality of ordered products and systems.

There are 34 performance factors that fall under these four categories.

Under the "quality of delivery" category, GTE evaluates on-time delivery, on-time delivery without constant follow-up, lead-time competitiveness, whether the proper items and quantities are being delivered, accuracy of documentation, and willingness of the vendor to handle emergency deliveries.

Under "quality of pricing", we rate:

- Competitiveness of pricing, where a vendor's pricing is compared to that of competitors' for comparable products.

- Price stability, whether prices fluctuate from one purchase order to the next.

- Price accuracy, comparing the invoice to the actual contract or purchase order price.

- Advance notice of price changes, whether GTE is notified or must discover the change through the invoice or acknowledgement.

"Quality of customer service" rates a number of factors such as:

- Is there compliance to the payment and performance terms of the contract or purchase order?

- How effectively does the vendor handle complaints?

- How well do distributors provide feedback to and from the manufacturer, and pass that information along to GTE?

- Other factors, such as strong inside sales support, helpfulness, and market insight.

"Quality of customer service" includes a number of other considerations, such as training, technical support, emergency shipment and support, and invoicing. GTE considers all customer service factors to be very important.

The category of "quality of ordered products and systems" is broken down into various types of telecommunications equipment. Customer premises equipment is judged on product reliability, durability, and meeting specifications. The measurement is the number of defects as a percentage of the total products that have been issued to the field.

Printing wiring cards are separated into line and common PWC's. Their quality is evaluated on their reliability and durability during the initial turn-up, as well as during normal maintenance.

Systems are also evaluated for their reliability and durability for normal maintenance. We look at new system feature introductions separately, and closely.

Warranty repairs are measured by means of a ratio of acceptable warranty repairs and replacements to the total amount of defects sent in for repair.

The final factor is a subjective rating on the product or system's state of the art.

Now, how are these evaluations conducted? There are several ways. The factors I have been discussing are all part of a vendor evaluation questionnaire. Evaluators could come from any of nine different departments within the seven telephone operating companies, depending on the specific criterion. This ensures that when a vendor receives a quality evaluation, several points of view are represented.

Ratings include "Excellent", "Acceptable", "Marginal", and "Unacceptable". All evaluations are submitted to a central vendor quality group, which compiles data and writes a summary report. Each of the four categories -- quality of delivery, pricing, customer service, and products and systems -- is given a mean rating. These are rolled into a composite rating.

A composite rating of "Excellent" places a vendor in our "preferred" category. Lesser ratings are discussed by GTE and the vendor. The evaluation may help a vendor to uncover an area needing improvement, even when the vendor is making a concentrated effort to ensure quality. GTE works closely with its vendors to help as many as possible achieve the "preferred" status. When vendors show significant improvement or achieve a rating of "Excellent", GTE recognizes their performance with awards and commendations.

There are other ways in which GTE evaluates quality. Our own standardization management evaluation professionals -- located at GTE's modern lab facilities in Lexington, Kentucky -- conduct technical evaluations of a product's ability to meet published specifications.

We also conduct audits of our vendors' design, engineering, and manufacturing processes and facilities in order to assess how capable they are of producing a reliable product. These audits rely on questionnaires completed by the vendor management teams, as well as on-site visits by our own standardization management people.

Working together, an individual vendor and GTE develop their own individually-administered performance improvement targets for mature embedded base products, as well as process improvement objectives for new products. These targets and objectives are reviewed and revised each year.

Finally, given our cost and quality performance "drivers", GTE Telephone Operations wants to utilize those products that offer the best life-cycle cost performance. Life-cycle cost elements include:

- Capital, non-recurring, one-time charge, initial purchase cost, installation charge, out-of-box failures.

- Expense. An annual maintenance cash outlay repair charge with or without warranty, handling and postage, diagnostic and restoration costs.

- External failure cost. Customer goodwill lost because of excessive system downtime, revenue loss, and so forth.

Our systematic analysis of these three factors utilizes a Lotus program called Life-Cycle Cost Estimation, or LCCE.

To conclude, I would say that the Partners In Quality program is designed to be thorough, constructive, and effective. It is not a "quick fix" to quality-related problems. Instead, it is a long-term commitment to work with vendors as partners. The success of this process has already become evident -- in the gains experienced by GTE as well as by its preferred vendors.

As partners, both are benefitting from the achievement of quality.

TELECOMMUNICATIONS QUALITY: YOU'VE GOT TO KEEP THE CUSTOMER SATISFIED

Sharon L. Nelson
Chairman

Washington State Utilities and
Transportation Commission
South 1300 Evergreen Park Drive SW
Olympia, WA 98504

Since the early 1970's, "quality" has become a shibboleth among American producers. In the auto industry we are told that "quality is job one". Quality circles have spread across the plant floor. Still, I think the new focus on the quality of telecommunications service is one the most fascinating by products of recent industry changes. For years, high quality telecommunications service was taken as a given. Ma Bell was widely recognized as bringing us "the best telecommunications system in the world". Since divestiture, however, quality of service has come to the fore as a critical issue for the future. At the federal and state levels, virtually all proposals for regulatory reform explicitly include a quality of service element. In the market place telecommunications providers, such as U.S. Sprint, attempt to make quality a major selling point. Finally, conferences such as this one are addressing the issue of quality as a key attribute telecommunications managers must address.

What is really happening with quality of service? Are we really seeing a decline? Is there really something to worry about? My preliminary assessment is that it is too early to tell. Much of the evidence is anecdotal and contradictory. Therefore, I would like to spend my time today sketching some of the reasons I think that quality has become an important issue in telecommunications, and offer some preliminary observations on how the issue may develop.

I think quality has become a major issue for two fundamental reasons. The first reason is the changing economic structure of our country. It is trite but true that we are moving to an information age.

Increasing proportions of our economy are dependent upon the generation and distribution of information. In Washington state, anywhere from 30 to 40 percent of the work force can be reasonably classified as occupying information intensive jobs. Even basic extractive industries, such as timber, are becoming more information intensive with increasing use of computerized manufacturing and distribution facilities. The reason for this change is simple, as pointed out in a recent paper issued by the Harvard Program on Information Resources Policy. According to the paper, of all manufacturing inputs, only the capital cost of information is declining. Therefore, firms which can substitute information for other inputs in the manufacturing process can secure cost advantages and increased competitiveness. In addition, government and others facing resource constraints are increasingly turning to information technologies to improve service delivery and reduce cost. For example, our state is beginning to explore distributing state benefits, such as unemployment compensation through bank automatic teller machines. The authors of the Harvard study contend, and I would agree, that we are likely to see this trend accelerate over the next few years.

Another key factor driving the information revolution is demographics. As the baby boom goes bust, we are likely to see a shortage of skilled labor in many parts of the country. By using information to reduce labor intensity of jobs, manufacturers can cope with this new work force. Further, some employers are using information technology to make up for a lack of basic computational and communication skills in the work force. By turning calculations over to a machine, the employer can use a wider range of people in data entry jobs. I do not think this is a trend to be applauded, but it is a trend which will drive adoption of information technologies.

Information networks are the backbone of this new economy. In the past, telecommunications expenses were simply a cost of doing business. Now because of greater competitive choices and technological advances, these costs not only can be controlled, they represent an opportunity to create new profit centers and to exploit market niches. The increased importance of information technologies has led to increased concerns about their quality. The Mothers Day fire in Chicago, which knocked out a major switching center, points out the vulnerability of the system. I think most observers would find the failure of that switching office unacceptable. Certainly the businesses who are losing thousands of dollars and the residences enduring incredible inconvenience would agree. The Washington Post quoted the Hinsdale, Illinois Village Manager as saying, "I don't think anyone in the outside world understands what has happened here. They understand losing your phone service is an inconvenience. But phones are a necessity when you're trying to call your doctor, the fire department, or the school to see if your kid got there. Some of the day-to-day essentials we can't do here. Banks can't make transactions, businesses can't run their computers, stores can't get approval for credit card purchases. Burglar alarms don't work. People can't call the police." This lesson will serve to reinforce the need for a reliable and high quality telecommunications system.

Earlier I mentioned that under Ma Bell it was widely perceived we had the best, most reliable telephone system in the world. That perception, I fear, is no longer shared by many observers. Structural and economic changes in the industry have led to a situation where quality is becoming a real concern. For the most part, traditional application of rate of return regulation, in the context of a fairly tight and unchallenged monopoly, led to substantial redundancy in the system. Why put in one pair of wires when you could put in two? There was simply no real penalty for installing excess capacity or a more elaborate and exotic plant. With technology improving and unit costs falling, regulators had little incentive to police the prudency of major telephone company investments. The price was right and the service was good, so there was little reason to dig in and see if the system was being engineered in the leanest possible fashion.

Competition changes all of that by rewarding the low cost provider. One way to become a low cost provider is to reduce over-engineering of the network. Another way to reduce cost is to reduce maintenance and other expenditures -- to run the operation a little closer to the bone. In 1984, when I headed the staff of the Washington State Legislature's Joint Select Committee on Telecommunications, one of our more thoughtful members identified the problem precisely. He said that in a competitive market it might be inevitable that quality would decline because we may have been paying for a higher level of quality than a competitive market would sustain. It is interesting to note that all of the "market based" alternatives to rate of return regulation we are seeing, such as social contract and price caps, recognize that if a company has incentives to cut costs to increase profit, maintenance and service quality may be among the first areas to suffer. Because of previous over-engineering, we may not see deteriorating service from that cost cutting for some time. However, once deterioration occurs, the screams from the customers are likely to be loud and protracted, and the cost of improving the system at that point may be substantial. Thus, changing economic incentives in the industry, brought about by increased competition and higher profit desires are beginning to cause concerns about continued high service quality.

I think it is also important that when we discuss the word "quality" we define the term broadly. Certainly the provision of steady, quick dial tone is an element of quality. So is the clarity of voice and data transmission. But quality also includes customer perceptions about the overall bundle of services provided by a telephone company. If a company offers services that are not considered state of the art, no matter how well they perform by objective engineering standards, that company will not be perceived as providing high quality service. Let me give you an example, admittedly anecdotal, which illustrates my point. On the east side of Lake Washington we have a high technology corridor. Many new computer and software companies are located there along with several established industry giants such as Microsoft. Microsoft occupies the same business park with the Washington Community College Computing Consortium. Because of franchise boundaries, Microsoft is served by one local exchange company and the computing Consortium is served by another. Microsoft has access to a full array of ISDN-type services, while the Computing Consortium has difficulty getting adequate digital data lines. The lines the Computing Consortium receive are good, high quality lines, but they do not receive the same array of services as Microsoft, which they can see from their office windows. Another example comes from rural Washington. Many areas of rural Washington continue to have a high percentage of party lines. The Washington State Grange, among others, is beginning to press strongly to convert all party line service to one-party service. This is largely driven by the need for farmers to be able to tap into computer networks. In addition there are concerns that enhanced public safety services such as 911, are not available with party line service. Thus, a quality of service which was adequate in past times may not be adequate in the future. As more information age services become available, I expect these quality concerns to increase.

I do not mean to imply that we face an imminent crisis in service quality. When I was preparing for this talk, I asked a representative of one of our major industrial telecommunication users if he thought the quality of service was deteriorating. He said that he thought the quality of telephone service on the the public switched network was as good or better than it has ever been. Indeed, in our state, U.S. West Communications has invested heavily in digital technology - in all central offices, rural as well as suburban and urban. For the large industrial customer, which can afford a telecommunications manager and which is actively courted by competing telecommunications firms, the current environment offers an uprecendented array of choices and quality. This same manager also noted that for smaller firms and residential customers, the demise of end-to-end service could well lead to a perception that quality is decreasing. Again, our local BOC has attempted to counter this perception by extending hours of service for installation and repair work for residential customers. Further, he noted that big users have substantial concerns with implementation of open network architecture. Unless we are careful in implementation, ONA could make it difficult for firms to build an efficient, coordinated system.

During the years of the Bell System monopoly, AT&T was a de facto standards agency, setting high quality telecommunications standards followed by all companies. Since divestiture, standard setting has become more fragmented and no government agency has stepped in to play the role. I think that is a major concerns. I am a believer in the benefits of competition. I think competition forces companies to bring us better products at lower cost. On the other hand, competition can also lead to incompatible standards as companies try to carve out a market niche. While we may be able to live with Beta and VHS standards in the videocassette industry, I doubt people will tolerate any significant incompatibility in telecommunications. This concern was echoed in a recent issue of Rural Telecommunications. There it was reported that Bell Atlantic CEO Tom Bolger has been warning of the danger that "the public switched network will become "Balkanied," that is, broken up into smaller entities, possibly incompatible with each other." The article also noted that "prior to divestiture (standards setting) decisions were at least strongly influenced by AT&T. Now in the post MFJ world, investment and standards-setting decisions have been diffused."

So where do we go from here? While I do not think the evidence supports the notion that we are in a crisis of quality, there are legitimate concerns that need to be addressed. I think you are likely to see state and federal regulators begin to explicitly adopt service quality standards and begin to more aggressively monitor the quality of telecommunications services provided. I think you are likely to see large customers "vote with their feet" and penalize companies perceived to offer lower quality of service by shifting business elsewhere. For customers without the ability to switch companies, I think you are likely to see them agitating for high quality service in any forum they can-- regulatory, legislative or media. The telecommunications industry, as it becomes an ever more significant part of our economy, will be under increasing pressure to deliver higher quality service. If telephone bills take up a high proportion of the corporate or family budget, customers will demand greater value for their dollar and will become more vocal if they do not receive it. As the nation continues its experiments with deregulation and competition in the telecommunications industry, we should seek to avoid diminution in service quality such as that which occurred in the deregulated airline industry. The national goals of service quality, reliability, and appropriate redundancy remain important to consumers and to our overall national competitiveness.

PQR-10

NEW SOFTWARE DEVELOPMENT PROCESSES

Cyrenus M. Rubald, Chairperson
Department Head
5ESS® Switch System Integration Department

AT&T Bell Laboratories
1200 E. Warrenville Road
Naperville, IL 60566

ABSTRACT
The ever-increasing demand for new and complex communications software will continue for the foreseeable future. To meet this need of the industry, software development processes which are cost-effective, yet support rapid implementation, exceptional quality, and high productivity are needed. This seminar presents four sessions which deal with process innovations of the kind needed to move the industry to its challenging goals. A process to measure, manage, and influence software product quality is analyzed. Three case studies in high-leverage areas are presented: simulators for software testing; expert systems for engineering change problems; and a consolidated, improved method of software integration.

Henti Tung   - AT&T Bell Laboratories

Bernie Sander   - AT&T Bell Laboratories

Judd Ostle   - Northern Telecom, Inc.

Suresh Borkar   - AT&T Bell Laboratories

PROJECT MANAGEMENT - INCREASING FOCUS ON QUALITY

Henti Tung
Member of Technical Staff
5ESS Switch System (5E5) Project
Management

AT&T Bell Laboratories
1200 E. Warrenville Road
Naperville, IL 60566

ABSTRACT

This paper describes a quality management process which is used for a large switching software development project. The project has an established quality goal to reduce the expected customer-found fault density after product is delivered. The main focus in this discussion is the fault detection and removal activities of each phase in the software life cycle. The monitoring of the fault detection activities starts at the beginning of the project and continues throughout the software product development life cycle. Quality metrics are established and tracked for each development phase to ensure that the product quality is satisfactory at each phase and is moving towards the overall quality goal. To assure that all detected known problems are resolved, a fault tracking mechanism is used to record and track such problems. Boundaries between the software life cycle phases are clearly defined and formalized so that transition from one phase to the next is easily tracked with measurable quality. The project management organization is charged with the quality management responsibilities to monitor and analyze the quality data and to control the product quality trend with respect to the overall quality goal.

INTRODUCTION

Managing for Quality

Product quality is defined by the customers to whom the product is for. The customers have a set of expectations toward the product and their satisfaction level is based on the ability of the product to meet or exceed these expectations. For a software product, the elements upon which the overall quality assessment may be based are:

- the software product itself,

- the related documentation,

- software services including product installation, maintenance, operation, field updates, and reliability, etc.

An objective assessment of the customers satisfaction level can be made by counting the number of customer complaints toward the product during the product life cycle. The complaints may cover a wide range of problems from operational software, and documentation, to services and procedures. Some of these complaints may be customer specific and are problems only to certain customers for whatever the particular situations they might be in. Most of the other complaints are more general types of problems and can be traced back to the design and development flaws which did not get uncovered and corrected before the product is delivered to the customer. This latter class of problems are the ones we hope to eliminate or to reduce through the quality management process. In order to deliver to the customer a clean and quality product, free from faults and errors, it is necessary that we detect and correct all the faults prior to the delivery of the product. On one hand, it seems to be a very expensive proposal because of the amount of testing effort it would require to fully test a large software product. The situation will become worse as the number of remaining design faults and errors increases. The amount of testing and regression testing required can become prohibitively costly and time consuming. On the other hand, if we can assume that the software product is reasonably free from design errors and faults when it is being tested, the testing would become relatively straightforward. In other words, the testing simply verifies the fact that the software product worked exactly according to its design. The following is a set of principles which should be followed in order to have a high quality design:

- do it right the first time,

- catch faults and errors early,

- eliminate root cause of faults and errors.

In this project, the software development process is divided into a number of phases based on the software life cycle model. Each of the phases is clearly defined as far as its requirements and conditions and the tasks that need to be completed. Extensive development methodology and process descriptions are used to help the developers to complete the tasks in each phase. To assure that quality is designed into the product, various verification and validation techniques are used to check the quality of the output of each phase. Quality metrics are established to evaluate the quality data and the effectiveness of the fault detection and removal activities of each phase. The quality management responsibility is given to the project management organization. It provides the necessary monitoring and control functions to ensure the integrity of the development process and that the process output satisfies its customer.

QUALITY PLAN AND GOALS

In a quality management system, one of the most important elements is to have a quality plan. The quality plan is:

- a mechanism and approach to accomplish quality goals,
- a way to systematically manage quality improvement,

- a way to focus resource on quality.

The major quality improvement goal is to reduce the amount of customer found fault density. In order to achieve this goal, two approaches are taken. One approach is to improve the process so that less faults are introduced in the development of the product. The other approach is to increase the effectiveness of fault detecting activities in the development phases. The objective is to find the problems as early as possible.

THE PROCESS

The development phases in a software life cycle model can be described as:

- generic/feature planning,

- architecture,

- capability requirements,

- capability design,

- unit design,

- coding,

- unit testing,

- capability testing,

- integration/system test,

- site testing.

PROCESS DESCRIPTIONS/
DEVELOPMENT METHODOLOGY

One of the critical aspects of process quality is consistency. A complete and accurate process description represents a consensus of current understanding of the process and the associated requirements and conditions.

- With the process descriptions the project members can have a consistent view of the entire process.

- It allows each project member to follow the same path through the development process.

- It provides a unified base for quality comparison and evaluation.

- It helps to assure consistent results on quality.

- It provides the basis for process improvement.

- Clarification of work activities

- Systematic identification and removal of the root cause

- Problem prevention

- Reduced fire-fighting

- Achievement of quality objectives in less time and less effort.

PROCESS OUTPUT

There are four types of output from the development process.

- Documents - Documents are generated in the planning, requirement, design, and unit design phases. These documents represent the results of a sequence of translation steps which converts the external customer requirements to the detailed system implementation. The quality of these documents in terms of its conformance to the customer requirements has a great impact at the subsequent phases. A formal review process is used to provide the quality check of the documents.

- Software code - The output of the coding phase is the software code. An accurate coding is vital in order to convert the paper design into machine executable form while maintaining all the design quality obtained in previous phases. The accuracy and functionality of the software code is checked with a formal code inspection.

- The number of tests executed and passed - From the unit testing to site testing, each phase is required to have a set of tests written and executed to verify the software functionality and customer documentation appropriate for that level. The number of tests passed represents the level of completion of that phase and the quality of the product.

- Quality Index - The testing spans multiple test phases. It uses runs to measure the system performance level by exercising all of the functions of the software under a sustained load for a period of time. This is done to demonstrate that the software is reasonably free of serious or numerous errors. Under this test, the software should be stressed to its designed capacities and beyond in order to ensure that the system operates with an acceptably low level of system error messages. An index is computed at the end of runs to provide product quality index.

PROCESS CONTROLS

The development process may be controlled through the following:

GUIDELINES

Guidelines are important for the in-process controls. It provides directions for the process activities and can be modified and adjusted based on new information obtained in the process.

ENTRY AND EXIT CRITERIA

The entrance and exit criteria for each process phase are established to formalize the process boundaries. These are the conditions that must be satisfied before the task in a phase can begin or end.

PHASE TRANSITION

In order for the transition from one stage to the next to occur, the specific criteria must be met and satisfied. Control of the phase transition can ensure that the necessary quality is obtained at each phase before the output of one phase may be passed to the next phase for processing.

PHASE OUTPUT VALIDATION

- Reviews

  A formal peer level review is held to ensure the accuracy and the quality of the document produced in each phase. All reviewers are required to sign-off on the review report and to indicate their recommendation for disposition (rating). The disposition of the document is based on the lowest or the worst rating given by the reviewers. If the final disposition is not acceptable, then rework or re-reviews may be needed. If the rating is acceptable, then the final check is provided by passing the document through a committee with representations from all areas.

- Code Inspection

  A code inspection is held after the coding has been completed, and any compiler detectable errors have been corrected. The code inspection should be performed before any unit test activities. The inspection is done at the peer level and an overview meeting may be held to help inspectors to become familiar with the code and the design. Several other non-traditional code inspection techniques such as code walk-through, interface inspections, and unit test scenario walk-through, etc., are sometimes used to increase the effectiveness of the inspection.

- Test Completion

  Each test phase requires a certain percentage of planned tests to be executed and passed before the phase may be considered

SUPPORTING SYSTEMS

- Test Control System

  The test control system is used to track the test progress. It helps to document and keep track of tests by keeping the test scripts and record of test status on-line. It provides

1490

automated test status reports which can be used as a tool by developers and management. It offers a permanent record of completed tests and the associated test details which can be used for future reference and regression testing.

- Coverage Monitor

A coverage monitor is a computerized system for measuring which lines of computer software have been executed. It can be done with a hardware monitor system which does non-interfering monitoring or a software monitor system which modifies and interferes with the software being tested. In any case, the purpose of this system is to provide indicator of code coverage during testing to ensure that all legs of code have been tested. A full coverage of the code is required for the completion of unit testing phase.

- Problem Tracking

All the problems reported in the product life cycle are maintained in a problem tracking database. It keeps a complete record of the problem descriptions, the error conditions, the generic and the development phase in which the problem was found, the priority status, and other information such as the date when the IMR was opened. The problem is closed when it is solved with a modification request to the generic. The problem tracking database provides a problem tracking mechanism from "open" to "close" of any problem. The number of "opened" problems at any given point in time represents the number of unsolved known problems remaining in the system.

- Quality Database

The measured quality data are stored in a computer database which is easily accessible to members in project management. This database is periodically audited to assure its accuracy. The quality data are used in various types of quality analysis and the results of the quality analysis may be used for the following purposes:

- overall quality assessment of the product

- understand trends of the software product performance

- provide feedback to project members

- understand the source of errors and faults

- identify high risk areas

- new process improvement

- identify needs for new metrics and tools

The software product quality indicated by the quality data and metrics should be verified with the actual product performance. It is important that the metrics reflect the product quality as closely and accurately as possible. The metrics may be evolved on an ongoing basis based on the past history and new information.

RESPONSIBILITIES

Achieving quality requires a team working spirit among project members. No one organization can single-handedly work to achieve quality.

Development organizations need to produce good product quality by design. To do this, developers should have good knowledge of the customer requirements, the feature, the methodology, the development process and environment, the quality process guidelines, criteria, and metrics, and adequate training to fully understand the system. Prior to handing the product over to testers, developers should have the product tested to the extent that feature level functionalities have been verified.

The test organizations take the product and run it through a rigorous set of tests to integrate features into a generic, to shake down any problems developers are not capable of finding, to stress test under load condition, to perform quality runs and obtain the index, to test customer documentation, and to perform site testing. In the end, the test organization would have verified the quality of the product by thoroughly testing it under various conditions and to assure the customers of high quality product with a high stability.

The project management organization acts independent of the development and test organizations. It should have sufficient authority and freedom to perform quality-related tasks. These include:

- To issue quality guidelines and criteria for the process,

- To ensure that the quality process is adhered to and followed during product life cycle,

- To perform product trend analysis and exercise control,

- To provide quality feedback in weekly status meeting,

- To perform other project management functions.

It is important for project management to show its support to the project community. It should encourage and act on feedback from project members regarding the quality process and to actively seeking process simplification without sacrificing quality.

PROJECT MANAGEMENT FOCUS ON QUALITY

The following are some examples of project management activities to focus on quality issues.

- Use project benchmark tracking to enforce the formal transition between development phases and to assure that the entry and exit criteria are satisfied.

- Review quality - The quality data obtained from each review process are applied to a process model for evaluation. If the results are not satisfactory, then feedback will be given and re-review may be recommended.

- Code inspection quality - The results of each inspection and its quality data are applied in a remaining coding error estimate model. Based on the model, the quality of the code and the amount of remaining error density may be estimated. An re-inspection may be recommended if the model indicates that the remaining error density is higher than the acceptable level. The current results have shown that the re-inspection effort is effective in uncovering additional faults which would otherwise be found in the testing.

- Development phase quality history - A history of errors found in each phase is kept in the quality database. The data may be used in various ways to show the product quality trend, the effectiveness of the fault detection activities, and to identify the new quality data or metrics that might be needed.

- Problem tracking - In addition to being a tracking mechanism of known faults, problem tracking data may be used to provide some product quality indication and to identify the risk areas. For example, the open/close rate, the number of "opened" problems at various phases, the areas that have the most number of problems, and so forth.

- Status report - Organize weekly project status meetings to provide reports to the project on the project status and quality issues. Through this forum, the project members are encouraged to focus on quality issues in the discussion to raise awareness of quality.

CONCLUSION

A quality management process model for a large software project is discussed. The underlying development process uses extensive methodology support plus the verification and validation techniques such as formal reviews and code inspections to assure that product quality is "built-in" from design inception and implementation rather than "added-on" through last-minute testing. With quality metrics and entry/exit criteria the output of each phase is examined to determine if the expected quality has been achieved. The product quality is monitored by project management which is independent and charged with project quality responsibilities. The overall objective of the process is to detect and remove errors early in the product development phases and thereby to minimize the number of customer found errors.

A SWITCH SIMULATOR FOR SOFTWARE INTEGRATION

Bernard T. Sander
Supervisor
AP and Attendent Recent Change Group

AT&T Bell Laboratories
1200 E. Warrenville Road
Naperville, IL 60566

ABSTRACT

A switch simulator of the 5ESS Switch was provided as a cost-effective alternative to a system laboratory for testing much of the software in a recently released generic. The simulator was used most extensively in strip debugging of Recent Change software and in verifying the Office Dependent Data for System Laboratory. It was also used extensively in testing and debugging the call processing software developed for ISDN Business Residential Customer Services, Operator Services and Toll features.

This session provides a summary of the functionality provided by the simulator in supporting the above testing. Use of the simulator in the different phases of the development process is described. The paper closes with a review of usage patterns, cost effectiveness and plans for future evolution.

INTRODUCTION

System laboratory tests models for testing code associated with new features on the 5ESS Switch are expensive both to purchase and to maintain. To control costs and to improve developer productivity in the test phase, significant effort has been devoted to providing a simulator of the 5ESS Switch. The use of this simulator in the development of a recent 5ESS Generic is described.

The first section provides an introduction to the 5ESS Switch and the construction of the simulator. The software development process and the role of the simulator in that process are described in the next two sections. The fourth section provides a summary of support effort required and economies associated with the use of this simulator. The final section is a summary and a view of further extensions to a successful tool for software development.

SIMULATION OF THE 5ESS SWITCH

The architecture of the 5ESS Switch contains a number of loosely coupled processors. There are many levels of processors, but we shall limit the discussion to the Administrative Module and the Switch Modules. The processors excluded from this discussion provide a large number of other functions like input/output, links to operational support systems, digital service circuits, line unit control, etc. These processors are all interconnected to the system through either the administrative module or one of the switch modules.

The administrative module handles many of the global functions required by the switch - path hunt, routing, billing, traffic reports, centralized maintenance, etc. The switch modules provide for all the functions associated with the lines, trunks and service circuits terminated on the switch module. These functions include scanning, hardware control, diagnostics and port-associated data.

The administrative module and the switch module are loosely coupled through the communication module. Each of these processors has its own operating system and communicates via messages through the communication module with other processors in the multiprocessor environment of the 5ESS Switch.

A typical 2-party call (line-to-line, trunk-to-line, or line-to-trunk) requires that functions be performed by three of these processors - the administrative module and two switch modules. Multiway or other complex calls may require functions in more than three modules.

Terminal processes with associated data are created in each of the switch modules serving the ports between which the call is to be made. Messages are passed between them to/from the global process in the administrative module in handling a call from initial recognition of the off-hook to tearing down the path.

The simulation of this multiprocessor environment is accomplished by creating a process on the simulator for each of the processors in the switch. These processes are then coupled or linked by passing messages through a shared memory segment. Additional processes created on the simulator provide for emulation of the ISDN Customer Premise Equipment, links to signal transfer points, etc. Both simple analog and very complex ISDN calls can be made (simulated) using the configurations supported on the simulator.

The processes built for the simulator do not include all of the code included in building loads for the 5ESS Switch. Specifically, most of the code associated with hardware and its maintenance is not included in the simulation. Thus, code providing functions like diagnostics are fault recovery cannot be tested using the simulator. The exclusion of this code and associated functionality was done to reduce complexity and size of files on the simulator. It also facilitated an emphasis on providing a high-quality, cost-effective environment for the areas where most testing is done on the simulator - specifically Recent Change and Call Processing.

The test tools and the user interface to these tools are almost identical to those available to developers in system test laboratories. These test capabilities included tracing tools, quick fix or patch capabilities, and facilities for use of private products. This requirement of sameness is viewed as essential to the success of the simulator. Developers must find it easy to move between the "real" world of a system laboratory and a simulation of that environment.

Access to the simulator was provided through Datakit to 5ESS Switch software developers. Thus, an individual developer can work at his/her desk by logging into the simulator, setting up a desired test configuration and testing. Problem discovery in functional areas supported on the simulator was more immediate and thorough than in areas where laboratory time needed to be scheduled.

THE SOFTWARE INTEGRATION PROCESS

The software development process utilized in the development of features for the 5ESS Switch follows a methodology much like that used in most large software development projects.

The development process consists of a design, coding, and testing phases. The design process is a top-down process starting with high-level requirements and moving to the lowest level of requirements and design. The three levels are features, capabilities, and design units, with the design unit level being the lowest level in the top-down process. The number of elements tends to increase through the process, i.e., there are many more design units than features. Features are typically broken into capabilities and capabilities into design units, though it is not required to maintain a strict tree structure. Many to many mappings are permitted in the methodology and are, in fact, frequently used in the design process. A design unit is constrained to specification of changes within a single subsystem. Subsystems are defined along functional boundaries - like audits, feature control or Recent Change. Requirements and design documentation is prepared and reviewed at all phases of the design process.

The coding phase includes the writing and inspection of the code changes in the subsystem. The implementation follows the specifications of the design unit documentation as approved by the review process of the design phase. The code inspection utilizes a rigorous procedure to ensure that high-quality code which satisfies specifications is being introduced. All code changes must be inspected before being introduced into the load line.

The testing phase parallels the design phase, but moves from the lowest level of design unit testing to feature level testing. Test plans based on requirements/design at each level of the design phase are prepared, reviewed and executed as design units are built into capabilities and capabilities into features.

To support this software development process, a load line is supported in the test laboratories and the simulator. The loads supported in this load line are periodically updated by incorporating additions and fixes. A new load is built, brought up in the laboratory and the simulator and then distributed to all test models. The bringup process includes extensive regression and stability testing. Mechanisms for including patches and fixes during the bringup process ensure that existing functionality in the load is maintained and that developers can continue to be productive, i.e., concentrate their efforts on new features.

Strong links were established between the bringup of loads in the system laboratories and the bringup on the simulator. These ties were used to ensure commonality between the loads available in the two environments. These same ties were used in frequently updating the Office Dependent Data available on the simulator. This commonality was another of the elements critical to making the simulator a productive environment for developers as they moved between the laboratory and simulator environments.

DEVELOPMENT USE OF THE SIMULATOR

The simulator was used most successfully in testing at the lowest level (Design Unit) phase of the software development process, though it was also successfully used in several other areas - such as capability testing, problem resolution, verification of fixes, and Office Dependent Data verification. This section provides a brief summary of some of the ways the simulator was used in the development of ISDN Business Residential Customized Services, OSPS features, and Toll features.

Recent Change is the 5ESS functional area (subsystem) which provides the switch craft the ability to modify the Office Dependent Data for additions/deletions of units or ports to the switch or to make changes in the features active on a given port. Extensive development was done in the Recent Change subsystem for all areas in which new features were developed - Business Residential Customized Services, Operator Services, and Toll. The correlation between the laboratory and simulator environment is highest for the Recent Change subsystem. As a consequence, a methodology has evolved in which most testing in this subsystem is done on the simulator. This includes almost all design unit level testing and some capability level testing. Most Recent Change problems are debugged on the simulator. The emphasis on using the simulator rather than a laboratory test model permits rapid turnaround of fixes and early testing of new code. Use of the simulator in this subsystem accounted for approximately one-half of the total usage of the simulator in the generic release.

Extensive testing in other subsystems was also done. The development of ISDN Business Residential Customized Services made use of the simulator for design unit level testing in the feature control subsystem for debugging of some feature problems and for pretesting of fixes with the simulator prior to verification on a system laboratory test model. The pretesting of fixes included extensive regression testing and resulted in much more efficient use of the expensive laboratory test models and higher quality fixes being submitted to the load integration process.

A methodology utilized in the development of Operator Services provided for a "common" load on the simulator with untested changes from a pool of developers. This "common" load was built on top of the supported load line by building a new load with these additional changes and then rerunning regression tests. The new, untested code was then tested in this "common" load prior to submission to the supported load line. Both Recent Change and Operator Service functionality was integrated through this methodology. The process provided a very stable and cost-effective mechanism and resulted in very high-quality Operator Services code. This methodology was used in other areas, particularly Business Residential Customized Services, but not as successfully as in the development of Operator Services. The difference in success appears to be due to differences in complexity and number of interfaces.

The development of Toll features utilized less total simulator time than other features, but did successfully use it to emulate a large number of trunk types, including trunks with common channel signaling links. Loop-around trunks and a signal transfer point emulator were used in setting up the desired test configurations.

An area which made extensive use of the simulator was verification of the Office Dependent Data for system test laboratories during the final phase of feature testing. The Office Dependent Data is the data base of features associated with lines and trunks on the switch. A mechanism was provided by which Office Dependent Data bases for the system test laboratory could be transported between the two environments - system test laboratory model and simulator. The simulator was then used to verify proper population of relations in the data as well as special test configurations. These were then saved and moved to the system laboratory for testing of features.

A GENERIC DEVELOPMENT EXPERIENCE

This section summarizes briefly the overall support required in the successful use of the simulator in the development and integration of a recent generic providing business, residential, Operator Services and Toll features. There were two peaks in weekly usage. The first occurred during the design unit test phase and provided test facilities equivalent to approximately eight system test models.

The second peak occurred much later in the cycle and was due to two important

factors - use of the simulator to either debug problems or verify fixes and the use of the simulator to verify system laboratory Office Dependent Data. In this peak period, the equivalent of four to five system test models were provided by the simulator. Since a simulator test hour is approximately one-seventh the cost of a test hour in a system test model, the use of this simulator contributed significantly to controlling the development cost associated with testing this complex generic with many new features.

The extensive use of a simulator for the 5ESS Switch in the development of feature software required a number of changes in culture and methodology. To facilitate this, significant effort was devoted to ensuring the quality of the test environment on the simulator. User meetings to introduce new capabilities and discuss problems were held at frequent intervals. Help lines and beepers were used to ensure that problems could be quickly resolved and questions answered immediately. Groups in critical areas were "adopted" with special support and dedicated interfaces. A special interface with frequent contact was established with the computer center providing the machines on which the simulator was provided.

SUMMARY

The simulator for the 5ESS Switch described in this paper provides a cost-effective vehicle in the development of Recent Change and Call Processing functionality. It was used extensively and successfully in the development of a recent generic software release for the 5ESS Switch containing ISDN Business Residential Customized Services, Operator Services, and Toll features.

A number of extensions to the simulator are currently under active development. Among the more interesting are additional audit testing capabilities, interfaces to automated call simulators, and new test capabilities for data services and primary rate interfaces.

EXPERT SYSTEMS: THE PROMISE AND THE

REALITY

Judson Ostle
Director
Business Systems Meridian Business Systems

Northern Telecom Inc.
2305 Mission College Boulevard
Santa Clara, CA 95054

ABSTRACT

This paper will describe the reasons for selecting an Expert System approach to a multi-location engineering change management problem. The original expectations were that this developmental approach would take less time, cost less money, require less maintenance, and deliver the needed functionality across many divisions located in the United States and Canada. The majority of our expectations have been met or exceeded, and we are exploring new ways to apply this technology.

INTRODUCTION

Project Background

The results of a division-wide business data model study suggested our engineering change process should be given a more detailed analysis.

In mid 1985, a project leader was hired and a formal requirements phase was launched. After 6 months of hundreds of interviews, a twenty foot process flow chart was developed which described the many activities, and processes that were involved in handling engineering changes in the division. Now, for the first time, we knew how the process worked, which organizations participated in what activities and, most importantly, the relationships between these activities.

When we stepped back and looked at it, we found we had three different processes, 48 major activities, and entirely different engineering change systems for different product lines. The next step was to simplify, or synthesize, these diverse approaches to proceeding an engineering change in order to develop a solution that could be handled by an information system. A requirement specification incorporating this synthesis was completed and approached in December 1985. Because there was a high level of interest throughout the company in how to more effectively handle engineering changes, other divisional inputs were solicited. As a result of differing business requirements from one division to another, a single change process useable by all could not be defined. Instead, a flexible system was needed that could be easily modified at each division to reflect local business and process needs. Each site was encouraged to document their existing processes, then simplify them.

After incorporating other divisional inputs, an RFP and External Specification was issued to a number of software vendors in mid 1986. As envisioned, the system would have to (1) become a repository of process knowledge, (2) process text and graphics "pages," (3) provide queries and reports, (4) integrate with IEDB (an SQL/DS Relational Database) and the Product Administration System, and (5) run on IBM mainframes under VM. Their responses ranged from $300K - $1M and would take six to nine months to complete the project. One of the bidders commented, "Do you realize you have written a specification for an expert system?"

PROTOTYPE PHASE

The cost of the various bids was far in excess of the funds available to continue the project, so based on the bidder's suggestion we conducted a review of expert systems as a less expensive alternative. A vendor was selected to construct a prototype to verify that an expert system was the appropriate development approach and that it would deliver the functionality to meet our requirements. The Expert System software was installed in January 1987 and the prototype was completed in just 72 days by a knowledge engineer and one software engineer. After a company-wide technical review, the Expert System approach was approved, and we began to develop the first generation production system.

DEVELOPMENT PHASE

ECM Phase 01, our first production system, was completed by a team of one knowledge engineer and three software engineers in 3 months and turned over to the users for acceptance testing in November 1987. To verify its' functionality another division installed and tested this same version, and found that it met 75 percent of their needs. This same version was also used to demonstrate the tremendous velocity that can be gained in digital design transfer.

In March of this year, we began development of an enhanced version of ECM, Phase 02. The delivered product will be fully integrated with the Product Structure Manager, at the application and data base levels, incorporate advanced graphics capabilities, and provide expanded user and system manager functionality.

LESSONS LEARNED

Expert System projects can be divided up and managed much like traditional system development projects. In the development phase, Expert Systems tends to be much more iterative than traditional system projects.

Knowledge acquisition will take longer than originally planned. Therefore, the knowledge engineers· expertise at constructing valid and logical rules is vital to this process. Knowledge bases, or the collection of rules, are best segmented from a design and processing efficiency standpoint. Our first attempt in developing ECM was to create a single knowledge base of over 200 rules. This not only lead to inefficient processing, but unnecessarily complicated the effort to make changes to the knowledge base. We have subsequently divided the single knowledge base into 28 separate knowledge bases.

Accurately estimating computing resources, particularly CPU demand, are difficult at best. Backward and forward chaining activities can consume more CPU resources than originally expected.

Finally, select the application first, then the tool. The ideal application should have the following characteristics: well understood, preferably a small, self-contained problem.

CONCLUSION

Expert Systems are a viable tool for developing flexible solutions for complex processing problems. When we decided to use an Expert System for this application, our expectations were that the development system could be reduced; the resulting architecture would be flexible enough to be used throughout the corporation; and the on-going maintenance effort would be considerably less than systems developing using conventional languages. To date, the elapsed development time and total cost for ECM has been roughly one half of the amount of time and cost of a traditional system project. ECM is currently installed in three locations, one of which has markedly different engineering processes than the other two. Our current maintenance effort amounts to the equivalent of two people, much less than would be needed for support of a traditional system project of this size. For us, Expert Systems have kept their promises, and we are looking for other opportunities to extend their potential.

REFERENCES

1. "Expert Systems for Business", B. Silverman, Addison-Wesley, 1987.

2. "Putting Expert Systems Into Practice", R. Bowerman and D. Glover, Van Norstrand Reinhold Company, 1988.

3. "Expert System: Tools and Applications", P. Harnon, John Wiley, 1988.

PROCESS IMPROVEMENT FOR SOFTWARE INTEGRATION IN A DISTRIBUTED ENVIRONMENT

Suresh R. Borkar
Supervisor
Large Systems Development Department

AT&T - R&D (EUO)
1100 E Warrenville Road
Naperville, IL 60566

ABSTRACT

The development activity for a typical computer product generally involves several tasks being carried out over a distributed network of computers and a combination of manual procedures and integration load building tools. This note identifies two major areas of software integration process improvement relating to such a distributed environment - a set of automation tools and a consolidated development and integration environment based on the use of the AT&T 3B^{TM}4000 computer.

INTRODUCTION

AT&T has recently introduced a highly-coupled high end minicomputer called the AT&T 3B4000 [1]. The development of a typical large computer system like the 3B4000 computer and similar other developments involve the complex steps of integrating various hardware, firmware, and software modules. As part of the continuing effort of quality and process improvements being carried out in the R&D laboratories for various projects, the process of integration of software for the 3B4000 computer was monitored, evaluated, and recommendations for further improvements were generated. The results can be applied to the projects of similar scope. The intent of this paper is to share the experience gained in this effort to-date.

The next section summarizes the terminology and a description of a typical integration process. The analysis of the data obtained during the monitoring of the integration process is indicated next. The recommendations based on the analysis of the data are covered subsequently followed by concluding remarks.

TYPICAL INTEGRATION PROCESS

The critical initial step for process improvement [2] requires the definition and identification of customer requirements. Typically for the integration activity, the vendors are the developers who submit the code as per the requirements of their subsystems. The output of the integration activity is then delivered to the customers. The customers are the testers and the developers who in turn may carry out further development and modifications. The first step in integration involves the process of building the software system, e.g., the UNIX^{TM} system with its associated kernel and commands. Subsequent to this load building activity, the second step involves installing and testing the load on the computer hardware laboratory. The load may then be delivered to the customers after it passes the necessary exit criteria (see Fig. 1).

The first step in this sequence of events involves the development of code by developers under a project change management system. Depending upon the size of the project and the modularity of the system, the development and integration environment may involve a set of computer resources interconnected via a network, e.g., the members of the 3B family of computers [3] connected via the AT&T 3BNET[TM] [4] or the AT&T STARLAN[TM] [5] network (See Fig. 2). The delivery of the developers' code into integration must pass a set of entrance criteria mutually agreed to by the development community and the integration team. These criteria generally include a measure of the quality of the code in terms of absence of errors during the building of the subsystems and the passing of component tests performed by the developers.

Subsequent to the completion of the deliveries by the developers, the first step in the integration activity may involve the collection of the source code changes on to a centralized load building computer. Several manual and automated load building steps are then carried out by the integration team to build the software system called the "load". Generic load building steps include (See Fig. 3)

● a mechanism for accepting a list of changes from the developers and the associated information pertinent to the subsystem and its impact on other subsystems,

● a screening step to verify that the developer deliveries meet the integration entrance criteria,

● the step of reformatting and/or filtering the information received from the developers to make it suitable for load building,

● a sequence of manual or automated steps to build the load, and

● the final steps of building the file systems so that the load can then be installed and tested on the system hardware.

After the load is built, the load testing phase is initiated. This usually is the first time the subsystems with all their changes are built into a combined system. Any problem encountered during the installation and operation of the load on the hardware is either fixed by

incorporating additional changes or deferred, depending upon the severity of the problem. The passage of the load to the customers depends on the successful completion of a set of exit criteria typically involving a minimum set of functional capabilities.

In general, the measure for a process involves the quality of the delivery to the customer and the timeliness of this delivery. The integration process, in a general sense, provides a filter function by verifying the basic sanity or functionality of the software system and identifying inconsistencies between the changes made by different developers. Hence the quality of the integrated system delivered to the customers depends primarily on the quality of the "raw material" (i.e. software changes) delivered by developers. For this process, therefore, timeliness of the delivery is of primary interest and is within process boundaries. The quality of the delivery is part of the overall software development process. Only the first issue of timeliness is being addressed here.

DATA COLLECTION AND ANALYSIS

After the process and the customer requirements are defined, the next step involves the identification of the control points in the system and the establishment of the mechanisms for measurements at these control points. During the development of the 3B4000 computer, the integration process summarized above was divided into a controllable number of distinct activities with their associated input and output boundaries. A template was generated to document the data. The start and end times, the problems encountered, and the resolutions for each of the problems were then documented for a series of loads built and tested.

The data collected over a series of loads indicated that the process was in statistical control (see, e.g., P. 65 of [6]). This implied that individual errors need not be individually scrutinized and corrected, but the underlying process needed to be studied in detail for improvements. In other words, the steps of defect analysis had to be carried out so that the underlying reasons for "classes" of errors rather than the specific errors could be identified. The errors encountered and the time for resolution for each of the errors were grouped into several bins and the Pareto analysis technique [6] was used to identify improvement opportunities.

RECOMMENDATIONS

The primary emphasis for improvement was identification of areas within the process boundaries. The major areas for improvements were reduction of the elapsed time for procedures and human interfaces and the improvement in the machine environment for software development and integration.

The reduction of elapsed time involves the automation of various interfaces and procedures. This is a series of tools, each taking the output from the previous tool and providing the input to the next one (See Fig. 4). The intent is to automate the developer-to-integration interface, perform appropriate checkpoints, and eliminate manual procedures.

The first of these series of tools (the deliver tool) automates the developer-to-integration delivery procedure. The next one, called the screening tool, reduces the time taken to check the acceptance criteria for load building and making other validity checks. In addition to performing various audit functions, this tool also provides data on the deliveries back to the developers. The pre-process tool reformats and filters the developer deliveries into a form suitable for load building. This tool does the sorting functions for each subsystem build and provides the build instructions in their final form for load building purposes. The last load build procedure tool then interactively carries out the actual steps of the load building procedures.

The other major area for improvement addresses the problems encountered due to networking in a distributed development environment. It also provides a speed up of the integration procedures via the use of a faster processor. The AT&T 3B4000 computer [1] was identified as the system which meets both of these needs because of its unique architecture. The 3B4000 computer consists of a host processor and a set of adjunct processors interconnected via a fast packet bus (See Fig. 5). The current adjunct processors can easily be used for their specialized functions. The Adjunct Communications Processor (ACP) is used for allowing connections for developers, integration engineers, and other users. The developer activity can be carried out on the other adjuncts, specifically the Enhanced Adjunct Data Processor (EADP) which supports user file systems and provides processing power. The architecture of the 3B4000 computer allows isolation of the load building activity to a specific EADP which can be declared "private" so that the load building activity is minimally affected by the developer activity being carried out elsewhere in the system. This facility in the 3B4000 computer can even be extended to subsystem developments so that the environment can be optimized for any mix of development types. The 3B4000 computer also allows a single machine view of the development environment to the user.

CONCLUDING REMARKS

Based on the systematic approach of process quality management and improvement, two major areas for integration process improvement have been identified - the use of automation tools for load building and consolidation of development and integration activities on to a computer system which allows specialized functions and at the same time allows efficient sharing of data and information, viz the 3B4000 computer. These steps are part of a continuing emphasis at AT&T for quality and productivity improvement.

ACKNOWLEDGEMENTS

This paper is based on the efforts of a task force at AT&T R&D (EUO) in Naperville, IL. Tariq Badsha was the process owner and the members of the team were Betty Cox, Roger Hortin, Bill Spanogle, and Jim Valastro, all from AT&T. Their contributions are sincerely acknowledged.

REFERENCES

1. "Documentation, Training, and Support Guide for the AT&T 3B4000 Computer", AT&T

2. R.B.Ackerman, R.J.Coleman, E.Leger, and J.C.MacDorman, "Process Quality Management & Improvement Guidelines", AT&T Bell Laboratories, 1987.

3. "3B Application Software Packaging Guide", AT&T

4. "AT&T 3BNET Overview", AT&T

5. "AT&T STARLAN NETWORK - Technical Reference Manual", AT&T

6. W.S.Scherkenbach, "The Deming Route to Quality and Productivity", CeePress, Washington, D.C.

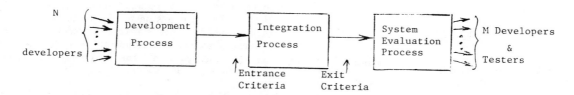

Figure 1: Overview of Integration Process

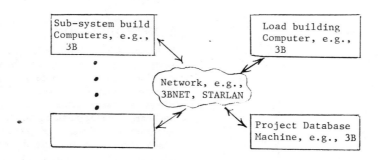

Figure 2: A Typical Distributed Development
and Integration Environment

Figure 3: Typical Load Building Steps

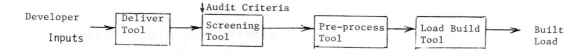

Figure 4: Series of Automation Tools

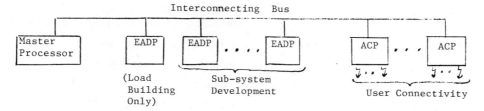

EADP: Enhanced Adjunct Data Processor
ACP : Adjunct Communications Processor

Figure 5: AT&T 3B4000 Computer as a Development and
Integration Machine

1500

PQR-11

MANAGING SOFTWARE DEVELOPMENT FOR QUALITY & PRODUCTIVITY

D. P. Smith
Head, Switching System
Quality Department

AT&T Bell Laboratories

1200 East Warrenville Road
Naperville, IL 60566
(312)979-1383

ABSTRACT

Software development quality and estimation is a major business priority issue. The ability to accurately estimate the duration, schedule and quality of a software development is one of the first issues that must be dealt with in a successful software project. Models and prediction algorithms must be based both on past experience and a reasonable estimate of the new conditions of a proposed development. Methodology for improving the quality of the developing software product is the next critical issue faced in any large software development. The details of code inspection preparation, review rates, and meeting dynamics are important methodology issues which must be factored into the development. Attendees of this seminar learn about practical techniques that optimize and predict the cost, quality and development interval of large software systems.

Niel L. M. Davies	- Hewlett-Packard Co.
William R. Francis	- AT&T Bell Laboratories
Irene Sokolowski	- AT&T Information Systems
Weider D. Yu	- AT&T Bell Laboratories

IMPROVING THE QUALITY OF SOFTWARE COST ESTIMATION

Weider D. Yu

Switching Systems Quality Department
AT&T Bell Laboratories

200 Park Plaza
Naperville, Illinois 60566-7050

ABSTRACT

With software development viewed more as an art than a science, it has been difficult to study the cost factors which affect software projects and predict accurately software development costs. Poor estimates are at the root of the difficulty in meeting commitments and achieving high quality software.

This paper will describe a new software cost estimation modeling process used in the largest telecommunication project at AT&T Bell Laboratories. The model estimation approach has improved the quality of estimates and the productivity of planning estimation process.

1. INTRODUCTION

Software cost estimation is an important task in large scale software development projects. With software development viewed more as an art than a science, it has been difficult in studying the cost factors which affect software projects and predicting accurately software development costs. In order to improve the accuracy of software cost estimation, the estimation tasks should be performed periodically during the planning and development stages of a software project.

Large projects can involve many hundreds of developers. If the software development process is closely coupled to parallel development of special hardware which is required for the execution of the software programs, the estimation tasks can be complicated. Such projects require estimation models and estimation process specifically designed to the environment. Commercial models provide minimal guidance on the estimation solution required in these cases.

In this paper, a new software cost estimation process used in the 5ESS® project at AT&T Bell Laboratories is discussed.

2. ESTIMATION NEEDS IN THE R&D ENVIRONMENT

2.1 The Software Life Cycle

Software estimation is based on a model of software development and can be best constructed using a project life cycle decomposition. A software life cycle is a series of events occurring during the life time of a software product and is defined in an IEEE standard to include the following phases:

- Concept and Definition
- Requirement Analysis
- Design
- Implementation
- Integration and Test
- Installation
- Operations and Maintenance
- Retirement

Each phase can be viewed as an independent process that consists of a sequence of activities leading to the completion of a major project milestone.

A software life cycle can be further divided into three specific sub-cycles, a planning sub-cycle, a development sub-cycle, and a maintenance sub-cycle. The planning sub-cycle includes the "Concept and Definition" phase; the development sub-cycle includes the phases "Requirement Analysis," "Design," "Implementation," and "Integration and "Test"; and the maintenance sub-cycle includes the phases "Installation," "Operation and Maintenance," and the "Retirement". The software estimating technology referred to in this paper is developed for the *development sub-cycle*.

To achieve accurate estimates, the software development process used on a software product should be well understood and the software estimation process should be closely linked to this development process.

2.2 Difficulties in Estimation

Depending on the availability of information, it may be necessary to generate estimates for a software product several times during its life cycle.

During the planning phase, the information which drives effort, staff, and schedule estimates is unstable and not well-understood. During the development phase, a better knowledge of the product makes it possible to give detailed estimates of these values.

The needs on resource estimates at planning and development phases are different. For instance, planning estimates may provide just the total development effort and schedule. Development estimates, on the other hand, should provide detailed development effort and schedule by major activity, such as requirements, design, coding, and test.

3. ESTIMATION MODELS

3.1 The Components of Estimation Technology

Familiarity with the software development *process,* the development *environment,* and the characteristics of the software *product* to be developed are three major influences on estimation for the software product. These three influences and the factors into which they are decomposed form the framework of models used in our estimation technology.

Estimation technology contains five major components: estimation target, estimation model, estimation process, historical project database, and estimation tools. These components are constructed based on the knowledge on software development process, development environment, and the major characteristics of the software product.

Estimation targets identify the desired results of the estimation process, such as the development effort, cost, and schedule. The estimation model is a set of algorithms which produce the estimation target values by modeling the software development process, the development environment, and the characteristics of a software product. The estimation process is a set of procedures used to generate the estimation targets for a software product. The historical project database is a collection of completed projects with identified effort, staffing, and schedule results as well as known environmental values. Estimation tools provide a user friendly way of accessing the historical database and of generating requested estimates.

3.2 Industry Models

Historically, models used in the software industry assume a waterfall life cycle and can be viewed as consisting of two parts. One part provides a base estimate as a function of high level parameters such as project size and type, e.g. military, commercial. A second part modifies this base estimate to account for the influence of supplementary factors, such the experience of the staff. As an illustration, Barry Boehm's[1] COCOMO model provides a formulation with lines of code, representing size, raised to a power between 1.05 and 1.20. It uses this value to derive a base effort estimate. The specific exponent used from the above range is determined by whether the project is simple, average, or complex. Fifteen supplementary factors are identified covering computer, personnel, and project attributes and these are assumed multiplicative and independent in the resulting effort estimation algorithms. Schedule and staffing are derived from the effort estimate and the other previously used project characteristics.

The Jensen[2] and Putnam[3] models are more complex formulations than the COCOMO model and are based on a Rayleigh curve representation of effort over the life cycle. These models include a dis-economy of scale effect not necessarily reflected in other models. In these models staff months of effort increases as the schedule is compressed. Boehm, Jensen, and Putnam provide a single model of a project so that life cycle phases such as design or system test are derived from this single model.

The Capers Jones SPQR/20[4] approach is somewhat different in that he models each life cycle function separately, i.e. planning, design, implementation, test, user documentation/training, and project management. Additionally, each of these model project staffing separately from effort. The mathematical formulation, while not in the public domain, appears to be similar to the Boehm approach. Because of the use of many separate models, the Jones approach affords more flexibility where it is desired to tune parameters to the local environment.

SPQR/20 and the ESTIMACS model of Rubens[5] includes an alternative to the size metric of lines of code. Since lines of code is frequently difficult to estimate early in a project, these models provide for optional use of "function points" to identify size. (Function points are an empirical measure of functionality and include counts of inputs, outputs, inquiries, interfaces, and files. This concept was introduced in 1981 by Alan Albrecht of IBM. For real time applications it is not directly applicable because major processing functions are not so coupled to the inputs and outputs of the system.) A version of function points is currently used on the 5ESS project to develop an estimate of product size in lines of code.

3.3 Building an Estimation Model

The following process was used in establishing the estimation model:

1. Review estimation needs with project personnel.

2. Establish a fundamental productivity and quality understanding of the software products and the development environment.

3. Identify commercial models to be used as references in building models for the AT&T R&D processes.

4. Choose a general model and identify the factors that influence software productivity and quality using developer input and commercial references.

5. Establish data collection standards.

6. Collect historical project data and analyze the results.

7. Establish factor influence levels based on industrial experience, judgement of project personnel, and analysis of historical data.

8. Calibrate or provide calibration algorithms for the estimation models to adjust results based on historical information.

9. Refine the estimation process and models using data on recently completed projects. This includes adjusting basic productivity relationships, adjusting factor weights, and adding new factors to the model.

The input questions of the estimation model shown in Table 1 have been generated based on the cost estimation factors found in the 5ESS development organization.

4. THE ESTIMATION PROCESS

The 5ESS switch is a modern digital electronic switching system with a distributed hardware and software architecture. The size of the latest 5ESS generic software delivered to customers has reached millions of lines of source code. At present there are many hundred software engineers involved in the development process. It is one of the largest software products in the AT&T history.

The generic planning estimation process is illustrated in Figure 1. In the process of estimating a feature, the system engineer who is responsible for the feature, provides the feature definition in a document. This document serves as the basis for a high level design proposal. The hign level design proposal is provided by the architectural engineer or experienced development engineer assigned to the feature. These documents are the basis for an estimating meeting used to review and finalize inputs to the estimation model.

The strategy to embed the major input required by the model in the high level design document is proved to be successful. It has saved time and effort in collecting input to the model.

Before the estimation meeting and before generating the model estimates for a feature some key development engineers are normally contacted to refine the input to the model. The model estimates are usually developed before the estimating meeting held for the feature.

In the estimating meeting, the system engineer and architectural engineer present the major information in the feature definition and design proposal documents. Because the expertise for the feature is concentrated in one place, most of the open issues related to the feature can be resolved effectively in the estimating meeting. The meeting enables the finalization of information that is used to derive a lines of code estimate.

If there are some differences found on the impacts from the feature during the discussion in the meeting, the model input is revised and the model estimates are generated again. The model estimates for the feature are then presented to compare with the estimates from development engineers. If there are any large discrepancies between the model estimates and engineer-generated estimates, a reasonable explanation on what caused the differences between the two is necessary.

Project results are reviewed and added to a project database.

5. SUPPORT TOOLS

A tool for 5ESS called the 5ESS SIZER assists in developing size estimates, in lines of code, and in providing planning estimates. It is called the 5ESS SIZER. It includes a 5ESS project database and makes reference to this data when making new estimates. Each estimation session is automatically recorded in an "estimation worksheet" file for further file retrieval and cross reference.

The 5ESS SIZER is developed in the UNIX environment and written in FRANZ LISP language. It is available for 5ESS project managers and feature estimators. The tool is designed with an interactive user-friendly interface.

The expertise gained from the development and application of the 5ESS SIZER has been used to aid in the development of the 5ESS DEVELOPMENT ESTIMATOR. The 5ESS DEVELOPMENT

ESTIMATOR will give the detailed development estimates on effort and schedule at each development stage. It can make use of the inputs to the 5ESS SIZER but requires additional inputs to develop the more detailed estimates.

6. RESULTS FROM USE OF SOFTWARE ESTIMATION TECHNOLOGY

The new estimation technology has recently been introduced and the impact is just beginning to be felt. Input has been received from the 5ESS user community. Feedback from users is summarized below.

6.1 More Thorough Planning

During the estimation process of a system or feature on 5ESS , the users of the estimation model have found that the input questions allow them to systematically reconsider major planning. This includes (1) the impact that the feature can produce on the total 5ESS system, (2) alternative feasible implementations of the feature, and (3) restrictions on the implementation of the feature. These restrictions include such things as the resources available for the development and the experience of the staff.

6.2 Establishing Data Collection Standards

In the past on 5ESS, the tasks of collecting project data and analyzing historical results have been complicated by the lack of guidelines and standards. Since defining the standards and methods to accommodate our estimation needs and developing a set of systematic data collection tools, the tasks of collecting and of using historical information have been simplified. Standards have been defined for counting lines of code and for counting development effort among others. Because of these new standards the quality of historical project data has greatly improved.

6.3 Use of Historical Records

In the new process, history information on completed projects is recorded and has been found useful by project managers. This includes both the use of this data to calibrate general productivity as well as the use of this data to develop understandings about areas that could and should be improved.

6.4 Productivity Studies

With a set of well-defined software productivity metrics, projects can be tracked and comparisons made between projects. Furthermore, the influence of cost factors on productivity can be studied and the model updated as appropriate. Also goals for certain factor values can be set.

6.5 Model Estimation Accuracy

Two measures of the success of the model relate to (1) the comparison of estimates generated for completed projects against the actuals experienced on these projects and (2) the relationship of the model derived estimates to independently derived estimates from the development engineers. In the former case the historical estimation results were within 5-20% of 5ESS actuals.

On the comparison to developer-generated estimates the model estimates have been consistent with the developer-generated estimates. Although individual minor subsystem or activity estimates were occasionally off significantly, the total estimates usually agreed with the estimation results within 20%.

6.6 User Expense

Because the input questions of the estimation model are generated from the locally derived cost estimation factors found in the 5ESS organization, users can easily understand the questions and promptly respond. The task of giving responses to the input questions has never been viewed as a burden for the users.

7. REFERENCES

[1] [Boehm, 1981]. Barry W. Boehm, *Software Engineering Economics*, Prentice-Hall Inc., Englewood Cliffs, N.J., 1981

[2] [Jensen, 1981]. R. W. Jensen, "A Macro-Level Software Development Cost Estimation Methodology," *Proceedings - Fourteenth Asilomar Conference on Circuits, Systems, and Computers*, IEEE, New York, 1981

[3] [Putnam, 1980]. L. H. Putnam, *Software Cost Estimating and Life Cycle Control: Getting the Software Numbers*, IEEE, New York, 1980

[4] [Rubens, 1987]. Howard A. Rubens, "Productivity and Quality Strategies for Measurement," *Fifth National Conference on Measuring Data Processing Quality and Productivity*, Quality Assurance Institute, Orlando, Fla. 1987

[5] [Jones, 1986]. T. Capers Jones, *Programming Productivity*, McGraw-Hill, Inc., New York, 1986

TABLE 1 - INPUTS TO 5ESS SIZER MODEL

- FEATURE REQUIREMENTS
- FEATURE HARDWARE IMPACT
- FEATURE DEVELOPMENT PROCESS
- FEATURE COMPLEXITY
- PERFORMANCE CONSTRAINTS
- FEATURE NOVELTY
- WORK ENVIRONMENT
- STAFF EXPERIENCE
- 5ESS SOFTWARE ARCHITECTURE IMPACT
- FEATURE INTERACTION
- 5ESS STATIC AND DYNAMIC DATA IMPACT

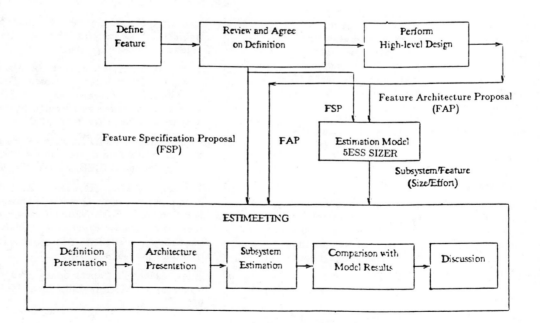

Figure 1 - NEW 5ESS PLANNING ESTIMATION PROCESS

INNOVATIONS IN SOFTWARE QUALITY AT HEWLETT-PACKARD

Niel L. M. Davies

HEWLETT-PACKARD COMPANY
Roseville, California

ABSTRACT

This paper describes the quality practices in use at the Office Systems Division of Hewlett-Packard. The Office Systems Division produces software which allows users of personal computers (PC's) to tap into the power of their pre-existing departmental computers for centralized printing, plotting, data access and back-up.

The paper describes how software quality is categorized into a number of different attributes which are collectively known as FURPS (Functionality, Usability, Reliability, Performance, Support).

The paper then continues to describe the key philosophical underpinnings to our whole quality improvement program and then to explain, including the definition of what metrics are collected and when, how these philosophies are deployed through the software development lifecycle. The role of the quality department is then explored and the paper closes with a discussion of our plans for the future.

1. What do we mean by SOFTWARE QUALITY?

It is our opinion that many of the quality measures that are about to be outlined in this paper are unduly subjective in nature. However you must recognize that this is the opinion of America's foremost maker of test and measurement instruments and that our expectations for accuracy may be too high for the relatively imprecise world of software.

It is also necessary to recognize that a customers perception of quality is affected by much more than the basic attributes of product quality that I will be concentrating on in this paper. For example we are doing a large amount of work to improve the quality of our sales and installation processes for our software. One of our conclusions to date is that the quality of the process of setting customers expectations during the sales cycle has a far bigger effect on customer satisfaction than any basic reliability problems. The majority of our hot-sites still come from miss-set customer expectations - not defects.

Even within the realms of pure product quality it is worth noting that the product is much more than the software itself. The customer also judges on items such as the documentation, training etc. as well as on less tangible characteristics such as overall product consistency, price etc.

Having made these caveats how do we measure product quality at HP? At the Office Systems Division we believe that quality should be measured under 5 headings which we refer to as FURPS.

F is for Functionality.
Functionality refers to the basic activities that the product undertakes to do for it's users. For example a word processor has to allow for typing, spelling correction, tabs, filing etc. We measure functionality through subjective customer evaluations and of course by comparison with our competitors.

U is for Usability.
Usability refers to the quality of the user interface to the product. How easy was the product to learn? How good were the manuals? Was the user interface intuitive or did you need to consult the help screens at every turn? How good was our training?

We measure usability by a combination of subjective user ratings using surveys and customer visits and through formal usability testing in our labs.

R is for Reliability.
Reliability refers to how often the product breaks or does not perform to specification. This is the classic measure of product quality for the software industry.

This is the area that the majority of our effort has been traditionally devoted to within Hewlett-Packard. Once again by comparison to our hardware reliability measurement program it is our feeling that our software metrics are in need of serious improvement and yet again we believe we are at the forefront of industry in our use of these measures today. The key measures that we use today are:

— Number of critical and serious defects in our software.

— Number of defects that are detected in the first year of product life. (normalized by lines of non-comment source statements x 1000 - (KNCSS))

P is for Performance.
Another key element in overall customer satisfaction with our software products concerns their satisfaction with our performance. Does the software load fast enough? Are you always typing ahead of the ability of the computer to deal with your input? Can you get answers when you need them.

Performance is relatively easy to measure but it is very difficult to understand the break point between acceptable and unacceptable. At this time we continue to rely upon subjective user views of performance for our evaluations.

S is for Support.
Quality in our software business does not stop when we have finished building the product. How well do we support the product is another vitally important factor in the equation. Support to us implies: how easy is it to install our products; can our customers get answers to those questions that cannot be answered by our documentation; how well are training courses delivered;

etc.

Once again our metrics on the issue of support are subjective but they are closely watched. We carry out regular surveys of customer satisfaction as well as watching some of the key industry polls such as DataPro. Additionally we measure many variables concerning response time to customers, mean time to fix etc.

2. What are the major planks in our software improvement programs?

Our basic philosophy for improving both productivity and quality in our software is the same as that used in manufacturing - namely Total Quality Control (TQC). Unfortunately we cannot use the letters TQC.

Software engineers see themselves as the last bastions of creativity in an increasingly bureaucratic world and they have typically seen TQC as being a manufacturing only solution. In consequence we have adopted the subterfuge that we are not using TQC but instead we are doing lifecycles (processes), metrics (measurements), postmortems (cause and effect), and are promoting customer visits (awareness of customer needs).

Our challenge in the use of lifecycles is that each project is different from previous projects in total yet clearly could be made easier in many areas by learning from past experiences on previous similar projects. In order to deal with this challenge we have used the concept of a "meta methodology." In this concept each project is required to formally state what procedures it will follow and the total package can only be constructed from "pre-approved" components of "good practice". Project teams accept that this allows them to have some degree of freedom whilst in practice we find that 85% of projects follow the "standard project development lifecycle". (Note it is very difficult to measure adherence to a lifecycle and these comments are subjective only.)

Our basic philosophies for metrics come from the views of Lord Kelvin, the famous English mathematician:

"I often say that when you can measure what you are speaking about and express it in numbers you know something about it. But when you cannot measure it, when you cannot express it in numbers, your knowledge is of a meager and unsatisfactory kind."

and from Tom DeMarco:

"Rational men and women can work effectively to maximize any single observed indication of success."

Fundamentally this translates into a belief that if we set the right quantitative measures and consistently observe and act upon the results of those measures we will improve any process. (It is assumed that we do not hire any irrational people!)

One of the key planks in our quest for improved quality is the concept of defect analysis and correction of process based on the results. Our way of achieving this is through a process we call the postmortem. Typical software projects consist of about 8 major (and sometimes overlapping) phases (investigation, external design, internal design, construction, testing, delivery, obsolescence). At the end of each project phase we carry out a formal postmortem to understand what went well and what went badly about the recently completed activities. Some of the items which are raised by the project team are items which can be remedied within the project team itself before the next phase of the project is undertaken, e.g., better attendance at team meetings. The majority of the items however cannot be fixed on a single project basis. In these cases the quality department maintains a record of what problems were detected/what practices worked best and publishes a quarterly record of the consolidated view of the whole division. We have a standing committee which then reviews these items and considers how/whether to incorporate them into our lifecycles.

Another of our key planks towards improving the overall quality of our software is continuous interaction between our designers and their customers.

3. What are we doing and what results are we seeing?

3.1 General programs not related to project phases.

Customer awareness: We have a number of ways in which we achieve this. First, every R&D engineer has a quota that they must personally visit or interact with at least 2 different customers per year. Second, we continuously survey our customers to get their opinion of our products (this is a service provided by the quality department). Third, we maintain a continuous defect tracking system with regular communications with our customers.

Estimating quality factor calculation: It is our belief that a major, though unquantified, impediment to quality in a finished product is the fact that most projects take about twice as long as they were originally estimated to require. This in turn puts extra pressure on project teams to deliver at any price. We have a program in place to try and improve the quality of our estimates through a program of measuring how accurately we estimate and an analysis of what factors caused the variance. To do this we are using a metric called Estimating Quality Factor.

Our experiences with the estimating quality factor show some very simple correlations of the kind that you would expect. Namely, the more overall effort that is required to produce an E.S. the more likely we are to have serious problems with inaccurate estimates.

3.2 Investigation phase

The correctness of the investigation/product definition phase of product development has potentially the highest impact on our overall productivity and quality. All projects develop "momentum" towards a perceived goal no matter how correct it is - and it is very difficult to correct a project's direction after it has been established.

Unfortunately this process is the one which is most subject to "genius" and the least susceptible to process analysis and improvement. The metrics that we have in place to measure this process today are very simple.

- Number of customers talked to
- Readability index for the investigation report
- "comfort" of the project team

Our experiences here are that the typical project exits this phase with too little investigation having been completed for a number of reasons:

- the time allotted to the investigation had been used up.
- the project team itself develops a "let's get something done instead of all this investigating" philosophy.

Inherently this leaves us with the most difficult of problems to solve. Namely, one where neither management nor project engineers have a desire to solve it. Clearly what we have to do is develop some clear criteria for recognizing when enough investigation has been completed with some high correlation to the eventual success of the product. Today no such measures exist.

3.3 External design phase

The external design phase of a Hewlett-Packard project is intended to be the time during which every aspect of the "customers view" of a project is defined. All screens, error messages, dialogs etc. are expected to be in their final form and they are NOT expected to change during the internal design and alpha/beta testing processes that follow. Obviously at this stage we will have some clear ideas on how to implement the algorithms of the project BUT there is still some flexibility left for the project designers to improve on this.

In theory at this stage we could have our writers start to produce manuals, our trainers start to produce courses, and our translators could start to translate our products into local languages. Unfortunately our external specifications are not yet good enough to make this happen but this is the direction in which we are headed.

Within Hewlett-Packard there are two main avenues of thought as to how to improve the quality of the work done at the external design phase of a project. One school uses the techniques of formal structured analysis and design as it's main plank to ensure that External Designs are complete and accurate. The other school believes that the construction of working prototypes is the best way of achieving the same result. The Office Systems Division is a believer in the prototyping route.

The main metrics that we use to ensure quality of our external designs are:

- User reaction to prototype F.U. ratings (note reliability and support are not judged from protos; performance is not currently judged from protos)
- Number of defects in the investigation report
- Readability index for the External Specification

We are most excited about our FUS measurements on our prototypes and yet to date do not have any data to support their use other than the excitement of both the engineers and the users at being able to react to a model so early in the development lifecycle. Clearly one of the key things we have to do is to establish the correlation between good prototyping and good products. Historically there have been many attempts to use prototyping which have failed due to - inadequate funding or lack of discipline in following and improving the prototyping process. Some lessons we have learned to date are that the prototype must be sufficiently robust to allow us to let the user play with it themselves otherwise we see the "Oh, I didn't realize you meant that" syndrome.

Our analysis of changes of "concept" discovered in the External Specification process is an interesting example of the complex interaction of factors that need to be resolved before we can truly address these problems. Basically we have found that in 100% of the projects (only 3 in total) where there was a serious difference between the concepts in the investigation report and those which were delivered in the E.S. both the project team and the management team were very aware that the investigation was not solid and still proceeded to the next step. Why? A mixture of trying to meet what we thought were the expectations of our next level of management and of trying to meet perceived market windows of opportunity.

The question we must now ask is, "Is the problem soluble or even worth solving?". There may be a variety of different correct answers depending upon the volatility of the market and the degree to which the "more correct" answer could have been determined during the investigation phase. A great deal more data collection and analysis is needed here before we can draw any conclusions as to whether a better solution is available.

3.4 Internal Design Phase

This is the area where I believe we in the Office Systems Division have fewest project metrics in place. We have no formal checkpoints in place for the completion of this phase.

On the other hand this, together with the construction and testing of our software, is probably the area at which we are best. Therefore, we are investing the majority of our resources to improve the areas of our process where we are weaker.

3.5 Code construction and testing phase

We have a large number of metrics in place which allow us to measure the quality and completeness of our efforts in this phase of our projects:

- Code stability
- Code defect density
- Critical and serious defect counts
- Defect arrival rates
- FURPS ratings from our Alpha and Beta sites
- Path Flow Analysis
- External Specification Error counts.

The main purpose of these metrics is to predict the quality of the product after it has been released. Generally, the reliability metrics are excellent predictors and we have now institutionalized them as part of our sign-off criteria which must be met before a product can be released to general distribution to our customers. The broader metrics of customer acceptability (FURPS) are in the early stages of use and whilst we believe strongly that they will be excellent predictors of eventual quality, they have not been in use for a sufficiently long period of time for us to have any hard data yet. We do have formal release criteria for FURPS and any product which does not rate very good or better (on a scale from unacceptable to excellent) on 4 out of 5 of the criteria and which does not rate very good or better overall will not be released without significant rework. Our only significant problem with our FURPS metrics to date has been that our customers have a tendency to evaluate what is there and often are unable to tell us (other than by failing to purchase the product) about the things we have left out.

We carry out similar ratings for our documentation and training, both for customers and for our own field (whose training is every bit as important as that of our eventual customers).

We have a number of key techniques that we use

in order to help us achieve our goals for each of these metrics.

- Code inspections - design walkthroughs
- Usability testing on documentation
- Automated regression test harnesses
- Path flow analysis
- Alpha and beta testing
- Focus groups
- Defect prone code rewrite program (partial)

3.6 Post release

The post release processes in software are possibly unique in respect to quality and what to do about defects. The typical product warranty program for a regular product allow for repair/replacement/recompense for products which fail to meet specification. However I believe that software is unique in the fact that we try to repair major omissions of functionality (i.e. the product didn't do what you wanted) as part of the warranty program. We are now critically examining whether this "de facto" practice really makes sense in terms of providing for long term customer satisfaction. Would customers be better off if we no longer hid the costs of updating existing products - at least the existing customer would have a better lever through which to influence our choice of new features to add to our products.

We have a number of key metrics by which we judge the quality of our software after it has been released :

- number of queries per kncss
- mean time to fix defects
- error detection efficiency ratio (a measure of testing effectiveness)
- defects detected in the first year after release
- sales dollars
- number of hot sites
- customer satisfaction (FURPS) surveys

The majority of these measures are in fact lagging measures of the product development process and do not provide us with any data upon which we can act. However the two-edged sword of software does mean that we can address major customer dissatisfiers and get "new and improved" software to our customers. The metrics which are used at this time are primarily those which deal with support quality. If mean time to fix slips outside it's control limits, then we know that we have to bring additional support resources to bear. If number of hot sites increase, then we know we have a problem with either our sales process (expectations

1509

being set badly) or our support processes (product is being badly installed).

The results of the lagging measures are fed back via the lifecycle into the software development lifecycle by the defect analysis done by the quality department. A postmortem is held approximately one year after product release. We examine what results we have actually achieved under the sometimes harsh scrutiny of our real world customers and then determine what was the earliest point at which we could have detected problems that we missed during the development process. From there, what checks/metrics we could add to our lifecycle in order to prevent the re-occurrence of this class of defect in future.

4. What is the role of a quality department?

We at Hewlett-Packard believe that we are on the forefront of the evolution of the role of a quality department in American software. Much of this evolution closely follows the changes that have occurred to the role of a quality department within the manufacturing sectors of American industry. Here we have seen quality assurance evolve from the role of "testers" and "hurdles over which product teams must jump to ship product" into process improvement experts, teachers, and facilitators.

The role of the quality department in the Office Systems Division of Hewlett-Packard is :

- to own, and continuously improve upon, our lifecycles (processes)

- to act as consultant on key issues of reliability, etc.

- to provide productivity and quality enhancing tools for our engineers

- to measure quality and determine what progress we are making

- to provide quality engineering services to our projects

- to advise the project leader on what lifecycle processes to use on this particular project

- to advise the project leader on what metrics to produce

- to carry out and publish the agreed measurements

At Hewlett-Packard the creation of new software is normally carried out by a multi-disciplinary project team formed specifically to develop a particular product or enhancement. Each team typically consists of a project leader (almost always from R&D), several R&D engineers, a product manager, one or more writers, a support engineer, and a quality engineer. What does the quality engineer do? Why do we have one on the project team?

In our opinion the presence of a quality engineer on each project team has been the single most important factor in our success in improving our quality practices at the Office Systems Division. There are a number of reasons as why this is true.

The first factor is that the quality engineer is now an integral and necessary part of the team that produces our products. The engineer has real deliverables that have to be completed before the product can be released. The engineer is working for the project manager NOT the quality department. This factor alone has improved the ability of that engineer to influence the project's adoption of leading edge quality practices. It has also eliminated some of the negative feedback that quality engineers were not aware of the "real world" of project development and were always seeking solutions that were too idealistic.

The second factor is that the quality engineer now has control of the key documents that specify how to improve our processes. First the engineer writes the document that specifies the methodologies to be used for this project (quality plan) and second the engineer actually gathers most of the metrics which also ensures that they get done.

The third factor is that the quality engineer is seen as a "free" resource to the project manager and can therefore concentrate on lifecycles and metrics without being a drain on project resources. One of the major difficulties with any kind of process improvement activities in software has been that the extremely long cycle time of the development process. This has always deterred any significant investment in measurement because any resource spent today would only slow down the current project phase and would not produce any benefit until the next iteration of that phase which might be as much as 2 years away. By providing a "free" resource we get over this problem.

5. What results are we actually achieving?

For the type of code that we write (subsystems/low level applications) we believe that the measures that we have undertaken have produced products whose reliability is amongst the leaders today. (we actually achieve a post release defect density of approximately .2 defects (any type) per kncss in the first year of our software's release to our customer base).

It is our belief that our major opportunities for improvement lie in the area of the human interface and in getting the basic functionality right for our products.

6. Where are we going in the future?

Hewlett-Packard is known as being an industry leader in quality and merely being among the leaders in reliability is not enough. We have set ourselves the goal of improving our reliability by a factor of 10 in the next 5 years.

The main methods by which we plan to achieve these goals are basically evolutions of the program that we have in place today. Better measures, earlier measures that are better predictors of where we need to change our products, etc.

Some key areas where we are already planning to improve our processes and measures include:

- more sensitivity to customer needs by using the DTFTS concept (Defects times Frequency times Severity)

- earlier measurement of Functionality acceptability through Quality Function Deployment

- usability defect stability metrics

- error prevention through code reuse and automatic integrity checking during code construction

- standardized architectures and components

For the longer term we believe that there may be substantial benefits to using a combination of expert systems and production line methods for writing new software. Our belief is that the original ideas for the creation of software may be best improved by using the techniques of expert systems to nurture the creativity of the individual engineer but the the majority of the construction and testing activities will eventually become very specialized and automated activities in a "software factory".

7. Conclusions

Overall we believe that we are making major strides towards being able to measure what are the biggest factors which inhibit our producing high quality products the first time. Unfortunately, we are finding that some of the biggest factors were ones that we were already aware of and which are sociological rather than technological in nature. These problems will not be solved overnight.

Or to quote from Tom DeMarco

"the truth will set you free but it may also make you miserable"

8. References

[1] Tom DeMarco - Controlling Software Projects - Yourden Press - 1982

CODE INSPECTIONS IN THE DEVELOPMENT OF A LARGE MULTIPROCESSING SYSTEM

Irene Sokolowski

AT&T INFORMATION SYSTEMS

Naperville, IL   60566

ABSTRACT

Code inspections have been utilized extensively in software development to improve the quality of the software product. Code inspection management techniques, such as control of inspector preparation effort and inspection rate have improved the results of code inspections, as measured by the percentage of errors found.

Guidelines for the amount of inspector preparation and the rate of inspection have been offered in the literature [1,2], but these may not apply universally. The problems associated with developing software for large multiprocessor operating systems are different than those in developing other types of software. The relative costs of fault removal in the various development phases are probably different as well. We found that an average of 30 staff-hours of inspection effort per thousand non-commentary sources lines (KNCSL) of code found slightly over 80% of the coding errors, and was cost effective in our environment.

INTRODUCTION

The importance of producing quality software has been emphasized in response to the Japanese challenge, competitive market and customer requirements, among other factors.

The routine production of software products of specified quality within budget and on schedule continues to be an elusive goal. The main cause of the difficulty is the fact that software development is a labor intensive process which admits many opportunities for the introduction of errors that can degrade the quality of the final product [3]. In addition, the techniques employed in the development are not specified precisely, and the quality of resulting products is variable. By contrast, in the more mature hardware development, quality can be monitored and measured without much difficulty, since methods have existed for years.

Initially, the process of monitoring the quality of software was testing before it "goes out the door." Defect detection was almost totally dependent upon testing during development and by the user. This has changed, since 1972 [2] code inspections and walk-throughs have assumed the defect detection burden, and the quality of inspections are a direct contribution to product quality. Error detection and error correction are now considered to be the major cost in software development [4,5].

Code inspections have been successfully used within AT&T Bell Laboratories [6], IBM [2], and many others [7]. The accelerated rate of adoption of inspection throughout the software development industry is an acknowledgment of its effectiveness. Experience over the last 16 years has shown [2,6,7] code inspections to be an efficient defect detection technique, finding 60 to 90 percent of all defects.

Outlined in this paper are experiences with code inspection during development of a UNIX®/C based multiprocessing system.

DESCRIPTION OF THE ENVIRONMENT

The software project that served as a base for collection of code inspection data was a large UNIX based multiprocessing system, identified as Product "A". At the time of collection of the data, Product "A" consisted of approximately 670,000 lines of C and some Shell language code and was in the second release phase. Approximately 70 developers, and the same number of testers were involved in the project. Product "A", like most large software products, was not developed from scratch. It evolved from existing product, so the size of Product "A" is a function of new and modified code. The "new" code is defined as code in newly developed files, while "modified" means code added to existing files.

The execution of an inspection was specified as a trackable project milestone, and was not at developer's discretion. Each inspection meeting was expected to be carried out according to the internal inspection guidelines and meet quantified standards for inspection rate and amount of preparation time per 1000 lines of noncommentary code. The standards are as follows:

1. 10 hours of preparation per 1000 NCSL to be inspected (total preparation time for the team)

2. Inspection rate not higher than 300 lines per hour

3. A single inspection meeting should not last longer than 2 hours

The objectives of the code inspection process were defined as follows:

1. To find errors in the code in a formal and efficient manner

2. To ensure that the code, data base files, and interfaces are in agreement with the design

3. To verify that the developed code conforms to the project programming standards

Verifying that the code, data files, and interfaces match the design can generate an immediate cost savings by reducing the number of errors in the code/program. Enforcing conformance to standards is a long-term process designed to reduce maintenance costs by insuring that the code is human understandable.

This paper will examine parameters of the inspection process in order to develop an understanding of their impact on the number of errors found.

SUMMARY OF COLLECTED DATA

The analysis described in this paper is based on results from 456 inspection meetings. All meetings were formally structured; conducted by team of peers, involving preparation, active participation and synergy, vigorous "reading" of the code, defect detection and recording, and objective decision on the disposition of the code. The inspection team, on the average, consisted of four peers: author, moderator/scribe, reader and inspector. The moderator was chosen from the "approved" list of moderators. All moderators, on the list, had attended an inspection workshop. The other participants of the meeting were technically competent people; majority of them also had attended an inspection workshop. The moderator was leading the meeting with emphasis on detection of faults, and not discussion of programming styles. If something was *wrong*, it was not a question of style, and if something could make the product *difficult to maintain*, it was not considered a question of style, either.

The data from each meeting was reported on the Inspection Summary Form. It included names of the participants, the number of non-commentary source lines (NCSL) of code inspected, the total time spent by the inspectors preparing for the meeting, the length of the meeting, and the number and type of errors found.

The input to all inspections was clean compiled code. In the 456 inspection meetings, 80,766 lines of code were inspected and 1,407 faults were found. The total effort spent in these inspections amounted to 2,357 staff hours, which is the sum of preparation time and duration of inspection meeting for each participant. The average error density amounted to 17.4 errors per KNCSL.

In all analyses, errors and preparation time are normalized to error rates per thousand lines of code and hours per thousand lines of code, respectively.

ANALYSIS TO BE PERFORMED

Collected data was then analyzed. The objectives of the analysis were as follows:

1. Identify predominant types of errors detected in code inspections

2. Emphasize the importance and low cost of inspections

3. Evaluate parameters of the inspection process, and possibly

4. Determine effectiveness of the inspection process.

The first step in the analysis was to examine distributions of preparation time, inspection rate and size by testing for skewness and kurtosis. The rationale for this was that some of them were highly skewed with large variances. To correct the problem, log10 transformation was used. The log10 transformation process tends to eliminate skewness by reducing the disproportionate impact of a relatively few extreme values for a variable [8].

The major limitation of the analysis concerns the accuracy of preparation time reporting. Members of the inspection teams were not required to log their time while preparing but to submit the number of hours to the moderator at the beginning of the meeting. Consequently, some unexplained variance could be attributed to reporting error.

CODE INSPECTION ERROR TYPES

The overall breakdown of fault types for all the faults found in inspections is presented in Figure 1. The three most frequently encountered errors are as follows in the order of frequency: Logic, Functionality and Maintainability. They account for 52.4 percent of all software faults found by inspection of this product.

It is worth mentioning that new and modified code have the same type of error frequency distribution. It appears, that whether we inspect new or modified code, the effort is concentrated on detecting FN and LO errors in particular. These errors will produce incorrect results but otherwise precipitate no obvious malfunction of the given program. Normally, those are often the last to be found. The success in detection of those errors in our environment, can be probably attributed to the formal structure of our inspection meetings. By requiring preparation for the meeting, all inspectors coming to the meeting already know or are familiar with the functionality and logic of the code to be inspected; then it is much easier to find these types of errors.

The FN and LO errors were detected with some regularity, the detection of the remaining types of errors varied widely from individual to individual.

The distribution of detected fault densities for each error type is shown in Figure 2. Error types are listed in the same sequence as they appear on inspection forms. Since not all inspections are being conducted according to the guidelines, Figure 2 illustrates the difference in discovered error densities between inspections having preparation time less than the recommended 10 hours per KNCSL (197 inspections) which averaged at 5.35 hours/KNCSL, and those having preparation times in excess of 10 hours (259 inspections) which averaged at 18 hours/KNCSL. The overall density of detected errors rose by 209 percent with a factor of 3.36 increase in the preparation time. All errors have some impact on software reliability, but logic (LO) and functional (FN) errors are probably more "lethal" than most others. The additional preparation time increased the detected density of these errors by a factor of 4 (FN) and a factor of 2 for LO, respectively.

COST OF CODE INSPECTIONS

In the analysis of the overall effort involved in inspections, two components are being considered:

1. the combined preparation time of all participants, and

2. the time taken by all participants during the inspection meeting.

Figure 3 shows the breakdown of the total effort involved in all inspections. The overall average effort was approximately 29.2 staff hours per KNCSL. Average inspection and preparation efforts were 19.47 and 9.7 hours per KNCSL, respectively.

PARAMETERS OF THE INSPECTION PROCESS

There are number of factors which one can identify as having an impact on effectiveness of code inspections. Parameters such as moderator skill, code size, preparation time and inspection rate will be examined next.

Value of "Approved" Moderator: In Release 2 of the project, the idea of approved moderator was introduced. The concept behind it was that some moderators are more effective than others in steering the meeting, so more errors can be detected. In all inspections, there were 40 unique moderators. Comparisons between the data from different moderators, indicate that moderator is not the significant variable that has an effect on the number of faults found in inspection. Using ANOVA for unbalanced designs, it was determined that variable moderator explains less than 13.1 percent variation in the density of detected errors. That amount of variation is not significant and can be explained by pure randomless. In order to verify the finding, a designed experiment would need to be performed.

Preparation Time, Inspection Rate and Code Size: The variables which are significant in the detection of errors are preparation time per KNCSL and inspection rate.

Figure 4 shows a log-log scatter plot of discovered error density and the amount of preparation per KNCSL. Both, the preparation time and inspection rate were found to be affected by the size of the code being inspected, as illustrated in Figure 5.

In part (A) of Figure 5, the solid line shows the logarithmic mean of the error density distribution, which amounts to 15.43, and the dotted lines indicate one standard deviation on either side of the mean. In addition, part (A) shows that as the size of the inspected code increases, the density of errors decreases. The coefficient of correlation between log (size) and log (density) is at -0.7844 which indicates strong negative correlation. The average size of the inspected code was 310 lines, while the median was 141 lines.

In part (B) of Figure 5, the dotted line shows the recommended level of preparation of 10 hours per KNCSL. The coefficient of correlation between log (size) and log (preparation time per KNCSL) is at -0.6927, which indicates significant negative correlation. This means that as the size of the inspected code increases, the amount of preparation time per KNCSL decreases.

As was mentioned earlier, inspection rate is one of the factors that determines the effectiveness of inspection From part (C) of Figure 5, it can be seen that larger pieces of code tend to be inspected more rapidly. The dotted line shows the recommended rate of 250 to 300 lines per meeting hour.

Code Inspection Effectiveness: In our environment, inspections are typically done after developer's test, so fault density discussed here does not reflect all faults in the code. On the average, code inspections were effective on removing 81.9 percent of errors found in inspection and testing. Fraction of errors found in inspections is defined as follows: Error density found in inspection divided by the total error density, where the total error density is a sum of inspection error density per KNCSL and MR density per KNCSL. MR, or modification request, is issued when a code error is found after inspection.

Figure 6 illustrates the fraction of errors detected at each inspection, versus the total amount of preparation per KNCSL. We found that for our environment, it does not pay off to spend more than 10 hours per KNCSL in preparation. The cost of finding additional error in code inspection is probably higher than finding it in the test area.

CONCLUSIONS

In our environment, code inspections proved to be an effective and inexpensive method of detecting coding errors. The amount of preparation time per thousand lines of code and inspection rate were found to be two key metrics of the inspection process. If these two parameters are monitored properly, and size of the code brought to the meeting is limited to approximately 600 lines of code, efficiency of code inspections can be increased independently of who is moderating the meeting. It is important however, to have a moderator who is in charge of the meeting and provides proper emphasis on error detection.

REFERENCES

[1] M. E. Fagan "Advances in Software Inspections," IEEE Transactions on Software Engineering, Vol. SE-12, No. 7, July 1986.

[2] M. E. Fagan "Design and Code Inspections to Reduce Errors in Program Development," IBM System Journal, Vol. 15, No. 3, 1976.

[3] Julia V. Bukowski, University of Pennsylvania, Philadelphia "A Software Design Assistance Tool," Proceedings Annual Reliability Symposium, 1985.

[4] B. Boehm, et al., "Information Processing/Data Automation Implications of Air Force Command and Control Requirements in the 1980's (CCIP-85)," Space and Missile Syst. Org., Los Angeles, CA, February, 1972.

[5] B. Boehm, "Software and Its Impact: A Quantitative Assessment," Datamation, Vol. 19, pp. 48-59, May, 1973.

[6] A. F. Ackerman, P. J. Fowler, and R. G. Ebenan "Software Inspections and the Industrial Production of Software," Software Validation, H. F. Hausen (editor), Elsevier Science Publishers B. V. (North-Holland), 1984.

[7] R. Peele, "Code Inspections at First Union Corporation," Proceeding of COMPSAC, pp. 445-446, 1982.

[8] N. Draper, H. Smith, "Applied Regression Analysis," Second Edition, Willey Series in Probability and Mathematical Statistics.

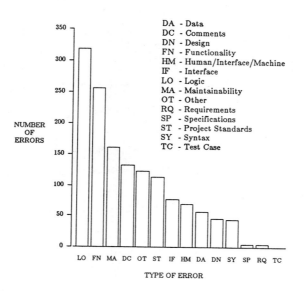

FIG. 1 - DISTRIBUTION OF CODE INSPECTION ERROR TYPES

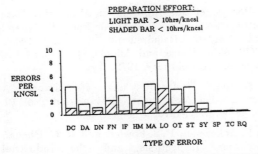

PREPARATION EFFORT:
LIGHT BAR > 10hrs/kncsl
SHADED BAR < 10hrs/kncsl

FIG. 2 - DENSITY DISTRIBUTION OF INSPECTION ERROR
TYPES FOR DIFFERENT EFFORT LEVELS

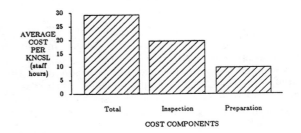

FIG. 3 - AVERAGE COST OF CODE INSPECTIONS
FOR PRODUCT "A"

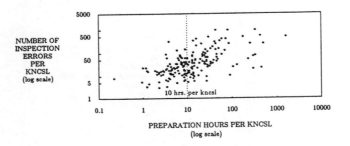

FIG. 4 - DENSITY OF CODE INSPECTION ERRORS
VERSUS PREPARATION EFFORT FOR
PRODUCT "A" CODE INSPECTIONS

1515

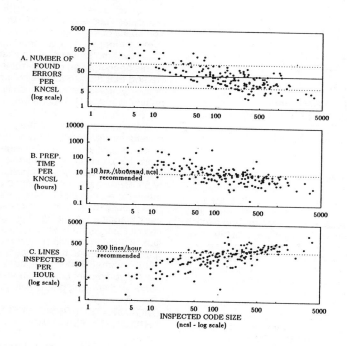

FIG. 5 - ERROR DENSITIES, PREPARATION EFFORT, AND INSPECTION
RATE VERSUS CODE SIZE FOR PRODUCT "A" CODE INSPECTIONS

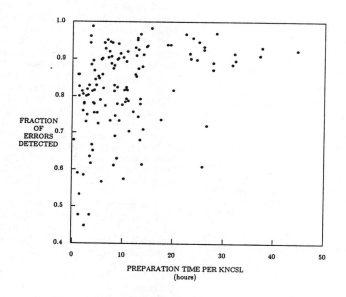

FIG. 6 - INSPECTION EFFECTIVENESS VERSUS PREPARATION
TIME FOR PRODUCT "A" CODE INSPECTIONS

TOTAL QUALITY COMMITMENT

Konstanty E. Krylow
Director, Quality Assurance
GTE Communication Systems Corp.
400 North Wolf Road
Northlake, Illinois 60164

ABSTRACT

Total quality commitment in any business must address the current products and services as well as the future offerings. To accomplish this there must exist an overall quality system – a structure on which all actions can be based. There must also exist well defined plans and procedures encompassing explicit quality requirements for developing, releasing and putting new products or services into being. For the already deployed products or services, machinery must exist to permit effective, efficient and rapid quality improvement based on customer feedback. This seminar will discuss these topics with emphasis on implementation, pitfalls and successes.

Thomas P. Huizenga   — Juran Institute
Phil M. Scanlan   — AT&T Information Systems
Don Schmidek   — Northern Telecom
Frank Voehl   — Florida Power & Light

PLANNING FOR QUALITY IN PRODUCT DEVELOPMENT

Thomas P. Huizenga
Vice President

Juran Institute, Inc.
88 Danbury Road
Wilton, CT 06987-4409

ABSTRACT

Today, because of increasing global competitive pressures on producers of products and services, new techniques are being utilized by organizations in planning for quality for the purpose of meeting customer needs and for bringing high quality products to market faster. This paper will explore reasons why planning for quality is affected by traditional organizational relationships, it will review recent literature on new techniques being applied to enhance product development efforts and will recommend specific actions to be taken to make a product development process more effective.

INTRODUCTION

U.S. companies from a multitude of industries are faced with a crisis in quality today and for the foreseeable future. Many companies have come to the realization of the need to examine their approach to managing for quality. Historically, U.S. companies have had little or no foreign competition, or have hidden behind the temporary security of patent protection. The results of this lack of competition were competitive complacency and a lack of focus on customer needs. Manufacturers sold products on the basis of pre-determining customer needs with the attitude that the customers will always buy what is designed for them.

Product development is the lifeblood of companies that provide goods and services. New products create opportunities for growth and profits. Competition and advances in technology are requiring companies to respond with shorter product development cycles and better quality. Typical U.S. practice has been to compress development cycles but at the expense of lower quality products. Quality problems are typically discovered late in product development, and the pressure to ship and meet schedules causes many products to be released to market early. The ability of engineers to follow through after product release is often hampered by demands for new products which does not allow time to fix newly released or existing products. Due to this phenomenon of early release and pressure to move on, we find that the product development process is the hatchery of quality problems, which is evidenced by the high costs of poor quality in many U.S. companies today.

Planning for quality in the product development process—developing products and processes to meet the needs of external as well as internal customers—is a competitive requirement for survival. As companies review their approaches to managing for quality, an important finding has been that quality problems have been planned that way. This arresting statement is meant to emphasize the fact that many of the deficiencies in our products and processes have had their origin in deficient planning for quality.[1] This paper will explore reasons why product development efforts are affected by traditional organization relationships, will review recent literature on new techniques being applied to enhance product development efforts and will recommend specific actions to be taken to make the product development process more effective in meeting customer needs and bringing products to market faster with better quality.

ORGANIZATION DESIGN EFFECTS ON QUALITY PLANNING

As if we needed another lesson from Japan, Ishikawa reports that in the late 1950's, Japan began quality assurance with an emphasis on new product development. At each stage of the way from planning for new products to after service, evaluation was to be tightly conducted and quality assured.[2] He also points out the Japanese dedication to customer satisfaction, use of market research to discover customer needs and participation by all employees in quality related activities.

Traditional organization design and practices have hampered U.S. companies in their efforts to meet customer needs and produce better quality. With respect to planning for quality, the first organizational issue that raises its head is traditional focus on control within departments causing sub-optimization. Sub-optimization is a widespread problem within companies due to the practice of establishing departmental budgets and goals and then judging the performance of managers based on departmental performance against such goals. Sub-optimization causes problems when departmental performance is measured on output rather than on the effect of this output on the user.[3] Chronic interdepartmental quality problems originate from the boundary or interface between one department and another.[4] In developing products, the classic example of sub-optimization also causes problems in planning processes which cross organization boundaries, due to lack of cooperation among departments who feed each other in a process.

The second organizational issue affecting planning for quality is responsibility for new product planning. Typically, this responsibility rests with R&D/Engineering, Marketing or a Corporate Development function. A typical example is shown in Figure 1 where R&D and Marketing are involved throughout the development process and the other important functions (Manufacturing, Quality, Service) get involved later in the process. Lack of participation early on in design generally means that changes to improve quality cannot be made in time for shipments to customers according to schedule.

The third organization issue is the absence of goals for quality and the subsequent delegation of responsibility for quality to the Quality department. Upper managers focus on the language of money, but the costs of poor quality are usually buried in financial reports; hidden in standard costs and overhead rates. Unless these "hidden factory" costs can be identified, there will be no opportunity for upper managers to act on problems.

A fourth issue is the organization reward system. In the U.S., the dominant system for rewarding performance is merit pay. The problem with this system with respect to quality is that it focuses on individual performance and creates competition among individuals within a company. In managing large processes like product development, cooperation is required by the departments responsible for the development effort. In merit pay systems team performance is usually not rewarded and the focus of competing outside with a shared sense of common fate is diminished.

A fifth issue is the separation of planning from execution. Planning is often done by people who will not have responsibility for carrying out the plans in actual operations. The classic problems here are the lack of manufacturability or servicability of designs.

Each of the above has a major impact on an organization's ability to build in quality in the product development process. The next section will review recent literature on corporate efforts in planning for quality which reveal how some companies face these organization issues.

REVIEW OF RECENT LITERATURE ON QUALITY IN PRODUCT DEVELOPMENT

A review of recent literature on the subject of planning for quality in product development reveals some new trends in planning for quality. These are as follows:

- Explicit product development processes defined using a flow diagram of activities.

- Use of the customer-producer-supplier model to improve process performance and communication.

- Early involvement by all major departments in product design and manufacture.

- Market research to discover customer needs in specifying product design features.

A discussion of these points follows.

1. Product Development as a Process

A process is a systematic series of actions directed towards the achievement of a goal.[5] Organizations reporting on defining product development as a process include Hewlett-Packard, IBM, AT&T, Perkin-Elmer and the Department of Defense.[6,7,8,9,10] A review of the papers referenced here indicates the following benefits from managing product development as a process:

- Use of flow diagrams to define the activities of the process helps to increase communication within the organization by defining activities at each step of the process and the inputs and outputs of the process. Figures 2 and 3 are examples of process flow diagrams.

- Breakdown of traditional organization barriers and elimination of departmental sub-optimization are facilitated by defining the customer-processor-supplier relationships involved in the process. By conducting this evaluation at each step of the process, needs of internal customers are identified and planned into the process.

- Checkpoints are provided in the process to review progress and evaluate results.

- A greater understanding of the whole process is achieved by formal documentation of the process. This becomes an aid for those involved who work within the process to know how their work ties into the whole and helps managers understand progress of a project by knowing where a development team stands with respect to the process.

2. Teams and Early Involvement

Organizations are reporting on use of multifunctional teams empowered to develop products from the product concept stage to customer shipments. The multifunctional team concept reflects the fact that many departments within a company are required to make a product successful.

Early involvement in product design using the multifunctional team approach allows for problems to be detected early in the development cycle with adequate time to correct them. The potential benefits are better product quality and faster development cycles. Design for manufacturability analysis is being incorporated into product development efforts to minimize parts and make designs easier to manufacture and service. Benefits from this are better quality/reliability due to fewer parts, lower overhead costs, faster development cycles, shorter manufacturing cycle time and better customer service.

3. Market Research to Discover Customer Needs

Customer input to the process of product development is beginning to be recognized as a first step in defining product features and product quality. Discovering the needs of customers has been a cornerstone in Japanese product development.[11] Since 1949, the Japanese Union of Scientists and Engineers has sponsored 43 different courses in quality related matters starting with the Quality Control Basic Course (for engineers). The second course was—Market Research.[12]

In conducting quality related market research, the fundamental issues are:

- What is the relative importance of quality-related factors that influence the purchase decision, as seen by the users?

- As to these quality-related factors, how do your products compare to those of competitors, as seen by the users?

- What is the significance of those quality differences, to your company, in money and other ways that might be important to you?

Not much has been written on how companies go about conducting such research. Two excellent papers on this subject include a paper on an approach used at General Electric outlined in a paper by L.J. Utzig, and a paper written by Dr. F.M. Gryna.[13,14] Another recent paper on market research and quality was written by P.E. Plsek, a former AT&T employee.[15]

This emphasis on discovering customer needs within the product development process is a recognition that the definition of quality encompasses the ideas of freedom from deficiencies (product dissatisfaction) and product performance (product satisfaction). Companies need to concentrate on both aspects of quality to ensure customer satisfaction.

CONCLUSIONS

U.S. industries are faced with a serious quality crisis today and for the foreseeable future. In order to compete on the basis of quality, companies must examine their existing approach to managing for quality. Planning for quality in the product development process is essential for an ability to compete on the basis of quality. Prior planning practices are the cause of lower product quality, chronic quality problems within organizations and inability to get the right products to market in a timely fashion.

Traditional organization design has an adverse effect on planning for quality in product development. Managers are forced to focus on control within their respective departments and are rewarded for optimizing activities within, with the frequent consequence of sub-optimizing performance for the company. Merit pay systems focus competition among individuals within the organization when the real competition is external. Teamwork is not promoted within traditional organizations due to the focus on departmental control and particular power bases of responsibility such as the Marketing and R&D departments which typically control product development efforts. Top management does not generally have a good idea on how to manage for quality throughout the company, how to set management goals and build these goals into the business plan.

A review of recent literature on the subject of planning for quality in product development offers insight into approaches being used to address competitive and organizational shortcomings that block the way for competitive products that meet customer needs.

RECOMMENDATIONS

Companies considering ways to become competitive in managing for quality and planning for quality in product development should be required to undertake the following activities:

- Conduct a study on the costs of poor quality in their organization. This study will provide upper management with the knowledge of the financial impact that quality has on the organization. Since these costs for U.S. companies are usually high (in the area of 20% of sales), top management attention is almost assured.

- Treat product development as a major business process and replan the process to facilitate improved quality and faster product development cycle times. Several process planning models are available on the market and an investigation of these would be in order. The reference papers can help explain some of these. Once the process is complete a formal product development guide should be written and distributed to management and department employees involved in the process.

- In replanning the process, the flow diagram should be used as a tool to define process steps, to define the inputs and outputs of each step, and to identify internal customers and their needs at each step. This exercise will help the development team understand where key quality activities need to take place and where opportunities for optimization can occur. The customer-processor-supplier mode is useful in this exercise.

- The tools of market research should be used to discover customer needs for quality as part of the product development process. The reference papers in this report provide a good understanding of how this process works.

- An analysis of design for manufacturability to look for and eliminate unnecessary parts and to review the design for ease of assembly should be built into the process. Various techniques are available to assist teams in such reviews. Referenced papers provide information on these techniques.

- An element of lessons learned from previous product development efforts should be built into the design process. Such a review should identify carryover of failure prone designs or components, poor vendors, inadequate manufacturing processes, etc.

These activities are far reaching, are by no means easy to achieve in a short period of time, and require a great deal of initiation and coordination within an organization. However these activities do represent some of the vital things necessary to attain a competitive edge in quality.

REFERENCES

1. J.M. Juran, Juran On Planning For Quality, The Free Press, 1988, p. vvi.

2. K. Ishikawa, What Is Total Quality Control? The Japanese Way, Prentice-Hall, Inc., 1985, pp. 19-20.

3. E.H. Melan, "Quality Improvement In An Engineering Lab", Quality Progress, June 1987, pp. 18-25

4. Ibid, p. 20.

5. Juran, op. cit., p. 273

6. C.H. House, "Product Development By The Numbers", Engineering Manager, April 1985, pp. 27-30

7. Melan, op cit., pp. 18-25

8. G.J. Surette, AT&T Technical Journal, June 1986.

9. T.P. Huizenga, K. Liepins, and D.J. Pisano, Jr., "Early Involvement", Quality Progress, June 1987, pp. 81-85.

10. W. Bodensteiner and J.W. Priest, "Designing Quality Into Defense Systems", Quality Progress, June 1987, pp. 93-96.

11. Ishikawa, op. cit., pp. 176-179.

12. F.M. Gryna, Jr., "Marketing Research and Product Quality", 1983-ASOC Quality Congress Transactions-Boston, p. 342.

13. L.J. Utzig, "Quality Reputation—A Precious Asset", 1980-ASOC Technical Conference Transactions—Atlanta, pp. 145-154.

14. Gryna, op. cit., pp. 385-392.

15. P.E. Plsek, "Defining Quality At The Marketing/Development Interface", Quality Progress, June 1987.

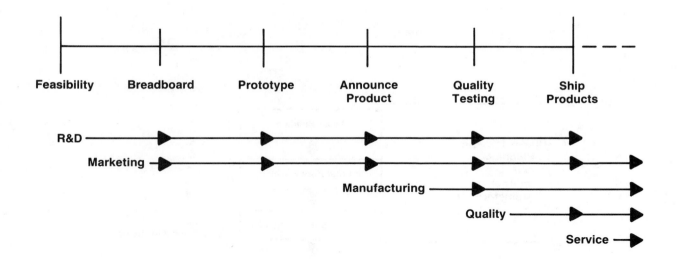

Fig. 1. Old Development Process

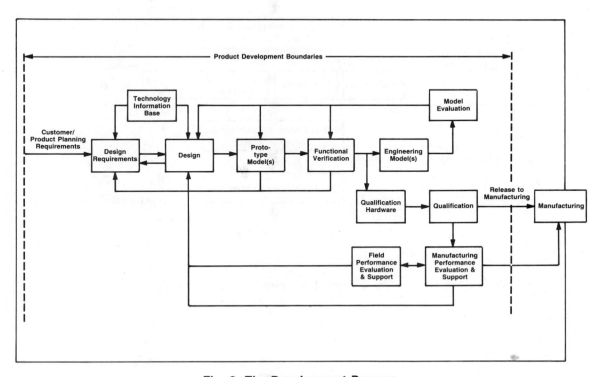

Fig. 2. The Development Process

1520

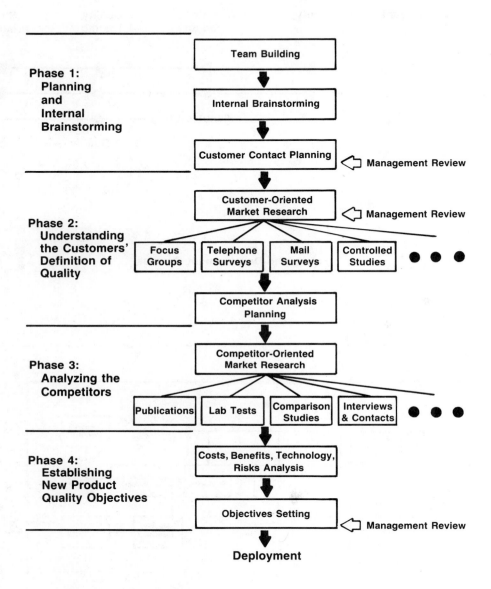

Fig. 3. Market Research Study on Quality

AT&T'S PERSPECTIVE ON QUALITY

Phil M. Scanlan
Director-AT&T Corporate Quality Office

AT&T Information Systems
55 Corporate Drive
Berkeley Heights, New Jersey

INTRODUCTION

For more than a century, AT&T has enjoyed a reputation for providing high-quality products. That reputation has endured because of a clear focus on quality control and quality assurance in the company's manufacturing operations. Indeed, many of today's quality fundamentals were established by AT&T. To name but a few, these include:

— Quality assurance acceptance inspection of "telephone appliance" that began in 1882.

— Walter Shewhart's development of statistical quality control chart at Bell Laboratories in 1925—the very foundation of statistical quality analysis.

— The development and publication of Inspection Sampling Tables by Harold Dodge and Harry Romig of Bell Labs in 1944.

— Publication in 1956 of the *Western Electric Statistical Quality Control Handbook,* which was developed by a team of manufacturing engineers led by Bonnie Small. Some 30 years after its first printing, this is still recognized as **the** book on statistical process control methods.

— And finally, many people think of AT&T as the very birthplace of quality, referring to the pioneering work of W. Edwards Deming and Joseph W. Juran at Bell Labs.

Parallelling these developments were AT&T's intangible accomplishments, which served to engender a lasting vision and a methodology for achieving quality. In its first 50 years—i.e., before 1925—AT&T.

— Identified quality as a core value of its business.

— Recognized that customer satisfaction drives quality.

— Saw that inspection alone was inadequate to assure the quality required by the company and its customers.

— Recognized that doing the job right the first time called for a scientific base for quality assurance—and developed that base.

— Acknowledged that achieving quality required linking the designer with the manufacturer.

While AT&T is justly proud of its quality heritage, the company knows that laurels are better built upon than rested upon. No company in the annals of American business can be more acutely aware than AT&T of a new era that has dawned. Our marketplace is now global and fiercely competitive, and throughout AT&T there is a growing recognition that in order to succeed as a competitor in that global marketplace, the company nust view quality as a strategic asset and implement a quality program throughout every aspect of its operations.

In other words, the heritage of high-quality products must seed a complementary tradition of high-quality service as well. Because there exists more parity in technology than ever before, it is increasingly difficult to differentiate among products. It is therefore not product superiority alone that makes for a loyal, satisified customer. Rather, studies have shown that market share and profitability in a highly competitive marketplace are directly related to two customer-based judgements:

— Does this product/service offer high value compared to cost?

— Will I be satisfied with delivery, performance, and support of this product/service?

The vaildity of a corporate strategy of high customer satisfaction with relatively low internal costs has been repeatedly demonstrated by those companies—frequently Japanese—that have achieved significant growth in market share and "best in class" reputations in a global marketplace. The simple lesson learned, or rediscovered, by American industry in this decade is that a company that provides excellent service to its customers—in addition to a high-quality product—will gain an increasing advantage over its competitors.

As service and product support are becoming the new standards by which companies are being judged, AT&T, like many other businesses, is emphasizing quality of service—i.e., attention to the customer—in addition to technical product quality; both are key strategies for moving toward a market-based enterprise.

This is not to ignore the fact that AT&T has traditionally focused on customer service. The company's "Spirit of Service" heritage dates from its earliest days. In the words of a senior AT&T manager, however, "The systems, processes, and management approaches that allowed us to provide high-quality service so well for so many decades [are] too costly, cumbersome, and fragmented for long-term success in a competitive environment."

In other words, AT&T recognizes that in order to sustain a competitive advantage in the marketplace, the company must not only focus attenton on services to the end customer, but must also pay strict attention to the quality and efficiency of **all** internal processes and customer support systems. Every business process must be viewed within the context of the whole, if AT&T is able to deliver high-quality products and services to its end customers.

A NEW APPROACH

Clearly, what is called for is an **integrated** approach to quality—i.e., a system that ensures that a consistent concern for quality underlies everything the company does. And in response to the challenges it faced following divestiture—challenges to enter new markets and maintain high standards for products and services in a competitive environment—that is exactly what AT&T has developed, an integrated quality system.

For AT&T, *quality* is the ability of a product or service to satisfy customers at the lowest overall cost to the company. Managing for quality means incorporating a specific, systematic, and consistently applied program into everyday operations in order to:

— Establish product or service requirements, based on customer needs and world-class performances, which can be measured and verified.

— Define and structure operations that can meet these requirements efficiently, across organizational boundaries.

— Measure, analyze, control, and improve products or services and the operations that produce them.

An integrated quality system is the formal structure for managing quality, end to end across the operation. Such a system unifies operations throughout the company by identifying and coordinating all quality-related activities. It clarifies the role of management and the responsibilities of employees, while building quality-related activities into the company's total management system. Finally, an integrated quality system links business processes to customer needs and expectations.

Quality at AT&T is a matter of top-down concern. The Quality Policy, signed by the company president and chief operating officer, established responsibilities and a course of action that allows each AT&T employee to contribute to the realization of the company's overarching goal of customer satisfaction. Specifically, the Quality Policy states, "Quality excellence is the foundation for the management of our business and the keystone of our goal of customer satisfaction. It is therefore our policy to:

— Consistently provide products and services that meet the quality expectations of our customers.

— Actively pursue ever-improving quality through programs that enable each and every employee to do his or her job right the first time."

The vision of service excellence that is articulated in the AT&T Quality Policy serves as the starting point for building a service quality strategy for the company. Inherent in the policy statement is the recognition that the quality of the customer service provided rests largely with the individual employee—every employee, not only those with direct customer-service responsibility.

AN ARCHITECTURE FOR QUALITY

AT&T believes that managing quality as the top business priority is a strategy that supports all other goals. Accordingly, the AT&T Quality Policy fixes responsibility for product and service quality within each of the company's business units. An Integrated Quality System Architecture translates the intent of the Quality Policy into a design for implementation. The architecture links activities across and within organizational boundaries to meet customers' expectations and achieve major improvements in profitability.

In treating quality as a strategic business variable, the architecture provides a structure that enables upper management in each business unit to assume overall responsibility and leadership for quality. A Business Unit Quality Council in each AT&T organization includes the business unit president, all senior managers within the unit, and senior managers of important related business functions outside the unit.

Within a functional organization, the architecture defines two levels of quality-related activity:

— High-level quality leadership and management, which is the responsibility of the functional organization quality steering committee.

— Quality-related activities that have a direct impact on customer satisfaction and profitability improvements, which are implemented at the level of business processes.

In terms of the quality architecture, a business process refers to a group of interrelated operations or activities that together generate a well-defined set of outputs from a well-defined set of inputs and have a single "owner" with primary responsibility for process management and improvement. Using a customer-driven approach to quality managment ensures that the outputs of one's job satisfy his or her customer and that the process is responsible to changes in customer requirements.

AT&T's Process Quality Management and Improvement (PQMI) methodology is based on a customer/supplier model (see figure 1). It operates under the premise that everyone has customers—either inside or outside the company—who use the outputs of their job. At the same time, according to the model, everyone has suppliers, who provide the inputs to their job. This model provides a framework for establishing and maintaining effective relationships with customers and suppliers. Applying the customer/supplier model forces the user to seek answers to several categories of questions, including:

— Questions about issues pertaining to the relationship with one's customers.

— Questions to solicit feedback pertaining to process performance.

— Questions to solicit feedback pertaining to one's relationship with suppliers.

The PQMI methodology is based on the customer/supplier model and is used by process owners and managers to improve the quality of product and service delivery to customers. The methodology consists of seven steps that operate as a cycle, which is managed and improved and continuously repeated. The seven steps include activities to be performed at each of four distinct stages, as described below:

Stage I—Ownership.

The purpose of the ownership stage is to ensure that someone is in charge of the process and that a team exists to carry out day-to-day management activities. The key objectives of this state are:

— To identify an overall process owner who is ultimately accountable for the process and who can manage the process across functional or organizational boundaries (Step 1).

— To define roles and responsibilities and ensure that everyone involved in the application of process quality managment and improvement works as a team with personal ownership of the performance of the process (Step 1).

Stage II—Assessment.

The purpose of the assessment stage is to assure that the process is clearly defined, that customer expectations are clearly understood, and that measures are in place to determine how well the process is satisfying customer requirements and internal business objectives. The key objectives of this stage are:

— To understand how your process operates (Step 2).

— To identify your customers' needs in measurable terms (Step 2).

— To determine what elements of the process should be measured and controlled to meet customer requirements (Step 3).

— To test and then implement appropriate new measures or validate existing measures on a wide scale (Step 3).

— To gather data on process performance (Step 4).

— To control and stabilize process performance (Step 4).

— To assess process performance against customers' requirements (Step 4).

Stage III—Opportunity Selection.

The purpose of the opportunity selection stage is to understand how internal process problems affect customer satisfaction and cost, and to identify and rank order opportunities for process improvement. The key objectives of this stage are:

— To identify critical internal process problems that are affecting customer satisfaction and cost (Step 5).

— To identify process simplification opportunities (Step 5).

— To rank improvement opportunities based on customer satisfaction and business objectives (Step 6).

— To set appropriate quality improvement and performance targets (Step 6).

— To identify quality improvement projects to pursue (Step 6).

Stage IV—Improvement.

At the heart of AT&T's Quality Policy is a commitment to **continuous** quality improvement. The purpose of the improvement stage of the PQMI methodology is to achieve and sustain a new level of process performance by implementing an action plan for realizing opportunities identified in the previous stage. The key objectives of this stage are:

— To organize quality improvement teams that will develop action plans to address opportunities for process quality improvement (Step 7).

— To identify and remove root causes of problems (Step 7).

— To control and monitor the process at the improved level of performance (Step 7).

— To monitor and assess process performance on an ongoing basis (Step 7).

RESULTS

Organizations throughout AT&T are using the PQMI methodology to manage and improve operations as diverse as computer technology development, provisioning of AT&T PhoneCenter Stores, vendor management, support services, telemarketing, payroll processing, human resources policy development and deployment, material and information distribution, library support services, occupational staffing, appraisal process design and management, sales order methods and procedures development, executive speechwriting, intellectual property licensing and management, and a variety of other service and administrative processes.

At all times, a key focus is in managing and improving internal work processes in order to ensure the final delivery of high-quality products and services to AT&T's end customers.

CONCLUSION

In developing the Process Quality Management and Improvement guidelines to be used as a tool in implementing a customer-focused service strategy, AT&T has taken measures to ensure customer satisfaction with the quality of its service by providing people throughout the enterprise with a blueprint for action. AT&T's senior management has also recognized that it will take focused and committed leadership, supported by effective human performance and measurement systems, as well as education and training, to make this goal a reality.

To borrow a line from the AT&T Quality Policy: "Quality will continue to be a major, strategic thrust in AT&T. It lies at the heart of everything we do." AT&T has embarked upon a journey toward continuous quality improvement. The mission is engaging. The possibilities are exciting. The prospects are bright.

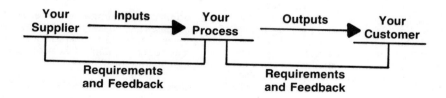

Fig. 1. Customer/Supplier Model

NEW PRODUCT INTRODUCTION
QUALITY PROCESS

Don Schmidek
Director
Reliability & Quality Assurance

Northern Telecom Inc.
Meridian Communication Systems
2305 Mission College Boulevard
Santa Clara, California 95054

ABSTRACT

This paper presents Northern Telecom/BNR's highly successful, complex, but practical aspects and methods, concerning the introduction of new products. From concept definition, to development and manufacture, and on to the market place the product proceeds via a structured and controlled process and methodology.

The applied principles are fundamental and consist of a multiphase step process, called the Gates Process. The one key element which differentiates this methodology from others is the application of quality assurance precepts to the entire process, where checks and balances are applied to each phase. During early planning it is determined where quantifiable and thus measurable results are expected and what are the ultimate criteria for passage.

INTRODUCTION

In todays rapidly evolving and highly competitive market environment, introduction of new products on a weekly basis — both hardware and software — fully meeting customer requirements, exceeding competition's offerings, at the required quality levels, on time and at the projected cost levels, is fundamental to success.

Traditionally, the new product introduction process in the regulated telecommunication industry, specifically in the period before divestiture, used to be an extremely thorough, but leisurely process. In 1976 Northern Telecom was the first manufacturer to introduce a complete range of digital telecommunication products for central switching as well as for private branch exchange (PBX). These products were based on the latest microelectronics techology and raised the criticality of software in the development of products and features. With the introduction of the new generation of products, and the phenomenal evolution of the post divestiture telecommunication market, it became rapidly evident that previous management policies, practices and methods for new product introduction could not satisfy the required pace, quality levels and the market place requirement. Product introduction cycles had to shrink, quality had to be right the first time, and product performance had to be ever improving. The complexity required that new products and programs be well integrated across a variety of interdisciplines and multifunctional interfaces.

In the early 80's, Northern Telecom and Bell Northern Research, (the R&D arm of NT), addressed the issue of a New Product Introduction and developed a fundamental process, which could lend itself to all divisions and to all types of products, including software. The break-through was based on a number of basic precepts, which are fundamental to good quality assurance concepts, i.e.:

— Define the System.

— Understand the supplier/customer relationship.

— Define the objectives and deliverables.

— Measure where you are vs. the objectives.

— Focus on continuous improvement.

These precepts have been developed in what is now called the:

"GATES PROCESS"

The Gates Process (see Figure 1) consists of 5 phases, each one culminating in a formal review. There the decision is made as to the appropriateness of continuing, adjusting the process by acceleration/delaying, adding/reducing resources or changing the decision point at which the transition to the next step will take place.

Each Gate requires that a certain "deliverable" be completed at a predefined quality level. Each function must complete the specified task and provide the results by the Gate. Quality Assurance has the responsibility for assessing the adequacy of each of the deliverables, and to make recommendations as to Gate status and overall acceptability. The Gate is considered passed if the key participants including the General Manager deem it so.

The process has been in place for two years at all Northern Telecom and BNR Divisions. It has proven to be a highly successful tool to facilitate the new products process and to validate and meaure the probability of product introduction at the predefined quality, cost, and schedule.

Since its inception two years ago, the Gate success rate has risen from a 35% to 85%. At the same time, the quality level of new products has increased by a significant margin, as have the customer satisfaction levels, because all the required deliverables have been available when needed at the appropriate and defined levels.

The Gates Process, as it was developed and has evolved, is based on the following fundamental quality assurance precepts and definitions:

1. **System** — A set of 5 key gates which control the transition between the 6 key introduction steps, i.e.: Product Definition, Product Development, Design and Verification, Preproduction and Qualification, Production, and the Customer.

2. **Supplier & Customer** — For each of the Gates a set of suppliers and customers were identified. The supplier, for instance, for Gate 1 would be Marketing while the customer may be Design. Each of these had to deliver and/or accept the "deliverables".

3. **Objectives & Deliverables** — The objectives for each deliverable and for each function were the hardest to adequately define and to quantify in quality terms. The requirements are still an ever evolving process. The goal is to obtain a sufficiently complete "deliverable", without overkill, or semblance of bureaucracy, while still satisfying the necessary requirements.

4. **Measurement** — A set of acceptance criteria for each deliverable was developed to measure and control the process. The belief that "if you know where you are, you will get to where you are going" has been the motto and method of operation.

5. **Improvement** — Having developed the system with its defined practices and methods, some major factors such as: cycle time, quality of deliverable, and a number of pro-

cess and system shortcomings became measurable. With this knowledge in hand, the process was adjusted, the deliverables were better defined, and ultimately, the quality of the process was increased and the cycle time dramatically reduced. The evolution still continues.

GATES STRUCTURE

The Gates Process, is intended for projects of all sizes, but some judiciousness is necessary. For larger projects, the Gates must be followed explicitly, requiring that the Gate reviews be attended by senior management – Director level and above.

Some projects of special critical nature or size require Executive Gate reviews which provide visibility of progress to the highest echelons of the Corporation via direct participation and involvement.

Smaller projects are managed at a less formal level, but require that the Project Plan define the conditions up-front. These are attended by Senior Engineers & Managers, and can be combined and abbreviated. None of the key issues – those of performance, cost and completeness – can be neglected.

GATE RELEASE & APPROVAL

All Gates must be approved by the principal recipient of the Gate deliverabes, as well as the Directors or alternates of Product Management, Development and Quality Assurance. For some Gates, approval from the Directors of Manufacturing, Service and Project Management is also required. The key gates require that the General Manager approve the release.

The process stipulates that the Quality function provides an overall assessment of the deliverables, based on predefined acceptance criteria and deliverable content. In addition to the deliverables, an assessment is made of the results of testing, the degree of project completion, the cost projections, and the customer satisfaction levels during beta tests.

The gates release is formally approved via a gate release authorization, which in cases of passed gates, will indicate passing, and if needed, identify the minor conditions which need to be satisfied or completed at a certain predefined time. For gates which have failed, the reason for failure is stated. Those Gates are rescheduled based on the completion date of the tasks which have caused the failure.

For a Gate 0 failure, the product will not be authorized and additional definition work is not warranted. In cases of a Gate 1 failure, the development process cannot be initiated and development funding will not be released. For a Gate 2 failure, the product will not be authorized for preproduction and Beta test, while a Gate 3 failure will preclude production and release for customer sales.

THE GATES DEFINED

Each Gate has its objectives, key milestones and deliverables. The following are the principal and fundamental items which need to be formally presented and discussed at each Gate. All items must be in an appropriate document (deliverables), duly structured, reviewed and approved. For products with multi marketing applications, full concurence from all the Product Primes (managers responsible for the product) must be obtained. Quality Assurace has a dual role in all the Gates. It must provide the Quality Project Plan, on par with the other plans which Design, Manufacturing, etc. provide, and it also must assess the adequacy of the other plans. QA has to "suggest" to the Chairman of the Gate, whether or not the requirements for the Gate have been met, and recommend whether or not the Gate should be passed.

GATE 0

Product Concept Identification

The objective of the Gate is to obtain approval of the initialization for the product development from the conceptual and definitional prospective. This is the stage when Marketing puts forth the proper rationalization for the needs of a new development, including market needs and penetration estimates. Preliminary development feasibility estimates, product costs and profit rates are also reviewed at this time. The following are the items which must be completed and reviewed by the proper parties, and must be judged to be of adequate merit to allow further corporate investment.

Gate 0

General Deliverable	Responsible Function
• Market Needs	Marketing
• Market Size – Available & Share	Marketing
• Competition Offerings	Marketing
• Marketing Strategy	Marketing
• Product Description	Marketing
• Service & Reliability	Marketing
• Technical Approach	Development
• Schedule & Risk	Development
• Resources & Investment	Project Management

GATE 1

Product Definition & Requirements

This Gate is one of the most critical as it is the one which actually launches the new product process. By this gate the Marketing product requirements have to be finalized, the marketing strategy completely defined and the product properly positioned. This Gate is also the culmination of the design feasibility where the development groups defined the technological approach, the software and the product size. The development plans, cost and schedules are also finalized by this Gate, as is the overall Project Plan. The Project Plans define the product introduction schedule, and set the dates for the other Gates and the date for the product release. The development costs and capital equipment needs are reviewed and fundamentally approved. Manufacturing plans are completed prior to this Gate and the highlights and the overall intergration are reviewed and approved at the Gate. The Beta Test plans are defined and the required sites and site profiles identified. Service plans and strategy, are validated against the marketing objectives. Finally the Quality Assurance Program Plans must tie in all the design, development, procurement, product qualification, process control and the software requirements, to assure that the overall customer expectations are met.

GATE 1

General Deliverable	Responsible Function
• Commercial/Product Specification	Marketing
• System Requirements & Reliability	Marketing
• Customer Satisfaction Attributes	Marketing
• Revenue Plan	Marketing
• Market Segments	Marketing
• Product Design Spec	Design/Development
• Technology Selection	Design/Development
• Software Sizing & Complexity	Design/Development
• Development Plan	Design/Development
• Verification Plan	Design/Development

• Component Plan	Design/Development
• Development Quality Plan	Design/Development
• Reliability Estimates	Design/Development
• Manufacturing Plan	Manufacturing
• Procurement Plan	Manufacturing
• Production Test & Yield Plan	Manufacturing
• Value Analysis Plan	Manufacturing
• Manufacturing & Product Costs	Manufacturing
• Quality Program Plan	Quality Assurance
• Supplier Quality Program	Quality Assurance
• Software Quality Plan	Quality Assurance
• Reliability Test/Audit Plan	Quality Assurance
• Quality Targets – Hardware & Software	Quality Assurance
• Service & Support Plan	Field Service
• Project Plan	Project Management
• Project Funding & Schedule	Proejct Management
• Team Structure Resource Needs	Project Management

GATE 2

Design, Verification and Preproduction Qualification

This Gate is fundamental and is the culmination of the design and development cycle. At this time the product – hardware and/or software – and all the associated processes and documentation must be in their final versions. This Gate authorizes two key events: the transfer of product design information to manufacturing for preproduction and production, and secondly the start of formal Beta Tests, or Field Trials, in a number of customer locations. This gate assures that the product is viable in a manufacturing sense, that it meets the market requirements and expectations and that the costs are on target.

The process requires that a significant number of major milestones be completed. A number of functions must indicate that they are ready to start the deployment phase of the product. A list of the prime requirements to pass the Gate are as follows: successful completion of hardware and/or software verification and qualification of preproduction products; qualification of all sourced items and their suppliers; process qualification of all critical new manufacturing processes; availability of Manufacturing Test capability; validation of preliminary process test yields and burn-in results; quality assessment of first product preproduction runs; completion of all customer required documentation; full definition and plans for Beta Tests (field trial tests and required site profiles); completed development of Service Training cources for product support and for end users; sales forecasts and lead customers identification; marketing announcement plans, pricing, advertising, product introduction phasing and documentation; availability of Beta Test sites/customers satisfying all the required product configurations and loading factors.

Gate 2

General Deliverable	Responsible Function
• Project Plan	Product Management
• Investment Status	Product Management
• Design Verification Reports	Development
• Design Documentation	Development
• Software Contents & Test Report	Development
• Design Qualification Report	Development
• Open Problems – Hardware & Software	Development

• Component Qualification Status	Development
• Market Introduction Program	Marketing
• Sales Forecast	Marketing
• Lead Customers & Beta Test Sites	Marketing
• Marketing Communication	Marketing
• User Documentation	Marketing
• New Process Qualification	Manufacturing
• Test & Burn-In Capacity	Manufacturing
• Product Costs	Manufacturing
• Manufacturability Assessment	Manufacturing
• Manufacturing Build Plan	Manufacturing
• Supplier Qualification	Manufacturing
• Product Assessment	Quality Assurance
• Yield Analysis	Quality Assurance
• Process Capability Analysis	Quality Assurance
• Reliability Assessment	Quality Assurance
• Assessments Vs. All Targets	Quality Assurance
• Service & Training Program	Service

GATE 3

Product General Market Release

Based on satisfactory final qualification results and successful Beta Test conclusions of hardware and/or software, the product can be released. The release allows that either controlled sales or uncontrolled sales take place. Controlled sales occur only in cases where special market considerations are needed, i.e.: when customer configuration requirements need more intense validation; during the initial stages, to assure that the order and sales process is under full control; when product is of limited availability. Uncontrolled sales release is applicable where product sales and support does not need checks and balances by Marketing.

The product qualification requirements, which have been defined prior to Gate 2, must have been fully met, and all the tests completed on the latest product configurations. This is especially true for products modified as a result of field trials or some other inputs.

The manufacturing process must reflect capability to produce at the projected yields, as measured by mechanical/visual and electrical/test, including product burn-in. The outgoing quality levels must meet the predefined requirements, as measured by an independent quality test and acceptance process.

The Beta Test results must have shown positive results in a number of areas. The installation quality must have met all the following requirements: ability to install the product per installation documentation; troubleshooting and diagnostic ability; DOA projected rates in the first 7 to 30 days; performance to expected and specified levels relative to features, etc.

The key objective of the Beta Test is to validate that the **entire** product performs to objectives, in a number of real world applications, and especially in conditions which cannot be well simulated in laboratory environments. Thus, these tests must be conducted at sites which represent all the intended product applications – software feature applications and end use consideration are key for this selection.

The most critical part of this phase is the customer response to the product. This is achieved via a Customer Satisfaction

Survey of the product users, and is obtained from a valid cross-section of Beta site users. The objective is to achieve a satisfaction level of users in the high 90's and to validate the original, pre Gate 1 expectation.

Gate 3

General Deliverable	Responsible Function
• Project Investment	Project Manager
• Project Plan/Schedule	Project Manager
• Life Cycle Revenue/ Profitability	Project Manager
• Sales Forecast	Marketing
• Orders Received	Marketing
• Market Expansion Strategy	Marketing
• Documentation & Communication	Marketing
• Advertising & Promotion	Marketing
• Beta Test Satisfaction Report	Marketing
• Qualification Test-Final Results	Development
• Environmental & Regulatory Tests	Development
• Design Change History	Development
• Configuration Control	Development
• Final Documentation Release	Development
• Field Trial Results	Development
• Field Installation Manuals	Development
• Reliability Design Analysis (Final)	Development
• Manufacturing & Test Capacity	Manufacturing
• Manufacturing Ramp-Up Plan	Manufacturing
• Test Yield	Manufacturing
• Process Qualification	Manufacturing
• Product Costs	Manufacturing
• Supplier Base & Part Availability	Manufacturing
• Repair Capacity & Plans	Manufacturing
• Installation Group Qualification	Service
• User & Maintenance Training	Service
• Support Group Availablity	Service
• Distributor Qualification/ Readiness	Service
• Spares Requirements	Service
• Supplier & Parts Qualification	Quality Assurance
• Process Qualification	Quality Assurance
• Incoming Acceptance Readiness	Quality Assurance
• Reliability Test Results	Quality Assurance
• Burn-In Requirements	Quality Assurance
• Field Trial Results Analysis	Quality Assurance
• Preproduction Part Failure Analysis	Quality Assurance
• Field Trial Returns Analysis	Quality Assurance
• Field Returns Plans	Quality Assurance
• Installation Quality Audit Plans	Quality Assurance
• Customer Satisfaction Plan	Quality Assurance

GATE 4

Post Market Release Evaluation

This Gate is a validation that the product and processes as finalized at Gate 3 are performing at the defined levels. Key attributes assessed at this stage are in the areas of delivery, market penetration, revenues, distribution, competitive positioning, sales, profitability, design stability & status, manufacturing yield, costs, performance, service, service documentation, field performance, reliability and customer satisfaction.

Results of the Gate are used to learn and to improve the product and the process. Key issues, as identified, and action plans are defined and scheduled.

MEASUREMENTS

A number of Gate deliverable measurement practices and standards have been established.

One practice hinges on a Index, which is based on a minimum acceptable rating, by deliverable. The contents, by section of each deliverable, are assigned weight factors, and are scored accordingly. Then the weighted scores for all are added and these in turn are added for each scored document. The process is quite thorough, but it lacks the required product or program uniqueness adaptation.

Another practice, is to assess the deliverables, using criticality factors, and only where significant deficiencies are noted, would the deliverable be considered as not acceptable. This approach was found more acceptable, but requires that senior and knowledgeable people assess each deliverable, and define their acceptability. The method is better understood by all the functions involved, as major discrepancies are generally more easily conveyed and rationalized.

The most important benefit of the Gating Process is that it has become measureable and quantifiable. Success factors, as well as causes for failure, can be defined and measured. Similiarly the primary causes of Gate failure can be extracted, and plans developed to improve the future success probability. The process has brought about a consciousness among all the groups involved, and a significant improvement and success rate has been the net effect.

The items which are still not well understood, are the causes of delays or failure, either in the definition or delivery. These will be a source of study – root cause study – to define how the process of definition, estimation and scheduling can be improved.

At all Northern Telecom/BNR locations, this process has been embraced and well implemented. We have learned, that the process must be customized by each Group and Division, to fit their organizational structure, their products and their customer environment.

We can summarize that the process has been effective and we can state with confidence that the Gates Process has been the:

"GATE TO SUCCESS"

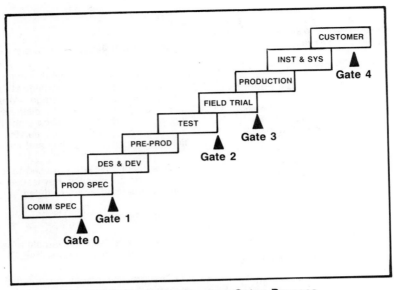

Fig. 1. The New Product Gates Process

TRANSFORMING YOUR ORGANIZATION
THROUGH QUALITY IMPROVEMENT

Frank Voehl
Director
Quality Services

Florida Power & Light's QualTec
11300 U.S. Highway
Suite 500
Palm Beach Garden, Florida 33408

Let me begin by declaring what I have often said in the past:

The quality improvement imperative is not a fad. A lot of us thought it was, when it was first introduced into our company. As someone said to me a few years ago; ''We thought that if we kept quiet, it would go away''. But it hasn't. In fact, I believe it's the most valuable management system ever employed by our company. The return on your investment in quality improvement begins the very instant that your company makes a commitment to do things right – not just better, but right.

What are we talking about when we say ''quality improvement?'' Understanding the concept is crucial to knowing how and why it needs to be institutionalized as a transformational process and not just another fad. Indeed, what do we mean by ''quality''?

At FPL we define quality as meeting our customers' valid requirements. That includes many facets: cost of service, reliable service, accurate billing, safe generation of power and prompt response to service problems. We ascertain those requirements by listening to our customers. We may negotiate some of the requirements, making them ''valid''. Obviously, we couldn't offer all the service a customer wanted and charge only a dollar a year; that is an example of an invalid requirement.

In applying our definition of quality to other industries, a quality automobile would be one that was reliable to the degree customers demanded it to be, at a given price. I think most of you would agree that at no price would a customer be satisfied with a car which would not start 20% of the time, or an airplane which stayed aloft only 50% of the time. There are some minimum benefits which a customer expects to receive when he buys or uses a product or service.

With this understanding of quality, I think it is clear that quality improvement means trying to make existing levels of quality better. Even that statement may be too simple because quality improvement is not a target or a final destination. Quality improvement is a process, a mechanism, of doing things in a certain manner; it is a non-ending journey, not a destination. That is precisely why quality improvement must be institutionalized for it to be effective.

For a while, we presumed what many others have presumed, that quality if free. But we discovered that quality is about as free as clean air and about as difficult to grasp. In 1981 we began a revival of quality awareness at FPL, with a company-wide movement centered on a Quality Improvement Program which we simply called QIP. We went to our employees and asked them how their work units could perform better, providing better service to their customers, both external – rate payers – and internal – other work units they interact with. Today the quality improvement teams are a dynamic mechanism for making significant improvements in our operations, from allowing us to refuel nuclear plants ahead of schedule to handling power lines more safely.

We have worked hard at getting our teams to function well. Training, heavy use of data collection and analysis is required. Systematic problem solving techniques are employed. While membership on the teams is voluntary, 56% of our employees are directly involved on teams. Teams typically meet one hour per week. Sometimes they may need months to solve a given problem or determine the best way to take advantage of an opportunity.

We broadened our quality improvement efforts in 1984 with Policy Deployment. Whereas quality improvement teams may work on matters affecting their own work units, Policy Deployment is more concerned with major issues which affect the company as a whole. The process seeks areas that are so significant that it pays for the company to mobilize all of its resources to achieve. A lot of planning is required for Policy Deployment and a major benefit is the communication and coordination among departments, divisions and top management which results. Through a series of Executive Visitations, each FPL executive visits annually at least one of the company's plants and departments to discuss with employees their department's and company's objectives. Every six months, each department head reviews his department's activities with the President and Chairman, using quality process methods; we refer to this process as Presidential Reviews. Probably the biggest contribution which Executive Visitations and Presidential Reviews achieve is the focusing by all levels of employees on their respective priorities and roles within the company.

But what is the return on investment of producing quality – and when do you start seeing the results? Who benefits, and how is it measured? The initial investment that I alluded to – the idea of doing it right – is something more valuable than money. That is a difficult concept for some of us to accept and perhaps even more difficult for some of our shareholders to understand. But how do we attach a price to a complete change of attitude? A changing corporate culture that espouses not only a philosophy with a new respect for quality, but a new respect for the customer as well? How much is it worth to you, and to the stockholders, to be able to create within your company an environment where positive change is encouraged and quality performance is expected, where waste and inefficiency are viewed as undesirable and unacceptable by virtually every employee? Such an environment, in my mind at least, is priceless. It's the commitment to quality that I believe is essential not only for the bottom line, but for our very survival as a business, and perhaps as a nation.

FPL has a major goal, a mission, to be the best managed electric utility in the United States by the end of the decade, a well managed company overall and to be recognized as such. It is important that all levels of employees be marching to the same tune, toward that mission.

In 1986, we added the third part of our quality improvement triangle, Quality in Daily Work. This segment concentrates on improving quality in daily work activities. It starts by each employee identifying his customers and their requirements. Part of the process involves direct negotiation between employees and their customers, to determine which requirements are valid. Through the process, each employee determines the best way to meet his customer's valid requirements by re-examining his individual work process. When the same kinds of work are being performed by different employees, the most efficient techniques are duplicated. Although Quality in Daily Work is still relatively new to us, it will ultimately be a useful tool to serve our customers better and, therefore, provide quality service.

We're a rapidly changing industry, in a rapidly changing world. We're no longer a monopoly in the classical sense. Competition is charging towards us. And the best way I know to hold on to a customer is with quality – a quality product, quality service, and quality management. Our company-wide Quality Improvement Program is only five years old, but I'm proud to point out that already it has become an internationally recognized, award-winning program. We have had more than 400 American companies and organizations visit our company to seek guidance in their own effort towards quality improvement.

Is quality improvement worth the effort? Obviously, FPL thinks it is. Although some may think a regulated utility need not be concerned with cost and productivity. I can assure you that profits are not guaranteed. Indeed, it was made clear to

us in the 1970's that survival wasn't even guaranteed. Regulatory agencies will not rubber-stamp rate increases. In the case of FPL, we had to find a way of becoming more productive and provide better service at a lower cost. Quality Improvement has been our way to do just that. Do we want to stay with our process? Would any company which found success using an effective program want to continue to use it?

While the answers to both questions are obviously positive, it's not all that easy to accomplish. How many management philosophies have gone by the wayside when the top man in the company retired or was replaced? Or, how many practices were discontinued after a halfhearted attempt was made to use them?

But we knew we had a tiger by the tail in QIP; the trick was to get the tiger into the tank. We needed more than just a tune-up or an oil change, we needed a major overhaul. We had to change not only the way we did things, but the way we thought about doing things. And initially we looked at the very simple things, the problems on which our people could develop their skills in QIP.

Today, we're seeking break-throughs, innovative ways of doing business that can help keep the increase in rates at or below the consumer price index, as well as provide an increased return on investment to our stockholders. And by the first part of 1989, we expect to be looking for break-throughs that will help us solve major problems and expand to new opportunities. You know, "break-through" is kind of a corporate buzzword today. I don't believe it's anything much more than a new idea – or sometimes even an old idea with new applications. And it doesn't take very many such ideas to achieve success. As Albert Einstein admitted, he had only one great idea in his entire lifetime, but his theory of relativity kept him in pipe tobacco for a heck of a lot of years.

While we may be some distance away from achieving the major break-throughs that are the ultimate stepping stones of quality, the program is more than paying its own way, even at these early stages. While our costs will continue to come down as our training takes effect, our savings will continue to go up as our people become more efficient and more knowledgeable about quality. Furthermore, we expect major break-throughs in the future to add to our savings.

Getting back to the issue of why you have to institutionalize a quality improvement process is that you want to give it sufficient time to prove that the process works. You want the process to outlive the current management. You want the process to be as much a part of the company's culture as its basic business. Does anyone think that when our top management retires, FPL will not be in the energy business? We want everyone to view our quality programs with the same degree of permanence. Quality improvement has to be part of a company's institution. Serving customers and generating electricity is our business. Quality improvement is the way we manage the business, the dynamic structure that makes things happen.

It's our intention to infuse the process and the philosophy of QIP into every corporate cubbyhole at FPL, to weave the process and philosophy so deeply into the fiber of doing business that it becomes second nature to each and every employee. Lately, the idea of American quality has become somewhat of a myth, and the trouble with myths is that someone might begin to believe them. And I don't think we can accept that myth as a company – and I know that we cannot accept it as a nation – if we wish to maintain and indeed build upon our role as a world economic force.

How is quality improvement made part of the institution? We have found that just as the success of the process depends on top management support, its continued success also requires such support. I don't mean lip service. Top management has to employ the process in the management of the company at all levels. The process has to be built into the way decisions are made. The process can't be isolated for "special occasions". Top management must commit to quality as a priority and make its stand known throughout the company, that it demands and expects quality to improve. Quality processes have to be used everyday, despite the temptation to take shortcuts. Employees at all levels must be trained in quality processes and learn that quality achievement is synonymous with cost effectiveness, not the opposite.

Quality permanence requires continuous promotion and reinforcement. Success stories have to be publicized. Even the most enthusiastic quality achiever needs a boost. The process needs attention or it will be taken for granted and it's benefits overlooked. Unfortunately, you always have an element in any company that is waiting to pounce on the failure of some department or idea. As soon as there is a sign of a discouraging word, these cynics will be for dropping the process, to "save" the money that quality wastes. It never ceases to amaze me how some people talk of quality's affordability, as if they were discussing the purchase of a new computer system. They might ask if they can afford to go out of business. To me, quality means survival. Customers will pay for quality. Provide quality and utilize quality processes and profits won't be too far behind.

As I previously mentioned, our quality program has taught us, among other things, that we must be customer-driven, that we must put aside our egos and let the customer be in charge – and if there's one thing that customers demand today, it's quality. I believe the cost of quality must be weighed against the consequences, and while it's still too early in our case to determine the exact impact on the bottom line, we've already received a return on investment far greater than we had ever anticipated. For one thing, the number of customer complaints has decreased substantially, over 40% in some categories. In our latest customer attitude survey, we achieved the highest rating in our history.

Our service representatives have taken to heart the idea of staying with the problem – and the customer – until the problem is solved and the customer is satisfied. Those are the kinds of results that we're looking for in QIP – the kinds of return on investment that may not show up on the ledger but are vital to our company's future well-being. A part of our quality improvement program features a corporate vision which is simply this: during the next decade, we want to become the best-managed utility in the U.S. and to be recognized as such. In 1986 we were fortunate enough to be named winner of the Edison Award – the highest honor given within our industry – and QIP was highlighted as the single most significant contribution to serving our customers effectively.

The Edison Award brings to mind the fact that Edison, like a number of you, have been a customer of a utility for many years. I'm not sure, if Edison were alive, that I'd have the nerve to send him a bill. Instead, I might send him a note thanking him for the bit of advice he gave so many years ago – I suppose it wasn't so much a piece of advice as a directive: "There is a better way. Find it."

Finally, let me close with some thoughts on management's role. Management must be willing to support teams through budgeting decisions and be willing to provide the people as resources for team meetings. Management must take the approach that solving problems the teamway is the normal way. Team solving efforts must become as much a part of the institution as the coffee break.

When there are barriers to quality efforts, management must step in and remove those barriers. It has to be ready to do this in day one of the process or day 10,000. It must be alert to the need for such support. Quality improvement is a dynamic process, with many subtleties. Breakdowns are not always apparent. At FPL, we have a staff of quality specialists, the Quality Improvement Department. The Departments function is to assist other departments when breakdowns occur. But, it is important that the Quality Improvement Department act as internal consultants. It is not up to this department to make the quality process work. Rather, it is the responsibility of all employees. Once all employees recognize their obligation to the process, a company has gone a long way toward institutionalizing that process.

When a quality improvement process is just beginning, there are usually some levels of management which resist, especially if it appears to them that a team is encroaching on management prerogatives. Top management support means reeducating such managers or moving them. Continued success requires that the same commitment by all managers be demanded in hiring and promoting.

A good example of our top management's commitment to Policy Deployment is this year's requirement that certain of the quality processes and procedures must be employed as part of each department's budget approval process. In front of top management and his management peers, a manager must use quality charts and quality indicators in the prescribed manner or his department will have no funds appropriated. With that, is the implication that unless the manager does the process correctly and procures his appropriation, his replacement will surely be able to. Believe me, it would be just as easy for top management to stick to the same annual reviews, as many companies have been doing for fifty years. By making this requirement, however, it is a major step of impressing upon everyone that the quality process is with us to stay, and is part of the way we manage our business.

At FPL we're a long way from reaching the end of our journey toward total quality, but I believe we are beginning to see the light at the end of the tunnel. And though I can't predict when quality improvement will give you the return on investment you may be looking for, I sincerely believe that the quality concept can mold the corporate future of America.

PQR-13

INTRODUCTION OF THE QUALITY PROCESS

INTO THE WHITE COLLAR ENVIRONMENT

Kurt E. Knuth - Chairperson
Department Head
Technology Development & Computer Resources

AT&T - Data Systems Group
5555 W. Touhy Ave.
Skokie, IL 60077

ABSTRACT

When the subject of Quality is introduced, one tends to relate to manufacturing of a product or provision of a service. Quality and its partner Productivity are as important in the White Collar environment as in the factory or field. This seminar focuses on applying modern quality processes to such an environment to cause the desired cultural changes. Some theories and practical applications of Quality and Productivity will first be presented, followed by specific presentations relating to the Sales environment, the Engineering environment and the Product Development environment. This expansion of the Quality Process into the White Collar environment will be a necessary attribute of the successful business.

Mike Bechtold	-- Hewlett Packard
Emory Christiansen	-- Hewlett Packard
Dick Knudtsen	-- Hewlett Packard
George Henry	-- Tatham Process Engineering
John Sebeson	-- AT&T

CULTURAL CHANGE AND WHITE-COLLAR PRODUCTIVITY

Michael Bechtold
Region Quality Manager

Hewlett Packard
5201 Tollview Drive
Rolling Meadows, IL 60008

ABSTRACT

"I'm not going back to America. If you establish your own sanity, you don't have to worry about other people's sanity. And so many Americans are going stone insane."
- Ronald Bierl, a young American expatriate in Turkey. From "Future Shock," by Alvin Toffler.

"We call some societies primitive because of their desire to remain in the same state in which gods or ancestors created them at the beginning of time, with a demographic balance which they know how to maintain and an unchanging standard of living protected by their social rules and metaphusical beliefs."
- Claude Levi-Strauss, 1983. International Symposium on Productivity in Japan. From "Kaizen," by Masaaki Imai.

We have all seen and heard a great deal of discussion about how the geometrically increasing rate of technological change is driving social and political change in our American society. Some change is positive, and some is negative, with the jury of history still out on the net impact but, the costs of change are many: confusion, inefficiency, even clinical depression.

Those of us charged with managing and promoting change in our organizations must understand the nature of the beast if we are to optimize the return on our change investments. We must view change as a process and manage it as such, and effectively.

One analysis of change is presented by Leon Martell in his book on "Mastering Change." Leon points out that human change is usually of two types: cyclical or structural. This analysis is important because it points the way toward some basic strategies of managing such changes.

Cyclical changes are those whose basic structure is repetitive. Two examples might be commodities prices and ladies' hemlines: they go up and down with time, and can be expected to continue to do so. (those of you who have a demonstrated ability to time these Cycles should chat with me privately before you publish.) Our strategies for managing these changes should obviously take advantage of this known aspect of their behavior.

Structural changes are those that do not repeat. They occur as random events without a great deal of predictability until they are well underway, and do not go away after some period of time. One example might be the historically recent increase of the percentage of women in the workforce. The change took place because of some very deep social and opinion shifts; the increase will not go away anytime soon. In this case, our strategy for coping will obviously be quite different than before.

A second aspect to be considered is not the type, but rather the rate of change. I believe that Alvin Toffler was the first to point out this fact in his book on "Future Shock." Again, our strategy for coping should bear in mind that the direction of the change is irrelevant; it is its rate that creates the strongest opposition.

But all of these are aspects of change that we cannot easily control. If we are charged with implementing positive change (such as instituting a quality improvement culture), what strategies or models will help us facilitate that shift with minimum cost and damage to our human resources and yet with all possible speed?

STRUCTURAL MODELS

Noel M. Tichy conducts an excellent discussion of models in his work on "Managing Strategic Change." He begins by noting that many managers often use "'implicit models' composed of their own somewhat subjective and biased views of the managerial problem. This can easily bring on conflict about what course of action to take in a change effort. Such implicit models create a great deal of difficulty in resolving differences. The differences generally emerge during disagreements of what to do. This is because in the absence of an accepted model, it is difficult to explore the underlying reasons for various actions."1

Tichy goes on to reinforce the concept of model creation and agreement by noting that "Organizational models filter and focus perception."2 And further that ". . .the change manager must examine and ultimately alter the underlying conceptual frameworks used to make decisions about organizational change."3

The issue here does not seem to be one of semantics, but one of people attempting to communicate from the bases of entirely different assumptions about how the organization does or should operate. These underlying assumptions must be clarified before any productive discussion can begin. It is interesting to note that the PDCA quality improvement cycle used by many quality-conscious managers is an excellent tool to begin with, since it can help to establish the proper focus to begin with.

Tichy then posits three models for our consideration to create, as it were, a vocabulary of model elements to discuss with. They are as follows:4

THE CLASSICAL/MECHANISTIC MODEL

The first is the classic hierarchal organization first referred to as the mechanistic model by Burns and Stalker in 1961. Its internal rules include the following:

1. Differentiated into specialized functional tasks.
2. Subordinates should pursue individual tasks with concern only for the completion of their narrowly stated tasks.
3. Rigid chain of command (one man, one boss).
4. Detailed and exhaustive job descriptions.
5. The overall picture of the organization is only relevant to those at the top of the hierarchy.
6. Interaction follows vertical lines along the chain of command.
7. Behavior is governed by superiors.
8. Emphasis is on narrow, specialized knowledge rather than general, complete knowledge.

McGregor (1960) referred to this sort of an organization as a "Theory X" type. Typical examples of this sort of organization are governmental and military bodies.

HUMAN RESOURCES ORGANIC MODEL

The human resource, or again from McGregor, the "Theory Y" organization, is shown to have the following characteristics:

1. A network structure of control, authority, and communication.

2. Continual adjustment of tasks through interaction with the whole.
3. Commitment to the organization as a whole.
4. Lateral as well as vertical interaction.
5. Communication of advice rather than orders.
6. Sanctions derived from within the community (peers and superiors) indicating a concern for the whole organization.
7. Jobs not formally defined.

Tichy goes on to list the various assumptions underlying this form of the organization, which is common in the electronics industry today. In the author's opinion, this model is strongly supportive of the Deming view of the organization as a system with stochastic behavior. The strategies that prove the most effective are those that place power in the hands of the process owners, and that encourage cooperation among the various individuals and groups that make up the organization.

THE POLITICAL MODEL

The political model is one in which "Organizations can be viewed as political arenas in which multiple coalitions vie for control of the organization's resources and the uses for which they will be put."5 Henry Mintsburg developed a way of looking at such organizations that breaks up the political environment into external factions (governments, special interest groups, and the general public), and internal factions (line managers, staff, top management, unions, operators, and so forth). The recommended strategy becomes a political one by which change is negotiated between the conflicting groups vying for control.

THE ADOPTER MODEL 6

Everett Rogers provides a model from a very different perspective, one that treats the organization as a distribution of personalities. Such a model is particularly useful from the perspective of one-on-one relationships. The author has found this model of particular use in his own "Theory Y" type of organization; but it should be of great use to others as well. Briefly, the model posits five categories of "adopters," or people who embrace organizational change. (Figure 1) They range from the "innovators," who actively seek new and unique approaches to things, to the "late adopters," whose primary motivation seems to be fear. Summarizing:

1. Innovators are primarily characterized as venturesome, or eager to try new ideas. They are highly mobile people, and have personal networks that range far beyond their local peers. They think conceptually, and are capable of dealing with a high degree of uncertainty.
2. Early adopters are a more integrated part of the company's social system, and as such, tend to have a greater effect on the generally prevailing cultural opinion. Potential adopters look to this group for advice on new ideas; their discretion is appreciated and respected.

3. The early majority is the great middle that embraces an idea just before the statistical average. Because of their position, they are an important bridge between the "early radicals" and the "late conservatives."

4. The late majority are the skeptics that adopt new ideas fairly late in their cycle. They are cautious, and peer pressure is needed as well as proof of utility before new ideas are adopted.

5. The late adopters are the traditionalists who oppose change simply because it's different. They are suspicious of innovation, very local in their outlook, and very difficult to convert. If placed in positions of authority, they can often stall innovation for long periods of time.

THE S-CURVE OF ADOPTION

Rogers also did research on the rate of change of innovation, and posited an S-curve as shown in figure 2. The curve rises slowly at first, because only the relatively small number of early adopters and innovators are involved. The rate of change then accelerates through the organization, only slowing down when the late adopters are finally involved.

Rogers' work has several conclusions that are of note:

1. Word of mouth will always be the most important method of insuring that an idea gets adopted.

2. Innovators seldom invent their ideas; they get them from their outside networks.

3. The rate of awareness is much steeper than the rate of adoption. Typically, awareness must reach a 25-50% level before a 5-10% level of adoption is reached. The average length of the time between awareness and adoption varies widely among organizations.

4. There is no correlation between adopter category and level in the organization.

Rogers also posits a six-stage model of adoption. We at Hewlett-Packard routinely discuss change in terms of four, and in terms of a process: the manager moves from opposition to neutrality to involvement to support. It is important to note that a change agent cannot move an individual more than one step at a time! To do so will cause the individual to "dig in" and stall progress until the next step is properly achieved.

5. Rogers goes so far as to posit that, once a change has been adopted by 20% of the organization, it becomes inevitable, a true "force of history." Thus change agents cannot afford to waste their efforts trying to convert single high-level managers. The winds of change can blow up the organization from below!

TACTICS AND EXPERIENCES

The author's personal experiences in facilitating change in a large sales organization using the above models as bases for strategies and tactics might be summarized as follows:

1. People like to be talked to. Memos tend to be ignored. As a result, change agents absolutely must own and practice excellent verbal persuasion skills. Success is corelated as much with the amount of face-to-face time spent talking to managers as it is with who in the organization they are persuading.

2. The most effective change planning strategy is to create a matrix of people in the organization. On one axis, we list the political or hierarchal level of influence each individual commands in the organization. On the other axis, we plot their adopter category. The "strategy" then becomes one of focusing resources on the most influential innovators to start with. To put things another way, go for the "easy sell" first, and ignore the rest of the organization. Focus your efforts to make that first sale! Then and only then should you begin to identify the next target.

3. Change agents are scarce resources. It is absolutely crucial that they leverage their efforts if they are to be successful. Remember, "real people" in the organization will carry more influence than the change agents themselves. Thus, by focusing effort on innovators and early adopters, the change agent will find "the force of history" on his or her side.

4. The best size for a change agent organization is small, but more than one individual. The change agent needs other commited individuals to help with his or her change process, but not too many! Too many people to manage absorbs too much of the change agent's time in administration and dilutes the required focus.

5. People are ambiguous about success, but never about failure. When you are championing new ideas in an organization, don't ask for wholesale change, but rather for small pilot projects. Pilots can be used to demonstrate success just as well as large organizations, and their smaller scale and ease of management reduce the risk of failure.

6. Change agents must be absolute masters of their concepts. Credibility is vital; do not ignore your own self-development.

Despite all these difficulties, change agents are vital for the continued survival of their organizations, perhaps even more so than general managers. Enjoy your role!

1. "Managing Strategic Change: Technical, Political, and Cultural Dynamics." by Noel M. Tichy. John Wiley & Sons, 1983. Page 39.

2. Ibid, page 40.

3. Ibid, page 40.

4. Ibid, pages 42-49.

5. Ibid, page 47.

6. Internal Hewlett-Packard document summarizing Rogers' work.

OTHER REFERENCES INCLUDE:

"The Change Masters," by Rosabeth Moss Kanter, Simon & Schuster Inc., New York, 1983

"Future Shock," by Alvin Toffler, Random House, 1970

"Communication of Innovations," E.M. Rogers and F.F. Shoemaker, 1971

"Diffusion of Innovations," E.M. Rogers, 1983

"Kaizen," by Masaaki Imai, Random House, 1986

"Mastering Change," by Leon Martel, 1983, Simon & Schuster

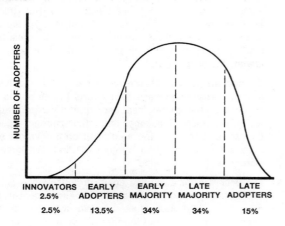

FIGURE ONE: ADOPTER CATEGORIES vs TIME

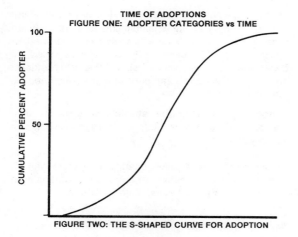

FIGURE TWO: THE S-SHAPED CURVE FOR ADOPTION

Emory Christensen
Chair
R&D Productivity Steering Council
Corporate Engineering

Hewlett-Packard Company
P.O. Box 39
Boise, ID 83707

ABSTRACT

This paper discusses some basic elements of engineering productivity, their importance as an ingredient of a strategy to gain a competitive advantage, and their relationship to the quality of work life. The discussion particularly focuses on the most critical of the elements, people, and their role in the productivity equation.

INTRODUCTION

R&D productivity presents a major challenge in the marketplace since it is a critical element of American industry's ability to remain technically competitive and to deliver timely, new products. This paper discusses basic ideas regarding quality of work life and engineering productivity.

Basically, productivity includes people (labor), capital investment, materials, and energy resources. While historically, the processes and measurement of capital investments, materials costs, and energy resources have been reasonably well understood, people resources have been the most variable and therefore, the most difficult to quantify and manage. People therefore also usually provide the largest opportunity for return.

A major factor influencing the opportunity for productivity gain among engineers is quality of work life (QWL). Subsequent sections of this paper will discuss engineering and QWL, process control's application to and positive influence on QWL, and elements of an engineering productivity strategy.

QUALITY OF WORK LIFE

What is QWL? One useful explanation is: ". . . those actions taken by management to improve the feelings of employees about their employment relationship." 1 This encompasses several major areas, including management style, supervision, communications, rewards (both monetary and non-monetary), job design, working conditions, tools and training, technology, company characteristics, and company demographics.

2 Management styles vary widely, ranging from autocratic control to employee involvement. The use of each depends on the answer to the question: Is management's role to make decisions and set goals or to see that decisions are made and goals met? Although seemingly a subtle difference, the implications of each choice are major. One of the key benefits of the more participatory style is the employees' acceptance or

ownership of their job. This especially impacts productivity improvement because employees' involvement adds many insights and positive suggestions for improvement. On the other hand, it's well known that a rigid management style stifles creativity. Since the reward system is controlled by management, such creativity may actually adversely affect an individual's performance assessment. Ultimately, the results of autocratic management may range from the loss of creative productivity to the loss of individuals, with the resultant loss of knowledge, technical expertise, leadership, and understanding of product strategies. Individually or collectively the sum total is usually a heavy cost.

Organizations using autocratic management styles are usually oriented toward methods referred to as production-oriented. On the other side of the spectrum are those oriented around the quality of work life. Figure 1 illustrates the continuous spectrum between the contrasting styles and how the balance between them impacts productivity. It also depicts how an organization's global objectives provide the focus for its managerial style and determines the resultant productivity. Too great an emphasis on either quality of work life or on production reduces productivity.

Communications, when used constructively, can be an effective productivity tool to direct the entire organization, transmitting company objectives, directions, values, progress, challenges, and successes to build a sense of pride and adopted ownership. Communication may also bind the organization together, instilling a unique indentity which includes pride and a sense of belonging. Conversely, ineffective communication raises barriers which subtly saps productivity. W. Edwards Deming stresses removing those obstacles which prevent employees from taking pride in their work as a means of unleashing creative productivity. Such a feat of management can only be achieved if constructive channels of communication exist.

Communication can also help manage change. Strategies can be elucidated, course corrections explained and changes discussed. Managing an organization without such communications is similar to giving a commercial airline pilot one course bearing and the cutting off all contact with crew, passengers, and tower.

Reward structures are also essential to productivity. It is especially important to consider what types of behavior are desirable. People seldom do anything without some motivation to achieve certain "desirable" results. This must not be construed to be strictly monetary in nature. Money, a motivator to some degree, eventually loses its impact as a productivity motivation for most technical professionals. However, improperly administered monetary rewards can be a powerful de-motivator and a significant producer of negative productivity.

Non-monetary rewards should also be considered and applied. Recognition of individual behaviors and successes send strong value signals to the rest of the work force. Other "perks," such as flexible work hours, occasional "comp" time, or other small concessions may also cultivate good will and improve productivity. It is here that process oriented management becomes an important tool for enhancing non-monetary rewards and QWL.

PROCESS MANAGEMENT FOR PRODUCTIVITY

Process management is widely accepted as a proven method for effectively managing manufacturing. Management of people involved in research and development, where technology and creativity are fundamental, is considered by many to be an improper application of process management. The uniqueness of the technical work being done is an argument frequently set forth. It is time to set this mentality aside. Substantial evidence abounds that there is a process methodology useful for understanding and improving the engineering productivity in a creative organization. Specifically, this process is for managing product development and is comprised of several basic components. It should be applied hierarchically, beginning with a global view and narrowing to specifics.

The initial element to be defined is the end-product or desired result of the object process. What exactly is being developed and what constraints have been imposed? In this case, the object being addressed is the management process itself. In order to ascertain a reasonable objective or desired result, experience and examination of past performance will probably indicate what most needs of improvement. It is particularly helpful to have several capable individuals at various levels who provide input regarding the specific problem areas, and a Pareto (order of relevant significance) listing to help determine priorities. Realistically limit the number or magnitude of items targeted for change.

The existing process or methodology should be listed with its related set of deliverables, including a given level of technical development, documentation, manufacturing preparation, test plan, etc. Next, a metric or set of metrics should be identified that will motivate behavior producing the desired result. Carefully test the selected metrics and insure that they provide the proper visibility, elegance, balance and timeliness. The most difficult parameters to identify are those which predict change before it occurs. 3 The balance of all four tests is required to avoid encouraging extreme behavior in any particular direction. For example, a new product development metric which may seem beneficial is project development time or time to market. But if not used with other metrics to provide better balance, many decisions may be made which will get the product out the door with a good time-to-market but still culminate in failure due to poor product definition, poor quality, or high cost due to poor manufacturability. A much better metric for this case might be break-even-time (BET). [Figure 2]. It shows both the cost-versus-time of the project investment as well as the return-gained-by-the-product and how long it takes to recover the product development costs.

Upon completion of a balanced set of metrics, a practical system for collection must be determined. Simplicity should be stressed. One effective approach is to define a method of manual collection that can be implemented during startup. As this process is understood, automating the system of collection is usually straightforward. Trying for too much elegance at the beginning may doom the project to failure at the start.

Once information and results are available, they may be evaluated to compare delivered results with expected results. Deviations should then be understood, correlated, and prioritized using Pareto techniques. Changes to the process or to the set of applied metrics should then be determined, and a plan for implementing the changes constructed. The plan is implemented and the procedure is repeated. In many cases, a thorough examination of the actual process leads to a much better understanding of many costs induced by the bureaucracy and overhead structures inherent in large organizations. Another opportunity for improvement that comes up is the chance to apply better tools to help overcome or offset other deficiencies. This repeated examination and improvement of the process is also known as total quality control (TQC).

When this process control methodology is used for managing technical projects, it's important to retain the information of past project histories. Over time, histories provide two important functions: 1) a baseline from which to evaluate progress and 2) an indicator of relative movement. In some cases, it may indicate the results of specific efforts or programs, if carefully tracked and understood. Such data may be used to temper future project or program planning. FOr example, if the historical data indicates that program productivity has been improving at an annual rate of 3-5 percent, and a program is being proposed that would require a 25 percent annual improvement, it's obvious that, unless major changes are made, the proposed 25 percent improvement is unrealistic and probably unattainable. Frequently, however, management places pressure on product development teams to make improvements well beyond their historical abilities. So, if no historical information has been kept, the management goals usually become the official project goals. And yet, such goals will probably receive little more than lip service from the engineering staff who now feel they have had a schedule forced upon them. Conversely, if presented past data showing their schedule demands are unrealistic, management must reconsider and choose alternative courses of action.

What does implementation of this approach entail? Many things:

1. Implementation requires the involvement of all layers within the organization. Involvement by many individuals in activities with common goals inevitably fosters closer working relationships, increased communication, and hence, improved understanding. This focusing effect also brings about a heightened sense of belonging and shared identity.

2. Implementation requires management commitment and follow-through, connoting concern for all and a desire to grow and improve.

3. Improvements identified and implemented often reduce frustrating and time-wasting road blocks. This effectively reduces some of the demotivating factors and thus enhances the QWL accordingly.

4. Formalizing and documenting the existing processes communicates a clearer picture of the challenges to all by reducing ambiguities that promote diverging perspectives. This improved understanding enables everyone to focus on the same process definition and realize many of the same solutions. These solutions are subsequently better understood, accepted as reasonable, and bought into by all.

5. The well-defined metrics now provide a framework for applying the acquired parameters to necessary decisions. Good information and increased understanding leads to a corresponding improvement in the quality and timeliness of decision-making at each level. This positive influence then begins to have global impact on attitudes and support. Scheduling, resource planning, and new product definitions particularly benefit from higher quality decision-making. These three factors are usually tightly coupled with an infinite number of choices. By understanding scheduling and past staffing profiles more fully, project completion dates can be better estimated. This allows a more realistic feature set to be defined and implemented within a specific market window. It also means more timely addition of planned resources. This results in more competitive new products which should increase market share over time.

6. Accompanying the improvement in the decisions is a correlated second order effect yielding higher quality products as a result of increased pride in the engineers' work.

7. Another improvement from better decision-making is the reduction of waste arising from more stable processes. This reduces not only physical expenditures for material and equipment but reduces thrashing and time wasted communicating dissatisfaction when questionable decisions are handed down.

8. Finally, communication channels are clarified and improve as individual confidence arises in engineers' acceptance and ability to make substantive contribution.

The positive effects and benefits to be gained as this methodology is applied have the potential for dramatic improvements on the perceived QWL.

Job design is yet another aspect influencing the technical employees' productivity. Job design is the structuring of tasks and opportunities in relation to individual skills and interests. For example, requiring an engineer with specialized expertise to focus on assignments not utilizing those skills demotivates and wastes the engineer's acquired expertise. Failure to provide support for many routine, non-technical activities is similarly counterproductive and demotivating.

Tools and training is an investment area with great opportunity, but also one that can easily be fraught with snares and "gotcha's." It is currently estimated that the half-life of an engineer's knowledge is five years, necessitating continual investments in training to keep up with technological advances. Tools should only be considered once the related processes have been thoroughly outlined and understood. Many tools when selectively applied can provide huge returns through reduced human error, a more complete understanding of the parameters and problems being addressed, and more rapid design completion.

Interestingly, tools are devised and follow a progressive path from inception during the R&D phase, prototyping and testing during a leading edge phase, and widespread application during the best practices and standards phases as detailed in Figure 3. Providing tools in early development for a risky, critical project can only complicate and slow down its progress. Yet, there may be situations where leading edge tools are required to deal with leading edge technologies and although fiscally costly, it may be absolutely essential to the success of the project. Whatever course of action or set of tools is selected for application, an adequate training plan and course of migration from existing tools is a fundamental necessity. Using prudence and substantial input from those closely involved in the design process can also contribute its share to improve the quality of work life and bolster the spirits of those involved who see the willingness of management to provide tools as a test of their true interest for the design community. Few things are as demoralizing as setting high expectations with demanding technical challenges without providing a supportive atmosphere and the necessary tools.

How then should an organization proceed to begin the process of change and to establish a productivity program for its professional resources? First, a high level executive should be assigned the responsibility of chief productivity officer (CPO). 4 Second, the CPO should study both the organization and the overall company objectives to use as a basic framework for describing a vision of future capabilities and goals. Third, a strategy should be developed containing the particulars of a program for achieving the productivity vision. The strategy should contain a minimum of a five-year intermediate range plan with supporting tactical objectives in the form of a Hoshin plan where responsibilities, tactical objectives, and a specified time frame for periodic review are all clearly outlined. This program should be clearly understood and supported from the highest levels of management so that expectations and supporting values can be communicated top-down. Without upper managements involvement or support, the program is doomed to limited successes with marginal credibility. With management's their active support, a heightened sense of productivity awareness and improved quality of work life can be cultivated.

SUMMARY

In conclusion, the importance of improving the quality of work life and its relationship with engineering and professional productivity is essential. Many of the key factors that should be taken into consideration include an organization's management style, reward system, communications policies, job design, tools and training, and working conditions. A methodology for applying

process control with effective metrics and employee involvement to improve productivity in technical program management has been described. Its correlation to improved QWL was also explained and, finally, the basic elements for generating a productivity strategy within an organization were briefly explained.

BIBLIOGRAPHY AND FOOTNOTES

1. William A. Ruch and William B. Werther, Jr., Proceedings, "Hewlett-Packard Productivity College", May, 1988, pg 29.

2. Ibid., pg 15.

3. Chuck House and Marv Patterson, "Managing R&D Productivity in HP", February, 1988, pg 5.

4. William A. Ruch and William B. Werther, Jr., "The Chief Productivity Officer", National Productivity Review, pp 397-410, Autumn 1985.

**QWL AND PRODUCTIVITY:
THE LINKAGE IS MANAGEMENT STYLE**

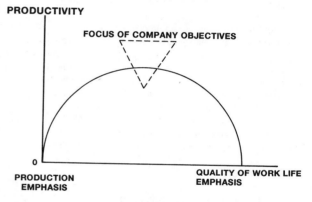

THE RETURN PICTURE

PROJECT CONTROL GRAPH

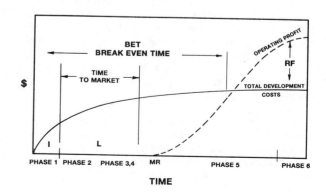

TECHNOLOGY TRANSITIONS

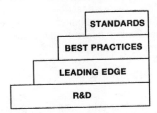

- LEADING EDGE PROJECTS TEND TO BE LOCAL AND INFORMAL
- BEST PRACTICES TEND TO BE FORMAL WITH DEMONSTRATED RESULTS
- STANDARDS USE PROVEN RESULTS WITH FORMAL AND GLOBAL DISTRIBUTION

APPLICATION OF PROCESS QUALITY MANAGEMENT AND IMPROVEMENT METHODS TO PRODUCT DEVELOPMENT

John M. Sebeson
Head, Computer Engineering Information Department

AT&T Data Systems Group
1100 E. Warrenville Road
Naperville, Illinois 60566

ABSTRACT

Product development is an important area for continuous improvement of "white collar" quality. We describe here a process model for product development and a technique for improvement, called Process Quality Management and Improvement (PQMI). We have applied this model and PQMI to product development in the AT&T Data Systems Group. We have discovered that early attention to process definition, customer requirements, and process control are important prerequisites for improvement. An example of a factor-of-10 improvement in process quality is discussed.

INTRODUCTION

Quality, in a broad sense, has become a critical differentiating factor in the marketplace. In the past, the meaning of quality was often associated with attributes of a manufactured product, and thought to be primarily a problem for the factory floor. Today, however, there is a wider significance to quality. Any task, any activity, can be viewed as being carried out for the benefit or use of a customer. The customer could be, and often is, another task or activity. The goal of quality is the ever increasing satisfaction of the needs of the customer in this general sense. Therefore, the concept of quality and the application of quality improvement theory and technology is now seen to extend beyond the factory floor to the offices and design laboratories of a business enterprise.

As organizations develop this new awareness of the scope of quality, they may struggle with how to apply quality improvement principles in a non-manufacturing situation. Are these principles and techniques, statistical methods for example, relevant to services or product development?
The answer is yes, provided one is guided by a conceptual model.

ATTRIBUTES OF A PROCESS

Manufacturing is a good place to start in developing a quality improvement model, because manufacturing is a particular instance of a more general situation. Everyone would agree that in manufacturing we start with raw materials or components and turn them into something else. We would also agree that this is a process, meaning "steps conducing to an end." Actually this process requires more than materials; it also requires equipment, methods and standards, people, and an environment. These five things are the inputs to the process [1]. The process produces an output. Inputs come from suppliers while outputs go to customers. A supplier to a process could include management, by providing the environmental conditions or the methods and standards for the process. The output may not be what is desired. The manufacturing process may produce a defective output or it may produce something of no use or value to a customer even if fabricated correctly. To detect such conditions, the process requires feedback. Moreover, the process has certain statistical characteristics. There may be variation in the input and variation in the process steps, leading to variation in the output. Most manufacturing operations are carried out with a set of operational definitions or requirements. Operational definitions convey clear meaning for a concept or expectation, usually by specifying tests, and criteria for the judgement and use of the results of such tests. Operational definitions are the means for clear communication between customer and suppliers, while "methods and standards" refer to the set of procedures within a process. Poor quality in many processes can often be traced to lack of proper operational definitions [2].

PRODUCT DEVELOPMENT AS A PROCESS

The manufacturing example helps us see that almost all tasks and activities have the attributes of a process. There is no doubt that product development is a process in the sense of "steps conducing to an end." Furthermore, we can describe the product development process in terms of the attributes discussed above.

The process requires the same five generic inputs of any process. The "material" for the start of the process and many of the subsequent steps may be information, in the form of an idea or studies on market opportunities, instead of physical material. The equipment ranges from pencils and paper to computer aided design systems and experimental test facilities. The environmental input is more than offices and laboratories; it also includes the structure of the organization, the policies and behavior of management, the shared values (culture), the reward and performance appraisal systems, and other such factors. People are essential to the process, and bring in such factors as the necessary technical disciplines, degrees of training and experience, cultural diversity, and pride of professionalism and workmanship. Product development usually has established methods and standards such as software inspections or a structure for engineering documentation.

The output, the product itself, may be "correct" and find a market, or it may not. On the other hand, the development process may produce errors in design or an inadequate set of features, which would be the equivalent of a "manufacturing defect."

Operational definitions are important in product development. They appear as testable requirements at various stages and in the statement of what is expected when information is passed from one function to another.

The actual process steps in product development are, of course, specific to the particular product and development organization. There is a different set of detailed steps for developing a fuel additive versus a computer. There is the possibility that the process is not planned, in which case the process steps take on the appearance of a random walk rather than a deliberate and directed activity.

The development process, like any process, will have certain statistical characteristics and display variation even if it is well-planned. The idea that a process such as development is statistical in nature rather than deterministic is often difficult to understand. However, any product developer can describe the effects of variation in the process, when even with the best of plans, schedules can be missed and certain outcomes unpredicted. If one looks at the process inputs, one begins to appreciate that there can be tremendous variation in all of them. Much day-to-day energy in development is often spent coping with such variation. In fact, one of the aims of quality in development is to effectively find and reduce sources of variation in the process.

The process model applies not only to the product development process as a whole but also to its various components or sub-processes. The process model still holds, only the parameters change. For example, hardware design may have as its supplier systems engineering and the material it receives from this supplier is in the form of product definitions and requirements. The hardware design process could be further broken down into a logic design process, an equipment design process, a design documentation process, and so forth. The basic attributes of a process remain descriptive of the tasks and activities of product development at almost all levels of detail.

THE NEED FOR CONTINUOUS PROCESS IMPROVEMENT

Having a process model for development is important because a fundamental principle of quality is that the quality of any result is determined by the process that produced the result. Improvement of quality requires improvement of the process.

Assuming for the moment that we know what attributes constitute "quality" in a given situation, there are three strategies for assuring that quality: inspection, prevention and continuous improvement. Inspection may prevent a defective output from reaching a customer, but it is the most costly strategy, and accepts waste as part of the process. Prevention, by finding the source of the defect in the process and correcting the process at that point, is a

better strategy, but by itself may not respond to changing expectations of the customer. The modern competitive environment requires the adoption of the strategy of continuous improvement, which is a constant search for opportunities to move the quality attributes of the output to higher levels, to reduce variation in the output ever further, and to reduce variation and cost in all process steps. Inspection and prevention may be needed but continuous improvement seeks to go beyond them. With the strategy of continuous improvement, customer satisfaction is not good enough. We instead search for ways to surprise and delight our customers with the excellence and value of our output and to anticipate ways to make the lives of our customers better and their jobs easier. In short, the continuous improvement of quality is a competitive strategy, required these days to stay in business. Moreover, all aspects of the business, development, manufacturing, sales, service, employee relations, and so forth need to adopt this strategy to maintain the edge in overall cost, productivity and performance of the enterprise.

In AT&T we are adopting the goal of continuous improvement of quality [3]. One of our methods for achieving that goal is called Process Quality Management and Improvement or PQMI [4]. The underlying theory of PQMI follows well established quality improvement principles and is a version of the Deming Cycle of Plan, Do, Check, Action or PDCA [5]. Within the AT&T Research and Development community, PQMI is beginning to be applied to the product development process.

PQMI IN PRODUCT DEVELOPMENT

The fundamental conceptual framework of PQMI is the process model discussed above. Application of PQMI methods allows the detailed description of the model for a specific process, aids in the assessment of the dynamic performance of the process, and guides the continuous improvement of the process.

We cannot describe here the details of PQMI, but will highlight some of its important features. PQMI consists of two basic pieces: control of a process and improvement of a process. We will focus on the control stage of PQMI because this is where we are learning some important lessons for quality improvement in product development. In a manufacturing process, the conditions and characteristics of "control" are often presumed to be present, and the emphasis turns immediately to "improvement." This is often not the case in product development.

In the control stage of PQMI, four steps are taken:

1. Establish Process Management Responsibilities. This step assigns an "owner" to the process who is responsible for guiding the control and improvement activities. This is a simple step, but has important effects. When management takes this step, it signals a serious intent to improve quality and a recognition that understanding processes is an important part. Knowledge of processes in product development is often fragmented and whatever improvement takes place is equally piecemeal. This step promotes a broader and

more comprehensive understanding. Training of process managers in the theory and practice of PQMI is an important part of this step.

2. Define Process and Identify Requirements. This is a critical step where the customers and suppliers are identified and where customer/supplier requirements are researched and precisely documented as operational definitions. The process boundaries are established and the inputs of material, equipment, methods and standards, people, and environment are defined. The process steps are described and flow-charted.

3. Establish Measurements and Controls. Using the requirements and operational definitions as guides, the process manager puts in place a system to measure attributes of the process relevant to customer needs and critical performance attributes such as task intervals or rework.

4. Control Process and Assess Performance. In this step the recognition of process variation and what to do about it are important. Using statistical methods, the process manager seeks to assess the state of statistical control of the process, that is, whether the measurements of the process show evidence of special variation, or whether the process is a stable, common cause, system [6]. This step is very important for continuous improvement and is often overlooked or misunderstood. A process that produces chaotic or unpredictable results cannot be improved in any fundamental way. (In fact, it calls into doubt whether we even have a "process.") It should first be brought "under control." The sources of instability should be found and corrected before further attempts at analysis and improvement. It could be, for example, that information or material from a supplier is never dependable or consistent. The methods and standards could be so lax that some task is always done in a different way. The people may lack training so that they don't really know how to execute some part of the process, or the work force may be too unstable. All of these conditions should be discovered and corrected at this stage. An out-of-control process will meet customer requirements only by chance. However, even if the process is stable or has been brought under control, it may not meet requirements. Data from the measurement system will indicate this, but it is important to remember that no measurement is meaningful when the process lacks statistical control.

The four steps of the control stage of PQMI are ways of getting the information needed for improvement in a disciplined and objective way. This is critical, because a common trap in quality improvement is to jump to a quality improvement project prematurely. Trying to improve a process where the customers and their requirements are poorly understood, for example, will waste resources and have little effect. Reducing the interval to produce an engineering drawing, when the drawing is unusable because of errors, is not an improvement for the customer of the drawing.

Our experience so far with PQMI in product development

suggests that the control stage is very difficult to get through. The notion of suppliers and customers in a development process is not natural and much confusion can result. It is not uncommon, for example, for a person or an organization to be, at the same time, both a customer and a supplier to the same process. This is the case when designers need a prototype from manufacturing. The designers must supply the manufacturing process with certain information, and in turn the manufacturer supplies the design process with their prototype. Thus, the designers are both suppliers and customers and the manufacturer is both a customer and supplier as well. What helps clear up the confusion is that the customer/supplier relationships are process relationships and not necessarily organizational relationships. Another area of difficulty is customer requirements. When asked to specify requirements for the process, the tendency is to specify either what the process is already capable of or what has historically been done. It is difficult to break out of "the way we've always done it." Process customers often live with whatever they get, precisely because they have never thought of themselves as "customers" who deserve quality and satisfaction.

We will not elaborate on the improvement steps of PQMI in this paper, because they are largely straightforward [4]. In brief, one uses the knowledge obtained in the control stage to investigate and prioritize opportunities for improvement and then set up improvement projects. The work involved in doing this should not be minimized, but the job is made vastly easier by proper attention to the control stage of PQMI. Maintaining knowledge and control of a process is a constant activity and provides the necessary foundation for continuous improvement.

AN EXAMPLE OF APPLICATION OF PQMI

In the development of the AT&T line of mini-computers, we are beginning to apply PQMI techniques to a broad range of processes, from early architectural design through introduction to manufacture, and including such areas as administrative support. In this section, we briefly review results obtained from one of these processes to illustrate principles discussed in this paper. This process is a common and routine part of almost all product developments: the production of engineering documentation.

The term engineering documentation refers to that set of information necessary for configuring, ordering, assembling and testing the product. It is also used as source material for operation manuals, service manuals, sales information and training courses. In the language of processes, engineering documentation forms part of the input material needed for several business processes subsequent to product development.

Production of engineering documentation was a process largely taken for granted. With the application of PQMI, however, we developed new knowledge which has allowed a significant improvement in quality over a relatively short period of time.

By assigning a process manager we were able, for the first time, to get a view of how engineering documentation is developed from start to finish. The process is complex enough that previously no one understood enough about the process to make large changes, and no one felt responsible for its overall quality. Before much detailed process analysis work was done, an assessment was made of the "quality" of the documentation. A team was assembled of people from design and manufacturing knowledgeable about documentation methods and standards to audit independently the output on a sample basis. They developed a system of scoring documentation in terms of weighted defects, assigning high weight to any problem that would seriously impact downstream use of the information. Conducted over a period of several months and analyzed by the process manager, it was found that the weighted defect density of the documentation was predictable within a range and stable. Even though it was common knowledge that these audits were occurring, there was no significant change in defect density over time. This was the signal of a common cause system where only fundamental changes in the process would improve quality in terms of this measure.

The process manager, assisted by others involved in the process, systematically studied the process steps, the customers of the documentation and their requirements, the levels of training, and other factors. Several problems surfaced. One was that customer requirements were nowhere recorded as operational definitions. There were expectations and needs for information to be conveyed in specific ways. Experienced engineers knew many of these rules, but others didn't and there was no method of training in place. The process operated in such a way that work was done piecemeal so that great potential existed for lack of consistency and missing information. The computer tools used for parts of the process were found to be deficient in critical areas.

These and other factors formed the basis for proposed improvements in the process. An experiment was set up to test the improvements on one project. Process steps were altered, the computer tools changed, and the appropriate engineers were trained in the customer requirements and process changes. The audit system for determining defect density was used as a control point to determine the effectiveness of the changes.

The immediate results were a factor of 5 reduction in the weighted defect density in engineering documentation produced by the project. Analysis of the results showed that some simple steps could reduce the defect level by another factor of 2. Thus, with application of PQMI to this process, a factor of 10 improvement in one important quality attribute was achieved in about a 6 to 8 month period of time.

CONCLUSION

Application of quality improvement theory and practice to product development is aided by viewing it as a process with attributes common to all processes. The modern competitive situation requires continuous improvement of the quality of all business processes including development. Process Quality Management and Improvement (PQMI) provides a discipline and technique for continuous improvement. In our early experience with PQMI, we have found the control stage to be of vital importance; namely, the assignment of process management responsibility, the understanding of customers and their needs, and the establishment of control over the process. By proper attention to the control stage, rapid and significant improvements in quality have been achieved.

ACKNOWLEDGMENTS

J.T. Gruenwald and R.A. Ogle of the AT&T Data Systems Group deserve much credit for their considerable effort and insight in translating PQMI principles into practice in our development environment. They provided me valuable help through their critical review of this paper. The improvement example was the work of K.L. Leach, our process manager for engineering documentation, and the members of his talented team.

REFERENCES

1. William W. Scherkenbach, The Deming Route to Quality and Productivity, CEEPress Books, George Washington University, 1987

2. H.L.M. Artinian and E.M. Baker, "Improving Quality: the Hidden Link," ASQC Quality Congress Transactions, Dallas, 1988.

3. AT&T Quality Policy Statement.

4. Process Quality Management and Improvement Guidelines, Quality Assurance Center, AT&T Bell Laboratories, 1987.

5. W. Edwards Deming, Out of the Crisis, MIT Center for Advanced Engineering Study, Cambridge, Mass., 1988.

6. W.A. Shewhart, Economic Control of Quality of Manufactured Product, D. Van Nostrand Co., New York, 1980 reprint.

INCREASING SALES FORCE PRODUCTIVITY

Richard Knudtsen
National Marketing Manager
U.S. Field Operations
Hewlett-Packard
10520 Ridge View Court
Cupertino, CA 95014

Applying TQC concepts to improving the selling process is new, yet has the potential to positively impact a large component of the white collar workhorse. This session reviews, from a management perspective, the approach being applied by Hewlett-Packard, including the implementation of portable computers and information access tools to increase the effectiveness and efficiency of HP's sales force.

CONTINUOUS PROCESS IMPROVEMENT IN ENGINEERING

George Henry
President
Tatham Process Engineering
2200 Lakeshore Blvd., West
Suite 308
Toronto, Ontario Canada M8V 1A4

Until recently, Total Quality Control (TQC) or Continuous Process Improvement (CPI) methodologies have been used mainly in the manufacturing environment. However, all business functions can be viewed as processes in which the tools and methodologies of CPI can be applied to improve productivity and quality. This seminar describes CPI and how it can be applied to a "white collar" engineering environment.

SOFTWARE QUALITY ASSURANCE

Mary P. Bakallis - Chairperson
Manager, Quality Assurance

AT&T Network Systems
6200 E. Broad Street
Columbus, OH 43213

ABSTRACT

The explosive growth in the software content of telecommunications products has created an ever-increasing need for the prevention of software defects early in design. The cost-effectiveness of this approach is astronomical compared to earlier methods where design and code were completed and system test was expected to clean up the errors. Emphasis on assuring that product requirements have been clearly defined, that reviews are held during each phase of the product development to assure conformance to those requirements and that changes are controlled and documented are all crucial to building quality into the software. This session presents different perspectives on how these concepts of defect prevention have been successfully applied.

Ashu Balpay	--	Bell Communications Research
Edward Crabill	--	AT&T Network Systems
James Harty	--	AT&T Network Systems
Younghee Kang	--	AT&T Network Systems
Michael Fabisch	--	Bell Communications Research
Roman Sikaczowski	--	Rockwell International

ANALYSIS OF SOFTWARE QUALITY FROM A USER'S PERSPECTIVE

Ashu Balpay
Member of Technical Staff
Quality Assurance Center

Bell Communications Research (Bellcore)
6 Corporate Place
Piscataway, NJ 08854

ABSTRACT

The quality of software is the integration of the resultant quality requirements obtained in each of the individual processes used throughout the total life cycle of the software. Analysis of software quality focuses on a supplier's ability to define the quality requirements for the various processes, manage the individual processes in order to attain these requirements, and manage the overall interfacing, sequencing, and evolution of the processes throughout the total life cycle. Bell Communications Research Inc.'s (Bellcore's) Quality Assurance currently uses four software quality analysis tools to support our client's needs in assuring quality software in the telecommunications network. These analysis tools provide a layered approach of increasing detail based on a standard Software Quality Analysis Framework.

1. INTRODUCTION

The maintenance of effective Quality Assurance/Control (QA/QC) programs has played an important role within the telephone network for many years. The application of effective quality programs to software, however, has gained momentum over the last few years with the formation of QA/QC groups within the software development organizations. This lack of previous concern over software quality becomes critical when one considers that within the next several years 80% of all telephone systems will operate under software control. In addition, there are numerous operations support software packages that could cause severe economic loss to the telephone network if operated at a substandard level.

Development and implementation of a comprehensive software quality assurance program, which covers the total software life cycle, including the development, deployment, and support processes, is required to assure the integrity of the network and other services provided by the telephone companies. Although the quality of hardware also impacts upon the integrity of the network, software has unique characteristics which makes its negative impact much more catastrophic:

1. Software operational errors of defects require that the software be modified for correction; it cannot be replaced with a spare as in hardware components.

2. A software operational error affects both the primary and back-up systems; a multiprocessor mode does not prevent loss of system operation.

3. The ability to predict the quality of delivered software through implementation of end-product inspections is significantly more difficult.

As generally perceived by the user, software is made up of a series of deliverable components which include:

1. Coded programs

2. Associated documentation

3. Associated user data

4. Related supplier services, such as installation, training, maintenance, and technical support.

The quality of a supplier's software relates to a much broader domain. In order to obtain quality software, a supplier must manage the quality of every process used throughout the total software life cycle, plus manage the software project as a whole.

2. BELLCORE'S APPROACH TO SOFTWARE QUALITY

Prior to AT&T's divestiture of the Bell Operating Companies, the quality of software used in the Bell System was determined largely by AT&T and its Bell Telephone Laboratories and Western Electric organizations. After divestiture, the seven Regional companies and their associated Bell Operating Companies assumed the responsibilities of evaluating, procuring, and assuring the quality of the software used in their telecommunication businesses. Software quality assurance is critical in today's post-divestiture telecommunications environment because current technologies rely heavily on software. Bellcore, being jointly owned by the seven Regional companies, supports its owners in the area of software quality assurance.

The Regional company users need well-defined, easily understood and comparable software quality standards. As the first step in meeting this goal, Bellcore has defined and proposed a Software Quality Analysis Framework [1] which consists of Elements (what to look at), Quality Requirements (what to look for), and Measurement Tools (how to look). The following is an outline of the Bellcore Software Quality Analysis Framework.

The Bellcore Software Quality Analysis Elements, which address generic processes used throughout the total life cycle, are:

1. Organization and Life Cycle Plans
2. Commitment to Quality
3. Standards, Procedures, and Practices
4. Software Development (Through Unit Testing)
5. Integration and Testing (To System Level)
6. Software Change (Mtce. and Modification)
7. Manufacture and Delivery
8. Site Installation and Testing
9. Supplier Support Environment
10. Configuration Management (SW/Doc. Control)
11. Quality Information
12. User Interaction
13. User Operational Information
14. Management Performance

Each of these Elements contains a number of individual attributes that are subdivided into a hierarchical structure according to increasing levels of complexity.

Bellcore's proposed Quality Requirements focus on each of the above Elements, and their associated hierarchy. The Bellcore Quality Requirements consist of four classes:

1. Correctness (preceding acceptance)
2. Reliability (performance after acceptance)
3. Usability (all user affecting characteristics)
4. Changeability (all changes during the life cycle)

These classes represent the set of elementary user requirements that, in Bellcore's view, form the basic definition of software quality. Each class contains specific quality attributes for each Bellcore Software Quality Analysis Element and its associated hierarchy.

The Bellcore Measurement Tools address each Element and the four classes of Quality Requirements. The Measurement Tools are divided into four categories:

1. Process Description Measures
2. Software Characteristics Measures
3. Personnel Performance Measures
4. Record/Documentation Measures

These measurements are the collimation of the expansion of the Elements, their associated hierarchy, and the Quality Requirements. These tools provide a generic set for analyzing the quality of software packages purchased by the Regional companies and their respective Bell Operating Companies. These Bellcore Measurement Tools address quality in all the various processes associated with software throughout its total life cycle and can be applied to various types and sizes of software packages.

This approach provides the framework necessary to perform comparable analyses of the variety of software systems purchased by Bellcore clients.

3. BELLCORE'S TOOLS FOR SOFTWARE QUALITY ANALYSIS

Due to the varying complexities of software and the requirement to meet the needs of customers in terms of analysis cost and contractual time frames, Bellcore uses four separate, yet related, tools to conduct Software Quality Analyses. This layered approach to Software Quality Analysis utilizes Software Facility Reviews, Software Quality Program Analyses, In-depth Software Quality Analyses, and on-going Software Quality Audits (Fig. 1). A Software Facility Review is a relatively brief review of a supplier's resources and their quality activities dealing with planning, creation, and support of their software. A Software Quality Program Analysis (QPA) is a detailed analysis (typically one week on-site) of a supplier's software quality system as it applies to the total life cycle of their software. An In-depth Software Quality Analysis is an extension of the Software QPA, which normally covers a period of several months and focuses on tracking and resolution of identified deficiencies. Software Quality Audits consist of Software Inspections and Software Quality Surveillance that are on-going and address the ability of the supplier to maintain a quality process over the long term.

3.1 Software Facility Review

The Software Facility Review is Bellcore's simplest Software Quality Analysis Tool that consists of a relatively brief review of the supplier's resources and software quality program. The Software Facility Review is normally conducted when a Regional company seeks a quick analysis of factors which may be relevant to its estimation of the supplier's capability to produce quality software. The Bellcore Software Facility Review performs two basic functions:

1. Examines the supplier's facilities and resources that are used for development, deployment, and support of software to determine if the basic resources exist to produce and support software throughout its total life cycle. This is accomplished through a series of questions that address the size, components, control mechanisms, and limitations of the supplier's physical resources.

2. Reviews the supplier's current Software Quality Program, as it applies to the total software life cycle. This consists of checking to see if the supplier's program addresses the Bellcore Software Quality Analysis Elements, but due to time constraints, does not use the Bellcore Measurement Tools to analyze their program and verify that the supplier's organizations adhere to their quality plan.

Following the review, a report of the findings is issued to the Regional company customers for use within their procurement process. Should the customer decide to proceed with contractual arrangements, the more formal Software QPA is recommended.

3.2 Software Quality Program Analysis

The Bellcore Software Quality Program Analysis is an intense analysis normally reserved for more complex software systems such as digital central office switching equipment, public packet switching systems, and operational support systems. The Software QPA activities normally cover a period of approximately one month and is conducted by a team of Bellcore Quality Assurance Engineers. The Software QPA utilizes the full Software Quality Analysis Framework to address a supplier's quality program as it is used to assure control of software quality throughout the software's total life cycle. Prior to the start of the on-site analysis, the analysis team obtains supplier documents relating to the software quality program currently in use, which include standards and guidelines that direct the processes and descriptions of organizational responsibilities. The initial stages of conducting a Software QPA focus on resolving the following questions:

1. Based on the specific software being analyzed, do all the Bellcore Software Quality Analysis Elements apply?

2. How far into the hierarchy of each Element should the analysis proceed?

The resolution of these questions defines the scope of the Software QPA and enables the analysis team to select the applicable set of measurement tools. The analysis team conducts a formal opening conference with the supplier, then performs the QPA using the measurement tools to determine:

1. How the supplier's quality program addresses the processes defined in the appropriate Bellcore Software Quality Analysis Elements and associated hierarchy.

2. What the supplier's software quality requirements are and how these match the Bellcore Quality Requirement classes.

3. How the supplier adheres to their program and controls their processes in order to achieve their quality requirements.

The analysis team conducts daily feedback sessions with the various supplier organizations during the analysis to identify areas of concern and clarify details. Prior to leaving the supplier's site, the team presents its findings and recommendations to the supplier in a closing conference. After the conclusion of the analysis, the team drafts a report, which includes information regarding the logistics of the analysis, an overview of the analysis team's findings, and details of the supplier's capabilities as they relate to the Bellcore Quality Analysis Framework. The analysis report is reviewed with the supplier prior to release to the customer. This review activity provides assurance that the analysis team has accurately portrayed the supplier's processes and that the supplier clearly understands the nature of any deficiencies.

After the supplier has indicated that corrective action has been taken on the deficiencies identified, a follow-up analysis is conducted and a supplemental report is issued.

3.3 In-depth Software Quality Analysis

An In-depth Analysis follows the same general procedures as a Software QPA, but involves additional time (approximately 3-6 weeks) at the supplier's site(s) to conduct a more extensive analysis. As deficiencies are identified in the supplier's quality program, a corrective action log is established that documents and focuses the dialog between the responsible supplier personnel and the analysis team. This log is utilized to track the on-going corrective actions and eventual resolution of deficiencies. In addition the log becomes part of the analysis report, which is written at the close of the analysis. Following the release of the analysis report, periodic status meetings are held to assure that the items in the corrective action log are being addressed. When closure is obtained on a sufficient number of log items, a follow-up analysis will be performed to verify the effectiveness of the corrective actions. At the conclusion of the follow-up analysis an addendum will be issued for the initial report describing the corrective actions initiated by the supplier.

3.4 Software Quality Audits

Once a Regional company customer has committed to purchase a software system in substantial quantities, Software Quality Audits can be used to assure that the supplier maintains an effective on-going quality program, and to alert the customer should evidence of poor quality be detected. These Software Quality Audits are implemented through the use of inspection and/or surveillance programs and are usually preceded by a Software QPA or an In-depth Software Quality Analysis.

Software quality inspection is defined as the activity of comparing a software package against an established set of standards on a statistical sampling basis and collecting the resultant data for analysis and report generation. Software Inspection uses the Bellcore Measurement Tools in the category of "software characteristics measures" which can be most easily applied to the life cycle stages of manufacturing and delivery, installation, operation and use, maintenance and modification. Some examples of inspection at the various stages are:

1. Verifying the correctness of software parameters and features of site-specific loads

2. Verifying the correctness and reliability of the software installation process

3. Checking for application of current software updates

4. Verification of delivery of all required user documentation

Bellcore Quality Engineers, after analyzing a specific supplier's processes, their associated software, and customer requirements, determine which supplier operations or functions have the most impact upon the resulting software quality and develop inspection procedures for these key areas. Normally inspections are performed using a random sample of the software, with the frequency dependent on the current quality level, the software's complexity, and the volume of software being generated.

Software surveillance is defined as the activity of monitoring a supplier's control of the various processes used by the supplier throughout the total life cycle of a software system. In contrast to the software quality inspection that focuses on the end quality of software, documentation, and services delivered to the customer, software surveillance can be used on the stages of the software life cycle. Generically, the supplier's control of a process entails data collection, analysis, and corrective action to eliminate deficiencies or enhance the process. Software surveillance uses the Bellcore Measurement Tools in the categories of "process description measures," "personnel performance measures," and "record/documentation measures."

The specific procedures of a software surveillance program are developed by Bellcore Quality Engineers, after analyzing the supplier's processes used throughout the total software life cycle, assessing the quality requirements, and selecting the appropriate measurement tools. Surveillance activity is performed on either a regular basis or tied to specific events in the software life cycle. Status reports on the surveillance process are periodically issued to the Regional company customers.

4. SUMMARY

The Bellcore Software Quality Analysis Tools provide a layered approach of increasing detail based on a standard Software Quality Analysis Framework that addresses generic processes used throughout the total life cycle, associated quality requirements, and related measurement tools. The analysis tools consist of:

1. The Software Facility Review that examines the supplier's resources necessary to support the software life cycle processes and reviews the supplier's quality program.

2. The Software Quality Program Analysis that examines the processes used by a supplier over the total life cycle; the quality requirements associated with each process; and performance of the supplier in following their program, meeting quality requirements, and managing the processes.

3. The In-depth Software Quality Analysis that expands on the Software QPA by providing detailed tracking to promote corrective action on software quality deficiencies.

4. Software Quality Audits, which provide an on-going program, that monitors the supplier's performance in managing their life cycle processes and meeting their process quality requirements.

These analysis tools provide essential data to our clients necessary for their respective evaluations of a supplier's software quality.

References

1. R. L. Braun, "*Providing User's A Framework For Software Quality,*" IEEE GLOBECOM'86.

2. J. L. Pence, "*The System and Methodologies of Bell Communications Research, Inc.'s Quality Assurance Function,*" IEEE GLOBECOM'84.

3. DOD-STD-2167, "*Defense System Software Development,*" June 4, 1985.

4. Bell Communications Research, Technical Advisory, TA-TSY-000179, "*Software Quality Program Analysis Criteria.*"

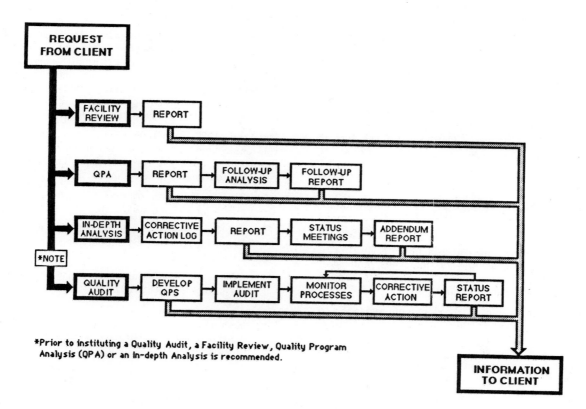

FIGURE 1

Bellcore's Software Quality Analysis Tools

THE QUALITY IMPROVEMENT
PROCESS - AN AT&T MODEL

Edwin F. Crabill
Strategic Planning Product Manager

James P. Harty
Senior Member - Information System Staff
Quality Assurance

Younghee K. Kang, Ph.D
Information System Staff Member
Project Engineering

AT&T Network Systems
2600 Warrenville Road
Lisle, IL 60532

A new product center at the AT&T Network Software Center was surveyed in 1987 by an AT&T Quality Assurance survey team. The eight high level recommendations they made, the Quality Improvement Process resulting from those recommendations, implementation results, and conclusions are presented in this paper.

INTRODUCTION

At the AT&T Network Software Center (NSC), there is a Quality Council composed of the location Vice President and his Engineering Directors. This Quality Council and the product center itself requested Quality Assurance (QA) to conduct an independent Software Development Survey (SDS) of their development process. The QA team interviewed selected members of the product center, including all management. The purpose was to assess the current quality processes, and formulate recommendations for improvements. The management team agreed that the survey would be useful in setting a quality direction for the young product line, and would be good preparation for the possibility of a Bellcore audit.

QA SOFTWARE DEVELOPMENT SURVEY PROCESS

In recent years, NSC QA survey teams have focused on improving the processes used by their client development, deployment and customer support organizations. Over forty organizations at NSC and/or AT&T Bell Laboratories have been surveyed by this QA group since 1984. Feedback from these organizations, especially during the survey postmortem, has continuously improved the QA survey process. After the survey team reviewed the external quality program standards and guidelines (as published by Bellcore and IEEE) as well as the various AT&T quality documents, we developed a survey plan that measured this product center against those standards and guidelines. The scope of the formal plan included:

1. An assessment of the product center's processes as documented in their methodology

2. The development and use of a questionnaire which was directed at the specific development process employed by this product center

3. The selection and subsequent interview of a representative sample of managers and staff from not only this product center but also its major interfacing organizations

4. The observation of development reviews and other project and quality management meetings to support the documented methodology, the cultural practices, questionnaire responses, interviewee assertions, and the survey team's own findings

5. Follow-up conversations and readings to rebut or verify assertions and survey team preliminary findings

6. Draft and final report findings and quality improvement recommendations as well as an executive summary distributed to selected audiences.

The informal survey team work plan employed several techniques designed to produce a positive impact on the product center not only during the survey process, but long after the survey was completed. The major emphasis was to:

1. Develop a partnership between the survey team and the product center

2. Improve quality and productivity a la the Hawthorne Effect

3. Energize the product center leadership

4. Celebrate the product center's successes while motivating continuous quality improvements

SURVEY EXECUTION AND RECOMMENDATIONS

While planning for this SDS began in late 1986, the survey execution was begun in February, 1987. A project management engineer was assigned as a central point of contact for the QA team. Although on the product center staff, this engineer was a participant in the survey team weekly meetings, which were held to review the survey scope, objectives and formal plan document during the survey planning phase.

Later, the weekly survey team meetings were used to assess survey progress against plan and redirect our focus as appropriate. Both formal and informal discussions and presentations were held with the product center quality working group (members), managers and other key personnel while the findings and recommendations were being formulated.

By April, 1987, recommendations were presented to the management team, that included 8 high level and 32 detailed quality improvements. The high level recommendations were as follows:

1. Elevate the level of management commitment and support for quality improvement.

2. Develop, review and implement an overall Project Plan and the supporting comprehensive detailed Product Development Plans (PDPs).

3. Write a comprehensive Software Quality Assurance Plan (SQAP).

4. Increase use of current in-process documentation, as described in the project methodology, and expand to include customer documentation.

5. Strengthen and improve the use of reviews and audits to evaluate the software product throughout its life cycle.

6. Increase the effectiveness of the phased approach to the testing process.

7. Commit to systematic data collection, analysis, and measurement of software quality across the total product life cycle.

8. Assign responsibility for tool coordination and development.

IMPLEMENTATION PROCESS FOR QUALITY PROGRAM

The SDS process and the results of the survey elevated management's attention to the quality program needs, and as a result, a full-time quality engineer was assigned to coordinate the implementation of the recommendations. A rejuvenated Quality Working Group, chaired by the Project Engineering Manager and supported by the Quality Council, regularly held meetings for brain storming, progress reporting, problem solving, and steering the quality improvement program. The SDS recommendations fell into two main categories: Increased Management Commitment, and Quality Assurance Planning.

A plan was formed with short-range (3-6 months), medium-range (6-12 months), and long-range (> 1 year) actions and goals.

Short-range goals were:

• Revise and document the product life cycle plan

- Characterize all processes, including entry/exit criteria
- Establish quality control processes with data collection points

Medium-range goals were:

- Document and publish all development processes and existing tools
- Provide staff training for the product and methodology
- Monitor compliance to the methodology

Long-range goals were:

- Collect data, analyze, and report
- Identify problem areas
- Implement improvement processes continuously

To implement the plan, goals were prioritized, Action Teams were formed, and implementation schedules were set. We used existing processes, teams, committees, and meetings where we could and created new ones where necessary. The strategy (in part) was to raise the quality consciousness of both management and staff as well as promote teamwork. This was a key; over time, more than 50 percent of the project staff were members of an Action Team. In that way, they became both developers and users of the improved processes.

QUALITY ASSURANCE PLAN

A comprehensive Quality Assurance Plan (QAP) was developed:

1. to ensure the quality of the product and services we provide to customers.
2. to improve communication throughout the project, and
3. to ensure consistency throughout the project.

The QAP was based on the 1984 IEEE-730 standard [1], as well as NSC guidelines [2,3]. After some customizing to fit our individual needs, the QAP included the following sections [4]:

— Introduction
— Purpose
— Management
— Documentation
— Standards, Practices, and Conventions
— Reviews and Audits
— Software Configuration Management
— Problem Reporting and Corrective Action
— Tools, Techniques, and Methodologies
— Source Code Control
— Media Control
— Supplier Control
— Record Collection, Maintenance, and Retention
— User Training and Support
— Sales Support

We received much help from existing Quality groups at the Network Software Center, including the Quality Council, the Product Center Managers/Branch Council, Quality Assurance, Quality Systems Engineering, and the Branch Quality Improvement Department. QA provided the SDS recommendations, tracked our progress, and participated to achieve improvements. QSE advised on AT&T Network Systems policies, supported our implementation of NSC Quality policies, and participated in our Quality Improvement Plan, especially in the reviews and audits. The Branch Quality Improvement department provided much of the data collection, metrics, analysis, and process improvement suggestions.

RESULTS

By June, 1988, 30 of the 32 recommendations had been implemented. Some of the qualitative accomplishments were as follows:

— Increased quality awareness
— Revised and documented the product life cycle plan
— Improved documentation of each phase
— Audited reviews and review documents
— Developed and provided in-house staff training
— Increased compliance
— Improved communication within the project
— Improved tool development process and documentation; published tool manual
— Improved data collection and report analysis
— Improved software product and service quality (figures 1-6)

The attached figures indicate that the number of faults per thousand non-comment source lines (kncsl) has been decreased by more than one third (figure 2), even with a larger product size (figure 1). In addition, the mean time to fix faults has been cut more than in half (figure 4). The data collected to date shows a quality improvement, with no decrease in productivity.

CONCLUSIONS

To achieve long-term sustainable quality improvements requires planning and management commitment. We are achieving success today because the management team is willing to dedicate time and resources, even when under extreme pressure to meet schedules. The time spent on analysis of our process and methodology, training, and documentation will pay even more dividends in the future.

Another key is assigning a dedicated person as quality coordinator. In our case, this was a full time job. While quality is part of everyone's job, sometimes we need a facilitator or catalyst to achieve our common goal. This is not a quality control auditor; rather, this is someone to interface with the QA and QC groups as well as management, to form plans, and to ensure good communication on the project through training, team activities, etc.

The final major key is to maximize the involvement in quality improvement activities. We had over 50 percent of the project staff directly involved in the Quality Action Teams and managers have led many Action Teams and Quality Working Group activities. This helped make everyone aware of the quality improvement process and increase the buy-in from team members, since they had played a major role in setting the policies and procedures.

In summary, we found the Software Development Survey to be a valuable process, both in analyzing our project to find ideas for improvement, and in preparing for possible future audits. We applied a shotgun approach to plant a seed for improvement in many different areas; this year we will be systematically attacking specific areas on a priority

basis. While the data collected to date is insufficient to finalize conclusions, a positive trend is clear. Improved responsiveness to our customers, represented by figure 6, was facilitated by product quality improvements, represented by figures 2 and 5.

The data does help to indicate the major problem areas and we will develop the quality improvement plan for the next phase based on the data collected. By analyzing our processes, planning, prioritizing, and focusing on improvement -- rather than control -- we have positioned ourselves for sustainable quality improvements for several years to come.

References

[1] ANSI/IEEE Standard 730-1984, *IEEE Standard for Software Quality Assurance Plans,* IEEE, Inc., 1984

[2] *NSC Quality Improvement Manual,* AT&T-NS Issue 2, November, 1985

[3] *Employee Guide to Quality Improvement,* AT&T-NS, December, 1986

[4] *[The project] Quality Assurance Plan,* AT&T-NS, Issue 1.0, February, 1988

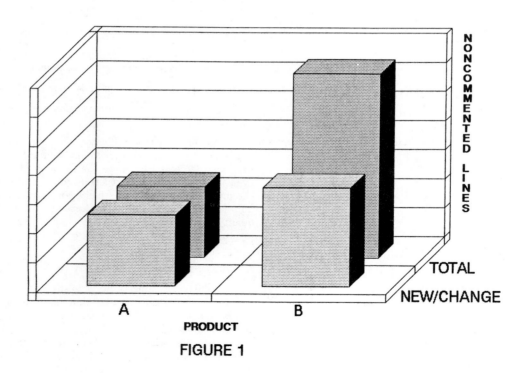

PRODUCT SIZE

FIGURE 1

CUMMULATIVE FAULT DENSITY

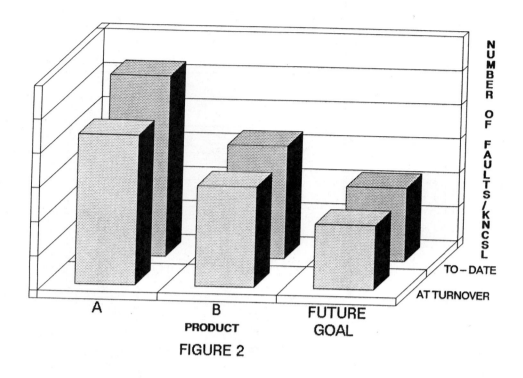

FIGURE 2

NON – TRIVIAL FAULTS

AFTER PRODUCT RELEASE

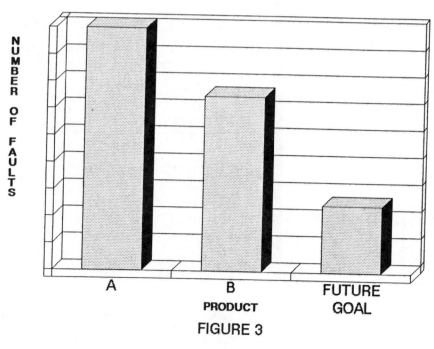

FIGURE 3

1552

MEAN TIME TO CLOSE FAULTS

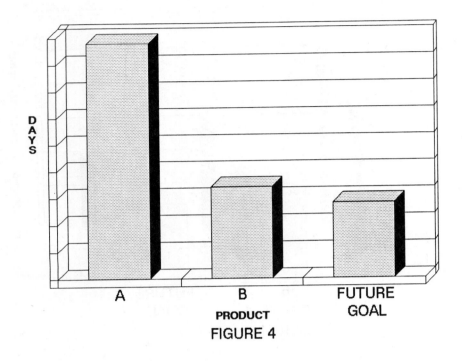

FIGURE 4

CUSTOMER REPORTED FAULT DENSITY

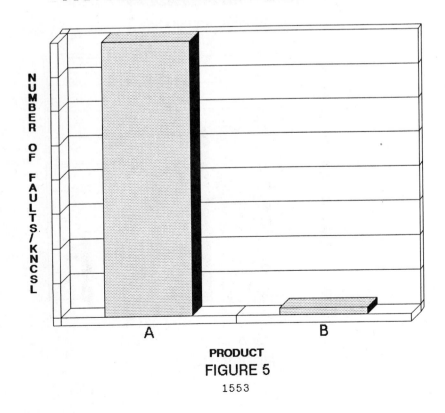

FIGURE 5

MEAN TIME TO RESOLVE ISSUES

CUSTOMER REPORTED PROBLEMS

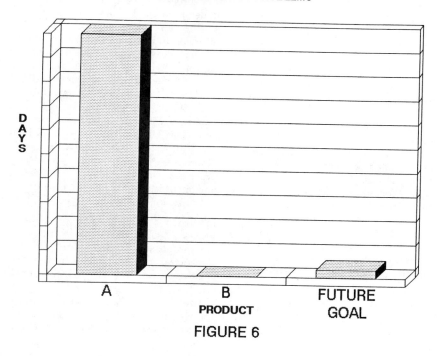

FIGURE 6

THE CHANGING OF THE GUARD IN SOFTWARE QUALITY

Roman O. Sikaczowski
Manager, Software Quality Assurance

Rockwell Communications Systems
Switching Systems Division
1431 Opus Place
P.O. Box 1494
Downers Grove, IL 60515

ABSTRACT

Many opportunities exist for Software Quality Assurance (SQA) to improve the productivity of a software development team. However, all too often, concentration on a "Policeman", testing or final approval authority role limits and even negates SQA's impact. This paper proposes returning the "policeman" and approval roles to developers and independent testers of the software product and discusses audits, metric collection, internal consulting, process analysis and other tasks which SQA should perform to improve product quality and software development productivity.

INTRODUCTION

The decades of the 70's and 80's have produced an ever increasing demand for computerization. Advances in hardware designs and components have given potential to computers far beyond what was possible even 10 years ago. The need for computer software has also risen in parallel to and because of hardware breakthroughs. Indeed, the need for software is often the limiting factor in how fast new computer applications are developed.

The amount of software developed by the industry each year has been rising to meet this demand and is predicted to continue doing so through the 90's and beyond. Along with this rise in software quantity a corresponding rise in software defects has also occurred. In fact, software maintenance costs have often equaled or even outweighed software development costs. In order to address this problem, software quality organizations were formed.

The software quality organizations evolved from the established hardware quality organizations. Hence, SQA charters were (and often still are) based on parallel hardware Quality Assurance charters. Perhaps the most significant effect of this was that SQA often did not get involved in the early phases of the software life cycle. Rather they concentrated on testing the software product *after* it came off the developer's "assembly line." This method did have some success in that more defects were discovered before products were shipped. However, the responsibility for software quality was diluted away from developers. Software developers sometimes became tempted to cut corners and not test their software adequately assuming SQA would find any defects later. This caused more defects to be hidden in the software. Correcting these and other defects found by SQA became costly and time consuming. SQA was always the bearer of bad news. Thus, the end effect of a talented, trained, conscientious SQA department was often an increase in defects in the software, missed schedules, forced overtime and cost overruns! SQA was rarely looked upon by management (especially software development management) as a benefit to the organization. Few people were satisfied working in SQA and few SQA groups survived. Changes in the way SQA operates were needed. This paper discusses some of these changes.

Throughout this paper it is assumed that an SQA organization is independent from the development organization and its management. This insures objectivity and freedom in reporting. Also, it is assumed that SQA personnel work across all projects rather than being dedicated to one at a time. This insures breadth of experience and knowledge.

THE SOFTWARE PROCESS

Software development is a process of steps. Major gains in quality and productivity can be realized by optimizing the process. Yet organizations often do not know where to optimize a process or even what process they are really using. There are "Fantasy" processes and schedules which are assumed before a project starts and then there are the "Reality" processes and schedules which in fact occur. Getting the "Fantasy" and "Reality" schedules to converge is often a matter of getting the "Fantasy" and "Reality" processes to converge. Yet without documenting proposed processes, capturing actual data on how the processes are implemented, comparing that data vs. the documented process, analyzing differences and inefficiencies, and finally implementing corrections, convergence is unlikely. The result has been not only repeatedly missed schedules and lower productivity, but also lower quality resulting from omitting or modifying process steps in order to meet schedules. The process, instead of being well planned and optimized, becomes an accident of the product and knowledge gained during the project often gets lost or stays with only one or two project leaders without any plan to use the information to improve the next development. To change this, a cycle must be implemented where you DOCUMENT, IMPLEMENT, CAPTURE, ANALYZE, and IMPROVE the process

on an ongoing basis. SQA's role in this, as part of the software development team, is described below.

DOCUMENT

The process by which software is developed must be understood and followed by all applicable groups within an organization. In an area such as telecommunications, there are thousands of interfaces during a software development project between various departments and individuals. Inputs and outputs are expected at certain times and in certain formats. Without documented standards and procedures to refer to, it is highly unlikely that everyone will understand the process the same way and that all the interfaces and handoffs will occur smoothly. It is also nearly impossible to determine differences between real processes and "Fantasy" processes if they are not written. Therefore, documentation of the process is essential if optimization is to be achieved.

In order to document the software development process, a high level framework for the process must be proposed. Then the standards, procedures, interfaces, guidelines and authorizations needed by each department must be identified, agreed upon and written. Often these involve interfaces and handoffs between various groups in an organization. A leader for coordinating the development of these procedures and standards is needed. SQA can fill this role very well.

SQA's independence and cross project experience allows them to create and propose a high level process framework which takes into account individual department concerns and experience and also addresses the efficiency and quality of the process as a whole. This proposed framework can then be reviewed and modified by performing departments until agreement on the framework is reached. SQA can moderate these sessions. Once this is done, the individual departments can identify their roles and create documents needed internally; for example, coding standards, requirements guidelines, system test procedure formats, etc. SQA can also have a major consulting role in this effort. They should insure that all interfaces are addressed and coordinated; that already existing standards and procedures within the company are identified and used where appropriate; that industry standards are implemented as necessary. In all, SQA can coordinate the effort necessary to create a complete, efficient, effective, detailed and documented software development process that all participants develop and agree to follow.

IMPLEMENT

The implementation of a software process is not as simple as distributing the associated documentation. Various organizations must implement training programs to teach their staff the detailed procedures management expects them to use and follow. The expected inputs to and outputs from the department must be clearly identified. Standards and guidelines must be explained. In addition, a training plan for new hires and transferees into the department should be put in place.

SQA should be an active participant in this training process. Since an active SQA department will have had experience working across several project boundaries and in coordinating the software process development effort, their involvement with the training programs will help keep methodology as consistent as possible within an organization. They can identify existing training material already written and proven useful on other projects. Since SQA is usually not in the critical path of software development schedules they may have more time to research and identify outside seminars, speakers or training programs on software development and provide recommendations on their scheduling. During the training process, SQA should also insure that software quality standards and guidelines are met by the training programs. Working across department boundaries SQA can help insure that training on the interface points of a project where handoffs occur is consistent and fully covered by all applicable departments. Finally, SQA can also give training classes themselves on appropriate topics such as coding guidelines or review, walkthrough and inspection rules and procedures.

Overall SQA should have a large involvement with documenting the development process and implementing training programs and plans. However, it must be stressed that this involvement consists of *helping* other organizations. SQA should not take execution responsibility away from the performing departments nor should they dictate that SQA rules override all others. Any such issues should be worked out with all concerned parties as they arise.

CAPTURE

After documenting and implementing a software development process, major productivity and quality gains will be realized. However, the process will still require constant monitoring and improvement. This is due to several ongoing factors. It is highly unlikely that a process can be optimized on the first pass. Actual results must be measured and captured for later analysis and comparison with other proposed processes. Technological changes will cause parts of processes to become obsolete or outdated. Processes will need to be eliminated, changed or added. It is also likely that parts of the overall documented process will be skipped or modified during the actual project life cycle. All of these factors must be captured in order to understand and improve the software development process.

The capture of process and resulting product data should be one of SQA's primary responsibilities. This responsibility can be divided into 2 major areas: Metrics and audits.

Metrics

The implementation of a metrics program is critical in making software engineering a science vs. an art. Yet few organizations have a robust, ongoing metrics program. This is often due to software developers' fear of being measured. Another factor is that the results of measurement programs are often screened and reported only if they show "good" results. This tends to eliminate their usefulness as indicators of problem areas to concentrate on and improve. Finally, the implementation, gathering and reporting of metrics is a non-trivial task. Many development schedules do not allow time for this activity since benefits accrue in the future but today's costs and schedules may override future considerations. SQA coordination and execution of a metrics program eliminates many of the above difficulties.

Specifically, what can SQA do? They should coordinate the development of a metrics program covering the entire software life cycle. This would include working with various management teams to identify and propose metrics and measures which would help them analyze and control their part of the software development process. Identification of where in the process metrics should be implemented and who will provide them must be agreed upon. SQA can at this point volunteer to start the collection process and provide periodic reports across all development projects to the proper management levels.

How can SQA overcome the previously mentioned difficulties? SQA's independence helps to insure objective reporting of metric results. At the same time, since it is process and product data *not* individual performance data that is needed, SQA can filter out names yet still provide accurate and useful numbers. Also, SQA can work during a project to collect and report metrics without disrupting developers from their day-to-day tasks and schedules.

Audits

Audits between software life cycle phases can provide consistent points in the software development process where metrics can be collected. However, process analysis cannot be done solely via collection and study of metrics. An involvement with the process and, more importantly, maintaining an awareness of variances from the "Fantasy" process is crucial. For example, it can be very misleading to compare data on coding errors found in system test before and after a new review process is implemented if the review process is not actually being followed. Thus real time audits of the conformance to documented processes must be performed and results reported. SQA is again an ideal candidate for this task.

SQA provides objectivity in audit reports that is crucial to their usefulness. SQA is able to, on a sampling basis, audit in process reviews or inspections and then compare processes actually implemented with those which are documented. Periodic reports listing variances, their causes and suggested recommendations for improvements can then be written. SQA should also audit areas such as conformance to coding standards, thoroughness of test plan coverage, currentness of design documents, configuration management and others. These audits can be done on a random, sampling basis in a relatively short amount of time. SQA can also attend or chair life cycle phase audits such as the Functional Configuration Audit (prior to release to field trial) or Physical Configuration Audit (prior to release to production). All of these audits and their resulting reports can then be analyzed along with metrics collected on the development process to provide a true indication of the current status of the process.

ANALYZE

A frequent occurrence in many organizations that evolve to the point of developing, auditing and measuring a software process is that the metrics and audit reports are not fully utilized. In some cases they are almost ignored, thus wasting the effort required to capture them. Each department in an organization should be required to quantify their performance during the software life cycle, analyze the results, compare them to goals and implement improvements as warranted. However, this can be very time consuming, especially if development or production schedules are tight. Again, SQA can help.

As mentioned previously, SQA can be chartered with collecting and reporting metrics within an organization. As they are familiar with the development process they should also be able to interpret the metrics and report any significant trends or variances. This provides several benefits. One is that this frees developers to do development work instead of metric analysis. Another is that an independent organization will not only look for "good" data but will also be more apt to find and report problem areas which otherwise may be left undiscovered or undocumented. A further benefit is that SQA should have data from various projects and thus may be able to more easily compare projects with one another or against a company or industry average. This, combined with a good understanding achieved by auditing the "Reality" process throughout the software life cycle can make SQA a key team member in proper analysis and understanding of the software development process and its strengths and weaknesses.

IMPROVE

At this point, strengths, weaknesses and inefficiencies of the real software development process should be obvious. The final stage of the process improvement cycle is the implementation of corrective actions. SQA can be used here as internal consultants to help in determining necessary corrective actions. SQA may call and chair project postmortems where all departments discuss and resolve issues identified by metrics, audits or other methods. However, responsibility for implementing improvements remains with each performing department.

CONCLUSION

The major responsibility of a good SQA organization should not be that of executing a "policeman" type role. Indeed this is often counter-productive and causes many SQA organizations to fail. Instead, there are ways to leverage SQA's independence and experience across projects by using SQA as internal software process consultants. This involves SQA participation in coordinating the documentation of software processes, implementation of training programs, execution of internal audits, metric implementation, process analysis and implementation of corrective actions. All of these actions, if properly done, will improve the software process and consequently the software product. This allows SQA to take more of a partnership role and be considered a productive team player in the software development process rather than just the stereotypical bearer of bad news.

EXPERIENCES OF THE SOFTWARE DEVELOPMENT AND SERVICES COMMITTEE

Michael P. Fabisch
Assistant Vice President
Software Technology and Systems

AVP - Bell Communications Research
3 Corporate Place
Piscataway, NJ 08854

The talk entitled "Experiences of the Software Development and Services Committee" covers how to improve software development quality without sacrificing productivity. The approach to improving quality involves trying to take advantage of local and incremental changes to process, procedure and technology, without cultural disruption and mass confusion.

Examples are given of the five wide-scope Bellcore programs:

- *Customer Service,* the procedures by which we interface with our customers and service our software products,

- *Development Process,* the procedures by which we plan and develop our software products, focusing particularly on reuse and standards,

- *Improved Technology,* the specification of the software development tools necessary to support cost-effective development,

- *Quality Assurance/Assessment,* the development and execution of product-specific programs to measure and improve quality and

- *Education,* the development and, at times, delivery of courses to support execution of the product and services quality program.

Each program is briefly discussed in context of its status of implementation, success or failure. Much of the talk revolves around the Software Development and Services Committee, an AVP-level group chartered with making the quality improvement happen. The committee is in its third year now, and deeply into the implementation of the five program areas.

Software Productivity And Quality

Experiences Of The Software
Development & Services Committee

Mike Fabisch

Fig. 1

The Quality Effort At Bellcore

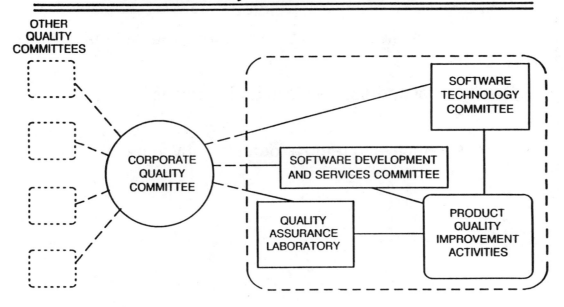

Fig. 2

A Three Pronged Attack

- Software design

- Software technology
  - Software Technology Committee

- Software development process
  - Software Development and Services Committee

Fig. 3

Quality Principles

• Customer satisfaction tied to customer expectations

• Quality must address services and products

• It is cost effective to remove defects early in development

Fig. 4

Cost Of Defects

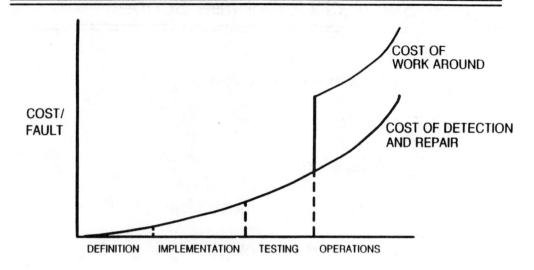

Fig. 5

Software Development And Services Committee

Purpose:

    To address ST&S software quality and productivity problems

Charter:

    To define and implement software development and customer service processes that will make Software Technology and Systems the best development organization in the world - producing high quality, cost effective and timely software systems and services.

Fig. 6

Software Development And Services Committee Scope

- Development process

- Customer services

- Education

- Quality improvement/assessment

- Improved technology

Fig. 7

Software Quality And Service Program

EDUCATION
    SOFTWARE QUALITY CURRICULUM
    MANAGING SOFTWARE DEVELOPMENT
    NEWSLETTER
    TALKS

QUALITY IMPROVEMENT/
ASSESSMENT
    SOFTWARE PROCESS AUDITS
    METRICS & GOALS
    QUALITY IMPROVEMENT PLANS
    ANALYSIS & FEEDBACK

SOFTWARE DEVELOPMENT
& SERVICES COMMITTEE
POLICIES
PROGRAMS

CUSTOMER SERVICES
    COMMITMENT LETTER
    JEOPARDY NOTICES
    SERVICE PLANNING
    SATISFACTION
    ASSESSMENT

IMPROVED TECHNOLOGY
    STANDARD DEV ENVIRONMENTS
    BELLCORE APPLICATION
    ENVIRONMENT
    PRODUCTIVITY TOOLS
    REUSE
    SOFTWARE TESTING

DEVELOPMENT PROCESS

TRACK & REPORT KEY MILESTONES
CUSTOMER INVOLVEMENT
PERFORMANCE MANAGEMENT
ECONOMIC MODELS
CODE INSPECTIONS & REVIEW PROCESS

DEVELOPMENT OF RELEASE PLANS
DOCUMENTATION
FRONT END PROCESS
(PLANNING, REQ'TS. & COMMITMENT)
PROJECT DEBRIEFING

Fig. 8

Quality Program Focus

1986 - Identify issues
     - Establish preliminary policies

1987 - Develop policies and guidelines
     - Launch policy trials

1988 - Policy implementation
     - Policy improvement

Fig. 9

Policies & Guidelines

Software Development Policies & Guidelines	
Introduction	1
Software Development Policies	2-3
Policy SME/Reference List	4-5
Product Policy Checklist	6
Major Software Product List	6
Software Product Development Guidelines	
Development Process	7-12
Reference Materials	
Key Milestone Form	13
Commitment Letter Outline	14
Jeopardy Notice Form	15
Code Inspection Information Form	16
QUIP Outline	17
SQPA Outline	18
Quality Measurement Charts	19
Maintenance MR Severity Definitions	20
BDE Product Chart	21
Prospectus Outline	22
Product Plan Outline	23
Development Plan Outline	24
Reference Documents List	25

- Facilitate buy-in

- Spread the word

- Hold line managers accountable

- Avoid bureaucracy

Fig. 10

Policy List

- Key milestones
- Customer involvement
- Economic model
- Commitment letter
- Jeopardy notice
- Performance model
- Code inspections

- Customer service plan
- Quality improvement plan
- Software quality program analysis
- Quality goals & measures
- Bellcore development environment
- Quality curriculum

Fig. 11

Policies

Affect All Systems
- Key Milestones
- Commitment Letter
- Jeopardy Notice
- Code Inspections
- Customer Service Plan
- Quality Improvement Plan (QUIP)

Affect Major Systems
- Customer Involvement
- Economic Model
- Performance Model
- Quality Goals & Measures
- Bellcore Development Environment (BDE)

Not System Specific
- Software Quality Program Analysis
- Quality Curriculum

Fig. 12

Commitment Letter

All software products will provide a commitment letter [*]
for each feature release, at the completion of design
or approximately six months prior to release shipment.

Contents:

- Executive Summary
  - New feature list
  - Benefits - short summary
  - Performance impact - short summary
  - Quality

- New features - descriptions
- Benefits
- Performance impact
- Quality commitment
- Schedule of deliverables

Fig. 13

Jeopardy Notice

A jeopardy notice will be issued to the customer
whenever a software product is in jeopardy of
missing a product or service commitment as defined
in the commitment letter or customer service plan.

NO.:	DATE
MILESTONE OR SERVICE JEOPARDY:	
DESCRIPTION	
ACTION PLAN	
PERSONS NOTIFIED	COPY TO

Fig. 14

Quality Goals And Measures

All major software products will have as their goal that each software release will improve in quality and service relative to the previous release. All major products will provide size/productivity, product quality and service metrics on a periodic basis.

Measures:

- System size
- Source lines productivity
- Field fault density
- Quality trends
- Mean time to repair for field faults
- Status of field faults

Fig. 15

Quality Improvement Plan (QUIP)

All software products will provide and implement a quality improvement plan (QUIP) to be updated annually that will be integrated into the project management process. A QUIP may cover a group of products.

Addressed:

- Prior-year review
- Management commitment
- Education and communication
- Process review
- Quantitative goals
- Measurement and analysis
- Corrective action
- Recognition
- Schedule

Fig. 16

Software Quality Program Analysis (QPA)

Selected software products will periodically undergo a quality program analysis (QPA) and periodic surveillance conducted by the Quality Assurance Laboratory.

In   1987 : 8 QPAs were conducted

For 1988 :

- Software Policy Review
- In depth product line support
- Metrics

Fig. 17

QPA Findings

Deficiency	Exemplary
Quality Data Analysis	Management commitment
Development Documentation	Automated development tools
Review policies	Customer involvement
Test methodology	Customer technical support
Procedure documentation	Release control

Fig. 18

What Has Changed?

- Product quality teams formed

- Formal development process initiated

- Customer interaction improved

- Software inspections started

- Development testing expanded

- Cooperative testing formalized

- Defect analysis initiated

- Quality is an active component of software schedules

Fig. 19

Quality Program Fundamental Ingredients

- Line (not staff) management and accountability
- Grass roots participation/buy-in
- Small not large (few key policies, small trials)
- Committed management participation/Strong Leader
- Visibility and communication (well documented, coherent, success stories)
- Angels/distribution of work
- Process analysis
- Quality goals, measures and analysis
- Customer satisfaction assessment
- Customer involvement
- Reuse of existing work

Fig. 20

PQR-15

MANUFACTURING ENHANCEMENTS

William S. Sedlacek - Chairperson
Vice President/General Manager
Reliable Electric/Utility Products
11333 Addison Street
Franklin Park, Illinois 60131

ABSTRACT

"World Class Manufacturing" is a status that must be achieved by American Manufacturers if we are to remain a part of the successful global corporations. The key to achieving this challenge is to successfully implement a series of manufacturing enhancements that will keep our organizations in step with the dynamics seen in today's environment. This seminar brings four exciting presentations and case studies on flexible manufacturing, impact on computer use in a JIT environment, paperless factory and integrating MRP in a JIT environment.

Joel D. Goldhar   -- Illinois Institute
                        of Technology

Vinod K. Kapoor   -- Challenger Electric
                        Equipment Corp.

Robert Storrs   -- A T & T

Richard Dworak   -- Tandem Computers Inc.

THE IMPACT OF FLEXIBLE MANUFACTURING ON PRODUCT INNOVATION AND COMPETITIVE STRATEGY

Dr. Joel D. Goldhar
Professor of Technology Management
School of Business

Illinois Institute of Technology
10 W. 31st Street
Chicago, Illinois 60616

ABSTRACT

The availability of computer integrated and flexible manufacturing technology allows us to create factories with new capabilities to handle low volume/high variety products without a loss of quality or increase in costs. In turn, this opens up new possibilities in product design and marketing strategies that are based upon the economy of scope exhibited by CIM/FMS Manufacturing.

INTRODUCTION - TRENDS AND EVOLUTION IN MANUFACTURING

Manufacturing, as a technology and as an industry, is undergoing substantial and significant changes. These changes must be viewed as both a logical extension of the trends and innovations in manufacturing since the industrial revolution and as a revolutionary discontinuity that will result in a new style of manufacturing operations and a new role for manufacturing as a competitive weapon and an integral component of the strategy of the business. This paper will review the evolution of manufacturing from craftsmen to CIM; the ongoing changes in product and market characteristic; the capabilities of CIM (essentially flexibility at low cost); and the competitive strategies that build upon the strength of CIM investments and operations.

Looking back over the history of industrial technology, we can observe three sets of trends:

A. A change in basic resources of manufacturing, from an initial dependence upon human labor and human intelligence to efforts to replace human labor with machines while still relying upon human intelligence to the replacement of human intelligence with machine intelligence and its integration with machine labor. In effect, the information technology revolution is applied to engineering and production.

B. An evolution in manufacturing policy from specialization to mechanization to automation to integration.
                        and
C. Changes in the available science and technology including:

° Machines that perform more tasks in one place

° Multi-purpose machinery and facilities

° Smart tools that can communicate

° Data intensive systems

° Design and process data in machine readable form

° New materials and processes

° Increased scientific understanding of material and process behavior

Most of these changes are made possible and/or accelerated by the availability of low cost, sophisticated electronic computing controls and communications technologies.

Together, these changes in resources, policy and technology lead to manufacturing processes with increased levels of certainty, predictability and controlability. These processes make possible highspeed, continuous flow, high variety, just-in-time, zero inventory, point-of-use production systems, factories that have economies of scope rather than scale high levels of integration without loss of flexibility and the ability to support very aggressive competitive strategies.

This is the evolution of the factory from a mechnical to an information system. One that substitutes _information_ for tooling, inventory, space, labor, supervision, time, movement and vertical integration. From a system where we manage people, materials and costs to one where we must manage information, change and speed. Thus, the CIM factory should be seen as botha logical continuation inthe historical evolution of the replacement of human capabilities with machines and as a revolution in which new technology that is fundamentally different from the traditional allows us to perform old tasks more efficiently _and_ to create goods and services not possible with traditional mechanical technology.

Manufacturing is in the midst of a very exciting time. Production processes are moving inexorably toward flexibility - driven by both the technology and the changes in products and markets that require flexibility and innovation. To a large extent, information technology is allowing manufacturing to become a service business!!!

THE PARADOX OF INNOVATION VERSUS PRODUCTIVITY

The technical and economic constraints that come with traditional manufacturing technology and operations management techniques forces most capital intensive businesses to regard innovation and productivity as a "trade-off". The general attitude in operations is that "change costs money." Therefore, if we minimize change of any kind: in the product, in the process, in the production schedule, in the people we deal with, and so on, and focus on the efficient use of our resources (doing tranditional tasks better), costs will be minimized and the business will be profitable. We achieve "productivity" by replacing human labor with machinery and human intelligence with special tooling and complex material handling devices that trade flexibility for the low production costs that come with long runs of a standard product.

The traditional "economy of scale" factory derives its productivity from a combination of physical and organizational _size_ which reduces the investment cost per unit of installed capacity, _volume_ which spreads fixed costs over a large number of units, _standardization_ which reduces both information and

technology requirements and _experience_ which reduces costs through _repetition_ (learning) over time. Unfortunately, this factory cannot respond to the rapid changes that are occurring in today's marketplace, the new competitive pressures and the increased complexity characteristic of the "augmented" (1) product needed today - the product that gives customers enhanced value through variety, uniqueness, customization, quality, fashionability, just-in-time delivery, and other such "intangibles."

The "generally accepted" strategic manufacturing rule has been, "as a product matures, we standardize the design and switch our innovation effort from product to process development" to developing a low cost, but utilizing traditional techniques, a relatively inflexible production system. We strive for a factory that operates with perfect reliability and predictability, minimum labor content, level production rates, high economic order quantities and balanced flows, high quality and high production rates. (2) Unfortunately, this highly productive factory often comes on-stream just as the product reaches the maturity stage of its life cycle. Soon we are left with a "perfect" but rigid factory and a rapidly aging product. This experience, repeated too often to be ignored in the decision making of most firms, has led to a trade-off between capital investment and both product and process innovation, because innovation obsoletes capital investment far too soon, especially if interest rates are high or capital scarce.

In turn, this leads executives to a trade-off between innovation and productivity. Innovation is just not compatible with productivity as we traditionally define it. Given the economics of traditional production technologies, large scale change has very high risks. These economics have led us to a risk averse and incremental approach to new technology and innovation. Figure 1 offers a visual summary of this problem.

In effect, the factory has become a barrier to further product innovation. Our response is marketing efforts that attempt to lengthen the product life-cycle through development of new market segments or small product changes. Efforts that will allow us to utilize a factory that has high capital investment, but low operating costs and is dedicated to a specific product design for a longer time period. This will increase the return on our original investment considerably. The marketing literature is filled with aricles on how to extend the life cycle of your product. (3) But, nobody really wants to keep an old product in the marketplace. What the marketing experts really offer is a set of techniques for keeping an old (or, in fact, not so old) process and distribution system that is rigidly designed for high productivity manufacturing and distribution of a particular product, useful for a longer period of time, whether or not the market still wants the product.

The premise of this paper is that the new manufacturing technology, the application of digital electronics to all aspects of manufacturing, physical process control, material handling, production planning and control and the entire knowledge work cycle of design, manufacturing and distribution, has fundamentally changed the economics of manufacturing from "scale to scope" and allows us to relax the traditional constraints and, in fact, to change the trade-off between volume and variety, between costs and flexibility. In the "Factory of the Future" continual innovation is productivity and is the only way to compete in the evolving global marketplace for both consumer and industrial products.

The problem is not one of being wrong about manufacturing decisions in the past. In fact, the choices of standardization, scale and long life cycle with few innovations were correct and highly profitable, given the available production technology. The danger lies in learning from experience. Continuing to do the things that were correct in the past in the face of changing market trends and a revolutionary discontinuity in production technology and economics. (4)

UNDERSTANDING CIM

To understand the implications of modern manufacturing, two basic ideas require consideration. The first is that the new manufacturing technology is fundamentally different in design, in operation, and in capability, from the equipment, process and technology that we are accustomed to in traditional factories. The new technology is smarter, faster, close-coupled, integrated, optimized and flexible. We are going to have to become accustomed to a whole new lexicon of buzz words, very different from those that we used in traditional manufacturing and engineering. The new factory not only does traditional tasks differently, it can perform tasks not possible in the traditional factory. This means that many of the opportunities that we face, the management styles we need to use, the strategic options that are available to us, and the production decisions that we have to make are going to be contrary to the experience of past successes.

Secondly, manufacturing is rapidly becoming a science-based activity, with high potential for revolutionary change - well beyond what is considered even today as the state of the art. We are about to go beyond the situation where to say, "I'm a manufacturing engineer," was a euphemism for not having a college degree and for coming up from the plant floor. The level of scientific and technical capabilities required to truly understand how to design, manage and optimize the kinds of factories we are discussing are well beyond even what most college-trained manufacturing engineers possess. Trends in materials science, control theory, and artificial intelligence, combined with the application of computers and communications technology and information science techniques will lead us to the new concept of manufacturing at its most powerful level.

Computer-integrated manufacturing (CIM) embraces fully integrated, close-coupled, high variety but continuous-flow systems in which lead times for new product introductions or improvements will be drastically reduced. Work-in-progress inventories will practically disappear; costly final-goods inventories, used to buffer the factory from the uncertainties of the marketplace, will not be as necessary; and both direct and indirect labor will be substantially reduced.

A word of warning is appropriate, however, the new technology is a computer-aided way to do the things we always recognizzed as necessary to run an effective factory. But, if management is not running an effective factory now, no amount of computer automation is going to help. If the industrial engineering is sloppy, if the standards are loose, if the layout is poor, if the production planning and control systems are not up to the standards of today's best practices, if the product designs are old - then simply putting everything on the computer is not going to help very much. The advent of the new technology allows us to do these things better, and provides a stimulus for thinking through proper methods, procedures and management techniques.

The CIM factory is a paperless factory. It is a combination of computer-controlled hardware that is adaptable, flexible and multi-functional, and paperless knowledge work capabilities that allow us to manage large amounts of information in real time; to handle variety, quick change, and flexibility, and to take advantage of the true power of the new factory hardware. One without the other is not sufficient. Quick-change hardware without an information system that allows one to keep track of variety will cause trouble, and a fancy information system that is faster than hardware can change is not going to deliver its full value.

We also need to rethink most of our traditional concepts of factory organization, plant layout, facilities location, choice of process technology and equipment, production planning and control techniques, degree of standardization of product designs, length of run, size of batch, line versus staff responsibilities, the factory's focus or lack of it, the means for introducing new technology into existing systems, how to measure productivity and performance, and the training and skills needed by managers and professionals. Everything is up for reappraisal.

That is not to say that everything is going to change. It is to say that everything has to be looked at with a fresh eye to find out whether or not it has to change. The science and technology of manufacturing are becoming much more complex and far more powerful. We are developing a better understanding of the scientific underpinnings of production. This comes from better knowledge of the behavior of solid-state materials under various process conditions. As an analogy, we might ask why chemical companies have been willing to invest hundreds of millions of dollars in relatively unproven new process technology plants. It is, in my view, because we know enough about the behavior of matter in the fluid state to be able to design and optimize a new process on paper and in the computer, and to build a test-scale pilot plant before companies make large-scale investments. We do not have many pilot plants for mechanical-based technologies; nor do we have a sense of confidence in our scale-up factors. But we are getting there. We are beginning to learn more about how to simulate factory operations. We are beginning to get better analytical tools. We certainly know more now about the behavior of materials than we are using in the design of factory and manufacturing systems. Control theory, artificial intelligence, measurement and sensing capabilities are all advancing at a very rapid rate.

This increasing scientific base overall is leading toward a factory with reduced process uncertainty. Information always reduces uncertainty; and this is what is happening in the CIM factory. We are moving toward what has been called data-intensive manufacturing. Data reduces uncertainty and that, in turn, makes the factory more predictable and more controllable, much more like a chemical plant, but as I will explain later, with some very important differences in its fundamental economics and technology.

The application of electronic computers, communications technology and information science to all aspects of manufacturing, from control of the physical conversion and movement of materials to the design, planning and managerial knowledge work of the factory, is, of course, becoming more common. Add to this the concepts of group technology and the availability of three-dimensional geometric models that link computer-aided design and engineering to computer-aided manufacturing and computer-assisted manufacturing; making factories predictable, controllable and subject to mathematical modeling and optimization - that is to say, a science-based manufacturing system.

This new manufacturing will be at its most powerful when the computer and communications technologies are used with increased scientific understanding of materials and processes to link production processes and management tasks in that fully integrated, close-coupled, continuous-flow, still utopian (but not for much longer) factory of the future. Computer-integrated manufacturing is central to the factory of the future - a combination of hardware and software and a data base describing the physical phenomena that allows someone to write a computer program that models the factory, and communications to provide on-line, moment-by-moment schedule and performance optimization, and dynamic reallocation of resources. It is, in a sense, the "perfect information" factory. We are not quite there yet, but at least now we can set the standard for the future.

We are switching from an era in which we produced large volumes of standard products on specialized machinery to systems for the production of a wide variety of similar products in small batches - even one at a time - on technology that is standard but multimission, flexible, and tailored to the particular design through software. When information is in machine-readable form, rather than built into conveyors or pipes or cams and gears, we have the flexible capabilities of the factories we are talking about. These combinations of computer systems and chemical-plant flows with their attributes of scope, flexibility and close-coupling will allow U.S. industry to respond to the market pressures of the future.

ECONOMY OF SCOPE AND FACTORY OPERATIONS

The key to understanding the opportunities presented by flexible manufacturing is a set of production economics concepts called economy of scope. Economy of scope allows for low-cost variety of output, and this means that the cost of producing a bundle of different product configurations on a particular piece of multimission equipment is the same as, or, more likely, less than the cost of producing the same number of pieces of identical design on specialized equipment designed for that particular product configuration.

The best example is a simple numerical control machine tool or CNC machining center. Such a tool can equally well make 12 of one product design in a row, or one each of 12 different designs in random order, provided those 12 different designs have been incorporated into its software. Essentially, this moves the fixed cost per design away from the plant floor and back to the engineering stage - and leads us to some generalizations on the design and characteristics of the factory of the future. A factory based on economy of scope rather than of scale will require a switch in management emphasis from minimum cost to maximum effectiveness and profitability. It will entail a very real change in the way we talk about productivity and in the role of the factory manager.

In practice, these factories could operate with an economic order quantity of one. Variety will have no cost penalty, at least on the production floor, but cost per unit will be very sensitive to volume because total costs are essentially fixed. The factory will be capable of high levels of accuracy and repeatability. However, these cost-of-variety advantages will do little good for a company that is selling long runs of standard products with (assumed) long life cycle.

The factory is going to be essentially unmanned, capable of rapid changes in design and in production rates - probably more capable than are its managers. Quality will be built in from the beginning. Product decisions will be based on "joint cost" rather than "marginal cost" economics. If the factory is thought of as a computer system, capacity additions will be in relatively small increments. Once the basic computer capability has been built, the software to add another milling machine or another robot card or another loop on the line can be in place quickly enough to eliminate any long--range capacity planning concerns. We are going toward what is essentially virtually unlimited capacity, analogous to "virtual memory" in a computer system.

"Traditional line managers "responsibilities for productivity will move to what we now consider "staff"; or, alternatively, we had better redefine who is staff and who is line and who is responsible for productivity. Management's attention will be focused on extensive and very expensive preproduction activities, rather than on the plant floor.

New concepts of traditional engineering and production management will be needed as well. The manufacturing manager of the future will have to shift attention from the traditional narrow focus on productivity and unit material and labor costs to: 1) integration within the factory and integration among R&D, engineering, the factory, marketing and distribution; 2) innovation, both process innovation and product innovation; and 3) strategy for the manufacturing function and the contribution of manufacturing to the strategic thrust of the firm as a whole. Let us examine briefly how the manager's working environment and decision-making structure will change.

For the old factory, sound operating principles and management techniques consonant with the old assumptions were developed. Centralization, large plants, balanced lines, smooth flow, standard product design, low rate of change, and inventory as a decoupler from the market were all desirable characteristics of the "good" factory.

The new factory will be marked by an entirely different set of desirable operating characteristics: decentralization, disaggregation, flexibility, rapid conversion of product lines produced, surge and "turn-aroundability," responsiveness to innovation, production tied to demand, multiple functions, and close-coupled systems. These represent sharp changes both for practitioners of manufacturing engineering and teachers of manufacturing management. The new factory will change the definition of productivity to one based on these variables; from a cost focus to a profitability focus.

Other demands to be put on the new factory and included in the definition of productivity are: minimal downtime for maintenance; maximum product-family range; the ability to adapt variability in materials and process conditions; the ability to handle increasingly complex product designs and technology into the existing systems with minimum disruption and minimum cost. The factory of the future is as likely to be a high-cost factory (capable of dominating the fashion market segment through rapid product design change) as a low-cost price leader. A narrow preoccupation with cost and traditionally measured productivity will not get us where we need to go. The good news, however, is that the new glogal marketplace demands flexibility and fast response that CIM technology offers and will, in the long run, penalize firms that do not invest in these capabilities.

THE CHANGING MARKETPLACE

A trend toward shorter product life cycles is the most important of the far-reaching changes taking place in the marketplace. We need to stop using the term "product life cycle" and start using the term "product half-life", defined as: "How many months will it be before half the units you are ever going to sell are going to be sold?" Not everything is going to a less than a year life cycle like a video-game or a microchip; but within the culture of a particular business we are seeing product life cycles shrinking to anywhere from one-half to one-third of their former lengths. Add to this much greater product variety and choice in the market-mostly driven by the internationalization of markets, sources of production, and sources of new product ideas and innovation (5).

There are many more competitors today and they complete on a global scale. They are matched by far more sophisticated customers who have little loyalty to their traditional suppliers. They demand innovation and reliability and just-in-time delivery, as well as quality, unique design and low price. We need only to look at the changes in the vendor-supplier relationship in the automobile industry to begin to see the trends that are developing. These trends add up to a more fragmented marketplace in which many of the segments are going to be too small to support a traditional factory based on the economies of scale.

The product is also changing as a result of far more complex technology; cameras that talk, appliances that include computers, engines that use ceramics, and, my favorite example, the running shoe. (The tennis sneaker and its evolution into the running shoe is a good example of what can happen in many traditional industries.) Finally, the product development cycle is shrinking - in some cases to as little as 20 percent of its former time. Months now replace years for a new product to emerge from R&D and engineering/design.

This poses an important challenge to manufacturing. There is less time to get ready to manufacture a product that you haven't seen before; and there is less time to recoup the investment in any specialized kind of equipment and tooling required to manufacture that product at a reasonable price. These are new demands that can only be met with sophisticated production processes that are more than a linear extension of the old ways of doing things. Speed and flexibility are the only possible solutions to this dilemma.

Today, we need to develop a strategy of adding value to the production ways that are deeply embedded into the manufacturing process. We need products that are hard, if not impossible, to copy without making an investment in sophisticated production processes. We need products that can't be "knocked-off" in a low, labor-cost environment. We see increasing customization, market fragmentation, and truncated product development and life cycles for the same reason.

These market and product changes require far more sophistication, capability and innovation on the part of the production process than is now typical. The good news is it is possible - not cheap, and not instantaneously available - but possible.

STRATEGIES FOR MAXIMIZING VALUE IN CIM BASED BUSINESSES

The changing marketplace plus the new operating characteristics and the changing criteria for manufacturing success lead to a set of new strategies for maximizing the value of investments in CIM technology that are "counter-intuitive" to what we usually teach in engineering and business schools and also to the things that worked well in the past.

It starts with: _invest_ _in_ _flexibility_ - not just in the flexibility of machining or assembly but in the flexibility of the organization as a whole - flexibility in research, engineering, marketing and distribution, and strategic planning.

Once you have that flexible capability, you have to take control of the marketplace. Deliberately _truncate_ _the_ _product_ _life_ _cycle_. Create a product life cycle that is so short that by the time a competitor has a "knock-off" product, it is clear to the customers that it is not the most advanced product available. If a slightly more advanced or a clearly newer product is available at a reasonable cost, people will buy it! And if you have a real economy of scope, flexible, manufacturing system, you don't have to trade off newness vs. product cost. Then, customers will stay with you and the rewards for imitation as opposed to innovation are going to decrease and the rewards for being innovative, for being the "first mover," are going to increase. Next, we need to _proliferate_ _the_ _range_ _of_ _products_ to the extent of customizing them one-by-one so that no customer ever has a reason _not_ to go to you for whatever they need. You don't allow "cherry picking" around the product niches and you don't allow "cherry picking" around the geographical niches; you deliberately _fragment_ _the_ _market_ into segments so small that they can't support a traditional economy-of-scale based factory. Do the things that prevent competitors from coming in and competing in your market without having to make the same high levels of investment; not just capital investment but the human and organizational investment, in flexibility.

Next, I would argue for deliberately complicating the product. It goes against everything that we learned and teach in value engineering and reliability engineering and production management. But if the product is simple, it is easy to copy and there are no barriers to entry and no switching costs. What I really mean by "complicate the product" is to gradually embed the uniqueness of the product more and more deeply into the manufacturing process, so that it can't be copied except by making that same kind of investment in flexibility. To add value through service and innovation capabilities of the process rather than of the product design and technology.

Finally, once you achieve flexibility at low cost, you clearly have to compete broadly across a wide range of market segments and a wide range of products in order to keep that flexible manufacturing system (and that flexible company) busy 24 hours a day, 7 days a week because you are working with an almost 100 percent fixed-cost manufacturing system. In turn, this will put tremendous burdens for managing variety and flexibility on the marketing and distribution capabilities of the firm.

In effect, this is a "service" strategy for manufacturing that depends for its success, on the inability of competitors to "clone" or imitate a service (such as Just-In-Time delivery) as compared to the relative ease of "reverse engineering" a product design - especially one that has been based upon the principles of simplification and "design for manufacturability." We must develop a new set of marketing tactics that are based upon manufacturing flexibility.

Management will have to ensure that marketing and R&D keep ahead of markets, controlling change if possible, dealing with new products, new processes and new relationships between the two.

Cherished marketing concepts like segmentation, positioning and penetration will have to go to rework - or scrap.

The question will no longer be "Can the factory make this for us?" It will become "Can marketing and R&D develop the most profitable mix and variety of products that can be sold?"

Further, these issues will have to be tackled in a market where:

° Production rates are closely tied to short-term fluctuations in demand, reduced inventory and warehousing costs.

° Distribution channels proliferate with direct sales, application engineers, systems houses, distributors, value-added resellers and mill supply houses.

° Advertising and promotion shift toward process and capability rather than product.

° More "skim" pricing and fewer "mature" products.

Many factory managers have gotten where they are today relying on a set of poorly articulated assumptions about what the factory can and cannot do. What these managers have done well is manage long runs of standard products over long periods of time. Change has been barred at the door.

The very principles that served them so well for so long are wrong for the future. But, it will be very difficult for these managers to reverse course. This is the challenge for the business schools, boards of directors, bankers, investment analysis (and venture capitalists), recognize the potential in CIM technology and to create the strategies and organizational structures and corporate cultures that can realize the full value of investments in flexible production technology.

MAKING IT HAPPEN

Achieving all this requires a top-down strategic approach. This kind of innovation is not going to bubble up from the plant floor. There has to be commitment; starting with the board of directors and implemented across the organization. This means that a firm must have a well-thought-out strategy before it can effectively justify and utilize a "factory of the future." We must ask: What business are we in or what business do we want to be in? And what must we be able to do well to be successful in that business? And then, how can we acquire the necessary skills?

The most important starting point is the realization that low cost (productivity in the traditional definition) is a necessary but not sufficient condition for competitive advantage and sustainable profitability. That a so-called "high cost" factory that offers rapid response to customer demand may be the most profitable one. And, that CIM technology <u>breaks</u> the linkage between volume and cost; and eliminates the factory as a barrier to rapid product innovation and aggressive customer service relationships. In summary, CIM allows manufacturing to become a "service business."

FOOTNOTES

1. For a discussion of the "augmented product concept" as a basis for production differentiation see "Theodore Levitt, <u>The Marketing Imagination</u>, New York; the Free Press, 1983 p. 81-84.

2. William J. Abernathy, <u>The Productivity Dilemma</u>, Baltimore: The Johns Hopkins University Press, 1978, p. 388.

3. See for example, Harry W. McMahan, "Like Sinatra, Old Products Can, Too, Get a New Lease on Life," <u>Advertising Age</u>, 25 November 1974, p. 32. A good article for putting this issue into context is "A Strategic Perspective on Product Planning," by George S. Day, <u>Journal of Contemporary Business</u>, Spring, 1975, pp. 1-32.

4. For a thorough discussion of this point, see Robert B. Reich, <u>The Next American Frontier</u>, New York: Books, 1983.

5. See <u>Fortune</u>, March 5, 1986, "High-Speed Management for the High-Tech Age" by Susan Fraker.

FIGURE 1

INNOVATION VS. PRODUCTIVITY IN THE PRODUCT AND PROCESS LIFE CYCLES

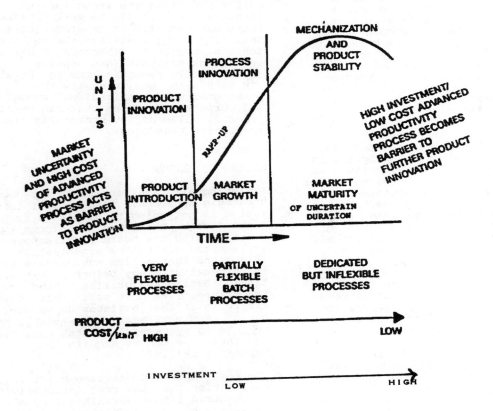

CHANGES IN COMPUTER USE AS JUST-IN-TIME WAS IMPLEMENTED IN A MANUFACTURING PLANT

Vinod K. Kapoor

Challenger Electrical Equipment Corp.

750 Boling Street
Jackson, MS. 39225

ABSTRACT

The purpose of this presentation is to share the changes in the use of the computer as a result of just-in-time implementation in the Westinghouse plant at Asheville, North Carolina during 1984 to 1987. Just-in-time enabled considerable simplification in the method of assembly, parts manufacture, storeroom management, engineering and keeping score. These changes had a profound impact on the plant's computer use.

INTRODUCTION

In June 1984, the Asheville plant of Westinghouse Electric Corporation made a commitment to embrace the just-in-time philosophy. I happened to be the plant manager when this decision was made and was closely involved with implementing the necessary changes.

Using just-in-time, the plant made giant strides over the next few years in:

- increasing on-time performance to over 90%
- reducing cycle times two to four times
- cutting product warranty costs by 60%
- increasing productivity by 70%
- reducing inventories by 60%
- and, freeing up more than half the plant.

As various concepts inherent to just-in-time manufacturing were implemented, one area that found itself playing a significantly different role, was the management systems department and the computer. Before I discuss these changes, let me give you some background information:

BACKGROUND

Prior to the conversion to just-in-time, Asheville was what one would call a conventional manufacturing plant. It was producing a multitude of control products for various customers. These products fell under the categories of medium voltage assemblies, low voltage assemblies, excitation assemblies, and control components. Our customers were spread throughout the United States.

Though a comparatively new plant, Asheville was using traditional manufacturing techniques to fabricate, machine and assemble parts into finished products. Further, these operations were spread throughout a plant and that was run on a cost center basis.

The system used to build products was also traditional. Typically, orders for the end products found themselves being held in the office. Once a month these were transformed into a firm shop load or schedule. These were then run through the computer based Materials Requirement Planning (MRP) system to generate material requirements. Feeder shop schedules and purchase orders followed. Assembly schedules for various cost centers were developed and, through a lot of coordination and effort, finished products eventually were shipped to customers.

Asheville's performance was about par with many American facilities producing similar products. But lately problems had started to surface. Inventories were considered high, cycle times long, product warranty costs excessive and customer service left something to be desired. Further, the business environment of the late seventies and early eighties, coupled with competitive pressures, had begun to erode into its profits.

As many of us can vividly recall, the seventies was the era when manufacturing experts throughout America were prophesying that those businesses would be competitive in future who had their plants highly mechanized. Further, these "factories of the future" were just around the corner. Many corporations heard this and quite a few started investing heavily in automation and computers.

Westinghouse-Asheville was no exception. To solve its problems, it too started to upgrade its manufacturing techniques by purchasing robots, computer controlled equipment, and high speed computers. Bigger computers were installed, numerous terminals placed throughout the factory, and the services of quite a few systems analysts sought. But, as time went by, it became evident that in spite of these large investments, payback was yet to materialize. It is worth pointing out here that Westinghouse-Asheville was not alone in this realization. Others in Corporate America had begun to learn the same lesson.

Also, the turn of the decade witnessed the surfacing of some new manufacturing ideas. These included the concepts of

KANBAN, PULL SYSTEM, SINGLE MINUTE EXCHANGE OF DIES, LOW LOT MANUFACTURE and QUALITY CIRCLES. Further, as the Japanese began to make in-roads into the American market, their success got attributed to their superiority in manufacturing. The phrase JUST-IN-TIME began to get heard more and more.

By early 1980, a couple of plants in Westinghouse had begun to experiment with just-in-time. These techniques, though originally planned to reduce inventories and improve productivity, began to show some other benefits -- improved on-time performance and shorter manufacturing cycle times. These successes and its disenchantment with the progress made to date, led Asheville to convert itself into a just-in-time facility.

During the months that followed, considerable simplification was achieved in the method of assembly, parts fabrication, storeroom management, purchase of parts, material control, engineering and accounting to name a few. Hardly an area was left untouched. Let us look at a few of these and notice the impact they had on the plant's computer use.

PRODUCT ASSEMBLY

Perhaps the best way to describe what we did is to look at a specific product line -- medium voltage assemblies, which is marketed under the trade name Ampgard.

Ampgard is a complex electrical product that is modular in design. It is custom engineered and built on a job-order basis. In the past its modules were manufactured in six different cost centers under six individual supervisors. Along with that went six different production schedules, each with their own start and stop dates.

By embracing the FOCUSED FACTORY concept of just-in-time, we took all the six operations and physically moved them to one area. Then by rearranging the work area, streamlining the order flow and using only one production schedule, we greatly simplified the method of manufacture.

Gone now was the need to create six production schedules. Gone also was the need to coordinate various sub-assemblies with the final assembly. Gone was the need to keep track of production of the six cost centers. Gone was the need to track work-in-process inventory as it moved from one cost center to another. Gone was the need to track efficiencies of the six production groups, etc., etc. The net result of this simplification was a reduction in the information requirements to assemble Ampgard. This in turn meant we could get by with less computer memory and fewer CRTs.

Let us now look at some of the specific improvements made.

By physically moving all the six operations into one, we created in effect a "factory within a factory". This mini-assembly plant -- as I prefer to call them -- had its own mini-storeroom, its own work stations, its own packaging area, and all of this connected by conveyers so as to minimize material handling.

Modular steel frames, fabricated daily in small lots, are today delivered from the feeder plant to the mini storeroom. Electrical components, sub-assemblies and wire harnesses are then put in each frame by a "picker". These kits are then ready to be sent down to one of eight assembly stations.

It is important to know that no orders in the "traditional" sense are issued to the sheet metal shop to build the four styles of frames. Instead, the KANBAN SQUARE concept of just-in-time was implemented in which space is reserved in the Ampgard mini-storeroom to accommodate only a specific number of frames for each style. Each day it is the responsibility of the frame welder to note how many frames have been used. This then is his signal to weld more frames -- with the quantity being only what was consumed the previous day. If no frames of a particular style were consumed yesterday, no frames are welded today.

The frame welder's area has been set up to accommodate all the parts necessary to build the different frame styles. Their replenishment was set up on a KANBAN system -- a just-in-time concept. As parts get consumed, depending on the usage of frames in the Ampgard mini-assembly plant, kanban cards are forwarded to the punch presses for part fabrication. It is the responsibility of the punch press operators to produce only the quantities specified on these cards and then deliver the parts to the frame welding station.

The fabrication of a part consumes raw material. This triggers raw material kanban cards into action and these then become the input for the purchasing department to order raw materials. Outside vendors were developed who could replenish daily only the quantity specified on these raw material kanban cards. Also, these materials had to be 100% good as all incoming steel inspectors had been eliminated.

With the above system, it is the need to build a customer order that triggers the usage of a frame. This in turn "pulls in" the need to weld a frame which in turn pulls in the need to fabricate the component parts and which in turn pulls in the need to purchase materials from outside vendors. Another name for all of this is the PULL CONCEPT of just-in-time. Unlike the traditional PUSH CONCEPT which would have scheduled every operation independent of when the assembly department needed the parts to build the end product, the pull concept makes the various operations only produce when the actual parts get consumed down a line.

As you can see, this is a far simple and more radically different system and one whose dependency on the computer is almost negligible. The use of this concept expanded to many more parts, reduced dramatically the need of the computer on Asheville's shop floor.

The ASSEMBLY VILLAGES are another integral part of every mini-assembly plant. They are used to supply harnesses and sub-assemblies. Unlike sub-assembly stations in a traditional environment, they are physically part of each focused factory and set up to handle the specific needs of their own mini-assembly plants. The various sub-assemblies were also set up on the pull system. Close coordination between the picker of the mini-storeroom and the assembly village operators ensures just-in-time delivery. These villages in turn get parts by kanban from the feeder department for those self-manufactured and the master storeroom for those bought-outside.

Each of the eight assembly stations is a self-contained area capable of complete assembly and wiring. They were efficiently designed to accommodate air tools, hardware bins and in future will have their own test box. Also, the work stations can be raised or lowered to facilitate individual assembly.

Each station was also designed to have its own pre set-down area or kanban square. Because of this there are always two units of work at each work station -- one on the work bench being assembled and another in the kanban square waiting to be worked on next. This ensures there will be no idle time due to lack of work -- an empty kanban square signaling the picker to send down one unit of work, non-emptiness saying "do not send any work".

The employees at the work stations are expected to assemble and wire and will in future also test -- unlike in the past where they performed only one specialized task. Getting people to perform MULTIPLE TASKS, another just-in-time concept, has not been easy. We have had to spend considerable time communicating and working with them so that they understand their new role.

Once the frames are assembled, they are moved to an intermediate staging area where various frame modules are bolted together to build the final Ampgard. Some more assembly and wiring is done and then the product is ready for final testing. After this it is packed and shipped to the customer.

The creation of the Ampgard mini-assembly plant and the use of various just-in-time concepts enabled us to:

- improve on-time performance to over 90%
- cut cycle times in half
- reduce product warranty 40%
- reduce space requirements 50%
- and improve productivity 50%.

Further, it significantly reduced the shop paperwork and information necessary to build Ampgards, resulting in reduced computer needs.

This process of creating focused factories, and applying other just-in-time techniques, was repeated over and over for the various families of products. The result was the creation of five mini-assembly plants, one feeder plant and one master storeroom.

PARTS MANUFACTURE

Let us look at in-house parts manufacture next.

Here we implemented MANUFACTURING CELLS. Instead of the traditional layout in which machines are grouped according to what functions they perform, e.g., all shears together, all punch presses together, all welders together, etc., manufacturing cells encourage machines representing different processes to be placed adjacent to one another. This concept allows one to focus directly on how to manufacture a part efficiently instead of using the indirect approach of improving the efficiency of each process independently and thereby hoping this will then result in the best method for parts manufacture. To illustrate the power of this just-in-time concept, let us look at an example.

Being a manufacturer of control assemblies, Asheville uses a lot of fabricated steel -- some of it low volume and some high volume. For the low volume steel parts, we decided to form a manufacturing cell. We connected our shears, mechanically controlled turret punch presses, press brakes and welders by a simple conveyor. Consequently there were now four separate machines operating as one. Today there are two such lines.

In the past, this equipment was spread all over the plant -- a factor which caused (i) excessive material handling between machines (ii) scheduling and follow-up of each machine independently (iii) bunching of orders and increasing of lot sizes (iv) long cycle times for part manufacture and (v) more importantly, inflexibility in handling emergencies. The introduction of the conveyor enabled us to make giant strides in resolving these problems.

For example, the shear operator is the only person given the production schedule. Sheared pieces flow to the turret punch press, the next machine on the line. Its important to note that the operator of this machine is given no schedule. That individual's job is to work on pieces as they arrive. The bending operation is next. Its operator too has no production schedule, but works on parts as they arrive. The welding operation -- next on the line -- works in a similar fashion. Final stop is the paint line. Completed parts are now ready to be delivered for assembly.

Through this process several things were learned. One was that there were too many raw material styles. Asheville began with 16 styles. Today, there are six. Another was the need to develop a JUST-IN-TIME VENDOR for sheet steel. Previously we purchased parts from five separate vendors, we often found machines with too much inventory or none at all, and we spent too much time expediting. Today, only one steel vendor is used who makes daily shipments. He visits the shop every noon and machine stoppages due to raw material stock-outs are indeed rare.

We also learned something about the importance of REDUCING SET-UPS -- another just-in-time concept. If the shear operator worked in low-lot quantities, the turret press operator was faced with a large number of set-ups. Work often backed up. This forced us to address the set-up issue. We found that we used over 90 different tools while our turret machine had room only for 32 at any one time. A TASK FORCE was formed from marketing, engineering and manufacturing with the explicit instruction not to leave the meeting until all parties had agreed on a common 32 tool configuration. Six hours later the meeting broke up with a recommendation that called for 31 tools -- one less than we had asked for.

With this accomplished there was no need to ever change tools. Whether the lot size was one or a hundred became less significant. It took us another 18 months to fully realize the benefits of this decision. This was because of the large number N.C. tape conversions that had to be implemented. As a side benefit, sizable savings are being realized today in lower total expenditure

for the purchase of tools. One further benefit -- engineering now designs parts so that the agreed turret needs no tool change. This is a major step towards PROCESS STANDARDIZATION -- another just-in-time concept.

Also, with the new line there was no need for an inspector. Each of the operators running their machines perform their OWN INSPECTION -- another just-in-time concept.

But as we were to find so often, the solution to one problem would often lead to another opportunity. No longer having the need to change tools, the turret punch press and press brake could be brought closer together. This allowed ONE OPERATOR TO RUN TWO MACHINES -- another just-in-time concept that further improved productivity. Also, we found that one shear could manage the load of two lines, allowing one to be removed! In fact, every month more ways were found to fine tune this line -- fine tuning that enabled us to reduce cycle times, reduce inventory, improve productivity, reduce rejects and be more flexible.

As can be seen from this example, adopting the manufacturing cell concept greatly simplified the information needs to manufacture low volume parts. Instead of scheduling ten machines and four work centers, now we were scheduling two lines! This in turn led to the simplification of routings on operation cards and resulted in reduced memory requirements for our computer's data base. Also, it was no longer necessary to track the work-in-process status of various parts as operations got completed at different machines. All of this helped to reduce our computer needs.

Further, to drive this low volume fabrication cell, we selected the kanban system. Since kanban was also the material replenishment system for the mini-assembly plants, one can now see the implementation of a simplified infrastructure to order and make materials that is solely driven by the rate at which customer orders get assembled and one that is totally under the control of hourly employees recycling kanban cards. The frequency at which parts get fabricated now did not have to depend on a computer generated schedule.

With this set-up, gone was the need for production planners. Gone was the need for production clerks. Gone also was the need for elaborate sheet metal schedules by machines and work centers. Gone was the need to track materials all over the fabrication shop. In fact, gone was the need for MRP to drive the feeder plant and this is the conclusion we came to one morning.

You can imagine the cultural shock in our organization when we decided to turn the MRP module off! Just a few years ago, it had been considered a key element in the building of our "factory of the future" and one to which considerable financial resources had been committed. It had played a very crucial role in the up-grading of our computer and had neces-sitated the build up of both management systems and other office staff to support its implementation. But once we turned the MRP module off, the days ahead showed that we could indeed operate a plant efficiently without it. In fact we found that kanban and manufacturing cells tied closely to the focused factories via the pull system, provided a more rewarding and cost effective alternative to running our plant.

MATERIALS STOREROOM

Prior to the implementation of just-in-time, Asheville had a centralized storeroom that received parts from outside vendors, in-house feeder operations and sub-assembly cost centers. Incoming inspectors insured that only good parts were stocked. The computer was used to designate material locations. As a result there existed multiple loca-tions for the same part. When materials were issued to the shop floor, the computer was updated by entering every item, the quantity and the job assigned to. To maintain system accuracy, the whole storeroom was fenced, with entrance restricted to authorized personnel only. As you may gather from this description, we had a random-storage-computer-con-trolled storeroom very much in vogue in many traditional plants.

Looking back at this, I can today point to some of its inherent drawbacks. First it was very big -- occupying a sizable portion of the total plant. Second it required a lot of resources in manpower, computer memory, and material handling equipment to run it. Third, its service response time was always a bone of con-tention between assembly personnel and storeroom attendants. And finally, it had become a bureaucratic institution more concerned with its own propagation and one that had lost sight of its true mission, namely, to supply materials to help ship products on time.

The implementation of just-in-time in the assembly and feeder operations impacted the physical layout as well as the modus operandi of this storeroom. What were these changes and what was their impact? Let us explore.

With the change to the focused factory concept, each mini-assembly plant ended up with its own mini-storeroom or MINI-MARKET as it is referred to in the

just-in-time jargon. This mini-market became the heart of the material flow system for its own mini-assembly plant. It receives material from the feeder plant, the main storeroom and the assembly villages -- with the replenish-ment system being kanban. For the Asheville plant this meant having five mini-markets.

The use of the cell concept in the feeder plant and the incorporation of the pull system between it and the mini-assembly plants made us set up a raw materials mini-market. The use of the kanban card to produce parts led us eventually to make each manufacturing cell person responsible to pull his own materials. With the development of just-in-time raw material vendors, we soon found that kanban raw material cards simplified material procurement dramatically and that the manufacturing cell personnel were the logical ones to turn these in. This meant that raw material issuing, ordering and replenishment could now be handled directly between feeder person-nel, purchasing and outside vendors and did not need the help of our traditional stores personnel.

Thus, the creation of mini-markets changed the role of the main storeroom dramatically. For the feeder plant, the main storeroom found itself providing no service at all, while for the mini-assembly plants it became a back-up source or SUPERMARKET as just-in-time implementors would like to call it.

With this new role of the main storeroom as a supermarket, it was natural for us to come to the conclusion that the best model for laying it out was the neighbor-hood grocery supermarket. That is, we should abandon the computer based random location system and use the GENERIC parts concept that emphasizes only one location per part with all parts belonging to the same family grouped together -- just like in the local grocery where there is only one location for a particular soup and all the different soups are grouped together.

Further, we found that as evolution progressed, we began to place more emphasis on VISUAL CONTROL rather than CRTs and computer printouts to tell us if we had materials in stock. In spite of our best efforts in the past, too often what the computer showed was actually not on the shelf.

The creation of the mini-markets and the supermarket, the use of kanban, and the introduction of generic layout and visual control, were to play a key role in help-ing us reduce inventories. As this happened, storeroom space shrunk from 54,000 square feet to 14,000 square feet

-- a 75% reduction; material handling vehicles were reduced from 67 to 22 -- a 67% reduction; the number of vertical racks came down from 450 to 90 -- an 80% reduction; and, one type of tote pan got reduced from 4,200 to 1,700 -- a 59% reduction.

Also, the dependence on the computer diminished. The elimination of the random storage concept meant there was no need to let the computer assign stockroom locations. Having fixed locations also meant one need not go to the CRT prior to picking a part to determine its possible locations. Since there was only one, employees ended up memorizing it by constant use. Visual control meant that rather than relying on computer prints, material could now be ordered by seeing when it was running low -- a method very similar to that used by housewives to replenish their kitchen supplies.

One more important development needs to be mentioned. As kanban became the recognized method of issuing parts to mini-markets, the traditional computer issue system to control inventories became very cumbersome. This was resolved when we implemented what we ended up calling FOUR WALL ACCOUNTING. Stated simply, it means that the four brick walls of a plant now become the new fences of the storeroom. This meant we no longer had to keep track of every move the material made -- right from the time it was received, through the various cost centers, until the product was finally shipped. We need now input only when materials are received in the plant and use the bill of material processor to electronically relieve inventory when a job gets shipped. This resulted in further reduction in computer use and helped free up clerical help to do more productive tasks.

In retrospect, the transformation of the traditional materials storeroom to a supermarket, the incorporation of various just-in-time techniques, and the use of four wall accounting, helped us reduce inventories, improve material availability and at the same time cut down the number of CRTs and computer memory to run the Asheville plant.

ENGINEERING

Making accurate information available and streamlining its flow was a natural evolution of creating mini-assembly plants. The focused factories made us develop information to fit their specific needs. For example, we found that the information needed to build a standard product was quite different from that needed for a custom engineered product. However, no matter what the product, the underlying emphasis was in three areas. First, providing minimum infor-mation to build it. Second, structuring this information to fit the method of manufacture. And third, developing a simplified order processing system to eliminate delays and inaccuracies.

Let us look at an example to illustrate this. In the case of one of our custom-engineered products -- air-conditioning controls -- our customers were eight mechanical OEMs. All of them sold air-conditioners into the same market. Yet due to their individual designs and unique approaches to the market place, each order got custom engineered by us. This caused the following problems: (i) long queuing delays in the office, (ii) numerous errors of interpretation with subsequent shop and field problems, (iii) constant customer complaints about deliveries and quality.

To address these issues, we formed a TASK FORCE of knowledgeable people from marketing, engineering and manufacturing. Their mission was to use a CLEAN SHEET approach and come up with a system that not only eliminated the drawbacks just described, but also complemented the modular method of assembly being used in the mini-assembly plant.

Asking themselves two questions: (i) what do our customers want? (ii) and how do we go about servicing them? led to the following system being implemented.

On receipt of an order, a check list called the input form is completed. Its purpose is to transform customer information into a uniform format. This process ensured that there is complete data to work with -- unfilled areas highlighting that information is incomplete and further clarification from the customer necessary.

The completed input forms are then entered into the computer to generate a top level bill of material. Enough checks were built in the system to safeguard wrong selection of parts.

This feature helped eliminate numerous engineering errors and encourage STANDARDIZATION in part selection -- a key just-in-time concept.

On receipt of the manufacturing infor-mation, the picker of the mini-assembly plant kits the necessary parts from the mini-market and sends them down the assembly line. Meanwhile in the computer, the top level styles get exploded into lower level parts and are assigned electronically to the specific job. Shop completion of the order is used to generate shipping papers, relieve inventory using the four wall accounting system, perform cost accounting transactions and print the invoice -- all within 24 hours.

As a result of implementing this, the number of engineers and technicians handling air-conditioning orders were reduced from seven to two -- a 71% reduction. Further, this streamlining helped cut the cycle times in the office two to six times. Many of our customers told us we were much more responsive now and able to deliver a higher quality product than ever before.

One such customer is McQuay - a division of SnyderGeneral Corporation. In the early eighties it decided to buy controls from one of our competitors. We made a strong effort after just-in-time implementation to regain their business. They liked our prices -- but were not sure of our ability to perform consistently as we now said we would. However, they agreed to give us a chance. All of that happened in mid-1986. I was pleasantly surprised when we received shortly thereafter a plaque recognizing our support and contribution.

KEEPING SCORE

The application of just-in-time enabled Asheville not only to improve its plant operations, but also simplify its system of keeping score.

We started by selecting a simple measurement system like output per day and displaying it openly. It was the responsibility of each mini-assembly plant supervisor to update this daily. A detailed chart was prominently displayed in each mini-assembly plant while another was placed outside the plant manager's office. Thus by walking to the various mini-assembly plants or going outside the plant manager's office, any employee knew precisely how we were doing.

To this, a few months later, was added the product warranty chart. Not only was a monthly graph displayed, but detailed charges incurred on specific jobs were also listed. To this was added the overtime chart. This showed the weekly overtime worked by every employee and the trend over the past year. Soon thereafter, a skills chart was added. This showed how cross-training efforts were progressing. In fact, more and more things got displayed in the open -- so much so that special bulletin boards were set up in every mini-assembly plant for this specific purpose.

In addition, monthly meetings were held with the plant manager. At these sessions I shared with all plant employees the prior month's sales, how much money was made, our on-time performance, the progress made to reduce inventories, improve product warranty,

etc. This dual approach of displaying VISUAL INFORMATION in the mini-assembly plants and monthly BUSINESS MEETINGS, helped our employees focus on a common goal and see that progress was being made on a continuous basis.

We also simplified many record keeping procedures. Let me share just three.

The labor reporting system was overhauled. In the past, employees recorded time they spent on various jobs. This was then input into the computer. Not only was this time consuming, but its accuracy was only as good as the effort taken to fill this conscientiously. It was too cumbersome to police and over the years had lost credibility as a source for making decisions. The creation of the mini-assembly plants enabled us to permanently assign employees to a mini-assembly plant. Now by charging all their salaries weekly to the respective mini-assembly plants, we had a far simpler and more accurate way of knowing the labor content of our various product lines.

The system of measuring cost center efficiencies was eliminated. In the past, we were busy trying to measure efficiencies of each plant section hoping this was the way to improve overall plant productivity. This approach served its time well. But now it had drawbacks. With the business environment the way it was, we could no longer allow section supervisors to produce parts so that they could generate high net allowed hours and thereby maximize their own efficiencies, not caring whether these parts were really needed. Also, we took this opportunity to eliminate the filing of transfer slips used as a basis to shift hours worked by direct hourly employees from productive to expense categories. Instead we concentrated on using total compensation as a percent of sales and sales billed per employee as a gauge to measure how productivity was improving.

The hourly payroll system was also simplified. In the past, a computer operator logged daily all the hours worked per employee. This formed the basis for payment. This was placed with an exception system. Now, once a week, the various shop supervisors turn in a report stating only the number of hours an employee was absent and the number he or she worked overtime. This report is signed by every employee prior to its being entered into the computer. The method of payment then boils down to subtracting from the base weekly wage the absence and adding in the overtime worked.

Today we can truly say that emphasis on visual reporting and the use of simplified accounting systems have complemented very nicely the many just-in-time concepts implemented in the shop. They helped us eliminate much paperwork and made us more efficient and cost effective.

CONCLUSION

The use of just-in-time at Westinghouse Asheville resulted in the gradual reduction of numerous non-value adding activities. As these were reduced or eliminated, the size of various departments got smaller. For example, for the materials department it meant reduction in the number of purchasing people, production planners, schedulers and storeroom attendants from 73 to 29 -- a 70% reduction. For the accounting department it meant reducing the size from 16 to 8 -- a 50% reduction.

Also, it meant that we did not need as big a computer system as we currently had. We found that we needed about 26 CRTs instead of 78 to run our business and that we could get by with less computer memory, allowing us to reduce our computer leasing costs by 75%. The need for six people to continuously update the data base was found to be redundant. In fact, we were pleasantly surprised to find that we could manage all plant MIS requirements with just two systems analysts, one computer operator and no business systems manager.

In conclusion, let me add that the use of just-in-time helped to simplify greatly the running of the Asheville plant. As one concept after another was implemented, we were continuously shocked to realize how complicated our original systems had become. Each implementation confirmed that this need not have been the case; that there was indeed a less complicated alternative, and one that in many cases was more effective and less costly.

Today, the computer plays a vital role in running the Asheville plant. But, instead of being the monster that it had once become, its power has been harnessed and being channeled daily to more productive use. Now it is helping Asheville become truly a "factory of the future" by making it accomplish its mission. And, that mission, incidentally, is: first, to be the best customer service plant in the industry; second, to have the reputation of building the highest quality products; and third, to turn in a respectable profit for Westinghouse.

BIOGRAPHICAL INFORMATION

Vinod K. Kapoor is Vice President of Standard Distribution Products Division, Challenger Electrical Equipment Corporation, Jackson, Mississippi, a wholly owned subsidiary of Westinghouse Electric Corporation. Prior to his current position he was Operations Liaison Manager for Westinghouse.

He received his MBA in Finance from Northwestern University. He holds a BS in Mechanical Engineering from the Indian Institute of Technology, Kharagpur, India and an MS in Industrial Engineering from the University of Wisconsin.

Since joining Westinghouse in 1968, he has held various management positions in Industrial Engineering, Manufacturing Engineering, Manufacturing Operations and Plant Management. During 1980 to 1987, while a Westinghouse Plant Manager, Mr. Kapoor successfully implemented two Just-In-Time conversions -- the first at Fayetteville, North Carolina and the more recent one at Asheville, North Carolina.

He is a dynamic speaker who has spoken to numerous organizations in the areas of Just-In-Time/Total Quality Control. He has also been published in several magazines, among them: Appliance Manufacturer, Production Engineering, Iron Age, Manufacturing Systems, Quality Progress, and Automation.

INTEGRATING MRP IN A JIT ENVIRONMENT

Robert Storrs
MRP II Implementation Manager

A. T. & T.
Denver Works
1200 West 120th Avenue
Westminster, Colorado 80234-3278

ABSTRACT

Just In Time (JIT) techniques have become the popular strategy for the turn around of American manufacturing. However, many firms have found that the best approach is the use of both Manufacturing Resources Planning (MRP II) and JIT. A.T.& T.'s Denver Works represents a successful user of both systems on its way to World Class Manufacturing status.

The modification and application of shop floor control to interface with a JIT pull system and the enhancements to the component storeroom are presented.

1583

INTRODUCTION

MRP II attempts to meet manufacturing objectives by detailed planning and tracking with continuous updates to plans based on feedback received through the system. It originated in the 1960s as a materials focused system called "small MRP" (Material Requirements Planning). During the 1970s, the system expanded its scope to become a closed loop system, Manufacturing Resources Planning (MRP II). Shop floor control and master production scheduling modules as well as formalized feedback loops were added.

Just In Time (JIT) manufacturing techniques were first collected as a comprehensive approach by Toyota Mfg. in the 1970s. JIT approaches many traditional problems with a new outlook and attempts to remove all waste and overhead in the production process. Quality, high velocity manufacturing, reduced inventory levels, pulling of inventory through manufacturing are basic concepts of these techniques.

Combining these two approaches to improving manufacturing has provided A.T.& T.'s Denver Works with special problems and far-reaching rewards.

A.T.& T. DENVER WORKS

A.T.& T.'s Denver Works is the sole manufacturing location for PBX (Private Branch Exchange) equipment for the A.T.& T. system. This product line includes the MERLIN family for small business, the System 25 for medium size business, the System 75 and the System 85 which will support customers requiring very sophisticated telecommunication needs with line sizes ranging from a few hundred to many thousands. Besides these major product lines, growth and service parts represent a significant part of the output of the factory.

The MERLIN family is a make-to-stock product while the rest of the major products are manufactured to customer order configuration. The products are primarily circuit packs, circuit pack carriers, cables, cabinets and consoles all assembled at Denver Works.

Denver Works was an early user of an MRP system. The original system implementation started in 1969 with the opening of the pilot factory. In 1985, however, the factory began a major project to replace that system with a modern, full featured MRP II system. After comprehensive evaluation, an internal AT&T system was adopted and installed. This installation and migration from the old system to the new system was the focus of materials management for 1986 and 1987. During this same time period, engineering introduced special projects to demonstrate a JIT pilot line in the factory.

Both systems saw much success and resulted in significant reductions in inventory levels. However, this success brought new challenges. How could we build on the successes and expand JIT to the rest of the manufacturing lines? How could we resolve the conflicts between JIT and MRP II to get the best of both worlds? When the path to JIT was going to take some time, how could we adapt MRP II to support many of the same goals?

COMPARISON OF JIT AND MRP

MRP II and JIT share many of the same goals. Both strive to fulfill the customer demand with high service levels. Both strive to keep inventory investment to a minimal level. Both attempt to smooth the flow of product through the manufacturing process. Both attempt to reduce overhead in support organizations. However, JIT goes beyond these common goals to assert itself in improving quality, reducing set-up times, ensuring machine operations via rigorous preventative maintenance and eliminating wasteful operations which have traditionally been seen as a natural part of the manufacturing operations.

Even in areas where the two systems share common goals, the methods used to accomplish these goals are often radically different. Traditional manufacturing has tried to reduce the cost of machine set-up per unit manufactured by running large lots and by using algorithms from MRP II to balance material carrying costs against the set-up cost to achieve the lowest cost balance. Contrast that with the JIT philosophy of working to reduce the set-up of the process until it is economic to run very small lots eventually, running mixed mode process with lot sizes of one. MRP II and traditional approaches have accepted problems and developed techniques to deal with them. JIT has taught us that we can change the solve problems. Many examples come quickly to mind. If a process has a quality problem, MRP II allows the user to assign a yield factor to insure planning is adequate for meeting established schedules. JIT gives us structure to examine the underlying quality problems and to work to resolve them. It is not true that traditional manufacturing does not try to solve such problems. But the methods are not part of an integrated philosophy. Additionally, allowing the systems to adapt to the problems reduced the visibility of the problems. A little additional inventory covers up the problem and "out of sight, out of mind."

MRP II and JIT also differ in approaches to controlling the flow of product through the manufacturing process. MRP II begins the control with a master production schedule which provides a forecast for independent demand and an explosion of dependent demand from higher levels in the bill of material. Shop orders are released. If storeroom picking is the first operation, material pick lists or "selects" are generated. The release of the select to the shop floor decrements storeroom inventory balance and increases work in process inventory for the assembly. A shop floor control module then schedules the shop work order against all other shop work orders and based on the techniques chosen provides the shop with a dispatching list. If all areas of the shop are able to follow the dispatch list, product will move through the shop in a smooth flow. If not, a replanning process must take place and new directions issued to the shop.

JIT focuses on planning only the final assembly process and tries to plan this operation to a predetermined rate which will meet the customer demand rate. This plan for final assembly is not only balanced to the customer demand, it is also smooth and constant over a short horizon. This allows manufacturing of the same items in the same quantities each day. Modification to these rates are made only when the customer demand rate changes. Once the final assembly operation is operating to a smooth program, pulling of subassemblies from supplying shops and vendors is begun. A pull system allows all operations to run at a matched rate without generating and updating complex plans.

While some might suggest MRP II be discarded and JIT installed in its place, one must recognize the strengths and weaknesses of each system. JIT is strong in managing the execution of short cycle manufacturing processes. This includes internal operations and outside vendors. However, MRP is strong in providing the planning necessary to manage long cycle manufacturing processes or long leadtime vendors. JIT is a path, not a system to be installed. Many of the conditions which make JIT work so smoothly do not happen overnight. MRP II is the tool for the transition.

The two approaches also have conflicts which make the application of MRP II and JIT to the same manufacturing operations a problem. JIT expects lot sizes to be equal to or less than the daily customer demand rate. Many MRP systems are still tied to weekly planning in weekly or greater lot sizes. "Bucketless" systems which attempt daily scheduling are driven to chaos by the fivefold increase paperwork.

DENVER WORKS STRATEGIES

While the basic approach taken at Denver Works may not be unique, many of the problems faced and solutions arrived at provide a look at how one factory was able to marry MRP II and JIT. As mentioned earlier, Denver Works found itself with two new systems, both of which had shown to be of value in obtaining our goals. We also found ourselves with new problems we had not expected. These problems were most acute in two areas. The first was the control of our ciruit pack production line. We modified shop floor control to march to the pull signals of a JIT final assembly process. The second was to enhance our component storeroom to support the increased demands put on its operation as we moved from weekly to daily schedules.

SHOP FLOOR CONTROL

After carrying out many manufacturing enhancements, the next step was to establish a daily final assembly schedule which allowed for a consistent production program in the assembly area and in the feeder shops (circuit pack assembly). A simple division of the weekly customer orders into five days resulted in a very unbalanced load on the circuit pack shop. To overcome this, a cabinet assembly sequencer was developed for us by Bell Laboratories. This program places the customer orders into a daily schedule trying to produce an even daily demand on all the circuit packs which can be ordered by a customer. The program makes multiple passes until the improvement between runs is not significant. This approach is an attempt to obtain a constant daily rate for circuit pack production - a basic requirement for successful JIT.

The next challenge was how to coordinate circuit packs production with the final assembly schedule. Traditionally, circuit packs have been made to a forecast, pushed to final assembly and expedited with hot list to meet actual customer order demand. JIT philosophy suggest the establishment of kanban queues between the circuit pack shop and final assembly also kanban queues within the circuit pack shop. Because of the variation in circuit pack demand and the large number of codes involved, the inventory in kanban queues would be substantial. Neither of these approaches appear satisfactory to us at that time. Pushing circuit packs through the process meant we never had the right packs in the right quantities while kanban would have meant buffer inventory larger than we wanted. Instead, we decided to modify the normal MRP II shop floor control module. First, all demand to shop floor control comes not from the master schedule, but from the actual daily customer order schedule. This assures the shop works to actual need and very quickly adapts to a new schedule if needed. Second, scheduling in SFC changed from critical ratio to earliest due. This helps insure that all the various circuit packs needed for one customer arrive at about the same time. Third, we removed priorities from the system, and the shop sees only what to do next based on product that has finished the previous operations. Fourth, the priorities of the shop are extrapolated into the storeroom to help insure that material selects are pulled and ready for the shop when they are needed.

What we have is a traditional SFC system that marches to a JIT drum. With reduced lot sizes, the circuit pack shop will make each day the exact customer need of each of the many codes.

STOREROOM

With the above processes in place, inventory levels were very quickly reduced. As many textbooks on JIT suggest, this will result in discovering rocks in the stream which block the smooth flow of production. We found a boulder. Our component storeroom was designed to pick weekly selects for each assembly and to complete that task within a specified week. Besides normal component picking operations, the storeroom also does the functions of sequencing taped, axial components, programming of PROMs, preforming component leads and kitting into presentation trays. As smaller lot sizes were introduced, the storeroom ran out of capacity. An evaluation of full JIT implementation for the shop showed that the storeroom needed to increase the component picks three-fold! Three times as many set-ups required on the machinery for sequencing, PROM programming and preforming! Not only was capacity a concern, an increase of threefold work in the storeroom would endanger the 98+% inventory balance accuracy level which had been achieved.

We looked at automatic storage and retrieval systems. However, few systems proved able to support the volume of picks required for daily schedules. The systems were also very costly and lacked flexibility for future directions in JIT. The JIT approach of eliminating the storeroom and delivering material directly to the shop floor was also judged impractical at this point. The decision was made to continue use of the traditional MRP supported storeroom, but to increase the capacity of the storeroom.

This effort took three directions. First, the set-up times for sequence machine were a bottleneck and required

reduction. Second, the actual component picking operation had to be done in less time. Third, operations in the storeroom had to be phased with daily shop schedules.

Sequence machines place in sequence on a taped reel, those specific components needed for insertion into a printed wiring board. The set-up involves removing components reels used in producing the previous sequence and mounting reels for the next sequence. These reels are mounted on heads. Even before small lots, set-up time was consuming half of the available time. To reduce set-up, two actions were taken. First, we installed two new machines and upgraded eight existing machines to eighty heads on each machine. This allowed for many more neads than any single sequence tape required. Second, Bell Laboratories developed software to minimize set-up y dedicating sixty of eighty heads on all machines. Sequences are then assigned to specific machines. The remaining heads are set up to specific requirements for the sequence being run. Set-up time was reduced to a maximum of 15 minutes with no more than five real changes for any sequence.

To reduce material pick time, new tools were developed for the storeroom. The heart of these tools is a computer controlled, select cart. The cart has electronic scales which can weigh components to over 99% accuracy. Attached also are a bar code reader and printer all controlled by a hand held computer mounted on the select cart. The hand held computer communicates with the central storeroom computer, an AT&T 3B2, via radio frequency transmission. A group of picks are down loaded to the computer which then begins to direct the work of the picker. The computer displays the next bin location. When the stock selector arrives at the location, he or she scans the bar code lable on the bin to validate the correct component. The computer loads the scale with the count and piece weight. The stock selector loads parts onto the scale until the correct quantity registers. A bar code label is printed and attached to the bag of parts for routing. This cart has reduced pick time by well over 50% with an increase in accuracy.

Having removed the major bottlenecks in the storeroom, the phasing of picking in the storeroom with the pull requests from the shop was next attacked. A special computer program was developed to match shop pull requests and daily schedules to open selects and provides the storeroom a schedule integrated with the shop demand. This eliminated "hot lists" and for the first time, put the storeroom on a daily schedule. With this report, the storeroom goal of providing a balanced 20% of the material picks each day could be accomplished. The next goal was to support the smaller and smaller lot sizes.

Often the exact daily demand cannot be predicted a week ahead when the demand is divided into lots and pick documents are created. This created imbalances between shop demands and the shop work order. We needed a change to the MRP II system! This change allows the master scheduler to release a material pick authorization for the entire week into a "bank account." Shop pull signals are then "withdrawn" from the bank account by the storeroom. The system produces the documents for the pick and down loads the information into the 3B2 computer for pick scheduling. By decoupling the master scheduler from the daily execution, the planning phases of MRP II do not have to deal with the complexities and volumes of details that daily schedules produce. The execution phases of MRP II and JIT are still able to run well in daily lot sizes.

RESULTS

Denver Works has seen many improvements over the past several years. Many have come as the result of MRP II implementation; many have come as a result of JIT implementation. But, all have come because of the extraordinary effort of people dedicated to success. Some of these improvements include:

Turn Over Ratio (TOR), the measure of how fast inventory is being transformed into final product for a customer, has moved from 2.5 to 10 at the end of last year. While this year has brought new problems, our goal is to exceed that level by the end of 1988.

Space needs in the factory and the storeroom have been reduced and have allowed us to take on additional work not previously done in the factory.

The cost of quality, a measure we use to track how effective we are in moving from an inspection based quality system toward "quality at the source", has been reduced. During this same time, our outstanding quality record has not suffered in the least.

Manufacturing lead times were reduced allowing us to change from an assemble to order environment to a manufacture to order environment by getting our manufacturing lead times less than our customer lead times. We have also been able to reduce our customer lead times by several weeks. Shipping performance has remained above our target goal.

In summary, JIT and MRP II have brought successes and new challenges. By learning to use the best of both and learning to let all the employees solve the problems, AT&T Denver Works has become a leader in becoming a World Class Manufacturer.

THE PAPERLESS FACTORY IN ACTION

Richard Dworak
Telecommunications Program Manager

Tandem Computers Inc.
19191 Vallco Parkway
Cupertino, California 95014-2525

ABSTRACT

Tandem Computers Inc., Watsonville, California plant has successfully increased capacity in a given plant size and continues to enhance their manufacturing capability. The paperless factory system was implemented to record and control labor, inventory, parts reorder, etc. and was a strategic key in significantly changing the business.

PQR-16

ENHANCING PROCUREMENT QUALITY AND RELIABILITY

Peter Krywaruczenko - Chairperson
DSG Manufacturing Sourcing & Planning Manager

AT&T
4513 Western Ave.
Lisle, IL 60532

ABSTRACT

Product life cycles have been drastically shortened and are futher complicated by rapid production ramp-ups. To successfully accomplish these rapid transitions the buyer must rely heavily on a vendors ability to deliver quality product. This seminar addresses methods and tools for assessing quality potential, from design through delivery, and assuring consistent quality from both the buyer's and seller's points-of-view.

R. F. Nicholson   - AT&T Bell Laboratories
D. S. Paul   - Hewlett Packard Co.
S. J. Amster   - AT&T Bell Laboratories
P. Saacke   - Bell Communications
                     Research
J. G. Bonito   - Rath & Strong, Inc.

QUALITY MANAGEMENT OF HIGH TECHNOLOGY PROCUREMENT

Roger F. Nicholson
Supervisor - Systems Quality Technology Group

AT&T Bell Laboratories
Crawfords Corner Road
Holmdel, NJ 07733

ABSTRACT

Principles of quality management and constant quality improvement have been long applied to factory manufacturing processes. Here they will be applied to the business process of procuring new, high technology communications products. Using customer/supplier models, process input and output requirements are identified. Various stages of the process are defined using the product life cycle concept.

RELIABILITY GROWTH MONITORING AS PART OF A DIVISION WIDE FOCUS

D. Scott Paul
Quality Engineer

Hewlett Packard Co.
Greeley Storage Division
700 - 71st Avenue
Greeley, CO 80634

For a new product, the continuing process of quality and reliability improvement is often extensive but not well quantified in terms of effort applied and results attained. A lot of engineering time and effort may be spent implementing changes to increase the quality and reliability of a device going to market. These efforts need to be managed, measured, and made visible through a dedicated and assiduously pursued Reliability Growth Program.

Demonstrated reliability growth data is also a valuable marketing tool. In a marketplace where competition is high and new products rush to meet tight budgets and demanding schedules, unsupported claims of quality and reliability are commonplace. Customers often require actual proof of reliability claims. The thoughtful vendor with demonstrated reliability data in hand has an edge on the competition.

J. T. Duane [1], in a paper published in 1964, analyzed the reliability improvements that are obtained through a test, analyze and fix process. Duane noted that many reliability prediction techniques did not take into consideration the time varying nature of reliability due to continual design improvements. He determined empirically that log-log plots of cumulative failure rate vs. cumulative test hours data showed remarkably similar trends. For a wide range of equipment types and complexities the data formed straight down-sloping curves (Figure 1). This relationship was easily expressed in mathematical terms. Duane observed that similar slopes of these curves indicated a uniform rate of reliability growth, and also that the relative vertical position of the curves was an indication of the initial design reliability of the device. Duane said that these curves could be used to monitor improvement toward a reliability goal, which may be derived from known reliability data for the individual components in the device. The curves could also be extrapolated to predict reliability growth trends and to plan reliability improvement programs. Duane theorized that the relationship would hold true as long as a constant reliability improvement effort was in place.

Four years later, Ernest O. Codier [2] published a paper adding several observations to the state of the art of reliability growth. He noted that the definition of a failure would have an affect on the vertical position of the curve, but not on the slope. One may conclude that the definition of a failure is semi-arbitrary, but should remain consistent throughout a reliability growth program. Codier also concluded that the value of the growth exponent 'alpha' would be in the range from 0.3-0.5 when a systematic and dedicated reliability improvement effort is in place. Codier was first to plot log MTBF vs. log test time, rather than log failure rate, giving the curves an upward slope rather than downward slope (Figure 2). He surmised that 'up is good', especially in management circles.

Patrick O'Connor [3] further quantified the rate of reliability growth 'alpha' (@), suggesting the following guidelines:

@ = > 0.4 Program dedicated to the elimination of failure modes as a top priority. Use of accelerated (overstress) tests. Immediate analysis and effective corrective action for all failures.

@ = 0.3-0.4 Priority attention to reliability improvement. Normal (typical expected stresses) environment test. Well managed analysis and corrective action for important failure modes.

@ = 0.2 Routine attention to reliability improvement. Testing without applied environmental stress. Corrective action taken for important failure modes.

@ = 0-0.2 No priority given to reliability improvement. Failure data not analyzed. Corrective action taken for important failure modes, but with low priority.

The reliability growth program in place at Hewlett Packard Co's. Greeley Storage Division, in Greeley, Colorado, incorporated the Codier enhanced Duane model. The model is being used to track reliability improvement of the HP 88780A, a new low-cost, auto-loading, GCR tape drive for 1/2" tape. The formulation of the Duane model is:

$$\log \textit{Øc} \sim \log \textit{Øo} + @(\log T - \text{Log To})$$

where - Øc is the cumulative MTBF (total hours/total fails)
T is the cumulative test hours (total hours)
Øo is the cum MTBF at the start of monitoring period
To is the cum hours at the start of monitoring period
@ is the slope 'alpha', of the growth curve

This gives:

$$\textit{Øc} = \textit{Øo}(T/To)^{@} \qquad (1)$$

The instantaneous MTBF is derived by differentiation of the above, and is given by:

$$\textit{Øi} = \textit{Øc}/(1-@) \qquad (2)$$

The instantaneous MTBF can be thought of as the MTBF of a currently produced product which has the benefits of all design improvements to date.

The instantaneous MTBF goal for the 1/2" tape drive was projected during early development stages. Historical failure rate data for all mechanical and electrical components were compiled, combined, and a potential failure rate for the entire product was calculated. This number, based on actual component data, was the expected reliability for the 1/2" tape drive at the time of it's release to manufacturing. A rate of continuing reliability growth was then assumed for the new product, based on the observed effect of ongoing improvements made to the previous generation tape product. The carryover of experienced engineering and manufacturing talent to the new product reinforced the expectation of continuing top priority analysis and effective correction of all failures. The reliability growth monitoring period started at initial release of the product and will continue until 18 months thereafter. Note that this phase of reliability growth monitoring takes place entirely while the device is in production. The projected failure rate number at the end of the monitoring period was then converted to an MTBF of 22,400 hours. This then was chosen as the instantaneous MTBF goal for the Duane chart.

Closely monitored test hours from five sources were chosen as input to the Duane model. These sources are:

1) Production final test and ambient burn-in of 100% of units.
2) Production environmental stress-life (strife) audit program. [4]
3) 100% of units shipped to European customers are audited enroute, at a sister division, Computer Peripherals Bristol, located in Bristol, England.
4) Close-tracking of several units used in our own factory computer center.
5) Close-tracking of a number of units at customer sites.

Accumulating test hours from only these sources has simplified the measurement process. Although the process is simple, we are tracking units directly off the production line, units that have been aged in Strife, units that have seen many transportation miles, and units that are in the hands of their end-users. A test hours forecast spreadsheet was created as the tool to track test hours and compare them to the projected hours from each source.

A very conservative starting point for the Duane plot was obtained by assessing the frequency of pre-production design changes along with the amount of closely-tracked test hours in stress and life tests, prior to manufacturing release.

With the final goal of 22,400 hr MTBF,

the start point determined, and a projected number of test hours (1,000,000 hr), a goal line was plotted on the Duane chart (Figure 3). The resulting aggressive slope of 0.57 is compatible with our top priority dedication to eliminate failure modes through the use of accelerated stress tests and immediate corrective action for all failures.

A simple way to define a failure was also implemented. For the measurement of reliability growth, only Class-type fails are counted:

1) Fail must be common to all units.
2) Fail requires an engineering change to be fixed.
3) Fail would likely cause units in the field to be upgraded.

The reasoning behind this definition is twofold. First, the finding and fixing of Class-type defects really drives reliability growth. Second, the method is easy, consistent and, according to Codier, should not affect the slope of the Duane graph. The fails are counted by noting the number of Class-type engineering changes that are implemented on the product.

When plotting MTBF data, one first divides cumulative test hours by cumulative failures to get cumulative MTBF. This MTBF and test hours data is added to previous cumulative data. Next, a linear regression is done on the logarithms of all the cumulative data weighting later points

increasingly greater. This produces the slope 'alpha'. Instantaneous MTBF is then calculated using eq. (2) above. Both cumulative and instantaneous MTBF are then plotted on log-log paper and progress is noted towards an instantaneous MTBF goal.

In summary, the reliability growth program for the HP 88780A 1/2" tape drive has proven beneficial in both the factory and marketing arenas. As class-type failures are found and fixed, growth in demonstrated MTBF is made highly visible. Promptly shared successes add to the momentum and enthusiasm for the program. Finally, the real moment of truth occurs when the customer can confidently make a knowledgeable product selection based on demonstrated quality and reliability.

REFERENCES:

[1] Duane, J.T., "Learning Curve Approach to Reliability Monitoring", IEEE Transactions on Aerospace, Volume 2, Number 2, April 1964, pp. 563-6

[2] Codier, Ernest O., "Reliability Growth in Real Life", presented at the 1968 Annual Symposium on Reliability, Jan. 16-18, 1968

[3] O'Connor, Patrick D. T., Practical Reliability Engineering, 1981, Heyden & Son Ltd, Philadelphia, pp. 203-9

[4] Bailey, Bob, "STRIFE Testing", QUALITY, Volume 21, Number 11, November 1982, pp. 53-55

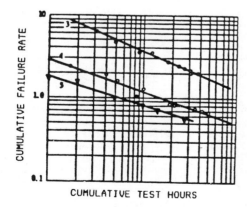

Figure 1 - Examples from Duane's Original Data

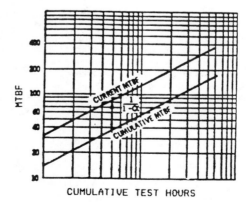

Figure 2 - Codier Enhanced 'Up is Good' Duane Plot

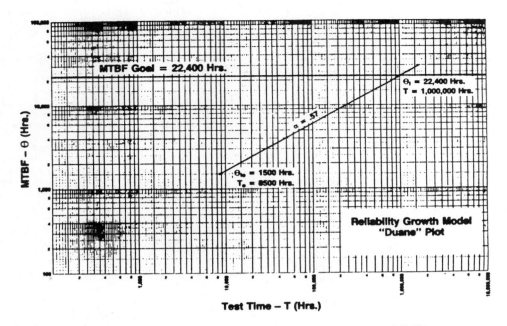

MTBF Goal = 22,400 Hrs.

Θ_1 = 22,400 Hrs.
T = 1,000,000 Hrs.

α = .57

Θ_{io} = 1500 Hrs.
T_o = 8500 Hrs.

Reliability Growth Model
"Duane" Plot

MTBF – Θ (Hrs.)

Test Time – T (Hrs.)

Figure 3 – Duane Plot for Hewlett Packard Co's 88780A
1/2" Tape Drive – showing
Reliability Growth Goal

STATISTICAL METHODS FOR RELIABILITY IMPROVEMENT

Sigmund J. Amster
MTS
Quality Theory and Technology Dept.

Jeffrey H. Hooper
Supervisor
Quality Theory and Technology Dept.

AT&T Bell Laboratories
Crawfords Corner Road
Holmdel, NJ 07733

INTRODUCTION

Statistical methods play an important role in the design and manufacture of reliable products. They are used to design, analyze, and present reliability improvement studies such as accelerated testing of critical parts, prototype testing, process design and qualification, first-office applications, and field-tracking studies.

This article defines statistical reliability methods, explains how a product-reliability program uses them, and presents an example of their use. It also explores available software tools, training materials, and future directions.

PRODUCT RELIABILITY

Reliability does not just happen in a product. It must be planned for and built into the product at each stage of the product-realization process.

A product-reliability program helps to ensure that the delivered product meets or exceeds its reliability objectives, and does so economically. Such a program comprises a coordinated set of activities (Figure 1) that begin at the early stages of system design and continue through design and development, implementation, manufacturing, and sales and support. Many of these activities involve statistical methods for designing reliability studies and analyzing and presenting reliability data.

During system design, for example, we determine the system architecture that can best meet the overall product-reliability objectives, and then allocate these objectives down to the subsystem and circuit-pack level. The allocation process, called reliability budgeting, provides designers and developers with meaningful reliability goals.

As the next step in the reliability program, we identify those parts or subsystems that are critical to the system's reliability. (Small changes in their reliability cause large changes in system reliability.) Additional engineering effort or testing will be devoted to these parts to ensure that they meet their reliability objectives. However, because no hardware exists that can be tested, statistical reliability methods are generally not useful at this stage.

During the design and development phase, early hardware begins to be available and statistical reliability methods become useful. We do accelerated life tests on critical parts at this early stage to determine if these parts will meet their reliability objectives. When designing these tests, we determine what stress levels to use and how many parts to test at each stress level.

Accelerated life tests are also used to evaluate competing designs and determine how to modify a given design to improve its reliability. At this stage, we may test completed prototypes, too, to find out if the subsystem or system can meet its reliability objectives.

During the implementation phase, reliability data are often collected to evaluate, improve, and qualify process designs. This is particularly true in component manufacturing. We also collect reliability data to qualify vendor products as meeting their reliability requirements.

In the manufacturing phase, we must determine whether the product performs as intended in the field, and then ensure that it continues to do so. Therefore, we collect and analyze reliability data from a first-office application and from factory testing. We also analyze factory test data to prove product reliability to customers.

Reliable performance in the field is essential for important new-technology products. If we monitor this performance with a field-tracking study, any departure from the reliability objectives will trigger reliability-improvement activity.

While repair data can be messy, routinely extracting reliability information from these data can be important. For example, we can use information on the current replacement rate for circuit packs to provide customers with up-to-date information on product reliability, and determine current needs for spare circuit packs.

In addition, component-reliability information can sometimes be pulled out of repair data. We can feed this information into the reliability-information database to improve the reliability prediction for the next generation of the product.

RELIABILITY MODELS

Many parametric reliability models have proven useful for analyzing reliability data. The models most frequently used are listed in Table I. All are special cases of the Generalized Gamma model, a fact we can use to determine which model is most appropriate for a given set of data.

It is possible to give a physical reason for using most of these models, [1] but the real justification is empirical. Because these models are flexible, we have found that they fit a wide variety of reliability data.

When several models fit a given set of data equally well, we can base our choice of model on conservative extrapolation, previous use in the same field, or other considerations. For example, the Weibull model eventually will predict a shorter probable failure time than the lognormal model.

The failure-rate function, $h(t)$, is frequently used to summarize a set of time-to-failure data. It describes how the instantaneous probability of failure changes with time. Because failure rate is a population quantity, a decreasing $h(t)$ may not imply that individual units are improving with age. The bathtub curve (Figure 2), or parts of it, characterizes many data sets.

When there is insufficient test time available to observe failures under use conditions, accelerated life testing is often employed. By increasing temperature, voltage, or other stress factors, it is possible to observe failures sooner. To extrapolate the data to use conditions, we have found two broad classes of models are effective: proportional-hazard (PH) models for T (time-to-failure) and accelerated-failure-time (AFT) models. [2,3]

The PH model is usually presented as

$$h(t/x) = h_o(t)e$$

where $h_o(t)$ is the baseline hazard or failure-rate function (when all $x_i = 0$); the β are unknown parameters; and $x = (x_1, x_2, ..., x_k)$ is a vector of k explanatory variables.

We can estimate β either from a parametric model for $h_o(t)$ or in a model-free (nonparametric) fashion. For a given change in the value of x_i, a larger β means a larger change in $h(t/x)$, the failure-rate function.

For example, with k = 1, the ratio

$$\frac{h(t/x_{i1})}{h(t/x_{i2})} = e^{\beta_1(x_{i1} - x_{i2})}$$

is independent of t. In general, for the PH model, the failure rates for two different values of an explanatory variable are in constant proportion, independent of time.

The AFT model is usually presented as:

$$\log T = \mathcal{M}(s) + \sigma e$$

where T is time to failure, s is stress, $\mathcal{M}(s)$ is the location parameter for the log T (log-failure-time) distribution, and σ is the distribution's scale parameter. That σ is independent of s is a consequence of the assumption that stress just speeds up time. We assume, as usual, that e follows a standard Gaussian (normal) model. When we can find a tranformation of stress, $x(s)$, such that $\mathcal{M}(s)$ is a linear function of stress, then the AFT model has the following highly intuitive interpretation.

As Figure 3 shows, if we increase the stress, the distribution moves down the straight line. Only in this case does the term **acceleration factor** mean simply a multiplier of time. An example of this is to use the Arrhenius relation for temperature stress, where β is just a known constant times the activation energy.

Some early failures may already have been dead at the start of the life test. A useful model for dead-on-arrival failures is

$$P[T<t] = p + (1 - p)F(t)$$

where p is the probability of a dead-on-arrival and $F(t)$ is a parametric model (exponential, lognormal, etc.). We can use the data to estimate p, as well as the parameters of $F(t)$.

RELIABILITY ANALYSIS

Because reliability data are often either censored or truncated, many standard data-analysis techniques cannot be used. **Censoring** means that we know exact failure times for few, if any, units. For all other units, we know only that the failure time falls somewhere in an interval. **Truncation** means that we do not know how many units started at time zero, because only those that survived the first t hours could be observed.

These special characteristics of reliability data make conventional statistical-analysis techniques inappropriate. For example, suppose we know some failure times, but we only know that three units live longer than 1000 hours. What is the average of the data?

A strategy that has proven useful in analyzing reliability data proceeds in three basic stages:

1. Nonparametric or model-free analysis to look at the data without restrictive model assumptions.

2. Graphical methods to choose the best parametric model.

3. Fitting the best parametric model and then using this fit to answer important reliability questions.

Without making any model assumptions, we can estimate cumulative-failure probability as a function of time. For example, the Kaplan-Meier estimate [2] can be used for data sets with only simple censoring, but the Turnbull estimate [4] is required when truncation or complex censoring is present.

We use the nonparametric estimate of cumulative-failure-probability to determine which parametric model, if any, best fits these data, without determining the model's specific parameters. Then, we take the best model and estimate the model parameters.

This gives us a single time-to-failure distribution that best fits the data. Usually we use the method of maximum likelihood. Then, we can use the resulting model to interpolate (smooth) the cumulative-failure-probability function over the range of the data and extrapolate this function beyond this point.

FUTURE DIRECTIONS

The latest methods for analyzing and presenting reliability data require both significant computation power and graphics capability.

Until recently, these methods were inaccessible to most engineers and technicians who need to analyze reliability data. Because they often used paper and pencils for analyzing studies, additional reliability information was not pulled out of the data.

Now, the latest reliability methods are readily available through STAR, a UNIX\ system software tool for the analysis and presentation of reliability data. AT&T engineers and technicians can use STAR throughout a product-reliability program. Panel 1 describes one application.

STAR is easy to use and guides a user, from data entry, through data analysis, to the creation of presentation-quality tables and plots. Thus, it can quickly turn reliability data into useful information.

In a three-day statistical reliability workshop, we teach participants to use STAR effectively to improve product reliability, and help them understand the most important reliability models and their underlying assumptions. The workshop emphasizes how to use the STAR software package to fit these models to reliability data and assess the goodness of this fit.

In workshop exercises, participants gain hands-on experience with STAR to analyze reliability data. In particular, they are encouraged to analyze their own data.

Soon, stand-alone tools like STAR will be integrated with other reliability tools like SUPER to form a workbench that will provide comprehensive support for a product reliability program. (SUPER stands for: the system used for prediction and evaluation of reliability.)

Another important step is to integrate these reliability tools into computer-aided engineering, design, and manufacturing (CAE/CAD/CAM) systems. This will plug important reliability improvement methods directly into the product-realization process.

The next stage of integration will be to integrate reliability tools into factory and industrial automation systems. Thus, these tools will become part of the normal way of doing business.

The next generation of statistical reliability technology will focus on ways to build high reliability into products in a cost-effective way. There currently appear to be at least two fruitful directions for this technology.

The first involves a closer coupling between the physics of failure and reliability models, by developing a set of models based on the physics of failure. In this way, knowledge about an appropriate reliability model would provide insight into the physics of failure and vice versa.

The other fruitful direction for statistical reliability technology concerns measured-degradation data. With the advent of microprocessor-controlled life tests, it is now economical to measure periodically the change in degradation of product parameter values. (Previously we simply checked the time when these parameter values exceed a threshold.)

Thus, much useful data is collected even on products that do not fail. This is especially important for some new high-reliability products where few units would fail during a life test.

In addition, if we know how a parameter value will change, we could compensate for this change in the product design, thus greatly improving product reliability.

Panel 1: Accelerated Life Testing, an Example

High-K ceramic capacitors were to be used in a new system under a 25V operating voltage stress. To determine warranty expenses, the probability of failure in the first year of operation, 8760 hours, was needed. Because only a small proportion of capacitors were expected to fail within the first year, an extensive accelerated life test was conducted.

During the test, groups of capacitors were subjected to a 50V, 100V or 150V accelerated voltage stress. First, the individual voltage-group data was examined to determine if the accelerated-failure-time model and the parametric time-to-failure model were adequate. Then, all the data were used to fit the AFT model.

As the first step in analyzing the data, a nonparametric estimate was obtained of the cumulative-failure probability as a function of time for each group. Then, probability plots were obtained for the parametric models that were considered candidates.

Because any model that fits the data well will plot as a nearly straight line, the plots were examined to determine which one was closest to linear. Simultaneous confidence bands furnish a quantitative measure of **goodness of fit** and usually provide evidence to eliminate models that fit poorly.

For the capacitor data, the lognormal distribution was selected and individual lognormal distributions were fit to the data at each voltage. The fitted distributions and nonparametric results, Figure a, give a visual measure of the equality of the slopes, which is an important assumption of the AFT model. (σ is the same at each voltage.)

Because voltage was the stress, the inverse-power-stress function was used in the AFT model. It was assumed that

$$e^{\mu(s)} = e^{\beta_0} s^{\beta_1}$$

or

$$\mu(s) = \beta_0 + \beta_1 \log s$$

and $\log (T(s))$ has a lognormal distribution with parameters $\mu(s)$, σ.

Then, maximum likelihood was used to fit all the data to this model and obtain estimates β_0, β_1, and σ of the unknown parameters. With these estimates, the original data was converted to estimated residuals. Every time, $T(s)$, was replaced with

$$\frac{\log(T(s)) - [\beta_0 + \beta_1 \log s]}{\sigma}$$

in Figure a and a normal probability plot was done with STAR, the statistical reliability analysis software.

When the modeling assumptions are true, if we subtract an estimate of $\mu(s)$ and divide by an estimate of σ, the data will reduce to a common $\mu = 0$ and $\sigma = 1$. In fact, the linearity of the residual probability plot indicates that both the AFT model and the inverse-power-stress function fit the data. The plot in Figure b should be linear within the 95-percent confidence bands, if all the assumptions hold.

Because this diagnostic check appears to be satisfied, the same $\mu(s)$ and σ are used to estimate $\mu(s)$ for 25V and get the result in Figure c. Here, the parallel lines are a consequence of the equal σ assumption.

Figure d shows the failure rates (in units of 10 hours) of the fitted distributions at the four voltages: 25V, 50V, 100V, and 150V. All lines would show that the failure rate initially increases for sufficiently small times. But, despite the apparent decreasing failure rates exhibited by all the test data, we expect capacitors operated at 25V to exhibit a slightly increasing failure rate over the first 10,000 hours.

From a STAR analysis, the probability that a high-K ceramic capacitor operating at

25V will fail in the first year is approximately 0.0063, with a 95-percent confidence interval of (0.00064, 0.059).

REFERENCES

1. N. L. Johnson and S. Kotz, Continuous Univariate Distributions, Vols. 1 and 2, Houghton Mifflin, Boston, 1970.

2. D. R. Cox, "Regression Models and Life Tables" (with discussion), Journal of the Royal Statistical Society, Series B. Methodological, Vol. 34, 19872, pp. 187-220.

3. J. F. Lawless, Statistical Models and Methods for Lifetime Data, John Wiley and Sons, New York, 1982.

4. B. W. Turnbull, "The Empirical Distirbution Function with Arbitrarily Grouped, Censored and Truncated Data," Journal of the Royal Statisitical Society, Series B. Methodological, Vol. 38, 1976.

Figure 1. Product reliability program activities. Starred (*) items involve statistical reliability methods: the design of reliability studies, and the analysis and presentation of reliability data.

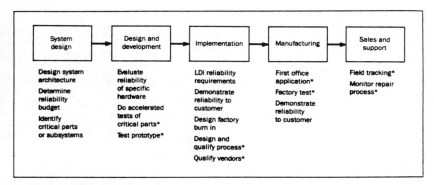

Table I. Most Frequently Used Parameter Models

Model	Probability (Failure Time $> t$)	Failure Rate
Exponential	$e^{-\lambda t}$	Constant
Gamma	$\dfrac{1}{\Gamma(k)} \displaystyle\int_{t}^{\infty} u^{k-1} e^{-u}\, du$	Decreasing, or increasing and then decreasing
Lognormal	$\dfrac{1}{\sqrt{2\pi}} \displaystyle\int_{\left(\frac{\log t - \mu}{\sigma}\right)}^{\infty} e^{-(u^2/2)}\, du$	Increasing and then decreasing
Weibull	$e^{-(\lambda t)^{\beta}}$	Decreasing or constant or increasing

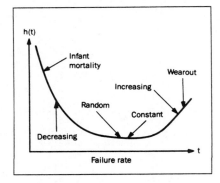

Figure 2. Plots of time-to-failure data usually produce the bathtub curve.

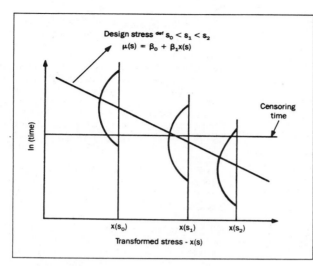

Figure 3. Accelerated-failure-time model. Assume that $\mu(s) = \beta_0 + \beta_1$ for $x(s)$, an increasing function of stress. Censoring time is the length of the experiment.

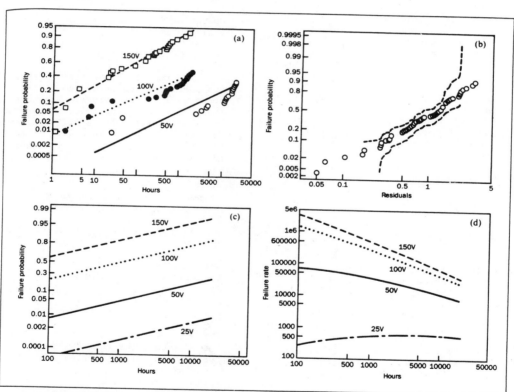

Lognormal failure probability for high-K ceramic capacitors. (a) shows the fitted distributions and the circles, dots, and squares give the nonparametric results. (b), a lognormal probability plot with 95-percent simultaneous confidence bands, shows the residuals. (c) shows the probability of failure for four voltages, and (d) shows the failure rates (in units of 10^9 hours) of the fitted distributions for these voltages.

THE BUYER SUPPLIER TEAM: VALUE AND PROFIT

Paul Saacke, District Manager
Quality Assurance Technical Information

Bell Communications Research
6 Corporate Place
Piscataway, NJ 08854

ABSTRACT

Increasingly, corporate consumers are discovering that supplier quality control, without buyer quality assurance, can result in quality and costs out of control. The companies who participated in the Bellcore study practice a diverse range of methods for "managing" suppliers -- from developing long-term relationships, to establishing rigorous requirements and standards, to weeding out poor performers.

This paper highlights results of studying 30 major companies that use methods like these in systematic programs to keep purchased quality under control. It profiles key attributes of the leading-edge Buyer Quality Assurance programs, the problems they address, how they address them, what resources they utilize, and what role they play in a company's total quality improvement effort.

The paper concludes by examining how any company might utilize study information to promote increased supplier quality responsibility -- and to improve its program in other areas where Buyer Quality Assurance is breaking new ground.

INTRODUCTION

A major American appliance maker estimates that 40% of its quality problems come from purchased parts; a Japanese firm had to recall 45,000 washing machines due to fires caused by a supplier's defective capacitors; and the investigations into the Challenger and Chernobyl accidents revealed procurement policies that often undermined quality. Supply setbacks like these have severly hampered many companies' otherwise noble efforts to upgrade quality and become more competitive. Yes, there are warranties that provide some compensation, and legal channels are available for redress -- but neither can begin to offset all the costs, anguish, and inconvenience of shoddy supply sources.

So why don't quality-conscious companies do a better job of selecting suppliers who share their commitment (thus avoiding such problems)? The answers are many: Price-based bidding competition that inevitably leads to corner cutting, quality problems that go unrecognized because they're buried in the cost of doing business, and a supplier commitment-competence gap that leaves the buyer short on quality. Yet, these answers are not the real problem -- a lack of buyer involvement. Quality seldom "happens" by itself. Quality must be defined by the buyer's requirements and must be assured by buyer monitoring (quality assurance) of the supplier's quality program (quality control).

Indeed, Buyer Quality Assurance (Buyer QA) is an idea whose time has come in what might be called the second wave of the "Quality Revolution Of The 80's." Successful companies have comprehensive programs. These programs seek to stimulate supplier quality performance and improvement through a variety of techniques. The particulars for a given company depend on a host of business factors. Consequently, Buyer QA program activities can differ considerably among practitioners, but in concept they all are based on a set of planned or systematic measures intended to provide adequate confidence that a purchased product or service will initially satisfy stipulated needs and that any problems are remedied effectively and expeditiously.

The study was conducted by Bell Communications Research (Bellcore). Since 1984, Bellcore has helped maintain quality standards for local telephone service by providing Buyer QA support for its owners (Bell Operating Companies, Regional Companies, and affiliates).

BUYER QA BASICS

The results of Bellcore's Buyer QA Study are derived from interview visits with corporate quality executives. The intent was to learn as much as possible, rather than formulate scientifically certifiable conclusions, so the approach was more akin to focus groups than to traditional study research. The following companies were interviewed:

Bausch & Lomb (Optics Center)
Centel Corporation (Telephone Operations)
Compaq
Eastman Kodak (Kodak Park Division)
Emerson Electric (Electronics and Space Division)
General Electric
Grumman (Aerospace Division)
GTE
Hewlett Packard
Hewlett Packard (Ultrasonic Division)
IBM
ITT-Telecom
Litton Industries (Data Systems Division)
Loral Corporation (Electronic Systems Division)
LTV (Aerospace Division)
Martin Marietta (Data Systems Division)
McDonnel Douglas (Aircraft Division)
Motorola
National Semiconductor (Semiconductor Division)
North American Phillips Corporation
Pitney Bowes (Business Systems Division)
Prime Computer
Raytheon (Missile Systems Division)
RCA (Communications Division)
Singer (Kearfoot Division)
Tandem Computer
Texas Instruments

3M Company
Xerox
Zenith Electronics (Consumer Electronics Divisions)

The first major conclusion is that companies who practice Buyer QA usually fall into three categories according to their normal modes of supplier interaction:

(i) Partnership - To the extent possible, companies in this category offer suppliers the financial security of a long-term relationship in exchange for supplier commitment reinforced by active buyer involvement. Partnership characteristics will be explored in a later section.

(ii) Prevention - These companies have the same technical orientation to quality as those in the first category, but they either can't, won't, or haven't yet used partnership. Although being "limited" to prevention does not necessarily make them less effective, their costs for assuring purchased quality as well as their costs over time are likely higher.

(iii) Inspection - These companies follow the traditional practice of combining lot sampling and various forms of piece inspection, depending on circumstances. In many cases, military standards required in government contracts drive this approach, but there are "progressive" companies in this category who are pushing for changes. These are the most expensive programs.

Although these categories make important distinctions, there are equally-important similarities (across categories) among the companies. Using three headings (**Philosophy, Strategy, Implementation**), these Buyer QA cross-category similarities are detailed in the following summary:

Common Philosophy

1. Buyer's Rights/Supplier's Obligations "Buyer Beware" doesn't cut it any longer. Most companies believe in a right to quality and reliability in products and services provided by suppliers, a right to assure that quality, a right to insist on defect prevention, and a right to expect constant quality improvement from regular suppliers.

2. Quality Assurance Doesn't Cost..Poor Quality Does - There remain responsible business people who talk about cutting quality control costs to become more competitive, but they are not to be found here. Even higher-cost, inspection-oriented Buyer QA programs were believed by respondents to cost decidedly less than the poor quality costs they eliminate.

3. Quality Control and Quality Assurance: Together But Separate - Most companies recognize that no matter how good their quality control, it may go for naught because of the garbage-in, garbage-out principle. In fact, the better their quality control, the more crucial it is for good (buyer) quality assurance to prevent defective purchased components from upsetting a finely-tuned manufacturing process.

4. Better Supplier Relationships - Companies in every category shared the belief that better supplier relationships are the key to better quality, although they markedly differ on what those relationships can or should be. Effective Buyer QA seeks to end supplier-buyer fingerpointing, and point the way to mutual achievement of quality goals.

Common Strategy

1. End Commodity-Based Purchasing - Study subjects have put an end to the traditional purchasing game, whose primary players were price and availability. Buyer QA is a whole new ball game that makes quality the primary pitch to suppliers, instead of a throw-in to sweeten a deal.

2. Wariness on Warranties...Contracts Aren't Crutches - The companies interviewed reject supplier contract concessions (if it isn't right, I'll charge you less) and "stronger" warranties as ways to better quality. Not all costs are warrantied, and litigation can last longer than the product.

3. Pay Now, Not Later - These companies are not quality idealists. Rather, they are financial pragmatists for whom quality is a means to an end --better results. By investing in Buyer QA up front, they reduce later, and much larger, hidden costs of poor (supplier) quality.

Common Implementation

1. Corrective Action - Right down the line, these companies put the responsibility for quality back where it belongs --with the supplier. Fundamental to their Buyer QA programs is that corrective action should take place before the buyer gets the product and at the instigation of the supplier.

2. Supplier Recognition - Buyer QA demands supply quality, but accomplishing that takes equal parts congratulations and criticism. Most respondents make liberal use of public awards to top-performing suppliers -- sometimes accompanied by hoopla and hurrahs.

3. Technological Sophistication Products and services that are increasingly based on software and electronics

require rapid advances in manufacturing skills and tools. The study found heavy investments in upgrading Buyer QA to work with suppliers in adapting to technological change.

4. Quality Improvement - To get suppliers in the quality fold, these companies lead by example --deploying extensive quality improvement programs in their own operations and providing training and consultation to help their suppliers do the same.

WHY NOT THE BEST?

Having examined the far-reaching similarities let us now devote attention to the substantial differences. To do this, we'll look at areas in which the partnership companies were clearly distinguished from companies in the other two categories. The findings below form a profile of the leading-edge practitioners of techniques for influencing supplier quality.

1. Supplier Reduction - Leading buyers typically have slashed supplier bases in half (one company cut several thousand down to less than one thousand), and have focused their business, and Buyer QA attention, on a few hundred preferred suppliers. The results has been closer, mutually-beneficial supplier-buyer relationships.

2. On-Site Presence - Major or critical contracts require first-hand knowledge of a supplier's capabilities, and visits to assure quality through involvement in both production planning and monitoring of actual production are common.

3. Emphasis On Process - Finding errors early or preventing them is simply much less costly, and that means focusing on the production process, rather than the end product.

4. Higher Quality Goals - Companies are ardent devotees of the Pygmalion Principle (adapted for Quality) --you get (from suppliers) what you expect.

5. Supplier Initiative - As buyer-supplier relationships have improved, buyers report additional benefits of supplier initiatives beyond the contract specifics. These might be classified under the umbrella of "value creation," where suppliers actively seek ways to reduce buyer cost -- not by reducing quality, but by constantly questioning what is needed and how it should be done.

BECOMING THE BEST

For Bellcore and its owners, these study findings have mainly served to validate what they're already doing, and to lend added credence to what they're planning. Nevertheless, some findings are being used to shape or modify both current Buyer QA practices, and plans. While Bellcore is a unique company in many respects, an overview of some of the circumstances in which Bellcore's QA program operates may prove helpful in identifying similarities and the potential for application to other company situations.

Prior to the Bell System breakup, Bellcore did not exist. Under AT&T ownership, the Bell Operating Companies (BOCs) purchased the bulk of their equipment from Western Electric. This equipment was manufactured to Bell Laboratories requirements, which in turn incorporated uniform quality standards. It was Bell Labs' express responsibility to look after the buyers' "quality interests". With divestiture the BOCs were not purchasing entirely from independent suppliers (including AT&T) --with a wide variety of requirements and standards for quality. The "new" companies now had another new responsibility.

In this new environment, Bellcore QA began supporting the BOCs in their separate dealings with suppliers, each BOC or Regional Company making its own procurement decisions and agreements with its particular suppliers. Thus, Bellcore is not a buyer for its owners, and cannot form "quality partnerships" with their suppliers. However, Bellcore can and does assist each of its owners with "stand alone" aspects of applicable partnership (and other leading-edge) approaches to Buyer QA.

MAKING THE BEST BETTER

The results of this study have enabled Bellcore and its owner/clients to envision a new horizon of quality improvement for client suppliers. There are a few clouds which must be circumvented in order to keep the rain off the ever-advancing supplier quality parade:

1. Improve Quality Cost Information - Probing in this area made it easier to believe a recent survey disclosing that most executives don't know what poor quality costs their companies. Even these "best companies" give less attention to "quality accounting' than to other types of expense tracking and analysis. But as gains come more grudgingly and international competition intensifies, more complete and detailed data is needed for closer quality cost comparisons and optimum utilization of Buyer QA resources.

2. Make Buyer Quality A Key Strategy - In recent years, top executives have become directly involved in implementing quality as a corporate strategy - spurring improvements that have bolstered both marketing and manufacturing competitiveness. But the survey reveals scant attention to the singular strategic implications of supply quality - e.g., most aspects of supply partnerships are handled by purchasing and other operations/administrative functions. It would seem a natural extension of management's

role in mergers, acquisitions, and joint ventures to make "supply quality partnerships" one of the strategic alliances that companies covet.

BUYER QA: A FINAL PERSPECTIVE

In this paper, we've looked at why Buyer QA is important, what Bellcore learned from a study of successful Buyer QA practitioners, how the results are being used, and areas for further improvements. But can anything definitive be said about Buyer QA? Perhaps so, by use of an analogy. Buyer QA can be thought of as a three-legged race. The movements (quality actions) of both buyer and supplier must be coordinated, or they work against each other and no progress is made. Hence partnership and/or other forms of cooperation are essential for accomplishing the ultimate objective of Buyer QA: for buyer and supplier to mutually confront quality issues instead of confronting each other -- so that both parties come out in front.

Using Task Teams to Improve Procurement Quality

Joseph G. Bonito
Consultant

Rath & Strong, Inc.
21 Worthen Road
Lexington, MA 02173

ABSTRACT

Improving procurement quality requires employees to feel "empowered" to get involved and one way is via a structure of task teams. Task teams are chartered with a specific business need focus that is significant, reasonable, achievable, and is integrated into the overall business strategy. This session will focus on the task team model utilized to improve customer/supplier relationships with quantifiable results from staffed teams composed of cross functional levels.

Why the Need

1. Long-term change deals with cultural and behavioral issue.

2. Get people involved who are closest to the problem.

3. Create commitment towards the habit of continuous improvement.

4. Leverage organizational resources.

Structuring for Change

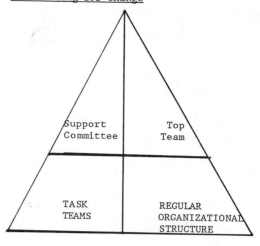

o Flexible
o Integrated
o Fixed Duration

The Process

PHASE 1 - Getting Started

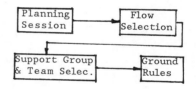

PHASE II - Initial Data Collection

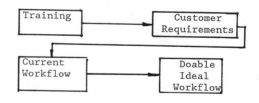

PHASE III - Implementing Improvements

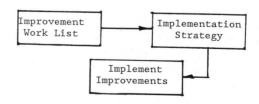

"TRUST THE PROCESS"

1600

Training & On-going Support

1. Team Building Training - creates energy, commitment and provides the upfront skill building.

2. Team Leader Training - creates a cadre of trained facilitators.

3. Technical Problem-Solving Skills - provides the right foundation of technical know-how.

4. Steering/Support Committee - eliminates obstacles and distractions for task teams.

5. Internal Charter/Outside Catalyst - provides the process with an objective third party resource.

Analyzing Team Effectiveness

HIGH

TASK MASTER	EFFECTIVE TEAM
DO NOTHING TEAM	COUNTRY CLUB TEAM

Concern for Task or Content

LOW   HIGH

Concern for people or Process

Benefits

1. Empower the organization towards continuous improvement.

2. Skill the organization to work in team oriented activities.

3. Achieve tangible results in a shorter time-frame.

PQR-17

PRODUCT TESTING STRATEGIES

C. R. GROSSMAN - Chairperson
Manager, Engineering - Process, Plant
& Works Services
AT&T
800 South River Street
Montgomery, IL 60538-0305

D. C. OPFERMAN - Chairperson
Director, Large Computer Systems
Laboratory
AT&T
1100 East Warrenville Road
Naperville, IL 60566

Products designed for the 90s will have
to fit in with both the manufacturing
disciplines of our modern factories
and the ever increasing standard of
quality demanded by the marketplace.
The role of testing, a pillar in the
quality architecture of the factory
of the past, is being redefined in the
new manufacturing environment. Total
Quality Control and high velocity manufacturing in the factory of the future,
along with new technologies, have given
rise to new test strategies. The trend
today is to reduce or eliminate the
dependency final tests for subassemblies
and systems and build a test strategy
around in-process performance and quality
verifications. Much of today's test
strategy involves both hardware and
software self test capabilities. These
new approaches have profound impact on
the product realization process.

This seminar will cover several approaches
to product testing in today's environment
and will touch on topics ranging from
component design architecture, production,
and field service test tools.
W. D. Ballew - AT&T
K. R. Berger - Northern Telecom, Inc.
P. Fleming   - Texas Instruments Corp.
D. T. McClean - Texas Instruments Corp.
G. R. Schultz - AT&T

HIERARCHICAL TESTABILITY

Donald T. McClean
Member - Group Technical Staff

Pete Fleming
Test Engineering Branch Manager
Texas Instruments Corporation
Mail Station 8407
P.O. Box 869305
Plano, TX 75086

ABSTRACT
This paper describes a test methodology,
hierarchical testability, which is designed to offset the detrimental effects
of advanced technologies on test. A
standard set of built-in-test elements,
embedded within the Unit-Under-Test (UUT),
and connected together with an industry
standard serial scan bus, provides the
necessary structure to implement a "divide
and conquer" strategy which allows the
individual testing of devices, boards, etc.
embedded within a complex system. Since
the hierarchical test elements are embedded
within the UUT, they can be reused at all
levels of test (IC, board, etc.) and can
be utilized at different test environments
(production test, depot, field test, on-
line test). The hardware test elements
can also directly contribute to tasks
other than test, such as design verifi-
cation/integration and software debug.
The implementation of hierarchical test is
incomplete without a set of tools designed
to ease the implementation and use of the
hierarchical testability architecture.

INTRODUCTION
The cost and complexity of testing current
and projected technologies is increasing
at a rapid rate. Advanced packaging
techniques and sub-micron geometries has
resulted in devices with the functionality
of earlier system. The resulting impact
on test includes:
. Excessive test generation costs
. Excessive test execution costs
. High fixturing costs

The size of a test pattern set for a given
Unit-Under-Test (UUT) tends to increase
exponentially with gate count. As test
patterns sets become larger, they take an
excessive amount of time to execute,
require an excessive amount of storage
space in Automatic Test Equipment (ATE)
memory, and are expensive to generate.
The complexity of the test generation
process often frustrates automatic test
generation tools, resulting in manual test
generation which is expensive, time-consuming, errorprone, and tedious.

Current testing techniques relies heavily
on obtaining physical access to key nodes
in the UUT. The growing use of surface
mount technologies in conjunction with
dual-sided Printed Wiring Boards (PWBs)
may preclude traditional in-circuit
testing due to cost and technical feasibility issues. The reduced geometries of
advanced packaged technologies may reach
the point where manual probing for functional tests is beyond the capabilities of
humans. In addition, the use of con-
formal coating has precluded the use of
in-circuit testing and probing techniques
at depots.

The current decade has seen a trend towards the implementation of structured
approaches for improving test controllability and observability. The structured
testability approaches include scan design
and embedded test pattern generation and
compression.

Structured testability techniques have
been successfully implemented in the IC

design and test world, but have not had a major impact on PWB and system testing. Even when ICs on a board or system have structured testability, it frequently cannot be utilized at the PWB or higher level. The failure to penetrate these areas of test can be attributed to the following factors:

. Lack of a standard approach
. Lack of a standard interface
. Undefined control structures
. Complexity of design
. Design impact (gate count, pin-count, timing)
. Inability to address non-scanned designs

Semi-conductor manufacturers have traditionally implemented testability features on devices with the goal of supporting test only in production environments without consideration of test problems in the PWB and system environments. The IC structured test capabilities present are usually accessed through special probe pads that are not bonded out in the packaged part. Even when IC testability features are accessible after packaging, testability features are frequently undocumented such that the end-user cannot utilize them. This results in the redundant development of test pattern sets which could have been avoided.

To address these test problems, the hierarchical testability methodology was developed. Subsequent sections of this paper will discuss the hierarchical testability methodology, and the components of hierarchical testability, which include hardware, Computer-Aided-Design and Computer-Aided-Testability (CAD/CAT) tools, and the real-time Maintenance Bus Support System (MBSS).

THE HIERARCHICAL TESTABILITY METHODOLOGY
Hierarchical testability refers to a combined methodology and system architecture intended to optimize the test process. This optimization is achieved by:

.Migrating considerations for PWB and system test down to the component level
.Providing a standard serial bus which all test structures are connected to
.Implementing a hardware test framework that supports all levels and environments of test
.Providing an integrated tool set to design, develop, and execute tests which maximum commonality of effort.

Figure 1 shows an example of the hardware implementation of the hierarchical test approach. All devices containing test features are equipped with a Joint Test Action Group (JTAG) serial interface and are connected together via a common bus. The JTAG bus consists of a 4-wire serial interface in which data is clocked from one device to the next. The JTAG bus has been endorsed by a number of American and European companies as a simple and efficient method for supporting boundary scan applications.

Boundary scan refers to the methodology whereby testability cells are placed at the perimeter of the IC die such that the input and output pins of the device can be controlled and observed via the JTAG serial scan bus. Boundary scan allows the partioning of a board or system into blocks which can be tested in either the "pins-in" or "pins-out" direction. "Pins-in" refers to the ability to test logic contained within a boundary scan ring. Patterns are applied via scan at the input of the UUT, and the resultant output patterns are captured, scanned out, and compared against the expected good values.

"Pins-out" refers to the ability to test the connections between neighboring components equipped with boundary scan. The interconnections between boundary scan equipped parts can be tested by controlling the output cells of one device to a known state, and observing the resultant patterns via the boundary scan cells of a neighboring device.

COMPONENTS OF HIERARCHICAL TEST
The principle components of hierarchical test are shown in Figure 2. Each is discussed below.

HARDWARE
The hardware components for hierarchical testability consist of testability cells, testability ICs, and test controllers.

An Application Specific Integrated Circuit (ASIC) library of Standard Controllability/ Observability Perimeter Elements (SCOPE) testability cells which support both boundary scan and other Built-In-Test functions has been made available for circuit designers. Although emphasis is placed on I/O, the SCOPE concept is well suited for inclusion in the core logic or for surrounding 'megacells'. In addition, the interface between boundary scan and internal scan (such as Level Sensitive Scan Design (LSSD) will be supported.

The testability ICs are designed to provide additional test control and observability to critical points in the circuitry and to provide the hooks required to test non-scannable and combinatorial logic on the PWBs. The test ICs perform the same function as parts normally implemented within the design, but also contain enhanced testability features. The initial implementation of the test ICs has targeted the high-volume commodity ICs (octal buffers, transceivers, latches, and buffers).

External control for SCOPE and the test ICs is distributed via the JTAG bus. Control is communicated via protocolled commands (opcodes) scanned into internal control registers. IC and PWB testing will use ATE to drive this bus, but system testing will require an embedded control capability. A pair of controllers are being developed to support efficient control/data transmission via the JTAG bus. The high-end controller will maximize throughput on the JTAG bus by having dedicated local memory which it can read and write via Direct Memory Access (DMA) capability. The low-end controller operates under direct control of a host microprocessor, trading off lower throughput with a lower cost-of-implementation.

An additional device, designated as the Device Select Module (DSM) is proposed to provide a switch capability for serial scan rings. This feature will significantly reduce the number of patterns required to access the hardware and provide additional isolation and fault tolerance.

COMPUTER-AIDED-DESIGN/COMPUTER-AIDED-TESTABILITY (CAD/CAT)

For engineers to properly implement testability, analysis tools must be provided to ensure proper specification, implementation, and simulation of the test capabilities. All CAD features currently provided for other cells and parts must also be provided for the test ICs and SCOPE. Schematic capture symbols, logic/fault simulation models, and any special models supporting CAD must be made available on design work-stations.

Proper implementation of testability, ad hoc or structured, involves proper, implementation, and evaluation. A series of work-station resident computer-aided testability tools are being developed to provide this information to the designer in his native environment.

MAINTENANCE BUS SUPPORT SYSTEM (MBSS)

Proper use of the hierarchical test becomes more complex as the test environment migrates from IC to PWB to system. Significant bookkeeping and concentration is required to understand the dynamically changing configuration and scan length of the scan paths. The number of ones and zeros required to exercise and monitor the hardware can easily overwhelm the designer or test engineer. The Maintenance Bus Support System (MBSS) is designed to have the computer maintain this knowledge, allowing the engineer to think in terms of registers and patterns without regard to the overhead of the serial interface.

MBSS will access the hardware test structures to provide engineers with the ability to support simulation, design verification, integration, troubleshooting, production test and BIT. Configuration files will allow the software to understand the proper control sequences to execute these operations.

CONCLUSION

Hierarchical testability offers advantages to the hardware design engineer, the software design engineer, the test engineer, and the product maintain. Hierarchical test offers a broad range of test capabilities with a structured approach for implementation and use. This approach overcomes the inherent uniqueness of ad hoc approaches, allowing efficient generation of design support tools, analysis tools, hardware/software interfaces, and computer-aided test generation.

Benefits will occur as hierarchical testability becomes entrenched in the engineering process. The learning curve for the engineering disciplines will be reduced. The performance impact of SCOPE and test ICs will be established, making it straightforward for hardware designers to incorporate them and simulate the functional performance of the design without regard to the test functions.

The hardware structures provide low-level control and visibility into the hardware design, improving not only test efficiency and performance, but the ability to troubleshoot and integrate systems. Because the test functions are blended in with functionality, the design penalty for power, real estate, reliability, and cost are reduced compared to ad hoc approaches. This will result in more efficient testability and, in many cases, the inclusion of testability that would not have been implemented otherwise.

Because the test features are applied at the IC level, common test approaches (and ideally, test program sets) can be achieved. This greatly reduces test generation cost and improves the repeatability of test results. Test vectors developed for the packaged part can be scanned in for use in PWB and system testing.

PWBs designed with the proper levels and implementation of hierarchical testability may be capable of being tested without requiring in-circuit fixturing. Functional fixturing may be greatly reduced, in some cases to the minimal connections to the maintenance bus, power, ground, and clocks. The partitioning and vertical testability provided by this approach will significantly reduce the size, execution times, and generation cost of test programs. Logic blocks may be limited to sizes adequate for automatic test pattern generation programs to be effective.

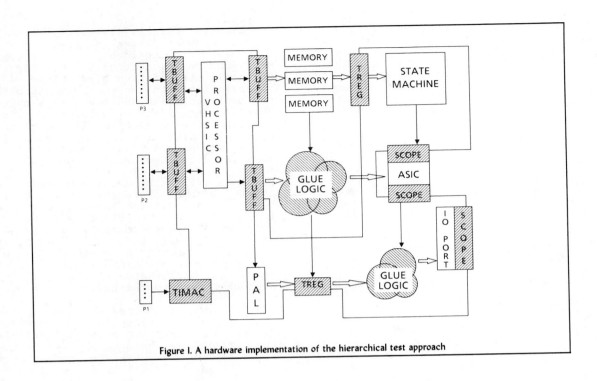

Figure I. A hardware implementation of the hierarchical test approach

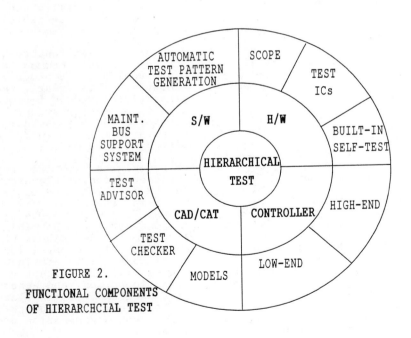

FIGURE 2.
FUNCTIONAL COMPONENTS
OF HIERARCHCIAL TEST

ANOTHER LOOK AT FAULT COVERAGE IN VOLUME MANUFACTURING

W. David Ballew
Network Circuit Pack Test
Engineering Manager
AT&T
7725 W. Reno Ave.
Oklahoma City, OK 73125

ABSTRACT
The increased speed and packaging density of telecommunications circuitry, along with more and more mixed-signal applications, cause the test engineer to look at the overall test strategy for the high volume factory. Total fault coverage and the loss of observability will be dealt with.

PROBLEM
In volume manufacturing, defects may be classified in several broad classifications:
1. Component Failures
   A. Failure to meet specification
   B. Infant mortality
2. Shorts and Opens
   A. Device level
   B. Board level
   C. System level
3. System Failures
   A. Parametric
   B. Functional

Unfortunately, there are no simple ways to determine where a particular class of defect is introduced or, consequently, can be removed from the product. Also, there are many restrictions based upon cost and available test equipment that impact overall test strategies. Defects should always be eliminated at the earliest and least costly point in the manufacturing process.

For the purposes of determining the effectiveness of a test audit and the risk of not performing an audit, the following definitions are given:

Failure - The loss of functionality of a device, board, or system such that the performance of the product is measurably different.

Fault Coverage - The ability to detect and observe any failure.

Detectability - The ability to measure a loss of functionality.

Observability - The ability to isolate a detectable failure and assign a root cause (usually by propagation to an output pin).

Total Test Orthogonality - 100% test fault coverage.

Partial Test Orthogonality - Less than 100% test fault coverage due to a loss of detectability, observability, or both.

TEST STRATEGIES
Within the product realization process, there are at least five opportunities to detect and observe failures. They are:
1. Chip Test
2. Incoming Test
3. Circuit Pack Test
4. Systems Test
5. Product Application

Today's product test strategies are designed to view the entire product realization process, from "Cradle to Grave" to achieve optimum test benefits at the highest level of vertical integration. Even very large companies with a high degree of vertical integration have difficulty managing high level test strategies. Some of the reasons this job is difficult are:
1. Managing technical information in standard format across my organizations.
2. Establishing test standards and test equipment that can be used in two or more of the five traditional test areas listed above.
3. Dealing with the three broad classifications of defects in the fault spectrum at successive stages in the manufacturing process.
4. Dynamics and variability of product attributes.

This paper will not attempt to deal with economic analysis. However, it has been shown for components that, at certain levels of incoming quality, incoming inspection may be eliminated or drastically modified based upon the downstream impact.[1]

OPPORTUNITIES FOR BREAKTHROUGH
Incoming component quality levels have fallen two orders of magnitude in the past three years, to below 100 PPM.[2] Also, during the same time frame, factory assembly and soldering processes have made significant improvements. These factors have altered the quantity and types of failures that must be removed from products prior to shipment.

Higher clock speeds, twenty-five mil lead spacing, increased integration at the silicon level, and double-sided surface mount technology all seem to demand new test strategies. Most of these changes demand new approaches to achieve detectability and observability. Design for testability (DFT) techniques point to built-in-self-test and other observability approaches as mandatory breakthroughs if some future designs are to be manufacturable.

The combination of constantly improving older technologies coupled with rapid introduction of new technologies, have placed a real burden on test strategies and implementations. It is not clear if these demands are in harmony or conflict with concepts such as just-in-time and total quality control. To be sure, there are very real demands that are pushing traditional manufacturing approaches. What we have is an excellent opportunity for breakthrough because the situation analysis demands one.

IMPACT ON THE FACTORY
Consideration must be given to the "New Fault Spectrum" which comes about as a result of the factors just described. How do the faults differ, both in quantity and type? The major impact comes in the following areas:

1. Loss of observability
2. Inability to test at speed
3. Difficulty in correlating results due to multiple test approaches
4. Absence of exhaustive, totally deterministic vector sets for very large digital designs

Given five traditional test areas in the Product Realization Process, and the four reasons that complete vertical integration is difficult to achieve, one can see that almost every area in the factory is impacted one way or another. Any test strategy that is to be successful, must deal with each of these issues simultaneously, or there is a risk of sub-optimization.

CONCLUSIONS
The ability to detect and observe all defects in each of the subclasses is mandatory if high quality products are to be manufactured. The total fault spectrum, where the defects are created, and their relationship to the entire product realization process must be analyzed simultaneously to achieve optimum results. Factors which influence product test strategies, vertical integration, and their impact on the factory were examined.

[1] W. D. Ballew, L. M. Streb, "Elimination of Incoming Test Based Upon In-Process Failure and Repair Costs", International Test Conference, September 1988.

[2] A. E. Dugan, W. D. Ballew, L. M. Streb, and G. D. Wade, "Improving Component Quality Through A Dynamic Vendor Interface", Juran Institute Conference Proceedings, November 1987.

CUSTOMER DRIVEN TEST/VERIFICATION PROCESSES: WAVE OF THE FUTURE

Kenneth R. Berger
Manager, RTP FAST Operations
Northern Telecom Incorporated
P.O. Box 13010
Research Triangle Park, NC 27709

ABSTRACT
The telecommunications revolution has challenged every vendor's methods and processes related to new product realization. The success of these new processes is strategically coupled with new product introductions, carefully integrated and targeted in meeting customer expectations. Within the test community, the balance between hardware and software is becoming increasingly significant related to achieving customer goals of product performance excellence. Generic hardware and software introductions and the integration of these test strategies for large central office telecommunications equipment will be overviewed during this session.

INTRODUCTION
Customer Service is the bottom line in meeting the customer requirements and expectations of product excellence. Successful companies in any highly competitive market place are constantly attempting to serve the customer's ever changing needs in an effective/responsive manner.

The value of customer driven product introduction or birthing, establishing and maintaining of related hardware and software integration test strategies for large central office telecommunications equipment has become increasingly significant. These integrated strategies are paramount in the ability to successfully deliver and sustain a complex telecommunications installed base.

HISTORY
The telecommunications product revolution has made great strides in catching up to space-age technology in recent years. There has been an evolution in the process of moving early product life design ambiguities previously discovered in the field environment to the earliest point in the process, with the targeted thrust of uncovering these early life opportunities in the design laboratory.

The history of large switching system introduction into the operating companies being one of "letting the customer find" and debug a manufacturer's new product is a very lengthy, intensive and expensive process. This previously accepted strategy is being tolerated less by the customer/operating companies for normal product roll out. Northern Telecom's leadership in providing product excellence to the industry and several related hardware and software processes utilized in "getting there" will be overviewed during this session.

SOFTWARE/HARDWARE TEST STRATEGY DEVELOPMENT

Conceptually, before any strategy is attempted to be developed, one must carefully analyze the overall industry direction. This analyzation permits any strategies that result to be very comprehensive and most importantly, able to address future customer requirements and expectations. (Fig. A)

The same type of strong leadership required to drive the overall industry toward telecommunications excellence is also needed in the area of test strategy development. Never in the history of the telecommunications industry has competition been keener, with time to market pressures and customer expectations of minimal (zero) defects absolutely must be taken into account as these strategies are exploited.

FUTURE PRODUCT REQUIREMENTS FOR THE COMPETITIVE EDGE

Several key areas of product evolution need careful review prior to any test strategy development. Increased focus on SILICON and SOFTWARE is seen as over-riding opportunities in the product arena.

Both SILICON and SOFTWARE concentration puts increased emphasis on ensuring that everything is done "right the first time". Both areas require working closely with the CUSTOMER in defining specific and desired functionality. Once the specification is documented, closing related hardware and software developments begin on a converging path toward implementation.

Basic product performance relates back to the accuracy of the specification, planning with the customer and the designers. The silicon can be measured for accuracy and performance by being "correct by construction", and software "defects per number lines of code" are industry accepted. As both silicon and software become dominant in the 1990s, along with increasing complexity and interdependence, what strategies must telecommunication vendors target to ensure product excellence?

KEYS TO PROCESS EXCELLENCE

Two key items that can significantly contribute to a customer driven test and verification process require continued commitment for use in the telecommunications industry. Item one is found at the beginning of the customer driven process in the use of hierarchical simulation for conceptualizing proposed designs and interactions. The second item ties the installed base customer reported problem system into either design, hardware or software processes for dynamic enhancement at the other end of the process.

The first area that is currently being investigated and where exploratory work is

being carried out is that of TOP DOWN (hierarchical) simulation. The use of hierarchical simulation can significantly contribute to the reduction in the TIME-TO-MARKET interval by providing the methodology and techniques to self-document a product design starting with the all-too-important customer at the highest level, working down level by level to the silicon components to effectively design by. This information can then be used in many areas, including the manufacturing process for test process development.

The customer problem reporting system must be sensitive to customer problems and allow for immediate problem resolution (short-term solution), and of equal importance; correlation of these problem areas in the modification of various processes by adjusting strategies (long-term solution). A knowledge based system can be "optimally" employed when a company has a large installed base which allows the customer reporting system to be increasingly effective and responsive to corrective process and strategy developments. (Fig. B)

HARDWARE TEST PROCESS: REQUIRED EVOLUTION

Historically, the manufacturing test processes have added multiple test steps in order to increase the fault coverage of the overall process. These increased number of test steps have proven costly to the bottom line, and marginally effective in preventing slippage into the customer base. (Fig C) Technology is tightly coupled with customer input to evolve a test process with less steps of an increased quality level.

There are three major areas (Fig. D) that must be addressed by the hardware manufacturing strategy to ensure cost effectivity: design simulated product, components, and process control. It has been demonstrated that process control in a high volume pack shop can be similar to successes in silicon foundry; that is, control of the processes, controls product yield.

A commitment by design management that 100% of all new designs will be simulated, ensures future product design centering, as this aspect is particularly critical with the thrust toward semi-custom silicon. As the industries' simulation capabilities become increasingly comprehensive, the need for verification of pack and system level device/pack interaction in manufacturing will dissolve once demonstrated product performance allows "out-of-box" installation.

With the inception of space-age microelectronics, the revolution in product capability and functionality has been integrated into custom and semi-custom (ASIC) silicon type devices. These silicon devices are beginning to dominate product portfolios and as such, test strategies must evolve to address this technical challenge.

Extensive vendor certification programs have been implemented which rewards the supplier by awarding a large percentage of the business to key suppliers and no longer at the lowest price. The historic need to test components at the incoming inspection test station now becomes significantly de-emphasized relating to overall test strategies with the advent and implementation of vendor/supplier certification programs.

Single stage pack level test strategies (Fig. E) must be able to verify the manufacturing integrity of the new product. This single stage concept focuses attention on the need to deliver the highest quality, "one-step" pack level test, which has shown the capability to target the entire fault spectrum, in an expeditious test time. There are several new techniques now under investigation and early deployment, one of the most promising uses Digital Signal processing integrated into the tests of ISDN type packs. (3)

The subsystem test strategy is critical to customer satisfaction. Early in a product evolution, the subsystem test function performs a "mini-design" assessment/ analysis in a lab environment. This assessment ensures the integrity of the earlier tests, components, processes and design using maintenance diagnostics in the first of a true hardware/software integration manufacturing test strategy. The software is used as a tool in verifying the hardware performance just as our customer would exercise diagnostics during in-service system operations.

The test engineering staff executes IM 925 installation testing procedures just as the customer will verify product performance in the field. These early stringent final lab tests, once the product is proven, move into an audit procedure in the Quality Audit Facility (QAF). (1)

SOFTWARE: DOMINANT TOOL FOR THE FUTURE
With software predicted to grow (Fig. F) at tremendous rates over the next decade, high technology companies must continue to adapt internal processes which effectively manage this software design/ introduction/general release. Northern Telecom manages its Batch Change Supplement (BCS) software developments through a series of milestone reviews (2), with established stringent release criteria.

As the installed base of hardware expands software dominance related to feature richness become a design/marketing tool to

offer this field population further attractive options. With millions of lines of code, and hundreds of thousands of lines added, changed or deleted lines during every BCS release, what strategies can be employed to achieve customer satisfaction of product excellence?

A multifaceted attack at reducing the number of potential software problems to an order of magnitude below accepted industry practice at product release starts with the design. Code inspection, increased test coverage both at the designer and initial system integration levels (1) plus overall attention to detail and striving to do the job right the first time are important to the foundation of many ongoing design process improvement programs.

Feedback to/from the other process stages and most importantly, the customer information must be maintained and properly managed. Valuable information which allows for existing process improvements and future process evolution is examined by many groups within Northern Telecom and BNR.

INTEGRATION OF SOFTWARE IN THE WORLD'S LARGEST NON-INSERVICE OFFICE; PRODUCT EXCELLENCE GOAL
The First Application System Test (FAST) represents the customer in terms of software application prior to any inservice office receipt. The FAST offices receive three iterations of every BCS release, starting with the Ready to Order-Not In Service (RTO-NIS). This RTO-NIS load is the first verification of BCS software and associated tools that will be used by in-service offices beginning with the release of RTO-In Service BCS during the verification office time frame. (Fig. G)

The FAST office experiences intense testing during the BCS verification. (Fig H) These various types of testing categories all are targeted at uncovering potential problem areas early enough in the BCS cycle to ensure correction prior to customer receipt of the BCS. Review of customer requirements for items like PM/CC compatibility with various BCS combinations are managed throughout each BCS period prior to software ramp.

A CUSTOMER PROBLEM IS BIGGER THAN A TEST CASE
The aforementioned referenced process feedback can be exemplified by customer service review of all Customer Service Reports (CSRs), using a knowledge based system to prioritize and sort these CSRs ensures consistent handling and prompt disposition which allows for possible process enhancements. Again, the customer input is extremely valuable in ensuring a closed loop test and verification process.

Test Strategy Development: The Foundation

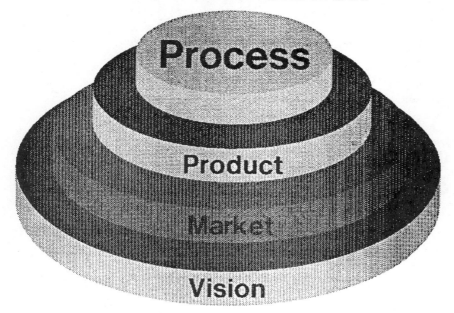

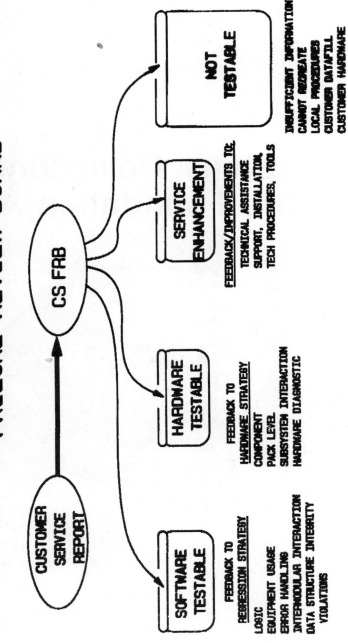

Fig. B

1611

Fig. C

Technology Drives Test Evolution

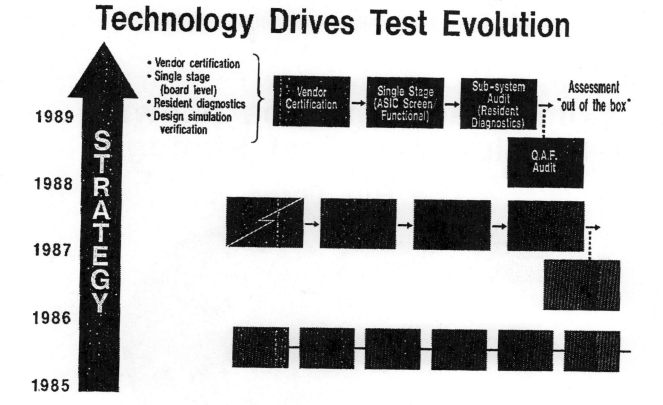

Committed Functions Allowing
Revolutionary Test Strategy

"The Big Three"

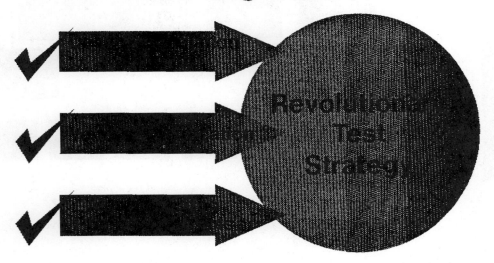

Single Stage Test

- **Highest quality assembled board level test/one handling step**
- **Integrates multiple levels of test**
  - **Incoming/vendor vectors/parameters**
  - **Classic manufacturing defects (shorts, opens)**
  - **Full functional test/product performance**

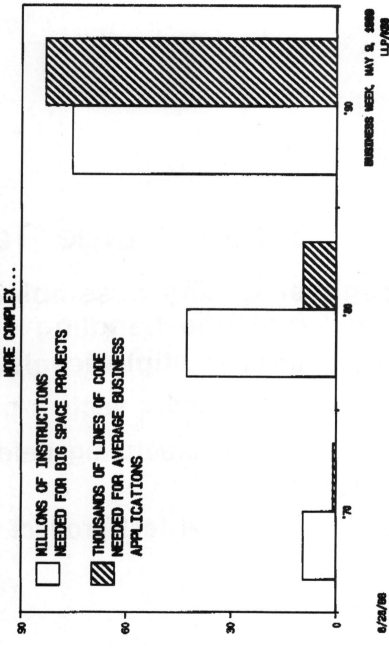

THE SOFTWARE CRUNCH

...PROGRAMS ARE GETTING
MORE COMPLEX...

□ MILLIONS OF INSTRUCTIONS
NEEDED FOR BIG SPACE PROJECTS

▨ THOUSANDS OF LINES OF CODE
NEEDED FOR AVERAGE BUSINESS
APPLICATIONS

BUSINESS WEEK, MAY 9, 1988
LLP/RB

6/28/88

Fig. F

INTEGRATED NETWORK SYSTEMS
CUSTOMER SERVICE

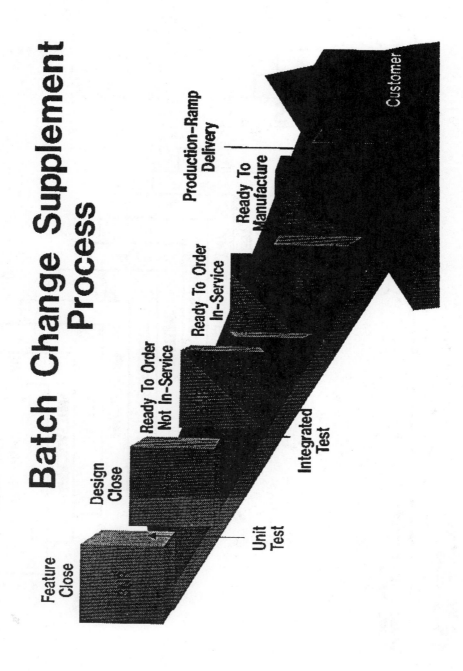

Fig. G

Batch Change Supplement Process

Feature Close

Design Close

Ready To Order Not In-Service

Ready To Order In-Service

Production–Ramp Delivery

Ready To Manufacture

Customer

Unit Test

Integrated Test

1616

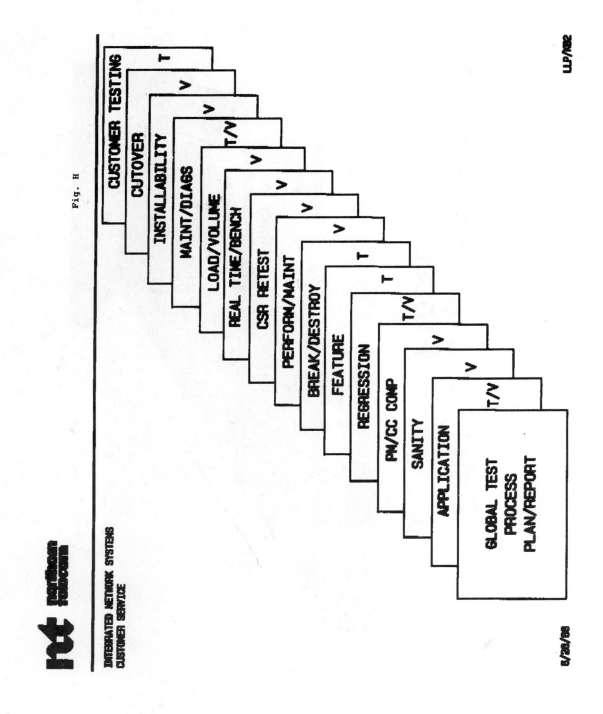

Fig. H

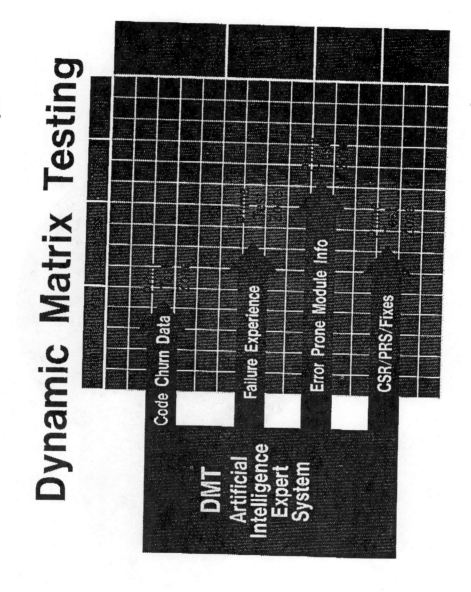

Dynamic Matrix Testing

DMT
Artificial
Intelligence
Expert
System

Code Churn Data

Failure Experience

Error Prone Module Info

CSR/PRS/Fixes

Fig. 1

Formula for Product Excellence

Fig. J

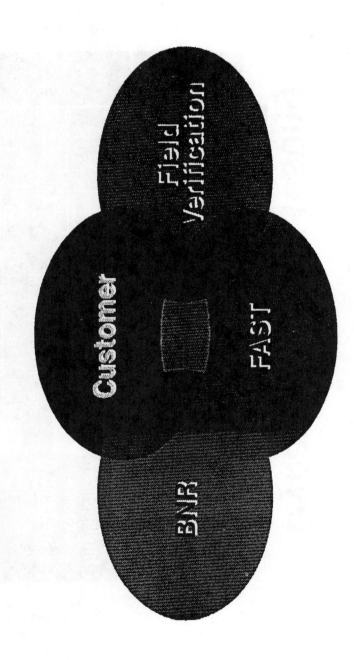

Any CSRs and potential field problems related to software and software slippage once selected by the knowledge base system, are carefully reviewed by FAST software test engineers. Although test cases are written immediately to enable capture of identical problems in the future, more importantly, a global regression strategy is carefully examined so that a much more comprehensive view of similar classes of problems are also captured internally. Once identified and properly classified, FAST personnel refer these problem areas with solutions to BNR for inclusion in their regression test package, in a continual effort to move problem resolution to the earliest point in the development cycle possible.

With projected growth of overall software requirements in systems like DMS, alternatives such as computer aided software engineering (CASE) must be invested in today to address critical future needs. Dynamic Matrix Testing (Fig. I) can be seen as an example of CASE, which incorporates various inputs like code churn data, past failure experience, and previous areas requiring fixed via CSR/PRS tracking. The shear volume of test case possibilities present the need to utilize CASE type systems to ensure customer satisfaction related to excellence in product performance.

SUMMARY
Successes in the telecommunications industry, past, present and future, can be largely attributed to working closely with the customer. Customer driven test/verification processes (Fig. J) are no exception to the rule. The integration of hardware and software test processes have been a key customer driven input ford product assurance, and end-user satisfaction.

With industry pressures to introduce cost effective measures due largely to the divestiture, there is one common thread running through the communications fabric the professionals in the industry all share; that is, the desire to provide excellence and innovation in every communications solution offered and implemented.

REFEENCES
1. Seaton, David B. PARTNERS IN QUALITY-- THE PAYOFF, 1987 National Communications Forum Vol. 41 No II.

2. Runyon, Stan, THE GREAT ASIC WAVE GATHERS FORCE, Electronics, August 6, 1987

3. Special Report, THE SOFTWARE TRAP; AUTOMATE - OR ELSE, Business Week, May 9, 1988, Page 142-154.

4. Berger, Kenneth R., TEST REVOLUTION: MIXED SIGNAL LAUNCH INTO THE FUTURE; ATE WEST PROCEEDINGS, Anahiem, CA, January 1988

TEST STRATEGIES FOR PRODUCT REPAIR IN A DEPOT ENVIRONMENT

George M. Schultz
Engineering Manager
Planning and Development -
Repair and Distribution
AT&T
400 South Woods Mill Road
Chesterfield, MO 63017

ABSTRACT
Developing a test strategy for a repair environment handling field returns is dependent on the repair strategy to be used and the test requirements for the product. The test requirements in repair are generally functional in nature since it is the primary job of repair test equipment to determine if the product requires repair or not. The repair strategy to be used is not as straight-forward since it is dependent on the predictability of the product failure modes and the volume of the repair expected. Due to these two variables and others there is not a single repair strategy for a repair depot. Due to the multiplicity of repair strategies, there is also a number of test strategies which must be supported. Out of all these repair strategies, those utilizing the Expert System technology seem to be providing a unifying influence on all of repair which should have a strong influence on unifying the test strategy.

INTRODUCTION
As the product realization moves from manufacturing to the field, the issue of handling product returned from the field for repair must be addressed. The product can be returned for a variety of reasons ranging from functional failures to general customer dissatisfaction with the product. In a large telecommunication company, product level repair cuts across all types of communication equipment ranging from voice and data terminals to switching and transmission equipment to office and engineering workstations, etc. All of these product groups carry with them different end point electrical requirements, many vintages, varying levels of appearance standards, and different customer expectations of repair. Regardless of the reason for returning the product or the type of product, it must pass a set of functional requirements before it can be returned back to stock or back to the customer. These functional requirements include a functional test which means test equipment which requires a test strategy. In a depot environment handling many different types of product, there are many repair strategies which have the effect of producing widely varying test strat-

egies. This paper shows how these varying strategies evolve through the product life cycle as the product moves from the factory to a field environment. The paper concludes with a discussion of the use of Expert Systems in repair and how this technology is having a unifying effect on the repair test strategies across product families.

THE EVALUATION OF REPAIR TEST STRATEGIES

The test strategies for repair tend to vary depending on where the product is in its life cycle. Early in the life cycle, considerable analyzation is performed on returned product to determine how the product failed so that design or manufacturing process changes can be made before manufacture ramp-up. The test strategy at this point is heavily oriented toward parametric testing in an effort to characterize the operation of the product to determine the root cause of the failure even below the replaceable module level. As the product moves deeper into the life cycle and becomes generally available, the test strategy shifts to a strong emphasis on functional testing to determine that the product meets all functional requirements. In this phase there is a strong emphasis on test and failure data collection to detect any weaknesses in parts used in the product or to detect any trends that need to be addressed by other organizations (field technicians, customer training, transportation, packing problems, etc.) While the need for test and failure data collection does not alter the test specifications for the product, the test equipment/procedure must be able to support this function.

As the product stabilizes in the field in terms of its design, manufacture, and customer acceptance, the final phase of the test strategy is encountered which carries through until the end of the repair life for the product. Generally speaking, the repair life extends for 5-10 years beyond the manufacture discontinue availability date depending on the projected life of the product. At this point in the life of the product, it is completely understood in terms of failure modes and no major design changes are expected. The test strategy in this part depends almost completely on functional testing and is heavily influenced by the major failure modes that are inherent in the product and the way the product is being used.

At this point there is almost a complete departure from the testing strategies used in manufacturing. The principle reasons for the departure:

1. It is assumed that the product worked once and there is little need to detect manufacturing problems.

2. Quantity is lower (different) set of economics).
3. Must be able to handle all vintages of the product, not just the current vintage.
4. Quality standards tend to be determined more by customer desires and needs in keeping with the design intent of the product.

While these reasons tend to drive apart the test strategies, the test specifications which define the functionality of the product remain closely interlinked. The way the specifications are met is driven by the test strategy which in turn is driven by the reasons stated above. For example, in a modern manufacturing facility operating a "Just-In-Time" mode tends to have their test function dispersed throughout the process where a repair environment would have all tests embodied into one test set.

In summary, the test strategies within repair tend to differ from manufacturing and tend to vary depending on where the product is in its life cycle. Once the product stabilizes from a design, manufacturing, and customer viewpoint, the repair test strategy stabilizes and becomes heavily influenced by the major failure modes of the product.

REPAIR TEST STRATEGY

First, every product exhibits some pattern in the way that it fails. This pattern of failures can range all the way from a uniform distribution of failures to extremely dominant or Major modes of failure. Our repair depots see products on both ends of this spectrum and all points in between so the way the product fails becomes a variable in determining the test strategy. Secondly, because of the reduced volume in repair (thousands rather than millions) the level of investment (capital and expense) that can be introduced is very sensitive to volume. The million dollar investment in a factory becomes 60-70 thousand dollars in a repair shop. Our test strategy is based on the distribution of these failure modes and the volume of the product to be repaired. These two variables (failure mode distribution and volume) are two of the many factors in forming a test strategy and form the graph shown in Figure One.

The dividing line between low and high volume on the vertical axis in Figure One is generally determined by the level of capital investment that the repair of a particular product can support in a repair environment. The level of capital investment can be calculated given that all the relevant costs and the earning requirements for the environment are known. The dividing line between Major and Uniform distributions is not as clearly defined but it generally follows the following rule of thumb:

If 20 percent or less of the parts in a product cause 80 percent of the failures, it is classified as falling into the Major failure mode category.

Given this diagram, we then determine for each of the following four quadrants the repair strategy to be used which in turn determines our test strategy.

Quadrant   I - Low Volume - Uniform distribution of failures
Quadrant   II - High Volume - Uniform distribution of failures
Quadrant   III - Low Volume - Product exhibits major failure modes
Quadrant   IV - Low Volume - Product exhibits major failure modes

Figure Two shows the same diagram with our repair strategy superimposed in each Quadrant. As can be seen from this diagram, a threefold repair stategy has been developed which has the following characteristics:

Low Volume - Uniform Distribution - Many of large digital motherboards tend to fall into this category. Our testing in this quadrant is oriented toward bench level instrumentation which can be used by highly trained technicians to troubleshoot the product. Digital instrumentation (logic analyzers, digital scopes, etc.) are the rule here. Technician training is paramount. System testing of the boards in their host machine dominates the test strategy.

High Volume - Uniform Distribution - Same types of product - digital in nature - motherboards - processors - memory boards. Use large bed-of-nail fixtures to do a combination of in-circuit, functional, processor emulation, and ROM emulation techniques to troubleshoot board to component level. Very capital intensive. Centralized repair. High engineering content.

Low Volume - Major Failure Mode/High Volume - Major Failure Mode - Products in this class tend to be terminal equipment. line cards, trunk cards, modems, etc. They tend to have predictable failure patterns. Use functional test sets to test the operation of the product. Use Expert Systems to troubleshoot product to component level. (Expert System described in next section.)

We are finding that more and more of our repair work is falling into the Major failure mode category and I believe there are three reasons why this is so.

1. The bulk of communication repair work is made of either terminal equipment or line and trunk equipment which tend to exhibit major failure modes.

2. The Expert System technology is so robust that it is driving its application line deeper into those products which exhibit more uniform failure modes.
3. When a product reaches its end of life, repair of the major failure modes only may meet the declining maintenance demand. This issue is becoming increasingly more important because individual product life is becoming shorter and there is a tradeoff between the use of new or repaired product to meet demands.

The remainder of this paper is directed toward our use of Expert Systems as a repair strategy.

EXPERT SYSTEMS TO REPAIR MAJOR FAILURE MODES

An Expert System is just what the name implies, that is, it is a collection of the knowledge, experience, rules of thumb, and do's and don'ts that a genuine, real life expert possesses.

In our case our expert is an engineer who has analyzed a number of defective units to determine a body of knowledge which consists of:

- major failure modes identification
- the "how-to's" to link symptoms to causes
- strategies for isolating the causes doen to specific components

This body of knowledge is then encoded into a special software system which can accept knowledge and generate troubleshooting instructions using that knowledge. This software package is then inputted to a computer which is linked to terminals at a repair technician's workplace. This software system is called an Expert System since it now possesses the knowledge or expertise of the engineer for that product.

This system is then accessed by a technician who inputs the symptoms and/or major failure modes in the computer and the system leads him through the troubleshooting of the unit. The technician can now perform the same function as our engineering expert.

The use of Expert Systems with AT&T's repair shops began in June 1987 for voice terminal repair. The original application was based on the OPS5 language running on an AT&T 3B02 computer system. At the present time, our applications are based on C5 which is a rule-based programming language. C5 is a superset of Forgy's OPS5 language, is written entirely in C, and is available for virtually all AT&T computers including the 6300.

Our use of Expert Systems can probably best be described by the process we go through to implement repair via this approach which is given in the following five step process:

Step 1 Develop a functional test set for the product to be repaired. The test set is controlled from a 3B02 computer via the General Purpose Interface Bus. The 3B02 is also responsible for interfacing to the repair operator via RS 232 interface. The 3B02 controller is driven at a high level by the C5 language which places the operation of the test set, all the instrumentation, and the interface to the operator under control of the Expert System software package.

Step 2 Identify major failure modes of the product through engineering analysis. This is usually accomplished through a detailed analysis of 200 units of product to determine the relationship between a component failure and a test step programmed into the functional test step. There is usually a fair amount of interaction between Step 1 and Step 2. Many times the failure mode data is available from the analysis performed earlier in the life of the product. Out of this comes a diagram similar to that shown in Figure Three.

Step 3 Develop a troubleshooting algorithm for each major failure mode. This generally takes the form of a tree which contains instructions to the operator and to the test set to diagnose that failure mode down to the component level. We generally find that one or two components in each of the major failure modes accounts for the bulk of the failures. For example, under Power Supply defects, one component, a capacitor, accounted for 70 percent of all the failures.

Step 4 Input to the Expert System and prove-in. The C5 package has provisions for inputting these troubleshooting trees.

Step 5 Deploy and train. Beside being a very efficient way of implementing repair, the Expert System is also an excellent training aid. There is a learn mode built into the system which describes to the operator in detail on how to do a particular task. It even explains how diodes are coded so test leads can be properly placed. In many cases, the operators after using the system for a few days will turn it off completely because they

have learned cause-effect relationships between functional failures and components. Also, the learn mode is very valuable for low volume repair where product knowledge cannot be mastered.

The use of the Expert System methodology has had the impact of simplifying our test strategy. Our test equipment does not have to carry the load of supplying detailed data for troubleshooting to the repair operators as this is now the responsibility of the Expert System. This has the impact of reducing equipment complexity (particularly software) and also its cost. The most dramatic impact is the use of the Expert System approach rather than the very costly bed-of-nails approach. Engineers can concentrate on how the product is failing and how to troubleshoot those failures rather than fixture development.

In general, this approach has had the effect of unifying our repair and test strategies. Repair engineers zeroing in on how product fails rather than test development, test set designers are seeing commonalities between products much greater than before because of the imperial nature of the Expert approach, our technicians are more involved, and our overall expenses, capital requirements, and development times have been reduced.

CONCLUSION

In a repair depot environment repairing many different types of product, the test strategies need to be flexible to accommodate the needs of each product and its set of customers. Over the past few years, the use of Expert Systems requires that we concentrate on how the product fails and how to develop a knowledge base to troubleshoot these failures and shift some of this burden away from our test equipment and test engineering. This is having the effect of unifying our test strategies which in turn reduces test equipment capital cost and test engineering expenses.

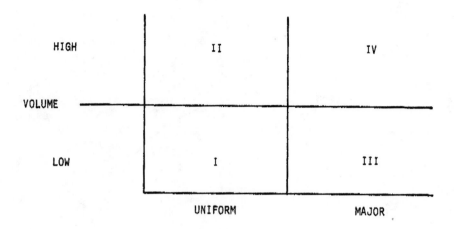

FAILURE MODE DISTRIBUTION

FIGURE ONE
FAILURE MODE DISTRIBUTION VERSUS VOLUME

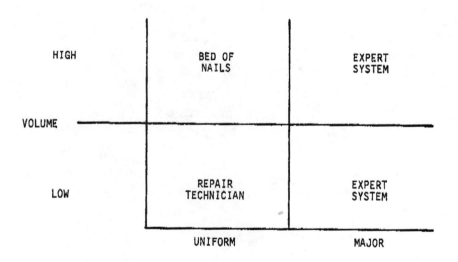

FAILURE MODE DISTRIBUTION

FIGURE TWO
REPAIR STRATEGY

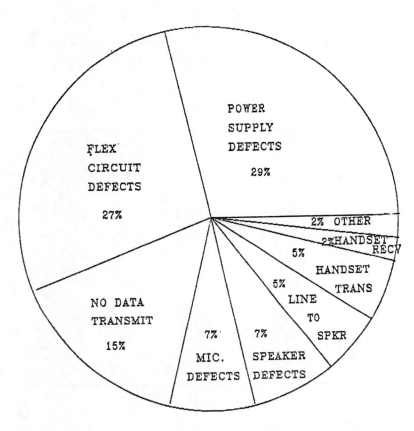

POWER
SUPPLY
DEFECTS

29%

FLEX
CIRCUIT
DEFECTS

27%

2% OTHER

2%HANDSET
RECV

5%

HANDSET
TRANS

5%

LINE

TO

SPKR

NO DATA
TRANSMIT

15%

7%

MIC.
DEFECTS

7%

SPEAKER
DEFECTS

FIGURE THREE
MAJOR FAILURE MODE DISTRIBUTION

OPTICAL SWITCHING AND COMPUTING
THE INDUSTRY PERSPECTIVE

Matthew F. Slana, Chairperson

Head, Software Development

AT&T Information Systems

1100 E. Warrenville Road
Naperville, IL 60566

ABSTRACT

Optical technology has been increasingly studied since the invention of the laser, a coherent source of single-frequency light. Initial investigations in the 1960's led towards use of lenses to form Fourier Transforms of functions. Later research has, especially in the past decade, led to increased use of optical components and techniques in both telecommunications switching and computing. The benefits of optical technology were first seen in fiber transmission systems, which have further spawned increased uses and applications in the 1980's. An increased flow of ideas and applications generated in research labs have in turn led to developments and commercial applications in transmission links. Optical computing, while slower in reaching the development labs from the initial Fourier Transform techniques based on laser/optical systems, has now reached the stage where devices capable of switching light beams and photons are available for researchers to study the use of these techniques in computers and switching systems. As these systems evolve further, the melding of switching, computing, and transmission devices are being studied with the possible end result of system architectures in which electrons are converted to photons in the customer terminals and transmitted as photons exclusively to the recipient.

This seminar provides an overview of the basic concepts associated with photonic switching and computing, followed by a brief exposition of switching and computing work now being performed in industrial laboratories. This seminar also provides the basics for the companion seminar TEC-02, "Optical Switching and Computing - The University Research Perspective," which describes some of the photonic switching and computing research now being undertaken in university laboratories.

This seminar begins with an overview of the impact which might be expected from photonic switching on optical communications and computing, describes the status of photonic switching devices, and projects the trends in future optical information systems. The second speaker extends this overview to photonic networks and architectural alternatives. The third paper deals with construction of optical switching matrices and implementation considerations, and investigates the interaction between photonic interconnection technology and optical crosspoints. The final paper then addresses the thrust of optical switching from initial use as an efficient interconnection technology through penetration to

optical gate interconnection and eventual switching of light by light.

K. D. Anderson -- Bell Northern Research

H. S. Hinton -- AT&T Bell Laboratories

Peter W. Smith -- Bell Communications Research

H. W. Willemsen -- Bell Northern Research

R. C. Williamson -- Lincoln Laboratory, Massachusetts Inst. of Technology

PHOTONIC SWITCHING: CURRENT WORK
AND FUTURE PROSPECTS

Peter W. Smith

District Manager, Ultrafast Optics and Optical Signal Processing Research

Bell Communications Research

331 Newman Springs Road
Red Bank, NJ 07701

ABSTRACT

There is at present a growing interest in developing photonic switching and signal-processing devices for future communications and computing applications. In this paper we will begin by explaining some of the reasons for this interest. We will then discuss some of the strong and weak points of photonic switching devices. After a presentation of some examples of current research of electro-optic and all-optical switching elements, we will conclude with a discussion of future prospects for photonic switching.

INTRODUCTION

Despite the fact that electronics technology continues to make substantial advances in speed, complexity, and reduced cost, there is at present a growing interest in developing photonic switching and signal-processing devices for future communications applications [1]. One reason for this interest is the major commitment that is being made for fiber optics for data transmission. As shown in Fig. 1, the demand for more and more sophisticated services continues to push the development of communications networks with increasingly high bit rate capacity. Fig. 2 illustrates the fact that we are now at the stage where lightwave communication networks are limited not by the fiber capacity, but by the limitations of the electronics used for the switching, routing, and signal processing. Because, as shown in Fig. 3, optical switching and routing devices can function in a time range inaccessible to electronics, it is tempting to suggest that photonic signal-processing elements will be used in future communications networks to eliminate the electronics "bottleneck". In this paper we will examine some of the attributes of photonic switching elements that make them attractive for these applications, and present some of the current research that is being done to bring the photonic network of the future closer to reality.

POTENTIAL

The field of optical switching and signal-processing is still in its infancy, and much work remains to be done before practical and reliable devices are available for widespread use. Nevertheless, it is possible to make some general observations.

The strong points of optical devices are:
1) Speed: optical devices are able to switch in sub-picosecond times -- far faster than any other technology.
2) Bandwidth: by maintaining a single mode channel for the optical signal, even relatively slowly-responding mechanical or electro-optic photonic switches are able to preserve the large bandwidth of single mode optical fiber.
3) Parallelism: many optical devices have an inherent capability to perform multiple simultaneous operations, and to perform complex interconnections.
4) Elimination of optics - electronics - optics conversions.
5) Freedom from electromagnetic interference.

The weak points of optical devices are:
1) High power is required for fast switching: this will cause thermal problems unless special precautions are taken.
2) Optical devices are generally much larger in size than their electronic counterparts.
3) Materials and processing technology for optical devices are in a relatively early stage of development.

Clearly much work remains to be done -- not only to develop useful photonic switching elements, but also to develop systems that are designed to take advantage of the unique capabilities of optics.

It is perhaps instructive to look at the past history of the adoption of new switching technologies. Fig. 4 shows that there has been a lag of 25 to 30 years between the laboratory exploration of a new switching technology and the large-scale utilization of this technology for telecommunications applications. Thus it is reasonable to expect that the major impact of photonic switching will not be felt until after the year 2000.

CURRENT WORK

There is at present a great deal of work on photonic switching, and international conferences are held on this topic. In this section I will attempt to review briefly the various types of photonic switching elements that have been studied, and give three examples of new results.

Table I shows three categories of photonic switches

and gives a picture of how close each category is to practical applications.

Mechanical switches for routing signals from one optical fiber to another have been available commercially for some time. Although switching times are in the millisecond regime, low loss operation can be obtained, and the bandwidth of the optical channel is preserved.

Electro-optic switching elements are usually based on integrated optical components fabricated using substrates of lithium niobate - a transparent electro-optic material. Waveguides can be formed in the material by the in-diffusion of titanium, and the optical properties can be controlled by the application of a voltage to electrodes deposited on the surface. Conventional devices of this type suffer from several problems: they are sensitive to the polarization of the light; they are sensitive to the wavelength of the light; and they are sensitive to fabrication tolerances. These problems are basically related to the fact that the voltage response of these switches looks like that depicted in Fig. 5a, rather than the ideal digital response shown in Fig. 5b.

In the last year, however, there has been a breakthrough in integrated optical switch design [2]. The new design, shown in Fig. 6a, operates on a new physical principle. As evidenced by the experimentally observed response curves shown in Fig. 6b, the device has an almost ideal digital response. This digital optical switch is insensitive to polarization and wavelength of the light, insensitive to control voltage fluctuations, and insensitive to fabrication tolerances. It represents a major step towards practical applications of electro-optic photonic switches.

Further into the future, all optical switching elements are likely to be favored because of their capability for ultrafast (sub-picosecond) switching. Recently, an all-optical switch which has the fastest switching time of any switching device was demonstrated [3]. The device consists of two closely-spaced optical waveguides in a nonlinear glass, as shown in Fig. 7. A change in light intensity can cause the light to switch from one output waveguide to the other. The results observed with one-tenth picosecond pulse excitation are shown in Fig. 8a. Because the switch response time is much faster than the pulse duration, the output observed with a (slow) electronic detector does not indicate the true switch response. Thus although complete switching occurs during the optical pulse, some average output is observed from both output ports. The data are in excellent agreement with a theory that assumes rapid complete switching and takes into account the slow detector response. These results give convincing evidence that nonlinear glass couplers may become the first practical all-optical switching elements.

The last example of novel photonic switching concepts I will discuss is an all-optical pulse encoding scheme that could make feasible an ultrahigh bit rate local area communications network without requiring fast electronics [4]. One possible use for such a network is shown in Fig. 9. The system is based on a pair of passive optical phase plates which serve to code and decode optical pulses. Each pulse, representing a data bit, is converted into a coded sequence of pulses called a "key", as shown in Fig. 10. At the receiver, a complementary code mask (the "lock") converts the coded pulse back to a replica of the input pulse. As the encoding/decoding process is unique to each pair of users, many subscribers could share a common single mode fiber without interference. Fig. 11 illustrates this coding and decoding with actual experimental results using picosecond optical pulses. This concept should make possible picosecond asynchronous optical code-division multiplexing, where multiple transmitters in the system can operate simultaneously without interference. Because such a system utilizes all-optical processing, channel capacities of hundreds of gigabits/sec should be possible without requiring high-speed modulators or electronics.

FUTURE PROSPECTS

What of the future? There are a number of indications that we are on the threshold of a photonics revolution. Sales projections suggest that the optics industry will grow dramatically in the next few years, and that the total revenues may approach those of the electronics industry before the end of this century. There are many exciting areas of photonics research that may influence our lives in the years to come. Optical computing and photonic implementations of neural networks may provide immense computing power for processing as well as new ways of accessing information.

It seems clear that optics will become a critical and pervasive technology. Fig. 12 illustrates this evolution in communications and computing.

In the more immediate future we can expect to see the interface between the optics used for transmission and the electronics used for signal-processing begin to recede. There will be some optical signal-processing performed before the optical signals are converted to electrical ones. Optics will also be used for interconnection and special-purpose functions. The fast response time and high bit rate capacity of optical devices will greatly enhance the capabilities of present-day communications and computing systems, and this will be an important step in the forthcoming photonics revolution.

REFERENCES

1. P. W. Smith, "On the Role of Photonic Switching in Future Communications Systems", Proceedings of the 1987 International Communications Conference, IEEE Press (1987)

2. Y. Silberberg, et al, "A Digital Optical Switch", Appl Phys Lett 51, 1230 (1987)

3. S. R. Friberg, et al., "Ultrafast All-Optical Switch Using a Dual Core Nonlinear Coupler", Appl Phys Lett 51, 1135 (1987)

4. A. M. Weiner, J. P. Heritage, and J. A. Salehi, "Frequency Domain Coding of Femtosecond Pulses for Spread Spectrum Communications", Proceedings of the 1987 CLEO Conference, Optical Society of America (1987)

	DEVICE DEMONSTRATION IN LABORATORY	SYSTEM DEMONSTRATION IN LABORATORY	DEVICE AVAILABLE COMMERCIALLY	INSTALLED IN OPERATING SYSTEM
MECHANICAL	✔	✔	✔	✔
ELECTRICAL	✔	✔	✔	?
OPTICAL	✔	?	—	—

TABLE I. Photonic switches.

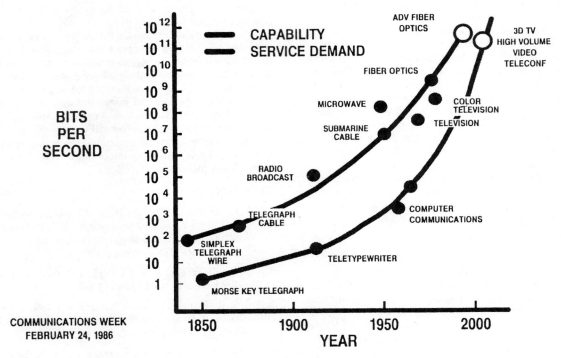

FIG. 1.   DEVELOPMENT OF DIGITAL
            TELECOMMUNICATIONS.

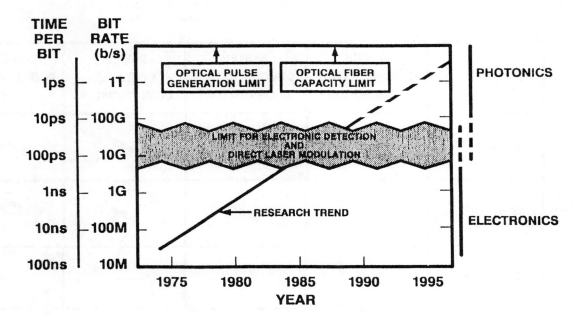

FIG. 2.   LIGHTWAVE COMMUNICATIONS
            SYSTEMS

1629

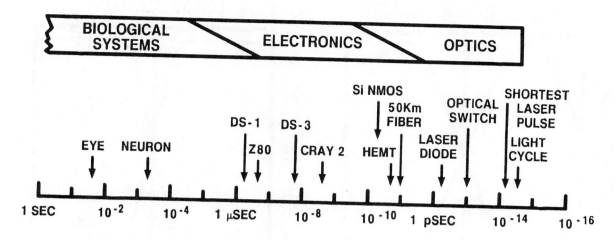

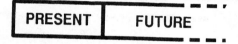

FIG. 3.   TIME SCALES.

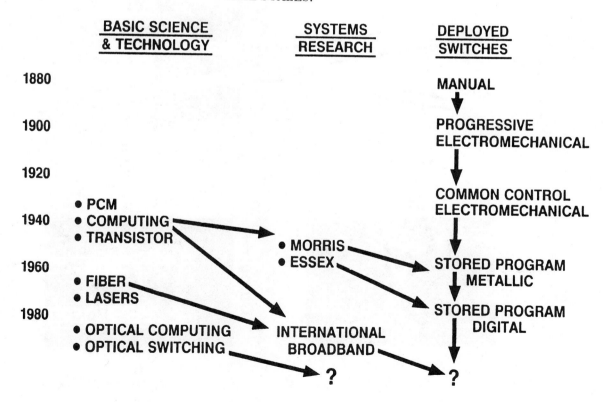

FIG. 4.   A BRIEF HISTORY OF SWITCHING.

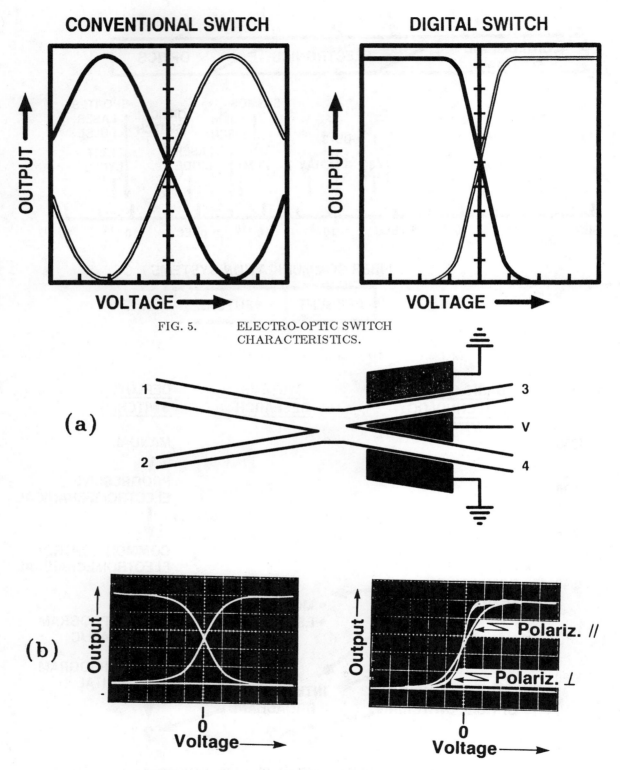

CONVENTIONAL SWITCH

DIGITAL SWITCH

OUTPUT

VOLTAGE

OUTPUT

VOLTAGE

FIG. 5.   ELECTRO-OPTIC SWITCH
CHARACTERISTICS.

(a)

1

2

3

V

4

(b)

Output

0
Voltage

Output

Polariz. //

Polariz. ⊥

0
Voltage

FIG. 6.   DIGITAL OPTICAL SWITCH.

1631

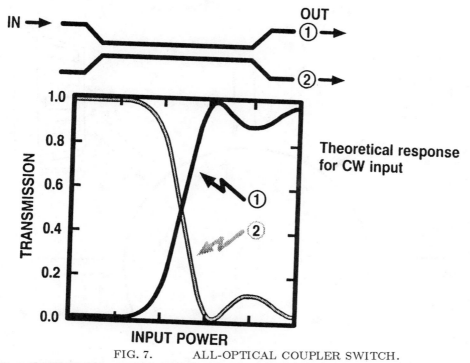

FIG. 7.   ALL-OPTICAL COUPLER SWITCH.

2 CORE FIBER ALL-OPTICAL SWITCH
1/10 picosecond pulses

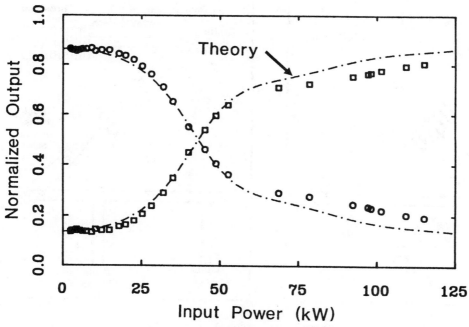

FIG. 8.   ALL-OPTICAL SWITCH EXPERIMENTAL RESULTS

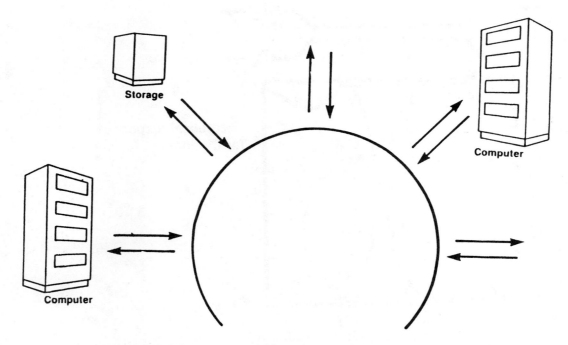

FIG. 9.   PICOSECOND OPTICAL NETWORK.

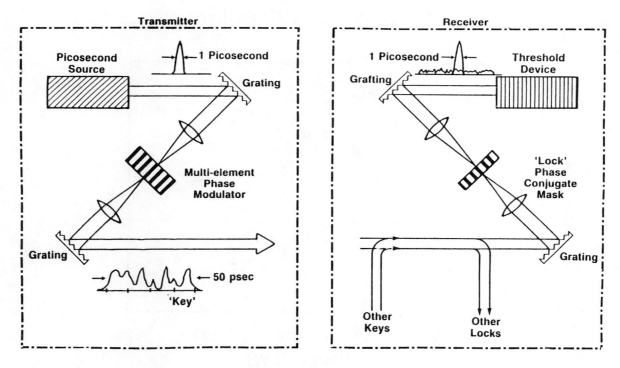

FIG. 10.   PICOSECOND OPTICAL
                MULTIPLEXING.

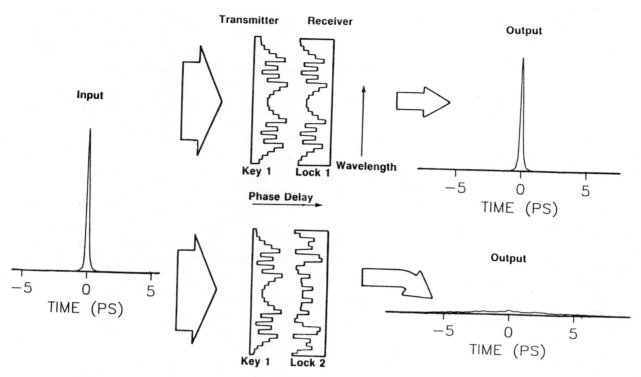

FIG. 11.   SPECTRAL CODES FOR
             PICOSECOND OPTICAL
             MULTIPLEXING.

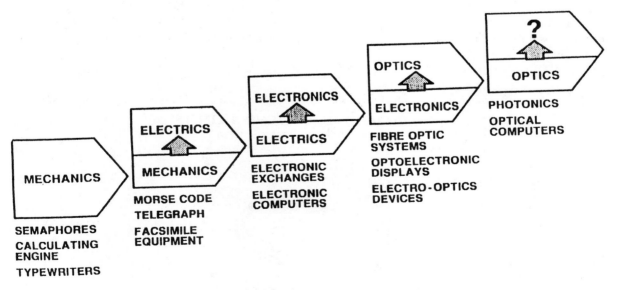

FIG.12.   THE EVOLUTION OF
             COMMUNICATIONS AND
             COMPUTING.

PHOTONIC SWITCHING IN TELECOMMUNICATIONS APPLICATIONS

H. S. Hinton

Supervisor, Photonic Switching
Technologies

AT&T Bell Laboratories

200 Park Plaza
Naperville, IL 60566

ABSTRACT

Some of the strengths and limitations of the photonic technology as applied to telecommunications switching will be presented. This discussion will define relational and logic switching systems and include some practical system design considerations.

INTRODUCTION

Within recent years, there has been a significant amount of interest in applying the new and developing photonics technology for telecommunications switching [1]. As the transmission plant has converted its facilities to fiber there is an economic interest in completing the optical path through the switching system to the terminal facilities without requiring optical-to-electrical (o/e) conversions. Several devices have emerged within the past few years that have the capability of meeting this goal. These devices can be arranged, according to the function they perform, into two major classes, relational and logic devices. The relationships between these devices and their potential uses will be described. The fundamental limits of switching devices will be explored to provide a base, as seen in Fig. 1.

RELATIONAL DEVICES

The first of these classes, called relational devices and shown in Fig. 2, performs the function of establishing a relation or mapping between the inputs and the outputs. This relation is a function of the control signals to the device and is independent of any signal or data inputs. An example of this type of device is the directional coupler as is it is used in switching applications. The information entering and flowing through the devices cannot change or influence the current relation between the inputs and outputs. The major weakness of relational devices is that they cannot sense the presence of individual bits that are passing through them.

LOGIC DEVICES

The second class of devices will be referred to as logic devices, as also shown in Fig. 2. In these devices, the data or information carrying signal that enters the device controls the state of that device in such a way that some boolean function is performed on the inputs. The upper bit-rate of a system composed of these devices is limited by the time required to make these devices change states or switch, since at least one device in the system will have to operate at the maximum bit-rate. This high speed requirement for logic devices limits the bit-rates of signals that can flow through these systems to less than those that can pass through relational systems.

SUMMARY

This paper reviews some of the proposed photonic switching systems that are based on optical relational devices. It will then focus on some practical considerations for directional coupler based systems. These practical considerations include packaging, optical amplifiers, and polarization maintaining fiber. Finally, there will be a brief discussion of optical logic switching systems. The key figures that will be used in the presentation are Figs. 3 through 12.

REFERENCES

1. H. S. Hinton, "Applications of the Photonic Switching Technology for Telecommunications Switching", ICC 1987 (June 7-10, 1987)

FUNDAMENTAL SWITCHING LIMITS
(After P. W. Smith, BSTJ, Oct. 1982)

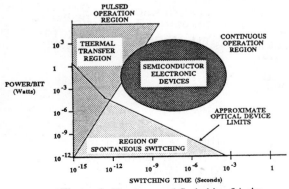

Figure 1. Fundamental Switching Limits

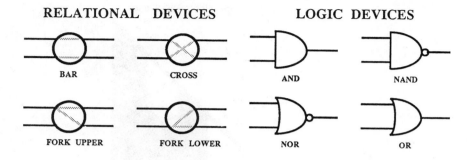

RELATIONAL DEVICES   **LOGIC DEVICES**

BAR   CROSS   AND   NAND

FORK UPPER   FORK LOWER   NOR   OR

Figure 2. Relational Devices vs. Logic Devices

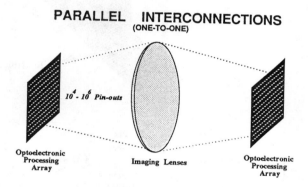

PARALLEL INTERCONNECTIONS
(ONE-TO-ONE)

$10^4 - 10^6$ Pin-outs

Optoelectronic
Processing
Array

Imaging Lenses

Optoelectronic
Processing
Array

HSH 1/30/87

Figure 3. Optical Parallel Interconnections

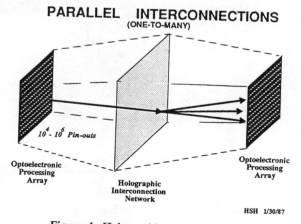

PARALLEL INTERCONNECTIONS
(ONE-TO-MANY)

$10^4 - 10^6$ Pin-outs

Optoelectronic
Processing
Array

Holographic
Interconnection
Network

Optoelectronic
Processing
Array

HSH 1/30/87

Figure 4. Holographic Interconnections

PARALLEL INTERCONNECTIONS
(Potential Optoelectronic Cells)

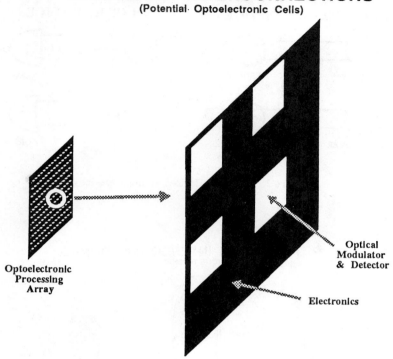

Figure 5. Smart Pixels

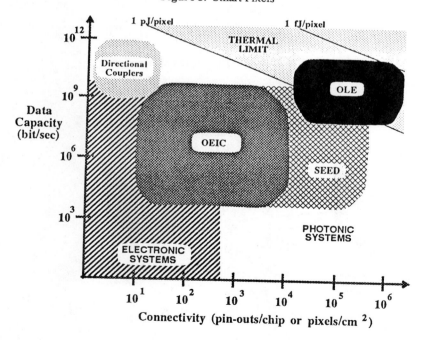

Figure 6. Device Capabilities

OPTICAL CROSSBAR NETWORK

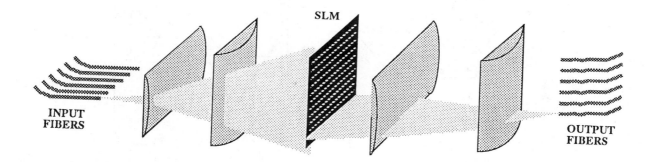

Figure 7. Optical Crossbar Interconnection Network

Wavelength-Division Interconnection Network

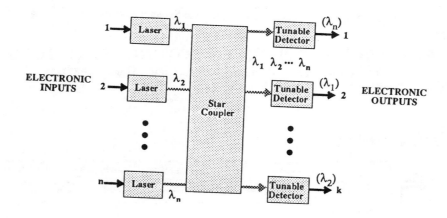

Figure 8. Wavelength Division Switching

32 Line Optical Space-Division Switching System
(Suzuki et al, OFC/IOOC å87)

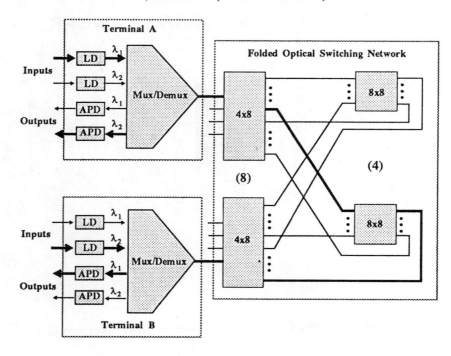

Figure 9. 32x32 Space-Wavelength Division Switching System

ELECTRONIC OVERLAY PHOTONIC SWITCHING
(A. deBoslo et al, Photonic Switch. Conf., March, 1987)

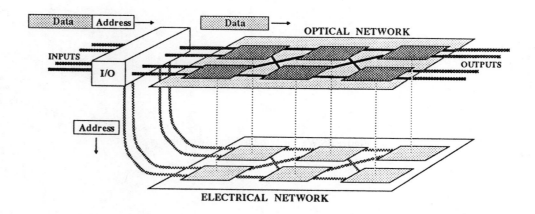

Figure 10. Photonic packet switching architecture

PHOTONIC MULTISTAGE NETWORKS

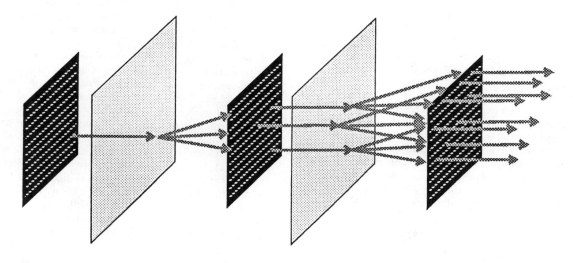

Figure 11. Free-Space Multistage Switching Network

PHOTONIC SHUFFLE NETWORK
(J. E. Midwinter, University College London)

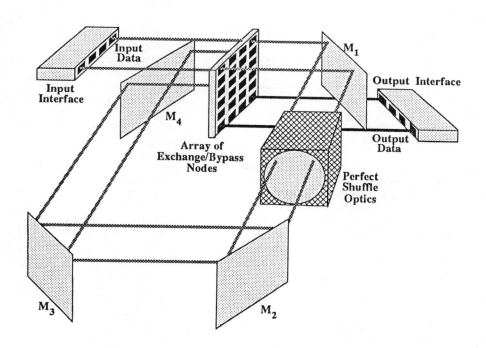

Figure 12. Proposed Free-Space Shuffle Switching Network

PHOTONIC TECHNOLOGY IN SWITCHING

H. W. Willemsen

Manager, Optoelectronics

K. D. Anderson

Bell Northern Research

P. O. Box 3511, Station C
Ottawa, Ontario, Canada K1Y4H7

ABSTRACT

Recent and expected advances in optical/optoelectronic/electronic devices has prompted widespread interest in the construction of small size electrically reconfigurable optical switching matrices. This paper discusses the implementation problems of such a switch matrix as a function of size and throughput, and appraises their impact on the evolution of near-term photonic interconnection technology and possible future optical crosspoints.

OPTICAL COMPUTING

R. C. Williamson

Head, Applied Physics Laboratory

Lincoln Laboratory, Massachusetts
Institute of Technology

Lexington, Massachusetts 02173-0073

ABSTRACT

The insertion of optical devices in digital systems is likely to evolve from initial use as efficient means for interconnections. The attractive ultimate goals for optics are the penetration of optical interconnections to the gate level and, ultimately, the switching of light by light. Prospects for optical computing are reviewed in terms of power levels, speeds, and new architectures and capabilities promised by optics.

INTRODUCTION

The use of optics for information processing has been a subject of great interest for many years. Recently, special attention has been paid to the use of optics in digital systems [1]. An examination of the history and the evolution of optical information processing and communications techniques indicates how this emphasis on "optical computing" has grown and how the use of optics in digital systems is likely to evolve from initial relatively simple applications in providing interconnections.

The use of optics in digital systems has followed two separate threads which are outlined in Fig. 1. With varying degrees of success, optical techniques for information processing have evolved from a variety of analog techniques including synthetic-aperture-radar (SAR) processing, spectral analysis and correlation of

signals, and image processing. In addition to these classic analog applications of optics, there has been a recent increase in interest in more complex nonlinear optical processing for pattern recognition and for the implementation of optical logic. The second thread is the development of optical communications. In almost all cases, the information transmitted over optical fibers is in digital form. The use of fiber optics for long-lines service is well established. The areas of penetration in the near future are for shorter distances including loop service and local-area networks. Examples exist of the use of fiber optics to interconnect computer modules spaced within meters of each other. The trend is toward employing optical communications over shorter and shorter distances. The ultimate evolution would be the use of optical techniques for interconnections down to the gate level. At this point, the optical techniques would play a significant role in defining the architecture and algorithms employed in the digital computer. The application of optics at this level can be described as optical digital logic. Therefore, both the information-processing and digital communications threads lead to a special interest in optical digital logic.

OPTICAL INTERCONNECTIONS

The penetration of optical interconnections into digital systems is likely to occur because of the attractive strengths of optics. One of these strengths is the high degree of parallelism provided. A trivial example of such parallelism is optical imaging in which millions of resolvable pixels are all manipulated in parallel by a simple lens. While conventional digital chips are viewed as two-dimensional layouts connected along their perimeters, optics promises the ability to employ the third dimension for large-scale interconnections between planes. Because photons don't interact, low interference is provided. Moreover, separate information-carrying optical beams can share the same physical space, a feature not provided by wires. Another attractive feature of optical interconnections is their ability to operate at very high speeds through fibers or through free space and with the same freedom from mutual interference. The depth of penetration of optics into digital systems will be strongly constrained by technology developments which will allow these strengths to be exploited.

Fig. 2 illustrates the use of optical interconnects at various levels in digital systems. Fiber optics may provide high-bandwidth links between digital modules such as CPU and memory or between the many processing units and shared memory in distributed computer systems. Fibers may replace wires down to the board, or even, chip level. However, free-space techniques may be favored at the inter- or intra-chip level.

It is possible to make a case for optical interconnections on the basis of power savings. For long lines, the power advantages of fiber optics over conventional cable are undisputed. How does this argument play out at shorter distances? The implications have been worked out in some detail for a particular set of assumptions associated with the interconnection of CMOS circuits [2]. It is assumed that information is being transmitted between two digital elements from the same CMOS logic family. The driver for a metal line of various assumed dimensions must provide enough power to yield adequate swing for switching the receiving element as shown in Fig. 3. Similarly, the power in the driver for a laser and in the receiving circuit must be adequate to yield the required logic switching levels. For a given interconnection length and assumed optical link efficiency, the required switching energy per bit as a function of rise time is shown on the left of Fig. 4. Calculations for two different lengths show that the energy required for a conventional metal interconnection is a strong function of distance, especially because of the need to charge the capacitance of longer lines. For an optical link, the switching energy is essentially independent of length. Therefore, for any rise time, there exists a breakeven length beyond which the optical interconnection operates with lower power. The breakeven length as a function of risetime is shown on the right of Fig. 4. Clearly, the optical interconnections are preferred for longer distances and faster rise times. This figure gets altered as different optical system efficiencies, laser thresholds, fan outs etc., are assumed. However, projected optical link performance for a range of reasonable assumptions indicates that optical interconnects should provide power advantages at lengths· down to a few mm for data rates in the few hundred megabit/s range. This conclusion predicts an optimistic future for the use of optical interconnections, perhaps all the way down to the chip and gate level.

For optical interconnections at the fine-grain level, new computer configurations are envisioned as shown in Fig. 5. Here, an array of electronic logic gates would communicate over optical beams generated on the chip to another gate array with the interconnection pattern established by a computer-generated hologram.

DIGITAL OPTICAL COMPUTING

If optical interconnections promise advantages down to the gate level, we need to examine what impact this is likely to have on the details of the operation of the logic elements and on the architecture of the computer. The most revolutionary approach would be direct switching of light by light in simple structures. This is the ultimate "pure" optical computer. However, these hypothesized computers might end up looking much more like a hybrid of optical and electronic switching. Will the introduction of optics result in higher switching speeds and higher throughput in a computer that has power and cost advantages?

All levels of the use of optics for interconnections share some common features. Whether it be at the computer, board, chip or gate level, optical encoded bits are detected and then they alter the state of the digital logic and the resultant bits are sent out over optical beams as indicated in Fig. 6. While fiber interconnection of main frames is already being readily adopted because such interconnections fit well into conventional computer architecture, the penetration of optical interconnections down to the chip and gate level will require major changes in the basic architecture.

To be useful at the chip and gate level, the functions of detection, logic, and optical modulation must be increasingly integrated. The ultimate optical logic device would be one that used no wires. A typical device of this type is shown schematically in Fig. 7. Such a device is structured so that the optical transmission is a strongly nonlinear function of the incident intensity. This is accomplished by forming a Fabry-Perot etalon around a material whose optical index is a nonlinear function of incident intensity. The optical powers P_1 and P_2 can be arranged to implement AND and OR gates. Many different materials have been investigated in such etalons. The great virtue of the all-optical switches is that they are relatively simple and can switch very fast. However, there exists a speed-power tradeoff as with conventional gates. Typically, the switching energies of optical switches have been too high to be attractive relative to conventional transistor gates [3]. Fast optical devices require very high powers. The list in Fig. 7 of desired features of digital logic contains several areas where the simple optical logic device is marginal or deficient. Such a device is two-terminal, not three terminal. Contrast is often poor and the output has a slope both above and below the switching threshold. In other words, the logic level is not restored and therefore tight control on power levels and thresholds is required. Although differential gain can be achieved near the switching threshold, fanout and cascading are difficult.

Further research may yet yield attractive all-optical logic, but progress in the field is not dependent on reaching this ultimate goal. Intermediate approaches which segment, but closely integrate, the functions of detection logic and modulation may well yield the winning approach. An example of this hybrid approach is the recent demonstration of a phototransistor placed in series with a multiple-quantum-well structure [4] as shown in Fig. 8. The structure is three-terminal with hard limiting and provides net gain from the control signal to the transmitted pump beam. Rapid progress is being made in increasing the speed and contrast of this type of hybrid device.

If the optics penetrates to the fine-grain level and optically activated logic devices replace conventional electronic gates, radical changes in the architectures and algorithms of computers will ensue. Many researchers in the optical-computing field have speculated as to what form the architecture of an optical computer would take on. The consensus is that optically-activated logic gates would be laid out in two dimensions. Data would enter as two-dimensional intensity patterns with each pixel representing a bit. The optics between the input and the planes of gates would route the bits and provide the basic structure of the computation [5] as shown in Fig. 9. Such highly-parallel free-space interconnections between planes and parallel logic operations within the planes would maximally exploit the special features of optics and potentially provide very high computational throughput. Fig. 10 shows two examples of the form of these hypothetical optical gate arrays or logic planes. The one on the left employs "pure" optical logic while the one shown on the right is composed of pixel elements which are small-scale hybrids of optical and electronic components which form "smart pixels". Note that there are no electrical connections to the edge of these planes, except possibly for dc power.

The overall configuration shown in Fig. 10 has the attractive feature of implementing a highly parallel computational structure with arbitrary interconnect capability. However, the optics required to implement a complicated interconnection pattern is very demanding. Even the best holographic techniques will be stressed to provide arbitrary interconnections between large arrays of optical logic gates. A regular and much simpler interconnection scheme is desirable. One of the potential ways to make a useful computer is to employ the algorithm of symbolic substitution [6]. A simple example of this process is shown in Fig. 11. The task is to search a pattern such as the example shown in the lower left for all occurrences of a particular reference pattern such as that shown in the upper left. When such a pattern is located, a mark (in this case, a white square) is placed in an intermediate plane as shown in the lower center of the figure. Then for each such mark, a new pattern such as that in the upper right is substituted. A large number of useful computational problems can be implemented by such techniques. The great attraction is that the pattern search can be implemented by relatively simple optics which performs a small number of shifts and superpositions of the original pattern. Such global shifting and superposition can be performed with relatively simple holograms or with beam splitters and tilt prisms as shown in Fig. 12. The first stage on the left can locate a three-pixel reference pattern by implementing three shifts and looking with an AND-gate array for the positions where three transparent pixels overlap. The optics on the right performs the substitution in an OR-gate array. Recently, this symbolic-substitution approach has received much attention [7].

Another potential scheme for optical implementation of general-purpose computational structures is through the use of a special type of hybrid optical/electrical logic which takes advantage of the ability of essentially analog optics to implement massively parallel AND and OR operations. In any digital computation or logic process, there must be some nonlinear element. In the configurations shown in Fig. 13, only one nonlinear element, an electronic threshold, is employed. An AND operation is implemented by asking whether a light source is on and whether a shutter (e.g. acoustooptic cell or spatial light modulator) is open. Cascaded shutters, operated electrically, implement a multiple AND operation. The stress in this approach is to make highly transmissive shutters that operate fast with a minimum of electrical power. Another approach which better utilizes the parallelism of optics is shown in the lower portion of Fig. 13. Here, the optical shutters operate in parallel and a lens gathers the light through all of the shutters and images the light on a detector. A multiple OR operation is implemented by determining whether light has come through any shutter. In this case, the shutters must have high contrast and the optical system must have low stray light. A flexible digital processor which computes logic functionals by means of the operations shown in Fig. 12 is being pursued [8]. Wide bandwidth acoustooptic cells are a near-term approach for implementing the fast shutters.

Studies of the information-processing structure of the brain and of the structure of electronic computers which emulate brain functions have been topics of interest for many years. The recent surge of renewed interest in neural networks has stimulated the optics community to investigate the role that optics may play in this unusual type of computer. Key features of neural processes are a high degree of connectivity and parallelism combined with repeated use of correlations between new and learned patterns. These features suggest that optics has a role. Optically nonlinear devices will be needed to provide the essential nonlinear feedback in these neural network schemes. An example of one type of optical neural network which implements a Hopfield associative memory is shown in Fig. 14. Each of the optical sources in the input row represents a neuron whose activity V_i is proportional to the output intensity. With cylindrical optics, each input "neuron" illuminates a vertical column of a mask. The transmission pattern T_{ij} for the pixels in the mask represents a stored pattern of interconnection strengths for the "synapses" which connect one neuron with another. All of the information concerning the stored patterns against which new patterns are being compared is stored in the interconnection or "synapse" strengths. With cylindrical optics, the light transmitted through each row is collected on a vertical set of detectors each of which represents the input to a neuron. This set of optics implements a vector-matrix process in analog form. The output of each detector is the dot product or correlation between the input vector and a row of the matrix. The activity of a neuron is a nonlinear function of the input and this nonlinearity tends to emphasize the stronger correlations which are fed back and cycled through the system until the neural net converges on the best match between the input and one of the stored patterns. The trick is in providing the nonlinear feedback. Initial demonstrations have taken the signal out of the detectors and sent the signal through conventional electronic thresholding gates [9]. Future systems might employ optically nonlinear elements along the output column and appropriate optics to rotate the image and add it to the input. There are many postulated variants on this basic scheme and all suggest the fascinating potential of a new type of information-processing system implemented with a novel and powerful new technology.

SUMMARY

Optical devices are very different from conventional electronic circuits and the development of optical computers is paced by the need for unusual and specialized components. A lot of thinking has gone into new architectures, algorithms, and devices for optical computing. However, most of these ideas are untested by actual implementations in a credible prototype computer. Lacking a clear view of what is the best approach for implementing optical logic, performance limits have not been studied in detail. More critical examinations of the performance limits imposed by any new optical technology are required. It may well be difficult to form useful optical logic gates from lumps of material which must combine the functions of detection, logic, and modulation. Even if these "pure all-optical-logic" components don't prove useful in their simpler forms, they are important stepping stones to hybrid structures. Optical computers may well be implemented with hybrid electrical/optical circuits, even at the gate level. Moreover, the input and output are likely to be electrical, although fibers offer an optical alternative.

Our world is faced with enormous computational requirements in applications such as artificial intelligence, signal processing, and modelling of complex physical phenomena. These applications-driven needs have pushed the development of new algorithms and computer architectures and have placed a heavy demand the technology to meet these needs. Conversely, new technologies such as optical computing will spawn thinking about new architectures and algorithms to exploit the technology. Will optics meet the stringent specifications driven by applications? Can new computer structures be fashioned out of optical components and matched to demanding applications? The answers are actively being sought.

ACKNOWLEDGMENT

The work at MIT Lincoln Laboratory in the areas of optical interconnections and computing is supported by the Departments of the Air Force and Navy and by the Defense Advanced Research Projects Agency.

REFERENCES

1. T. E. Bell, "Optical Computing: A Field in Flux", IEEE Spectrum, 23, 34 (1986)

2. M. R. Feldman, et al., "Comparison Between Optical and Electrical Interconnects Based on Power and Speed Considerations", Appl. Optics, 27, 1742 (1988)

3. P. W. Smith, "On the Physical Limits of Digital Optical Switching and Logic Elements", Bell Syst. Tech. J., 61, 1975 (1982)

4. P. Wheatley, et al., "A Hard-Limiting Opto-Electronic Logic Device", Digest of Topical Meeting on Photonic Switching, 88 (March 1987)

5. A. A. Sawchuk and T. C. Strand, "Digital Optical Computing", Proc. IEEE, 72, 758 (1984)

6. K. H. Brenner, "Programmable Optical Processor Based on Symbolic Substitution", Appl. Optics, 27, 1687 (1988)

7. See for example, special of Appl. Optics on Optical Computing, 27 (May 1988)

8. P. S. Guilfoyle, "Programmable Optical Digital Computing", Proc. of Asilomar Conference on Signals, Systems and Computers (November 1987)

9. D. Psaltis, "Optical Neural Computers", Digest of Topical Meeting on Photonic Switching, 12 (March 1987)

NOW   FUTURE

INFORMATION
PROCESSING

                    SAR PROCESSING
                            SIGNAL PROCESSING
                                    IMAGE PROCESSING
                                            PATTERN RECOGNITION
                                                    OPTICAL DIGITAL LOGIC

DIGITAL
COMMUNICATIONS

                LONG LINES
                        LOOP SERVICE
                                LOCAL AREA NETWORKS

                                        OPTICAL INTERCONNECTS
                                                OPTICAL DIGITAL LOGIC

FIG. 1.   EVOLUTION OF OPTICAL
             INFORMATION PROCESSING AND
             DIGITAL COMMUNICATIONS
             TOWARD OPTICAL DIGITAL
             LOGIC.

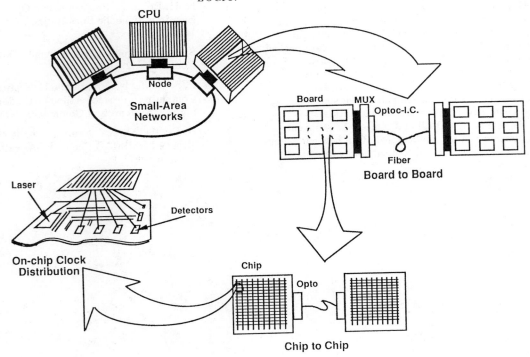

FIG. 2.   OPTICAL INTERCONNECTS AT
             VARIOUS LEVELS IN DIGITAL
             SYSTEMS.

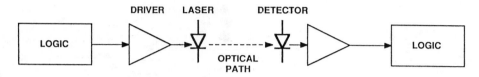

FIG. 3.   BASIC ELEMENTS OF ELECTRICAL
              AND OPTICAL INTERCONNECTS
              BETWEEN ELECTRONIC LOGIC
              ELEMENTS.

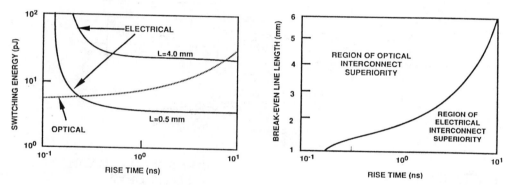

FIG. 4.   SWITCHING ENERGY, RISE TIME
              AND LENGTH TRADEOFFS FOR
              ELECTRICAL AND OPTICAL
              INTERCONNECTIONS (FROM
              REF. 2).

Computer generated hologram

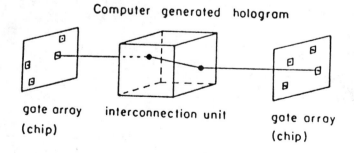

FIG. 5.   OPTICAL INTERCONNECTION OF
              GATE ARRAYS WITH A
              HOLOGRAM (FROM REF. 5).

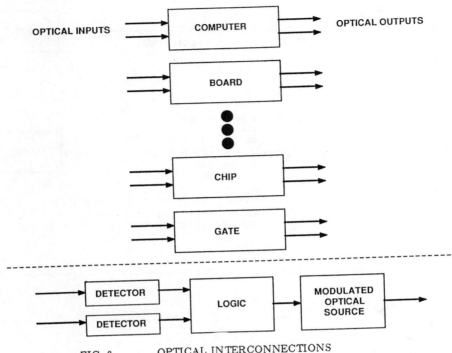

OPTICAL INPUTS → COMPUTER → OPTICAL OUTPUTS

BOARD

CHIP

GATE

DETECTOR → LOGIC → MODULATED OPTICAL SOURCE

DETECTOR

FIG. 6.   OPTICAL INTERCONNECTIONS
AND ELECTRONIC LOGIC AT
VARIOUS LEVELS IN DIGITAL
SYSTEMS. LOWER: COMMON
FEATURES.

FEATURES SOUGHT IN OPTICAL DIGITAL LOGIC

- FAST
- LOW POWER
- HIGH CONTRAST
- GAIN AND FAN OUT
- LOGIC LEVEL RESTORATION
- THREE TERMINAL
- CASCADABLE

GENERIC OPTICAL LOGIC DEVICE

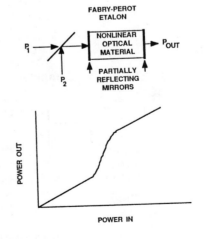

FABRY-PEROT
ETALON

P_1 → NONLINEAR OPTICAL MATERIAL → P_{OUT}

P_2

PARTIALLY REFLECTING MIRRORS

POWER OUT

POWER IN

FIG. 7.   DESIRED FEATURES AND
TYPICAL OPERATION OF AN
ALL-OPTICAL LOGIC DEVICE.

SCHEMATIC DIAGRAM OF DEVICE

INPUT-OUTPUT CHARACTERISTIC

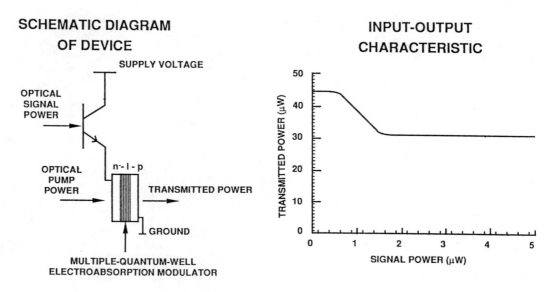

FIG. 8.   A HARD-LIMITING
OPTOELECTRONIC LOGIC DEVICE
(FROM REF. 4).

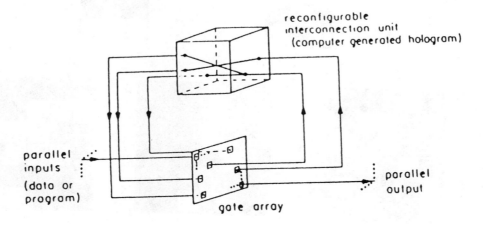

FIG. 9.   FUNCTIONAL BLOCK DIAGRAM
OF A SEQUENTIAL OPTICAL
LOGIC SYSTEM (FROM REF. 5).

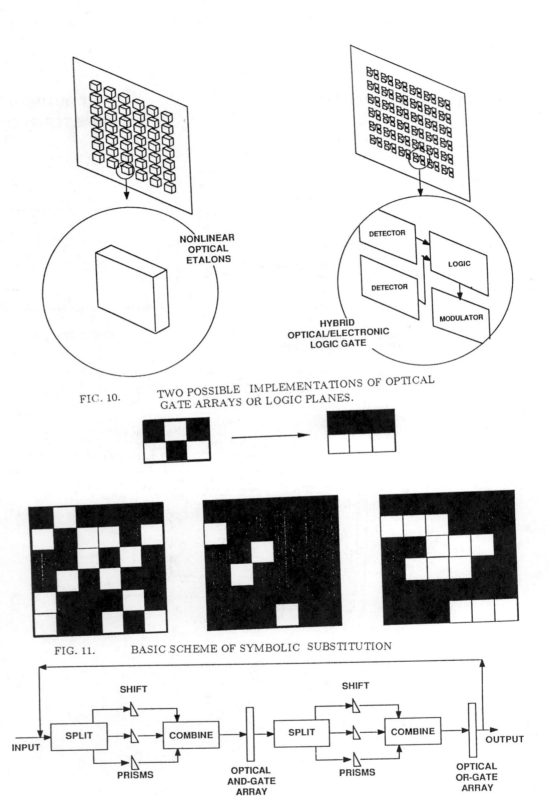

FIG. 10. TWO POSSIBLE IMPLEMENTATIONS OF OPTICAL GATE ARRAYS OR LOGIC PLANES.

FIG. 11. BASIC SCHEME OF SYMBOLIC SUBSTITUTION

FIG. 12. SIMPLIFIED OPTICAL SYSTEM

1649

MULTIPLE "AND" GATE

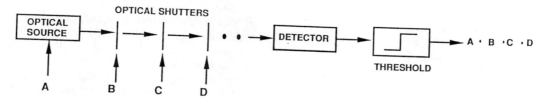

MULTIPLE "OR" GATE

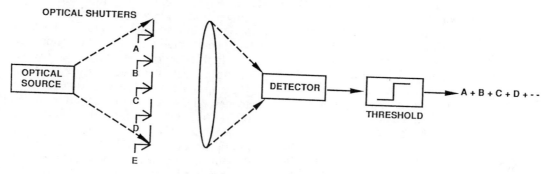

FIG. 13.   OPTICAL MULTIPLE-INPUT
              HYBRID LOGIC.

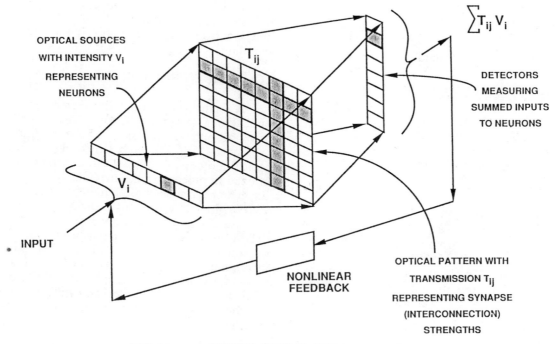

FIG. 14.   OPTICAL NEURAL NET BASED ON
              VECTOR-MATRIX MULTIPLIER.

OPTICAL COMMUNICATIONS AND COMPUTING -- A UNIVERSITY PERSPECTIVE

Karolyn Eisenstein, Chairperson
Assistant Director, Center for Compound
Semiconductor Microelectronics
University of Illinois at Urbana-Champaign
Urbana, IL 61801

ABSTRACT

In universities, as in industrial laboratories, researchers are exploring photonic technologies of the future. The National Science Foundation has funded three Engineering Research Centers to investigate optoelectronic systems critical to integrated, high-speed communications and computing. The Columbia University center is prototyping high-speed optical telecommunications networks. The Illinois center is applying compound semiconductor technology to the challenge of optical interconnection and switching. At the computing process level, the Colorado center is developing "proof-of-principle" machines to examine the advantages of photonics over electronics. This seminar surveys these emerging lightwave technologies and their potential impact on high-speed digital systems.

W. Thomas Cathey   Univ. of Colorado
Joseph Verdeyen   Univ. of Illinois, Urbana
X.-C. Zhang   Columbia University

HIGH-SPEED OPTICAL NETWORKS

X.-C. Zhang
Center for Telecommunications Research and
Electrical Engineering Department
Columbia University
New York, New York 10027

ABSTRACT

High-speed optical networks incorporating all-optical processing of medium access protocols are discussed, and performance results from several demonstration networks are presented. Novel opto-electronic and optical techniques (such as photonic switching) required for implementation of future opto-electronic and all-optical networks are discussed.

INTRODUCTION

The expected rapid increase in the operating speed of information exchange, handling, and computation has necessitated the use of photonic switching, optical computing, and optical communication networks. Increased speed and bandwidth offered by all-optical signal processing has been demonstrated. However, the optical devices and fiber technologies, in comparison to electronic devices and semiconductor technology, are immature. Although several well-developed photonic transmission techniques (such as fiber optics) have been widely used, many more crucial and certainly more difficult tasks still remain (such as digital optic and integrated-optic processing). Most of the photonic processing techniques are still limited to the device lab or have just moved to the optical communication systems research lab. Driven by the needs of future communication systems and scientific challenges, scientists not only replace some conventional electronic devices with fast optical devices, but also think at a higher level to design and build new architectures based on photonic techniques.

In this section, we will present several all-optical multiple access networks that we have demonstrated. They include synchronous time division multiple access (TDMA), code division multiple access (CDMA), and self-routing optical switching networks. We will discuss a two-dimensional multiple processor (2DMP) which can produce a two-dimensional ultrafast optical data matrix in free space and convert it into a one-dimensional data train with a bandwidth of several hundreds of Gbit/s. We will also discuss some applications of optoelectro-optical measurements for optical devices and circuits, using nonlinear optical effects, such as optical rectification and electro-optic effects for optoelectro-optical sampling.

LOCAL AREA NETWORKS

A dramatic increase in the aggregate capacity of optical area networks (OLANs) has been shown by using all-optical processing of the medium access protocols [1]. The high bandwidth of fiber and optical processors allows more bandwidth to be utilized in processing the medium access protocols. Asynchronous code division multiple access (CDMA) at 100 Mbit/s, sychronous CDMA, and sychronous fixed assignment time division multiple access (TDMA) at 12.5 Gbit/s have been proposed and demonstrated. These all-optical networks incorporate fiber-optic signal processors and optical interconnection fabrics to eliminate the processing bottlenecks caused by the bandwidth limitation of conventional electronic circuits, interfaces, and switches.

A time division multiple access (TDMA) optical network uses centrally distributed ultrafast optical pulses and fiber-optic delay line signal processing. TDMA protocols utilize the available bandwidth more efficiently than CDMA, but generally require global synchronization. This receiver-fixed assignment local area network has an aggregate capacity limited only by the ability to generate and threshold-detect ultrafast optical pulses, and currently supports more than 100 users at 100 Mbit/s transmission rate per user.

An optical local area network can use CDMA to multiplex and demultiplex information. Asynchronous, simultaneous communications are advantages of CDMA. Using a specially developed set of optical CDMA codes, a temporal bandwidth expansion of N^2 is required to achieve 10^{-9} BER for N simultaneous, asynchronous users.

A self-routing photonic switching system can route information on a bit-by-bit basis by using all-optical processing techniques to encode and decode destination information [2]. High switching speeds and throughput have been attained. Self-gating of 3 Mbit/s optical data through a $LiNbO_3$ integrated-optic waveguide modulator has been demonstrated. Optical code division multiple access (CDMA) is used to subcode data at 100 Mbit/s. The self-routing of 100 Mbit/s data through an 8*8 $LiNbO_3$ integrated-optical crossbar switch matrix using 12.5 Gbit/s CDMA subcoding has been achieved. Switching speeds of 1.3 GHz, extinction ratio > 15 dB, non-optical crosstalk < -12.3 dB and optical crosstalk < -23 dB have been measured. 12.5 Gbit/s optical data throughput is limited by the optical clock pulse width of the central laser. For bandwidth optimization, the dispersive properties of optical fiber and $LiNbO_3$ devices must be considered. With a fiber-grating pulse compressor, 1.6 psec optical pulses have been obtained, and a much higher throughput is possible.

2-D OPTICAL MULTIPLE PROCESSOR

Phase shift of optical data between data channels in an optical network using fibers as time delay units faces a timing accuracy problem. In a TDMA or CDMA network where multiple delayed optical channels are required, the timings between channels are extremely sensitive to fiber lengths and are therefore difficult to adjust. An extra fiber length of 1 mm generates approximately 5 psec delay time for propagated optical data. External temperature fluctuations or physical stress variations on the fibers can also cause timing jitter or phase shift of the optical information. This problem is difficult to compensate for and can seriously affect the stability and the bandwidth of ultrahigh speed optical networks.

A two-dimensional multiple processor (2DMP) has been proposed which produces an optical pulse train with an ultrahigh repetition rate and precise timing. The principle of 2DMP is based on multireflecting a laser beam consisting of ultrashort optical pulses, generated by a mode-locked laser, on two pairs of parallel specially-coated mirrors. The output from a 2DMP forms an array of beams, where the two-dimensional N*M array is scanned with sequential time delay and equal intensity. For a commercially available compressed CW mode-locked laser with 2 psec pulse width, 100 MHz repetition rate and 1 mm beam diameter, a beam array consisting of 1000 beams and a scan rate at 100 GHz could be smaller than 5*5 cm^2. The beam array can be focused to a waveguide or fiber by a spherical lens with a matching f number, and the 2-D pattern (parallel) is converted to a 1-D string (serial) without introducing any additional jitter.

Since the beam array of a 2DMP is in free space, parallel coding of this 2-D plane is easy to achieve using optics. Because each pixel on the enclosed plane is timed sequentially, the coding rate can be as slow as the repetition rate of the master laser, and a higher coding rate would not increase the data transmission rate. The maximum array size (N*M) depends upon the pulse width of the master laser, repetition rate, and beam diameter. If the space between two adjcent beams in the array is set to 1.5 mm, the size of the array will be 6.7*6.7 cm^2 for a 200 Gbit/s transmission rate. With suitable modulation on the 2-D plane, this 2DMP can be used to generate a highly synchronized optical clock or to code data for optical CDMA or TDMA with over 100 Gbit/s transmission rate. The applications of this 2DMP includes a 2-D image to a 1-D sting converter and ultrafast optical modulator.

OPTOELECTRO-OPTIC MEASUREMENT

When an optical device, such as a photonic switch, has a channel bandwidth comparable to that of the optical fiber, the measurment of device characteristics without degrading its performance is crucial. Noninvasive electro-optical sampling [3] has recently been developed and demonstrated for the characterization of semiconductor integrated circuits [4]. The sampling and detection method which uses ultrafast laser pulses has a real time display (< 1 psec time resolution and < 1 mV voltage sensitivity). Measurement of devices with optical input signal, compared with that of the electronic signal, is much more complicated and difficult to implement. It consists of optical amplitude (intensity) and timing (phase) parameters like the electronic technique, but, unlike electronics, it also includes the polarization, wavelength, and coherence length parameters in the measurement. The confinement of light in the waveguide (mode distribution) is different from that of the electrons in a conducting wire (such as the skin effect of a high frequency signal). Due to the fact that electronic processing in most cases does not compete with the bandwidth of optical processing, the best solution to pursue measurement of optical devices is optical probing. Optoelectro-optical sampling, similar to the electro-optical sampling for semiconductor circuits, is certainly the best candidate for the characterization of optical devices with comparable bandwidth.

The principal idea of optoelectro-optical sampling is based on the electro-optic effect of nonlinear optical materials and its inverse effect, optical rectification, or other mechanisms. It also can be understood as an excite and probe technique. The optical pulses (carrying data) propagate through a nonlinear material and generate (or excite) a traveling electric field along with the optical pulses by optoelectronic effect. The induced electric field will cause a change of birefringence in the material through the electro-optic effect, and the change of birefringence can be detected (or probed) by a synchronized beam. For electro-optic media, a Cherenkov cone of pulsed far-infrared radiation has been generated, and coherent detection of the electric field of this far-infrared pulse by electro-optic sampling has been demonstrated [5]. Both signal generation and detection are in the terahertz spectral range.

Measurements of an induced electric field on optical fibers have been performed. The peak electric field over 100 mV/cm crossing the fibers has been measured utilizing a picosecond laser setup and phase-sensitive detection. Optical rectification is the main source of the electric field generation. If this induced electric field can be detected optically, more accurate and larger bandwidth measurements are expected. More detailed research will explore the optoelectro-optic effect and its applications.

CONCLUSION

All-optical networks incorporating fiber-optic signal processors and interconnections eliminate the processing bottlenecks of the bandwidth limitation of conventional electronic circuits and interfaces. 2-D multiple processors can provide precise time delays for the optical networks. Optoelectro-optic measurement for high speed optical devices demonstrates superior bandwidth; it can be used potentially for "on-chip" and noninvasive diagnostics in optical integrated circuits.

ACKNOWLEDGMENTS

This paper is based partly on work done by P.R. Prucnal and D.J. Blumenthal, to whom I am most grateful. I also wish to thank D.H. Auston and P. Christianson for their encouragement and support, and S. Elby and Y. Yin for their collaborative assistance.

REFERENCES

1. P.R. Prucnal, M.A. Santoro, S.K. Sehgal, and I.P. Kaminow, "TDMA Fiber-Optic Network wih Optical Processing," Electron. Lett., vol. 22(23), 1218, 1986.
2. P.R. Prucnal, D.J. Blumenthal, and P.A. Perrier, "Self-Routing Photonic Switching Demonstration with Optical Control", Optical Engineering, vol. 26, 473, 1987.
3. IEEE Journal of Quantum Electronics, vol. 24, Special issue papers on ultrafast optics and electronics, 1988.
4. X.-C. Zhang and R.K. Jain, "Analysis of High-Speed GaAs ICs with Electro-Optic Probes", SPIE, vol. 795, Characterization of Very High Speed Semiconductor Devices & Integrated Circuits, 317, 1987.
5. D.H. Auston, K.P. Cheung, A. Valdmanis, and D.A. Kleinman, "Cherenkov Radiation from Femtosecond Optical Pulses in Electro-Optic Media", Physical Review Letters, vol. 53, 1555, 1984.

COMPOUND SEMICONDUCTOR DEVICE TECHNOLOGY IN INTEGRATED OPTOELECTRONIC CIRCUITS

Joseph T. Verdeyen
Center for Compound Semiconductor
Microelectronics and
Department of Electrical and Computer Engineering
University of Illinois
Urbana-Champaign, IL 61801

ABSTRACT

Compound semiconductor electronics forms the basis of an emerging technology involving devices which have no counterparts in conventional microelectronics. Heterostructure lasers and quantum-size effects, strained layers, impurity induced layer disordering, and real space transfer, are all topics which have surfaced through the III-V semiconductor route. Thus, while many have recognized the potential advantage of using photons rather than the transport of charges at the chip or board level, the configuration to optimize the speed, connectivity or parallelism has not been established. However, some rather unique devices, waveguides and switches and system analysis techniques have surfaced. The Illinois ERC has contributed to each topic and some of these highlights will be reviewed.

THE INTERCONNECT PROBLEM

The problem facing high-speed digital electronic information transfer is a fundamental one imposed by the relationship of inductance and capacitance on geometry. If one attempts to transfer and route charge from a source (a generic transmitter) to the next device (a generic receiver), one must live with the basic circuitry shown in Fig. 1.

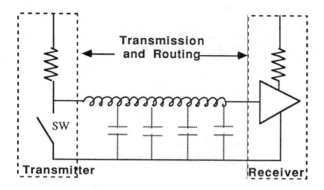

Fig. 1 A generic source and receiver

In constructing Fig. 1, we have assumed the simplest and most idealistic scenario imaginable --that of an infinitely fast switch driving a lossless transmission line and exciting the receiver which is another voltage controlled switch. If the source impedance R is equal to the characteristic impedance of the line and if the receiver is also matched to it, the limiting technology would be the speeds of the switch and the receiver. Seldom are the idealistic and "if" conditions satisfied. For instance, consider the case of a source communicating over a distance of 1 cm with a 1μm wide line deposited on an oxide ($E_r = 4$) of 1000 Å thickness. The characteristic impedance of such a line is 18.9Ω. If the source were connected to a 5 volt supply, it must switch 0.265 amp and 1.33 watts. Clearly the power requirements are excessive. If the receiver were not matched, the characteristic ringing frequency would only be 2.35 GHz. If one attempts to use a higher impedance source to reduce the switching power requirements, then the R (of the source) C (of the line and receiver) product becomes the limiting time scale. If one picks $R_s = 1k\Omega$, then $R_s C \sim 3.63$ ns or the data rate must be less than ~ 275 Mb/sec.

To achieve higher net data rates crossing a given plane, one resorts to a parallel architecture. While this is a fruitful strategy, there are significant

geometrical constraints on the packaging density. Since each source (or detector) would be more-or-less the same as any other in the parallel path, crosstalk due to inductive or capacitance coupling becomes a serious problem.

The above set of numbers are offered to illustrate the problem with the transport of charges. One cannot afford the power dissipation to match the interconnect. Any number of conventional devices have inherent switching speeds far in excess of the time scales noted above, but the geometrical factors, inductance, and capacitance are a most serious limitation.

As one final illustration of the interconnect problem, consider the Table I taken from a publication by R. Keyes which is a numerical description of a simple IC with 1496 gates. While the integration of that number of gates on a 0.566 x 0.566 cm chip is significant, note that such a chip has 4 meters ($\sim$ 12 ft) of wiring there also. Obviously, most of the real estate is devoted to the interconnections.

Table I

Characteristics of Integrated Logic Chip [1,2]

Chip size	0.566 x 0.566 cm
Max gate content	1496
Total wire length	4 m
Wire channel width	6.5 μm

However, that same publication and others [1,3-5] make a case that optical components will not supplant the conventional logic configurations except in specialized data processing applications. We subscribe to that view also and thus are concentrating on the problems of data links between chips or boards, and the requirements at the back plane of high speed digital computers.

Optical interconnects hold the promise of bypassing these geometrical problems. Figure 1 is quite adequate for the optical interconnect if the transmitter is identified with optical source and the receiver with a detector. Any imaginable optical transmission system is always much longer than a wavelength and thus functions as a waveguide with at most, annoying but not serious, discrete reflections. Furthermore, various parallel sources may be made orthogonal to each other so that the problem of crosstalk can, in principle, be completely eliminated, even with parallel sources sharing a common waveguide. Even loss can be compensated with broadband gain in integrated waveguides, as will be discussed below.

OPTICAL INTERCONNECTS

The field of fiber optics for telecommunications has virtually exploded in the last 10-15 years, especially for long haul applications (> miles), because of many well-known reasons: low loss, minimum dispersion, virtually crosstalk-free, and immunity to electrical interference. Many of those same features are present for the short haul applications such as those encountered in a computer, whether it is on-chip, between chips or boards, or at the backplane. Let's identify a few of the features of the optical domain and contrast it to wired link. Whatever the scenario envisioned, one must deal with the generic system shown in Fig. 2, which applies equally well to the conventional system involving charge transport in addition to photons. The main value of Fig. 2 is that it assigns a technological function to the various components, and defines various research problems to be addressed. The overwhelming problem impeding the application of this system is the ability to integrate the various devices and functions. (One can make the system with off-the-shelf components, but its performance would most likely be dismal, to say nothing about the cost and size.)

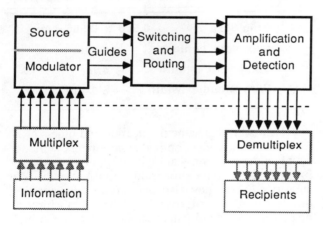

Fig. 2 The Optical Interconnect System.
The Center for Compound Semiconductor Microelectronics is focussed on those problems above the dashed line

The interconnect problem is the focus of the National Science Foundation Engineering Research Center (ERC) for Compound Semiconductor Microelectronics at the University of Illinois. The electrical and optical devices that are the necessary components for system, the technology and science necessary to make those components, the models of the devices for their incorporation into a global system analysis to evaluate its performance are the tasks of our three research thrusts shown in Fig 3.

While much of our effort is focussed towards optoelectronic components of the optical domain, we recognize that the entire system would fail without the high speed conventional electronic components. Thus significant work is in progress on high speed and novel electronic devices

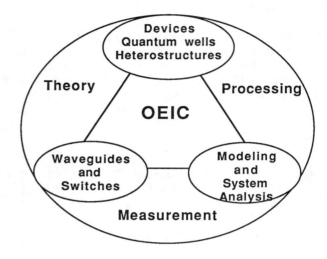

Fig. 3 Technological Thrusts of the University of Illinois ERC

1. Devices

The task of this thrust is to bring the emerging technology of heterostructures, quantum wells, and superlattices to bear on the system configuration. This has required us to invest considerable effort in the growth of materials either by MOCVD, MBE, or CBE and to ascertain the quality of the starting materials. Some of the notable accomplishments that have been made through this thrust are the achievement of the first CW laser in the AlGaAs system grown on silicon [6] and the invention of the heterostructure hot electron device (H2ED), an extremely fast switch [7]. The achievement of a CW laser on silicon was a noteworthy example of cooperation between industry (Texas Instruments and Xerox) and the university.

2. Waveguides and Switches

A most critical element or subsystem of the overall generic system shown in Fig. 2 is the guidance and the switching or routing of the photons. We feel that the quantum step in performance can only come if the photons themselves are routed rather than returning to baseband electrical signals, routing those, and re-converting to photons. The key technology upon which this thrust is based is impurity induced layer disordering a phenomena discovered at Illinois in 1981[8]. While this will be discussed in detail in the presentation, suffice it here to note that this technology enables one to construct (in principle) active as well as passive [9] optical waveguides and switches with a planar technology. Hence, it is quite reasonable to envision a universal chip which, with suitable masking and processing, could be made into a laser source, waveguide links, and an electro-optic routing switch.

3. Modeling and System Analysis

Our commitment to optical interconnects poses rather unique problems for a system analysis. Many of the devices are new with, at best, rudimentary phenomenological explanations. It is necessary to establish a first principle model based upon fundamental semiconductor theory. Furthermore, even their gross terminal characteristics do not fit those of conventional devices, and thus the system analysis must be general enough to incorporate the advances in devices without major surgery and the analysis tools.

The development of the simulation program MINILASE [10] is an advance towards the goal of a two dimensional, fully integrated theoretical description of a semiconductor laser which couples the photon with the charge carriers in a fundamental semiconductor environment. The iSMILE program, a general purpose simulation program for optoelectronic integrated circuits, was also developed under this thrust. It enables one to incorporate new devices in an optoelectronic interconnect system without months of code modifications.

INTEGRATION

The goals of all ERCs are to increase the competitive stature of U.S. industry, and we are attempting to focus our work in compound semiconductors towards that mission. While the discrete components mentioned above are most critical to the ultimate achievement of an OEIC, integration is the goal but is also the most difficult.

The task of integration of even a few of the necessary components is a formidable one and requires a considerable investment in process technology, characterization, and state-of-the-art measurements -- at the growth, process, and device stages. Our efforts concentrate on the engineering physics of the system, but we recognize that a critical aspect is packaging. Unfortunately, our resources do not allow an extensive effort in that direction, although it is not ignored and at least one advance was pioneered at Illinois. Since silicon has a higher thermal conductivity than GaAs (or other III-V's), the achievement of device quality material on Si is a significant contribution to the packaging issue.

Our vision is to start small and grow in cooperation with various U.S. industries. We have started the discussion of the technical issues of integrating high-speed detectors and electronics as a lowest level of integration, and are establishing groups to evaluate the routing and switching aspect. Ultimately, our goal is to integrate the entire generic system of Fig. 2.

REFERENCES

1. R.W. Keyes, Proc. IEEE, 69, 267, 1981.
2. R.J. Blumberg and S. Brenner, IEEE J. Solid State Circuits, SC-14, 818, 1979.
3. R.W. Keyes, IEEE J. Solid State Circuits, SC-14, 193, 1979.
4. R.W. Keyes, Optica Acta, 32, 525, 1985.
5. R.W Keyes, Science, 230, 138, 1985.
6. D.W. Nam, N. Holonyak, Jr., K.C. Hsieh, R.W. Kaliski, J.W. Lee, H. Shichijo, J.E. Epler, R.D. Burnham, T.L. Paoli, Appl. Phys. Lett. 51, 39, 1987. See also, D.G. Deppe, D.W. Nam, N. Holonyak, Jr., K.C. Hsieh, R.J. Matyi, H. Schichijo, J.E. Epler, H.F. Chung, Appl. Phys. Lett. 51, 1271, 1987.
7. K. Hess, T.K. Higman, M.A. Emanuel, and J.J. Coleman, J. Appl. Phys. 60, 3775, 1986. See also, T.K. Higman, J.M. Higman, M.A. Emanuel, K. Hess, and J.J. Coleman, J. Appl. Phys. 62, 1495, 1987. See also, J. Kolodzey,J. Laskar, T. Higman, M. Emanuel, and J.J. Coleman, IEEE Elect. Device Lett. (June 1988).
8. W. D. Laidig, N. Holonyak Jr., M.D. Camaras, K. Hess, J. J. Coleman, P. D. Dapkus, and J. Bardeen, Appl. Phys. Lett. 38, 776(1981)
9. F. Julien, P.D. Swanson, M.A. Emanuel, D.G. Deppe, T.A. DeTemple, J.J. Coleman, N. Holonyak, Jr., Appl. Phys. Lett. 50, 866, 1987. See also, P.D. Swanson, F. Julien, M.A. Emanuel, L. Sloan, T. Tang, T.A. DeTemple, and J.J. Coleman, Optics Lett. 13, 245, 1988.
10. D.S. Gao, A.T. Young, and S. Kang, 1988 International Symposium on Circuits and Systems. See also, A. Young, D.S. Gao, and S. Kang, International Conf. on Computer Design, Oct. 1987.
11. J. P. Leburton, U. Ravaioli, K. Hess, Private communication
12. S. S. Bose, B. Lee, M. H. Kim, G. E. Stillman, Appl. Phys. Lett. 51, 937, 1987; See also T. R. Lepkowski, R. Y. DeJule, N. C. Tien, M. H. Kim and G. E. Stillman, J. Appl. Phys. 61,4808, 1987

OPTOELECTRONIC COMPUTING SYSTEMS

W. Thomas Cathey, Director
Center for Optoelectronic Computing Systems
University of Colorado
Boulder, Colorado 80309-0425

ABSTRACT

There is a strong tie between computing and communications. Some of the common topics are an optical bit serial computer, optical signal processing for bandwidth compression, optical neural nets for speech and image recognition, high-speed optical switches, crossbars, and spatial light modulators.

INTRODUCTION

Historically, there has been a close relation between communications and computation. This is because of the common components and frequent overlap in role. Here, we explore the relation between optical communications and the projects within the Center for Optoelectronic Computing Systems. An overview of the research is given, highlighting the research done by the 26 faculty, 10 professional staff, and 53 students in the Center. The purpose of the paper is to tell the communications industry what potential benefits may come to them from the work in optoelectronic computing.

The objectives of the research are specified and the advantages of optoelectronics are reviewed. The level of effort given to the program is detailed and the individual thrusts most relevant to communications are delineated. To tie the research together in a focussed, systems-directed program, we are building three proof-of-principle machines. The Center is organized around these machines and the device and materials research needed to demonstrate feasibility of the concepts. Success in the bit serial computer project will eliminate the photon-to-electron and electron-to-photon conversions that are required when optical data must be processed electronically and then converted back to photons. The goal is to exploit the potentially high speeds that are possible with optics. The overriding computer architecture research is to explore architectures when the delays are not concentrated in the gates. The optical signal processing program has projects on cellular array processing for vector-matrix operations, bandwidth compression, and an image algebra that has promise for great bandwidth compression for image transmission. An optical artificial intelligence program contains reesearch on associative memory, pattern classification, and symbolic logic. The programs drive research on optical crossbars, spatial light modulators (SLM), lithium niobate optical

directional couplers, multiple quantum well devices for optical switches, and CCD-driven SLMs.

As a National Science Foundation Engineering Research Center, we have a charge to facilitate technology transfer to industry. The techniques to do this include industrial advisors, visiting scientists, a favorable patent licensing policy, and strong interaction with students.

RESEARCH OBJECTIVES IN OPTOELECTRONICS

One of the research objectives of the Center for Optoelectronic Computing Systems is to develop the understanding of optoelectronic computing systems. This includes architectures where the gate delays can not be assumed to be the dominant delay in the system; the time taken to execute a carry, for example may be greater than the time needed to perform an addition in a gate. Also included is a study of which connectionist models are best implemented optically. The optical signal processing program has a project to match algorithms for matrix operations to the capability of optics.

To develop this understanding, we plan to design and build proof-of-principle machines. The construction of these machines serves as a research driver and requires that the system architects and the device researchers work closely together. This approach also forces them to consider the problems involved in actually building a system. A paper study that can gloss over the realizibility of a system is not sufficient. The construction of a machine to demonstrate feasibility also provides benchmarks for the research and is a tremendous motivator of faculty and students. In the construction of the bit serial optical computer, we will explore and exploit the potential advantages of the speed of optics; the optical connectionist machine will use the high connectivity of optics; and the optical cellular array takes advantage of the natural parallelism of optics.

In the high-speed device and materials program, the research objective is to develop an understanding of optical devices and materials that can be used in optoelectronic systems and to design and build devices based on this understanding. In particular, multiple quantum well devices in GaAlAs and InP are being explored for optical switches; photo-addressed lithium niobate optical switches are being researched; and ferroelectric liquid crystals and amorphous silicon detectors are being used to build photo-addressed spatial light modulators.

The advantages of optoelectronics for computing and communications are much the same: low EMC/EMI, low dispersion and high bandwidth, reduced impedance matching problems, high fan out/fan in possibilities, highly parallel interconnects, and reduced clock skew. There is essentially no crosstalk from one optical beam to another, whether in free space or a fiber. The low dispersion is due to the fact that an optical pulse spreads several orders of magnitude slower than an electrical pulse. The problem of capacitive loading and high driving power associated with pin driving is eliminated. With imaging optics, the signal arrival times easily can be matched to better than a picosecond, and without too much difficulty, to better than a femtosecond. The predictions are that, while electronic computing systems can provide a 10 to 1000 increase in computing power, optoelectronic computing systems can provide a 10,000 to 1,000,000 increase in computational power. Both systems will almost certainly have superconducting components.

PROGRAM ORGANIZATION

Two universities are involved with the Center -- the University of Colorado and Colorado State University. The organization of the effort is shown in Fig. 1 where the four programs appear with the program managers. The Policy Board, made up of industrial cosponsors of the Center and the university administrators, approves the overall direction of the Center. The Scientific Advisory Board, made up of invited scientists and industrial representatives, evaluates the research, gives advice relating to priorities and future directions, and makes recommendations to the Director. The Executive Committee, made up of the director, managing director, associate director, program managers, and the heads of the departments principally involved in the Center meets at least twice monthly to coordinate the research and educational aspects of the Center. The program managers coordinate and guide the research within their programs.

DIGITAL OPTICAL COMPUTING

The project in this program most closely related to communications is the bit serial optical computer. The current problem is that data are frequently stored optically and transmitted optically but even the most trivial processing is done electronically. This requires photon-to-electron and electron-to-photon conversions at the interfaces as illustrated in Fig. 2. By doing the processing optoelectronically, the bottlenecks at these interfaces can be eliminated. At this time, however, there are no optical transistors and no optical VLSI. In the interim, simulations of architectures have been used for preliminary analyses. Simulation is not adequate, however, when the device parameters are not known. We are building and will operate a complete, stored-program optical digital computer. The approach is to use few, state-of-the art devices analogous to the early electronic computers. In the first phase, a basic

computer has been designed that uses 48 lithium niobate switches and uses optical fibers for data storage and as shift registers [1]. The signal level is restored and time synchronization is accomplished by switching in copies of the optical clock signal with another 20-30 switches.

This proof-of-principle machine will operate on optical data in optical form and not require conversions to electronic data format. It will have limited power, being roughly equivalent to an optical PDP 8 or PDP 11, but there are several applications where processors built using these same concepts could be very useful. One example is optical comunication systems where limited but high speed processing must be done on the data. At present, the data must be demultiplexed so that the electronic data processing system can handle the data rate and then reconverted to optical form for retransmission. A joint research project between the centers at Colorado and Columbia is directed at this particular problem.

OPTOELECTRONIC SIGNAL PROCESSING

The thrusts of this program most closely relating to communications have applications to bandwidth compression, reduced image representation, and cellular array processing of matrix operations. Specific applications include: signal processing and linear algebra at video rates and bandwidth compression of speech, images, and multidimensional data.

The approach in this program is to match the large number of potential algorithms for signal processing to the optical devices that can be made available. If one reviews the history of signal processing as given in Fig. 3, progress is seen to depend on the association of mathematical techniques with the advances in hardware. The promise for the future depends on the fusion of mathematical techniques and optical implementations.

One of the more interesting areas of research where this is being done is to replace images by "eigenimages" that can be used to represent the data in a greatly reduced data set [2].

OPTICAL ARTIFICIAL INTELLIGENCE

The property of optical techniques that is most useful in artificial intelligence implementations is high connectivity. With an imaging system or an optical crossbar, tens of thousands of processors can be connected without much difficulty. The increased power possible with optical systems can make practical such applications as speech and image recognition and automatic speech translation. Research is currently being conducted on optical pattern classification, optical associative memory, and optical symbolic logic. This research is not as close to implementation as research in the other programs, but it could have a major impact on communication systems of the future.

DEVICES AND MATERIALS

The researchers in this program are interacting closely with the systems researchers and are conducting research on optical devices for the proof-of-principle machines. They also are doing exploratory research on optical devices and materials. Some of the accomplishments of this research group are low-loss ferroelectric crystal (FLC) switches operating in 10 microseconds, photo-addressed FLC spatial light modulators (SLM) using amorphous silicon, lithium niobate optical switches, GaAs Mach Zehnder structures, and multiple quantum well (MQW) structures. Current research also includes new FLC materials, photo-addressing of lithium niobate switches, a GaAs optical switch, a charge-coupled addressed indium phosphide MWQ SLM, and diamond film.

The facilities include the only gas-source molecular beam epitaxy (MBE) machine in a U.S. university, MOCVD and plasma chemical vapor deposition facilities, and an organic synthesis laboratory. A wide range of materials characterization equipment is available including, for example, three scanning electron microscopes.

TECHNOLOGY TRANSFER

In a university center, the most effective technology transfers in students. In addition, we have close direct interactions with our industrial members. There are biannual meetings of the policy board and the scientific advisory board and these are very effective sessions, where the industrial members evaluate our research. Loaned scientists and visitors offer the closest interaction. For example, AT&T has loaned us one of their scientists to work on the optical bit serial machine. Center students also are spending one of their first summers in the Center at the facilities of industrial members.

The patent licensing policy gives priority to Center members and center membership fees are credited toward future license fees.

CONCLUSIONS

The use of optoelectronics can greatly increase the capability of communications systems in ways other than simply the use of fibers. All-optical packet switches, bandwidth compression, image transmission, intelligent communications systems, and new optical devices are on the way.

REFERENCES

1. V.P. Heuring, H.F. Jordan, and J.P. Pratt, "A Bit Serial Architecture for Optical Computing," submitted to IEEE Trans. on Computing.
2. L. Scharf, S. Voran, and M. Freeman, "Signal Processing with Spatial Light Modulators," submitted.

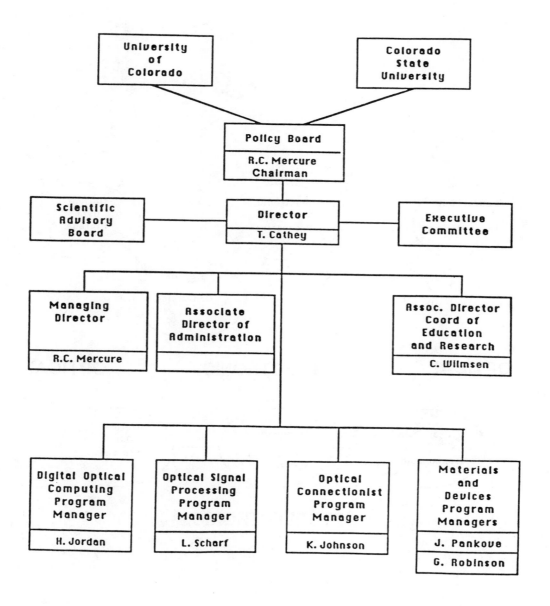

Fig. 1   Organization Chart of the Center for
Optoelectronic Computing Systems

1660

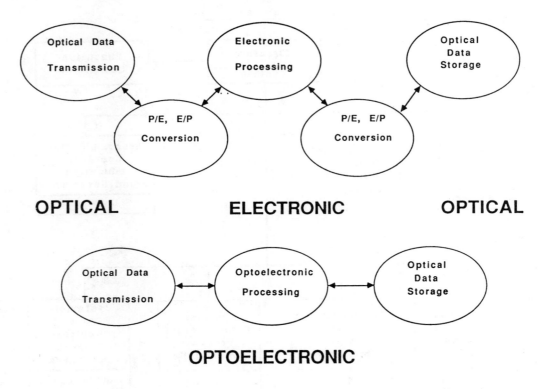

Fig. 2   Photon-to-Electron and Electron-to-Photon Interfaces

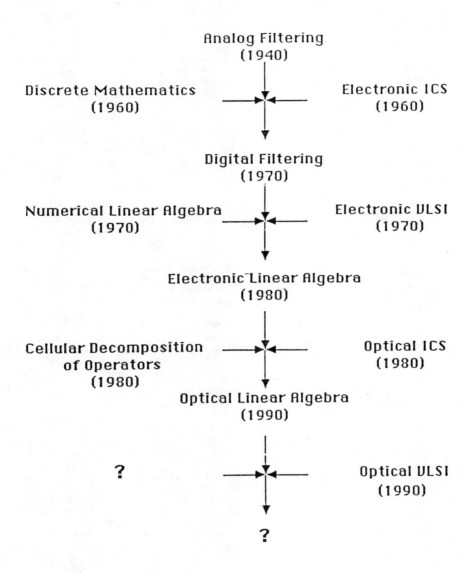

Fig. 3 Evolution of Ideas and Technologies for Signal Processing

TEC-03

IMPACT OF EMERGING TECHNOLOGIES
Paul F. Liao - Chairperson
Division Manager
Photonic Science and
Technology Research
Bellcore
331 Newman Springs Road
Box 7020
Red Bank, NJ 07701-7020

ABSTRACT

New technologies - what is now emerging? And what is the implication for communications? Past experience has shown that a steady flow of new materials and device technologies both produced and stimulated advances in capabilities and new services. Today, a host of new technologies are emerging from the research laboratory. Photonic switching promises to eliminate costly electrical-to-optical conversions, while neural networks offer systems with the reliability and intelligence found only in the human brain. Material advances include the ability to tailor semiconductor materials with single atom precision and Nobel prizes have been awarded for breakthroughs in superconductivity that promise revolutionary advances once thought difficult if not impossible. This seminar discusses these emerging technologies and their potential impact on telecommunications.

Stewart D. Personick - Bellcore

Fernand Bedard - National
Security Agency

Lester F. Eastman - Cornell Univ.

Lawrence D. Jackel - AT&T Bell Labs

PHOTONIC (OPTICAL) SWITCHING: TECHNOLOGY AND APPLICATIONS

Stewart D. Personick
Assistant Vice President
Network Technology

Bellcore

331 Newman Springs Road
Box 7020
Red Bank, NJ 07701-7020

ABSTRACT

In the last decade, optical fiber technology has made rapid advances in the transmission portions of telecommunications networks. More and more, signals are moved from point to point as pulses of light over fibers. A question which arises is whether the signals should be in optical form while being routed or converted to electrical form for switching. To answer this question, the session examines the use of photonic switching devices.

INTRODUCTION

In the last decade, optical fiber technology has made rapid advances in becoming a widely used method for implementing the transmission portions of telecommunications networks. More and more, signals are moved from point-to-point over optical fibers in the form of pulses of light modulated on and off. A question which arises more and more as applications of fiber optics increase is whether photonic devices should be used to build switches which keep the signals in optical form while they are being routed, rather than converting the optical signals to electrical form for switching purposes. To answer this question, it is helpful to review very briefly how one physically switches an optical signal between two paths. That is, we should first review the subject of photonic switching devices. Then we can explore the question of how these devices might be used to create switching systems.

I. Photonic Switching Devices

An optical crosspoint is a device which allows an incoming optical signal to be routed to one (or more) of several outgoing paths. There are several approaches which have been demonstrated or proposed to accomplish this function. One example is a mechanically activated optical switching crosspoint where a mechanical force moves an incoming fiber to one of two positions; causing it to couple to one of two corresponding outgoing fibers. The mechanical force can be generated by an electrically activated solenoid. Repeatable losses below 0.5 dB are obtainable for the paths through such a switch. Reconfiguration (switching) times are limited by mechanical considerations, and are in the range of milliseconds. Crosstalk (coupling to an unwanted output path) can be essentially negligible in this type of design.

In order to switch an optical signal between several possible paths, it is not necessary to use a mechanically activated device as described above. An alternative is an electrically activated optical directional coupler switch which works on the principles of the electro-optic effect. We begin with a substrate (slab of material) whose optical properties can be modified by the application of an electric field. In particular, the refractive index of the material can be modified slightly by the presence of a field produced between two electrodes when a voltage is applied to those electrodes. In the surface of this substrate we form (very accurately) regions of higher index of refraction by an ion exchange process. For example, if the substrate is made of the exotic material lithium niobate, we can form regions of higher refractive index in the surface by exposing the surface to titanium atoms. If the regions of higher index of refraction are in the shape of two parallel channels in the surface of the substrate, about a few micrometers wide and a micrometer deep, then these higher index regions form two optical waveguides. Light launched into one of the channels at one edge of the substrate will tend to be guided in the channel by total internal reflection. Furthermore, if the two channels are close together, light guided in one channel can couple across to the other channel via a coupled waveguide process. How much coupling takes place depends upon the details of the waveguides and how strongly they are coupled. Using two sets of metal electrodes formed on the surface of the substrate (above the waveguides) one can apply voltages which produce fields within the substrate which modifies its optical properties, and "tunes" the optical characteristics of the waveguides, and which in turn can control the coupling between the waveguides. With proper design, one can have nearly complete coupling (all the light launched into one waveguide couples to the other waveguide at the output end of the device) or no coupling - depending upon the values of voltages applied to the metal electrodes. Thus, we end up with a voltage controlled 2x2 optical switch. Typically directional coupler switches are polarization sensitive and they almost always require use of a light signal in a well defined single spatial field pattern (single mode excitation). Switches of this type have been demonstrated in the laboratory to be capable of reconfiguration (changing which path the light is directed to) in less than 100 picoseconds (one tenth of one billionth of one second). For carefully designed devices, the insertion loss associated with placement of the switch in a light path can be below 3dB. These devices have shown steady progress toward practical application, but are still considered to be in an exploratory state of development.

An even more exotic method of implementin an optical switching crosspoint is an optically activated optical switch, where an optical control signal causes another optical signal to switch between two paths. One can form an optical cavity by placing two nearly totally reflecting mirrors back to back as shown. Intuitively one would think that the combination of two mirrors, one behind the other, would produce an even more strongly reflecting mirror. However, this is not the case. If the spacing between the mirrors is related to the wavelength of the optical signal in precisely the right ratio (an even number of quarter wavelengths) then the combination of the two mirrors (one behind the other) will act as a transparent window. This can happen because a large light field builds up inside the cavity formed by the two mirrors. Light leaking through the mirrors from this stored field cancels the reflection we might intuitively expect, and produces a transmitted signal in the direction of the incoming light. On the other hand, if the mirrors are spaced by an odd number of quarter wavelengths, this field buildup does not occur inside the cavity, and the combination of two mirrors appears as a reflecting device.

Therefore, we can switch the device from the transparent to the reflecting mode of operation if we can somehow manage to change the "apparent" spacing of the mirrors. This is accomplished by placing a material in the space between the mirrors which is optically nonlinear. This means that its optical properties can be changed by the presence of an optical field. The "apparent" length of the gap between the mirrors is dependent upon the index of refraction of the material in the gap. If the index of refraction of this material can be changed by applying an optical field, then we can modify the apparent length of the gap, and thereby cause the device to switch from the transparent to the reflecting mode of operation. To switch the device, we apply an optical control signal. Optically controlled optical switches based on nonlinear optical effects have been demonstrated in the laboratory, but are considered to be in a very preliminary state of technology emergence. Nevertheless, they promise the possibility of exceedingly fast reconfiguration (switching) speeds less than one picosecond (one thousandth of one billionth of one second).

Whereas it is optical crosspoints that are the key devices in any switching system for optical signals, crosspoints alone are typically not sufficient. For example, a number of electrically activated 2x2 directional coupler optical switches can be simultaneously formed in the surface of an electro-optic material to form a switch with several inputs and several outputs. Any input can be switched to any output by applying appropriate control voltages to the electrodes above the individual 2x2 crosspoints. As a light signal passes from an input to an output through the sequence of paths and 2x2 crosspoints it accumulates certain degradations. There is loss of light (attenuation) due to inevitable imperfections in the waveguides formed in the surface of the substrate, absorption by the substrate material, radiation due to sharp bends in the waveguides, and light lost by scattering at the crosspoints due to their inevitable imperfections. In addition to the cumulative loss of light, there is leakage at each crosspoint into the undesired path (crosstalk) since the switching action is not perfect. This leakage of undesired signals into other signals accumulates in a large switching matrix to produce unacceptable levels of interference.

In electrical switching systems, the accumulation of loss and interference can be removed by amplifiers and regenerators (for digital signals). If we were going to fabricate an all-optical switching system with a large number of inputs and outputs, we may require the optical equivalents of electrical gain and regeneration. Devices which provide such functions have been demonstrated in the laboratory.

II. PHOTONIC SWITCHING APPLICATION

Having now briefly reviewed the technology of optical crosspoints, we can begin to examine how these photonic devices can be incorporated into switching systems on which fiber optic transmission systems terminate. Consider a hypothetical all-optical switch having an architecture similar to today's electronic digital switches. Each incoming fiber carries to the switch a sequence of optical pulses corresponding to an underlying digital bit stream. This bit stream is likely to be a multiplex of many information streams interleaved in time. Each of these information streams is likely to require different routing. Thus, the switch must separate out the individual pulse streams, route them to the proper different outputs, and then recombine all signals leaving the same output port on the switch for transmission on the corresponding outgoing optical fiber. In order to separately route various optical pulses, in this hypothetical all-optical switch, the incoming optical pulse streams will have to be synchronized to a common clock (phase synchronized) so that as they pass through an all-optical demultiplexer or an all optical time divided switch they can be routed bit-by-bit. Since the incoming optical pulses have suffered some loss in transmission to the switch, and since pulses arriving on different fibers may not be of the same power level, some sort of power level equalization will be required. As the optical pulses work their way through the optical switch matrix they will suffer some attenuation, and they will accumulate interference from the inevitable coupling of optical signals to unintended paths in the matrix. To remove these degradations some sort of optical regeneration including reclocking will be required.

All of these functions: synchronization, demultiplexing, separate routing of demultiplexed components, regeneration/amplification, and remultiplexing are done in conventional electronic switches. An all optical version of today's electronic digital switch would require all-optical components capable of doing these things. From a scientific perspective, it is possible to either imagine or construct devices that can do these functions. However, it is a consequence of the physics of optical devices that such devices tend to be large compared to their electronic counterparts. This is because photonic devices must have physical dimensions which are many times the wavelength of the light - many micrometers. Meanwhile electronic devices of great complexity are being fabricated today with dimensions of individual transistors in the micrometer range. The necessary large physical size of the photonic devices translates into problems in fabricating inexpensive photonic circuits of more than minimal complexity since the large individual devices use up expensive "real estate" on the optical substrates in which they are formed, and optical circuits occupying a large amount of real estate are more likely to be ruined by a small defect in the substrate anywhere within the boundaries of the circuit. Thus even if one were to develop simple photonic devices which could be manufactured at low cost, it is difficult to see today how one might make practical devices of the necessary complexity that could compete with their electronic counterparts in constructing a switching system using today's switching system architecture. Economics will ultimately prevail in chosing the technology to use in switching systems, and with today's architecture it would appear simpler and less expensive to convert the incoming signals from optical form to electronic form before performing the switching function. There are, however, some other possibilities for using photonic devices in switching - not necessarily as a substitute for electronic devices, but in conjunction with electronic devices. Whereas it is difficult and expensive to make complex all-optical circuits, photonic devices do have the potential for very high speed operation. Electronic circuits can be very complex, but their speed may not be as fast as what can be obtained with photonic devices. Thus it may be that one could use photonic devices for doing certain high speed functions in a switching system which are not too complex (e.g., demultiplexing an incoming optical signal into several lower speed optical bit streams) and use electrical components for doing the lower speed more complex functions (routing pulses through a large switching matrix). Alternatively one might see photonic switching devices used in entirely new switching architectures which are optimized to trade speed for simplicity.

Alternatively, consider a hypothetical switching architecture which uses a number of interconnected rings to route bit streams from various inputs to various outputs. Each access port on the switch transfers incoming signal bits onto a circulating bit stream using available time slots. These time slots may be allocated on a demand basis by a central controller as needed, or they may be competed for using some packet switching access protocol (or a combination of both). Bits are transferred between rings to their destination output ports by gateways. Since a time slot on a receiving ring may not be available when a bit arrives at a gateway from a transmitting ring some storage will be required in the gateway. If the gateway function were to be implemented in an all-optical fashion, then this would require all optical storage. Of course this architecture could also be implemented with electronic components. As a heavily time-divided switching architecture it trades speed for simplicity, and thus may be more favorable for an all-optical implementation. Whether photonic devices serve as high speed demultiplexing and multiplexing interfaces between optical fibers and future electronic switching matrices, or whether photonic devices work their way further into the switching matrix is an area of research investigation at this time. There is also some possibility that optical means might be deployed to solve problems associated with fixed interconnections between sub-elements of a switching system. This may take the form of either optical fiber interconnects or free-space optical interconnects using advanced imaging optics.

REFERENCES

1. P.W. Smith, "On the Physical Limits of Digital Optical Switching and Logic Elements," 61:1975-1993, October, 1982.

2. P.W. Smith and W.J. Tomlinson, "Bistable Optical Devices Promise Subpicosecond Switching," 18:26-33, June, 1981.

3. M. Kondo, Y. Ohta, M. Fujiwara, and M. Sakaguchi, "Integrated Optical Switch Matrix for Single-Mode Fiber Networks," QE-18:1759-1765.

POTENTIAL IMPACT OF HIGH TEMPERATURE SUPERCONDUCTORS ON TELECOMMUNICATIONS

Fernand Bedard
Research Physicist
Office of Research
National Security Agency
Fort George G. Mead, MD

ABSTRACT
Superconductivity at temperatures above 90 degrees K opens potential opportunities for electronics applications whose impact ranges from significant to unique. Now all superconducting systems can use highly efficient and reliable cryogenics. More importantly, high performance semiconductor electronics can be enhanced with superconductive components. Indeed, there are functions that can only be credibly done by using the best aspects of both semiconductor and superconductor technologies.

The discovery of superconductivity at temperatures well above 90K has caused an awesome surge of activity among physicists, materials experts, chemists and ceramists. The excitement has spilled over to the engineering community where applications in motors, generators, transportation and power transmission are clearly envision. In contrast, the electronics world, which has an easier time with these presently brittle materials is apparently more cautious, tentatively exploring where zero resistance might make a difference. However there was no immediately perceived, obvious, major application or opportunity begging for this solution. One reason for this hesitation is the comparative lack of experience in electronics "small scale" systems vis-a-vis "magnet" type uses. A second, and possibly more dominant reason, is the systems designer's antipathy toward refrigeration. Nevertheless, there are a significant number of electronics applications which offer sufficient and even tempting improvements. These uses cover both the analog and digital domain, the civilian and military sectors. Furthermore, they frequently make use of more than the obvious "zero resistance" property of super- conductivity.

Electronics should be operated at ambient, room temperature. Cryogenic temperatures should be invoked only when the performance gain exceeds the penalty of the cooling system--and is really needed. In general, performance means "high" performance -- then only if the performance--fast speed, low power, small size, reliability. Superconductivity does indeed offer many, and sometimes all, of these features.

Prior to "High T_c", the materials of choice for electronics had evolved to be niobium and niobium nitride, calling for bath temperatures of $\sim$ 4K (for Nb) and $\sim$ 8-10K (for NbN). The technology has indeed been exploited in many "niche" applications: ultra-high sensitivity magnetometers for sample measurements an bio-medical diagnoses, very low noise mm wave detectors and mixers for radio astronomy, precision voltage standards and, most recently, a commercial instrument- a 5 picosecond sampling oscilloscope. As important as these uses are, they do not, yet, represent a wide spread technology insertion.

The discovery of high temperature superconductive materials seems to promise a major change in acceptance. One can now consider all superconducting systems with cryogenic support systems, dewars or refrigerators, which are smaller and more supportable. Second, there are existing and proposed semiconductor electronics systems where performance can be enhanced by the addition of superconductive components. And finally, electronics systems engineers have needed and sought special functions which have been pursued by semiconductor electronics with great difficulty. There are configurations using the best features of both semiconductors and superconductors which show great promise in solving some of these problems.

We shall discuss examples of both analog and digital electronics which appear promising for further evaluation and possible exploration using high T_c materials, low T_c and semiconductors.

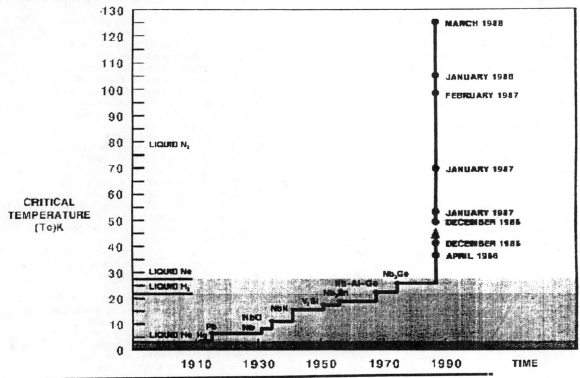

HIGH T$_c$

- **BETTER COOLING FOR "ALL SUPERCONDUCTING SYSTEMS"**
- **IMPROVED SEMICONDUCTOR SYSTEMS**
- **NEW SEMICONDUCTOR- SUPERCONDUCTOR SYSTEMS**

ELECTRONICS APPLICATIONS OF SUPERCONDUCTIVITY

- DRIVING FORCE
  - HIGH PERFORMANCE

- APPLICATIONS
  - ANALOG
  - DIGITAL

LARGE COMPUTER SYSTEM

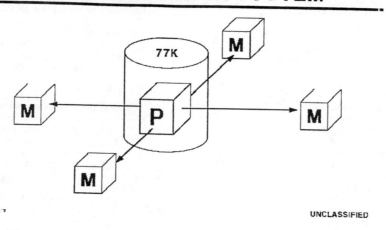

77K

CROSSBAR SWITCH

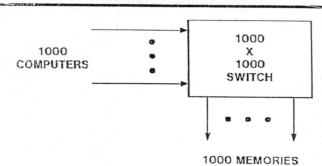

1000 COMPUTERS

1000
X
1000
SWITCH

1000 MEMORIES

SIZE: 6" CUBE (APPROXIMATELY)

ATOMIC LAYER ENGINEERING OF ELECTRONIC AND PHOTONIC DEVICES

Lester F. Eastman
Professor of Electrical
Engineering
Department of Electrical
Engineering

Cornell University
Ithaca, NY

ABSTRACT
The chemical composition and impurity doping of compound semiconductors are beginning to be controlled to single atomic layer precision. Electron beam and optical methods can be used in situ, along with molecular beam epitaxy and organometallic vapor phase epitaxy methods with single atom layer growth cycles. The impact of these techniques on improving transistors, tunnel devices, photodetectors, and lasers is discussed.

Advanced electron devices are now starting to take advantage of atomic layer engineering for better performance. The semiconductor chemical composition of compound semiconductors can be changed abruptly from GaAs to AlAs at an interface, for example. Dilute chemical impurities can be varied sharply also. The control of the abruptness depends upon the method of growing the layered crystal structure, but the physical limit of atomic-layer abruptness is being achieved.

These sophisticated layered structures are being used to improve the performance of transistors, for higher frequency microwave operation or for higher switching speed in logic devices. Photonic devices such as semiconductor lasers, and high speed optical detectors, also require such layered structures.

There are two methods of obtaining these layered structures. One is by molecular beam epitaxy (MBE), and one is by

1668

organometallic vapor phase epitaxy (OMVPE). An MBE machine is a large vacuum chamber with a set of heated crucibles containing the chemical elements of interest, such as gallium, arsenic, aluminum, indium, silicon, beryllium, and germanium. A polished, cleaned wafer of single-crystal GaAs substrate is heated in a position where the chemical beams, from the several crucibles, converge. Shutters are used to start and stop the chemical beams from the individual crucibles. By growing at a rate of about one atomic layer per second, it is possible to deposit as little as one atomic layer of any chemical. In normal growth of GaAs, the gallium and the arsenic beams impinge on the substrate together. Other chemicals, such as aluminum and indium ca be added by opening their shutters. The flow rates of these beams are controlled by precisely controlling the individual crucible temperatures. The second method of epitaxial growth of sophisticated structures, by OMVPE, uses streaming gases at or near atmospheric pressure. The substrate is heated in order to breakdown the gas molecules. Trimethyl gallium $(Ga(C_3)_3)$ is used for gallium deposition and arsine (AsH_3) is used for the arsenic deposition in this method. By quickly changing the composition of the gases, the chemical composition of the layers can be abruptly changed.

It is also possible to deposit exactly one atomic layer, and only one, at a time by alternately supplying the gallium and the arsenic. This technique, called atomic layer epitaxy, depends on the rejection of added layers of gallium or arsenic from the heated substrate, when they re alternately supplied in this manner.

Field effect transistors can make very effective use of such abrupt heterostructures with controlled doping profiles. Figure 1 shows the cross-section of such a transistor, with its source for electrons, the gate, and the drain for the electrons, Electrons flow in a potential depression in the pure GaAs. The electrons are attracted to the positive silicon doping ions in the AlGaAs, but a potential barrier, caused by the heterojunction, prevents them from joining these ions. With the electron separated the short distance from the doping ions, they can travel rapidly, without colliding with the ions. In recent devices, a thin layer if InGaAs has been placed between the GaAs and the AlGaAs at this heterostructure. in atom is larger than the Ga atom it replace, causing some strain. No defects result, however, if the fractional content of indium is traded off with the thickness of this InGaAs layer. Using 25% indium, and 75% gallium, in a layer 100 A thick, high performance has resulted. Electrons go along this channel 80% faster than they do in a doped GaAs channel, and this is 200% faster than they would in a silicon

channel. With gate lengths of .2 um, current gain up to 120 GHz, and power gain up to 200 GHz have been achieved. Other similar structures should allow current gains to over 250 GHz and power gains to over 500 GHz, when .1 pm gate lengths are used. Switching times of 6 picoseconds have been achieved to date in .2 pm gate heterojunction FET's, and eventually less than 4 picoseconds can be achieved with .1 pm gates.

Bipolar transistors with AlGaAs emitters, and GaAs base and collector regions, also have high performance. With the larger forbidden band gap in the AlGaAs emitter, the current gain is raised by preventing holes, from the base, from injecting back into the emitter. Thus very high base doping, up to $1 \times 10^{20}/cm^3$ is possible, to lower the base resistance without lowering current gain significantly. Current gains have been obtained to 105 GHz, and power gains to 175 GHz to date. With improved structure parameters and processing, the current gain should be able to re baised to 200 GHz, and the power gain to 200 GHz.

Semiconductor lasers can also be made for high performance using abrupt interfaces. Figure 2 shows the composition profile for a strained-layer, graded-index, separate-confinement, heterojunction laser. The electron energy profile is similar. The 40 A quantum well, responsible for the lasing action, is in $_{37}Ga_{63}As$ instead of the usual GaAs. Electrons, at high density, are injected from the n-type AlGaAs, and similarly holes are injected to a high density from the p-type AlGaAs. Light is wave guided by the graded AlGaAs regions due to the higher refractive index in these regions, compared with the regions with high, uniform aluminum content. This structure gave out light at .99 pm wavelength, rather than the more usual .83 pm wavelength characteristic of GaAs quantum wells. Thus, using atomic layer engineering, laser structures can be made to operate at different wavelengths for different applications. Future applications will involve integrated photonic, and integrated photonic and electronic devices for digital and microwave applications.

In conclusion, it has been shown that the epitaxial growth of doped compound semiconductors their heterojunctions with each other, can lead to very high performance transisperformance transistors and photonic devices. In order to achieve the best performance, the composition of these structures will be controlled with atomic layer precision. The use of MBE and OMVPE will be made to achieve this atomic layer engineering from the next generation of advanced electro. vices.

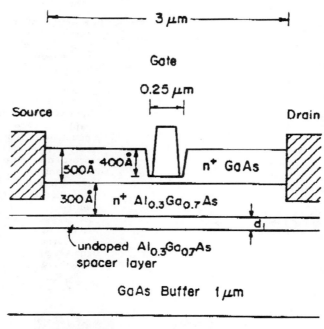

Figure 1

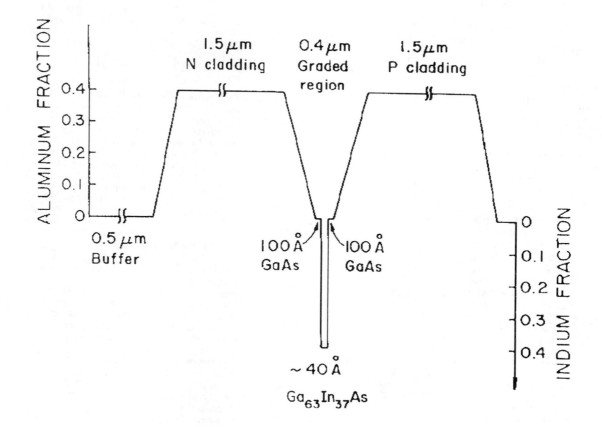

Figure 2

NEURAL NETWORK CHIPS

Lawrence D. Jackel
Department Head
Device Structure Research Dept.

AT&T Bell Laboratories
Holmdel, NJ

ABSTRACT

Research activity in electronic neural networks has exploded in the last few years. These networks are electronic circuits or computer programs loosely based on biophysical models of neural functions that seek to capture the strenghts of biological information processing. Analog VLSI neural-net chips have been developed that perform "neural arithmetic" at rates up to 10 billion bit operations per second. This session presents an overview of the field and a critical assessment.

INTRODUCTON

Early results from exploring alternative computer architectures based on hints from neurobiology suggest that networks of highly-interconnected, simple, low-precision processors may give us new tools for tackling problems that have been hard or impossible to do on standard computers. In this paper we describe an electronic neural model and we show this model is readily adapted for use in pattern recognition tasks. We also describe a chip, implementing this model, that is used for handwritten digit recognition.

A NEURAL MODEL

Figure 1a is a drawing of a neuron, or nerve cell, which can typically have 10^4 input and output connections. The input structure is a branching tree of fibers called dendrites that receive inputs from other neurons through adjustable connections called synapses. The output of the cell is sent along another set of fibers, called axons, to the synapses of other neurons. When a neuron is excited at its input synapses, it produces a train of pulses that travel along its axon. Inputs at excitatory synapses increase the pulse rate, while inputs at inhibitory synapses reduce the pulse rate. The output pulse rate depends on both the strength of the input signals and strength, or weight, of the synaptic connections. The memory and processing ability of this network are thought to lie in the pattern of these connections and their weights.

In a simple neural model the pulse rate is determined by a sigmoid function of a weighted sum of the inputs. This function can be built using traditional electronic components in an analog sum-of-products circuit, Figure 1b. In this circuit the variable pulse rate of the neuron is replaced by the variable output voltage of the amplifier and the synaptic connections are replaced by conductances. Input voltage signals supply current into the wire dendrite in proportion to the product of the input voltage and the synapse conductance. The sigmoid transfer function is provided by the saturating characteristics of the amplifier.

We can calculate the output pulsing rate of a neuron u_i as a function of its input signals v_i and their connection strengths W_{ij}:

$$u_i = f(\sum_j v_j W_{ij}) \ ,$$

(1)

were f is a sigmoidal function, such as tanh. Evaluation of the right side of Equation (1) is the major computation required of electronic "neural" processors. In our electronic circuit the W_{ij} are conductances connecting the inputs to the wire "dendrite". These elements are often more complicated than simple resistors because both positive ("excitatory") and negative ("inhibitory") connections are usually needed.

This basic circuit can be used as a building block for a variety of network architectures that can function as both memories and processors. The first of these, the "perceptron"[1] and the "adaline"[2] were proposed over 20 years ago and early prototypes demonstrated their potential for tackling simple problems. However, implementation (or even simulation) of large networks was not feasible until recently.

PATTERN MATCHING

Neural circuits excel in tasks of pattern matching and classifying large quantitites of noisy, low information content data into a limited number of categories. Suppose that we wish to determine the degree of match between some input pattern and a list of stored patterns, for example a set of handwritten digits. We could just compare the input pixel pattern to stored pixel maps of various examples of characters, but it is more effective to approach the problem in a hierarchal manner. First, we look for a representation of the image in terms of primitive features, like vertical lines or line ends, and then in a second stage of matching we compare this set of features to those expected for the prototypical examples of the characters. For example, a "2" would be expected to have line segments ending at the upper left and lower right of the image and have a horizontal line at the bottom.

In our notation, the input data to the network for the first task of recognizing features is a vector $\vec{v}$ with components v_j where each of the j's refer to one of the pixels in a small section of the image. In the simplest case, this vector can be just binary, only ones and zeros, each representing the presence of a black or white pixel. (In a more complex system, there could be analog representations of the pixel gray level).

Patterns are stored that represent the features to be extracted. Each stored pattern (say the i th) is represented by a vector $\vec{W_i}$ with components W_{ij} which is a template for pattern i. In our example, $\vec{W_2}$ would be the template for a particular feature, say a horizontal line, in the subsection of the image. Then, each u_i of Equation (1) is the dot product of $\vec{v}$ with $\vec{W_i}$. This means that each u_i is a projection of the input pattern $\vec{v}$ onto the template $\vec{W_i}$. If the value of its projection is greater than a predetermined threshold value, a feature is considered to be present.

Figure 2a shows an example of a handwritten character "2" and figures 2b-2d show examples of features that might be used as primitives to describe this image. The shading in the 7x7 image corresponds to the values of W_i for each of these features. Clear areas have no weight, while dark areas have a positive weight and shaded areas have a negative weight. This first feature corresponds to a line coming from the left and stopping in the dark area without extending to the shaded area. By "sliding" (convolving) these features over the image of the "2" we make a feature map indicating the location of various features.

A goal of our research is to build high-speed electronic hardware that can implement these pattern matching operations, and thus provide a key portion of the processing necessary for pattern recognition.

CMOS PROGRAMMABLE NETWORKS

The function described in Equation (1) can be implemented on conventional digital computers or special purpose digital hardward and there is a growing body of work describing classification schemes using this techniqui[3]. Since most pattern matching problems do not require the precision of digital computation, it can be more effective to use analog circuits with lower resolution, but greater speed and density to do this task. Figure 1b is an example of such an analog circuit where multiplications are done using Ohm's law at each resistor and the summation is done using Kirchhoff's law for summing currents on a wire. Thus the problem of calculating a sum of products (or, equivalently, dot products between two vectors) is reduced to summing currents through resistors attached to the input lead of an amplifier ("neuron").

We have used novel CMOS circuitry combined with static RAM cells to make a programmable neural net chip with 54 electonic "neurons" and about 3000 synapses[4]. To simplify the design (and reduce the size of the circuit) the synapses can only have a limited set of values. Rather than use resistors as shown in Fig. 1b, a transconductance cell combined with 2 bits of local memory is used to allow both signs of weights in Eq. 1. The basic synaptic unit is about 100 microns on a side. The unit is designed so that when the input from the axon rises to the 1 state, transistor switches connect the output dendrite to either a current source (excitation) or a current sink (inhibition). The kind of connection is determined by the states of the two RAM cells contained in the unit: a 1 stored in one of the cells specifies an excitatory connection, a 1 stored in the other specifies an inhibitory connection.

Up to 49 vectors of 49 bits each can be stored in on the chip and compared with an input test vector. The search for a match requires only about 1 microsecond, corresponding to 2.5×10^9 one-bit multiplications and additions per second. This chip can be used directly to perform the feature matching necessary for character recognition[5]. Geometrical features can be represented by 7x7 pixel maps as shown in Fig 2b and stored as 49 bit vectors. When a 7x7 segment of the image is presented as a test vector, the chip checks whether any of the stored features is a close match to the pixel pattern in this segment. Matches are stored in a feature map and a new section of the image is loaded into the chip and tested for the presence of the standard features. The resulting feature map can then be compared with similar maps formed from a broad set of sample characters and identification made. This process can be nearly 99% accurate for carefully written characters.

NETWORK MODELS AND LEARNING

The chip described above has externally programmed features inspired by studies of biological vision systems. This is essentially a "hard-wired" system. One of the key goals in the development of artificial neural networks has been to emulate the adaptability of biology. A learning network should be able to form or define categories on the basis of experience for problems in which the proper representations are not fully understood. A variety of networks and automatic learning rules have been studied, but there is still strong debate over efficacy of existing rules and the potential for developing new ones with more utility[3,6,7]. Hardware implementation of such learning systems will require chips like that described above, but with weights that have analog depth to accommodate incremental learning processes[8].

CONCLUSIONS

Neural networks provide a new way of looking at some classes of complex problems. Special-purpose VLSI chips are now being made that implement neural-net algorithms, providing a new tool to apply for computationally difficult tasks in machine perception.

Serious questions remain whether or not current neural algorithms and hardware offer substantial advantages over conventional approaches. Most of the computing power of electronic neural nets is obtained by building special purpose VLSI chips that implement the algorithms. To make a fair comparison, one must measure neural-net chips against special-purpose chips designed to implement conventional algorithms. We believe that the outcome of such a comparison hinges on the following considerations: within a given fabrication and packaging technology there is a fixed budget for chip area, chip power dissipation, and chip-to-chip communication. Only so many bits can be transferred on and off a chip each second, and only so many transistors can switch their states before the power dissipation budget is exceeded. The key to high performance is to get as much useful computation from each I/O operation and transistor switching event as possible. The promise of electronic neural networks is that the low-precision additions and multiplications of neural circuits coupled with their high connectivity will provide an economy that surpasses conventional circuits for problems with massive amounts of low-precision input data. Research now underway is attempting to see the realization of that promise.

REFERENCES

[1] F. Rosenblatt, "Principles of Neurodynamics: Perceptrons and the Theory of Brain Mechanisms", Spartan, Press, Wash., DC, (1961).

[2] B. Widrow, "Generalization and Information Storage in Networks of Adaline 'Neurons'," in "Self Organizing Systems", M. C. Yovits et al., eds., Spartan Press, Wash., D.C., pp. 435-461 (1962).

[3] For a sampling of current research in neural modeling and artificial neural nets see: Proceedings of the IEEE Conference on "Neural Information Processing Systems - Natural and Synthetic" Denver, Colorado, November 1987, edited by Dana Anderson, to be pub., the American Institute of Physics (1988).

[4] H. P. Graf et al, "VLSI Implementation of a Neural Network Model", IEEE Computer Magazine, 21, 41 (1988).

[5] L. D. Jackel et al, "An Application of Neural Net Chips: Handwritten Digit Recognition," Proc. International Conference on Neural Networks, San Diego Ca., (1988).

[6] J. S. Denker et al, "Automatic Learning, Rule Extraction, and Generalization", Complex Systems, 1, 877 (1987).

[7] R. P., Lippmann, "An Introduction to Computing with Neural Nets", IEEE ASSP Magazine, 4, 4, (1987).

[8] "Implementations of Neural Network Models in Silicon", S. Mackie et al, in Neural Computers, R. Eckmiller and C. v.d. Malsburg, ed., Springer-Verlag, Berlin, 1988.

FIGURE CAPTIONS

Figure 1. a) Drawing of a biological neuron b) Electronic analog.

Figure 2. The feature extraction process. a) shows an image of a handwritten character. b), c) and d)

show examples of feature templates, and
the resultant feature maps for the image
shown in a). In the templates, black is
excitation and gray is inhibition. b)
and c) check for line endstops, d) checks
for horizontal lines.

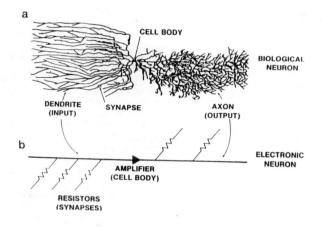

Fig. 1

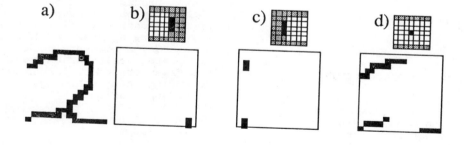

Fig. 2

TEC-04

SPEECH RECOGNITION AND RESPONSE TECHNOLOGIES - I

Robert E. Wohlford, Chairperson
Senior Director-Information Technology
Applied Technology and Development

Ameritech Services, Inc.
1900 E. GOlf Road
#750
Schaumburg, IL 60173

Significant progress has been made in moving speech recognition and response technologies from the traditional hands-and-eyes-busy market niche into a new and broad-based office information market. Recent advances in speaker independent speech recognition technology is poised for the next stage of market penetration - telecommunications. Small vocabulary speaker-independent connected speech recognition and speaker verification technology is fast approaching performance levels necessary for wide spread implementation of new telecommunications services. Continued improvements in speech coding and synthesis technology provide a spectrum of speech response options to the system developer. This seminar focuses on recent advances in these three speech processing technologies and demonstrates applications which will provide the basis for new telecommunications services.

Merrill. Solomon - Voice Processing Corporation

Jayant Naik - Texas Instruments, Inc.

SPEECH RECOGNITION

Robert E. Wohlford, Chairperson
Senior Director-Information Technology
Applied Technology and Development
Ameritech Services, Inc.
1900 E. GOlf Road
#750
Schaumburg, IL 60173

The state-of-the-art speech recognition technology is reviewed by a description of three approaches currently used in speech recognition products and laboratory systems. Strengths and weaknesses of these approaches are discussed for both speaker-dependent and speaker-independent applications. Recent advances in speaker-independent recognition over telephone networks is reviewed. The session concludes with a technology forecast indicating the challenges that need to be addressed before speech recognition is successfully deployed in broad-based applications.

SPEAKER-INDEPENDENT CONNECTED SPEECH RECOGNITION OVER THE TELEPHONE NETWORK

Merrill Solomon
President
Voice Processing Corporation
1 Main Street
Cambridge, MA 02142

A speaker-independent speech recognizer, based on acoustic phonetic rules, is described for naturally produced continuous speech input. Performance of the system for connected digit strings over a dialed telephone network is discussed. A live demonstration of the recognizer over a telephone network is provided.

SPEAKER VERIFICATION

Jayant Naik
Member of Technical Staff
Computer Science Center
Texas Instruments, Inc.
P.O. Box 226015
MS 238
Dallas, TX 75266

Speaker verification technology is finding a range of applications in controlling access to privileged resources and high cost transactions. Advances in digital signal processor and speech processing technology have made possible the design of fast, cost effective and high performance speaker verification systems. This session presents recent advances made in speaker verification technology and discusses practical issues involved in deploying this technology in telephone based applications.

TEC-05

SPEECH RECOGNITION AND RESPONSE TECHNOLOGIES - II

Matthew Yuschik, Chairperson
Advisory Technical Staff
Applied Technologies and Development

Ameritech Services, Inc.

1900 E. Golf Road
#750
Schaumburg, IL 60173

Significant progress has been made in moving speech recognition and response technologies from the traditional hands-and-eyes-busy market niche into a new and broad-based office information market. Recent advances in speaker independent speech recognition technology is poised for the next stage of market penetration - telecommunications. Small vocabulary speaker-independent connected speech recognition and speaker verification technology is fast approaching performance levels necessary for wide spread implementation of new telecommunications services. Continued improvements in speech coding and synthesis technology provide a spectrum of speech response options to the system developer. This seminar focuses on recent advances in these three speech processing technologies and demonstrates applications which will provide the basis for new telecommunications services.

Christopher Schcmandt - Massachusetts Institute of Technology

Gabriel Groner - Speech Plus, Incorporated

Paula Wilson - AT&T Conversant Systems

SPEECH SYNTHESIS

Matthew Yuschik, Chairperson
Advisory Technical Staff
Applied Technologies and Development
Ameritech Services, Inc.
1900 E. Golf Road
#750
Schaumburg, IL 60173

Speech synthesis has reached acceptable quality. However, improved naturalness and overall intelligibility are required before speech synthesis becomes widely used for speech response. Listener preferences have identified some of the problems and new approaches are being explored to overcome these deficiencies. This session presents an overview of synthesis technology, key issues, testing procedures and future expectations.

A VOICE RESPONSE SYSTEM

Gabriel Groner
Vice President, Engineering
Speech Plus, Incorporated
P.O. Box 7461
640 Clyde Court
Mountain View, CA 94039-7461

Voice response has gained increasing popularity in the telephone network. Because of limitations in current text to speech synthesis technology, a voice response system must provide a spectrum of voice response options, and software tools for translation of application requirements into an application program. A description of a voice response system architecture, its interface to the telephone network, and an interpreted language which provides a simple software interface is presented. Improvements in speech quality based on listener studies are also discussed.

INTEGRATION OF VOICE WITH ADVANCED WORKSTATION FUNCTIONS

Christopher Schmandt
Director, Speech Research
MIT Media Laboratory
Massachusetts Institute of Technology
Cambridge, MA 02139

The key for successful use of voice in advanced workstations is integration. Workstations and telephones must be interconnected to facilitate the interdependence between information storage and telecommunications, allowing the Workstation to intervene in voice traffic and provide remote access to local data. A prototype of a Workstation-based phone assistant demonstrating these concepts is described.

INTEGRATING VOICE TECHNOLOGIES WITH THE TELEPHONE NETWORK

Paula Wilson
National Account Manager
Marketing and Sales Division
AT&T Conversant Systems
6200 East Broad Street
Columbus, OH 43213

Automated voice-based services requires integration of various speech processing technologies such as speech recognition, speaker verification and speech coding. A system architecture, hardware platform and software tool set are described for the integration and development of voice based transaction services over telephone networks. Applications of automated services and field trial results are discussed.

TEC-06

HIGH-PERFORMANCE NETWORKING

James I. Cochrane, Chairperson
Director
Signaling and Data Network
Planning Center

AT&T Bell Laboratories
Crawfords Corner Road
Holmdel, NJ 07733

The speed and delay performance of local interconnection mechanisms – LANs, Rings, busses – within and close to computer centers continues to grow rapidly; several hundred megabit/second interconnections will soon be common. Can such performance be extended over longer distances both metropolitan and worldwide? Can the principles of ISDN – standard open interfaces and sophisticated signaling – be extended to the high speeds that will be needed? Can the telecommunications industry add functionality and value in this area of technology that has traditionally been led by the computer industry? In this seminar we show that very high performance networks can be constructed that meet the additional challenges of common-user networks – switching with "fair" sharing algorithms, distributed control, practical congestion control, and open standard interfaces.

Barry Goldstein - IBM Corporation

Scott C. Knauer - AT&T Bell Laboratories

Gillian Woodruff - Bell Northern Research

Robert L. Pokress - GTE Laboratories

DISTRIBUTED DATA PROCESSING

Barry Goldstein
Director-Large Systems & Communications
Thomas J. Watson Research Center
IBM Corporation
P.O. Box 218H3-D56
Yorktown Heights, NY 10598

High-performance interconnection of mainframes and work stations over long distances will make feasible a new generation of applications. This session shows how to configure such networks and highlights both the challenges and opportunities.

ULTRA HIGH-SPEED PACKET SWITCHES

Scott C. Knauer
Department Head
11251- Digital Architectures Research
AT&T Bell Laboratories
600 Mountain Avenue
3D-481
Murray Hill, NJ 07974

Interconnection of LANs and mainframes requires high-performance packet routing and switching. This session describes how a family of unbuffered packet switching elements can be configured to provide packet switches multi-megabit/second interfaces and gigabit/second total switching capacity with state-of-the-art VLSI.

END-TO-END CONTROL OF HIGH SPEED, PACKETIZED COMMUNICATION NETWORKS

Gillian Woodruff
Manager
Department 6K54
Bell Northern Research
P.O. Box 3511 Station C
Ottawa, Ontario, Canada

Future high speed networks will have to accommodate a wide range of user traffic requirements: continuous and bursty, narrowband and wideband. End-to-end network controls will be required to ensure the efficient and fair allocation of network resources between the users of the system, particularly when the network is heavily loaded. This session shows examples of controls, and illustrates their effectiveness with results from a simulation test bed.

Distributed Control Network Architecture

Robert L. Pokress
Director-Network Operations & Planning
Technology Center
GTE Laboratories
40 SYlvan Road
Waltham, MA 02254

Very high speed Ga/s technology has allowed Gb/s transmission systems in local and interexchange networks. Emerging database and software technologies promise to unlock the power of high-performance networking. A simple dispersed control switching and network architecture is demonstrated for high-performance value-added network capabilities. New architectures are shown that allow fault-free network performance objectives and open interfaces for ONA and CEI.

VIDEO COMPRESSION AND IMAGE PROCESSING

J. A. Bellisio, Chairperson

Division Manager, Digital Signal Processing Research

Bell Communications Research

331 Newman Springs Road
Red Bank, New Jersey 07701-7020

ABSTRACT

There is a revolution taking place in the processing of the television picture that rivals the introduction of color television in the late forties for sheer excitement and breath of new technology. At one end of the spectrum, low bit rate coding techniques make it possible to transmit full motion video over a digital network (ISDN) with picture quality that is appropriate for teleconferencing applications. At the other end of the spectrum, the possibility of sending a television picture that far exceeds the quality of today's television picture has energized research on the coding of the television image and the network transport. Recent research demonstrates the coding of a high definition (HDTV) component signal into 135 Mbps for distribution in a broadband ISDN environment on fiber. Alternatively, research also demonstrates the coding of NTSC video into a higher than normal quality image that is transportable over conventional broadcast channels, as well as fiber and satellite. Out of this complex fabric of competing television technologies there is an ongoing effort to reach some concensus on issues relating to standards, compression and transport that will carry television into the 21st century.

Hamid Gharavi — Bell Communications Research

Didier J. LeGall — Bell Communications Research

Arpad Toth — Philips Laboratories

Michael A. Isnardi — David Sarnoff Research Center

LOW BIT RATE TELEVISION ON ISDN

Hamid Gharavi
Member of Technical Staff

Bell Communications Research
331 Newman Springs Rd., NVC 3X-313,
Red Bank, NJ 07701-7020

ABSTRACT

This paper discusses a hybrid coding method for low bit-rate video transmission over the 2B channels (128 Kb/s) of ISDN networks. In this method the coding frame is divided into two dimensional m-by-m blocks where each block is further divided into smaller sub-blocks. Block classification and blockmatching motion estimation are based on the larger block size, while the transformation is performed on a sub-block basis. The transform coefficients are coded in such a way that the inter sub-block correlation can be efficiently exploited. As a result, for every block the sub-block coefficients are scanned by grouping all the first coefficients, followed by all the second coefficients and so on. The manner in which the sub-blocks are
scanned is called inter sub-block scanning. Three types of sub-block scanning are considered: zig-zag, horizontal and vertical scanning. The inter sub-block scanning is made adaptive by deciding which of the above scanning types is the most efficient. Consequently, this requires additional overhead to be sent to the receiver at the beginning of each block.

In our simulation the main block size of 16x16 and 32x32 is considered. In order to find the best sub-block size, four different sizes such as 2x2, 4x4, 8x8 and 16x16 are evaluated. The results using a few video sequences as the input show that a good quality video can be obtained at the transmission rates of 48 kb/s, 64 kb/s and 112 kb/s.

INTRODUCTION

The field of digital image and video processing is experiencing tremendous growth due to dramatic improvements in integrated circuits (IC) process technology. The recent advances in high capacity memory chips and VLSI technology have created a new horizon in low cost implementation of complex video compression algorithms. Consequently the transmission of video signals with an acceptable quality at very low rates is becoming feasible.

With the recent development of ISDN and the availability of 2B channel capacity (each B channel being 64 kb/s) the transmission of motion video coupled with its associated audio is becoming increasingly desirable. The success of ISDN depends not only on the nature of the service it is offering but also on the quality and cost of the service itself. The transmission of motion video at the basic rate of 48 kb/s (excluding 16 kb/s for audio) demands a compression rate of more than a thousand to one. Such high compression can not be achieved without employing the most sophisticated signal processing techniques.

Many applications in image compression involve the use of methods such as DPCM or transform coding [1]. For low bit-rate motion video signals the combination of the two, known as the hybrid coding [2,3,4], is considered to be the most efficient compression method. Figure 1 shows the block diagram of such an encoder with inter/intra frame prediction. For interframe, motion compensation predictions can also be used to improve the coding efficiency.

The coding efficiency of a hybrid encoder depends on the coding of the transform coefficients, the effectiveness of the motion compensated prediction, and the size of the transform block. Advantageously, a large block size achieves better compression since less overhead information need be transmitted per video frame of data as fewer blocks are required to be transmitted per frame. However, as the block size increases, the complexity of the circuitry required to perform the transformation of each block dramatically increases. This is especially true for complex transform methods such as discrete consine transform. Furthermore, as the block size increases, there is increased subjective degradation in the decoded video signal noted by the presence of block distortion in which the viewer perceives the outlines of the blocks.

In this paper we have expanded our hybrid coding method [5] by introducing adaptive scanning. The input signal arrives as two dimensional blocks of m $\times$ m PELs (main block) where each block is later divided into smaller sub-blocks n $\times$ n (n<m). The block classification and block matching motion estimation are performed on the main block basis whereas transformation, which takes place inside the hybrid loop (Figure 1), is achieved on a sub-block basis. In addition, an efficient adaptive scanning method to exploit the inter sub-block correlation is introduced.

BLOCK CLASSIFICATION

Before each block of data arrives at the hybrid encoder, it is characterized either as static interframe, dynamic interframe, or intraframe block.

The criteria in which the classification is achieved is based on absolute average block difference. Three types of average block differences are defined:

    i)   Non-motion Compensated Block Difference NCBD where

$$NCBD = \sum_{i}^{m-1} \sum_{j}^{m-1} |\, S\,(I + i, J + j, K) -$$

$$\hat{S}\,(I + i, J + j, K - 1)\,| \qquad (1)$$

    ii)   Motion Compensated Block Difference MCBD where

$$MCBD = \sum_{i}^{m-1} \sum_{j}^{m-1} |\, S(I + i, J + j, K) -$$

$$\hat{S}\,(I + i - m_i, j + j - m_j, K - 1)|$$

    iii)   Intra-frame Block Difference IBD where

$$IBD = \sum_{h}^{\gamma} \sum_{l}^{\gamma} \sum_{i}^{n-1} \sum_{j}^{n-1} |\, S(I + i + n\,h, J + j + n\,l, K) -$$

$$DC(h,l)\,| \qquad (2)$$

where

$$gmma = m/(m-1)$$

and

$$DC(h,l) = (\alpha_1/n^2) \sum_{i}^{n-1} \sum_{j}^{n-1} S[I + i + n\,(h-1), J + j + n\,l, K]$$

$$+ (\alpha_2/n^2) \sum_{i}^{n-1} \sum_{j}^{n-1} S[I + i + n\,h, J + j + n\,(l-1), K] \quad (3)$$

In the above equations, $S(I, J, K)$ and $\hat{S}(I, J, K)$ are the original and the reconstructed PEL values at the Ith row, J^{th} column and the Kth frame of a video sequence which is represented by a three dimensional signal array. m_i and m_j are the horizontal and vertical components of the estimated motion vector M. α_1 and α_2 are the horizontal and vertical weighting factors which are used in the two dimensional prediction of intraframe sub-blocks.

Once NCBD, MCBD and IBD are computed for each block of incoming data, the classification is performed in the following steps:

Step 1:

    If NCBD < (MCBD - t)   Block is static otherwise dynamic

Step 2:

    If IBD < (smaller of NCBD and MCBD)   Block is intraframe

Since the static block does not require the transmission of motion vectors, the threshold t is included to bias the decision towards static block.

INTERFRAME PREDICTION

The inter-frame predictor has two distinct modes: static and dynamic. In the static mode, the decoded data block from the same location on the previous frame is used to predict the coming block. Whereas for the dynamic block, a displaced block from a previously reconstructed frame is considered in the prediction. The estimated motion vector for each block is derived by applying the block matching motion estimation scheme [5].

INTRAFRAME PREDICTION

If the block is classified as an intraframe, the prediction is performed on a sub-block basis. Due to the smaller size of the sub-block, the intraframe prediction utilizes the correlation of the neighboring sub-blocks. Thus in the prediction the DC values of the previously decoded sub-blocks in both horizontal, A_{DC} and vertical B_{DC}, directions are considered.

In the actual coding each PEL in the sub-block is subtracted from the DC values of the two previous sub-blocks A and B.

$$E(I + i, J + j, K) = S(I + i, J + j, K) - (\alpha_1\, A_{DC} + \alpha_2\, B_{DC})$$

$$A_{DC} = 1/(n^2) \sum_{i} \sum_{j} \hat{S}(I - n + i, J + j, K)$$

$$B_{DC} = 1/(n^2) \sum_{i} \sum_{j} \hat{S}(I + i, J - n + j, K)$$

$$i, j = 1, 2, \ldots n - 1$$

$\hat{S}\,(\cdot)$ denotes the reconstructed PEL and $E\,(\cdot)$ is the error signal. The prediction error signals in the sub-block are transformed into a new domain where the coefficients are quantized and temporarily stored until all the sub-block coefficients within the block are scanned. Subsequently, these coefficients are quantized and coded in the same manner as in the case of interframe prediction. The significance of this type of intraframe prediction is that it can allow smaller blocks to be used which is not only efficient but also compatible with interframe prediction.

QUANTIZATION

A uniform quantizer with a center dead zone 'd' and step size 'Δ' is applied to quantize the transform coefficients. The parameters d and Δ are independent of each other and their values are different from one coefficient to another. For example, the lower transforms coefficients are quantized with a greater accuracy than the higher coefficients. The two dimensional distribution of various quantizers for the transform coefficients is performed by a masking file. The function of the quantized masking file is to assign a set of quantizers to each coefficient. For example $q_{h, \ell}$ is the quantizer which is assigned to the coefficient in the hth column and the ℓth row in the sub-block of n × n PELs. These quantizers differ in the value of their dead zone 'd'.

SCANNING AND CODING

The number of non-zero coefficients in a sub-block depends on the accuracy of inter/intra frame prediction as well as the size of the quantizer dead zone d. In general the transform coefficients, after being quantized, are scanned, entropy coded and transmitted to the receiver on a block by block basis. The consecutive non-zero and zero coefficients are transmitted by coding the non-zero coefficients followed by a 'run-length prefix' code and subsequently the coded length of zero coefficients [2]. For higher compression where the quantizer dead zones are large, this method with the following modification is preferred.

In this paper only non-zero coefficients with their corresponding positional information are transmitted. The non-zero coefficients are variable word length (VWL) coded, whereas positional information is run-length coded. In run-length coding each scanned block is considered as consecutive black and white runs. The black run corresponds to the length of the zero coefficients and the white run corresponds to the length of the non-zero coefficients. The end of block code is also applied to terminate the coding process once the last non-zero coefficient is transmitted. In this method the majority of the overall bits goes towards transmitting the run-length coded positional information and any attempt to improve the coding efficiency should be directed at improving the efficiency in which the positional information is coded. To achieve this objective, we have proposed a scanning method which can increase the average black and white runs and thus reduce the bits required for transmitting the positional information. In this method the transform coefficients are scanned in a way that can efficiently exploit the inter sub-block correlation. As a result, for every block, the sub-block coefficients are scanned by grouping all the first coefficients, followed by all the second coefficients and so on. We call the order in which each group is scanned Intra-sub-block scanning. Three types of Inter-sub-block scanning are proposed:

i) Zig-zag scanning where the sub-blocks are scanned in a manner shown in Figure 2-a.

ii) Horizontal scanning where the sub-blocks are scanned from left to right and top to bottom (See figure 2-b).

iii) Vertical scanning where the scanning is performed form top to bottom and left to right (see Figure 2-c).

The scanning can be made adaptive by deciding which of the above scanning types is more efficient. This will require an additional overhead to be sent to the receiver at the beginning of each block.

COLOR

In the case of color video the three primary colors, R G B, are transformed to Y, I, Q components. In the Y, I, Q domain most of the energy is concentrated in the luminance component, Y, with little energy in I and Q. This would suggest that the high energy component needs to be coded more accurately than the chrominance components. One method of coding chrominance signals is to reduce the spatial resolution. The lowered resolution chrominance components can be coded using the same method as for the luminance signal.

In this paper the chrominance signals have the same spatial resolution as luminance signals except that they are coded with a much lower precision. As a result, the quantizers dead zones for Y, I, Q are selected according to the energy distribution of Y, I, Q signals

$$dQ > dI > dY$$

dY, dI and dQ are the dead zones of the quantizers which correspond to Q, I and Y components respectively. In addition, the higher components are also discarded in the quantizer masking file. With regards to motion compensation, the I and Q signals have used the same motion vector derived from the Y component.

RESULTS

In our experiments we have used two video sequences; the one known as the "Trevor" sequence contains 75 frames with relatively fast motion. This is one of a test sequence used for evaluating 384 Kb/s CCITT video codecs [3]. The second sequence is "Mary" which was generated at Bellcore and contains 140 frames with slower motion but with close up head and shoulder. The spatial frame resolution for both sequences is 256×240.

In the coding process, each block was classified into intra-frame, static interframe or dynamic interframe. Table 1 shows a variable word length code which is used to encode the classification modes where the intraframe block has the longest codeword. The assignment of the VWL codes was made adaptive. For example, if the intraframe codeword (001) occurs in succession for a given number of times, then the codeword for the static block (1) is used to represent the next intraframe codeword. But if the next codeword is, in fact, the static block codeword, the 001 is selected. In our simulation the main block size of 32x32 and 16 × 16 was used. In order to find the best sub-block size, four different sizes were evaluated; 2 × 2, 4 × 4, 8 × 8 and 16 × 16. In this experiment by using Discrete Cosine Transform (DCT) we observed that the overall performance for sub-block size of 4 × 4 is slightly better than 8 × 8 and both are significantly superior to 2 × 2 and 16 × 16. The overall performance includes signal to noise ratio and subjective quality at a given bit-rate. In this evaluation, for a given block size, all the transform coefficients have used the same uniform quantizer. For each case the quantizer step size was selected according to the bit accuracy of the transform coefficients which depends on the size of the sub-block.

In the final stage of our simulation, the block size of 32×32 and the sub-blocks of 4 × 4 using adaptive inter sub-block scanning, was applied. The output buffer size was fixed at 16 Kbits. The buffer fullness, at three different levels, controlled the selection of the quantization masking files. Therefore, four different masking files were applied in the coding process. Each masking file represented the distribution of quantizers with different dead zones, in accordance with the importance of transform coefficients. Lower coefficients were quantized more accurately. The buffer output was fixed at a rates of 48, 64 and 112 kb/s including the multiplexed color data (I and Q). These rates were selected to meet the 1B or 2B channel capacity of ISDN when combined with audio. The real time display of processed sequences indicates very good and promising results for video phone application over ISDN network. This can be verified, to some extent, from figures 3 and 4. These figures show 16 consecutive decoded frames (with a transmission rate of fifteen frames per second) for each sequence at rate y 112 kb/s..

CONCLUSION

In this paper a hybrid coding method is presented for low bit-rate video transmission over the ISDN networks.

In this method each coding block was divided into smaller sub-blocks. To reduce the overhead information, the block classification and block matching motion estimation were performed on a main block basis. To reduce the hardware complexity and blocking effects the transformation was performed on sub-block basis. To improve the coding efficiency a method of inter sub-block scanning was introduced which can exploit the sub-block correlation within each block.

An intra-frame sub-block prediction method using the DC values of two previous sub-blocks along the horizontal and vertical direction was also discussed. Computer simulation results were presented for two video sequences showing several consecutive frames of each sequence. The coded sequences indicate an impressive performance at transmission rates of 48, 64 and 112 kb/s (particularly when displayed in real-time).

REFERENCES

[1] H. M. Musmann, P. Pirsh, and H. J. Gravoert, "Advances in Picture Coding", Proc. IEEE, Vol. 73, pg. 523-548, April 1985.

[2] A. Habibi, "An adaptive Strategy for Hybrid Image Coding," IEEE Trans. Commun., Vol. COM-29, pp. 1736-1740, Dec. 1981.

[3] W. Chen and W. K. Pratt, "Scene Adaptive Coder," IEEE Trans. Commun., Vol. COM-32, pp. 225-232, March 1984.

[4] S. Okubo, R. Nicol, B. Haskel, S. Sabri, "Progress of CCITT Standardization on nx384 kbits/s video codec," Globcom-87.

[5] H. Gharavi, "Low Bit Rate Video for ISDN," IEEE Transaction on Circuits and Systems, Feb. 88, Vol. CAS-35, No. 2.

[6] T. Koya, K. Iinuma, A. Hirano, Y. Iijima, and T. Ishiyuro, "Motion-compensated Inter-frame coding for Video Conferencing," in NTC 81, Proc. pp. G5.3.1 - G5.3.5.

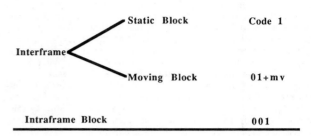

Table 1
Block Classification

Each block is classified into one of the of the following:

Static Block	Code 1
Moving Block	01+mv
Intraframe Block	001

Interframe

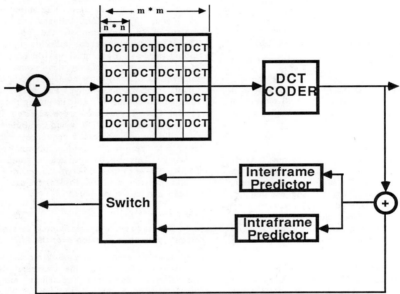

Figure 1. Hybrid Sub_block

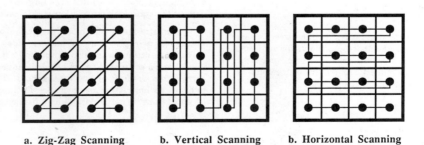

| a. Zig-Zag Scanning | b. Vertical Scanning | b. Horizontal Scanning |

Figure 2. Inter Sub_block Scanning

1681

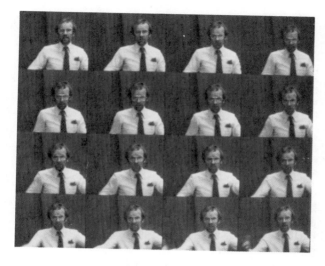

Figure 3. "Trevor" Sequence at a Rate of 112 kb/s.

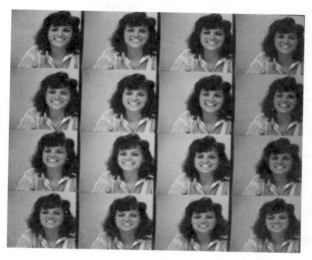

Figure 4. "Mary" Sequence Processed at a Rate of 112 kb/s.

TRANSMISSION OF HDTV SIGNALS UNDER 140 Mbits/s

USING A SUB-BAND DECOMPOSITION

AND DISCRETE COSINE TRANSFORM CODING

Didier Le Gall
Member of Technical Staff

Hugo Gaggioni
Member of Technical Staff

Cheng-Tie Chen
Member of Technical Staff

Bell Communications Research
435 South Street
Morristown, NJ 07960-1961

ABSTRACT

A technique to compress a HDTV signal at a bit-rate below 140 Mb/s has been developed. This scheme involves intrafield processing only and is based on splitting the signal into four narrow bands; the baseband signal is further transformed via DCT, quantized and entropy coded while the higher band signals are quantized and runlength coded. The band splitting technique uses low complexity filters permitting a simple hardware realization. Transmission of a signal of good quality both spatially and temporally is shown to be feasible.

INTRODUCTION

Digital transmission is a very promising solution for the delivery of High Definition television signal, especially when a high quality signal is needed. While a full Bandwidth PCM component HDTV signal requires as much as 1.2 Gbits/s, digital video coding makes transmission at much lower bit rate feasible. Among the possible service bit-rates defined on the emerging Broadband ISDN [1], the H4 access level rate of about 140 Mb/s seems the most appropriate for the transmission of High Definition Television. At this rate of 140 Mb/s we have pursued the investigation of a purely intrafield coding scheme for the following reasons: recent advances in signal processing and in VLSI have rendered high compression intrafields schemes feasible while, on the other hand, the cost of implementation of a truly motion compensated high quality inter-frame coder remains fairly high for HDTV.

In this paper we suggest a joint subband and transform coding approach that aims at fulfilling the following goals: 1) give a high quality, artifact free version of the original signal at below 140 Mb/s and 2) keep the need for high speed circuitry (at clock rate of above 50 MHz) to a minimum. An additional incentive for using a multirate signal processing approach (or sub-band) is the possibility of extracting a lower resolution television signal from a subchannel at 45 Mb/s.

SUB-BAND DECOMPOSITION

Sub-band coding refers to the class of techniques whereby parallel application of a set of filters, the input signal is decomposed into several narrowbands that are decimated and encoded separately for the purpose of transmission. In this paper we shall consider only separable filter banks applied first horizontally then vertically. Selection of a two-band one dimensional filter bank will give rise to an analysis of the image in four bands: horizontal low - vertical low; horizontal high - vertical low; horizontal low - vertical high and horizontal high - vertical high (Fig. 1). Encoding of each band will be performed according to each signal statistics. The filter bank has another advantage in terms of implementation: because the signals are decimated after filtering, the filter bank acts as a demultiplexer and all further processing occurs at one quarter of the HDTV clock rate.

Perfect reconstruction filterbanks can be designed with the implementation complexity in mind and the filters of [5] have been used successfully [6,7]. The derivation of perfect reconstruction filterbanks with short linear phase response is given in Appendix I. Alternatively one can also use the classical QMF filter bank of [8]. The short filter of [6] are particularly suitable for HDTV processing because they can be implemented using only a limited number of adders (Fig. 3). Table 1 gives the coefficients of some suitable FIR filter banks; the filter bank FB1 has been used in the simulation.

Encoding of the Baseband. Most of the information of the HDTV signal resides in the baseband signal. This signal forms an image with half the number of samples vertically and horizontally. Since HDTV has at least twice the vertical and horizontal resolution of 525 (625) lines system, this baseband (or a section of it) can be viewed as a compatible 525 lines sub-signal. Unlike digital video generated within the frequency constraints of CCIR Recommendation 601, the baseband produced by an exact reconstruction filterbank has a significant amount of information all the way to the Nyquist frequency.

This high frequency content of the baseband appears critical. In order to achieve a sufficiently high compression, the DCT is applied to the baseband of the luminance and the chrominance components with subsequent entropy coding of the transform coefficients.

In a sub-band coding scheme, the quality of the encoding of the baseband has to be very high since the interpolation process greatly increases the visibility of the artifacts. For this reason, the block size has been restricted to 4x4 and 8x4 for the luminance. (In the reconstructed image they correspond to 8x8 and 16x8 blocks respectively.) Also for this reason the same quantization step is used for all the coefficients i.e. no visibility threshold is used. For the chrominance signals a block size of 8x8 is used.

The encoding of the transform coefficient is carried out according to a variant of the scene adaptive coder of Chen and Pratt [8], with separate Huffman codebooks for the runlengths and the amplitudes values. Also no threshold is used and the quantizer step is the only control of the image quality.

Encoding of the High Bands. The encoding strategy for the high bands is a variation of the coding technique in [4]; a quantizer with deadzone is used and because the high bands fall within the deadzone most of the time the quantized data are encoded using run-length coding while the few non-zero values are encoded separately. A simple variable length code is used to further compress the non-zero values.

For very high quality reconstruction as is the case in HDTV coding, it is necessary to select a very small deadzone and in some cases the image noise produces a significant number of isolated dots in the highbands that contribute little to the signal, yet significantly degrade the performance of the run length coder. Those isolated dots can be removed by application of a very simple 3x3 nonlinear filter before the data is runlength coded.

SIMULATION RESULT ON A TEST SEQUENCE.

The test sequence used was "Kiel Harbor" and was provided by the Heinrich-Hertz Institut (HHI), Berlin, Germany. This sequence is a synthetic zoom and pan generated from a very high resolution still picture and contains a full 27 MHz of very busy information with extremely critical high frequency details. Despite the fact that this sequence does not have a 16:9 aspect ratio it was thought to be extremely interesting test material for the algorithm simulation in view of its high spatial and temporal frequency content.

The test sequence was R, G, B, sequence with equal bandwidth in the three components and before any encoding it was converted to luminance and chrominance components (Y, Cr, Cb) according to the specifications of CCIR Recommendation 601 and the color difference signals were filtered and subsampled by a factor of two yielding a signal that can be referred to as 16:8:8 in the family of the CCIR signals.

While it was anticipated that the baseband signal would fit into 45 Mb/s, it was found that for this test sequence much better results were obtained by allocating a 65 Mb/s channel for the baseband (Y, Cr, Cb) since the DCT coding artifacts are extremely visible after the interpolation (moving noise patterns). It was found that the higher bands for both luminance and chrominance never occupied more than a 50 Mb/s channel and a channel of 55 Mb/s was allocated to the higher bands for a total of 120 Mb/s. The data rate generated for a typical field (#2) is described in Table 2.

Display of the reconstructed sequence (one quarter of the full picture chosen where the content was thought most critical) through the Abekas A60 digital video showed a very satisfying picture undegraded in resolution and with no noticeable moving noise pattern.

Channel Rate Adaptation Strategy. In the light of the simulation results a rate buffer strategy was designed. Two parameters can be acted upon: the quantizer step for the DCT and the deadzone for the higher bands. We suggest to chose the DCT quantizer step as a function of the status of the buffer. For the higher bands, a two state coder with two deadzones (small and large) will provide the right degree of adaptation and the large deadzone should be used only in exceptional circumstances. The set-up of those parameters was such that for our test sequence the buffer was never close to its fullness status. A quality identical to that obtained on the test sequence should be available on a wide range of source material.

CONCLUSION

The coding scheme presented in this paper is a most promising result that proves the feasibility of high quality HDTV transmission at the rate of about 140 Mb/s with a simple intrafield coder.

APPENDIX I: Exact Reconstruction Linear Phase Filter Bank.

Exact reconstruction Linear Phase Filter Banks are analysis/synthesis systems that allow a perfect restitution of the original signal from its subbands in absence of quantization error. Fig. 2 depicts the principal elements of a two-channel analysis/synthesis filter bank system. As shown, the input signal $x(n)$, is filtered into two bands, which are then decimated by a factor of 2. At the synthesis side, the signals $y_0(n)$ and $y_1(n)$ are interpolated (i.e., by inserting zeros between successive samples), filtered and added together to reproduce the original signal. Output $Y(z)$ in this figure can be written as:

$$Y(z) = G_0(z) Y_0(z) + G_1(z) Y_1(z) \qquad (2.1)$$

where

$$Y_0(z) = \frac{1}{2} [H_0(z) X(z) + H_0(-z) X(-z)] \qquad (2.2)$$

$$Y_1(z) = \frac{1}{2} [H_1(z) X(z) + H_1(-z) X(-z)] \qquad (2.3)$$

Substitution of Eqs. (2.2)-(2.3) into (2.1) yields

$$Y(z) = 1/2 [G_0(z) H_0(z) + G_1(z) H_1(z)] X(z)$$

$$+ 1/2 [G_0(z) H_0(-z) + G_1(z) H_1(-z)] X(-z) \qquad (2.4)$$

From Eq. (2.4) it is easily seen that aliasing is removed if the synthesis filters are defined as

$$\begin{aligned} G_0(z) &= H_1(-z) \\ G_1(z) &= -H_0(-z) \end{aligned} \qquad (2.5)$$

For this class of synthesis filters, perfect reconstruction of the input signal requires that

$$H_0(z) H_1(-z) - H_0(-z) H_1(z) = 2z^{-m}. \qquad (2.6)$$

where m is the delay introduced by the combination of analysis/synthesis filter banks. Filters that satisfy those conditions have been described in [6] and appear to be quite appropriate for a high-speed implementation.

ACKNOWLEDGEMENT

The authors would like to thank Dr. R. Schaefer of HHI for kindly providing the digital test sequence. We also thank Scott Soper for his contribution to the simulation.

REFERENCES

[1] H. Gaggioni, and D. Le Gall, "Digital Video Transmission and Coding in the Broadband ISDN", IEEE Transaction on Consumer Electronics, February 1988.

[2] M. Vetterli, "Multi-Dimensional Sub-band Coding: Some Theory and Algorithms", Signal Processing 6 (1984), pp. 97-112.

[3] J. W. Woods and S. D. O'Neil, "Sub-Band Coding of Images", Proc. ICASSP 86, pp 1005-1008, April 1986.

[4] H. Gharavi, and A. Tabatabai, "Sub-band Coding of Digital Images Using Two-Dimensional Quadrature Mirror Filtering," Proc. SPIE, vol. 707, pp. 51-61, September 1986.

[5] D. Le Gall, "Subband Coding of Images with Low Computational Complexity", Picture Coding Symposium, Stockholm 1987, § 3.17.

[6] D. Le Gall and A. Tabatabai, "Sub-band Coding of Digital Images Using Symmetric Short Kernel Filters and Arithmetic Coding Techniques", Proc ICASSP 88, April 1988.

[7] M. Vetterli and G. Karlson, "Subband Coding for Packet Video", to be published Optical Engineering, to be published.

[8] W. H. Chen and W. K. Pratt, "Scene Adaptive Coder", IEEE Transaction on Communications, Vol. COM-32, pp. 225-232, March 1984.

[9] J. D. Johnston, "A Filter Family Designed for Use in Quadrature Mirror Filter Banks", Proc. of 1980 ICASSP pp. 291-294.

	LOW-PASS	HIGH-PASS
FB1	-1 2 6 2 -1	1 -2 1
FB2	-1 3 3 -1	1 -3 3 -1

Table 1: Filter Coefficients for Low Complexity Filter Banks

Mbit/ field	Baseband	Higher bands
Y	0.985	0.827
Cr	0.081	0.015
Cb	0.105	0.030
Total	1.171	0.872

Table 2: Data rate generated for field #2 (Mbits)

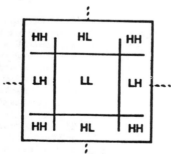

Figure 1: Four Band Split with Separable Filter Bank

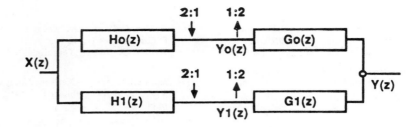

Figure 2: A Two-Band Analysis/Synthesis Filter Bank System

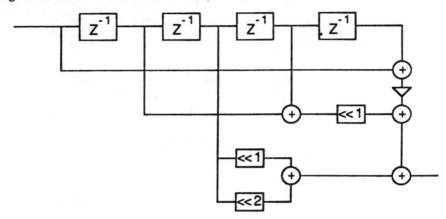

Figure 3: A possible realization of the filter bank (LP filter).

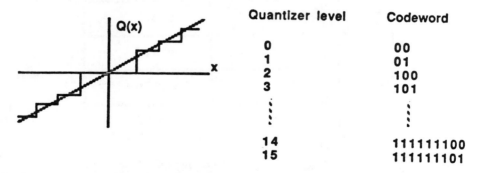

Figure 4: Quantizer and Variable Length Code for the Higher Bands

HIERARCHICAL HDTV TRANSMISSION,

A TOTAL SYSTEM APPROACH FOR NORTH AMERICA

Arpad G. Toth
Chief Scientist

Mikhail Tsinberg
Research Dept. Head of Advanced TV Research

Charles W. Rhodes
Principle Research Scientist

Philips Laboratories
345 Scarborough Road
Briarcliff Manor, New York 10510

ABSTRACT

High Definition Television (HDTV) has become a major worldwide event in the television arena. Since the early 1980s, when HDTV was first demonstrated by Japan, a number of alternate systems have emerged. These systems reflect clearly the business and political objectives of the particular countries or organizations. In North America, which is the largest single consumer market in the world, technical, business and political considerations are shaping the evolution of HDTV.

This paper describes a possible Advanced TeleVision (ATV) architecture for North America and defines its functional modules and corresponding interfaces. The developed model is recommended as a design tool for standardizing ATV in North America and analyzing interrelationships of the functional modules on the economic basis. The paper proposes a "hierarchical" ATV emission system with full NTSC compatibility and HDTV quality. Solutions are recommended for terrestrial broadcast CATV, and satellite. This work describes a total systems approach to HDTV called HDS-NA (High Definition System for North America). The two emission signals of HDS-NA: HDMAC-60 and HDNTSC are characterized. RF alternatives for the terrestrial broadcast of HDTV are also discussed.

GENERIC ATV ARCHITECTURE FOR NORTH AMERICA

For the purpose of identifying standard requirements of a North American ATV system, we have developed a system plan, as shown in Fig. 1.1, that identifies major functional modules of an ATV system and their functional and physical interfaces. According to this plan, the North American ATV system can be subdivided in the following main modules: production environment, emission environment including feeder and distribution systems, and consumer environment. Each functional module is separated by *interface ports* which could be subject to standardization:

- Ultimate HDTV Production Standard: HDP-U (Interface Port "A")

- North American HDTV Production Standard: HDP-NA (Interface Port "B")

- North American HDTV Common Emission Standard: HDE-NA (Interface Port "C")

- ATV Feeder Signals (Interface Port "D")

- ATV Distribution Signals (Interface Port "E")

- ATV User Port (Interface Port "F")

Within the consumer equipment to ensure modularity for cost effective design, user flexibility and interconnection of devices from different suppliers, the following *internal interface ports* are also important to define as standard interfaces:

- "F.1" -Baseband Unprocessed - Video/Sound/Data/Control Access Port

- "F.2" -Baseband Processed Component Video/Sound/Data Control Access Port

- "F.3" -Baseband Analog Stereo Sound Access Port

HDTV Program Production Environment. The current state of technology in the HDTV production environment will further improve and evolve to an ultimate production standard based on progressive scan and higher line rate. Fig. 1.1 illustrates this evolution by defining Interface Port "A" as a standard for ultimate worldwide HDTV production: HDP-U. It would be desirable to select a production standard: HDP-NA in North America (Interface Port "B") identical with HDP-U. However, due to international business and political considerations plus time constraints, this goal may never be realized. Therefore, it appears more realistic if we define HDP-NA according to the North American technical and business requirements.

HDP-NA can interface with HDTV production standards of other countries and can also be converted to the North American common HDTV emission standard: HDE-NA. For technical and economic reasons, commonality between HDP-NA and HDE-NA signals should exist. This involves common video parameter values: field rate, aspect ratio, number of horizontal lines, common digital sound format, etc. Table 1.1 attempts to illustrate and compare four alternatives of HDP-NA. The table compares ATV key baseband parameter sets at each interface port for applications explained below.

ATV Feeder System. Commonality among the baseband parameter values of the different emission signals is critical for economic and business reasons. This would eliminate the necessity of expensive format converters (signal processing with field-rate change) and would minimize format transcoding

(signal processing without field-ratio change) complexity. Emission systems and TV receiver costs are highly dependent on the location of the format converter. For this cost reason, it is desirable to eliminate field rate conversion completely in the emission and consumer environments. In addition, NTSC will remain an important emission standard well into the 21st century. Consequently, field-rate relationship between the new ATV emission standards and NTSC is also important.

The analog encoder between Ports "C" and "D" present baseband ATV emission signals to the various analog channel modulators. Channel characteristics and modulation techniques may be widely different in the emission systems used for television (e.g., terrestrial broadcast, satellite, fiber optics and Direct Broadcast Satellite - DBS). Modulation techniques could be analog and digital. A number of technology options exist for analog feeder transmission of HDTV. Currently, the most common NTSC feeder system is satellite based. Technical requirements for a Fixed Satellite Service (FSS) to support high quality HDTV feeder transmission in the USA must be developed based on the consideration of using similar techniques for DBS.

In case of digital feeder transmission, the common digital HDE-NA emission signal at Port "C" is recommended to be transmitted over a bit rate reduction process for the purpose of bandwidth conservation. The output of this digital processing could then be encoded to formats optimum for the appropriate digital feeder emission system environments. Future studies should focus on the necessity of integrating the bit rate reduction function between Ports "C" and "D" and Ports "D" and "F". The question mark in the diagram at Port "D" indicates this problem. Coupling with Broadband-integrated Services Digital Network (B-ISDN) standards and digital VCR development activities is also essential.

TV Distribution System. Interface Port "E" represents a number of interfaces to ATV distribution emission systems optimized according to their technical characteristics and requirements. Modulation schemes, signal multiplexing techniques could be different from emission format to emission format. However, according to Port "C" requirements, baseband parameter values are common for each Port "E" signal. This will guarantee simple transcoding at Port "E" between the output feeder ATV signal and the input ATV distribution signal as required.

ATV Consumer Equipment. Future ATV consumer products will be different from conventional NTSC in a number of aspects:

- Modularity for multiple emission signals (Port "F") reception capability

- Modularity for user equipment interconnection capability at the best interface level to reach maximum performance

- Modularity for upgrading capability so that even first generation ATV systems can be easily upgraded to future applications and new emission formats

- Multi-service capability (video, sound, data)

- Human-friendly control capability

- Simple computer controlled tuning, adjusting and equipment testing capability

To implement the features listed above, the ATV consumer receiver is desirable to have three internal functional and physical interface Ports: "F.1", "F.2" and "F.3" as shown in Fig. 1.1.

According to the distribution channel requirements, input processors of the ATV receiver will decode the signal to an unprocessed video signal, unprocessed digital sound signal and data (Teletext, Videotex) plus control signals. Port "F.1" signal is then presented to the picture and sound processors and controller. These processors generate output signals matching the image and sound reproduction devices requirements. Ports "F.2" and "F.3" add extra flexibility to the user for access.

Fig. 1.1 includes also connection of add-on consumer devices: VCR (Video Cassette Recorder), CDV (Compact Disc-Video), TV camera, ESP (Electronic Still Picture photography), computer keyboard and remote controller.

HIERARCHICAL EVOLUTION OF ATV-A PHILIPS APPROACH

We believe ATV developments in the USA should pursue HDTV as a quality goal for all applications of ATV. Compatibility with the NTSC installed base should be maintained and NTSC as a standard should also be retained. Major evolution stages of ATV should hierarchically relate to one another on the basis of signal parameter values as shown in the following list:

- NTSC - today's technology base

- INTSC - Improved Definition Television System, also called as Improved Definition Television (IDTV). We believe, NTSC standard will continue to exist well into the 21st Century. INTSC is fully compatible with the NTSC emission signal. Changes occur only in the receiver by signal post-processing and introduction of new features (e.g., picture-in-picture, digital receiver electronics, comb filter, etc.). INTSC receivers are the reality of today's marketplace.

- EDNTSC - Enhanced Definition Television System Conventional NTSC and INTSC TV receivers could be fully compatible with the EDNTSC emission signal. Signal improvement can be achieved by luminance and chrominance resolution enhancements, noise reduction, progressive scanning at both the camera and receiver but retaining transmission in interlace format, extension of the 4:3 aspect ratio up to 16:9.

- HDNTSC - High Definition Television System Conventional NTSC, INTSC and EDNTSC TV receivers could be fully compatible with the HDNTSC emission signal. Characterization of HDNTSC will follow.

- HDMAC-60 - High Definition Television System Conventional NTSC, INTSC, EDNTSC and HDNTSC TV receivers could be fully compatible with the new HDMAC-60 emission signal because the signal decoder will have HDT/EDTV/NTSC baseband component and NTSC RF outputs. Characterization of HDMAC-60 will follow.

HDTV Emission Feeder System - Analog. HDMAC-60 is a high definition multiplexed analog component television transmission system. It is a master feeder signal between interface Ports "D" and "E" designed and optimized for satellite transmission. It is also the basis to define a signal for DBS. It is "NTSC-friendly" because it has the parameter values of NTSC: 525 lines, progressive scan, 16:9 aspect ration and 59.94 Hz frame rate; therefore it can be easily (at low cost) transcoded to NTSC wherever it is necessary within the emission and consumer environments.

HDTV Emission Feeder System - Digital. Digital broadband transmission over fiber optics has been gaining rapid acceptance mostly in the telephony network environment. The multi GB/s capacity of a single mode fiber optic trunk cable and the increasing availability of broadband network switching could enable the use of this telephony trunk network for ATV feeder applications.

Such a network could essentially emulate the current satellite feeder system used for FSS applications including the delivery of any form of digital video cost competitively. Once a nationwide fiber trunk network infrastructure is in place, the long-haul carriers could offer video trunk transmission services to major networks, pay-TV providers, special program providers, etc. The key feature of such a fiber trunk network could be its customer controllable capability, i.e., the broadcaster could determine trunk routing requirements without human interaction of the Bell Operating Companies (BOCs) and the long-haul carriers. The system would be superior over satellite considering robustness, reliability, lifetime, rerouting capability, service flexibility and signal transmission quality.

Digital feeder transmission requires overall signal coordination between Interface Ports "C" and "F". Bit rate reduction functions, transmission bit rate and interconnection between the feeder and distribution environments in the digital domain require careful analysis and coupling into the B-ISDN standardization activities. HDTV digital recording and play-back techniques should also accommodate to standard video bit rates of the B-ISDN.

ATV Physical Feeder and Distribution System. For the purpose of physical distribution of prerecorded magnetic tape and laser disc programs, physical routing of the prerecorded master HDE-NA is essential to points where the consumer tapes and discs are manufactured. For redistribution directly to consumers, conventional sales or rental outlets are appropriate. In the longer term, when B-ISDN access will fully evolve, network distribution of prerecorded program in the form of on-demand video service could become cost effective and more practical.

ATV Emission Distribution Signal - Terrestrial Broadcast and CATV. For the purpose of terrestrial broadcast and CATV distribution of HDTV, we have designed an emission signal called HDNTSC (High Definition-NTSC). The signal is fully compatible with NTSC and delivers an HDTV quality signal to the homes over a maximum of (6+3) MHz band. Described below are the signal and possible RF alternatives for HDNTSC terrestrial broadcast.

If the market demand exists for the parallel introduction of Enhanced Definition Television (EDTV) with HDTV, we believe that any EDTV technique adopted for television broadcast in North America should be fully compatible with NTSC. Hence, we call this emission signal: EDNTSC. This signal should have minimum impact on the studio environment and little, if any, impact on the NTSC emission standard.

It should be noted that the validity of the basic ideas underlying our concepts of HDMAC-60 and HDNTSC are relatively independent of the selection of candidate EDTV alternative(s) as long as full NTSC compatibility is retained for EDTV. EDTV systems proposed for wide aspect ratio video transmission within the current 6 MHz channel spectrum with NTSC compatibility require careful RF investigation prior to concluding its viability.

PHILIPS HDTV SYSTEM EMISSION FOR NORTH AMERICA: HDS-NA

Our earlier studies (Refs. 1,3,4,5,7 and 8) resulted in the development of basic techniques essential to the HDNTSC concept which is a high definition NTSC compatible television system.

In April 1987, we presented a progress report of our research results to the North American industry including public demonstrations at out research laboratories. Since that time, we continued our efforts to demonstrate the total emission system concept HDS-NA including terrestrial broadcast, CATV distribution and satellite transmission of HDTV. In September 1987, we communicated the results of the baseband HDTV studies [3] and in November, we presented *comments* to the Federal Communications Commission in reply to its Notice of Inquiry on HDTV [9].

HDMAC-60 Television Signal. Conventional MAC transmission systems (e.g. B/C/D/D-2/-MAC/MUSE) are intended for satellite transmission of television signals. They are a time-multiplex of compressed luminance, chrominance and data plus sound. The HDMAC-60 signal for feeder and DBS applications is also designed for satellite transmission. To deliver HDTV image quality, bandwidth reduction techniques are required. The source signal is progressively scanned with 59.94 Hz frame rate (as well as field rate). It has 525 lines in each field and 16:9 aspect ratio. The active line time is 26 μsec.

The HDMAC-60 signal carries spatially and temporally a balanced distribution of detail that is well suited to the characteristics of the human visual system. The progressively transmitted HDMAC-60 carries the video information with a spatial resolution of at least 480 TV lines/picture height (TVL/PH) in vertical direction and 495 TVL/PH resolution in the horizontal direction if derived from a high line rate studio signal, such as 1050, 2:1 interlace or 1:1 progressive and displayed on a high line rate display. It is an "NTSC friendly" system based on parameters that provide easy transcodability to NTSC and HDNTSC.

HDMAC-60 carries CD quality multi-channel digital sound, data, plus control and could accommodate encryption for secure signal transmission similar to conventional MAC systems. The approach in HDMAC-60 is to send the most important detail of the spatial spectrum (i.e. strictly vertical or horizontal resolution) at full field-rate (59.94 Hz), while suppressing the high frequency diagonal luminance and chrominance detail or by sending it at lower rates. A Line Differential (LD) signal transmits the vertical/temporal high frequency detail of the luminance component. HDMAC-60 applies different compression and expansion ratios for different components in different source lines. The ratios are defined such that each signal component is balanced for carrier-to-noise ratio requirements in the RF domain. Efficient packaging of the increased number of signal components in a MAC format necessitates the use of a time multiplex block that equals two (instead of one) NTSC lines in duration. Refs. 2, 3 and 4 describe HDMAC-60 baseband signal components in detail.

HDNTSC Television Signal. The HDNTSC signal is fully compatible with NTSC and delivers an HDTV quality signal to the homes over terrestrial or CATV broadcast delivery systems.

HDNTSC has been designed to carry the information contained in HDMAC-60 and maintain a spatial resolution of at least 480 TVL/PH in vertical direction and 495 TVL/PH resolution in the horizontal direction if derived from a high line rate studio signal, such as 1050, 2:1 interface or 1:1 progressive and displayed on a high line rate display. HDNTSC is based on a 525/1:1/59.94/16:9 parameter set which is identical to the parameter set of HDMAC-60. The transcoding of HDMAC-60 into HDNTSC is simple and can be accomplished without introducing artifacts. The baseband HDNTSC information is packaged in two signals: the first being the NTSC Signal Package (NTSC-SP) and the second being the Augmentation Signal Package (ASP). The NTSC-SP is purely NTSC and carries the conventional 4:3 aspect ratio, 525 line 2:1 interlace television signal with 59.94 Hz field-rate. The ASP provides the extra information required to deliver an HDTV service to the home. This extra information includes the side-panels to extend the 4:3 aspect ratio of NTSC to 16:9, information to increase the spatial and temporal resolution, plus digital multi-channel sound.

The basic transmission scheme of HDNTSC is progressive and free of motion artifacts. Possible alternatives for the terrestrial broadcast of HDNTSC are discussed below. HDNTSC is intended to be transmitted over conventional CATV distribution systems by using any 6 MHz channel band of the cable spectrum while sharing a second 6 MHz channel between two HDNTSC augmentation signals. The 6 MHz NTSC-SP and 3 MHz ASP channels can be placed anywhere in the CATV spectrum.

The HDNTSC system produces a spatially and temporally balanced distribution of detail that is well suited to the human visual system similar to the HDMAC-60 signal. Due to the common parameter values of HDMAC-60 and HDNTSC and the applied signal packaging technique, the transcoding between the two signals is accomplished without signal degradation.

HDNTSC supports multi-channel CD quality digital sound, while retaining analog sound compatibility with conventional NTSC receivers. It provides the capability for encrypted transmission of video, sound and data by the use of conventional techniques.

TERRESTRIAL BROADCAST OF HDTV

We believe that a terrestrial broadcast spectrum plan is possible that will permit VHF and UHF broadcasters to use HDNTSC without a material change in the current RF spectrum assignments. The following is a brief description of some of the spectrum plans we have examined in support of HDNTSC terrestrial broadcasting considering digital transmission option for the ASP. Full analog RF techniques may also be developed to distribute the two HDNTSC signal packages: NTSC-SP and ASP. In both analog and digital cases, the ASP requires 3 MHz of the RF spectrum. This permits the shared use of a 6 MHz taboo band between two HDTV program channels as described below.

The results are preliminary in nature and simulation work is ongoing to refine this plan. Propagation and interface characteristics of a 3 MHz digitally modulated ASP signal are also studied.

Digital Modulation of ASP with Analog NTSC-SP. A spectrum solution is to apply digital modulation for the ASP while retaining analog modulation for the NTS-SP. Digital modulation allows power to the augmentation signal 15-20 dB below the power needed for analog modulation of main channel. Digital modulation at lower power also allows the service area coverage of the augmentation channel to be equal to the coverage of a main NTSC channel at higher power. This result would not be possible if both channels used analog modulation.

While digital modulation is in may ways attractive, it does require sophisticated bit rate reduction techniques to be employed at the transmitter and HDTV receivers must be able to receive and process the digital signal. However, the consequent digital signal processing is consistent with the expected evolution of digital receiver technology supported by high speed VLSI techniques.

At this stage of our work, we see two RF spectrum engineering implementations of a digitally modulated augmentation channel. The first involves channels adjacent to the main NTSC channel (i.e., n-1 or n+1 where "n" equal the channel to which the receiver is tuned). The second involves spectrum in non-adjacent channels above the main channel (UHF channels n+14 and n+15) which are especially attractive as these taboo frequencies are protected for 60, 75 miles around "n". Other taboo frequencies such as n±2,3,4,5 are protected to only 20 miles from "n". In each of these cases, the utilized extra band falls into the taboo bands of the terrestrial television broadcast.

Digital Modulation Using Adjacent Channel. The radiated augmentation signal, with its carrier component suppressed, could be placed in half of channel n-1 in which case the augmentation signal would exhibit a flat energy density. As a result, interference into "n" would appear as only a slight increase in the random noise level, not as channel print through or as a beat pattern. Channel n+1 requires a different scheme but can also be used.

Digital Modulation Using Channels n+4 or n+15. The radiated augmentation signal could also be placed in UHF channel n+14 or n+15. In this implementation, all VHF and UHF licensees would have the same even-handed opportunity to participate in HDTV. Below channel 55, all UHF channels have a TV channel: n+14 and n+15. However, for UHF channels 56 and above, neither channel n+14 or n+15 exists. Today, there are 168 UHF licensees at channel 56 or above. If those 168 UHF licensees were allowed to use channel n+15 in a given serving area, there would be 722 channels left for the augmentation signals of the 680 current VHF licensees.

Taboos. The HDTV spectrum plans discussed above introduce sideband energy into taboo channels n-1, n+1, n+14 or n+15. This sidebank energy will be rejected by the IF selectivity characteristics of most existing television receivers in the case of n-1. For channels n+14 and n+15, the RF selectivity of present receivers appears adequate to reject the n+14, n+15 signals which are about 15 dB lower in level. The power characteristics of the digitally transmitted augmentation signal will prevent interference with the main channel on all existing sets. These results are preliminary. Once the industry has focused on specific options for HDTV spectrum use, studies should be undertaken to determine precisely the effects of HDTV signals in the n-1, n+14 and n+15 taboos and the effects of these signals on NTSC receivers of all ages.

CONCLUSIONS

This paper introduces a generic ATV architecture as a design tool and approach for ATV emission standards setting.

A hierarchical NTSC compatible ATV system called HDS-NA is described with the objectives of delivering ATV quality video signal to the user. The signals of HDS-NA: HDNTSC and HDMAC-60 are defined. We propose HDTV emission signals which should have common parameter values with NTSC for the purpose of simple transcodability or direct compatibility within the emission and consumer environments. The NTSC compatible evolution approach recommends a smooth transition to HDTV by the broadcasters, CATV operators and other signal carriers and permits harmony with the NTSC consumer equipment base.

ACKNOWLEDGEMENTS

The authors wish to acknowledge the effort of all those at North American Philips Corporation who have been contributing to the implementation of the HDTV system. In particular, effort by C. Basile and A. Cavallerano are appreciated.

REFERENCES

[1] M. Tsinberg, "HDTV Transmission System", US Patent 4694338, Philips Laboratories, North American Philips Corporation, April 1986.

[2] A. G. Toth, M. Tsinberg, C. W. Rhodes, "NTSC Compatible HDTV System", IEEE Trans., Consumer Electronics, March 1988.

[3] A.G. Toth et al, "A Hierarchical Advanced Television System for the NTSC Environment" - WHITE PAPER, Philips Laboratories, North American Philips Corporation. August 1987.

[4] M. Tsinberg, "NTSC Compatible HDTV Emission System", Philips Laboratories, North American Philips Corporation, HDTV'87 Colloquium, October 1987.

[5] A. G. Toth, "Hierarchical Evolution of HDTV", Philips Laboratories, North American Philips Corporation, HDTV'87 Colloquium, October 1987.

[6] R. S. Proden, "Multidimensional Digital Signal Processing for HDTV", Philips Laboratories, North American Philips Corporation, HDTV'87 Colloquium October 1987.

[7] A. Cavallerano, "Decomposition and Recomposition of a Wide Aspect Ratio Image for ENTSC Two-Channel Television", Philips Laboratories, ICCE'87 Proceedings, June 1987.

[8] C. Basile, "Channel Matching Techniques for Two-Channel Television", Philips Laboratories, ICCE'87 Proceedings, June 1987.

[9] E. Goldstein, et al, "Comments of North American Philips Corporation - Reply to the FCC Notice of Inquiry", North American Philips Corporation, November 1987.

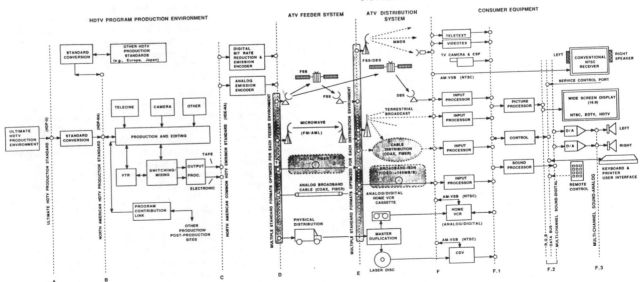

FIGURE 1.1: ADVANCED TELEVISION SYSTEM ARCHITECTURE FOR NORTH AMERICA.

ATV OPTION / INTERFACE PORT	OPTION 1	OPTION 2	OPTION 3	OPTION 4	DESIRABLE CHARACTERISTICS	COMMENTS
"A" (HDP-U)	TO BE DEFINED				progressive scan, "film-friendly", fully compatible with digital TV hierarchy	
"B" (HDP-NA)	1050 1:1 59.94 16:9	525 1:1 59.94 16:9	1050 2:1 59.94 16:9	1125 2:1 60.00 16:9		
"C" (HDE-NA)	525 1:1 59.94 16:9			1125 2:1 60.00 16:9		
"D" (ATV FEEDER)					progressive scan, fully compatible with digital TV hierarchy and NTSC baseband parameter values	potential bottleneck if parameter values not compatible with NTSC baseband parameter values
"E" (ATV DISTRIB.)	525 1:1 59.94 16:9 / NTSC	525 1:1 59.94 16:9 / NTSC	525 1:1 59.94 16:9 / NTSC	525 1:1 59.94 16:9 / NTSC	1125 2:1 60.00 16:9	
"F" (ATV CONSUMER EQUIPMENT)						
BEST OPTION		1050 1:1 59.94 16:9		1125 1:1 60.00 16:9		

TABLE 1.1: ATV PRODUCTION STANDARD ALTERNATIVES AND THEIR RESULTANT EMISSION PARAMETER SETS.

COMPATIBLE METHODS FOR ADVANCED TELEVISION BROADCAST

Michael A. Isnardi
Member of Technical Staff

David Sarnoff Research Center
Princeton, NJ 08543-5300

ABSTRACT

This paper reviews several compatible methods for transmitting additional video information in a standard NTSC television signal. Compatible encoding methods are challenging because they must meet two conflicting requirements. First, they must ensure that the extra information does not degrade the picture quality on NTSC receivers under normal viewing conditions. Second, they must ensure that the extra information can be properly decoded by special receivers. Highlighted in this paper is the Advanced Compatible Television System, developed by the David Sarnoff Research [1], [2]. In this system, a novel combination of encoding methods is used to reconstruct a wider, sharper picture in a compatible manner.

INTRODUCTION

In recent years, the television industry has witnessed the development of high-definition TV (HDTV) equipment capable of displaying impressively realistic widescreen images with spatial resolution rivaling 35-mm film. This technology will soon be available to U.S. consumers in the form of HDTV playback media, such as VTRs and optical disks. To remain competitive, the broadcasting industry is vigorously supporting research to find a practical method for delivering high-quality widescreen images to the home.

A major problem faced by broadcasters is the basic incompatibility between the current NTSC standard and the proposed HDTV standard. Compared to NTSC the proposed HDTV format has more than twice the number of lines per frame, a slightly higher field rate, a wider aspect ratio, and over five times the luminance bandwidth [3]. In recent years, a number of encoding methods have been proposed to deal with the many practical problems of delivering improved images to the home. Each has benefits and drawbacks.

Single-channel incompatible methods, such as MUSE [4] and others [5], have the potential for producing images with the highest quality and fewest artifacts. However, the transmitted signal cannot be displayed on standard NTSC sets without a converter. *Two-channel compatible* methods [6], [7] can provide service to NTSC sets in the first channel and can produce high-quality images on two-channel receivers, but broadcasters must find additional spectrum for the augmentation channel. *Single-channel compatible* methods [1], [2], [8], [9] are attractive to the broadcaster because they can provide continuing service to NTSC sets and improved image quality to enhanced-definition widescreen receivers. However, the constraints imposed by NTSC compatibility limit the transmission efficiency and may compromise the ultimate quality of the enhanced-definition widescreen picture.

This paper examines the challenges and compromises of several single-channel encoding techniques. Explored in the next section are unused or inefficiently used "subchannels" in the NTSC signal that may be exploited to transmit additional video information [10]. The final section discusses how these subchannels are used to send widescreen and high-detail luminance information in the Advanced Compatible Television System.

EXPLOITABLE SUBCHANNELS IN THE NTSC SIGNAL

In this section, three unused or inefficiently used subchannels in the NTSC spectrum will be described. These channels may be used to transmit additional video information that is physically or perceptually hidden on NTSC sets.

Normal Overscan Regions. The normal overscan regions in the NTSC signal may be exploited to physically hide additional information. Overscan is the portion of the active picture that is not displayed on home TV sets. Consumer picture tubes are intentionally overscanned in both the horizontal and vertical directions to allow for shrinkage of the raster with age. Because of this, important scene content and text are kept within a "shoot-and-protect" zone.

Most home sets in the United States have at least 2% overscan on each edge of the picture, as shown in Fig. 1 In terms of data capacity, 2% overscan yields about 20 52-μs segments and 920 1-μs segments per frame, for a total of about 2 ms per frame. Additional video information having 4.2 MHz of horizontal resolution and full vertical-temporal (V-T) resolution may replace normal picture material in these regions.

Two straightforward modifications to the overscan method are possible. One extension is to invade the horizontal and/or vertical blanking regions [7], [11]. However, this might cause synchronization problems in some consumer sets, and the signal would not survive processing by NTSC equipment that stripped and regenerated sync and blanking. Another extension is to invade the *displayed* picture area. Systems described by Lippman et al. [9], Iredal [12], Glenn [7], and NHK [11] reduce the height of NTSC picture to achieve a wider aspect ratio and to provide a channel for augmentation information. Although a high-capacity channel is formed, compatibility issues are raised concerning the visibility of the "black" or "noisy" bars at the top and bottom of the picture.

Quadrature RF Carrier. Another channel that might be exploited is the double-sideband region around the RF picture carrier, as shown in Fig. 2. A video signal of approximately 1 MHz in bandwidth with full V-T resolution may be modulated in quadrature with the main picture carrier and recovered by a synchronous detector at the ATV receiver [13].

Several drawbacks of this scheme must be mentioned. If the quadrature signal is spatially uncorrelated with the main signal, it may be visible on NTSC sets with RF envelope detectors. In the U.S. most existing sets use this form of RF detection. Multipath may cause compatibility problems even in sets with synchronous detectors. If the quadrature baseband signal has a DC term or contains significant energy below 100 KHz, then the phase modulation of the picture carrier may degrade the quality of intercarrier sound and BTSC stereo. Finally, this channel only exists at RF. A separate channel must be used to record the quadrature signal and to carry it around the studio.

The "Fukinuki Hole". When analyzed in 3-D frequency space, four of the eight octants opposite the modulated chroma regions contain high-frequency, low-energy components corresponding to moving diagonal luma detail. These "holes" comprise a subchannel in the 3-D NTSC spectrum that was first used by Fukinuki to send extra luma detail [14]. An additional phase-controlled subcarrier is needed to modulate additional video information into this sub-channel. The new subcarrier can be created by inverting the phase of an interlaced carrier on alternate fields. V-T phase and frequency diagrams are shown for an interlaced carrier in Fig. 3a and for a Phase-Alternate Field (PAF) carrier in Fig. 3b.

To reduce crosstalk at the ATV receiver, the main NTSC signal should be bandstop filtered in the spectral regions opposite chroma, and the auxiliary baseband signals should be lowpass filtered in all three dimensions before modulation. For best results, the ATV receiver should use matched 3-D filters to extract the modulated chroma. If the modulated information is spatially uncorrelated with the main signal, special techniques must be used to minimize crosstalk in the ATV receiver.

The visibility of the PAF carrier on existing NTSC sets depends on the level at which the auxiliary information is inserted, the spectral placement of the carrier, and the degree of spatial correlation between the main and auxiliary signals. When visible, the artifacts will appear as a fine crosshatch pattern moving down the screen (if decoded as luma), or as flickering patches of complementary color (if decoded as chroma). A good choice of parameters will cause the auxiliary information to be *perceptually hidden* on standard NTSC sets.

THE ADVANCED COMPATIBLE TELEVISION SYSTEM

A novel combination of the above encoding methods is used in the Advanced Compatible Television System to transmit a wider, sharper picture in a compatible manner. Shown in Fig. 4 is a pictorial block diagram of the Advanced Compatible Television single-channel encoder. An original widescreen 525-line progressive scan signal is digitized and separated into four components.

Component 1 is the main 525-line interlaced NTSC signal. It contains the central 4:3 portion of the widescreen picture with standard NTSC resolution. In addition, it contains the side panel low frequencies compressed into 1 μs strips on the ends of each line. On NTSC sets, these strips will be physically hidden by the normal horizontal overscan.

Component 4 is a 750-KHz luma "helper" signal that assists the Advanced Compatible Television decoder in the conversion from interlace to progressive scan. The helper signal represents the error that would occur if pure temporal interpolation were used to synthesize the missing progressive scan samples. This low-energy signal is transmitted in quadrature with the main RF picture carrier. This signal will be physcially removed on NTSC sets with synchronous detectors. Because it is spatially correlated with the main signal, it will be perceptually hidden on NTSC sets with envelope detectors.

Component 2 contains the side panel high frequencies that have been NTSC-encoded and time expanded to fill the central 50 μs of each active line. Component 3 contains the extra horizontal luma detail between 5.0 and 6.0 MHz that has been shifted to DC and time compressed from 52 μs to 50 μs. Components 1, 2, and 3 are digitally prefiltered by a process known as *intraframe averaging,* which is explained in more detail below. This linear time-varying filtering process creates a spectral response of Components 2 and 3. These latter two components are quadrature modulated at reduced amplitude by a 3.1 MHz PAF carrier into the spectral hole of Component 1. On standard NTSC sets, the modulated components produce dot crawl and color flicker artifacts that are not perceived at normal levels of chroma saturation and sharpness.

Fig. 5 describes intraframe averaging in more detail. In the intraframe averaging process, mutually exclusive pixel pairs 262 lines apart within a frame are averaged, and the original values are replaced by the average. This averaging can be done on a composite signal without destroying chroma, because the color subcarrier is in-phase for pixels 262 lines apart. When a PAF carrier is used to quadrature modulate baseband signals that have also been intraframe averaged, the new signal has pixel pairs 262 lines apart of the form M+A and M−A, where M is a sample of the main composite signal (above 1.5 MHz), and A is a sample of the auxiliary modulated signal. At the Advanced Compatible Television decoder, it is a simple matter to separate the "M" samples from the "A" samples by averaging and differencing pixel pairs 262 lines apart. Thus, intraframe averaging is an effective way of prefiltering two signals so that they may be separated free from crosstalk at the receiver, even in the presence of motion.

At the Advanced Compatible Television decoder, the inverse operations are performed to recover the widescreen enhanced-definition image with greatly reduced cross-color, cross-luma, and interlace artifacts. Compared to standard NTSC luminance resolution (350 lines/picture height vertically, 330 lines/picture height horizontally), the Advanced Compatible Television decoder recovers over 450 lines vertically and 400 lines horizontally.

CONCLUSIONS

This paper has described three subchannels in the NTSC signal that may be used to send additional information in a compatible manner: the normal overscan regions, the quadrature RF region, and the spectral region opposite chroma. In the Advanced Compatible Television System, these subchannels are used to transmit widescreen information and high-frequency luma detail in a single channel.

ACKNOWLEDGEMENTS

This paper could not have been written without the contributions of many talented people at the David Sarnoff Research Center. Special thanks go to my colleagues Terry Smith and Charlie Dieterich for reviewing this paper.

REFERENCES

[1] M. A. Isnardi, J. S. Fuhrer, T. R. Smith, J. L. Koslov, B. J. Roeder, and W. F. Wedam, "Encoding for Compatibility and Recoverability in the ACTV System" *IEEE Trans. Broadcasting*, **BC-33** No. 4, Dec. 1987, pp. 115-123.

[2] M. A. Isnardi, T. R. Smith, and B. J. Roeder, "Decoding Issues in the ACTV System", *IEEE Trans. Consumer Electronics*, **CE-34**, No. 1, Feb. 1988, pp. 111-120.

[3] T. Fujio, "High Definition Television Systems: Desirable Standards, Signal Forms, and Transmission Systems", *IEEE Trans. Commun.*, **COM-29**, Dec. 1981, pp. 1882-1891.

[4] Y. Ninomiya, Y. Ohtsuka, and Y. Izumi, "A Single Channel HDTV Broadcast System - the MUSE", NHK Laboratories Note No. 304, Sept. 1984.

[5] W. F. Schreiber, A. B. Lippman, A. N. Netravali, E. H. Adelson, and D. H. Staelin, "Noncompatible 6-MHz High-Definition TV Distribution System", presented at the 22nd Annual SMPTE Television Conference, Nashville, Tennessee, Jan. 29-30, 1988.

[6] M. Tsinberg, "ENTSC Two-Channel Compatible HDTV System", *IEEE Trans. Consumer Electronics*, **CE-33** No. 3, Aug. 1987, pp. 146-153.

[7] E. G. Glenn and K. G. Glenn, "HDTV Compatible Transmission System", *SMPTE J.*, Vol. 96, No. 3, March 1987, pp. 242-246.

[8] R. J. Iredale, "A Proposal for a New High-Definition NTSC Broadcast Protocol", *IEEE Trans. Consumer Electronics*, **CE-33**, No. 1, Feb. 1987, pp. 14-27.

[9] A. B. Lippman, A. N. Netravali, E. H. Adelson, W. R. Neuman, and W. F. Schreiber, "A Single-Channel Backward-Compatible EDTV System", presented at the 22nd Annual SMPTE Television Conference, Nashville, Tennessee, Jan. 29-30, 1988.

[10] M. A. Isnardi, "Exploring and Exploiting Subchannels in the NTSC Spectrum", presented at the 129th SMPTE Conference, Los Angeles, Oct. 31-Nov. 4, 1987.

[11] NHK, "HDTV and ADTV Transmission Systems: MUSE and Its Family", presented at the 1988 NAB Convention, Las Vegas, April 11, 1988.

[12] R. J. Iredale, "A Proposal for a New High-Definition NTSC Broadcast Protocol", *IEEE Trans. Consumer Electronics*, **CE-33**, No. 1, Feb. 1987, pp. 14-27.

[13] Y. Yasumoto, S. Kageyama, S. Inouye, H. Uwabata, and Y. Abe, "An Extended Definition Television System Using Quadrature Modulation of the Video Carrier with Inverse Nyquist Filter", *IEEE Trans. Consumer Electronics*, **CE-33**, No. 3., Aug. 1987, pp. 173-180.

[14] T. Fukinuki, Y. Hirano, and H. Yoshigi, "Experiments on Proposed Extended-Definition TV with Full NTSC Compatibility", *SMPTE J.*, Vol. 93, No. 10, Oct. 1984, pp. 923-929.

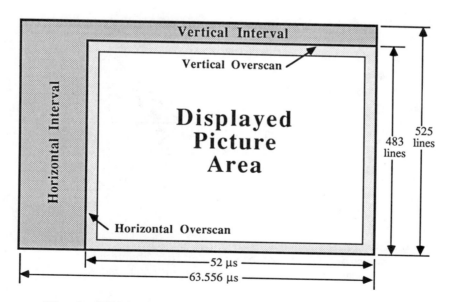

Fig. 1 NTSC raster showing blanking intervals, overscan regions, and displayed picture area.

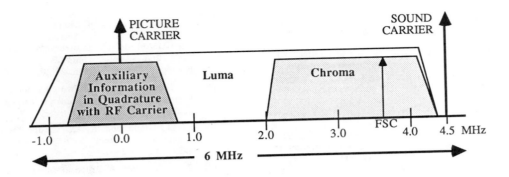

Fig. 2 Spectrum of 6-MHz NTSC channel showing quadrature subchannel around RF picture carrier.

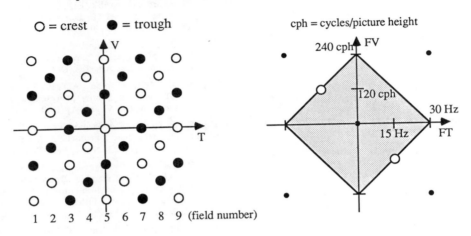

(a) These phase relationships are for an interlaced subcarrier, whose frequency is any odd multiple of half the line rate.

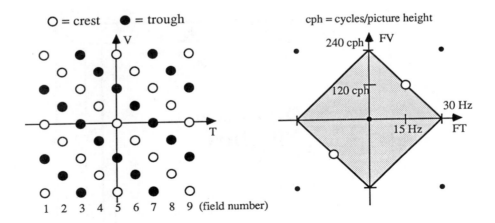

(b) These phase relationships are for a phase-alternate field (PAF) subcarrier, which may be generated from an interlaced subcarrier by inverting the phase on alternate fields.

Fig. 3 V-T phase diagrams (left) and FV-FT frequency diagrams (right) of interlaced and PAF subcarriers.

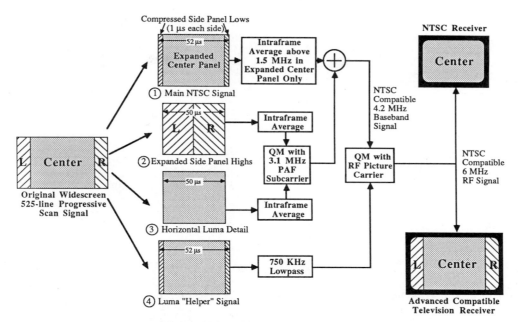

Fig. 4 Pictorial Block Diagram of
Advanced Compatible Television Single Channel Encoder.

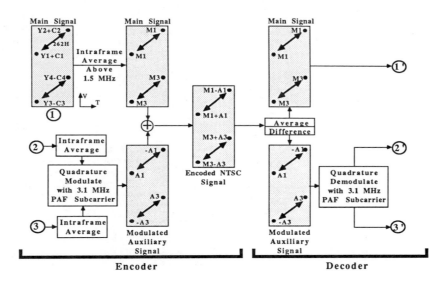

Fig. 5 The intraframe averaging process.

TEC-08

COMPUTATIONAL SCIENCE -- ADVANCES IN SUPERCOMPUTING APPLICATIONS

Michael W. Rolund - Chairperson
Department Head
Data Systems Group

AT&T
1100 East Warrenville Road
Naperville, Illinois 60566

ABSTRACT

This seminar will focus on the advanced computational and visualization work being done at the National Center for Supercomputing Applications at the University of Illinois at Urbana-Champaign. The NCSA is a multidisciplinary research institute built around a state-of-the-art computing technology environment. This world-renowned facility brings together the world's most powerful computing systems and minds to find answers to questions posed in the natural sciences, engineering, economics, medicine, agriculture, art, music, and many other fields. The NCSA is committed to advancing knowledge and strengthening the competitiveness of American industry.

Larry Smarr   -- University of Illinois
Donna Cox   -- University of Illinois
Robert Haber   -- University of Illinois
Charles Catlett   -- University of Illinois
John Stevenson   -- University of Illinois

COMPUTATIONAL SCIENCE

Larry Smarr
Director

National Center for
Supercomputing Applications
University of Illinois
605 East Springfield Ave.
Champaign, Illinois 61820

ABSTRACT

This session includes a major presentation on Computational Science by the NCSA's Director, Larry Smarr. Dr. Smarr is considered by many as this nation's leading spokesperson for supercomputing applications.

CONVERGENCE OF ART AND SCIENCE

Donna Cox
Professor of Art and Design

National Center for
Supercomputing Applications
University of Illinois
605 East Springfield Ave.
Champaign, Illinois 61820

ABSTRACT

This session addresses the blending of art and science in a supercomputing environment.

ADVANCED COMPUTING AND VISUALIZATION

Robert Haber
Professor of Civil Engineering

National Center for
Supercomputing Applications
University of Illinois
605 East Springfield Ave.
Champaign, Illinois 61820

ABSTRACT

This session focuses on the expanding opportunities for supercomputing via advanced visualization.

BRINGING THE SUPERCOMPUTER TO YOUR DESKTOP

Charles Catlett
Remote Access Coordinator

National Center for
Supercomputing Applications
University of Illinois
605 East Springfield Ave.
Champaign, Illinois 61820

ABSTRACT

This session deals with interconnecting the user and the supercomputer.

SUPERCOMPUTING BENEFITS AND PROGRAMS

John Stevenson
Corporate Officer

National Center for
Supercomputing Applications
University of Illinois
605 East Springfield Ave.
Champaign, Illinois 61820

ABSTRACT

This session addresses the programs established between the National Center for Supercomputing Applications and interested industrial partners.

TEC-09

USER INTERFACES FOR FUTURE SERVICES

Catherine Marshall - Chairperson
Director, Advanced User Interfaces
U S WEST Advanced Technologies
6200 S. Quebec St. Suite 320
Englewood, CO 80111

ABSTRACT

Advances in hardware and software technology are making possible a myriad of new telecommunications services with potential to enhance both person-to-person communication and individual access to information. Increasingly, tele-communications service providers and equipment manufacturers are realizing that to be successful in the market-place, they must emphasize good user interface design. The "user interface" has often been thought of as a thin surface layer that can be applied to a product or service during the final stages of design, rather like paint. This seminar will present an alternative point of view, describing ways in which fundamental decisions regarding technologies to be deployed and functionality to be provided can have a significant impact on the design of the user interface and subsequent customer acceptance. State-of-the-art methods for user interface design and evaluation will also be discussed.

Christine Riley	--	Bell Communications Research
Teresa Roberts	--	U S WEST Advanced Technologies
Frederick Chang	--	Pacific Bell
Clayton Lewis	--	University of Colorado

USER ACCEPTANCE OF NEW SERVICES

Christine A. Riley
District Manager
Network Services Specification Research

Bell Communications Research
445 South Street, Room 2E-274
Box 1910
Morristown, New Jersey 07960-1910

ABSTRACT

Future communications products and services must be both useful to and usable by the intended customer population if they are to meet with broad acceptance and market success. Products and services based on new technology have sometimes failed, and other times have succeeded beyond all expectations. This session will examine examples of successes and failures, to illustrate the individual, organizational, and societal factors that influence user acceptance.

INTRODUCTION

The service capabilities that will be available in tomorrow's networks are very exciting to the technologists who understand them. There is widespread belief that these capabilities will be of great benefit to customers. In my view, such a belief is a necessary act of faith on the part of scientists and engineers. However, the literature on technological innovations is replete with stories of dashed expectations. (See Kraut, 1987a, on the sad history of predictions.) What we would really like to be able to do, of course, is to predict the future - to know which technology-based services will be successful. Since I am no better at predicting the future than anyone else, I will try to provide some understanding of the complex issues that affect user acceptance by examining some past successes and failures. My overriding message is that we must respect the customers/users of our technology and listen to what they are telling us.

The telephone and television are examples of remarkably successful technology. Unquestionably, the telephone and television provide useful and usable communications services. Both have reached a penetration of nearly 100% of all households in the United States. In the case of the telephone, it took about 100 years to reach this level of success. In the case of television, most of the growth took place during a single decade, the 1950's. Both the telephone and television show a similar growth pattern, the "S-shaped" curve that often describes the diffusion of innovation. Growth was slow at first, followed by a period of rapid acceleration, and then finally deceleration when penetration approached the asymptotic level.

The growth of television now provides the model for forecasting the growth of almost any new product or service. Everyone predicts tremendous growth within the coming decade. When this does not happen, the model is not abandoned. The assumption is made that we are still in the initial slow growth phase, and the growth will be seen in the next decade. The following statement is prototypic: "_____, while slow in growing in the past, is poised for dramatic growth as vendors become aggressive in their marketing, and potential users come to recognize the benefits." This statement has been made about office automation, teleconferencing, telecommuting, videotex, voice mail, and many other technology-based innovations. Sometimes a service *is* still in the slow growth phase, but more often the potential customers/users are telling us something by their lack of use. In general, it is safe to assume that a useless service won't be used, a useful service won't be used unless is usable, and a useful, usable service won't be used if it costs too much.

While usability, thus a well designed user interface, is important for a successful new product or service, it is important to go beyond the individual user in order to understand the context into which the product or service is being introduced. In particular, we must look at the product or service and the individual user in larger organizational and societal contexts, as illustrated in figure 1.

When trying to predict user acceptance of a new service, questions such as the following should be addressed:

Utility

- Is it useful to the individual?
- Is it easy to integrate into the individual's life?
- Does it make sense in a large organizational and societal context?

Usability

- Can it be used without learning new skills?
  Can it be used without taxing human perceptual or cognitive abilities?

- Does it provide reasonable support (error correction and help)?

Cost

- How much?
- Who pays?
- Is there a big up-front investment?

USER INTERFACES TO NETWORK SERVICES

A major theme of our work at Bellcore has been to view the future public telecommunications network a facilitator of universal communications service that is independent of place, time, and medium. Individual subscribers to this network will have options for personalized, and personally programmed, communications services that will presumably result in more communications with those they want to communicate with, and less with those they do not. (See Herman & Riley, 1988.) This vision of the network as an intelligent facilitator of communications is very powerful, and we expect this network can provide services that customers will find useful. Let's accept, for the moment, that users of this network will want increased control over their communications environment. Will the service be accepted? In this case the answer will certainly depend upon how the user does the "personal programming;" upon whether the services are usable.

Today the user interface to most voice communication services is via the touchtone pad of a standard telephone set, where user input is dialed digits and the system response is various tones. Limited programming capabilities exist now, such as the call forwarding and speed dialing services provided through the central office or on a PBX. Experience has shown that customers have difficulty using even these relatively simple services. Results from the early trials of services with somewhat more functionality, such as selective call forwarding based on the originating telephone number, indicated that the touchtone interface is completely inadequate to support widespread use of these services. Using voice prompts rather than tones leads to somewhat greater use of the services, but voice prompts alone cannot undo the complexity and awkwardness of providing program input via a 12-button keypad. In trying to evaluate the results of trials of new services, it is important to keep in mind that we cannot assess the utility of a service if it is not usable. And services such as those made possible by the future intelligent network will not be usable unless the interface to the service is something better than a touchtone pad.

At Bellcore we have done research exploring alternative user interfaces for network services. Among the promising approaches are the use of speech technology, such as speaker identity verification, speech recognition, and speech synthesis, the use of graphics displays and direct manipulation interfaces, like the user interface on the Apple Macintosh, and the use of intelligent software to provide user assistance through smart error correction and help functions. It is essential that we take most of the burden off the users. Users must be able to program the system in a way that does not require them to read volumes of instructions, that does not tax their memory or perceptual abilities, that gives them feedback about the consequences of their actions, and that provides system status information. An example of a direct-manipulation graphic interface to selective call routing that we believe satisfies the above criteria is shown in figure 2. If we pose a difficult task to the users before they can start to experience a service, it is unlikely many will get past that obstacle and discover whether or not the service has utility to them.

ORGANIZATIONAL AND SOCIETAL FACTORS INFLUENCING USER ACCEPTANCE OF SERVICES - THE CASE OF DISTRIBUTED WORK

Starting around the time of the Arab oil embargo in the early seventies, there has been much interest in what has been labeled the "transportation - telecommunications tradeoff" (See Nilles *et al.*, 1976). The replacement of travel by teleconferencing or telecommuting yields a tremendous potential market for communications services. Teleconferencing and telecommuting have been the subject of many optimistic forecasts, but explosive growth has yet to be seen. I believe that organizational and societal factors, not the lack of technology, have been responsible for the lack of growth.

For example, forecasts made around 1975 suggested that 75% of all face-to-face meetings would be displaced by teleconferences within the decade. Obviously, that did not happen. In 1985 we saw forecasts that "dramatic growth will come when users come to learn the benefits and overcome their discomfort." It is important to understand why people continue to travel and teleconference when economic factors would appear to drive them to avoid travel. Analysis of face-to-face meetings shows that important communication takes place that transcends the "information exchange" that is the surface agenda of most meetings. This communication ranges from informal strategy sessions at the coffee break to subtle revelations of organizational culture and power relationships gained through observation of interpersonal interactions. Meetings have multiple agendas, some implicit and some explicit, and despite statements by participants that such meetings are a waste of time, almost no one is willing to conduct such meetings through a teleconference. There are always informal and relational messages being exchanged, and some of these messages are essential to individual and organizational success. To continue to push "meetings" as the market for teleconferencing, or to say that reduced cost or improved technical quality will lead to user acceptance, is to ignore a major organizational reason why teleconferencing is not accepted. (See Egido (1988) for a detailed review and analysis.)

We shouldn't reject the concept of teleconferencing, however. There are many situations in which individuals work together using telecommunications. What is needed is a different model. Teleconferencing should be viewed as a means of *communications augmentation*, rather than *travel substitution*. Work is done over the telephone everyday. We can view all 2- and 3-way telephone calls as teleconferences. We should look for ways to exploit emerging capabilities for integrated voice/data/graphics/video communications on the desk top to facilitate the sorts of remote communication that already occur in the workplace. Research on desk top conferencing is now being energetically pursued under the theme of computer-supported cooperative work, and it appears to have considerable promise as an accepted communications service.

Telecommuting, or telework, provides a similar case. Forecasts made in the mid-1980's suggested that 20 to 40% of all workers would work at home within the decade. We believe that this prediction, too, will not come true. The view of telecommuting provided by the popular press is that of the professional/management employee of a large corporation working at home with a flexible schedule and no time wasted in commuting. Like the travel substitution model described above, this can be viewed as *workplace substitution*. The reality of workplace substitution today is that it rarely occurs. Census data show that the percent of (non-farm) workers in the U.S. working at home has been declining for several decades, and that people who work at home are typically part-time workers or the self employed. There are many reasons why workplace substitution does not occur, including organizational concerns about the management of home workers and individual concerns about their roles in the organization, their visibility and opportunities for promotion.

The labor movement has a very different image of work at home. Here the image is of clerical workers doing piece-work data entry or similar tasks. These workers, mostly women with small children, work at home because they have no alternative. The unions are concerned that electronic home work provides an opportunity for work exploitation similar to garment industry work earlier in this century. The AFL-CIO and the National Organization of Working Women (9 to 5) have called on the U.S. Labor Department to institute a ban on home clerical work. Thus, in the case of telecommuting, there are societal concerns about work vs. family life that may also affect the acceptance of technology on a wide scale. (See Kraut (1988) for a detailed review and analysis.)

Again, the problems with the workplace substitution model of telecommuting does not mean that there is no opportunity for the use of technology for work at home. Research conducted by Kraut (1987b, 1988) showed that in a high-technology company, the professional and management workers who spent the most time working at home were the very same people who spent the most time working at the office. That is, busy people take work home in their briefcases.

Here the model of *workplace augmentation*, of providing workers with electronic briefcases, may yield insights for successful service opportunities.

In summary, the success of technologically-based services depends on many nontechnological factors. These factors include the usefulness of a service to an individual and the usability of the service. They also include the organizational and societal context in which the service is to be deployed.

References

Egido, C. Videoconferencing as a technology to support group work: A review of its failure. *Proceedings of the conference on Computer Supported Cooperative Work - CSCW '88.* Portland, Oregon, September, 1988.

Herman, G. & Riley, C. A. (1988) Services for the next generation network: Experience with a network services testbed. *Proceedings of EUROINFO '88.* Amsterdam: North-Holland.

Kraut, R. E. (1987a) Social issues and white-collar technology: An overview. In R. E. Kraut (ed.) *Technology and the Transformation of White-Collar Work.* Hillsdale, N. J.: Lawrence Erlbaum Associates, 1-21.

Kraut, R. E. (1987b) Predicting the use of technology: The case of telework. In R. E. Kraut (ed.) *Technology and the Transformation of White-Collar Work.* Hillsdale, N. J.: Lawrence Erlbaum Associates, 113-133.

Kraut, R. E. (1988) Telework as a work-style innovation. In B. R. Ruben (ed.) *Information and Behavior, vol 2.,* 116-146.

Nilles, J., Carlson, F. R., Gray, P., & Hanneman, G. (1976). *Telecommunications/transportation tradeoffs: Options for tomorrow.* New York: Wiley.

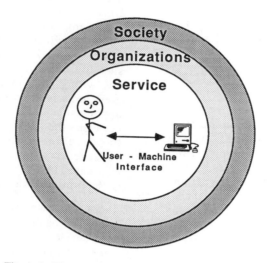

Figure 1. The context for acceptance of new services.

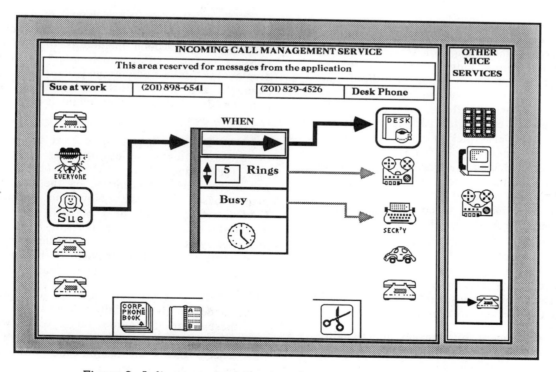

Figure 2. A direct manipulation interface for selective call routing

MATCHING THE INTERFACE TO THE SERVICE

Teresa L. Roberts
Member of Technical Staff
User Interface Research

U S WEST Advanced Technologies
6200 S. Quebec Street
Englewood, Colorado 80111

Summary:

The usability of advanced communications services will be greatly influenced by the input and output technologies upon which those services are based. For example, a voice mail service based on dial-pad input and tone feedback is likely to be less usable that a similar service offering the same functionality via voice I/O or handwritten input and display screen output. This session will discuss technology selection and user interface design.

Introduction

Now that deregulation and competition are allowing and encouraging telephone companies to expand their range of service from the simple connections they've provided in the past, we're beginning to see a wealth of new features. The phone system on one college campus, for instance, allows functions ranging from conference calling to "parking" a call and letting someone else pick it up at *any* phone set on the campus. In some cases, new features are provided by capabilities incorporated into telephone sets or in equipment designed to be attached locally to telephone sets; examples include speed dialing services and answering machines. In other cases, the incorporation of sophisticated, software-controlled equipment into the telephone network makes it possible to provide new features centrally, as can been seen in a network-based voice messaging service field tested in the Denver area in 1987.

In this environment of rampant functionality, the phone service provider is left with the problem of how to enable the user to access all of the capability. In the past, services that have been provided centrally have tended to be designed with the assumption that the equipment available to the user would be an ordinary 12-button phone set. As a result, the designers of those services have squeezed the commands for accessing the functionality into what can be expressed with those twelve buttons. And because of constraints in the network itself, user feedback in services has often consisted solely of abstract tones. Under the circumstances, we do not find it surprising that the usage of the new telephone services is disappointingly low. Our hypothesis is that the market surveys showing that the functionality is desired are not wrong, but that the functionality goes unused because it is too *hard* to use. We further hypothesize that the difficulty in use is not because the designers weren't clever enough to develop a decent user interface, but because it is impossible to develop an adequate user interface given equipment of such limited "bandwidth".

There are two potential ways to increase the effective bandwidth of the user interface for new services. One is to keep the same customer premise equipment -- the 12-button phone set -- but to incorporate into the network additional "intelligence" for handling both input and output: for example, to recognize speech for input and synthesize speech for output, allowing the richness of language to compensate for limited sensory and motor channels. The second method is to base new services on new CPE, which might include a display to take advantage of the visual channel, and also allow richer input with pointing devices and other methods for input of instructions.

Work at Bellcore began to look at the effects of different technologies on user interfaces (see, for instance, Root and Chow (1987)), but has moved on to concentrate on the design of display-based systems. Now the Advanced User Interfaces group of U S WEST Advanced Technologies is embarking on a project specifically to study the magnitude of the effect that the interface technology has on the usability of advanced telephone functions.

This paper presents an ongoing pilot study being done to give us initial feedback on our hypotheses and to guide larger-scale work. (Such a pilot study is very desirable; there have been cases in which the intuitively expected large differences between systems have *not* shown up in empirical studies. An especially clear example of this phenomenon is Whiteside et al.'s (1985) study of command-based, menu-based, and iconic operating systems.) In this study, we have chosen a small but representative subset of the kind of advanced functionality that is being offered now and in the near future, we have prototyped user interfaces to such functionality on various systems representing the different technologies, and we are now running usability experiments.

The Functions

The three representative functions that we are concentrating on for this pilot study are the following:

Call routing: This is the function is which the user preprograms the phone system to ring the phone at a different number when a given number is called. The simplest call routing is unconditional: it directs all calls to the new number until it is explicitly turned off. More complex call routing can be based on conditionals such as the number of the calling party, the date and time, and whether the original destination phone is busy or wasn't answered.

Call screening: Call screening is a general title for capabilities that allow the recipient of the call to know who's calling, in order to decide what to do about it. For this exercise, call screening is implemented with the capability of allowing distinctive ringing depending upon the number that the call is coming from, and for ringing a different number of times before an answering service feature takes the call.

Message retrieval: This is the process of listening to any messages that have been left by callers. Messages can be listened to in any order and can be deleted individually.

The Devices and Designs

The space of possible technologies on which the functionality might be based is large. We chose three points that span the space and that are representative of the technologies on which phone services are or might be offered.

While the choice of technology significantly constrains the user interface that can be built on it, there is still considerable design latitude -- in fact this is just the point at which the process of user interface design often begins. Even though we are mostly considering the larger design space in which not even the base technology is a given, we still need to do a credible job in designing the interfaces on the specific platforms. The general style of the interfaces on each platform is described below along with the platforms.

Twelve-button phone set

This device has twelve buttons for input, each of which emits a DTMF tone into the system. Output is in the form of tones, which can have different pitches, quality, and duration.

The user interface consists of typing codes keyed to mnemonic letters, and receiving positive or negative tones in response.

Twelve-button set plus speech output

The second device has the same twelve DTMF buttons for input, but additionally provides speech output. For the pilot study we are using synthesized speech. It sounds computerish but is easily decipherable; we recognize that human recorded voice may be preferable in a real system.

Speech output offers a range of advantages over tone-only output: the system can prompt the user for applicable input, the system can give information that's already in its database, and the system can confirm the correctness of changes by giving its interpretation in natural language of what the user did.

We have developed two user interfaces based on this technology. One is a standard prompting interface. The second, in response to the complaint that the prompting interface is too aggressive, is a user-driven interface in which the voice output is used mostly for feedback and confirmation.

Display-based system

Attached to the normal phone is a small bitmapped display with a keyboard for typing and mouse for pointing. (A real product might replace the mouse with a touchscreen or the keyboard with a handprinting recognizer.)

Two primary advantages that such a configuration has over one based on speech output are that the user can scan the information in the system at his or her leisure, and that the user can change things by manipulating them directly rather than by issuing commands.

The user interface developed on this hardware is based on icons and tables. Different groupings of functionality are hidden in different preset icons. To access a set of functionality, the user opens the icon into a window, and its contents are displayed in a table.

About the Experiment

The experiment is being run using people from the community as the subjects. Each subject learns how to use one version of the system by watching a videotape, and then performs a set of tasks of increasing difficulty. We videotape them, recording the time it takes them to do the tasks and the problems that they have.

The subjects return for a second day of tasks, to see how well they remember how to use the system. We record their performance in the same way as on the first day, and then ask them to rate how well they liked their system. Finally, they are shown video demonstrations of the other versions of the system, including an operator-assisted service, and they rate how easy each new system seems to be, compared to the one they used.

Use of the Results

The data we will be obtaining take three forms: time required to perform the tasks, problems the subjects had while using the interfaces, and the subjects' attitudes toward the systems and the services.

The data on time and problems will be useful to us in designing interfaces in the future. We will know what sort of situations to avoid. But certain problems can't be avoided completely in certain kinds of interfaces, such as forgetting the details of data stored in a non-visual system; such occurrences will be the basis of our comparisons between technology platforms. Attitude data tend to be "noisier" since different subjects focus on different sorts of things in forming their preferences, but such data are vital to a prediction of public acceptance.

These results will be used mostly as input to the next phase of our work: mockups of systems that are more realistic both in their functionality and in the robustness of their interfaces. The technology platforms we choose to use for the next step will be those shown to be more successful in the pilot testing, and the details of the interfaces will also be based on the pilot results.

Implications

The results of both the current pilot study and the future larger study will be important to the design of telecommunications services meant for the general public. The public that might buy advanced services is a large enough market that offering services that they find useful and usable can be quite rewarding, but mistakes can be similarly costly. It is vital to learn as early as possible what network capabilities will be needed to support the user in using new functions. In addition, we need to know to what extent supporting devices will be needed in the home. In this way, the telecommunications industry as a whole, comprising both equipment vendors and service providers, can offer services that are usable, and hence will actually be used.

References

Root, Robert W., and Ching-Hua Chow. Multimode Interaction in a Telecommunications Testbed: The Case of Memory Dialing. In G. Salvendy (ed.), *Cognitive Engineering in the Design of Human-Computer Interaction and Expert Systems* (1987), Amsterdam:Elsevier, 399-406.

Whiteside, John A., Sandra Jones, Paula S. Levy, and Dennis Wixon. User Performance with Command, Menu, and Iconic Interfaces. *Proc. CHI'85 Human Factors in Computer Systems* (San Francisco, April 1985), New York:ACM, 185-191.

THE ROLE OF BEHAVIORAL RESEARCH AND USABILITY TESTING IN SOFTWARE DEVELOPMENT

Frederick R. Chang
Director, Information and Decision Sciences

Pacific Bell
2600 Camino Ramon, Rm. 3N301
San Ramon, CA 94583

ABSTRACT

This session will discuss the role of behavioral science research in the design of user interfaces for Information Age services.

Particular emphasis will be placed on describing the methods to be employed and the benefits to be derived from usability tests. Videotaped examples will also be presented.

INTRODUCTION

Recently, while waiting for a table at a restaurant, I overheard a bright, articulate woman commenting on her new VCR and how difficult it was for her to use. She mentioned that it took her four hours to set the clock on her new machine and that she thought the designer should be shot. More generally, it turns out that over half of the people who own VCRs cannot program them to record a future program. People clearly have the desire to perform certain tasks on their VCRs but evidently the way the technology is currently designed does not facilitate efficient use.

In this talk, I will describe why and how behavioral research techniques can be used to improve people's use of sophisticated software systems. I will discuss some basic methodological concerns and highlight a few key issues using examples from our own research conducted at Pacific Bell. Some of the examples will be supported by videotape which helps to illustrate the points. Our primary goal is to design and test "Information Age" software that is maximally usable for our users.

USUABILITY IS IMPORTANT

The goal of most computer programmers and software developers is to produce clean, efficient code that is easy to integrate with other code, easy to modify and importantly, easy to maintain once written. Indeed, in support of these goals, the software will undergo considerable testing that examines logic, structure, and performance, among other things.

The usability of the software (or how the software will be used by people) is a concern to programmers and software developers; however typically much less systematic emphasis is given to usability, particularly as regards testing.

In an explanation for why the above situation seems to be the case Tom Landauer of Bell Communications Research uses the term the "egocentric intuition fallacy," which has two parts: First, programmers think that what is correct for them must be correct for other people. That is, since they (the programmers) can figure out how to use a particular function to perform a task, everybody should be able to figure it out. Second, people believe that they know the reasons and causes of their own behavior. Unfortunately, people's intuitions are frequently wrong. Related to both of these points is the fact that people untrained in the behavioral sciences may not have a good feeling for the wide variability in human behavior. In trying to design software products for use by a large target audience, variability in human use is of critical importance.

USUABILITY TESTING

At Pacific Bell we have constructed a sophisticated usability laboratory in which we have trained professionals testing and improving the usability of software. I will briefly describe our laboratory, but one does not have to have access to a lab as sophisticated as ours to conduct useful, less formal usability tests.

In our lab we try to simulate as closely as we can the actual environmental conditions under which a person will be using a software system in the "real world." People are brought into the lab and interact with a prototype of a software system we are developing. People are asked to perform tasks on the system much like those they would perform when using the system at home or in the office. The people we bring into the lab are very carefully selected to represent a broad cross-section of the users who we expect to use the system. We work closely with our marketing colleagues to identify the population who will be using information services.

We make use of "rapid prototyping tools" that allow us quickly to simulate a service (its user interface) and make changes based on data collected in our studies. We work with tools pertinent to both audio and video services; more will be said about iterative testing below.

Regarding data collection, we have the capability to keep a timed log of all keystrokes entered by the user during a testing session. We also have an extensive videotaping facility where we can tape up to three simultaneous views of the user interacting with the software. In the case of video services, one view is of the screen so that we can see what the user sees. Another view is of the person seated in front of the computer so that we can see what the user is doing (e.g., facial expressions, pointing at the screen). A third view is from overhead looking down onto the work surface so that we can see the users' hands on the keyboard, documentation and mouse use if required by the software. A good clean audio track accompanies the video. Finally, we frequently administer pre- and post-session rating scales in which we ask users about their subjective impressions of the software.

Our usability testing is heavily performance oriented, so from the data we collect we are very interested in such things as task performance time, task error rate, task learning time, and task retention. Working closely with our marketing colleagues, we establish human performance objectives for our software. That is, just like other aspects of the software we set up certain task performance goals (related to task performance time, errors and the like) that we require our users to meet. Through a process of iterative design we work to meet those performance objectives.

Iterative design (also known as formative evaluation) involves bringing in a sample of users for a certain version of the user interface and conducting usability tests on that version. Based on data collection and interpretation, a new design is created and then implemented using the rapid prototyping tools. We have found this technique to be most useful in improving usability. Our Voice Mail user interface represents the result of a series of iterative usability tests and we have been able to show rather impressive increases in usability. While we conducted extensive testing and design on our Voice Mail product, in general, one does not have to use huge numbers of participants or a huge number of iterations to show appreciable improvements in usability.

While quantity of participants is not the overriding concern, I can't overstate how important the issue of participant type is in designing usable software. If you don't choose the right users for the usability test, you may well end up designing a good, usable system, but for the wrong users. In our tests, we typically bring in a wide range of users and have found that what proves to be helpful for one type of user sometimes proves harmful,

in terms of performance, for another type of user. Designing usable software involves numerous tradeoffs.

CONCLUSIONS

Increasingly, industry is recognizing the need to design software that is usable by people. Behavioral research and usability tests as I've described can go a long way toward improving usability. It has been our experience that if you start early in the software development cycle usability tests can actually save on software development costs. If conducted properly, the results from the tests will accurately reflect what would have happened had you released the software without the testing. Detecting and fixing problems early and often prior to final release is certainly better and more cost effective than waiting for the end users to find the problems and then complain to you about them.

BEYOND EMPIRICAL TESTING

Clayton H. Lewis
Associate Professor, Department of Computer Science and Institute of Cognitive Science

University of Colorado
Campus Box 430
Boulder, CO 80309

ABSTRACT

Empirical testing of user interfaces is expensive. It also produces findings that are difficult to generalize, and hence provides limited guidance in an ongoing design process. Detailed paper scenarios and theoretical models of user interactions can provide complements to empirical testing which help to solve these problems. This session will describe these techniques and present examples of their application to the design of future telecommunications services.

TEC-10

NEW TECHNOLOGIES: WIRELESS DISTRIBUTION TECHNOLOGY

Thomas C. Campbell, Chairperson

Executive Director-Technology Assessment

SBC Technology Resources, Inc.

One Bell Center
St. Louis, MO 63101

OVERVIEW

Portable Communications has permeated the marketplace in various forms. This is evidenced by the increasing customer demands for wireless services such as cellular, paging, and cordless phones. Digital technology and digital signal processing will improve the efficiency by which scarce radio frequencies are utilized. Customers are alert to new wireless services, and are interested in applying these services in their communication networks to increase flexibility and/or lower cost. This session will explore the concept of portable communications, as well as the technologies that will be employed to make future wireless communications more affordable and ubiquitous.

Dr. Peter E. Jackson
SBC Technology Resources, Inc.

Mr. Robert J. McGuire
Rockwell International

Mr. Thomas M. Taylor
Bell Communications Research, Inc.

Dr. Andrew Motley
British Telecom Research Labs

Dr. Kaveh Pahlavan
Worcester Polytenic Institute

PORTABLE COMMUNICATION

Peter E. Jackson
Vice President-Applied Technology

David A. Deas
Director Transport & Delivery

SBC Technology Resources, Inc.
One Bell Center
St. Louis, Missouri, 63101

Abstract

Portable communications has permeated the marketplace in various forms. This is evidenced by the increasing customer demands for wireless services such as cellular, paging, and cordless phones. Digital technology and digital signal processing will improve the efficiency by which scarce radio frequencies are utilized. Customers are alert to new wireless services and are interested in applying these services in their communication networks to increase flexibility and/or to lower cost. This paper will explore the concept of portable communications as well as the technologies that will be employed to make future wireless communications more affordable and ubiquitous, and conclude with a vision of a portable communication network.

Application

As you arrive at the check-in desk at the airlines, you notice your scheduled 4:30 pm flight has been delayed until 6:00 pm. You are scheduled to meet your wife and children at your destination, but now you are going to arrive at least an hour and a half late. Your mind begins to race for an answer to your dilemma. How can you get a message to them? They may be in transit to the airport. A portable communication network of the future is a solution to this problem. The scenario goes something like this:

You proceed to call your spouse's personal access number (PAN) on your portable cellular telephone and enter the following alphanumeric page via your attached keyboard, "My plane is delayed one and a half hours. I will take taxi home if you do not wish to wait." In less than one minute, the network locates your wife in her car and delivers the message. You receive a response back in less than five minutes from your spouse stating, "Got your message, I will wait for you at the airport."

This scenario, or one like it, is played out almost daily by people on the move. Their ability to get messages to and from family and work associates is essential.

Portable communications for people on the move can take many forms. These forms extend from simple one-way tone and alphanumeric pages to services comprised of full two-way voice and facsimile transmissions. Portable communications is the ability for individuals to get information to others, regardless of location or time.

Attributes of Portable Communication

A portable communication network will require individual users to be uniquely addressed through a logical access number. Much like the telephone number in the public switched telephone network which provides for a physical access mechanism today, the portable communication network must provide the customer with access on a real time basis independently of the customer's temporary physical position.

In order to provide a dynamic mapping between physical and logical access points, a portable communication network must allow users to notify the system of their location on a periodic basis. Locating a subscriber whose absolute position within the network is unknown poses new and challenging network opportunities. Intelligent devices which notify the network of their status and location will be advantageous in improving network efficiencies. The term "follow me" communications has been coined to describe the basic function of the portable communication network in tracking customer locations (with their help).

The portable communication network must be embedded in an overall communication network environment which has an evolved intelligence. It is this intelligence which will provide underlying feature capabilities to add network level features such as "follow me" database mapping, and customer service option choices which move with the customer throughout the day rather than being tied to specific physical access lines. Technical aspects of portable communications are addressed in an accompanying paper, Network Programmability: A Technology Perspective, also presented at NCF88.

Elements of Portable Communication

Future demand for portable communication will take off from a solid platform as evidenced by products and services customers purchase today. Portable communication currently takes many forms, and is constantly being employed in the home and work place.

Two-Way Radio

Two-way radio and SMR (Specialized Mobile Radio) are two of the earliest forms of portable communications. With its roots in satisfying the need for wireless communication for public service agencies, such as police and fire, SMR has grown into a huge industry. It is limited, however, in capacity and range. Privacy is virtually nonexistent, but cost is reasonable. SMR and two-way radio networks are predominately voice, but emerging technologies are opening the avenue for data transmission.

Paging

Paging has grown at a fast pace in recent years. Although the technology to deliver paging is not new, this service is now affordable for the business user, as well as the individual. The service is reliable and covers large geographic areas. Some paging services cover the continental United States, making it extremely popular. Paging today, however, is restricted to one-way transmission and is limited in the amount and type of information that can be sent.

Cordless Phones

Cordless phones are an example of what the marketplace states it wants in portability. Cordless phone sales have grown at a high rate. The residential consumer has shown a demand for an untethered connection to the public switched telephone network within their homes. Despite shortcomings of range and reliability, cordless phones are a highly sought item in consumer electronics.

Cellular Phones

Cellular phones are in high demand. Since spectrum and capacity were limited in the Improved Mobile Telephone Systems (IMTS) costs were high and penetration low. But cellular radio service has become a relatively economic and effective means by which mobile, point-to-point voice communication is delivered. Cellular phones provide a reliable form of portable communication locally, and nationwide. Current limitations include ease of roaming (transparency to the user) and capacity. Currently, cellular service within the United States does afford nationwide compatibility. Extensions and enhancements of the cellular network, including an evolution to full digital service, are viewed as the basis for the portable communication network in the nineties.

Rural Radio

Telephone companies have long awaited an efficient radio telecommunication system for providing rural telephone service which offers cost savings over traditional copper plant. With new innovations in digital signal processing and digital radio design, rural radio is becoming an economic reality for telephone companies. The use of radio over physical plant has stemmed from the rising cost of copper, rather than the need for an untethered communications link.

Air-To-Ground

Recently, a new service has been offered to the public which provides access to the public switched telephone network from aboard a commercial aircraft. This service provides reliable communication while in flight, but the market demand is currently unknown. Air-to-ground radio does not employ new technology, but is a new application of existing technology that is seeking a position within the marketplace. The FCC has issued a developmental license for the purpose of assessing the demand and the technology employed in delivering this service.

Satellite

Communicating via satellite is not new. However, there are new applications of satellite technology. Prototypes of portable satellite terminals are being demonstrated which provide voice communication via satellite from devices the size of a briefcase. Satellite communication research has also contributed to technical advances in ultra-high frequency (GHz range) radio designs which will be used in the portable communications RF links of the future.

Intelligent Networks

Intelligent networks and portable communication networks are related. Intelligent networks today provide customers with a form of portability over the public switched telephone network. Call forwarding is the classic example of a communication service which gives customers control in directing their calls. Voice messaging and calling number identification services are other examples of how intelligent networks can satisfy emerging customer demands. Extension of intelligent networks will be the "glue" that binds seemingly unrelated networks together and provides the end user a singular interface with a host of new network services.

Portable Communication - A Customer's Perspective

Benefits

Any service supported by a network must offer value to the potential users. The services offered must be independent of time and space. Information must be relayed between locations and within a time period acceptable to the user.

Convenience is of utmost importance. A user must not need a separate device for each of the several networks in a portable communications environment. The interconnection between dissimilar networks must be done internally with the customer having access and control from a single, compact, low cost device.

Access to the portable communication network must be large in scope. Nationwide coverage should be provided with international access possible through the public switched network.

Requirements

A portable communication network must have a minimum set of interface standards. Since services must be easily accessible from a single device, it is envisioned that more complex services will require peripheral devices. Thus, making an interface standard necessary.

The cost of the services must match a perceived level of value to the customers. Customers should be able to select and activate services when needed and be charged for services only when used.

The control of information in the portable communication network will be an important issue as customers will want the flexibility to control the delivery of information at their discretion.

Portable Communication - A Service Provider's Perspective

The goal of every service provider is to make a profit and to satisfy their customers. To do so, service providers must evolve their networks over time in such a way as to provide efficiently the new services customers demand.

Existing wireless networks must be extended to serve the customer's demand for mobility. This extension will take two forms: one, of increased capacity, such as the current move to a next generation cellular network; and two, an increase in coverage area. This added capacity will be needed to handle the increased demand for wireless services for both voice and data.

Existing wired networks must be incorporated. The public switched telephone network along with cellular, paging, and a newly overlaid intelligence based network will be integrated and managed as a single network to meet the needs of the customers served by various communications providers.

Integrating the embedded networks will not be enough unless new value-added services are provided. Customer demands for portable communication will be met with services which can be more efficiently implemented over an integrated network.

The integration of networks required to support portable communication will not evolve overnight. Service providers must have a common view of this futuristic network, and along with manufacturers, make a common transition in their network architectures to meet this objective. The basic elements which will make a nationwide portable communication network possible are standard network interfaces, open architectures, and distributed intelligence within the networks.

Technology Issues

New technologies will play a large role in the portable communication network of the future. Four technology areas are viewed as directly affecting the successful evolution of existing networks to a ubiquitous portable communication network. The four areas are digital RF technology, wireless distribution systems, power sources and devices, and intelligence within the network.

Digital RF technology

The application of digital technology in the radio frequency (RF) environment is making radio services more cost effective. Digital RF technologies which have impact on a portable communication network are listed.

- Access methods (FDMA, TDMA, CDMA)
- Digital modulation techniques
- Voice coding
- Error detection and correction
- Gigahertz RF technology

The two basic types of digital modulation are constant envelope such as FM, and linear modulation such as AM. Constant envelope modulation schemes typically vary phase or frequency, and are less spectral efficient, offering today around 1-2 bits/hertz. Linear modulation techniques combine both amplitude and phase in encoding information. They are more spectral efficient (2-6 bits/hertz) than constant envelope techniques. Linear modulation schemes require either an ultra-linear power amplifier (to prevent phase and amplitude distortion) or a class AB power amplifier used in its linear operating region. Due to development on low power linear RF amplifiers and high bits/hertz efficiency, a linear modulation scheme like 16-QAM will probably be used in a future portable communication network.

Good quality voice has been encoded at bit rates of less than 4 kbits/sec. Current voice codec techniques under consideration today are:

- SBC-APCM (Sub-band coder with adaptive PCM)
- SBC-ADPCM (Sub-band coder with adaptive DPCM)
- MPE-LTP (Multi-pulse excited long-term prediction)
- RPE-LPC (Regular-pulse excited LPC)

By the mid-nineties, 8 kbit/sec speech coding will be standard. The coding algorithm selected for speech coding will be selected on the basis of subjective testing and ease of implementation.

The error detection and correction techniques used are impacted by the RF environment (inside and outside) and the services delivered by the radio system (voice or data). Error detection and correction is important in a radio environment due mainly to both Rayleigh fading and "shadowing". Error detection and correction techniques will be employed to improve carrier-to-noise and carrier-to-interference ratios, and their use will provide a more robust radio system.

Another important area of research is the application of digital RF techniques in the gigahertz frequency band. RF spectrum is a scarce resource and so must be used efficiently. RF technologies in the gigahertz range (1-3 GHz), where spectrum is available, must be mastered not only at the device level, but also at the system and network levels. The use of gigahertz RF technology in connection with a microcell frequency reuse architecture will provide sufficient capacity to meet any level of forecasted demand for wireless services.

Wireless Distribution Systems

Propagation of an RF signal in the megahertz and gigahertz ranges will require designers to employ new wireless distribution systems. Different distribution technologies will be employed inside and outside buildings. Distribution systems, characterized by microcells or "leaky cables", will ensure efficient and reliable distribution of RF within the portable communication network.

Power

Efficient use of power in network equipment and customer owned devices will become extremely important in making a portable communication network a reality. Given that a customer must be able to interface the network via a small lightweight device that will easily fit in a shirt pocket or purse, powering of the device becomes an important consideration. The device must be able to "power down" circuitry until it is needed and power sources used must be small and efficient.

Intelligent Networks

Intelligence, as it applies to the portable communication network, implies a distributed control mechanism of independent network elements.

Distributed processing within the network will be a key element of the intelligence needed in the portable communication network. Control of the network is distributed from the highest level down to and including the customer device. Using single chip computers in the customer device, network protocols, services, and access capability may be "down loaded" as a service request is initiated.

An overlaid signalling network, which communicates with all networks supplying various services to the customer, is essential. The intelligent signalling network will provide messages between different network elements, identify users and their service levels, update billing databases, monitor network trouble, and provide customers a unified access to all communication networks.

The intelligence network will have databases which are linked via the signalling network. New services and protocol updates will be distributed to various network elements by means of updating specific databases from a master file. Network elements will access these databases to provide the customer access to new services and features.

These technology issues are by no means the only ones; however, they are key technologies that must be further developed for a portable communication network to become a reality. These technologies must evolve with the view of a futuristic network which will be more efficient and flexible than networks of today. It is important that thought be given to these concepts and ideas, particularly as researchers, manufacturers, and service providers work to transition to the next generation of networks. By focusing on the needs of a portable communication network today, the transition of networks over the next 10 to 15 years could result in an architecture that could easily support the demands of a highly mobile, information based society.

One View of a Portable Communications Network

One potential view of a portable communication network is shown next. Four areas of the network are discussed: Architecture, Distribution, Intelligence, and Terminal. The description presented is one realization of a portable communication network, and assumes the absence of legal and regulatory restrictions which today might prevent integration of various networks.

The three networks in place today most likely to evolve into an integrated portable communication network are: the public switched telephone networks (PSTN), the cellular networks, and the paging networks.

Architecture

Cellular networks of the future will be digital both in the switching and RF environment. The base stations will be "rehomed" into the local telephone company switches. Service generics and signalling systems will be part of a separate network by which customers will derive their services. Wireless service will be an extension of the wired service link provided today via the public switched telephone network.

Cellular networks will come in at least two planes. The first plane is a microcell plane used by subscribers who are on foot, within buildings, on the street, or in underground tunnels such as subways. The second plane is a macrocell plane for use by vehicles. It has larger cell area to reduce inter-cell switching requirements for fast-moving terminals. (Figure 1)

Distribution

Distribution of RF in a microcell network will be done from small roof top antennas. Propagation will be limited over cell areas of 100-300 meters. Macrocell RF distribution will be performed in a manner similar to today's cellular system.

Microcell architecture will be used inside buildings. Media such as "leaky cables" or infrared transceivers are candidates for distributing RF within buildings depending on the distance, reliability, and services involved. (Figure 2)

Intelligence

Intelligent nodes are planned which serve to update local network elements. These nodes, by means of a signalling network (initially SS7), will transmit the customer's level of service and activate those services at home and distant locations. Intelligence will be embedded in the public switched telephone network, which will be accessed by the cellular and paging networks. Intelligent nodes will also serve functions such as billing, fault detection, information routing, and other network management activities. Figure (3)

Terminals

Customer equipment or terminals are key to a portable communications network of the future. These terminals will be very small and power efficient. They will be all digital and use single chip computers with resident ROM and RAM storage capabilities. Depending on location, the customer's device, when activated, will request network acceptance. The network will respond by querying the intelligent node for validity of the customer and level of service subscription. Once authenticated, the local switching node will "down load" the unique system protocols to resident RAM on-board the terminal. The terminal is a totally digital transceiver which employs digital signal processing and consists largely of VLSI. The resulting terminal will be reliable and inexpensive. The basic transceiver will have multiple peripheral devices that can be purchased to enhance its functionality. For example, the basic terminal will be very similar to today's portable cellular phones, but with peripheral devices that can be purchased for the home or car to convert its use to a cordless phone (used over the PSTN) at home or a fully functional mobile phone in the car. The paging function will be a network service, and the terminal will have a display for receiving pages and returning short alphanumeric responses. An attachable keyboard will be available enabling customers to type data directly into the system. (Figure 4)

Conclusion

A portable communication network is possible if service providers and manufacturers work closely to define interface standards and architectures that will allow for the evolution of today's existing networks into fully functional components. Research into micro-cell-based frequency reuse technologies must progress in harmony with development of radio technologies in the gigahertz range. A robust, highly functional, open architecture signalling overlay network must be specified capable of supporting not only the switched network, but also the cellular and paging networks. In addition, a low cost, highly reliable wireless terminal must be developed to provide the customer a user friendly access to the network.

ARCHITECTURE

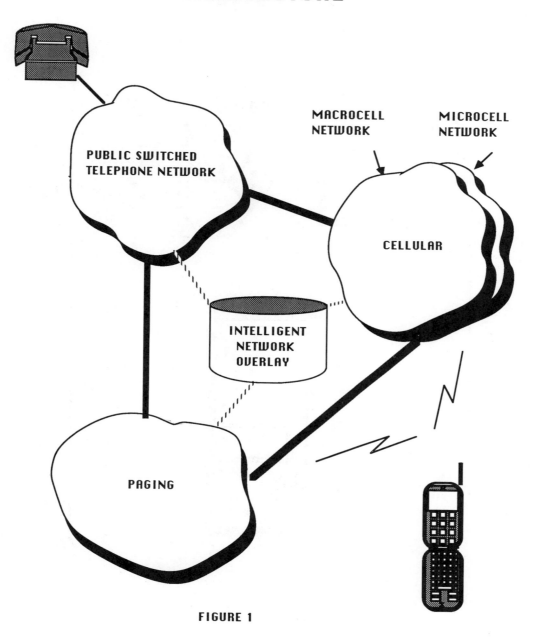

FIGURE 1

DISTRIBUTION

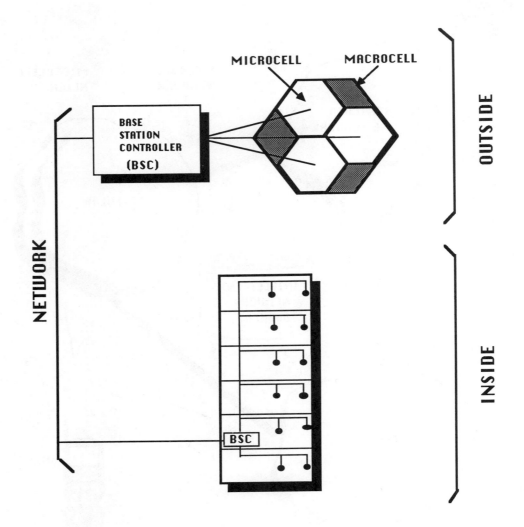

FIGURE 2

1711

INTELLIGENCE

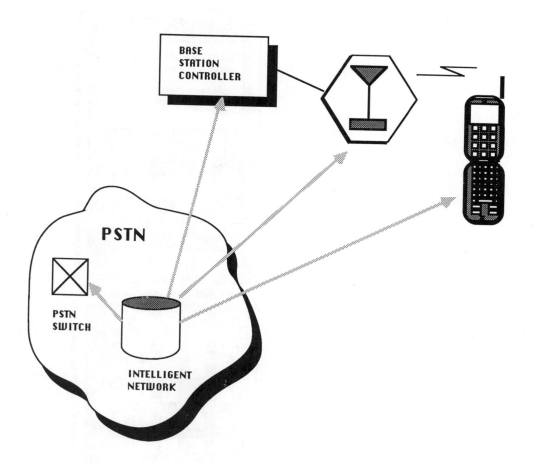

Figure 3

TERMINAL

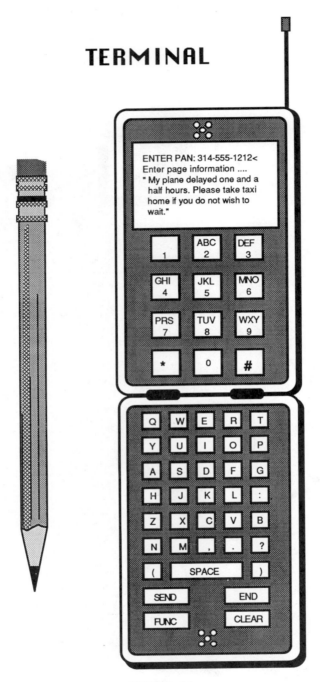

ENTER PAN: 314-555-1212<
Enter page information ....
" My plane delayed one and a
half hours. Please take taxi
home if you do not wish to
wait."

	ABC	DEF
1	2	3
GHI	JKL	MNO
4	5	6
PRS	TUV	WXY
7	8	9
*	0	#

Q W E R T
Y U I O P
A S D F G
H J K L :
Z X C V B
N M , . ?
(SPACE)
SEND   END
FUNC   CLEAR

FIGURE 4

BASIC EXCHANGE TELECOMMUNICATION RADIO (BETR) TECHNOLOGY

ROBERT J. McGUIRE
Manager, Local Loop Products
Rockwell International
Network Transmission Systems Division
P.O. Box 568842
Dallas, Texas 75356-8842

ABSTRACT

The architecture for a point to multipoint digital radio system, designed to operate in the 450 MHz band, allocated by the FCC for Basic Exchange Telecommunications Radio Service (BETR), will be discussed. Radio design considerations will be presented for a system which is sized to provide toll grade, telephone service for up to 24 subscribers. The use of TDM, TDMA and FDMA radio access technologies will be illustrated.

INTRODUCTION

A new radio service, known as Basic Exchange Telecommunications Radio Service (BETR), was recently established by the FCC (CC Docket 86-495) to improve rural telephone service. The new service will operate in the 150 MHz, 450 MHz and 800 MHz bands. This service, which is implemented using a point-to-multipoint radio technology, provides an alternative to copper wire for providing telephone service to subscribers. Some of the major considerations which influenced the design approach of a 450 MHz, exchange radio system will be presented.

Exchange radio equipment, designed for use in the 450 MHz band, operates with a frequency plan originally intended for Public Land Mobile Service (PLMS). BETR systems are required to co-exist with installed base and mobile radio communication equipment. The exchange radio system should provide a high quality of telephone service to a variety of users. It must be easy to engineer and install so that it operates with existing central office switches and subscriber telephone equipment. It must also be economically competitive with existing forms of equipment now providing this service, including copper wire, cable, carrier systems, radio or fiber optics. Typical copper wire installation costs per subscriber line as a function of loop length are shown in figure 1.

An exchange radio system, consisting of a base station, subscriber terminals and repeater, is illustrated in figure 2. The base station is connected to the local exchange using either vf cable pairs (one pair per subscriber) or a digital facility such as a T1 Repeatered Line. Subscriber radio terminals connect to the end-user's standard Protector/Network Interface Unit (RJ-11 jack) which is mounted at the customer premise location. Subscriber terminals may connect to a single end user or to a cluster of two or more end users using vf cable pairs. A repeater may be necessary to circumvent obstructions between base station and some of the subscriber terminals.

A typical network of subscribers which are linked to the base station by radio is shown in figure 3. The base station terminal is equipped with an omni directional antenna while subscriber antennas are directional. The radio system employs concentration and as a result, the number of subscribers normally exceeds the number of available radio trunks. During idle periods, subscriber receivers are tuned to the control channel frequency and transmitters are switched off. When a call is initiated at the subscriber or central office, the time division multiple access (TDMA) control channel is used to establish the trunk on an idle radio channel.

Frequency division multiple access (FDMA) methods are used to connect a trunk on an available radio channel. The traffic between the central office and a subscriber terminal consists of voiceband signals plus the signaling data needed to support the various subscriber options of POTS, Coin and Multiparty services.

CHARACTERISTICS OF THE 450 MHZ BAND

Technical operating requirements for rural radio service are provided in Part 22.601, Subpart H of the FCC Code of Regulations. Some of the technical standards issued by the FCC in part 22 are summarized as follows:

	Central Office or PLMS Base	Subscriber or PLMS Mobile
Transmit Carriers (26)	454.025 to 454.650 MHz	459.025 to 459.650 MHz
Frequency Tolerance	.00025%	.00025%
20 kHz Emissions	F1D, F1E, F3C, F3E	Same
Maximum Power	2000 watts	500 watts
Modulation Requirements	See figure 4	

Although the emission types for signals having 20 kHz of bandwidth are shown to be frequency modulated (FM) signals, the FCC permits the use of phase or amplitude modulation for digital signals provided the emission falls within the mask shown in figure 4. The authorized bandwidth permits digital emissions with symbol rates up to 18 kilobaud.

MODULATION TECHNIQUES

Exchange radio service could be provided using either analog or digital modulation methods. Mobile radiotelephone users, who also occupy the 450 MHz band, employ FM which is typically used for transmitting a single channel on each carrier frequency.

Digital modulation was chosen over analog for exchange radio service. Cost factors which influence this choice are:

Privacy of radio signal in a fixed station environment.

Robustness of radio signal in high noise.

Multiple subscribers per carrier.

Signaling and control channels.

Concentration circuits at base station.

Digital connectivity into telephone network.

Digital signal processing (DSP) technology.

TDMA/FDMA

Complexity of linear and non-linear radios.

1714

Figure 5 illustrates the possible information rates which can be transmitted over one of the 26 available channels in the 450 MHz band, using various digital modulation schemes[1]. When a digital signal is applied to a channel, the maximum available bandwidth of the channel is approximately 18 kHz. Transmission rates up to 36 kb/s are possible using 4-FSK or 4 QAM. The use of 16-QAM or 16-PSK permits channel data rates of up to 72 kb/s, while 32 QAM affords the opportunity to transmit up to 90 kb/s on a single carrier. The higher modulation levels, of course, reduce system gain because of their higher signal to noise requirements.

SYSTEM GAIN[2]

The path calculations for a typical exchange radio system, using 16 QAM or 4 QAM modulation, are given below. Elevation of the base station, omni antenna is assumed to be 100 feet, while the subscriber antenna elevation is 50 feet. Transmitter power is assumed to be +23 dBm.

Transmitter Output	+ 23.0	dBm
100 Ft. Transmission Line Loss	− 1.5	dB
Transmitter Antenna Gain (Omni)	+ 6.0	dB
15 Mile Free Space Loss	−113.5	dB
Receive Antenna Gain (Directional)	+ 10.0	dB
50 Ft. Transmission Line Loss	− 0.75	dB
Receiver Signal Level	− 76.75	dBm
Receiver Signal Level for BER at 10^{-3}	−105.0	dBm
Free Space Fade Margin (16 QAM)	28	dB
Free Space Fade Margin (4 QAM)	34	dB

With 20 dB of fade margin, 99.9% availability is provided for a 450 MHz radio channel. A transmitter operating at +23 dBm provides margin for shadow and defraction losses. Additional margin against interference and variable path lengths between the subscriber terminals and the base station can be achieved by employing automatic power control (APC)[3].

DIGITAL CODING OF VOICE BAND SIGNALS

Two coding algorithms are considered to be toll quality for transmitting voice band signals over the digital network. The most common algorithm used in telephone networks in North America is 64 kb/s mu-law PCM. The second algorithm, which is a recognized international standard, is the 32 kb/s ADPCM algorithm specified in CCITT Recommendation G.721[4]. The ADPCM algorithm was designed so that synchronous conversions can be made from PCM to ADPCM to PCM without introducing cumulative distortion. The capacity of transmission equipment can, therefore, be doubled by equipping 64 kb/s interfaces with 32 kb/s ADPCM codecs in order to compress digital voice band signals into a smaller bandwidth. This bandwidth compression technique is compatible with the digital network because speech quality is maintained and because no significant degradations occur to voiceband data (up to 4800 bps), DTMF and facsimile signals.

Other voiceband coding algorithms have been developed which operate at bit rates in the range of 12 to 24 kb/s[5]. The channel capacity of an exchange radio system can be increased using these low bit rate coders; however, telephone network compatibility is sacrificed. Several coding algorithms, designed to operate at 14.4 and 16 kb/s, are ranked at near toll quality when subjective tests on the perceived speech quality are conducted. Circuit quality is reduced however when these coders are introduced into the network because of their long processing delays, incompatibility with voiceband data signals, and the cumulative distortion introduced when these coders are cascaded.

GRADE OF SERVICE[6]

Since call blocking can occur in a system employing concentration, the system must be engineered to provide a grade of service. The grade of service normally required in exchange radio applications is .01, which specifies the probability that a call will be blocked during the busy hour at 1%. After the calling rate of each subscriber is established, and the number of subscribers to be served by a base station is known, the Erlang B equation can be applied to establish the required number of radio trunks. Six radio trunks provide for a traffic intensity of 1.91 Erlangs which is adequate to serve 24 subscribers, if the calling rate for each subscriber is .06 Erlang during the busy hour (3.6 minutes/busy hour).

Consider the multiplex strategies which can now be employed to provide toll quality exchange radio service. The data rate (R) selected for one 32 kb/s ADPCM trunk is:

$$R = 32 \text{ (voice)} + 1.33 \text{ (signaling)} + 1.33 \text{ (overhead) kb/s}$$
$$= 34.67 \text{ kb/s}$$

The modulation required to provide various subscriber services on a single RF channel is summarized below:

Subscriber Rates	Modulation	450 MHz Service on 1 RF Channel
1. 32 kb/s	4 QAM	POTS, voice or data Coin 2 Party ANI
2. 32 + 32 kb/s TDM Mode	16 QAM	2 co-located subscribers Voice + Data, 1 subscriber
3. 64 kb/s	16 QAM	POTS, Coin Clear channel
4. 32 + 32 kb/s TDMA mode	32 QAM	2 subscribers, any location

The TDMA mode provides the advantage that two subscribers at any location may access a radio channel, and as a result, three RF channels can accommodate 6 trunks for any arrangement of subscriber terminals. One disadvantage is that a less robust form of modulation is required.

The TDM mode provides an economical approach for connecting more than one co-located subscriber to a radio terminal, however more RF channels may be required depending on the cluster arrangements. If 24 subscribers are clustered at one subscriber terminal, for example, TDM provides the same grade of service as TDMA using the same number of RF channels. If no subscribers are co-located, 6 RF channels are required for the same grade of service.

EXCHANGE RADIO IMPLEMENTATION

The architecture of the Rockwell CXR 424 Exchange Radio, designed to provide network quality service, is illustrated by the block diagrams of the base station and subscriber terminals given in figures 6 and 8.

The base station is designed to simultaneously occupy any 6 RF channels in the 450 MHz band. Subscriber terminals are frequency agile and terminals are designed for 1 or 2 subscriber lines on any channel assigned by the base station. Terminals are equipped with automatic power control (APC) in order to permit carriers to be transmitted at levels ranging from +20 to +29 dBm.

Concentration at the base station is accomplished by converting voiceband signals into a 64 kb/s mu-law signals, using Dual Channel Units (DCU). Alternatively, the base station may be equipped with a Line Interface Unit (LIU) if the central office connection is at the 1.544 mb/s rate. 64 kb/s traffic is time division multiplexed onto PCM and signaling busses. Modems are capable of selecting traffic from one or two time slots which are assigned by the Base Processor. Modems are equipped with 32 kb/s ADPCM voice compression circuits for up to two subscriber lines. Voice compression is disabled if a subscriber line is provisioned for 64 kb/s traffic. The operating mode of each modem is dynamically changed to 4 QAM or 16 QAM when a call is initiated, depending on the number of lines connected to the subscriber terminal. The other modules at the base station combine the traffic from up to six modems. A frequency agile synthesizer module permits a signal from any modem to be translated to any of the 26 channels in the 450 MHz band.

The Subscriber terminals may be equipped for 1 or 2 subscriber lines. Service options are selected by equipping the terminal with the appropriate channel unit. The modem in the subscriber unit is also processor controlled so that it can be configured to operate in the same mode as the base station modem when a call is processed. The modem signals are placed on the appropriate RF channel by a frequency agile synthesizer. Frequencies are established at the base station and synthesizer commands are transmitted to the subscriber terminal over the control channel. When the subscriber lines are idle, the power amplifier is switched off in order to permit other terminals in the system use of the rf frequencies. During idle periods the subscriber receiver is tuned to the control channel frequency so that calls can be initiated at either end of the system using the control channel.

The protocols used by the CXR 424 are demonstrated in figure 9, which illustrates signals that are transmitted over the control channel and one of the traffic channels. Figure 9 illustrates the use of two RF channels over a period of time in which a call is initiated at the central office.

Control channel transmissions from the base station to all subscriber terminals are continuous TDM signals consisting of various commands such as poll or call initiate. The continuous signal allows all subscriber terminals to synchronize to the system clock and carrier frequencies. Control channel responses from the subscribers are timed with the base station commands so that collisions do not occur when a call is initiated. Subscribers access the control channel by switching on its PA and transmitting a data packet when status is requested or a call is initiated at the subscriber end of the system.

If a call is initiated at the base station from subscriber 14, for example a call initiate packet is transmitted to the appropriate terminal. After receiving an acknowledge packet from the subscriber terminal, the base station processor provisions a modem which is assigned to operate on an idle RF channel. After the terminal is synchronized to operate on its assigned channel, signaling data from the central office rings the subscriber. The call is connected when a subscriber off hook signal is detected. The call is terminated when on hook is detected at either end of the system and the RF channel returns to idle so that it is available for another call.

CONCLUSION

An exchange radio system which operates in the 450 MHz band can provide network quality telephone service to rural subscribers. Reliable operation in the 450 MHz band requires the use of a robust form of modulation in order to co-exist with current users of the band and to maintain quality trunks. A digital radio system provides the necessary immunity to noise and the privacy required for the telephone network. Network quality trunks can be provided over the system by using 64 kb/s mu-law PCM or 32 kb/s ADPCM for voiceband signal compression. Six trunks are normally required for 24 subscribers. An example of the operation of a toll quality exchange radio system was presented using the CXR 424 Exchange Radio, manufactured by Rockwell International.

REFERENCES

1. P. R. Hartmann, *"Radio Technology - Present and Future"*, Proceedings of the National Communications Forum, 1987, Volume 41, No. 1, PP 443.
2. Kenneth Bullington, *"Radio Propogation Fundamentals"*, Bell Systems Technical Journal, Volume 36, No. 3, May 1957, PP 593-626.
3. W. A. Conner, *"Automatic Power Control in Microwave Communications"*. Proceedings of the National Communications Forum, 1987, Volume 41, No. 11, PP 957-961.
4. CCITT Recommendation G721, *"32 kbit/s Adaptive Differential Pulse Code Modulation (ADPCM)"*, Red Book, October 1984.
5. Nuggehally S. Jayant, *"Coding Speech at Low Bit Rates"*, IEEE Spectrum, PP 58-63, August, 1986.
6. Roger Freeman, *"Reference Manual for Telecommunications Engineering"*, PP 1-18, John Wiley and Sons, 1985.

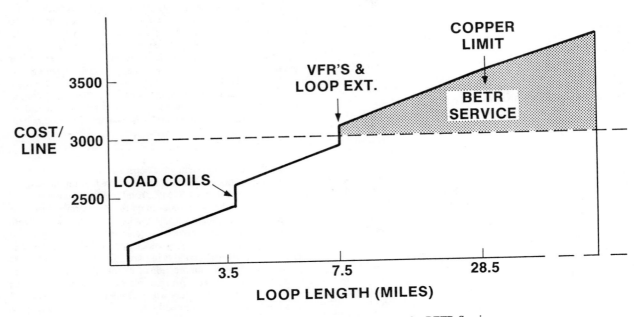

Figure 1. Economical "Prove-In" Chart for BETR Service.

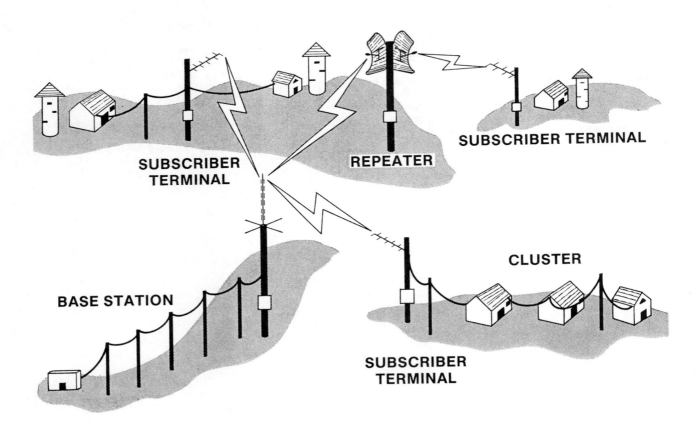

Figure 2. Basic Exchange Telecommunictions Radio (BETR).

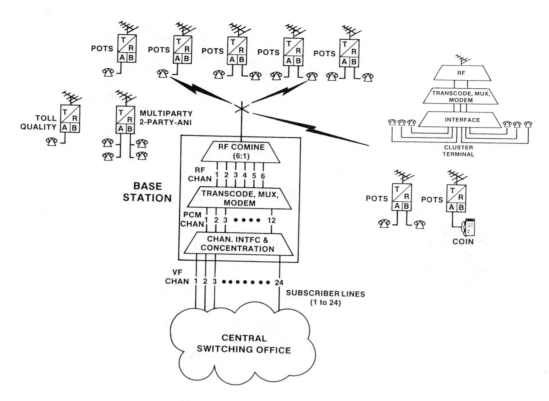

Figure 3. Central Switching Office.

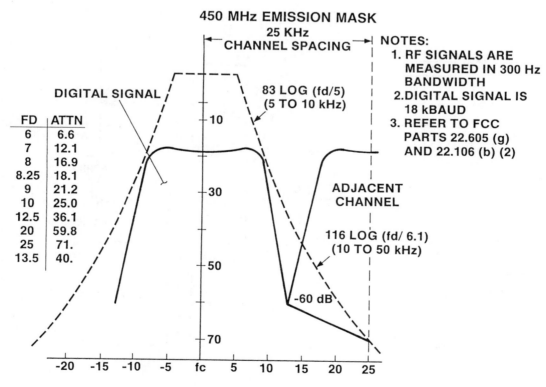

450 MHz EMISSION MASK

25 KHz CHANNEL SPACING

DIGITAL SIGNAL

83 LOG (fd/5)
(5 TO 10 kHz)

ADJACENT CHANNEL

116 LOG (fd/ 6.1)
(10 TO 50 kHz)

-60 dB

NOTES:
1. RF SIGNALS ARE MEASURED IN 300 Hz BANDWIDTH
2. DIGITAL SIGNAL IS 18 kBAUD
3. REFER TO FCC PARTS 22.605 (g) AND 22.106 (b) (2)

FD	ATTN
6	6.6
7	12.1
8	16.9
8.25	18.1
9	21.2
10	25.0
12.5	36.1
20	59.8
25	71.
13.5	40.

Figure 4.   450 MHz Emission Mask.

1718

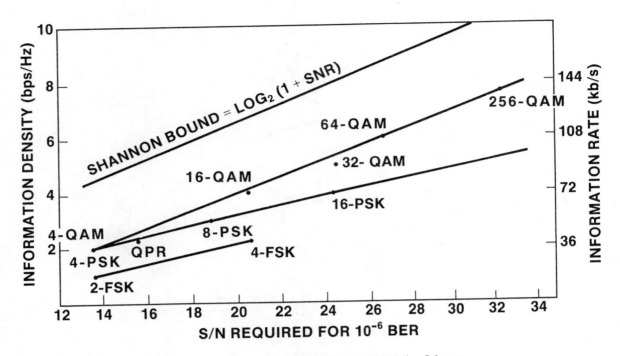

Figure 5. Channel Capacity for Various Modulation Schemes.

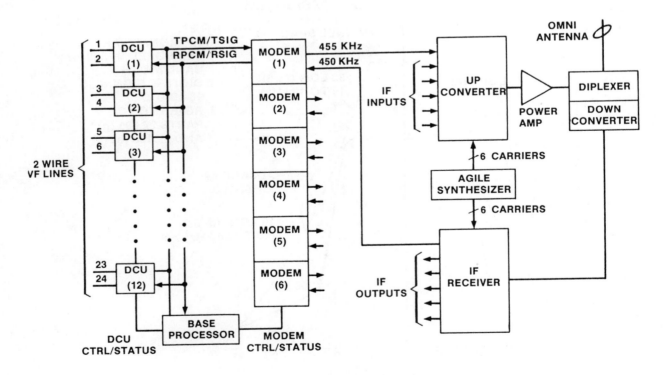

Figure 6. CXR 424 Base Station.

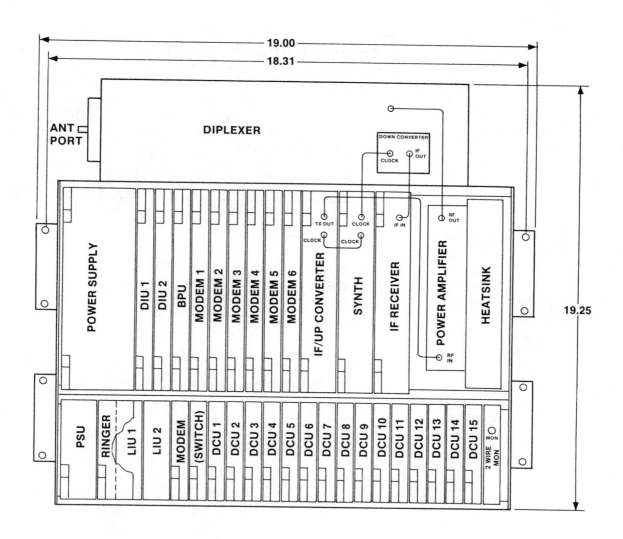

Figure 7. CXR-424 Base Station Unit

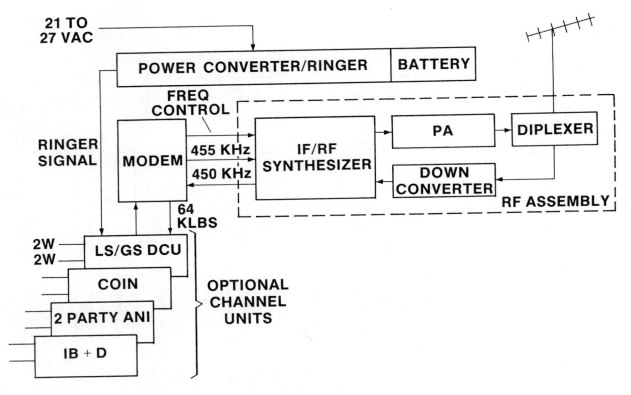

Figure 8.   CXR 424 Subscriber Unit.

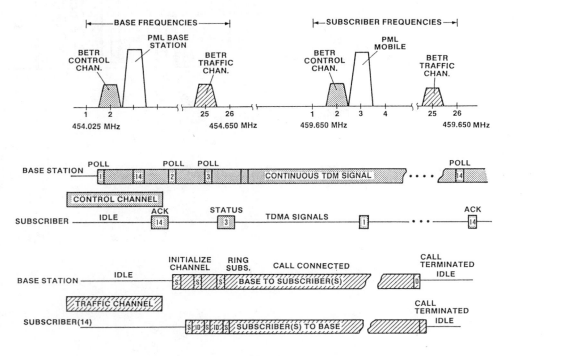

Figure 9.   CXR 424 Protocol.

1721

POWERING ISSUES

Thomas M. Taylor

District Manager-Energy Systems Technology

Bell Communications Research

435 South Street
Morristown, NJ 07960

Some key elements of portability are size and weight. The power consumption of a portable terminal figures prominently in affecting the terminal's bulk because each watt of power consumption requires 8 cubic inches for electrochemical energy storage. There is an accompanying pound of weight associated with the watt. In what follows, a brief look will be taken at what some new battery technologies may offer towards reducing this size and weight. Then energy conserving designs will be described. These enable the battery to be reduced for the same amount of operation between charging. The impact of some new technologies that could potentially revolutionize the portable terminal will then be described.

A rule of thumb in electrochemical technology is that in terms of energy storage density, a given system in maturity only attains about 20 percent of its theoretical maximum. This is true of lead-acid today, and it is becoming true of nickel-cadmium. Lithium systems currently on the market are at about ten percent of their theoretical limits in volumetric storage efficiency. If the same 20 percent threshold holds true for lithium batteries, and there is every indication that it will, then the most we can expect is a doubling of energy density over that of products being manufactured today.

Consequently, we should not expect anywhere near an order-of-magnitude improvement in battery size over the next decade. We will have to reduce power consumption by prudent circuit design, judicious selection of components and topologies and by developing new technologies which facilitate lower power communication.

Energy conservation has never been a concern on the part of manufacturers of telecommunications equipment. Work at Bellcore centered around the modification of a modern digital loop carrier, (DLC), system which demonstrated that the particular manufacturer could provide the same function at one third the monthly electric bill. Furthermore, the peak power and attendant power processing equipment could have been reduced by 25 percent. The manufacturer's savings in this equipment would have more than paid for any extra component costs required. Reliability was favorably affected because heat removed from the rack lowered component temperatures. The methods employed to accrue these savings did not require any new invention or leading edge technology. We turned off idle circuitry, substituted lower power components for ones that had to be on much of the time and in light traffic hours we packed traffic into a few carrier lines so that the others, along with their repeaters, could be powered down. A Bellcore Technical Seminar on Digital Loop Carrier Energy Utilization was held on December 10, 1987. Many of the techniques employed with DLCs can be applied to portable terminals. Some of these and others are in fact being utilized in equipment on the market today.

Polling of a receiver on a low duty-cycle basis permits a portable terminal to conserve battery while 'on-hook'. This allows the battery to be rated in terms of call-minutes rather than simply recharge interval. Pulsed carrier operation, in conjunction with packetizing of data, facilitates powering of the transmitter on a low duty cycle basis during transmit intervals. Choice of a low power device technology for digital signal processing functions is essential. In general, every quantum of energy needs to be scrutinized carefully with the aim of reducing or eliminating it.

Some new developments in technology offer promise for the future. Superconducting antennas could lead to more efficient drive circuits and perhaps higher antenna gain. As carrier frequencies rise, microprocessor controlled phased arrays may become more realistic for the portable terminal. As these and other developments facilitate more efficient battery utilization, the concept of staged portability will be very much in vogue.

REFERENCES

[1] Taylor, T.M., Tuhy, F.P. Jr., "Scrutinizing Digital Loop Carrier Energy," Bellcore Digest, October 1987.

RADIO COVERAGE IN BUILDINGS

Dr. Andrew J. Motley
Executive Engineer
Amanda J. Martin

British Telecom Research Labs

Martlesham Hoath
Ipswich IP5 7RE
England

ABSTRACT

For future advanced cordless telecommunications services, a very high standard of radio coverage within buildings will be essential. This can be achieved using either distributed antennas or radiating cables. In either case, simple prediction models are required to make the planning and installation of these systems as easy and cheap as possible. Appropriate models are presented here and compared with measured radio coverage at 900 MHz in a typical office building.

INTRODUCTION

There is a mounting demand for greater flexibility, mobility, and improvement in the range of services provided by telecommunications products used in the home, office or in public places. This is particularly so in the case of cordless telephones (CT), where at present, they only replace the cord of a normal simple telephone with a radio link. This enables mobility of use up to, typically, between 50 and 200 m, depending on location. Such CTs use conventional analogue modulation over the radio link which results in a low level of privacy, and as there are only a small number of fixed radio channels available, the user densities are low. This has limited the present cordless market to mainly the residential sector.

The need for an advanced cordless telecommunications service (ACTS) offering a secure service with a range of flexible facilities and which permits very high user densities has been recognized by many [1]-[8]. In particular, this has been endorsed within Europe by the Conference of European Postal and Telecommunications Administrations (CEPT) through the production of a recommendation [8] on the services and facilities required by future generations of cordless products.

This has fuelled the development of a digital second generation CT, known as CT2. This uses FDMA with 40 channels, each 100 kHz apart, and bothway speech sent in bursts (time division duplex) over single radio channels. Its greatly improved user capacity, call security and privacy, as well as its increased service flexibility and performance, are ideally suited to the various needs of the business market, and this together with large demand for domestic products and services will realize large volume, low-cost equipment.

Probably the most challenging cordless application is the Wireless-PBX (WPBX) [9] or what has been more generally called the Cordless Business Communication System (CBCS). It is a particularly demanding service to provide in a high user density environment where both good spectrum efficiency and high performance are essential. This means that highly reliable radio coverage is necessary with system flexibility to cope with all user requirements, particularly localised peak demand in an office complex.

There are two basic techniques available to provide this high quality coverage. The first uses distributed antenna around the customer's site, in the form of a miniaturised three dimensional cellular radio layout. This has come to be known as a picocellular approach, due to its very small coverage zones from each antenna. The second technique is to guide and tailor coverage through the use of radiating cables. Here poorly screened coaxial cables are laid, say along central corridors to direct signals from and to offices either side, together with covering the passageways in between.

In some cases, a combination of both techniques would be used to give optimal coverage in a varied environment at minimal cost.

The dimensioning of a CBCS using picocellular of radiating cables will critically depend on the radio coverage each provides. This coverage can change dramatically from building to building due mainly to the differences in construction [10, 11]. However, to minimise the installation costs and subsequent expansion of the system, there needs to be a very simple planning tool to enable the installer to easily and quickly determine the correct system layout for each customer's premises. This ideally requires, say, a personal computer to be used with a few key parameters entered by the installer, say building type, sizes, etc., and the computer output then provides the siting of base units.

The major requirement for the computer planning tool to be effective is the availability of accurate coverage prediction modelling, which takes account of the effects of different types of buildings. How this can be achieved for both antennas and radiating cables is the subject of this paper.

MODELLING ANTENNAS PROPAGATION

The relationship between transmitted and received power for mobile radio applications is typically expressed [12] (see Figure 1) as

$$\bar{P}_r = P_t - L - 10n \, \text{Log}_{10} \, d \tag{1}$$

where $\bar{P}_r$ = Mean received power (dB)
P_t = Transmitted power (dB)
L = Clutter loss (dB)
d = Distance between transmitter and receiver
n = Signal decay rate

The clutter loss is the extra signal attenuation, above the plane earth prediction, due to the surrounding environment. This is a particularly important factor within buildings, where walls, furniture and people all add to the path loss. The received signal suffers from rayleigh fading when moving around, with $\bar{P}_r$ being the mean level obtained over an area of several wavelengths. However, there is also a shadowing effect present, due to obstacles within a building which causes the clutter loss, L, to vary around the site. In outside mobile communication, this variation is lognormally distributed with a certain variance. This has also been found to be the case within buildings, and so L in equation (1) should be replaced by the mean, $\bar{L}$, of a lognormal distribution with a variance, v, which needs to be characterised for different buildings. Hence, equation (1) becomes

$$\bar{P}_r \, (\text{Rayleigh}) = P_t - \bar{L} \, (\text{Lognormal, v}) - 10n \, \text{Log}_{10} \, d \tag{2}$$

or simply

$$\bar{P}_r = P_t - \bar{L} \, (v) - 10n \, \text{Log}_{10} \, d \tag{3}$$

The spread in L can be reduced if the major obstructions can be separately identified. The floors of a building are one such factor and to account for these, equation (3) is modified as follows

$$\bar{P}_r = P_t - \bar{L}_A \, (v) - 10n \, \text{Log}_{10} \, d - kF \tag{4}$$

where F is the signal attenuation through each floor and k is the number of floors traversed. Fire walls also provide significant losses and could be added to equation (4) together with other major obstacles. However, for simplicity, these other factors will not be considered here.

MODELLING RADIATING CABLE PROPAGATION

Radio coverage from a radiating cable can be modelled in a similar fashion to antennas, except now, as shown in Figure 2, there is the cable attenuation to take into account. So equation (4) now becomes

$$\bar{P}_r = P_t - \bar{L}_c \, (v) - 10n \, \text{Log}_{10} \, d - kF - xA \tag{5}$$

Here A is the cable's coaxial attenuation per metre and x is the distance from the nearest point on the cable to the receiver in Figure 2. The clutter loss for antennas is now retermed coupling loss for cables,

$\bar{L}_c \, (v)$. This is the signal strength 1m from the cable (as for antennas) which varies along its length due to building and cable affects. This variation is again taken to be lognormal with a certain variance.

MEASUREMENTS

These propagation models have been obtained from coverage measurements in many buildings, primarily at 900 MHz. However, as an example here, results from one typical modern office block will be used to identify the parameters required in the models.

The building is 50m long by 15m wide and built of reinforced concrete with plasterboard internal partitioning walls. A typical floor layout is shown in Figure 3. For the antenna measurements, the receiver was placed on the third floor attached to a dipole antenna, and in each case, a portable transmitter using quarter wavelength with ground plane antenna was carried around several rooms throughout the building. The same was repeated for a radiating cable positioned in the ceiling void on the sixth floor and attached to the measurement receiver as shown in Figure 3. The cable had a loosely braided screen and semi-airspaced dielectric, with coaxial attenuation of 0.3 dB/m and 75Ω characteristic impedance. Further details on the measurement techniques can be found in references [10] [11] [13] [14].

ANTENNA RESULTS

The results from the antenna measurements are shown in Figures 4(a) without correction for floor attenuation. Here the decay rate is 7 and the clutter loss is13 dB.

In Figure 4(b), the signal levels are corrected for floor attenuation. This is done by increasing each data point by the appropriate kF. The value of F was identified by finding the value which minimises the variance in the data. As Figure 4(b) shows, this gave a floor attenuation of 5.4 dB, with decay rate 4 and clutter loss of around 30 dB. The variation in the mean signal level about the straight line decay rate was found to be lognormal with a standard deviation of about 4 dB. Also, the localised signal variations were rayleigh distributed, except when in the same room as the receiver.

This has characterised the antenna radio coverage within a building such that predictions to within ±5 dB can readily be made with a high degree of confidence.

RADIATING CABLE RESULTS

The signal variations alongside the cable are shown in Figure 5. These results were with the transmitter on the same floor as the cable, and they have been corrected to account for slight difference in the separation from the cable, to remove path loss variations. The straight line shows the cable attenuation, and as can be seen, the received signals fall close to this line. It is interesting to note the long standing wave which is prominent in the result. This is due to interaction between different propagation modes present with the radiating cables. This affect could possibly be included in the model to improve predictions.

Looking now at the signal decay away from the cable, the results in Figure 6 were obtained. Here, the signal levels have been corrected for both cables attenuation and floor losses. In the latter case, the appropriate floor factor was again derived from the value which minimised the variances in the data about the best fit straight line. Not surprising, the values obtained of 6 dB is virtually the same as for antennas, allowing for accurate measurements.

The decay rate is 3 and the mean coupling loss $\bar{L}_c$ (v), is around 60 dB. Again, the variations in this value around the building are lognormally distributed with a standard deviation, in this case of 3 dB. Also, the localised signal variations were rayleigh distributed.

Again, the building has been characterised, but in this case for radiating cable radio coverage. This will provide predictions to within ±5 dB with a slightly higher degree of confidence than antennas.

CONCLUSIONS

It has been shown that radio coverage within buildings can be predicted with a high degree of accuracy and confidence. This will enable future advanced cordless telecommunications services, such as the cordless business communication system, to be dimensioned correctly and installed simply and cheaply.

ACKNOWLEDGEMENT

Acknowledgement is made to the Director of Research and Technology, British Telecom, for permission to publish this paper.

REFERENCES

[1]   R.S. Swain, "Cordless telecommunications in the UK," Brit. Telecom Technol. J., vol 3, no 2, pp 32-38, Apr 1985.

[2]   D.C. Cox, "Universal portable radio communications," IEEE Trans Veh. Technol., vol VT-34, pp 117-121, Aug 1985.

[3]   Pactel International, "Future mobile communications services in Europe," Report to the Eurodata foundation on the systems and opportunities for services to the year 2000, Sept 1981.

[4]   J.E. Padgett, "Cordless telephones: Present and future," in Proc. Nat. Commun. Forum, 1984, Professional Education Int. Inc., vol 38, pp 151-155.

[5]   P.D. White, M.K. Gurcan and R.J.G. MacNamee, "900 MHz digital cordless telephone," Proc. IEE, vol 132, pt F, pp 425-432, Aug 1985.

[6]   M.J. Carey, A.J. Anderson, D.J. Mobley and M.A. Munro, "An onsite mobile business communications system using spread-spectrum modulation," in Proc. 3rd Int. Conf. Land Mobile Radio, Dec 1985, IERE pub 65.

[7]   British Standard: Apparatus Using Cordless Attachments (Excluding Cellular Radio Apparatus) for Connection to Analogue Interfaces of Public Switched Telephone Networks, British Standards Institution BS6833 parts 1 and 2 1987.

[8]   CEPT, "Services and facilities aspects of 2nd generation cordless telephones, Recommendation T/SF 42, 1986.

[9]   A.J. Motley, "Advanced cordless telecommunications services," IEEE Trans. on Selected Areas in Com., vol SAC-5, pt 5, pp 774-782, June 1987.

[10]   S.E. Alexander, "Radio propagation within buildings at 900 MHz," Electron. Lett. vol 18, no 21, pp 913-914, Oct 1983.

[11]   , "Characterising buildings for propagation at 900 MHz," Electron. Lett. vol 19, no 20, p 860, Sept 1983.

[12]   R.J. Holbeche, "Land mobile radio systems," IEE Telecoms. series 14, chapter 3, Peter Peregrinus Ltd., 1985.

[13]   A.J. Motley and D.A. Palmer, "Directed radio coverage within buildings," in Proc. Conf. Radio Spectrum Conversation Techniques, Sept 1983, IEE Conf. Pub 224.

[14]   K.J. Bye, "Leaky feeders for cordless communication in the office," Conf. Proc. Eurocon 88, Stockholm, June 1988.

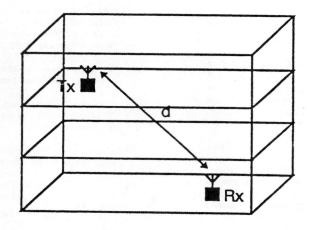

Building Schematic for Antennas

Figure 1

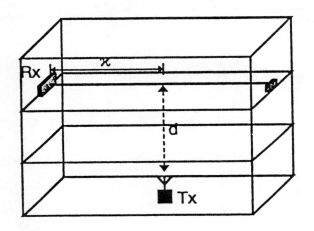

Building Schematic for Radiating Cables

Figure 2

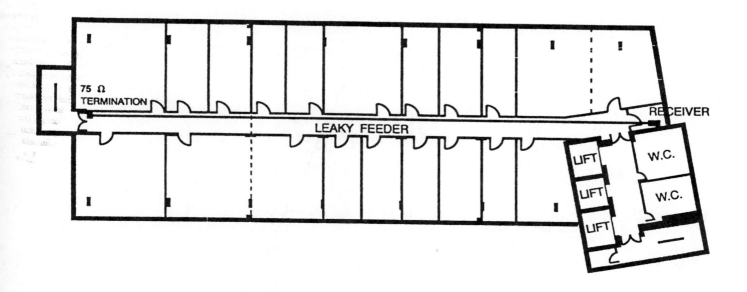

Floor Plan of Test Building

Figure 3

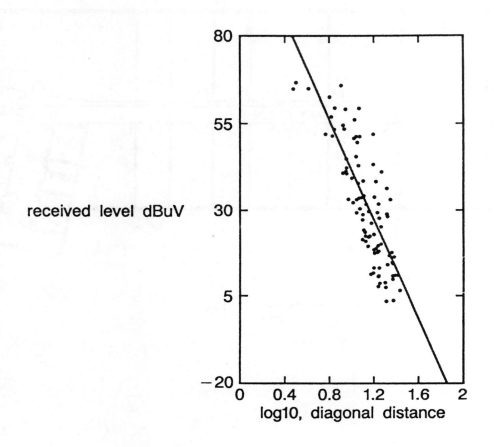

received level dBuV

Antenna Results

Uncorrected for Floor Attenuation

Figure 4a

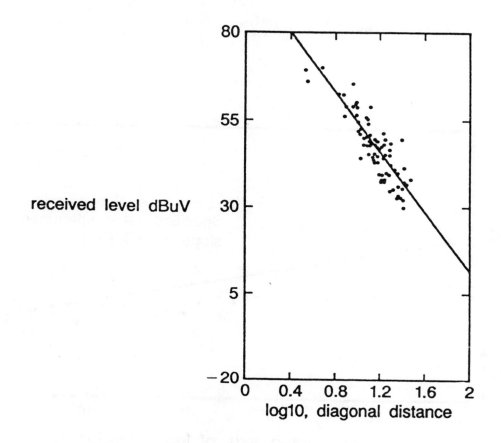

received level dBuV

Antenna Results

Corrected for Floor Factor = 5.4 dB

Figure 4b

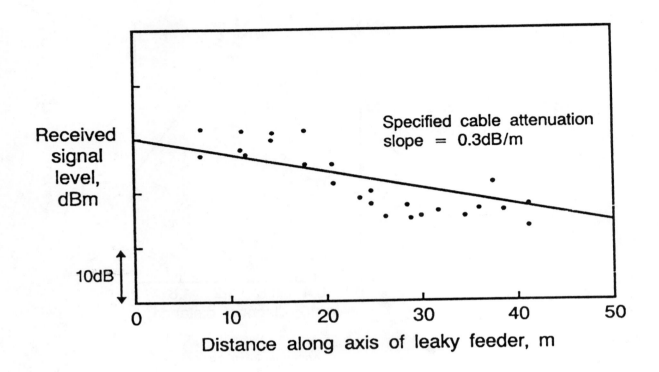

Longitudinal Signal Variation

Figure 5

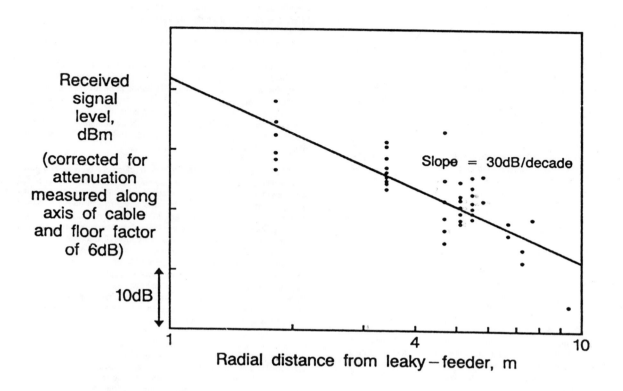

Radial Signal Variation

Figure 6

TECHNOLOGIES FOR WIRELESS INDOOR NETWORKS

Kaveh Pahlavan

Associate Professor, Electrical Engineering Department

Worcester Polytenic Institute

Worcester, MA 01609

Abstract

This paper addresses the existing and growing demands for wireless local area network (WLLAN) for application in offices and manufacturing floors. Similarities of these networks with mobile radio, cordless phones, packet radio, and data radio are discussed; and the radio frequency (RF) and infrared (IR) communication technologies are examined as candidates for implementation of such networks. For RF networks, characteristics of the indoor radio channel for radio wave propagation are given. Data rate limitations for the standard radio modems and spread spectrum modems are assessed, methods to increase the data rate are introduced, and practicality of various multiple access techniques are discussed. For IR networks, effects of ambient lights and the data rate limitations for diffused and directed beam optical signals are presented and examples of the architecture of the network are given. Finally, various systems are compared in terms of supportable number of users within a cell of a cellular architecture, cost efficiency, mobility, detectability, and range.

Introduction

Recently, application of wireless indoor networks for manufacturing floors and office environments has attracted tremendous attention [1,5]. The main motivations for using such networks are to provide communication with mobile terminals (such as AGVs, mobile robots, and portable phones) and to avoid expensive installation and relocation costs of the wired LANs [1,4]. Researchers both in the industrial laboratories and educational institutions are studying the behavior of such networks as a potential candidate to replace (either completely of partially) the existing wired networks in manufacturing floors and office environments. The behavior of radio/optics wave propagation, the architecture of the networks, and the performance of various transmission techniques are under study. This paper presents a tutorial overview of the existing work in wireless indoor networks.

Wireless communications in an indoor environment could be carried out by the use of radio frequencies (RF) or optical infrared (IR) radiation [1,4]. Infrared and radio signals both employ electromagnetic waves, with optical frequencies ranging approximately 10^5 GHz, and practical radio signals at frequencies below 300 Ghz range. The depth of penetration of electromagnetic waves is inversely proportional to the frequency. As a result, IR signals can not pass through most objects while radio signals can. The choice between IR or RF wireless office information networks depends on the building architecture, construction materials, and the purpose the network is designed for. For example, for office buildings with metal partitioning or offices located in or close to manufacturing floors with extremely high power man-made noise at radio frequencies, IR networks are more attractive. For an office building with many small offices, signals must pass through the walls; and radio networks are more appropriate. The IR equipment is less expensive than the RF equipment. However, the RF technology at the present time is more mature and well understood.

To provide full coverage of the building and to fight the data rate limitations for wireless indoor modems, the architecture of a wireless indoor network must be cellular (regardless of the technology). Otherwise, the number of terminals supported by wired LANs would be much higher than the wireless LANs (WLLAN). The size of the cell and the method used for interconnecting the cells depend on the technology used for transmission. For IR wireless networks, a cell must be limited to a room; in RF wireless networks, the definition of the cell depends on the frequency band and maximum power allowed by federal regulations. Interconnection between the cells could be provided by either wires or radio signals, and if line of sight between two cells exists, a high power narrow beam optical signal may be used.

Indoor Radio Networks

The dependence of a wireless system on effective radio propagation demands measurement and modeling of the radio wave propagation to characterize the communication channel. The results of these measurements and modelings are used for assessing feasibility of different network architectures and transmission techniques.

CHARACTERISTICS OF INDOOR RADIO CHANNEL

Most of the recent measurements for indoor radio communications have been performed in or around 1 GHz [1,5]. From a technical standpoint, frequencies around 1 GHz seems to be the best for indoor communications. Higher frequencies have difficulty passing through the walls (for a few tens of GHz, the signal is almost confined in the room). In lower frequencies, available bands are more restricted, longer antennas and wider separations are required, and the interference from high power ignition systems is high.

Radio propagation through indoor channels is very complex because usually the direct shortest path between transmitter and receiver is blocked by walls, ceilings, or other objects. There are many paths with different power which transfer radio waves from transmitter to the receiver. The difference in the arrival time of the signal from various paths is proportional to the length of the path and consequently, the size and the architecture of the office and location of the objects around transmitter and receiver. The strength of such paths depends on the attenuation caused by passing through or reflection from various objects in the path. A deterministic analysis of propagation mechanisms in such an environment is not feasible and one has to determine statistics of the channel parameters. The statistics of channel parameters are obtained from measurements collected from various locations of the transmitter and the receiver in a building.

Channel characteristics required for narrowband and wideband signaling are different. For narrow band signals, such as cordless telephone or low speed data, the emphasis is on the statistics of the received power while for high data rates or inherently wideband communications, such as spread spectrum, the multipath characteristics of the channel are also important. The first step in this line is to measure the so called power distance law to determine power requirements for the communications. If the channel is susceptible to fading, the fading characteristics of the channel should be measured. Then, one needs to determine the coherent bandwidth of the channel which provides a rough estimate for the maximum supportable data transmission rate for narrowband signaling over that channel. The coherent bandwidth is the inverse of the measured multipath delay spread of the channel. Finally, a statistical model and a computer simulation should be developed for the channel as a tool to analyze the performance of various communication techniques and network architectures.

In indoor radio, one of the earliest statistical measurements of the amplitude fluctuations have been reported in [6] for cordless telephone application. The statistics in this experiment were collected by fixing the transmitter and moving the receiver in various locations in a multi-room office environment. The result of these measurements suggests that the fluctuations of the amplitude of the received signal for various locations in an office building form samples of a random variable with Rayleigh distribution. This conclusion is confirmed by some others [7] while some recent works suggest a Rician distribution [8].

The received signal power is inversely proportional to the distance between transmitter and receiver, raised to a certain power. In free space radio propagations, this power factor is two. The power factor inside the office depends on the architecture of the office and the material used for the building. The available intra-office measurements for the center frequencies of around 1 GHz reports power factors even smaller than two, up to values as large as six [6,7]. The smaller values correspond to hallways which act as waveguides for radio propagations, and the large values are related to buildings with metalized partitioning.

The first multipath delay spread measurement within buildings were reported recently in [9,10] and followed in [7]. The multipath delay spread is dependent on room size and the material used for construction of the building; and if there are windows, the relative position of the building in the neighborhood. Multipath delay spreads as high as 400ns for indoor areas larger than a hundred meters, and as low as 30ns for rooms smaller than ten meters have been reported [11].

Statistical channel modeling for indoor data communications is in its early stages. The only attempt made so far is the one recently reported in [7], which is based on a limited data base with eight rooms in a building. While confirming the power-distance law and measuring the multipath delay spread, this work suggests a statistical model for the channel. The model suggested in [7] is based on a limited data base and uses several assumptions for simplicity which harms the validity of the model for some applications.

RADIO TRANSMISSION TECHNIQUES FOR WLLANs

The wireless media has its own limitations in supporting the data rate and these limitations are reduced if more complex transmission techniques are employed. Research in transmission involves performance analysis for various modulation, coding, and receiver structures to determine the optimum transmission scheme to support the maximum data rate for the media. Either average probability of error or probability of outage are normally used as performance criteria for communications over fading multipath channels. Probability of outage is the fraction of time in which the probability of error exceeds a given threshold. For indoor communications, probability of outage represents the percentage of locations in a large area for which a fixed terminal experiences a higher error rate than the given threshold. For portable terminals, it represents the percentage of time the user experiences an error rate above a certain level, while moving in a large area.

With narrowband signaling and single diversity, the maximum supportable data rate for QPSK modulation is in the order of fractions of a percent of the coherent bandwidth of the channel (around few hundred Kbps). This data rate can be improved if the receiver uses diversified reception, adaptive equalization, multi-rate modems, or multi-amplitude/phase modulation and coding techniques. If dual or quadruple diversities are used, the theoretical data rate can improve by an order of magnitude [11,23]. However, n indoor radio channels providing independent diversified channels are practically hard, and the predicted data rates can not be achieved in practice. Adaptive equalizers can improve the data rate limitations over fading multipath channels by another order of magnitude [24]. The decision feedback equalizer has been shown to have a superior performance over various fading multipath channels such as the troposcatter, HF, and microwave LOS. The drawback in this case is that the implementation of a DFE modem at high data rate is expensive with the current technology. Another simple system to improve the data rate is the use of a multirate modem. These modems have two data rates, and as the situation in the channel deteriorates, the lower data rate is used. It can be shown that the theoretical maximum throughput of such modems in fading multipath indoor radio channels is an order of magnitude higher than for one data rate modems [39]. The application of multi-amplitude and coding techniques (such as QAM and TCM) over voice band channels has been extremely successful [38]. Using these techniques, the data rate of the voice band modems has increased form 2400 bps to 19.2 kbps which is approximately another order of magnitude improvement for the data rate. The implementational issues, such as timing and phase recovery for radio channels are more complicated than for voice-band telephone channels. Besides, at high data rates of the radio modems, implementation of sophisticated techniques, such as trellis code modulation, is expensive with the existing technology.

In addition to standard narrowband modulation techniques, wideband spread spectrum communications has attracted considerable attention for indoor communications. Recently, application of spread spectrum technology for non-government users has been encouraged by the FCC [20], making this technology more interesting for indoor applications. Spread spectrum is resistant to intentional and unintentional interference (e.g. caused by machinery in manufacturing environments). Spread spectrum use can reduce the effects of multipath caused by reflections from the walls and, consequently, can increase the mobility of the terminal or telephone sets. The low spectral power density of spread spectrum increases the possibility of overlay with certain existing systems and reduces the sensitivity to health related issues in high-power transmission. Spread spectrum improves interception resistance and hence, traffic privacy. The general problem with this type of communications is that it requires much larger bandwidth than standard systems; thus it reduces the potential number of users for a given bandwidth. To overcome this problem, it is possible to use code division multiple access (CDMA) [4]. In CDMA, all terminals use the same bandwidth at the same time, a set of orthogonal codes are assigned to the users and each user is identified with a unique code. Work on the behavior of CDMA systems in indoor environments [1,21,22] has been concentrated on the transmission side, which evaluates the probability of error versus SNR for a given number of users and code lengths.

There are several interesting facts about the spread spectrum in fading multipath indoor channels. In CDMA spread spectrum, other users are the major source of the noise. As a result, the number of supportable users in a given bandwidth will increase if the requirement on the error rate decreases. For lower error rates, the channel can be disturbed with more noise. Consequently, more users can exist in the channel at the same time. The spread spectrum systems can take advantage of the multipath in the channel and use it as a source of internal diversity to improve its performance (increase the number of users); while in traditional communication techniques, multipath always degrades the performance. The theoretical data rate per terminal for a spread spectrum system in fading multipath channels is around the coherent bandwidth of the channel. However, these data rates require unreasonably high bandwidth. The practical data rate limitation for spread spectrum communications is due to the bandwidth availability rather than the amount of multipath spread. In a given bandwidth, the data rate could be adjusted by employing different code lengths. For example, for the 25 MHz bandwidth assigned by the FCC, a code of length 255 provides a data rate of 100 Kbps while a code of length 127 can provide 200 Kbps per terminal. The major problem in spread spectrum communication is the low bandwidth efficiency for the fading channels. This can be improved by using multiple codes per station in an M-ary signaling scheme [26].

NETWORK ARCHITECTURE AND RELATED ISSUES

The details of the architecture of the wireless networks for manufacturing floors and office environments is unknown at the present time. To develop an understanding about the existing issues for investigation, it is helpful to look at the existing radio systems. There are two classes of systems: the preliminary services for indoor applications and radio networks for outdoor use.

The preliminary services for indoor applications are cordless phones (for limited number of short range voice) and the so called data radio [1] (an introductory service for local wireless data terminals). Cordless phone and data radio are primitive wireless connections (not networks) which by no means exploit the existing opportunities for wireless indoor networking.

Modulation for cordless phones is analog FM, and the multiple accessing technique is FDM. These cordless phones are not a part of an integrated system, and each phone operates as an independent low power terminal with limited range. The current frequency available in the U.S. supports up to ten duplex channels, and there is no available strategy to avoid simultaneous usage of two terminals at the same time in nearby locations (except that some manufacturers have a sort of automatic checking for free channels). As a result, even if less than ten users are in the system, they may interfere with each other. This limitation on the number of simultaneous users may not have a very serious impact on a single family residential area. However, for the office environment and manufacturing floors where a number of office workers may use their telephones at the same time, the current cordless telephone system is impractical. In addition, the cordless phones are limited to the connection between handset and base unit, and indoor wiring is required to connect the base unit to the telephone network. If the connection is used for data communication, it has the limitation of all voice band data communication modem, which restrict the data rates to below 19.2 kbps [38]. In spite of these severe limitations, 20 million of these cordless phones have been sold in the U.S. by mid-1986 [5], which indicates the extensive demand for wireless resources for indoor applications.

Data radio systems are designed for transferring data between various terminals. In these systems, one or a few digital radio channels are shared on a contention basis among a number of terminals. A radio channel is assigned between two users after an introductory hand shaking process, and after data transfer is terminated, the channel is released for other users. These terminals use relatively high power to cover an area of up to several miles, and the high power raises questions of health hazards. These services have limited data transmission capabilities (currently compatible with voice band modems) and are not suitable for longer periods of connection for voice communications. Since they are designed for high power application, the frequency reuse in an office environment can not be applied; as a result, the system can not support many users. A preferred way would be low power transmission in a cellular architecture, which can support more users.

The existing radio networks are mobile radio networks (exclusively designed for voice communications) and packet radio (designed basically for data communications), both for outdoor applications. In the mobile radio networks, the existing systems are cellular; while in the packet radio environment, access to the remote terminals is by using multi-hop networks [12]. In mobile radio, the current analog FM modulation systems use FDMA, while the trend in the future is toward digital modulation with TDMA. In packet radio, spread spectrum is the preferred transmission technique, and the access to the channel is through contention based algorithms, such as ALOHA, CSMA/CD, and BTMA (busy tone multiple access) [13].

The difference in modulation and multiple accessing techniques arises from the fact that each of these networks are designed for either basic data or voice. In the voice communications, the ratio of the average to peak packet arrival rate is small, the volume of information is high, and quality requirement on transmission is low (packet loss of 1% has no significant effect on the quality of the voice). As a result, bandwidth efficient narrowband modulation techniques and TDMA or FDMA are more attractive for voice dominated networks such as mobile radio. The data packets are bursty, and the requirement on the quality of transmission is higher than voice. As a result, more reliable transmission (spread spectrum) with contention based multiple access techniques (such as ALOHA, CSMA, or BTMA) are more attractive for primarily data oriented networks such as packet radio. For indoor networks primarily designed for voice users to connect to the telephone network, a cellular TDMA and narrow band communications is interesting. However, for a WLLAN, the architecture is not known and it requires further studies. One possible architecture for an integrated voice data network using polling techniques is described in [26]. In this architecture, voice packets are served as they arrive, while the data packets are kept in a queue. The time is divided into frames and each frame is divided into slots. The length of the frame is selected to provide a maximum of 100-200 msec delay between packets of each slot. The slots are divided between voice and data packets. The number of voice slots is determined so that the voice packets can not suffer more than a 1% loss. The transmission technique is a double rate modem. It is shown that in an ideal condition for two order of diversity this system can support 65 voice users with 6,900 packets of data per second.

Given the variety of multiple accessing techniques used in networks which are similar to wireless networks in manufacturing floors and office environments, one can realize the demand for a serious study of the behavior of various multiple access techniques and network architectures for indoor applications. Besides, particular issues such as connectivity and security have to be addressed in the design of such networks.

Recently, some works have been initiated to address the structure of indoor networks [14,15] and the performance analysis of the multiple accessing techniques in fading multipath indoor channels [16,19].

IR Networks In Office Environment

Several features of IR communications are well suited for wireless office networks. Transmitter and receiver for IR systems require light emitting diodes (LED) and photo sensitive diodes. These diodes are inexpensive as compared with RF equipment and cost compatible with wires regardless of the installation cost. IR does not interfere with existing RF systems, and is not subject to FCC regulations. The IR signal does not penetrate the walls, providing privacy within the office area. The only way for IR signals to be detected outside the office is through the windows, which can be covered with a curtain or a shade. In addition to privacy, this feature of IR systems allows concurrent usage of similar systems in neighboring offices without any mutual interference. Therefore, in a cellular architecture, all units can be identical, as opposed to RF connections in which the center frequency of neighboring cells has to be different. In an IR network, terminals within a cell communicate with a node or satellite installed on the ceiling, and these nodes are interconnected to the rest of the network with wires, cables, radio, or fiber optics lines [27,29]. The cell could be a smaller office or a part of a large open office, depending on the architecture of the building.

IR communication is dominating the low speed remote control market, and is available for cordless phones [30] and connections between keyboard and terminal in personal computers [31]. However, for wireless office networks, the successful applications of IR networks need further work. The major problems for IR in wireless networks are its data rate limitations, extensive power fluctuation, and the interference from ambient lights. In particular, a reliable multiple access technique for IR systems to counteract the effects of ambient lights and moving objects close to the transmitter or receiver is not easily possible.

In the past decade, most of the efforts in wireless IR communication have been concentrated in diffused radiation. The advantage of this type of radiation is that it does not require a direct line of sight between the transmitter and the receiver [32]; the receiver can collect a transmitted signal through the reflection from the walls, ceiling, or other objects in the room. The problem in this type of radiation is that in simultaneous two-way communications, each receiver collects its own transmitted reflections which are stronger than the transmitted signal from the other end of the connection.

Recently, the application of directed optical beams for wireless office information networks has been investigated [29,33,34]. The advantage of this method is that it needs less optical power for communication and can handle bidirectional communications better than diffused radiation.

IR CHANNEL CHARACTERIZATION AND DATA RATE LIMITATIONS

There are three limitations for IR communications: interference from ambient lights, multipath characteristics of the channel for diffused communications, and transient time of the IR devices. The rise time and fall time of the inexpensive LEDs limit the data rate to 1 Mbps. Explanation of the other two limitations requires more detail which follows.

Effects of Ambient Lights

The infrared content of ambient light can interfere with IR radiations and, if extensive, can overload the receiver photo diode and drive it beyond its operating point. Three sources of ambient lights are the following: daylight, incandescent illumination, and fluorescent lamps--all of which potentially interfere with IR communications. Incandescent light, being rich in long wavelength (red) light, has the worst effect because its spectrum peak overlaps that of the GaAs diode spectral center.

Daylight contains less IR radiation, but if sunlight falls directly on the receiver lens, whether it is indoors or outdoors, it may jam an IR link. Fluorescent light normally has a small amount of IR radiation and during turn-on time emits a 120 Hz interfering baseband signal rich in harmonics which may reach up to 50 KHz [35].

The effects of ambient light are reduced by modulating the transmitted IR signal. The modulation carrier frequency should be at least several hundred KHz to avoid being compressed by fluctuation of the ambient light.

Multipath Characteristics

The above discussion implies that IR communication in an office environment is performed through many different paths. Thus, the IR propagations in an office environment form a multipath channel. The multipath causes a spread of the transmitted symbol in time, and the resulting intersymbol interference restricts the digital transmission rate. Similar to radio propagations, as room dimensions become larger, the multipath spread is increased, and the supportable bit rate is decreased. The theoretical limitation for the transmission rate is 260 Mb-meter/s [32]. Therefore, for a room with a length of 10 meters, one expects a transmission rate of 26 Mb/s, if multipath is the only cause of data rate limitation.

TRANSMISSION AND MULTIPLE ACCESSING

The most common applications of IR communication in the past decade include remote control, hearing aid and wireless audio systems, cordless phones, wireless connections between keyboards and terminals, and WLLANs. Various modulation and multiple access techniques have been examined for these systems with various manufacturers. Details of various modulation and multiple accessing techniques are provided in [4]. Here, an updated summary of these techniques is provided.

The AM/FM modulation is standard for continuous time audio and cordless phones. The FM modulated message is AM modulated over IR radiations. The bandwidth of the transmitted FM signal is normally around 50 KHz and carrier frequency is 95 KHz. Modulation over a carrier reduces the effects of low frequency ambient light interferences, and FM modulation eliminates the effects of extensive amplitude fluctuations of the channel in the information bearing signal. With this approach, up to nine channels are frequency division multiplexed for multichannel audio equipment [35]. Another modulation technique used for cordless phones is the pulse position modulation [30]; the sampling rate for this application is 9K samples/sec.

For low speed data, the remote control and wireless keyboard applications are very similar. In wireless keyboards, the number of alphabets are larger and are used more often than the remote control keys. For remote control, various modulation techniques have been examined by different manufacturers; the most commonly used modulation technique is on-off shift keying in which a tone is turned on and off to represent the ones and zeros in the data [36]. For wireless keyboards, digital pulse position modulation is used in which the RF pulse is transmitted at the beginning or at the middle of the bit duration interval to represent transmission of one or zero bits [31]. The 40 MHz carrier is almost a standard for both applications, and the data rate is below 2400 bps. The use of several remote control systems in one room is unnecessary. The wireless keyboards are used very close to the terminals with directed lights, and several of them can work in the same

room; therefore, in both cases, the multiple accessing technologies are not needed.

The WLLANs or wireless PBX systems require many users in a multiple access mode and much higher data rate for transmission of information. Therefore, more investigations are required for these applications. Pulse code modulation with data rate of 125 Kbps has been experimented with diffused IR high speed data communications [32]. In the vicinity of ambient lights, this system has shown a poor performance due to interference at low frequencies. To avoid this problem, the PSK system with a data rate of 64 Kbps has been examined in continuation of the same experiment. In a multiple access environment, the FSK modulation has been experimented with a CSMA environment. In this experiment, the up-link and down-link are separated in frequency domain. They use 200 KHz and 400 KHz center frequencies respectively, and data rates up to 100 Kbps have been supported by this system [37]. In this experiment, transponders are installed in the ceiling and communication between terminals and transponders is made with an IR link, while transponders are connected with fixed wires to the controller. The wired portion of the network, in this case, does not necessitate relocation expenses, and terminals can be relocated without cost. None of these systems have been successfully marketed.

Recently, direct optical beams have been examined for wireless office communication. The multiple access technique in this system is CSMA, and the data rate supported by the system is 1 Mbps. The experimental IR networks are designed for data communication; and for voice, the single user cordless phone has been successful in some markets. Current direction of research in this area is toward higher order data rates, tens of Mbps, using directed beam optical signals.

Conclusions

Because of the increasing installation and relocation costs of the wired indoor equipment and the decreasing cost of wireless connections, offices and the manufacturing floors of the future are expected to include wireless networks. The wireless offices and manufacturing floors would provide new portable services and would improve the performance of existing networks. Both IR and RF are expected to influence future wireless indoor networks, with IR more for limited range and RF for larger range. A cellular architecture, in both cases, is expected to connect various equipment in different offices. The following table provides a comparison between different techniques.

References

1. K. Pahlavan, "Wireless Intra-Office Networks", ACM Trans. on Office Inf. Sys., Jan. 1988.

2. M. Marcus, P. Ferert, and K. Pahlavan, "The Wireless Office", MIT Communication Form, Sept. 1985.

3. K. Pahlavan, "Wireless Intra-Office Communications", invited lecture, IEEE Commun. Thy. Workshop, April 1987.

4. K. Pahlavan, "Wireless Communications for Office Information Networks", IEEE Comm. Mag., pp. 19-27, June 1985.

5. D.C. Cox, "Universal Digital Portable Radio Communications", Proceedings of the IEEE, April 1987.

6. S.E. Alexander, "Radio Propagation within Buildings at 900 MHz", Proc. of ICAP, pp. 177-180, 1983.

7. A.M. Saleh and R.A. Valenzuela, "A Statistical Model for Indoor Multipath Propagation", IEEE JSAC, pp. 128-137, Feb. 1987.

8. R.J.C. Bultitude and S.A. Mahmmoud, "Estimation of the Indoor 800/900 MHZ Digital Radio Channel Performance Characteristics Using Results from Radio Propagation Measurements", Proceedings of the IEEE ICC, June 1987.

9. D.M.J. Devasirvatham, "Time Delay Spread Measurements of Wideband Radio Systems Within a Building", Electronics Letters, pp. 949-950, November 1984.

10. D. Devasirvatham, "Time Delay Spread Measurement of 850 MHz Radio Wave in Building Environment", Proceedings of IEEE Globecom, pp. 32.1.1-32.1, Dec. 1985.

11. J.H. Winters and Y.S. Yeh, "On the Performance of Wideband digital Radio Transmission Within Building Using Diversity", Proceedings of Globecom, pp. 32.5.1-6, Dec. 1985.

12. F. Tobagi, "Modeling and Performance Analysis of Multihop Packet Radio Networks", Proceedings of the IEEE, Jan. 1987.

13. IEEE Proceedings, Special issue in packet radio, Jan. 1987.

14. E.S. Chien, D.J. Goodman, and J.E. Russel, "Cellular Access Digital Network (CADN): Wireless Access to Networks of the Future", IEEE Comm. Soc. Mag., June 1987.

15. A.S. Acampora and J.S. Winters, "System Applications for Wireless Indoor Communications", IEEE Comm. Soc. Mag., Aug. 1987.

16. B. Ramamurthi, A.A. Saleh, and D.J. Goodman, "Perfect Capture ALOHA for Local Radio Communications", IEEE JSAC, June 1987.

17. D.J. Goodman and A.M. Saleh, "Local ALOHA Radio Communications with Capture and Packet buffers", Proc. Globecom, pp. 32.4.1-7, December

18. R. Ganesh, "Multiple Accessing in Local Area ALOHA Networks in the Presence of Capture", M.S. Thesis, WPI, June 1987.

19. R. Ganesh and K. Pahlavan, "Multiple Accessing in Local Area ALOHA Networks in the Presence of Capture", Proceedings of 1987 conference on Information Science and Systems, John Hopkins University, Baltimore, MD, March 1987.

20. M.J. Marcus, "Recent U.S. Regulatory Decisions on Civil Uses of Spread Spectrum", Proceedings of IEEE Globecom, pp. 16.6.1-3, Dec. 1985.

21. M. Kavehrad and P. McLane, "Performance of Low-Complexity Channel Coding and Diversity for Spread Spectrum in Indoor, Wireless Communication", BSTJ, pp. 1927-1965, October 1985.

22. K. Pahlavan, "Spread Spectrum for Wireless Local Networks", Proceedings of IEEE PCCC, Feb. 1987.

23. T. Sexton and K. Pahlavan, "Effects of Multi-Cluster Delay Spectrum on Wireless Indoor Communications", Proceedings of 1987 conference on Information Science and Systems, John Hopkins University, Baltimore, MD, March 1987.

24. T. Sexton and K. Pahlavan, "Delay Densities and Adaptive Equalization of Indoor Radio Channels", Proceedings of IEEE MILCOM, Nov. 1987.

25. M. Chase and K. Pahlavan, "Spread Spectrum Multiple Access Performance of Orthogonal Codes in Fading Multipath Indoor Channels", Proceedings of IEEE MILCOM, Nov 1987.

26. K. Zhang and K. Pahlavan, "An Integrated Voice/Data System for Wireless Local Area Networks", Proceedings of Annual conference in Information Sciences and Systems, Princeton, 1988.

27. F.R. Gfeller, "Infrared Microbroadcasting for In-House Data Communications", IBM Technical Disclosure Bulletin, pp. 4043-4046, 1982.

28. R. Mednick, "Office Information Network: An Integrated LAN", Proceedings of IEEE Globecom, pp. 15.2.1-5, Dec 1985.

29. C.S. Yen, and R.D. Crawford, "The Use of Direct Optical Beams in Wireless Computer Communications", Proceedings of IEEE Globecom, pp. 39.1.1-5, Dec 1985.

30. E. Braun and S. Schon, "A Cordless Infrared Telephone", Telecom Report, Vol. 3, No. 2, pp. 83-86, 1982.

31. B. LaReau, "IR Unit Runs Computer Remotely", Elect. Week, November 12, 1984.

32. F.R. Gfeller and U. Bapst, "Wireless In-house Data Communication Via Diffuse Infrared Radiation", IEEE Proc., pp. 1474-1486, 1979.

33. Y. Nakata, et. al., "In-House Wireless communication Systems Using Infrared Radiations", Proc. of the Int. Conf. on Comp. Comm., pp. 333-338, Sydney, 1984.

34. T.S. Chu and M.J. Gans, "High Speed Infrared Local Wireless Communication", IEEE Comm. Soc. Mag., Aug 1987, pp. 4-10.

35. H.A. Ankerman, "Transmission of Audio Signals by Infrared Light Carrier", SMPTE Journal, pp. 834-837, 1980.

36. S. Ciarcia, "Use Infrared Communication for Remote Control", Byte Pub. Inc., April 1982.

37. F.R. Gfeller, H.R. Miller, and P. Vettiger, "Infrared Communications for In-House Applications", IEEE Compcon, pp. 132-138, Washington, 1979.

38. K. Pahlavan and J.L. Holsinger, "Voice Band Data Communication, A Historical Review: 1919-1987", IEEE Comm. Soc. Mag., Jan 1988. This is a test program for the folder system.

39. A. Acampora and J. Winters, "A Wireless Network for Wide-Band Indoor Communications", IEEE JSAC, June 1987.

Comparison Between Radio and IR Systems				
Technique	D F / I R	D B / I R	R F	R F / S S
Data rate	< 1 Mbps	< 50 Mbps	.1 - 10 Mbps	100 kbps (50 terminals)
Cost efficiency	Low	Medium	Medium	Medium
Mobility	Good	Non	Better	Best
Detectability	Non	Non	Some	Little
Range	Low	Low	Medium	Medium

TABLE 1

TEC-11

NEW COMPUTER ARCHITECTURES

Michael W. Rolund - Chairperson
Department Head
Data Systems Group
AT&T
1100 East Warrenville Road
Naperville, Illinois 60566

ABSTRACT

Despite the consolidation of the computer industry around a few "standard" architectures, especially IBM and DEC, the pace of architectural innovation has actually intensified over the past several years. Notable efforts to exceed the traditional limits on computer performance fall into two broad categories: (a) parallel processing, including vector processing as a subset; and (b) RISC, or Reduced Instruction Set Computers. This seminar provides an overview of recent developments in parallel processing, vector processing, and RISC.

Omri Serlin   -- ITOM International
NEW COMPUTER ARCHITECTURES

Omri Serlin
Head
ITOM International
P.O. Box 1415
Los Altos, California 94022-0222

ABSTRACT

The quest for enhanced performance in computer systems has recently focused on two diverse (but not mutually exclusive) approaches. RISC (reduced instruction set computer) is one such approach; it seeks to gain speed by simplifying the architecture of a given processor. Parallelism takes on many forms, including pipelining (employed in vector processors); replication of functional units (as in Long Instruction Word or LIW machines); and a variety of multi-processor arrangements.

RISC

Origins and Current Status of RISC

Although the term RISC was coined in 1980 at U.C. Berkeley, earlier manifestations of some aspects of RISC philosophy were incorporated in the IBM 801 project (which strongly influenced the architecture of the microprocessor in the IBM RT/PC). The MIPS (Microprocessor without Interlocking Pipe Stages) project at Stanford U. is also regarded as an early RISC development; it directly influenced the chip set from the MIPS Computer company.

Some pre-1980 designs are now recognized as having followed some RISC tenets; among those are the CDC 6000 line, designed by Seymour Cray, which was one of the earliest to employ the "load-store architecture" (see below).

Among other commercial systems claiming RISC features are the recently-announced Sun 4 models, which are based on a microprocessor dubbed SPARC (Scalable Processor ARChitecture). The key features of SPARC closely resemble the Berkeley RISC ideas. The Hewlett Packard Spectrum project used RISC principles as the basis for a family of minicomputers now used as the high-end of the 3000 series of commercial machines, running the proprietary MPE operating system; and the 9000 series of technical systems, which use HP-UX, a Unix-based operating system.

RISC claims have also been made by minicomputer makers Pyramid Technology and Ridge Computers. The Motorola 88000 microprocessor family, due for initial shipments late this year, combines RISC ideas with parallel processing concepts to achieve very high projected performance.

What's Wrong with CISC?

RISC does not denote any specific architecture; rather, it was proposed as a counter-philosophy to the prevailing computer design ideas, which for contrast are termed CISC (complex instruction set computer). The IBM 370 architecture, DEC VAX line, Motorola 68000 and Intel 80X86 families are widely regarded as prime examples of CISC. An often-cited "extremely-CISC" case was the Intel 432 microprocessor, a later version of which is at the heart of a product line soon to be announced by BiiN, the joint venture of Intel and Germany's Siemens.

Patterson and his students argued that the CISC mind set developed at a time when memory was very slow compared to the processor's logic. Good performance depended on minimizing the number of memory accesses, by including as many functions as possible in each instruction fetched.

Key RISC Ideas

The fundamental idea in RISC is to obtain performance by reducing the complexity of the instruction set the CPU hardware must execute. The hardware is to support only a small subset of the most commonly used and simplest instructions. Functions that are deemed too complex (e.g., any register instruction that requires more than one cycle), or that are encountered infrequently, are to be delegated to software (e.g., HP's millicode).

RISC proponents argue that the decoding of complex instructions and computation of complex addressing modes penalize all instructions. Complex instructions often are ignored by the compilers; sometimes a sequence of simple instructions can accomplish the same function quicker. Well-known examples of this exist in the IBM System/370 and DEC VAX architectures.

Limiting a processor's hardware to support just a small set of instructions with simple addressing modes and a minimum of side-effects results in a small, regular control structure, which is critically important in microprocessors, where "real-estate" (chip area) considerations are paramount.

High-level language compilers for a RISC machine are expected to make up for the simplicity of the hardware by creating software subroutines for the more complex functions, and by optimizing the use of registers. In some designs (e.g., MIPS, Multiflow), the compiler is aware of the CPU's pipeline characteristics, and generates code that will never result in a pipeline conflict. This simplifies the hardware design by eliminating the need to use hardware interlocks. The compiler may also be entrusted with the explicit management of caches, again simplifying the hardware design.

In order to reduce memory accesses, RISC designs typically employ a register-intensive, "load-store" architecture. In such designs, all computations are expected to be performed between registers; only explicit load and store instructions are allowed access to memory. This is in contrast to conventional, CISC designs, in which virtually all computational instructions assume one operand is in memory.

If a large enough register bank is present (some machines, e,g, Pyramid, offer hundreds), operands could be brought in once, and manipulated several times, before results need to be sent back to memory; this reduces memory accesses, and takes good advantage of the speed of register-to-register operations. The cpai (cycles per average instruction) of a well-designed RISC machine should come much closer to 1 than is possible with CISC designs of comparable cost.

In order to put to good use the wait time entailed in memory accesses, most RISC designs support variations of the "delayed branch" concept, where the time slot following the memory access is available for executing another instruction (a rudimentary form of parallelism). The compiler is responsible for finding an appropriate instruction above the branch (or memory access) that can be moved to this time slot.

Some RISC designs employ overlapping "windows" (another form of parallelism). In such designs, each procedure can be allocated a private register set from the general register bank. Some registers in this set are visible to both calling and called procedures. This permits very rapid procedure calls, since registers typically needn't be saved, and parameters can be passed in the window without actual data transfers. However, some have argued that this feature can also be implemented in conventional architectures, and hence isn't a logical part of the RISC philosophy. A large register bank also creates a problem when registers must be saved and restored, as happens on context switches, or when more procedures are called than there are register sets.

Is RISC Worth It?

Taking advantage of the lack of a standard definition of the term, virtually all new computers and microprocessors introduced in the past two years or so have claimed RISC heritage. In doing this, they attempt to capitalize on the mystical implications of the RISC design philosophy, often ignoring the only issue that really matters: performance.

RISC designs to date have not demonstrated conclusively that they result in a dramatic enough performance advantage over conventional designs. Such a clear-cut advantage is essential, since every RISC design creates a major software dislocation. Mips figures quoted for some RISC machines are impressive, but they are not necessarily comparable to mips measurements on conventional architectures where the average instruction presumably accomplishes more work.

Even when the measurements are based on equivalent work, doubts remain due to the very sloppy ways in which manufacturers report benchmark results: they usually neglect to specify completely the environment, thus making it impossible to evaluate competing claims. For instance, mips claims obtained with such simplistic, CPU-bound tests as the Dhrystone benchmark are highly-suspect, not just due to the various existing versions of this benchmark, but also because it is so small that it can easily fit within the cache of most modern systems, bypassing all memory references.

Worse still, mips figures obtained with CPU-intensive benchmarks give no clue to the multi-user performance of the system, where the efficiency of disk I/O and the operating system's scheduling mechanisms usually are far more critical than raw CPU power. Mips figures obtained by assuming the VAX 11/780 equals 1 mips are overstated by more than a factor of two: the 11/780 actually rates 0.47 mips. (See Major Performance Discrepancy Discovered, *The Serlin Report on Parallel Parallel Processing*, No. 7, December 1987).

Arguments Against RISC

There is no general agreement on what constitutes a true RISC design; so far, no two designs claiming RISC heritage are alike in their instruction sets and other features. For instance, not all RISC proponents have accepted the overlapped register windows and the delayed branch features as essential elements of the RISC concept.

The most fundamental argument against RISC is that computer history has shown that software development is more error-prone than hardware; so moving complexity to the software seems a bad idea.

A semi-conceptual proof that RISC doesn't work well is that no RISC machine to date has been able to delegate to software the execution of floating point or decimal arithmetic operations, without incurring a substantial performance penalty. RISC systems sold in technical environments typically add conventional (CISC) arithmetic hardware.

Two attempts to measure the value of the RISC design philosophy separate from such unrelated factors as compiler efficiency have been reported. (See Computers, Complexity and Controversy, *IEEE Computer*, September, 1985; and And Now a Case for More Complex Instruction Sets, *IEEE Computer*, September, 1987. Both found little tangible benefits to the RISC ideas.

Negative Impact of RISC

A rather negative outcome of RISC has been the re-emergence of proprietary architectures. For several years now the industry seemed to be heeding an overwhelming users' desire for standards, exemplified by the rise of UNIX; the success of the "single family" concept pushed by DEC; and by the earlier success of the IBM 360-370 architectural standard. In the microprocessor arena, the Motorola 68000 and Intel X86 families have succeeded in establishing common architectures that have benefitted enormously computer manufacturers, ISVs, 3rd party add-on vendors, and users. Consider, for example, the success of the Intel-based IBM PCs and clones.

The fascination some vendors have acquired for RISC is in direct opposition to this trend. Each RISC design is unique, proprietary, and incompatible with any other system, RISC or CISC.

This has already created massive dislocations for at least one vendor. The difficulties HP has been having in porting its entire software arsenal from the HP 3000 line to the Spectrum is a good example. Despite a well-thought-out migration strategy, HP could not completely isolate its current HP 3000 users from the architectural differences in the new line.

Another negative impact of the preoccupation with RISC is that it has diverted designers' attention to the relatively-simple problem of developing new instruction sets, while ignoring more important (and more difficult) issues, especially the design of multiprocessor systems. Multiprocessor systems offer rich opportunities for innovation; for example, in assuring cache coherence; in quantifying the benefits of message-based vs. procedure based operating systems; and in devising effective distributed systems. None of these problems are getting any attention from designers who are busy re-inventing instruction repertoires.

CISC is Catching Up

Meanwhile, CISC is catching up, invalidating one of the favorite contentions of RISC partisans: the argument that, once the initial step-function improvement in RISC performance is realized, RISC would be able to at least maintain, if not expand, its lead over CISC designs forever. In particular, it was argued that RISC designs would be able to come close to 1 cpai (cycles per average instruction), while those based on CISC would remain entangled in multi-cycle cpai figures.

The reality is that, with the aid of pipelining, caches, and branch- prediction logic, CISC designs are rapidly narrowing the cpai gap vis.-a- vis. RISC. Edge Computer, which emulates the CISC design of the Motorola 68020, has broken the 2 cpai barrier and is competing head-on with the best of the RISCs. Of course, Edge is a multi-board design which is far more expensive than single-chip RISC microprocessors. But Intel for one has been dropping heavy hints that its next generation 486 microprocessor will come close to the 1 cpai goal, without giving up compatibility with the X86 CISC architecture.

Although commercial interest in RISC ideas is high, no specific RISC implementation has emerged as a credible alternative to the key existing architectural standards (IBM S/370, DEC VAX, Motorola 68000, Intel x86, and Cray). RISC-based machines are most likely to succeed as single-user workstation, where RISC disadvantages and software compatibility issues are currently less important.

PARALLEL PROCESSING

Applied to computer technology, the term "parallelism" implies some form of hardware duplication and concurrency of operations. Parallel designs today come in three main flavors:

o Interconnection of multiple, conventional processors
o Replication of functional units within a processor
o Pipelining and chaining of processor functional units

Multiple Processors

Architectures employing SIMD (Single Instruction stream, Multiple Data streams) and MIMD (Multiple Instruction streams, Multiple Data streams) organizations are an increasingly important form of parallelism. Examples of SIMD systems include the Connection Machine (from Thinking Machines Corp.) and the Matrix systolic array computer from Saxpy.

MIMD parallelism is used to achieve one of two aims. One is improved system throughput, i.e. the ability to process more unrelated tasks per unit time by assigning each task to a separate processor. This is typical of commercial environments, especially on-line transaction processing. The other objective is to reduce the run time of a long-executing task, such as those typically encountered in scientific and engineering applications, by dividing it into a number of sub-tasks that can be executed concurrently.

Examples of MIMD architectures designed for throughput improvement are the IBM 3090 series, the DEC 8800 and 6200 series, the Tandem and Stratus systems, among many others. MIMD architectures that can be used for both throughput and run-time improvements include the systems from Sequent, Encore, and Elxsi. MIMD architectures specialized for run-time improvement include the hypercube systems from Intel; the multi-stage network based Butterfly and Monarch systems from BBN; and the tree-network based, relational database machine from Teradata.

Granularity is one way to describe the nature of a parallel system. The more lines of code each processor must execute in order to minimize the communications overhead, the more "coarse grained" is the system (or the application). At the logical extremes, systems designed for greater throughput by processing concurrently multiple, unrelated tasks may be thought of as very-coarse-grained; while LIW and vector machines (see below) may be thought of as fine-grain parallel systems.

Multiprocessor systems can also be characterized by the nature of the interconnect mechanism. The most popular choices today are bus, multi-port memories, cross-bar, near-neighbor (e.g., hypercubes), and multi-stage shuffle network. Each has its own set of advantages and disadvantages. In general, bus and cross-bar interconnects are useful only when the number of interconnected elements (processors, memories) is small, say 20-30. Sequent, Encore, and Elxsi build such systems, using bus interconnect. In its FX series, Alliant Computer employs both bus and cross-bar, with up to 12 terminal processors and eight vector engines. Encore Computer is building for DARPA a 128-processor system using a clever, two-level bus scheme; and Evans & Sutherland Computer Division plans to use a cross-bar interconnect in its 128-processor parallel supercomputer.

In multi-port memory designs, each processor is physically attached by a separate bus to each memory bank. Logic built into the bank performs arbitration among conflicting concurrent requests. The cost of this scheme escalates very rapidly with the number of processors and memory banks; it is employed by all current supercomputers and most large mainframe computers.

Massively parallel systems, which employ hundreds or thousands of processors, typically use either the hypercube or the multi-stage shuffle interconnect schemes. The hypercube interconnect is used by Intel's iPSC, FPS T-Series, and the Connection Machine. Multi-stage schemes are used in BBN's Butterfly, and in IBM's RP3 and TF-1 experimental systems. Occasionally, other forms are employed: for example, Teradata's back-end database machine uses a binary tree network, in which each processing node attaches to at most three other nodes; Ametek's 2010 uses a planar interconnect, in which each processing element is attached to four immediate neighbors. This is also the preferred interconnect for Transputer-based multiprocessor designs; the basic Transputer microprocessor supports four communications channels for this purpose.

A key architectural characteristic of multiprocessor systems is the memory usage. In loosely-coupled or local memory systems, each processor owns its private memory and executes its own copy of the operating system and applications code; communications between processors is via messages. Loosely-coupled systems can admit a large number of processors (depending on the interconnect mechanism), and are fault-resistant in that one processor's failure need not affect others. Communications overhead is the key disadvantage of such systems. In tightly-coupled or global memory systems, all processors have access to a common memory system, and may execute the same copy of the operating system and applications.

Shared memory may be used as a very-fast interprocessor communications mechanism; having applications data accessible to all processors directly is another significant advantage. Tightly-coupled system are, however, more fragile in that a processor contaminating shared memory can bring down other processors or the entire system. Also, the number of processors sharing a common memory effectively is limited by the memory bandwidth as well as by the interconnect scheme.

Pipelining, Vectorization and Amdahl's Law

Pipelining is the key concept in vector processing, one of the most important current forms of parallelism, which is present in conventional supercomputers from Cray, ETA, NEC, Fujitsu/Amdahl; and in minisupers from Convex, Alliant, and SCS.

A pipelined functional unit, like a factory production line, performs an operation as a series of sub-tasks. Once the pipe is full, a complete result is produced on every clock, even though the complete operation may have required n clocks. A speed-up of n is thereby obtained. The longer the vector (array of data items to be processed), the more efficient pipelining becomes, because the pipe-fill overhead becomes relatively smaller.

While vector operations have been the staple of supercomputing since Cray started shipping in 1976, their ultimate usefulness is increasingly being questioned. A recent report found that, after years of optimizing for supercomputers, production codes at the Los Alamos and Livermore National Laboratories average only 60%-70% vectorization (meaning that 60%-70% of their arithmetic content can be processed using the vector facilities). This may appear at first blush to be a high proportion; in fact, it is a disappointing figure.

What makes it disappointing is Amdahl's Law, a tenet originally proposed in 1967 in a very loose form by Gene Amdahl, a designer of large-scale IBM machines and later the founder of Amdahl Corp., Trilogy Ltd., and Andor. Amdahl in effect observed that if a program contains, say, 40% code that cannot be parallelized in some form (the so called "junk" or serial code), then no matter how effective the parallelization facilities, the program will never run faster than 2.5 times its all-serial execution. Thus the substantial investment in specialized vector facilities doesn't begin to pay off until the percent of vectorization reaches into the 80%-90% range. The fact that few programs today exhibit such high vectorization levels encourages those who propose other approaches to parallelism, such as VLIW and dataflow systems.

Long Instruction Word (LIW)

Functional unit (FU) replication or proliferation is the key concept in the superminis from Floating Point Systems, Multiflow, and Cydrome/Prime; it is also present in the basic processor in the CDC Cyberplus system. The term Long Instruction Word (LIW) is an appropriate description of these approaches to parallelism. In these systems, the processor may contain several adder-subtractors, floating point units, address calculation units, and multiple memory read-write pipes. A fully-stuffed "long instruction" will have some operation for each of these FUs. Although the functional units in LIW machines are usually pipelined, the key speed-up comes from the system's ability to execute concurrently multiple unrelated operations. The compiler is responsible for scheduling the use of the multiple functional units.

Dataflow Machines

While there are those who regard multi-processor configurations as being "non-Von-Neumann", dataflow machines are really the only class of reasonably-practical parallel architectures that fall outside the classical or Von Neumann computer concepts.

The key idea in dataflow systems is to treat the user's application as a collection of operations (e.g., add, multiply) and operands. The order of execution is determined not by explicit instructions written down by the programmer, (as in conventional architectures); but rather by the availability of input operands. Operations are scheduled for execution whenever the operands they need have been produced by previous operations. The precedence relations specifying the order in which operations must occur are implicit in the programming language, such as Id.

The hardware to support such a concept basically consists of multiple functional units or processors, connected through a routing network in such a way that a result (called "token") produced at the output of any FU can be routed back into an input of any FU. The machine's control must determine, by examining each token, which subsequent operations are now enabled and should be scheduled.

Dataflow machines promise to extract a good deal more parallelism from user programs than is possible with conventional systems. The key disadvantage of such systems is that they require completely new programming languages; existing "dusty decks" cannot be processed by a dataflow machine.

At MIT, Arvind and others have developed a tagged-token dataflow machine concept, whose hardware realization is dubbed Monsoon. It also requires a new programming language, called Id. MIT would like industry partners to help fund the development of a miniature, four processor dataflow machine in the form of a plug-in board for a Sun workstation; followed by a more ambitious, 256-processor stand-alone Monsoon architecture machine.

Other dataflow designs have been realized in experimental hardware at Manchester University (U.K.), and at Japan's Electro-Technical Laboratory.

Performance of Parallel Systems

There is a substantial difference between peak theoretical performance and between "delivered" or sustained performance in parallel systems. Peak performance is computed assuming that all vector pipes and/or all processors in the system run at their maximum possible speed. This condition is, of course, rarely achieved in practice for any length of time. Indeed, peak performance claims should be treated as that level of performance which the manufacturer guarantees will never be exceeded.

Delivered or sustained performance is much more difficult to measure; but as a first approximation, performance on some reasonably useful benchmarks, such as Argonne Labs' Linpack or the Livermore Loops, can be taken as delivered performance. Defining the efficiency of a machine as the ratio of delivered to peak performance, most current models exhibit no more than 5-10% efficiency. For example, each processor of a 4-processor, 10.5 ns ETA 10-E is rated by ETA at a peak of 857 mflops; but on the 100x100 all-Fortran Linpack, the processor achieves just 52 mflops, a 6% efficiency factor.

Software for Parallel Processing

Lack of easy-to-use tools for developing applications on parallel processing systems is widely recognized as the key hurdle holding back widespread use of such systems.

There are, of course, parallel architectures which hide their complexity from the casual users. For example, all vector machines provide vectorizing Fortran compilers. Such compilers analyze conventional Fortran code, and substitute vector operations where possible. Conventional Fortran coding is also possible with such LIW machines as the Multiflow and Cydrome systems.

Some Fortran compilers are even capable of automatic parallelization for multiprocessor systems. This is generally done at the DO-loop level: successive iterations of the loop are executed concurrently by the multiple available processors. Variations of this scheme are present in the Fortran compilers for the Alliant FX line, Convex C2 line, and in the IBM Parallel Fortran for the 3090 multiprocessors. Cray is developing an automatically-parallelizing version of its CFT77 compiler.

In general, automatic vectorization and DO-level parallelization do not yield as dramatic performance benefits as those that result from algorithmic modifications; i.e., by allowing the user to restructure the logic of the program to take advantage of the presence of multiple processors. There are several attempts under way to create standard Fortran calls which will enable casual users to do this: SCHEDULE from Argonne and FORCE from U. of Colorado are examples.

Why is software development for parallel processing so much more difficult than for conventional, scalar architectures? There are several reasons.

First, the variety of parallel processing architectures is overwhelming. Because these architectures are so different from each other, there is no way that an effective piece of software, be it a compiler or an application code, can be developed without taking into consideration the characteristics of the target architecture.

Second, in those parallel processing architectures employing a large number of interconnected processors, conventional scalar development and debugging techniques are ineffective. None of these machines currently offer software that automatically allocates pieces of the application to the various processors or parts of the system. Yet that is precisely what the system must do if it is to offer the same detachment from hardware details that is supported by compilers and development tools for scalar machines.

Furthermore, when the parallel application bogs down, as it is wont to do in the early development phases, the user usually has no clue as to which processor or part of the system failed to do the right thing. A "core dump" sometime helps on a uniprocessor; but how would you like to slog through 128 or 256 or 1024 core dumps? Currently, the only solution offered (if any) is a simulator of the parallel system, running on a conventional machine. The simulator can be used to verify that the logic of the parallel program is correct. Unfortunately, such a simulator is likely to be so slow that no realistic applications could be seriously developed using it. A better way has to be found.

Worse still, the operating software offered on some current parallel systems is rudimentary to the point of being antediluvian. Most supercomputers and some parallel systems, for example, do not support the concept of virtual memory. The usual justification is that paging is incompatible with the goal of high-speed arithmetic. Some parallel systems do not offer the kind of common memory protection that prevents users from accidentally destroying the operating system. These, and other deficiencies make for a very unstable and error prone environment, which is not conducive to rapid software development.

Third, conventional operating systems are simply not suited for supporting configurations with a large number of processors. If each task allocated to each processor has to be treated by the operating system as a separate "user", there will be no time left for processing: it will all be used for scheduling. The emerging solution is the concept of "light-weight objects": sub-tasks within a process that share resources allocated to the main process, and can therefore be scheduled much more rapidly. This is the essence of the threads in the MACH system from Carnegie Mellon. Similar artifices are present in the operating systems for the Ardent and Stellar "personal supercomputers".

Real progress in fulfilling the promise of parallel processing isn't likely to happen until one of the many available hardware solutions becomes a clear winner. Once the key architectural features of the target machine are fixed, software developers could focus their attention on developing automatic applications parallelizers and effective debugging tools, which in turn would encourage widespread use of parallel processing technology.

TEC-12

2000 AND BEYOND -- A FUTURISTIC VIEW OF TOMORROW'S TELECOMMUNICATION NETWORK

Robert W. Bellin - Chairperson
District Manager - New Technology

Wisconsin Bell
722 N. Broadway
Milwaukee, WI 53202

ABSTRACT

Emerging technology trends offer opportunities in telecommunications far beyond today's network capabilities. Tomorrow's network will offer infinite and virtually "free" bandwidth based on next generation switching and fiber optic transport mediums. Emerging medical diagnostic systems based on advanced non-invasive techniques will be linked to remote expert computer systems. This will allow for cost effective medical care of the highest quality to be provided from walk-in clinics. Weather monitoring sensors will record such items as wind speed and lightning stroke information across the country and provide instant analysis and warning of potential hazards, such as wind shear for aircraft and hazardous storm conditions for local population. Independent voice recognition and language translation capabilities will provide the ultimate "gateways" to unlimited information bases, video media and computer systems. Video on demand capabilities will provide interactive entertainment and education services for a new generation of consumer products based on advanced image technology such as holography projection. These trends will also offer a new opportunity for the legal and regulatory structure to provide a balance between adequate safeguards and technology opportunities.

John Lemay -- Bell Northern Research

Henry D. Levine -- Morrison & Foerster

Walter D. Sincoskie -- Bell Communications Research

David Valack -- AT&T Bell Labs

Stephen B. Weinstein -- Bell Communications Research

BROADBAND PACKET SWITCHING

W.D. Sincoskie
Division Manager, Packet Communications

Bell Communications Research
445 South Street
Morristown, NJ 07960-1910

ABSTRACT

This session will discuss tomorrow's networks and their infinite provision of bandwidth. Solutions for voice and data services are a major concern of the future, therefore, this presentation will examine the integrated high speed packet transport as one possibility.

INTRODUCTION

Broadband packet technology has evolved in response to a perceived need. The need is not, as many think, to provide specific video or data services to customers of the Broadband

Integrated Services Digital Network (BISDN), but rather to provide a single technology capable of providing a plethora of services through a single integrated network to future customers of the BISDN. The definition of the problem is crucial, for if it is wrong, broadband packet technology may become a solution searching for a problem. If, for example, the market for communications in the 1990s and later requires mainly voice services, with penetrations in the data and video markets remaining small, a different technology may be more appropriate. If, as we suspect, the market for communications becomes much less monolithic than it is today, with a plethora of very different services being demanded by the customers, then broadband packet technology is the best known solution.

Why is it necessary to make such a radical change in the technology upon which the telephone network is based? Simply, the BISDN is not being designed to be a telephone network. Rather, it is better termed an information network. Today's network was designed with one thing in mind: providing affordable, reliable voice communications. Indeed, the name "telephone company" implies this primary service. Our operating assumption for the future network is that the availability of an abundance of channel capacity will stimulate new and highly demanding uses for the network in forms such as data, video, telemetry and facsimile transmissions, all moving simultaneously with traditional voice traffic. We should not put ourselves in the position of designing a network around a particular application. The future network will have to be enormously flexible, in order to deliver communications services of all types. In this environment, packet switches have a decided advantage over circuit switches because of the tremendous efficiencies gained in the elimination of fixed channels between transmitting and receiving points.

TDM VERSUS PACKET NETWORKS .

To understand how a broadband packet switch provides extremely flexible communications channels, let us compare the way information is arranged in a packet transmission channel to a traditional time division multiplexed (TDM) channel. Figure 1 shows the channel format for a TDM system quite similar to those used in today's telephone network. The channel is divided into frames, and each frame contains a number of slots. One telephone call is transmitted in each slot, and the same pattern of slots is repeated in every frame. When a new call is added to the system, a free slot is allocated, and the switching equipment is instructed to route information from this call into the appropriate slot.

TDM systems were invented decades ago, in a time when bandwidth was very expensive, and transmission efficiency was the paramount concern. A TDM system transmits nothing other than the information involved in the calls. The routing information, which tells switching systems how to direct the information from the source to the destination, is computed once, at call setup time, and then stored in the memory of the switches.

A packet transmission system, shown in figure 2, is really just a variant of TDM. A packet system may not have frames, since the pattern of information in the slots changes very rapidly. Each slot, or packet, contains information from one call, but also contains a header which contains the routing information, namely the source and destination, for the packet. Thus, the routing information which was formerly computed once and stored in the switching system is now computed on the fly and transmitted with the packet.

How does a packet system compare to a traditional TDM system? The major advantage packet has over TDM is that bandwidth can be allocated with extreme flexibility, which translates into a system which can carry a rapidly varying mixture of traffic. TDM systems must allocate their bandwidth in fixed rates, which are multiples of some basic rate. Bandwidth flexibility is really the compelling reason which is driving researchers worldwide into considering broadband packet technology as the basis for BISDN.

To appreciate the impact packet technology has upon the architecture of a BISDN system, consider figure 3. This figure shows a possible architecture for a BISDN central office using a mix of technologies. A new network must be constructed for each type of communication provided. At a minimum, different switches and networks are needed for voice, data, and video. The complexity of maintaining multiple different networks, one for each class of traffic, rapidly becomes overwhelming. Interworking of the different networks is nearly impossible. Figure 4 shows a much simpler architecture, in which all traffic is eventually carried by the broadband packet switch. There is also a

reasonable migration path from where we are today. The entry of broadband packet switching is justified by new services, either data or video based. As existing switches are phased out, voice traffic is integrated into the broadband packet network.

Obviously, we are not getting all of the advantages of broadband packet technology without some cost. Some of the traditional problems associated with packet networks have been: low efficiency, large delay, and low speed, complex switches. Fortunately, considerable progress has been made in each of these areas.

Consider the efficiency of a packet system compared to TDM. The transmission efficiency of a TDM system exceeds 99 percent in many cases. Efficiency in a packet system is determined mainly by the ratio of the header to body size of the packet. Table 1 shows the range of packet sizes currently being considered by international standards bodies. It can be seen that, while the efficiency of packet networks is not quite as good as TDM, efficiencies of over 90 percent are achievable. Fortunately, the impact of fiber optic technology upon the loop and trunk plant has reduced the cost of transmission sufficiently that losses of 5 to 10 percent are now acceptable.

Delay has been a problem, especially in traditional low speed packet switching systems. Total delay in a packet network is made up of 3 components: propagation delay, switching delay and packetizing delay. In a broadband packet system, propagation delay will be the dominant factor, ranging from 0 to 270 ms. Switching delay is caused mainly by the queuing of packets to reduce contention and other problems in the switch. This delay is inversely proportional to the bit rate. Traditional packet switching networks, operating at speeds of 50 to 100 Kb/s can incur switching delays of as long as 1 second. However, at rates of 100 Mb/s and above, switching delays will drop to less than 1 ms, small enough to be overwhelmed by propagation delay. Table 1 shows that packetizing delay for 64 Kb/s voice is in the range of 4 to 16 ms, again small compared to the propagation delay. So, total delay for packet voice in a broadband packet network will be in the range of 5 to 287 milliseconds. Echo cancelers are only necessary when interfacing between a broadband packet voice service and existing analog POTS services. They will be located in the interworking unit shown in figure 4.

Current packet switches, which interface to trunks at speeds of 64 Kb/s, are much too slow to even carry significant amounts of voice. Local area network (LAN) technology can switch packets at speeds of 10 to 100 Mb/s, but even this is not nearly enough to consider handling hundreds of video channels at rates of 150 Mb/s and above. The next section describes some recent technological advances in broadband packet design.

BROADBAND PACKET SWITCH TECHNOLOGY

In order to achieve the enormous throughputs necessary for a packet switch based BISDN, it was necessary to reexamine the methods used in building traditional packet switches. Many current packet switches are built using a general purpose computer, which read a packet into memory, interpret the headers, and then write the packet onto an output trunk. This method, called a memory switch, suffers from two drawbacks. First, the general purpose computer must execute hundreds of instructions to switch a single packet. If this problem is solved by

replacing the general purpose computer with specially designed hardware, then the bandwidth of the memory becomes the limiting factor. Memories with bandwidths of 5 Gb/s have been built, and in fact used as small prototype BISDN switches. However, these switches cannot be easily expanded to the 1000 Gb/s or so necessary for a full scale BISDN central office. Another approach, popular in the data communications market, is to use a bus or ring to switch packets. Most current LANs and MANs (Metropolitan Area Network) use this approach. MAN speeds of 1 Gb/z have been demonstrated at Bellcore, but speeds much above this rate are difficult to achieve. The bus or ring acts much like the memory above in limiting the ultimate growth of the system.

The approach being taken at Bellcore is to build a broadband packet switching fabric based on the Batcher-banyan (B-b) switch. A B-b switch is one of a class of parallel switching fabrics being considered in a number of research labs worldwide. These switching fabrics do not show the bottleneck characteristic of memory or bus switches, and have no fundamental limits to their growth (technology limitations always define the upper bounds of the growth of these switches). A B-b switch is built around a 2x2 (2 input, 2 output) switching cell. This cell connects the inputs to the outputs in one of 2 ways (pass or cross), depending upon the information contained in the headers of the packets appearing on its inputs. A VLSI implementation of a 2x2 cell requires approximately 100 transistors. Switching cells can be arranged into larger switches. Figure 5 shows a 4x4 non-blocking Batcher-banyan switch. It is fairly easy to build small switches, but as the switches grow, the interconnection patterns begin to dominate, as can be seen in the 64x64 switching network in figure 6. In order to reduce the complexity of the interconnection of these networks, researchers at Bellcore have developed a novel 3-dimensional package. By placing adjacent columns of switches (the vertical columns of circles in figure 6) onto circuit boards mounted orthogonally, the wiring complexity is vastly reduced.

Bellcore researchers have designed custom VLSI chips in order to demonstrate the feasibility of this approach to broadband packet switching. A single chip was recently demonstrated operating as a 32x32 packet switch, with each input (and output) line running at 140 Mb/s, for an aggregate bandwidth of 4.48 Gb/s, a world record for a single chip packet switch. The 3-D package, when completed, will hold approximately 100 Bellcore-designed VLSI chips, and implement a 256x256 B-b fabric, for a total throughput in excess of 35 Gb/s. Current research efforts are centered around the design of central office scale switches, consisting of several hundred 3-D switching modules, providing over 10,000 lines at 150 Mb/s and throughputs of over 1000 Gb/s.

WHAT'S NEXT?

There is an enormous amount of work yet to do. Research will continue on very large switches, traffic theory for broadband packet networks, and the implementation of various broadband services. In the meantime, technology must be transferred to manufacturers, standards must be developed and written, and then products useful to operating companies must be defined and developed. The time involved for this process can span more than a decade. It will be an exciting decade, though, as we will be building the infrastructure upon which the information industry of the next century will reside. Telephones, computers, videophones, television, and applications not yet conceived can be all integrated into and interwork through this network.

Table I. Packet Sizes

	Header	Body	Efficiency	Voice Packetization Delay
TDM	0	1	100%	125 MS
PACKET	2	32	94%	4 MS
PACKET	10	130	93%	16 MS

(SIZES IN BYTES, 1 BYTE = 8 BITS)

Figure 1 - Time Division Multiplexing

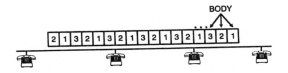

- Routing information implicit in position
- Low overhead
- Poor efficiency for variable rate traffic
- Low delay

Figure 2 - Packet Multiplexing

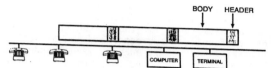

BODY   HEADER

COMPUTER   TERMINAL

- TDM variant
- Routing Information contained in packet header

Figure 5 - 4x4 Batcher - banyan Switch

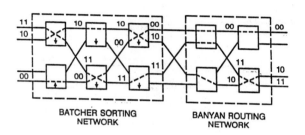

BATCHER SORTING
NETWORK

BANYAN ROUTING
NETWORK

Figure 3 - Circuit - based Network

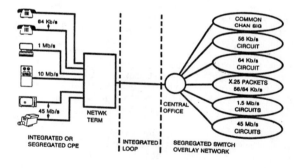

Figure 4 - Packet Switched Network Architecture

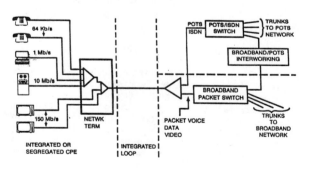

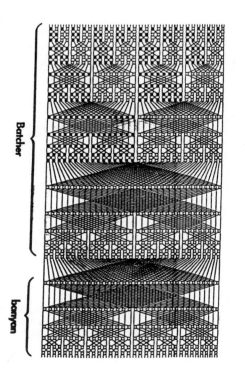

Figure 6

A MANUFACTURER'S PERSPECTIVE

David Valack
Department Head
Exploratory Wideband Switching

AT&T Bell Labs
Room 1U102
200 Park Plaza
Naperville, IL 60566-7050

ABSTRACT

Future networks promise virtually "free" bandwidth. This session analyzes the potentialities and implications of such an environment.

NETWORK SERVICE ARCHITECTURE EVOLUTION

John Lemay & Richard Gillman
Manager of Future Network Services

Bell Northern Research
Dept. 6K20 PO Box 3511
Station C Ottawa, Ontario
Canada K1Y4H7

ABSTRACT

The Telephone Companies (TelCos) have a number of objectives which result in considerable impacts on today's network, particularly on its complexity. This paper proposes that the key factor which will enable the TelCos to achieve their objectives is a well-structured network architecture. The important concepts for future network architectures are identified, and a Network Functional Architecture (NFA) which uses those concepts to meet the TelCos' objectives is outlined. Within the NFA a Network Service Architecture is defined, together with a transition strategy to achieve it. The utility of the transition architecture is demonstrated by means of an example of an enhanced service provider gateway service.

INTRODUCTION

The ability of local and inter exchange Telephone Companies (TelCos) to succeed in the advanced network of the future will be dominated by their ability to rapidly and economically deploy new services. This must be done in the context of an increasingly complex and competitive network environment. This environment will be characterized by increased service complexity and scope, multi-vendor networks and service competition between network providers. In addition, the TelCos must support the smooth and increasingly rapid introduction of new system and technologies and allow for the customization of services and related OAM.

The design and deployment of a network that achieves this vision and provides the flexibility needed to meet these goals is a significant challenge. There are many factors for success, but three key enabling factors are identified.

The first factor is a flexible and product independent network functional architecture. The architecture is the structure by which network functions are described and allocated to network elements. It enables vendor independent product requirements and open network interfaces to be defined.

The second factor is flexible network elements (e.g., Switching Systems (SS), Service Control Points (SCPs), etc.). The next generation of network elements must be designed with flexibility as a primary focus. They must be logically and physically partitioned to allow the introduction of new technology (e.g., integrated switching fabrics, new terminal types, etc.) with minimum system and service disruption. They must provide standardized system interfaces that allow the customization of services by OTC personnel and possibly by end users and their resources must be dynamically provisionable to allow OTC responsiveness to rapidly changing service demands.

The third factor for success is the introduction of automated tools and processed for the design and deployment of network services. Current intervals of two or more years for the design and standardization of services, such as Enhanced/800 or networked Call Completion to Busy Subscriber (CCBS), will not be acceptable in the competitive network. Automated tools which capture and validate distributed network designs and speed implementation will be needed to reduce these intervals.

This paper expands on the first enabling factor, Network Functional Architecture. The important concepts for future network architectures are identified, and a Network Functional Architecture (NFA) which uses those concepts to meet the TelCos' objectives is outlined. Within the NFA, a Network Service Architecture is defined, together with a transition strategy which identifies access services as the first class of services which can be implemented in conformance to the target architecture. The utility of the access service transition architecture is then demonstrated by means of an example of an enhanced service provider gateway service.

NETWORK FUNCTIONAL ARCHITECTURE CONCEPTS

Of the three factors outlined for OTC success we believe that a Network Functional Architecture is initially the key enabling factor because of its potential power to formalize the product requirements capturable on Computer Aided Design (CAD) tools. However, to realize that potential, the architecture needs to be based on sound and formal principles. Specifically, as an increasing number of new network services are provided in terms of software, a view of network architecture which encompasses a view of the software in the network physical elements is essential.

The basic structuring concepts which any formal network architecture should use are Layering, Partitioning and Domains.

Layering provides the means to structure the network so as to maximize re-use of functionality/capabilities and is also a means to hide functionality in one layer from another. This principle of layer separation means that the software or hardware realizing the entities in one layer may be changed without impact on the other layers. So, for example, service providing applications of the network can be made independent from the underlying technology of the Switching Systems.

Partitioning provides the means to structure functionality, within a layer. The partitioning rules developed for a layer should define how to break-up complex designs (e.g., for some services) into manageable parts which can then be distributed into different network physical elements. A systematic technique, which allows successive levels of decomposition of the layer (e.g., like an object-oriented class hierarchy) is needed.

Domains are containers for the functional entities defined within the network architecture (e.g., a Switching System). A more concrete example of domains within systems are processors, memory and disks. These entities by themselves provide only an environment in which to support or store the functional entities. The concept of domains is important because it enables functional requirements and the functional architecture to be defined, initially, without regard for physical distribution (e.g., placement in domains). This ultimately means TelCos would be free to pursue their own optimum physical network architectures and intelligence deployment strategies, by controlling the mapping of the defined entities into their domains.

NETWORK FUNCTIONAL ARCHITECTURE

In the past, we have presented some proposals (Ref:1) for a Network Functional Architecture which uses the concepts specified and enables the OTC objectives to be met. The layered view of the proposed NFA is shown in Figure 1:

1. The Physical Resource Layer is the lowest layer and is partitioned into functional entities which represent different physical resources realized by hardware (e.g., tone generators, tone receivers, announcers, conference bridges, and physical transport links).

2. The Logical Resource Layer is built on top of the Physical Resource Layer and is partitioned into functional entities which represent the different logical resources realized in software (e.g., common channel signaling network, protocol entities, network databases, frame transport subnets, packet transport subnets and logical terminals).

3. The Network Service Layer is partitioned into different functional entities which represent the applications used to realize services in the network, by exploitation of the network logical resources. These services are provided to a Service User which accesses them through an application in the Network Service Layer which acts as the Service User's agent.

A layered OAM functional architecture is also included within the scope of the NFA.

NETWORK SERVICE ARCHITECTURE (NSA)

The Network Service Architecture (NSA) defines the structure of the Network Service Layer of the NFA. The NSA is the most important part of the NFA in helping to achieve the rapid definition and deployment of new services, as it deals with the control and complexity of advanced multi-user, multi-media distributed services.

The major source of complexity in distributed services is the need to arbitrate interactions between services and users. Service processing complexity increases with the number of users in the call, the number of features invoked by these users, and the distribution of control. As new services are introduced, interactions with existing services must be specified. For example, mutually incompatible features must be screened and the orderly execution of features maintained.

The approach taken in NSA to simplify management of service interactions is to classify services. Interactions between services within a class are dealt with in a single optimum way for each class. Relationships between services in different classes are also specified and managed in other ways. For example, in the CCITT OSI and ISDN standards forums (Refs: 2 & 3) functional models have been produced for different services (e.g., for Teleservices, such as X.400 Message Handling; and ISDN Bearer Services, such as the basic ISDN call service and supplementary services). It is our contention that the NSA should act as a "meta-model" and show the relationship between the functional models developed of these classes of services and the individual services in the same class.

Our analysis of the traditional telecommunications Bearer Services, which carry information, shows that the basic and supplementary services naturally fall into two broad classes: access services and core services. At a certain level of functional decomposition of the NSA, overlayed onto a particular set of domains, this gives rise to the NSA model shown in Figure 2.

USER is the Service User's agent in the Network Service Layer. It receives Service User's service requests and indications, and then converts them into the corresponding service control invocations. In the physical example represented in Figure 2, the User defines the application functionality in the phone supporting the Service User (e.g., human) Man Machine Interface.

ACCESS hides all real terminal/user characteristics from the services so that they can work for any terminal/user by converting and interpreting the signaling control messages. It also authorizes the User's invocation of bearer services depending on a service user's subscriptions, and current terminal and interface capabilities. It then "triggers" the invocation of the relevant service providing applications. Thus, it is the interaction control point between different services invoked for the user.

ACCESS SERVICES are bearer service application factors that are provided to a single user and do not require coordination with other users. In general, these applications are invoked by users while establishing and disconnecting calls (i.e., while the call is single-ended and only one user is involved).

CORE SERVICES are bearer service application functions that are provided to a set of related users which must be coordinated. Some form of policy is required to arbitrate the different user's requests (e.g., for users related by a call or one or more connections) and handle the interactions between those services. In general, these services (e.g., set up call, release call, hold call, transfer call, etc.) modify call or connection objects, which are jointly controlled by the inter-connected users. In Figure 2, call and connection control functions of core services are shown distributed between Switching Systems/Network Nodes across the network (as they are today).

Relationship (r1, r2, etc.) entities model the information flow dialogues between the functional entities shown. All of the primitives are related to the request or indication of services.

ACCESS SERVICE TRANSITION ARCHITECTURE

The NFA and NSA presented in this paper show a number of inter-layer interfaces (fig. 1) and intra-layer partitions (fig. 2). Most of today's network products and architectures do not exhibit the architectural structure proposed for the future, consequently some form of transition strategy is needed. Such a transition needs to accommodate an evolutionary, rather than revolutionary approach. Thus, the only way to achieve transition is to identify which are the key layers or partitions to break-out and implement first. In making such decisions, both commercial value and technical difficulty needs to be taken into account and balanced.

Most of the "Intelligent Network" services (e.g, Enhanced 911, Automatic Call Distribution, Screening Services, PVN, etc.), or at least a significant component of those services that the TelCos are contemplating for the early 1990s, can be classified as access services.

Although all Switching Systems exhibit some form of proprietary layering in their architectures, our analysis shows that the most benefit and simplest first step would be realized by separating access services from the rest of call processing. In addition, switch call processing has a number of existing capabilities, including the existing service base, which could be exploited and re-used by access services.

As nearly all access services only require an underlying database resource, and because they exhibit limited service interactions between themselves and other classes of services, they show good potential for being distributed into other network elements, such as the Service Control Points (SCPs) identified in the Intelligent Network physical architecture.

From these arguments, Figure 3 shows the first step transition architecture for access services.

The Call Processing Sub-System (CPSS) represents the existing call processing functionality and underlying resource control functionality of the Switching System (i.e., CPSS is an entity combining switch access, call processing "core" services (e.g., Centrex services) and layered resource control). CPSS in existence today conform to the vendors' own proprietary architectures which probably cannot be retroactively standardized without significant revolution to the switches. However, a high level vendor independent call model is needed to identify the Point in Call (PICs) where access services may be introduced.

The Service Switching Point (SSP) should contain the functionality to "trigger" and route service requests to and from the Access Service Applications (ASAs). The ASAs may reside in external, centralized Service Control Points, integrated SCPs within a node, or simply on other applications processors within the Switching System. The SSP does not appear in the target architecture as service independent triggering is proposed to be a future function of access. The SSP is introduced into the transition architecture because of the vendor dependent nature of existing CPSS, and the need to clearly and separately define the additional requirements to support access services.

Relationships r1, r2, etc., represent the contents of standardized CCS7 TCAP transaction (invokes and replies) between the SSP and individual ASAs. As the CPSS is vendor specific and both the CPSS & SSP are within the switching system, then the relationship rX will be vendor specific. However, both the CPSS and SSP are network visible functional entities and would be assigned different CCS7 addresses (e.g., sub-system numbers). These addresses would be used when the Switching System is accessed externally by the CCS7 network protocols.

Knowledge of some Intelligent Network/1 access services, such as 1-800 and Credit Card, has already been embedded in vendors' CPSS (as represented by relationship r1). Other service specific triggers could be added to CPSS although it is proposed that new access services would be added through "datafill" of the SSP's service independent "trigger tables."

ACCESS SERVICE EXAMPLE

In order to illustrate the utility and benefits of breaking-out access services more clearly, an example is given. In the current United States regulatory environment there is increasing opportunity for the TelCos to sell gateway services to Enhanced Service Providers (ESPs). Many of these services may be classified as access services.

In the example, shown in Figure 4, the ESP is providing a 1-900 information service, which is provided on a simple answering machine.

The user dials the 1-900 number which gets routed to a particular Switching System. At a particular point in the call processing, which can be armed for particular ESPs, the SSP is invoked. The SSP determines, perhaps from an IN/2-type Trigger Table, what if any access services should be invoked and addresses a transaction to the "GlobalTitle" of the related application. In this case, the trigger condition may be the 1-900 number which would cause the 1-900 application to be invoked.

The 1-900 application provides a service to the ESP. The first function shown is screening. The calling user's Directory Number (DN) could be on the ESP's screening list to disallow access to the service. This could be at the request of the calling user to prevent the user's children calling the number without inputting a password/ customer number; or the ESP could have made the entry to reject certain users (e.g., who may not have paid their ESP bills). Secondly, the service translates the

1-900 number onto a valid terminating resource for the destination ESP.

The important thing to notice about the example, however, is the nature of transaction response from the 1-900 ASA to the CPSS.

The ASA, SSP and CPSS are both in the same peer service layer (e.g., no "diagonal" relationships between layers to underlying resources across the network). The CPSS is in control of the call and associated resources (e.g., user, terminals, trunks, lines, etc.) at all times, and so is in a position to resolve resource contention problems, keep track of the resource states and solve interaction problems with other switch-based services (e.g., on-hook while the transaction is outstanding).

The returned CP instructions manipulate the call on behalf of, in this case, the called user (ESP) as it's the ESP's access service (i.e., access services are not like a "3rd party" controlling the call, but have a "single-ended" view of the call and do something on behalf of one of the users involved, or to be involved, in the call). A single call processing instruction is returned (e.g., reject the call, queue the call, forward the call, deliver the call). These instructions can be treated as if issued by the ESP itself and hence normal switch billing, authorization, interaction and arbitration mechanisms may be used to interpret them. In fact, many of the CP instructions that are useful for access services may be already existing core services (e.g., call forward).

CONCLUSIONS

This paper has proposed an advanced Network Functional Architecture, with sound layering and partitioning concepts, which will strongly contribute towards meeting the TelCos' objectives.

The Network Service Architecture, part of the NFA, partitions the service layer into classes of service, and derives the distributable applications which provide the services themselves. This technique allows the service interaction and complexity issues to be well managed and controlled, while at the same time being "open-ended" about what new service classes and applications are introduced.

Access services are proposed as the initial transition step towards the target architecture. By way of relating the access service transition architecture to Intelligent Network services, and by the ESP gateway service example, the potential short-term commercial benefits and relative technical simplicity was demonstrated.

REFERENCES

(1) John Lemay & Jim McGee. "A Distributed Network Architecture for the Competitive

Network Environment." Proceedings of ISS87.

(2) CCITT Recommendations X.200, X.400, et al. on OSI and OSI applications.

(3) New CCITT Study Group XI/WP5 Recommendations Q.65, Q.71, Q.80-Q.87 on ISDN Stage 2 Service Definitions.

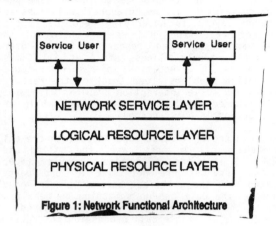

Figure 1: Network Functional Architecture

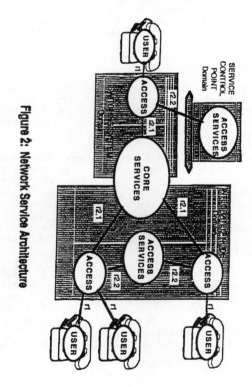

Figure 2: Network Service Architecture

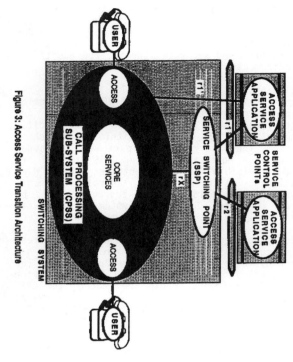

Figure 3: Access Service Transition Architecture

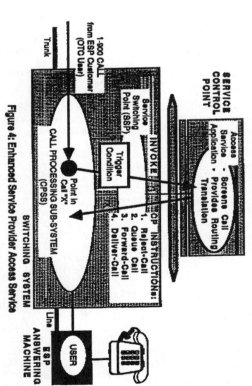

Figure 4: Enhanced Service Provider Access Service

COMMUNICATION SERVICES OF THE FUTURE

Stephen B. Weinstein
Division Manager - Network Services Research

Bell Communications Research
Room 2E283
445 South Street
Morristown, NJ 07960-1961

ABSTRACT

Tomorrow's network will offer many services not possible today. This session will discuss potential applications and services of the future.

INTRODUCTION

"Communication" will have a different meaning in the future, when major networks and the equipment connected to them will resemble huge, distributed computer systems. Another paper in this conference (1) describes the access structure of BISDN designed to flexibly accommodate the multiple media and, often, multiple connections required for future services. The connection protocols for realizing multimedia multipoint communications are also receiving attention (2-4), and Broadband ISDN is evolving quickly in both technical and services concepts (5-8). But network operators need to do much more than offer connection services and transmission channels, however broad (high capacity), from one point to another. They must plan an infrastructure that will complement or merge with office information systems, home entertainment electronics, personal computers and workstations, and existing communications devices and networks to remove geographic and media obstacles from everyday personal and business interactions. The network will provide some services directly and facilitate many more, bringing together providers and users of a large variety of services and applications.

The public communications industry has future markets in the information, entertainment, and educational needs of businesses and individuals as well as in extensions of today's telephone and data communications services. A very wide range of capabilities are to be integrated - functionally, if not always physically - in the lightwave networks whose architectures and components are being researched and prototyped today. To offer such capabilities, these networks must become not only broadband, offering a wide range of transmission capacities at reasonable cost, but also intelligent, with services and operations under flexible software control through a ubiquitous signaling network. Interworking among networks and terminals, private and public, will be a key element of this communications future. The intelligence may reside partly in the network and partly at its periphery (9).

The term "Broadband Integrated Services Digital Network" (BISDN) has come to denote the architecture and services concepts of a future public network providing the whole spectrum of communication capabilities. In the long-range view, all of the functions of today's separate telephone, cable television, and data communication networks - plus many new functions - are to be provided in BISDN, which could become widely deployed early in the twenty-first century. Channel data rates in the region of 150 Mb/s are proposed with flexible allocations of bandwidth to accommodate almost any mix of traffic.

The services aspirations of the public network to be realized in BISDN and designed for the evolving "information society" of the world's economically advanced countries, could be described as "universal communications" (10) consisting of:

. Communication among people anywhere, at any time, in any medium or combination of media, and at acceptable cost.

. An "information community" retrieving and sharing information from dispersed sources and in multiple media.

. An entertainment, educational, and cultural environment offering choice and quality, including some forms of video on demand.

This paper describes several examples of the personalized, multimedia communications services implied by these aspirations, not all requiring broadband transmission. The services embody concepts of communication among individuals, not telephone numbers; media groupings and conversions; network "mediation" of working communications and information processing sessions among people and machines; messaging as well as real-time communications in multiple media; choice, quality, and personalizations in entertainment services; and "browsing" through multimedia information on the basis of visual as well as textual attributes. The time may come when users of communications services, not only providers, will write and execute computer programs coordinating network resources in ways which are only dimly perceived today. This prospect of a truly "open network," a very large, complex distributed computer system, offers many challenges to designers.

Telephone companies have progressed toward universal communications in the normal course of building more reliable and economical communication networks. The economics of digital lightwave communication all the way to the subscriber, and of independent software control of communications resources, are expected to become favorable in the not-too-distant future. The cost of replacing the vast existing copper wire plant will, of course, have to be spread out over many years, and questions of regulation and industry structure resolved.

NEARER-TERM ISDN SERVICES

If it is not leapfrogged by BISDN, the Integrated Services Digital Network, ISDN, will provide direct digital access to the individual subscriber with a 144 Kb/s interface consisting of three channels, two offering 64 Kb/s transmission in both directions, and the third carrying 16 Kb/s control and data traffic. The two 64 Kb/s channels will accept digital telephones, higher speed data, graphics and facsimile terminals, data transfers from personal computers, and even highly compressed video. The 16 Kb/s "D" channel will be connected into the out-of-band signaling network through which switches and other network elements are to be controlled.

Although ISDN is still "narrowband," it encourages possibilities for multimedia communication and information retrieval (11-14). It will make it relatively simple to realize a single call with simultaneous voice and document (facsimile, text and graphics) transmission, in which the connected parties could annotate the document as they discussed it. It will offer sufficient capacity for 5-second-per-page facsimile, transmission of color pictures, and "super videotex" information services in multiple media. It will support wide-bandwidth (7KHz) audio and limited forms of videotelephony. The 1.5 Mb/s Primary Interface ISDN, which will be offered to business users, will permit flexible consolidation of multiple voice and data channels, and, hopefully, provide local area network (LAN) interconnection services.

Of course, many "ISDN services" are possible without ISDN. Media integration can, for example, be realized through the logical integration of a PBX or Centrex system providing voice channels, with a LAN carrying information and signaling data. The market viability of ISDN has been questioned for this and other reasons. There appears to be some consensus among business and institutional communications users that ISDN is attractive for cutting down on wiring costs at customer locations with a moderate number of users, and for making integrated services available to outlying locations and smaller users.

NETWORK "INTELLIGENCE"

ISDN and BISDN have revolutionary implications for the establishment and control of communications sessions. The separate network signaling system is part of the concept of network intelligence which is so important to future services. Network intelligence implies software definition and control of services and personal communication environments (15). Call placement in the intelligent network is not necessarily a connection to a certain subscriber line, but can be an inquiry, through the common channel signaling network, to a database in which a services script has been programmed. One example of an intelligent network service already exists. Each of the 4 billion toll-free "800" calls made in the United States each year is an inquiry to a database which is "translated" into an actual telephone number. The number may depend on the location of the caller, the time of day, and other factors. During the daytime, for example, someone calling a credit card issuer might be connected to a local servicing center. At night, when the local servicing center is closed, the caller is routed to a more distant 24 hour servicing center.

In the future, the instructions in the database may relate not only to the physical connection, but also to translating a personal identification of the called party into a destination number and implementing the treatment that the called party wants to give to the particular calling party. For example, a professional leaving the office for an automobile trip may request that an urgently expected text message from a colleague be forwarded to his or her car. In this example of selective call forwarding, only a message from that particular colleague would be forwarded. Network intelligence, aware that the car has a telephone and not a data terminal, would synthesize a spoken version. The message would be addressed not to a certain location, as telephone calls (except for "800" calls) are today, but to the lifetime number of a certain individual, regardless of where that individual is. An advanced user interface would facilitate giving forwarding instructions to the network in a simple, intuitive, and fast way.

The intelligent network concept implies a separation of network elements, such as switches, signaling units, and media conversion devices, from the higher-level software controlling them. It will give network services designers great flexibility in configuring or changing services quickly, as well as allowing customers to change bandwidth, number assignments, and other parameters of their services. Large corporate users will be able to create "virtual private networks" within the public network, replacing or complementing privately-owned facilities.

Just as computer system operators may buy applications software from a variety of vendors, network operators may mix and match the applications software used to control network elements. A network Services Control Point could include a software package from one vendor defining a dialing from terminal service, a package from a second vendor for a multi-party conferencing service, and software from a third vendor for data communications for a hybrid CATV system. The communications industry could change significantly as development of services creation software becomes a growing and highly competitive business, ending the era of services definition in the software of large switching systems.

An even larger impact could result from making the software-controlled network elements directly available to outside parties. As "Open Network Architecture" (ONA), with standard interfaces to network building-block capabilities, evolves, it will very likely lead to a proliferation of communications services packagers and repackagers, and eventually, as suggested earlier, to end-user programming of the public network as if it were a personal computer.

THE BROADBAND NETWORK

The BISDN deployment strategy assumes a "learning curve" of decreasing costs (5). Larger business locations, with a large bulk of consolidated voice, data, and (in the future) video traffic, would get the first installations and pay a relatively high monthly connection charge.

One of the most requested broadband business services is interconnection of high-speed LANs on which workstations, computers, printers, and other information-handling devices are connected to local environments. Higher speed optical LANs, such as the Fiber Distributed Data Interface (FDDI) (16), a proposed American National Standard for a 100 Mb/s token ring, are nearing commercial availability. Standards for dedicated interconnection networks, called Metropolitan Area Networks (MANs), are being debated in international standards bodies. One of the current questions in the development of broadband communication is the integration of the BISDN and MAN perspectives, which have come from the telephone and computer communications communities respectively. MANs can and must be realized within BISDN to meet business needs. A two-way, 150 Mb/s access channel is adequate for this and most other present business needs.

For the residential subscriber, many operators believe that the fiber must carry video entertainment services, as well as ordinary telephone calls and whatever new interactive services might be salable, to justify the installation cost, even late in the learning curve (17). Rather than bring 35 or 50 video channels simultaneously into each home, as cable television does today, a single fiber might deliver two or three channels selected by the subscriber through interactive communications and switched by the network. A pair of fibers could provide these switched digital (at rates up to 150 Mb/s) downstream (broadcast) channels, plus a two-way 150 Mb/s channel for everything else. Close coordination with progress in terminal equipment is essential. If network operators someday reach agreement with home

electronics manufacturers, the hand-held TV remote control will communicate with the network's video switch rather than only a channel switch inside the television set.

Replacement of existing CATV and telephone service by a fiber subscriber line could be driven by a significant consumer demand for HDTV (high-definition television), which cable operators may find difficult to deliver with high quality through their coaxial cable plant. The demand could arise with the introduction of HDTV videocassette players, HDTV television sets, and HDTV projection systems over the next twenty years, with a penetration of perhaps 15 million HDTV sets by 2008 (18). Digital transmission at 100-150 Mb/s could offer excellent HDTV quality. Given this assumption, an early 21st century perspective for lightwave communications to most homes is reasonable. With the right mix of technological, economic, and regulatory events, cable operators may one day become service providers on this general purpose public lightwave network.

A CLOSER LOOK AT SERVICES

Message communications and real-time communications complement one another, allowing call completions not possible with real-time communications alone. Messaging is also important as a "record communications" medium. Facsimile is finally, after many decades, becoming a mass-market service, led by Japan, where 2 million facsimile terminals help overcome the difficulties of messaging with non-alphabetic characters. High-speed communicating copiers, facsimile-accessed information services, and color capabilities will become part of facsimile service.

Various telematic services, communicating text, data, and visual materials, will displace most present-day movement of paper and magnetic media (19). Simultaneous use of multiple media will be essential for communications among individuals who want to share documents, pictures, drawings, data files and other materials used in face-to-face meetings. Electronic communication will go well beyond "hard" media with its potentials for searching, filtering, transforming, composing, editing, and interpreting information (20), although transformations between paper formats and "soft" screen displays will be widely used. Facsimile, for example, will be generated at or delivered to computer terminals as well as normal facsimile machines.

Videotex, a generic name for information and transactional services in which subscribers access a variety of services providers through network facilities and get back text and graphics displays on their terminal screens, has used 1200 b/s telephone line or packet network channels up to now. The difficulty of doing attractive photographic, animated, and audio-accompanied screens, with reasonable response times, at this rate may be one of the reasons videotex has failed so far in the United States and Britain, but is probably not the main reason. In France, where the government gave away hundreds of thousands of Minitel terminals and provides transmission and billing services for about 5,000 independent service providers, there are more than 2.5 million users and general agreement that the venture is a success. There is evidence that Minitel users may be more interested in personal communications and social interaction than in information services. "Super videotex" at 64 Kb/s ISDN rates and higher, with rapidly-displayed color photographs, music and voice accompaniment (21), may help build consumer interest, but will not in itself drive information services.

Outside of the unique French experience, information services are more likely to be directed toward professional and business users, and will have a different character from videotex. A user may wish, on the basis of a fairly general query, to transparently retrieve and browse a large body of materials from distributed sources, viewing full materials in multiple media, rather than searching an index for a particular item from a particular source (22, 23). Another user may wish to browse a specialized data base on the basis of visual attributes, digging behind the pictures for more information as needed (20). Intelligent machine intermediaries will be available in advanced systems to help users sharpen their requests and gather relevant materials from diverse sources. In many applications, particularly residential ones, users may simply wish to "graze" (29), passively letting information flow by and picking up interesting items. Advertisers will wish to target electronic ads (which will be associated with information to keep the cost to the subscribers low) to individual profiles.

Combining information access with multimedia communication, collaborative work in shared electronic workspaces could find significant professional applications. In these sessions, users would share several computer applications simultaneously through multiple "Windows" on the screens of their individual workstations and personal computers. Participants in a multipoint desktop conference (24) would be able to open and close computer applications just as in a local environment, retrieve information, invoke computer processing, jointly edit and design in multiple media (25), and share and store results. Wideband audio and small moving pictures of the other parties would help the interaction, subconferences apart from the main meeting would be possible, and machine "advisors" and facilitators would be consulted as needed. In this picture, communications will be used to enhance and extend the electronic work and social environments coming into existence now in companies, institutions, schools, and government agencies.

DISTRIBUTION SERVICES

The major distribution services are video programming, primarily movies, news, and sports as we know them from broadcast television and CATV.

The existence of 8,000 cable systems in the United States, with 50 million subscribers, shows that wired delivery of broadband programming meets a very strong consumer demand (25). In addition to the higher quality epitomized by HDTV, BISDN would introduce opportunities for much greater choice and convenience in broadcast entertainment.

Existing forms of pay-per-view television deliver a scheduled single event, such as a movie or boxing match, to the paying customers. There is still nothing approaching video on demand, getting what you want when you want it (26). Even BISDN would be -hard pressed to deliver movies precisely on demand, for that would require a vast number of very high speed channels. A more realistic service would offer a selection of perhaps 500 movies delivered to every distribution office serving subscriber fiber lines. The movies might be available at two-hour intervals. This arrangement would not be strictly on demand - the subscriber might have to wait an hour or two - but could supply a large number of popular movies on something close to demand. A few on-demand channels might be provided for viewers willing to pay a premium to see less popular movies. Another option is "democratic TV," a concept, from France, of subscribers voting on what movies to see. There is no escaping the basic principle: in the absence of unlimited transmission capacity, even in the BISDN world, service comes closest to "on-demand" delivery when many other subscribers want the same thing.

This does not rule out the deferred delivery, in off hours and perhaps at lower - or higher than normal rates, of individually selected video material. A movie, or, for that matter, a college lecture or other audio/visual program, could be ordered by a subscriber and downloaded by the provider to a VCR or other local storage device (such as rewritable digital optical memories) for later viewing. Electronically-accessed video libraries may be as common in the future as videocassette rental stores are today.

The development of consumer-priced digital video technologies, such as digital VCRs and very large capacity digital optical storage devices, would encourage creative new video delivery techniques. Some observers see a tremendous potential in video compression codecs (code-decoders). With no compression, a normal television signal might encode into a 90 Mb/s data stream. With a 1.5 Mb/s codec, a full movie might be stored on a CD-ROM. Movie distribution on CD-ROMs could become practical with symmetric codings: the analog-to-digital encoding is complex and is done on a large computer, but the decoding is fast, cheap, and realized in very compact electronics (27). If such highly compressive codings are successful, video on demand could have a new lease on life.

Customized transmission and storage goes beyond simple delivery of a requested program. Intelligent interpreters programmed in the subscriber's equipment, if not in the network's Service Control Point, might compose personalized magazines consisting of news, professional information, and entertainment, e.g., by selection of camera views of a sports field, one of several parallel sessions from a conference, or one of several endings to a movie, would be possible. Information services could be combined with video distribution services, so that a viewer wanting, for example, background information on a particular team or player in a sports event, beyond what the announcer is offering, could call it up on a window insert within the moving picture. The exchange of video programs among subscribers is still another possibility.

THE CERTAIN FUTURE

Communication networks must meet people's expectations, raised by advancing home and office communications, information, and entertainment systems, for higher quality and more flexible services. Lightwave, software, and television technologies are making this possible, and manufacturers have already made major investments. The intelligent, broadband network that only a few years ago was a dream, has become a future certainty, unfolding in the next several decades as technical, economic, and political questions are resolved.

REFERENCES

(1) Bussey, H.W., "Integrating Services in broadband networks - the challenge and the future," National Telecomm Forum, Chicago, October, 1988.

(2) Kano, S., "ISDN user-network interface layers 2 and 3 protocols: new developments after 1984," Proc. 1986 IEEE Internat. Conf. on Commun. pp. 341-345.

(3) Minzer, S.E. & Spears, D.R., "New directions in signaling for broadband ISDN," IEEE Communications Magazine (to appear).

(4) Adachi, M., Chow, CH., "How ISDN terminals access intelligent network services", Proc. Int. Conf. on Data Commun, Singapore, D. 1988

(5) White, P.E., "The Broadband ISDN - the next generation of telecommunication network," Proc. IEEE Internat. Conf. on Commun. (ICC)

June, 1986.

(6) Kahl, P., "The Broadband ISDN, an upward-compatible evolution of the 64 kb/s ISDN," Proc. IEEE Internat. Conf. on Commun. (ICC), Seattle, June, 1987, pp. 0609-0613.

(7) IEEE JSAC Issue on Broadband Communications, July, 1986.

(8) Armbruster, H., & Arndt, G., "The evolution of broadband services," IEEE Communications Magazine, November, 1987.

(9) Huber, Peter, The Geodesic Network, (a report prepared for the U.S. Dept. of Justice),U.S. Govt. Printing Office, Jan, 1987.

(10) Weinstein, S.B., "Telecommunications in the coming decades," IEEE Spectrum, November, 1987.

(11) CCITT Red BOok, Vol. III, fascicle III.5 Integrated Services Digital Network (ISDN), Recommendations of the Series I, VIIIth Plenary Assembly, Malaga- Torremolinos, 8-19 Oct. 1984, Issued in Geneva, 1985.

(12) O'Toole, T.J., "ISDN: A larger user's perspective," IEEE Communications Magazine, vol. 25, #12, December, 1987, pp. 40-43.

(13) Anderson, C.P., "ISDN market opportunity," IEEE Communications Magazine, vol. 25 #12, December, 1987, pp. 55-59.

(14) Chen, C.H. et.al., "Integrated services workbench: a testbed for ISDN services," Proc. Globecom '87, Tokyo, November, 1987.

(15) Hass, R.J. & Humes, R.W., "Intelligent Network/2: A network architecture concept for the 1990's", Proc. Int. Switching Symposium, Phoenix, Arizona, March, 1987.

(16) Ross, Floyd, "FDDI A Tutorial", IEEE Communications Magazine, May, 1986, pp. 10-17.

(17) Judice, C., Addeo, E., Eiger,M.,& Lemberg,H. "Video on..." IEEE Int. Conf. on Commun., Toronto, June, 1986, pp 1735-1739.

(18) Darby, L.F., "Economic potential of advanced television products," April 7, 1988 (prepared for the National Telecommunication & Information Administration).

(19) Judice, C.N. & Legall, D., "Telematic services - are we ready?" IEEE Communications Magazine, July, 1987.

(20) Irven, J.H., Nilson, M.E., Judd, T.H., Patterson, Y.S. & Shibata, Y., "Multi-media

information services: a laboratory study," IEEE Communications Magazine, June, 1988.

(21) Sugimoto et.al., "Videotex: Advancing to Higher Bandwidth," IEEE Communications Magazine, Vol. 26, #2, February, 1988, pp. 22-30.

(22) Schatz, B.R., "Telesophy: A System for manipulating the knowledge of a community," Proc. Globecom '87, Tokyo, November, 1987.

(23) Caplinger, M., "An information system based on distributed objects," Proc. ACM OOPSLA '87, Oct. 4-8, 1987.

(24) Addeo, E.J., Gelman, A.D. & Massa, V.F., "A Multi-media teleconferencing bridge," Proc. Internat. Switching Symposium, Phoenix, Arizona, March, 1987.

(25) Weinstein, S.B., "Getting the Picture: A guide to CATV and the new electronic media" IEEE Press, New York, 1986.

(26) Judice, C.N., "Communications in the year 2001: the third age of video," Radio-Electronics, May, 1987.

(27) "RCA Labs' Video Compression Breakthrough Gets Ovation," Electronic Engineering Times, March 9, 1987.

(28) Lippman, Andrew, "News and Movies..." Proc. IEEE Globe., Tokyo, Dec. 1987, pp 1976-1981.

(29) Egido, Carmen, personal communication.

TELECOMMUNICATION REGULATION IN THE YEAR 2000 AND BEYOND: Thomas Hobbs Meets Karl Marx

Henry D. Levine
Partner

Morrison & Foerster
2000 Pennsylvania Avenue, NW.
Suite 5500
Washington, DC 20006

ABSTRACT

This paper discusses the prospects for long-term regulatory change in the communications industry in the wake of the technological and economic revolution of the last decade. It considers two scenarios, one involving the disappearance of the local exchange bottleneck, and the other assuming that the bottleneck survives.

If the bottleneck dissipates, the present legal and regulatory structure governing telecommunications can be largely eliminated. If the local bottleneck continues, however, significant regulatory controls will still be required. These could include protection for low income consumers and rules/safeguards to prevent local exchange carriers from abusing their market power. Prohibitions on local exchange carrier entry into particular lines of business will almost surely disappear, but complex rules designed to prevent anticompetitive behavior -- e.g., a requirement that LECs unbundle monopoly services and purchase them at the same tariffed rates as others -- may well endure.

INTRODUCTION

Karl Marx predicted that with the triumph of socialism, the state would "wither away." Thomas Hobbs, an earlier philosopher, took a more somber view: emphasizing the darker side of the human personality, he concluded that strong governmental institutions would always be needed to check man's baser impulses.

Over the last fifteen years, and particularly since the beginning of the present decade, technological advances (such as the introduction and widespread deployment of digital switching and optical fiber) and legal/regulatory changes (notably the AT&T divestiture and the virtual elimination of entry restrictions in most communications markets) have combined to create a "sea change" in the industry. Regulation has advanced as well, but many in the industry -- particularly the Regional Holding Companies ("RHCs") -- believe that it has not kept as a result, they believe, anachronistic regulation is inhibiting the deployment of new services and technologies. Can the legal and regulatory structure accommodate and adjust to the technical advances of the next quarter century and beyond?

THE BOTTLENECK

The critical question for the long-term prospects for communications regulation is the local exchange bottleneck. There are essentially two scenarios for the industry over the next twenty years. In the first, one finds continued technical advances, leading to enriched features and functions both within and outside the public network, but the monopoly of local exchange carriers over switched local service and access remains in place. The second scenario is exactly the same, except that the local PSN bottleneck falls victim to the evolution of cellular telephone service, expanded CATV functionality, the success of Digital Terminations Service ("DTS"), or other technical advances not yet envisioned.

If the local switched bottleneck disappears, the rationale for communications regulation as we know it will largely disappear. There is no need (in theory or reality) to control the prices or terms of service of carriers that lack market power. With the exception of regulation of "lifeline" service or service in rural areas where competition is acknowledged to be infeasible, communications industry could move to where the trucking, railroad and airline industries have moved over the last decade. There would be neither entry nor exit restrictions, and any existing or potential entrant in the industry could offer any service in any place.

EVOLUTION, NOT REVOLUTION

The problem with this scenario is that in the view of many -- including this author -- it is not likely to come to pass. Instead, the communications industry in the first part of the 21st century is far more likely to resemble the electric or natural gas industries than data processing, railroads or airlines, because local exchange carriers will retain their monopoly over local switched service and access, and with it the power (absent regulation) to control price and/or leverage their bottleneck into adjacent markets.

That is not to say that the deregulatory trends of the 1980s will be halted or reversed. Change will continue, but it will be quantitative not qualitative, and key elements of the present regulatory regime will remain in place.

Thus, I anticipate that the line of business restrictions in the MFJ will disappear, though not as quickly as the RHCs would like (or, for that matter, as slowly as interexchange carriers and equipment manufacturers would prefer). Before 1995, Judge Greene will be out of the communications business, and the FCC will once again take control over all aspects of domestic communications policy at the national level.

In place of line-of-business prohibitions, we may see a variety of mechanisms designed to prevent LEC abuse of the local bottleneck. At one extreme, one can envision a revival of the separate subsidiary concept if the nonstructural safeguards promulgated by the FCC in the Third Computer Inquiry are ineffective or unworkable. At the other extreme, most present regulation will "wither away" in favor of antitrust litigation -- or the threat thereof -- as a check on predation, price squeezes, refuses to deal, and other anticompetitive tactics. In this scenario, the Department of Justice becomes the principal regulator of the industry, and the FCC becomes a technical caretaker whose role is largely limited to handing out (and policing the use of) radio spectrum.

The middle scenario -- which I confess to viewing as the most likely -- is an extrapolation of current trends. Thus, the requirement of accounting separation of monopoly and competitive enterprise continues, and nonstructural rules or safeguards remain in place to prevent competitive abuse. For example, LECs may be allowed to offer any service, but will be required to purchase basic services out of tariffs (or at least published price lists) whenever they plan to use them to offer a complex or enhanced service. "Price parity" of this kind is relatively easy to envision and enforce. The tougher problem is price regulation to assure not only that all competitors pay the same price for monopoly services, but that those services by priced in a manner that prevents the monopoly provider from reaping monopoly profits on them.

In this area, as in many others, the first halting steps to reform are now being taken. Even those with little faith in "price caps" as an alternative to traditional rate of return regulation believe that rate of return regulation can be substantially simplified to the benefit of regulators, regulated companies, competitors, and consumers. The year-long rate case is already a thing of the past, and the development of flexible returns, with an emphasis on accounting review rather than litigation as an economic control, seems to be proceeding a pace.

CONCLUSION

Technology occasionally advances by revolution, but absent a real revolution (i.e., a war), law and regulation never do. That is true in communications as in everything else, and it suggests that the "Marxists" among the communications industry are overly optimistic (or overly ambitious) when they predict the disappearance of regulation as we know it. For the industry as a whole, middle-term prospects are for diminishing -- but still significant -- regulation of bottleneck services, but deregulation of almost everything else.

MOLDING THE NETWORK VIA
CUSTOM PROGRAMMING

John P. King, Chairperson
Director, Application Technology

Northern Telecom Incorporated

4001 E. Chapel Hill-Nelson Hwy.
P. O. Box 13010
Research Triangle Park, N. C.   27709
(919) 992-4504

ABSTRACT

Never has there been such an exciting challenging time in the Telecommunications industry as it pushes toward the goal of free market competition in both telecommunications and information services. Rapid market and technology changes surround us, but so do new business opportunities. Many of these opportunities manifest themselves as customized software features and services requirements on the telecommunication network, molded to meet a specific service provider or end customer unique requirement.

The traditional vendor approach to address network and customer needs has been by selling products and services. However, as the complexity and diversity of the network increases and the network moves toward an open architecture, a more open and dynamic approach is required from communications vendors. Custom Programming promises to be a key for delivering advanced network services in a highly competitive environment and enables the telephone operating companies to define and implement their own market specific applications.

This seminar examines three distinct and different perspectives of custom programming. We will first examine an operating company view of the market need and benefits addressable by the custom programming capability that allows an operating company or end user to define and implement extensions to the functions provided by the product vendor. We will then look as an example at the custom programming implementation plans of Northern Telecom, on its DMS SuperNode and related products to provide a highly levered environment for customers to implement custom programmed applications. The session describes the approach, tools and lab functions being put in place to support customers utilizing the custom programmability capability. The final session is an interesting and inspiring technical look into the future at the computer aided software engineering tools under development for speeding up and simplifying the custom development of distributed real-time applications in the 1990's.

Mark Beckner - Ameritech Services
Fahim Ahmed - Northern Telecom Incorporated
Jim McGee - Bell Northern Research

USER NEEDS FOR
NETWORK SERVICE CUSTOMIZATION

Mark Beckner
Senior Director
Switching Technology

Ameritech Services, Inc.
1900 East Golf Road
Schaumburg, Illlinois

ABSTRACT

For network providers, the abilities to rapidly develop and deploy new services and to customize new or existing services to the individual needs of customers is perhaps the most important of the current Intelligent Network developments. This ability has been broadly referred to as "service creation".

Vendors are beginning to offer low-level service creation capabilities by defining and implementing extensions to the functions provided in their systems and creating development environments so that network providers or third parties can develop applications. While this is not the complete service creation capability sought by network providers, Ameritech in particular, custom programmability of vendor systems will be a necessary part of a complete service creation environment.

BACKGROUND

In general, the switched telephone network has undergone significant change over the last 20 years. While some of these changes have been at the network level - e.g., common channel signaling, 800 service, etc. - most have been associated with advancements in the architecture and functionality at the network node level.

At the network node level, evolution to stored-program control switching systems has given switch developers tremendous flexibility in providing new switch-based features and functionality - custom calling features for residential and small business users and Centrex capabilities for large businesses are typical examples. Stored-program control has also given network providers a limited ability to configure specific instances of services that are generically implemented in a switching system.

In addition to changes in the control structure of switching systems, there has also been significant evolution in the transport capabilities offered by switching systems. Perhaps the most notable of these is the evolution from analog space-division architectures to digital time or time-and-space architectures. This evolution, in conjunction with evolution occurring at the network level, now is the process of offering end-to-end digital capabilities to end users via the establishment an integrated services digital network (ISDN).

Not only technological change has occurred. Changes in the structure of the telecommunications industry and, in particular, the industry regulation has resulted in network elements based on industry standards and supplied by a variety of equipment vendors. While this has generally been an overall benefit, it has often made the integration of these separate network elements a challenging task for the network provider whose customers prefer to view the network as a seamless whole.

To summarize, the general evolutionary trend - driven on three fronts by technology, service requirements, and industry structure - has been one of making telecommunications networks more flexible and, by doing so, transforming them from telecommunications networks to information networks. This trend must continue if the needs and expectations of network users are to be met.

THE MOTIVIATION FOR SERVICE CREATION

There are three motivating factors that clearly define the need for standard network service creation capability.

First, a multiple vendor industry structure is and will continue to be a necessity. Hence, current and future end user service requests will be met by a network constructed of elements from multiple vendors. In today's environment, this means either that new switch-based services must be developed more than once - i.e., once by each vendor - or that parts of a network based service must be developed by different vendors. And while standards help narrow the differences between these developments, services that are built on a base of new technology - e.g., ISDN services - often have measurable differences due to the immaturity and, hence, lack of common implementation of the technology base. By equipping network elements with functionality that will help to disassociate the underlying transport technology from the service being developed, a common service creation capability can be implemented.

Second, a standard service creation environment will permit services to be developed by parties in addition to the vendors of network elements. Hence, a further degree of freedom is permitted network providers in both the cost of developing new services and the rate of introduction of new services. More service creators should result in more services, effectively faster development of new services, and development costs that approach true costs.

A third motivator is that service creation will permit more rapid development of a portfolio of services for new transport technologies, helping to hasten both the technology deployment and arrival at the point where cost benefits due to wide deployment are realized.

THE ROLE OF CUSTOM PROGRAMMABILITY

Custom programmability currently is offered in different forms by different vendors. Each version of custom programming is tightly coupled to the operating environment or equipment offered by that vendor. Also, the degree of custom programming functionality varies among vendors. As such, it will be difficult for network providers to base their service creation environments on these individual custom programming environments unless vendors could agree to some standards for these environments.

If a standard platform could be agreed to and implemented by multiple vendors, or at least if individual vendor platforms could be constructed with industry standard components - i.e., programming languages, operating systems, computing systems, etc. - then there is the possibility of developing applications once for implementation in multiple operating environments. Hence, a smooth evolution to an intelligent network service creation capability could be envisioned.

Custom programmability will have an important role to play in adding functions of network elements beyond the intelligent network capabilities that are currently invisioned. One view is that network element functions developed for an intelligent network implementation, taken globally, define a "network operating system" on which a variety of new applications and services can be constructed. Custom programmability will be a necessary and useful tool to make changes or additions to this network operating system.

SUMMARY

Custom programmability is a necessary and useful tool in the continuing development of the intelligent network. Although in its current forms it does not provide a complete service creation capability, it may be if some basic standards could be agreed to among vendors who offer custom programmability.

DMS SUPERNODE
CUSTOM PROGRAMMING THRUST

Fahim Ahmed
Director, Custom Programming
Integrated Network Systems

NORTHERN TELECOM INC.
4001 E. Chapel Hill-Nelson Hwy.
Research Triangle Park, NC, 27709-3010

ABSTRACT:

The post-divestiture market dynamics have created a need for faster delivery of new services by the Telephone Operating Companies. This in turn dictates a need for a greater degree of control by the Operating Companies in the definition and direction of products being developed by the switch vendors.

This paper describes the mechanisms being put in place by Northern Telecom in response to this very real need. The paper discusses the resources, facilities, technologies and the support services that are available to our customers.

INTRODUCTION

In the post divestiture era, the velocity and size of business opportunities available to the Telephone Operating Companies requires a re-definition of the traditional relationship between the operating companies and the equipment vendors. The new, and as yet emerging, market dynamics have created a need for new customized services accompanied with the speed of delivery of these services. This implies a closer coupling of the Telephone Operating Companies' requirement with the product definition and development activities of the switch vendors, and the independence from the scheduled BCS feature releases of the vendors.

Northern Telecom's answer to the needs of our customers is provided by the establishment of a Custom Programming Facility. In simple terms, Custom Programming can be defined as the availability of the methods, technology and the processes by which the Telephone Operating Companies can control the capabilities of our product, in order to meet their diverse and independent market requirement.

THE PROCESS

When a service opportunity is identified, a specialist project team is formed to conduct a preliminary business and technical analysis. The team would consist of subject matter experts from Northern Telecom and the Telephone Operating Company,

The outcome of the preliminary analysis provides a go-no-go division point early in the process without too much commitment of resources, yet is sufficient to determine the commercial and technical feasibility of the opportunity. A go recommendation will result in an expansion of the analysis activity, and the formal commitment of resources by both parties, working to a schedule. The deliverables would be a detailed definition of the product requirements, deployment strategies and schedules, V.O. site identification, pricing and contact terms. A second check point is provided at the end of this activity by the signing of a formal agreement, before product development will commence.

The terms of the agreement and partitioning of responsibilities is tailored to the specific needs of each individual Telephone Operating Company.. On one extreme the Telephone Operating Company may choose to define the requirement and contract NT to design, test and verify. On the other hand, it may choose to undertake all aspects of the product from definition to deployment, with NT providing consultation and training.

THE PLATFORMS

Northern Telecom's Custom Programming offering consists of three Platforms. The Services Platform, the Programming Platform and finally, the Execution Platform.

The Services Platform is a comprehensive portfolio of services to support customized features from the definition to the deployment stage. The Service package is in itself customized to the needs of the individual Telephone Operating Company. The System Design Service consists of a pool of technical experts to work jointly with the Telephone Operating Company's Marketing & Technology staff during the definition stages. Customer Training and Documentation services provide the necessary transfer of knowledge to the managerial and technical staff of the Operating Company to assist them in the selection of architectural trade-offs and options. A Custom Programming Laboratory provides secure customer office areas and workstations for use by customer staff. Also provided are facilities for the verification and testing of custom applications, through Northern Telecom's FAST II and DMS Captive offices. Project Management and Field Trail Support Services provide the processes used internally by Norther Telecom to ensure the integrity of product and schedules.

The Programming Platform is a complete service creation/development environment to enable customer design staff to design custom applications either for test marketing of services or their final deployment. The environment consist of an industry familiar operating system and programming languages. The necessary support tools to allow for the debugging program library and configuration management, and testing of applications is part of the platform.

Finally, the Execution Platform, on which the application will be deployed, offers several options. Dependant in the nature of the application the execution vehicle could be an application processor integral to the DMS SuperNode or attached to the SuperNode via a well defined interface, called DMS-API.

SUMMARY

Northern Telecom's commitment to Custom Programming is a recognition of the reality of today's and tomorrow's marketplace. A marketplace where the canned approach of feature delivery by the switch vendors is not responsive enough to the new competitive pressures. It is a recognition of the fact that each Telephone Operating Company's market and product needs are unique.

NETWORK SERVICE DESIGN - A 1990'S VIEW

Jim McGee

Bell Northern Research

P. O. Box 3511, Station C
Ottawa, Ontario, Canada   K1Y4H7

ABSTRACT

ISDN will enable an evolution from simple network services such as calling line number delivery and display to sophisticated services such as multimedia calling. However, with these services comes the potential for a complexity explosion. to address this, BNR is exploring the application of new computer-aided design technologies to the specification, design and development of network architectures and services.

INTRODUCTION

It is generally accepted that software consumes 75% or more of the development resources of modern digital communications vendors. Currently, large switching machines may have upwards of 10 million lines of source code for service applications, system functions and associated OA&M. Given this code bulk, and the realtime performance and reliability criteria, switching machines already constitute some of the largest and most complex software projects in the world.

A look at some of the current trends in network environment provides a clear indication of the potential for a massive software complexity explosion.

Single Node Services & OAM->Multinode
    Services & OAM
Single Node Control   ->Distributed
    Multinode Control

Single Media Services   ->Multimedia
    Services
Single Vendor Services   ->Multivendor
    Services

Even the most conservative estimates would place the software complexity of the year 2000 network at 100 to 1000 times greater than today's single node switching systems. This network will contain millions of coordinated, co-operating software programs with literally hundreds of millions of lines of source code.

Given this context and the assertion that the software systems of the next generation network will be beyond human comprehension and control with current manual design methods, BNR researchers are exploring the application of new computer-aided design technologies to the specification, design and development of network architectures and services. This paper will briefly discuss the importance of network architecture and then concentrate on the network service lifecycle and associated design tools.

NETWORK SERVICE COMPLEXITY

A network service is any functionality offered by service providers to end users. Basic circuit switched service, packet switched service, speed calling and call waiting are all examples of network services.

In the 1960's it was recognized that large software applications had to have structure to isolate the relationships between modules to well defined, relatively narrow interfaces. These structuring concepts have evolved to form the basis of modern distribution and fault tolerance. Of course all successful switching system vendors have applied structured software design techniques to their products.

Curiously, despite the emphasis on multivendor distributed network services, no architecture exists to provide an application level framework for the software modules that will be needed to implement these services. In addition, with a few exceptions [GrMcCh88], [LeMc87], there seems to be little recognition in the industry of the necessity of such an architecture despite the overwhelming evidence from thousands of large software projects. It is not enough to define the location and low level primitives for network service processing [HaHu87]. This is like saying the definition of the system calls between an application and an operating system is sufficient to address application design issues. In large switching systems the semantic relationships between applications are by far the dominant design issues.

The most complex network design and standardization issues are associated with the controlling, managing, and accessing of distributed network services and not the transport, protocol or processing functions. The upper limit on the design, development and deployment of new network services will be based on the limitations of distributed network control theory and its associated software implementation and not on new transmission, line card or switching fabric technology.

ARCHITECTURE

In communications systems the term *architecture* is a synonym for *structure* . In the simplest sense an architecture consists of:

a set of objects of various types,
a set of inter-object relationships,
a set of rules for object interconnection,
a set of design principles or axioms.

Typically the design principles are used to validate the design rules and pertain to the integration or separation of the objects into layers of the architecture where a layer is a type of relationship between objects. An example architectural principle is "separate call control objects from connection control objects".

In a *functional architecture* the objects specify *what* functions are to be performed in terms of messages or signals sent or received and computations performed but now *how* they are to be implemented in hardware or software design decisions are made to implement each function in the functional architecture.

To have any lasting value, architectural rules must be enforced during the specification, design and implementation phases of the lifecycle. These rules cannot be pragmatically enforced manually. Architecture tools must capture architecture in a formal, machine readable manner. Computer based tools must assist the user in creating specifications and designs that are compliant with the architecture.

NETWORK SERVICE LIFECYCLE

The creation and deployment of network services can be modeled in a simple lifecycle view (Figure 1). Service velocity is the rate that new service functionality is added to the network. Service velocity should be weighted according to the value of the service functionality to the end user. Service interval is the time between the conception of a new or modified network service and its deployment (ubiquitous) and operation in the network.

Currently the average interval from conception to operation is about 4 years for relatively simple services such as network automatic callback. (More complex multivendor network services such as multimedia calling have yet to be defined.) An analysis of the components of the interval indicates that approximately 60% of the time is spent in the front end of the lifecycle on the activities of service conception, analysis, specification and high level design. This is typically a joint effort between the Service Providers and the equipment vendors.

Specifications and high level designs are often imprecise and ambiguous. This is usually discovered during the product design phase. In some cases the discovery is during product interworking trials between machines from different vendors. The cost of correcting an error during the deployment phase of the lifecycle is in the order of 1000 times the cost of correcting the same error during the specification or high level design phase. Poor specifications result in an increase in interval during subsequent phases.

Our industry targets should be to reduce the average interval to one year and increase the service velocity by a factor of ten by 1995 while maintaining the trend towards zero defect products. This can only be done by bringing computer-assisted technology to all phases of the network service lifecycle since an unbalanced reduction in any phase will leave bottlenecks in other phases. It is proposed that the formal capture of architecture and the massive reuse of specification and design components are critical to achieving these improvements.

ADVANCED NETWORK ENVIRONMENT

The exploitation of new computer aided system technologies will take place in the context of a environment of co-operating intelligent machines assisting highly skilled persons in the lifecycle activities associated with the creation and operation of network services (Figure 2). While the generic components will be mostly evolved versions of those of today, the degree of computer interworking within and between the lifecycle activities will eliminate our current reliance on informal and inefficient systems for the transfer and understanding of information.

The network environment will consist of advanced computer based toolsets for all elements of the network service lifecycle, with full electronic interworking between the toolsets. Included in the network design toolset will be the capability for the formal capture of network architecture at all logical and physical levels. This formal architecture will be the primary model for the semantic exchange of information between tools. In addition to providing a master framework for the creation, deployment and operation of network services it will be the single greatest factor in the reduction of network complexity. It is critical that this architecture be complete. In addition to specifying the interfaces between the physical layer network elements the architecture must provide definitions of the necessary interfaces between the software programs that constitute the control elements for distributed network services.

NETWORK SERVICE DESIGN

The design of a network service may be split into two stages (Figure 3). The first stage is a functional specification and design defining what the service is to do but not how it is to be implemented in a product. The output from this stage is a validated functional design which is fed to various product design and development environment. The output from the second stage is a validated and tested set of product hardware and software designs for eventual deployment in a multi-vendor network. As indicated above, the design of the service including its interaction with or dependencies on other services is constrained by the rules of the network functional architecture. In the product design stage a service design must be compliant to both the network and product architectures.

While functional network designs are primarily at a black box level they must be executable and subject to computer validation for correctness in terms of freedom from deadlock, starvation and critical race as well as compliance to performance requirements. The network and product design environment contain similar computer assisted capabilities for the specification, design, simulation and analysis of architectures, services and protocols (figures 4 and 5).

ADVANCED TOOLSET ARCHITECTURE

Our vision is a communications services toolset consisting of a family of tools interworking via an intelligent database (Figure 6). The most fundamental capabilities are those for the capture of the structure (architecture), behavior, data and protocols associated with a service design. The power of the toolset is based on the user's capability to directly manipulate, through graphical interfaces, large system design concepts such as multidimensional layers, hierarchical decomposition, concurrent finite state machines and abstract data types. The fact that many designs share common components is exploited using an object oriented approach. The object database serves as a storehouse of reusable specification, design and implementation components. Reuse is of critical importance since in the absence of any killer technology, reuse is likely to be the dominant means of increasing productivity in the 1990's.

CONCLUSION

Advances in large system software technology have not kept pace with advances in hardware technology. Software technology limits will put an upper bound on vendor's and service provider's abilities to deliver new services to end users. We must exploit the experience we have gained through hard lessons in large software system development and realize that there is no such thing as an application or service independent network architecture. The desired functions of the network at all levels must be structured and enforced via network functional architectures. The scope of the problem demands that a set of tools be constructed to achieve the formal, electronic capture of architecture. Service designers may then use a set of computer assisted design tools for the rapid and reliable development of network services, making maximum reuse of a common set of design components. Only then will the development of services for the intelligent network be intelligent.

REFERENCES

[HaHu87] R. Hass, and R. Humes, 'Intelligent Network/2: A Network Architecture Concept for the 199', *Proceedings ISS,* June 1987.

[GrMcCh88] S. Greenspan, C. McGowan, M. Chandra Shekaran, 'Toward an Object-Oriented Framework for Defining Services in Future Intelligent Networks', *IEEE Proceedings ICC88,* June 1988.

[LeMc87] J. Lemany, J. McGee, 'A Distributed Network Architecture for the Competitive Network Environment', *Proceedings ISS,* June 1987.

Network Service Lifecycle

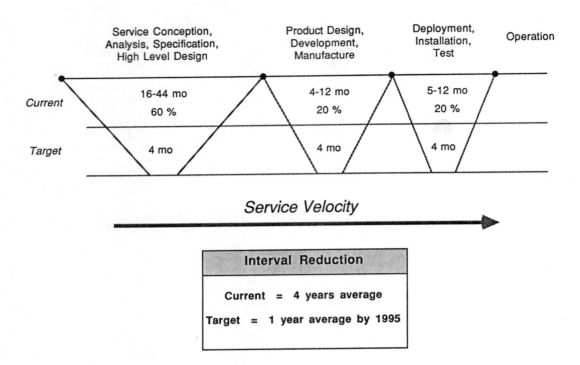

Service Conception, Analysis, Specification, High Level Design

Product Design, Development, Manufacture

Deployment, Installation, Test

Operation

Current

16-44 mo
60 %

4-12 mo
20 %

5-12 mo
20 %

Target

4 mo

4 mo

4 mo

Service Velocity

Interval Reduction
Current = 4 years average
Target = 1 year average by 1995

Advanced Network Environment - Vision

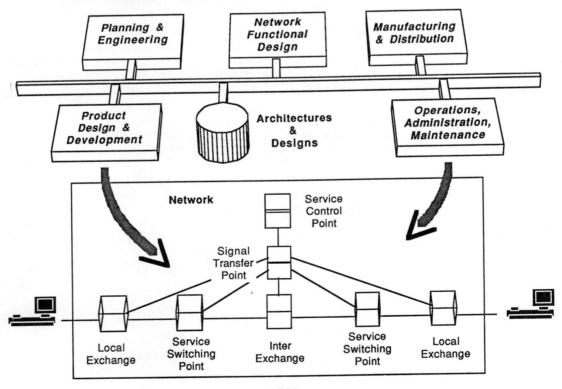

Planning & Engineering

Network Functional Design

Manufacturing & Distribution

Product Design & Development

Architectures & Designs

Operations, Administration, Maintenance

Network

Service Control Point

Signal Transfer Point

Local Exchange

Service Switching Point

Inter Exchange

Service Switching Point

Local Exchange

1765

Advanced Network Environment - Design

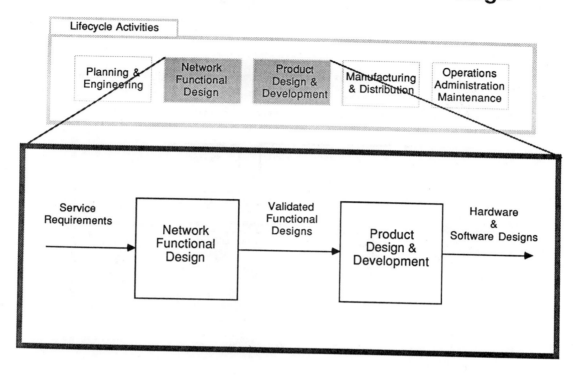

Network Functional Design Environment

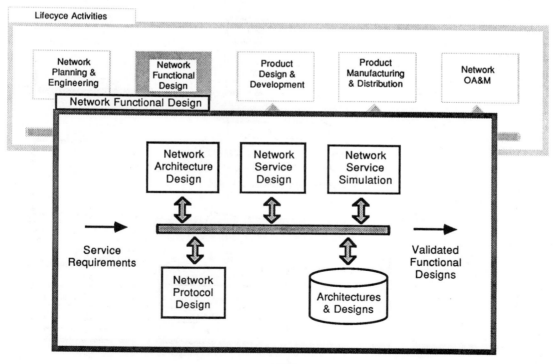

Product Design & Development

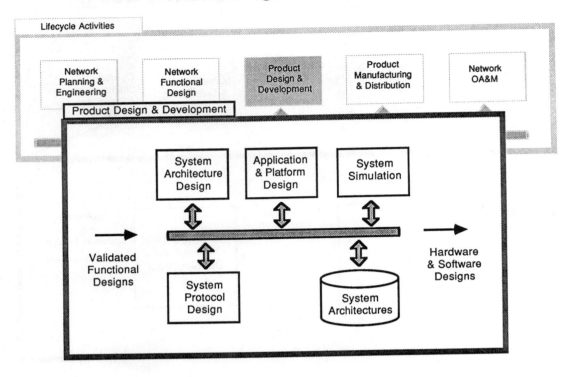

Advanced Toolset Architecture

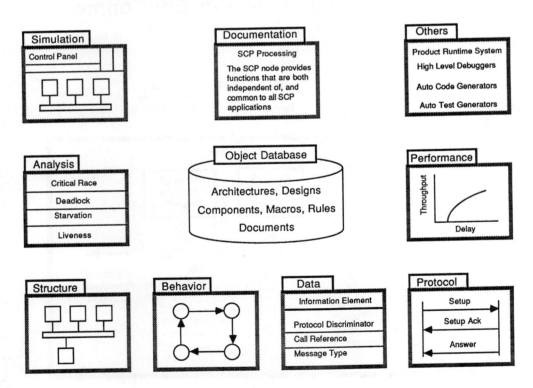

AI AND EXPERT SYSTEMS

Sushil G. Munshi - Chairperson
Vice President
Technology Planning

United Telecommunications, Inc.
2330 Shawnee Mission Parkway
Westwood, KS 66205

ABSTRACT

In recent years Expert systems have been introduced in the telecommunications field. This seminar explores issues in deploying the expert system technology for practical applications. The first session is an introduction to expert systems covering potential application domains and considerations for selecting an application. The second session addresses one of the key issue, knowledge acquisition. Third session gives an assessment of the available tools, hardware and software, for mainframe to PC based development. A telephone company's approach to identify and initiate the development of a practical applications is given in session four. The seminar concludes with a discussion of real application.

Jean C. Zolnowski-- Bell Communications
Research

Robert Stepp, III -- University of Illinois

Peter Politakis -- Digital Equipment
Corporation

Sushil G. Munshi -- United Telecommunications,
Inc.

John C. Thomas -- NYNEX Corporation

FROM EXPERT SYSTEMS FEASIBILITY PROTOTYPE TO FIRST APPLICATION: A CASE STUDY

Adam E. Irgon
Member - Technical Staff

Jean C. Zolnowski
District Manager - Human Computer Technology

Bell Communications Research
444 Hoes Lane
Piscataway, NJ 08854 USA

INTRODUCTION

The Bellcore AI Team (BAIT), a joint venture of the Bellcore Computer Technology Transfer project and various development organizations within Bellcore, has provided a unique opportunity to both explore and transfer expert system technology. At this point in its life cycle, BAIT also now provides the opportunity to assess how well the expert system technology worked. The purpose of this paper is to provide a brief description of one of the BAIT expert system projects and a short retrospective of what was required for its development.

FAST-FACS ADVISOR FOR SYSTEM TUNING

● **The Domain**

The FACS Advisor for System Tuning (FAST) is an expert system for tuning the performance of application and system software associated with the Facility Assignment and Control System (FACS). The FACS application consists of close to one million lines of C source code, making it one of the largest software systems in the world. FACS requires a dedicated mainframe configured with two or three 7 MIP processors, 50 Megabytes of main memory, and up to 75 disk packs on seven dual controllers. FACS is operational in many Bell Operating Companies, and site requests for tuning FACS have grown dramatically over the last two years.[1] The FAST expert system encodes large amounts of application and system tuning expertise to assist production FACS sites in analyzing and improving the performance of their systems.

● **Problem design**

FAST reasons over data gathered by various performance monitors to identify the cause of performance problems concentrated in the following three areas: 1: Mistaking a poorly tuned system for one that is out of cpu capacity, 2) Inadvertent introduction of queueing delays, 3) End-user habits or system setup causing performance problems on systems *with spare cpu capacity*.

Each of these categories of problems breaks down into other categories. For example, queueing delays, which are particularly insidious, can be traced to the I/O subsystem, data management routines, application data bases, application caches, or software setup parameters. For certain problems, such as I/O subsystem imbalances, FAST will; recommend explicit fixes for the problem: for example, file balancing recommendations.

Large amounts of various types of performance data are required to analyze FACS performance problems. A time-consistent snapshot of the FACS system is created by invoking performance monitoring tools, and the data produced is the input to the FAST expert system running on a high-end workstation, as pictured in Figure 1.

---

[1]. This growth in tuning requests is commensurate with the growth in workload and conversion to the FACS software.

The picture shows further that this data is analyzed by FAST, and tuning recommendations that would, if implemented, result in a tuned FACS system are made. FAST is not a realtime monitor, but rather is invoked to solve existing performance problems or to tune a FACS system to prevent future performance problems, much like domain experts are called upon to address problems.

AI ASPECTS OF THE PROBLEM AND SOLUTION

The multiparadigm implementation of FAST includes frame-based knowledge representation with multiple inheritance, data driven reasoning for diagnosis, and assumption-based reasoning for determining optimal performance tuning recommendations. The multiparadigm programming environment greatly facilitated the implementation of this system, since a large amount of information with many interactions had to be represented in order to make possible a straightforward implementation of the diagnostic behavior required.

Put another way, without powerful knowledge representation capabilities, there would have been an explosion of the number of special-case production rules, rather than the relatively few, generic production rules which are actually used. The problem solving knowledge base is very compact because the data representation facilitates this problem solving. For another part of the FAST system, making repair recommendations, the difficulty of solving the I/O subsystem file balancing problem would have presented a daunting challenge without the ability to do assumption-based reasoning for hypothesizing file moves and comparing alternative solutions.

DEVELOPMENT PERSPECTIVES ON THE PROBLEM

This project began by gauging the problem-solving behavior we wanted to achieve for FACS performance tuning, and translating this into a development schedule. Development of expert systems is by nature something of a free-wheeling process which cannot be pinned down as neatly as that of conventional systems, characterized by high-level requirements, detailed requirements, coding, unit testing, and integration testing. The following sections highlight key points in the evolution of FAST from feasibility prototype to "production system".

- **Training**

  The official programming training period for the FAST project using the multiparadigm tool was two weeks for a vendor course. However, the inevitable startup costs involved in working in any new software environment are especially great for multiparadigm tools, and the gradual training in this tool, which happened during the development of the system, stretched out the development time for each phase. We have found that even for a person with experience in AI, it can take months to be comfortable with the nuances of using the multiparadigm tool. For a person who doesn't have experience in AI, and specifically the Lisp programming language, this period will be even longer, since the multiparadigm tool is built on Lisp, and non-trivial applications inevitably involve "dropping down" into Lisp for some processing.

- **Knowledge Acquisition and Domain Modeling**

  For the FAST project, knowledge acquisition activities were structured around an "operational principles" document which specified the problem solving behavior desired (in the form of heuristics) and the performance data which would be needed to enable this problem solving. This document formed the high-level requirements for the system, and facilitated knowledge acquisition by providing a reference point for discussions between the domain expert and knowledge engineers, both for understanding the required behavior of the expert system and for understanding FACS performance tuning concepts. The seeming simplicity of the problem solving specified often belied the ultimately complicated implementation which was required (involving, for example, advanced reasoning strategies) to implement the specified behavior. Also, there were subtle errors and omissions which did not become evident until the expert system was tested thoroughly. Nevertheless, *this was a very affective means of transferring domain knowledge which we would not hesitate to employ on any expert system project where it is practical.*

  It was important that there not be fixed requirements describing the structure of the implementation, because the design of the knowledge base is an experimental, iterative process aided by the development facilities of the programming environment. The "getting it right" part of expert system development is undeniably something of an acquired talent; this process is less easily explicated than the process of development of conventional systems, but the factors we are discussing here have been instrumental in our success in implementing FAST. Happily, too, the process of "getting it right" is aided by a corpus of development tools in the multiparadigm environment. The environment encourages finding solutions to problems experimentally, and generally the penalty for design mistakes is not large.

- **Integration Issues**

  The FAST expert system has to get data from production FACS systems, but not in real time, and so some of the thorniest types of integration issues have been avoided. Because this is not a real-time application, integration has not been a large problem for the FAST project, but rather gathering consistent snapshots of various types of performance data from production FACS machines has been our biggest problem. Also, we have had to allocate time to the development of software to automate the collection and transfer of data, in order to alleviate the problem of human error.

- **Testing**

  Generally, four tiers of testing are appropriate for expert systems: unit testing by knowledge engineers, to ensure results consistent with their current understanding of the domain; rigorous testing by the domain expert; testing by other domain experts, to reach a consensus on the system's behavior; testing by the end-user(s) of the system.

  Testing of FAST has been accomplished by having the domain expert examine the performance statistics being used by FAST, and independently deciding what tuning is appropriate. These recommendations have been compared with FAST's recommendations, and the system has been modified to account for inconsistencies. *This iterative development and testing of the knowledge base is typical of expert systems, and is time consuming and essential.*

  Further testing of the system is also being done by other domain experts to ensure that the system is unbiased (that is, it reflects the common wisdom of a group of performance tuning domain experts). Also, an end user is testing prior to soak.

- **Enhanced User Interface Facilities**

  To help ensure acceptance of the system, we decided to build a much more ambitious user interface than we had originally intended. Features include widespread use of interactive graphics, and explanation upon request (in restricted English) of the reasoning used by FAST to reach any of the presented tuning recommendations. In retrospect, *we feel that the spiffy user interface has been vital in attaining the widespread acceptance of FAST which we have experienced. In particular, the explanation facility has been important because it allows end users to understand the system's reasoning,* thus avoiding "black box syndrome."

- **Advanced, Debugged Problem Solving**

  FAST uses assumption-based reasoning to solve the complex problem of relocating identified problem files in a FACS I/O subsystem. The high-end tool we used provides an elegant method for implementing this problem solving, which might not otherwise be attempted, through their version of an Assumption-based Truth Maintenance System (ATMS), but the facility is non-trivial to use, especially for novice expert system developers.

CONCLUSIONS

FAST has been extremely successful experiment, but not wholly for technological reasons. Other reasons why it is successful stand out. First, FAST was a well-conceived project. That is, we undertook a problem that *really needed to be solved*, and that was especially well-suited for implementation using expert system technology. Also, it was a proper approach to use a high-end expert system development tool, but there were significant training costs associated with these environments, even for a developer well-versed in AI concepts. This time must be built into the development schedule.

Second, a team of people who complemented each other well (domain expert, experienced and apprentice knowledge engineer) worked on the project, and the FACS organization supported the project well. The availability of a willing, insightful domain expert has been one of the most important factors in making this project successful. In the case of FAST, the expert interpreted the knowledge of a group of domain experts, and provided that knowledge in a comprehensible format, thus allowing us to skirt the difficult issue of knowledge acquisition from multiple domain experts, and also do knowledge acquisition quickly.

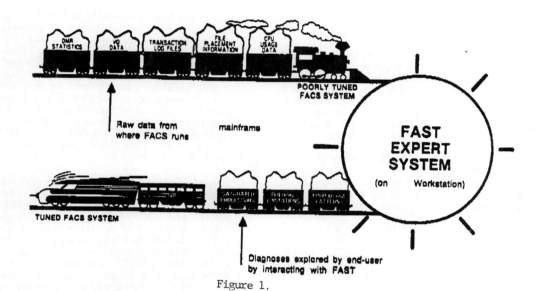

Figure 1.

TOOLS FOR AI APPLICATIONS

Robert Stepp, III
Coordinated Science Laboratory

University of Illinois
1101 W. Springfield, Avenue
Urbana, IL 61801

ABSTRACT

In the information age, knowledge is a commodity that may soon be more precious than gold. As observed long ago, the difference between information and knowledge is that knowledge has utility (by being digested so it can support inference and problem solving) for solving complex intellectual tasks, for designing and inventing, and for explaining. Managing knowledge (collecting, repairing, generalizing, organizing, or applying it) requires AI tools. The size of useful knowledge bases far exceeds the capabilities of human or regular data processing techniques. The issues for selecting/building AI tools include hardware size, speed, and cost as well as software comprehensiveness and human engineering. In this paper the current frontier of AI knowledge management tools is explored with attention to a few of the emerging trends.

INTRODUCTION

The economy, corporate finance, customer assistance, product design, system configuration, fault diagnosis, etc. are but a few of the business areas that have become so complex that achieving real progress is very difficult without computer assistance. Conventional programming and database applications are adequate when limited to handling isolated and well defined problems:

- a database of customer accounts can be established easily but the modes of querying the database are greatly constrained at the time of database design--only limited flexibility is usually provided and it was not possible to *teach the database new tricks*.

- a program to simulate network traffic can be put together to exercise a programmed model of the traffic dynamics and give a report--the nature of the network model is highly constrained by the programming and the system has little ability to interpret and explain the results of the simulation--that is left solely to the network analyst.

AI techniques are being used in the attempt to bring more diverse knowledge to bear on solving problems. Rather than have tools that are limited by their design to a single method appropriate only to certain subproblems, many AI systems have scores of *rules* in their knowledge bases to handle a wide variation of situations. With AI systems, it is anticipated that the knowledge governing the behavior and utility of the system will evolve (though perhaps slowly) and be improved. This has the promise of yielding both a more robust system, and one that rather gracefully gets better as additional knowledge is added.

Many applied AI problem solving systems are instances of so called *expert* systems. These systems are mostly used to do fault diagnosis (analogously derived from the early expert systems that were developed to do disease diagnosis). Expert systems are also being used to do system configuration and product design, but these two tasks are inherently more difficult, with product design being the most difficult.

An expert system must hold knowledge (and information) and process it to conclude a decision (or set of decisions) within a reasonable length of time. Knowledge and information are stored in the form of inference rules (e.g., *if X is true and Y is true then conclude Z*), relational data tables (e.g., lines of data arranged in columns such as *salesman-name, total-sales, office-number*, etc.), or frames (e.g., *part-123 ISA line-amplifier, with gain=50, output-impedance=50-ohms, power-consumption=35-watts*). A cousin of the frame is used in the currently popular *object-based/object-oriented* approaches. An *object* is like a frame in that each object is described by the values of its *slots* (like "gain" above; slots on objects are often referred to as the object's *instance variables)*. An object, unlike a frame, also operates as a procedure that understands *messages* that request the computation of defined functions.

An expert system uses inference rules to deduce the best decision that is indicated from the available facts. Non-trivial expert system applications often involve massive amounts of stored information and produce decisions that are based ultimately on the application of hundreds of inference rules. Current computer workstation technology is called on to address both the issues of memory size and processing speed.

From their name, expert systems are supposed to function as an expert would; they need to incorporate accurate and comprehensive knowledge (usually as inference rules) that will yield the same (or fundamentally similar) decisions as an expert would produce. The bottleneck is the problem of *knowledge acquisition*: how to get the rules to put into the expert system. This problem is confounded by the fact that an *expert* in our society is a person who demonstrates a high level of proficiency at a particular skill but is not necessarily good at explaining *how* the expertise should be applied or codified. Although most expert systems are built by debriefing experts (getting them to tell their problem solving recipes a task they are not often well suited to perform), AI research into the areas of automated knowledge acquisition and learning from examples is starting to provide a better alternative.

THE HARDWARE FRONTIER

An AI System can be written in any computer language (even ADA) and executed on any computer system, but nearly all AI systems do extensive amounts of symbolic computation that is especially well suited to the LISP and/or PROLOG programming languages. Thus there is special interest in hardware environments for LISP and PROLOG.

AI applications are usually both memory and processor intensive. The typical AI system will have many megabytes of RAM memory and a virtual address space of nearly a quarter gigabyte or more. Symbolic computing programs (e.g., LISP programs) are aided by hardware that has *tagged memory*. Most LISP machines use this memory architecture; personal computers and mainframes do not; symbolic computing on general-purpose computers sacrifices a measure of performance that may or may not be warranted by the equipment price differential.

Computation speed is the other major factor. All the current processor technologies (parallel processing, instruction/data caches, pipelined operations, high clock speed, wide data paths) can be applied to improve performance. Some manufacturers have analyzed the atomic operations that are most prevalent in symbolic computing and are developing RISC (reduced instruction set computer) processors that are optimized for blinding speed through the use of fewer and simpler types of machine instructions.

The user environment is often significant in determining how productive a workstation will be. LISP machines have been way ahead in having a supporting user environment. The development of LISP-based systems and knowledge-based systems does involve much symbolic information that is often arranged in rather arbitrary ways. LISP machines have large multiple window displays for simultaneous editing and testing of new functions. The system kernel supports *break for inspection* that causes the program to pause to permit the user to probe its structure to find out whether it is behaving as expected. Then regular execution can be resumed or the function aborted. There are also aids for managing large programs. General purpose systems have not yet been able to offer the same quality of LISP development friendliness. For already completed expert systems that are being consulted to solve some decision problem, some of the built in user-friendly support is not greatly needed.

- **Some hardware tools available now**

    A large number of different AI workstations are available. Certainly they all cannot be mentioned here, but instead classes of workstations will be described. At the top of the machine taxonomy, there is the distinction between LISP machines and AI workstations that (among other things) can run LISP.

- **LISP machines**

    A LISP machine is presently a computer system whose processor is specifically designed to run LISP. Often these machines have tagged memory, writeable/loadable microstores (permitting the software engineer to redefine machine instructions), a LISP oriented keyboard with numerous special function keys, and a large graphic display with a resolution of about 1000 by 1000 dots on which there are multiple windows. The system software on a LISP machine is written in (compiled) LISP. The better known LISP machines are made by Symbolics and Texas Instruments. The list price varies with the configuration, but is typically about $60,000 for a basic system. Options can extend this price upwards of $100,000 per system.

    RAM memory size varies, with 16 megabytes being that of a "modest" system. It is not uncommon to see system specifications that provide for RAM memory options extending up to 128 megabytes. Presently, most LISP machines have a RAM memory size of 8 to 32 megabytes--this reflects the current price vs. desired system performance sentiment. One should note that the current cost of RAM memory is inflated by U.S./Japan trade discussions and reactions.

    LISP machines are almost always acquired with modest to large disk storage capacities. The LISP software itself is large (about 100 megabytes) and disk space must be reserved for the paging area that supports the virtual memory (at least 100 megabytes) and for application files. Each LISP machine thus has disk space that may range from a modest 300 megabytes to a more robust 1 gigabyte, or more.

    Present day LISP machines run Common-LISP (and usually another older LISP, and PROLOG). The low-level details of their graphic displays are unique to the different brands, and applications that provide fancy screen displays must be ordered for a particular system. Comprehensive expert system tools, such as ART and KEE are often run from LISP machines.

    The Texas Instruments EXPLORER II and the Symbolics 3650 are presently the top-spec models from each company. Both are fast LISP processing systems, with some users feeling that the EXPLORER II is faster than the 3650 but the 3650 supports "really huge" applications by virtue of its larger virtual memory. Because of the high workstation price, both companies are defending their interests with low-cost compatible workstations with reduced performance. Texas Instruments has introduced the MICRO-EXPLORER which is a special TI LISP chip on a processor board that installs in a Macintosh. Symbolics has plans to introduce a LISP chip of its own for a product in this class. Cost for a complete system (e.g., Macintosh plus special LISP board) is about $20,000 list. The performance of the MICRO-EXPLORER is rumored to be roughly half that of the EXPLORER II.

- **LISP workstations**

Powerful general purpose workstations have appeared on the market in the last year. They can be considered in three group: SUN workstations (and other high performance workstations including Apollo workstations and DEC micro-vax workstations), personal computers in the PC family, and personal computers in the Macintosh family. In each case, the underlying system kernel is no written in LISP (the language"C" is popula today) and the computer's architecture is no optimized for LISP.

The SUN family of systems spans a very wide range of performance/cost figures. At the top end, the SUN-4 system uses a high speed RISC architecture that yields a machine that can perform 10 million instructions per second (10MIP). LISP programs on this machine are said to execute as fast or a little faster than on the EXPLORER II. There has been a major difference between LISP machines and LISP workstations: the LISP user environment/support on LISP workstations has been much inferior to that on the LISP machine. This is a matter of mature software rather than hardware difference and Sun has announced its solution to this deficiency as being the Symbolic Programming Environment (SPE) which is a set of comprehensive aids for the development of artificial intelligence applications. The new tools are designed to improve productivity and ease LISP program development in the manner of the LISP machine programming environment. A SUN-4 workstation configured for LISP programs (large RAM memory--32 megabytes) has a list price in the $70,000 range. For about one fourth of this price you can get another model that runs about one third as fast and for about one eighth this price you can get a diskless model that runs about one fourth as fast.

In the IBM PC world (in which dozens of companies are marketing look-alike systems) LISP is available as an add-on language, or by the attachment of an auxiliary processor (such as the add-on "Hummingboard" offered by Gold Hill Computers). LISP on a PC is usually limited to the execution of programs developed on more powerful systems, although with the introduction of the PS/2 line of 80386-based systems (and non-IBM look alikes) the performance can be roughly one third (or a bit more) of the SUN-4. There are several expert system tools that are marketed to the PC user (see following sections). PROLOG is available for the PC, and occasional AI systems are written in "C" or PASCAL for the PC.

LISP and PROLOG are available for the Apple Macintosh itself, and for the TI MICRO-EXPLORER that is an add-on to the

Macintosh II. The Mac alone (depending on the model) has performance that ranges from that of a PC to that of the lower performance SUN workstations. Of course, the Mac has multiple windows and a graphics oriented display and menu-oriented mode of operation--all qualities that fit well to its use as an AI system.

- **Mainframe computers**

For AI applications, the bulk of novel applications are targeted for workstations rather than for mainframes, although "Common LISP and PROLOG (and of course "C" AND PASCAL, etc.) are available from most vendors. Many expert system shells (written in LISP) are thus available for mainframes. Of special interest is LISP on supercomputers. Several projects are being pursued towards providing Common LISP on supercomputers (such a Cray II machines) with networking hookups to workstations (such as SUN or Macintosh) to make AI applications on the supercomputer appear like workstation applications, only 100 times faster.

- **Networking**

No discussion of AI hardware tools could be complete without mentioning networking. Networking of AI workstations is commonplace and is considered a standard part of any system (unless it is physically isolated from other systems). TCP/IP is the most widely used network protocol, with LISP machines, SUN workstations, PC's (with ethernet boards), and Macintoshes (with ethernet boards) able to communicate with each other at effective transfer rates of up to 100,000 characters per second. At major universities and research centers, national and international network communication is possible at little cost. This has greatly aided the sharing of information and ideas.

Some future hardware prospects

The hardware for AI applications has been getting steadily more powerful without much change in price. Watch balance of trade negotiations with the Japanese as it affects the price and availability of memory chips. Memory prices had been falling gradually until recent economic tensions caused them to jump up. AI applications remain memory hungry and there will be benefits to the continuing decline in memory chip costs.

Several microprocessor manufacturers are developing RISC processor chips, some of which (like the Motorola 88000) may be cast into specialized versions for symbolic computation. Workstations may soon have multiple processor chips, perhaps dozens of identical processor chips to enable parallel processing of large problems. There will be more really high speed add-on boards (such as the MICRO-EXPLORER). Symbolics is working on its "Ivory" chip set and some smaller companies are doing likewise. Gradually the development support environment found on LISP machines will be more generally provided on a range of LISP workstations.

Networking will play an increasingly important role. Shortly, AI systems will begin to be configured so that they can cooperate with each other, managed collectively via the network to solve larger and more complex decision-making/planning/designing tasks.

THE SOFTWARE FRONTIER

Although much current basic AI research will have only eventual peripheral impact on expert system science and engineering, it is the concept of the so called *expert system shell* that has spawned dozens of commercial products. An expert system shell provides the mechanization for acquiring knowledge and information (providing storage schemes for rules, data tables, frames, and objects, depending on which formalisms a particular product supports), for aiding the evaluation of the accuracy, completeness, and consistency of the knowledge and information, for repairing the knowledge where it is determined to be faulty, and for managing the interaction with the end user. Some of the better known shells include Goldworks, ART, and KEE.

Vendors of expert system shells (for example Gold Hill Computers, Inference Corp., IntelliCorp, and many more) are active in porting their systems to the popular hardware configurations, especially to support the lower cost workstations that are often used in a company's initial adventure into AI.

Sales of ART and KEE (both large expensive systems) account for about half of the expert system shell market. In the PC arena, there are a number of smaller software tools. Popular systems include TI's Personal Consultant Plus, RuleMaster, KES, M.1, Exsys, Level Five, and GURU. Additional systems are hitting the market all the time.

Some software tools available now

Of the systems named above, GURU, Level Five, and Personal Consultant Plus are sometimes mentioned as the PC-size systems that are most versatile. Versatility can mean the difference between being able to integrate the expert system (that is usually rule driven) with conventional databases and software that is procedure or data driven. The developer appreciates systems that are equipped with a wide range of knowledge representation and processing options, particularly when the options are well thought out and are sensible to use. It is sometimes critical that the AI tool be usable by non-programmers and/or non-knowledge-engineers.

Relatively few AI tools have been developed specifically for the Macintosh although many tools written in LISP can be easily ported by the user (if the vendor cooperates). With the introduction of the reasonably affordable MICRO-EXPLORER, the Macintosh community will have the same tool alternatives as the LISP machine community: virtually all major tools are likely to be offered.

Here is a very brief incomplete list of some expert system shells, along with the name of the developer, the systems on which they run, and a few characteristics of the system. With the rapid development of systems, this listing is sure to be out of date. Many expert system developers will be showing improved systems at the 1988 conference of the American Association for Artificial Intelligence (AAAI) in August.

▸ ART (Inference Corp): For LISP machines, VAX; frames and relational tables; multiple viewpoints; TMS (truth maintenance system); higher cost.

▸ EMYCIN (Sumex): For Interlisp systems; interactive explanation capability; confidence factors; less flexible control over rules.

▸ ExperOPS (ExperTelligence, Inc.): For Macintosh; faster than OPS5.

▸ Exsys (Jeffrey Perrone & Associates): For PCs; implemented in "C"; multiple modes of uncertainty factors.

- Goldworks (Gold Hill Computers): For Hummingboard PC add-on; on-line tutorial.

- GURU (Micro Data Base Systems, Inc.): For PCs and VAX; database management; spreadsheet; easy interface to conventional programs.

- KEE (IntelliCorp): For LISP machines; object-oriented; frames; TMS; rule tracing, higher cost.

- KES (Software Architecture and Engineering, Inc.): For Common LISP or C; Bayesian statistics; rule analyzer.

- Knowledge Craft (Carnegie Group): For LISP machines and VAX; frames; database manager; object-oriented; logic programming; multiple rule contexts.

- Knowledge Workbench (Silogic, Inc): For SUN workstations; PROLOG based; relational database; higher cost.

- Level Five (Level Five Research): For PCs; implemented in PASCAL; lower cost; menu display; for smaller applications.

- M.1 (Teknowledge): For PCs; implemented in PROLOG; for experienced users.

- Nexpert (Neuron Data): For PC, VAX, SUN, Macintosh; object-oriented; links to conventional programs; bidirectional inheritance.

- OPS5 (Franz, Inc.): For Franz LISP; object-oriented; user provides most of the control mechanism; general purpose; widely used; fewer special features.

- OPS83 (Production Systems Tech.): For VAX or PC; more flexible, more expressive, faster than OPS5.

- Personal Consultant Plus (T1): For PC and EXPLORER; based on EMYCIN; flexible interface to conventional programs; frames; object-oriented.

- RuleMaster (Radian Co.): For C-based UNIX systems; knowledge acquisition from examples; fuzzy-set uncertainty; pipes to conventional programs.

Besides expert system shells, there is a growing market for LISP interpreters, many which come with low-level AI tools such as support for object-oriented programming. Lucid Common LISP is said to be providing LISP for IBM mainframes and the PS/2 computer families. Their Common LISP is also available on SUN workstations. Franz, Inc. now markets a Common LISP system for SUN workstations. Much of the PC LISP market has been captured by Golden Common LISP from Gold Hill Computers. Part of this popularity is an on-line LISP tutorial, and the fact that they entered the PC LISP market early. There are several other LISP vendors for the personal computer market. One that also runs on the Macintosh is Le LISP by ACT Informatique. PROLOG systems are available for all the popular workstations and personal computers. PROLOG is not presently very popular in the US although it remains so in Europe and in Japan.

- **Some future software prospects**

So far, most of the expert systems business has been in the marketing of expert system shells (i.e., general purpose knowledge-free development environments), rather than in complete, knowledge-rich systems. This is beginning to change. Look for major vendors to begin to offer domain-customized systems that come with knowledge sets, acquisition tools, and user interfaces that are specifically designed for one area of expertise.

In the future there could well be a mushrooming of knowledge-for-sale businesses with ready to go expert systems for many business and engineering problem settings. There are many such systems now available, for example the RS-232 Consultant (from Human Edge) can advise you about how to make RS-232 connections. The AI system Goldworks AXLE (from Gold Hill Computers) can teach you about building expert systems. After having bought (or built) many diverse expert systems, the future challenge will be how to hook them together to "sum" their knowledge. This problem of interacting expert systems is at the early research stage.

In the more immediate future, one will soon begin to see expert systems accompany complicated machinery rather than complicated diagnostic manuals. When there is a problem, the expert system will guide the engineer towards the required repairs. The trend towards flexible systems that offer multiple knowledge representation strategies will accelerate. Such systems work with rules, frames. data tables. and object-based representations. There will always be important computations performed outside the AI system (such as simulations and database queries) so that interface options to conventional programs will remain important. This is already driving some systems towards the C++ object-oriented extension to the "C" programming language. This trend will likely continue, especially with the introduction of high performance C-based UNIX workstations (such as the SUN-4 family). Object oriented languages are presently highly non-standard but work is well along towards a standard approach. This will further accelerate the trend towards object-oriented expert systems.

CONCLUSION

The expert system industry was forecast to experience considerable growth in 1987. Because of general economic problems, this did not happen to the degree projected. The strong growth forecast for 1987 is now expected this year. A steady wave of new hardware and software tools will likely carry the interest in AI systems along projected dimensions as more and more business, engineering, and manufacturing tasks are fitted with AI solutions.

REFERENCES

1. P. Harmon and D. King, *Expert Systems,* John Wiley, New York, 1985.

2. P. Harmon, *Expert Systems Strategies,* Cutter Information Corp., San Francisco, Vol. 4, 1988.

KNOWLEDGE ACQUISITION AND REFINEMENT FOR DIAGNOSTIC CLASSIFICATION TASKS

Peter Politakis
Eng. Mgr. - External Consulting Group, Select

Digital Equipment Corporation
290 Donald Lynch Blvd.
Marlboro, MA 01749

ABSTRACT

This session discusses the knowledge acquisition process from the perspective of types of problems suitable for expert system technology. Methods for constructing and facilities for validating rule based systems, for diagnostic classification problem solving are discussed. Two systems are reviewed that facilitate knowledge acquisition and rule refinement, respectively. Examples are taken from applications in network troubleshooting and medical diagnosis.

KNOWLEDGE ACQUISITION

Knowledge acquisition for diagnostic activities usually includes the formalization of a human expert's empirical knowledge, rules of thumb, and known laws governing the problem domain. Over the past several years, a plethora of expert system "shells" have appeared on the commercial market. Their intent is to provide simple facilities for the development of expert systems, targeted to those not well versed in the traditional AI languages such as OPS and LISP. The drawback in this approach, however, is that by creating a shell with simple features much expressive power may be lost. On the contrary, if the shell provides complex features, the increased expressive power may be accompanied by an increased difficulty in coding the rules.

To circumvent these problems we have developed ESSA [2], an *Expert System Shell Assistant*, that creates an interface between the developer (a domain expert) and EXPERT [4], the expert system shell (and target language). It's purpose is to provide *intelligent* assistance to the expert, aiding in the formalization of experiential knowledge and in the utilization of the shell's features. The initial motivation for the design of this facility was to enhance the knowledge acquisition for the Network Troubleshooting Consultant (NTC), a rule-based expert system providing interpretive analysis for Ethernet/DECnet related problems. The generality of the ESSA facility, however, makes it applicable to other diagnostic problems.

The domain of problems to which ESSA is well suited is approximately the classification-type problems. These, therefore, define the class of problems that ESSA can handle effectively. ESSA builds a diagnostic problem solver, which infers diagnoses based on evaluating rules relating symptoms to diagnostic statements. In ESSA, the formulation of rules is done entirely in a graphical language while automatic translation is provided to the target implementation language EXPERT. ESSA guides the user with the following capabilities: *i* a divide-and-conquer methodology that facilitates a decomposition of the domain into rules for certain diagnostic problems. *ii* a language sensitive editor that allows the expert to concentrate on formulating rules in a graphical form. *iii* logical analysis checks are inherent in formulating rules with ESSA. These capabilities form a basis of an intelligent interface between a domain expert and an emerging knowledge base of rules. This presentation reviews the design of ESSA and presents examples of its performance in developing a diagnostic system for troubleshooting computer network problems. Traditionally, the requisite knowledge base for a rule-based expert system, regardless of whether that system is being developed with a shell or in a general programming language, is produced by an individual via a text editor and a working knowledge of the target language syntax and semantics. In addition, the domain expert is required to explicitly formulate his knowledge into rules of the form:

- IF cond_{1} & cond_{2} & ... & cond_{n} - > conclusion

Our experience in dealing with experts in the networking domain indicates that they do not naturally formulate their empirical knowledge into such a structure. While the "if-then-else" clause may seem quite natural to the knowledge engineer or computer programmer, it appears to be an awkward knowledge representation mechanism for others. The reasons for this seem rooted in the kind of troubleshooting techniques that a network specialist employs. For instance, much of our experience with these individuals indicates a sequential diagnostic process for ruling in and ruling out candidate diagnoses within the network domain; and the flow diagram is a natural form for expressing troubleshooting criteria for this kind of diagnostic process. ESSA was developed to provide an intelligent interface to the EXPERT system [4] for developing rule based consultation systems. The tractability of the scoring function can be complex in developing large knowledge bases. Only detailed analysis of the knowledge base reveals the order in which questions are asked and conclusions are reached. In an application for advising about network troubleshooting, a knowledge base with 700 rules involving 250 symptoms and 200 conclusions is complex for maintenance. This complexity, left in the hands of a domain expert, results in either inadequate or improper use of EXPERT'S facilities. It is here that ESSA makes a major contribution by managing the complexities, providing intelligent assistance to the domain engineer.

KNOWLEDGE REFINEMENT

Knowledge refinement is an important subpart of the knowledge acquisition problem. It may also be viewed as the second of a two-phase process for acquiring rules. The ESSA system may be viewed as addressing the first phase, i.e., the acquisition of entire rules, indeed entire sets of rules, for concluding various hypotheses. The second phase, called the refinement phase is characterized not so much by the acquisition of entire rules but by the addition, deletion, and alteration of rule-components in certain rules in the existing KB, in an attempt to "fine tune" the system's performance. Obviously the foregoing description of KB construction is an idealization. In practice the line between these two phases is not as sharply drawn. The SEEK family of systems are described that aid knowledge base designer in the refining rules for diagnostic classification. In the original SEEK system [3] and successor SEEK2 [1] systems, case knowledge is used to drive a process involving empirical analysis of rule behavior in order to generate plausible suggestions for rule refinement. Case knowledge is given in the form of a data base of correctly diagnosed cases, i.e., each case contains not only a record of the case observations but also a record of the expert's conclusion for the case. Empirical analysis of rule behavior involves gathering certain statistics concerning rule behavior with respect to the data base of cases; suggestions for rule refinements are generated by the application of knowledge base refinement heuristics that relate the statistical behavior and structural properties of rules to appropriate classes of rule refinements. SEEK's control strategy is a combination of "divide and conquer" together with a goal-directed backward chaining mechanism. We assume that the expert and knowledge engineer can identify a finite set of final diagnostic conclusions or "endpoints"; these are the conclusions that the expert uses to classify

the given cases. One can then confine one's attention to the refinement of rules that are involved in concluding a particular endpoint, e.g., if the domain is Rheumatology one may decide to work on refining those rules involved in concluding the single final diagnosis Rheumatoid Arthritis.

SEEKS knowledge base consists of heuristic rules for refinement that relate statistical and structural properties about rules, for a particular domain, e.g., Rheumatology, and to give advice about generalizing or specializing these rules. The heuristic rules are applied only to a proper subset of the rules in the domain KB. The goal-directed backward chaining mechanism comes into play once an endpoint has been chosen. If our chosen endpoint is Rheumatoid Arthritis, for example, we begin by applying the heuristics to all the rules in the KB that directly conclude Rheumatoid Arthritis, i.e., rules whose right hand side is this conclusion. A rule that directly concludes some endpoint will, in general, have components on its left hand side that themselves are the conclusions of some other rules; such components are called intermediate hypotheses. The rules that conclude intermediate hypotheses will themselves include components that are intermediate hypotheses, and so on. Whenever our refinement heuristics suggest deleting an intermediate hypothesis IH from some rule, the rules that conclude IH are thereby implicated as candidates for refinement.

- **Generalizing and Specializing Rules**

At the highest level, refinements of production rules may be thought of as falling in one of two possible classes: generalizations and specializa-tions. By a rule generalization we mean any modification to a rule that makes it "easier" for the rule's conclusion to be accepted in any given case. A generalization refinement may be accomplished by deleting or altering a component on the left hand side of the rule or by raising the confidence factor associated with the rule's conclusion. By a rule specialization we mean modifications to a rule that make it "harder" for the rule's conclusion to be accepted in any given case. A rule specialization is accomplished by adding or altering a component on the left hand side or by lowering the confidence factor associated with the rule's conclusion. Thus any particular piece of evidence suggesting a rule's refinement will either favor generalization or favor specialization. On the side of evidence for rule generalization, one of the concepts we have employed in both SEEK and SEEK2 is a statistical property of a rule computed by a function that we call Gen(rule). Gen(rule) is the number of cases (in the case knowledge data base) in which (a) this rule's conclusion should have been reached but wasn't, (b) had this rule been satisfied the conclusion would have been reached, and (c) of all the rules for which the preceding clauses hold in the case, this one is the 'closest to being satisfied." A measure of how close a rule is to being satisfied in a case, based on the number of additional findings required for the rule to fire, is easily computed given the case data.

On the side of evidence for rule specialization, one of the concepts we have defined is a statistical property of a rule that is computed by a function we call (SpecA(rule). SpecA(rule) is the number of cases in which (a) this rule's conclusion should not have been reached but was, and (b) if this rule had failed to fire the correct conclusion would have been reached, i.e., the correct conclusion was the "second choice" in the case (due to its having the second highest confidence), and the only circumstance preventing its being the "first choice" is the fact that this rule is satisfied. If there is more than one satisfied rule that concludes the incorrect first choice then none of these rules has its SpecA measure incremented; instead we have defined an additional concept to cover this situation called SpecB(rule): each of these rules has its SpecB measure incremented.

This presentation concludes with a review of the limitations and extensions of the SEEK and SEEK2 systems.

REFERENCES

1. Ginsberg, A., Weiss, S., and Politakis, P. "Automatic Knowledge Refinement for Classification Expert Systems." (to appear) Artificial Intelligence (1988).

2. Hannan, J. and Politakis, P., "ESSA: A Knowledge Acquisition Facility for Diagnostic Expert Systems." In IEEE, Proceedings of Artificial Intelligence Applications, (1985).

3. Politakis, P. and Weiss, S. "Using Empirical Analysis to Refine Expert System Knowledge Bases." Artificial Intelligence. 22 (1984) 23-84.

4. Weiss, S., and Kulikowski, C. "EXPERT: A System for Developing Consultation Models." In IJCAI-79. Tokyo, Japan, 1979, 942-947.

AN APPROACH FOR INTRODUCING EXPERT SYSTEM TECHNOLOGY IN THE TELECOMMUNICATION INDUSTRY

Sushil G. Munshi
Vice President
Technology Planning

United Telecommunications, Inc.
2330 Shawnee Mission Parkway
Westwood, KS 66205

INTRODUCTION

Artificial Intelligence Technology has made significant progress in recent years. It has emerged from the pure research environment of early years to the real world with some practical applications. AI technology in the broad sense includes a number of application fields; viz. robotics, machine vision, speech recognition, natural languages and expert systems. Even though speech recognition and natural languages are strategically important for communications in the long run, from our industry's perspective, at least for now, expert systems, appear to be of greater importance. The executive management of our company, recognizing the importance of expert systems technology, formed a committee to address the following:

*   Define those areas in the telecommunications industry of interest to UTI that could benefit from AI/Expert systems technology.

*   Survey current and past projects at UTI which illustrate the application of expert systems techniques.

*   Recommend high-priority projects that should be undertaken in the near future utilizing an expert systems approach.

EXPERT SYSTEMS IN TELECOMMUNICATIONS INDUSTRY

Expert systems are built upon "If------Then " rules. The rules are acquired by interrogating an "expert" in a particular field under consideration. Consequently, expert systems are generally amenable to problems where there exists a definable set of symptoms, and based on the knowledge of the expert, inferences could be made regarding cause and perhaps possible corrective actions. This characteristic explains the early success of expert systems in the medical field.

In the past few years, major switch vendors have caught on to this characteristic of expert systems and have developed products for switch diagnostics and maintenance, e. g. AT&T #5 ESS, NTI DMS,GTE #2 EAX, etc. The manufacturer is in a better position to develop such applications than the end user due to the amount of details, software as well as hardware, required. However, the users should insist that the vendor deploy the latest technologies to facilitate the maintenance and reduce the associated labor cost.

Another promising area where the expertise is becoming scarce and complexity is ever increasing, is Network Planning. However, the domain is too broad to allow a realistic application using expert systems. Instead of tackling the problem in its entirety, a number of tools using expert systems can be developed to assist the network designers and to facilitate exploration of many alternatives and what-if scenarios. The programs can also be used to train new staff in this area. This approach is particularly attractive considering the evolving telecom network of the future where rules for the "optimum" network design are expected to change.

Network management and maintenance are two other obvious areas where this technology has a vital role to play. For the maintenance arena one can specify the routine tests and expected results, from which the problems can be diagnosed, and corrective actions can be suggested. It can also be a valuable tool for preventive maintenance. As different transmission media, switching systems, interface devices, etc. are deployed in the network the task of network maintenance takes on added dimensions; expert systems could be of great help. Network management, from the routing point of view, is another area where expert systems are applicable. Demand for variable bandwidth, alternate routes based on time of the day, DNHR, recovery under failure, SS#7, associated routing schemes, and intelligent peripherals create an excellent opportunity for the expert systems techniques.

In addition, this technology is very suitable in some operations related problems, for example, financial reporting, FCC rules and their impact on rates and tariffs, data center operations, analysis of acquisitions and/or divestiture of business, portfolio management, personnel management, etc. In future, when natural language interfaces and speech recognition technologies are adequately matured, one can see a large number of applications to support executive decision making.

CURRENT AND PAST PROJECTS

Like many large organizations, a number of groups in our corporation were engaged in developing expert systems applications. However, these were individual efforts and there was no cohesive approach to direct the activities with an overall strategic perspective. The corporate technology group was attempting to provide the needed leadership. The corporate group was initially responsible for bringing technology awareness to various business groups and continues to keep up with the developments to identify future applications. The management decision to establish the committee was a key factor in looking at this new technology from the corporate strategic importance.

PROJECT IDENTIFICATION AND SELECTION

- **Process**

In order to identify projects which can utilize expert systems throughout the corporation, it was decided to solicit input from as many departments as possible. It was also assumed that an introduction to AI/Expert-Systems and exposure to current applications in the industry would help stimulate the thought process.The process was formalized as follows:

- Discussion meeting: Intro-duction to AI/Expert systems.
- Application Suggestions from the participants within two weeks following the meeting.
- Review submitted applications and prepare a short list of high priority projects.
- Request and acquire a detailed description of the projects in the short list.
- Rank order the short list.
- Recommendations.

- **Discussion Meeting**

About 20 participants from 16 departments attended the discussion meeting. Background material covering AI/Expert systems was sent to each participant prior to this meeting. At the meeting, video tapes on AI (Expert Systems) gave an excellent overview of the technology. This was followed by presentations from various UTI groups engaged in AI related activities. A number of invited vendors demonstrated real applications. Each participant was asked to submit at least one application within two weeks.

- **Suggested Applications**

The response from the participants was very encouraging. About 45 applications were suggested and they covered a wide variety of areas, viz. tax advisor, finance, tariff, network management, network planning assistant, stock options, budget, data centers automation etc. All of these applications required the use of an expert's knowledge or an existing set of rules and procedures. That is to say that each one of these applications could benefit from the use of expert systems technology, some appear to have a closer alliance to expert systems techniques while for some the traditional programming techniques seem to be most appropriate. Note that the terminology assistant and the like reflects the nature of applications selected, i.e. they are tools to support the person to do the job and not replacement for the person doing the job.

Selection Of High Priority Projects

Even though AI research began almost twenty five years ago, the potential of this technology is just beginning to be realized. The increased computing power and advances in memory devices together with success of early expert systems are major factors for this enormous interest in the technology. It is reasonable to assume that AI techniques will play a dominant role in telecommunications industry in the future. The strategic importance will depend upon the type of business. In the service industry such as UTI, which is by and large a deployer of technology, the benefits will be derived as a result of increased efficiencies, reduced cost of operations, improved decision making, and the availability of information and analyses in the right format. Many applications which can create new revenues and strengthen competitive positions are possible when intelligent networks (SS#7) begin to proliferate in the public switched networks.

It is very tempting to select the application based on its economic benefits, e.g. rate of return on investment. At this stage it will not be in the best interest to spend time to determine ROI, there is not enough hard data available to carry out this exercise. We are relying on our subjective judgment to asses the value of the application. It should be noted that, regardless of the final outcome, the process by itself is useful; it forces everyone involved to formalize the problem solving technique. Past experience indicates that this was helpful in uncovering deficiencies in the solution techniques and inconsistencies. In addition, the problem solving technique is now well documented.

Key considerations for the selection focused on the relative value of the project, complexity, availability of in-house expert familiar with problem domain and solution, and the degree to which AI techniques are appropriate. Review of all the suggested applications by the committee resulted in five projects. A series of applications were in the automation of data center and were classified as one project. Other areas were network planning assistant, access service tariff cost, trouble report analysis and tax analysis assistant.

These five applications offer a good mix of different areas with practical benefits.

REVIEW BY AN OUTSIDE CONSULTANT

An outside consultant organization, was retained to review the five applications selected by the Task Force. After their review, they gave a presentation addressing the key issues; complexity, development estimates, hardware and software cost, and approach to expert system developments to the committee members. Principal contributors to the five applications were also present and provided more details of each proposed application. Overall, the consultant did a very good job of advising on the expert system development.

All applications were ranked of equal importance by the consultants. This was partly due to the measures used to assess the potential; possibility of prototyping in a short time played a heavy role in the evaluation. That is to say that all applications were worth prototyping in three to six months. The cost of hardware could range from 10K to 50 K based on whether a PC or a workstation is utilized for the development. Software can run anywhere from a few thousand to tens of thousands. The main message was to keep domain narrow, followed by utilizing available knowledge from practices and documents and from experts in the field. Once the prototypes have been developed, the final product may evolve from the users reaction and will lead to deciding which of these applications should receive priority and emphasis.

RECOMMENDATIONS

The committee recommendations resulted in the start of two projects with a prototype to be completed by the end of this year. It was also suggested that additional applications should be considered for prototyping in 1989. The committee also suggested that there is a need for a corporate wide program to increase awareness of this technology and its potential.

CONCLUSION

This paper has described an approach taken by a service provider in deploying new technology into their business where beneficial and a key for future success. Few points are worth noting, they are applicable for the introduction of any new technology. First, it is very important to have the support of top management. Second, is that the business units must be partners in the total effort, i.e. users should feel that they are partners and that can happen only if they are convinced of the benefits. Third, it takes a concerted effort to increase the awareness of the new technology and its potential advantages and limitations.

Title

John C. Thomas
Director Artificial Intelligence Lab

J. Euchner
Supervisor Expert Systems Development

NYNEX Corporation
500 Westchester Avenue
White Plains, NY 10604

ABSTRACT

It would seem obvious that Expert Systems could have tremendous application within the telecommunications industry. Expert Systems, compared with traditional systems, require a slightly different project management process, different software, and in some cases, different hardware. The question then arises how one may introduce expert systems effectively into a telecommunications company. In this talk, I will describe the overall mission and objectives of the Artificial Intelligence Laboratory at NYNEX. I will then describe our strategy for introducing Expert Systems. In describing this strategy, we will first specify our objectives and secondly specify a number of situational factors. Together these provide constraints on the strategy initially chosen. Our strategy dealt with three factors: project identification, technology transfer, project and personnel management. After describing the general strategies, I will talk more specifically about the particular tactics that we are employing at NYNEX and how successfully these tactics are being employed through a look at some specific projects.

OBJECTIVES AND ASSUMPTIONS

The mission of the NYNEX Artificial Intelligence Laboratory is to utilize artificial intelligence technology to solve problems, create opportunities, and improve customer service for NYNEX and to advance AI technology in areas of strategic importance. Since we want to solve real problems, this means we have to pay attention to organizational issues, consider delivery and integration, and involve all our relevant users and customers in our projects. In order to maximize our chances for success, we developed a strategy for introducing AI technologies into NYNEX. We periodically review our strategy and tactics to determine how to change them in the light of changes in the context and objectives.

Initially our objectives included establishing credibility within the parent organization developing internal expertise, developing working relationships with a large number of family units, and transferring expert systems technology to the family units. As a new organization, we felt it important to establish our credibility as an organization capable of dealing with very advanced technology and yet able to identify relevant challenges within the company and provide quality solutions. The development of internal expertise was chosen as an objective because it was felt that artificial intelligence technologies will be of continuing importance within NYNEX into the foreseeable future and that a competitive advantage can be gained from these technologies. Furthermore, increasing competitiveness will characterize the future of the telecommunications industry. We wished to develop working relations with a large number of family units because we felt we needed a broad base of political support and time to gain experience to see where the greatest leverage in expert systems might be. Our intuition was that the application of expert systems to telecommunication systems problems would

outstrip our ability to identify and implement solutions with our likely headcount growth. For this reason, we also set technology transfer as an objective; thus, family units themselves would be able to begin building Expert Systems.

In developing a set of strategies for dealing with Expert Systems to meet these objectives, we considered a number of background assumptions dealing with our particular situation. Other companies in other situations would require a different set of strategies. Our particular background assumptions are outlined below. We wanted to provide solutions to real problems for real people in the real world. We were not interested in, nor was NYNEX interested in, the development of "toy" systems such as chess-playing machines or wine tasting expert systems.

Another assumption was based on our analysis of Expert System Failures based on the literature, personal experience, and consulting. We found these failures not typically due to technical failures but due to such factors as organizational issues, poor user interface, and integration with existing systems. Another assumption was that existing tools for the development of Expert Systems provides efficient flexibility for a wide variety of useful applications within telecommunications. Coupled with this was the realization that tool building is a difficult and long term undertaking Another assumption concerned person power. Ph.D.'s in computer science with extensive artificial intelligence experience are rare. We also assumed that Expert Systems technology could be used very widely throughout NYNEX.

Our assumption about credibility was that it only follows local success. In other words, the fact that other companies had successfully used Expert Systems would not in itself guarantee any credibility for Expert Systems within NYNEX

There were a number of other factors internal to the artificial intelligence laboratory that had to be considered in the development of a strategy. First of all, the laboratory was new. There was no established culture, and the laboratory had no image with clients. There was also significant manpower growth planned during the first few years of the Artificial Intelligence Laboratory. We assumed that most of the personnel from the artificial Intelligence Laboratory would be new to NYNEX, and in fact, most would be new to the Bell System. We also assumed that NYNEX would be willing to commit substantial corporate resources to artificial intelligence in the near term but that monetary support from the operating units would be required within a few years. Incidentally, all of these assumptions have been subsequently substantiated.

There were also a number of factors external to the artificial intelligence laboratory that had to be considered. Artificial Intelligence technology is moving rapidly. Another assumption about the field is that the turnover of Artificial Intelligence professionals is high. Regarding NYNEX itself, it is still predominately a public utility with an established culture but undergoing significant changes including rapid diversification. Cost reduction is important for NYNEX. NYNEX has a large installed hardware-software base and this has implications for integration. In addition, we assumed the telecommunications business would become increasingly competitive and that new business opportunities would be opening up to NYNEX due to deregulation in the years ahead. Combining our assumptions with our objectives led to the strategies outlined below.

PROJECT IDENTIFICATION STRATEGY

One important aspect of our overall strategy is the identification of projects to work on. We decided to work with the family units to identify possible projects. We felt it was important to take a broad-based approach to project identification rather than focusing all of our efforts on a particular family unit. Therefore, we met with the management of many of the operational units of NYNEX to present the concepts of Expert Systems, why they were useful, what they were, and how to identify potential applications. We then challenged people in the various units to identify possible project opportunities. From a large number of potential projects we moved onto the second stage which was to have a more detailed meeting in which we looked into potential applications in more depth. In this meeting, we tried to assess technical as well as political factors that would weigh for or against a particular project. Initially, our bias was to select projects that were fairly straightforward from both a technical and a political standpoint. The reasons for this were as follows. First, we were a new organization and wanted to establish credibility quickly. Second, most of the personnel in the Artificial Intelligence Laboratory were new to the Bell system and would consequently need to spend a considerable amount of time learning about the domain as well as about company procedures. Third, there were a number of labor intensive processes involved with starting up any new organization; for example, we had to order and install hardware and software systems. We also needed to spend a fair amount of time during the initial few years on recruiting, establishing appropriate business procedures and administrative procedures, and further publicizing and searching for potential projects. Fourth, we were interested in delivering real systems that would be used by the real users. We found that most Expert Systems existed as nifty prototypes that "worked" but for some reason beyond the control of the developer were never actually used in the field. We recognized then, that a considerable amount of effort would be required to insure integration, acceptance by users and management, and avoidance of a number of "political" factors that other people had cited as reasons (excuses?) that prevented the actual use of "perfectly good" systems. Our criteria for success

however, included the actual deployment and use. Few people, we found, had extensive experience in this process of fully deploying systems. Given these a priori challenges, it would seem absurdly risky to overlay these unavoidable difficulties with the additional difficulty of attempting something that was a technological breakthrough. We tended to look therefore for fairly well-defined domains in stable environments. And, we looked for diagnosis and classification problems rather than planning or design problems. We tried to avoid additional technical challenges such as real-time Expert Systems or the necessity for combining the information of multiple experts.

NYNEX was an early investor in Teknowledge, one of the first companies to specialize in Expert Systems. We wanted to leverage our investment by using Teknowledge as a consultant, when appropriate, to help us identify projects and to review our project identification strategy. In fact, based on their experiences with other companies, a number of possibilities for introducing Expert Systems were discussed. One alternative strategy was the "thousand flowers" strategy. In this strategy, a wide-spread if superficial education about Expert Systems is accompanied by the widespread distribution of a low--end development and delivery vehicle such as M-1 on a personal computer. The notion is that "bottom up", a large number of projects will be attempted and a small proportion of these will be successful. The successful projects, under such a scheme, however, would then become highly visible and motivate people to find additional opportunities for Expert Systems technology. We felt that such a strategy was not appropriate for NYNEX, however, for a variety of reasons. First, within the corporate culture, most people tended to have well-defined and demanding jobs. It was difficult for people outside of Science and Technology to find time away from their defined jobs for education in something like Expert Systems, the time to identify a potential application, and then the time to develop such a system and publicize the results. We also felt that our review of other Expert Systems pointed to the importance of a good user interface. We had both a commitment within the Artificial Intelligence Laboratory to produce usable systems, and the expertise and experience to make this a likely reality. Individual programmers on the other hand, would be unlikely to have a systematic plan for attacking such issues.

A quite different strategy for project selection is the "flagship" approach. In this approach, a management consensus is reached at a high level on a large scale highly visible, high payoff project. A number of factors convinced us not to adopt this strategy. First of all, we wanted to give our personnel time to develop expertise in identifying and developing Expert Systems, as well as experience in managing the business and political processes within our company. Also, as previously stated, there were a number of time-consuming activities that would involve our staff in the first few years of existence. This would make it even more difficult to pursue a large-scale project requiring the cooperation of many professionals. Furthermore, we wanted to test the waters with a number of family units to determine the receptiveness to such systems and the availability of people within those organizations who could serve as technology transfer agents. We were too inexperienced with the company, which itself was in dynamic flux, to be assured of an appropriate environment if we put all of our resources on one project.

A third alternative strategy for project identification would be to have our central group serve essentially as educators and facilitators. In this role, we would train DP professionals in other family units who would actually do most of the development work. Such an approach would be antithetical to the basic philosophy of setting up a centralized science and technology facility. In addition, it was felt that the credibility necessary to effectively allow a central organization to control projects throughout the company would require a local history of success. Obviously, since we were a new organization, this was impossible.

The strategy we did chose was to begin with several small projects and then become more ambitious as our people became more experienced and the organization more stable.

Another aspect of our project selection strategy was to choose projects that would both provide some short-term benefit to NYNEX and advance technology in ways that were of strategic importance. If one took the extreme strategy of selecting a very ambitious long term goal, we would not meet our objective of establishing credibility. It would be doubtful in today's business climate that a portfolio of projects selected on such a basis would be tolerated. Conversely, one could select projects purely on the basis of short term benefit, concentrating wholly on projects with a short-term feedback regardless of any advancement in the technology. While this would be beneficial to the company in the short run, it was felt that such a strategy would ultimately not advance the position of NYNEX.

One of the specific technological issues that we felt would be important is the rebuilding of knowledge bases in related domains. Traditionally, Expert Systems are built using an inference engine for the logical aspects of the problem but begin from scratch with regard to the knowledge base, however, there are a number of factors in the telecommunications business which would be common across many possible applications. While concentrating on a number of individual projects, we have also taken a view toward building up a general knowledge base of rules applicable to network issues generally. At some point in the future, we will focus a specific effort on providing an underpinning for building Expert Systems in network planning, diagnosis, and data interpretation. Such a foundation could speed the development of specific projects in the future. In addition, we can envision that when a specific Expert System cannot solve a problem on the basis of its specific rule base, it could fall back on reasoning from "first principles".

Although this paper focuses on the deployment of Expert Systems technology in NYNEX, it may be instructive, in the context of this project identification strategy, to illustrate how short term benefits and technological advancement interplay in some of the other areas of Artificial Intelligence technology. In the speech recognition area, for example, we have been working with operator services in areas where over-the-telephone, speaker independent, small vocabulary speech recognition could enhance the productivity of operators. We feel that speech recognition is a strategic technology for NYNEX and that with moderate advances combined with intelligent deployment, there are some short term benefits to be gained. In some rural areas, for instance, an operator must ask customers for the number dialed when that number has been changed or disconnected. We feel that there is reasonable chance that a combination of touch-tone input and speech recognition could aid this process. As a first step, we simulated automated equipment and collected speech samples of real customers over the network. The purposes of this study were to test various dialog structures, record a substantial amount of speech data under real field conditions, and to gauge customer acceptance. We are now in the process of testing various recognizers against this database. We are also working on advancing the technology in this area by building a knowledge-based speech recognition system. Such a system will enable us to much more quickly develop specialized vocabulary.

Another technology that we feel may be of strategic importance in the computer and communication industry, is neural network technology. If successful, such a technology could help ease the "software bottleneck" and could be of use in automatically optimizing a communications network. Rather than doing abstract, basic, or toy world research, we are attempting to explore, advance, and implement this technology in a real near term application. New York Telephone receives hundred of thousands of checks each day and the amount must be entered into a computer system. We are attempting to use neural network technology to read the courtesy amount on some proportion of these checks.

TECHNOLOGY TRANSFER

We estimated that the number of useful applications for Expert Systems technology would fast outpace the number of people we would have available to develop such systems. Therefore, it was important to develop a strategy for transferring this technology to other family units. We decided to implement this in a number of phases. In phase one, we would concentrate on identifying and succeeding at three or four useful projects; this would give us experience and credibility. Only following such local successes could we count on people within the family units being motivated to learn and use this new technology. It also implied that it was necessary to monitor the revenue, expenses, cost savings, and/or customer service-improvements resulting from such projects.

Once these projects were successful, we would then begin an awareness and education program, spending part of our resources to train people from other areas of NYNEX to learn the technology and also to make people broadly aware of the capabilities of this new technology. At this point we would then help primarily in the identification of new projects and operate on a coaching and consulting basis while people from the family units did most of the development work. We would also at this point begin to undertake problems and opportunities within NYNEX that were higher risk and higher payoff. Such projects would now be more feasible because we would have developed the experience and expertise as well as the necessary infrastructure. Another aspect of the technology transfer structure was the actual rotation of personnel from family units through science and technology.

PERSONNEL STRATEGY

The third important aspect of our general strategy was a personnel strategy. There are several aspects of this. Highly experienced people in all phases of expert system development are rare. We were fortunate to have access to highly experienced technology personnel for coaching and training early in the history of the laboratory. We spent considerable time and effort in recruiting and selecting personnel. In the personnel selection process, we looked for evidence of not only computer skills but people that would be able to deal with implementation, integration, and even political issues revolving around the actual deployment of Expert Systems. We wanted to minimize turnover and work on progressively harder projects to develop expertise internally. This meant setting aside substantial time and money for continued training and other experiences promoting professional development.

PROGRESS TO DATE

A number of projects are in various stages of development. One project, the Merchandise Classification system, has been delivered on schedule within budget and met the requirements that we established. Materiel Enterprises is that part of NYNEX that does internal warehousing, ordering, and vendor selection. When items are ordered through Materiel Enterprises, a merchandise classification number needs to be assigned. In most cases, this was not done automatically by existing computer systems; rather, a printout was produced each day that listed items for which no classification number could be assigned. At this point an expert with 40 years experience in the Bell system looked at the item description and the vendor name and wrote down by hand a merchandise classification number. This number was later keypunched into the system and used for determining pricing and for financial tracking. This introduced delays in processing orders and inconsistencies in pricing. In addition, the entire system relied on the expertise of a particular individual who would soon retire.

Personnel from the Artificial Intelligence Laboratory identified this project as a potential for Expert Systems technology after seven projects were identified with management at Materiel Enterprises as possibilities for Expert Systems deployment. Each of these was further explored with operational personnel and number of issues were discussed. We considered the possible integration of the Expert Systems with other systems, the likely evolutionary paths of systems within Materiel Enterprises, and how users would interact with the expert system.

The Artificial Intelligence Laboratory personnel then, in conjunction with Materiel Enterprise personnel, decided on the Merchandise Classification system as the initial application. Over the next few months, extensive interviews with the expert system were undertaken, and a prototype developed using M-1 on the IBM personal computer. Later, a working system was built in AION and integrated into EAS, the main processing system of Materiel Enterprises. This Expert System met its goals for coverage and accuracy. After using the system for several months, the rules of the expert system were decentralized and incorporated into a job aid used by the sales people in Materiel Enterprises. While human performance using the job aid is not so accurate as the expert system, this manual system allows the customer to be quoted a price immediately. In this case then, the overall process of knowledge engineering, formalization, prototyping and deployment ultimately resulted in a restructuring of the work flow and the widespread dissemination of expert knowledge in a manual system with the computer program itself as a back-up.

A larger scale project for which a prototype has been developed is an expert system to aid in the interpretation of mechanized loop test data. This project was identified with the help of Service Company personnel. The mechanized loop test is designed to diagnose problems in the local loop. The existing program reduces extensive of electrical test data to a two digit verification code; this is then used in conjunction with a Bell systems practices book to determine the most likely cause of the problem and the appropriate personnel to fix the problem. Highly experienced maintenance personnel, however, do not always rely solely on this verification code, but instead, also consider the raw test data. In this way, they make a more accurate determination and avoid sending the wrong personnel, the wrong tools, or people to the wrong location, a greater proportion of the time. We have extensively interviewed personnel, primarily one expert, in conjunction with this project and built a prototype. We are now in the process of integrating this with the existing maintenance center systems.

Another specific system that has been developed in conjunction with the Wireless Communications Laboratory at NYNEX is a system to find nearest neighbors for cell sites in the NYNEX Mobile communication network. The New York metropolitan area offers unique challenges when one attempts to understand how to optimize a cellular radio network. "This is because of the density and mobility of the population and the topography. The Wireless Communications Laboratory at NYNEX has been involved in several projects to improve utilization and performance in the mobile phone network. The Artificial Intelligence Laboratory has been involved in developing an intelligent interface for one of these projects--a mobile surveillance system that allows operators of the system to view the status of the system graphically.

A more extensive project is currently underway to help with current facilities planning in the operating companies. Additional efforts in the Expert Systems area have included interpretation programs for network statistics, consulting for a pagination project, and intelligent interpretation for employee benefits, and in conjunction with the speech recognition group in the Artificial Intelligence Laboratory, a knowledge based speech recognition system that builds on the work of Victor Zue at MIT.

LESSONS LEARNED

While a great deal of thought went into devising an appropriate strategy, we periodically review our successes, failures, and partial successes to determine how we could have done better. Such reviews can result in changes of strategy, or more specific recommendations for how to implement the strategy more effectively.

Several of our experiences in developing specific Expert Systems have lead us to the conclusion that, other things being equal, we should avoid situations in which a third party vendor has a significant interest. Many software development houses, for example, see a new revenue opportunity in the development of Expert Systems, and, currently lacking expertise in these areas, may attempt to draw us into a project in order to learn about Expert System. In such cases, however, there will be a conflict of interest with respect to the identification of additional projects, and the ongoing maintenance and enhancement of existing systems.

A second lesson learned is that in the NYNEX context at least, it is necessary to have support for a project at all levels from the working level to the highest management level - anyone whose decisions can have an impact on the project. We have evolved a change in procedure to get higher management involved earlier in the overall identification and development process. This helps insure that family unit resources will be available in the family unit for which the project is being developed for training, maintenance, installation, and appropriate methods and procedures. In addition, it helps insure that the necessity for the expert system under consideration will not be cancelled by a more widespread change in operations or structure. Such considerations might lead one to the strategy of involving higher management from the very inception of a project. There are several other factors however, which mitigate against this extreme approach. For one thing the technical feasibility of a project and the resource level required cannot accurately be determined without some fairly extensive discussions with the expert. Until such preliminary knowledge engineering takes place, it is unclear what the breadth and depth of the reasoning process is, and the extent to which it is verbalizeable. One does not want to waste the time of higher executives by getting approval for numerous projects that, upon closer examination, turn out to be unworkable. Furthermore, in some cases, the proposed system and its potential impact are difficult to visualize in the absence of a proof-of-concept prototype. In light of these two sets of counter-veiling factors, the decision about what levels of management to involve then remains a judgment call which must be made on a case by case basis.

A new proposal aimed at addressing some of these issues is to form a higher management committee to help identify high leverage opportunities for Expert Systems technology. We discussed such a possibility previously but feel that it is now more appropriate to attempt this process for a number of reasons. First of all, we have many working prototypes which can be used to illustrate concretely to higher management what an expert system is and how it can positively affect the telecommunications business. This simultaneously demonstrates our credibility and helps them visualize similar possibilities within their own scope of responsibility. Second, the Artificial Intelligence Laboratory personnel are themselves now much more familiar with NYNEX and with its business thus making conversation about potential applications more productive.

In this paper, we have described the AIL approach to project selection, technology transfer, and personnel. We outlined the assumption underlying our approach and described some specific projects. Finally, we specified some modifications to our initial strategy based on our actual experience.

BUILT-IN SELF-TEST

Rodham E. Tulloss, Chairperson
Supervisor, BIST/Boundary-Scan Program Management
AT&T Bell Laboratories
Engineering Research Center
P. O. Box 900
Princeton, NJ 08540

ABSTRACT
Design for Testability is recognized as a critical component of product design in many firms. Costs of testing and introduction of packaging techniques that make physical probe contact impractical have led to increasing interest in using a product as its own tester. At-speed testing, high fault coverage, improved diagnostics, reduced investment in system diagnostic software, reduced inventory in field repair depots, and speedy product prove-in have been reported as benefits. However, if every manufacturer of ICs were to produce a unique approach, the most lucrative applications (board and system/field testing) might be undesirably difficult to achieve. A common means of communicating to self-testing chips is needed. International efforts at standardization have been initiated to deal with this potential problem. This seminar provides a look at the IEEE P1149.1 proposal originated by the international, *ad hoc* committee known as the Joint Test Action Group (JTAG). The proposed standard will be described and methods of combination with BIST at the chip, board, and system levels will be explored.

Lee D. Whetsel	Boundary-Scan: A Proposed Standard
Scott Davidson	Merging BIST and Boundary Scan at the IC Level
Charles L. Hudson, Jr.	Integrating Boundary Scan & BIST at the Board Level
John Sweeney	JTAG Boundary Scan: Diagnosing Module Level Functional Failures

A PROPOSED STANDARD TEST BUS AND BOUNDARY SCAN ARCHITECTURE

Lee Whetsel
Member, Group Technical Staff
Texas Instruments Incorporated
Test Automation Department
P.O. Box 869305, M/S 8407
Plano, TX 75086

ABSTRACT
Companies that manufacture systems with leading edge technologies are beginning to view test from a different perspective. In the past, the testability aspects of a design were given a lower level of priority with respect to the design's functional requirements. Today, companies are becoming more aware of the role testability plays in the products they sell and are placing more emphasis on testability at the conceptual stage of product development. As a result, standards for a serial test bus and boundary scan framework are being well received in both the military and commercial sectors of the electronics industry.

INTRODUCTION

While advances in board interconnect technology, surface mount packaging and integrated circuit (IC) gate density are having a positive influence on the design of state-of-the-art electronic systems, they are adversely affecting system-level testability. It is becoming more difficult and costly for a manufacturer to test leading-edge board designs using traditional testing techniques. One of the test areas that is being critically affected by advanced technologies is in-circuit testing. Conventional methods of in-circuit testing rely on the ability to physically access a board, using probing fixtures, to apply stimulus and measure response form the circuit under test. However, as board layouts become denser, the space allocated for probing is being reduced, and in some cases, deleted altogether.

Anticipating the need for a change, the Joint Test Action Group (JTAG) developed a specification that describes a proposed standard test interface and boundary scan architecture. JTAG is an international group of companies promoting the standardization of boundary scan by merchant IC manufacturers to support the testing needs of systems companies. This paper describes the test interface and boundary scan architecture proposed in the JTAG 2.0 specification.

BOUNDARY SCAN OVERVIEW

Boundary scan is the application of a partitioning scan ring at the boundary of IC designs to provide controllability and observability access via scan operations. In Fig. 1, an IC is shown with an application logic section and related input and output, and a boundary scan path consisting of a series of boundary scan cells (BSC), one BSC per IC function pin. The BSCs are interconnected to form a scan path between the host IC's test data input (TDI) pin and test data output (TDO) pin, for serial access.

During normal IC operation, input and output signals pass freely through each BSC, from the normal data input (NDI) to the normal data output (NDO). However, when the boundary scan test mode is entered, the IC's boundary is partitioned in such a way that test stimulus can be shifted in and applied from each BSC ouput (NDO), and test response can be captured at each BSC input (NDI) and shifted out for inspection. Internal testing of the application logic is accomplished by self-test or by applying test stimulus form the input BSCs and capturing test response at the output BSCs. External testing of wiring interconnects and neighboring ICs on a board assembly is accomplished by applying test stimulus from the output BSCs and capturing test response at the input BSCs.

The application of a scan path at the boundary of IC designs provides an embedded testing capability that can overcome the test access problems predicted in future board designs. The application of boundary scan is not new; many companies currently use this technique to improve product testability. However, in most instances each company has a unique test interface to shift data and apply test in their IC designs.

The main challenge facing the standardization of boundary scan is the identification and implementation of a standard test interface that guarantees interoperability between different merchants' ICs. The test interface must be general enough to be an acceptable alternative to existing test interfaces used in various areas of the electronics industry. Once a standard test interface exists, IC manufacturers will be more responsive to requests for boundary scan in standard components.

TEST INTERFACE & ARCHITECTURE

The proposed standard boundary scan architecture described in the JTAG 2.0 specification is shown in Fig. 2. The architecture consists of an instruction register, a data register group, and a test interface referred to as a test access port (TAP). In Fig. 2, the boundary scan register (BSR), an addressable data register scan path composed of a series of BSCs, is shown at the input and output boundary of the IC—to illustrate the similarity between Figs. 1 and 2.

The instruction register and the data register group comprise separate scan paths arranged in parallel between the primary test data input pin (TDI) and primary test data output pin (TDO). This architecture allows the TAP to select and shift data through one of the scan paths, instruction or data, without disturbing the other scan paths. It also simplifies the development of software support tools by providing separation between instruction register and data register scan operations.

TEST ACCESS PORT (TAP)

The TAP responds to the test access protocol, applied via the test clock (TCK) and test mode select (TMS) inputs, to shift data through either the instruction register or a data register. The TAP consists of a small controller design, driven by the TCK input, which responds to the TMS input as shown in the state diagrams of Figs. 3 and 4.

The main state diagram (Fig. 3) consists of two steady states, test logic reset (TLRESET) and run test/idle (RTIDLE), and two temporary states, select data register scan (SELDRS) and select instruction register scan (SELIRS). A unique feature of this protocol is that only one steady state exists for the condition when TMS is set high: the TLRESET state. This means that a reset of the test logic can be achieved within six TCK clock cycles or less by setting the TMS input high. By blending the test logic reset function into the test bus protocol, it is possible to reduce the initial five pin test interface, proposed in the JTAG 1.0 specification, down to a preferred four pin implementation, while maintaining the capability of forcing a reset condition on the test logic.

Tap Operation

At power up or during normal operation of the host IC, the TAP will be in the TLRESET state. In this state, the TAP issues a reset signal that places all test logic in a condition that will not impede normal operation of the Host IC. When test access is required, a protocol is applied via the TMS and TCK inputs, causing the TAP to exit the TLRESET state and enter the RT/IDLE state. The TDO buffer is forced to a tristate condition by the ENABLE output of the TAP (Fig. 5) during the TLRESET, RT/IDLE, SELDRS, and SELIRS states.

From the RT/IDLE state, a data scan access protocol can be issued to move the TAP through the SELDRS state to enter the data register scan block (Fig. 3). After the TAP enters the data register scan block, additional protocol is issued (Fig. 4A) to accomplish a test operation in the currently addressed scan path of the data register. While the TAP is in the data register scan block, the TDO buffer is enabled. After the test operation is complete, the TAP controller can either return to the RT/IDLE state or select another data or instruction register scan operation.

From the RT/IDLE state, an instruction scan access protocol can be issued to move the TAP through the SELDRS and SELIRS states to enter the instruction register scan block (Fig. 3). After the TAP enters the instruction register scan block, additional protocol is issued (Fig. 4B) to install a new test instruction in the instruction register. While in the instruction register scan block, the TDO buffer is enabled. After the instruction has been installed, the TAP controller can either return to the RT/IDLE state or select another data or instruction register scan operation.

The state diagrams of the data and instruction register scan blocks (Figs. 4A and 4B) are mirror images of each other, which adds symmetry to the protocol sequences. The first action that occurs when either diagram is entered is a CAPTURE operation. In the data register, the CAPTURE state is used to preload the addressed scan path with test data. In Fig. 2, if the BSR were the addressed data register, the NDI inputs would be captured during this state. In the instruction register, the CAPTURE state is used to preload user specified status information into the instruction register.

From the CAPTURE state, the TAP can move either to the SHIFT or EXIT1 state. Normally the SHIFT state follows the CAPTURE state so that test data or status information can be shifted out for inspection. Following the SHIFT state, the TAP either returns to the RT/IDLE state via the EXIT1 and UPDATE states or enters the PAUSE state via EXIT1. The reason for entering the PAUSE state would be to temporarily suspend the shifting of data through either the data or instruction register while a required operation, such as refilling a tester memory buffer, is performed. From the PAUSE state, shifting could be resumed by re-entering the SHIFT state via the EXIT2 state; or it could be terminated by entering the RT/IDLE state via the EXIT2 and UPDATE states.

Upon entering the data or instruciton register scan blocks, shadow latches in the scan paths are forced to hold their present state during the capture and shift operations. In Fig. 2, if the host IC is in a boundary test mode, the NDO outputs of the BSR will hold their present state during capture and shift operations so that the ripple effect caused by these actions will not be propagated out to disturb the application logic or external neighboring ICs. After a data or instruction register scan operation is completed, the TAP passes through the UPDATE state. The UPDATE state causes the shadow latches to update with the new data that has been installed into either the data or instruction register. In Fig. 2, if the host IC is in a boundary test mode, the next boundary test pattern will be updated and applied from the NDO outputs of the BSR during the UPDATE state.

The development of this test access protocol has played a key role in the acceptance of JTAG as a viable test bus standard for both commercial and military applications. One pleasing aspect of the test access protocol for the commercial side of the electronics industry is that it requires only four device pins. This means that implementation of the test bus in standard components only increases the package size to the next available standard size (i.e., 24 pins to 28, 40 pins to 44, etc.).

The test access protocol is attractive for military applications because it is architecturally consistent with existing scan interfaces that support separate instruction and data register scan architectures. In addition, the protocol is fault tolerant to a single event upset while in the TLRESET state. If an upset occurs, causing a transition into the RT/IDLE state, a recovery will occur back to the TLRESET state within three TCK cycles, via the SELDRS and SELIRS temporary states (Fig. 3).

In Fig. 5, the TAP control ouput signals are shown along with the instruction and data register interconnects. Table 1 shows the condition of each TAP output for each state in Figs. 3 and 4.

INSTRUCTION REGISTER

The instruction register is responsible for providing the address and control signals required to access a particular scan path in the data register. The instruction register is accessed when the TAP receives an instruction register scan protocol. Duirng an instruction register scan operation, the SELECT output from the TAP (Fig. 5) selects the output of the instruction register to drive the TDO pin. A general instruction register architecture is shown in Fig. 6.

Instruction Shift Register

The instruction shift register (Fig. 6) consists of a series of shift register bits arranged to form a single scan path between the TDI and TDO pins of the host IC. During instruction register scan operations, the TAP issues control via the instruction register shift enable (IRSHIFT) and instruction register clock (IRCLOCK) signals to cause the instruction shift register to preload status information and shift data from TDI to TDO. Both the preload and shift oper-

ations occur on the rising edge of TCK; however, the data shifted out from the host IC from TDO appears on the falling edge of TCK. The status inputs are user defined observability inputs, except for the two most significant bits, which are used for scan path testing purposes. When activated, the RESETZ input sets the instruction shift register to "all ones."

Instruction Shadow Latch

The instruction shadow latch (Fig. 6) consists of a series of latches, one latch for each instruction shift register bit. During an instruction register scan operation, the latches remain in their present state. At the end of the instruction register scan operation, the instruction register update (IRUPDATE) input updates the latches with the new instruction installed in the instruction shift register. When activated, the RESETX input sets the latches to "all ones."

DATA REGISTER

The data register group (Fig. 7) contains the scan registers involved with test. To conform to the proposed JTAG specification the data register group requires two of the scan paths shown in Fig. 7 (boundary register and scan bypass register). A third register (device identification register) has a specified form, but is optional. The data register group is expandable to any number of additional scan paths. The scan registers in the data register group are arranged in parallel from the primary TDI input to the primary TDO ouput. The instruction register supplies the address that allows one of the scan registers to be accessed for a data register scan operation.

During a data register scan operation, the addressed scan register receives control via the data register shift enable (DRSHIFT) and data register clock (DRCLOCK) inputs to preload test response and to shift data from TDI to TDO. Both the preload and the shift operations occur on the rising edge of the of TCK; however, the data shifted out of the host IC from TDO appears there on the falling edge of TCK. During a data register scan operation, the SELECT output from the TAP (Fig. 5) selects the output of the data register to drive the TDO pin. When one scan path in the data register is being accessed, all other scan paths remain in their previous state.

Scan Bypass Register

The scan bypass register consists of a single scan register bit. When selected, the scan bypass register provides a single bit scan path between TDI and TDO. The scan bypass register allows abbreviation of the scan path through devices that are not being tested. The scan bypass register is selected when the instruction register is loaded with a pattern of "all ones" to satisfy the JTAG scan bypass instruction requirement.

Device Identification Register

The device identification register is an optional scan register defined by JTAG for the purpose of identifying the device's manufacturer, part number, revision, etc. according to the relevant JEDEC standard. Although the implementation of the device identification register is optional, JTAG has dedicated an instruction to selecting this scan register path. The device identification register is selected when the instruction register is loaded with a patter of "100...00", (1 is the most significant bit (MSB)). If the optional device identification register is not implemented, the scan bypass register is selcted by this instruction.

Boundary Scan Register

The boundary scan register consists of a series of boundary scan cells (BSCs) arranged to form a scan path around the boundary of the host IC (Figs. 1 and 2). The BSCs provide the controllability and observability features required to perform boundary scan testing as described in the Boundary Scan Overview section of this paper. Shadow latches in the BSCs, driving the NDO outputs remain in their previous state during a data register scan operation. At the end of a data register scan operation, the data register update (DRUPDATE) input updates the shadow latches with the new boundary test pattern to be applied from the NDO outputs of the BSCs. The DRUPDATE input causes the BSCs to output the new test pattern on the falling edge of TCK. The boundary scan register is selected when the instruction register is loaded with a pattern of "all zeros" to satisfy the JTAG boundary scan instruction requirement.

CONCLUSION

The test access port described in the JTAG specification meets the requirements for a standard serial test interface. The architecture is flexible enough to support test structures ranging from boundary scan to the sophisticated maintenance and support structures required in the high-end military and commercial arenas of the electronics industry.

There is growing support for the TAP interface and boundary scan in both European and North American electronics companies, and some companies have already started implementing the proposed standard into new IC designs. JTAG released its 2.0 specification proposal in April 1988, and it has found acceptance within the IEEE P1149 standards committee. An IEEE P1149 subset referred to as P1149.1 has been set up as equivalent to the JTAG 2.0 specification. Ballotting on the P1149.1 subset is expected to occur sometime in late 1988 to formally create a standard.

REFERENCES

1. *JTAG Boundary-Scan Architecture Standard Proposal Version 2.0*, 30 March 1988, 90pp. [Available from author.]

2. Maunder, C. and F. Beenker, "Boundary Scan: A Framework for Structured Design-for-Test," *Proc. IEEE International Test Conference*, Washington, 1-3 September 1987, pp. 714-723.

3. Beenker, F. "Systematic and Structured Methods for Digital Board Testing," *Proc. IEEE International Test Conference*, Philadelphia, 1985, pp. 380-385.

4. Whetsel, L. "A View of the JTAG Port and Architecture," *Proc. ATE & Instrumentation Conference West*, January 1988, pp. 385-401.

5. Pradhan, M. M., R. E. Tulloss, F. P. M. Beenker, and H. Bleeker, "Developing a Standard for Boundary Scan Implementation," *Proc. International Conference on Computer Design*, Rye, New York, 5-8 October 1987, pp. 462-466.

Table 1 TAP Output Condition for Each State of Figures 3 and 4

		IRCLOCK	IRUPDATE	IRSHIFT	RESETZ	SELECT	ENABLE	DRSHIFT	DRUPDATE	DRCLOCK
FIG3	TLRESET	HI	HI	LO	LO	HI	LO	LO	HI	HI
	RT/IDLE	HI	HI	LO	HI	HI	LO	LO	HI	HI
	SELDRS	HI	HI	LO	HI	LO	LO	LO	HI	HI
	SELIRS	HI	HI	LO	HI	LO	LO	LO	HI	HI
FIG4A	DRCAPTURE	HI	HI	LO	HI	LO	HI	LO	HI	CK
	DRSHIFT	HI	HI	LO	HI	LO	HI	HI	HI	CK
	DREXIT1	HI	HI	LO	HI	LO	HI	LO	HI	HI
	DRPAUSE	HI	HI	LO	HI	LO	HI	LO	HI	HI
	DREXIT2	HI	HI	LO	HI	LO	HI	LO	HI	HI
	DRUPDATE	HI	HI	LO	HI	LO	HI	LO	CK	HI
FIG4B	IRCAPTURE	CK	HI	LO	HI	HI	HI	HI	HI	HI
	IRSHIFT	CK	HI	HI	HI	HI	HI	HI	HI	HI
	IREXIT1	HI	HI	LO	HI	HI	HI	HI	HI	HI
	IRPAUSE	HI	HI	LO	HI	HI	HI	HI	HI	HI
	IREXIT2	HI	HI	LO	HI	HI	HI	HI	HI	HI
	IRUPDATE	HI	CK	LO	HI	HI	HI	HI	HI	HI

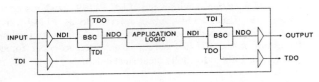

Figure 1 Boundary Scan Example

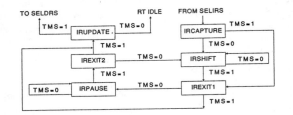

Figure 4B TAP Instruction Register Scan Diagram

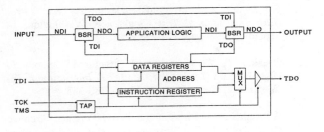

Figure 2 Standard Boundary Scan Architecture

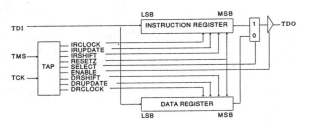

Figure 5 TAP Output Control Interconnect

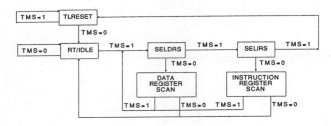

Figure 3 TAP Main State

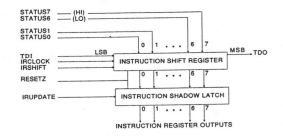

Figure 6 General Instruction Register Architecture

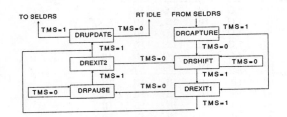

Figure 4A TAP Data Register Scan Diagram

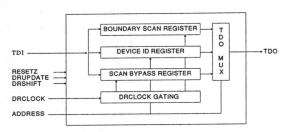

Figure 7 Data Register Architecture

INSERTING BUILT-IN SELF-TEST IN INTEGRATED CIRCUITS

Scott Davidson
Supervisor, Automatic Test Generation

AT&T Bell Laboratories
Engineering Research Center
P. O. Box 900
Princeton, NJ 08540

ABSTRACT

The increasing complexity of integrated circuits has made the testing of these circuits an increasingly difficult problem. One solution to this problem is to have hardware for the generation of tests and the capture of test results built in to the circuit. This is called *Built-in Self Test* (BIST). In this paper we give an introduction and motivation for the use of BIST, and briefly describe a system for the integration of BIST into integrated circuits. We also describe how BIST at the IC level can be used to ease the testing burden at the circuit board and system level. Subsequent papers in this section will describe testing at these levels in more detail.

INTRODUCTION

Products designed with digital logic are getting bigger and more complex in several dimensions. The number of transistors in an integrated circuit is growing as advances in manufacturing allow more circuitry to be packed into a given space. More integrated circuits are packed onto a printed circuit board. The complexity of systems and products is also growing rapidly as more functionality is demanded for a constant price. It is commonly said that the systems of yesterday are the boards of today, while the boards of yesterday are the integrated circuits of today. In fact, the systems of the day before yesterday are the ICs of today.

Unfortunately, the manufacture of ICs is still not a perfect process. Each IC made must be tested in order to verify that no defects have been introduced. This is called *testing,* and is distinct from testing to see if the circuit was designed correctly, which is called *design verification.* To test we must exercise every element of the IC. But it is not enough to confirm that every input of a logic gate that can be set to a one and a zero has been, and that every output can take on both the values of one and zero. We must also propagate the output of a gate to the output of the IC, where it can be observed by testing equipment. We must also control the inputs of gates from the inputs of the IC. The number of gates in an IC has grown faster than the number of input and outputs, which has meant that there is a myriad of logic paths to go through to control or observe a gate, which has made the writing of tests for ICs much more difficult. This has led to a reduction of the *fault coverage* of IC tests. Fault coverage is the percentage of faults in a circuit that are detected by a test. Lower fault coverage means that more bad ICs get through the screening process, which means more bad components in the printed circuit board or final system.

Increasing complexity has led to other problems. As there are more gates to test, test length gets longer. An accurate test should be supplied at the natural speed of the circuit, but ICs being designed today (for telecommunications systems, for example) may run at faster speeds than the test equipment supplying the test. Test equipment for state of the art ICs is getting more and more expensive in order to supply longer tests faster, and is already in the multi-million dollar range.

A solution to this problem is to build hardware for the generation of tests and the observation of test results into the circuit. Doing this is called *Built-in Self Test* (BIST).

There are several advantages to using BIST

- The test circuitry is closer to the logic to be tested, so it is easier to control and observe this logic.

- Since the BIST circuitry generates the test, we do not have to store the test on the test equipment. BIST can also be used to reduce the size of the test results, so less information on the expected results must be stored.

- Since the same technology being used for the IC is also being used for the test circuitry, and because the circuitry is right on the chip, the test will be applied at system speeds automatically. Further, expensive circuitry needed to interface the tester with the IC required for traditional approaches is reduced or not needed when BIST is used. There is therefore the possibility of using simpler, less expensive testers for circuits including BIST.

Certain logic blocks, such as memories, have easy to generate tests that may be extremely difficult to apply if the memory is deeply embedded within an IC. The use of BIST allows test circuitry to be added around these logic blocks, simplifying the testing problem. BIST techniques convert difficult to test sequential circuits into easy to test combinational circuits. This makes hardware based test generators possible, as well as making the automatic generation of tests easier. The alternative is long test generation times that can slow down product introduction.

The bottom line is that the use of BIST can make testing easier and faster. BIST is not free, however. The circuitry that must be added for BIST (typically 10-15% of the circuit transistor count) can decrease manufacturing yield and make the ICs more expensive. The added circuitry can also slow down the circuit. These costs must be compared to the savings gained in reduced testing costs throughout the product life cycle to determine if BIST is worthwhile for a particular IC.

BIST AND THE BOARD AND SYSTEM

So far, we have discussed the utility of BIST for the testing of ICs. With proper system design, this utility can be extended to the board and system level. A complete chip self test eliminates the need for a board tester to apply long strings of patterns to verify the operation of a chip after it has been placed on a board. When combined with Boundary Scan (Ref. 1) technology, a chip self test can be initiated from the board edge connector. If the entire board is designed with BIST and Boundary Scan, it might be possible to eliminate in-circuit test. In any case, a more thorough test of ICs on a board would be possible, especially important for boards returned after failing system test, or for boards returned from the field.

At the system level the advantages of BIST are even greater. Though a failing chip is difficult to diagnose after it has been placed on a board, it is an order of magnitude more difficult to diagnose when the board is placed in a system. In order to get the system running quickly, repair is usually done by board swapping. Often several boards are replaced to increase the probability of a correct repair. When BIST is included, the probability of a correct diagnosis to the failing board, and often to the failing IC, is much greater, allowing for faster more accurate repair with less inventory of spare boards. The subsequent papers will provide more detail on the subject of BIST at the board and system levels. While we will concentrate on BIST at the chip level, it must be remembered that BIST at the chip level is essential for BIST at higher levels of assembly, and that most of the economic impact of BIST will be from savings in the system and board areas.

IC LEVEL BIST TECHNIQUES

What kind of BIST should be used at the IC level? It depends in large part on the structure of the circuit. Parts of circuits are random logic, consisting of logic gates and flip flops. Other parts are regular structures, such as random access memory internal to the chip, read only memory, programmable logic arrays, and other large building blocks used by designers.

Regular structures will be used in many different ICs, so it is worthwhile to invest more in designing BIST techniques just for them. An example from AT&T is BIST for RAMs (see Ref. 2). A common example is BIST for ROMs. A ROM consists of an address register, in which the address of the word to be read from the ROM is placed, the ROM itself, and a data register in which the word read from the ROM is placed. BIST for a ROM (see Fig. 1) can consist of an additional counter and a signature analysis register, in which the result of the test is compressed into one word of data. Some multiplexers and control lines, to put the ROM into self test mode or system mode are also needed. To test the ROM, the counter counts through all addresses implemented by the ROM, the data in these words is read into the signature analysis register and compressed. When the test is complete, the signature is compared with a signature stored by the system that represents the contents of the ROM with no faults present. The signature depends both on the contents of the ROM and the order in which the contents are read, so errors in the addressing logic will be detected also. The actual implementation will probably be more sophisticated than this, for example the counter may be made to run backwards also for a more comprehensive test.

For random logic, a more general technique must be used.

We have chosen to convert a design automatically into a design using BIST. One of several BIST techniques can be used. One technique is to connect flip-flops in the circuit into a circular scan path, using the techniques proposed in Refs. 3 and 4. Another is to convert the flip-flops into test generators that will generate an exhaustive set of patterns for all inputs driving an output, a techniques called pseudo-exhaustive test (Ref. 5). Of course other techniques are possible.

An important issue is how to initiate and control the BIST. If there are many separate blocks in the circuit, there is a need for many control lines to start the BIST for each block. Each of these must be externally stimulated, which would require an excessive number of pins if no other technique were available. Fortunately, the JTAG boundary scan standard (Ref. 6) provides a solution. The *Test Access Port* (TAP) is a general purpose port providing access to test support functions built into the IC. The TAP consists of three input lines and one output line, and can be used to control boundary scan and BIST functions. For instance, the Instruction Register, which can be set externally from the TAP, can be used to initiate BIST for various blocks. Some blocks might be tested in parallel, some serially. In any case, all control is done by internal logic and signals. The results of the test can be captured by the boundary scan register or other register within the TAP, and provided to the outside world.

Boundary scan, then, provides a standard way of getting control signals to the parts of the chip designed with BIST. There are additional advantages. One is in getting control signals to the chip. In a board test environment, an in-circuit tester could be used, but this requires test pads for surface mount components, something which is getting harder to provide for dense circuit boards. Boundary scan allows these signals to be provided from the board edge connector, allowing functional testers to be used, or perhaps inexpensive PC-based testers. Boundary scan also allows the BIST on a chip to be easily initiated by a systems test or diagnostic routine, which may allow diagnosis and repair to a failing IC.

Another advantage of boundary scan is increasing the effectiveness of the BIST itself. The region between the IC inputs and the BIST flip-flops is not tested in the usual BIST technique except by deterministic patterns applied to the IC inputs. With boundary scan, the boundary scan flip-flops can be converted to BIST flip-flops, and be used to generate test patterns. This increases the fault coverage for the self test.

CURRENT WORK IN AT&T

AT&T is committed to BIST and Boundary Scan. There is wide management and engineering support for Boundary Scan standardization, since we see that industry standards are the best way to solve the testing problem in the area of greater density and less accessibility. At the Engineering Research Center we are working on a set of computer aided design tools for BIST. The CKT (Circuit Know Thyself) tool converts all or part of the flip flops in a circuit into a circular scan path, using a number of metrics (Ref. 7), runs fault simulation (Ref. 8) to determine the BIST fault coverage, and then uses an automatic test generator (Ref. 9) to add deterministic vectors to increase the fault coverage to a desired level. Fig. 2 shows the structure of CKT. An alternate method is a tool called PEST (Pseudo-Exhaustive Self Test) which converts circuit flip flops into pseudo-exhaustive test generators, and automatically adds test points so that the pseudo-exhaustive test is not too long. The advantage of PEST is that a 100% fault coverage test of the original circuit is guaranteed, without the need to do expensive fault simulation. Additional vectors are required to test the test circuitry. The advantage of CKT is that BIST overhead can be reduced by not including all flip flops on the scan chain, a technique called partial scan.

We have had some excellent results on real circuits with these techniques, and development of the tools and experimentation are continuing.

SUMMARY

As levels of integration and complexity increase, the problem of testing gets harder and harder. Built-in Self Test is an effective solution, but for full effectiveness it requires a set of support software and techniques. The development of this support is under way at AT&T. Though there are many advantages to BIST at the IC level, the major gains come from the later stages of the product life cycle. The evaluation of the cost effectiveness of BIST must take these into account. IC level BIST is the foundation for a complete test strategy for the products of the future.

REFERENCES

1. Maunder, C. M. and F. Beenker, "Boundary Scan: A Framework for Structured Design-for-Test," *Proc. 1987 International Test Conference*, Washington, 1-3 September 1987, pp. 714-723.

2. Jain, S. K. and C. E. Stroud, "Built-In Self Testing of Embedded Memory," *IEEE Design and Test of Computers*, Vol. 3, No. 5, Oct. 1986, pp. 27-37.

3. Krasniewski, A. and S. Pilarski, "Circular Self-Test Path: A Low-Cost BIST Technique," *Proc. 24th Design Automation Conference*, June 1987, pp. 407-415.

4. C. E. Stroud, "An Automated BIST Approach for General Sequential Logic Synthesis," *Proc. 25th Design Automation Conference*, June 1988, pp. 3-8.

5. E. J. McCluskey, "Verification Testing — A Pseudo-Exhaustive Test Technique," *IEEE Trans. Computers*, Vol. C-3, No. 6, June 1984, pp. 541-546.

6. *JTAG Boundary-Scan Architecture Standard Proposal Version 2.0*, 30 March 1988, 90 pp. [Available from R. E. Tulloss, AT&T Bell Labs, ERC, P. O. Box 900, Princeton, NJ 08540]

7. Pradhan, M. M., E. O'Brien, S. L. Lam and J. Beausang, "Circular BIST with Boundary Scan," *Proc. 1988 International Test Conference*, September 1988, to appear.

8. Davidson, S. and J. L. Lewandowski, "ESIM/AFS — A Concurrent Architectural Level Fault Simulator," *Proc. 1986 International Test Conference*, pp. 375-383.

9. Mallela, S. and S. L. Wu, "A Sequential Test Generation System," *Proc. 1985 International Test Conference*, pp. 57-61.

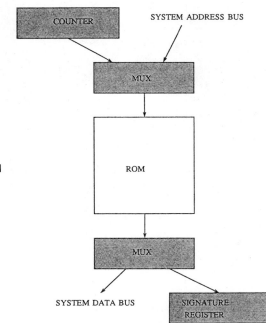

Figure 1. BIST Circuitry for ROM

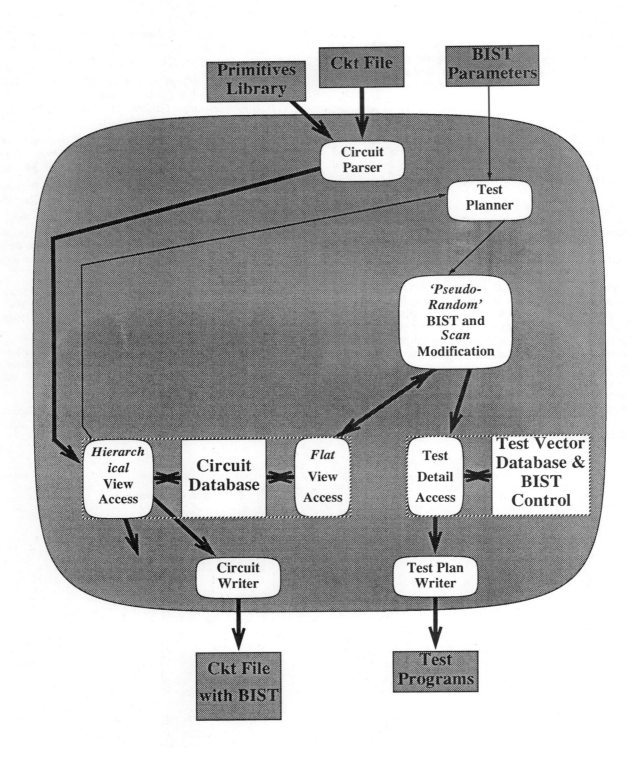

Figure 2. CKT BIST Tool

1795

INTEGRATING BIST AND BOUNDARY-SCAN ON A BOARD

Charles L. Hudson, Jr.
Manager, Design-For-Test

Honeywell, Inc.
Solid State Electronics Division
12001 State Highway 55
Plymouth, MN 55441

INTRODUCTION

Advances in processing and packaging technology have made accessing nodes within a design more difficult. Surface-mount technology eliminates many through-the-board holes, and the package-pin spacing and package-to-package spacing are shrinking. With unconstrained design, circuit boards densely-packed with extremely complex chips can quickly overwhelm conventional testing methods and the most sophisticated test equipment. The reduced accessiblity associated with increased complexity and new packaging technologies serves to reduce the inherent testability of new designs.

New design techniques and test methodologies are needed to overcome this reduction in inherent testability. Special features must be designed-in which will improve test access to the interior of the chip, board, or system being tested. Luckily, design-for-test techinques and standards are becoming available which can overcome many of the board and system test problems.

Boundary-Scan is one technique which, particularly when combined with design approaches such as Built-in Self-Test (BIST), can greatly improve board testability while reducing board testing costs. In adopting a Boundary-Scan testing strategy, the board test pattern generation costs can be reduced and the test coverage and fault isolation improved while reducing the cost of test equipment.

The development of Boundary-Scan standards and standard test interfaces will soon make the Boundary-Scan testing solutions available to a wide number of board manufacturers. This paper will introduce a number of ideas which will make it easier to implement a board testing strategy that uses Boundary-Scan.

BOUNDARY-SCAN

Boundary-Scan simplifies board-level testing by providing simple, serial access to the periphery of integrated circuits on a circuit board. By providing access from the edge of the board to the ICs, as shown in Fig. 1, one can test the components on the board separately from the interchip connections. These interchip connections can then be tested using the steps shown in Table 1.

The Benefits of Boundary-Scan

The ability to test the interchip connections separately from the internal logic of the ICs is the major benefit of Boundary-

1. Disable Chip Output Buffers
2. Make Boundary Shadow Registers Visible
3. Serial Shift In First Test Pattern
4. Switch Boundary Registers To Parallel Mode
5. Force Output Buffers Active
6. Single Functional Clock to Latch Test Results
7. Disable Output Buffers
8. Serial Shift Out Results/Shift in Next Pattern
9. Repeat Steps 4 - 8 Until Test is Complete

Table 1: Interconnect Testing Steps.

Scan. Many of the board-level defects that must be detected and isolated during manufacturing and maintenance are related to the interconnections. Since Boundary-Scan partitions the interchip connections away from the complex chip logic, it leaves a very simple circuit (consisting of the Boundary-Scan registers and interconnect) which can be easily and thoroughly tested.

Testing of this simple interconnect circuit will allow detection of most board-level defects. These defects can include defective (e.g., overdriven) output buffers, broken bonding wires, open or shorted interconnections, or defective input buffers (e.g., those damaged by electro-static discharge). As discussed later in this paper, a test-pattern set can be easily generated that will provide 100% coverage of interconnect stuck-at and bridging faults (Ref. 1). If these kinds of interconnect defects are expected, or fault isolation to an individual component is required, then Boundary-Scan is particularly useful.

Boundary-Scan will also allow thorough testing of the board without having to have a complete set of test vectors or simulation models of the individual components. If the user has difficulty obtaining chip test vector sets or chip simulation models, then he/she may be able to get by with a simple set of chip or board-wide functional vectors. If the chips include any chip-level BIST features, then using these features will eliminate the need to generate any functional vectors to test that component on the board. If the internal logic of the components have already been thoroughly tested prior to board assembly, then on-board testing of components would be used primarily to very the power supply and clock connections ot the individual components.

Boundary-Scan Design Overview

An integrated circuit with Boundary-Scan makes use of scannable flip-flops placed at the periphery of the chip which separate the chip application logic from the interchip connections. The IC will usually include some form of on-chip monitor (OCM) or test interface which controls the mode and operation of the Boundary-Scan cells. Fig. 2 shows the relationship of the OCM, Boundary-Scan logic, and the application logic. The chip-level test interface is usually a simple serial test interface which may control access to other design-for-test features in addition to Boundary-Scan. These interfaces may be the JTAG (Joint Test Action Group) test access port (Ref. 2) or perhaps the

VHSIC ETM bus (Ref. 3). A chip-wide output disable may also be provided to protect against conflicting three-state drivers on the same bus during power-up or while shifting the Boundary-Scan registers.

The key element to Boundary-Scan is the Boundary-Scan flip-flop placed at each I/O pin. These form Boundary-Scan registers which can be dedicated for testing or used both for functional and testing purposes. If the Boundary-Scan flip-flops are to be dedicated for testing, then they will include multiplexers, as shown in Fig. 3 so that they may be by-passed when the chips are in the normal, functional mode.

The Cost of Boundary-Scan

When Boundary-Scan is implemented using functional registers, the circuit overhead is that required to make the functional registers scannable. When shadow registers are used, the circuit overhead can be calculated using the equation:

$$\% \text{ Increase} = \frac{G_{BSCell} \cdot N_{I/O}}{G_{Total} - (G_{BSCell} \cdot N_{I/O})} \cdot 100\%$$

Where:
- G_{BSCell} = Number of gates in shadow registers
- G_{Total} = Total logic gates in design
- $N_{I/O}$ = Number of chip inputs & outputs

The area overhead as it affects the designer can be reduced by custom-packing Boundary-Scan cells in the periphery of the chip or by making use of existing functional registers in the design.

COMPONENT TESTING WITH BIST

The Boundary-Scan technique described above is an effective technique for self-test of the chip interconnect since only a few test patterns are needed for excellent fault coverage (Ref. 1). Many test strategies, however, will still require test coverage of the internal logic of the ICs on the board. BIST of individual components or at the overall board level is an effective way to provide this test coverage while minimizing test equipment and enhancing system maintainability. Some of the more commonly used BIST techniques are briefly described below.

Functional Self-Test

Functional self-test software routines (Ref. 4) are very attractive since they require little hardware overhead, are easily understood, and can be implemented at the end of the design cycle. In many cases, only a small amount of microcode memory is needed to implement the self-test routines. When used with Boundary-Scan, a board-wide functional self-test routine could be used to verify the clock and power connections of the individual components. These routines may also be used to verify "at speed operation" of critical paths within the design.

Although this is the most practical approach to board-level self-test, functional self-test does not usually allow for very high levels of fault coverage within the components. In addition, functional self-test alone usually will not test such items as microcode ROM contents accurately.

Enhancements to Functional Self-Test

Simple modifications to the functional self-test approach can help it to overcome some of its drawbacks. Addition of parallel input signature analysis registers can improve the visibility of points throughout the design and can improve self-test fault coverage. The addition of special self-test circuitry to blocks such as PLAs, ROMs, and RAMs can also improve the coverage by providing good test coverage of these blocks. This special test circuitry covers many transistor sites and helps manufacturing by separately testing function blocks which may significantly impact device yield. Although these enhancements improve test coverage, functional self-test still does not work for a wide class of digital designs and might not meet the fault coverage and fault isolation requirements of some applications.

Serially-Loaded Test Patterns

If the IC incorporates serial scan, serially-loaded pseudorandom test patterns may be a cost-effective self-test solution. In this case, a serial pseudorandom test pattern generator and serial signature analysis registers are connected to the application's serial scan path. To test the circuitry, a pseudorandom test pattern is loaded serially into the scan path. The scan registers are reconfigured into their normal functional configuration and the application is clocked once to latch the test results. The results are then scanned into the signature analysis register while the next test pattern is loaded into the scan path. This process is repeated several thousand times until adequate test coverage is obtained (Ref. 5). The test pattern generator and signature analysis register may be contained on-chip, on a board test-support chip, or off the board.

An interesting side note is that pseudorandom patterns may work effectively for testing interchip connections as well in certain cases. In designs where there are no three-state buses which may be forced to conflicting states, the pseudorandom patterns could eliminate the need to load boundary scan test patterns from off the board although precision of diagnosis of a failure is sacrificed.

Built-in Evaluation and Self-Test

Built-in Evaluation and Self-Test (BEST) uses parallel pseudorandom test patterns applied at the chip boundary to test the sequential logic array. The outputs of the array are then compacted into a checksum at the boundary output signals. This technique was first used by Control Data (Ref. 6) and has been used primarily on gate arrays (Ref. 7). This technique operates at full chip speed, provides good coverage of delay faults, and can be implemented at a reasonable cost. The technique is independent of the chip application, works well with Boundary-Scan designs, and at first glance looks as though it requires little effort by the designer.

Since the logic in the array is sequential, many thousands (or millions) of test patterns may be required to achieve the desired fault coverage. Also, it may be necessary to modify the sequential logic to improve the observability and/or controllability of nodes within the array in order to achieve the 95% single stuck-at fault coverage goal. Because of the large number of test patterns required and the possibility of losing fault information in the checksum, it is difficult to demonstrate that high fault coverage has been obtained.

Self-Test with BILBOs

There are also a number of promising self-test techniques which make use of Built-In Logic Block Observer (BILBO) registers (Ref. 8). In most of these techniques, functional registers in the chip designs are replaced with BILBO registers that can be configured as a normal functional register, a serial shift register, a pseudorandom test pattern generator (TPG), or a parallel signature analysis (PSA) register. Although these techniques are promising for testing embedded memory devices, they are not yet cost-effective for wide-spread use.

BOARD TESTING

If all of the components on the board contain Boundary-Scan, the design of a testable board is simple. The board is designed as it would be for a regular, functional board design; and then the test interfaces to each of the chips are connected in a loop as shown conceptually in Fig. 1. In addition to the serial data lines shown in the figure, the control and clock lines accompanying the serial test interface are also connected to all the components on the board.

Some chip designs may require a power-up reset signal to the test interface to ensure that the chip outputs are reset (thereby avoiding conflicts on three-state buses). This reset signal could be taken to the card edge or provided directly on the card.

Finally, when the serial test bus is not to be used for maintenance purposes in the system, it is important that the board be designed so that the serial bus signals are set to values that will not disturb proper operation of the board. One way that this can be done is to provide pull-up or pull-down resistors on the board for the serial test bus control lines. These pull-ups/pull-downs would be overridden by active drive during manufacturing testing so as to allow access to the serial test bus.

Test Setup

A properly designed test setup, such as that shown in Fig. 4, can dramatically reduce the test equipment costs for board testing. The elements of a simple test setup are an inexpensive testing computer with an instrumentation control bus (i.e., IEEE-488) and a serial test bus port, programmable power supplies, a load board/test fixture, and the board under test. In addition to being very inexpensive, this type of test setup could be easily expanded to handle testing of a number of boards simultaneously. The inexpensive nature of this test setup makes it useful for

manufacturing testing, burn-in, and other reliability testing of the boards.

One key to minimizing the test setup is proper design of the load board/test fixture. As shown in Fig. 5, the need for complex, functional, board testers can be eliminated by designing a load board that takes the board outputs and feeds them back into board inputs. This allows the boundary scan technique to apply test patterns that will verify the board to the very edge of the card. Additional signal loading can be added, if necessary, so that the board drivers are tested under loading conditions specified for the board.

A Test Procedure

Once the test setup is ready to go and test patterns have been gernerated, the test procedure for the board is quite simple. Following the steps in Table 2, the board can be quickly tested for most board-level faults. An important thing to notice is that thorough self-test is required if thorough coverage of delay faults is needed, since the boundary scan interconnection test is essentially a static test.

---

1. Power-up & Reset Components
2. Shift Test Bus To Verify Functionality of Bus
3. Shift To Verify The Boundary Paths
4. Load The First Serial Interconnect Test Pattern
5. Clock The Pattern Across The Interconnect
6. Shift Out & Compare Result / Shift In Next Pattern
7. Repeat Steps 5 & 6 To Fully Test Interconnections
8. Initialize Board For Self-Test
9. Run Self-Test & Check Result

Table 2: Board Testing Steps.

SYSTEM TESTING & MAINTENANCE

The fault coverage and fault isolation provided by boundary scan makes it extremely useful for system maintenance in addition to board testing. If the boundary scan is to be used at the system level, however, a few changes may be required.

The major change in the board design relates to the serial test interface. The JTAG (Joint Test Action Group) bus (also now to be known as the IEEE P1149.1 bus) is a serial test bus that primarily supports a loop configuration. If a multidrop backplane is required, it may be necessary to add a test-bus interface unit (TIU) between the on-board serial test bus and the backplane test bus as shown in Fig. 6. A TIU chip could be used for protocol translation, test sequencing, and other test or maintenance functions.

INTERCONNECT TEST PATTERNS

A major benefit of Boundary-Scan is the ease with which thorough test patterns can be generated for a board design. Complete stuck-at-one and stuck-at-zero testing of interconnect can be completed in two test patterns if

1798

multiple outputs are not wired together. If a maximum of K outputs are wired together, then 2·K patterns provide full stuck-at-zero testing interconnects (Ref. 1).

Fig. 7 shows a chip interconnect net with three sources and a single target. To test the top output buffer for a stuck-at-one condition, the top source output buffer is enabled while the other two are disabled. The top source is set to a logic zero; each of the disabled sources is set to a logic one; and the target is clocked to latch in the test result. To complete the stuck-at-one test of the net, the test described for the top source is repeated for the bottom two sources. When a source is disabled, the contents of the source flip-flop will be set opposite that of the enabled source. The process would be repeated, with values inverted, to obtain a stuck-at-zero test.

Testing for shorts with boundary scan is also very simple. The short shown in Fig. 8 can be detected by setting the top source flip-flop to a logic zero and the bottom source flip-flop to a logic one. The target flip-flops are clocked, and their contents are scanned out. If the contents of the two target flip-flops are the same (logic 1 for a wired-OR, logic 0 for a wired-AND), then a short is present.

$Log_2(n+2)$ test patterns are required for complete interconnect short testing, where n is the number of interconnection nets (Ref. 1). The intercconnect test patterns can be easily generated by computer, given an interconnection net list.

REFERENCES

1. Wagner, P. T., "Interconnect Testing with Boundary Scan," *Proc. IEEE International Test Conference*, Washington, 1-3 September 1987, pp. 52-57.

2. *JTAG Boundary Scan Architecture Standard Proposal Version 2.0*, 30 March 1988, 90 pp. [Available from R. E. Tulloss, AT&T Bell Labs, ERC, P. O. Box 900, Princeton, NJ 08540.]

3. Avra, L. J., "Honeywell's VHSIC Standard, On-Chip Test & Maintenance Controller," *GOMAC*, 1987, pp. 221-224.

4. Brahme, D. and J. A. Abraham, "Functional Testing of Microprocessors," *IEEE Trans. on Computers*, June 1984, pp. 475-485.

5. LeBlanc, J. J. "LOCST: A Built-In Self-Test Technique," *IEEE Design & Test of Computers*, November 1984, pp. 45-52.

6. Resnick, D. R., "Testability and Maintainability with a new 6K Gate Array," *VLSI Design*, March/April 1983, pp. 34-38.

7. Lake, R., "A fast 20K Gate Array with On-Chip Test System," *VLSI Systems Design*, June 1986, pp. 46-55.

8. Hudson, C. L., "Parallel Self-Test with Pseudo-Random Test Patterns," *Proc. IEEE International Test Conference*, Washington, 1-3 September 1987, pp. 954-963.

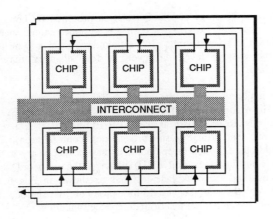

Figure 1.

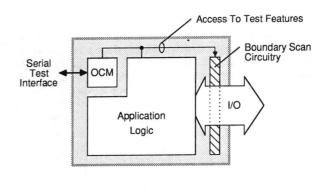

Figure 2.

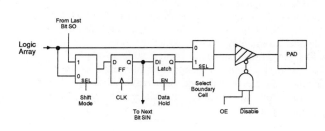

Figure 3. Boundary Scan Output Cells

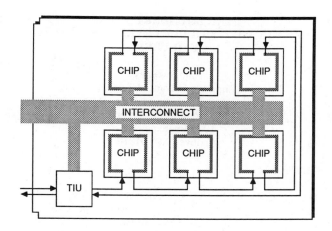

Figure 6.

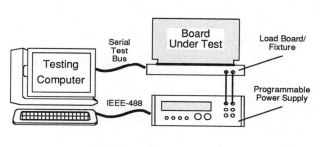

Figure 4.

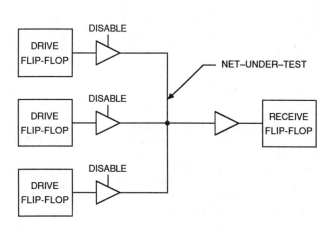

Figure 7.

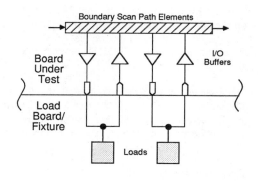

Figure 5.

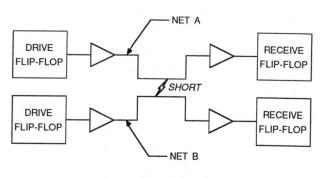

Figure 8.

JTAG BOUNDARY SCAN: DIAGNOSING MODULE LEVEL FUNCTIONAL FAILURES

John Sweeney
Principle Engineer, Advanced Test Technology

Digital Equipment Corporation
100 Minuteman Rd.
Andover, MA 01810

ABSTRACT

This paper will discuss a method for the use of JTAG boundary scan for testing and diagnosing functional or "at speed" failures on assembled modules. This can be accomplished if the Module Under Test (MUT), or the portion of it to be tested, can execute a repeatable test sequence and provide a trigger signal at the start of the test sequence. External test equipment or logic on the MUT can then activate the JTAG boundary scan latches within the devices on the MUT in their sample mode to capture the pin states of the devices on the module during the execution of the test sequence. By comparing this captured data with expected data, a test controller can classify the MUT as either "good" or "faulty". In the case of a faulty module, the captured data can be further analyzed to determine the faulty component on the module.

DESCRIPTION OF JTAG BOUNDARY SCAN "SAMPLE MODE"

A brief description of the JTAG "sample mode" functionality only will be presented here. For further details on the JTAG test logic and its other capabilities, please reference the latest JTAG specification (Ref. 1). While the JTAG boundary scan will be used during module test it must have been designed into the individual devices which will be present on the module.

The JTAG architecture specifies test logic for ICs which includes a four pin Test Access Port (TAP), an instruction register, a bypass data register and a boundary scan data register. The four pins of the TAP are Test Clock (TCK), Test Mode Select (TMS), Test Data In (TDI), and Test Data Out (TDO).

The JTAG boundary scan register can be thought of as a very wide parallel load, serial shift register. This register will be distributed around the chip edges with each bit in this register corresponding to either an input pin of the device, an output pin, or an I/O pin. The boundary scan register must be able to operate in a number of modes as determined by data previously shifted into the instruction register, one of these modes being "sample mode".

The boundary scan register latches will be physically inside the input or output buffers, i.e., they will sample the data that was actually received, or the data which is supposed to be driven. For an I/O pin the latch will sample the data which was read, or the data which is being driven, depending on the action the pin is taking in that cycle. In addition, for each I/O pin or set of pins, there is a boundary scan register cell which captures the direction of that pin or set of pins.

The goals of the JTAG boundary scan sample mode are to facilitate the performance verification of the MUT and aid in the goal of diagnostic accuracy to the faulty device for those devices containing JTAG boundary scan. To accomplish this, the JTAG boundary scan is able to capture the logic states at the physical boundaries of each of the selected devices on the module and then make these states available to logic on the module, external test equipment, or other diagnostic tools.

As specified, the operation of the JTAG boundary scan register does not interfere with the normal operation of the device on the module when operated in sample mode. This allows normal system or test program execution to continue after activation of the scan latches.

MODULE REQUIREMENTS

There are several requirements which must be met in order to implement this testing methodology. The first is that the test logic must be synchronized with the normal system logic in order to allow accurate sampling of device pin states. This can be easily accomplished if the system cycle time and the test clock (TCK) period are equal. This may not be possible if the test logic cannot operate as fast as the system logic. This situation would require some logic to allow TCK to be activated synchronous to the system clock in order to sample the device pin states into their boundary scan registers.

Another requirement is that the module logic must be able to execute a repeatable test sequence in order to stimulate the devices on the module. The fulfillment of this requirement allows samples captured in separate executions of the test sequence to be pieced together to reconstruct the entire test sequence. This test sequence can be provided by an on-board ROM based self-test (RBST) in most instances.

In addition, a stable trigger signal must be available which precedes the test sequence execution. In many instances, this trigger signal can actually be the module power-up reset signal because the de-assertion of the reset signal usually starts the execution of the RBST code.

A test controller must have access to the TAPs of the JTAG devices on the MUT in order to control the operation of the JTAG test logic and the execution of the RBST. This test controller can be external to the MUT or contained in the board logic.

The last requirement is that the majority of the devices on the module under test contain JTAG test logic. Obviously the higher the percentage of devices which implement the JTAG test architecture, the better the test and diagnosis will be.

CAPTURING THE PIN STATES

The following discussion assumes that the above

requirements have been met including the requirement that the test clock period and system cycle time are the same.

It will now be possible, during the execution of the RBST, to sample the pin state data of the JTAG devices from any particular cycle of operation by parallel loading it into the boundary scan register latches. This sampling is accomplished by manipulating the TMS and TDI signals such that the TAP controllers in all of the JTAG devices sequence into the boundary scan capture state. Then during subsequent cycles the sampled data is shifted out into comparison logic either on the module or in some external test equipment.

Because the activation of the JTAG boundary scan has not affected the system operation, once all the sampled data has been shifted, another set of data can be loaded and then shifted out. If there are a total of N boundary scan register cells in the devices on the module, and the TCK period is equal to the system cycle time, then the pin states can be sampled and shifted out every $N+X$ cycles where X is the number of cycles required to make the transition from the *SHIFT-DR* state, back to the *CAPTURE-DR* state (typically 4 cycles (Ref. 1)).

The procedure used to activate the scan latches involves using the ROM-Based Self-Test (RBST) resident on the board. One triggers the RBST, waits a certain number of cycles, loads pin state into the boundary scan register in one cycle, then starts shifting data out of the rings one cycle at a time. This sampling of data and shifting it out happens repeatedly through the RBST sequence. Because it does not allow testing of every cycle of test sequence in one pass through that sequence, due to the time spent shifting, the test needs to be repeated, each time starting the sampling operation later in the RBST sequence. This method of testing is called a "multiple pass test."

A "FRAME" of data is the set of logical values in the JTAG boundary scan cells during one system cycle. This data is "captured" by the JTAG boundary scan registers in one system cycle, then shifted out over the next $N+4$ cycles. Here N is the total number of boundary scan register cells in all of the JTAG devices on the MUT and the additional 4 cycles are required to get ready to sample again. Once the frame has been shifted out and the JTAG devices have been set into the *CAPTURE-DR* state, a new frame of data can be gathered and shifted out.

A "PASS" through the test sequence can gather multiple frames of data. Because the operation of the JTAG boundary scan register doesn't affect the execution of the test sequence, many frames of data can be collected in each pass through the test sequence.

The entire "TEST" consists of multiple "passes" through the test sequence, each pass varying which set of "frames" is collected. The set of frames which is sampled in any particular pass is determined by varying the delay from the trigger signal to the system cycle in which the first frame of data is sampled.

A visual representation of frame data collection for multiple passes is shown in Fig. 1. This figure is a visualization of the execution of a multiple pass test occurring on a module with a total of 100 JTAG boundary scan register cells. In pass 1, frames 0, 100, 200, etc. are collected, and in pass 2, frames 1, 101, 201, etc. are collected. This process is continued for 100 passes, collecting a different set of frames in each pass. After all of the 100 passes have been completed, the test has captured all of the frames of data for the entire test sequence operation, allowing diagnosis to the failing component.

Once all frames have been collected, it is up to the test controller to analyze the data and determine if the test passed or failed. If it is determined that the test failed, then further analysis of the frame data can be performed to indict the failing component.

This data capturing method can be thought of as a "sampling logic analyzer" which samples device pin states over a periodic function (the repeatable test sequence) in the same manner as a sampling oscilloscope samples voltages over a periodic waveform.

DIAGNOSIS OF FAILURES

The sequence of events executed in order to perform a diagnosis of a failing test are as follows:

1. Find the Earliest Failing System Cycle (EFC) or "frame of data" by repeatedly executing the following sequence:

    o   Read the data from the current pass through the test sequence to determine the First Failing Cycle (FFC) in that pass by comparing the actual frame data just captured against expected frame data. The expected frame data would have been previously generated via module level simulation of the test sequence or the capturing of the frame data from a known good module. If that FFC is earlier than the EFC, then make the EFC equal to the FFC from the current pass. It is not necessary to check frame data that occurs after the previous EFC.

    o   Determine if the Earliest Failing Cycle has been found by checking if all frames up to the current EFC have been checked. If the EFC has not been found, then execute another pass through the test sequence, selecting the appropriate frames to check on that pass. This is performed by setting up the test controller to vary the delay from the trigger signal which determines which set of frames to sample.

2. Once the Earliest Failing Cycle has been determined, then the failing frame corresponding to that cycle will be further analyzed to determine which bits of that frame are in error.

3. Because each bit in a frame represents the logical value of a device pin, the failing bits can be mapped to a failing component which can then be indicted. This mapping is

accomplished by utilizing first principles of the operation of the devices, along with the difference between the expected and actual pin states and pin directions.

One important aspect of the diagnosis is that the earliest failure must be analyzed in order to correctly diagnose the failing signal and component. If a later frame is analyzed, the *propagated effects* of the fault will be analyzed, possibly resulting in a misdiagnosis.

It should be noted that JTAG specifies that, for each I/O pin or set of pins, there is a boundary scan register cell which captures the direction of that pin or set of pins. (This detail has been left out of the above description of the boundary scan register for simplicity of presentation.) This direction information will be very important in the mapping of the failing bits to the failing component as it allows diagnosis not only to the signal, but to the particular component on that signal which is faulty.

LOGIC-ANALYZER-LIKE DISPLAYS

The test controller could allow the operator to utilize itf as a pseudo-logic-analyzer to observe the JTAG boundary scan latches in the MUT while the module is executing a test sequence. In this mode, the operator could specify signal names or device pins and a range of system cycles to observe; and the test controller would convert this request into a pass or series of passes through the test sequence, gathering a frame of data on each pass. This frame data would then be organized and displayed to the operator in the same way that a logic analyzer would, but without requiring physical access to signal networks. The sequence of events executed would be as follows:

1. The operator requests the signal(s) and system cycle(s), or frame(s), of the data which are to be observed. The test controller translates this request into one concerning which bits of the requested frames to display based on the selected nodes.

2. The test controller then executes a set of passes through the test sequence in order to collect all of the needed frames of data.

3. Once all the requested data have been collected, this data is displayed to the operator.

CONCLUSIONS

While the requirements of the logic to be tested are relatively strict, the use of sample mode testing can allow the diagnosis of functional failures without requiring physical access to the module under test. This will become more important as pin count increases and lead spacing decreases in future generations of surface mount packages.

REFERENCE

1. *JTAG Boundary-Scan Architecture Standard Proposal Version 2.0,* 30 March 1988, 90 pp. [Available from R. E. Tulloss, AT&T Bell Labs, ERC, P. O. Box 900, Princeton, NJ 08540.]

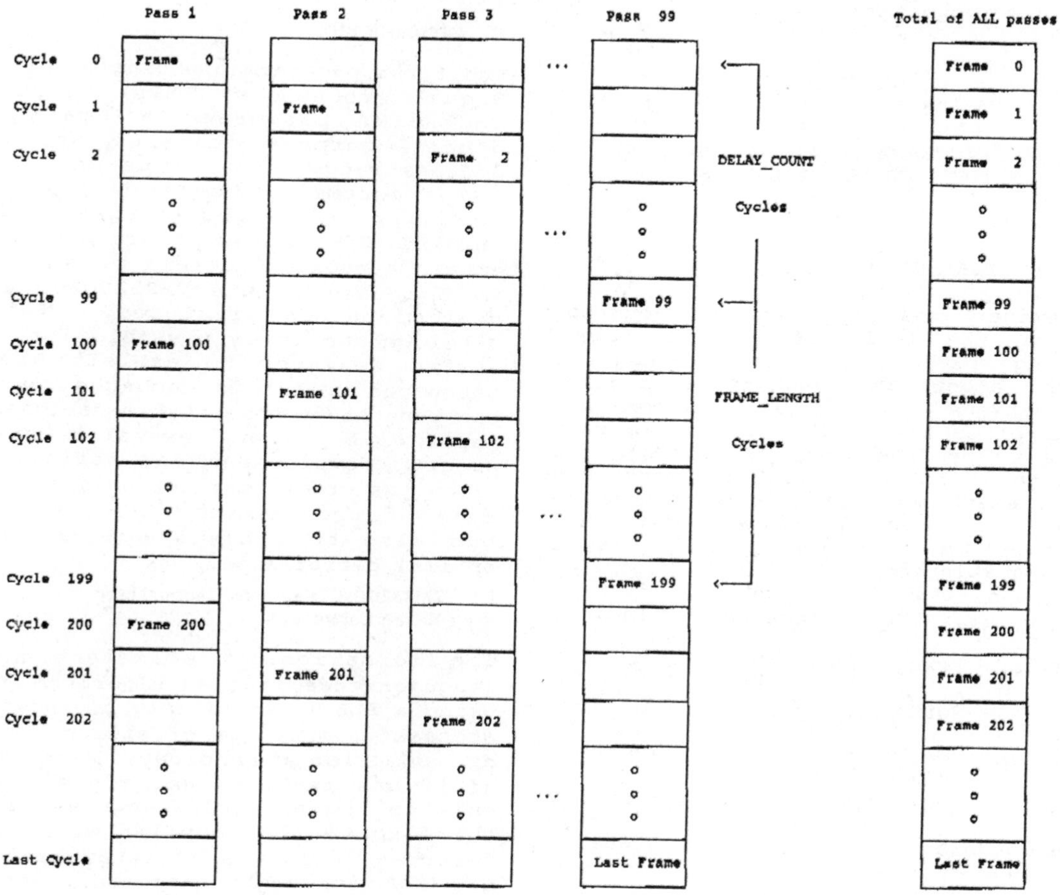

Pass 1
Pass 2
Pass 3
Pass 99
Total of ALL passes
Cycle 0
Cycle 1
Cycle 2
Cycle 99
Cycle 100
Cycle 101
Cycle 102
Cycle 199
Cycle 200
Cycle 201
Cycle 202
Last Cycle
Frame 0
Frame 1
Frame 2
Frame 99
Frame 100
Frame 101
Frame 102
Frame 199
Frame 200
Frame 201
Frame 202
Last Frame
DELAY_COUNT
Cycles
FRAME_LENGTH
Cycles

Figure 1.

TEC-16

"DIGITAL SIGNAL PROCESSING SESSION"

NEW TECHNOLOGIES INSTITUTE

J. R. KRONENBURGER
L. L. SHEETS

ROCKWELL INTERNATIONAL CORPORATION
DOWNERS GROVE, ILLINOIS

DIGITAL SIGNAL PROCESSING

This seminar presents important current topics in the field of Digital Signal Processing (DSP). The emphasis is on DSP hardware, algorithms, and implementation considerations applied in telecommunication applications. The seminar is very valuable to professionals responsible for the design of communication equipment that by requirement must precisely process an applied signal and possibly adapt that process as a function of the input signal's statistics.

Ray Simar, Jr. - Texas Instruments Inc.

Alan Davis - Texas Instruments Inc.

Greg K. Ma - Northern Illinois University

Sen Maw Kuo - Northern Illinois University

Pavan Gupta - Northern Illinois University

Sasan H. Ardalan - North Carolina State University

Gary L. Blank - Illinois Institute of Technology

A Study of the Application
of High-Level Languages to
Single-Chip Digital
Signal Processors

Ray Simar Jr. and Alan Davis
Texas Instruments, Inc.
P.O. Box 1443 M/S 701
Houston, Texas 77251-1443

ABSTRACT

This paper discusses strategies leading to the efficient use of High-Level Languages (HLLs) on single-chip Digital Signal Processors (DSPs). The paper takes the reader from the specification of a particular algorithm, through step-wise refinements, to an optimized implementation for the DSP. For the purpose of illustration, Texas Instruments' high-performance floating-point DSP, the TMS320C30, and its optimizing C-compiler are used. Further discussion is given to the execution of computationally intensive benchmarks where the TMS320C30 and its optimizing C-compiler combine to exceed the performance of a VAX 11/785 or a typical RISC processor.

1. INTRODUCTION

The first programmable single-chip Digital Signal Processors (DSPs), such as the TMS32010, possessed a small set of general-purpose features and a small address range ([1]). The principle mode for programming these devices is with assembly languages targeted for the specific DSP. Recent years have seen DSPs attain a greater address range, 64 Mbytes in the case of the TMS320C30, and more general-purpose features. With these developments it is possible for the DSP-system designer to exploit High-Level Languages (HLLs) in much the same way as the general-purpose system designer. This paper will present several techniques of program development and refinement that allow the programmer not only to enjoy the ease of programming attributed to HLLs but also to achieve optimal or near-optimal performance.

1.1 TMS320C30 Features Supporting High-Level Languages

The formation of efficient assembly-language code from an algorithm specified using a HLL is inevitably dependent upon a successful marriage of silicon technology and compiler technology. The TMS320C30 ([2]) has features which are useful not only to the assembly-language programmer but also to the compiler writer. These features include a register based 32/40-bit CPU with eight data and eight address registers, single-cycle floating-point operations, on-chip memory for local and global variable storage, an on-chip program cache, separate program and data buses, flexible addressing modes, and orthogonal instruction classes including three-operand instructions.

1.2 Description of the TMS320C30 Optimizing C-Compiler

The optimizing C-compiler for the TMS320C30 was designed with two major goals in mind:

1. For general-purpose C code, produce compiled code that performs nearly as well as hand-coded assembly.

2. Provide a simple and accessible programming environment so that applications demanding higher performance can be implemented using assembly language for critical code and still use C for general-purpose code.

First we will look at a few of the built-in optimizations the compiler performs. The optimizations include register tracking, jump optimizations, expression reordering , and dead-code removal.

1.2.1 Register Tracking

The compiler keeps track of the contents of registers so that it avoids reloading values if they are used again soon. For example, given the following code fragment:

```
int a = 10;
  c  = a + b;
```

The compiler, rather than generating

```
LDI    10,R0    will generate    LDI 10,R0
STI    R0, a                     STI R0, a
LDI    a,R1                      ADDI  b,R0

ADDI   b,R1
```

The compiler tracks variables, direct structure references, constants, and addresses of variables. The compiler also tracks register contents across branches.

1.2.2 Jump Optimizations

Often, the compiler generates branches to other branches. This happens when control structures are nested within each other. The compiler reduces branching chains to a single branch that jumps to the final destination. Therefore, rather than the compiler generating

```
L1:  ADDI R0,R0
BNZ  L2
LDI   a,R0
L2:  BR L1
```

the compiler generates

```
L1:  ADDI R0,R1
BNZ  L1
LDI   a,R0
BR   L1
```

1.2.3 Expression Reordering

In many cases, the compiler generates better code for an expression by reordering the expression. For example, -(a + b) is treated as if it were the algebraically equivalent -a - b and the compiler, rather than generating

```
LDI a,R0    will generate    NEGI    a,R0
ADDI b,R0                     SUBI    b,R0
NEGI R0
```

The compiler performs dozens of optimizations that involve reordering or distributing operations. Such optimizations are performed for logical,

pointer, relational, and assignment operations as well as the standard arithmetic ones.

1.2.4 Dead-Code Removal and Other Optimizations

Occasionally, a user writes a section of code that cannot be reached and so will never be executed. This section of code is referred to as *dead-code*. The compiler detects dead code and removes it.

The compiler performs numerous other optimizations to generate better code for various constructs. These are somewhat miscellaneous, but generally locally affect the code generated for a given operation or expression.

2. PROBLEM SPECIFICATION

Nothing could better illustrate our approaches to optimizing the performance of a DSP through the use of a HLL than a simple, concrete example. The particular example chosen is a C function rmvmul(). rmvmul() performs a multiplication between a real matrix A and a real vector x yielding the real vector y, that is $y = Ax$. rmvmul() has the advantage of being short enough to be considered in detail in this paper and sufficiently complex to describe several optimization strategies. rmvmul() and its arguments are defined as follows:

```
rmvmul (y, A, x, ncA, nrA)
float y[] Pointer to real output vector.
float A[] Pointer to real input matrix.
float x[] Pointer to real input vector.

int   ncA  Number of columns in matrix A
           and rows in vector x.

int   nrA  Number of rows in matrix A
           and rows in vector y.

           Returns -1 if nca ≤ 0 or
           nra ≤ 0.

           Otherwise, returns 0.
```

3. C VERSIONS OF rmvmul()

3.1 Plain-Vanilla Version of rmvul()

We will present several different versions of rmvmul(). Starting with our first version, the ``plain-vanilla'' version, we will follow a path of step-wise refinement in order to maximize the algorithm's performance. The plain-vanilla version is representative of the way one might write the routine without considering any optimization. The plain-vanilla version is shown in Figure 1. This version of rmvmul() executes in 24.36 µs on a TMS320C30 (@ 60ns/cycle).

The code in Figure 1 is divided into two portions. The first is the control portion of the code. This portion of the function checks for errors on the dimensions of the vector and matrices passed to it. If there is an error, rmvmul() returns -1. Otherwise, 0 is returned. This code is shown in Figure 2 and the resulting TMS320C30 assembly-language code is shown in Figure 3. This code is typical of the general-purpose code often found in a more sophisticated DSP-system. Notice that the compiler has produced extremely efficient code in this case.

The second major portion of the code is the computational portion of the code. This is the code contained within the for (i = 0; i < nrA; i++) {...} construct in Figure 1. Figure 4 shows the assembly-language code produced by the compiler for the statement sum += A[inca + j] * x[j]. It is in this eight lines of assembly-language code where most of the execution time is spent. While the compiler has produced extremely efficient code from the C code we provided, it is possible to significantly improve the performance of the function by simply modifying our C code to take advantage of register variables.

3.2 Using Register Variables

The TMS320C30, due to its register-based CPU, supports the C register type very efficiently. register variables are stored in CPU registers and do not have to be stored in memory. The result is these variables are then accessed very efficiently whenever they are needed. The TMS320C30 C-compiler user has available two CPU registers for variables of type register float, two CPU registers for variables of type register int, and four registers for pointer register-variables. If we rewrite rmvmul() to take advantage of these registers, then the variable definitions for rmvmul() appear as shown in Figure 5. This register version of rmvmul() executes in 19.08 μs. This dramatic improvement is due to, in large part, the shortened time necessary to calculate sum += A[inca + j] * x[j]. The TMS320C30 assembly-language code for this calculation is shown in Figure 6.

In the use of register variables, we followed one simple rule: *use register variables for data that is accessed often.* In this case, the pointers to the vectors and matrix were made register variables since these addresses are used often in the inner loop. Since the variable sum and the loop indices i and j are accessed every iteration, they were declared as register variables.

4. FURTHER OPTIMIZATIONS

Thus far we have focused only on the optimization of the C source-code by being smart about the way we write our algorithm. The next level of optimization involves optimization at the assembly-language level. The TMS320C30 C-compiler, assembler, and linker support several approaches for further optimization.

The C compiler supports the insertion of assembly-language code in the assembly-language output of the compiler from the C source-code level with the asm() function. For example, asm("ADDF R0, R1") will result in the assembly-language code ADDF R0, R1＋ being inserted directly into the assembly-language output of the compiler. This technique is particularly useful for TMS320C30 system-level functions such as enabling and disabling interrupts and enabling and disabling the cache. Since the output of the compiler is a TMS320C30 assembly-language source-file, this source file may be modified by the user. This approach may be a good starting-point for producing an optimized assembly-language module.

The third, and often best, way to optimize the C code, is to write time-critical functions in assembly language. By following the calling conventions of the C compiler, assembly-language functions can be written and called directly from the C source code. This approach is already common in the use of general-purpose microprocessors when speed is critical. This is the approach we will now follow.

4.1 Optimization With Assembly-Language Functions

As discussed previously, the heart of the rmvmul() function is for
(j = 0; j < ncA; j++)
/* Step across a row. */

sum += A[inca + j] * x[j];

This is the dot product between the vector x and row i of matrix A. The TMS320C30 supports the dot-product operation extremely efficiently, and since this is where most of the time in the algorithm is spent, this is a very reasonable point to optimize with an assembly-language function. We will call this function dotpr() and define it as follows:

float	dotpr(x, y, n)
float x[]	Pointer to real input vector.
float y[]	Pointer to real input vector.
int n	Integer input length of vectors.
	Returns the dot product of vectors x and y.

The assembly-language code for **dotpr()** is shown in Figure 7.

If we rewrite rmvmul() to take advantage of the assembly-language optimized **dotpr()** function, then we have the code shown in Figure 8. This version of rmvmul() executes in 14.22 microseconds.

Table 1 summarizes the results of the three different approaches we used in the step-wise optimization of rmvmul().

5. SOME 'PURE C' BENCHMARKS

More and more frequently, the system designer will find himself or herself wanting to write larger and larger portions of their programs in a high-level-language and exploit optimized subroutines where needed. In [3] we discussed the performance of the TMS320C30 on the Dhrystone benchmark and how it performed relative to several other microprocessors and computers. We found that it performed exceedingly well even exceeding the performance of a typical RISC processor. Notably, the Dhrystone benchmark is not a computationally intensive benchmark. What we will examine in this section is how the TMS320C30 and its optimizing C compiler perform on some computationally intensive tasks which are programmed in C.

For this several benchmarks, which are typical of computationally intensive tasks, were examined. These included the dot-product operation, vector-distance computation, and windowing.

The dot product operation occurs frequently in DSP applications. It is also important in graphics applications where vector transformations are performed. Many scientific routines (matrix inversion, solving differential equations, etc.) involve dot products. The C version of a dot product (**dotpr**) is shown in Figure 9.

The distance benchmark (Figure 10) computes the square of the Euclidean distance between two vectors. This operation occurs in graphics algorithms and in pattern-recognition algorithms.

The window benchmark (Figure 11) windows a vector using another vector. The result goes into a third vector. It does an element by element multiply of two vectors and places the result in a third vector. This operation is common as a preprocessing step in DFT-based frequency analysis. It is also used in forming the outer product of two vectors.

All three benchmarks were run on three different machines for comparison purposes. The machines benchmarked were a

16.66 MHz TMS320C30, a 16.66 MHz MIPS M/1000 (a typical RISC processor) and a VAX 11/785 (configured without a floating-point accelerator). Table 2 summarizes the relative speeds of the TMS320C30, the MIPS M/1000, and the VAX 11/785 on these three benchmarks. In all cases the TMS320C30 is faster.

Typically, performance is measured in terms of speed. Another important measure of performance is code size. In an embedded application, code size can be the deciding factor, all else being equal. Table 3 summarizes the code sizes, in bytes, of the TMS320C30 compiled code and the MIPS M/1000 compiled code for the kernel of each benchmark. In all cases the TMS320C30 code size is smaller.

6. CONCLUSION

The TMS320C30 and its optimizing C-compiler achieve very high levels of performance on not only numerically-intensive code but also general-purpose code. Given this, it is evident that HLLs are very useful tools for the DSP-system designer *when* the DSP and optimizing HLL compiler are jointly developed with the features necessary to support high-performance compiled code.

REFERENCES

[1] K. Lin, G. A. Frantz and R. Simar Jr., ''The TMS320 Family of Digital Signal Processors', Proceedings of the IEEE, pp. 1143--1159, Vol. 75, No. 9, September 1987.

[2] R. Simar Jr., T. Leigh, P. Koeppen, J. Leach, J. Potts, and D. Blalock, ''A 40 MFLOPS Digital Signal Processor: The First Supercomputer on a Chip,'' Proc. 1987 IEEE Int. Conf. on Acous., Speech, and Signal Processing, pp. 535--538, April 1987.

[3] R. Simar Jr. and A. Davis, "The Application of High-Level Languages to Single-chip Digital Signal Processors,'' Proc. 1988 IEEE Int. Conf. on Acous., Speech, and Signal Processing, pp. 1678--1681, April 1988.

Table 1:

Version	Time
Plain vanilla	24.36 μs
Register-variable optimization	19.08 μs
Assembly-language optimization	14.22 μs

Summary of the results of the approaches to optimizing rmvmul().

Benchmark	TMS320C30 C			MIPS M/1000			DEC VAX 11/785		
	Units/sec	MIPS relative	VAX relative	Units/sec	MIPS relative	VAX relative	Units/sec	MIPS relative	VAX relative
dotpr (Note 1)	2,083,333	1.7	40	1,234,567	1	24	52,356	0.04	1
distance (Note 2)	1,851,851	1.2	53	1,485,148	1	43	34,767	0.02	1
window (Note 3)	1,851,851	1.6	24	1,153,846	1	15	77,720	0.07	1

Note 1:   A unit is a sum += *x++ * *y++; .
Note 2:   A unit is a delta = *x++ - *y++; sum += delta * delta; .
Note 3:   A unit is a *z++ = *x++ * *y++; .

Table 2: Summary of Benchmark Results: Absolute performance numbers for the TMS320C30, MIPS M/1000, and the VAX 11/785 are given. Also the benchmark performance for all of the machines is expressed relative to the MIPS M/1000 and the VAX 11/785.

Benchmark	TMS320C30 code size in bytes	MIPS M/1000 code size in bytes
dotpr	20	36
distance	24	40
window	20	40

Table 3: Summary of Benchmark Code Sizes:
Absolute code-size numbers for
the TMS320C30 and MIPS M/1000 are given.

```
rmvmul(y, A, x, ncA, nrA)

float y[], A[], x[];
int   ncA, nrA;
{
    int   i,j;
    float sum;
    int   inca;

    /* Check for errors on dimensions. */
    if (ncA <= 0 || nrA <= 0)
        return(-1);

    for (i = 0; i < nrA; i++)     /* Step down a column. */
    {
        inca = i * ncA;
        sum  = 0.0;
        for (j = 0; j < ncA; j++) /* Step across a row. */
            sum += A[inca + j] * x[j];
        y[i] = sum;
    }
    return(0);
}
```

Figure 1: The plain-vanilla version of rmvmul().

```
/* Check for errors on dimensions. */
if (ncA <= 0 || nrA <= 0)
    return(-1);
    {
    /* computations */
    }
return(0);
```

Figure 2: C source for control portion of rmvmul().

```
_rmvmul: LDI      *-FP(5),R0    ;R0 = ncA
         BLE      LL3
         LDI      *-FP(6),R1    ;R1 = nrA
         BGT      L1
LL3:     LDI      -1,R0         ;return(-1)
         B        EPIO_2
L1:
    ; /* computations */
L3:      LDI      0,R0          ;return(0)
EPIO_2:  SUBI     4,SP
         POP      FP
         RETS
```

Figure 3: Resulting assembly-language code for the control portion of rmvmul().

```
        LDI     *-FP(3),R1      ;*-FP(3) = A[]
        ADDI    *+FP(4),R1      ;*+FP(4) = inca
        ADDI    R0,R1,AR0       ;R0 = j
        ADDI    *-FP(4),R0      ;*-FP(4) = x[]
        LDI     R0,AR1
        MPYF    *AR1,*AR0,R0    ;R0 = A[inca + j] * x[j]
        ADDF    *+FP(3),R0      ;R0 += sum
        STF     R0,*+FP(3)      ;*+FP(3) = sum
```

Figure 4: Resulting assembly-language code for sum += A[inca + j] * x[j]

```
rmvmul(y, A, x, ncA, nrA)

register float y[], A[], x[];
int ncA, nrA;
{
    register int i,j;
    register float sum;
    int inca;
    {
    /* Error checking and computations */
    }
}
```

Figure 5: Variable definitions for rmvmul()when using register variables.

```
        LDI     *+FP(1),R0      ;*+FP(1) = inca
        ADDI    R0,AR5,R1       ;AR5 = A[]
        ADDI    R5,R1,AR0       ;R5 = j
        ADDI    R5,AR6,AR1      ;AR6 = x[]
        MPYF    *AR1,*AR0,R1    ;R1 = A[inca + j] * x[j]
        ADDF    R1,R6           ;R6 = sum
```

Figure 6: Resulting assembly-language source for register version of sum += A[inca + j] * x[j]

```
; Initialization
_dotpr: PUSH    FP              ; Save the old FP.
        LDI     SP,FP           ; Point to the top of the stack.
        LDI     *-FP(2), AR0    ; AR0 = x
        LDI     *-FP(3), AR1    ; AR1 = y
        LDI     *-FP(4), RC     ; RC = n
        SUBI    1, RC           ; RC = n-1
        LDF     0.0, R0         ; R0 = 0
        LDF     0.0, R2         ; R2 = 0
; Dot product
        RPTS    RC
        MPYF    *AR0++, *AR1++, R0  ; R0 = x[i++] * y[j++]
||      ADDF    R0,R2               ; R2 = sum' = sum + R0
        ADDF    R0,R2               ; Last product.
; Return
        LDF     R2, R0          ; Put the result in R0.
        POP     FP              ; Pop the old frame pointer.
        RETS
```

Figure 7: Assembly-language routine dotpr().

```
rmvmul(y, A, x, ncA, nrA)

register float y[], A[], x[];
register int ncA;
int nrA;
{
    register int i;
    float dotpr();

    /* Check for errors on dimensions. */
    if (ncA <= 0 || nrA <= 0)
        return(-1);

    for (i = 0; i < nrA; i++)   /* Step down a column. */
        y[i] = dotpr(x, &A[i * ncA], ncA);

return(0);
}
```

Figure 8: C source of rmvmul()which uses the
          assembly language optimized
          routine dotpr().

```
main()
{
register float *x, *y;
register float sum;
register int i, N;

sum = 0.0;

for (i = 0; i < N; i++)
    sum += *x++ * *y++;
}
```

Fig 9 The dotpr benchmark.

```
main()
{
register float *x, *y;
register float sum;
register float delta;
register int i, N;

sum = 0.0;

for (i = 0; i < N; i++)
    {
    delta = *x++ - *y++;
    sum += delta * delta;
    }
}
```

Figure 10: The **distance** benchmark.

```
main()
{
register float *x, *y, *z;
register int i, N;

for (i = 0; i < N; i++)
    *z++ = *x++ * *y++;
}
```

Figure 11: The **window** benchmark.

A FEASIBLE APPROACH IN GENERATING
EFFICIENT SOFTWARE FOR
DIGITAL SIGNAL PROCESSORS

Greg K. Ma and Sen M. Kuo
Department of Electrical Engineering
Northern Illinois University
Dekalb, Illinois 60115

ABSTRACT

This paper presents the development of a code generator software package which generates optimized assembly programs that implement adaptive filters on DSP-32-based systems. The filter structures and adaptive algorithms supported by the code generator are also presented. To validate the code generator output, testing results of a number of adaptive filter programs with different structures and algorithms are given. These testing results are obtained by running the programs on DSP32 software simulator. A real-time application to line enhancement is presented and evaluated under real-time conditions.

INTRODUCTION

Intensive research on adaptive systems has produced a number of adaptive algorithms and structures. However, the amount of manpower and time spent on implementing these algorithms and structures on digital signal processor (DSP) systems is considerably large. This is due to the difficulty of assembly language programming. Assembly language programming for DSP is a non-trivial task since the architecture of most DSPs is highly pipelined and parallel, some powerful addressing modes are unavailable, and the number of data registers is limited. It is thus of our interest to have some automatic means to generate efficient assembly code for use in developing adaptive filter systems. Although some digital signal processor packages come with libraries of routines that support one or two filter structures and several adaptation algorithms, these libraries are not complete, and the users still need to code the main routine for adaptive filter applications. The interactive code generator not only can be used by engineers to evaluate different algorithms in real-time over and over again without going through the cumbersome process of coding and debugging assembly program, it can also be used by signal processing engineers without assembly language background.

DSP32 comes with a C compiler which compiles C source program into DSP32 assembly source program or load file. We do not question the flexibility of the C compiler. However, the line-of-code of the assembly program produced by the C compiler is almost three times as much as the code generated by the code generator.

AT&T DSP32 digital signal processor is a 32-bit high-speed, mask-programmable integrated circuit. It features 2 Kbytes of ROM and 4 Kbytes of RAM, both on chip, and 56 Kbytes of addressable space [1]. The architecture of DSP32 includes two processing units, a control arithmetic unit (CAU), and a data arithmetic unit (DAU). The DAU is the main execution unit for signal processing algorithm. It performs four million floating-point instructions of multiply/accumulate operations and data type conversions per second. The CAU is used to generate addresses to memory, perform logic and control operations, and execute 16-bit integer instructions. DSP32 also provides serial and parallel DMA operations and input/output conversion instructions to speed up the throughput.

Because of the highly pipelined and parallel architecture of DSP32, certain latency and pipeline effects do exist. They should be carefully taken into considerations when writing assembly programs for DSP32.

CODE GENERATOR DEVELOPMENT

1. CLASSIFICATION AND ORGANIZATION

Based on the degree of complexity and flexibility, code generator can be classified into two categories.

The first type of code generator generates assembly source code from scratch. It does not require any filter structure source file. Since no database is required, all necessary information (instruction set, filter structures, and algorithms) are built in the code generator itself. To develop such a code generator is both time and resource consuming. The size of the code generator program tends to be huge, the software is difficult to maintain, and the flexibility is limited.

The second type of code generator requires some basic filter structure source files. The assembly code generated is based on a specific source file and user supplied parameters such as filter's order, initial conditions, convergence factor, update algorithm, input/output configuration, etc. Each source file supports one filter structure and several algorithms for a variety of applications. Since each source file can be used to produce adaptive filters with different algorithms for different applications, the code generator has to determine, based on algorithm selected and user supplied parameters, which lines of code in the filter structure source file will be presented in the output assembly code. When a user wants to update the algorithms supported by the code generator package, he/she only needs to change the related filter structure source file, not the code generator.

We chose to develop the second type of code generator since its more flexible, more reliable, and easier to maintain.

The block diagram depicts the organization of the code generator can be found in Figure 1. The code generator provides the user a menu driven, interactive, and error checking interface. When the user brings up the code generator program, he/she will be prompted to select the filter structure, the adaptation algorithm, and the output code type. Three types of code can be generated. The input/output of the first type of code is configured to run in real-time. For the second type of code, the I/O is configured to run in simulator. The third type of code does not have input/output configuration set up, the user must explicitly configured the filter I/O for his/her specific application. After the selections have been done, the user is then asked to enter appropriate parameters based on the structure and algorithm chosen. A parameter file containing the parameters is created by the code generator. Then the code generator uses this parameter file and a filter structure source file to generate desired DSP32 assembly program.

2. DEVELOPMENT AND TESTING ENVIRONMENT

The entire code generator package is developed on an AT&T 6300 plus personal computer. The code generator program is written in C language, and compiled using Microsoft C Compiler. The assembly programs produced by the code generator are tested in two modes, real-time mode and simulation mode. In real-time mode, DSP32-PC is used as testing device. This device is a half size PC add-on card which features a DSP32 chip, 32 Kbytes of memory, an 8-bit codec, and analog I/O connectors. In simulation mode, DSP32 simulator program is used for testing. This program allows us to run DSP32 executable programs on a virtual DSP32 under the control of a command language driven user interface.

Figure 2 shows our experiment setup. In this setup, data used for real-time testing are sinusoid generated by TEKTRONIX FG504 Function Generator embedded in white noise generated by HP Precision Noise Generator, and data used for simulation testing are generated by software programs or digitized real data.

3. DEVELOPMENT PROCESS

The development of DSP32 code generator involves the design of code generator and the implementation of adaptive filter systems.

The code generator consists of two major parts. The first part of the code generator deals with user interface, i.e. obtaining input from the user. The second part deals with assembly code generating. This part is actually the heart of the code generator program. The code generating routine parses a filter structure source file, discards unnecessary lines, fills in appropriate parameters, and output the desired assembly code to the disk. The assembly code can then be used for the specific application.

The implementation of adaptive filter can be divided into five stages. Figure 3 shows the flow chart of this implementation.

In the first stage, algorithm design and study is performed on the AT&T 6300 plus PC. Once the algorithm is understood, the filter is implemented using C language program.

In the second stage, the C language program is rewritten such that it emulates the same sequence of operations with the same parameters and state variables as will be implemented on DSP32. This program will then serve as detailed outline for the DSP32 assembly language program.

The third stage is to develop DSP32 assembly program and to test the program using DSP32 software simulator. Output from the simulator is compared against the equivalent output of the C program in second stage. Since the simulator requires data file be in ASCII format, certain precision is lost during data conversion. Once the agreement within tolerable range between the two outputs is obtained, it is assured that the DSP32 software is essentially correct.

The fourth stage is to download the assembled and linked DSP32 program onto DSP32-PC device for real-time testing. The real-time debugging process is primarily constrained to debugging of the I/O timing structure of the algorithm, not the algorithm itself.

In the final stage of implementing adaptive filter systems, assembly programs of same filter structure but different adaptation algorithms are combined into one filter structure source file. Certain decision making key words, to be used by the code generating routine to determine which lines in the source file will present in the output, are added into this source file. Variables to be replaced by user supplied parameters are also added into the filter structure source file.

ADAPTIVE FILTER STRUCTURES AND ALGORITHMS

The general form of an adaptive filter is shown in Figure 4. With different input/output configuration, this adaptive filter can be applied to a number of applications. One example is the Adaptive Line Enhancer (ALE). In this application, $x(n)$ is the delayed version of the input signal $d(n)$, $y(n)$ is the enhanced output, and en) is the error signal used to update filter coefficients. Another example is the Adaptive Noise Canceller. In this application, the input signal $d(n)$ is corrupted by a primary noise which is correlated to the reference noise source $x(n)$, $y(n)$ is the predicted primary noise, and $e(n)$ is the output with noise being cancelled.

Many aspects of adaptive filter design and implementation are governed by the applications which give several practical constraints. For a particular application, adaptive filters can be implemented in a variety of structures, such as transversal (tapped delay line), symmetric transversal, lattice, and infinite impulse response (IIR) structures. Once the filter structure is chosen, an adaptation algorithm must also be chosen. Several alternatives are available, such as Least Mean Square (LMS), Leaky LMS (LLMS), Normalized LMS (NLMS), Sign-Error LMS (SELMS), Sign-Data LMS (SDLMS), Sign-Sign LMS (SSLMS), Kalman, Fast Kalman, Recursive Least Square (RLS), and Fast RLS algorithms. These structures and algorithms generally exchange increased complexity for improved performance.

The DSP32 code generator supports three filter structures, namely transversal (tapped delay line), symmetric transversal, and lattice. For transversal and symmetric transversal structures, six algorithms are supported. These algorithms are LMS, NLMS, LLMS, SDLMS, SELMS, and SSLMS. For lattice structure, the first three of these algorithms are supported.

A single input adaptive transversal filter structure is depicted in Figure 5 [2]. In this diagram, x(n) is the delayed version of filter input as previously described, $w_i(n)$ are the filter coefficients, and y(n) is the filter output which is obtained as follows:

$$y(n) = \sum_{i=0}^{N-1} w_i(n)x(n-i)$$

where N is the filter order.

This filter structure is sometimes realized as finite impulse response (FIR) nonrecursive filter structure. Only feedforward multipliers are used. It guarantees unconditional stability [3].

The DSP32 code generator supports six update algorithms for transversal filter structure. These algorithms are LMS, NLMS, LLMS, SELMS, SSLMS, and SDLMS. Descriptions of these algorithms follow.

The LMS algorithm is also known as stochastic gradient algorithm [4]. This algorithm considerably reduces computation requirement by using a simpler mean square error (MSE) estimator [2]. Instead of calculating the true gradient for estimating MSE, the square of the error signal (e(n) in Figure 5) is used as the estimator. The update of the filter coefficients is as follows:

$$e(n) = d(n) - y(n)$$
$$w_i(n+1) = w_i(n) + \mu e(n) x(n-i), 0 \le i \le N-1$$

Where μ is the convergence factor.

The LMS algorithm suffers from the constraint that the convergence factor must be in the range that's inversely proportional to the product of filter order and input signal power [2]. When input signal power is high or the filter order is high, the applicable range for convergence factor is very limited and we have to use a very small μ. Small μ usually means slow convergence speed, higher round-off noise, and will terminate adaption before algorithm converges to optimal solution. To solve this problem, NLMS algorithm is proposed [4,5]. This algorithm uses time-varying convergence factor $\mu(n)$ instead of constant μ. $\mu(n)$ is calculated as follows:

$$p(n) = \alpha p(n-1) + (1-\alpha)x^2(n) ---- (A)$$
$$\mu(n) = (1-\alpha) / p(n) ------------- (B)$$

equation (A) is used to calculate average power, and equation (B) is used to normalize $\mu(n)$ for each iteration. The initial power p(0) is preset by the user. α is the forgetting factor, $0 << \alpha < 1$.

In a fixed-point arithmetic environment, the accumulation of quantization noise and round-off noise must be considered by the engineers when implementing adaptive filters. Eventually these noises may cause the accumulator an overflow exception. The LLMS algorithm is used to solve this kind of problem [4,6]. This algorithm updates filter coefficients as follows:

$$w_i(n+1) = \beta w_i(n) + \mu e(n) x(n-i), 0 \le i \le N-1$$

where N is the filter order and β is the leaky factor slightly less than 1.

The other LMS-like algorithms are sometimes called simplified LMS in a sense that they simplify the multiplication operation for update algorithm [5]. These algorithms are SELMS, SSLMS, and SDLMS. The update equations for these algorithms are as follows:

Sign-Error LMS:

$$w_i(n+1) = w_i(n) + \mu x(n-i), \qquad e(n) \ge 0$$
$$w_i(n+1) = w_i(n) - \mu x(n-i), \qquad e(n) < 0$$

Sign-Sign LMS:

$$w_i(n+1) = w_i(n) + \mu, \qquad e(n) \ge 0$$
$$w_i(n+1) = w_i(n) - \mu, \qquad e(n) < 0$$

Sign-Data LMS:

$$w_i(n+1) = w_i(n) + \mu e(n), \qquad x(n) \ge 0$$
$$w_i(n+1) = w_i(n) - \mu e(n), \qquad x(n) < 0$$

As we can see from the above equations, the number of multiplication operation is reduced. The SDLMS requires one multiplication for each iteration to update all the coefficient since $\mu e(n)$ is constant for that iteration. The SSLMS does not even require multiplication. When implementing on fixed-point arithmetic DSP, if the convergence factor chosen is the power of two, then the multiplication can be replaced by a shift operation and leave only addition operation. These simplified LMS algorithms may look promising and they are being used in VLSI implementation.

However, the performance of these simplified LMSs is poor compared with standard LMS, and the decision of sign can break the instruction pipeline and severely reduce the execution speed on the DSP.

Figure 6 shows the symmetric transversal filter structure. This filter structure is desired when the application requires linear phase response in the frequency domain [5]. The symmetric transversal filter is actually an FIR filter with impulse response reflects about center tap. The output of the filter is obtained as follows:

$$y(n) = \sum_{i=0}^{N/2-1} w_i(n) [x(n-i) + x(n-N+i+1)]$$

One may notice that with this filter structure the multiplication operations are reduced by half. However this advantage is not so obvious to DSP32, since DSP32 takes equal amount of time for multiplication and addition (floating-point arithmetic) operations. Another advantage of this filter structure is that the storage requirement is also reduced by half. This advantage may be more concerned when memory is limited. All algorithms supported for the transversal filter structure are supported for symmetric transversal filter structure.

The next figure (Figure 7) depicts a general adaptive lattice filter. Lattice structure is an alternative FIR filter realization]7]. It can be considered as a cascade of single stage prediction error filters. Lattice filter is widely used in speech synthesis and spectrum estimation. The mathematical derivation for adaptive lattice filter can be found in [8,9].

In the following adaptive lattice filter implementation, $f_m(n)$ indicates forward prediction error, $b_m(n)$ indicates backward prediction error, $k_m(n)$ indicates reflection coefficient, $g_m(n)$ indicates filter coefficient, n is the time index, and M is the number of cascaded stages.

$$b_m(n) = b_{m-1}(n-1) - k_m(n) f_{m-1}(n)$$
for $0 \leq m \leq M$

$$f_m(n) = f_{m-1}(n) - k_m(n) b_{m-1}(n-1)$$
for $0 \leq m \leq M$

$$K_m(n+1) = K_m(n) + \mu [f_m(n) b_{m-1}(n-1) - b_m(n) f_{m-1}(n)]$$
for $1 \leq m \leq M$

$$e_1(n) = d(n) - b_0(n) g_0(n)$$

$$e_m(n) = e_{m-1}(n) - b_{m1}(n) g_{m-1}(n), \quad 2 \leq m \leq M+1$$

To implement ALE and Channel Equalization, y(n) is obtained as follows:

$$y(n) = \sum_{i=0}^{M} g_i(n) b_i(n)$$

For noise cancellation application, $e_{M+1}(n)$ corresponds to e(n) in Figure 6.

EXAMPLES

In this section we present some of our experiment results based on our experiment setup depicted in Figure 2.

The first example is the implementation of an Adaptive Line Enhancer using transversal structure and LMS algorithm. The filter order is 64, convergence factor (update stepsize) is 0.0001. The input signal used is sinusoid embedded in white noise. The normalized frequency of the input signal is 0.2, and signal to noise ratio os 9 dB. The first plot in Figure 8 plots the input test data and the outputs from C program and DSP32 assembly program (run using simulator). The difference between two outputs can hardly be seen. The second plot is the spectra of input signal and DSP32 program output. It is clearly seen that the noise level in the output is significantly reduced.

In the second example, we perform an Adaptive Predictor using lattice structure and LMS algorithm. The filter order is 3, and the convergence factor is 0.1. The input signal used in this example is a second order AR process [4] with eigne value spread ratio equals to 100. Similar to the first example, a plot of input data set and outputs from C program and DSP32 program can be found in Figure 9. Although the eigne value spread ratio is high (100), the convergence performance is still considered good. This is one of the advantages of lattice filter.

In our last example, we perform transversal LMS ALE in real-time. The filter order is 64, convergence factor is 0.01. The real-time input signal is analog sinusoid at 2700 Hz embedded in white noise. The input and output spectra (estimated by HP Dynamic Signal Analyzer) can be found on Figure 10. From the spectra plots we can see that the signal-to-noise ratio is improved.

CONCLUSION

The assembly program produced by the DSP32 code generator is guaranteed to be optimized since the code optimization has already been done while implementing adaptive filter systems. The DSP32 code generator has some other advantages such as simplicity, ease of use, and ease of maintenance, etc. The number of applicable adaptive filter structures and algorithms is huge. To our interest it is impractical trying to include all of them in one package. The DSP32 code generator does not incorporate a full set of filter structures and update algorithms, but it can be easily expanded to support more. The expandability is yet another advantage of this code generator. There is no doubt that the code generator is a good choice to implement adaptive filters on DSP-based systems.

5. REFERENCES

[1] AT&T, "WE DSP32 Digital Signaling Processor Information Manual," September 1986.

[2] B. Widrow and S. D. Stearns, Adaptive Signal Processing, Printice-Hall, 1985

[3] C. F. N. Cowan and P. M. Grand, ed., Adaptive Filters, Printice-Hall, 1985.

[4] S. Haykin, Adaptive Filter Theory, Printice-Hall, 1986.

[5] J. R. Triechler, C. R. Johnson, Jr., and M. G. Larimore, Theory and Design of Adaptive Filters, John Wiley & Sons, 1987.

[6] R. D. Gitlin, H. C. Meadors, Jr., and S. B. Weinstein, "The Tap-Leakage Algorithm: An Algorithm for the Stable Operation of a Digitally Implemented, Fractionally Spaced Adaptive Equalizer," Bell Sys. Tech. J. 61,8(1982)

[7] R. A. Roberts and C. T. Mullis, Digital Signal Processing, Addison-Wesley, 1987.

[8] B. Friedlander, "Lattice Filters for Adaptive Processing,"Proc. IEEE, vol. 70, pp. 829-867, August 1982.

[9] V. U. Reddy, B. Egardt, and T. Kailath, "Optimized Lattice-Form Adaptive Line Enhancer for a Sinusoidal Signal in Broad-Band Noise," IEEE Trans. Acoust. Speech. Signal Processing, vol. ASSP-29, pp. 702-709, June, 1981.

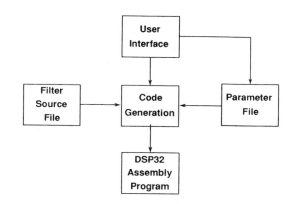

FIGURE 1. CODE GENERATOR ORGANIZAION

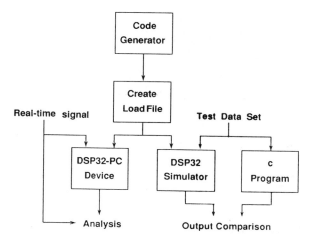

FIGURE 2. EXPERIMENT SETUP

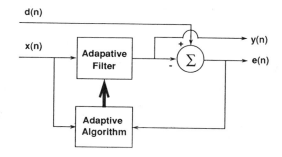

FIGURE 4. GENERAL FORM OF ADAPTIVE FILTER

1818

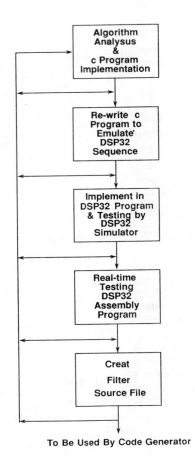

FIGURE 3. ADAPTIVE FILTER SYSTEMS IMPLEMENTATION

To Be Used By Code Generator

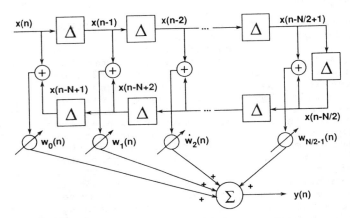

FIGURE 6. SYMMETRIC TRANSVERSAL FILTER STRUCTURE

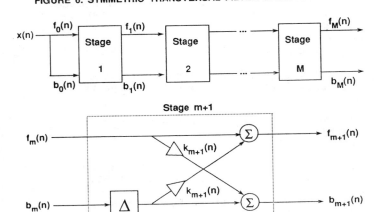

FIGURE 7. LATTICE FILTER STRUCTURE

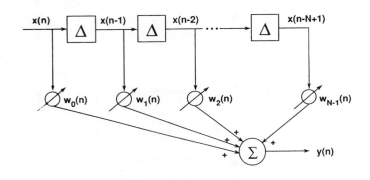

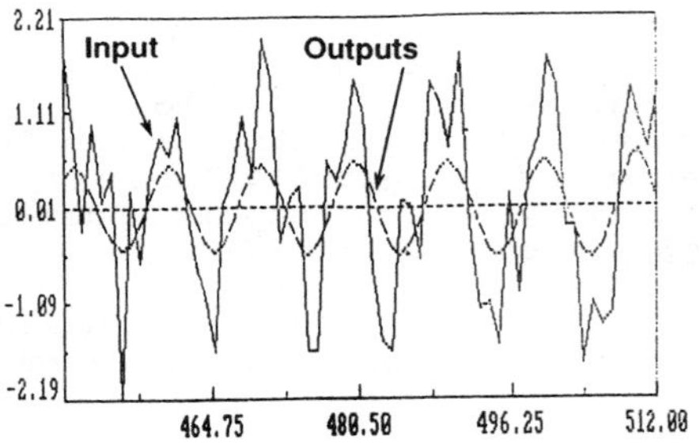

FIGURE 5. TRANSVERSAL FILTER STRUCTURE

Input & output signals

FIGURE 8. TRANSVERSAL LMS ALE

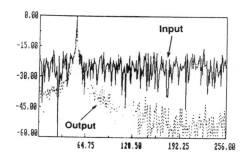

Input & output spectra

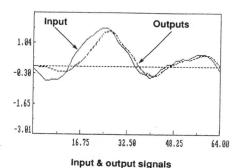

Input & output signals

FIGURE 9. LATTICE LMS ADAPTIVE PREDICTOR

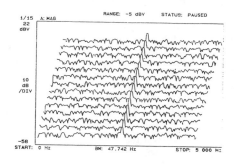

Three-dimensional plot of input spectra

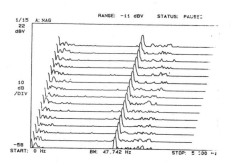

Three-dimensional plot of output spectra

FIGURE 10. TRANSVERSAL LMS ALE IN REAL-TIME

MULTIPLE DSP SYSTEMS FOR ADAPTIVE SIGNAL PROCESSING APPLICATIONS

Pavan Gupta and Sen M. Kuo
Department of Electrical Engineering
Northern Illinois University
DeKalb, IL 60115

ABSTRACT

Many problems encountered in communications and signal processing involve removing noise and distortion due to physical processes that are time varying or unknown or possibly both. These types of processes represent some of the most difficult problems in transmitting and receiving information. Adaptive digital filters present the most effective solution to these problems. Many of the signal processing applications require higher speed and throughput rates. A single processor may not be able to provide with sufficient speed and throughput requirements of a particular application. As such, many signal processors are connected together in a multiprocessor environment in order to meet these requirements. Two multiprocessor systems with TMS32020 as the central processing unit are presented. Both of these systems have been built with the use of two processors and the implementation of adaptive line enhancer (ALE) with cascade or parallel form of infinite impulse response (IIR) filter has been done on these systems.

INTRODUCTION

Adaptive filtering techniques, using transversal filters, have many applications, such as equalization for data transmission, echo and noise cancellation, prediction in waveform coding, spectral estimation, on-line system identification, and adaptive antenna arrays [1]. Most current coefficient updating algorithms are either well known least mean square (LMS) algorithm or appropriate variations. In addition to transversal filters, adaptive lattice filters have received recent attention; and there has also been considerable interest in developing computationally efficient least squares adaptation algorithms for rapid adaptation of transversal filter coefficients [2-3]. The hardware complexity of adaptation algorithms is usually given as the number of multiplications (or equivalently the multiplication rate). This reflects the dominant role of multiplier hardware at earlier stages of large scale integrations. Contemporary, high-density

1820

digital circuits (particularly the programmable processors) are particularly important in this regard. Depending upon the application, implementation of signal processing algorithms on a single processor can become quite computationally intense. As such, in order to obtain high arithmetic rates, the desired algorithm can be implemented in a multiprocessor environment [4-6]. Not only higher speed and throughput rates are achieved, large number of weights can be accommodated in a transversal filter and updated within one sampling period, when implemented on multiprocessor systems. Two such schemes for multiprocessor systems have been developed. The one is pipelined multiprocessor system, where all the processors are connected in a cascade array fashion. The other scheme uses master-slave configuration, where each slave processor is able to communicate to one master processor. Most of the signal processing algorithms can be easily implemented on these systems.

A PIPELINED MULTIPROCESSOR SYSTEM

The architecture of the pipelined multiprocessor system is shown in Figure 1. There are N microcomputers, denoted as M(1), M(2),...,M(N). Each microcomputer consists of a TMS32010 signal processor and a bank of program memory. These processors are cascaded such that the data output from i-th processor, M(i), can only be input to the next processor, M(i+1), or to the digital to analog converter (D/A), and also, M(i) can input data only from the previous processor, i.e., M(i-1). The head processor, M(1), can input data from an analog to digital converter (A/D), and the tail processor, M(N), can output data only to a D/A converter. Thus each processor has one input port (PA1) and two output ports, namely PA0 and PA1, one for the D/A converter and the other for the next processor in pipeline. Input port for the head processor, M(1), is PAO (A/D converter). Communication between any two processors is achieved through a link. These links are denoted as L(1), L(2),...L(N). Each of these links consists of a data buffer, a one bit register to indicate if the buffer is full or empty, and some control circuits. In order to achieve synchronization between the processors, the following constraints are applied:

1) The processor, M(i), cannot output the data to M(i+1) if the buffer is full.

2) The processor, M(i), cannot input the data from M(i-1) if the buffer is empty.

3) The failure to output or input the data for any processor, M(i), will hold it until the buffer is empty or full.

These constraints will assure a smooth data flow and will avoid any possibility of the data deadlock. The $\overline{BIO}$ pin and BIOZ instruction are used to realize the synchronization constraints. When a low is present on the $\overline{BIO}$ pin, execution of the BIOZ instruction will cause a branch to occur. While the program is being executed, each processor checks its $\overline{BIO}$ pin two times within one sampling period, once to check if the input buffer is full, and the second time to check the emptiness of the output buffer.

Design of the Link, L(i)

Each link consists of a data buffer, a one bit flag to indicate if the buffer is full or empty and some multiplexing circuit. The processor, M(i), polls its $\overline{BIO}$ pin before it can input the data from the processor, M(i-1), and also before it can output the data to the processor, M(i+1). That means for processor, M(i), to input the data it should connect its $\overline{BIO}$ pin to the output of the associated register in order to check if the input buffer is full (i.e., data is available at the buffer). Also, before outputting the data to M(i+1), the processor, M(i), should connect its $\overline{BIO}$ pin to the output of the associated register in order to check the emptiness of the output buffer. This suggests that some kind of multiplexing technique is needed which will connect the $\overline{BIO}$ pin of the processor, M(i), to the two different register outputs at appropriate times. In order to output the data, each processor executes the following set of instructions:

```
LOOP1     BIOZ      OUTPUT
          B         LOOP1
OUTPUT    OUT       X,PA1
```

and to input the data, a processor executes the instructions that follow:

```
LOOP2     BIOZ      INPUT
          B         LOOP2
INPUT     IN        X,PA1
```

The problem can be stated in words like this: When the processor, M(i), outputs the data, its $\overline{BIO}$ pin, $(\overline{BIO})_i$ should go to high state and the $\overline{BIO}$ pin of the processor, M(i+1), $(\overline{BIO})_{i+1}$ should go to low state, so that the processor, M(i+1) can input the data. Inputting data from M(i+1) should cause BIO_i to change to low state again (as

1821

output buffer is empty). The truth table for the link, L(i) is given in Table 1. It should be noted that each time a processor inputs the data, it expects to output the data before it can input something again.

The circuit diagram for the link, L(i), is shown in Figure 2. Use of D flip-flops makes the design of the multiplexing circuit simple. In the beginning all the flip-flops are reset. OUT(i) and IN(i) are pulses generated when a read/write occurs combined with the appropriate port address. Whenever the processor, M(i-1), outputs the data on to the data buffer, a high to low going pulse appears on OUT(i-1), and as such, $\overline{BIO}$ pin of the processor, M(i), $\overline{BIO}_i$, goes low. This causes the processor, M(i), to input the data and a IN(i) pulse is generated. At this moment, the $(\overline{BIO})_i$ pin is connected to Flag B, while the processor, M(i), is testing if the output buffer is empty. Having known the emptiness of the output buffer, it outputs the data and this causes $(\overline{BIO})_i$ pin to get connected back to Flag A, where it checks if the input buffer is full. At the same time, this will cause the $\overline{BIO}$ pin of the processor, M(i+1), $(\overline{BIO})_{i+1}$ to go to low state so that it can input the data through the data buffer.

The design of the head link, L(1) for processor, M(1), and that of the tail link, L(N) for processor, M(N), is slightly different, as the input source for the head processor is the A/D converter and the only output source for the tail processor is the D/A converter. The head processor, M(1), loads the sampling period (f_s) into a counter connected to its bus and reads through its I/O port. This counter sends at $1/f_s$ intervals, start of conversion pulses to A/D converter. The end of conversion (EOC) pulses are used to make the processor accept the input data once in each iteration loop. In order to use this pipelined system in an efficient manner, the tasks related to signal processing should be distributed to all the microcomputers as evenly as possible.

A pipelined system consisting of two processors has been constructed and is completely operational. Evaluation modules (EVM) are used as microcomputers and analog interface boards (AIB) are used to connect these microcomputers to the external world. Expansion ports on both the analog interface boards are used as the common bus and the data buffer between the two processors. The port address for the A/D and D/A converters is PA2, while the port address for the common data bus (expansion port) is PA3. The implementation of cascade form of IIR ALE (two stages) has been done on this system and is discussed later in this paper.

A Master-Slave Configuration for Multiprocessor System

The pipelined multiprocessor system discussed above has the disadvantage that the processor, M(i) can not send the data to the processor, M(i-1). This problem is overcome in part by choosing a master-slave configuration, where each of the slave processors, S(1), S(2) ..., S(N), can communicate to one master processor, M(0). The architecture of such a scheme is shown in Figure 3. Communication between master and slave processors i achieved through the links, L(0), L(1), ...,L(N), over a global data bus. Each link again consists of a data buffer, an one bit flag to indicate if the buffer is full or empty, and some control circuit. The definite advantage of the master-slave architecture over the pipelined architecture is that the data can be broadcast from the master to all the slave processors. Input data to the master comes from an A/D converter and the output can be sent to the D/A converters connected to slave processors. Two I/O ports are defined, one for the A/D and the D/A converters, namely PA0, and the other port, PA1, to address the global data bus. The synchronization between the processors is achieved by applying the following constraints.

1) Master, M(0), cannot output the data over to the data bus if the output buffer is full.

2) Output to master from slave processors is done sequentially, i.e., S(i) cannot send the data to master until master has accepted the data from S(i-1).

The problem can be stated as follows. Master processor gets the data from an A/D converter and knowing the emptiness of the output buffer, transfers it to the global data bus. At that instant the slave processors receive the data as the buffer is full. Now the master is expecting data from the first slave processor, S(1), before it can output to global bus again. Also, S(1) cannot send data to master until the last slave processor, S(N), has accepted data from master which has been there already on the global bus. Data transfer from slaves to master is done sequentially, i.e., S(N) cannot send data until the master has received it from S(N-1). The truth table for a system consisting of a master and two slave processors is given in Table 2.

Design of the Links

The design of the links depends upon the number of the slave processors used in the system. Considering a system with two slave processors three links are needed, namely L(0): the link between master processor and global bus, L(1): the link between S(1) and master, and L(2): the link between S(2) and master. The circuit diagrams of these link, L(0), L(1), and L(2) are shown in Figure 4, Figure 5, and Figure 6 respectively. Considering these three circuits as one and putting them together will make the understanding of the system easier. This circuit works as follows. Initially all the flip flops are reset and as such the $\overline{BIO}$ pin of the master is connected to end of conversion (EOC) pin of the A/D converter (Figure 4) and the BIO pins of the two slave processors, S(1) and S(2) are at high level (Figures 5 and 6). When M(0) accepts the data from an A/D converter (port PAO), a low to high going pulse is generated at the clock input of the flip flop L2 (Figure 4). At that moment $\overline{BIO}$ pin of M(0) gets connected to FLAG A, where it checks if the output buffer for M(0) is empty. Having found the emptiness of the output buffer, M(0) sends the data over to the global bus (port PA1) and a pulse is generated at the clock input of the flip flops A and L1 (Figure 4) and also at the clear input of the flip flop E (Figure 6). At this instant the $\overline{BIO}$ pin of S(1) connects to FLAG C while $\overline{BIO}$ pin of S(2) is already linked to FLAG E. Looking at the truth table in Table 2, it can be seen that this causes the BIO pins of the slaves to go to the low state and thus enables them to input the data and also the $\overline{BIO}$ pin of master gets connected to FLAG B, which tells the master if the data from slave processors is available on the data bus. Inputting the data to S(1) resets flip flop A (Figure 4), sets flip flops C and D (Figure 5) and thus makes its $\overline{BIO}$ pin to go the high state. This is done in order for S(1) not to transmit data to the master until S(2) has accepted the data already available on the global bus. Thus inputting the data to S(2) resets the $\overline{BIO}$ pin of S(1) to the low state again so that S(1) becomes ready to output the data to the master processor. It should be noted that at this instant the $\overline{BIO}$ pin of S(2) sets to the high state again (Figure 6). Now that the global data bus is available, slave processor, S(1), outputs the data to master (port PA1), which generates a pulse at the clock input of the flip flop F, and $\overline{BIO}$ pin of S(2) connects to FLAG F (Figure 6) while the $\overline{BIO}$ pin of S(1) connects to FLAG C and sets itself (Figure 5). Input to master resets the

$\overline{BIO}$ pin of S(2) (Figure 6), and thus enables it to transmit data to the master. As soon as the master inputs the data from S(2), flip flop L3 resets, $\overline{BIO}$ pin of M(0) links to FLAG A and is ready to check the emptiness of the output buffer (Figure 4). This whole process repeats itself if the processors want to communicate again. At the end of the sampling loop, the slave processor, S(1) issues a dummy command "OUT 0,PA5", this resets all the flip flops and the $\overline{BIO}$ pin of the master connects back to EOC and is thus ready to accept another data point from the A/D converter. The following set of instructions explains the sequence of operations that would take place in the master processor.

```
WAIT      BOIZ     INPUT
          B        WAIT
INPUT     IN       X,PAO
LOOP1     BIOZ     OUTPUT
          B        LOOP1
OUTPUT    OUT      X,PA1
LOOP2     BIOZ     INPUT1
          B        LOOP2
INPUT1    IN       X,PA1
```

The following sequence of instructions would be executed in the slave processor, S(1).

```
LOOP1     BIOZ     INPUT
          B        LOOP1
INPUT     IN       X,PA1
LOOP2     BIOZ     OUTPUT
          B        LOOP2
OUTPUT    OUT      X,PA1
          OUT      X,PAO
          OUT      X,PA5
```

It should be noted that every time the master processor sends data to the slaves, it expects response from slaves in a sequential manner, before it can transmit the next data. However, this sequence can be broken at any time by executing the dummy instruction, "OUT 0,PA5", in the slave processor, S(1), which will reset all the flip flops.

A system with a master processor and one slave processor has been constructed and is completely functional. Evaluation modules are used as the microcomputers and analog interface boards are used as A/D and D/A interface. The expansion ports available at AIBs are used as the global data bus and data buffers. Since unlike the pipelined system, the second processor (the salve) also sends data back to the master, two buffers (one for input and the other for output) are needed at each side of the data bus. The implementation of parallel IIR ALE (two stages) has been done on this system and is discussed later.

ENHANCEMENT OF MULTIPLE SINUSOIDS WITH CASCADE IIR ALE

A structure for removing multiple lines (three in this case) is shown in Figure 7. Each "stage" is composed of an IIR adaptive line enhancer like that in Figure 8. For stage i, $x_i(k)$ represents the input (sinusoid(s) plus noise), $y_i(k)$ corresponds to the enhanced output, and $e_i(k)$ is the error output [7]. Conceptually, the structure works as follows. If we assume the initial input, $x_1(k)$ to be comprised of 3 sinusoids in white noise, then it can be verified that the resulting error surface for stage 1 has three unique minima, one corresponds to each of the sinusoids. The gradient search technique in stage 1 will converge to one of the minima, causing the corresponding sinusoid to be removed from $x_1(k)$. As a result, $e_1(k)$, the input to the next stage, is composed of the two remaining sinusoids and the noise from the first stage. The second stage then proceeds to remove one of the two remaining sinusoids, and the third stage adapts to the last one. The enhanced outputs appear at $y_1(k)$, $y_2(k)$, and $y_3(k)$.

To illustrate the behavior of this structure, a real-time implementation with two stages is done on the pipelined multiprocessor system with two processors. In order to distribute the task evenly among the two processors, each processor computes one "stage". For both the stages, the value of the pole radius, r, is equal to 0.9, convergence parameter, μ is 0.01, and the sampling frequency is 10 KHz. The value of the initial adaptive weight in the two stages is kept different, which is 0.2795 for the first stage, and 0.559 for the second stage. These initial weights correspond to the center frequencies of 2000 Hz and 1200 Hz respectively. The first processor takes the input from the A/D converter, computes the IIR ALE algorithm, and sends the error signal to the second processor while the enhanced output is sent to the D/A converter. The second processor computes another IIR ALE with the error signal as the input and sends it enhanced output to the D/A converter. The input signal contains two sinusoids with frequencies of 1020 Hz and 2680 Hz embedded in white noise with SNR 0 db. The frequency spectra of the input and that of the enhanced outputs, $y_1(k)$ and $y_2(k)$, are shown in Figure 9. We note that the lower frequency shows up as a noise component in the enhanced output for Stage 1. In Stage 2, only lower frequency remains, and hence, the enhanced output contains only that frequency.

ENHANCEMENT OF MULTIPLE SINUSOIDS WITH A PARALLEL IIR ALE

This scheme uses a recursive IIR ALE which is implemented as the sum of constrained second-order bandpass filters. To obtain a stable H(z) during adaptation, the transfer function is broken into the sum of second order sections as shown in Figure 10. That is,

$$H(z) = H_1(x) + H_2(z) + ... + H_n(z)$$

where each $H_i(z)$ is a second order section. In this way simple constraints can be made on the denominator coefficients of each section to insure that the poles remain inside the unit circle [8]. Using prior knowledge of the problem, namely the input has sinusoidal components, further constraints are applied to the second order sections, $H_i(z)$, so that the frequency response of each is that of a bandpass filter whose peak is allowed to vary adaptively. Conceptually then, the adaptive algorithm will attempt to align the peak of the various filters with the frequencies of the incoming sinusoids. In this way each of the sinusoids is enhanced separately. The implementation of this structure with two parallel stages is done on the master-slave multiprocessor system, with a master and one slave processor. Each of the master and the slave processors executes IIR ALE algorithm. The master processor takes the input from the A/D converter, sends it to the slave processor and then computes the enhanced output, $y_1(k)$. Meanwhile slave processor receives input data from the master and computes its enhanced output, $y_1(k)$ and sends it to the master. Master receives $y_2(k)$ from slave, computes the global error and sends it to the slave and also updates its adaptive weight. Slave receives the global error and updates its own adaptive weight. After the end of each iteration, slave processor executes the dummy instruction "OUT X,PA5" in order to reset the flip-flops while master processor waits for another input from the A/D converter. The pole radius in each IIR ALE is 0.9, convergence parameter is 0.01, and the sampling frequency is 10 KHz. The initial values of the adaptive parameter for the two stages should be different, otherwise the two processors will give the identical results. If the approximate input frequencies are known a priori, it is advisable to initialize the different sections so that their peaks are near these frequencies. If not, a comb pattern is suggested where the different stages are initialized, so their peaks begin at equally spaced intervals along the frequency axis covering the range from d.c. to Nyquist. The two adaptive weight values are selected a 0.559 and 0.2795.

The input signal contains frequencies of 910 Hz and 3140 Hz embedded in white noise with SNR 0 db. The spectra for the input and output from each processor are shown in Figure 11.

CONCLUSION

Two multiprocessor systems with the use of TMS32010 digital signal processor as CPU have been presented. Many signal processing algorithms can be easily implemented on these systems. Choice of the multiprocessor system is made based upon the particular application requirements. The design mythology adopted in these systems is quite simple, and such these multiprocessor systems can be further modified to suit specific application. The systems have been built with two processors and real-time implementations of cascade and parallel forms of IIR ALE has been done.

REFERENCES

1) B. Widrow and S. D. Stearns, _Adaptive Signal Processing_, Englewood Cliffs, NJ: Prentice-Hall, Inc., 1985.

2) J. Cioffi and T. Kailath, "Fast Recursive-Least-Squares Transversal Filters for Adaptive Filtering", _IEEE TRANS. ON ASSP_, April 1984.

3) D. Slock and T. Kailath, "Numerically Stable Fast Recursive Least-Squares Transversal Filters", _IEEE INTERNATIONAL CONF. ON ASSP_, New York, April 1988.

4) D. P. Morgan and H. F. Silverman. "An Investigation into the Efficiency of a Parallel TMS320 Architecture: DFT and Speech Filterbank Applications", _PROC. IEEE_, 1985, pp. 1601-1604.

5) T. K. Miller and S. T. Alexander, "An Implementation of the LMS Adaptive Filter Using an SIMD Multiprocessor Ring Architecture", _PROC. IEEE_, 1985, pp. 1605-1608.

6) V. B. Lawrence and S. K. Tewksbury. "Multiprocessor Implementation of Adaptive Digital Filters", _IEEE TRANS. ON COMMUNICATIONS_, Vol. Com-31, No. 6, June 1983.

7) N. Ahmed, D. Hush, G. R. Elliot, and R. J. Fogle. "Detection of Multiple Sinusoids Using an Adaptive Cascade Structure", _PROC. ICASSP_, 1984.

8) D. Hush and N. Ahmed. "Detection and Identification of Sinusoids in Broadband Noise via a Parallel Recursive ALE", _PROC. ICASSP_, 1984.

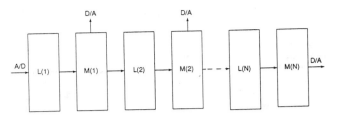

Figure 1. The architecture of pipelined multiprocessor system

Instruction	AQ	BQ	CQ	$\overline{(BIO)}_i$	$\overline{(BIO)}_{i+1}$
Reset	0	0	0	1	1
OUT(i-1)	1	0	0	0	1
IN(i)	0	1	0	0	1
OUT(i)	0	0	1	1	0
IN(i+1)	0	0	0	0	0

Table 1. Truth table for the link, L(i) in pipelined system

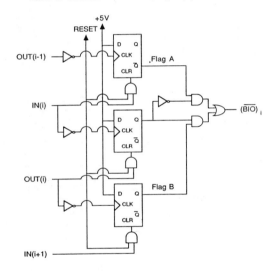

Figure 2. The Circuit diagram of the link, L(i).

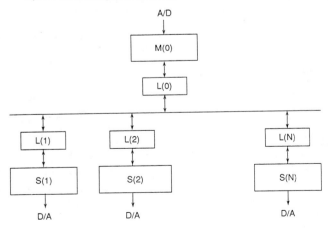

Figure 3. The architecture of master-slave multiprocessor system

1825

Table 2. Truth table for links, L(0), L(1), and L(2) in master-slave system

Processor	Instruction	AQ	BQ	CQ	DQ	EQ	FQ	GQ	L1Q	L2Q	L3Q	BIQ M(0)	BIQ S(1)	BIQ S(2)
	Reset	0	0	0	0	0	0	0	0	0	0	EOC	1	1
M(0)	IN X,0	0	0	0	0	0	0	0	0	1	0	0	1	1
M(0)	OUT X,1	1	0	0	0	0	0	0	1	1	0	1	0	0
S(1)	IN X,1	0	0	1	1	0	0	0	1	1	0	1	1	0
S(2)	IN X,1	0	0	1	0	1	0	0	1	1	0	1	1	1
S(1)	OUT X,1	0	1	0	0	1	0	0	1	1	0	1	0	1
M(0)	IN X,1	0	0	0	0	1	1	0	1	1	0	0	1	1
S(2)	OUT X,1	0	1	0	0	1	0	0	1	1	0	1	1	0
M(0)	IN X,1	0	0	0	0	1	0	1	0	1	1	0	1	1
M(0)	OUT X,1	1	0	0	0	0	0	1	1	1	1	1	0	0
S(1)	IN X,1	0	0	1	1	0	0	1	1	1	1	1	1	0
S(2)	IN X,1	0	0	1	0	1	0	1	1	1	1	1	0	1
S(1)	OUT X,5	0	0	0	0	0	0	0	0	0	0	EOC	1	1

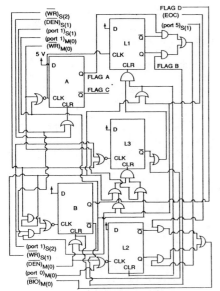

Figure 4. Circuit diagram of the Link, L(0)

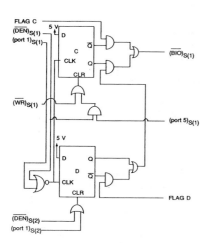

Figure 5. Circuit diagram of the Link, L(1)

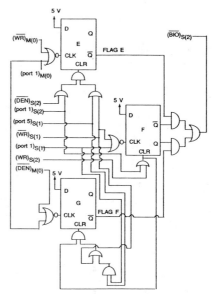

Figure 6. Circuit diagram of the Link, L(2)

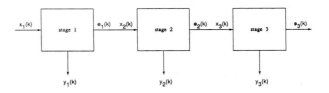

Figure 7. Casacded structure for enhancement of multiple (3) sinusoids

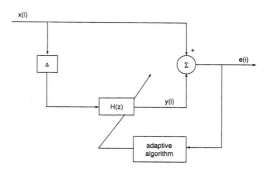

Figure 8. General form of Adaptive Line Enhancer

1826

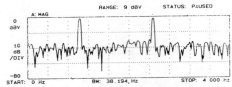

Figure 9 (a). Frequency spectrum of the input to cascade IIR ALE

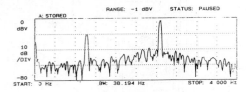

Figure 9 (b). Frequency spectrum of the output from "stage 1"

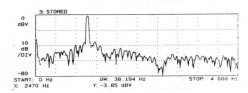

Figure 9 (c). Frequency spectrum of the output from "stage 2"

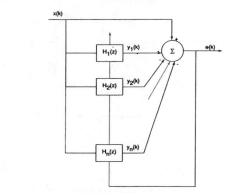

Figure 10. Parallel structure for the enhancement of multiple sinusoids

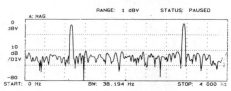

Figure 11 (a). Frequency spectrum of the input to parallel IIR ALE

Figure 11 (b). Frequency spectrum of the output from master processor

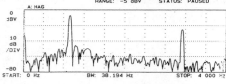

Figure 11 (c). Frequency spectrum of the output from slave processor

DESIGN ISSUES IN THE FINITE PRECISION IMPLEMENTATION OF ADAPTIVE FILTERING ALGORITHMS

Sasan Ardalan
Box 7914
Center for Communications
and Signal Processing
Dept. of Electrical and
Computer Engineering
North Carolina State University
Raleigh, NC 27685-7914

ABSTRACT

Adaptive filtering algorithms are playing a significant role in telecommunications. For example, in both the full duplex high speed voice-band modems and baseband 192 kbps ISDN U-interface echo cancellation and equalization algorithms are employed. In these applications, noise due to roundoff and truncation errors need to be analyzed in order to determine the required wordlength in the digital implementation of these algorithms. Furthermore, finite precision errors cause stability problems in some algorithms. In addition, for correlated signals, various algorithms deviate significantly from the expected high precision performance. Other issues involve dynamic range considerations and overflow prevention. In this paper, the results of current research in the analysis of roundoff errors is presented. Emphasis is placed on design issues.

I. INTRODUCTION

Many adaptive filtering problems can be cast as a systems identification problem. See Figure 1. Consider the desired signal d(n) which is a linear mapping of the sequence x(n) by the wrights w_i*,

$$d(n) = \sum_{i=0}^{N-1} x(n-i)\, w_i{}^* = \mathbf{x}^T(n)\, \mathbf{w}^*$$

where,

$$\mathbf{x}(n) = [\, x(0), x(1), ..., x(N-1)\,]^T$$

and

$$\mathbf{w}^* = [\, w_0^*, w_1^*, ..., w_{N-1}^*\,]^T$$

As an example, in echo cancellation d(n) represents the echo, x(n) the echo generation signal, and w_i* represents the coefficients of the echo path impulse response. In this case the adaptive filtering algorithm estimates the weights

$w_i(n)$ at each iteration in order to adapt to the echo path impulse response defined by $w*$. In the Recursive Least Squares algorithm [1], the weights $w_i(n)$ are calculated such that the accumulated sum of the error residuals is minimized. The error residual is the difference between the desired response and an estimate of the desired response obtained from $w(n)$.

$$w(n) = [w_0(n), w_1(n), \ldots, w_{N-1}(n)]^T$$

In Figure 1, $v(n)$ represents ad additive noise source which corrupts the desired response. Table 1 presents the conventional RLS adaptive filtering algorithm. The so-called Kalman gain vector $k(n)$ is computed from the NxN matrix $P(n)$. The updating of $P(n)$ requires order N^2 operations. Hence, the conventional RLS algorithm is too complex for large N. Faster RLS algorithms requiring order N operations were derived in [5],[2], and [3]. The RLS algorithm achieves very rapid convergence, and in high precision arithmetic, the convergence is independent of input signal correlation.

In the Least Mean Squares (LMS) algorithm, instead of computing $P(n)$, it is replaced by γI where γ is a constant. This approximation greatly simplifies the algorithm, however, at the cost of losing performance. In particular, by replacing $P(n)$ with γI in the LMS algorithm, a tacit assumption is made that the input signal

is white and uncorrelated. In this case, as n becomes large, $P(n)$ approaches a diagonal matrix. Thus, the LMS algorithm does not perform well for correlated signals. Other variants of the LMS algorithm exist but are not considered in this paper [17].

Table 1 Adaptive Filtering Algorithms

$$\hat{d}(n) = x^T(n) \, w(n-1)$$
$$e(n) = d(n) - \hat{d}(n)$$
$$w(n) = w(n-1) + k(n) \, e(n)$$
$$k(n) = P(n) \, x(n)$$

$$P(n) = \frac{1}{\lambda} \left[P(n-1) - \frac{P(n-1) \, x(n) \, x^T(n) P(n-1)}{\lambda + x^T(n) P(n-1) x(n)} \right]$$

$$P(0) = \delta^{-1} I$$

LMS Update Formula

$$w(n) = w(n-1) + \gamma \, x(n) e(n)$$

II. FIXED POINT ARITHMETIC

In this section, the effects of fixed point roundoff errors on the performance of the RLS and LMS algorithms is presented. The fixed point error analysis of the LMS algorithm received attention in the literature [11],[12],[15],[8] and [14]. In most analysis, the roundoff error of fixed point multiplication is modeled as an additive noise process after an infinite precision multiplication. Thus,

$$fi[x \, y] = x \, y + \varepsilon$$

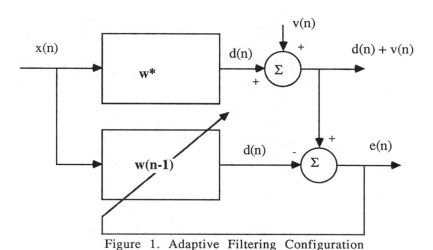

Figure 1. Adaptive Filtering Configuration

where ϵ is a uniformly distributed zero mean white random process uncorrelated with x, y and x y. If we include this model for the roundoff error into the RLS algorithm we obtain,

$$d'(n) = \mathbf{x}^T(n)\, \mathbf{w}'(n\text{-}1) + \epsilon(n)$$

$$e'(n) = d(n) - d'(n)$$

and for the weight vector element updates,

$$w_i'(n) = w_i'(n\text{-}1) + k_i(n)e'(n) + \mu_i(n)$$

The primes denote the finite register quantities. The quantities $\epsilon(n)$ and $\mu_i(n)$ are uniformly distributed zero mean white random variables. We have,

$$\sigma_\epsilon^2 = \frac{2^{-2B_\epsilon}}{12}$$

$$\sigma_\mu^2 = \frac{2^{-2B_\mu}}{12}$$

B_e and B_m are the number of bits used to represent the fractional part of the estimated desired response, and the weight vector coefficients.

The computation of (6) assumes that roundoff occurs after the accumulation of partial results in the vector inner product. In the above formulation we assumed that quantized versions of the Kalman gain vector calculated with infinite precision are available. Table 2 shows the results of fixed point roundoff error analysis obtained in [8] for the RLS algorithm and [11] and [19] for the LMS algorithm. In the table, the vector

$$\theta(n) = \mathbf{w}'(n) - \mathbf{w}^*$$

is termed the weight error vector. If the adaptive filter converges then $E\{||\theta(n)||_2\}$ approaches zero. The effects of the additive noise and roundoff error in the computation of the estimated desired response are combined in the term,

$$\sigma_\eta^2 = \sigma_v^2 + \sigma_\epsilon^2$$

Table 2. Fixed Point Roundoff Error Analysis Results

RLS Algorithm $\lambda < 1$

$$E\{\| \theta(n) \|^2\} = \frac{\sigma_\mu^2}{2(1-\lambda)}N + \frac{1}{2}N(1-\lambda)\frac{\sigma_\eta^2}{\sigma_x^2}$$

RLS Algorithm $\lambda = 1$

$$E\{\| \theta(n) \|^2\} = \frac{n}{3}\sigma_\mu^2 N + \frac{1}{n}\frac{\sigma_\eta^2}{\sigma_x^2}N$$

LMS ALgorithm

$$E\{\| \theta(n) \|^2\} = \frac{\frac{1}{\gamma}\frac{\sigma_\mu^2}{\sigma_x^2}N + \gamma N^2 \sigma_\eta^2}{[2 - \gamma(N+2)\sigma_x^2]}$$

In deriving the results of Table 2, it is assumed that the input is a white gaussian process and that the algorithm does not terminate updating. Early termination of weight vector updating results when the prediction error e'(n) is smaller than the quantization level of the rounding arithmetic. A number of issues are involved in the early termination of updating. One issue is the determination of $E\{||\theta(n)||^2\}$ for this case which may differ from the results of Table 2. Secondly, after how many iterations does updating terminate. In [12], [11], and [8] these issues are addressed in more detail. It is important to note that the number of iterations after which updating terminates increases with additive noise or by decreasing λ for the RLS algorithm and increasing γ for the LMS algorithm.

A number of interesting points can be observed by careful examination of Table 2.

(1) When additive noise is present, the RLS algorithm with $\lambda=1$ and obtain an unbiased estimate of the optimum weights w* in the absence of roundoff errors in the weight coefficients, i. e. $\sigma_\mu^2 = 0$. For the LMS algorithm this is not possible unless $\gamma \to 0$ which degrades convergence considerably.

(2) Due to roundoff error in the weight vector coefficient update calculation, the RLS algorithm with $\lambda=1$ diverges as the number of iterations increases. (as long as updating does not terminate.)

(3) Decreasing λ stabilizes the conventional RLS algorithm, however, at the cost of increasing noise due to additive noise and roundoff noise in the calculation of the desired response estimate. The optimum value for λ is,

$$\lambda_{opt} = 1 - \frac{\sigma_\mu \sigma_x}{\sigma_\eta}$$

expression 13 here.

Therefore, the effects of additive noise and roundoff noise can be minimized by choosing the above value for λ. Clearly, as the additive noise is increase, λ must be chosen closer to one.

(4) The term $(1-\lambda)$ in the RLS algorithm is analogous to γ in the LMS algorithm. Decreasing λ increases the tracking capability of the RLS algorithm while increasing γ does the same for the LMS algorithm (as long as the stability criterion is maintained). An interesting discussion on the selection of λ and γ and when to use an RLS algorithm appears in [14].

To compute the mean square prediction error with fixed point roundoff implementations, substitute the value for $E\{||\phi(n)||^2\}$ in the expression below.

$$\sigma_e^2(n) = \sigma_x^2 \, E\{||\theta'(n)||^2\} + \sigma_\eta^2$$

Figure 2 shows fixed point simulation results of the norm squared of the difference vector between the infinite precision weights, w(n) and the fixed point weights, w'(n).

In the simulation, 9 bits were used to represent the fractional part of the weights. ($B_m = 9$). The data samples were 14 bits. Clearly, the theory accurately predicts the linear growth of the mean of the weight error vector norm squared as predicted in Table 2.

$$E\{||\zeta(n)||^2\} = \frac{n}{3} N \sigma_\mu^2$$

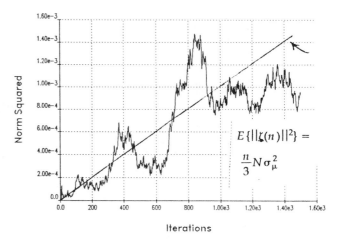

Figure 2. Fixed Point Simulation

III. FLOATING POINT ARITHMETIC

In floating point arithmetic, roundoff errors occur for both multiplication and addition in contrast to fixed point arithmetic. However, overflow problems are relaxed and complex scaling mechanisms are not required. In the results presented below we show that floating point addition in the weight vector update recursion leads to divergence in the RLS algorithm for $\lambda=1$.. First, however, the floating point roundoff error models are introduced. For multiplication,

$$fl[xy] = xy(1+\varepsilon)$$

where ε is a relative error, zero mean white random variable independent of x, y and (x.y). The variance of ε is related to the number of bits in the mantissa, B_e,

$$\sigma_\varepsilon^2 = E(\varepsilon^2) \sim (0.18) \, 2^{(-2B\varepsilon)}$$

For addition,

$$fl[x+y] = (x+y)(1+\delta)$$

where, δ is a zero mean white random variable with variance σ_δ^2

The results of the floating point roundoff error analysis [9] for the RLS and LMS algorithms appear in Table 3. In the Table, σ_μ^2 is the variance of the floating point error due to the addition of the correction term in the weight vector update. The additive noise component is contained in the σ_η^2.

1830

Similar remarks apply to the concerning the floating point case as was discussed in the fixed point case.

Table 3. Floating Point Roundoff Error Results

RLS Algorithm ($\lambda < 1$)

$$E\left\{\|\theta(n)\|^2\right\} = \sigma_\mu^2 \frac{e^{\chi(1-\lambda)}}{2(1-\lambda)} \|w^*\|^2 + \frac{1}{2} N(1-\lambda) \frac{\sigma_\eta^2}{\sigma_x^2} e^{\chi(1-\lambda)}$$

LMS Algorithm

$$E\left\{\|\theta(n)\|^2\right\} = \sigma_\mu^2 \frac{1}{2\gamma\sigma_x^2} \|w^*\|^2 + \frac{1}{2}\gamma N \sigma_\eta^2$$

IV. FURTHER ISSUES

The above results are useful in computing the necessary precision for a required bias in the weight vector, or signal to noise ration. However, other important issues such as scaling to prevent overflow, dynamic range considerations, transient behavior, and the effects of signal correlation need to be addressed.

The fast RLS algorithms [2],[3], and [5], exhibit stability problems in particular for λ<1 in contrast to the conventional RLS algorithm discussed above. This was recognized and discussed in [4] with further elaboration in [10]. Attempts were made to stabilize the fast RLS algorithm in [6], [7], and [18] for example. The work of [7] with new extensions presented in [18] managed to achieve stability for a large number of iterations.

Signal correlation cause adaptive filters to deteriorate in performance compared to white uncorrelated signals in finite precision implementations. An added complexity in adaptive filters with correlated signals is that the magnitude of the norm of the various vectors depends on signal correlation. For example [8], shows that the norm of the Kalman gain vector, $\|k(n)\|$, increases inversely with the minimum eigen value. In [2], the effects of correlation during the initial convergence of the RLS algorithms where the norm may become very large is discussed. This implies that more bits are required when dealing with correlated signals such as speech.

V. REFERENCES

[1] L. Ljung and T. Soderstrom, <u>Theory and Practice of Recursive Identification</u>, MIT Press, 1983.

[2] John M. Cioffi and A. Thomas Kailath, "Fast, Recursive-Least-Squares Transversal Filters for Adaptive Filtering" <u>IEEE Transactions on Acoustics, Speech, and Signal Processing</u>, Vol. ASSP-32, No. 2, April 1984, PP. 304-337.

[3] G. Carayannis, D.G. Manolakis, N. Kalouptsids, "A Fast Sequential Algorithm for Least-Squares Filtering and Prediction", <u>IEEE Transactions on Acoustics, Speech, and Signal Processing</u>, Vol. ASSP-32, No. 2, April 1984, pp. 304-337.

[4] S. Ljung and L. Ljung, "Error Propagation Properties of Recursive Least-Squares Adaptation Algorithms," <u>Automatica</u>, Vol. 21, No. 2, March 1985.

[5] D. D. Falconer and L. Ljung, "Application of Fast-Kalman Estimation to Adaptive Equalization," <u>IEEE Transactions on Communication</u>, Vol. COMM-26, No. 110, Oct. 1978.

[6] M. Bellanger and C. C. Evci, "Coefficient Wordlength Limitation in FLS Adaptive Filters", <u>Proceedings of ICASSP 86</u>, April 7, 1986, Tokyo, Japan, pp. 3011-3014.

[7] J. Botto, "Stabilization of Fast Recursive Least Squares Transversal Filters for Adaptive Filtering," <u>Proceedings IEEE ICASSP 87</u>, Dallas, Texas. pp. 403-407.

[8] Sasan Ardalan, S. T.Alexander, "Fixed Point Roundoff Error Analysis of the Exponentially Windowed RLSA Algorithm for Time-Varying Systems," <u>IEEE Trans. on Acoustics Speech and Signalling Processing</u>, Vol. ASSP-35, No. 6, June 1987.

[9] Sasan H. Ardalan, "Floating Point Roundoff Error Analysis of the RLS and LMS Adaptive Algorithms", <u>IEEE Trans. on Circuits and Systems</u>, Vol. CAS-33, No. 12, December 1986, pp. 1192-1208.

[10] John M. Cioffi, "Limited Precision Effects in Adaptive Filtering", <u>IEEE Trans. on Circuits and System</u>, Vol. CAS-34, No. 7, July 1987.

[11] Christos Caraiscos, Bede Liu, "A Roundoff Error Analysis of the LMS Adaptive Algorithm," <u>IEEE Trans. on Acoustics, Speech and Signal Processing</u>, Vol. ASSP-32, No. 1, February 1984.

[12] R. D. Gitlin et al, "On the Design of Gradient Algorithms for Digitally Implemented Adaptive Filters," IEEE Trans. on Circuit Theory, vol. CT-20, pp. 125-136, March 1973.

[13] Sasan Ardalan, "On the Sensitivity of RLS algorithms to Perturbations in the Filter Coefficients," IEEE Trans. on Acoustics, Speech and Signal Processing, November 1988.

[14] John M. Cioffi, "When Do I Use an RLS Adaptive Filter?", Asilomar Conference on Communication, Control, and Computers, Monterey, CA, November 1986.

[15] N. J. Bershad, "Dynamic Range and Finite Word Effects in Digital Implementation of the LMS Algorithm", Int. Symposium on Circuits and Systems, June 1988.

[16] Maurice G. Bellanger, "Computational Complexity and Accuracy Issues in Fast Least Squares Algorithms for Adaptive Filtering", Int. Symposium on Circuits and Systems, June 1988.

[17] J. M. Cioffi, "Precision-Efficient Use of Block Adaptive Algorithms in Data-Driven Echo Cancellers", Int. Conference on Communications (ICC88), June 1988.

[18] D. T. M. Slock and T. Kailath, "Numerically Stable FAst Recursive Least-Squares Transversal Filters", Int. Conf. on Acoustics, Speech and Sig. Proc. (ICASSP88), April 10988.

[19] Sasan Ardalan, "Finite Wordlength Analysis of the LMS Adaptive Filter Algorithm", CCSP Technical Report, CCSP-TR-84/4, Dept. of Elect. and Comp. Eng., NC State University, February 1984.

IMPLEMENTATION CONSIDERATIONS IN KALMAN FILTERING

Gary L. Blank

Department of Electrical and Computer Engineering
Illinois Institute of Technology
Chicago, Illinois 60616

ABSTRACT

As the demand for faster and more efficient algorithms for digital filtering increases, more interest has evolved in the area of Kalman filtering. The original Kalman filter is relatively complex and requires a large number of matrix operations and calculations. The fast Kalman algorithm is less complex and requires a smaller number of operations. Although the number of operations is relatively high for both, the rapid convergence of both algorithms makes them very useful in practical situations.

INTRODUCTION

R. E. Kalman [1] published a paper describing a recursive technique for solving the discrete-data version of the least--squares smoothing and prediction problem.

Many algorithms have been devised to do least squares filtering, among them are the conventional Kalman and the fast Kalman algorithms. In finite precision implementations, the performances of both algorithms are degraded. Periodic reinitialization of the fast Kalman algorithm, and the use of the covariance fast Kalman algorithm have both been successful [2].

This paper describes the implementations of both the conventional and the fast Kalman filters. Comparisons of the calculation burden and the speed of convergence are made for both algorithms and for the stochastic gradient method. The application used for the comparison test is an adaptive signal processor. Since the Kalman algorithms make better use of all the past available information than the stochastic gradient methods, their start-up and convergence are faster [3].

THEORY OF KALMAN FILTERS

Let $r(n)$ be a p-dimensional vector representing the new elements in the input signal vector $x(n)$. The signal has accumulated M components over the past N samples where $M=Np$. Then

$$x(n) = [r(n)^* \ldots, r(n-N+1)^*] \qquad (1)$$

where * denotes transpose. The output of the system is

$$y(n) = c(n-1)^* x(n) \qquad (2)$$

where $c(n-1)$ is the M-dimensional coefficient vector which was last updated at n-1.

The desired output signal is $d(n)$. The difference between the desired output signal and the true output is

$$e(n) = d(n) - y(n) \qquad (3)$$

It is desired to minimize the trace of the least-squares cost function

$$\sum_{k=o}^{n} w^{n-k} [d(h) - c(n)^* x(k)]^2 \qquad (4)$$

where w is a geometric weighting factor.

Differentiating (4) with respect to $c(n)$ and equating the resulting expression to zero yields the discrete time Wiener-Hopf equation for the coefficients $c(n)$

$$A(n)c(n) = v(n) \qquad (5)$$

where

$$A(n) = \sum_{k=o}^{n} w^{n-k} x(k) x(k)^* + w^n \delta I$$

$$= wA(n-1) + x(n)x(n)^* \qquad (6)$$

A small positive definite matrix δI is included to ensure positive definiteness.

$$v(n) = \sum_{k=o}^{n} w^{n-k} x(k) d(k)^*$$

$$= wv(n-1) + x(n)d(n)^* \qquad (7)$$

Substitution of the result of (5) into (4) yields

$$e(n) = E(n) - v(n)^* c(n) \qquad (8)$$

where

$$E(n) = \sum_{k=o}^{n} w^{n-k} d(k) d(k)^*$$

$$= wE(n-1) + d(n)d(n)^* \qquad (9)$$

Equations (6) and (7) describe a recursive definition of $A(n)$ and $v(n)$. This permits a recursive algorithm for finding the optimal coefficients.

RECURSIVE UPDATES

From Equations (5) and (7) it follows that

$$A(n)c(n) = wA(n-1)c(n-1) + x(n)d(n)^* \qquad (10)$$

Using Equations (3) and (6),

$$c(n) = c(n-1) + A(n)^{-1} x(n) e(n)^* \qquad (11)$$

and

$$c(n)^* v(n) = [c(n-1)^*$$

$$+ e(n) x(n)^* A(n)^{-1}] v(n) \qquad (12)$$

From equations (5) and (7),

$$c(n)^* v(n) = wc(n-1)^* v(n-1) + c(n-1)^* x(n)d(n)$$

$$+ e(n)x(n)^* c(n) \qquad (13)$$

$$= wc(n-1)^* v(n-1)$$

$$+ d(n)d(n)^* e(n) [x(n)^* c(n) - d(n)] \qquad (14)$$

$$= wc(n-1)^* v(n-1)$$

$$+ d(n)d(n)^* - e(n)e(n)^* [1-S(n)] \qquad (15)$$

where

$$S(n) = x(n)^* A(n)^{-1} x(n) \qquad (16)$$

CONVENTIONAL KALMAN

The conventional Kalman algorithm uses the recursive definition of Equation (6) and the matrix inversion relationship

$$A(n)^{-1} = w^{-1} [A(n-1)^{-1}$$

$$- A(n-1)^{-1} x(n) x(n)^* A(n-1)^{-1} / D(n)] \qquad (17)$$

where

$$D(n) = w + x(n)^* A(n-1)^{-1} x(n) \qquad (18)$$

If we define

$$P(n) = A(n)^{-1} \qquad (19)$$

then the Kalman algorithm becomes

$$c(n) = c(n-1) + g(n)e(n)^* \qquad (20)$$

where $g(n)$ is the Kalman gain,

$$a(n) = P(n-1)x(n) \qquad (21)$$

$$g(n) = a(n) / (w + x(n)^* a(n)) \qquad (22)$$

$$P(n) = w^{-1} [P(n-1) - g(n)a(n)^*] \qquad (23)$$

$$y(n) = c(n-1)^* x(n) \qquad (24)$$

$$e(n) = d(n) - y(n) \qquad (25)$$

THE FAST KALMAN ALGORITHM

The fast Kalman algorithm can be summarized by the following nine equations.

$$f(n) = r(n) - F(n-1)^* x(n-1) \quad (26)$$

$$F(n) = F(n-1) + g(n-1) f(n)^* \quad (27)$$

$$f(n)^1 = f(n)[1 - g(n-1)^* x(n-1)] \quad (28)$$

$$E(n) = wE(n-1) + f(n)^1 f(n)^* \quad (29)$$

The extended Kalman gain $g(n)$ is calculated as follows

$$g(n) = \begin{bmatrix} E(n)^{-1} & f(n)^1 \\ \\ g(n-1) - F(n)E(n)^{-1} & f(n)^1 \end{bmatrix} \quad (30)$$

Equations (26) through (29) update the forward predictor, Equation (30) computes the extended Kalman gain, and Equations (31) through (33) update the backward predictor. Partition Equation (30) as

$$g(n) = \begin{bmatrix} g(n)^1 \\ ------------ \\ u(n) \end{bmatrix} \quad (31)$$

$$b(n) = r(n-N) - B(n-1)^* x(n) \quad (32)$$

$$B(n) = [B(n-1) + g(n)^1 b(n)^*][I - u(n)b(n)^*]^{-1} \quad (33)$$

To initialize the conventional Kalman algorithm all variables are set to zero except $P(0) = 1/d\$ I$ to avoid a problem in inversion.

And the updated Kalman gain is determined from

$$g(n) = g(n)^1 + B(n)u(n) \quad (34)$$

To complete the algorithm Equations (2), (3), and (22) must be included.

To initialize the algorithm, set

$$F(0) = B(0) = 0$$

$$x(0) = g(0) = c(0) = 0$$

and

$$E(0) = \delta \ I$$

EXAMPLES OF DIFFERENT IMPLEMENTATIONS

Three methods are used for comparison. These are (a) the stochastic-gradient method, (b) the conventional Kalman algorithm, and (c) the fast Kalman algorithm.

The application chosen for this comparison is an adaptive signal processor (equalizer). Two cases are examined, viz., a symbol-spaced equalizer and a T/2- spaced equalizer.

SYMBOL-SPACED EQUALIZERS	(a)	(b)	(c)
No. of multiplications in implementation	63	1519	315
No. of iterations to converge to-15DB MSE	140	75	75
No.of iterations to converge to-20DB MSE	400	125	125

T/2-SPACED EQUALIZERS			
No. of multiplications in implementation	127	6045	1199

CONCLUSION

The implementation of Kalman filters requires some careful considerations. The Kalman and the fast Kalman are both very efficient requiring substantially less iterations than the gradient algorithm. The fast Kalman is less complex. Care must be taken to examine the problems of finite-precision implementation. When the algorithm is degraded because of finite-precision, it is possible to do a periodic reinitialization.

REFERENCES

(1)   R.E. Kalman.   "A New Approach To Linear Filtering and Prediction Problems" *Transactions of the ASME-Journal of Basic Engineering*, pp.35-45, March 1960.

(2)   D.W. Lin.   "On Digital Implementation of the Fast Kalman Algorithms," *IEEE Transactions on Acoustics, Speech, and Signal Processing*, Vol. ASSP-32, No. 5, pp. 998-1005, October 1984.

(3)   M.S. Mueller.   "Least-Squares Algorithms for Adaptive Equalizers," *The Bell System Technical Journal*, Vol. 60, No.8, pp. 1905-1925, October 1981.

CEL-01

THE CELLULAR REVOLUTION - THE BIG PICTURE
SUMMARY

Martin Cooper - Chairperson
Chairman

DYNA, INC.
1165 N. Clark St., Ste. 601
Chicago, IL 60610

ABSTRACT

Cellular radio has become a national institution, even an international one. With 1,500,000 subscribers in the U.S. alone, the investment (over 5 billion dollars) and the annual revenues (almost 3 billion dollars) are sufficiently large that cellular now means real business. The challenges of the industry have gradually shifted from building the network to sustaining profitable growth. Some persistent problems remain and new opportunities continue to appear.

THE PROBLEMS

Not all cellular systems have achieved satisfactory profit levels. Cooper's first rule of commerce states that "There are no easy businesses." Those cellular operators who run tight ships; who maintain low overheads; who balance growth with quality; are making money regardless of their size. All cellular systems have the potential but, as always, some people learn faster than others.

Cellular fraud has loomed into a significant problem. Roamer verification is partially in place but still not running smoothly. More serious is the fraud problem created because some manufacturers have made their phones less tamper free than they should be.

Quality of service is still inadequate in a number of cities. Cellular engineering has yet to solve the performance equation in all cities -- especially where rapid growth continues to be a factor.

THE CELLULAR SUBSCRIBER

The nature of the cellular subscriber has been gradually changing as the perception of the cellular phone changes from a high level perquisite to an important tool for productivity. The rapid and continuing drop in the price of cellular phones has contributed to the increased use of cellular phones by sales people and service representatives, while growth continues in the professional and management market segments. Surprisingly, the new categories of users generate as much air-time revenue as their wealthier predecessors.

NEW OPPORTUNITIES

A new service has been introduced by GTE Mobilnet that provides for "follow me roaming". A subscriber to this service can receive calls when in cities other than his or her phone city. The caller need only call the home cellular number; "follow me roaming" locates the subscriber and forwards the call.

Rural cellular systems are appearing more frequently wherein many of the phones in a system are fixed and substitute for the local-loop. In most cases, these phones use ordinary telephone sets interfaced electronically to the cellular radiotelephone.

The cellular pay phone market is maturing. Increased numbers of phones are being placed in limousines and taxis as well as intercity busses trains, and on off-shore oil drilling rigs.

Specific proposals for digital cellular radio have been introduced. A gradual cut-over will probably commence in the early 1990's in the large cities.

The use of cellular portables is being markedly stimulated by the entry of lower cost units and by improved service in some cities. The trend of lower price will accelerate.

CONCLUSION

The growth of cellular radio continues to be exciting but the industry is maturing. There is less experimentation and "wheeling and dealing" and more professional management and marketing. There is still room, however, for creativity and innovation in cellular technology.

James P. Caile   - Motorola, Inc.

Harold W. Clark   - Motorola, Inc.

Jesse E. Russell   - AT&T Laboratories

Mark O. Ripley   - GTE Mobilnet Inc.

CELLULAR IN THE U.S.

James P. Caile
General Marketing Manager
Cellular Division
Motorola Inc.
1501 Shure Drive
Arlington Heights, IL 60004

The U.S. cellular market continues to grow at 30% annually. Instead of stabilizing, a number of factors have been contributing to radical change and often turmoil. The factors discussed in this session include increasing dominance of the Regional Operating Companies and consolidation of non-wire line interests, new low cost equipment suppliers, deeper market penetration and the problems encountered by carriers in managing the growth.

CELLULAR SYSTEM PERFORMANCE

Mark O. Ripley
Vice President-Networks
GTE Mobilenet
616 FM 1960 West 8400
Houston, TX 77090

The product of the cellular industry is communication - almost always person-to-person. The quality of service in cellular and elsewhere has been demonstrated to have profound effect upon the acceptance of the service by the public. This session discusses the present services, its successes and shortcomings and the proposals for the future.

AN INTERNATIONAL PERSPECTIVE

Harold W. Clark
Strategic Product Manager
Cellular Division

Motorola Inc.
1501 W. Shure Drive
Arlington Heights, IL 60004

Although the cellular concept was born in the U.S., its first implementation was overseas. While the bulk of the market is in the U.S. today, the international market grows more rapidly; within 5 years there will be as many subscribers overseas as in the U.S. There are about 70 countries now proposing some form of cellular. The adoption of digital transmission will be a horse race between the U.S. and the rest of the world.

FUTURE DIRECTIONS OF CELLULAR TECHNOLOGY: BEYOND 1995

Jesse E. Russell
Director
Cellular Telecommunications Laboratory
AT&T Bell Laboratories
Whippany Road
3G-324
Whippany, NJ 07981-0903

ABSTRACT

Since the beginning of commercial cellular service in 1983 in the U.S., the market growth has exceeded industry expectations. Major U.S. cities are fast approaching capacity limits in terms of the ability to add new users to their network. As a result of this rapid growth, the U.S. cellular industry is evaluating proposals for a more spectrum efficient technology. As a result, several manufacturers have proposed second generation cellular RF technology for application within the U.S. While many of these proposals will more than adequately meet the immediate capacity needs of the U.S., there is a need to begin discussing third generation RF technology. This need is primarily driven by a worldwide demand for personal communications that will permit end users the freedom to move from country-to-country, network-to-network and maintain continuity of cellular service. The demands that personal communications will place on RF technology will require the technology to support high-density urban applications in major metropolitan cities throughout the world by 1995 and beyond.

This paper will overview some of the technologies that are currently being proposed for second generation systems within the U.S., as well as some of the issues associated with introducing these technologies. It will also discuss various technologies that are beginning to emerge in the research community that could serve as third generation cellular system to meet the growth demands for personal communications throughout the world. Also discussed within this paper will be many network considerations as well as technology transition issues to permit a graceful evolution between current second generation and possibly third generation RF technologies.

CEL-02

THE VALUE OF CELLULAR

Michael V. Patriarche, Chairperson
Vice President
Cellular SYstems

Northern Telecom Inc.

2435 N. Central Expressway
Richardson, TX 75080

The "value" of cellular has been one of the most highly debated issues in the telecommunications industry. This seminar provides a business and market perspective on the "value" of cellular as it relates to each of the major stakeholders in the cellular industry. The four perspectives captured in the seminar are:

- End User Perspective: Value of services to the end user
- Service Provider Perspective: Service providers' ability to enhance the value of services to the end user;
  Vendor Perspective: Technology's ability to enhance the value of the service providers' markets; and
  Wall Street Perspective: Changes and trends in the market valuation of cellular franchises.

Dr. John Berrigan - Booz Allen & Hamilton

Nancy J. Anderson - NYNEX Mobile Communications

Piyush Sodha - Northern Telecom Inc.

Dennis H. Leibowitz - Donaldson, Lufkin & Jenrette

THE CELLULAR PHONE MARKET: CHALLENGES FACING THE INDUSTRY

Dr. John Berrigan
Vice President
National Analysts
A Division of Booz Allen & Hamilton Inc.
400 Market Street
Philadelphia, PA 19106

ABSTRACT

The demand for cellular phones and service is expected to accelerate during the next decade. Major anticipated factors contributing to this growth are: decreased price of equipment, new enhanced features of equipment and service, and the introduction of residential customers into the market. The expected rapid market growth and the changing mix of buyers present several challenges to the cellular industry. This paper discusses three major issues that the industry will face within the next several years: (1) What equipment and service pricing mix will yield optimal levels of capacity demand within acceptable rates of return? (2) What service and equipment feature enhancements are likely to have the largest incremental impact on service and equipment demand? and (3) In what ways is the cellular market likely to re-segment itself, and what promotional and advertising strategies are likely to be the most effective for service and equipment providers? Market research data relevant to these issues will be presented during the seminar.

INTRODUCTION

Cellular phones and cellular service have become increasingly attractive to consumers, and the demand is expected to accelerate in the next decade. The growth in the number of equipment purchasers and subscribers will not be confined to business customers; residential customers are expected to play a significant role in the industry's growth.

According to surveys conducted by CTIA (1), there were 91,000 subscribers to cellular phone service in January, 1985 and 1.2 million subscribers in December, 1987 -- a 13-fold increase during this three-year period. Moreover, CTIA estimates that for each of the first five months of 1988, more than 60,000 subscribers have been added to the cellular system in the U.S. Industry analysts (2,3) predict 3 million subscribers in 1989 and somewhere between 8 and 12 million subscribes by 1992.

Several factors lead us to believe that accelerated growth in cellular service adoption will continue:

- Expanding availability of service. Service for cellular phones is expanding. In the beginning of 1985, there were 32 operating systems covering a small percentage of the U.S. population, whereas by the end of 1987, 73% of the population was served by 312 operating systems (4). If cellular installations continue at this rate, cellular service will be available universally by 1992.

- Decreasing cost of equipment. The price of cellular equipment is a major factor that currently drives customer demand. This trend is likely to accelerate, and prices are expected to drop even further. The price of cellular phones is expected to drop even further. The price of cellular phones is expected to reach the $500 level within the next five years (5).

- Improving quality of service. Industry analysts predict a major improvement in cellular service when transmission is converted from analog to digital. The conversion is expected to increase cell capacity, improve quality of signals and eliminate dead spots. Digital transmission will probably be available commercially sometime in the 1990s (6).

- Increasing product enhancements. Compact, light, ultra-portable cellular units -- no larger than a wallet -- are expected to be available shortly. Other product enhancements will include features such as data ports and voice recognition. By extending access and functionality, these product enhancements should stimulate a further expansion of the customer base, as well as increased usage.

- Accelerating awareness and acceptance of cellular technology. As cellular penetration increases among business and non-business primary users, word-of-mouth can be expected to erode perceived barriers to acquisition of both equipment and service. As was the case within the PC and VCR markets, rapid growth occurs after the innovators successfully test the technology.

The expected rapid market growth and the changing mix of buyers present several challenges to the cellular industry.

Major issues that the industry will face within the next several years are discussed in the next section.

ISSUES

What equipment and service pricing mix will yield optimal levels of capacity demand within acceptable rates of return?

Historically, the cost of technology, the high first-run fixed costs and the lack of critical mass resulted in an initial price for an installed unit approximately $2,000. Coupled with subscription fees and usage costs, the price of cellular service had the effect of containing demand, thereby permitting rational construction and distribution of cellular transmission systems. In fact, some industry analysts would argue that if equipment and service price had been lower at the outset, demand would have outstripped capacity, thus creating blocking problems similar to those that plagued the mobile phone system. More importantly, high rates of demand, concentrated in primary urban areas, would have forced a rapid and uneven construction of the cellular system.

Now, five years later, the urban analog cellular system is virtually complete. Improved technology and the availability of critical mass demand is forcing equipment prices down to levels affordable to the mass of potential buyers. As a consequence, cellular equipment purchases have accelerated within the last six months. In some cases, manufacturers are reporting two and threefold increases in monthly sales. In contrast, the cost of service has remained at the same relatively high rates.

The most immediate effect of the discrepancy between the price of equipment and the cost of service is likely to be a dramatic increase in already high rates of disconnected service. That is, when unsuspecting buyers of low-cost equipment, lured by advertising offering low trial service rates, later discover their monthly service bills to be unacceptably high, many will disconnect service. The net effect will be to create a growing discrepancy between the penetration rates of equipment and service, as illustrated in Figure 1. Such a gap presents both risk and opportunity to the cellular industry.

For equipment providers, the risk is that consumers will become aware of the real service cost prior to equipment purchase, and current accelerated rates of penetration will quickly flatten. For service providers, there are several risks. In the first place, frustrated consumer demand could lead to a regulatory backlash. In this situation, service providers may be unable to manage the structuring of rates; consequently, rates of return could suffer. A second, even more significant risk exists. It is common knowledge that service providers are anxious to transition from analog to digital service. The most important driver of the timing of regulatory approval for this conversion will be evidence that demand for cellular service will exceed analog capacity. If the cost of service remains constant and if the gap between the price of equipment and the cost of service widens, subscription penetration rates will lag significantly behind current industry estimates. Consequently, the critical mass required for digital conversion will not accumulate at rates consistent with service providers' planning horizons. In the worst case scenario, digital conversion will be delayed into the 21st century or may never occur because frustrated consumers refuse to buy equipment, and cellular demand will flatten or decline.

Given the magnitude of these risks, it is likely that service providers will respond to the challenge by seizing the opportunity stimulated by declining equipment prices. The issue the providers confront is to accurately determine price/demand elasticity rates that will promote rates of growth in sustained subscriptions and minutes of usage, consistent with expected rates of return and planned digital conversion horizons.

What service and equipment feature enhancements are likely to have the largest incremental impact on serviceand equipment demand?

Equipment manufactures and service providers alike will attempt to attract buyers and differentiate themselves by offering feature/functionality enhancements. The array of candidate enhancements is rather extensive. For example, equipment enhancements may include:

- compact, lightweight, pocket-sized portable units for use in vehicles or other locations

- data ports for fax, information service access. data entry, word processing or graphics

- voice recognition system for verbal dialing

- an incoming display board to register incoming call numbers

- a message board which records messages from unanswered calls

- a no-frills model with limited features.

Among enhanced service features, several options will be available:

- priority service which permits calls even during emergency conditions, such as snowstorms

- privacy service which provides secure voice transmission

- multi-party service for conference calls

- extension phone service

- geolocation service which identifies the location of a cellular unit on command

- a low-cost, restricted-area service linking cellular service to only one geographic area.

Before vendors invest in the design, development and commercialization of feature enhancements, it is imperative that they evaluate price/demand elasticities for each feature. Such as assessment will not only promote more

effective pricing, but will also enable them to filter and prioritize features/functionalities, based upon expected rates of incremental demand and return on investment.

In what ways is the cellular market likely to re-segment itself, and what promotional and advertising strategies are likely to be most effective for service and equipment providers?

The initial market for cellular service consisted primarily of business-related functional segments, complemented by a small, affluent group of innovators. Early target segments included former mobile phone users, senior executives, principals and owners, sales/marketing/service/maintenance personnel and gadget lovers. The needs and benefits driving interest in cellular technology tended to focus upon improvement in personal productivity, ability to stay in touch, competitive advantage, ability to be more timely in response to customer needs, status and system quality improvements. Virtually all advertising an promotional activities focused on the needs of these segments./ Moreover, early distribution channels tended to reflect these target segments.

Now, as the price of equipment falls and cellular service becomes more accessible to the mass market, a re-segmentation of the market is occurring. As new, populous markets open up, market segmentation becomes more complex for those formulating advertising, promotional, sales and distribution strategies. Who are the new target markets seeking to satisfy with cellular service?

Preliminary market research indicates that although traditional segment needs remain, such as increased productivity, cost effectiveness and staying in touch with customers, a new set of more pedestrian needs is driving the bulk of emergent purchases. These needs include cost, status, convenience, keeping up-to-date, accessibility in emergencies and flexibility -- the ability to make changes at the last minute.

To effectively exploit this shift in the segmentation of the cellular market, equipment and service providers alike will have to alter their advertising, promotion, distribution and sales tactics. We can expect mass media, such as television, to become a more prevalent message medium. Moreover retail outlet sales can be expected to increase. Advertising messages from equipment suppliers will focus on price and status, while service providers repeat an old, familiar refrain: "Reach out and touch someone -- from your car."

CONCLUSION

Market research evidence suggests that the demand for cellular technology has finally reached the takeoff stage. As the price of equipment falls, a new mass market is emerging. Effective exploitation of this explosive opportunity presents serious challenges to the industry. Equipment and service providers alike face critical choices in pricing, feature/functionality enhancements, product line extensions and distribution channel selection, as well as advertising and promotional strategies and tactics. Success will depend on a careful assessment of price/demand elasticities, emergent consumer needs/benefits, and proper selection channels and media.

Although acquisitions, mergers and shakeouts will create temporary disruptions as the market transitions, the critical challenge facing the industry may well be the cost of service. If the cost of service remains high in the face of an accelerated growth of equipment purchases fueled by lower prices, it may well be that voluntary disconnections and spreading consumer awareness of subsequent high cost service will prematurely truncate the future of cellular service.

REFERENCES

(1) State of the business. Cellular Business, June, 1988, pp. 16-17.

(2) Titch, Steven. Cellular plight will last until 1990s. Communications Week, February 2, 1987, pp. 29 ff.

(3) Booker, Ellis. Cellular service: A prime market. Telephony, September 21, 1987, pp. 46-47.

(4) Ibid., (1).

(5) Hello anywhere: The cellular phone boom will change the way you live. Business Week, September 21, 1987, pp. 84 ff.

(6) Ibid., (3).

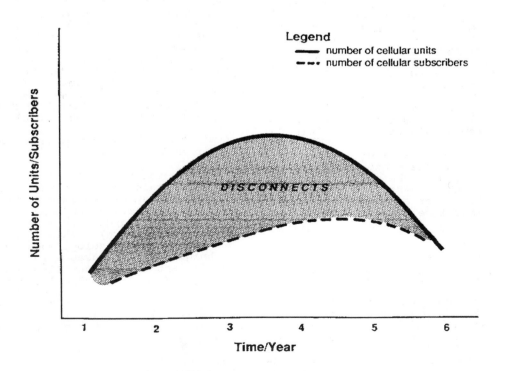

FIG. 1. POTENTIAL GAP BETWEEN EQUIPMENT AND SERVICE SUBSCRIPTION PENETRATION

THE VALUE OF CELLULAR: SERVICE PROVIDERS
PERSPECTIVE

Nancy J. Anderson
Vice President
Marketing and Technology
NYNEX Mobile Communications Company
One Blue Hill Plaza
Pearl River, NY 10985

This session presents the perspective of
the cellular service provider on specific
customer needs and applications. The
focus of the session is on the end user of
cellular-related services and how service
providers can enhance the value of these
services.

THE VALUE OF CELLULAR - VENDOR PERSPECTIVE

Piyush Sodha
Director
Business Development
Cellular Systems
Northern Telecom Inc.
2435 N. Central Expressway
Richardson, TX 75080

ABSTRACT

Market dynamics, regulatory events, and
limitations of the current technology have
set the industry in pursuit of future
cellular technologies. Before the
industry launches into discussion of
modulation techniques, coding techniques,
and the like, it is important to
understand the economic impact of future
cellular technologies. A quantitative
assessment of the impact of future
cellular systems will facilitate the
industry in selecting the optimal next
generation technology.

This paper focuses on the economic
implications, to the service provider, of
migrating from an analog to a digital
cellular system. Specifically, this paper
discusses the limitations of analog
cellular systems; the economic impact of
these limitations to the cellular service
provider and the industry; advantages of
digital systems over analog; and the
impact of digital cellular systems.

APPROACH

In late 1987, Northern Telecom undertook
the development of an economic model of
the cellular service providers business to
better assess the impact of digital
cellular systems in light of the cost
structure and variations in the supply and
demand economics. The supply economics
model was built from individual sub-models
associated with each of the major expense
and investment categories of the service
provider's business. These individual
sub-models were regression models that
explained variations in expenses as a
consequence of key drivers. The drivers

that explained the supply economics can be
grouped into three major categories 1)
Market characteristics (e.g., Coverage in
Square miles, Populations) 2) Technology
characteristics (e.g., number of
subscribers per cell, minimum cell size)
3) Service provider characteristics (e.g.,
Service price, Market share, Debt to
Equity ratio). For example, (See Fig. 1)
variations in network maintenance expense
across different markets can be explained
by the number of subscribers and the
number of cells in the system. These two
drivers are capable of explaining 97% of
the variation in expenses across markets
of differing size. Each of the individual
sub-models was derived from data on the
actual expenses incurred by differing
service providers in the industry.

The individual sub-models provided a
quantified understanding of the economies
of scale associated with the different
expense and investment categories. The
supply model was verified by comparing it
to actual market data (for markets that
were not used in deriving the
relationships). The comaprison indicated
that for differing market sizes the model
could explain more than 80% of the
variation in expenses and investments (see
Fig. 2).

The demand economics was modeled assuming
a "log-log" relationship between average
annual revenue per subscriber and market
penetration (in % population). Based on
market penetration behavior to date, a
demand curve was forecasted (see Fig. 3).
The model showed that at an average annual
revenue per subscriber of $700, a
penetration of 6.2% of the population
could be expected. Impact of variables
such as disposable income, market
maturity,and advertising effort were not
factored into the demand model.

Limitations of Current Technology and
Their Implications

There are three main limitations with the
existing analog cellular technology.
First, the typical maximum number of
subscribers that can be handled per cell
is 900 (assuming uniform 7 cells non-
sectorized pattern). This is primarily
due to the FM technology modulation
technique, which causes a relatively
inefficient use of the allocated spectrum.
The second major practical limitation is
that it is difficult to make the minimum
size of a cell less than 3 square miles
(i.e., 1 mile in radius). The first and
second limitations translate to the
technology's inability to accommodate more
than a maximum of about 220 subscribers
per square km. Lastly, the cost of radio
equipment makes the investment per
incremental subscriber high.

Analysis (from using the economic model)
indicated that, given the current

technology limitations, the cellular service providers had no economic incentive to reduce the price of cellular service. It was found that the average annual revenue per subscriber, where service providers maximized the value of their markets, was around $1,200 (see Fig. 4). However, the demand model indicated that an average annual revenue of $1,200 per subscriber will limit the penetration of cellular subscribers to 3-4 million in the United States. In fact, in certain large markets, prices translate to about $1,500 annual revenue per subscriber -- a reflection of the capacity limitation facing the service providers.

Digital Cellular Technology

The goal of future cellular technology should be to enable the service providers to enhance the value of their markets, and simultaneously be motivated to reduce the annual price to subscribers to around $500. It is believed that these goals can be achieved (over time) by digital cellular technology.

The major impact from digital cellular technology comes from increases in capacity (i.e., number of subscribers per cell, number of subscribers per square km). It is assessed that initial digital cellular systems (1991 time frame) could be capable of capacity increase of about 6 times over current analog systems (assuming an identical grade of service

and quality of speech). This assessment of capacity increase is based on a narrow-band (30 kHz) TimeDivision Multiple Access (TDMA) digital cellular system with 16 k bits per second speech coding. A times 12 improvement in capacity can be achieved by migrating the system to 8 k bits-per-second speech coding.

Assuming that the cost-per-channel is identical to that of current analog systems, as a consequence of this capacity improvement alone, the service provider will now maximize the value of his franchise at $700 annual revenue per subscriber (see Fig. 5). Assuming a transition of 6 years from analog to digital, the service provider should be capable of increasing the value of the franchise by 50%.

It is also expected that narrow-band TDMA digital cellular systems will b4e capable of reducing the incremental investment per subscriber by about 50% over analog systems. This cost improvement, coupled with the expected improvements in capacity, should motivate the service provider to operate at an annual revenue-per-subscriber of about $500. In this scenario, the service provider will increase the value of the franchise by about 100% (see Fig. 5).

The cost effectiveness of digital cellular systems over analog systems will enable the service provider to expand the portfolio of services from voice and voice-related services to other enhanced services. Some examples of near-term enhanced services are SS#7-related services such as Caller Identification; low speed data services such as alarm services; high speed database access and retrieval services, and facsimile services. Examples of futuristic services are locational and navigational services for automobiles.

In summary, digital cellular systems will allow service providers to reduce their cost of providing voice service - both from an investment as well as an expense point of view. In addition, the service providers will have the opportunity to provide new enhanced service economically.

Conclusions

The economic model developed at Northern Telecom provided the following understanding about the cellular service providers' economics:

- Significant economies of scale exist in the cellular service providers expense categories.

- However, the limitations of analog cellular systems do not allow for the service provider to reap the benefits of these economies.

- In fact, with analog cellular systems the service provider is motivated to operate at an average revenue-per-subscriber of around $1,200 per annum.

- Capacity and cost improvements from digital cellular technology (assuming a narrow-band TDMA system) will motivate the service provider to (over time) operate around an average annual revenue of $500 to $700 annually. If the service providers seek to maximize the value of their franchises, there will be about 15 to 18 million subscribers on the cellular network by 1996.

Based on this understanding of the service providers' economics it is Northern Telecom's belief that the industry should seek a solution, for the next generation cellular technology, that not only enhances the capacity of the systems significantly, but also brings about substantial cost improvement.

NETWORK EXPENSE

NETWORK EXPENSE* PER SUBSCRIBER PER YEAR
VERSUS TOTAL SUBSCRIBERS & NUMBER OF CELLS

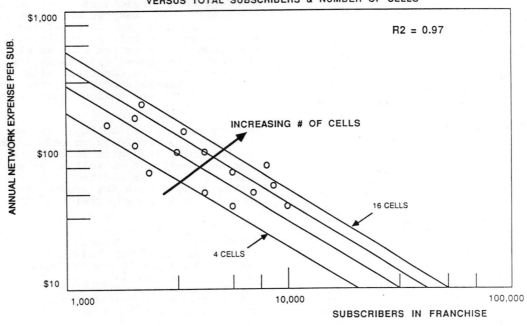

FIGURE 1

MODEL VALIDATION

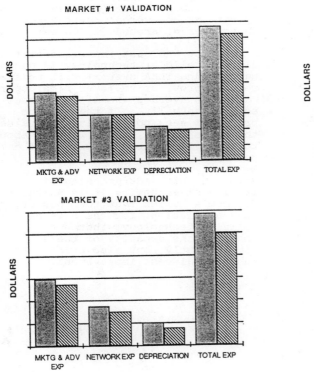

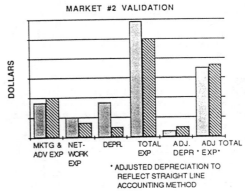

FIGURE 2

ANALOG CELLULAR

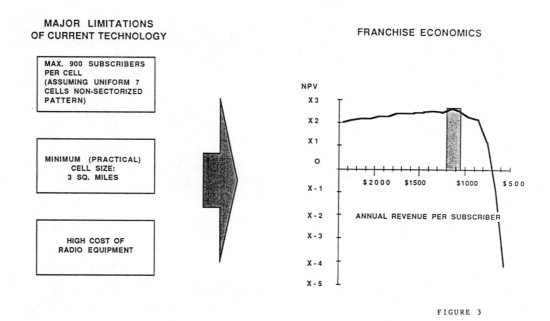

MAJOR LIMITATIONS
OF CURRENT TECHNOLOGY

FRANCHISE ECONOMICS

MAX. 900 SUBSCRIBERS
PER CELL
(ASSUMING UNIFORM 7
CELLS NON-SECTORIZED
PATTERN)

MINIMUM (PRACTICAL)
CELL SIZE:
3 SQ. MILES

HIGH COST OF
RADIO EQUIPMENT

NPV

ANNUAL REVENUE PER SUBSCRIBER

FIGURE 3

END USER CELLULAR DEMAND

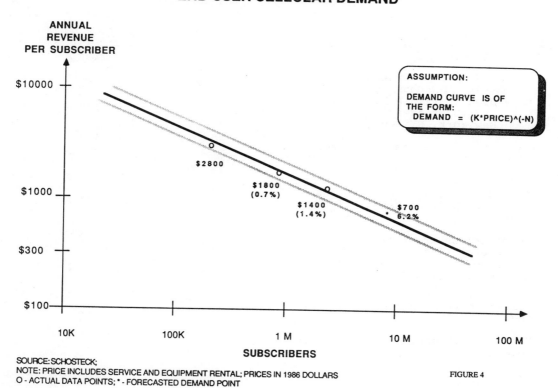

ANNUAL
REVENUE
PER SUBSCRIBER

ASSUMPTION:

DEMAND CURVE IS OF
THE FORM:
$$DEMAND = (K \cdot PRICE)^{-N}$$

$2800

$1800
(0.7%)

$1400
(1.4%)

$700
6.2%

SUBSCRIBERS

SOURCE: SCHOSTECK;
NOTE: PRICE INCLUDES SERVICE AND EQUIPMENT RENTAL; PRICES IN 1986 DOLLARS
O - ACTUAL DATA POINTS; * - FORECASTED DEMAND POINT

FIGURE 4

DIGITAL CELLULAR IMPACT

CAPACITY (SUBS. PER CELL)	COST (CELL SITE INV. PER SUB)	OPTIMAL PRICE (ANNUAL REVENUE PER SUBSCRIBER)	FRANCHISE VALUE (NORMALIZED NPV)
900	$500	$1300	1.0
5400 - (X6)	$500	$700	1.5
5400 - (X6)	$250 - (X2)	$500	2.0

BOTH CAPACITY AND COST ARE CRITICAL ...

FIGURE 5

THE VALUE OF CELLULAR: WALL STREET
PERSPECTIVE

Dennis H. Leibowitz
Senior Vice President
DOnaldson, Lufkin & Jenrette
140 Broadway
New York, NY 10005

This session addresses the Wall Street
perspective on the "Value" of cellular.
Analyses included are:

- Public values are based on discounts to private transaction
  trends;

- Transactions are reflecting im-
  balance of rising demand and
  downgrading supply, as well as,
  strong fundamentals;

- Values will move to cash flow
  multiples from "per pop" values;
  and

- Market excitement over open-ended
  potentials.

CEL-03

NEW DEVELOPMENTS IN DIGITAL RADIO
FOR DISTRIBUTION

Hamilton W. Arnold, Chairperson
District Manager
Radio Research Division
Bell Communications Research
331 Newman Springs Rd.
Red Bank, NJ 07701-7020

The emergence of viable wireless telecommunications distribution systems is being driven by technology, market demand, and spectrum availability. New technologies and novel system architectures together can yield radio distribution systems having high performance and reliability. The high cost of wiring (and rewiring) in the present distribution plant can make radio alternatives economically attractive. The popularity of tetherless distribution services in office, residential, and rural environments is evidenced by the large and growing vehicular mobile and cordless telephone markets. Current regulatory proceedings are facilitating the application of new wireless distribution technologies to a wider range of markets.

Dag Åkerberg
Ericsson Radio Systems AB

Katherine M. Falkenthal
Bell Communications Research

Richard G. Saunders
International Mobile Machines Corporation

Philip T. Porter
Bell Communications Research

DIGITAL RADIO DISTRIBUTION PLAN
FOR PERSONAL COMMUNICATIONS

Philip T. Porter
District Manager
Radio Research Division

Bell Communications Research
331 Newman Springs Road
Red Bank, N. J. 07701-7020

ABSTRACT

A system plan for providing widespread personal radio communications for business and residential usage is described. The reasons behind various system choices are given, and research results leading to a feasibility study are summarized.

INTRODUCTION

The history of mobile communications dates to the beginning of radio. The earliest mobile usage was on ships (eg. the SOS from the Titanic), and one needed a platform the size of a ship to carry the equipment. We've come a long way since then:

— experimental vehicular public safety radio from the '20s,

— ship-to-shore telephone from the early '30s,

— the "walkie-talkie" of WWII,

— manual mobile telephone from 1946, and its successors -- automatic mobile telephone, paging, and air-ground -- from the '60s,

— finally, "cellular" and "cordless" phones of the '80s.

But this talk is not about the past; it's about the future. I want to describe for you the vision of the future of personal communications that we in Applied Research at Bellcore have, what we've been doing to try to make it happen, and what else has to fall into place first. Don Cox talked[1] here at NCF back in 1984 about the concepts I'll be describing; I will hope to bring you up-to-date on our recent activity.[2] This is an extremely active field, so I can't possibly cite all recent authors here and abroad. In addition to the references mentioned here, see the IEEE Vehicular Technology Conf., the Nordic Conf. on Digital Land Mobile Radio, Globecom, and others.

The first issue in any new service conception is WHY?. *One* reason is the public's apparently insatiable *demand* for freedom and mobility. Since their inception early in the '80s, cordless telephones, which only partially provide this freedom, have sold to the tune of several million per year and have passed cumulative sales of 25 million units; this happened without any real system plan or significant frequency allocation and with only minimal standards. Cellular telephone, designed with vehicles in mind, provides a much wider range of coverage, and although more expensive than "cordless", is well past its millionth customer in only 4+ years; it is blessed with basic standards of interworkability. Learning from both of these services, we can easily see that, with lower prices and attention to designing for public acceptance, we can have a major impact on how the average person will communicate and use a telephone in the next decade.

A *second* reason why we turn to radio is *cost*. The loop distribution plant of a typical telco looks like the diagram on the left of Figure 1. A customer wire pair fans out from the central office in a tree of smaller and smaller cross-section, via cable splices, culminating in the house wiring of a user. While the pair itself is incrementally inexpensive, the poles, buried ducts, cable splices, house wiring, etc. are a significant investment and a source of major maintenance activity and record-keeping. Contrast this with the right side of Figure 1, where the basic radio distribution portion of our new plan is shown. The final portions of the distribution plant -- distribution cable, drop wire, and house wiring, plus the per-user portion of the feeder plant -- are replaced by a single shared facility plus a Radio Port (ie. mini-base station). The electronics in the box labeled Radio Port is sophisticated, but is amenable to VLSI and is shared among many users. It is easily plausible that the net cost of this shared facility, including maintenance, is less than the per-user cost of individual cable pairs, especially for new housing developments and commercial buildings; areas where distribution has already been paid for, of course, are harder to justify solely on cost.

Given the two good reasons for radio distribution -- public demand and telco cost -- you may then ask *why not* use the cordless and vehicular systems already in place. Answer: (1) cordless telephone extensions, unfortunately, are not geared to the business world, they aren't private, they're useful only in areas of low demand, and they can't be used far from their own base units; however, since European and Japanese planners have national allocations available, as you will hear from other speakers, they are making progress to cure some of these shortcomings. (2) Vehicular systems have different attributes; they are well designed for outdoor usage but fall short in several respects for personal communications:

— indoor and outdoor usages don't mix efficiently in radio systems because of the handhelds' building penetration problems (20-30 dB more attenuation),

— vehicular and personal units have different power source capabilities (eg. battery capacity) and they also differ in antenna size and orientation,

— people with portables offer a lot more traffic (factor of 5),

— the calling methods, the type of modulation, and other aspects of the current vehicular system could be improved, using 1988 state-of-the-art advances.

— 850 MHz. cellular network ownership rules in the U. S. are not amenable to economical system integration with the PSTN/ISDN at the loop level.

Other services -- paging, call forwarding, etc. -- also offer to the user a degree of mobility not found in simple telephone service; however, they fall far short of giving the complete freedom found in 2-way real-time services.

FACTS OF LIFE -- PROPAGATION

Systems of the sort we're discussing would be very spectrally economical and easy to design if radio coverage[3] were well behaved. Unfortunately, that is not the case.

Attenuation: On the average, received radio signal strength falls off with distance from a transmitter roughly as $1/r^4$. However, there is a very wide statistical standard deviation (8 to 10 dB) of what we call this "local mean" (the signal averaged over a few square meters) about this average, such that (for example) the strongest 5% of the local mean signals

at 2500 meters are stronger than the weakest 5% at 500 meters. This variability is caused by the random shadowing of buildings, walls, and hills. Furthermore, the instantaneous signal strength fluctuates widely about the local mean because of the addition or cancellation of the many reflected paths with random phases of the received field; it can change by 20 to 30 dB (a factor of 100 to 1000) in the space of only a few centimeters. [Typically, one percent of the area within a square meter has signal strength 20 dB or more below the local mean.]

This latter variability (called Rayleigh fading) can conveniently be mitigated to a great extent by "antenna diversity" -- selecting the strongest of the signals from two or more antennas which are a few centimeters apart or which have different polarities. The variability caused by the larger "shadows" can be made tolerable by means of "handover". That is, a metropolitan area would be served by many Ports, and system logic would route the call through the best one, not necessarily the closest; if/when the user moves his location during a call, again system logic would see that the user's unit is tuned to the best radio Port. This is another form of antenna diversity.

Delay spread: In addition to random amounts of attenuation, the various components of the signal undergo random propagation time-delays[4]. This effect is analogous to acoustic echoes which distort the output of a public address system in a stadium. In a digital radio system, the result is "intersymbol interference", placing an upper limit on the symbol rate that the channel can support before successive symbols interfere with each other and increase the error rate. For low power systems with low antennas, this delay spread can be as much as 400-500 nanoseconds, dictating a lower limit of about 2 microseconds for the symbol period, without adaptive equalization.

Fortunately, the same diversity methods which help amplitude fading also help alleviate delay spread's effects. Equalization can also be effective, but it consumes extra power and can be costly using today's state-of-the-art.

FACTS OF LIFE -- OBJECTIVES

Over the years, customers have developed high expectations regarding wireline telephone service today, and future radio-based service must meet these if we want to see it accepted as a replacement for the known performance of wire loops. These customer-dictated goals are:

— high speech quality (low noise, delay, distortion, etc.)

— high reliability (availability in space and time, no calls cut off)

— privacy

— low monthly cost, comparable to customary wire-line rates

— public safety features (eg. 911 service)

— unobtrusive personal unit (light-weight and small, plus low cost)

— variety of special services, including data.

Furthermore, the FCC expects high spectrum efficiency, the community insists on environmental acceptability, and the vendors want a system design that lets them employ reasonable technology.

A SYSTEM PLAN

The basic concept is to replace the end of the wire loop with a radio link, as shown in Figure 1. A digital approach to transmission has been Bellcore's first priority, although a conventional analog, single-channel-per-carrier plan is not to be ruled out.

Services: The basic service clearly is speech transmission, both for the residence and the business markets. However, data services are also a "must", especially in the business sector. Concepts borrowed from ISDN can be used, including the goals of "capacity on demand" and "end-to-end digital connectivity"; other network-provided services are straight-forward.

Speech Coding: 16 kb/s speech coding has progressed to the point where it can seriously be considered; 8 kb/s coding is still in the research phase. The need for rates between 8 and 16 kb/s is not clear, since this would open up network incompatibility issues. Factors of importance are: basic quality, robustness to errors, cost, delay, and dc power drain. Within these qualitative constraints, Bellcore intends to keep an open mind as to which specific speech coding algorithm to choose; CCITT (Consultative Committee for International Telegraph and Telephone) is beginning to work on standards at 16 kb/s for a variety of uses.

Since the radio channel has a bursty character, it is inevitable that occasional intervals of speech will be lost. One important technique[5] to combat this loss is extrapolation from previous speech information. Clearly, this process must be applied carefully so as not to introduce distortion or noise that the brain will perceive. Furthermore, this technique cannot be successfully applied beyond 30-50 msec.

Data Transmission: Since data service does not have the real-time constraint of speech, yet has more stringent accuracy demands, the technique to be used to counter noise in a data message is that of Automatic Repeat Query (ARQ). Error-detecting coding must be used to detect when errors are made, and an ARQ message issued. Again, this topic has been studied in other contexts, and a variety of protocols are in use. Specific proposals for this service will be forthcoming.

Privacy: Since the user, especially the business sector, expects privacy to be at least as good as that of wireline service, link encryption of the radio channel is called for. Again, the factors of speech

quality, cost, delay, and dc power are major issues. Bellcore proposes that a record of each user's key be kept in a "Home" data base, along with the other basic information about a customer, to be sent on request to any area where a user may show up. At the transmitter/receiver, this pseudorandom key can be added to the radio link bit stream being used by the customer to encipher/decipher the information.

Channel coding: A large technical literature exists on channel coding topics. However, in a portable radio frequency-reuse context[6] where C/I is controlling and where noise arrives in infrequent but long bursts (for slow-moving personal units), channel coding must be used carefully. In general, for slow-moving personal units, because of the Rayleigh fading, either the channel is very good (hence coding is not needed) or very bad (hence coding is not effective). The system planner has the choice of using part of the frequency allocation either for coding redundancy or for more channel reuse distance. In most instances, error-detecting coding is more useful that error-correcting coding, under conditions of antenna diversity and slow Rayleigh fading; the bandwidth saved can be used to get more channel reuse distance (ie. more C/I). For some types of digital speech algorithms, it has been proposed to use forward error-correcting only for 25-35 of the more significant bits of the speech frame.

Multiplexing: The multiplexing of individual channels is proposed to be:

— down-link -- Time-Division Multiplex (TDM), similar in concept to that used in digital microwave or subscriber loop carrier.

— up-link -- Time-Division Multiple Access (TDMA), coordinated with the down-link TDM, ie. with a half-frame offset, as diagrammed in Figure 2.

Several of these wide-band TDM/TDMA channels would be deployed in a planned frequency-reuse pattern (FDM) similar to the state-of-the-art at 850 MHz.

Some of the reasons behind this choice are: flexibility to give "capacity on demand," simplicity of channel combining, no need for a diplexer in the portable unit, fewer total radios at the Port.

For a lab experiment[7], Bellcore uses a 16 msec. frame period, 450 kb/s, and 40 time slots per frame; two time slots are required to send 16 kb/s. Of course, these parameters can change as we gain experience. The error-detecting means is a (161,147) code.

Modulation: The chief features of our modulation technique are:

— coherent demodulation[8] is being given serious consideration, since it increases spectrum efficiency somewhat.

— Quadrature Amplitude Modulation is also used; while this requires linearity in the transmitter, this is not a large problem at the power levels being considered, it is easy to generate and to filter, and has a compact spectrum. Furthermore, its delay spread performance is very good. Bellcore workers have shown that higher-level modulations beyond 4 do not provide more channel capacity, under conditions of Rayleigh fading and co-channel interference.

Radio plan: Facts about the proposed radio plan are:

— Outdoor antennas mounted at reasonable height (about 30-40 feet) in order to remain acceptable to local residents. For coverage in larger buildings, indoor antennas evenly placed within the buildings or leaky feeders along hallways.

— High probability of good reception:

a. antenna diversity[9] against Rayleigh fading, both at the portable and at the Port.

b. true loop replacement requires a high probability of finding a good signal (>99%); this will result in a reuse distance somewhat larger than that of 850 MHz. vehicular service (which typically accepts 90%).

— the precise location of a possible allocation is not known. But since common-carrier mobile service has never been allocated spectrum above 1 GHz., a leap beyond about 3 GHz. is not felt to be feasible from propagation and from circuit design considerations.

— from field studies[10] in suburban areas, a Port spacing of at least 2000 feet (7 Ports or fewer per square mile) looks possible for coverage into homes from outdoor Ports. In-building[11] spacing of up to 200 feet looks reasonable, but is heavily dependent on building construction.

— 5-10 mw. average transmitter power (100-200 mw. peak) per channel, kept low to (a) conserve dc power drain (ie. small, lightweight), (b) stay far below any possible radiation hazard limits, (c) simplify circuit/component design (including use of convection-cooled Port equipment), and (d) generally increase reliability and repairability. A listing of tentative parameters (Up-link) is as follows:

Gains	
Portable peak power (5% powered on)	20 dBm
Net antenna gains	4 dB
Port rcvr. sensitivity	-(-107) dBm
Total radio link gain	131 dB

Losses	
Free space atten. (1500 feet)	94 dB
Excess atten. (1500 feet)	32 dB
Margins, with diversity	
-multipath	5 dB
-shadowing	10 dB
Total radio link loss	131 dB

Call processing: The intent is to make this loop replacement service as fully integrated with the PSTN/ISDN as possible, while at the same time introducing a personal quality to the service. The alerting signal must be some form of radio paging. A method under investigation has evolved from a service known as Directed Call Pickup, using SS7 common channel signaling. The user would be paged, via either (a) one of several conventional paging systems or (b) a special paging system designed for and co-located with the Ports. He/She may answer on either the conventional PSTN/ISDN, or a vehicular system, or the wireless personal portable system; if the latter is chosen, the set would be energized, identification would be automatic, and SS7 would transmit information between the originating and the answering central offices to set up the connection. Call Forwarding and Call Waiting are inherent features of this plan.

The proper beginning of a call (initial access[12]) is crucial to its overall quality, as is the related process of handing over control of a call to some other than the initial Port as conditions change. This supervisory task should be handled by the portable itself, to make comparisons easy, and can involve measurement of signal strength, modem eye opening, and/or error rate. Bellcore is in the process of studying a variety of algorithms and protocols suitable for the noisy radio environment of portable units, with the goal of optimizing performance while keeping system overhead low. Computer simulation of this process is the only way to understand what can happen, short of a full-scale field trial with a sizeable allocation, a wide coverage area, and many users.

On-going Call Supervision: As indicated in Figure 2, about 1200 b/s (ie. 19/0.016) are tentatively reserved for system control and supervision; this function includes on/off supervision, handover control, ARQ requests, etc. Detailed design of this important process will take place later in the system design cycle, with a goal of reducing this overhead.

FUTURE DIRECTIONS

In general, we believe that the feasibility of personal communications in this harsh environment has been demonstrated, as has the public's demand for communications freedom. What remains to be done is:

— find space for an allocation,

— set standards,

— design equipment,

— deploy the infrastructure.

This is a large, costly process. But it also can be made a gradual process, just as the evolution of the wired plant took place over decades and the growth of the 850 MHz. vehicular service over several years. Bellcore, its seven regional owners, and other U. S. entities need to work within both domestic and international standards organizations (CCIR, CCITT, ANSI, TIA, USTA, etc.) and with the FCC and all interested parties so that the U. S. public of the 21st century will have the communications freedom they want.

ACKNOWLEDGMENT

The system plan described here is a product of the experience and innovation of many people in Applied Research at Bellcore. Most of them are named in the reference listing; their contributions are appreciated. The support of Bellcore's seven owners is also gratefully acknowledged.

REFERENCES

1. D. C. Cox, "Universal Portable Radio Communications", *Proc. Nat. Comm. Forum*, Sept. 1984.

2. D. C. Cox, H. W. Arnold, and P. T. Porter, "Universal Digital Portable Communications: A System Perspective", *IEEE J. Sel. Areas in Comm.*, Vol. SAC-5, No. 5, June 1987.

3. D. C. Cox, "Universal digital portable radio communication," *Proc. IEEE*, April 1987.

4. D. M. J. Devasirvatham, "Multipath time delay jitter measurements at 850 MHz. in the portable radio environment", *IEEE J. Sel. Areas Comm.* SAC-5, No. 5, June 1987.

5. V. K. Varma, "Performance of sub-band and RPE coders in the portable radio environment", *Proc. Int'l Conf. on Land Mobile Radio*, Coventry, U. K., Dec. 1987.

6. L-F. Chang, "Block-coded modulation for digital radio communications system," *IEEE Int'l Conf. on Comm. '88*, Philadelphia, June 1988.

7. L-F. Chang and N. R. Sollenberger, "The use of cyclic block codes for synchronization recovery in a TDMA radio system," *3rd Nordic Seminar on Digital Land Mobile Radio Communication*, Copenhagen, Sept. 1988.

8. J. C-I. Chuang, "Comparison of coherent and differential detection of BPSK and QPSK in a quasi-static fading channel", *IEEE Int'l Conf. on Comm. '88*, p. 749-758, Philadelphia, June 1988.

9. A. Afrashteh and D. Chukurov, "Performance of a novel selection diversity technique in an experimental TDMA system for digital portable radio communication," *IEEE GLOBECOM'88*, Ft. Lauderdale, Dec. 1988 (to be published).

10. D. C. Cox, R. R. Murray, and A. W. Norris, "800 MHz. attenuation measurements in and around suburban houses, *Bell Labs Tech. J.*, July-Aug. 1984.

11. S. E. Alexander. "Characterising buildings for propagation at 900 MHz.", *Electronics Letters*, 28 Sept. 1983.

12. R. C. Bernhardt, "An improved algorithm for portable radio access," *38th IEEE Veh. Tech. Conf.*, Philadelphia, June 1988.

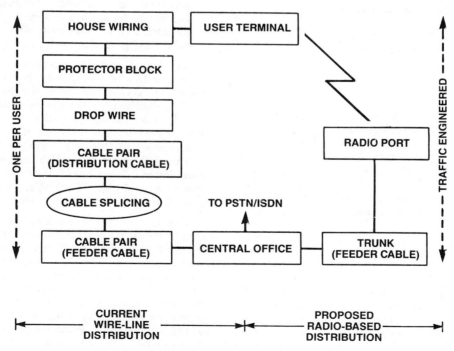

Figure 1. User Signal Distribution Plan

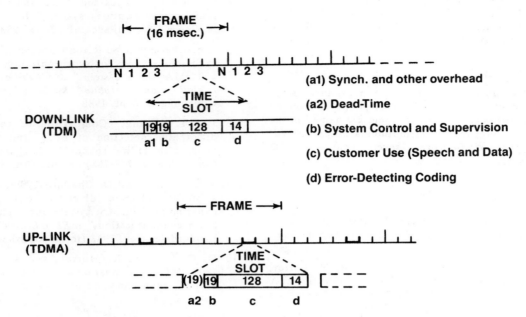

Figure 2. Experimental TDM/TDMA Format

EUROPEAN ADVANCES IN CORDLESS TELEPHONY

Dag Åkerberg
Manager Cordless Telephones and Paging
Radio Research Department

Ericsson Radio Systems AB
S-164 80 Stockholm, Sweden

ABSTRACT

CEPT has decided to base the new standard for European Digital Cordless Telecommunications, DECT, on Time Division Multiple Access/Time Division Duplex (TDMA/TDD), using frequencies in the 1.6 GHz band. This session discusses this effort and describes the radio link architecture of a TDMA/TDD pico-cellular cordless telephone system employing decentralized dynamic channel allocation and handover.

INTRODUCTION

Cordless telecommunications has only recently been recognized as a possible cost effective complement to mobile radiotelephony, and therefore as a potential market of tens of million units throughout Europe. In addition to the well known one base/one portable unit instrument intended mainly for use in homes, two other directions of applications are envisaged today:

- Pico-cellular systems in (large) industrial, office, leisure, construction, etc., sites, generally referred to as cordless PABXs or business cordless telecommunication (BCT) systems.

- Regional or national networks of cordless coinboxes to allow an owner of an appropriate portable unit to make calls without using ordinary callboxes, generally known as telepoint service.

Present day European analogue cordless telephones according to the CEPT T/R 24-03 standard (better known as "CT1") operate in the 900 MHz band and are intended mainly for use in residences. They do not provide enough capacity, security, quality or grade-of-service for BCT or telepoint applications. The capacity of "low-band" devices using a few pairs of channels in the 1.6 MHz and 47 MHz bands is even lower. "Low-band" instruments are in use in France and in the UK legally, and probably in all other European countries illegally.

During the last years, working parties in CEPT and among industrial organizations have made studies on the next generation of European cordless telephone systems(1). A future standard for cordless telecommunications must benefit from today's advances in digital technology, and considerable discussion arose about the way the radio channel should be accessed by different users. Two solutions were discussed: Frequency Division Multiple Access/Time Division Duplex (FDMA/TDD) and TDMA/TDD.

In January 1988 FCEPT/R decided to base the standard for medium and long term applications of advanced Digital European Cordless Telecommunications, DECT, on TDMA/TDD. FDMA and TDMA portables are supposed to be equal in cost, while TDMA can give better system features and lower fixed station costs.

The TDMA system will operate on a (low) number of radio carriers on frequencies common for Europe around 1.6-1.7 GHz. First products are expected on the market in early 1990's. (UK who proposed the FDMA/TDD system (6), and Sweden that proposed the TDMA/TDD system (2), will both implement their own system as a national interim solution in the 900 MHz band.)

This paper presents the status of the work in CEPT as well as properties of a TDMA/TDD pico cellular cordless telephone system concept. The concept has been proposed to CEPT by the Sweden PTT (2) and ESPA (European Manufacturers of Pocket Communication Systems) (3) as a basis for DECT. The possible applications range from PABX with wireless extensions, wireless PABX, wireless key systems and residential telephone systems to telepoints. See Fig. 1. Initial studies have been made on the 900 MHz band, but can with some care also be used to estimate the behavior on 1.6 GHz, where the main DECT allocation will be.

The market for business office systems is regarded as the most important. TDMA is very well suited for pico cellular office systems using decentralized dynamic channel allocation and hand over.

TOWARD A EUROPEAN DIGITAL CORDLESS TELECOMMUNICATIONS STANDARD

CEPT has recently been reorganized. The work is going on within the new RES (Radio Equipment Specification) Working Group 3, in close co-operation with manufacturers associations like ESPA and ECTEL.

Some of the requirements to be met are:

- Satisfy the needs for pico cellular office systems, basic cordless telephony and public telepoint access.

- Allow inexpensive technology to favor a large consumer market as well as a large professional market.

- Increased spectrum efficiency compared with the CEPT CT1.

- Duplex operation in one frequency band to ease frequency allocation and to avoid expensive duplex filters.

- Speech and flexible data services (ISDN compatible).

- Dynamic channel allocation in order to avoid traditional frequency planning and channel allocation.

The radio interface specification is suggested to consist of two levels. Level 1 is a mandatory minimum specification that assures co-existence on the same band of systems from different manufacturers. E.g., the frame cycle time must be common for all systems. This will allow freedom for private (business) systems to modify the air interface according to changes in needs, cost and technology as long as the co-existence is not adversely effected. E.g., introduce lower bit codecs, data services etc. Level 2 is on optional detailed air interface specification (speech service) for public use. A few adjacent 2 MHz bands can be allocated for private systems and a few bands for the larger public cells.

It is generally considered wise to have the two levels of specification. However, it was decided that basic parameters of the levels 2 specification shall be available at the time for release of the level 1 specification. This is to avoid the risk that manufacturers who make early level 1 developments, will have difficulties to later agree on the level 2 specification.

The following time table was set at the last RES-3 meeting in May 88:

- Sketch for level 2 air interface spec.   Spring '89
- Level 1 co-existence spec.   Spring '89
- Level 2 spec. air interface to permit telepoint services   Autumn '89
- Further optional level 2 spec.   Autumn '90
- Confirmation of the specification   Autumn '91

Start of development of private system is possible Spring '89.

SYSTEM DESCRIPTION

The system has 16 time duplex channels (time slots) on a 2 MHz wide frequency channel. For simplicity we describe the single carrier case. Fig. 2 shows an example of the TDMA frame and on the traffic slot. This frame allows the use of 32 kbps speech codecs. The fixed stations (FS) at each pico cell will be inexpensive, since one TDMA transceiver can communicate simultaneously on all channels.

Dynamic channel allocation

The channel (time slot) allocation is dynamic and decentralized to each pico cell and each portable. When a speech channel is wanted the portable communicates with the closest (strongest field strength) fixed station, FS, and they choose the channel with the least interference at the position of both the portable (PS) and of the FS. The PS identifies the strongest FS by reading the FS identification code in the S/ID part of each slot. Each FS is active at all times on at least one slot.

Since all the stations (also the portable at their positions) have continuous information of the status on all channels, the dynamic channel allocation can be made very efficient and fast. Also handover from one FS to another in the same office, can be made very efficient, fast and with no interruption of the speech. The portable can communicate with the old FS on one time slot, while building up the communication to the new FS on another slot.

The same speech channel (time slot) can be reused within the same office. The larger the office, the more cells, the more reuse and the higher the capacity. The range is C/I limited. Thus the capacity can be increased by installing the FS closer and closer.

It is not only possible to reuse the channels (slots) within a system. Different systems can use the same radio frequency channel, with no frequency planning.

Substantial signalling capacity in each slot

The preamble and the S/ID part of each slot make it possible for the FS and the PS to resynchronize and identify the transmitting station or receive a message from one single slot. This seems to be a key feature for good protection against time dispersion, for quick effective dynamic channel allocation with handover, for good power saving procedures for the portables and for effective control of the switched antenna diversity employed at the fixed stations.

Other features

The system performs very well with antenna diversity and needs no time dispersion equalization (8). The concept allows adjacent systems to co-exist without need for common frame synchronization, as long as the frame clocks are reasonably stable (7). Modest echo control is needed on each trunk to the PABX or PSTN if 2-wire connection is used. Full 4-wire connection needs no echo control (9, 10).

TRAFFIC CAPACITY

Simulations have been made for a pico cellular office system in a six storeyed modern building with a floor plan according to Fig. 3. 9 or 14 fixed stations (FS) per floor are placed as the x and o indicate.

The propagation model

Fig. 4 shows the propagation model used. The two curves indicate the space for a 20 dB shadow variation with even distribution. Rayleigh distribution is added. The model is derived from propagation measurements in the building made with the FS transmitter in the middle of corridors and the receiver in rooms along the corridor or along other corridors on the same storey and on other storeys. The model covers statistics from a line along a corridor as well as 45 degrees across the house on the same storey. The added isolation between the floors was in average at least 15 dB except for rooms that were located parallel across the open space between the houses. To compensate for that the added isolation between the floors was set to 10 dB. In the vertical direction all channels can be reused (at least in average) every three storeys. Thus the simulation is made for 3 storeys only.

Telephone density and traffic presumptions

Total traffic for 3 storeys: 100 E
Traffic per storey: 33.3 E
Telephones per storey (0.1 E per telephone): 333
Total area per storey: 4000 m^2
Telephone density: 1/12 m^2
Traffic density per 3 storeys: 12 500 E/km^2 (50% built)
The simulation is made for 10 E, 30 E, 70 E and 100 E, corresponding to 10%, 30%, 70%, or 100% of the telephones being wireless.
Call length: Average 100 sec. Exponential distribution
Call interval: Average 4 calls per tel and hour. Poisson distribution.

Radio characteristics

21 dB C/N corresponds to 89 dB attenuation in the propagation model, Fig. 4. Antenna diversity is used at the FS.

Test system

A small scale test system with 2 mobiles and up to 5 FS has been built. It is connected to a PABX and uses decentralized dynamic channel allocation with hand over, FS switched antenna diversity and no time dispersion equalizers. The system offers duplex speech service and functions very well.

Procedures

The procedures used are very similar to those we are testing in the test system. The portables are evenly distributed over the three floors. The portables are randomly selected for calls. For a call setup the portable chooses the strongest FS and then the channel is chosen that has the lowest field strength both at the FS and at the portable unit.

The interfering field strength to the portable is added up from all the FS that transmit on the chosen channel. The interfering field strength to the FS is added up from all portables (in their actual positions) that transmit on the chosen channel. The value of the field strength is calculated by deciding the distance between the receiver and the transmitter and for this distance taking a random attenuation sample within the 20 dB (shadowing) window of the propagation model. From this attenuation the average received field strength is derived. Two random samples of the Rayleigh distribution are added, and the best sample is chosen.

For a call setup C/I (or C/N) must be above 21 dB. There is then only 1% risk that a slowly moving portable receives less than 11 dB C/I. A call is terminated if C/I (C/N) is below 11 dB for more than 10 sec. For every new call setup and call termination, the C/I is recalculated for all active receivers, and if C/I is below 21 dB, a channel change and perhaps base change is initiated and if needed repeated.

In the table below blocked means that a call setup does not succeed, and interrupted means that an ongoing telephone call is forced by a new call setup to change channel, but does not succeed to find a new channel. Each of the 11 simulation runs contains 10,000 calls. Thus 0.01% corresponds to 1 call.

The number of channels is 16 or 32. For 32 channels 4 MHz is needed and each FS uses two 16 channel 2 MHz radios, 2 MHz separated. The portables can scan all 32 channels.

The traffic and the number of FS is for three storeys. The number of wireless telephones is ten times the traffic C.

Comments to the results in the Table

The simulation indicates that for one 16 channel system up to 30% of all telephones can be wireless, and that all can be wireless if a 32 channel system is used, when a 0.1 to 0.2% blocking limit is used.

The average number of used channels per FS station is derived by dividing the total traffic in E by the total number of FS stations. It is interesting to note that this average number is around 1 for the 16 channel system and 2 for the 32 channel system.

The 32 channel system is supposed to use two 16 slot radios on different carriers with 2 MHz spacing. Adjacent channel attenuation between the radios is estimated to be only 30-40 dB. Thus it is unlikely that the same slot can be used simultaneously on the two frequencies at the same FS. Runs 4b, 5b and 6b prohibit this use of the same slot at a FS, and show hardly any penalty. The reason is that on average only one slot is active per 16 shots. Thus transmission on the same slot can be inhibited by the system and no combiner is needed for the 32 channel case.

Runs not included in the Table show that 10 dB increase of the transmitter power increases the mean C/I, but has hardly any influence on blocked calls. This proves that the range is C/I limited.

The results of this simulation must not be generalized without care. At least the influence of close-by adjacent system has to be considered. Suppose that the building is surrounded on all three floors by adjacent systems, as in squares in Fig. 3. If all systems have their frames synchronized, the traffic capacity decrease due to adjacent systems is estimated to be no more than 5-25%. If the adjacent systems are non-synchronized the capacity decrease is estimated to be 10-30% (7). These figures must be verified by further simulations.

Later possible introduction of 16 kbps codecs will increase the capacity to 32 duplex channels per 2 MHz frequency channel.

It is reasonable to propose some 2 MHz channels for private residential and office use and a few adjacent 2 MHz channels for public telepoint use, totally about 10 MHz.

Comparison with an FDMA system

The results in the Table are also applicable to an FDMA system, but in this case each fixed station FS will need i complete radios and a combiner. See Fig. 5. If i is chosen to give no worse than 0.5% extra blocking per FS, than i equals the figures in the last column of the Table. Thus an FDMA system with a least 16 or 32 channels needs 3-5 times more FS radios than the TDMA system. A comparison between this TDMA system and a FDMA system has also been made by ECTEL (5).

CONCLUSIONS

CEPT and industrial organizations in Europe are currently specifying a medium and long term application of advanced digital cordless telecommunications. The application ranges from basic cordless telephones, pico- cellular office systems to Pan-European public telephone. Products are expected in the early 1990's, starting with private business office systems which are regarded as most important.

The specification will allow flexibility to develop private systems within the mandatory Level 1 specification (co-existence), as well as an optional (more detailed) Level 2 specification intended for public telepoint speech service.

The basic channel access principle will be multicarrier TDMA/TDD, allocated around 1.6-1.7 GHz.

It is very essential to avoid traditional frequency planning and channel allocation for individual (private) systems. The solution is Dynamic Channel Allocation, which avoids frequency planning for individual systems and permits system sales on a general (not individual) license.

From simulations and trials with a test system we have demonstrated the following:

- TDMA/TDD is well suited for speech and data pico-cellular office systems using decentralized dynamic channel allocation and fast handover, since one single radio can listen or communicate on all time slots simultaneously. This also gives inexpensive fixed stations (typical 4 times fewer radios than in a FDMA system) and avoids need for careful planning of the number of channels needed per fixed station.

- Dynamic channel allocation in combination with C/I-limited signal strength measurements, that ensure that each portable is connected to the closest fixed station, gives a stable frequency efficient system.

- Simple procedures ensure that the rate of interrupted calls is about 10 times below the grade of service for new calls.

- The system can temporarily assign more than one slot to a user if high data rate is needed.

- Simulations indicate that 6 to 10 MHz can provide densities of 30,000 E/km^2 or over 100,000 telephones/km^2 at 0.1-1% grade of service.

- Switched antenna diversity performs very well, in an environment with slow movements. No time dispersion equalization is needed.

- Slot synchronization between adjacent systems is desirable, but not necessary. The penalty is a graceful capacity reduction in the interference areas.

- Modest echo control is needed on each trunk to the fixed network, but only if 2-wire interconnection is used.

ACKNOWLEDGEMENT

The author would like to sincerely thank Mr. Bengt Stavenow who made the traffic simulation.

REFERENCES

1) H. Ochsner, "Cordless Telecommunications: Towards a Digital Standard." Eurocon '88. 8th European Conference on Electronics, Stockholm 1988.

2) Specification 8211-A130: Technical requirements for connection of digital cordless telephones to the public switched telephone network. Swedish Telecommunications Administration, Stockholm, Sweden.

3) ESPA. "Business Cordless Telephone." Publication No. 5.2, Sept. 1987. ESPA c/o Willems, Kapittelweg 10, NL-4827 HG Breda, The Netherlands.

4) D. Åkerberg, B. Persson, "A digital TDMA micro cell system for business cordless telephones." Report TY 86:1076. DMR II. Rev. C. Ericsson Radio Systems AB, S-164 80 Stockholm, Sweden.

5) ECTEL, "Report on business cordless telecommunication systems (BCT)." Doc. ECTEL/TCS 14/88. 11, Rue Hamelin, F-75783 Paris, Cedex 16, France.

6) BS 6833 - Parts 1 and 2 British Standard - Apparatus using cordless attachments (excluding cellular radio apparatus) for connection to analogue interfaces of public switched telephone networks. British Standards Institution, London, United Kingdom.

7) D. Åkerberg, "On time synchronization needs within and between TDMA systems." Report TY 87:2077. Ericsson Radio System AB, S-164 80 Stockholm, Sweden.

8) D. Åkerberg, "Tests of speech quality versus RMS delay spread for a digital TDMA cordless telephone system without use of time dispersion equalizers." Report TY 87:2091 Rev. B. Ericsson Radio Systems AB, S-164 80 Stockholm, Sweden.

9) D. Åkerberg, "Echo considerations in design of a BCT with a delay T." Report TY 86:2001 Rev. C. Ericsson Radio Systems AB, S-164 80 Stockholm, Sweden.

10) D. Åkerberg, "On echo control when a BCT with TMS inherent one way delay is connected via a satellite link." Report TY 87:2017. Ericsson Radio Systems AB, S-164 80 Stockholm, Sweden.

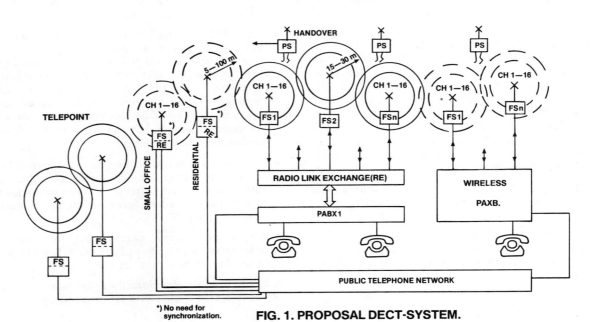

*) No need for synchronization.

FIG. 1. PROPOSAL DECT-SYSTEM.

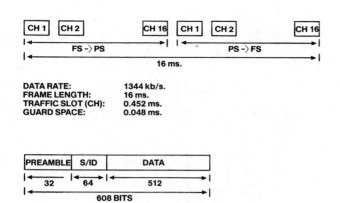

DATA RATE: 1344 kb/s.
FRAME LENGTH: 16 ms.
TRAFFIC SLOT (CH): 0.452 ms.
GUARD SPACE: 0.048 ms.

PREAMBLE	S/ID	DATA
32	64	512

608 BITS

PREAMBLE: Bit- and burst-synchronization.
S/ID: Signalling, FS-identification and quality monitoring.
DATA: Speech data.

FIG. 2. TDMA FRAME AND TRAFFIC SLOT.

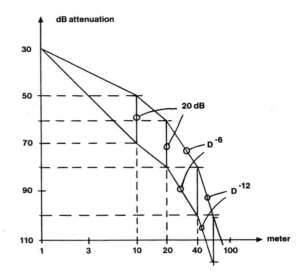

FIG. 4. THE PROPAGATION MODEL.

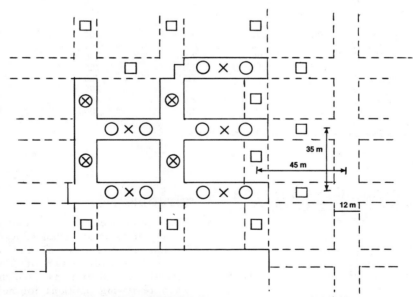

FIG. 3. FLOOR PLAN OF MODERN BUILDING WITH 6 STORIES.

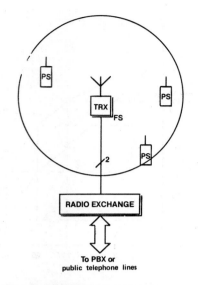 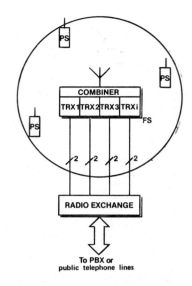

FIG. 5. SINGLE CELL TDMA
(max. 16 simultaneous channels)

SINGLE CELL FDMA
(max. i simultaneous channels)

Run no	No of chan.	Traffic % or E	C/I mean	No of FS	Blocked calls	Interrupted calls	Average no of used ch/FS	No of wireless telephones	No of channels per FS to give 0.5 % G.O.S.
1	16	10	53dB	27	-	-	0.4	100	3
2	16	30	42dB	27	1.4 %	0.25 %	1.1	300	5
2b	16	30		27	1.5 %	0.3 %	1.1	300	5
3	16	30	45dB	42	0.2 %	0.01 %	0.7	300	4
3b	16	30		42	0.2 %	0.02 %	0.7	300	4
4	32	70	45dB	27	0.7 %	0.04 %	2.6	700	8
4b	32	70		27	0.8 %	0.1 %	2.6	700	8
5	32	70	48dB	42	0.01 %	-	1.7	700	6
5b	32	70		42	-	-	1.7	700	6
6	32	100	46dB	42	0.1 %	0.01 %	2.4	1000	8
6b	32	100		42	0.1 %	-	2.4	1000	8

Table. Grade of service as function of traffic and other parameters.

NEW ALLOCATION CONSIDERATIONS FOR EXCHANGE TELECOMMUNICATIONS RADIO SERVICE

Katherine M. Falkenthal
Member of Technical Staff
Regulatory Research & Technical Analysis Division

Bell Communications Research
290 W. Mt. Pleasant Avenue, Room 2B233
Livingston, New Jersey 07039

ABSTRACT

This session describes considerations used by the Federal Communications Commission in determining the merits of allocating radio spectrum. It describes status of allocation proceedings such as Basic Exchange Telecommunications Radio Service (BETRS) and rural use of cellular mobile radio.

INTRODUCTION

This seminar deals with some of the "electropolitical" aspects of radio spectrum allocation. Specific topics include an overview of the rulemaking process followed by a discussion of "traditional" frequency allocation considerations used by the Commission when reviewing petitions for new allocations. This approach will then be compared with the Commission's new philosophy toward spectrum allocation and assignment known as the "flexible spectrum plan." It will include Basic Exchange Telecommunications Radio Service and rural use of Cellular Mobile Radio Service proceedings.

REGULATORY ASPECTS OF THE SPECTRUM ALLOCATION PROCESS

Although the Radio Act of 1912 was the first legislation dealing with domestic spectrum allocation issues, it wasn't until 1949 that the Federal Communications Commission established formal

1857

guidelines for the allocation of spectrum. In late 1944, the Commission initiated a rulemaking proceeding in Docket 6651 addressing the allocation of spectrum for the land mobile services. The Commission in its 1949 Report and Order established the traditional approach to spectrum allocation based on six guidelines or principles which are still in use today.

Because of the lack of available spectrum, it is necessary to understand how these six allocation principles are applied within the framework of the rulemaking process. Before the Commission would even consider the allocation of a new portion of spectrum or a reallocation of an existing frequency band, a great deal of effort is required to provide the appropriate information satisfying the six allocation principles. In addition, because of the short time frames for response in rulemaking proceedings, especially those concerning the politically sensitive subject of spectrum allocation, an understanding of the rulemaking process itself is important.

The Rulemaking Process

Since adoption of the Report and Order in Docket 6651, the allocation of spectrum for non-government use has been initiated by the establishedment of a rulemaking proceeding. A rulemaking proceeding may be instituted by either the Commission through a Notice of Inquiry (NOI), Notice of Proposed Rulemaking (NPRM), or by an applicant's Petition for Rulemaking requesting the allocation of frequencies for a particular radio service. Because of the Commission's obligation to determine the public interest in many cases it takes years to allocate the necessary spectrum.

Petition for Rulemaking (PRM)

The first step in a rulemaking proceeding involves the submission of a request to the Commission requesting an allocation and providing justification for its intended use. If the request appears unreasonable or inappropriate at the time, the Commission may dismiss the petition with a Memorandum Opinion and Order (MO&O), or it may decide that the intended use of the spectrum has some merit and therefore place the petition on public notice for comment.

The request is assigned a rulemaking (RM) number and placed on public notice; the public is then given 30 days to file comments either supporting or opposing the new allocation. Once comments have been filed, an additional 15-day period is allowed for the submission of reply comments.

The Commission then may continue the proceeding by adopting a Notice of Proposed Rulemaking, or it may terminate the proceeding.

Notice of Proposed Rulemaking (NPRM)

Based on its analysis of response to the RM the Commission may issue a Notice of Proposed Rulemaking (NPRM). Because the NPRM is in preparation for the adoption or modification of the Commission's rules, the issues addressed in the NPRM are usually more refined than those requiring response in the RM. As a result, participants should be in a position to provide detailed comments and data in response to the proposals. Because the NPRM affords the last official opportunity for public comment, some commenters may withhold information in the earlier phase for presentation at this time. Specific comment and reply comment due dates are established by the Commission.

Report and Order (R&O) or Memorandum Opinion and Order (MO&O)

The last stage of a rulemaking proceeding concerns the dismissal of the proposal via Memorandum Opinion and Order (MOO) or the adoption of the new rules via Report and Order (R&O). In most cases, when rules are established by an R&O, the new rules are adopted 30 days after publication in the Federal Register. Use of the Federal Register date is generally adhered to in cases where a new service is established or a significant portion of the spectrum is allocated or reallocated for a new use. There are exceptions, however, when the actual adoption date is stated in the R&O rather than basing adoption on the date of the Federal Register. Although the proceeding is terminated with publication in the Federal Register, the public is allowed a 30-day period to file Petitions for Reconsideration. As a last resort, the Court of Appeals could be asked to overrule any decision made by the Commission.

It should be noted that with the exception of the phase involving the Petition for Rulemaking, each of the phases listed above may require several iterations before completion. For example, a Second or Further NPRM may be released supplementing information presented in the earlier NPRM. Also of significance, but outside the normal rulemaking process, are other forms of involvement with the Commission and its staff. These lobbying efforts such as the use of ex parte presentations could significantly affect the outcome in a rulemaking proceeding.

Frequency Allocation Considerations

The 1949 R&O in Docket 6651 established the following list of allocation considerations which are used by the Commission to determine if a radio service merits the allocation of spectrum:

1. Whether radio is necessary or whether non-radio alternatives provide a practical substitute.

2. Whether the proposed radio service has social and economic benefit and, in particular, whether the service will be used for public safety purposes.

3. Whether many people would benefit from the proposed service.

4. Whether the proposed service is viable from a social, technical and economic standpoint.

5. Whether the requested frequencies are the most appropriate for the proposed service.

6. Whether existing users or the public, or both, would incur unacceptable costs in accommodating the new service.

Additional Technical Considerations

In addition to the six allocation principles detailed above, the Commission considers technical standards for the proposed service. The development of technical standards not only helps to determine the ideal place in the spectrum, but also allows for the orderly development of the service within the spectrum under consideration. In addition, the adoption of technical standards is a requisite for assuring compatibility with existing technologies. Areas requiring the development of technical standards include frequency limits, channel bandwidth, emission limits, frequency stability, modulation type, transmitted power, antenna characteristics, spectrum efficiency and the requirement for frequency coordination based on the potential for radio frequency interference.

THE COMMISSION'S NEW PHILOSOPHY CONCERNING SPECTRUM ALLOCATION

Over the past several years, the Commission's philosophy concerning the allocation of spectrum has undergone a radical change. Based on recent decisions in two different rulemaking proceedings, the Commission has implemented two separate allocation schemes which were developed to encourage the further sharing of spectrum. Neither is based on the traditional approach to spectrum allocation.

On September 9, 1983, the Commission adopted the First Report and Order in its proceeding addressing the use of certain bands between 947 MHz and 40 GHz. In its R&O, the Commission expanded eligibility in the 18 GHz band to include private users and others with requirements similar to common carriers, for whom the band had been allocated. Expanding use of the band to other licensees providing similar types of service was the Commission's first attempt at allocating spectrum on a "type of use" basis. Under a "type of use" scheme, spectrum is shared by licensees from different classes of radio service, i.e., Common Carrier, Cable, Private or Broadcast, which is different from the traditional approach where a specific portion of the spectrum is allocated on an exclusive basis by "class of user."

The Commission's second decision involves the allocation of spectrum based on the "flexible spectrum plan". Going a step further than the "type of use" scheme, flexible spectrum allocation principles have been adopted in the mobile radio services in frequency bands below 947 MHz.

Flexible Spectrum Allocation

On September 26, 1986, the Commission released a Report and Order in Docket 84-1231 allocating 2 MHz of spectrum in the 901-902 and 940-941 MHz bands for the General Purpose Mobile Radio Service (GPMRS). Known as the flexible spectrum plan, it allows licensees in these bands to be granted exclusive assignments which could be used to provide any type of mobile service using any type of technology. The flexible spectrum plan differs from the traditional approach to spectrum allocation in one major aspect. The allocation of frequencies under the flexible spectrum plan is based on the assumption that the spectrum is a commodity which has value in the marketplace and can, therefore, best be allocated by applying the law of supply and demand. Because of its value, the Commission asserts that the public interest would best be served by selling the rights for use of the spectrum. Once purchased through auction, the licensee could use the spectrum for any purpose including selling all or a portion of it to a third party. The only technical constraint is that objectionable interference not be caused to radio services using adjacent frequencies or, if assigned to different licensees on a geographical basis, that no objectionable co-channel interference result.

Although allocation of spectrum per the flexible spectrum plan might eliminate some of the roadblocks encountered under the traditional approach to allocation, it also presents problems for services requiring an exclusive nationwide allocation. The Commission recognizes the need for certain nationwide services as can be seen in its allocation of 6 MHz in the 821.0-824.0 and 866.0-869.0 MHz bands for public safety. Therefore, although generally supporting the use of flexible allocation principles, the Commission does still recognize the need for using the traditional approach, a point which should be kept in mind for many services.

STATUS OF RULEMAKING PROCEEDINGS

Basic Exchange Telecommunications Radio Service (CC Docket No. 86-495)

On January 19, 1988, the Commission released its R&O in the above proceeding. This was in response to a Petition for Rulemaking filed on May 9, 1986. The Commission established a new radio service known as the Basic Exchange Telecommunications Radio Service (BETRS) within the existing Rural Radio Service.

To accommodate BETRS the status of the Rural Radio Service was changed from secondary to co-primary with Public Land Mobile Radio Service in the 150 and 450 MHz bands. In addition, 50 private radio channels will now be available on a co-primary basis for BETRS outside major population centers.

The Commission also limited eligibility to state certified local exchange carriers and established bi-level interference standards.

On March 7, 1988 United States Telephone Association (USTA) and Pacific Bell and Nevada Bell filed Petitions for Reconsideration and Clarification of the Commission's Order. The petitioners requested the Commission to streamline the application approval process, to adopt a liberal waiver policy, and to make sure that frequencies were available when needed, especially in the 850 MHz range.

Liberalization of Technology and Auxiliary Service Offerings in the Cellular Radio Service

(CC Docket 87-390)

On October 15, 1987, the Commission released a NPRM in the above proceeding. In its NPRM, the Commission proposed relaxing current technical standards in the Domestic Public Cellular Radio Telecommunications Service (DPCRTS), for the purpose of introducing advanced cellular technologies and providing auxiliary services.

Referred to as the cellular radio service option, the Commission proposes special provisions which would remove restrictions on channeling schemes, types of emissions and modulations and certain other technical standards normally applied to cellular radio. In the Commission's view this would give cellular licensees more freedom to provide new technologies and services.

The Commission's action in this rulemaking proceeding is another example of implementing its philosophy concerning flexible use of the spectrum. As mentioned in its NPRM, technical and administrative rules have been relaxed for "the television auxiliary broadcast service, FM Subsidiary Communications Authority service, teletex service, private microwave service, General Purpose Mobile Radio service and Direct Broadcast Satellite service." By relaxing some of the technical standards for the DPCRTS, the Commission feels that new services can more easily be provided through the implementation of new technologies.

Perhaps the major issue in this proceeding is whether the development of technical standards inhibits or promotes the introduction of new technologies. In this instance, the Commission feels that new technologies might be implemented more readily in an unstructured environment, one open to full competition with few technical restraints. Although it is generally recognized that competition promotes innovation, standards may still be necessary and desirable, especially when considering the nature of the service provided and the potential for interfering with existing users.

ULTRAPHONE_R

WIRELESS DIGITAL LOOP CARRIER SYSTEM_TM

Richard G. Saunders
Senior Vice President
Engineering & Manufacturing Division

International Mobile Machines Corporation
100 North 10th Street
Philadelphia, PA 19103

BACKGROUND

The effort to develop an all digital, spectrum efficient communications system capable of providing service to subscribers in fixed, mobile and portable applications commenced in 1983. The technology in the system will support all three of these operational uses. In fact, the system has been tested in fixed, mobile and airborne applications. However, the primary initial application for the Ultraphone system is as a Wireless Digital Loop Carrier System (WDLCS) to provide local loop service for telephone company customers.

In December 1987, local loop telephony and the use of radio in the local loop received a real boost when the FCC issued the decision on Basic Exchange Telecommunications Radio Service (BETRS) and provided 94 channels for this application. IMM has been providing BETRS systems for over a year and a half supporting telephone operating companies in the United States and Canada.

SYSTEM ADVANTAGES

The Wireless Digital Loop Carrier System (WDLCS) is radio based and is designed to provide service comparable to cable as well as an alternative to cable in local loop applications. Radio in the loop offers several operational advantages for Telephone Operating Companies. Radio does not operate on a specified route, but provides the capability to meet customer needs on a area basis. It integrates well with other technologies and provides the unique capability to attack high cost difficult to reach areas. Changes in serving area requirements can be adapted to quickly and easily by modularly adjusting the equipment at a central location, thus reducing the need to oversize the system in anticipation of growth. Radio provides the capability to respond rapidly to unforeseen communications service requirements either in a permanent or temporary/emergency situation. Additionally, when service is no longer required, the equipment can be recovered and redeployed to provide support in other locations.

The system is tailor made to bypass difficult terrain features and other obstacles.

SYSTEM CONFIGURATION

The Ultraphone WDLCS consists of two major subsystems: the Network Station and the Subscriber Station. The Network Station consists of the Central Office Terminal (COT) and the Radio Carrier Station (RCS). The COT is located at the telephone Central Office and provides interconnect to the Public Switched Network. The RCS can be collocated with the Network Station or remoted by a T1 facility and placed in a location for good radio interconnect with the Subscriber Stations. Subscriber Stations are located at the customers' locations and consist of the transceiver unit, Power Supply and Antenna. The location of these subsystems and a comparison of a typical Subscriber carrier system architecture with that of the Ultraphone system is noted in Figure 1. Each system has a COT; each system has a remote terminal. However, in the case of the Ultraphone, the remote terminal or sub-terminal is the RCS. At this point, the difference between the two systems architecture is revealed. In the WDLCS loop, the connection to the Subscriber is made via spectrum efficient digital radio on an area basis.

CHARACTERISTICS & FEATURES

The Ultraphone 100 system is capable of operating on any of the 26 frequencies in the 454-459 MHz band and provides four voice circuits per frequency on a fully trunked basis. The system provides service up to 40 miles from the RCS location. The inherent ULtraphone 100 technology provides several key features. The most significant feature is the efficient use of the radio spectrum. The same digital technology also provides over-the-air privacy that does not exist in analog systems. The system provides transparent interface so that subscribers are unaware that digital radio is providing the transmission media. The system supports single line service and 300/1200 baud voice band modems.

NEW TECHNOLOGY

The technology embodied in Ultraphone comprises new technology developed and patented by IMM as well as older technology that has been combined in a unique way to provide the Ultraphone system. The spectral efficiency of the Ultraphone is achieved through the use of three principal technologies.

Digital speech compression to provide toll quality speech at a channel rate of less than 16 Kbps.

Time Division Multiple Access (TDMA) which subdivides the channel into four 16 Kbps slots.

Digital Multi-Level Differential Phase Shift Keying which enables the system to achieve a 64 Kbps channel rate within a 20 KHz occupied bandwidth.

The voice coding system converts analog voice signals to a 64 Kbps PCM format through the use of a standard codec. The output of the codec is fed into the system's Residual Excited Linear Predictive (RELP) transcoder which reduces the data rate to less than 16 Kbps. The addition of certain overhead and control bits raises the channel rate to 16 Kbps.

The use of TDMA subdivides the channel into time slots, thus providing up to four simultaneous 16 Kbps circuits on a single 64 Kbps radio channel. The system is capable of providing various combinations of conversations per channel ranging from 4 down to 2. The number of conversations per channel is determined by the modulation level used on a particular channel. At QPSK, two conversations per channel are possible. At a combination of QPSK and 16-DPSK, three conversations per channel are available and at 16-DPSK exclusively four conversations per channel are available. The modulation level is adjusted in response to path conditions to provide the desired reliability. Figure 2 summarizes the characteristics of the TDMA implementation.

Figure 3 depicts the TDM/TDMA system frame structure. The Network Station operates on a full duplex TDM basis whereas Subscriber Stations operate in a TDMA mode synchronized to the Network Station.

Analog radio in use today provides one conversation per radio channel. The digital multi-level phase shift keying technique used in Ultraphone is easily implemented in fixed and mobile, provides inherent security and provides 64 Kbps data in a 20 KHz occupied bandwidth. The dynamic adaptive multi-level DPSK was selected for system application due to its ease of implementation in a mobile scenario. As noted earlier the modulation level is dynamically adaptable to support a high grade of service under varying signal conditions.

The Ultraphone system concept is depicted in Figure 4. A single Ultraphone system consisting of one COT will support up to 570 lines. The system can be expanded by modularly adding COT and RCS equipment.

One of the circuits in the system is reserved for control purposes. This circuit is designated the Radio Control Channel (RCC). For example, a six RF channel system would provide 24 full period over the air trunks/circuits. One of these is reserved for control leaving 23 traffic circuits or trunks. All subscriber transceivers when idle are tuned to the RCC. If a subscriber goes off-hook a call request message is sent to the Network Station over the RCC initiating the call request sequence. If a channel is available, the Network Station assigns the subscriber to the channel frequency and time slot. The subscriber transceiver dynamically translates to the frequency and time slot where dial tone is returned to the subscriber premise equipment form the Class 5 switch. This call processing sequence is summarized in Figure 5. A similar process takes place for an incoming call to a subscriber.

APPLICATION

Application of the WDLCS fall into four principal areas.

> Providing service to areas that are uneconomical to serve utilizing standard wire and cable.
>
> Integrate with other facilities to support the planned upgrade of multi-party subscribers to single party.
>
> Support special services, events or emergency operations.

As of June 30, 1988, Ultraphone systems have been installed or are on order for twelve customers. Systems in support of BETRS have been operating for over two years. The systems in operation with the Federal Government have been modified to provide a transportable Network Station configuration. A certain number of these systems have also been modified to support the transmission of fully encrypted signals.

The successful implementation of an Ultraphone system to provide high quality service to telephone company subscribers is directly related to the quality and reliability of the equipment as well as the Telco planning. An important planning considerations is the number of subscribers to be initially served. The number of subscribers and the grade of service will determine the number of frequencies required to support the customer base. The terrain and location of the subscribers will determine the best location of the RCS for good area coverage. Growth can be dealt with in an incremental fashion and need not be expensed in the beginning. If growth is anticipated, it is only necessary to ensure that the Central Office and the facility housing the RCS have sufficient building space to add additional equipment.

To fully appreciate the flexibility and growth options offered by a WDLCS, consider the scenario depicted in Figure 6. Shown is a typical wire center in rural America. Initially the wire center had a requirement to serve unserved subscribers along the river in the upper portion of the figure designated by the black diamonds. A system was installed to support these users and sized to meet their needs. Subsequently, a requirement arose to upgrade multi-party wireline subscribers to single party subscribers as noted in the lower righthand portion of the figure represented by the black triangles. To support this requirement, it was merely necessary to add additional RF channels to the existing RCS and line cards to the COT. No additional outside plant construction was required. Again, new requirements developed to support a housing development in the center of the figure and a new factory on the righthand side of the figure represented by the black stars. Here again, it was

not necessary to install new cables or facilities in order to serve these new customers, but merely to add additional channel capacity to the existing Network Station and install the Subscriber Stations at the locations. A fourth situation is a bad feeder cable shown in the upper center portion of the figure. Here a number of subscribers represented by the black circles with white stars are without service. The telephone company is faced with the decision to replace the feeder cable or serve these subscribers with the existing WDLCS by merely installing additional Subscriber Stations and possibly adding channels if required. Thus, it can be seen that the initial installation of an Ultraphone WDLCS to serve unserved subscribers provided the capability as time progressed to serve additional subscribers under different conditions without the necessity to invest large sums in outside plant.

To gain a better appreciation of the Ultraphone system traffic handling capability, Figure 7 provides an indication of the number of RF channels required to serve subscribers under various load conditions. For example, a six RF channel Ultraphone system providing 23 traffic circuits will serve a community of approximately 130 subscribers with an offered load of 3.6 CCS and a .5% blocking.

STANDARDIZATION

Product standardization has historically been a long and tedious process within the Telephone Operating Companies. The Ultraphone 100 WDLCS standardization process was initiated in the second quarter of 1988 with analysis being performed by Bellcore under sponsorship of a Bell Operating Company. This analysis program consists of three phases:

> Phase I - Digital Loop Carrier Test
>
> Phase II - Voice Quality Analysis
>
> Phase III - RF Impairment

As of June 30, 1988, Phase I has been completed and Phase II is well under way with Phase III to be initiated in July 1988 for completion later in the year.

The difficulty associated with testing a new product such as the Ultraphone is that no generic requirement exists especially for this capability. In lieu of a generic requirement, Phase I testing was accomplished against the requirements of TR-TSY-000057, "Functional Criteria For Digital Loop Carrier Systems". IMM considers the results of the testing against this criteria very favorable and furthermore, these results have provided a significant input into the writers of the Generic Requirements Document. As a separate action, Bellcore has established and is chairing a committee to write a Generic Requirements Document for a Wireless Digital Loop Carrier System. Membership on this committee has been provided by five of the seven Regional Holding Companies. In advance of the Phase I field testing, IMM conducted extensive tests in its laboratories against TR-57 and provided that information to the Bellcore testers. The results of the field tests and analysis compared favorably with the tests conducted by IMM.

SUMMARY

The BETRS decision has clearly validated the market for a Wireless Digital Loop Carrier System and provided the spectrum resources necessary to support continued deployment and utilization by Telephone Operating Companies. The use of this technology clearly offers Telephone Operating Companies a reliable and cost effective alternative to the use of wire and cable in the local loop. IMM is pleased to have played a role in the development of this technology and providing this capability to the end user.

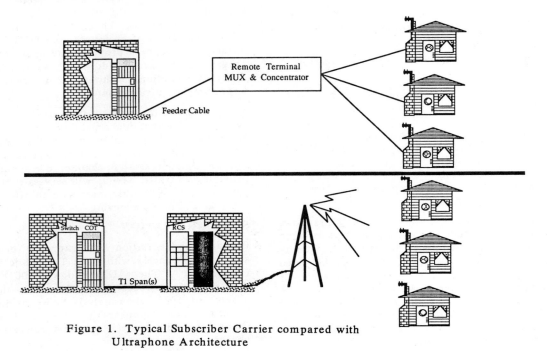

Figure 1. Typical Subscriber Carrier compared with Ultraphone Architecture

Network Station

- **TDM Transmission on Lower Frequency of Full Duplex Pair**
- **Channel Divided Into Time Slots**
- **Frame Length Equals Constant Number of Symbols**
- **Number of Slots Within Frame Dependent on Modulation Level**

    QPSK = 2 Slots/Frame

    16-DPSK = 4 Slots/Frame

- **TDMA Reception of Subscribers**

Subscriber

- **Transmission on Upper Frequency of Duplex Pair**
- **Reception and Transmission Slots Offset in Time**
    (Allows Full Duplex Operation w/o Duplexer)

Figure 2. Time Division Multiple Access Characteristics

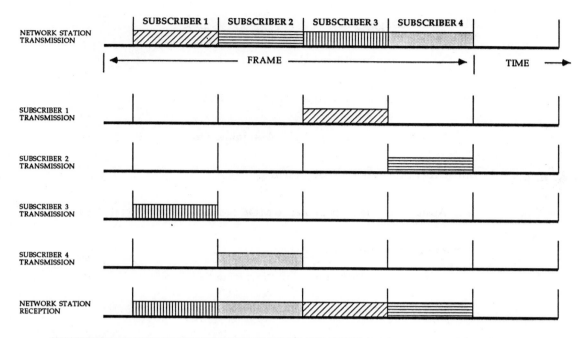

SUBSCRIBERS ARE SYNCHRONIZED TO THE FRAME TIMING SIGNALS FROM THE NETWORK STATION

Figure 3. TDMA Frame Structure

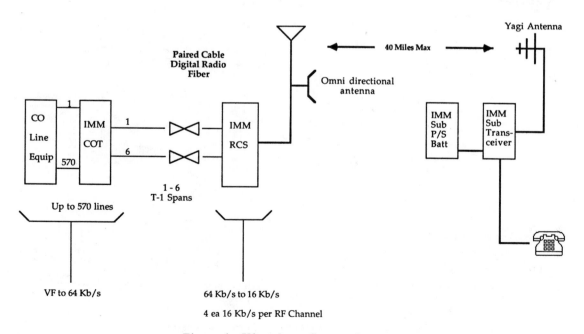

Figure 4. Ultraphone System Concept

Call Processing Sequence:

All Subscribers Tuned to RCC

Off-Hook Sends A Call Request to N.S. via RCC

N.S. Assigns A Frequency and Slot Assignment to Sub via RCC

Subscriber Moves to Its Assignment

N.S. Assigns A Line Appearance to MDF

Communication Link is Established

Figure 5. Ultraphone Call Processing Sequence

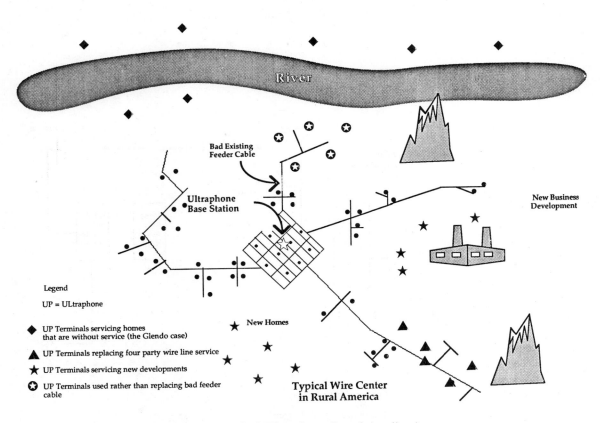

Figure 6. Typical Ultraphone Rural Applications

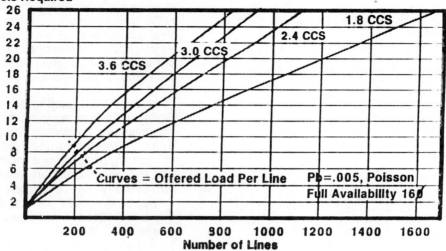

Figure 7. Ultraphone 100 Traffic Capacity

CEL-04

MICROWAVE RADIO ADAPTS TO CHANGES

Alan C. Walker - Chairperson

Director, Government & Industrial Relations

HARRIS CORPORATION
FARINON DIVISION
1691 Bayport Avenue
San Carlos, CA   94070

ABSTRACT

Advancing technology impacts the role that microwave radio plays in our communications networks. There are fields where the solutions available favor microwave radio. More sophisticated designs involve higher order modulation, automatic power control and its affect on frequency coordination. Angular diversity and transversal equalizers provide additional options to frequency or space diversity. RF repeaters provide other options in ranges from 900 MHz to 18 GHz. This seminar reviews these topics as employed in the telecommunications environment.

Paul A. Kennard   Radio Design Group
                              Bell Northern Research

Craig M. Skarpiak   Design Engineer
                              Andrew Corporation

Richard U. Laine   Systems Engineering
                          Harris Corp./Farinon Div.

Edward R. Johnson   Peninsula Engineering
                                         Group

FORWARD ERROR CORRECTION FOR
HIGH CAPACITY DIGITAL MICROWAVE
RADIO

P.A. KENNARD, J.D. MCNICOL
P.J. STOOP

BNR
P.O. BOX 3511, Station C
Ottawa, Ontario, Canada
K1Y 4H7

ABSTRACT

This paper describes the role of forward error correction (FEC) in 64 QAM digital radio transmitting in excess of 135 Mb/s. The application of FEC has resulted in enhanced performance monitoring capabilities and the ability to correct background bit errors.

Choice of FEC coding for high capacity digital radio is a complex process. Factors that influence code selection include coding gain, implementation considerations, efficiency, performance monitoring, delay and the behavior when faced by amplifier non-linearity and multipath fading. The merits of the most popular form of codes will be discussed with respect to these issues. FEC is considered to be an essential ingredient of future systems employing higher order modulations.

INTRODUCTION

This paper discusses the choice of Forward Error Correction (FEC) for use with 64 QAM digital radio. There are many types of FEC codes to choose from and there are many factors that influence this choice. The proper choice will lead to a system that has enhanced performance, can facilitate maintenance, and has improved monitoring capabilities.

The last several years have seen a large increase in the installation of 64 QAM digital microwave radio. This established base had proved the reliability of this high capacity product.

While it has been shown [1] that FEC is not required to achieve error-free operation (Bit Error Ratio < 10^{-13}) in 64 QAM digital radio, FEC can provide significant operational advantages.

FEC provides the operator additional margin against equipment degradation or misalignment. For modest impairments, errors can be detected and corrected and maintenance action completed without errors becoming visible to the customer.

Similarly, FEC enhances frequency diversity protection switching; often allowing switch transfer before the onset of DS-3 errors.

This paper discusses the issues related to the choice of FEC for 64 QAM radio. There are many types of FEC codes, each with differing performance and implementation considerations. The principle factors in the choice are performance, overhead (efficiency), complexity and delay.

Proper choice of these parameters will produce coding gain (enhanced performance) and increased robustness to normal system degradations such as equipment imperfections. Background bit errors will be effectively eliminated through the use of FEC coding.

FEC CODING

Forward error correction coding is a means of identifying and correcting errors due to the transmission medium without retransmission from the source. This is done through the use of redundancy which is added at the transmitter and removed at the receiver. This redundancy takes the form of parity bits that are added to the data. These parity bits allow a FEC decoder to identify and correct errors. These overhead bits require that the bit rate be increased.

In high capacity digital radio it is important that the overhead be kept to a low value (<5%). Increased overhead adversely affects filtering, adjacent channel interference and ability to meet the FCC mask.

There are two main types of codes: block codes and convolutional codes.

Block coding simply divides data up into fixed length blocks, appends the parity of that block to the end of the block and sends the block out. Successive blocks are treated identically with parity bits being derived from each block. At the receiver, the received block is processed in such a way that errors are identified and corrected up to the error correction ability of the code. If this ability is exceeded, the errored block continues through uncorrected and one or two extra errors may be added.

On the other hand, convolutional coding does not process the data in discrete blocks. Memory in the encoder and decoder retains information from previous symbols to help perform the error correction. Redundant bits are added to the data stream at the transmitter. The receiver processes incoming data along with previous data to determine whether errors exist. When an uncorrectable error pattern is received, there is a potential for a burst of errors.

The main cost of FEC is the expansion of the bit rate. This widens the signal spectrum and either adds more power to the adjacent channels or forces the filter roll-off factor to be reduced. Another factor to be considered is the time delay required to decode the received blocks. For a block code, this delay is roughly equal to one block. For a convolutional code, the delay is a function of the type of decoding procedure. The delay per hop should be held to an acceptable level such as 10 to 20% of the free space propagation delay of one radio hop.

The extra hardware and power required for FEC coding must be assessed. For codes operating in parallel at the symbol rate (20-30 MBaud) and implemented in CMOS LSI, there is minimal penalty. But codes operating serially at rates of 135 MB/s can have cost and power penalties, as they demand the use of ECL higher power technology.

Many of the general codes can be tailored to fit a certain need. Block lengths can be shortened to accomodate various data formats. This flexibility is important when considering future modulation schemes and data formats.

Each type of block code (such as BCH codes), has a defined error correction ability. This is simply the number of correctable errors per block, such as single error correction and double error correction. Once this is chosen, the overhead required and the block length become mathematically related. The normal trade off is a lower overhead for a longer block length. A doubling of the block length approximately halves the overhead percentage. but due to the fixed error correction ability in a doubled length, the performance will degrade. This exemplifies the trade-offs inherent in the choice of a particular code.

To see the full effect of FEC on BER performance, the ideal curve of BER vs SNR is normally used. See Figure 1. For all BERs better than 10^{-3}, the BER is improved dramatically. Single error correction will remove all single errors, and therefore two errors per block will dominate performance. Therefore the corrected curve will have a slope twice as steep as the uncorrected case. Double error correction will correct singles and doubles, so the corrected BER curve will have triple the uncoded slope. Due to this sharpening of the curve, there is a dramatic improvement in the residual BER after error correction.

BCH CODING

One important type of block code is the BCH (Bose-Chaudhuri-Hocquenghem) code. This is a random error correcting code that is very flexible, has low overhead and is straight-forward to implement at high speeds. It is usually implemented in single and double error correction. It is normally transparent to phase inversion, and is systematic, meaning that the data bits are uncoded (unchanged). Parity checks on various combinations of the data are added as redundancy [2].

At the BCH decoder, each block is re-encoded. This resulting parity word is used to determine error locations. This re-encoding requires the whole block, therefore there is a one block delay. The remaining algebraic processing takes several symbols, and then the block is corrected serially as it leaves the decoder.

This coding can be done independently in parallel on each modem bit line at the symbol rate or on the data lines after serial-to-parallel conversion from the DS-3 rate. Both of these methods work very well. The flexibility of BCH coding imposes minimal constraints on data formats and modulation choices.

The algorithm for double error correction (DEC) is relatively simple. For DEC twice the number of parity bits are needed than for SEC. For a fixed data block this would require twice the percentage overhead. The remedy is to double the block length. This gives approximately the same overhead, but with a much superior performance in all respects. The choice

for each case is the BCH (255, 247) SEC code with 3.2% overhead, and BCH (511, 493) DEC with 3.6% overhead. In the case of DEC, 493 data bits on a bit line are appended with 18 parity bits to form 511 bit blocks. This block is integral to the system framing format. At the receiver, one or two errors in each 511 bit block will be corrected, independent of the error locations.

CONVOLUTIONAL CODING

A second important type of coding is convolutional coding. As stated earlier, the data is not treated independently in block, but in a continuous fashion. Decoding can be done in a classic soft decision Viterbi decoder or in simpler decoders. The Viterbi decoder is extremely complex to implement and any simpler decoder has a poorer performance than with Viterbi decoding.

For a code with a lower overhead (4%) the decoder delay is large (3000 bits). Therefore to realize an acceptable time delay, this code must be implemented on serial data such as 135 Mb/s. This is a moderate concern for cost and complexity. For the same overhead as a BCH code, a convolutional code with a Viterbi equalizer gives identical coding gain at 10^{-3} BER, but requires at least ten times as much hardware to implement. A simpler decoder at 135 Mb/s has an inferior performance to BCH. Therefore in most respects BCH is superior to convolutional coding.

One example of a convolutional code suitable for 135 Mb/s implementation is the (19,18) double error correcting code [3].

SYMBOL CODES

Symbol codes are a non-binary type of block code. A binary code uses a signal set of 0 and 1. A symbol code processes multiple bit lines together into a non-binary symbol. For 64 QAM each symbol is composed of six bits. An errored six bit symbol is corrected independent of whether only one of the bits is in error, or all six. An advantage of symbol codes is that for the same block length, the required overhead usually decreases. The best known type is the Reed-Solomon symbol code.

In a Gray-coded system where a constellation symbol error usually generates only one or two errors, the advantage of being able to correct all six bits is lost. Therefore there is no advantage to these codes. In terms of BER peformance they are slightly inferior to BCH binary codes.

All of the above decoders operate to minimize an error function called the Hamming distance. This is one way of specifying the distance between two valid coded sequences. Another function, called the Lee distance, or Lee metric, minimizes in a slightly different fashion. These Lee Metric symbol codes are more inflexible than BCH codes.

Single error correcting Lee Metric codes have been implemented [4]. Double error correcting Lee Metric codes do not extend in a simple fashion such as in BCH coding. The inflexibility of these codes makes them somewhat undesirable. Codes with similar overheads to BCH DEC give slightly inferior residual BER performance in a thermal noise channel due to the fact they are only single error correcting codes.

BER PERFORMANCE

The use of FEC improves the BER over uncoded system. This allows a FEC-coded system to operate at a lower signal-to-noise ratio (SNR) for a particular BER. This improvement in SNR is defined as the coding gain. The coding gain at 10^{-3} BER is of some importance since the system gain is measured at 10^{-3} BER. Curves of BER versus SNR show that the coding gain increases as the BER improves. See Figure 2. It is also evident that FEC improves the residual BER.

There are two important types of distortion to which a system is exposed. There is linear distortion such as inter-symbol interference (ISI) caused by non-ideal filtering, and non-linear distortion normally caused by the power amplifier.

Linear distortions can be hardware imperfections in filters and equalizers, or channel imperfections such as multipath fading. The effect of linear distortion is similar to the effect of additive white gaussian noise (AWGN). Fading will produce this thermal noise. Therefore testing in a thermal noise environment is a standard method of characterizing the effects of linear distortion.

Non-linear distortion is introduced by the amplifier. In practice the power amplifier is pre-distorted to compensate for this, however time and temperature drifts may produce some residual non-linearity. The proper choice of FEC can help mitigate the effects of this residual non-linearity.

EFFECTS OF LINEAR DISTORTION

The effect of linear distortion is measured by the addition of thermal noise which produces randomly-occuring errors. All of the candidate codes are random error correcting codes, meaning they perform best in this environment. For the BCH (511,493) DEC code the ideal relation between the raw BER (p) and the corrected BER is

$$BER (FEC) = 2 \times 10^5 p^3 \qquad (1)$$

This is closely met in a linear channel with AWGN.

Normally the length of the code influences the coding gain at 10^{-3} BER. Shorter codes have good coding gain at 10^{-3} BER. Double error correction will have a steeper curve than single error correction, meaning the residual BER will be better.

Several codes which are being used, or are proposed for microwave radio are presented. The improvement on an ideal curve of BER versus SNR is shown for each code. The distance (in dB) between the ideal curve and each FEC curve is the coding gain at a specific BER. This is measured in a AWGN channel.

The codes that are compared are the convolutional (19, 18) DEC code [3], the single Lee error correcting (72, 70) symbol code [4], BCH (498, 488) SEC code [5] and the BCH (511, 493) DEC code [2].

It can be seen that the shorter block length codes have a slight advantage in the region of 10^{-3}. As the BER improves the extra correction ability of the DEC codes becomes evident and these codes give a much steeper curve and a better residual BER. The BCH DEC code has the same performance as the (19, 18) convolutional code, with a much lower overhead.

Multipath fading is a linear distortion that causes ISI and eye closure. This ISI has the same effect on FEC as AWGN. The tolerance of the equipment to multipath fading is described by the equipment signature [6]. FEC improves the signature. See Figure 3 for an example of a signature with and without FEC.

EFFECTS OF NON-LINEAR DISTORTION

Non-linear distortion introduced by the power amplifier can never be fully removed. Due to time and temperature drifts, or pre-distortion misalignment, a residual non-linearity will be present. FEC performance under these conditions is a real maintenance concern.

In general non-linear distortion causes some correlation between errors, so they no longer appear randomly in time. This slightly bursty error generation degrades random error correcting codes. In simple terms, multiple errors per block appear more frequently than in a AWGN channel. This severely degrades the performance of all single error correcting codes. Even moderate amounts of non-linear distortion reduce the coding gain of SEC to virtually zero.

For double error correcting codes, this effect is not as severe. Almost all of the theoretical coding gain can be achieved in moderately non-linear conditions. Coding gain is reduced significantly only in severely non-linear conditions.

Our measurement has shown DEC to be superior to SEC under non-linear conditions. This is shown in Figure 4, which is a plot of the ideal and measured performance of BCH DEC and BCH SEC.

PERFORMANCE MONITORING

FEC has the advantage that when correction is taking place, an indication is available which can be used as a monitor. In this way, a degraded channel (or equipment degradation) can be detected before the onset of bit errors. In this case counter measures such as protection switching can be taken.

In particular, DEC gives a good indication of degrading conditions before the errors are propagated through the system. An uncorrected BER of 10^{-6} is corrected to 10^{-13} by the BCH DEC code. This BER can be detected very quickly (1 second) while the corrected BER is still error-free. This gives potential for error-free protection switching.

This sensitive performance monitoring can also be used to detect the need for equipment maintenance, while still holding the BER to an acceptable level.

IMPLEMENTATION CONSIDERATIONS

The design complexity of each of the above FEC codes is discussed here. The choice of whether each code is implemented on serial or parallel data is examined.

The Lee single error correcting symbol code is a relatively complex code. This is implemented with one codec per I and Q axis at the symbol rate, therefore it can be manufactured in low cost CMOS VLSI.

Convolutional codes could be implemented either at the symbol rate, or at the serial bit rate. But due to delay considerations a simple decoder will have a long delay, and therefore serial implementation must be used. This requires the use of high speed logic such as ECL. This is costly and requires more power and space. On the other hand, the decoder delay can be eliminated through the use of a Viterbi decoder, but this is a very complex and expensive alternative.

BCH SEC codes have a very simple decoding procedure. DEC is slightly more complex. They give the best performance when implemented at the symbol rate. This can be easily done in low cost CMOS.

HIGHER ORDER SYSTEMS

The use of higher modulation levels will emphasize the need for FEC. The uncorrected residual BER will be poorer, and FEC will be needed to correct this. To attain maximum channel utilization, the filter roll-offs will be decreased. This tight packing of the signal spectrum into the channel will make the need for a low overhead FEC code more apparent.

As system bit rates increase, the use of serial FEC will become less desirable compared to parallel implementations.

Due to system gain requirements a higher power output will be required. Due to D.C. power and cost constraints, attempts will be made to operate nearer to the saturation point of the power amplifier. This will increase the possiblity of non-linear distortion.

SEC is felt to be inadequate in the presence of non-linearities. The residual BER of DEC is also superior to SEC. Therefore a low overhead double error-correcting BCH in a parallel implementation is felt to be a good choice for higher order modulation systems.

CONCLUSIONS

Due to system constraints such as overhead, complexity and decoder delay, BCH double error-correcting codes are a good choice for high spectral efficiency radio systems.

BCH DEC has the capability to give some coding gain at 10^{-3} BER and also maintain a good residual BER. Double error correction is superior to single error correction under non-linear conditions. The performance monitoring capabilities are suitable for monitoring and maintenance procedures consistent with the next generation of high capacity digital radio.

REFERENCES

[1] J.D. McNicol et al., Design and Application of the RD-4A and RD-6A 64 QAM Digital Radio Systems, ICC 1984.

[2] W. Peterson and E. Weldon, Error-Correctiong Codes, MIT Press, 1971.

[3] G.D. Martin, Implementation of Nondifferential Coding in QAM Digital Radio Systems with FEC, Globecom 1986.

[4] Y. Yoshida et al., 6 GHz 140 MBPS Digital Radio Repeater with 256 QAM Modulation, ICC 1986.

[5] H. Nakamura et al., A 256 QAM Digital Radio System with a Low Rolloff Factor of 20% for Attaining 6.75 BPS/Hz, Trans. of IEICE, Jan. 1988

[6] P.A. Kennard et al., Fading Dynamics in High Spectral Efficiency Digital Radio, ICC 1986.

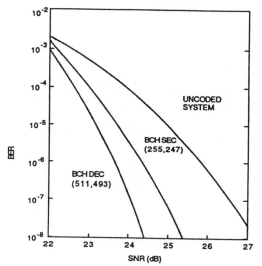

FIGURE 1 - BER Performance of FEC

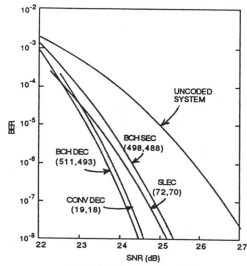

FIGURE 2 - Comparison of FEC Codes

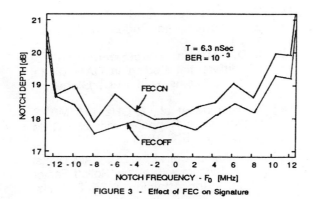

FIGURE 3 - Effect of FEC on Signature

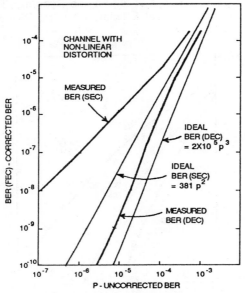

FIGURE 4 - Effects of Non-linear Distortion

ANGLE DIVERSITY ANTENNAS

Craig M. Skarpiak
Antenna Design Engineer

Andrew Corporation
10500 W. 153rd Street
Orland Park, Illinois 60462

Abstract

As digital radio evolves to levels of higher order modulation, the implementation of a effective countermeasure to protect against deep dispersive fading caused by multipath propagation becomes more imperative. Traditionally, this protection has been realized by the utlization of multiple antennas in a space diversity configuration supplemented by time or frequency domain adaptive equalization. However, in digital environments where space diversity could not be implemented due to tower wind loading, spatial or economic constraints, system bit-error-rate performance may have suffered from the lack of protection against multi-

path fading. Angle diversity techniques via a single aperture dual beam antenna allows diversity protection to be realized in these situations. For this reason, the understanding and integration of single aperture angle diversity antennas has become important in the terrestrial microwave communications community. The basic mechanism behind angle diversity will be reviewed with emphasis directed towards the design and implementation parameters for dual beam angle diversity antennas.

INTRODUCTION

The bit-error-rate (BER) performance of digital line-of-sight terrestrial microwave links can be severely impaired by multipath propagation. Multipath reflections are produced by terrain scattering, diffraction from objects along the path or when horizontally stratified atmospheric layers create discontinuities in the gradient of the refractive index. If these multipath rays arrive at the antenna with the correct amplitude relationship and out of phase with the direct ray, the resultant will be a deep frequency selective dispersive fade.

As higher order modulation techniques and increased channel loading are implemented in long and short haul digital microwave systems, an effective countermeasure against frequency selective fading becomes necessary. Space diversity has been the most common countermeasure used by the terrestrial community. During fading conditions, space diversity, which utlizies two antennas with large vertical separation, allows for amplitude and phase decorrelation of the direct and indirect rays incident at one of the antennas. However, in situations where space diversity either produces insufficient protection or implementation has not been possible, system designers have yearned for a new technique.

It has been shown that angle diversity implementation by the use of dissimilar aperture antennas [1], small antenna vertical offset angles [2,3], and dual beam antennas [4] produces significant diversity improvement for digital radio. Recent measurements of BER performance on high capacity 135 Mb/s 64 QAM digital radio links [4,5,6] incorporating dual beam antennas have reported improvement factors in the order of 1000 as compared to an unprotected system. The inherent economic and physical advantages associated with the dual beam antenna approach to angle diversity has stimulated substantial interest in this technique.

BASIC THEORY OF ANGLE DIVERSITY

In digital radio systems, the In Band Power Difference (IBPD) has been used as a measure of system performance. The IBPD is a measure of the difference in signal amplitude over the channel bandwidth and represents the dispersion within that channel. During normal non-fading conditions, the IBPD is small. However, during a frequency selective fade (notch fade), under conditions when the direct and indirect rays arrive with equal amplitudes and in antiphase, the IBPD within a channel can significantly increase. Diversity allows for the facility of "switching" to a secondary antenna port which exhibits significantly reduced IBPD during periods when the primary port is experiencing maximum IBPD.

Space diversity utilizes large vertical spacing between receive antennas to decorrelate the components of the fading signal by modifying the phase term of the relationship between the direct and indirect rays. This is accomplished by changing the relative path length of the two rays at the secondary antenna by a fraction of a wavelength, sufficient to avoid a deep fade. Typically, this delay is at least 1/8 wavelength and ideally 1/2 wavelength. Figure 1 shows the space diversity configuration.

By contrast, angle diversity relies upon the ability of the secondary beam to modify the amplitude terms (and possibility the phase terms) of the relationship between the direct and indirect rays. The difference in the vertical directive gain (radiation characteristic) of the secondary beam relative to the primary beam in the direction of the two incident rays is the fade decorrelation mechanism.

To quantify the diversity characteristics of an angle diversity configuration, E.H. Lin et. al. [4] introduced the concept of the Discrimination Ratio. This ratio considers the difference in elevation radiation characteristics at discrete angles of arrival of the direct and indirect rays as shown in figure 2. The ratio is defined as:

$$d = | (A1/B1) / (A2/B2) | \qquad (1)$$

where :
A1, A2, B1, B2 are functions of the antenna radiation pattern and the incident elevation angle for the direct and indirect rays, r1 and r2.

In decibel notation :

$$D = | 20 \times \log_{10}(d) | \qquad (2)$$

The Discrimination Ratio is a useful quantity which characterizes the diversity action of a particular angle diversity configuration. As the discrimination ratio becomes greater in magnitude, the system becomes less sensitive to selective fading. However, because of the simplistic nature of this ratio, some deficiencies exist:

• The ratio only considers the relative change in amplitude and does not consider the relative change in phase due to the antenna pattern.

• The ratio only considers the improvement in IBPD of the system and not the possible amplitude change of the received signal by switching to the secondary port.

• The ratio does not directly consider fading due to a three ray process. 1

• It does not consider angle diversity's dependence on the interrelationship between

antenna performance and radio system response.

Even with these deficiencies, the discrimination ratio is a useful indicator of the probable diversity benefit for the configuration and may be utlizied as a system qualifier.

RADIATION PATTERN ANALYSIS OF THE DUAL BEAM ANTENNA

To implement angle diversity into a single antenna radio system, the antenna must be capable of producing multiple beams disposed along the elevation plane of the antenna. A multiple aperture prime focus feed system within a parabolic reflector is capable of the required multiple beam operation.

It is well known that lateral displacement of a prime focus feed system within a parabolic reflector produces canting of main beam relative to the boresight of the reflector in the direction opposite to the feed displacement. Within the dual beam antenna, a pair of feed systems can be displaced equally but in opposite directions from the centerline of the reflector along the vertical plane of the antenna. With this configuration, each of these feeds produces a canted beam along the elevation plane of the antenna, one above and one below the boresight of the reflector. Figure 3 shows the dual feeds and their relationship to the canted beams from the antenna. Figure 4 displays the radiation characteristics of the dual beam antenna relative to the boresight of the reflector. The actual amount of beam canting is a function of feed system displacement, which is limited by the physical size of the feed horns, and the focal length of the parabolic reflector.

By applying monopulse radar techniques to the dual beam antenna, another mode of operation can be realized. This mode relies on

---

1) There is evidence that fading may often be a three ray process.[7,8]

---

the facility of the dual beam antenna to be utlizied as a phased array with two vertical elements. By simultaneously processing the signals from each of the individual beams in sum and difference modes, the resultant radiation characteristics of the antenna can be substantially modified. By processing the signals in this manner, the antenna is converted into a tri-beam antenna. The sum mode has a maximum power position at the boresight of the reflector. The difference mode has two lobes in the vertical plane, symmetrically displaced relative to reflector boresight and a deep null on boresight. Figure 5 displays the elevation radiation charactertics of the antenna in the sum and difference mode.

A magic tee hybrid junction can be used as the diplexer to implement the sum and difference mode. Because of its inherent symmetry to both even and odd field structures, the hybrid junction is a perfect candidate.

When a matched, lossless hybrid junction is attached to the outputs of the individual beam antenna, the response of the even and odd mode ports of the hybrid junction can be expressed as:

$$V_{sum}(\theta) = \frac{V_1(\theta) + V_2(\theta)}{2} \quad \text{(even mode)} \quad (3)$$

$$V_{diff}(\theta) = \frac{V_1(\theta) - V_2(\theta)}{2} \quad \text{(odd mode)} \quad (4)$$

where:
V_1 and V_2 are the normalized voltage radiation characteristics of the individual beams as a function of angle.

An important parameter in the design of a dual beam antenna is the maintenance of the sum port gain. By evaluating equation (3), the gain of the sum port at boresight is equal to the individual gain at the beam cant angle when the voltage ratio for both individual beams at boresight crossover (0 degrees) becomes:

$$V_1(0) = V_2(0) = 1/\sqrt{2} \quad (5)$$

As the crossover level deviates from the above relationship, the sum mode gain also deviates with a 1:1 correlation. As with the individual beam cant angle, the sum mode gain is a function of feed displacement and reflector focal length.

In either mode of antenna operation, angle diversity is derived from the availability of a secondary beam with radiation characteristics in the direction of the direct and/or indirect rays which are significantly different from those of the primary beam. As discussed previously, the discrimination ratio is a measure of this difference.

DISCRIMINATION RATIO ANALYSIS OF THE DUAL BEAM ANTENNA

Within this section, an analysis of the the Discrimination Ratio for the two operational modes of the dual beam antenna will be presented. Graphs of the antenna Discrimination Ratio as a function of angle-of-arrival (AOA) of direct ray and the difference between the AOA of the direct and indirect rays will be shown. This will allow an understanding of angle diversity's sensitivity to changes in the AOA of the rays incident at the dual beam antenna. The results shown were calculated using the actual 6.175 GHz radiation patterns from a 10' single polarized 5.925 - 6.425 GHz dual beam antenna.

First, the Discrimination Ratio results from the sum and difference mode will be presented to allow an insight into why it may be the most efficient operational mode of the antenna. Second, the results from the individual beam mode will be analyzed for several of the antenna alignments possible with this mode.

1) Sum and Difference Mode:

As shown in the previous section, the sum and difference mode inherently produces three characteristics which are extremely important to angle diversity performance and which affect the Discrimination Ratio curves of the antenna. These charactertics are:

- Concurrent positioning of the sum beam peak and the difference beam null near the boresight of the reflector.
- Low level of difference signal at boresight of reflector.
- Steep amplitude gradient of the difference beam around the boresight of the reflector as a function of elevation angle.

These characteristics are essentially, independent of frequency and polarization.

Figure 6 displays the Discrimination Ratio results for various AOA (α_1) of the direct ray as a function of the difference in AOA ($\alpha_2 - \alpha_1$) of the direct and indirect rays. These results assume that the antenna is aligned to the difference null position with a 25 dB null depth.

As can be seen, the Discrimination Ratio rapidly increases as the AOA of direct and indirect rays separate. Also, for the case where $\alpha_1 = 0.0°$, the response of the antenna is symmetrical for indirect rays above and below the primary path. However, as the AOA of the direct ray deviates from the orginal alignment point (possibly due to changes in the path "K" factor or antenna misalignment), the gradient of the discrimination ratio decreases and becomes asymmetrical.

Within figure 6, one of the deficiencies of the discrimination ratio, as it applies to actual system performance, becomes apparent. For the cases where $\alpha_1 = +0.1°$ and $+0.2°$, the discrimination ratio goes to zero at $(\alpha_2 - \alpha_1) = -0.2°$ and $-0.4°$, respectively. These zeros occur when the amplitude of the direct and indirect rays, due to the radiation characteristics of the antenna, are equal and assumed to be in antiphase.

This result predicts that both primary and secondary beams are concurrently exhibiting selective fading. However, if the antiphase relationship is modified by the relative phase change due to the antenna characteristics, a selective fade will not occur on the secondary beam. In the limit, where the relative phase change is 180 degrees, the signals will add constructively and double the output.

This relative phase change due to antenna performance is an important benefit to system performance which is not identified by the Discrimination Ratio.

2) Individual Beam Mode

In individual beam mode, there are three possible antenna path alignment positions each of which has its own performance characteristics. The direct ray can be aligned on:

I) Beam crossover position
II) Low or high beam peak position
III) First sidelobe null position

The results within this section were calculated based on radiation patterns in which the peak of the first sidelobe is at -13 dB and the first sidelobe null is at -35 dB, both relative to the peak of the mainbeam.

I) Beam Crossover Position

Figure 7 displays the Discrimination Ratio curves for the beam crossover position. As can be seen, the slope of the discrimination ratios are much less then those of the sum and difference mode. However, these curves remain relatively symmetrical and insensitive to changes in the AOA of the direct ray below +0.4°. Note, however that this alignment, because of the positioning of the antenna along the slope of the main beam, may produce varying receive signal levels caused by tower twist and sway.

II) Low or High Beam Peak Position

The results for the low beam peak positioning of the antenna are shown in figure 8. Note that the response of the antenna positioned to the high beam would be a mirror image of those shown in figure 8. As displayed in figure 8, the Discrimintation Ratios are widely varing as a function of AOA of the direct ray and, for two cases ($\alpha_1 = 0.0°$ and $+0.2°$), very asymmetrical. However, for the case where $\alpha_1 = +0.1°$, the Discrimination Ratio curve shows improved performance and symmetry against indirect rays from above and below the primary path. After analysis of the actual antenna pattern, the reason behind the improved performance of the $\alpha_1 = +0.1°$ case becomes apparent. In this case the direct ray is arriving at or near the first side lobe null of the high beam. This result leads to the third possible choice of alignment.

III) First Sidelobe Null Position

Figure 9 shows the resulting Discrimination Ratios when the antenna is aligned on the side lobe null. As shown in this figure, the results mimic those results produced in sum and difference mode (figure 6). In essence, the antenna is utilizing the same characteristics as sum and difference mode; namely, a null with steep amplitude slopes in both directions. However, to obtain across-the-band performance, this alignment requires that the depth and position of the first sidelobe null be independent of frequency and polarization which is not normally the case. Also, to maintain constant receive signal level on the primary beam, the first sidelobe null of one beam should be near the peak of the other beam.

OPERATIONAL MODE ADVANTAGES AND DISADVANTAGES

Each operational mode of the dual beam antenna has its own set of inherent performance advantages and disadvantages.

Sum and Difference Mode

Advantages:

- High levels of discrimination ratio

- Consistent across-the-band discrimination ratio independent of frequency and polarization.

- Symmetric response to indirect rays arriving above and below the primary path.

- Ease of path alignment (alignment to the difference null).

Disadvantages:

- Possible sum mode gain reduction

- Reduced sidelobe suppression as compared to individual beam mode.

- More complex waveguide components when compared to individual beam mode.

Individual Beam Mode

Advantages:

- Maintenance of antenna gain.

- Improved sidelobe suppression as compared to sum and difference mode.

Disadvantages:

- Discrimination ratio dependent on frequency and polarization.

- Reduced discrimination ratio depending on alignment used.

CONCLUSION

Test results as reported by several other papers have shown that, for digital systems, diversity protection against dispersive multipath fading may be realized by the use of a dual beam antenna in either individual beam or sum and difference modes.

Utilizing the discrimination Ratio as the figure of merit for the antenna, this paper has shown that the sum and difference antenna mode, because of its frequency and polarization independent characteristics, would be the most desirable for paths which exhibit severe dispersive fading. However, the ability to coordinate this antenna mode into todays terrestrial environment is very much at issue.

The coordination of the individual beam antenna mode is much less of an issue because of its improved sidelobe suppression. However, the characteristics of the antenna which govern the Discrimination Ratio response are very much dependent on frequency and polarization. Dependency on frequency and polarization produces a reduction in the across-the-band diversity performance from the system. This antenna mode is most likely to be implimented into a system where coordination is an issue and path conditions do not warrant maximum diversity improvement.

Further analysis and field measurements on angle diversity systems are still required to evolve to the truly optimum antenna configuration for different fading conditions and modulation schemes.

REFERENCES

[1] Gardina, M.F. and Lin, S.H., "Measured Performance of Horizontal Space Diversity On a Microwave Radio Path", GlobeCom November, 1985.

[2] Balaban, P., Sweedyk, E.A., and Axeling, G.S., "Angle Diversity With Two Antennas: Model and Experimental Results", ICC June, 1987.

[3] Dekan, P.M., Berg, J.H., and Evans, M., "Aperture diversity Using Simular Antennas", ICC June, 1987.

[4] Lin, E.H., Giger, A.J., and Alley, G.D., "Angle Diversity On Line-Of-Sight Microwave Paths Using Dual Beam Antennas.", ICC June 1987.

[5] Alley, G.D., Peng, W.C., Robinson, W.A., and Lin, E.H., "The Effect On Error Performance Of Angle Diversity In A High Capacity Digital Microwave Radio System., GlobeCom November 1987.

[6] Allen, E.W., "Angle Diversity Test Using A Single Aperture Dual Beam Antenna", ICC June 1988.

[7] Merritt,T.S., Webster, A.R., and Wong, H., "Experimental Determination Of The Structure Of Multipath Propagation On Terrestrial Microwave Links", Final Report, D.S.S. Contact 36001-603532/01-ST, Centre For Radio Science, The University of Western Ontario, London, Canada, December 1987.

[8] Webster, A.R. and Scott A.M., "Angles-of-Arrival and Tropospheric Multipath Microwave Propagation", IEEE Transactions On Antenna And Propagation, VOL. AP-35, NO. 1, January 1987.

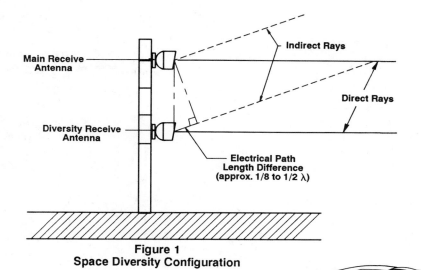

Figure 1
Space Diversity Configuration

Main Receive Antenna

Diversity Receive Antenna

Indirect Rays

Direct Rays

Electrical Path Length Difference (approx. 1/8 to 1/2 λ)

$$d = \left| \frac{A_1/B_1}{A_2/B_2} \right|$$

r_1 r_2

A_1 B_1

B_2

A_2

Signal Amplitude

Elevation Angle

(–)   (+)

Figure 2
Discrimination Ratio

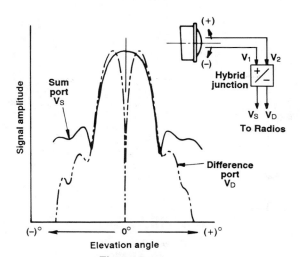

Low beam

High beam

Dual-beam feed

Antenna horizontal axis

Antenna vertical axis

Figure 3
Canted Beams Produced by Dual-beam Feed

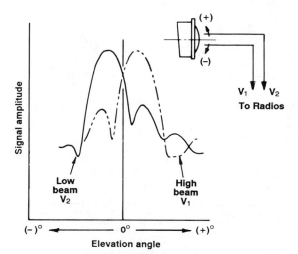

Signal amplitude

(+)
(–)

V_1 V_2
To Radios

Low beam V_2

High beam V_1

(–)°   0°   (+)°

Elevation angle

Figure 4
Radiation Pattern of Dual-beam Antenna in Individual Beam Mode

Signal amplitude

(+)
(–)

V_1 V_2

Hybrid junction
+ / –

V_S V_D
To Radios

Sum port V_S

Difference port V_D

(–)°   0°   (+)°

Elevation angle

Figure 5
Radiation Pattern of Dual-beam Antenna in Sum and Difference Mode

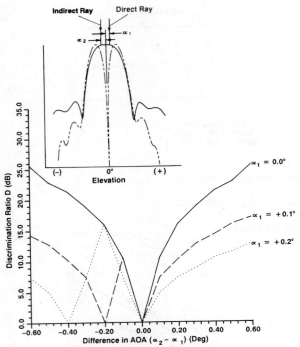

Figure 6
Discrimination Ratio
Sum and Difference Mode
Aligned at Null

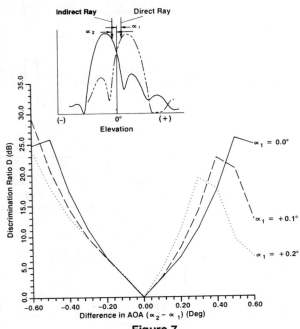

Figure 7
Discrimination Ratio
Individual beam Mode
Aligned at Crossover

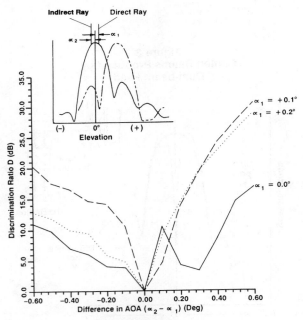

Figure 8
Discrimination Ratio
Individual beam Mode
Aligned at Low Beam Peak

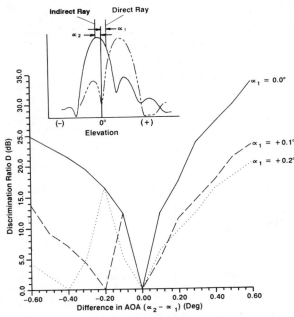

Figure 9
Discrimination Ratio
Individual beam Mode
Aligned at First Side Lobe Null

64 QAM DISPERSIVE FADING COUNTERMEASURES

Richard U. Laine

Harris Corporation/Farinon Division
San Carlos, California

ABSTRACT

An evaluation of the field performance of 64 QAM 6.7 GHz digital microwave radios over a long 44.57-mile path traversing San Francisco Bay is presented. The measured link performance was found to be asymmetrical, with one direction influenced heavily by urban area terrain scatter interference and atmospheric duct generated flat fade activity.

INTRODUCTION

The field performance evaluation of a 64 QAM microwave digital radio link on a 44.57 mile path between San Francisco and Mt. Vaca commenced in November 1987 and continued through a very heavy fade period until the end of March 1988. This was one of a series of 64 QAM tests conducted by this organization to characterize the field performance of a new 45 Mb/s digital radio operating in the 6.7 GHz OFS band over a wide variety of terrain, climatic, environmental, and installation conditions using a combination of equipment and space- or angle-diversity countermeasure techniques against destructive multipath fade activity.

This on-going 64 QAM test series is conducted in California, Washington, Texas, Utah, and Ohio, venues selected for one or several diverse and often detrimental path characteristics.

The San Francisco - Mt. Vaca Test Link locale (Figure 1) was selected not only for its well-known atmospheric duct-related difficult propagation characteristics, but also an adverse interference environment. Interference will tend to have increasing impact upon composite fade margins (and, therefore, upon propagation availabilities) in new digital radio links extended into urban areas, thus identifying this as an important test objective. Concerns completely satisfied for this and the other field tests were ready access to existing microwave facilities (rooms, battery plants, antennas, etc.) and the interest and support of the host organizations.

TEST OBJECTIVE

The objective of this propagation test was to quantize the performance of a DVM6-45 microwave radio link (with baseband time domain and IF amplitude slope adaptive transversal equalization and space diversity protection with errorless switching) in a field environment marked with occasionally severe duct-generated fade activity and urban-area terrain scatter interference.

RESULTS SUMMARY

The test period was 122 days (4 months) inclusive of 84 days with two-way space diversity (SD) protection, 35 days of non-diversity (ND)

operation towards Mt. Vaca, and 3 days of radio turn-down. The resulting one-way availabilities, bit error rates (including interference and fading), and space diversity improvement factors (I_O) measured during the conduct of this test are summarized below.

Availabilities	San Francisco to Mt. Vaca	Mt. Vaca to San Francisco
Objective	99.99909524%	Same
ND, measured	99.99679784%	Same
ND, computed	99.99047619%	Same
SD, measured	99.99898566%	99.99989632%
SD, computed	99.99989652%	99.99942851%
I_O, measured	3	30
I_O, computed	92	16
Measured ES floor*	3.27×10^{-18}	1.25×10^{-14}
Dribbling ES rate	7.78×10^{-12}	4.03×10^{-12}
Total ES (w/burst)	1.03×10^{-11}	5.60×10^{-12}

*Average derived from computerized CNR field measurements (per HP Journal, 7/87)

It is evident that the diversity outage toward Mt. Vaca was almost 10X that expected, although the non-diversity outage time was only 1/3rd the computed value. Conversely, the diversity outage in the San Francisco direction was only 1/5th that of the computed outage. The space diversity improvement factors follow (and exaggerate) these computed vs. measured differences. The two reasons for the increased outage towards Mt. Vaca were the degradation in composite fade margin (CFM) with terrain scatter RF interference off San Francisco urban area buildings and a less than optimum Mt. Vaca diversity antenna spacing to counteract deep flat fade activity.

PERFORMANCE DEFINITIONS AND OBJECTIVES

The performance of this digital radio Test Link is tied to circuit availability, that percentage (or actual amount) of time the derived voice, data, or television channels maintain continuity and are usable. Usable however, remains a rather subjective term to those more familiar with assessing analog radio or digital span line performance. Unlike analog microwave systems whose performance is demonstrated mainly by busy-hour noise and baseband outage, a number of terms kindred to the bursty nature of this medium are applicable to the evaluation of digital radio performance with most associated more with the quality of service than to circuit availability.

Availability and Outage Terminology

Microwave Link Outage occurs with a less than 2.5 second loss of DS1/DS3 frame synchronization (sync loss) with a bit error rate (BER) exceeding about 10^{-3}. Digital microwave link outage is in Severely Errored Seconds (SES)/year or other period, then converted to a % Availability. Such outages quickly clear with all telephone and other circuits remaining connected and little note taken of this transient event. Microwave outages are mostly propagation related (especially in non-diversity links), but may occur with a module switch to a standby unit. The venerable "Bell System" short-haul multipath outage objective widely accepted in industry is 1600D/250 = 6.4D one-way SES/year, where D is the path or system length in miles, or 285 SES/year for this 44.57-mile Test Link.

Very Severe Bursts (VSB) of errors result from microwave link (or other) outage durations of more than 2.5 seconds triggering DS1 trunk alarms, disconnecting all derived circuits, and otherwise blocking access to the system for at least 10 seconds per VSB event. This catastrophic event occurs with extended rain and multipath outage in vulnerable links assigned low fade margins without propagation redundancy. The performance objective is, of course, no VSB events in any microwave link.

Availability is that percentage of time with no microwave link outage. The computed annual availability objective for this Test Link is therefore $100 - 100 (285/31.5 \times 10^6$ sec/year) = 99.99909524%.

Unavailability is the measure of service outage, conditionally synonymous with **Probability of Outage**. The allocated unavailability for this Test Link is $285/31.5 \times 10^6 = 9.05 \times 10^{-6}$. Unavailabilities, probabilities of outage, and seconds are added directly on tandem digital links to derive a system value.

RSL's, fade margins, etc. to an easily measured (with an RF attenuator) 10^{-6} BER steady-state **Operating Point** are used to spec, evaluate, or compare digital radio factory and field performance without sync loss (outage). This (or other) low BER should never be used as a "threshold" for availability (outage) computations since the bursty, random ES seen in a fading radio link cannot be converted to a steady-state BER to confirm such performance.

Quality Terminology

An **Errored Second (ES)** is any measurement second with one or more bit errors.

Dribbling Errored Seconds are ES with a single error. These are contributed randomly by the microwave equipment (usually the transmitter PA in QPR and QAM links), interference and propagation-related RF spectrum stress.

Error Burst Seconds are ES with 2 or more bit errors, but without DS1/DS3 sync loss (perhaps less than 100 errors at DS1). Non-hitless module switching, interference, and propagation typically cause this random non-outage event. Such error burst seconds are included in the ES totals for performance evaluation purposes.

Error Free Seconds (EFS) define that percentage of seconds with no dribbling or burst ES over a measurement period (24 hours or more is

typical). AT&T DS1 ACCUNET 1.5 objectives are 98.75% EFS in a customer to serving office circuit, or 96.6% EFS between customer-customer locations separated by less than 250 airline miles for 1080 and 2940 allowable DS1 ES per 24 hours respectively (39 and 106 ES in a 56 kb/s data line). These higher DS1 ES rates mirror harsh span line and switching office environments, and may be compared to perhaps 2 ES/24 hour per-hop (20 ES/24 hour for a 10 hop 250-mile section) field performance typical of a well-engineered digital microwave system (10^{-11} BER/hop).

Errored Second Groups are short term increases in the number of ES over a given (few minutes to several hours) period, as caused by an increase in RF interference with atmospheric duct activity or terrain (intersection or urban area) scatter. There is no performance objective for such a transient event.

Errored Second Floor, defining the background ES contribution of the microwave equipment alone, is usually specified in the 10^{-11} or lower BER range (typically 10^{-12} to 10^{-18} per-hop). This is usually an insignificant contributor to the overall EFS performance of a longer digital microwave link operating in a moderate to heavy fade or interference environment.

PROPAGATION TEST PATH GEOMETRY

The San Francisco - Mt. Vaca Test Link is a high/low 44.57 mile path traversing San Francisco Bay with minimal ($0.6F_1$) clearance over intervening hills at k = 1 (Figure 2). These same hills effectively block long-delayed direct reflections off the Bay over all values of k. The transmission performance of this 64 QAM link is controlled, therefore, by the occurrence of destructive multipath signals via atmospheric boundary layer (ABL) reflection and refraction routes dominated by clear air multipath refraction at night.

The longest such multipath delays are very short, less than about 2 ns (about 2 feet) from a reflection off a presumed surface duct boundary some 200 feet above the Bay (Figure 3). Any other path geometry (refractive routes through an elevated ABL as shown in Figure 4, for example) result in even shorter multipath delay times. The resulting short-delayed multipath notch produces the equipment static signature curve, Figure 5, from which a 71 dB dispersive fade margin (DFM) for this 64 QAM Test Link is derived. This is insignificant compared to thermal and interference contributors to the 36 dB Test Link CFM, so is effectively excluded from the availability calculations.

A variation in a daytime k from 4/3rds to infinity in a nocturnal ABL causes only 0.25° upward movement of the path arrival angle (Figure 6) at San Francisco, well within the 1 dB points of the 10 foot parabolic antennas. With properly aligned (slight upward tilt) dishes, this eliminates any nighttime loss of fade margin due to k-factor antenna decoupling as a major contributor to heavy multipath fade activity.

ABL formation was a dominant factor in the heavy fade activity seen on the Test Link in February and March. (These were unseasonably warm drought months in this area.) The high/low path geometry dictated the passage of the direct ray (and the generation of refractive multipath routes) through these layers. Slow direct ray power fades ("defocusing") were seen with the partial isolation of the antennas by the ABL, and this temporary loss of fade margin contributed to the 3 flat fade multipath outages recorded towards San Francisco as well as most of the Mt. Vaca outages.

The 10-ft diversity antenna separations are 20 feet at San Francisco and 47 feet at Mt. Vaca. While these compute to space diversity improvements of 16 towards San Francisco and 92 towards Mt. Vaca, high/low path geometry and interference tended to reverse these numbers as discussed under **Measured Performance**.

PREDICTED PERFORMANCE

The annual one-way outage (to 10^{-3} BER sync loss) predictions for the Test Link are based upon Vigants' procedures and parameters [BSTJ, January 1975]. The results are on an annual basis, but with nearly all outage presumed to occur during a 3 month **fade season**. It isevident from the test results that the fade season started in early February and was on-going through the March 25th shutdown of the propagation test.

The annual one-way non-diversity outage time using Test Link coefficients is given by

$$T = 0.4 \ c \ f \ t \ D^3 \ 10^{-CFM/10}$$

where

    T = One-way non-diversity outage, SES/year
    c = terrain/humidity factor, 1
    f = 6.725 GHz
    D = 44.57 miles
    CFM = 36.0 dB composite fade margin
        (in the absence of interference)
    t = average annual temperature, 50°F.

Therefore
    T = 3000 SES/year
        (99.99047619% availability).

Since T greatly exceeds the 285 SES/year outage objective, space diversity protection against multipath fade outage is used. The predicted outage reduction factor with space diversity is

$$I_0 = 7\times10^{-5} \ f \ s^2 \ 10^{CFM/10}/D.$$

Therefore
    I_0 = 16 at San Francisco (s = 20 feet)
       = 92 at Mt. Vaca (s = 47 feet)

and the computed annual one-way outages with space diversity reduce to

    180 SES/year at San Francisco
    (99.99942851% availability)

    33 SES/year at Mt. Vaca
    (99.99989652% availability).

MEASURED PERFORMANCE

With almost 13 times more outage in the Mt. Vaca direction than towards San Francisco, the measured outage on the Test Link differed dramatically from the above predicted values. Some reasons for these discrepancies are evident:

- The measured non-diversity Test Link outage towards Mt. Vaca (193 SES) excluded much of the fade season; the November-December 1987 period was especially quiet with minimal fade activity.

- The measured performance with two-way space diversity encompassed the fade season with fade activity enhanced by the unseasonably warm days and cooler nights of one of the driest, warmest winters on record. Surface and elevated ABL formation was a dominant factor in the heavy fade activity seen during this period.

- The interference level into Mt. Vaca (from San Francisco area building reflections) was occasionally high, reducing CFM 5 dB and more. This increases outage and ES x3 (ND) to x10 (SD) during such periods. San Francisco, looking outbound from this urban scatter, was not similarly affected.

- The path geometry (Figure 6) is high/low, precipitating Fresnel nulls/peaks widely spaced (about 113') at Mt. Vaca causing more simultaneous flat fade outage to diversity dishes spaced only 47'. The Fresnel null/peak separation at San Francisco is little more than 6' for excellent diversity action between 10-foot dishes spaced 20', effectively reducing outage activity in that direction.

Non-Diversity Outage

The non-diversity test period towards Mt. Vaca was 35 days (3.02×10^6 seconds), during which there were 193 total two-way (looped DS1) outages. With no one-way outage recorded at the San Francisco space diversity terminal during this period, all 193 outages (half of which occurred on two days) were toward the Mt. Vaca non-diversity site. This multipath fade outage is but a fraction of the 1127 non-diversity outages computed for the path over this period (1/3rd of the fade season). Most of this 35-day test period preceded the fade season, however, with its increasingly severe fade activity reaching peak intensity towards the end of the space diversity (normal configuration) part of the propagation test.

Diversity Outage

The two-way space diversity part of the test was 84 days (7.25×10^6 seconds). However, instrumentation/equipment disconnect time and other exclusions from this total time reduce the valid space diversity test period to after 2/4/88. The space diversity time prior to 12/24/87 was a quiet fade period excluded from the final results (less than 8 two-way outages were measured in this initial one-month period).

Mt. Vaca to San Francisco Outage

Only three outages attributed to propagation were recorded (1 on 2/15/88 and 2 on 3/22/88). This computes to a 99.99989632% availability over an 803 hour test period, and is insignificant compared to the 180 SES/year computed outage.

San Francisco to Mt. Vaca Outage

Thirty eight outages (inclusive of 16 on the 2/15/88 severe fading day) were counted over a 1040-hour space diversity period. This computes to 99.99898566% availability, and was already higher than the computed outage of 33 SES/year with the fade season yet to finish.

Dribbling and Total ES and BER's

The test period is the same as for the space diversity period (803 and 1040 hours respectively in the SF and Mt. Vaca directions). The measured (ES per one-way DS1 line during these periods are

	Mt. Vaca to SF	SF to Mt. Vaca
Dribbling ES	18	45
Dribbling ES Rate	4.03×10^{-12}	7.78×10^{-12}
Total ES (Incl. bursts)	25	59
Total ES Rate	5.60×10^{-12}	1.03×10^{-12}

It is seen that the ES towards Mt. Vaca are over double the number to San Francisco, a result of the higher interference floor at Mt. Vaca. None of the errors was associated with very active receiver diversity switching. The errorless DS3 switch is activated below 10^{-9} BER by IF slope stress (as well as other alarms) which anticipates a degrading path condition before it contributes bit errors or outage.

ANTENNA FEEDER SYSTEM REQUIREMENTS

The antenna feeder system VSWR requirements for these 64 QAM digital radios are relaxed at least 10 dB as compared to that of an analog radio connected to a long waveguide run (from 26-28 to 16-18 dB return loss). These 6 GHz field test radios have variously been connected through long 1/2" heliax coaxial cables, standard (untuned) elliptical waveguide, analog radio waveguide branching networks, and couplers to standard VSWR dishes with no measurable impairment to the ES floor or any other performance parameter noted.

INSTRUMENTATION

Figure 8 shows the DVM6-45 Test Link digital microwave block diagrams with the instrumentation points and equipment used for these propagation tests. RF attenuators measured flat fade margins at local receivers and, by reducing the local PA output, the flat plus interference fade margins at the distant receivers. All important activity in the Test Link was monitored on BERTS printers, analog recorders, and the computer 40 MB hard disk for evaluation.

One data collection problem was at Mt. Vaca, where for 60 days the diversity receiver and all instrumentation were connected to an unprotected (no generator backup), unregulated AC wall plug susceptible to extended power outage and wide voltage fluctuations. The on-line transmitter and main receiver were on the -24 Vdc battery plant for the test period.

DIGITAL RADIO DISPERSIVE FADE COUNTERMEASURES

It was verified early in the test that all propagation-related (rather than "cockpit error") outages and BER degradations were traced to flat fading and external interference. Dispersive fade activity evident from the adaptive equalizer stress voltage recordings did not affect the performance of the Test Link.

The reason for this is evident from the DVM6-45 10^{-3} BER equipment signatures (Figure 5) which were measured and the dispersive fade margins (DFM) computed for multipath notch delays of 2, 6.3, and 25.5 ns. The 16.3 ns recommended by Rummler [BSTJ, May-June 1979] as that minimum notch delay for a 10 MHz RF bandwidth (bandwidth x delay product less than 1/6) was not used, but its effect could be scaled from these signatures. The computed DFM for the Test Link with its 2 ns maximum multipath echo notch delay was 71 dB. Since the CFM is 36 dB (degraded at Mt. Vaca to below 30 dB on occasion by urban area terrain scatter interference), dispersive fade activity was inconsequential to the performance of the Test Link.

The DVM6-45 modules central to the immunity of this Test Link to dispersive-type fade activity are the IF adaptive slope amplitude equalizers (ASAE) and the baseband adaptive time domain equalizers (ATDE) which continually compensate for amplitude and phase anomalies in the incoming signal that would otherwise generate intersymbol interference (ISI). Both are 3-tap transversal-type filters driven by recursive decision feedback tap control voltages. The ASAE, operating in the frequency domain, corrects for IF slope and is transparent to minimum/non-minimum path delay characteristics. The time domain ATDE uses a zero-forcing algorithm to eliminate ISI by optimizing the decoded eye patterns directly.

CONCLUSIONS

A 64 QAM field experiment with a 45 Mb/s digital radio operating in a 10 MHz-wide 6.7 GHz OFS channel over a long 44.57-mile fading microwave path is described. The performance of this link into the San Francisco metropolitan area exceeded expectations, while the outbound direction was degraded by interference and non-optimum diversity dish separation to heavy flat fade activity. No outage due to dispersion was seen because of the favorable path geometry and effective equipment countermeasures. Angle diversity tests on the San Francisco-Mt. Vaca Test Link commenced in July 1988.

ADDITIONAL REFERENCE

Woolley, B.G. et al, "A 64 QAM System for the Special Requirements of 2 GHz and 6 GHz Private Radio Applications ", ICC 87 Seattle.

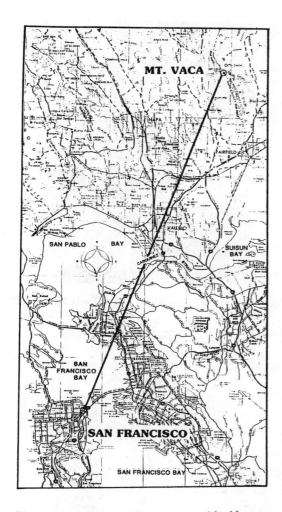

Figure 1. The San Francisco – Mt. Vaca 64 QAM Test Link

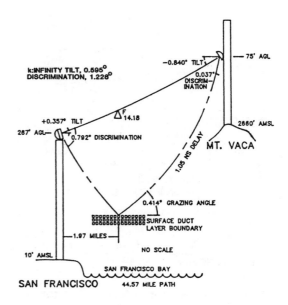

Figure 3. Path geometry at k:4/3rds.

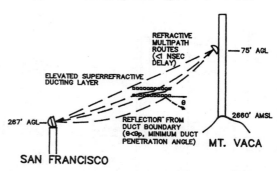

Figure 4. Multipath propagation through an atmospheric boundary layer.

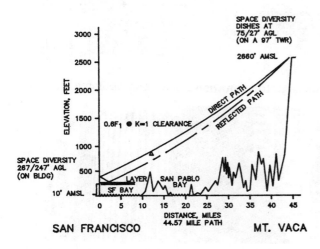

Figure 2. The Test Link path profile

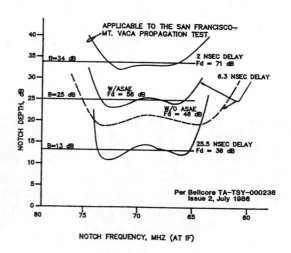

Figure 5. DVM6–45 signature curves at 10–3 BER for 2, 6.3, and 25.5 ns notch delays.

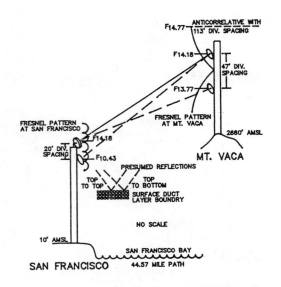

Figure 6. Fresnel interference patterns

Figure 7. A DVM6–45 64 QAM Test Link radio

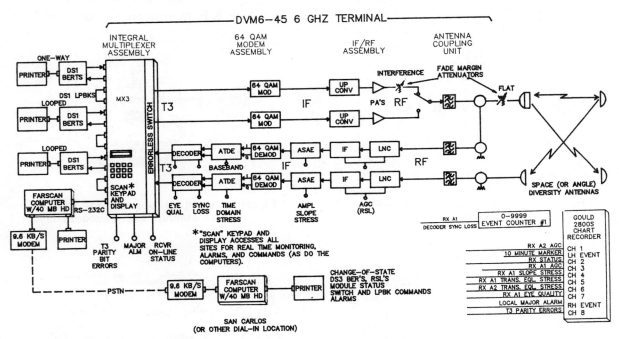

Figure 8. Path test radio block diagram showing instrumentation points and equipment

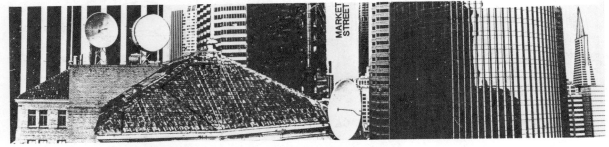

Figure 9. Westerly view down Market Street of the San Francisco
main (center) and diversity (right) Test Link dishes.

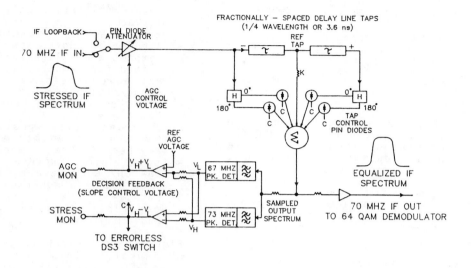

Figure 10. The DVM6-45 IF Adaptive Slope Amplitude Equalizer (ASAE) incorporating a delay-transparent 3-tap transversal filter.

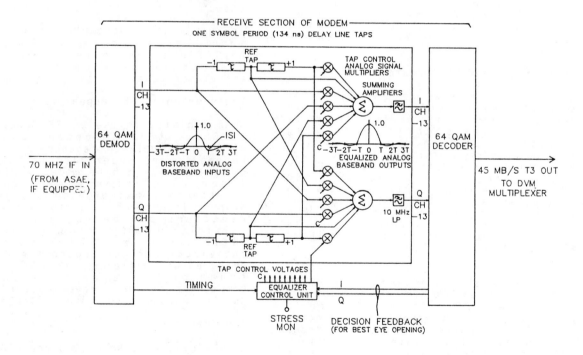

Figure 11. The DVM6-45 Adaptive Time Domain Equalizer (ATDE). The decision feedback to the control taps maintain the optimum I and Q channel eye openings.

ENGINEERING 18 GHz MICROWAVE PATHS
USING LINEAR RF REPEATERS

Edward R. Johnson
Vice President of Engineering

Peninsula Engineering Group, Inc.
1091 Industrial Road
San Carlos, CA 94070
(415) 593-2400

Abstract

Linear RF Repeaters have been used in recent years at frequencies from 800 MHz to 8 GHz to extend range and overcome obstructions at low total station cost. This class of Repeater equipment is now available at 18 GHz. Linear RF Repeaters provide great economic advantages due to their simplicity and reduced infrastructure costs. Engineering Linear RF Repeaters into new microwave routes involves an understanding of their differences from regenerative repeater stations. The differences of system gain, RF power, terminal modulation, prime power sources and remote monitoring are reviewed. Special emphasis is placed on range extension in the presence of rain fading. Advantages of low power consumption, solar power and all weather, wide environment operation are explained.

What are Linear RF Repeaters?

Linear RF Repeaters are Low Cost, full duplex (bi-directional) through repeaters used in microwave radio relay applications such as extending transmission range or clearing obstructed microwave radio paths. These RF Repeaters provide 50 to 60 dB of linear gain, band limited to reduce adjacent interference. RF Repeaters are transparent to the terminal radios when operated within design limits. Any terminal radio's modulated signal is received, amplified and retransmitted without changing its characteristics or frequency.

With the excellent antennas available today, operating an on-frequency repeater without self interference is very practical. Overshoot of a repeater is easily controlled with a slight "dog-leg" in the path and with the selection of cross polarization per hop where needed.

Linear RF Repeater stations are lower cost in both their equipment and in total when compared to regenerative repeater stations. RF Repeaters are simple in concept which makes them simple to make. Since an RF Repeater does not modulate, demodulate, or change carrier frequencies, no sensitive oscillators, mixers or modems are needed. This inherent product simplicity translates into an 18 GHz repeater that has these features:

- Power consumption only 3.2 amperes at 12 Vdc.
- Easily solar powered or by other alternative power sources.
- Compact and lightweight -- ideally suited for remote sites that do not have access to roads or commercial power.
- Wide Temperature Operating Range, -40 C - +60 C.
- Environmentally protected, suitable for use at unimproved sites anywhere in the world.
- Lowest infrastructure costs of any 18- GHz microwave radio repeater station. All equipment is outdoor rated.
- Compatible with any type of 18-GHz radio terminal.

Figure 1 is a block diagram of an 18-GHz RF Repeater. This shows a full duplex configuration with one internally redundant linear amplifier per RF channel. The amplifiers are provided with directional couplers for in-service RF output power measurements. The output power for a specific modulation type is maintained by the AGC/ALC circuit within the amplifier to correct input fades and reduce overload. Amplifiers can be replaced without disrupting service through the circulator access ports provided.

Engineering 18-GHz Repeaters

When deciding to use an RF Repeater at 18 GHz, it is important that the differences between regenerative and RF repeaters are understood so that the correct choice can be made. The most important difference is that RF repeaters do not provide any traffic drop or insert access while regenerative repeaters can be equipped with a multiplex traffic drop. The other differences are technical in the individual designs and cost. Cost is the greatest difference between the two types of repeater stations. A comparison summary between regenerative and RF repeaters is shown in Table I.

Applications

18-GHz Linear RF Repeaters are effective when used to clear an obstructed path where no drops are required at the repeater, to improve the reliability or range of a rain limited path and to reduce outage due to atmospheric multipath caused dispersive fading. Obstructed paths are the easiest to understand, the intended path is blocked by terrain or by structures. Solving the obstructed path can require either tall towers, another path or a repeater in the path. The RF Repeater can be placed on or near the obstruction if it provides line-of-sight to both end points.

More than one RF Repeater can be used in tandem to span greater distances. Often the total cost of a system can be less when multiple RF Repeaters are used instead of regenerative repeaters or stations with tall towers. The high waveguide loss at 18-GHz and poor accessibility make tall towers unfavorable choices.

Heavy rainfall is frequently the limiting factor in determining range and reliability of 18-GHz microwave paths. RF Repeaters can provide the intermediate relay points needed to shorten the individual hops and improve fade margins over longer direct links. RF Repeater paths referenced here are calculated assuming independent fading on each hop. Because the AGC/ALC range of the RF Repeater is not equal to the fade margin, it is possible that some degree of outage correlation between hops will exist. This correlation may be a subject of a future paper.

The path data sheets, Figures 2 and 3, show an example of how an RF Repeater can be used to improve the reliability of a rain limited path in Los Angeles, CA. Figure 2 shows a 12 mile path spanned directly with 18-GHz terminals. Outage time for the direct path is nearly 1900 seconds per year. Figure 3 shows the use of an 18-GHz RF Repeater with the same terminals to serve the same end points. The path was given a "dog-leg" to minimize overshoot making the total span 13 miles. Annual outage time is reduced to less than 630 seconds, a three fold improvement.

Performance

When considering a multiple hop microwave link, it is helpful to think in terms of annual outage per unit distance. This allows an overall outage budget to be allocated per each link and the engineer can then observe if an individual link is over or under budget.

If we calculate the hop length for terminal to terminal direct that would produce the same annual outage per mile as the 13 mile repeatered link shown in Figure 3, using the same conditions and antennas, we find the distance to be 6.5 miles which is the same as each hop of the RF Repeatered span. This indicates that a linear RF repeater as described can perform as well as a pair of terminal radios or a regenerative repeater.

A direct path with the same conditions as Figure 3, that has 630 seconds of outage (same as the repeatered link) would be 8.1 miles long with an annual outage per unit distance of 78 seconds/mile. The repeatered path compares favorably with 628 seconds of outage, 13.0 miles long and 48.3 seconds per mile outage annually.

Effect of RF Repeaters on Fade Margins and System Noise.

RF Repeaters provide linear RF amplification with gains from 50 to 60 dB typically. The gains provided are less than the terminal system gains of 100 to 120 dB. In normal installations, the RF repeater output power will drop when the input power fades beyond the downfade AGC reserve (10 dB Typ). PEGI determines repeater fade margins by determining the sum of noises added by the repeater(s) and the terminal receiver. When the total noise added equals the terminal threshold C/N for given noise or BER, the link system is at threshold.

The following equation is used to determine the Minimum Signal Level at an RF Repeater and then Fade Margin.

$$MSLr = MSLt - NFt + 10*LOG(10^{\wedge}(NFr/10) + 10^{\wedge}(-((Gr-NPL-NFt)/10)))$$

MSLr : Repeater Minimum Signal Level, dBm
MSLt : Terminal Minimum Signal Level, dBm
NFr : Repeater Noise Figure, dB
NFt : Terminal Noise Figure, dB
Gr : Repeater Gain at MSLr, dB (Normally = Max Gain)
NPL : Net Path Loss from Repeater to Terminal.

With tandem RF Repeaters, the RF Repeater closest to the terminal is calculated per above, the RF Repeater preceeding that one will use the results of MSLr as MSLt, NFr as NFt, NPL between repeaters.

Example:

MSLt = -80 dBm, NFt = 6 dB, NFr = 8 dB,
    Gr = 50 dB, NPL = 60 dB
MSLr = -80 - 6 + 10*LOG(10^(8/10)
    + 10^(-((50-60-6)/10)))
MSLr = -86 + 10*LOG(6.3096 + 39.8107)
MSLr = -86 + 16.6389
MSLr = -69.3611 dBm ... -69.4 dBm

Fade Margin is Repeater Nominal RSL - MSLr.

Power Requirements

Linear RF Repeaters are simple in design, using few total components as compared to terminal radios. The power requirements are generally low.

Depending on frequency band, power output and gain, the requirements range from 15 Watts to 50 Watts for a duplex protected repeater. The RF Repeater described can operate from dual +12.6 volt systems with 1.6 Amperes per +12.6 volt bus for a total current of 3.2 Amperes. This repeater can draw power from either source should one source fail. The +12.6 volt primary power was chosen to allow easy use of solar power. There are no elaborate power converters or conditioners to reduce efficiency.

The repeaters can also be powered from AC with battery backup. A pair of 3 Amp chargers (A + B battery) plus a 100 AH storage battery per charger bus is adequate. A pair of 100 AH batteries will operate the RF Repeater for 50 hours without recharging.

Typical solar power calculations are shown for Los Angeles County and New York City area. Estimated cost for solar power and battery equipment is $7400.00 for LA and $9040.00 for NYC. This amount can often be less than the cost of installing new power lines to a repeater site.

Monitoring System

The ability to remotely monitor the status of an RF Repeater improves the system operator's ability to maintain top performance, minimize outages, and schedule maintenance trips. One of the key advantages of a monitor system is that if there is a problem with a solar power system, the system operator can have several days advance warning before the batteries would fail. This gives the time needed to fix the problem before it results in a service outage.

An RF Repeater Monitor and Alarm System allows RF Repeater operators to monitor key repeater parameters such as amplifier status, battery voltage and temperature, etc. Major alarms are provided when the amplifiers fail, or the battery voltage drops dangerously low. The monitor has the flexibility to allow system operators to designate additional alarm monitor points. The monitor has dry contacts at the receiver which allow the operator to tie the system into a standard supervisory system.

Key features of an RF Repeater Monitor are:

-Operates over the microwave carrier being repeated.
- Provides sufficient alarm and monitor points.
- Extra customer designated alarm points.
-Real-time battery temperature telemetry -40 to +65 C.

- Voltage telemetry of 9 to 19.9 volts.
- Low Transmitter Power consumption for solar.

The repeater monitor consists of a set of transducers for monitoring the equipment, a transmitter at the repeater which generates the data signal and modulates the RF carrier, and a receiver at the microwave repeater or terminal which decodes the data stream, provides a local display, and provides dry contacts for further remoting of the alarms.

The alarm transmission is by means of a low bit rate telemetry signal amplitude modulated on the RF carrier passing through the repeater. The data rate is 32 baud (16 bits per second). The Amplitude Modulation is approximately 1 dB. The slow data speed and low level modulation insures that the monitor's signal will not interfere with normal radio link performance of virtually any type of analog or digital microwave radio. Amplifier status is detected through the use of a current comparator circuit. As a general rule when there is a problem in an amplifier the current drain will either increase or decrease. An alarm is provided if the current drain on any one of the amplifiers is significantly different than the others.

Conclusion

Linear RF Repeaters provide a cost effective means of overcoming path problems at 18-GHz. Rain limited paths can be made practical and reliable at low overall system cost. Engineering of RF Repeaters is similar to regenerative repeaters with the different considerations of no traffic drops, on-frequency repeating and flexibility in site selection when using solar power.

Table I. Comparison of Regenerative Repeaters and RF Repeaters

Item	Regenerative	RF Repeater
Modulate	yes	no
Demodulate	yes	no
Change Frequency	yes	no
Drop Traffic	yes	no
Shelter required	yes	no
System Gain	90-100 dB	50-60 dB
Power Output	+10 -- +20 dBm	+10 -- +20 dBm
Power Consumption	400 Watts *	40 Watts *
Solar Power cost	$100,000	$10,000
Monitor Systems	yes	yes
Variable Capacity	no	yes
Mid Air Meet	no	yes...always
Repeater Site cost	$300,000	$80,000

* Protected Duplex Configuration

1889

Figure 1
RF REPEATER BLOCK DIAGRAM

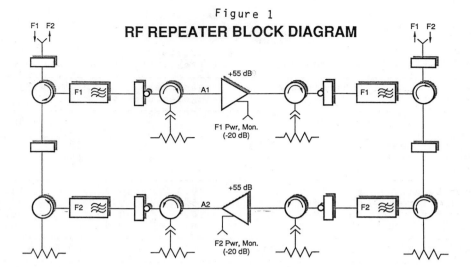

Figure 2.
Path Data Sheet for Microwave Radio
Terminal: Digital, FSK, 12 Mb/s

```
------------------------------------------------------------
Site                  Terminal A         Terminal B
Name  NCF88             Los Angeles County
------------------------------------------------------------
Tx Frequency    MHz 18605.0              18945.0
Path Length     mi            12.0
Free Space Loss dB           143.7
Absorption Loss dB             0.3
Path Loss       dB           143.9
------------------------------------------------------------
Feeder Length   ft    13.0               13.0
Loss/100 ft     dB     5.9                5.9
Feeder Loss     dB     0.8                0.8
Total Fixed Loss dB    0.8                0.8
------------------------------------------------------------
Total Losses    dB           145.5
------------------------------------------------------------
Antenna Type    :     Solid              Solid
Antenna Size    ft     4.0                4.0
Antenna Gain    dB    44.9               44.9
------------------------------------------------------------
Total Gains     dB            89.8
Net Path Loss   dB            55.7
------------------------------------------------------------
Transmit Power  dBm   18.0               18.0
Nom RSL(+/-2dB) dBm  -37.7              -37.7
Receiver Thresh. dBm -75.0              -75.0
Min C/I Required dB
Rec. Noise Figure dB   9.0                9.0
Min Rec. Power  dBm  -75.0              -75.0
Fade Margin     dB    37.3               37.3
Per Hop Rel.(MP) %  99.9991%           99.9991%
Per Hop Rel.(Rain)%  A <-> B   99.9958%
One Way Path Rel. % 99.9949%           99.9949%
------------------------------------------------------------
Reliability Data..........:

Terrain roughness factor, W:  50.0 Average terrain
Climate Type...............:     1 Coastal, hot, humid
Climate / Terrain Factor...:  2.000
Mean Temperature, degrees F:  60.0
Fading Season,........days : 111.7     1=A  4=D1  7=E  10=H
                                       2=B  5=D2  8=F
Rain Climatic Region (1-10):     8 F   3=C  6=D3  9=G

Multipath Outage/year, A receive :    292.6 Seconds
Multipath Outage/year, B receive :    292.6 Seconds
Rain+Multipath Outage/year, 2 Way:   1897.9 Seconds

      Path Length, End to End :     12.0 Miles
          Annual Outage/mile :    158.2 Seconds/mile
```

```
                          Figure 3.
                Path Data Sheet for RF Repeaters
            Repeater: RF-18000  Terminal: Digital, FSK, 12 Mb/s
------------------------------------------------------------------------
Site                  Terminal A          Repeater           Terminal B
Name  NCF88                           Los Angeles County
------------------------------------------------------------------------
Tx Frequency     MHz18605.0                                      18945.0
Path Length      mi       6.5                              6.5
Free Space Loss  dB     138.3                            138.3
Absorption Loss  dB       0.2                              0.2
Path Loss        dB     138.5                            138.5
------------------------------------------------------------------------
Feeder Length    ft    13.0          10.0       10.0           13.0
Loss/100 ft      dB     5.9           5.9        5.9            5.9
Feeder Loss      dB     0.8           0.6        0.6            0.8
Total Fixed Loss dB     0.8           0.6        0.6            0.8
------------------------------------------------------------------------
Total Losses     dB    139.8                            139.8
------------------------------------------------------------------------
Antenna Type     :    Solid         Hi Perf    Hi Perf        Solid
Antenna Size     ft     4.0           4.0        4.0            4.0
Antenna Gain     dB    44.9          44.9       44.9           44.9
Front/Back       dB                  60.0       60.0
------------------------------------------------------------------------
Total Gains      dB    89.8                             89.8
Net Path Loss    dB    50.0                             50.0
------------------------------------------------------------------------
Transmit Power   dBm   18.0                                      18.0
Repeater Input   dBm                -32.0      -32.0
Input Pad        dB                   0.0        0.0
Repeater Max Gain dB                 60.0       60.0
AGC              dB                   8.0        8.0
Amplifier Power  dB                  20.0       20.0
Output Pad       dB                   0.0        0.0
Repeater Output  dBm                 20.0       20.0
Nom RSL(+/-2dB)  dBm  -30.0                                    -30.0
Receiver Thresh. dBm  -75.0                                    -75.0
Min C/I Required dB
Rec. Noise Figure dB    9.0           9.0        9.0            9.0
Min Rec. Power   dBm  -75.0         -74.6      -74.6          -75.0
Fade Margin      dB    45.0          42.6       42.6           45.0
Per Hop Rel.(MP) %   99.9999%      99.9999%   99.9999%       99.9999%
Per Hop Rel.(Rain)%         A <-> R 99.9991%   99.9991%R <-> B
One Way Path Rel. % 99.9981%                                 99.9981%
------------------------------------------------------------------------
Repeater Antenna Coupling
Feed Point Sep.  ft                  10.0
Antenna Sep Loss dB                  50.7
Antenna XPD Loss dB                  20.0
Receive C/I,Rptr dB                  42.1       42.1
------------------------------------------------------------------------

              Reliability Data...........:

              Terrain roughness factor, W:  50.0 Average terrain
              Climate Type...............:     1 Coastal, hot, humid
              Climate / Terrain Factor...: 2.000
              Mean Temperature, degrees F:  60.0
              Fading Season,........days : 111.7    1=A  4=D1  7=E  10=H
                                                    2=B  5=D2  8=F
              Rain Climatic Region (1-10):     8 F  3=C  6=D3  9=G

              Multipath Outage/year, A receive :    21.7 Seconds
              Multipath Outage/year, B receive :    21.7 Seconds
              Rain+Multipath Outage/year, 2 Way:   628.0 Seconds

                   Path Length, End to End :    13.0 Miles
                       Annual Outage/mile :     48.3 Seconds/mile
```

```
                          Figure 4.
            Solar Electric Battery power for RF Repeaters
----------------------------------------------------------------------
Customer: NCF88                    Repeater :RF 18000
Location: Los Angeles County       Map Code :181
Latitude: 34N                      Longitude:118W
----------------------------------------------------------------------
Panel Factor        :      5.65    Battery Factor    :        131
Module model        : AS M75 SF    Battery model     : GNB 5000
Current, Amps       :      2.94    Capacity A/H      :        100
Voltage             :     16.0     Autonomy, days    :          7
Tilt Angle, deg     :     55 S     Minimum Temp, C   :          0
                                   Temp Comp         :          1
----------------------------------------------------------------------
Load                :   East (A)      :  West (B)
Current, Amps       :     1.60       :     1.60
Daily Load, A/H     :    38.40       :    38.40
----------------------------------------------------------------------
Array Size         Regulator Battery Size                   Cap A/H
A modules      4      1     A batt:          4                 400
B modules      4      1     B batt:          4                 400
----------    ---          ----------
Total   :      8      2     Total  :         8
----------------------------------------------------------------------
Autonomy, days (calculated)      A:      7.5        B:      7.5
```

```
                          Figure 5.
            Solar Electric Battery power for RF Repeaters
----------------------------------------------------------------------
Customer: NCF88                    Repeater :RF 18000
Location: New York City            Map Code :192
Latitude: 41N                      Longitude:74W
----------------------------------------------------------------------
Panel Factor        :      8.36    Battery Factor    :        146
Module model        : AS M75 SF    Battery model     : GNB 5000
Current, Amps       :      2.94    Capacity A/H      :        100
Voltage             :     16.0     Autonomy, days    :          7
Tilt Angle, deg     :     65 S     Minimum Temp, C   :        -10
                                   Temp Comp         :        1.1
----------------------------------------------------------------------
Load                :   East (A)      :  West (B)
Current, Amps       :     1.60       :     1.60
Daily Load, A/H     :    38.40       :    38.40
----------------------------------------------------------------------
Array Size         Regulator Battery Size                   Cap A/H
A modules      5      1     A batt:          5                 500
B modules      5      1     B batt:          5                 500
----------    ---          ----------
Total   :     10      2     Total  :        10
----------------------------------------------------------------------
Autonomy, days (calculated)      A:      8.1        B:      8.1
```

CEL-05

CELLULAR MARKETING - NEW CHALLENGERS FOR A GROWTH INDUSTRY

Daniel R. Croft - Chairperson

General Sales/Marketing Manager
Centel Cellular Company

8725 Higgins Road
#250
Chicago, IL 60631

The cellular industry is rapidly moving through the various stages of an industrial life cycle. Most metropolitan areas across the United States have cellular availability and expansion into the rural areas is becoming a reality. As the cellular industry matures, new marketing programs must evolve. This seminar addresses the marketing issues of a growing and a maturing business. Will service rates change and subscriber product continue its price declines? Can churn be dealt with effectively? The addition of service in the rural statistical areas will most certainly affect this industry not only in small towns and interstates, but also the manner in which cellular service is marketed in existing metropolitan areas.

Ronald F. Bills - Motorola Inc.

Daniel P. Norman - BellSouth

Herschel Shosteck - Herschel Shosteck
Associates, Ltd.

THE EVOLVING CHALLENGE

Daniel R. Croft
General Sales/Marketing Manager
Centel Cellular Company
8725 Higgins Road
#250
Chicago, IL 60631

Marketing cellular service has continued its evolvement. While fears of little opportunity beyond pent-up demand have subsided, customer churn, for example, is now a major threat to a successful cellular operation. This session addresses the key points of a marketing program that addresses the changing cellular industry.

SUBSCRIBER PRODUCTS AND NATIONAL DISTRIBUTION

Ronald F. Bills
Marketing Manager
Cellular Subscriber Product
Motorola Inc.
1501 W. Shure Drive
Arlington Heights, IL 60004

Subscriber product and national distribution subscriber product in a few short years has already evolved through numerous generations. A burgeoning demand for portable cellular telephones will have a vast impact on the marketing of cellular service. As portables proliferate, even greater attention will be focused on nationwide service offerings. This session examines the impact of product development and its effect on effective distribution methods.

MARKETING FOR TOMORROW

Daniel P. Norman
Director of Sales
BellSouth
5600 Glenridge Drive
#600
Atlanta, GA 30342

Subscriber demand has reached unprecedented levels in some markets while in others it remains a struggle. Competition remains fierce at all levels. Service in the RSAs is imminent. These factors and others will have a major impact on the price of the cellular service. This session focuses on the outlook for carrier rate structure as well as the role of subscriber product in the carrier's marketing plans.

THE LONG RANGE DEMAND FOR CELLULAR SERVICE

Herschel Shosteck
President
Herschel Shosteck Associates, Ltd.
10 Post Office Road
Silver Springs, MD 20910

With the proliferation of cellular service across the United States and decreasing equipment prices, new demand curves may be in the cellular industry's future. This session presents current statistical analysis of growth projections for cellular telecommunications. Long range opportunities and limitations confronting the cellular industry are examined.

CEL-06

DESIGNING, OPTIMIZING AND EXPANDING CELLULAR SYSTEMS

Neil E. Cox - Chairperson
Director, Engineering

Ameritech Mobile Communications
1515 Woodfield Road, Suite 1400
Schaumburg, Illinois 60173

Abstract

Early cellular systems had virtually
no frequency reuse. Since each
initial cell was relatively large,
the total number needed to serve the
desired area did not exceed the
allocated channel sets; therefore,
interference was low and call quality
was very high. However, growth in
cellular has caused changes to be
made to these designs to keep the
customers' expectations on call
quality the same as the initial
systems. This seminar will look at a
variety of methods for designing,
optimizing and expanding mature
cellular systems.

Thomas R. Crawford - Integrated
Telecom
Corporation

M. K. Detrano - AT&T Bell
Laboratories

Ray Dolan - NYNEX Mobile
Communictions
Company

Barry J. Leff - Peninsula
Engineering
Group, Inc.

Russell Patridge - GTE Mobilnet
Incorporated

DESIGNING A CELLULAR NETWORK FOR THE PORTABLE USER

Raymond P. Dolan
Manager - Frequency Planning
and Design

NYNEX Mobile Communications Company
One Blue Hill Plaza
16th Floor
Pearl River, NY 10965

Abstract

The demand for cellular
communications has far exceeded the
initial forecasts by system
designers. As a result, the focus in
most large systems has been on
increasing capacity through cell
splitting, with some enhancements to
coverage as well. The penetration of
portable 600mw cellular phones,
however, has added an additional
criteria to system design. This
paper will propose a method of
providing quality service to low
power portable customers while
continuing to serve the mobile user
as efficiently as possible.

OPTIMIZING COVERAGE WITH CELLULAR REPEATERS

Barry J. Leff
President

Peninsula Engineering Group, Inc.
1091 Industrial Road
San Carlos, CA, 94070

Abstract

As cellular systems mature beyond the initial
push to provide basic service in an area, more attention focuses on optimizing and improving
coverage. This is a very important topic, since
one of the major points that cellular companies
compete on is quality of coverage.

Cellular repeaters have become an accepted technology to use in filling in shadow areas caused
by terrain or buildings, and to provide service in
tunnels and convention centers. The economics
are compelling: a cellular repeater, capable of
carrying 30 - 40 channels at 250 mW ERP/chan-
nel can typically be installed for under $40,000
complete; this is approximately 10% of what it
would cost to install a cell site.

A paper at last year's NCF described cellular rf
repeater technology in general; the purpose of
this paper is to present some "real-life" examples
demonstrating the system engineering used in installing cellular repeaters. The examples given
include stretches of freeway, golf courses, tunnels, and convention centers.

Freeway Coverage

On heavily traveled freeway corridors, even
small shadow areas may be intolerable if they
cause calls to drop and customers to complain.
The application described here is a stretch of Interstate 5 between Olympia and Tacoma,
Washington. One interesting feature of this particular application is that only 45 dB of repeater
gain was required; showing that in many instances the full 70 dB available is not required.

Prior to installing the repeater, there was a 1/4
mile stretch of the freeway at Nisqually where
calls dropped out due to loss of coverage. With
the repeater there is continuous coverage through
this area.

The Peninsula Engineering Group CMRF-800
cellular repeater was installed on a 70' wood

pole, at the base of the pole, in a driveway of a private residence amongst trees. The antenna toward the donor cell is a Scala PRBB-850, 17 dB gain, 12° directional parabola, mounted at the top of the pole. The antenna toward the coverage area is another Scala PRBB-850 mounted at the 30' level on the pole. LDF5-50A feeder line was used.

The donor cell is a Northern Telecom system, loaded with 11 channels located 6.5 miles from the repeater site. A 10 dB omni no tilt antenna is used at the donor cell. The coverage area is a 1/4 mile stretch of I-5, 2 lanes North and South, located 2.5 miles away from the repeater site.

The cell site ERP is 100 Watts; signal level at the top of the pole is -50 dBm. The repeater gain has been padded down from the maximum 70 dB to +45 dB; with two 17 dB gain antennas, ERP/channel is +23 dBm. Repeater gains are adjusted taking into account maximum power authorized by the FCC, antenna decoupling available, and number of channels at the donor cell (maximum repeater output power varies with the number of channels going through the repeater to keep intermodulation products down).

Golf Course Coverage

Golf courses in general are an interesting application for repeaters. They are generally situated in areas where terrain and distance from the city center may make coverage difficult. There is also a strong desire on the part of relatively affluent golfers to be able to use their mobile phones on the course.

We have two golf course applications to describe, both somewhat similar, one in Phoenix, Arizona, one in Kent, Washington. In both cases, prior to installing the repeater there was NO coverage at the course due to the course being in a valley below a bluff that was blocking coverage. The coverage area in Kent is a .5 x 1 mile 18 hole golf course; in Phoenix it was desired to provide coverage along a commuter route as well, so the coverage area is 2 miles x 2 miles, with a 1/4 mile minimum distance to the repeater.

In both cases the donor cell was part of a Northern Telecom system located 6 - 6.5 miles from the repeater. In both cases the donor is providing 100 Watts ERP with an omni antenna.

At both Phoenix and Kent the repeater site itself is at a private residence. In Phoenix the PEGI CMRF-800 repeater was mounted in a pool-side closet with one Celwave PD10085 10 dB 65° panel antenna mounted on the front of the house pointing at the donor cell and another panel antenna mounted on a fence on the back of the house toward to coverage area. The panel antennas were selected for their "low profile" in a residential neighborhood. The signal from donor

in Phoenix was at a level of -59 dBm; with 10 dB of antenna gain on both sides and 65 dB of repeater gain, output toward the mobiles is 250 mW (+24 dBm) per channel.

In Kent the repeater and antennas were installed on a 60' ham tower at a private residence. Even though the repeater is a little closer to the donor cell than in the Phoenix installation, incoming signal to the repeater is down to -80 dBm (the trees in the Seattle area absorb lots of rf energy). In this case a 17 dB gain Scala parabola was chosen toward the cell site, and a 10 dB Celwave PD 10085 panel toward the coverage area. With full 70 dB of gain at the repeater, output toward the coverage area is +11 dBm per channel.

In both of these cases, the repeater allows portable coverage in an area where there was no coverage before. They also represent two different extremes in climate; Phoenix in the desert, with no trees to reduce signal levels, and wet, heavily forested Seattle.

Tunnel Coverage

Tunnels are difficult to provide coverage in with conventional technology; rf does not propagate into the mouth of the tunnel very well. While it is annoying not to have coverage in tunnels, in most cases it would not be economically justifiable to put a cell site in to cover a single tunnel. Cellular Repeaters make it economical to cover tunnels.

Peninsula Engineering Group worked with Cellular One in Pittsburg to provide coverage in three tunnels: Squirrel Hill, Fort Pitt, and Liberty tunnel. The tunnels range in length from 3600 to 5900 feet. Prior to the repeater installation there was only coverage near the portals; no coverage in the main sections of the tunnels. With the repeaters installed there is complete coverage in the tunnels (there are occasional problems at the far end of the Ft. Pitt tunnel, which is the shortest, at a curve).

The cellular system is Ericsson. The donor has 100 Watts ERP with omni antenna. The antenna used toward the donor cell was selected based on gain required to get a good signal into the repeater; antennas used were a 12 dB yagi at Squirrel Hill, a 17 dB Scala parabola at the Liberty tunnel, and a 26 dB gain 10 ft. Mark grid dish at Ft. Pitt. With 65 dB repeater gain and either a 9 or 12 dB Celwave yagi in the tunnel ERP per channel in the tunnel is +22 - +24 dBm.

At Squirrel Hill and Liberty the Peninsula Engineering Group CMRF-800 Repeater was installed on an outside wall; at Ft. Pitt the CMRF-800 was installed in the ceiling ventilation area.

All repeaters provide good coverage even in heavy traffic. The overall system dropped call rate improved by 25% with the advent of tunnel coverage.

Convention Center Coverage

Cellular operators can generate substantial revenue by being able to provide coverage inside convention centers, allowing the use of portable phones during trade shows. However, as is the case with tunnels, it would be difficult to cost justify a cell just for a convention center.

Many convention centers are built partly underground, or with construction techniques that do not allow good coverage inside from a signal outside. The Moscone Convention center in San Francisco is a concrete structure, largely underground. Without the repeater there was no coverage whatsoever.

Two PEGI CMRF-800 Cellular Repeater are used; with the repeaters installed there is portable coverage throughout the underground facility. Two repeaters were necessary because there are two halves of the convention center, with no conduit available to run a coax line and an antenna from one side to the other.

The cellular system in use is Ericsson; as this is in downtown San Francisco, the donor cells are relatively heavily loaded. The repeater are fed from different donors, both with 45 channels and three sectors. One donor is 2 miles from the convention center; the other is 3/4 mile. One donor has 91 Watts ERP, the other 87. Both result in a signal at the convention center of -75 dBm.

The repeaters are installed on the wall of utility closets. One repeater has a Sinclair 4R60 donor site antenna with 150' of LDF 5 - 50 feedline. With 65 dB repeater gain in the CMRF-800 and 200 - 300 feet of coax driving three KAT7402127 (9 dB gain, 105°) Katraine Panel antennas ERP per channel is approximately 10 dBm.

The other repeater has a Celwave PD10040 Panel Antenna (8 dB gain, 60°) toward the donor cell, and three panel antennas run off of 40 - 350' of coax, yielding similar signal levels.

The interesting thing to note in this installation is the use of multiple antennas in the convention center to provide even coverage. In both cases the two closer antennas were split off of one coax run, and the furthest antenna, 300 - 350' from the repeater, was on its own coax line.

The best coverage would be provided by using leaky coax around the building; however at $5-6 per foot, that is expensive. Our experience has shown that several antennas on regular coax provides nearly the quality of coverage that would be expected with leaky coax at much lower cost.

Conclusion

These examples show some of the flexibility of Cellular Repeaters. They can be used to improve coverage on a cost effective basis in rural areas, downtown in major cities, in all types of environments from desert to heavily forested regions. The systems described herein using the CMRF-800 Repeater have been virtually maintenance free since installation over a year ago.

INTEGRATING TRANSMISSION TECHNOLOGIES FOR CELLULAR NETWORKS

Thomas R. Crawford
Product Manager/Industry Specialist

Integrated Telecom Corporation
630 International Parkway
Richardson, TX 75081

Abstract

Providing transmission of voice and data is a primary requirement of a cellular network. This transmission must be done reliability yet cost effectively. Various technologies are available for use in implementing transmission networks with these considerations in mind. As cellular operators look to make network changes for long term growth and profitability, these technologies can be integrated into their networks.

Importance of Transmission

Transmission is often viewed as a necessary evil to the cellular network. However, its importance as a key ingredient in the successful operation of the cellular business should not be underestimated for three key reasons. First, good quality and reliable transmission can be an important ingredient in maintaining a marketing edge over the competitor. A second reason is that if a transmission path is down for any reason, lost calls and the resultant lost revenue can be staggering. Finally, while the cost of not having good quality, reliable transmission facilities is lost revenue and unhappy customers, the cost of maintaining these facilities is quite high. The average cellular operator spends between 20% and 50% of his operating budget maintaining these transmission facilities.

Emphasis on gaining better cost and operational control of transmission facilities is becoming increasingly important due to the maturation of many of the cellular networks. The licensing nature of the industry and the terms of those licenses dictate that MSA networks be built as expediently as possible with market coverage, market share and revenue growth being the immediate goals. Once these goals are approached, network profitability and reliability become the primary goals. As the network matures, the operator accumulates working knowledge of the network and can anticipate changes farther out into the future. Despite the best preplanning, the operators usually find differences between his existing network and the desired long term network. Many networks are now reaching a maturation stage where the operators are consolidating or redesigning the network to migrate towards the desired network.

Available Transmission Technology

The basic transmission requirements for cellular networks are simple. Voice traffic must be transmitted from its origination point, be it a cell site or a POP, to a MTSO. Once switched at the MTSO, this voice traffic must then be transmitted to the destination point, another cell or POP. In addition to the voice, relatively low speed data must be sent around the network. All of these transmission requirements can be satisfied with the proper combination of a small set of building blocks. They are: wide band transmission trunks, voice and data multiplexers, cross-connect devices, compression capabilities and network management.

Transmission Technology – Transmission Trunks

Transmission trunks of almost any bandwidth can be designed and implemented. However, various industry standards have developed through the years for telephone (primarily voice) transmission. These transmission standards are the analog transmission line, T1, T1C, T2 and T3. Since the breakup of AT&T, these standards have been followed by most carriers as well as by equipment vendors of most voice equipment.

The analog transmission line is designed to pass analog signals in the range of 300 hz to 3,300 hz. While its analog nature makes it prone to noise, this type of channel is used extensively throughout the non-cellular telephone networks. T1 is a digital standard for the transmission rate of 1.544 Mbps, of which 1.536 Mbps are useable by the customer. It was made available to private users by tariff in 1982 and has enjoyed considerable growth in usage since then. The other standard transmission trunks commonly used in

cellular networks are T1C, T2 and T3. These three standards are based on multiples of the basic T1 rate; T1C carriers twice the capacity of a T1, T2 four times the capacity and the T3 carries twenty eight times the capacity of a T1. Unlike the T1 trunk, T1C, T2 and T3 are not commonly available from carriers throughout the country.

Anticipated traffic patterns and network topology are key factors in determining the transmission standard to use. However, the choice of a transmission trunk standard usually comes down to tradeoffs between quality, reliability and cost. Other than the analog voice channel, all the other standards are digital and should be of equal quality. It is wise to check local references to validate this. With reasonable quality and reliability parity, the decision often centers on cost. Here dramatic savings can be achieved if traffic warrants it. Table 1 shows a comparison of recurring costs for the various trunk standards of carrier leased transmission facilities. The cellular operator can overlay the bandwidth requirements with the trunk cost comparison to indicate the preferred transmission trunk standard.

Transmission Technology – Multiplexers

Multiplexers are used to combined multiple channels for transmission over a single transmission trunk. While there are many multiplexing technologies, most cellular networks use the standard transmission trunks which are designed around time division multiplexing or, in the case of the analog trunk, no multiplexing.

In cellular networks, the bulk of the traffic to be transmitted originates in analog form (voice). In order to transmit these channels over digital "T Carrier" facilities, the analog sources must be converted to digital streams. In conjunction with T1, a standard for this conversion has been established whereby analog telephone signals are converted to a 64 Kbps digital signal. Once conversion of the analog telephone signals has been accomplished, the multiplexer combines multiple digital streams into a single digital aggregate for transmission. Most voice multiplexers adhere to standards defined in the AT&T Technical Publication 43801 by multiplexing of 24 channels, each 64 Kbps onto a T1 digital stream. The 24 channels fill the usable bandwidth available in the T1. This type of voice multiplexer is called a channel bank and is a commonly available product used in cellular networks (and elsewhere) for multiplexing voice. Multiplexers for data are also available but unlike the channel bank, there is no universal standard for multiplexing data; connectivity between different vendor's equipment is not always guaranteed. The channel bank aggregate is at T1. Multiplexing to T1C, T2 or T3 requires multiplexing equipment that can provide an aggregate at those rates.

Most multiplexers are used at the endpoint of a high speed trunk to demultiplex the entire trunk. Often the network designer merely wishes to add on or take off a few of the channels on a high speed trunk as the stream goes through a location. In this situation, a Drop and Insert Multiplexer may be used. Such a multiplexer is simply a multiplexer with two aggregates. The bulk of the channels do not terminate at the multiplexer, but rather enter through one aggregate and exit through the other. The few channels which do terminate at the multiplexer are dropped off from or inserted into one of the two aggregates for transmission to remote locations.

Transmission Technology –
Cross-Connect Devices

Many types of networks have juncture points where channels which had been sharing a transmission trunk must now be separated for transmission over separate transmission trunks. This situation requires the use of a cross-connect device, which can digitally split out single or groups of channels on one wide band trunk and route them to other wide band trunks. The routing is programmable, providing flexibility for easy changes and additions. Because the various wide band standards (T1, T1C, T2, T3) are all based upon the 64 Kbps channel as being the basic increment of bandwidth, most cross-connect devices are designed to switch single or groups of 64 Kbps channels. Proprietary multiplexing schemes (which do not segregate channels into 64 Kbps streams) will not be able to use cross-connect devices to switch the individual channels; any such multiplexed trunks must be switched as whole trunks.

Transmission Technology – Compression

In order to improve bandwidth utilization, as much traffic as possible should be placed in any given bandwidth. Filling unused channels is one means of increasing band width utilization. This

process, called "groom and fill", uses a cross-connect device to combine multiple, partially filled, parallel trunks into several completely filled, parallel trunks.

Once all the available channels are filled, attention focuses on reducing the bandwidth used by each channel. This is called compression. Compression algorithms are based on the predictability of the information being sent. For data, the predictability is relatively low and hence compression is not as easily accomplished. Voice patterns, on the other hand, are highly predictable. Further, unlike data equipment, the human ear can tolerate a significant amount of distortion or noise and still understand. There are numerous compression algorithms which can be used to provide dramatic bandwidth reductions. These algorithms can often be set to provide different amounts of compression, reducing voice channel bandwidth from 64 Kbps to 32 Kbps, 24 Kbps or even 12 Kbps. It is not surprising that as more compression is attempted, the quality of the voice erodes. This perceived voice quality is subjective. There is an industry term known as "toll quality" which is used to indicate a voice quality with no perceptible difference from a full 64 Kbps channel. A standard has been set for toll quality compressed voice using 32 Kbps ADPCM. Other non-standard algorithms offer toll quality voice but validation of this claim is recommended before any implementation is attempted. With the standard 32 Kbps ADPCM compression, a 2:1 bandwidth improvement is accomplished, effectively reducing the cost per channel by half.

Network Topologies

The most common network topologies are point to point, hub and spoke, ring and mesh. While the point to point topology is limited in its capabilities, its simplicity is attractive. Hub and spoke networks (multiple outlying nodes all connected to a central site) are typical where a large central resource must be accessed or shared, as in the MTSO for a cellular network. The hub and spoke networks often result from a series of point to point links all sharing a common central point. Ring (nodes arranged in a ring or loop fashion, each connected to its neighbor with transmission lines) and mesh (multiple nodes each with connectors to many or all other nodes) networks are more complicated networks which can provide multiple paths between any two points to improve the reliability of the network by providing for alternate routing around a failed trunk. With these alternate paths, network flexibility to deal with traffic peaks, maintenance outages or new equipment installation is provided.

Networks tend not to be static. The typical cellular network changes as more cells are added, more POPs are accessed and roaming connections are added. While each cellular network is different, most have developed in a similar fashion. This similarity has resulted in most cellular networks developing into a hub and spoke or extended spoke topologies. The hub and spoke topology is usually chosen because of the main focal point, the MTSO through which all traffic has to be switched. Figure 1 shows that the vast majority of cellular networks have relatively few cells. For these networks, the hub and spoke offers the simplest design. Even for larger networks, the hub and spoke design is the development path of least resistance because of the serial fashion with which cells are usually added. A cellular network designer usually estimates where to place the initial cells then uses the traffic patterns from these initial cells to pinpoint future cell locations. This pattern of adding sites does not lend itself to a precise topology plan in the early stages of a network.

Another tendency in cellular networks is the use of extended spokes. These spokes typically follow high density traffic patterns produced by major highways or population developments. As the development progresses outward, the spoke extends further.

Integration of Transmission Technologies

With the maturation of cellular networks, cost issued and control have become key concerns. Many of the transmission technologies outlined earlier may be used to address these issues. Integration of these technologies during network consolidation-redesign can result in improved, more cost effective networks.

Cost reduction through integration of these technologies can be achieved at all the key locations: the cell site, the remote hub, the extended spoke and the MTSO. Most techniques for cost reduction at the cell site are already widely practiced. Comparison of transmission trunk costs from carriers in a given MSA with the typical voice channel requirements usually indicate that T1

is the transmission trunk of choice. Where the traffic from a particular cell requires more than one T1 trunk, voice compression should be examined to "squeeze" the required traffic onto a single T1 trunk and still maintain toll quality.

The remote hub is an extension of the hub and spoke topology. As Figure 2 illustrates, most cells do not have enough voice traffic to completely utilize the bandwidth of a T1 trunk. Hence, even though T1 may be the most cost effective transmission trunk, part of the T1 leased bandwidth is unused. By integrating a cross-connect device at a remote location, or "remote hub", traffic from several cells may be combined to completely fill one or more T1 trunks for transmission to the MTSO. Voice bandwidth can be further reduced by integrating both a cross-connect device and voice compression at the remote hub location. Figure 3 illustrates this technique.

These same transmission technologies may be integrated in an extended spoke topology to reduce costs. Without some way to consolidate traffic, parallel trunks from all the cells must be connected to the MTSO. Maximized bandwidth utilization is accomplished by locating a cross-connect device and voice compression at points where the bandwidth of the spoke backbone is filled up with successive parallel trunks. Consolidation and compression of traffic will reduce trunk requirements as illustrated in Figure 4.

If appropriate measures have been taken at the cell, remote hub and extended spokes, all that need be done at the MTSO is to uncompress the channels and combine them in appropriate groups for switching by the MTSO. If the switch has T1 interfaces, the transmission trunks need only be presented in T1 form; demultiplexing to the analog voice level is not necessary. The number of T1s presented to the switch may not have to match the number of T1s originating from the cells. The groom and fill technique can consolidate the traffic into full T1 trunks for the switch.

The integration of various transmission technologies discussed thus far have dealt with cost reduction. Network control, flexibility and reliability are also key goals with a maturing network. The primary ingredients needed to accomplish these goals are: good network monitoring and diagnostic equipment, redundant communications paths and equipment, and the means of switching traffic onto alternate communication paths when needed. Network management ability to communicate among the components to fully utilize them is also required.

Network monitoring and diagnostic equipment varies considerably in terms of monitoring detail, reporting capabilities, diagnostics, speed and cost. While a detailed discussion of the available capabilities will not be given here, the basic requirement for the selected system is to allow monitoring at a central site of all key parts of the network to quickly pinpoint trouble.

While built in redundancy in equipment is a normal requirement, redundancy in communications trunks is less frequently specified. As we have seen in communications, paths alone are quite expensive. Providing redundancy for the paths compounds the expense. Despite this expense, redundancy may be warranted on paths with heavy or critical traffic. If full redundancy is to be provided, the trunks should be routed over different paths. Partial redundancy (maintaining n + 1 independently routed paths when n are needed) can be implemented with proportionately less cost while maintaining a high degree of redundancy.

Additional increases in network reliability are available by spreading traffic from several cells across different trunks. Any trunk failure results in partial service degradation from each cell rather than the full loss of service of any individual cell. Integrating both the cross-connect device and voice compression carries this capability one step further. Voice compression may be activated in the event of a trunk failure to squeeze all the traffic over the remaining trunks. This approach further increases redundancy without increasing the transmission channel costs. When considering trunk redundancy for a cellular network, the topologies tend to be more ring or mesh orientated. These are the topologies which offer redundancy in paths between network points.

Conclusion

A cellular telephone company's "business" is the transmission and switching of voice and data. Providing the necessary transmission is a major part of a cellular company's costs. However, any disruption in these transmission facilities results in significant lost revenue and disgruntled customers. Any network design involves the tradeoff between adequate, reliable transmission facilities and minimum transmission costs. Cellular networks are usually forced to develop quickly without the ability to preplan all geographic locations. As many cellular networks mature, changing priorities force a revisiting of the networks implementation. This presents an opportunity to make many changes required for the long term development of the network.

Several transmission technologies are available for use in making these changes. These technologies are: transmission trunks, multiplexers, compression, cross-connect capabilities, and network management. By integrating these technologies together in the network, enhanced flexibility and reliability can be obtained. Equally important, network operating costs can be decreased, often dramatically, Implementation of these technologies is dependent on the existing and desired long term topology of the network, and tradeoffs between features and costs. The resulting network can more efficiently match the long term requirements for the cellular business.

References

1. Based on interviews with numerous cellular operators by author.

2. Information contained in _Cellular Business_, June 1988, Volume 5, #6. Published by Cellular Business, P.O. Box 12901, Overland Park, Kansas 66212-0930.

3. Based on customer provided information and industry interviews by author.

Type of Trunk	Voice Channel Capacity[1]	Typical Relative Trunk Costs[2]	Typical Relative Cost[2] per Voice Channel
Leased Line	1	1	100
T1 (1.544 Mbps)	24	5–12	20–50
T1C (3.152 Mbps)	48	N/A[3]	N/A[3]
T2 (6.312 Mbps)	96	N/A[3]	N/A[3]
T3 (44.736 Mbps)	672	35–65	5–10

[1] Assuming No Compression
[2] Costs are typical only. Exact costs vary widely depending on carrier, distance and boundary crossings.
[3] N/A = Not Widely Tarriffed

TABLE I.   STANDARD TRANSMISSION TRUNK COMPARISON

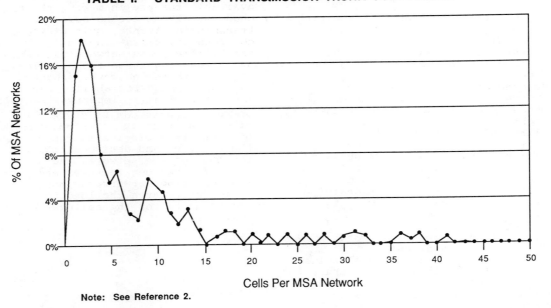

Note: See Reference 2.

Fig. 1.   Breakdown of Cells per MSA for Top Operating 305 MSA

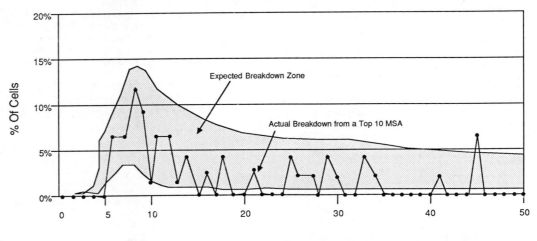

Note: See Reference 3.

Fig. 2.   Voice Per Cell Channel Trunk Breakdown

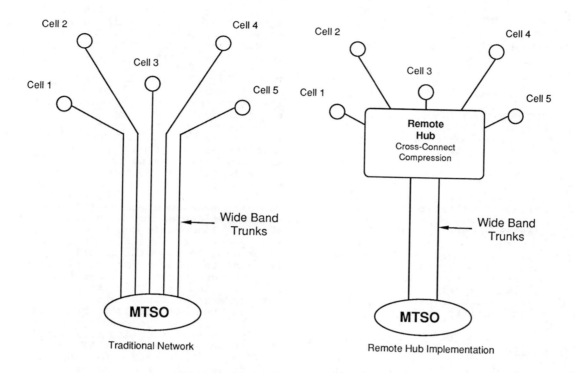

Fig. 3. Using a Remote Hub to Reduce Trunk Costs

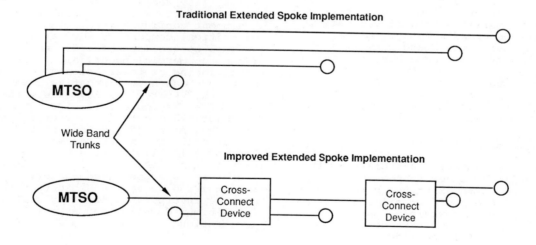

Fig. 4. Improved Extended Spoke Implementation

CELLULAR SERVICE QUALITY EXPECTATIONS

Russell Patridge
General Manager-Midwest Region

Keith Kaczmarek
Manager
Advanced Technology Planning

GTE Mobilnet Incorporated
6060 Rockside Woods Blvd.
Cleveland, Ohio 44131

Abstract

This paper addresses quality expectations of cellular telephone service as achieved primarily through system design, optimization and ongoing operations. The maturing process of the cellular industry has been characterized by the development of practices, procedures and the sophisticated support systems required to design, construct and operate high quality cellular networks.

Introduction

Cellular service quality expectations focus primarily upon the essential system performance characteristics, areas of coverage and availability of desired features. The objective of all carriers is to create a competitive advantage by offering high levels of service quality.

The cellular industry is now more than five years old with well over a million subscribers. Throughout this development process most carriers within a market have achieved parity in areas such as coverage, price, product performance and network reliability. Consequently, the only differentiation to the customer is overall quality of service. The significant practices and procedures used by carriers to develop and maintain quality networks.

System Design/Optimization

The initial activity associated with the design of a new system or the expansion of an existing system is the development of a preliminary growth plan. Growth plans are based primarily on demographic data, principal traffic corridors and forecasts for future demand. This data then becomes the basis for the specific design parameters of a new or expanded system. Plans are normally developed for both mobile and portable coverages. The reason for distinguishing between the two types of coverage is that portable coverage requires closer cell spacing for higher signal strength (stronger than - 85 dBm) and more gain in the talkback path (through the use of low noise amplifiers and 17 dB gain sector receive antennas) when compared to mobile coverage.

The design of a system in terms of cell placement consists of an iterative analyzation process of topographical maps, computer generated propagation patterns and actual transmission test patterns. This process is often repeated numerous times due to the unavailability of optimum cell site locations.

Capacity management is a critical element of design for a quality system. Inadequate capacity management will result not only in blocked calls but will greatly increase the chance for interference and poor audio quality. Blocking increases the potential for interference on directed retry as well as when attempting to hand-off to a busy cell. The result is that service is then provided from a cell that is sub-optimal for that location. The blocking probability that is designed into a network is at a level of two percent (P.02). Techniques used to increase capacity and minimize interference include use of additional levels of split cell sites, sectoring for closer frequency reuse, downtilt antennas for RF control and enhanced system control such as overlay/underlay and power control.

Reliability design goals must also be factored into switch and cell site equipment configurations. The loss of critical components such as switch or cell controllers, facilities links, commercial power, air conditioning or tower/antenna structure can have a negative impact on overall system quality (i.e., the loss of a busy core cell site cannot be tolerated due to its impact on the frequency plan and the loss of a remote cell site might result in the loss of all cellular service to an area for an extended period of time). Therefore, equipment redundancy, facilities diversity and backup power must be incorporated into the system for minimum downtime and system degradation.

Network interconnection facilities are designed and constructed using conventional digital circuits as well as fiber-optics where available. This configuration provides the benefits of digital quality from the cell sites through the cellular network and into the public telephone network. Trunk circuits are designed at a blocking probability of one percent (P.01).

Voice channel and trunk capacity is continuously monitored and studied to ensure that the blocking probability thresholds specified above are never exceeded. The result is that "fast busy" and interference related complaints are minimized.

Long-range (5 year) growth plans are developed based on operational feedback after implementing the above coverage capacity plans. These long-range plans are used to evolve coverage and capacity while minimizing the disruption to a system which occurs with a major system re-tune or when there is inadequate capacity in an area.

Implementation

A most critical element of network implementation within the cellular industry is the requirement to construct quickly and efficiently. This objective is being realized through programs such as standardized cell site designs (cookie cutter approach), automated design systems for non-standard cell site designs, pre-packaged portable cells and pre-installation of equipment in buildings prior to placement of the building. The overall results of these programs are that the efficiency and timeline of the construction process are significantly improved.

System Operations/Maintenance

The quality of service offered by a cellular network is influenced as much by the operation and maintenance as by the design and optimization. Consequently, many carriers have established elaborate pro-active maintenance programs. These programs identify and correct potential problems before they become evident to the customer.

The following are examples of elements of a preventative maintenance program employed to sustain high quality network performance:

o   The periodic complete inspection and alignment of cell site equipment;

o   Frequent cell site visits to assure consistent call quality;

o   Automated testing on every channel at specified intervals;

o   The periodic testing of trunk circuits that provide connection to the PSTN (Public Switched Telephone Network);

o   Verification of switching system performance;

o   Sweep testing of antenna and transmission lines over their dynamic range of operation.

In some networks outboard personal computer systems are used to evaluate system performance on a real-time basis. This process allows a network technician to detect both potential and actual problems and to respond appropriately. The systems also identify individual mobile problems which allow the carrier to advise customers of requirements to have their units serviced.

An additional test unit used by some carriers is the SMART (System Monitor And Radio Test) car which automates that process of gathering signal strength data. The data collected is used to determine the requirements for new cells and/or the modification to existing ones. This information is also used to fine tune hand-off topology resulting in more consistent performance throughout the system.

Planning For Future Customer Requirements

There are three primary areas of focus required to satisfy future customer quality expectations. Those areas include: high audio quality, increased coverage and additional enhanced services.

High audio quality is dependent upon maintenance of system capacity and the control of external interference. This condition can best be realized through the use of the "expanded" spectrum. The FCC's allocation of this additional 10 MHz of spectrum, to the cellular industry, will provide the ability to cost effectively meet the capacity requirements of most markets through the early 1990's. The requirement to continually provide more coverage will necessitate the expansion of current networks into new service areas as well as the development of interface capabilities between systems. The majority of the Metropolitan Statistical Areas (MSA's) will be in service by the end of 1988. Expansion into the Rural Service Areas (RSA's) is anticipated in 1989.

With increased portable usage the ability to easily roam in other systems becomes even more critical. An interim solution offered by some carriers forwards calls to the city the cellular customer is in. The next step will be implementation of a more sophisticated system interface standard (EIA IS-41) which will allow inter-system hand-off and eventually call delivery.

Enhanced cellular services that rival the capabilities of a business landline telephone are anticipated for future availability. These capabilities include: integrated voice messaging, higher levels of voice privacy, high-speed data transport, alpha-numeric paging, calling party display and other ISDN-type services.

Conclusion

The quality expectation benchmark of the cellular customer will continue to be that quality level experienced when using a landline facility. The demand of the cellular industry will be to continually upgrade network performance through new and improved procedures used to design, build and maintain cellular systems.

CELLULAR OPERATIONS TOOLS IN THE 1990s

R. L. Brown
M. K. Detrano

AT&T Bell Laboratories
One Whippany Road, Room 1C-350
Whippany, New Jersey 07981

Abstract

Cellular networks are expanding at a breathtaking pace. Tools and methods developed for the early systems of three or four years ago are quickly becoming obsolete. The complexity of these new networks, together with the growing capacity needs, demand increasingly sophisticated tools and systems. This trend will only become more important in the future. This session looks into the 1990s at how some of these future tools and systems could operate.

Historical Perspectives

The cellular phone business has grown at a rate that was not predicted by many. Only five short years ago in the U.S. domestic market, the first commercial systems were coming alive.

A few cells, huddled around the local MTSO, constituted those first systems. Coverage was the aim. The more coverage the better. Customers bought their service from a local provider and used the service locally. Expectations about service outside their home areas were modest. They were delighted when out of town to be be able to use the mobile to make a call. Receiving calls was not an expected reality. Cellular was very much an exclusive business service or an expensive toy that the customer had to be willing to pay for. They had survived without it all these years; the necessity of the service had not been established.

The service providers of those early systems were generally telco wireline subsidiaries, set up with a pioneering management structure and with an independent bottom line. They had few employees, each of whom had far reaching responsibilities, and very little experience operating a business involving switching, transmission, and radio technologies. Revenues were scarce at best and operations were streamlined. Those service providers that were not telco subsidiaries were generally entreprenurial communications companies, frequently from the broadcasting or paging industry. Their operations were similarly streamlined from necessity. Neither type of service provider could afford the elaborate structures set up in the local regulated phone companies. There was a scramble to put in place operations tools and work flows needed to run the business. Varieties of solutions emerged, tailored to specific local needs and experience.

Three distinct areas in the realm of O, A, and M (operations, administration, and maintenance) began to take shape. These can roughly be described as the customer services area, the traditional telco operations area, and the new cellular-specific area associated with managing the RF network.

Customer services, of course, deals with the marketing, provisioning, and the billing of cellular services. Here, most cellular providers relied on existing systems to provide their mechanized support, buying either computing services from an in-house parent data center or from a third party vendor. These systems were used to record service orders, and to rate and bill cellular calls. There was no connection between the service order system and the activation of the customer's service in the cellular switch through translations or recent change transactions.

The traditional telco operations area centered heavily on processing switch traffic data and in the surveillance and maintenance of cellular systems and facilities. By law, the FCC mandated 24 hour/day monitoring of all RF transmission equipment. As a result, this gave rise to a number of mechanized systems and service designed to receive and process equipment alarms and maintenance message data.

The needs of the RF engineer in the early operating environments were focused on providing adequate RF coverage as widely as possible and in trying to manage the quality of the service provided by the cellular network. Most service providers used regular reuse patterns of channel frequencies and were not forced to deal with the problems of capacity of cochannel interference. Many of the engineering and analysis processes were manual and extremely time consuming. Experience and insight grew with the industry.

Somewhat surprisingly, the industry has grown from its infancy to vigorous youth, almost behind our backs. Both wireline and non-wireline systems are now in service in most major markets, with RSA coverage being the next challenge. Most large cities today are faced with everyday problems of both switch and RF capacity as well as cochannel and adjacent channel interference. The problem is no longer one of adequate coverage but one of direct competition, placing increased emphasis on managing quality, features, capital investment in next generation technology, and in product differentiation. An no longer is the customer content to operate a mobile phone solely in the car in the home area. Improved performance for handheld units and wide area paging with call delivery and custom feature availability is expected in the population corridors of the U.S. and Canada.

Future Directions

It is unlikely that the service order process with change substantially in the next five years or so since the concept of providing service will be largely unchanged. The areas of credit checks, accounts receivable, billing records, and statements of billable services will still require mechanized support and will be integrated into a flow through process, if it is not already. Two areas are likely to change, though, as advanced cellular systems with more intelligent base stations and support tools emerge. The first area already beginning to change is to establish a direct, mechanized interface between the service order system and the cellular MTSO for the purposes of entering subscriber recent change information needed by the MTSO. Today this is a relatively straightforward procedure, whether manual or mechanized. However, as roamer service becomes more sophisticated, it will be necessary to establish or change customer service characteristics broadly across many systems at once. The concept of a national registration database (whether actually centrally located or distributed throughout the network) will be implemented, introducing the notion of "call following", i.e., calls will be able to follow you (actually your mobile, and more likely a small portable) across the country, finding you wherever you are without the calling party having to know that you have left your home area.

The other area of customer services change will follow as digital channels are deployed and flexible use of those channels is introduced. Billing criteria will become complex when a subscriber is no longer billed for just the minutes of air time but for the bits of air time (bandwidth) that is consumed. Packetized voice, and the availability of integrated voice/data services requiring

variable amounts of bandwidth will trigger this rethinking. The area of traditional operations focusses mainly on the day-to-day responsibilities for operating and maintaining the system. In the early 90's this activity will be extremely important since by then cellular telecommunications will be much more a part of everyday life of the average consumer and an essential service to the business community and the public safety network.

By the early 90's, mechanized tools and intelligent monitoring systems will be required components of any cellular telecommunications network. Unlike today's tools which are essentially passive, i.e., they report alarms, log maintenance messages, etc., the next generation of tools will be much more actively involved in the well-being of the system, and to a large degree integrated into it. To begin with, sophisticated built-in self test circuitry will be an integral part of digital cellular equipment. Self-diagnosis and self-correction (more accurately self-reconfiguration) will be available. Supplementary to that, the ability to reconfigure the system remotely and in real time will be a manual fallback strategy, allowing the network operator to deal directly with an outage of any level from that of a single radio to the loss of an entire base station. On line configuration data available through real time color graphics displays will be easily manipulated through the use of graphics editors and the like. But even more impressive will be the ability of these systems and tools to integrate system performance data in real time with configuration and maintenance data in order to provide an "expert" understanding of the situation and to feedback recommendations appropriate to the exact nature of the problem at that specific time. For example, suppose part or all of a base station is knocked out of service. The operator must adjust neighbor lists, thresholds and other parameters to compensate for the loss. Depending on the time of day and on the traffic patterns at that hour, the operator might want to vary the compensation plan. A system and tool set that automatically provides the traffic and real time load situation as well as the "best situational scenario" recommendation will optimize the changes of providing continuity of service.

Finally, the third area of cellular specific operations processes and tools will see significant changes. The introduction of an intelligent base station with digital channel technology will facilitate major alterations in today's cellular network topology. Existing cell site locations will be equipped with hundreds of narrower, more efficient digital channels, but will likely be operated in "mixed technologies mode" for quite some time as existing 30KHz FM channels are gradually mined out and replaced with newer technology. With the availability of remote radio frames, new cell site locations will be much easier to obtain and far less restrictive in terms of zoning required for antenna installation. This will result in wide deployment of "micro cells" in dense urban areas, with trunk groups ranging in size from very small (several

channels per street corner), to extremely large (several hundred channels providing wireless PBX services in a major office building). Highway corridor coverage using remote radio frames will become economically feasible, creating much larger geographic coverage areas and broader deployment for standardized cellular networking.

As RF technology and network topologies change, significant enhancements to the planning tools used by cellular engineers will be introduced. Propagation models which predict coverage and interference will model the characteristics of both today's FM channels as well as the newer digital channels. This will allow service providers to plan the orderly introduction of new RF technology with an understanding of expected performance in areas where multiple channel technologies are in use simultaneously. These tools, and the associate base station equipment, will allow such things as engineering of multiple independent server groups within a single base station. This will permit distinct groups of channels to be engineered independently using whatever reuse pattern is optimal for the channel technology being used. These models will provide reliable results in dense urban areas served by low powered micro cells using significantly lower antenna heights. They will also accommodate advanced antennas currently being designed to control coverage and interference more closely. Additionally, tools which characterize in-building RF propagation and the ability to serve primarily portable units will be required as networks evolve in these directions.

An increased demand for efficient transmission facilities will come with the dramatic increase in the number of radios deployed in a system due to the introduction of digital technology. Tools will be available to assist in planning the optimum interconnection of transmission, switching, and network equipment, which will take into account the large variations in trunk group size as well as the highly distributed nature of a cellular system.

Changes in planning tools will accompany the need for enhanced cellular system software to control calls in the new environment.

Improvements and increased flexibility in handoff algorithms, for example, will be used to optimize performance. This is particularly important for portables being served by micro cells and inside buildings, a situation commonplace in the 1990's.

Similarly, call control logic will react in real time to changes in the traffic demand patterns. Initially, traffic pattern analysis was performed by large, rigid, mainframe based tools that executed in batch, off-line mode. Once results were available, changes in allocation of system resources required visiting the affected base stations. Today, these analysis tools are moving toward user definable, PC based modules integrating traffic, maintenance, and configuration data. In the future, digital base station technology will be software controllable, thereby permitting remote reconfiguration. Once refined, these software modules will be incorporated directly into the system call control software and used to provide real time analysis and system reconfiguration in response to changes in traffic demand and availability of system resources.

In Summary

The precise time frame for these changes is not important. What is inescapable is that the cellular industry will continue to mature at a breathtaking rate. Planning now is vital to both the service provider and the manufacturer if each is to remain viable at the next crossroad. This includes the tools and processes by which the cellular networks are operated, a technology unto itself that must keep pace with that of the network.

CEL-07

CELLULAR – THE FUTURE TECHNOLOGIES

William C. Y. Lee, Chairperson

Vice President, Corporate Technology and
Planning

PacTel Mobile Companies
2355 Main Street
Irvine, CA 92713

Digital cellular will be the new
technology for U.S. cellular systems in
the 1990s. Since the mobile radio
environment has introduced both severe
signal fading and time delay spread along
the transmission, the outcome of future
digital cellular systems will be heavily
based on today's thorough designing and
planning. This seminar addresses, what is
digital cellular, why we need it, as well
as issues involving transition, co-
existing, speech coding, interconnection
with ISDN are also examined.

Bo Hedberg – Ericsson Radio Systems AB
Valy Lev – Motorola Inc.
Piyush Sodha – Northern Telecom Inc.
Reed Thorkildsen – AT&T Bell Laboratories
Edward Chien – Southwestern Bell

DIGITAL CELLULAR, WHAT AND WHY

William C. Y. Lee

ABSTRACT

This paper has described the general requirement
of digital cellular. Also, Lee's radio capacity
formula is used to compare the spectrum
efficiency between digital cellular systems and
analog FM systems.

I. INTRODUCTION

The reason that the digital cellular system
is different from the analog cellular system is
that the former transmits digital voice, and
the latter transmits analog voice. Today's
world cellular systems are analog systems. In
North America, the system provides 416 channels;
among them 21 are setup channels and 395 are
voice channels.

For the increase of spectrum efficiency in
cellular we use frequency again and again with
geographical separations. Those cells using the
same frequencies are called co-channel cells.

In designing a cellular system, we need to
have adequate coverage and minimum interference.
These two are always running against each other.
More adequate coverage in one area presents more
interference in neighboring areas. Therefore, we
use separation of co-channel cells and
sectorization in each cell to reduce interference.
However, interference is very hard to control by
the analog system. Therefore, we need to find
some other systems which can reduce and control
the interference, increase the spectrum
efficiency, and provide other new features.

II. DIGITAL CELLULAR

The requirement of a digital system used in
cellular is different from that used in other
applications. Mobile cellular environment
presents a very severe fading medium[1].
Therefore, digital cellular needs to pay
attention in the following areas;

1. Digital Voice –
   (a) It is for commercial use – needs a toll
       quality voice
   (b) It is in a moble radio environment (a
       multipath fading environment) application
       – needs a code protection

2. Speech Coding – there are many digital coding
   schemes. The requirement of speech coding is
   to have a low bit rate code which takes a
   narrow bandwidth, yet the voice has to be
   good.

Tested elements
   1) Different sex (male and female)
   2) Different age groups

Testing requirement
   1) speech recognition – toll quality
   2) speaker recognition –
      a) recognizing the speakers
      b) no distortion in voice due to the
         digitizing process

3. Channel code – to protect the speech code from
   contamination due to fading phenomenon

Tested elements
   1) different vehicle speeds
   2) different environments

Testing requirement
   1) speech recognition – toll quality
   2) speaker recognition –
      a) recognizing the speakers
      b) no distortion in voice due to fading

4. Modulations:

   There are two general types of modulations
   1) Constant envelope modulations – which are
      chosen because of the fading nature in the
      mobile radio environment. THe signal is
      not modulated on the envelope. This type
      of modulation usually takes a wider
      bandwidth.
   2) Linear modulations – linear modulation is
      always treated as a narrower bandwidth
      modulation . When a linear modulation is
      used for a analog signal, the envelope of
      the carrier is modulated by the signal.
      After the signal is received at the receiv-
      ing end, it is distorted by the fading.
      Therefore a replica of fading information
      should be generated solely at the receiver
      and used to recover the faded signal.

   When a linear modulation is used for a
   digital signal, such as shaped OPSK or OAM,
   the former has kept its signal information
   in the four phases of the carrier but the

latter has kept its signal information in both phase and envelope of the carrier. None of digital signals has its signal information kept merely on the envelope of the carrier as the analog signal. As a result, the radio fading only distorts the shape of the waveform but not the signal information itself in the shaped OPSK. The linear modulation's need for proper linear RF amplifiers is a challenging task.

5. Multiple Access Schemes
CDMA has proven to be not a superior scheme for spectrum efficiency, yet it is more complicated to implement. FDMA and TDMA theoretically are no different in comparing their spectrum efficiency usage. However, in reality, FDMA does show a slight advantage over TDMA because of the excessive overhead bits used in TDMA. Besides the spectrum efficiency issue we should also look into other areas such as linear amplification, co-existance, transition, weight, size and cost for comparing these two multiple access schemes.

III. Radio Capacity in Cellular
An equation derived by Lee[4,5,6] as he called it radio capacity is expressed as follows:

$$m = B_c \frac{B_t}{\sqrt{\frac{2}{3}\left(\frac{C}{I}\right)_s}} \quad \text{numer of channels/cell} \quad (1)$$

Where B_t is the total allocated bandwidth, B_c is the channel bandwidth, and $(C/I)_s$ is the required carrier-to-interference for a desired voice quality. The radio capacity is a measure of spectrum efficiency which depends on B_c and $(C/I)_s$. However, B_c and $(C/I)_s$ are dependent parameters which are determined by the voice quality. If B_c reduces, $(C/I)_s$ increases for maintaining a same quality of voice.

If the blocking probability grade of service P_b is defined, then the value in Erlang A can be found from Erlang B model from m and P_b.

$$A = A (m, P_b) \quad \text{Erlang/cell} \quad (2)$$

If the cell area is defined, then Eq(2) can be expressed as

$$A = (m, P_b) \quad \text{Erlang/mile}^2 \quad (3)$$

Therefore, Eq(1) is a fundamental equation.

IV. Why Digital
The digital cellular systems can provide more spectrum efficiency. The answer is given by Eq(1). We may take two approaches.

1) Let the channel bandwidth reduce:
In FM systems B_c = 30 kHz $(C/I)_s$ = 18 dB
$$m = (B_t/194) \times 10^{-3}$$

In digital systems[7,8], B_c = 10 kHz and $(C/I)_s$ 18 dB

$$m = (B_t/65) \times 10^{-3}$$

2) Let the $(C/I)_s$ reduce
In FM systems B_c = 30 kHz, $(C/I)_s$ = 18 dB
$$m = (B_t/194) \times 10^{-3}$$

In digital systems[9] B_c = 30 kHz, $(C/I)_s$ 10 dB

$$m = (V_t/77) \times 10^{-3}$$

In these two approaches, we can see that the digital cellular provides the better spectrum efficiency.

V. Conclusion
In this paper, we have described the digital cellular systems in general, and we also used Lee's radio capacity equation to show the spectrum efficiencies between digital and analog FM. The digital cellular is more spectularly efficient than the analog FM.

References

1. W. C. Y. Lee, Mobile Communications Design Fundamentals, Howard W. Sams, Indianapolis, 1986, Chapter 2.

2. W. C. Y. Lee, Mobile Cellular Telecommunication Systems, McGraw Hill, 1988, Chapter 4.

3. J. A. Tarallo and G. I. Zysman, "Modulation Techniques for Digital Cellular Systems" 38th Vehicular Technology Conference record, Philadelphia, PA June 15-17, 1988, pp.245-248.

4. W. C. Y. Lee, Spectrum Efficiency: A Comparison Between FM and SSB in Cellular Mobile Systems, presented at the office of Science and Technology, FCC, August 2, 1985. Also Telephony, Nov. 11, 1985, p. 82.

5. W. C. Y. Lee, How to Evaluate Digital Cellular Systems, presented to the FCC, Sept. 3, 1987. Also Telecommunications, Dec., 1987, p. 45.

6. W. C. Y. Lee, Spectrum Efficiency and Digital Cellular, 38th IEEE Vehicular Technology Conference record, Philadelphia, PA June 15-17, 1988, pp. 643-646.

7. AT&T Demonstration of a proposed digital cellular system in Chicago, IL held in March, April, 1988.

8. W. C. Y. Lee, Digital Cellular: AT&T Demonstration Report Mobile Radio Technology, June, 1988, p. 26.

9. J. Swerup and J. Uddenfeldt, "Digital Cellular", Personal Communications Technology, May, 1986, pp. 6-12.

TRANSITION ISSUES IN DIGITAL CELLULAR WITH TDMA

Bo Hedberg
Radio Research Department
Ericsson Radio Systems AB
S-164 80
Stockholm, Sweden

Introduction

A new digital system offering increased capacity in cellular systems is under development. Methods for speech coding, channel coding, digital modulation and multiple access are discussed and proposed.

A system concept based on 30 kHz TDMA is proposed. The problems with introducing this new system to operate together with the existing system will be analyzed.

Requirements

It is required to provide increased capacity in the major urban areas e.g. New York City and Los Angeles. Substantial capacity increase is required without adding new sites. Outside the major urban areas there is no capacity problem and less need to introduce new technology. This makes a concept with combined digital/-analog mobiles (dual mode) very attractive. The analog mode will provide Pan-American compatibility.

A critical issue is to provide hand held stations with long operational time and small size.

In addition the new system must co-exist with the present analog 800 MHz equipment in the same band and the transition to digital must be smooth and flexible.

Speech codec choice

Speech quality is of major importance. Therefore it must be ensured that
1) the speech codec bit rate is high enough to provide good quality,
2) error reduction techniques are used so that very few users suffer from high BER.

The Pan-European GSM work has resulted in the specification of a 13 kb/s RPE codec (RPE stands for Regular Pulse Excitation which is a simplified form of multi puls excitation). This provides a speech quality that has barely noticable speech degradation when compared to the quality of 64 kb/s PCM.

The complexity of a 13 kb/s codec is low enough to allow a power consumption of 100 mW which is necessary to the quality handportables.

Codecs operating at bit rates below 10 kb/s have not yet shown satisfactory speech quality in the mobile environment. Furthermore, cost and power consumption could be obstacles for introducing codecs below 10 kb/s.

However, 8-10 kb/s codec technology will be available in a few years time. It is therefore proposed to design the system in such a way that it is based on 8.7 kb/s codec but with the possible option to allow a 13 kb/s for early market introduction.

Channel codec choice

Modern interleaved channel codecs such as Reed-Solomon and Viterbi convolutional are very powerful in reducting the impact of fading. With a moderate bandwidth expansion of 50 %, coding gains are of the order 7-10 dB in carrier-to-interference (C/I) radio. This shows that channel coding is efficient from a capacity point of view.

Punctured convolutional coding (PCC) is very powerful code since it allows bit selective coding. This means that different parts of speech coder information can be coded with different coding rates. In the GSM system this method has been selected with three different classes of speech coding bits. Another advantage of convolutional coding is that soft decoding can be performed. The selected code has constraint length 5 and a soft decision 16 state Viterbi decoder is used.

It is proposed to use punctured convolutional coding with bit selective coding similar to the GSM system. An efficient channel code shall have an average rate around 2/3. Accordingly, the data rate after channel coding is proposed to be 13 kb/s with a speech codec operating at 8.7 kb/s.

Radio modulation choice

Modulation shall be chosen so that a data rate of 14 kb/s per user (including signalling and synchronization) can be accomodated in either 10 kHz equivalent band width 1.4 bps/Hz for an adjacent channel protection equal to the present 30 kHz analog FM system (i.e. around 30 dB).

This precludes constant envelope modulation methods (e.g. GMSK) and makes quasi-linear modulation methods necessary.

In addition there is requirement on C/I-performance. The digital system shall be capable of operating with the same or denser reuse cluster size as analog.

It is proposed to use QPSK which can achieve at least 1.4 bps/Hz. Power efficiency can be made good with offset modulation. There is no problem to provide good performance with existing re-use cluster plans even with differential demodulation. In fact a C/I of 14 dB should be possible to use.

FDMA/TDMA choice

The two most interesting multiple access methods are 30 kHz TDMA and sub-30 kHz FDMA. The difference between 30 kHz TDMA and sub-30 kHz FDMA is not dramatic from a cost or capacity point of view. Both methods make the dual-mode concept viable.

However, there are some system aspects which are very different.

Co-existence

There is a difference between FDMA and TDMA in the amount of spectrum that must be replaced at a time. With TDMA it is possible to replace channel by channel at individual sites i.e. only 30 kHz has to be released at a time. This is very flexible and directly gives more channels.

With FDMA this is not possible unfortunately. The reason is that when a 30 kHz channel is divided into several FDMA carriers these new carriers will be adjacent frequencies to each other in the same cell sector. This will require an adjacent carraier protection of 50-60 dB. This is not possible to use in the direction from mobile to base since it results in too low power efficiency of the mobile transmitter. This will ruin the battery lifetime of a handportable and will also add considerably to the volume of the handportable. It is therefore required to use an adjacent channel protection of 25-30 dB (similar to AMPS).

For FDMA it is thus necessary to replace a whole analog channel group of typically 21 frequencies (630 kHz) at a time. This is not attractive as the whole frequency plan is affected. This affects the co-channel interference situation also outside the sites where channels are replaced. Thus all analog channels operating in the 630 kHz band must be removed at all sites. Furthermore, it is also necessary to use new combiners at all the sites where digital is introduced.

For the TDMA-solutions no new combiners are needed and 30 kHz channels can be replaced one-by-one. Thus, the co-existence requirement makes the TDMA-system much more attractive than FDMA.

Services

The system should cope with a scenario where 8.7 kb/s speech coding is the basic rate but terminals using 13 kb/s speech codecs could also possibly be allowed. This is very simple to handle in TDMA.

For FDMA this is not so simple since it would mean to start with 15 kHz carrier spacing and then later convert to 10 kHz carrier spacing. This means that the co-existence problems mentioned will have to be dealt again when converting from 15 to 10 kHz.

There has been discussion of service called 2I + C where two information channels and one control channel is available per user. For FDMA it is not possible to transmit two carriers from the mobile equipment. Therefore a 2I + C service with full rate channels can only be handled with TDMA unless excessive cost of mobiles is accepted.

Proposal

As mentioned earlier it is risky to base the system on 8-10 kb/s speech codec technology due to both quality and complexity reasons. It is proposed to make the system in such a way that it is based on a 8.7 kb/s speech codec and can possibly support 13 kb/s speech codec.

This means that the analog FM 30 kHz carriers are divided into 3 channels as the basic.

Transition

When introducing the new system we have to face several problems. The most important are listed below.

- Compatibility between old and new systems.

- Is it possible to use the same infra structure as the existing i.e. the same frequency plan, sites, combiners, etc.?

- Implications for mobile and handportable equipment.

- Does the introduction of the new system imply degraded service for the old customers?

- The incentive for the new customers to buy potentially more expensive equipment for the new system.

Compatibility

Since no new frequency band will be available for the new system, introduction has to be made by substituting old channels for new ones. In the beginning this will be made in areas with a capacity problem i.e. centers of big cities. To ensure coverage offered by the existing system the mobile equipments have to be compatible with both systems, dual-mode, which implies more expensive and bulkier equipments. Eventually with good coverage from the new system, equipment designed for the digital system only might be acceptable.

Infra structure

With the system proposed a C/I of 14 dB will be achieved. This means that we can use the existing frequency plan based on a C/I of 17 dB. In fact, if it is acceptable to change the frequency plan, a 4/12 plan could be used to further almost double the spectrum efficiency compared to the existing 7/21 plan.

The required transmit peak powers will be roughly the same in a TDMA 3-split system as for the existing system. Thus the same sites may be used.

Also in a TDMA-system the channel separation and IF bandwidth will be the same as for the analog system. The radio part of the transceivers will therefore be very similar to the existing with the exception of the linear PAs needed for the linear modulation proposed. New modulators that have accurately controlled modulation index for digital modulation are also required.

The digital signal processing part of the transceiver comprises channel codec, speech codec and the baseband part of the modem.

Mobile equipment

The dual-mode requirement mentioned above will make mobile equipments more expensive, more power-consuming and bulkier which becomes a major problem for handportables. With the system proposed the increases in cost and size compared to pure analog handportables can be limited to between 10-20 % which is still significant and can make introduction difficult even though speech quality is superior and the customer will experience a lower blocking rate.

Degraded service

When introducing the new system at least one analog channel has to be substituted at a time, thereby increasing the blocking rate for the analog customer. For example, starting with 15 analog channels and a blocking rate of 5 % and substituting one channel leads to an increase in blocking rate to 7 %. This can be solved by trading in old equipment to some extent for new dual-mode mobiles.

Another solution is to have dual-mode base station transceivers in the start-up phase of the new system until the trunking efficiency for the digital channels has increased to an acceptable level.

Customer incentive

Mobile equipments for the new system will certainly be more expensive. If the cost has to be paid by the customer, some extra features in addition to the superior speech quality and higher degree of service are needed. Secure communication by enciphering and data communication service are possible choices. The question is: Are sufficient number of customers willing to pay the increase in equipment cost for these new features?

Another alternative is that the operator subsidizes the additional cost for a digital equipment which is hopefully a low investment for increased future revenues.

There is also a problem with new features and dual-mode mobiles since the new features are only supplied in the digital mode of operation.

Conclusion

A new digital system has been proposed. The system is designed to facilitate the transition from the existing analog system and also make full benefit of the capabilities of digital transmission.

The problems connected with the transition are identified and solutions are suggested.

TRANSITION ISSUES WITH FDMA

V. Lev
Senior Resource Manager
Cellular Infrastructure Division
Motorola Inc.
1501 W. Shure Drive
Room 2300
Arlington Heights, IL 60004

Various possible solutions and approaches are examined, e.g. FDMA vs. TDMA, constant envelope vs. linear modulation, etc. Next, an FDMA solution for a digital cellular system is presented including transition issues from present analog cellular. Additional issues relevant to digital cellular systems are also presented.

THE CO-EXISTENCE ISSUES

Piyush Sodha
Director Business Development
Cellular Systems Division
Northern Telecom Inc.
2435 N. Central Parkway
Richardson, TX 75080

During 1991-1996, analog and digital cellular technology will co-exist. This session addresses the business and technical issues associated with the co-existence of the two technologies.

SPEECH CODING IN CELLULAR

Dr. Reed Thorkildsen
Supervisor, Speech Processing Design
Cellular Telecommunications Division
AT&T Bell Laboratories
Whippany Road
Whippany, NJ 07981

ABSTRACT

Speech coding is defined as a digital representation of a speech waveform. The objective of any speech coding system simply put, is to achieve an acceptable level of distortion of the original speech at the least possible encoding rate given a set of implementation constraints. The goal of this paper is to give the audience an appreciation of the elements of the speech coding system objectives, high speech quality and low bit-rate, in light of the unique constraints placed upon the system by the cellular environment. These constraints include

° Robust performance in the presence of errors caused by the channel

° Low delay

° Low cost

INTRODUCTION

Speech has always been the main method of communication between people. What better example of this exists than today's telephone network. Like the landline network, the cellular network has been an "analog" one in which the acoustic waveform is represented by a corresponding electrical waveform. And, like the landline network, the cellular network is moving towards digital representation of information.

One reason for the move to digital is the desire for consistency in handling both voice and data. The cellular system is also faced with the problem of nearing capacity limits in high traffic areas. Since spectrum is a resource which has little chance of being expanded, cellular service providers must be able to increase the number of subscribers that the system can handle by being more spectrally efficient...i.e. by using narrower channels or assigning multiple users to a channel. Squeezing speech into smaller bandwidths is easier with digital technology than with analog technology. This is where a digital cellular system, and in particular speech coding technology, is important. High quality speech coders that operate at the lowest possible bit-rate play a key role in the development of more spectrally efficient digital cellular systems.

Developers of speech coding algorithms and hardware are faced with a challenging problem of balancing the trade-offs between a number of speech coding issues in designing for a digital cellular system. The key issues are:

* How is the speech quality measured

* What are the **relationships** between bit-rate, quality and complexity

* How does **coding delay** affect the system

* What are the **effects** of the cellular environment on the speech coder

* What is the **better choice** of DSP or VLSI **implementation** considering cost, **size, power** consumption and development time

Subsequent sections of this paper will discuss these issues. In addition, other speech processing tasks that may be of importance in cellular will be described.

SPEECH QUALITY MEASURES

The quality of **encoded speech** is the aspect of a digital **cellular system** that the end customer **will have to** deal with each time a call **is placed** and is thus an important one. Both objective and subjective measures of quality are useful. It is generally agreed that controlled listening to a speech coder gives a better evaluation of the quality of the coder than objective measures. On the other hand, objective measures are usually easier to obtain than subjective ones. For this reason, objective measures are usually used during the initial simulation and development stages of coder design to compare the coder with previously developed coders of known performance or to compare variations within the same coder design. Once a "good" system has been chosen, formal subjective testing is used to validate the performance. It should be noted that informal subjective tests, with just a few listeners, are also useful in the early stages of coder design.

An example of **an objective** test is the segmental signal-to-noise ratio, SEGSNR. To compute the SEGSNR the speech waveform is divided into segments of 15-20 ms and the signal-to-noise ratio is determined for each segment. The SEGSNR is then the sum of the signal-to-noise ratios for the individual segments divided by the total number of segments.

Subjective tests have been developed over many years which explore various perceptual attributes of a speech coder which are important for communications systems. Among these attributes are word intelligibility, speaker recognizability, and male/female performance. Some tests, such as the Diagnostic Rhyme Test (DRT), only test one attribute...in this case intelligibility. Other tests, such as the Diagnostic Acceptability Measure (DAM) and the **Mean Opinion Score** (MOS) attempt to **provide more of an** overall quality measure. **The MOS has been the** most widely used **subjective quality** measure. This technique uses a large number of **listeners** each of whom is asked to individually rank a system on an absolute **scale from 1 to 5** where the meaning of **the grades** are

        5 - excellent (imperceptable degradation)
        4 - good
        3 - fair
        2 - poor
        1 - bad (objectional degradation)

The MOS is then as it's name implies, the mean of the individual rankings. The designer, or evaluator of a speech coder must be aware of two issues when reviewing MOS test results. First, the test should include a well characterized coder from previous testing. The variability of human perception is reflected in the fact that the MOS score for a particular coder will vary from one test to the next. Incorporation of a coder that has been repeatedly tested will give a baseline to the scores for a particular test. The quality range of coders included in the test is also important. Incorporating coders that are very different from the coder under actual test, with quality either much better or worse, will cause the subject coder quality rating to be biased, low or high respectively

QUALITY, BIT-RATE, COMPLEXITY and DELAY

Fig. 1 shows a plot of quality, as measured in MOS testing, vs. bit-rate for a number of **classes** of speech coders. The **goal** of a speech coding system is to maintain the highest quality while achieving the lowest possible bit-rate. In addition, the choice of a speech coder is constrained by the allowable complexity of the system. Table I indicates the relative complexities of several speech coding algorithms.

Another important aspect of the speech coding **system, shown here,** is the coding delay. This difference in time between speech input and decoded speech output may become important when added to other communication system delays. An example of the **consequences of large delays** in a communication channel are satellite systems which **frequently exhibit** "doubletalk"

Here, delays on the order of 500 ms one way through the channel cause both parties to begin speaking simultaneously when one party erroneously interprets a long pause as an ending. As indicated in the table, the coding delay is not necessarily a function of complexity. Rather, it is a property of the algorithm class. For example, the LPC coders have the same delay because they use the same frame lengths...the amount of speech processed at a time.

Of course, the plots and numbers given here are subject to change, especially in the lower bit-rate - higher complexity areas. The goal of speech researchers is to discover new ways to take advantage of the redundancies in speech and provide high quality at ever lower bit rates. The developer of speech coding systems would like to find the most efficient ways of implementing the algorithms, reducing the system cost.

SPEECH CODING IN CELLULAR

BIT RATE AND QUALITY

With this brief introduction to the general issues one must deal with in designing a speech coding system, we may now look at the particular problem of selecting a speech coding system for the cellular application. The first constraint is bit-rate. The bandwidth of the channel and the modulation scheme will determine the number of bits-per-second that will be available to the coder designer. The total number of bits-per-second thru the channel is the sum of bits used by the speech coder, channel coder ("parity" bits added to the speech bits for error protection...discussed below), and overhead for channel management. Thus, the number of bits-per-second available to the speech coder may be anywhere from 45% to 70% of the total. For the digital cellular systems under consideration today this number corresponds to between 4000 bits-per-second (4Kbps) and 16 Kbps.

The speech coding delay for some of the higher quality coders is a tradeoff with bit-rate. As the bit-rate is reduced, the delay increases. Delay has been mentioned before as the cause of "doubletalk". Another problem associated with excessive delay is echo. Echo occurs at any point in the network where there is an impedance discontinuity, e.g. a hybrid to interface a two-wire to a four-wire line. Large coding delays exacerbate echoes in the communication channel.

The next issue is speech quality. Cellular subscribers have become used to the quality of the current analog FM systems, so a lower limit on the desired speech quality of a digital system might be that provided by FM. On a strong, clear channel the MOS for the analog FM system is approximately 4.0. Combining the requirements for high quality with bit-rates below 16 Kbps has focused coder development on the class of high-complexity hybrid coders.

This, however, points out an additional concern in cellular...quality versus channel signal-to-noise. As the bit-rates of speech coders drop, the more important the bits are. The loss of bits of information can mean serious degradation in speech quality. For this reason, digital cellular systems require some degree of error detection and correction known as channel coding. The channel coding scheme used in the cellular environment must be capable of handling bursts of errors caused by the fading of the channel in addition to the more typical random errors introduced by noise in the channel.

Of the many techniques used in channel coding schemes for cellular, one of the most powerful is matching the strength of error protection to the requirements of the speech coder. It turns out that in many speech coders, the bit stream output may be prioritized; that is, some bits are more important than others. An efficient channel coder could give more protection to the speech bits that are more important, and less protection to less important bits.

A channel coder that provides unequal error protection to the speech information bits is known as a variable-rate channel coder, while one that gives all speech bits the same protection, is called a fixed-rate channel coder. Fig. 2a shows a plot of bit-error rate versus channel signal-to-noise ratio for a system with and without channel coding. The bit-error rate is loosely associated with speech quality in that as the error rate increases, the quality of the speech is adversely affected. The goal for the relationship between speech quality and channel signal-to-noise ratio for a speech coder with and without channel coding compared to the existing FM system is shown in Fig. 2b. The speech coder designer, with help from a channel coding expert, seeks to give equivalent or better speech quality as compared to the FM system at high signal-to-noise ratios, and to maintain that quality at lower signal-to-noise.

Another important aspect of the speech coder quality is its response to other typical sounds in the automobile environment. For example, the coder should be tested for response to coughs, sneezes, whistles, fan noise, multiple conversations, and DTMF tones.

A final consideration in the quality of a speech coder is the effect of multiple encodings, called tandem coding. As the number of tandem encoding/decoding pairs increases, the quality of the speech degrades. A simple mobile-to-land call would normally entail a single encoding/decoding of speech. A mobile-to-mobile call would require two encoding/decoding pairs. A long distance call might add multiple encoding/decoding pairs as the speech moves through the long-distance network.

CODER IMPLEMENTATION

When candidate speech coders are identified as appropriate for cellular in terms of bit-rate and quality, the implementation of each coder must also be taken into account. The key parameters are cost, size, power consumption, and development time. These parameters, particularly the first three, are significant in cellular mobile and hand held terminals.

Speech coder technology is being driven by advances in Digital Signal Processing (DSP) and VLSI devices. In either case, the low power requirements in cellular demand the use of CMOS devices. The decision to use a DSP, a more general-purpose device, versus a VLSI, a more application specific device, to implement a coder design is based upon the maturity of the algorithm and the market. A VLSI device will most likely be lower in cost, size, and power consumption than a DSP. The drawbacks to using a VLSI are longer development time and less flexibility. Thus, if an algorithm is mature and the market for the device is a large, long term one, a VLSI implementation is a good choice. A DSP implementation, on the other hand, allows for low cost, rapid modification of an algorithm. In this way implementation improvements to a new coding algorithm may be easily incorporated. A DSP may also be capable of performing a wider range of speech processing tasks, such as speech recognition, than a VLSI device. Finally, the cost advantage of a VLSI implementation may not be as great as imagined, since the DSP implementation may take advantage of the volumes associated with use of the DSP in many other areas.

As was mentioned before in connection with Table I, coder complexity in terms of millions-of-instructions-per-second (MIPS) can span several orders of magnitude. Today's DSP devices are approaching 40 MIPS in a single, fixed-point device, making a single chip DSP implementation possible for highly complex coders. An additional complexity consideration might be floating-point versus fixed point implementation. While state-of-the-art floating point DSP's operate in the

15 MIPS range, less than the fixed-point devices, the use of floating-point can greatly reduce the computational overhead associated with parameter scaling required to satisfy dynamic range constraints in fixed-point devices. Also, while the floating-point devices tend to be larger and more expensive, the development time required for a floating-point realization of a coding algorithm may be much less than that for a fixed-point.

OTHER SPEECH PROCESSING TASKS IN CELLULAR

As was indicated above, a DSP implementation of a speech coding algorithm allows the possibility of performing other speech processing tasks for cellular. The coding algorithm itself, or a slightly modified version that would include extra features such as silence compression, could be used to provide a digital "answering machine" capability for cellular subscribers. The DSP could also be used to encrypt the speech information giving the subscriber anywhere from simple privacy to complex security. Other uses of a DSP might include a speakerphone function including acoustic echo cancellation and an eyes-free, hands-free speech recognition function for voice dialing.

CONCLUSIONS

The need for more efficient use of allocated spectrum has caused a move toward development of digital cellular systems using low bit-rate speech coding techniques. An understanding of speech quality measures, the relationships between quality, bit-rate, and complexity, and the effects of the cellular environment on speech coders, is important for the evaluation of speech coding technology. Achieving high speech quality at 16 Kbps and 8 Kbps using the latest high-complexity hybrid coders, while maintaining low implementation cost, can be successfully accomplished through the use of efficient algorithms in current CMOS DSP's.

GLOSSARY and REFERENCES

The following speech coders were mentioned in this paper:

ADPCM - Adaptive Differential Pulse Code Modulation

ASBC - Adaptive Subband Coding

CELP - Code Excited Linear Predictive also known as Stochasticly Excited Linear Predictive (SELP or SE-LPC)

LPC - Linear Predictive Coding

MP-LPC - Multipulse LPC

PCM - Pulse Code Modulation

These speech coders and others, as well
as a general discussion of speech
coding principles may be found in the
following excellent texts:

Flanagan, J. L.,SPEECH ANALYSIS,
SYNTHESIS AND PERCEPTION. New York:
Springer-Verlag 1972.

Jayant, N. S., "Digital Coding of Speech"
in DIGITAL COMMUNICATIONS. T. C. Bartree,
Editor. Indianapolis, IN: Howard W.
Sams & Co. 1986.

Papamichalis, P. E., PRACTICAL APPROACHES
TO SPEECH CODING. Englewood Cliff, NJ:
Prentice Hall, 1987.

TABLE I. SPEECH CODER COMPARISONS

Coder	Bit Rate (Kbps)	Complexity (MIPS)	Delay (ms)
PCM	64	<1	0
ADPCM	32	<1	0
ASBC	12 - 16	1-2	25
MP-LPC	8	10	35
CELP	4 - 8	50 - 100	35
LPC	2	1	35

Note: See glossary for expanded coder names.

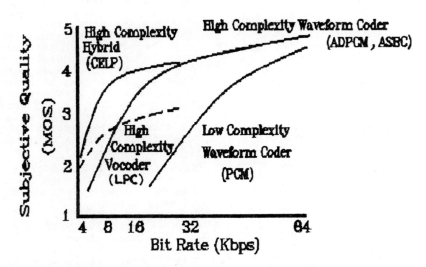

Fig. 1   Speech Quality vs. Bit Rate

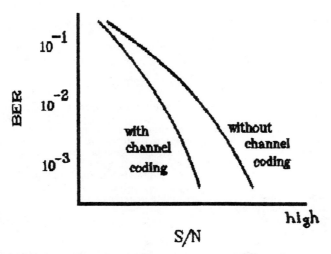

Fig. 2a Bit Error Rate vs. Signal-to-Noise

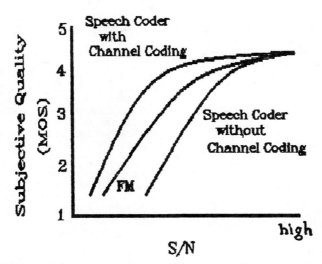

Fig. 2b Speech Quality vs. Signal-to-Noise

INTERWORKING BETWEEN CELLULAR AND ISDN

Edward Chien
Executive Director
Systems Technology
Southwestern Bell
1 Bell Center
Room 36-N-40
St. Louis, MO 63101

Interworking between cellular and ISDN is essential. Data transmission and service features of future digital cellular may be benefited by ISDN; therefore, the interworking needs to be planned.

CEL-08

CELLULAR ROLE IN THE

NATIONWIDE NETWORK

Mark J. Nielsen

Director, Marketing

Cellular Business Systems

1661 Feehanville Drive
Mount Prospect, IL 60056

ABSTRACT

The impact of cellular on the future of the nation's telecommunications network is both exciting and fraught with controversy. In only five years since cellular's introduction into commercial service, numerous controversies have begun to surface on how extensive cellular's role should be in replacing or enhancing existing telecommunications systems. This seminar provides a comprehensive look at some of the key controversies surrounding cellular including the use of cellular as a possible replacement for the local loop, the creation of "super systems" spanning multiple cities with interconnected cellular switches, the myths and facts of nationwide roaming across cellular systems, the potential for integrating paging with cellular phones and systems, and the feasibility of creating a nationwide cellular network. Recognizing both the engineering and business implications of these controversies, this seminar straddles and explores both the technical considerations as well as the financial and public policy concerns.

William D. Hays	-- Special Projects Manager, Mobile Communications Corp. of America
David E. Hogan	-- President, Century Telephone Enterprises Inc.
Mark J. Nielsen	-- Director, Cellular Business Systems
Michael Schwartz	-- Vice President, American Cellular Network Corporation
James M. Williams	-- Principle Staff Engineer, Motorola

THE EXPANDING WEB OF CELLULAR

Michael Schwartz
Vice President

American Cellular Network Corp.

Verona Boulevard, Suite 400
Pleasantville, NJ 08232

ABSTRACT

This session explores the technical and financial considerations of the growing interconnection of cellular systems and creation of regional or super systems. The discussion highlights both the business and engineering problems and opportunities with intertwist handoffs, wide area coverage, and the ability for a subscriber to both place and receive calls no matter on which system in the region he might happen to be located.

RURAL CELLULAR AND THE LOCAL LOOP

David E. Hogan
President

Century Telephone Enterprises, Inc.

P.O. Box 4065
Monroe, LA 71211

ABSTRACT

As cellular licenses are granted and construction begins in rural service areas (RSAs), the lanolin telephone company and others are asking whether or not cellular may be an attractive alternative to current wirelike services in these areas. Does cellular represent a threat or simply a resale opportunity to local exchange carriers? Will cellular become the technology of choice in rural America or will other signal-based communications such as BETR or mobile satellite systems be preferred?

ROAMING: THE GOOD, THE BAD AND THE UGLY

Mark Nielsen
Director-Marketing

Cellular Business Systems

1661 Feehanville Drive
Mount Prospect, IL 60056

ABSTRACT

This session examines the myths and realities of roaming across different cellular systems by both "bandits" and normal users. The revenue opportunities as well as the potential liabilities are explored, including an examination of current methods for stopping roamer fraud and allowing intercarrier settlement and clearing among various cellular operators.

SHOULD CELLULAR AND PAGING BE MERGED?

William D. Hays
Special Projects Manager

Mobile Communications Corp. of America

P.O. Drawer 2367
Jackson, MS 39225

ABSTRACT

Many people in companies are now investigating the feasibility of incorporating pages with cellular phones. As the portable phone becomes more prevalent, many ask why someone should also carry a separate pager. This session highlights the technical considerations as well as both sides of the public policy argument.

NATIONWIDE CELLULAR NETWORK:

FACT OR FOLLY?

James M. Williams
Principle Staff Engineer

Motorola, Inc.

1501 Shure Drive
Arlington Heights, IL 60004

A multitude of switch manufacturers, disputes over standards, varying regulatory requirements and competing owners make the dream of a nationwide cellular network often seem only a dream. Despite these barriers, this session explores a solution to providing a full-featured, fully automatic national cellular network.

SPEAKER/CONTRIBUTOR	SEMINAR	PAGE
Michael Ahdieh	DSW-05	1229
Fahim Ahmed	TEC-13	1760
N. Jean Airey	DSW-02	1167
Dag Akerberg	CEL-03	1851
Raymond F. Albers	LTW-07	306
Raymond F. Albers	DSW-11	1293
Hrair Aldermeshian	NET-29	700
Ronald G. Aldridge	OPS-08	1060
Jukka Alho	NET-09	511
Sig J. Amster	PQR-16	1591
Charles Anderson	NET-25	657
J. Trevor Anderson	NET-27	679
Nancy J. Anderson	CEL-02	1841
Philip J. Anthony	LTW-06	305
Sasan H. Ardalan	TEC-16	1827
Eve C. Aretakis	BUS-16	114
Lance Arnder	NET-32	742
Hamilton W. Arnold	CEL-03	1846
Elbert R. Ashbaugh III	NET-13	541
William Ashley	BUS-28	202
Donald E. Auble	NET-18	591
Richard N. Aurin	DSW-15	1344
Donald J. Bache	LTW-10	374
Karen S. Baer	NET-03	444
John Bain	BUS-12	77
Ashutosh Balpay	PQR-14	1544
Mary P. Bakallis	PQR-14	1544
W. David Ballew	PQR-17	1606
Alan J. Balma	NET-31	728
Mark E. Balmes	LTW-10	374
Ashu Balpay	PQR-14	1544
Marybeth Banks	BUS-08	55
Andrew C. Barrett	LTW-08	340
Bert E. Basch	LTW-06	298
Vincent L. Bates	USE-04	773
Kim Batho	NET-29	709
Donald V. Batorsky	LTW-05	280
Donald V. Batorsky	NET-29	703
David S. Bauer	ISS-09	888
Colin Beasley	NET-25	658
James R. Beatty	BUS-29	209
W. Michael Bechtold	PQR-13	1532
Mark W. Beckner	NET-03	452
Mark W. Beckner	DSW-16	1373
Mark W. Beckner	TEC-13	1759
Fernand Bedard	TEC-03	1606
Michael Begun	ISS-07	872
Robert W. Bellin	TEC-12	1743
Jules A. Bellisio	TEC-07	1678
George A. Benington	USE-06	787, 788
Herbert D. Benington	USE-06	787
Joan E. Berger	BUS-14	80
Joan E. Berger	BUS-17	127
Kenneth R. Berger	PQR-17	1607
John Berrigan	CEL-02	1837
Behram H. Bharucha	NET-04	459
James Bielanski	OPS-05	1020
John A. Bigham	LTW-09	358
John A. Bigham	LTW-10	386
Ronald F. Bills	CEL-05	1893
Richard D. Birckbichler	NET-16	551

SPEAKER/CONTRIBUTOR	SEMINAR	PAGE	
John Bjelland	USE-04	780	
Walter B. Blackwell	PQR-07	1453	
Gary L. Blank	TEC-16	1832	
William J. Blatt	BUS-25	173	
Jack Blount	NET-23	647	
Rodney J. Boehm	LTW-04	258	
J. Kenneth Boggs	DSW-08	1258	
Despina K. Boinodiris	USE-04	777	
Heidi Bomengen	OPS-08	1069	
Joseph G. Bonito	PQR-16	1600	
G. Kevin Borders	NET-21	616	
Suresh R. Borkar	PQR-10	1497	
Jane Bortnick	BUS-08	55	
Mark H. Bowers	LTW-08	328	
Barbara C. Bowie	ISS-14	922	
F. W. Boyd	BUS-07	51	
Gerald R. Boyer	NET-21	624	
William C. Boyken	LTW-02	220	
Stephanie M. Boyles	NET-19	605	
H. Paul Brant	ISS-02	831	
H. Paul Brant	ISS-12	912	
Sharon A. Brant	BUS-23	162	
Robert S. Braudy	PQR-01	1375	
Robert S. Braudy	BUS-07	54	
Michael T. Brennan	NET-25	660	
Douglas A. Brown	PQR-03	1405	
Douglas A. Brown	PQR-04	1405	
Peter Brown	ISS-01	1800	
R. L. Brown	CEL-06	1905	
Thomas E. Browne	NET-06	484	
Richard B. Brownfield	DSW-10	1290,	1293
Vicky Bruggeman	BUS-07	54	
Donald R. Brusk	USE-01	760	
Charles H. Bultmann	BUS-18	137	
Jayne Bunting	ISS-10	895	
Walter J. Burmeister	ISS-07	872	
James Burrows	BUS-08	55	
John H. Bush	BUS-15	106	
Howard E. Bussey	NET-04	459	
Gerald J. Butters	DSW-09	1272	
Thomas P. Byrne	LTW-03	230	
William R. Byrne	NET-29	700	
James P. Caile	CEL-01	1835	
Arthur J. Caisse	NET-27	687	
Arthur J. Caisse	ISS-13	913	
George F. Calcei	USE-05	786	
Thomas Campbell	TEC-10	1706	
Philip E. Cannata	ISS-11	911	
Anthony W. Capuano	BUS-13	79	
Donald C. Caramell	OPS-10	1100	
Joseph A. Carfagno	ISS-07	872	
James B. Carpenter	NET-05	475	
Richard G. Carr	DSW-01	1166	
Lou Carrion	BUS-04	21	
Bruce A. Cassidy	NET-27	680	
W. Thomas Cathey	TEC-02	1657	
Charles Catlett	TEC-08	1695	
Frederick R. Chang	TEC-09	1703	
Nim K. Cheung	LTW-06	290	
Edward Chien	CEL-07	1918	
Swee-Joo Chin	NET-19	605	

SPEAKER/CONTRIBUTOR	SEMINAR	PAGE	
Yauchau Ching	LTW-05	260	
Emory Christensen	PQR-13	1535	
Harold W. Clark	NET-14	542	
Harold W. Clark	CEL-01	1836	
Joanne Clawson	NET-30	716	
James I. Cochrane	TEC-06	1677	
Larry J. Cody	BUS-13	79	
Edward E. Cohen	NET-32	754	
Roberta Cohen	USE-03	767	
Thomas Cohen	BUS-08	55	
Warren Cohen	LTW-07	308	
Rita E. Collins	NET-31	728	
Charles S. Cooper	BUS-25	171	
Charles S. Cooper	BUS-26	194	
Martin Cooper	CEL-01	1835	
Michael H. Cooper	NET-10	514	
Kenneth M. Corcoran	OPS-14	1154	
David P. Cox	DSW-09	1280	
Donna Cox	TEC-08	1695	
Neil E. Cox	CEL-06	1894	
Edwin F. Crabill	PQR-14	1548	
Raymond G. Crafton	NET-26	674	
John R. Crankshaw	BUS-11	72	
Thomas R. Crawford	CEL-06	1896	
Daniel R. Croft	CEL-05	1893	
Norman L. Cubellis	OPS-10	1097	
David E. Curry	OPS-08	1057	
James J. Daley	BUS-27	199	
Edward A. Dalton	BUS-28	202,	204
Robert A. Dantowitz	ISS-14	914	
Jnan Dash	ISS-08	873	
Nancy R. Daspit	DSW-03	1182	
James Daughton	BUS-29	209	
Scott Davidson	TEC-15	1792	
Neil M. Davies	PQR-11	1506	
Alan Davis	TEC-16	1805	
Christopher L. Davis	OPS-10	1100	
Stewart O. Davis	PQR-02	1393	
John P. Delatore	DSW-04	1202	
Albert J. DellaBitta	BUS-19	138	
Robert P. DelPriore	DSW-14	1343	
Robert Deming	NET-08	497	
Dean L. Denhart	ISS-02	822	
Frank J. Denniston	OPS-12	1111	
Kathy Detrano	CEL-06	1905	
Hugh J. Devine Jr.	BUS-18	137	
William A. DeVor	NET-16	572	
Nikhilesh Dholakia	BUS-05	32	
Richard Dillon	DSW-10	1292	
Dimitri Dimancesco	PQR-02	1403	
Donald P. Dineen	NET-11	520	
George H. Dobrowski	NET-10	516	
Mary J. Doherty	BUS-17	127	
Ray Dolan	CEL-06	1894	
William J. Donnelly	ISS-10	903	
Michael A. Dougherty	USE-03	766	
John L. Draheim	OPS-07	1040	
Gary G. Drook	BUS-19	138	
Joe F. Drzewiecki	OPS-12	1127	
Victoria N. Duckworth	ISS-06	870	
Francis P. Duffy	DSW-07	1255	

SPEAKER/CONTRIBUTOR	SEMINAR	PAGE
J. Michael Dugan	NET-02	441
Tim A. Dunar	DSW-08	1267
Richard Dworak	PQR-15	1587
W. Dyczmons	NET-09	506
Elizabeth D. Eastland	OPS-05	1004
Lester F. Eastman	TEC-03	1668
Gwen C. Edwards	ISS-12	912
Gwen C. Edwards	ISS-13	913
Theodore A. Edwards	BUS-06	50
Karolyn Eisenstein	TEC-02	1651
William H. Eliot	LTW-03	232
Martin C. J. Elton	NET-04	456
Robert S. Emerson	ISS-12	912
Paul Eng	OPS-07	1040
Andre L. Engel	ISS-08	873
Stuart B. Erskine	ISS-13	913
Leo J. Esposito	NET-23	647
Glenn H. Estes	NET-22	646
Wylie E. Etscheid	OPS-08	1057
Evelyn Eubank	NET-12	531
Scott Evans	ISS-06	866
Melvin W. Evers	LTW-03	254
Michael P. Fabisch	PQR-14	1557
Katherine M. Falkenthal	CEL-03	1857
Michael A. Fekety	BUS-16	109
Roger D. Feldman	NET-30	718
Wayne J. Felts	NET-25	661
Al Fenn	NET-10	515
Glover T. Ferguson Jr.	ISS-11	911
Davis L. Fisher	BUS-09	56
Karen E. Fitzgerald	NET-24	649
Karen E. Fitzgerald	NET-25	649
Jerome S. Fleischman	ISS-02	815
Pete Fleming	PQR-17	1602
Donald W. Flynn	LTW-08	322
James Flynn	BUS-04	21
Mary A. Foley	BUS-25	181
Lee K. Foote	USE-02	762
Lenard J. Forys	DSW-15	1348
Rose Foss	DSW-01	1166
William R. Francis	PQR-11	1501
Ronald E. Froehlich	NET-31	739
Frederic E. Fulmer	BUS-10	63
John B. Gage	PQR-02	1400
Thomas P. Gallagher	ISS-10	895
Linda Garbanati	LTW-09	347
David Gardiner	ISS-06	866
Grant K. Garnett	PQR-05	1424
William S. Gaskill	USE-01	760
Robert A. George	LTW-03	230
Gary A. Getz	BUS-14	84
B. K. Pete Geurts	BUS-15	85
B. K. Pete Geurts	NET-05	478
Hamid Gharavi	TEC-07	1678
Carl Giallombardo	ISS-07	872
Michael A. Gibbens	BUS-05	32
Michael A. Gibbens	BUS-14	80
Patrick M. Gibbons	NET-31	732
Mark A. Gicale	OPS-08	1077
William E. Gilbert	ISS-04	848
Eileen Gillespie	OPS-02	957

SPEAKER/CONTRIBUTOR	SEMINAR	PAGE
James A. Goetz	ISS-14	920
David V. Golden	NET-12	535
Joel D. Goldhar	BUS-08	55
Joel D. Goldhar	PQR-15	1568
Barry C. Goldstein	TEC-06	1677
Barry C. Goldstein	NET-14	542
Deepak K. Goyal	ISS-04	855
Frank A. Graff	OPS-03	986
J. Arthur Graham	LTW-05	260
Michael Gray	DSW-07	1248
John W. Greene	BUS-14	83
Robert F. Griffith	DSW-04	1202
Gerald W. Grindler	ISS-09	892
Michael G. Grisham	OPS-05	1009
Gabriel Groner	TEC-05	1676
Alan H. Grossman	ISS-03	843
Charles R. Grossman	PQR-17	1602
John G. Gruber	OPS-12	1114
Wid Guisler	BUS-04	23
Howard J. Gunn	BUS-27	196
Pavan Gupta	TEC-16	1820
Joseph R. Gustafson	NET-10	514
Juan C. Gutierrez	OPS-13	1133
Robert Haber	TEC-08	1695
Herman Haberman	BUS-08	55
Michael A. Hall	ISS-01	810
Dennis S. Hamill	PQR-06	1436
David H. Hanneman	BUS-21	151
Richard P. Harrison	OPS-13	1133
S. Brad Harsha	OPS-06	1025
Paul R. Hartmann	NET-02	433
James Harty	PQR-14	1548
Greg Hawkins	PQR-01	1375
Charles S. Head	NET-03	443
Richard J. Hebda	USE-07	798
Bo Hedberg	CEL-07	1911
Robert H. Helgesen	NET-28	697
Marilyn A. Henderson	NET-17	573
Fran Henig	OPS-08	1067
George Henry	PQR-13	1543
Herbert Herrmann	NET-09	506
Stephen D. Hester	NET-23	647
Stephen D. Hester	NET-16	572
Earl Hewitt	PQR-02	1393
George M. Hickman	NET-17	577
George W. Hicks	LTW-10	374
Steven R. Hilbert	NET-21	637
Harvard Scott Hinton	TEC-01	1635
Lorne C. Hinz	DSW-05	1214
Teresa M. Hirsch	BUS-18	137
Donald J. Hoffman	OPS-13	1133
Phyllis L. Hoffman	NET-13	539
David E. Hogan	CEL-08	1919
Samuel B. Holcman	ISS-14	917
Joseph G. Holland	ISS-10	900
F. Timon Holman	BUS-10	63
Johnnie L. Holt	BUS-19	138
Lew Holt	NET-24	649
William L. Honig	ISS-01	800
Quentin V. Hovland	NET-24	655
Roger J. Howe	BUS-29	209

SPEAKER/CONTRIBUTOR	SEMINAR	PAGE		
Nian Chyi Huang	DSW-13	1326		
Charles L. Hudson Jr.	TEC-15	1796		
Paul V. Hughes	OPS-13	1140		
Thomas P. Huizenga	PQR-12	1517		
Robert W. Humes	NET-03	442		
Tetsuhiko Ikegami	LTW-06	286		
Theodor Irmer	NET-09	502		
Michael A. Isnardi	TEC-07	1690		
Sridhar S. Iyemgar	ISS-11	911		
Lawrence D. Jackel	TEC-03	1671		
Peter E. Jackson	DSW-11	1298		
Peter E. Jackson	TEC-10	1706		
Steven W. Jackson	USE-04	770		
Joel E. Jakubson	LTW-05	273		
Gail R. James	NET-23	647,	648	
Robert M. Janowiak	BUS-01	1		
James A. Jenkins	ISS-05	865		
Donald J. Jester	PQR-08	1454		
Bruce Johnson	NET-26	672		
Edward R. Johnson	CEL-04	1887		
Henry C. Johnson	BUS-07	51		
J. L. Johnson	NET-05	475		
Walter Johnston	LTW-07	312		
Douglas Jordan	BUS-27	199		
Keith Kaczmarek	CEL-06	1903		
William H. Kalbfleisch	BUS-11	65		
Luke D. Kane	OPS-05	1015		
Younghee Kang	PQR-14	1548		
William Kania	BUS-24	170		
Kathy M. Kaplan	NET-18	603		
Vinod Kapoor	PQR-15	1576		
William F. Kehoe Jr.	NET-13	539		
Myron L. Keller	LTW-09	354		
Barbara Kemp	NET-17	573		
Paul Kennard	CEL-04	1867		
Leonard Kennedy	NET-09	511		
Michael G. Kern	OPS-03	981		
Ian H. Kerr	OPS-02	970		
David L. Kessell	ISS-06	866		
David L. Kessell	ISS-03	835		
David L. Kessell	ISS-04	848		
David A. Kettler	NET-22	639		
John P. King	TEC-13	1759		
C. Fred Klein	DSW-06	1238,	1239,	1243
Robert W. Klessig	NET-10	516		
Scott C. Knauer	TEC-06	1677		
Dick Knudtsen	PQR-13	1542		
Kurt E. Knuth	PQR-13	1532		
David Ko	LTW-08	318		
Denny P. Ko	DSW-05	1221		
Michael E. Koblentz	ISS-09	882		
Michael E. Koblentz	ISS-04	861		
Jagdish C. Kohli	NET-07	493		
Barbara A. Kraemer	NET-12	531		
Michael H. Kraft	NET-30	716		
Richard A. Kraus	OPS-09	1080		
Patrick Krause	OPS-02	950		
Karen A. Krepps	OPS-06	1025		
John R. Kronenburger	TEC-16	1805		
Konstanty E. Krylow	PQR-12	1517		
Peter Krywaruczenko	PQR-16	1588		

SPEAKER/CONTRIBUTOR	SEMINAR	PAGE
Patrick Marino	NET-24	656
J. Thomas Markley	BUS-28	207
Barry L. Marks	BUS-04	26
Jeff Marr	BUS-18	137
Richard J. Marsh	BUS-05	34
Catherine Marshall	TEC-09	1696
Richard J. Martin	BUS-03	19
Ronald G. Martin	PQR-09	1474
David J. Marutiak	NET-03	444
Steven P. Mathews	BUS-22	157
Gordon Matthews	BUS-07	51
Phillip Matthews	ISS-01	806
William Maybaum	BUS-22	157
Susan Mazonson	BUS-26	183
Donald T. McClean	PQR-17	1602
W. Edward McConaghay	BUS-16	107
David L. McCrosky	OPS-06	1027
Robert W. McDarmont	DSW-04	1213
Robert W. McDarmont	DSW-09	1283
Tommy W. McEaddy	OPS-09	1089
John E. McElhany	BUS-29	209
Stephen A. McGaw	NET-05	481
James R. McGee	TEC-13	1762
Robert J. McGuire	TEC-10	1714
Dennis L. McKiernan	PQR-03	1405
Dennis L. McKiernan	PQR-04	1405
Thomas McManus	PQR-02	1382
Gale P. McNamara	NET-15	550
J. D. McNicol	CEL-04	1867
Steven B. Meadows	BUS-05	40
Steven B. Meadows	BUS-13	79
Steven B. Meadows	BUS-28	204
Steven B. Meadows	USE-06	790
Kenneth E. Means	USE-01	760
Allison B. Mearns	NET-06	484
Carol J. Meier	BUS-12	77
Arthur R. Meierdirk	PQR-07	1450
Donnie Mekins	NET-21	630
Ronald C. Menendez	LTW-01	211
Craig Mento	ISS-11	911
Robert A. Mercer	NET-18	602
A. Methiwalla	DSW-13	1326
Edward E. Meyer	NET-01	399
Richard F. Michael	NET-31	736
Douglas L. Michels	ISS-05	865
Clifton Miller	PQR-09	1482
Jo Anne H. Miller	PQR-08	1454, 1470
M. Peter Miller	USE-07	794
Robert A. Miller	DSW-15	1356
Kevin L. Mills	ISS-03	841
Paul Miner	BUS-10	63
James Mollenauer	NET-04	464
Ernest J. Moore	OPS-01	930
Mitchell S. Moore	DSW-10	1290
Thomas B. Morawski	NET-29	700
Thomas V. Moresco	NET-06	492
M. B. Morris	BUS-26	183
Wendy Morris	OPS-07	1052
John Morton	DSW-01	1166
Lornia R. Moseley	NET-06	484
Marvin Moser	NET-03	452

SPEAKER/CONTRIBUTOR	SEMINAR	PAGE	
Andrew Motley	TEC-10	1722	
M. J. Muller	ISS-05	865	
Jane E. Munn	ISS-04	856	
Sushil G. Munshi	TEC-14	1768,	1779
John A. Muntean	USE-05	786	
Brian Murphy	NET-26	669	
William Murphy	DSW-14	1339	
Anthony T. Murray Jr.	BUS-03	20	
J. David Murray	DSW-03	1181	
Rodney Murray	LTW-03	249	
..Jeffrey M. Musser	OPS-14	1156	
Edmund H. Muth	ISS-08	879	
Sudhesh Mysore	LTW-02	213	
Jayant Naik	TEC-04	1675	
Vijay Naik	BUS-16	121	
John E. Nast	PQR-05	1415	
Jerry L. Neal	OPS-06	1036	
Michael E. Nedzel	BUS-15	97	
Gary A. Nelson	NET-04	456,	470
John A. Newell	USE-05	786	
Thomas E. Newman	NET-17	582	
Roger F. Nicholson	PQR-16	1588	
Mark J. Nielsen	CEL-08	1919	
David S. Niles	DSW-03	1178	
Daniel P. Norman	CEL-05	1893	
Thomas A. Nousaine	BUS-23	158	
Gene R. O'Brien	BUS-03	19	
G. Kelly O'Dea	BUS-03	19	
Colton O'Donoghue	LTW-10	386	
Eric Offerman	NET-10	515	
Burgess G. Oliver	PQR-08	1464	
Randi L. Olsen	OPS-11	1105	
Lyndon Y. Ong	NET-19	614	
D. C. Opferman	PQR-17	1602	
Mark Orenstein	NET-10	514	
Brian A. Ostberg	DSW-15	1359	
Jud R. Ostle	PQR-10	1495	
Mil Ovan	BUS-27	196	
Bill D. Pack	BUS-23	162	
Kaveh Pahlavan	TEC-10	1731	
Bob Panoff	BUS-07	54	
Michael G. Parfett	ISS-07	872	
Stephen Parker	ISS-02	831	
Mark A. Pashan	NET-22	646	
Roger R. Patel	PQR-08	1459	
Michael V. Patriarche	CEL-02	1837	
Russell E. Patridge	CEL-06	1903	
C. Clement Patton	BUS-24	170	
D. Scott Paul	PQR-16	1588	
Alan Pearce	BUS-02	13	
Jim Pearce	NET-32	742	
Richard L. Peck	BUS-06	50	
John L. Pence	BUS-19	138	
William C. Pennington	DSW-16	1373	
James A. Peponis	BUS-11	64,	74
Steven E. Permut	BUS-20	142	
Stewart D. Personick	TEC-03	1663	
John W. Peters	LTW-02	223	
Harry F. Petty III	PQR-01	1375	
Louis B. Phillips	OPS-14	1153	
Lynn W. Phillips	BUS-03	19	

SPEAKER/CONTRIBUTOR	SEMINAR	PAGE	
Linda Pierce	NET-30	724	
Edward Pillman	ISS-13	913	
Gary L. Pinkham	DSW-12	1321	
Mark D. Pitchford	NET-21	624	
Robert L. Pokress	TEC-06	1677	
Peter Politakis	TEC-14	1777	
Philip T. Porter	CEL-03	1846	
Michael K. Pratt	PQR-02	1388	
Robert S. Preece	NET-27	684	
John Racioppi	LTW-07	312	
Daniel P. Rafferty	PQR-06	1431	
P. Venkat Rangan	ISS-09	886	
Barbara T. Reagor	OPS-03	981	
Joyce M. Rector	OPS-11	1101,	1102
Dennis E. Reese	NET-03	444	
Michael P. Ressler	ISS-09	882	
Edward D. Reynolds	DSW-13	1326	
Jerry L. Rhattigan	DSW-11	1293	
Michael B. Ribet	USE-02	762	
Richard J. Riccoboni	NET-30	718	
David R. Richards	DSW-04	1213	
Evan B. Richards	OPS-02	950	
Richard C. Ricks	PQR-02	1383	
Christine A. Riley	TEC-09	1696	
Mark O. Ripley	CEL-01	1836	
Derek Ritson	DSW-08	1261	
Robert A. Rivenes	NET-32	754	
Teresa L. Roberts	TEC-09	1701	
Kenneth G. Robinson	BUS-12	77	
Richard W. Robinson	NET-32	742	
Thomas W. Robinson	LTW-02	213	
Richard B. Robrock	BUS-25	171	
Stephen L. Rogers	USE-01	760	
Michael W. Rolund	TEC-08	1695	
Michael W. Rolund	TEC-11	1737	
Richard K. Romanow	DSW-09	1283	
Ken E. Ross	OPS-03	983	
Kermit L. Ross	PQR-06	1431	
Cy M. Rubald	PQR-10	1488	
Philip E. Rubin	LTW-06	286	
Joseph G. Rudolph	DSW-07	1247	
Joseph G. Rudolph	DSW-08	1247	
Michele S. Ruetty	DSW-03	1196	
Vicky Ruggeman	BUS-07	54	
Jeff Rulifson	ISS-12	912	
C. Thomas Rush	BUS-07	51	
Jesse E. Russell	CEL-01	1836	
E. G. Russo	NET-29	709	
Anthony N. Rybczynski	NET-27	675	
Paul Saacke	PQR-16	1597	
Shaker Sabri	NET-05	483	
Bernard T. Sander Jr.	PQR-10	1492	
Dennis J. Sassa	OPS-07	1044	
Richard G. Saunders	CEL-03	1860	
Phillip M. Scanlan	PQR-12	1522	
Scott Schaefer	NET-25	657	
William D. Schindel	PQR-07	1450	
Christopher M. Schmandt	TEC-05	1676	
Don I. Schmidek	PQR-12	1525	
Bernard V. Schneider	NET-16	572	
Thomas Schnepp	BUS-26	185	

SPEAKER/CONTRIBUTOR	SEMINAR	PAGE
Charles Schott	BUS-08	55
George R. Schultz	PQR-17	1620
Roger A. Schwantes	DSW-11	1304
Michael Schwartz	CEL-08	1919
John M. Sebeson	PQR-13	1539
William S. Sedlacek	PQR-15	1568
Harry Semerjian	BUS-23	169
Omri Serlin	TEC-11	1737
Mo Shabana	DSW-12	1312
Barry A. Shaffer	PQR-03	1405
Barry A. Shaffer	PQR-04	1405
Edward G. Sharp	ISS-05	865
Laurence L. Sheets	TEC-16	1805
Daniel Sheinbein	NET-28	698
D. Sid Shelton	NET-15	543
D. Sid Shelton	ISS-12	912
Howard Sherry	LTW-07	306
Robert A. Sherry	DSW-04	1207
Joan L. Shine	DSW-03	1192
Herschel Shosteck	CEL-05	1893
Pierre Sibille	DSW-05	1214
Steven A. Siegel	ISS-02	815
Roman O. Sikaczowski	PQR-14	1554
Ray Simar Jr.	TEC-16	1805
Robert L. Simms	NET-26	665
Walter D. Sincoskie	TEC-12	1743
Martin H. Singer	PQR-07	1450
Douglas D. Sink	DSW-12	1306
Craig Skarpiak	CEL-04	1873
Florence R. Skelly	BUS-14	83
Matthew F. Slana	TEC-01	1626
Rosetta M. Slavin	USE-07	794
Larry Smarr	TEC-08	1695
D. Paul Smith	PQR-11	1501
Peter W. Smith	TEC-01	1626
William L. Smith	NET-22	639
William W. Snell	BUS-09	56
Harold Sobol	NET-02	427
Piyush Sodha	CEL-02	1841
Piyush Sodha	CEL-07	1913
Irene Sokolowski	PQR-11	1511
Merrill Solomon	TEC-04	1675
Richard J. Solomon	NET-14	542
Loren Southwick	NET-27	679
Ronald A. Spanke	DSW-13	1332
Scott A. Spayde	ISS-11	911
James H. Spencer	DSW-12	1325
James J. Stahl	NET-12	533
Grace L. Stahlschmidt	NET-24	655
John J. Stangland	BUS-05	37
Russell C. Stanley	LTW-11	390
James H. Starr	NET-32	742
Marian Steeples	OPS-04	998
Carl J. Stehman	DSW-12	1306
Roger Steiner	BUS-16	114
William D. Stephenson	BUS-16	121
Robert Stepp III	TEC-14	1772
John Stevenson	TEC-08	1695
Alan Stewart	BUS-15	87
George R. Stiglich	NET-29	706
Michael Stillwell	BUS-04	24